GENERAL MOTORS | CENTURY/LUMINA/GRAND PRIX/INTRIGUE 1997-00 REPAIR MANUAL

Covers all U.S. and Canadian models of
Buick Century and Regal, Chevrolet Lumina and
Monte Carlo, Oldsmobile Cutlass Supreme
and Intrigue, Pontiac Grand Prix

by Robert E. Doughten

PUBLISHED BY **HAYNES NORTH AMERICA, Inc.**

AUTOMOTIVE
PARTS &
ACCESSORIES
ASSOCIATION MEMBER

Manufactured in USA
© 2000 Haynes North America, Inc.
ISBN 0-8019-9317-2
Library of Congress Catalog Card No. 00-132212
1234567890 9876543210

Haynes Publishing Group
Sparkford Nr Yeovil
Somerset BA22 7JJ England

Haynes North America, Inc
861 Lawrence Drive
Newbury Park
California 91320 USA

ABCDE
FGH

4J2

Contents

Contents

SAFETY NOTICE

Proper service and repair procedures are vital to the safe, reliable operation of all motor vehicles, as well as the personal safety of those performing repairs. This manual outlines procedures for servicing and repairing vehicles using safe, effective methods. The procedures contain many NOTES, CAUTIONS and WARNINGS which should be followed, along with standard procedures to eliminate the possibility of personal injury or improper service which could damage the vehicle or compromise its safety.

It is important to note that repair procedures and techniques, tools and parts for servicing motor vehicles, as well as the skill and experience of the individual performing the work vary widely. It is not possible to anticipate all of the conceivable ways or conditions under which vehicles may be serviced, or to provide cautions as to all possible hazards that may result. Standard and accepted safety precautions and equipment should be used when handling toxic or flammable fluids, and safety goggles or other protection should be used during cutting, grinding, chiseling, prying, or any other process that can cause material removal or projectiles.

Some procedures require the use of tools specially designed for a specific purpose. Before substituting another tool or procedure, you must be completely satisfied that neither your personal safety, nor the performance of the vehicle will be endangered.

Although information in this manual is based on industry sources and is complete as possible at the time of publication, the possibility exists that some car manufacturers made later changes which could not be included here. While striving for total accuracy, the authors or publishers cannot assume responsibility for any errors, changes or omissions that may occur in the compilation of this data.

PART NUMBERS

Part numbers listed in this reference are not recommendations by Haynes North America, Inc. for any product brand name. They are references that can be used with interchange manuals and aftermarket supplier catalogs to locate each brand supplier's discrete part number.

SPECIAL TOOLS

Special tools are recommended by the vehicle manufacturer to perform their specific job. Use has been kept to a minimum, but where absolutely necessary, they are referred to in the text by the part number of the tool manufacturer. These tools can be purchased, under the appropriate part number, from your local dealer or regional distributor, or an equivalent tool can be purchased locally from a tool supplier or parts outlet. Before substituting any tool for the one recommended, read the SAFETY NOTICE at the top of this page.

ACKNOWLEDGMENTS

Portions of materials contained herein have been reprinted with the permission of General Motors Corporation, Service Technology Group.

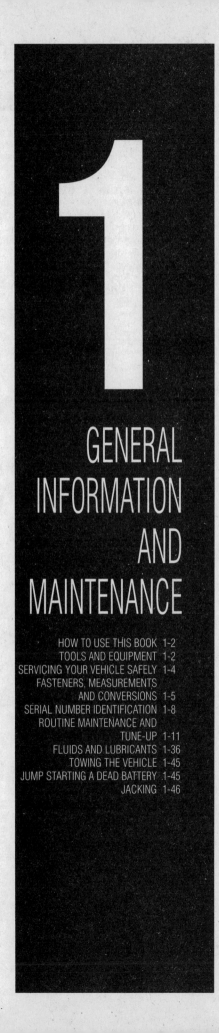

1

GENERAL INFORMATION AND MAINTENANCE

HOW TO USE THIS BOOK

Chilton's Total Car Care manual for the 1997 Oldsmobile Cutlass Supreme, 1998–00 Oldsmobile Intrigue and 1997–00 Chevrolet Lumina and Monte Carlo, Buick Regal and Century, and Pontiac Grand Prix, is intended to help you learn more about the inner workings of your vehicle, saving you money on its upkeep and operation.

The beginning of this book will likely be referred to the most, since that is where you will find information for maintenance and tune-up. The other sections deal with the more complex systems of your vehicle. Operating systems from engine through brakes are covered to the extent that the average do-it-yourselfer becomes mechanically involved. This book will not explain such things as rebuilding an automatic transaxle for the simple reason that the expertise and the investment in special tools that would be required, make this task uneconomical. This book will, however, give you detailed instructions to help you change your own brake pads and shoes, replace spark plugs, and perform many more jobs that can save you money, give you personal satisfaction and help you avoid expensive problems.

A secondary purpose of this book is a reference for owners who want to better understand their vehicle and to be able to communicate more intelligently with their professional automotive technician. In this case, no tools at all are required.

Where to Begin

Before beginning any procedure, read through the entire procedure. This will give you the overall view of what tools, parts and supplies will be required. There is nothing more frustrating than having to walk to the bus stop on Monday morning because you were not able to complete a maintenance procedure on Sunday afternoon. So read ahead and plan ahead. Each operation should be approached logically and all procedures thoroughly understood before attempting any work.

All sections contain adjustments, maintenance, removal and installation procedures, and in some cases, repair or overhaul procedures. When repair is not considered practical, we tell you how to remove the part and then how to install the new or rebuilt replacement. In this way, you at least save labor costs. "Backyard" repair of some components is just not practical.

Avoiding Trouble

Many procedures in this book require you to "label and disconnect . . ." a group of lines, hoses or wires. Don't be lulled into thinking you can remember where everything goes—you won't. If you hook up vacuum or fuel lines incorrectly, the vehicle may run poorly, if at all. If you hook up electrical wiring incorrectly, you may instantly learn a very expensive lesson.

You don't need to know the official or engineering name for each hose or line. A piece of masking tape on the hose and a piece on its fitting will allow you to assign your own label such as the letter A or a short name. As long as you remember your own code, the lines can be reconnected by matching similar letters or names. Do remember that tape will dissolve in gasoline or other fluids; if a component is to be washed or cleaned, use another method of identification. Even professional technicians will often make a quick pencil sketch of an unfamiliar installation, such as the often confusing routing of serpentine drive belts before beginning disassembly. A permanent felt-tipped marker or a metal scribe can be very handy for marking metal parts. Remove any tape or paper labels after assembly.

Maintenance or Repair?

It's necessary to mention the difference between maintenance and repair. Maintenance includes routine inspections, adjustments, and replacement of parts which show signs of normal wear. Maintenance compensates for wear or deterioration. Repair implies that something has broken or is not working. A need for repair is often caused by lack of maintenance. Example: draining and refilling the automatic transaxle fluid is maintenance recommended by the manufacturer at specific mileage intervals. Failure to do this can shorten the life of the transaxle, requiring very expensive repairs. While no maintenance program can prevent items from breaking or wearing out, a general rule can be stated: MAINTENANCE IS CHEAPER THAN REPAIR.

Two basic technician's rules should be mentioned here. First, whenever the LEFT side of the vehicle or engine is referred to, it is meant to specify the driver's side. The RIGHT side of the vehicle means the passenger's side. Second, screws and bolts are removed by turning counterclockwise, and tightened by turning clockwise unless specifically noted.

Safety is always the most important rule. Constantly be aware of the dangers involved in working on an automobile and take the proper precautions. See the information in this section regarding SERVICING YOUR VEHICLE SAFELY and the SAFETY NOTICE on the acknowledgment page.

Avoiding the Most Common Mistakes

Pay attention to the instructions provided. There are 3 common mistakes in mechanical work:

1. Incorrect order of assembly, disassembly or adjustment. When taking something apart or putting it together, performing steps in the wrong order usually just costs you extra time; however, it CAN break something. Read the entire procedure before beginning disassembly. Perform everything in the order in which the instructions say you should, even if you

can't immediately see a reason for it. When you're taking apart something that is very intricate, you might want to draw a picture of how it looks when assembled at one point in order to make sure you get everything back in its proper position. We supply exploded views whenever possible. When making adjustments, perform them in the proper order. One adjustment possibly will affect another.

2. Overtorquing (or undertorquing). While it is more common for overtorquing to cause damage, undertorquing may allow a fastener to vibrate loose causing serious damage. Pay attention to torque specifications, especially when dealing with aluminum parts. Use a torque wrench during assembly, whenever possible. If a torque figure is not available, remember that if you are using the right tool to perform the job, you will probably not have to strain yourself to get a fastener tight enough. The pitch of most threads is so slight that the tension you put on the wrench will be multiplied many times in actual force on what you are tightening. A good example of how critical torque is can be seen in the case of spark plug installation, especially where you are putting the plug into an aluminum cylinder head. Too little torque can cause a loose fit and allow leakage of combustion gases and consequent overheating of the plug and engine parts. Too much torque can damage the threads or distort the plug, changing the spark gap.

There are commercial "threadlocking compounds" for ensuring that fasteners won't come loose, even if they are not torqued just right (a very common brand is Loctite®). If you're worried about getting something together tight enough to hold, but loose enough to avoid mechanical damage during assembly, one of these products might offer substantial insurance. Before choosing a threadlocking compound, read the label on the package and make sure the product is compatible with the materials, fluids, etc. involved.

3. Crossthreading. This occurs when a part such as a bolt is screwed into a nut or casting at the wrong angle and forced. Crossthreading is more likely to occur if access is difficult. It helps to clean and lubricate fasteners, then to start threading the bolt, spark plug, etc. with your fingers. If you encounter resistance, unscrew the part and start over again at a different angle until it can be inserted and turned several times without much effort. Keep in mind that many parts, especially spark plugs, have tapered threads, so that gentle turning will automatically bring the part you're threading to the proper angle. Don't put a wrench on the part until it's been tightened a couple of turns by hand. If you suddenly encounter resistance, and the part has not seated fully, don't force it. Pull it back out to make sure it's clean and threading properly.

Be sure to take your time and be patient, and always plan ahead. Allow yourself ample time to perform repairs and maintenance. You may find maintaining your car a satisfying and enjoyable experience.

TOOLS AND EQUIPMENT

◆ **See Figures 1 thru 14**

Without the proper tools and equipment it is impossible to properly service your vehicle. It would also be virtually impossible to catalog every tool that you would need to perform all of the operations in this book. Of course, it would be unwise for the amateur to rush out and buy an expensive set of tools on the theory that he/she may need one or more of them at some time.

The best approach is to proceed slowly, gathering a good quality set of those tools that are used most frequently. Don't be misled by the low cost of bargain tools. It is far better to spend a little more for better quality. Forged wrenches, 6 or 12-point sockets and fine tooth ratchets are by far preferable to their less expensive counterparts. As any good mechanic can tell you, there are few worse experiences than trying to work on a vehicle with bad tools. Your monetary savings will be far outweighed by frustration and mangled knuckles.

Begin accumulating those tools that are used most frequently: those associated with routine maintenance and tune-up. In addition to the normal assortment of screwdrivers and pliers, you should have the following tools:

- Wrenches/sockets and combination open end/box-end wrenches in sizes from ⅛ –¾ in. or 3–19mm, as well as a ¹³⁄₁₆ in. or ⅝ in. spark plug socket (depending on plug type).

➡ **If possible, buy various length socket drive extensions. Universal-joint and wobble extensions can be extremely useful, but be careful when using them, as they can change the amount of torque applied to the socket.**

- Jackstands for support.
- Oil filter wrench.
- Spout or funnel for pouring fluids.
- Grease gun for chassis lubrication (unless your vehicle is not equipped with any grease fittings—for details, please refer to information on Fluids and Lubricants, later in this section).

- Hydrometer for checking the battery (unless equipped with a sealed, maintenance-free battery).
- A container for draining oil and other fluids.
- Rags for wiping up the inevitable mess:

In addition to the above items there are several others that are not absolutely necessary, but handy to have around. These include Oil Dry® (or an equivalent oil absorbent gravel—such as cat litter) in case of fluid spills, and the usual supply of lubricants, antifreeze and fluids, although these can be purchased as needed. This is a basic list for routine maintenance, but only your personal needs and desire can accurately determine your list of tools.

After performing a few projects on the vehicle, you'll be amazed at the other tools and non-tools on your workbench. Some useful household items are:

TCCS1200

Fig. 1 All but the most basic procedures will require an assortment of ratchets and sockets

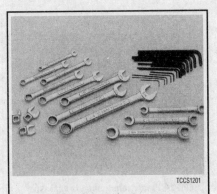

TCCS1201

Fig. 2 In addition to ratchets, a good set of wrenches and hex keys will be necessary

TCCS1202

Fig. 3 A hydraulic floor jack and a set of jackstands are essential for lifting and supporting the vehicle

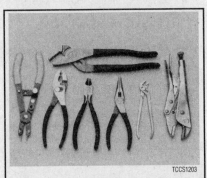

TCCS1203

Fig. 4 An assortment of pliers, grippers and cutters will be handy for old rusted parts and stripped bolt heads

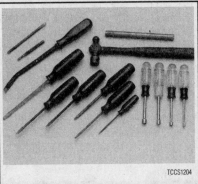

TCCS1204

Fig. 5 Various drivers, chisels and prybars are great tools to have in your toolbox

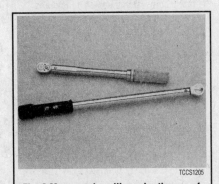

TCCS1205

Fig. 6 Many repairs will require the use of a torque wrench to assure the components are properly fastened

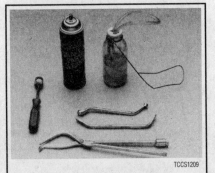

TCCS1209

Fig. 7 Although not always necessary, using specialized brake tools will save time

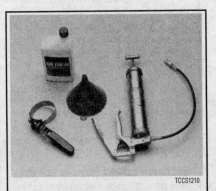

TCCS1210

Fig. 8 A few inexpensive lubrication tools will make maintenance easier

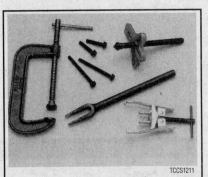

TCCS1211

Fig. 9 Various pullers, clamps and separator tools are needed for many larger, more complicated repairs

Fig. 10 A variety of tools and gauges should be used for spark plug gapping and installation

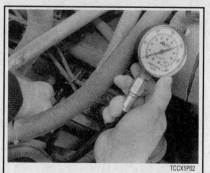

Fig. 11 A screw-in type compression gauge is recommended for compression testing

Fig. 12 A vacuum/pressure tester is necessary for many testing procedures

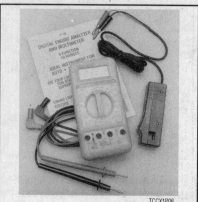

Fig. 13 Most modern automotive multimeters incorporate many helpful features

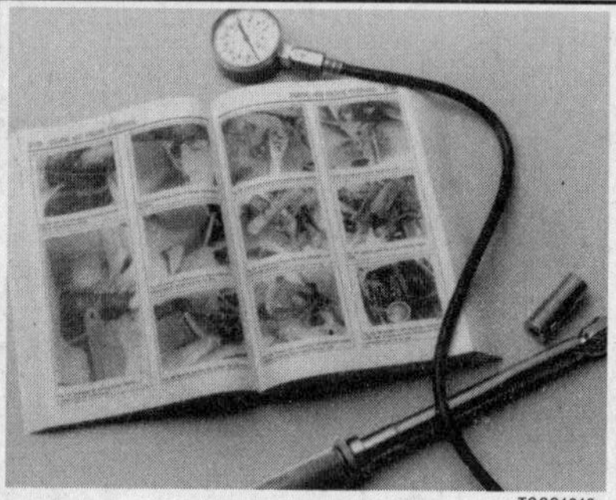

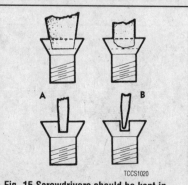

Fig. 14 Proper information is vital, so always have a Chilton Total Car Care manual handy

a large turkey baster or siphon, empty coffee cans and ice trays (to store parts), ball of twine, electrical tape for wiring, small rolls of colored tape for tagging lines or hoses, markers and pens, a note pad, golf tees (for plugging vacuum lines), metal coat hangers or a roll of mechanic's wire (to hold things out of the way), dental pick or similar long, pointed probe, a strong magnet, and a small mirror (to see into recesses and under manifolds).

A list of more advanced set of tools, suitable for tune-up work, can be drawn up easily. The key to these purchases is to make them with an eye towards adaptability and wide range of use. In addition to these basic tools, there are several other tools and gauges you may find useful. These include:

• Spark plug wrench and gapping tool.
• Compression gauge. The screw-in type is slower to use, but eliminates the possibility of a faulty reading due to escaping pressure.
• Manifold vacuum gauge.
• 12V test light.
• A high-impedance digital volt/ohmmeter (commonly called a DVM)

• Induction Ammeter. This is used for determining whether or not there is current in a wire. These are handy for use if a wire is broken somewhere in a wiring harness.

As a final note, you will probably find a torque wrench necessary for all but the most basic work. The beam type models are perfectly adequate, although the newer click types (breakaway) are easier to use. The click type torque wrenches tend to be more expensive. Also keep in mind that all types of torque wrenches should be periodically checked and/or recalibrated. You will have to decide for yourself which better fits your pocketbook, and purpose.

Special Tools

Normally, the use of special factory tools is avoided for repair procedures, since these are not readily available for the do-it-yourself mechanic. When it is possible to perform the job with more commonly available tools, it will be pointed out, but occasionally, a special tool was designed to perform a specific function and should be used. Before substituting another tool, you should be convinced that neither your safety nor the performance of the vehicle will be compromised.

Special tools can usually be purchased from an automotive parts store or from your dealer. In some cases special tools may be available directly from the tool manufacturer.

SERVICING YOUR VEHICLE SAFELY

♦ See Figures 15, 16 and 17

It is virtually impossible to anticipate all of the hazards involved with automotive maintenance and service, but care and common sense will prevent most accidents.

The rules of safety for mechanics range from "don't smoke around gasoline," to "use the proper tool(s) for the job." The key to avoiding injuries is to develop safe work habits, think ahead, plan the procedure and to take every possible precaution.

Do's

• Do keep a fire extinguisher and first aid kit handy.
• Do wear safety glasses or goggles when cutting, drilling, grinding or prying, even if you have 20–20 vision. If you wear glasses for the sake of

Fig. 15 Screwdrivers should be kept in good condition to prevent injury or damage which could result if the blade slips from the screw

Fig. 16 Using the correct size wrench will help prevent the possibility of rounding off a nut

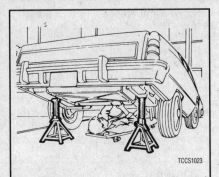

Fig. 17 NEVER work under a vehicle unless it is supported using safety stands (jackstands)

vision, wear safety goggles over your regular glasses.

- Do shield your eyes whenever you work around the battery. Batteries contain sulfuric acid. In case of contact with the eyes or skin, flush the area with water or a mixture of water and baking soda, then seek immediate medical attention.

- Do use safety stands (jackstands) for any undervehicle service. Jacks are for raising vehicles; jackstands are for making sure the vehicle stays raised until you want it to come down. Whenever the vehicle is raised, block the wheels remaining on the ground and set the parking brake.

- Do use adequate ventilation when working with any chemicals or hazardous materials. Like carbon monoxide, the asbestos dust resulting from some brake lining wear can be hazardous in sufficient quantities.

- Do disconnect the negative battery cable when working on the electrical system. The secondary ignition system contains EXTREMELY HIGH VOLTAGE. In some cases it can even exceed 50,000 volts.

- Do follow manufacturer's directions whenever working with potentially hazardous materials. Most chemicals and fluids are poisonous if taken internally.

- Do properly maintain your tools. Loose hammerheads, mushroomed punches and chisels, frayed or poorly grounded electrical cords, excessively worn screwdrivers, spread wrenches (open end), cracked sockets, slipping ratchets, or faulty droplight sockets can cause accidents.

- Likewise, keep your tools clean; a greasy wrench can slip off a bolt head, ruining the bolt and often harming your knuckles in the process.

- Do use the proper size and type of tool for the job at hand. Do select a wrench or socket that fits the nut or bolt. The wrench or socket should sit straight, not cocked.

- Do, when possible, pull on a wrench handle rather than push on it, and adjust your stance to prevent a fall.

- Do be sure that adjustable wrenches are tightly closed on the nut or bolt and pulled so that the force is on the side of the fixed jaw.

- Do strike squarely with a hammer; avoid glancing blows.

- Do set the parking brake and block the drive wheels if the work requires a running engine.

Don'ts

- Don't run the engine in a garage or anywhere else without proper ventilation—EVER! Carbon monoxide is poisonous; it takes a long time to leave the human body and you can build up a deadly supply of it in your system by simply breathing in a little every day. You may not realize you are slowly poisoning yourself. Always use power vents, windows, fans and/or open the garage door.

- Don't work around moving parts while wearing loose clothing. Short sleeves are much safer than long, loose sleeves. Hard-toed shoes with neo-

prene soles protect your toes and give a better grip on slippery surfaces. Jewelry such as watches, fancy belt buckles, beads or body adornment of any kind is not safe working around a vehicle. Long hair should be tied back under a hat or cap.

- Don't use pockets for toolboxes. A fall or bump can drive a screwdriver deep into your body. Even a rag hanging from your back pocket can wrap around a spinning shaft or fan.

- Don't smoke when working around gasoline, cleaning solvent or other flammable material.

- Don't smoke when working around the battery. When the battery is being charged, it gives off explosive hydrogen gas.

- Don't use gasoline to wash your hands; there are excellent soaps and convenient waterless hand cleaners available. Gasoline contains dangerous additives which can enter the body through a cut or through your pores. Gasoline also removes all the natural oils from the skin. Dry hands will absorb oil and grease.

- Don't service the air conditioning system unless you are equipped with the necessary tools and training. When liquid or compressed gas refrigerant is released to atmospheric pressure it will absorb heat from whatever it contacts. This will chill or freeze anything it touches.

- Don't use screwdrivers for anything other than driving screws! A screwdriver used as an prying tool can snap when you least expect it, causing injuries. At the very least, you'll ruin a good screwdriver.

- Don't use an emergency jack (that little ratchet, scissors, or pantograph jack supplied with the vehicle) for anything other than changing a flat! These jacks are only intended for emergency use out on the road; they are NOT designed as a maintenance tool. If you are serious about maintaining your vehicle yourself, invest in a hydraulic floor jack of at least a 1½ ton capacity, and at least two sturdy jackstands.

FASTENERS, MEASUREMENTS AND CONVERSIONS

Bolts, Nuts and Other Threaded Retainers

♦ See Figures 18, 19 and 20

Although there are a great variety of fasteners found in the modern car or truck, the most commonly used retainer is the threaded fastener (nuts, bolts, screws, studs, etc.). Most threaded retainers may be reused, provided that they are not damaged in use or during the repair. Some retainers (such as stretch bolts or torque prevailing nuts) are designed to deform when tightened or in use and should not be reinstalled.

Whenever possible, we will note any special retainers which should be replaced during a procedure. But you should always inspect the condition of a retainer when it is removed and replace any that show signs of damage. Check all threads for rust or corrosion which can increase the torque necessary to achieve the desired clamp load for which that fastener was originally selected. Additionally, be sure that the driver surface of the fastener has not been compromised by rounding or other damage. In some cases a driver surface may become only partially rounded, allowing the driver

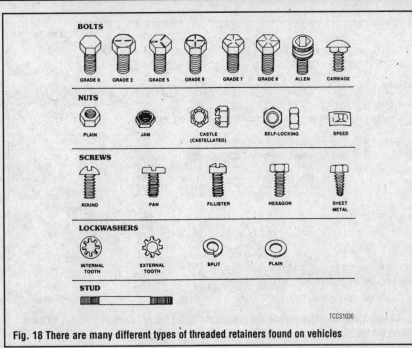

Fig. 18 There are many different types of threaded retainers found on vehicles

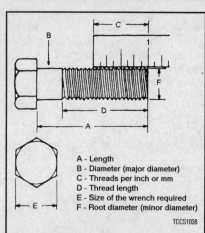

A - Length
B - Diameter (major diameter)
C - Threads per inch or mm
D - Thread length
E - Size of the wrench required
F - Root diameter (minor diameter)

TCCS1038

Fig. 19 Threaded retainer sizes are determined using these measurements

to catch in only one direction. In many of these occurrences, a fastener may be installed and tightened, but the driver would not be able to grip and loosen the fastener again. This could lead to difficulties at a later date should that component ever need to be disassembled again.

If you must replace a fastener, whether due to design or damage, you must ALWAYS be sure to use the proper replacement. The vehicles covered by this book are of metric design. Care must be taken when obtaining replacement fasteners to make sure they will fit properly. There are different thread pitches on metric fasteners and the they must not be mixed. In all cases, a retainer of the same design, material and strength should be used. Markings on the heads of most bolts will help determine the proper strength of the fastener. The same material, thread and pitch must be selected to assure proper installation and safe operation of the vehicle afterwards.

Thread gauges are available to help measure a bolt or stud's thread. Most automotive and hardware stores keep gauges available to help you select the

proper size. Another way to check threads is to use another nut or bolt of known size, for a thread gauge. If the bolt being replaced is not too badly damaged, select a match by finding another bolt which will thread in its place. If you find a nut which threads properly onto the damaged bolt, then use that nut to help select the replacement bolt. If, however, the bolt being replacing is so badly damaged (broken or drilled out) that its threads cannot be used as a gauge, look for another bolt (from the same assembly or a similar location on your vehicle) which will thread into the damaged bolt's mounting. If the other bolt can be used as a sample to select a nut; the nut can then be used to select the replacement bolt. In all cases, be absolutely sure you have selected the proper replacement.

✺✺✺ WARNING

Be aware that when you find a bolt with damaged threads, you may also find the nut or drilled hole it was threaded into has also been damaged. If this is the case, you may have to drill and tap the hole, replace the nut or otherwise repair the threads. NEVER try to force a replacement bolt to fit into the damaged threads.

Torque

Torque is defined as the measurement of resistance to turning or rotating. It tends to twist a body about an axis of rotation. A common example of this would be tightening a threaded retainer such as a nut, bolt or screw. Measuring torque is one of the most common ways to help assure that a threaded retainer has been properly fastened.

When tightening a threaded fastener, torque is applied in three distinct areas, the head, the bearing surface and the clamp load. About 50 percent of the measured torque is used in overcoming bearing friction. This is the friction between the bearing surface of the bolt head, screw head or nut face and the base material or washer (the surface on which the

fastener is rotating). Approximately 40 percent of the applied torque is used in overcoming thread friction. This leaves only about 10 percent of the applied torque to develop a useful clamp load (the force which holds a joint together). This means that friction can account for as much as 90 percent of the applied torque on a fastener.

This shows the need to always have clean threads when assembling parts. Old sealer, rust and corrosion on threaded parts open to the cooling system and age can all cause build-up or damage to threaded fasteners.

TORQUE WRENCHES

▶ See Figures 21 and 22

In most applications, a torque wrench can be used to assure proper installation of a fastener. Torque wrenches come in various designs and most automotive supply stores will carry a variety to suit your needs. A torque wrench should be used any time we supply a specific torque value for a fastener. A torque wrench can also be used if you are following the general guidelines in the accompanying charts. Keep in mind that because there is no worldwide standardization of fasteners, the charts are a general guideline and should be used with caution. Again, the general rule of "if you are using the right tool for the job, you should not have to strain to tighten a fastener" applies here.

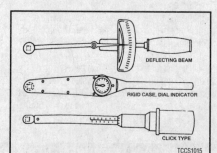

DEFLECTING BEAM

RIGID CASE, DIAL INDICATOR

CLICK TYPE

TCCS1015

Fig. 21 Various styles of torque wrenches are usually available at your local automotive supply store

Beam Type

▶ See Figures 23 and 24

The beam type torque wrench is one of the most popular types. It consists of a pointer attached to the head that runs the length of the flexible beam (shaft) to a scale located near the handle. As the wrench is pulled, the beam bends and the pointer indicates the torque using the scale. Many technicians still use this type of torque wrench especially the smaller ⅜-drive wrenches, when low torque settings are specified that would be difficult to set-up on a click-type foot-pound wrench. For example, a specification of only 6 ft. lbs. would be difficult to set on most click-type foot-pound wrenches. The solution is to multiply the ft. lbs. specification by 12 (6 ft. lbs. x 12 = 72 inch lbs.) to get an inch lbs. specification, as demonstrated here.

Click (Breakaway) Type

Another popular design of torque wrench is the click type. To use the click type wrench you pre-

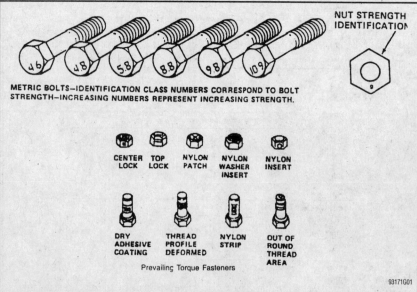

NUT STRENGTH IDENTIFICATION

METRIC BOLTS—IDENTIFICATION CLASS NUMBERS CORRESPOND TO BOLT STRENGTH—INCREASING NUMBERS REPRESENT INCREASING STRENGTH.

CENTER LOCK | TOP LOCK | NYLON PATCH | NYLON WASHER INSERT | NYLON INSERT

DRY ADHESIVE COATING | THREAD PROFILE DEFORMED | NYLON STRIP | OUT OF ROUND THREAD AREA

Prevailing Torque Fasteners

93171G01

Fig. 20 Metric bolt identification and the types of prevailing torque fasteners that may be found on your GM vehicle

adjust it to a torque setting. Once the torque is reached, the wrench has a reflex signaling feature that causes a momentary breakaway of the torque wrench body, sending an impulse to the operator's hand.

Some torque wrenches (usually of the click type) may be equipped with a pivot head which can allow it to be used in areas of limited access. BUT, it must be used properly. To hold a pivot head wrench, grasp the handle lightly, and as you pull on the handle, it should be floated on the pivot point. If the handle comes in contact with the yoke extension during the process of pulling, there is a very good chance the torque readings will be inaccurate because this could alter the wrench loading point. The design of the handle is usually such as to make it inconvenient to deliberately misuse the wrench.

➡ It should be mentioned that the use of any socket wrench universal joint, wobble extension or extra length extension will have an effect on the torque readings, no matter what type of wrench you are using. For the most accurate readings, install the socket directly on the wrench driver. If necessary, straight extensions (which hold a socket directly under the wrench driver) will have the least effect on the torque reading. Avoid any extension that alters the length of the wrench from the handle to the head/driving point (such as a crow's foot). A socket wrench universal joint, or wobble extensions can greatly affect the readings; avoid their use at all times.

Rigid Case (Direct Reading)

A rigid case or direct reading torque wrench is equipped with a dial indicator to show torque values. One advantage of these wrenches is that they can be held at any position on the wrench without affecting accuracy. These wrenches are often preferred because they tend to be compact, easy to read and have a great degree of accuracy.

TORQUE ANGLE METERS

▸ **See Figure 25**

Because the frictional characteristics of each fastener or threaded hole will vary, clamp loads which are based strictly on torque will vary as well. In most applications, this variance is not significant enough to cause worry. But, in certain applications, a manufacturer's engineers may determine that more precise clamp loads are necessary (such is the case with many aluminum cylinder heads). In these cases, a torque angle method of installation would be specified. When installing fasteners which are torque angle tightened, a predetermined seating torque and standard torque wrench are usually used first to remove any compliance from the joint. The fastener is then tightened the specified additional portion of a turn measured in degrees. A torque

Class	Diameter mm	Pitch mm	Specified torque					
			Hexagon head bolt			Hexagon flange bolt		
			N·m	kgf·cm	ft·lbf	N·m	kgf·cm	ft·lbf
4T	6	1	5	55	48 in.·lbf	6	60	52 in.·lbf
	8	1.25	12.5	130	9	14	145	10
	10	1.25	26	260	19	29	290	21
	12	1.25	47	480	35	53	540	39
	14	1.5	74	760	55	84	850	61
	16	1.5	115	1,150	83	—	—	—
5T	6	1	6.5	65	56 in.·lbf	7.5	75	65 in.·lbf
	8	1.25	15.5	160	12	17.5	175	13
	10	1.25	32	330	24	36	360	26
	12	1.25	59	600	43	65	670	48
	14	1.5	91	930	67	100	1,050	76
	16	1.5	140	1,400	101	—	—	—
6T	6	1	8	80	69 in.·lbf	9	90	78 in.·lbf
	8	1.25	19	195	14	21	210	15
	10	1.25	39	400	29	44	440	32
	12	1.25	71	730	53	80	810	59
	14	1.5	110	1,100	80	125	1,250	90
	16	1.5	170	1,750	127	—	—	—
7T	6	1	10.5	110	8	12	120	9
	8	1.25	25	260	19	28	290	21
	10	1.25	52	530	38	58	590	43
	12	1.25	95	970	70	105	1,050	76
	14	1.5	145	1,500	108	165	1,700	123
	16	1.5	230	2,300	166	—	—	—
8T	8	1.25	29	300	22	33	330	24
	10	1.25	61	620	45	68	690	50
	12	1.25	110	1,100	80	120	1,250	90
9T	8	1.25	34	340	25	37	380	27
	10	1.25	70	710	51	78	790	57
	12	1.25	125	1,300	94	140	1,450	105
10T	8	1.25	38	390	28	42	430	31
	10	1.25	78	800	58	88	890	64
	12	1.25	140	1,450	105	155	1,600	116
11T	8	1.25	42	430	31	47	480	35
	10	1.25	87	890	64	97	990	72
	12	1.25	155	1,600	116	175	1,800	130

TCCS1041

Fig. 22 Torque wrenches with pivoting heads must be grasped and used properly to prevent an incorrect reading

93176P09

Fig. 23 This inch pound beam-type torque wrench is being used because the low torque settings specified would be difficult to set-up on a foot pound wrench

93176P10

Fig. 24 Simply multiply a ft. lbs. torque specification by twelve to get the inch lbs. equivalent and read it off the pointer scale

TCCS1043

Fig. 25 Some specifications require the use of a torque angle meter (mechanical protractor)

angle gauge (mechanical protractor) is used for these applications.

As an example of the importance of always using the correct fastener is the cylinder head bolts. These bolts are designed to permanently stretch when tightened. The correct part number must be used to replace this type of fastener. Do not use a bolt that is stronger in this application. If the correct bolt is not used, the parts will not be tightened correctly. The components will likely be damaged. It is good practice to always use new, factory service replacement head bolts.

Standard and Metric Measurements

▶ See Figure 26

Throughout this manual, specifications are given to help you determine the condition of various components on your vehicle, or to assist you in their installation. Some of the most common measurements include length (in. or cm/mm), torque (ft. lbs., inch lbs. or Nm) and pressure (psi, in. Hg, kPa or mm Hg). In most cases, we strive to provide the proper measurement as determined by the manufacturer's engineers.

In some cases, that value may not be conveniently measured with what is available in your toolbox. Fortunately, many of the measuring devices which are available today will have two scales so the Standard or Metric measurements may easily be taken. If any of the various measuring tools which are available to you do not contain the same scale as listed in the specifications, use the accompanying conversion factors to determine the proper value.

The conversion factor chart is used by taking the given specification and multiplying it by the necessary conversion factor. For instance, looking at the first line, if you have a measurement in inches such as "free-play should be 2 in." but your ruler reads only in millimeters, multiply 2 in. by the conversion factor of 25.4 to get the metric equivalent of 50.8mm. Likewise, if the specification was given only in a Metric measurement, for example in Newton Meters (Nm), then look at the center column first. If the measurement is 100 Nm, multiply it by the conversion factor of 0.738 to get 73.8 ft. lbs.

CONVERSION FACTORS

LENGTH–DISTANCE

Inches (in.)	x 25.4	= Millimeters (mm)	x .0394	= Inches
Feet (ft.)	x .305	= Meters (m)	x 3.281	= Feet
Miles	x 1.609	= Kilometers (km)	x .0621	= Miles

VOLUME

Cubic Inches (in3)	x 16.387	= Cubic Centimeters	x .061	= in3
IMP Pints (IMP pt.)	x .568	= Liters (L)	x 1.76	= IMP pt.
IMP Quarts (IMP qt.)	x 1.137	= Liters (L)	x .88	= IMP qt.
IMP Gallons (IMP gal.)	x 4.546	= Liters (L)	x .22	= IMP gal.
IMP Quarts (IMP qt.)	x 1.201	= US Quarts (US qt.)	x .833	= IMP qt.
IMP Gallons (IMP gal.)	x 1.201	= US Gallons (US gal.)	x .833	= IMP gal.
Fl. Ounces	x 29.573	= Milliliters	x .034	= Ounces
US Pints (US pt.)	x .473	= Liters (L)	x 2.113	= Pints
US Quarts (US qt.)	x .946	= Liters (L)	x 1.057	= Quarts
US Gallons (US gal.)	x 3.785	= Liters (L)	x .264	= Gallons

MASS–WEIGHT

Ounces (oz.)	x 28.35	= Grams (g)	x .035	= Ounces
Pounds (lb.)	x .454	= Kilograms (kg)	x 2.205	= Pounds

PRESSURE

Pounds Per Sq. In. (psi)	x 6.895	= Kilopascals (kPa)	x .145	= psi
Inches of Mercury (Hg)	x .4912	= psi	x 2.036	= Hg
Inches of Mercury (Hg)	x 3.377	= Kilopascals (kPa)	x .2961	= Hg
Inches of Water (H_2O)	x .07355	= Inches of Mercury	x 13.783	= H_2O
Inches of Water (H_2O)	x .03613	= psi	x 27.684	= H_2O
Inches of Water (H_2O)	x .248	= Kilopascals (kPa)	x 4.026	= H_2O

TORQUE

Pounds–Force Inches (in–lb)	x .113	= Newton Meters (N·m)	x 8.85	= in–lb
Pounds–Force Feet (ft–lb)	x 1.356	= Newton Meters (N·m)	x .738	= ft–lb

VELOCITY

Miles Per Hour (MPH)	x 1.609	= Kilometers Per Hour (KPH)	x .621	= MPH

POWER

Horsepower (Hp)	x .745	= Kilowatts	x 1.34	= Horsepower

FUEL CONSUMPTION*

Miles Per Gallon IMP (MPG)	x .354	= Kilometers Per Liter (Km/L)	
Kilometers Per Liter (Km/L)	x 2.352	= IMP MPG	
Miles Per Gallon US (MPG)	x .425	= Kilometers Per Liter (Km/L)	
Kilometers Per Liter (Km/L)	x 2.352	= US MPG	

*It is common to covert from miles per gallon (mpg) to liters/100 kilometers (1/100 km), where mpg (IMP) x 1/100 km = 282 and mpg (US) x 1/100 km = 235.

TEMPERATURE

Degree Fahrenheit (°F)	= (°C x 1.8) + 32
Degree Celsius (°C)	= (°F – 32) x .56

TCCS1044

Fig. 26 Standard and metric conversion factors chart

SERIAL NUMBER IDENTIFICATION

Vehicle

▶ See Figures 27 and 28

All of the vehicles covered by this book are built on a similar platform; GM calls them a W-Body. Other GM vehicles have their own platform designations. The Vehicle Identification number (VIN) plate is located on the left upper instrument panel and is visible from the outside of the vehicle at the lower left (driver's side) of the windshield. The VIN consists of 17 characters. Each sequential build unit number is prefixed by eleven letters and numbers. These numbers are an important source of identification for your vehicle and its equipment. The fourth and fifth positions of the VIN identify the model (series, this case, W-Body) and body style

93171P89

Fig. 27 The VIN is visible through the windshield of your vehicle

of the vehicle. The eighth digit is the engine code and the 10th letter represents the model year (in this case, V=1997, W=1998, X=1999, and Y=2000).

Engine

▶ See Figures 29, 30, 31 and 32

The eighth VIN position identifies the engine. This is important since many parts books require the engine VIN to correctly identify the engine. For example, this book covers a 3.8L (VIN K) engine and a 3.8L (VIN 1) engine. The VIN K engine is normally aspirated while the VIN 1 engine is supercharged. Knowing the correct VIN of the engine is key to getting the correct replacement parts.

VEHICLE IDENTIFICATION CHART

Engine Code

Code	Liters	Cu. In. (cc)	Cyl.	Fuel Sys.	Eng. Mfg.
M	3.1	191 (3135)	6	SFI	GM
X	3.4	204 (3350)	6	SFI	GM
E	3.4	196 (3206)	6	SFI	GM
H	3.5	212 (3474)	6	SFI	GM
1	3.8	231 (3791)	6	SFI/SC	GM
K	3.8	231 (3791)	6	SFI	GM

Model Year

Code	Year
V	1997
W	1998
X	1999
Y	2000

SFI-Sequential Fuel Injection

SFI/SC-Sequential Fuel Injection/Supercharged

Note: Engine VIN is 8th digit of the Vehicle Indentification Number (VIN)

Model Year VIN is the 10th letter of the Vehicle Identification Number (VIN)

93171C01

GENERAL ENGINE SPECIFICATIONS

Year	Model	Engine ID/VIN	Engine Displacement Liters (cc)	No. of Cyl.	Engine Type	Fuel System Type	Net Horsepower @ rpm	Net Torque @ rpm (ft. lbs.)	Bore x Stroke (in.)	Compression Ratio	Oil Pressure @ rpm
1997	Cutlass Supreme	M	3.1 (3135)	6	OHV	SFI	160@5200	185@4000	3.51 x 3.31	9.5:1	15@1100
	Cutlass Supreme	X	3.4 (3350)	6	DOHC	SFI	215@5200	220@4400	3.62 x 3.31	9.5:1	15@1100
	Grand Prix	M	3.1 (3135)	6	OHV	SFI	160@5200	185@4000	3.51 x 3.31	9.5:1	15@1100
	Grand Prix	X	3.4 (3350)	6	DOHC	SFI	215@5200	220@4400	3.62 x 3.31	9.5:1	15@1100
	Grand Prix	1	3.8 (3791)	6	OHV	SFI/SC	240@5200	280@3200	3.79 x 3.39	8.5:1	60@1850
	Grand Prix	K	3.8 (3791)	6	OHV	SFI	195@5200	220@4000	3.79 x 3.39	9.4:1	60@1850
	Lumina	M	3.1 (3135)	6	OHV	SFI	160@5200	185@4000	3.51 x 3.31	9.5:1	15@1100
	Lumina	X	3.4 (3350)	6	DOHC	SFI	215@5200	220@4400	3.62 x 3.31	9.5:1	15@1100
	Monte Carlo	M	3.1 (3135)	6	OHV	SFI	160@5200	185@4000	3.51 x 3.31	9.5:1	15@1100
	Monte Carlo	X	3.4 (3350)	6	DOHC	SFI	215@5200	220@4400	3.62 x 3.31	9.5:1	15@1100
	Regal	M	3.1 (3135)	6	OHV	SFI	160@5200	185@4000	3.51 x 3.31	9.5:1	15@1100
	Regal	K	3.8 (3791)	6	OHV	SFI	195@5200	220@4000	3.79 x 3.39	9.4:1	71@3000
	Century	M	3.1 (3135)	6	OHV	SFI	160@5200	185@4000	3.51 x 3.31	9.5:1	15@1100
1998	Grand Prix	M	3.1 (3135)	6	OHV	SFI	160@5200	185@4000	3.51 x 3.31	9.5:1	15@1100
	Grand Prix	1	3.8 (3791)	6	OHV	SFI/SC	240@5200	280@3200	3.79 x 3.39	9.4:1	60@1850
	Grand Prix	K	3.8 (3791)	6	OHV	SFI	195@5200	220@4000	3.79 x 3.39	9.4:1	60@1850
	Lumina	M	3.1 (3135)	6	OHV	SFI	160@5200	185@4000	3.51 x 3.31	9.5:1	15@1100
	Lumina	K	3.8 (3791)	6	OHV	SFI	200@5200	225@4000	3.79 x 3.39	9.4:1	60@1850
	Monte Carlo	M	3.1 (3135)	6	OHV	SFI	160@5200	185@4000	3.51 x 3.31	9.5:1	15@1100
	Monte Carlo	K	3.8 (3791)	6	OHV	SFI	200@5200	225@4000	3.79 x 3.39	9.4:1	60@1850
	Regal	M	3.1 (3135)	6	OHV	SFI	160@5200	185@4000	3.51 x 3.31	9.5:1	15@1100
	Regal	K	3.8 (3791)	6	OHV	SFI	195@5200	220@4000	3.79 x 3.39	9.4:1	60@1850
	Regal	1	3.8 (3791)	6	OHV	SFI/SC	240@5200	280@3600	3.79 x 3.39	8.5:1	60@1850
	Century	M	3.1 (3135)	6	OHV	SFI	160@5200	185@4000	3.51 x 3.31	9.5:1	15@1100
	Intrigue	K	3.8 (3791)	6	OHV	SFI	195@5200	220@4000	3.79 x 3.39	9.4:1	60@1850
1999	Grand Prix	M	3.1 (3135)	6	OHV	SFI	160@5200	185@4000	3.51 x 3.31	9.5:1	15@1100
	Grand Prix	1	3.8 (3791)	6	OHV	SFI/SC	240@5200	280@3200	3.79 x 3.39	9.4:1	60@1850
	Grand Prix	K	3.8 (3791)	6	OHV	SFI	200@5200	225@4000	3.79 x 3.39	9.4:1	60@1850
	Lumina	M	3.1 (3135)	6	OHV	SFI	160@5200	185@4000	3.51 x 3.31	9.5:1	15@1100
	Lumina	K	3.8 (3791)	6	OHV	SFI	200@5200	225@4000	3.79 x 3.39	9.4:1	60@1850
	Monte Carlo	M	3.1 (3135)	6	OHV	SFI	160@5200	185@4000	3.51 x 3.31	9.5:1	15@1100
	Monte Carlo	K	3.8 (3791)	6	OHV	SFI	200@5200	225@4000	3.79 x 3.39	9.4:1	60@1850
	Regal	K	3.8 (3791)	6	OHV	SFI	200@5200	225@4000	3.79 x 3.39	9.4:1	60@1850
	Regal	1	3.8 (3791)	6	OHV	SFI/SC	240@5200	280@3600	3.79 x 3.39	8.5:1	60@1850
	Century	M	3.1 (3135)	6	OHV	SFI	160@5200	185@4000	3.51 x 3.31	9.5:1	15@1100
	Intrigue	K	3.8 (3791)	6	OHV	SFI	195@5200	220@4000	3.79 x 3.39	9.4:1	60@1850
	Intrigue	H	3.5 (3473)	6	DOHC	SFI	215@5600	230@4400	3.52 x 3.62	9.3:1	29@2000
2000	Grand Prix	M	3.1 (3135)	6	OHV	SFI	175@5200	195@4000	3.51 x 3.31	9.5:1	15@1100
	Grand Prix	1	3.8 (3791)	6	OHV	SFI/SC	240@5200	280@3200	3.79 x 3.39	8.5:1	60@1850
	Grand Prix	K	3.8 (3791)	6	OHV	SFI	200@5200	225@4000	3.79 x 3.39	9.4:1	60@1850
	Lumina	M	3.1 (3135)	6	OHV	SFI	160@5200	185@4000	3.51 x 3.31	9.5:1	15@1100
	Lumina	K	3.8 (3791)	6	OHV	SFI	200@5200	225@4000	3.79 x 3.39	9.4:1	60@1850
	Monte Carlo	M	3.1 (3135)	6	OHV	SFI	160@5200	185@4000	3.51 x 3.31	9.5:1	15@1100
	Monte Carlo	E	3.4 (3206)	6	OHV	SFI	180@5200	205@4000	3.62 x 3.31	9.6:1	60@1850
	Monte Carlo	K	3.8 (3791)	6	OHV	SFI	200@5200	225@4000	3.79 x 3.39	9.4:1	60@1850
	Regal	1	3.8 (3791)	6	OHV	SFI/SC	240@5200	280@3200	3.79 x 3.39	8.5:1	60@1850
	Regal	K	3.8 (3791)	6	OHV	SFI	200@5200	225@4000	3.79 x 3.39	9.4:1	60@1850
	Century	M	3.1 (3135)	6	OHV	SFI	160@5200	185@4000	3.51 x 3.31	9.5:1	15@1100
	Intrigue	H	3.5 (3473)	6	DOHC	SFI	215@5600	230@4400	3.52 x 3.62	9.3:1	29@2000

93171C02

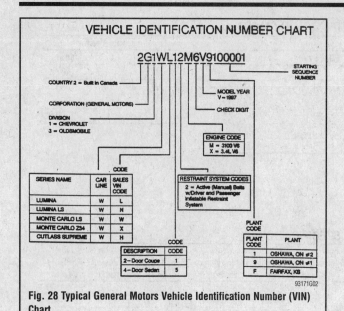

Fig. 28 Typical General Motors Vehicle Identification Number (VIN) Chart

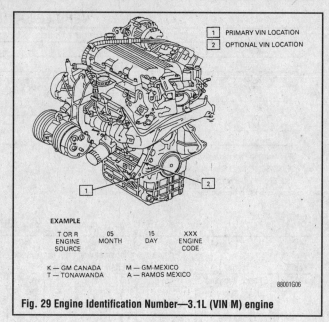

Fig. 29 Engine Identification Number—3.1L (VIN M) engine

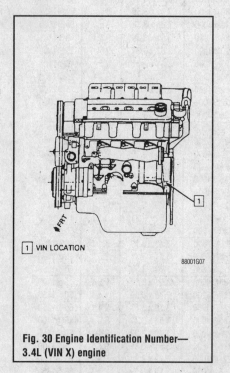

Fig. 30 Engine Identification Number— 3.4L (VIN X) engine

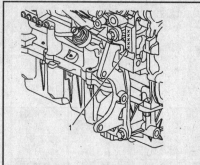

The Vehicle Identification Number (VIN) Derivative is located on the right front side of the engine block (1) and is a nine digit number stamped or laser etched onto the engine at the vehicle assembly plant. If reading the identification number the following information can be obtained:

- The first digit identifies the vehicle division.
- The second digit is the model year.
- The third digit identifies the assembly plant.
- The fourth through ninth digits are the last six digits of the Vehicle Identification Number (VIN).

Fig. 31 Engine Identification Number— 3.5L (VIN H) engine

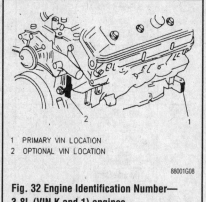

Fig. 32 Engine Identification Number— 3.8L (VIN K and 1) engines

Transaxle

♦ See Figure 33

All transaxles are stamped with a partial Vehicle Identification Number. The stamping contains nine positions. Transaxle model and serial number identification can be found on the transaxle identification plate and the Goodwrench® tag.

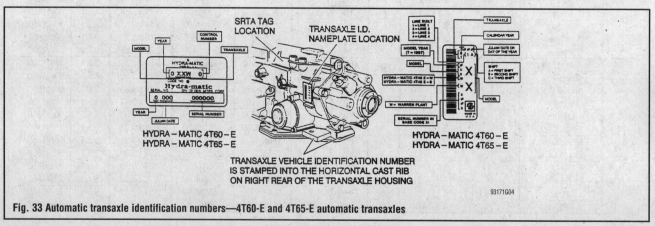

Fig. 33 Automatic transaxle identification numbers—4T60-E and 4T65-E automatic transaxles

ROUTINE MAINTENANCE AND TUNE-UP

▶ See Figures 34 and 35

UNDERHOOD MAINTENANCE COMPONENT LOCATIONS—3.5L ENGINE

1. Battery
2. Engine oil fill cap
3. Engine oil dipstick
4. Engine struts (wishbones)
5. Diagonal braces
6. Upper radiator hose
7. Air cleaner assembly
8. Brake fluid reservoir
9. Transaxle fluid dipstick
10. Coolant reservoir
11. Engine cosmetic/acoustic cover
12. Power steering reservoir fill cap

93171PX3

UNDERHOOD MAINTENANCE COMPONENT LOCATIONS—3.8L (VIN K) ENGINE

1. Battery—
2. Radiator cap (do not open hot)
3. Spark plug wires (coil ends)
4. Engine struts (wishbone)
5. Engine oil dipstick
6. Engine oil fill cap
7. Engine cosmetic/acoustic cover
8. Upper radiator hose
9. Air cleaner assembly
10. Coolant reservoir
11. Diagonal braces
12. Brake fluid reservoir
13. Transaxle fluid dipstick
14. Accessory drive belt
15. Belt routing label
16. Windshield washer fluid reservoir

93171PX4

UNDERHOOD MAINTENANCE COMPONENT LOCATIONS—3.8L (VIN 1) ENGINE

1. Battery
2. Radiator cap (do not open hot)
3. Belt routing label
4. Spark plug wires (coil ends)
5. Engine struts (wishbones)
6. Engine oil dipstick
7. Engine oil fill cap
8. Engine cosmetic/acoustic cover
9. Upper radiator hose
10. Air cleaner assembly
11. Diagonal braces
12. Brake fluid reservoir
13. Transaxle fluid dipstick
14. Coolant reservoir
15. Accessory drive belt
16. Supercharger drive belt

Proper maintenance and tune-up is the key to long and trouble-free vehicle life, and the work can yield its own rewards. The vehicle's Powertrain Control Module (PCM), a computer that controls most driveline related functions, controls many of the functions that at one time, were considered part of a standard tune-up. Mixture adjustment and engine ignition timing are now all controlled by the PCM. No adjustment is possible on these systems. Engine valves no longer need periodic lash adjustment since they are hydraulic and no adjustment is required. So underhood tune-up has taken on a new meaning, generally being centered around engine oil and filter changes, spark plug changes and

maintaining the cooling system. Owners are encouraged to set aside time to check or replace items which could cause major problems later. Keep a personal log of services performed, how much the parts cost and the exact odometer reading at the time of service work. Keep all receipts for such items as engine oil and filters, so that they may be referred to in case of related problems or to determine operating expenses. These receipts are the only proof you have that the required maintenance was performed. In the event of a warranty problem, these receipts will be valuable.

The literature provided with your vehicle when it was originally delivered includes the factory recom-

mended maintenance schedule, found in the owner's manual. If you no longer have this information, replacement copies can usually be ordered from the dealer. A maintenance schedule is provided later in this section, in case you do not have the factory literature.

A number of labels will be found underhood with warnings, cautions, fluid specifications for coolant and accessory drive belt routing. A few examples are given here.

Air Cleaner (Element)

REMOVAL & INSTALLATION

3.1L Engine—Type I

▶ See Figures 36 thru 43

There are several air cleaner types used on these vehicles with this engine. The procedure is similar and the air filter element is easily serviced on all vehicles.

1. Disconnect the retainer clips (or remove the screws, depending on the vehicle) in the air cleaner cover and separate the cover from the air cleaner housing.
2. Remove the air filter element.

To install:

3. Clean the air cleaner housing to remove dirt and debris. Inspect the filter element for excessive dirt and dust. Replace if necessary.
4. Position the filter element in the housing using care to see that it is properly seated.

Fig. 34 The larger of the labels shown here is the Vehicle Emission Certification Information (VECI) label which also includes some tune-up specifications

Fig. 35 Late-model GM products use a special long-life coolant called DEX-COOL® that can NOT be mixed with other brands or types of coolant

Fig. 36 On this 3.1L engine, unfasten the retaining screws . . .

Fig. 37 . . . then lift the lid and remove the air cleaner element

Fig. 38 On this 3.1L engine, the clamp retaining the flexible air intake hose was loosened with a screwdriver so the hose could be disconnected from the upper lid of the air cleaner housing

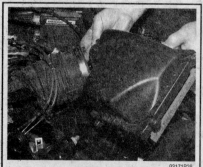

Fig. 39 The upper lid of the air cleaner housing was removed and separated from the air intake hose

Fig. 40 The air filter element simply lifts out of the lower part of the air filter housing

Fig. 41 The air filter element looks like it was overdue for a change and was covered with dirt

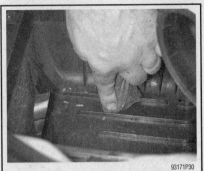

Fig. 42 An air filter element change isn't complete without a thorough cleaning of the air filter element housing

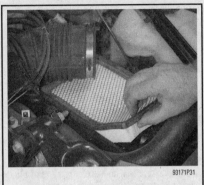

Fig. 43 A new air filter element is installed and the housing reassembled

Fig. 44 On this 3.8L Grand Prix, the air filter housing is held together with clips

5. Place the cover into position on the housing and secure with the latching clips.

3.1L Engine—Type II and 3.8L Engine

▶ See Figures 44 thru 48

1. Locate and disconnect the Intake Air Temperature (IAT) sensor electrical plug.
2. Locate and disconnect the Mass Air Flow (MAF) sensor electrical plug.
3. Loosen the air intake duct/MAF sensor hose clamps and remove the duct/MAF sensor assembly.

4. Carefully remove the air inlet hose from the throttle body and air cleaner cover.
5. Remove the two housing cover retaining clamps.
6. Remove the air cleaner cover and remove the air filter element.
7. Inspect the housing cover, seal assembly and air ducting for damage. If a problem is found, replace as necessary.

To install:

8. Clean the air cleaner housing to remove dirt and debris. Inspect the filter element for excessive dirt and dust. Replace if necessary.

9. Carefully install the air filter element into the air cleaner assembly.
10. Reinstall the housing cover and housing cover retaining screws.
11. Install the air inlet hose to the throttle body and air cleaner cover. Tighten the clamp.
12. Install the air intake duct/MAF sensor assembly and tighten the hose clamps
13. Carefully plug in the MAF and IAT sensor electrical connectors.

3.4L (VIN E and X) and 3.5L (VIN H) Engines

▶ See Figure 49

1. Locate and remove the four retaining screws and the housing cover from the air cleaner assembly.
2. Carefully remove the air filter element.

To install:

3. Clean the air cleaner housing to remove dirt and debris. Inspect the filter element for excessive dirt and dust. Replace if necessary.
4. Install the replacement air filter element into the air cleaner assembly.
5. Install the housing cover and the four retaining screws on the air cleaner assembly.

Fuel Filter

▶ See Figure 50

⁕⁕ CAUTION

Observe all applicable safety precautions when working around fuel. Whenever ser-

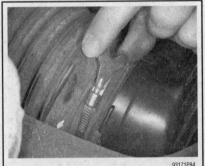

Fig. 45 The clamp retaining the flexible air intake hose has a wing nut-like fitting so no tools are required to loosen the clamp that secures the hose to the upper lid of the air cleaner housing

Fig. 46 As you can never know what to expect, this low-mileage 3.8L Grand Prix had an opening in the flexible air intake hose, apparently chewed through by mice. This large hole was on the clean side of the air filter which means unfiltered air was getting into the engine

Fig. 47 This debris left by the mice meant that the air filter housing had to be removed for a thorough cleaning

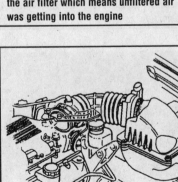

Fig. 48 Another variation of the air induction arrangement and filter housing

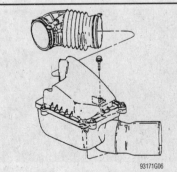

Fig. 49 Air filter housing. 1997 Lumina, Monte Carlo and Cutlass Supreme with 3.4L (VIN X) engine

vicing the fuel system, **always work in a well ventilated area. Do not allow fuel spray or vapors to come in contact with a spark or open flame. Keep a dry chemical fire extinguisher near the work area. Always keep fuel in a container specifically designed for fuel storage; also, always properly seal fuel containers to avoid the possibility of fire or explosion.**

A fuel filter is used in the fuel feed pipe ahead of the fuel injection system. The fuel filter housing is steel with a quick-connect fitting at the inlet of the fuel filter and a threaded fitting at the outlet of the filter. The threaded fitting is sealed with an O-ring, which is replaceable. The filter element is paper and is designed to trap particles suspended in the fuel that may damage the injection system. The fuel filter on these vehicles is attached to the underbody, in front of the fuel tank. Note that there are no service intervals for in-line fuel filter replacement. Only replace the filter if performance problems or troubleshooting indicates the filter is restricted.

Care is required when working around the fuel feed and return pipes. Many vehicles now use nylon fuel pipes, designed to perform the same job as steel or rubber fuel lines. Nylon pipes are constructed to withstand the maximum fuel system pressure, exposure to fuel additives and changes in temperature. Two sizes are used: 5⁄16 in. I.D. for the fuel return and 3⁄8 in. I.D. for the fuel feed. Nylon fuel pipes are somewhat flexible and can be formed around gradual turns. However, if forced into sharp bends, nylon pipes will kink and restrict fuel flow. In addition, once exposed to fuel, nylon pipes may become stiffer and are more likely to kink if bent too far. Special care should be taken when working on a vehicle with nylon pipes.

Quick-connect type fittings provide a simplified means of installing and connecting fuel system components. Depending on the vehicle model, there are two types of quick-connect fittings, each used at different locations in the fuel system. Each type of quick-connect fitting consists of a unique female connector and a compatible male fuel pipe end. O-rings, located inside the female connector, provide the fuel seal. Integral locking tabs, or fingers, hold the quick-connect fitting together. For addition information on quick-connect fittings and nylon fuel pipes, please see Section 5 of this manual.

❋❋ CAUTION

To reduce the risk of fire and personal injury, it is necessary to relieve the fuel system pressure before servicing any fuel system component. If this procedure is not performed, fuel may be sprayed out of the connection under pressure. Cover the fuel hose connections with a shop cloth before disconnecting to catch any residual fuel that may still be in the line. Always keep a dry chemical (Class B) fire extinguisher near the work area.

REMOVAL & INSTALLATION

▶ **See Figures 51, 52, 53 and 54**

The fuel filter is located in the fuel feed line attached to the underbody, directly in front of the fuel tank.

1. Relieve the fuel system pressure using the procedure outlined in Section 5. Also remove the fuel tank cap to relieve any residual fuel pressure in the tank which could force out fuel when the fuel lines are disconnected.
2. Raise the vehicle and safely support with jackstands.
3. Locate the fuel filter. Clean the area around the fittings, especially on the plastic quick-disconnect fittings. Use a bristle brush and/or compressed air, if available. A small amount of penetrating oil can be used on the steel threaded fitting only. This may be helpful, especially on high-mileage vehicles or where the filter has not been previously serviced.
4. Disconnect the fuel lines from the filter. The quick-connect end may have a dust cover over the end of the fitting. If used, slide the dust cover back over the fuel line to expose the fitting. For more information on servicing the quick-connect fitting, please refer to Section 5. To reduce fuel spillage, place a shop towel over the fuel lines before disconnecting.
5. Remove the filter from its bracket

To install:
6. The replacement fuel filter should come with a new plastic connector retainer. Install the new plastic connector retainer on the filter inlet.
7. Slide the filter into the mounting bracket.
8. Apply a few drops of clean engine oil to the male pipe ends. This will ensure proper reconnection and help prevent possible fuel leaks. During normal operation, the O-rings located in the female connector will swell and may prevent proper reconnection if not lubricated. New O-rings are recommended and should come with the filter kit.
9. Using new O-rings, install the fuel lines to the filter. Pull on the quick-connect fitting end to verify that the locking tabs are properly engaged. If used, reposition the dust cover onto the fitting.
10. Tighten the steel fitting end of the filter. Use a backup wrench to keep the filter from turning. Torque the fittings to 22 ft. lbs. (30 Nm).
11. Lower the vehicle. Retighten the fuel filler cap.
12. Connect the negative battery cable. Start the engine and check for leaks.

PCV Valve

The Crankcase Ventilation Valve, also known as the Positive Crankcase Ventilation or PCV Valve, is part of the system used to consume crankcase vapors in the combustion process instead of vent-

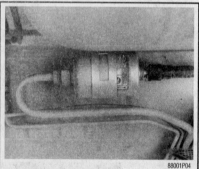

Fig. 50 Location of the fuel filter. Note a threaded fitting on the inlet and a quick-connect fitting on the outlet end

88001P04

Fig. 51 Unfasten the mounting bracket if necessary, to make fuel filter removal easier

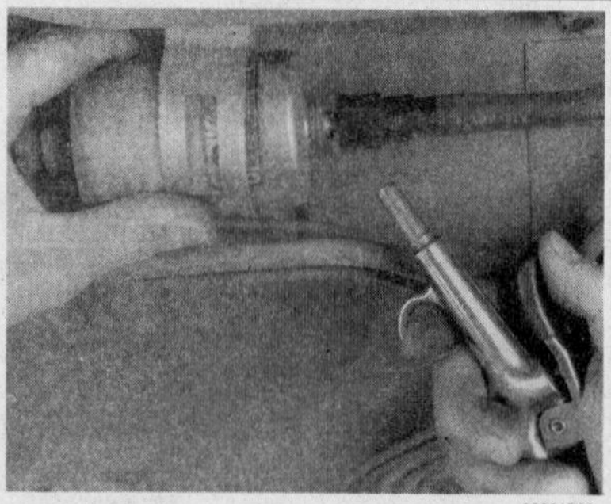

88001P05

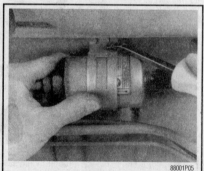

Fig. 52 Either use a clean cloth or compressed air to clean the area around the quick-connect fitting

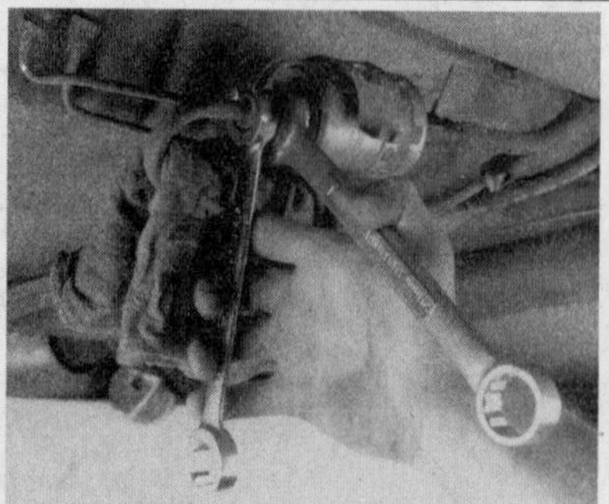

88001P06

Fig. 53 Always use a backup wrench when loosening the threaded fitting

88001P07

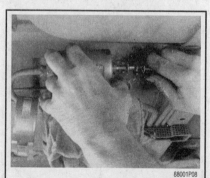

Fig. 54 Disengage the quick-connect fittings, then remove the filter from the vehicle

88001P08

ing them to atmosphere. Fresh air from the throttle body is supplied to the crankcase, mixed with blow-by gases, and then passed through the crankcase ventilation valve into the intake manifold system. The primary control for this system is the crankcase ventilation valve which meters the flow at a rate depending on inlet vacuum. To maintain idle quality, the valve restricts the flow when inlet vacuum is low (idle or low rpm operation). If abnormal operating conditions arise, the system is designed to allow excessive amounts of blow-by gases to back flow through the crankcase vent into the throttle body to be consumed by normal combustion.

A plugged valve may cause a rough idle, stalling or slow idle speed, oil leaks and sludge in the engine. A leaking valve would cause a rough idle, stalling and high idle speed. Another area to watch is the rubber grommet which retains most PCV valves. These deteriorate from their constant exposure to engine oil and heat. If the grommet shows signs of cracking or has deteriorated to the point where the PCV valve is not a tight fit, it should be replaced.

The crankcase ventilation valve should be inspected every 30,000 miles (50,000 km) for proper operation. To check, remove the valve, and operate the engine at idle. Place your thumb over the end of the valve to check for vacuum. If there is no vacuum, check for a plugged hose, a clogged manifold port or suspect a failed valve. Turn off the engine and remove the valve and shake it. Listen for the rattle of the check needle inside the valve. If the valve does not rattle, replace it

In general, crankcase ventilation valve service is relatively simple. While the valve can be cleaned in many cases, replacement is recommended.

REMOVAL & INSTALLATION

3.1L (VIN M) and 3.4L (VIN E) Engines

▶ See Figures 55, 56 and 57

1. Locate the vacuum hoses that run to the fuel pressure regulator and the Positive Crankcase Ventilation (PCV) valve. They should run parallel to each other. It may be necessary to disconnect both hoses, depending on the model and the brackets. The vacuum hose to the ventilation valve terminates on the valve which is pressed into a rubber grommet mounted on one of the valve rocker covers.

2. Pull the vacuum hose off of the valve. The valve should be easily pulled from its grommet.

Fig. 56 The PCV valve on this 3.1L engine was contaminated with and oil/coolant mix that resulted from intake manifold gasket failure

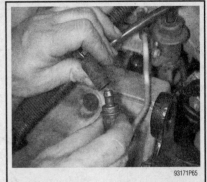

Fig. 57 A new PCV is connected to its vacuum hose then simply inserted back into the rubber grommet in the rocker arm cover

3. Install the replacement valve into the grommet. Make sure it is seated properly so there will be no vacuum leaks.

4. Connect the vacuum hose(s) to the crankcase valve as well as the fuel pressure regulator, if removed. Verify the hoses are secure.

3.4L (VIN X) Engine

▶ See Figure 58

1. Locate the crankcase ventilation valve in its location in its molded rubber connection on the lower side of the intake manifold.

2. Remove the valve from its vacuum hose connection.

To install:

3. Install the replacement valve. Make sure it is seated properly so there will be no vacuum leaks.

4. Connect the vacuum hose to the crankcase valve. Test run the engine to verify no vacuum leaks.

3.8L (VIN K) Engine

▶ See Figures 59 thru 66

1. The cosmetic/acoustic engine cover is called the fuel injector sight shield. Remove this cover by first turning counter-clockwise the tube/oil fill cap from the valve rocker arm cover. Lift the fuel injector sight shield up at the front and slide the tab out of the engine bracket.

2. Locate the Manifold Absolute Pressure (MAP) sensor at the end of the intake manifold. Remove the MAP sensor by disconnecting the electrical connector. Carefully bend the locking tabs holding the MAP sensor to the PCV valve cover just enough to remove the sensor. Pull the MAP sensor straight out of the PCV valve cover.

3. Use a 16mm socket to press the access cover down and rotate ¼ turn counter-clockwise. Remove the access cover.

4. Remove the PCV valve and the O-ring from the intake manifold.

To install:

5. Inspect the O-ring. It should be replaced, if necessary. Install the replacement PCV valve. Install the access cover.

6. Inspect the seal on the MAP sensor. It should

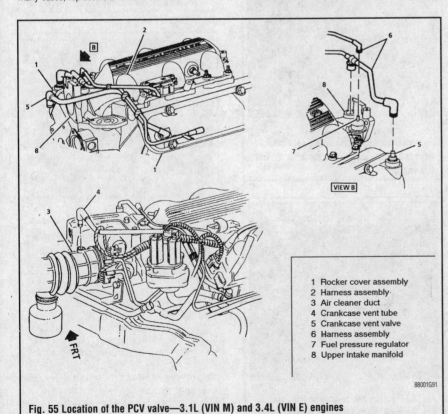

1	Rocker cover assembly
2	Harness assembly
3	Air cleaner duct
4	Crankcase vent tube
5	Crankcase vent valve
6	Harness assembly
7	Fuel pressure regulator
8	Upper intake manifold

Fig. 55 Location of the PCV valve—3.1L (VIN M) and 3.4L (VIN E) engines

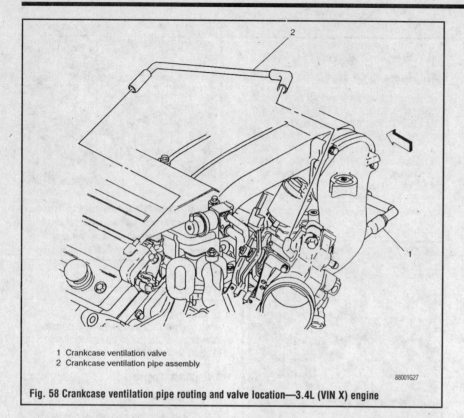

1 Crankcase ventilation valve
2 Crankcase ventilation pipe assembly

88001G27

Fig. 58 Crankcase ventilation pipe routing and valve location—3.4L (VIN X) engine

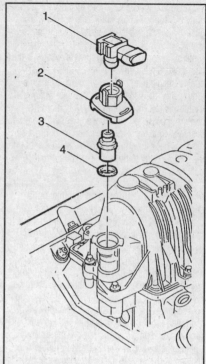

1. MAP sensor
2. Cover
3. Crankcase Ventilation Valve
4. O-Ring

88001G25

Fig. 63 On the 3.8L (VIN K) engine, you must first remove the MAP sensor to access the crankcase ventilation valve

93171P59

Fig. 59 The engine cover shown here must be removed for almost any engine maintenance. Dirt that collects around the oil fill tube opening must be removed or it will fall into the engine when the cover is removed

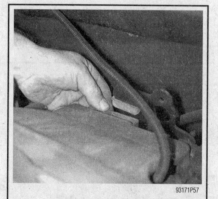

93171P57

Fig. 61 Disengage the cover's rear tab from the metal bracket on the back side of the engine

93171PA6

Fig. 64 On this 3.8L engine, after the MAP sensor is unclipped, the plastic PCV cover needs about ⅛ turn to disengage it from the base

93171P58

Fig. 60 The plastic oil fill tube is the primary cover retainer. Twist the plastic oil fill tube to disengage it. You can see how dirt and debris, if not cleaned off, could easily enter the engine

93171P56

Fig. 62 Remove the cover and set aside in a safe place. Install the oil fill tube temporarily to keep dirt out of the engine

be replaced, if necessary. Position the MAP Sensor to the PCV cover. Make sure the locking tabs engage to hold the MAP sensor to the PCV cover. Plug in the electrical connector.

7. Insert the tab of the fuel injector sight shield under the engine bracket. Place the hole of the shield onto the oil fill neck of the valve rocker arm cover. Install the tube/oil fill cap onto the valve rocker arm cover and twist clockwise in order to lock.

Fig. 65 The PCV valve is seated in the lower housing and is retained by a silicone O-ring

Fig. 66 View of the PCV valve and O-ring seal once removed from the 3.8L (VIN K) engine

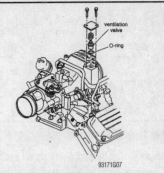

Fig. 67 On the 3.8L (VIN 1) supercharged engine, the crankcase ventilation valve is found under a cover plate

3.8L (VIN 1) Engine

▶ See Figure 67

1. The cosmetic engine cover, also called the fuel injector sight shield, must be removed. Remove this cover by first turning counter-clockwise the tube/oil fill cap from the valve rocker arm cover. Remove the nut holding the shield to the fuel injector rail brace std. Lift the fuel injector sight shield up at the front and slide the tab out of the engine bracket.

2. On this engine, the crankcase ventilation valve is under an access cover at the throttle body end of the intake manifold. The cover is under a small pressure from a spring underneath the cover. While holding down the valve access cover, remove the two cover bolts.

3. Remove the access cover, then remove the crankcase ventilation valve, the spring and O-ring.

To install:

4. Install the replacement valve with a new O-ring. Position the spring and install the cover.

5. While holding down the ventilation valve access cover, install the cover retaining bolts.

6. Install the engine cover by inserting the tab of the cover under the engine bracket. Place the hole of the cover onto the oil fill neck of the rocker arm cover.

7. Install the tube/oil fill cap into the rocker arm cover and twist clockwise in order to lock.

8. Install the nut holding the cover to the fuel injector rail brace stud and snug down to just 18 inch lbs. (2 Nm).

Evaporative Canister

▶ See Figure 68

The basic Evaporative Emission (EVAP) Control system used on these vehicles is the charcoal canister storage method. This method transfers fuel vapor from the fuel tank to an activated carbon (charcoal) storage device (canister) to hold the vapors when the vehicle is not operating. When the engine is running, the fuel vapor is purged from the carbon element by the intake air flow and consumed in the normal combustion process.

The EVAP purge solenoid valve allows manifold vacuum to purge the canister. The Powertrain Control Module (PCM) supplies a ground to energize the EVAP purge solenoid valve (purge on). Poor idle, stalling and poor driveability can be caused by: a malfunctioning purge solenoid, a damaged canis-

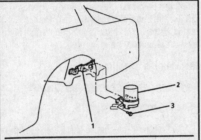

| 1 | CANISTER MOUNTING BRACKET | 3 | BOLT/SCREW |
| 2 | CANISTER | | |

Fig. 68 The evaporative canister on W-Body vehicles can be found on the left rear of the vehicle, behind the wheel well lining (inner fender panel)

ter; hoses and lines split, cracked or not connected properly (perhaps after rear end collision body work to the vehicle).

SERVICING

The evaporative canister is not a serviceable unit. If found to be defective, replace the entire unit. On all of these vehicles, the EVAP canister is located in the wheel well behind the driver's side rear wheel. The canister and valve can be serviced only by replacement. For further information, please see Section 4.

Battery

PRECAUTIONS

✳✳✳ WARNING

Before removing or disconnecting the battery on these vehicles, record all of the vehicle preset radio stations (if applicable). Record the radio's THEFTLOCK code (if applicable). Turn all lamps and accessories OFF. Always disconnect the negative battery cable first, and reconnect last.

Always use caution when working on or near the battery. Never allow a tool to bridge the gap between the negative and positive battery terminals.

Also, be careful not to allow a tool to provide a ground between the positive cable/terminal and any metal component on the vehicle. Either of these conditions will cause a short circuit, leading to sparks and possible personal injury.

Do not smoke, have an open flame or create sparks near a battery; the gases contained in the battery are very explosive and, if ignited, could cause severe injury or death.

All batteries, regardless of type, should be carefully secured by a battery hold-down device. If this is not done, the battery terminals or casing may crack from stress applied to the battery during vehicle operation. A battery which is not secured may allow acid to leak out, making it discharge faster; such leaking corrosive acid can also eat away at components under the hood.

Always visually inspect the battery case for cracks, leakage and corrosion. A white corrosive substance on the battery case or on nearby components would indicate a leaking or cracked battery. If the battery is cracked, it should be replaced immediately.

GENERAL MAINTENANCE

A battery that is not sealed must be checked periodically for electrolyte level. You cannot add water to a sealed maintenance-free battery (though not all maintenance-free batteries are sealed); however, a sealed battery must also be checked for proper electrolyte level, as indicated by the color of the built-in hydrometer "eye."

Always keep the battery cables and terminals free of corrosion. Check these components about once a year. Refer to the removal, installation and cleaning procedures outlined in this section.

Keep the top of the battery clean, as a film of dirt can help completely discharge a battery that is not used for long periods. A solution of baking soda and water may be used for cleaning, but be careful to flush this off with clear water. DO NOT let any of the solution into the filler holes. Baking soda neutralizes battery acid and will de-activate a battery cell.

Batteries in vehicles which are not operated on a regular basis can fall victim to parasitic loads (small current drains which are constantly drawing current from the battery). Normal parasitic loads may drain a battery on a vehicle that is in storage and not used for 6–8 weeks. Vehicles that have additional accessories such as a cellular phone, an alarm system or other devices that increase parasitic load may discharge a battery sooner. If the vehicle is to be stored for 6–8 weeks in a secure area and the alarm system, if present, is not necessary, the negative battery cable should be disconnected at the onset of storage to protect the battery charge.

Remember that constantly discharging and recharging will shorten battery life. Take care not to allow a battery to be needlessly discharged.

BATTERY FLUID

▶ **See Figures 69 and 70**

Check the battery electrolyte level at least once a month, or more often in hot weather or during periods of extended vehicle operation. On non-sealed batteries, the level can be checked either through the case on translucent batteries or by removing the cell caps on opaque-cased types. The electrolyte level in each cell should be kept filled to the split ring inside each cell, or the line marked on the outside of the case.

If the level is low, add only distilled water through the opening until the level is correct. Each cell is separate from the others, so each must be checked and filled individually. Distilled water should be used, because the chemicals and minerals found in most drinking water are harmful to the battery and could significantly shorten its life.

If water is added in freezing weather, the vehicle should be driven several miles to allow the water to mix with the electrolyte. Otherwise, the battery could freeze.

Although some maintenance-free batteries have removable cell caps for access to the electrolyte, the electrolyte condition and level on all sealed maintenance-free batteries must be checked using the built-in hydrometer "eye." The exact type of eye varies between battery manufacturers, but most apply a sticker to the battery itself explaining the possible readings. When in doubt, refer to the battery manufacturer's instructions to interpret battery condition using the built-in hydrometer.

➡ Although the readings from built-in hydrometers found in sealed batteries may vary, a green eye usually indicates a properly charged battery with sufficient fluid level. A dark eye is normally an indicator of a battery with sufficient fluid, but one which may be low in charge. And a light or yellow eye is usually an indication that electrolyte supply has dropped below the necessary level for battery (and hydrometer) operation. In this last case, sealed batteries with an insufficient electrolyte level must usually be discarded.

Checking the Specific Gravity

NON-MAINTENANCE-FREE BATTERIES

▶ **See Figures 71, 72 and 73**

A hydrometer is required to check the specific gravity on all batteries that are not maintenance-free. On batteries that are maintenance-free, the specific gravity is checked by observing the built-in hydrometer "eye" on the top of the battery case. Check with your battery's manufacturer for proper interpretation of its built-in hydrometer readings. The owner's manual should have more specific information for your vehicle.

✳✳ CAUTION

Battery electrolyte contains sulfuric acid. If you should splash any on your skin or in your eyes, flush the affected area with plenty of clear water. If it lands in your eyes, get medical help immediately.

The fluid (sulfuric acid solution) contained in the battery cells will tell you many things about the condition of the battery. Because the cell plates must be kept submerged below the fluid level in order to operate, maintaining the fluid level is extremely important. And, because the specific gravity of the acid is an indication of electrical charge, testing the fluid can be an aid in determining if the battery must be replaced. A battery in a vehicle with a properly operating charging system should require little maintenance, but careful, periodic inspection should reveal problems before they leave you stranded.

As stated earlier, the specific gravity of a battery's electrolyte level can be used as an indication of battery charge. At least once a year, check the specific gravity of the battery. It should be between 1.20 and 1.26 on the gravity scale. Most auto supply stores carry a variety of inexpensive battery testing hydrometers. These can be used on any non-sealed battery to test the specific gravity in each cell.

The battery testing hydrometer has a squeeze bulb at one end and a nozzle at the other. Battery electrolyte is sucked into the hydrometer until the float is lifted from its seat. The specific gravity is then read by noting the position of the float. If gravity is low in one or more cells, the battery should be slowly charged and checked again to see if the gravity has come up. Generally, if after charging, the specific gravity between any two cells varies more than 50 points (0.50), the battery should be replaced, as it can no longer produce sufficient voltage to guarantee proper operation.

MAINTENANCE-FREE BATTERIES WITH BUILT-IN HYDROMETER

1. Make sure the vehicle is parked relatively level.
2. When checking the hydrometer, make sure the top is clean. Use a light in poorly-lit areas.

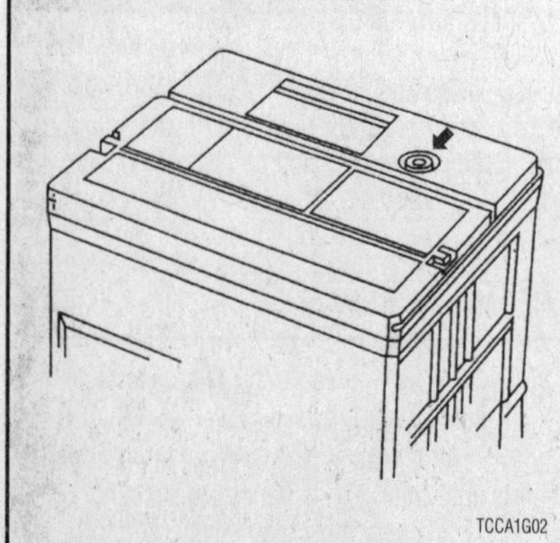

![Figure 69 battery diagram] TCCA1G02

Fig. 69 A typical location for the built-in hydrometer (note arrow) on maintenance-free batteries

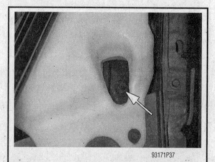
93171P37

Fig. 70 Since the maintenance free batteries used on the vehicles covered by this manual are hidden away under the windshield washer reservoir, the reservoir has an opening so the battery "eye" can be checked

TCCA1P07

Fig. 71 On non-maintenance-free batteries, the fluid level can be checked through the case on translucent models; the cell caps must be removed on other models

TCCA1P08

Fig. 72 If the fluid level is low, add only distilled water through the opening until the level is correct

TCCA1P09

Fig. 73 Check the specific gravity of the battery's electrolyte with a hydrometer

3. Tap the hydrometer lightly on the top to dislodge any air bubbles that might give a false indication. Normally, one of three things might be seen:

a. GREEN EYE: If any green can be seen in the hydrometer, the battery is at about 65% state of charge or above and may be tested. This is considered a normal indication.

b. BLACK OR DARK EYE: If the green dot cannot be seen and there is a problem cranking over the engine to start, the battery should be charged.

c. CLEAR OR LIGHT YELLOW EYE: If the hydrometer appears clear or light yellow, the fluid level is below the level of the hydrometer. This can be caused by excessive or prolonged charging, a broken case or excessive tipping causing electrolyte to leak out thorough the vents. If this happens, it could mean high charging voltages caused by a problem in the charging system. Do not attempt to charge or test a battery whose hydrometer is clear or light yellow. Replace the battery.

CABLES

▶ **See Figures 74 thru 81**

Once a year (or as necessary), the battery terminals and the cable clamps should be cleaned. Loosen the clamps and remove the cables, negative cable first. Clean the terminals with a wire brush until all corrosion, grease, etc., is removed. A small deposit of foreign material or oxidation there will prevent a sound electrical connection and inhibit

either starting or charging. Special tools are available for cleaning side terminal batteries, although a small wire brush works well.

After the terminals are clean, reinstall the cables, negative cable last. Check the cables at the same time that the terminals are cleaned. If the cable insulation is cracked or broken, or if the ends are frayed, the cable should be replaced with a new cable of the same length and gauge. Original equipment cables are recommended. Also, make sure that the replacement cable is routed in exactly the same way as the original. The factory routing normally keeps the cable clear of heat and moving components that could damage the cable. It is good practice to route and secure the cables in the same manner as the originals. Note too, that ground

straps are commonly used to provide an electrical connection between the body, frame, engine and transaxle. Always reinstall any disconnected ground straps and replace any broken ground straps to insure

CHARGING

Fig. 74 This diagonal brace, which runs across the coolant reservoir, must be removed before reservoir removal. The brace on the other side (not shown) must be removed to access the battery

Fig. 75 The diagonal brace is retained by three bolts. Use care at installation not to strip the threads in the body

Fig. 76 Loosen the battery cable retaining bolt . . .

Fig. 77 . . . then disconnect the cable from the battery. Always remove the negative cable first

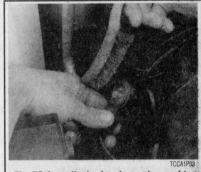

Fig. 78 A small wire brush may be used to clean any corrosion or foreign material from the cable

Fig. 79 The wire brush can also be used to remove any corrosion or dirt from the battery terminal pad

Fig. 80 The battery terminal pad can also be cleaned using a solution of baking soda and water, applied with a stiff brush

Fig. 81 Before connecting the cables, a thin coat of dielectric grease (not chassis grease) can be applied to the battery terminal pad

tilation and take appropriate fire safety precautions when connecting, disconnecting, or charging a battery and when using jumper cables.

A battery should be charged at a slow rate to keep the plates inside from getting too hot. However, if some maintenance-free batteries are allowed to discharge until they are almost "dead", they may have to be charged at a high rate to bring them back to "life". Always follow the charger manufacturer's instructions on charging the battery.

REPLACEMENT

When it becomes necessary to replace the battery, select one with an amperage rating equal to or greater than the battery originally installed. Deterioration and just plain aging of the battery cables, starter motor, and associated wires makes the battery's job harder in successive years. The slow increase in electrical resistance over time makes it prudent to install a new battery with a greater capacity than the old one.

Drive Belt

INSPECTION

▶ See Figures 82, 83, 84 and 85

Inspect the belts for signs of glazing or cracking. A glazed belt will be perfectly smooth from slippage, while a good belt will have a slight texture of

fabric visible. Cracks will usually start at the inner edge of the belt and run outward. All worn or damaged drive belts should be replaced immediately. It is best to replace all drive belts at one time, as a preventive maintenance measure, during this service operation.

ADJUSTMENT

Belt tension is maintained by the automatic tensioner and is not adjustable.

REMOVAL & INSTALLATION

❊❊ WARNING

Before removing or disconnecting the battery on these vehicles, record all of the vehicle preset radio stations (if applicable). Record the radio's THEFTLOCK® code (if applicable). Turn all lamps and accessories OFF. Always disconnect the negative battery cable first, and reconnect last.

3.1L (VIN M) Engine

▶ See Figures 86 and 87

1. Disconnect the negative battery cable.
2. Remove the drive belt shield.
3. Fit a ⅜ inch breaker bar or ratchet to the square hole in the tensioner. Lift, or rotate the tensioner off of the drive belt. When the tension on the belt is removed, slide the drive belt from the pulleys.

To install:

4. Taking care to follow the proper routing of the belt, slip the belt onto the pulleys. As a help, note that the water pump pulley is usually driven from the back (smooth side) of the belt.
5. Fit a ⅜-inch breaker bar or ratchet to the square hole in the tensioner. Lift, or rotate the tensioner and, with the belt in place, gently release the tensioner.
6. Verify that the belt is correctly routed and aligned in the proper grooves of the accessory drive belt pulleys. Inspect the drive belt length scale on the drive belt tensioner for the proper indicated length. If the drive belt length scale does not indicate the proper installed length, the belt may be incorrect, incorrectly installed, worn out or the tensioner may be defective.
7. Connect the negative battery cable. Start the vehicle and verify correct operation.

3.4L (VIN X) Engine

▶ See Figure 88

1. Disconnect the negative battery cable.
2. Remove the coolant recovery reservoir.
3. Using a box-end wrench of the appropriate size, rotate the drive belt tensioner clockwise to remove the tension on the drivebelt.
4. Remove the drive belt

To install:

5. Taking care to follow the proper routing of the belt, slip the belt onto the pulleys.
6. Using the same box-end wrench, rotate the tensioner and slip the belt over the tensioner pulley. Slip the belt over the power steering pulley last.

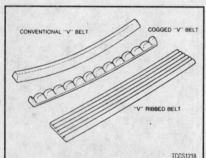

Fig. 82 There are typically 3 types of accessory drive belts found on vehicles today. Only the wide, v-ribbed belt is used on the vehicles in this book

Fig. 83 Installing the incorrect belt, or failing to install the belt properly will give this result

Fig. 84 The belt routing for your vehicle should be found on an underhood label

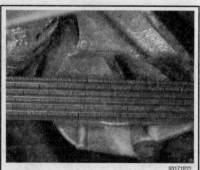

Fig. 85 This high-mileage Lumina's accessory drive belt is showing signs of distress but is still serviceable

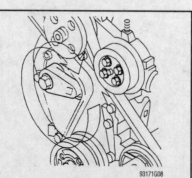

Fig. 86 Remove the drive belt by rotating the tensioner off the belt using a ⅜ in. breaker bar or ratchet

Fig. 87 This label shows the accessory belt routing on a Lumina with a 3.1L engine

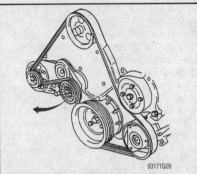

Fig. 88 Rotate the drive belt tensioner clockwise with a box-end wrench—3.4L (VIN X) engine

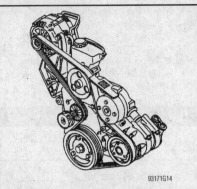

Fig. 89 Accessory drive belt routing—3.4L (VIN E) engine

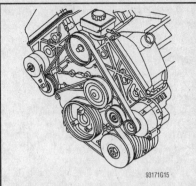

Fig. 90 Accessory drive belt routing—3.5L (VIN H) engine

7. Install the coolant recovery reservoir.

8. Connect the negative battery cable. Start the vehicle and verify correct operation.

3.4L (VIN E) Engine

▶ **See Figure 89**

1. Disconnect the negative battery cable.

2. Rotate the drive belt tensioner in order to release the pressure on the drive belt.

3. Remove the drive belt from the vehicle.

To install:

4. Taking care to follow the proper routing of the accessory drive belt, slip the belt onto the pulleys, except the alternator pulley.

5. Rotate the drive belt tensioner to install the drive belt over the alternator pulley last.

6. Make sure the belt is correctly routed.

7. Verify that the mark on the drive belt tensioner is in range, as indicated on the tensioner housing.

3.5L (VIN H) Engine

▶ **See Figure 90**

1. Disconnect the negative battery cable.

2. Rotate the drive belt tensioner in order to release the pressure on the drive belt. Note that there are two square holes in the tensioner bracket, accepting either a 3/8 or 1/2 inch breaker bar.

3. Remove the drive belt from the vehicle.

To install:

4. Rotate the drive belt tensioner, and, taking

care to follow the proper routing of the accessory drive belt, slip the belt onto the pulleys.

5. Inspect the drive belt and pulleys to verify proper alignment.

3.8L (VIN K) Engine

▶ **See Figures 91 and 92**

1. Disconnect the negative battery cable.

➡The drive belt path on the 3.8L (VIN K) engine is somewhat complicated. An underhood sticker should show the correct routing. If the label is missing or unreadable, make a sketch of the belt's path. A minute spent now can save much time later.

2. Using a 15mm box-end wrench on the pulley nut, lift, or rotate the drive belt tensioner to take the pressure off of the belt. Remove the drive belt.

To install:

3. Taking care to follow the proper routing of the belt, slip the belt onto the pulleys.

4. Using the same box-end wrench, rotate the tensioner and slip the belt over the tensioner pulley. Slip the belt over the power steering pulley last.

5. Connect the negative battery cable. Start the vehicle and verify correct operation.

3.8L (VIN 1) Engine

▶ **See Figures 93, 94, and 95**

The supercharged 3.8L (VIN 1) engine uses two drive belts. The outer belt drives the supercharger. The inner belt drives the alternator, power steering

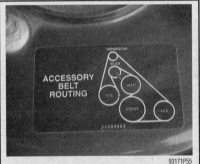

Fig. 91 This label shows the accessory belt routing on a Grand Prix with a 3.8L engine

Fig. 92 Rotate the tensioner off the drive belt using a 15mm box-end wrench on the pulley nut—3.8L (VIN K) engine

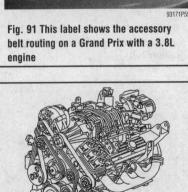

Fig. 93 The 3.8L (VIN 1) supercharged engine uses two drive belts. The outer drives the supercharger, the inner drives most accessories

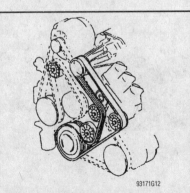

Fig. 94 Supercharger belt routing—3.8L (VIN 1) engine

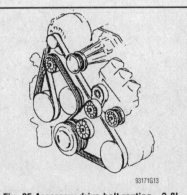

Fig. 95 Accessory drive belt routing—3.8L (VIN 1) engine

pump, coolant pump and air conditioning compressor. Each belt has its own tensioner.

1. Disconnect the negative battery cable.

2. Using a 15mm box-end wrench on the supercharger drive belt tensioner pulley nut, lift, or rotate the drive belt tensioner to take the pressure off of the belt. Remove the supercharger drive belt.

3. Using a 15mm box-end wrench on the accessory drive belt tensioner pulley nut, lift, or rotate the drive belt tensioner to take the pressure off of the belt. Remove the accessory drive belt.

To install:

4. Taking care to follow the proper routing of the accessory drive belt, slip the belt onto the pulleys.

5. Using the same 15mm box-end wrench,

rotate the accessory drive belt tensioner and slip the belt over the tensioner pulley.

6. Using the 15mm box-end wrench again, rotate the supercharger drive belt tensioner and slip the supercharger belt over the tensioner pulley.

7. Connect the negative battery cable. Start the vehicle and verify correct operation.

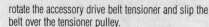

Timing Belt

INSPECTION

▶ **See Figures 96 thru 101**

Only vehicles with the 3.4L (VIN X) Double Over Head Camshaft (DOHC) engine use a timing belt in

conjunction with a timing chain. All other engines use combinations of sprockets and timing chains. Any engine's valve timing is critical to the engine's operation. This is especially the case of any belt-driven over head camshaft engine. In the 3.4L (VIN X) engine, the combination of four camshafts, 24 valves, and tight clearances means that if the belt should slip or otherwise get "out of time", expensive engine damage will result. The timing belt should be inspected for cracks, wear and other damage at 60,000 miles (100,000 km) and then every 15,000 miles (25,000 km). Replace the belt and/or tensioner as needed.

For the timing belt removal and installation procedure, please refer to Section 3 of this manual.

Hoses

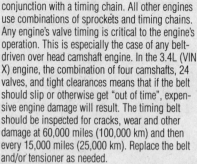

✳✳ CAUTION

These vehicles are equipped with electric underhood cooling fans. An electric fan can start up even when the engine is not running and can injure you. Keep hands, clothing and tools away from any underhood electric fan.

INSPECTION

▶ **See Figures 102, 103, 104, and 105**

Upper and lower radiator hoses, along with the heater hoses, should be checked for deterioration, leaks and loose hose clamps at least every 15,000

TCCS1242

Fig. 96 Do not bend, twist or turn the timing belt inside out. Never allow oil, water or steam to contact the belt

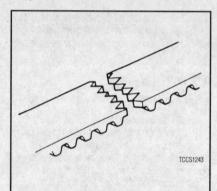

TCCS1243

Fig. 97 Check for premature parting of the belt

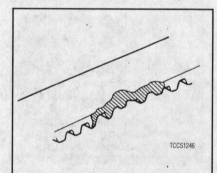

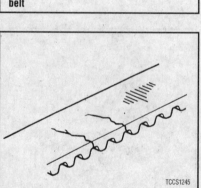

TCCS1244

Fig. 98 Check if the teeth are cracked or damaged

TCCS1245

Fig. 99 Look for noticeable cracks or wear on the belt face

TCCS1246

Fig. 100 You may only have damage on one side of the belt; if so, the guide could be the culprit

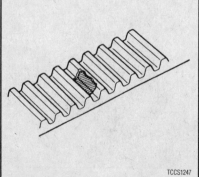

TCCS1247

Fig. 101 Foreign materials can get in between the teeth and cause damage

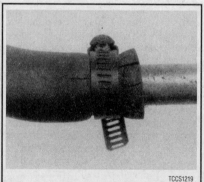

TCCS1219

Fig. 102 The cracks developing along this hose are a result of age-related hardening

TCCS1220

Fig. 103 A hose clamp that is too tight can cause older hoses to separate and tear on either side of the clamp

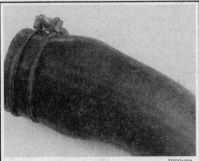

Fig. 104 A soft spongy hose (identifiable by the swollen section) will eventually burst and should be replaced

Fig. 105 Hoses are likely to deteriorate from the inside if the cooling system is not periodically flushed

Fig. 106 CV-boots must be inspected periodically

miles (24,000 km). It is also wise to check the hoses periodically in early spring and at the beginning of the fall or winter when you are performing other maintenance. A quick visual inspection could discover a weakened hose which might have left you stranded if it had remained unrepaired.

Whenever you are checking the hoses, make sure the engine and cooling system are cold. Visually inspect for cracking, rotting or collapsed hoses, and replace as necessary. Run your hand along the length of the hose. If a weak or swollen spot is noted when squeezing the hose wall, the hose should be replaced.

REMOVAL & INSTALLATION

✳ CAUTION

Never remove the pressure cap while the engine is running, or personal injury from scalding hot coolant or steam may result. If possible, wait until the engine has cooled to remove the pressure cap. If this is not possible, wrap a thick cloth around the pressure cap and turn it slowly to the stop. Step back while the pressure is released from the cooling system. When you are sure all the pressure has been released, use the cloth to turn and remove the cap.

All of the vehicles covered by this book were originally filled at the factory with GM Goodwrench DEX-COOL®. DEX-COOL® is an ethylene-glycol coolant that was developed to last for 150,000 miles (240,000 km), or 5 years, whichever occurs first. It is recommended that only DEX-COOL® be used when coolant is added or changed. A 50/50 mixture of this ethylene-glycol coolant and water should be used, providing freezing protection down to -34°F. (-37°C), boiling protection to 265°F (129°C), and rust and corrosion protection for the system. A solution stronger than 70% antifreeze is not recommended and pure antifreeze will freeze at only -8°F (-17°C).

1. Remove the radiator pressure cap.
2. Position a clean container under the radiator and/or engine draincock or plug, then open the drain and allow the cooling system to drain to an appropriate level. For some upper hoses, only a little coolant must be drained. To remove hoses positioned lower on the engine, such as a lower radiator hose, the entire cooling system must be emptied.

✳ CAUTION

When draining coolant, keep in mind that cats and dogs are attracted by ethylene glycol antifreeze, and are quite likely to drink any that is left in an uncovered container or in puddles on the ground. This will prove fatal in sufficient quantity. Always drain coolant into a sealable container. Coolant may be reused unless it is contaminated or several years old.

3. Loosen the hose clamps at each end of the hose requiring replacement. Clamps are usually either of the spring tension type (which require pliers to squeeze the tabs and loosen) or of the screw tension type (which require screw or hex drivers to loosen). Pull the clamps back on the hose away from the connection.
4. Twist, pull and slide the hose off the fitting, taking care not to damage the neck of the component from which the hose is being removed.

→ **If the hose is stuck at the connection, do not try to insert a screwdriver or other sharp tool under the hose end in an effort to free it, as the connection and/or hose may become damaged. Heater connections especially may be easily damaged by such a procedure. If the hose is to be replaced, use a single-edged razor blade to make a slice along the portion of the hose which is stuck on the connection, perpendicular to the end of the hose. Do not cut deep so as to prevent damaging the connection. The hose can then be peeled from the connection and discarded.**

5. Clean both hose mounting connections. Inspect the condition of the hose clamps and replace them, if necessary.

To install:
6. Dip the ends of the new hose into clean engine coolant to ease installation.
7. Slide the clamps over the replacement hose, then slide the hose ends over the connections into position.
8. Position and secure the clamps at least ¼ in. (6.35mm) from the ends of the hose. Make sure they are located beyond the raised bead of the connector.
9. Close the radiator or engine drains and properly refill the cooling system with the clean drained engine coolant or a suitable mixture of ethylene glycol coolant and water.
10. If available, install a pressure tester and

check for leaks. If a pressure tester is not available, run the engine until normal operating temperature is reached (allowing the system to naturally pressurize), then check for leaks.

✳ CAUTION

If you are checking for leaks with the system at normal operating temperature, BE EXTREMELY CAREFUL not to touch any moving or hot engine parts. Once temperature has been reached, shut the engine OFF, and check for leaks around the hose fittings and connections which were removed earlier.

CV-Boots

INSPECTION

▶ **See Figures 106 and 107**

Front wheel drive vehicles use drive axles (also called halfshafts) which are flexible shaft assemblies that transmit the rotational forces from the transaxle to the front wheel assemblies. The axle assembly is made up of an inner and outer Constant Velocity Joint (commonly called a CV-Joint) connected to an axle shaft. The inner joint is completely flexible and can move in-and-out as the suspension also moves. The outer joint is also flexible but cannot move in-and-out. These CV-joints are expensive, precision-made assemblies and are protected from the elements by flexible covers called CV-boots. If the boot becomes damaged or torn, the

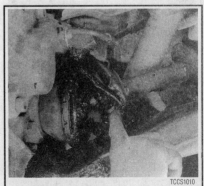

Fig. 107 All torn boots should be replaced immediately

special CV-joint lubrication can run out and dirt, water and debris will get in, damaging the precision surfaces and quickly ruining the joint.

The CV-boots should be checked for damage every time the oil is changed and any other time the vehicle is raised for service. Heavy grease thrown around the inside of the front wheel(s) and on the front brake caliper can be an indication of a torn boot. Thoroughly check the boots for missing clamps and tears. If the boot is damaged, it should be replaced immediately. Please refer to Section 7 for the procedure.

Fig. 108 Remove the through bolt from the engine side of the strut

Fig. 109 Make sure to save the bolt and the special locknuts

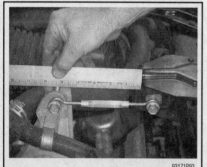

Fig. 112 Another method is to obtain a turnbuckle and install it between the two engine strut through bolts. The ruler helps indicate how much the engine will be rotated

Rotating The Engine

▶ **See Figures 108 thru 114**

Today's vehicles have extremely cramped engine compartments. The Front Wheel Drive (FWD) design allows for more room in the passenger compartment and a lower, sleeker front profile. Unfortunately, this has made engine components more difficult to access.

Unlike the engines used in older, rear drive cars where the engine mounts were placed on the sides of the engines to minimize shake, the V6 engines covered by this manual have a different arrangement. These engines have their engine mounts installed on the crankshaft centerline, balancing the engine between a mount just behind the crankshaft pulley and just ahead of the flywheel. This means the engine has limited movement front (radiator side) to rear (firewall side). To stop engine shake, the vehicle has two wishbone-shaped engine struts to limit engine movement. If these struts are removed, the engine can be pulled forward giving at least a little more access to the firewall side (rear) of the engine. This is especially important for spark plug service and other firewall side service work on the engine. Even an inch or two makes a lot of difference when changing spark plugs on the right side (rear, or firewall side) of the engine.

Fig. 110 Remove the through bolt from the body-side bracket. Note the "wishbone-shape" of the engine struts

Fig. 113 Simply tighten the turnbuckle. Our $1.19 hardware store turnbuckle gently pulled the engine back, "rotating" it away from the firewall

Naturally, special tools are available for "rotating" the engine. Some are levers, others are ratcheting straps. The non-professional may have to improvise. The following may be helpful.

The engine struts are at the front of the vehicle, bolted on one end to brackets attached to the radiator support and on the other end to strong brackets on the engine.

1. Remove the through bolts from the engine side of both struts.
2. Remove the through bolts from the body side brackets and remove both engine struts.
3. Reinstall just the bolts and nuts on the engine-side brackets.
4. Attach a pulling device between the engine side bolts and the body side bracket. This could be a chain and lever or a hardware store turnbuckle.
5. Pull or "rotate" the engine away from the firewall and toward the radiator to give a little more clearance at the back of the engine.
6. When service work is complete, reinstall the engine struts.

Spark Plugs

A typical spark plug consists of a metal shell surrounding a ceramic insulator. A metal electrode extends downward through the center of the insulator and protrudes a small distance. Located at the end of the plug and attached to the side of the

Fig. 111 It is possible to use a chain and lever to pull the engine forward, securing the chain on the body-side engine strut bracket. Use care not to damage anything and make sure the chain is secure to prevent injury

Fig. 114 When the turnbuckle bottomed out, the engine had been "rotated" nearly 1¼ inch. Experimenting with different length screw eyes for the turnbuckle, a few links of chain and/or different anchor points may yield even more working space at the back of the engine

outer metal shell is the side electrode. The side electrode bends in at a 90° angle so that its tip is just past and parallel to the tip of the center electrode. The distance between these two electrodes (measured in thousandths of an inch or hundredths of a millimeter) is called the spark plug gap.

The spark plug provides a gap across which the current can arc. The coil produces anywhere from 20,000 to 50,000 volts (depending on the type and application) which travels through the wires to the spark plugs. The current passes along the center electrode and jumps the gap to the side electrode, and in doing so, ignites the air/fuel mixture in the combustion chamber.

SPARK PLUG HEAT RANGE

♦ See Figures 115, 116, 117 and 118

Spark plug heat range is the ability of the plug to dissipate heat. The longer the insulator (or the farther it extends into the engine), the hotter the plug will operate; the shorter the insulator (the closer the electrode is to the block's cooling passages) the cooler it will operate. A plug that absorbs little heat and remains too cool will quickly accumulate deposits of oil and carbon since it is not hot enough to burn them off. This leads to plug fouling and consequently to misfir-

ing. A plug that absorbs too much heat will have no deposits but, due to the excessive heat, the electrodes will burn away quickly and might possibly lead to preignition or other ignition problems. Preignition takes place when plug tips get so hot that they glow sufficiently to ignite the air/fuel mixture before the actual spark occurs. This early ignition will usually cause a pinging during low speeds and heavy loads.

The vehicles covered by this book use resistor type, tapered seat spark plugs on all engines. No gasket is used on these tapered seat plugs. When replacing the spark plugs, use only the type specified.

A **normally worn** spark plug should have light tan or gray deposits on the firing tip.

A **carbon fouled** plug, identified by soft, sooty, black deposits, may indicate an improperly tuned vehicle. Check the air cleaner, ignition components and engine control system.

This spark plug has been **left in the engine too long,** as evidenced by the extreme gap- Plugs with such an extreme gap can cause misfiring and stumbling accompanied by a noticeable lack of power.

An **oil fouled** spark plug indicates an engine with worn poston rings and/or bad valve seals allowing excessive oil to enter the chamber.

A **physically damaged** spark plug may be evidence of severe detonation in that cylinder. Watch that cylinder carefully between services, as a continued detonation will not only damage the plug, but could also damage the engine.

A **bridged or almost bridged** spark plug, identified by a build-up between the electrodes caused by excessive carbon or oil build-up on the plug.

TCCA1P40

Fig. 115 Inspect the spark plug to determine engine running conditions

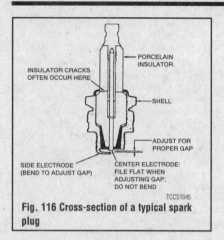

Fig. 116 Cross-section of a typical spark plug

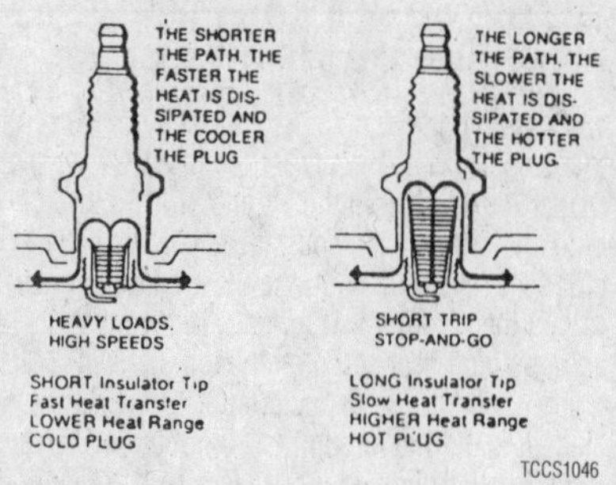

Fig. 117 Spark plug heat range

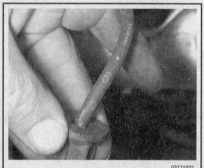

Fig. 118 A variety of tools and gauges are needed for spark plug service

REMOVAL & INSTALLATION

♦ See Figures 119 thru 125

A set of spark plugs usually requires replacement after about 20,000–30,000 miles (32,000–48,000 km), depending on your style of driving. Top quality (platinum) plugs in a well-maintained engine may go as many as 100,000 miles (160,000 km) between change intervals. On some engines, hard parts such as the intake manifold may need to be disassembled. On V6 engines, the firewall side spark plugs will be difficult access, so spark plug changes have become more of a challenge than in times past, another reason manufacturers have gone to longer change intervals. On a practical note, many technicians feel that letting spark plugs stay in the engine that long will make removal very difficult and may even damage the cylinder head, especially aluminum heads.

Some sources feel, that in normal operation, plug gap increases about 0.001 in. (0.025mm) for every 2,500 miles (4,000 km). As the gap increases, the plug's voltage requirement also increases. It requires a greater voltage to jump the wider gap and about two to three times as much voltage to fire the plug at high speeds than at idle. The improved air/fuel ratio control of modern fuel injection combined with the higher voltage output of modern ignition systems will often allow an engine to run significantly longer on a set of standard spark plugs, but keep in mind that efficiency may drop as the gap widens (along with fuel economy and power).

There are a number of points to keep in mind when changing spark plugs.

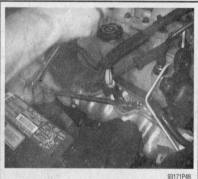

Fig. 119 Although the original spark plug wires may have identification numbers on them, it is good practice to use small tags to identify the spark plug wires before removal, to avoid improper installation

Fig. 120 A flex-head ratchet, along with a suitable extension and spark plug socket help with spark plug removal and installation

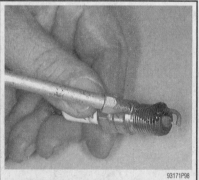

Fig. 121 The small protrusions on this spark plug's electrodes identify it as a platinum tipped spark plug that can be regapped but must not be filed or the platinum tips will be damaged

Fig. 122 For spark plugs being installed in cast iron cylinder heads, apply a small amount of clean engine oil to the spark plug threads

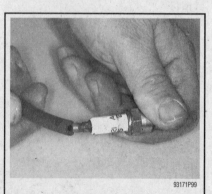

Fig. 123 For spark plugs being installed in aluminum cylinder heads, it is important to apply a small amount of anti-seize compound to the spark plug threads

Fig. 124 It can be hard to start the threads, so slip a piece of tight-fitting vacuum hose over the end of the spark plugs, then install the plug, turning with the hose

Fig. 125 This spark plug wire has a heat shield

• When you're removing spark plugs, work on one at a time. Don't start by removing the plug wires all at once, because, unless you number them, they may become mixed up. Take a minute before you begin and number the wires with tape. If the vehicle has been run recently, allow the engine to thoroughly cool.

• Carefully twist the spark plug wire boot to loosen it, then pull upward and remove the boot from the plug. Be sure to pull on the boot and not on the wire, otherwise the connector located inside the boot may become separated.

• Using compressed air, blow any water or debris from the spark plug well to assure that no harmful contaminants are allowed to enter the combustion chamber when the spark plug is removed. If compressed air is not available, use a rag or a brush to clean the area. Use a spark plug socket that is equipped with a rubber insert to properly hold the plug.

✳✳ WARNING

Be sure not to use a flexible extension on the socket. Use of a flexible extension may allow a shear force to be applied to the plug. A shear force could break the plug off in the cylinder head, leading to costly and frustrating repairs.

• Use care when threading the plug into the bore by hand. If resistance is felt before the plug is almost completely threaded, back the plug out and begin threading again. In small, hard to reach areas, an old spark plug wire and boot could be used as a

threading tool. The boot will hold the plug while you twist the end of the wire and the wire is supple enough to twist before it would allow the plug to crossthread.

✳✳ WARNING

Do not use the spark plug socket to thread the plugs. Always carefully thread the plug by hand or using an old plug wire to prevent the possibility of crossthreading and damaging the cylinder head bore.

• Use care when tightening the spark plug. The vehicles covered by this manual all use tapered seat plugs. They do not require as much torque as plugs with crush gaskets. Tighten the plug to specifications provided by the vehicle or plug manufacturer. GM original equipment spark plug wires have a coating on them and GM no longer recommends putting silicone dielectric compound on the end of the spark plug lead or inside the spark plug boot to prevent sticking, since they feel this leaks to carbon tracking and spark plug misfire. Carefully install the boot to the spark plug and push until it clicks into place. The click may be felt or heard, then gently pull back on the boot to assure proper contact.

3.1L (VIN M) and 3.4L (VIN E) Engines

▶ See Figures 126, 127 and 128

1. Turn the ignition switch to the **OFF** position, then disconnect the negative battery cable.

2. Remove only one spark plug wire at a time to avoid mixing up the wires. Each must be returned to its original location. Note the position of the spark plug wires before removing them. The high energy in these ignition systems can cause induced voltages to fire in adjacent spark plug wires. For this reason, the factory engineers take care to position the wires to minimize "crossfire." Wires should be returned to their exact locations and secured with whatever clips or loom components were originally installed.

3. Spark plug boots tend to stick firmly to the spark plug insulator. DO NOT pull on the spark plug wire. Pull on the spark plug boot or heat shield only, twisting a half-turn to release the seal while removing. Do not pull on the spark plug wire or it may be damaged.

4. Using the proper size spark plug socket, remove the plug from the cylinder head.

To install:

5. Verify that the spark plug is clean, properly gapped and that the threads are lightly lubricated with clean engine oil.

6. Be sure the plug threads smoothly into the cylinder head and is fully seated. Use a "thread chaser" if necessary to clean the threads in the cylinder head. Cross-threading or failing to fully seat the spark plug can cause overheating of the plug, exhaust blow-by, or thread damage. Follow the recommended torque specifications carefully. Some technicians will place a small piece of rubber tubing (like a piece of vacuum line) on the terminal end of the spark plug and use it to turn the plug, by hand. In this way, if the plug is not threaded properly, not enough torque can be placed on the plug to do any damage, especially on engines such as the 3.1L that have aluminum heads.

7. Torque the spark plug to 11–15 ft. lbs. (15–20 Nm).

8. Install the spark wire to the spark plug, making sure the connector engages the spark plug and the boot is fully seated.

3.4L (VIN X) Engine

1. Disconnect the negative battery cable.
2. Turn the ignition switch to the **OFF** position.
3. Remove the upper intake manifold, as outlined in Section 3 of this manual.
4. Remove only one spark plug wire at a time to avoid mixing up the wires. Each must be returned to its original location. Note the position of the spark plug wires before removing them. The high energy in these ignition systems can cause induced voltages to fire in adjacent spark plug wires. For this reason, the factory engineers take care to position the wires to minimize "crossfire." Wires should be returned to their exact locations and secured with whatever clips or loom components were originally installed.

5. Spark plug boots tend to stick firmly to the spark plug insulator. DO NOT pull on the spark plug wire. Pull on the spark plug boot or heat shield only, twisting a half-turn to release the seal while removing. Do not pull on the spark plug wire or it may be damaged.

6. Using the proper size spark plug socket, remove the plug from the cylinder head.

To install:

7. Verify that the spark plug is clean, properly gapped and that the threads are lightly lubricated with clean engine oil.

Fig. 126 When removing the spark plug wires, pull on the boot, NOT on the wire itself

Fig. 127 Use a socket and suitable extension . . .

Fig. 128 . . . then remove the spark plug from the cylinder head

8. Be sure the plug threads smoothly into the cylinder head and is fully seated. Use a "thread chaser" if necessary to clean the threads in the cylinder head. Cross-threading or failing to fully seat the spark plug can cause overheating of the plug, exhaust blow-by, or thread damage. Follow the recommended torque specifications carefully. Some technicians will place a small piece of rubber tubing (like a piece of vacuum line) on the end of the spark plug and use it to turn the plug, by hand. In this way, if the plug is not threaded properly, not enough torque can be placed on the plug to do any damage, especially on engines with aluminum heads such as the 3.4L.

9. Torque the spark plug to 11–15 ft. lbs. (15–20 Nm).

10. Install the spark wire to the spark plug, making sure the connector engages the spark plug and the boot is fully seated.

11. Install the upper intake manifold. Please refer to Section 3.

3.5L (VIN H) Engine

▶ **See Figure 129**

This procedure requires the removal of the engine cosmetic/acoustic cover and the removal of the ignition coil assembly. This engine does not use spark plug wires. The ignition coils plug onto the spark plug tops.

1. Turn the ignition switch to the **OFF** position. The engine must be cool before removing the spark plugs. Attempting to remove the spark plugs from a hot engine may cause the plug threads to seize, causing damage to the cylinder head threads.

2. Remove the ignition coil assembly. For this procedure, please refer to Section 2.

3. Remove the spark plug boots from the

plugs using GM tool J 43094, or an equivalent tool. GM specifically warns against using pliers or other makeshift tools to remove the spark plug boots.

4. Clean the spark plug recess area before removing the spark plugs. Failure to do so could result in engine damage because of dirt or foreign material entering the cylinder head, or by contamination of the cylinder head threads. The contaminated threads may prevent the proper seating of the new plug. Use a thread chaser to clean the threads of any contamination.

5. Remove the spark plugs from the engine.

To install:

6. Use only the spark plugs specified for use in this vehicle. Do not install spark plugs that are either hotter or colder than those specified for the vehicle. Installing spark plugs of another type can severely damage the engine.

7. Check the gap of all new and reconditioned spark plugs before installation. The pre-set gaps may have changed during handling. Use a round feeler gauge to ensure an accurate check. Installing the spark plugs with the wrong gap can cause poor engine performance and may even damage the engine.

8. Use care installing the spark plugs. Be sure the spark plugs thread smoothly into the cylinder heads and that the spark plug is fully seated. Cross-threading or failing to fully seat the spark plug can cause overheating of the plug, exhaust blow-by, or thread damage.

9. Tighten the spark plugs to 15 ft. lbs. (20 Nm).

10. Install the spark plug boots to the ignition coil assembly.

11. Install the ignition coil assembly following the procedure in Section 2.

3.8L (VIN 1 and K) Engines

▶ **See Figure 130**

1. Turn the ignition switch to the **OFF** position, then disconnect the negative battery cable.

2. On the 3.8L (VIN K) engine, the cosmetic/acoustic engine cover, also called the fuel injector sight shield, must be removed. Remove this cover by first turning the tube/oil fill cap counterclockwise from the valve rocker arm cover. Lift the fuel injector sight shield up at the front and slide the tab out of the engine bracket.

3. Remove only one spark plug wire at a time to avoid mixing up the wires. Each must be returned to its original location. Note the position of the spark plug wires before removing them. The high energy in these ignition systems can cause induced voltages to fire in adjacent spark plug wires. For this reason, the factory engineers take care to position the wires to minimize "crossfire." Wires should be returned to their exact locations and secured with whatever clips or loom components were originally installed.

4. Spark plug boots tend to stick firmly to the spark plug insulator. DO NOT pull on the spark plug wire. Pull on the spark plug boot or heat shield only, twisting a half-turn to release the seal while removing. Do not pull on the spark plug wire or it may be damaged.

5. Using the proper size spark plug socket, remove the plug from the cylinder head.

To install:

6. Verify that the spark plug is clean, properly gapped and that the threads are lightly lubricated with clean engine oil.

7. Be sure the plug threads smoothly into the cylinder head and is fully seated. Use a "thread chaser" if necessary to clean the threads in the cylinder head. Cross-threading or failing to fully seat the spark plug can cause overheating of the plug, exhaust blow-by, or thread damage. Follow the recommended torque specifications carefully. Some technicians will place a small piece of rubber tubing (like a piece of vacuum line) on the end of the spark plug and use it to turn the plug, by hand. In this way, if the plug is not threaded properly, not enough torque can be placed on the plug to do any damage.

8. Torque the spark plug to 11–15 ft. lbs. (15–20 Nm).

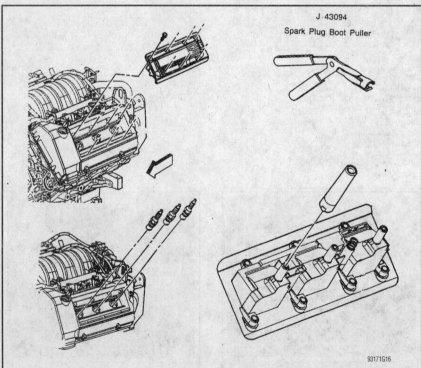

J 43094
Spark Plug Boot Puller

93171G16

Fig. 129 On the 3.5L engine, the spark plugs are located directly under the ignition coil "cassette". No spark plug wires are used

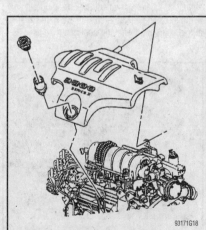

93171G18

Fig. 130 The cosmetic/acoustic engine cover must be removed for access to the spark plugs—3.8L engine

9. Install the spark wire to the spark plug, making sure the connector engages the spark plug and the boot is fully seated.

10. On the 3.8L (VIN K) engine, install the cosmetic/acoustic cover. Insert the tab of the fuel injector sight shield under the engine bracket. Place the hole of the shield onto the oil fill neck of the valve rocker arm cover. Install the tube/oil fill cap onto the valve rocker arm cover and twist clockwise in order to lock.

INSPECTION & GAPPING

▶ **See Figures 131, 132 and 133**

Check the plugs for deposits and wear. If they are not going to be replaced, clean the plugs thoroughly. Remember that any kind of deposit will decrease the efficiency of the plug. Plugs can be cleaned on a spark plug cleaning machine, which can sometimes be found in service stations. These machines are small abrasive blasters and some authorities feel, that since it rounds off the edge of the electrode, it actually raises the voltage requirements to fire the spark plug. While you may be able to do an acceptable job of cleaning with a stiff brush, keep in mind that spark plugs are relatively inexpensive and if there is any question as to their condition, replace them. If the plugs are cleaned, the electrodes must be filed flat. Use an ignition points file, not an emery board or the like, which will leave deposits. The electrodes must be filed perfectly flat with sharp edges. A spark jumps better from a sharp edge

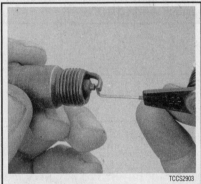

Fig. 131 Checking the spark plug gap with a round wire spark plug gauge

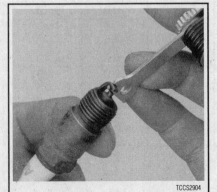

Fig. 132 Adjusting the spark plug gap

Check spark plug gap before installation. The ground electrode (the L-shaped one connected to the body of the plug) must be parallel to the center electrode. Using a wire feeler gauge, check and adjust the spark plug gap. When using a gauge, the proper size should pass between the electrodes with a slight drag. The next larger size should not be able to pass while the next smaller size should pass freely.

Always check the gap on new plugs as they are not always set correctly at the factory. Do not use a flat feeler gauge when measuring the gap on a used plug, because the reading may be inaccurate. A round-wire type gapping tool is the best way to check the gap. The correct gauge should pass through the electrode gap with a slight drag. If you're in doubt, try one size smaller and one larger. The smaller gauge should go through easily, while the larger one shouldn't go through at all. Wire gapping tools usually have a bending tool attached. Use that to adjust the side electrode until the proper distance is obtained. Absolutely never attempt to bend the center electrode. Also, be careful not to bend the side electrode too far or too often as it may weaken and break off in the engine, likely burying itself in the relatively softer metal of the piston top the first time the engine is started.

Spark Plug Wires

Use care not to damage the spark plug wires (more properly called the secondary ignition wires) or the spark plug boots. Rotate each boot about one half turn to dislodge it from the plug or coil tower before removing it from either the spark plug or the ignition coil. Never pierce a secondary ignition wire or boot for any testing purposes. Future problems are guaranteed if pinpoints or test lights are pushed through the insulation for testing.

The spark plug wiring used with these ignition systems is a carbon impregnated cord conductor encased in a 7mm or 8mm diameter silicone rubber jacket. The silicone jacket is designed to withstand very high temperatures. The silicone spark plug boots form a tight seal on the plug. The boot should be twisted one-half turn before removing. Care should also be used when connecting a timing light or other pick-up equipment. Do not force anything between the boot and wiring, or through the silicone jacket. Connections should be made in parallel using an adapter. Do not pull on the wire to remove.

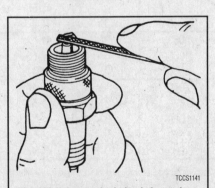

Fig. 133 If the standard plug is in good condition, the electrode may be filed flat—WARNING: do not file platinum plugs

Pull on the boot, or use a tool designed to remove spark plug boots.

TESTING

▶ **See Figure 134**

At every tune-up/inspection, visually check the spark plug cables for burns cuts, or breaks in the insulation. Check the boots and the nipples on the distributor cap and/or coil. Replace any damaged wiring.

Every 50,000 miles (80,000 Km) or 60 months, the resistance of the wires should be checked with an ohmmeter. Wires with excessive resistance will cause misfiring, and may make the engine difficult to start in damp weather.

To check resistance, disconnect the spark plug end and coil end of one spark plug wire. Connect an ohmmeter to lead to each end of the spark plug wire's terminals. A general rule is to replace the wire if the resistance is over 30,000 ohms. It should be remembered that resistance is a function of wire length and a longer wire may have more resistance. Today's vehicles are factory equipped with top quality spark plug wires since they must carry enormous amounts of energy, and, if treated carefully, generally give little trouble for the life of the vehicle.

REMOVAL & INSTALLATION

▶ **See Figures 135, 136 and 137**

➡ **If all of the wires must be disconnected from the spark plugs or the ignition coil pack at the same time, be sure to tag the wires to assure proper reconnection.**

When installing a new set of spark plug wires, replace the wires one at a time so there will be no mix-up. Start by replacing the longest cable first. Twist the boot of the spark plug wire ½ turn in each direction before pulling it off. Install the boot firmly over the spark plug. Route the wire exactly the same as the original. Insert the nipple firmly onto the tower on the ignition coil. Transfer any boot heat shields, plug wire conduits and retaining clips to the new wires. On some V6 engines, the front engine mount strut must be removed and the engine rotated, or pulled forward in its mounts to access the rear spark plug wires. For details regarding rotating the engine, please refer to the procedure located earlier in this section.

Fig. 134 Checking individual plug wire resistance with a digital ohmmeter

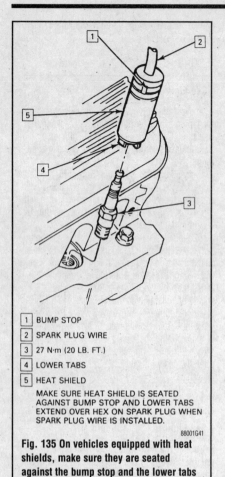

1. BUMP STOP
2. SPARK PLUG WIRE
3. 27 N·m (20 LB. FT.)
4. LOWER TABS
5. HEAT SHIELD

MAKE SURE HEAT SHIELD IS SEATED AGAINST BUMP STOP AND LOWER TABS EXTEND OVER HEX ON SPARK PLUG WHEN SPARK PLUG WIRE IS INSTALLED.

88001G41

Fig. 135 On vehicles equipped with heat shields, make sure they are seated against the bump stop and the lower tabs extend over the plug's hex

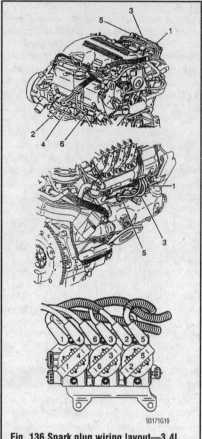

93171G19

Fig. 136 Spark plug wiring layout—3.4L (VIN E) engine shown, 3.1L (VIN M) engine similar

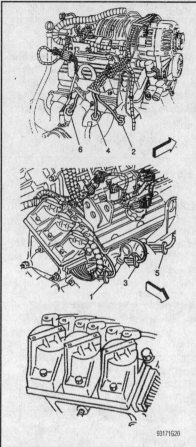

93171G20

Fig. 137 Spark plug wiring layout—3.8L (VIN K) engine shown

ENGINE TUNE-UP SPECIFICATIONS

Year	Engine ID/VIN	Engine Displacement Liters/cc	Spark Plug Gap (in.)	Ignition Timing	Fuel Pump (psi)	Idle Speed (rpm)	Valve Clearance In.	Valve Clearance Ex.
1997	M	3.1 (3135)	0.060	①	41-47	②	HYD	HYD
	X	3.4 (3350)	0.045	①	41-47	②	HYD	HYD
	1	3.8 (3791)	0.060	①	48-55	②	HYD	HYD
	K	3.8 (3791)	0.060	①	48-55	②	HYD	HYD
1998	M	3.1 (3135)	0.060	①	41-47	②	HYD	HYD
	1	3.8 (3791)	0.060	①	48-55	②	HYD	HYD
	K	3.8 (3791)	0.060	①	41-47	②	HYD	HYD
1999	M	3.1 (3135)	0.060	①	41-47	②	HYD	HYD
	1	3.8 (3791)	0.060	①	48-55	②	HYD	HYD
	K	3.8 (3791)	0.060	①	41-47	②	HYD	HYD
2000	M	3.1 (3135)	0.060	①	41-47	②	HYD	HYD
	E	3.4 (3348)	0.060	①	48-55	②	HYD	HYD
	H	3.5 (3474)	0.060	①	41-47	②	HYD	HYD
	1	3.8 (3791)	0.060	①	48-55	②	HYD	HYD
	K	3.8 (3791)	0.060	①	41-47	②	HYD	HYD

Note: The Vehicle Emission Control label reflects specification changes during production and must be used if they differ from this chart.

HYD: Hydraulic

① Distributorless Ignition System-No adjustment is possible

② Idle speed is computer controlled-No adjustment is possible

93171C03

Ignition Timing

All of the vehicles covered by this manual are equipped with distributorless ignition systems. Ignition timing is controlled by the Powertrain Control Module (PCM) and is not adjustable.

Valve Lash

All engines in the vehicles covered by this manual are equipped with hydraulic valve lifters and do not require periodic valve lash adjustment. Adjustment to zero lash is maintained automatically by hydraulic pressure in the lifters.

Idle Speed and Mixture Adjustments

Idle speed and mixture for all engines covered by this manual are electronically controlled by the Powertrain Control Module (PCM). Idle speed and mixture cannot be adjusted.

Air Conditioning System

SYSTEM SERVICE & REPAIR

➡️**It is recommended that the A/C system be serviced by an EPA Section 609 certified automotive technician utilizing a refrigerant recovery/recycling machine.**

The non-professional should not service his/her vehicle's A/C system for many reasons, including legal concerns, personal injury, environmental damage and cost. The following are some of the reasons why you may decide not to service your own vehicle's A/C system.

According to the U.S. Clean Air Act, it is a federal crime to service or repair (involving the refrigerant) a Motor Vehicle Air Conditioning (MVAC) system for money without being EPA certified. It is also illegal to vent R-134a refrigerant into the atmosphere.

State and/or local laws may be more strict than the federal regulations, so be sure to check with your state and/or local authorities for further information. For further federal information on the legality of servicing your A/C system, call the EPA Stratospheric Ozone Hotline.

➡️**Federal law dictates that a fine of up to $25,000 may be levied on people convicted of venting refrigerant into the atmosphere. Additionally, the EPA may pay up to $10,000 for information or services leading to a criminal conviction of the violation of these laws.**

When servicing an A/C system you run the risk of handling or coming in contact with refrigerant, which may result in skin or eye irritation or frostbite. Although low in toxicity (due to chemical stability), inhalation of concentrated refrigerant fumes is dangerous and can result in death; cases of fatal cardiac arrhythmia have been reported in people accidentally subjected to high levels of refrigerant. Some early symptoms include loss of concentration and drowsiness.

Also, refrigerants can decompose at high temperatures (near gas heaters or open flame), which may result in hydrofluoric acid, hydrochloric acid and phosgene (a fatal nerve gas).

R-134a refrigerant is a greenhouse gas which, if allowed to vent into the atmosphere, will contribute to global warming (the Greenhouse Effect).

It is usually more economically feasible to have a certified MVAC automotive technician perform A/C system service to your vehicle. While it is illegal to service an A/C system without the proper equipment, the home mechanic would have to purchase an expensive refrigerant recovery/recycling machine to service his/her own vehicle.

PREVENTIVE MAINTENANCE

Although the A/C system should not be serviced by the non-professional, preventive maintenance can be practiced and A/C system inspections can be performed to help maintain the efficiency of the vehicle's A/C system. For preventive maintenance, perform the following:

• The easiest and most important preventive maintenance for your A/C system is to be sure that it is used on a regular basis. Running the system for five minutes each month (no matter what the season) will help ensure that the seals and all internal components remain lubricated.

➡️**Most new vehicles automatically operate the A/C system compressor whenever the windshield defroster is activated. When running, the compressor lubricates the A/C system components; therefore, the A/C system would not need to be operated each month.**

• For efficient operation of an air conditioned vehicle's cooling system, the radiator cap should have a holding pressure which meets manufacturer's specifications. A cap which fails to hold these pressures should be replaced.

• Any obstruction of or damage to the condenser configuration will restrict air flow which is essential to its efficient operation. It is, therefore, a good rule to keep this unit clean and in proper physical shape.

➡️**Bug screens which are mounted in front of the condenser (unless they are original equipment) are regarded as obstructions.**

• The condensation drain tube expels any water, which accumulates on the bottom of the evaporator housing, into the engine compartment. If this tube is obstructed, the air conditioning performance can be restricted and condensation buildup can spill over onto the vehicle's floor.

SYSTEM INSPECTION

As stated earlier, although the A/C system should not be serviced by the do-it-yourselfer, preventive maintenance can be practiced and A/C system inspections can be performed to help maintain the efficiency of the vehicle's A/C system. For A/C system inspection, perform the following:

The easiest and often most important check for the air conditioning system consists of a visual inspection of the system components. Visually inspect the air conditioning system for refrigerant leaks, damaged compressor clutch, abnormal compressor drive belt tension and/or condition, plugged evaporator drain tube, blocked condenser fins, disconnected or broken wires, blown fuses, corroded connections and poor insulation.

A refrigerant leak will usually appear as an oily

residue at the leakage point in the system. The oily residue soon picks up dust or dirt particles from the surrounding air and appears greasy. Through time, this will build up and appear to be a heavy dirt impregnated grease.

For a thorough visual and operational inspection, check the following:

• Check the surface of the radiator and condenser for dirt, leaves or other material which might block air flow.

• Check for kinks in hoses and lines. Check the system for leaks.

• Make sure the drive belt is properly tensioned. When the air conditioning is operating, make sure the drive belt is free of noise or slippage.

• Make sure the blower motor operates at all appropriate positions, then check for distribution of the air from all outlets with the blower on HIGH or MAX.

➡️**Keep in mind that under conditions of high humidity, air discharged from the A/C vents may not feel as cold as expected, even if the system is working properly. This is because vaporized moisture in humid air retains heat more effectively than dry air, thereby making humid air more difficult to cool.**

Windshield Wipers

ELEMENT (REFILL) CARE & REPLACEMENT

▶ **See Figures 138, 139 and 140**

For maximum effectiveness and longest element life, the windshield and wiper blades should be kept clean. Dirt, tree sap, road tar and so on will cause streaking, smearing and blade deterioration if left on the glass. It is advisable to wash the windshield carefully with a commercial glass cleaner at least once a month. Wipe off the rubber blades with the wet rag afterwards. Do not attempt to move wipers across the windshield by hand; damage to the motor and drive mechanism will result.

To inspect and/or replace the wiper blade elements, place the wiper switch in the LOW speed position and the ignition switch in the **ACC** position. When the wiper blades are approximately vertical on the windshield, turn the ignition switch to **OFF**.

Examine the wiper blade elements. If they are found to be cracked, broken or torn, they should be replaced immediately. Replacement intervals will vary with usage, although ozone deterioration usually limits element life to about one year. If the wiper pattern is smeared or streaked, or if the blade chatters across the glass, the elements should be replaced. It is easiest and most sensible to replace the elements in pairs.

If your vehicle is equipped with aftermarket blades, there are several different types of refills and your vehicle might have any kind. Aftermarket blades and arms rarely use the exact same type blade or refill as the original equipment.

Regardless of the type of refill used, be sure to follow the part manufacturer's instructions closely. Make sure that all of the frame jaws are engaged as the refill is pushed into place and locked. If the metal blade holder and frame are allowed to touch the glass during wiper operation, the glass will be scratched.

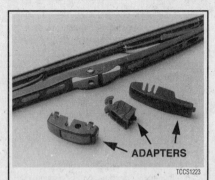

Fig. 138 Most aftermarket blades are available with multiple adapters to fit different vehicles

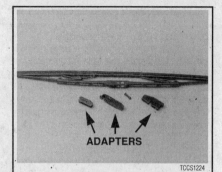

Fig. 139 Choose a blade which will fit your vehicle, and that will be readily available next time you need blades

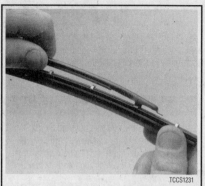

Fig. 140 When installed, be certain the blade is fully inserted into the backing

Tires and Wheels

Common sense and good driving habits will afford maximum tire life. Fast starts, sudden stops and hard cornering are hard on tires and will shorten their useful life span. Make sure that you don't overload the vehicle or run with incorrect pressure in the tires. Both of these practices will increase tread wear.

➡️ **For optimum tire life, keep the tires properly inflated, rotate them often and have the wheel alignment checked periodically.**

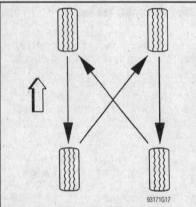

Fig. 141 GM's recommended rotation pattern for front wheel drive cars. DO NOT include the "Temporary Use Only" spare tire in the rotation

Inspect your tires frequently. Be especially careful to watch for bubbles in the tread or sidewall, deep cuts or underinflation. Replace any tires with bubbles in the sidewall. If cuts are so deep that they penetrate to the cords, discard the tire. Any cut in the sidewall of a radial tire renders it unsafe. Also look for uneven tread wear patterns that may indicate the front end is out of alignment or that the tires are out of balance.

TIRE ROTATION

◆ See Figures 141, 142 and 143

Tires must be rotated periodically to equalize wear patterns that vary with a tire's position on the vehicle. Tires will also wear in an uneven way as the front steering/suspension system wears to the point where the alignment should be reset.

Rotating the tires will ensure maximum life for the tires as a set, so you will not have to discard a tire early due to wear on only part of the tread. Regular rotation is required to equalize wear.

Some styled or "mag" wheels may have different offsets front to rear. In these cases, the rear wheels must not be used up front and vice-versa. Furthermore, if these wheels are equipped with unidirectional tires, they cannot be rotated unless the tire is remounted for the proper direction of rotation.

➡️ **The compact or space-saver spare is strictly for emergency use. It must never be included in the tire rotation or placed on the vehicle for everyday use.**

TIRE DESIGN

◆ See Figures 144 thru 148

For maximum satisfaction, tires should be used in sets of four. Mixing of different types (radial, bias-belted, fiberglass belted) must be avoided. In most cases, the vehicle manufacturer has designated a type of tire on which the vehicle will perform best. Your first choice when replacing tires should be to use the same type of tire that the manufacturer recommends.

When radial tires are used, tire sizes and wheel diameters should be selected to maintain ground clearance and tire load capacity equivalent to the original specified tire. Radial tires should always be used in sets of four.

✳️ WARNING

Radial tires should never be used on only the front axle. Radial tires must be used on all four positions.

When selecting tires, pay attention to the original size as marked on the tire. Most tires are described using an industry size code sometimes referred to as P-Metric. This allows the exact identification of the tire specifications, regardless of the manufacturer. If selecting a different tire size or brand, remember to check the installed tire for any sign of interference with the body or suspension while the vehicle is stopping, turning sharply or heavily loaded.

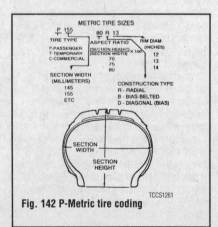

Fig. 142 P-Metric tire coding

Fig. 143 Tires with deep cuts, or cuts which bulge, should be replaced immediately

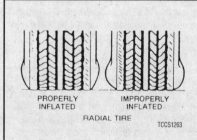

Fig. 144 Radial tires have a characteristic side wall bulge; don't try to measure pressure by looking at the tire. Use a quality tire gauge

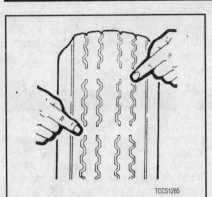

Fig. 145 Tread wear indicators will appear when the tire is worn

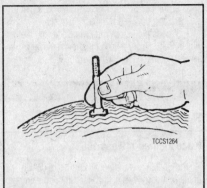

Fig. 146 Accurate tread wear depth indicators are inexpensive and handy

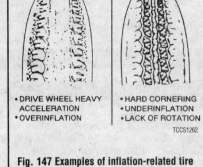

- DRIVE WHEEL HEAVY ACCELERATION
- OVERINFLATION
- HARD CORNERING
- UNDERINFLATION
- LACK OF ROTATION

Fig. 147 Examples of inflation-related tire wear patterns

CONDITION	RAPID WEAR AT SHOULDERS	RAPID WEAR AT CENTER	CRACKED TREADS	WEAR ON ONE SIDE	FEATHERED EDGE	BALD SPOTS	SCALLOPED WEAR
EFFECT							
CAUSE	UNDER-INFLATION OR LACK OF ROTATION	OVER-INFLATION OR LACK OF ROTATION	UNDER-INFLATION OR EXCESSIVE SPEED*	EXCESSIVE CAMBER	INCORRECT TOE	UNBALANCED WHEEL OR TIRE DEFECT *	LACK OF ROTATION OF TIRES OR WORN OR OUT-OF-ALIGNMENT SUSPENSION.
CORRECTION	ADJUST PRESSURE TO SPECIFICATIONS WHEN TIRES ARE COOL ROTATE TIRES		ADJUST CAMBER TO SPECIFICATIONS	ADJUST TOE-IN TO SPECIFICATIONS	DYNAMIC OR STATIC BALANCE WHEELS	ROTATE TIRES AND INSPECT SUSPENSION	

*HAVE TIRE INSPECTED FOR FURTHER USE.

Fig. 148 Common tire wear patterns and causes

Snow Tires

Good radial tires can produce a big advantage in slippery weather, but in snow, a street radial tire does not have sufficient tread to provide traction and control. The small grooves of a street tire quickly pack with snow and the tire behaves like a billiard ball on a marble floor. The more open, chunky tread of a snow tire will self-clean as the tire turns, providing much better grip on snowy surfaces.

To satisfy municipalities requiring snow tires during weather emergencies, most snow tires carry either an M + S designation after the tire size stamped on the sidewall, or the designation "all-season." In general, no change in tire size is necessary when buying snow tires.

Most manufacturers strongly recommend the use of 4 snow tires on their vehicles for reasons of stability. If snow tires are fitted only to the drive wheels, the opposite end of the vehicle may become very unstable when braking or turning on slippery surfaces. This instability can lead to unpleasant endings if the driver can't counteract the slide in time.

Note that snow tires, whether 2 or 4, will affect vehicle handling in all non-snow situations. The stiffer, heavier snow tires will noticeably change the turning and braking characteristics of the vehicle. Once the snow tires are installed, you must re-learn the behavior of the vehicle and drive accordingly.

➡**Consider buying extra wheels on which to mount the snow tires. Once done, the "snow wheels" can be installed and removed as needed. This eliminates the potential damage to tires or wheels from seasonal removal and** installation. Even if your vehicle has styled wheels, see if inexpensive steel wheels are available. Although the look of the vehicle will change, the expensive wheels will be protected from salt, curb hits and pothole damage.

TIRE STORAGE

If they are mounted on wheels, store the tires at proper inflation pressure. All tires should be kept in a cool, dry place. If they are stored in the garage or basement, do not let them stand on a concrete floor; set them on strips of wood, a mat or a large stack of newspaper. Keeping them away from direct moisture is of paramount importance. Tires should not be stored upright, but in a flat position.

INFLATION & INSPECTION

The importance of proper tire inflation cannot be overemphasized. A tire employs air as part of its structure. It is designed around the supporting strength of the air at a specified pressure. For this reason, improper inflation drastically reduces the tire's ability to perform as intended. A tire will lose some air in day-to-day use; having to add a few pounds of air periodically is not necessarily a sign of a leaking tire.

Two items should be a permanent fixture in every glove compartment: an accurate tire pressure gauge and a tread depth gauge. Check the tire pressure (including the spare) regularly with a pocket type gauge. Too often, the gauge on the end of the air hose at your corner garage is not accurate because it suffers too much abuse. Always check tire pressure when the tires are cold, as pressure increases with temperature. If you must move the vehicle to check the tire inflation, do not drive more than a mile before checking. A cold tire is generally one that has not been driven for more than three hours.

A plate or sticker is normally provided somewhere in the vehicle (door post, hood, tailgate or trunk lid) which shows the proper pressure for the tires. Never counteract excessive pressure build-up by bleeding off air pressure (letting some air out). This will cause the tire to run hotter and wear quicker.

✳✳ CAUTION

Never exceed the maximum tire pressure embossed on the tire! This is the pressure to be used when the tire is at maximum loading, but it is rarely the correct pressure for everyday driving. Consult the owner's manual or the tire pressure sticker for the correct tire pressure.

All tires have built-in tread wear indicator bars that show up as ½ in. (13mm) wide smooth bands across the tire when $^1/_{16}$ in. (1.5mm) of tread remains. The appearance of tread wear indicators means that the tires should be replaced. In fact, many states have laws prohibiting the use of tires with less than this amount of tread.

CARE OF SPECIAL WHEELS

If you have invested money in magnesium, aluminum alloy or sport wheels, special precautions should be taken to make sure your investment is not wasted and that your special wheels look good for the life of the vehicle.

Special wheels are easily damaged and/or scratched. Occasionally check the rims for cracking, impact damage or air leaks. If any of these are found, replace the wheel. But in order to prevent this type of damage and the costly replacement of a special wheel, observe the following precautions:

- Use extra care not to damage the wheels during removal, installation, balancing, etc. After removal of the wheels from the vehicle, place them on a mat or other protective surface. If they are to be stored for any length of time, support them on strips of wood. Never store tires and wheels upright; the tread may develop flat spots.

• When driving, watch for hazards; it doesn't take much to crack a wheel.

• When washing, use a mild soap or non-abrasive dish detergent (keeping in mind that detergent tends to remove wax). Avoid cleansers with abra-sives or the use of hard brushes. There are many cleaners and polishes for special wheels.

• If possible, remove the wheels during the winter. Salt and sand used for snow removal can severely damage the finish of a wheel.

• Make certain the recommended lug nut torque is never exceeded or the wheel may crack. Never use snow chains on special wheels; severe scratching will occur.

FLUIDS AND LUBRICANTS

Fluid Disposal

Used fluids such as engine oil, transmission fluid, antifreeze and brake fluid are hazardous wastes and must be disposed of properly. Before draining any fluids, consult with your local authorities; in many areas, waste oil, antifreeze, etc. is being accepted as a part of recycling programs. A number of service stations and auto parts stores are also accepting waste fluids for recycling.

Be sure of the recycling center's policies before draining any fluids, as many will not accept different fluids that have been mixed together.

Fuel and Engine Oil Recommendations

FUEL

➡**Some fuel additives contain chemicals that can damage the catalytic converter and/or the oxygen sensors. Read all of the labels carefully before using any additive in the engine or fuel system. The owner's manual should also be consulted.**

All of the vehicles covered by this manual are designed to run on unleaded fuel. The use of a leaded fuel in a vehicle requiring unleaded will plug the catalytic converter and render it inoperative. It will also increase exhaust backpressure because the material in the converter will tend to collapse and plug the exhaust, severely reducing engine power. The minimum octane rating of the unleaded fuel being used must be at least 87, which usually means regular unleaded, but some high performance engines may require higher octane ratings. Fuel should be selected for the brand and octane which performs best with your engine.

➡**All of the engines covered by this manual require a fuel with an octane rating of 87 or higher, except for the 3.8L (VIN 1) supercharged engine which requires premium fuel with an octane rating of 92 or higher.**

The use of a fuel too low in octane (a measure of anti-knock quality) will result in spark knock. While the computer controlled ignition system uses knock sensors to detect knock and then electronically adjust the ignition timing to compensate, there is a limit to the system's adjustment capability. Since many factors such as altitude, terrain, air temperature and humidity affect operating efficiency, some light knocking (usually on acceleration) may result and is even considered normal. But if persistent knocking occurs, it may be necessary to switch to a higher grade of fuel. Continuous or heavy knocking may result in engine damage.

ENGINE OIL

♦ **See Figures 149 and 150**

The Society of Automotive Engineers (SAE) grade number indicates the viscosity of the engine oil and thus its ability to lubricate at a given temperature. The lower the SAE grade number, the lighter the oil, the lower the viscosity, and the easier it should be to crank the engine in cold weather. Oil viscosities should be chosen from those oils recommended for the lowest anticipated temperatures during the oil change interval. With the proper viscosity, you will be assured of easy cold starting and sufficient engine protection. The information found in your owner's manual will give you the best recommendations for your vehicle.

Fig. 149 Look for the API oil identification label when choosing your engine oil

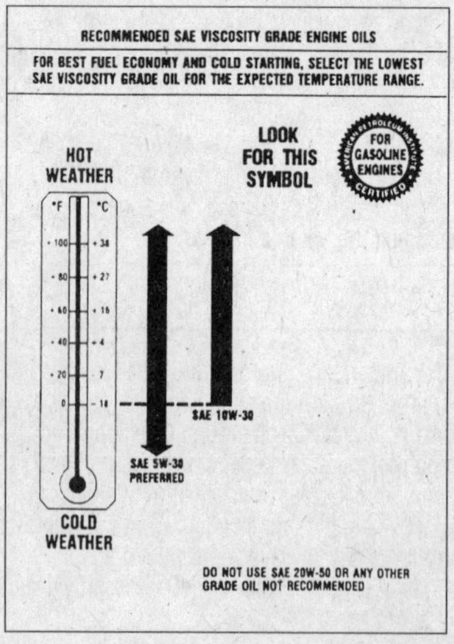

Fig. 150 Recommended SAE engine oil viscosity grades for gasoline engines

Multi-viscosity oils (5W-30, 10W-30, etc.) offer the important advantage of being adaptable to temperature extremes. They allow easy starting at low temperatures, yet they give good protection at high speeds and engine temperatures. This is a decided advantage in changeable climates or in long distance driving.

The American Petroleum Institute (API) designation indicates the classification of engine oil used under certain given operating conditions. Only oil designated for Service SJ, or the latest superseding oil grade should be used. Oils of the SJ type perform a variety of functions inside the engine in addition to their basic function as a lubricant. Through a balanced system of metallic detergents and polymeric dispersants, the oil prevents the formation of high and low temperature deposits and also keeps sludge and particles in suspension. Acids, particularly sulfuric acid, one of several by-product of the combustion process, are neutralized by the additive package in the oil. Both the SAE grade number and the API designation can be found on the side of the oil bottle.

Synthetic Oils

There are excellent synthetic and fuel-efficient oils available that, under the right circumstances, can help provide better fuel mileage and better engine protection. However, these advantages come at a price, which can be significantly more than the price per quart of conventional motor oils.

Before pouring any synthetic oils into your vehicle's engine, you should consider the condition of the engine and the type of driving you do. It is also wise to again, consult the owner's manual.

Generally, it is best to avoid the use of synthetic oil in both brand new and older, high mileage engines. New engine require a proper break-in, and some sources feel that the synthetics are so slippery, that they can impede the normal wear engines need for break in. Some manufacturers recommend that you accumulate at least 5,000 miles (8,000 km) before switching to a synthetic oil. Conversely, older engines are looser and tend to lose more oil; synthetics will slip past worn parts more readily than regular oil. If you engine already leaks oils (due to worn parts or bad seals/gaskets), it may leak more with a synthetic oil.

Engine

OIL LEVEL CHECK

♦ **See Figures 151 thru 157**

The engine oil level indicator (dipstick) is located at the front center of the engine compartment. The oil level indicator handle generally has a yellow loop design or a T-handle, for easy identification.

1. At each fuel fill, turn the engine **OFF** and give the oil a few minutes to drain back into the oil pan.

2. Pull the dipstick out of the dipstick tube, clean it with a paper towel or cloth to remove splash oil, then fully reinsert the dipstick all the way.

3. Remove the dipstick again, keeping the tip down, and check the level. The dipstick should either have a crosshatched area, or marks indicating the maximum (FULL) and minimum (ADD) oil levels. Approximately one quart of oil will raise the oil level from the ADD mark to the FULL mark. Do not overfill.

✳✳ WARNING

DO NOT overfill the crankcase. It may result in oil-fouled spark plugs, oil leaks caused by oil seal failure or engine damage due to oil foaming.

➥Vehicles equipped with the 3.8L (VIN 1) supercharged engine use a special oil in the supercharger. The supercharger lubrication system is a sealed system and does not use engine oil. The supercharger oil level should be checked every 36 months or every 30,000 miles (48,000 km), whichever occurs first. Use only GM Supercharger Oil Part Number 12345982.

OIL & FILTER CHANGE

▶ See Figures 158 thru 168

✳✳ WARNING

To prevent leakage around the oil filter, it is very important that the installation instructions are closely followed or engine damage may result.

1. Raise and safely support the vehicle using safety stands.
2. Position a drain pan of at least 5 quarts capacity under the oil pan. Wipe road dirt and debris from around the oil drain plug with a cloth.

Fig. 151 This 3.4L (VIN X) engine uses a dipstick with a loop handle

Fig. 152 Another engine, but the dipstick location is similar—3.1L Engine

Fig. 153 The 3.8L engine uses a T-handle dipstick

Fig. 154 Wipe the dipstick with a clean cloth to remove splash oil, then reinsert for an accurate level reading

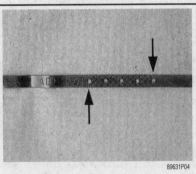

Fig. 155 The oil level should be within the crosshatched area on the dipstick (between the photo's arrows)

Fig. 156 If the oil level is low, remove the fill cap . . .

Fig. 157 . . . then add the correct amount of oil through the opening in the valve cover

Fig. 158 Loosen the drain plug using the proper size wrench

Fig. 159 Quickly withdraw the drain plug and move your hands out of the way

3. Loosen the drain plug using a ratchet, short extension and socket or a box-end wrench. Turn the plug out by hand, using a cloth to shield your fingers if the engine oil is hot. Keep inward pressure on the plug as you unscrew it, so oil won't escape past the threads and you can remove it without being burned by hot oil.

4. Quickly withdraw the drain plug and move your hands out of the way. Do not drop the drain plug. Allow the engine oil to drain completely. Clean the drain plug thoroughly, and inspect the gasket. If it is damaged, it should be replaced. Reinstall the cleaned drain plug. Do not overtighten the plug.

5. Move the drain pan under the oil filter. Use a strap-type or cap-type wrench to loosen the oil fil-ter. Remove the oil filter by rotating it counterclockwise. It contains nearly a quart of dirty oil and should be allowed to drain into the pan.

6. Using a clean, lint-free cloth, wipe off the oil filter mounting surface where the rubber O-ring will seat.

7. Lightly oil the replacement oil filter O-ring with clean engine oil. This is important since the oil will react with the rubber and cause the seal to slightly swell after installation. This means the filter will seal well without having to over-tighten the filter, causing removal difficulties next oil change. Install the oil filter by rotating it clockwise. After the oil filter O-ring contacts the oil filter mounting surface, continue to tighten ¾ to 1 full turn. If necessary, use a cap-type wrench or strap-type wrench with a swivel handle to insure proper installation. DO NOT OVER-TIGHTEN.

8. If raised, carefully lower the vehicle.

9. Refill the engine with the correct amount of fresh engine oil. In nearly all cases, this will be five quarts of oil. Check the Capacities Chart in this section for the specifications for your vehicle.

10. Check the level on the dipstick to verify the correct amount of oil has been added. It is normal for the level to be above the FULL mark until the engine has been run and oil has filled the filter. With the engine oil at the proper level, run the engine for about three minutes and thoroughly check the oil filter, oil pan, drain plug and surrounding areas for leaks.

11. Used engine oil should be properly recycled. Do not dump drain oil.

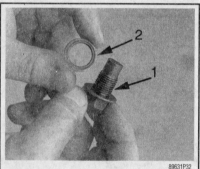

Fig. 160 Clean the drain plug (1) and inspect the gasket seal (2). Replace, if necessary

Fig. 161 Allow the oil to completely drain from the pan, then reinstall the drain plug

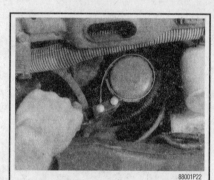

Fig. 162 Use an oil filter wrench to loosen the oil filter. A strap-type wrench was used here

Fig. 163 On this engine, the oil filter is being removed with a special pliers-type gripping tool

Fig. 164 Oil filter removal can be messy, so protective gloves may be a good idea

Fig. 165 Clean the oil filter mounting area with a clean, lint-free cloth before installing a new filter

Fig. 166 Before installing a new oil filter, lightly coat the rubber seal with clean engine oil

Fig. 167 Remove the oil fill cap on the valve cover to refill the engine with oil

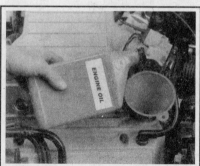

Fig. 168 Using a funnel prevents spills. Oil should be kept off all rubber parts, especially hoses and rubber drive belts

➡Many of the vehicles covered by this manual use an oil change indicator or oil life monitor which must be reset.

Oil Change Indicators and Monitors

These vehicles use systems that inform the driver when an oil change is needed. This indicator should be reset after every oil change. There are some variations to the reset procedures depending on the make, model, year and the vehicle's optional equipment. The vehicle's owner's manual should be consulted because it will help identify the system used on your specific vehicle, engine and option combination.

One version of the system is called the Change Oil Soon Indicator. It predicts when the oil's remaining life is almost up. The system predicts remaining oil life using travel distances, coolant temperature, engine RPM, and vehicle speed inputs. This indicator alerts the driver to change to oil on a schedule consistent with the vehicle's driving conditions.

Another variation is called the Oil Life Monitor. The oil life monitor shows the percentage of the oil's remaining useful life. The system predicts remaining oil life using travel distances, coolant temperature, engine RPM, and vehicle speed inputs. This monitor should also be reset after every oil change.

CHANGE OIL SOON INDICATOR

1997 Grand Prix, Century and Regal

▸ See Figure 169

The CHANGE OIL SOON indicator should come on as a bulb check when the engine is first started. If this indicator stays on for approximately 20 seconds when the ignition is first turned **ON**, change the engine oil and filter. When to change the engine oil depends on driving habits and conditions because they affect engine speed, coolant temperature and vehicle speed. Because of this, the CHANGE OIL SOON indicator may come on as early as 2,000 miles (3,200 km) or less under harsh driving conditions. Reset this indicator after every oil change using the following procedure

1. Turn the ignition to the **ON** or **RUN** position, WITHOUT STARTING THE ENGINE.
2. Fully press and release the accelerator pedal three times within five seconds.
3. If the CHANGE OIL SOON indicator flashes two times. The system is reset.
4. If the CHANGE OIL SOON indicator comes

FUNCTION MONITOR
WASHER FLUID
LOW COOLANT
LOW FUEL

SECURITY
DOOR HOOD
TRUNK AJAR

LIGHT CHECK
HEAD HI BEAM
TURN SIGNAL
BRAKE TAIL LIGHT

SERVICE REMINDER
CHANGE OIL
OIL FILTER
ROTATE TIRE
TUNE UP
MILES KM

88800

89631G18

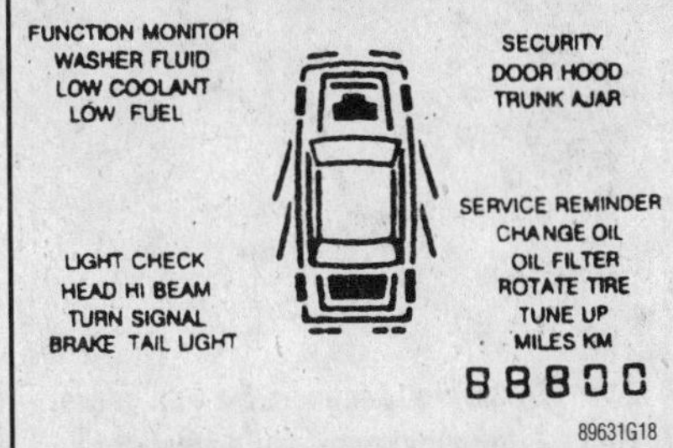

Fig. 169 Typical Driver Information Center (DIC) display

on and stays on for five seconds, try the reset system again.

➡If the vehicle is equipped with a Driver Information Display (DIC) in the instrument panel cluster, the system may be reset by pressing the DIC RESET button for five seconds while OIL LIFE is displayed.

OIL LIFE MONITOR

1998–00 Vehicles

➡This procedure covers all 1998–00 vehicles, except for the vehicles with the specific option packages outlined below. It also does not cover the 2000 Monte Carlo, which is outlined below. To determine which procedure to use, first read through all of the procedures and decide which one fits your vehicle and option package.

These vehicles are equipped with an engine oil life monitor. The engine oil life monitor will show when to change the engine oil and oil filter. This will usually occur between 3,000–7,500 miles (4,800–12,000 km) since the last oil change. Under severe conditions, the indicator may come on before 3,000 miles (4,800 km). Never drive this vehicle more than 7,500 miles (12,000 km) or 12 months without an oil and filter change. The engine oil life monitor will not detect dust in the oil. If the vehicle is driven in a dusty area, be sure to change the oil and filter every 3,000 miles or sooner if the CHANGE OIL indicator comes on. Reset the oil life monitor when the oil and oil filter has been changed. Use the following procedure.

1. Turn the ignition switch to the **ON** position, but DO NOT START THE ENGINE.
2. Fully depress and release the accelerator pedal slowly three times within 5 seconds.
3. If the CHANGE OIL (some instrument panels may have a variation of this warning, such as CHANGE OIL SOON, or CHG OIL SOON) indicator flashes (usually two times), the system is resetting.
4. Turn the ignition switch to the **OFF** position after the indicator has finished flashing, then start the vehicle. If the CHANGE OIL indicator comes back on, the engine oil life monitor has not been reset. Repeat the procedure.

1997–98 Century and Regal and 1999–00 Intrigue

If the vehicle is equipped with the U20 option, which is an instrument cluster containing gauges for oil, coolant, temperature, volts, trip odometer, tachometer and fuel data display, the vehicle has an oil life monitor. The oil life monitor shows an estimate of the oil's remaining useful life. When the oil life index is less than 10%, the display will show OIL LIFE LOW. Reset this monitor after every oil change using the following procedure.

1. Locate and press the Driver Information Display switch RESET button.
2. Hold the reset button for more than five seconds while the oil life monitor is being displayed, or until the oil life percentage changes to 100%.

1997–00 Grand Prix

If the vehicle is equipped with the U40 option, which is the Direct Digital Display Readout option

(Trip Computer), the vehicle has an oil life monitor. The oil life monitor shows the percentage of the oil's remaining useful life. The system predicts remaining oil life using travel distances, coolant temperature, engine RPM and vehicle speed inputs. Reset this monitor after every oil change using the following procedure.

1. Press the trip calculator MODE button until the light appears next to OIL LIFE.
2. Press and hold the trip calculator RESET button until the oil life percentage changes to 100%.

2000 Monte Carlo

Follow this procedure to reset the GM Oil Life System• on vehicles equipped with the DE 100 Series Radio®.

1. Turn the ignition switch to the **ACC** or **ON** positions and the radio off.
2. Press and hold the DISP button on the radio for at least five seconds until SETTINGS is displayed.
3. Press and seek up or down arrow to scroll through the main menu.
4. Scroll until OIL LIFE appears on the display.
5. Press the PREV or NEXT button to enter the submenu. RESET will be displayed.
6. Press the DISP button to reset. A chime will be heard to verify the new setting and DONE will be displayed for one second.
7. Once the message has been reset, scroll until EXIT appears on the display.

Automatic Transaxle

FLUID RECOMMENDATIONS

When adding or refilling the transaxle, DEXRON® III Automatic Transmission Fluid is preferred. DEXRON® IIE is an acceptable substitute. It's a good idea to purchase a quart or two of GM DEXRON® III Automatic Transmission Fluid from an authorized GM dealer so the correct transmission fluid is always available.

LEVEL CHECK

▸ See Figures 170, 171 and 172

1. Park the vehicle on a level surface. Apply the parking brake and block the wheels.
2. Start the engine and operate the vehicle for 15 minutes or until the transaxle fluid reaches operating temperatures; about 180–200 °F (82–93°C). The end of the dipstick will be too hot to hold comfortably.
3. While the engine is idling and with your foot on the brake pedal, move the shift lever through each gear range, ending in Park.
4. Locate and pull out the transaxle dipstick, located at the rear of the engine and wipe off the splash fluid.
5. Push the dipstick completely in the filler tube, wait three seconds, then pull the dipstick out again.
6. Check both sides of the dipstick. Generally, an area of etched lines designed to retain fluid, called the crosshatch area, shows the acceptable range of fluid level. The fluid level is acceptable if it is anywhere within the crosshatch area. The fluid level does not have to be at the top of the cross-

Fig. 170 With the engine idling, remove the automatic transaxle dipstick, wipe clean and reinsert it fully

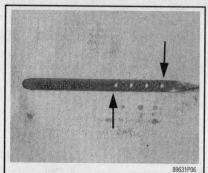
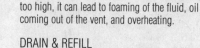

Fig. 171 DO NOT add fluid if the level is anywhere within the crosshatched area on the dipstick

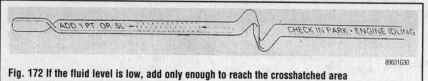

Fig. 172 If the fluid level is low, add only enough to reach the crosshatched area

hatch area. DO NOT add fluid unless the level is below the crosshatch area. The fluid level will be higher on the dipstick when the transaxle is cold; the level will drop at operating temperature.

7. The fluid color should be light brown. Transmission fluid may turn dark with normal use. This does not always indicate oxidation or contamination. If the fluid is foamy, the transaxle may be overfilled. If the fluid color is a milky, non-transparent pink, there is likely contamination from the engine's cooling system by way a failed transmission oil cooler in the radiator. Since coolant will adversely affect the seals and friction plates in the transaxle, this requires immediate replacement of the transmission oil cooler (usually a complete radiator replacement) and a complete drain and refill of the transaxle fluid.

8. If the fluid level is low, add only enough DEXRON® to bring the level into the crosshatch area. It generally takes less than a pint. Do not overfill an automatic transmission. If the fluid level is too high, it can lead to foaming of the fluid, oil coming out of the vent, and overheating.

DRAIN & REFILL

▶ **See Figures 173 thru 181**

The fluid should be drained when warm so contaminants are in suspension in the transaxle fluid.

1. Raise and safely support the vehicle on safety stands.
2. Place a suitable drain pan under the transaxle fluid pan.
3. There is no drain plug for changing the transaxle fluid, so fluid change on most automatics is messy. Draining the fluid involves loosening some bolts, removing others, and, after the pan is loosened, letting the fluid run out from the joint between the pan and gasket and the transaxle body. Use a drain pan with a large enough opening to accommodate draining the fluid from a large section of the pan.
4. There are twenty oil pan bolts. Loosen and remove only the bolts from the front and sides of the pan.
5. Loosen the rear bolts about four turns.

Fig. 173 Installed view of the automatic transaxle pan

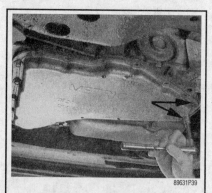

Fig. 174 Remove the bolts from the front and sides of the pan

Fig. 175 Tap or pry the pan loose, then allow the fluid to drain completely

Fig. 176 After all the fluid has drained; unfasten the remaining bolts and remove the transaxle fluid pan

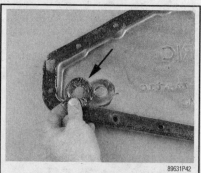

Fig. 177 Remove the pan magnet and inspect it for metal chips, which may indicate excessive wear

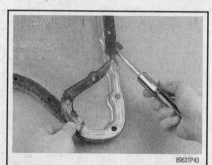

Fig. 178 Carefully remove the pan gasket. Some late-model pans use a steel-core gasket, which, if in good condition, can be reused

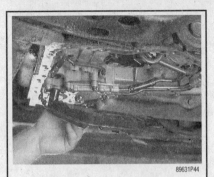

Fig. 179 Removing the filter from the transaxle

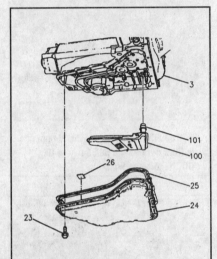

3 TRANSAXLE CASE

23 BOLT

24 OIL PAN

25 BOTTOM PAN GASKET

26 MAGNET, CHIP COLLECTOR

100 FILTER

101 SEAL

Fig. 180 Exploded view of the automatic transaxle fluid pan, gasket and filter

Fig. 181 Use a long-neck funnel to add fluid through the automatic transaxle dipstick tube

✻✻ WARNING

Do not pry between the oil pan and the aluminum transaxle case. A prying tool could mark, scratch or gouge the gasket sealing rail making it impossible for the replacement gasket to provide a satisfactory seal.

6. Lightly tap the pan with a rubber mallet to loosen and allow the fluid to drain.

➡️**If the transaxle fluid is very dark or has a burnt smell, transaxle damage is indicated. Have the transaxle checked professionally.**

7. Remove the remaining bolts, the pan and the gasket. Hold the pan level to keep a small amount of fluid in the bottom. This allows you to check the sediments in the pan for contaminants. Remove the pan and set aside.

8. The transaxle oil filter has a small neck that is a press-fit into the transaxle case. It should pull straight out. A little careful prying may be required. The rubber grommet that accepts the neck on the filter will likely remain in the transaxle case. Use a small screwdriver to carefully remove the seal. Use care not to damage the case sealing surface.

9. Inside the pan should be a small magnet. Inspect the oil pan magnet for small bits of steel. The factory places the magnet here to trap stray metal particles. Excessive amounts of steel shavings indicate internal transmission damage. A small amount of sediment in the pan is normal as the friction elements wear.

10. If desired, use side cutters to open up the transaxle oil filter assembly by cutting or prying the metal crimping away from the top of the filter and by pulling the filter apart. Inspect the filter for excessive amounts of the following: clutch plate assembly fiber material, indicating clutch distress; bronze slivers, indicating bushing wear; steel particles, indicating internal transaxle wear.

To install:

11. Clean all parts well. Clean all traces of old gasket off of the oil pan gasket rail as well as the sealing surface on the transaxle. Use care not to damage the sealing surface on either area.

12. Inspect the oil pan for damage to the sealing surface and dents or cracks in the pan.

13. If the oil filter seal came out of the case, install it using a socket as a driver. Gently tap in with a plastic mallet. Using the same plastic mallet, gently tap the filter neck in place.

14. The design of the steel-core factory gasket is such that it may be reusable, if not bent or otherwise damaged. Note that most replacement transaxle oil filters come with a new gasket. Lay the oil pan gasket on the pan and install the pan to the case. Normally, no sealer is used. Start a few bolts at the ends of the pan to hold it and to keep the gasket from moving out of position. Install all 20 bolts and tighten to 97 inch lbs. (11 Nm). Do not overtighten or the gasket could be squeezed out of position and/or the bolt threads in the aluminum transaxle case could be damaged.

15. Lower the vehicle to the floor.

16. To refill the transaxle from just a bottom pan removal, 7.4 quarts of DEXRON® IIE or DEXRON® III

will be required. Use a funnel to reach the filler/dipstick tube. Use care not to spill fluid in the engine compartment.

17. Check for leaks.

Cooling System

The engine is kept cool by coolant circulating through the engine to a radiator where the heat to transferred to the air. The coolant is circulated by a pump driven by the engine accessory drive belt. The complete cooling system consists of a radiator, recovery system, cooling fans (electric on these vehicles) thermostat, pump and the serpentine drive belt.

FLUID RECOMMENDATIONS

See Figure 182

All of the vehicles covered by this book were originally filled at the factory with GM Goodwrench DEX-COOL®. DEX-COOL® is an ethylene-glycol coolant that was developed to last for 150,000 miles (240,000 km), or 5 years, whichever occurs first. It is recommended that only DEX-COOL® be used when coolant is added or changed. It's a good idea to purchase a gallon container or two of DEX-COOL® from an authorized GM dealer so the correct antifreeze is always available. A 50/50 mixture of this ethylene-glycol coolant and water should be used, providing freezing protection down to -34°F (1°C), boiling protection to 265°F (265°C), and rust and corrosion protection for the system. A solution stronger than 70% antifreeze is not recommended and pure antifreeze will freeze at only -8°F (-22°C).

Fig. 182 Late-model GM products use a special long-life coolant called DEX-COOL® that can NOT be mixed with other types of coolant

LEVEL CHECK

◆ **See Figures 183 and 184**

A pressure vent radiator cap is used on all models to allow a buildup of 15 psi in the cooling system. This pressure raises the boiling point of coolant to approximately 262°F. at sea level. DO NOT remove the radiator cap to check the engine coolant level.

Always check the coolant level by looking through the "see through" area of the coolant recov-

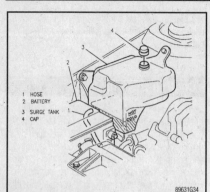

1 HOSE
2 BATTERY
3 SURGE TANK
4 CAP

Fig. 183 The coolant reservoir is normally located on the fenderwall

Fig. 184 Coolant level should be between the FULL HOT (A) and ADD (B) marks, depending on the coolant temperature

ery reservoir. Coolant should be added ONLY to the reservoir, after the system cools. Because a radiator cap, loosened when the engine is hot, will cause a loss of pressure and immediate coolant boiling, possibly with explosive force, most car makers, including GM, have designed the radiator cap in such a way that it is not easy to get a grip, to discourage inadvertent removal. Embossed on the cap is a caution against its being opened and arrows indicating the proper closed position. During routine maintenance, ALWAYS check the coolant level (and add, if required) at the coolant recovery reservoir. Refilling coolant at the radiator should only be required if the radiator and/or the cooling system has been drained.

DRAIN & REFILL

▶ See Figures 185 thru 191

1. With the engine cool, remove the radiator cap by slowly rotating the cap counter-clockwise to the detent (a stop that will prevent further turning). Do not press down while rotating the pressure cap. Wait until any residual pressure (indicated by a hissing sound) is relieved. After all hissing stops, continue to rotate counter-clockwise until the cap is removed.

➡Dispose of used coolant in a proper fashion, such as recovering the coolant and storing the used coolant in a container for recycling. NEVER POUR USED COOLANT DOWN A DRAIN. Ethylene glycol is a very toxic chemical. Dis-

posing of it into the sewer system or ground water is illegal and ecologically unsound. Keep children and pets away from open containers of coolant.

2. Place a drain pan under the vehicle to collect all of the drained coolant.

3. Open the radiator drain valve located at the bottom of the radiator tank. For procedures requiring the cooling system to be partially drained, opening the radiator drain valve should provide sufficient draining and no further action should be necessary.

Fig. 185 The radiator caps used on these vehicle have no handles to discourage removing the cap when the engine is hot

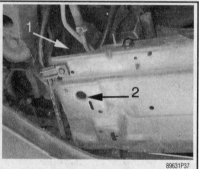

Fig. 186 Location of the drain valve (1) and drain hole (2)

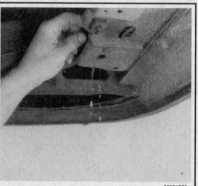

Fig. 187 When draining the cooling system, placing a piece of tubing over the drain valve may help control spills

4. Locate and open the air bleed vent(s). They are generally located on the thermostat housing. The air bleed vent should be opened two to three turns.

5. Allow the coolant to completely drain from the radiator.

6. Close the radiator drain valve.

7. Slowly fill the cooling system through the radiator neck using the following procedure:

a. If the coolant system has been flushed (block drains opened), first add 100% DEX-COOL®.

Fig. 188 Fill the radiator to the bottom of the filler neck with a 50/50 mix of DEX-COOL® and clean water

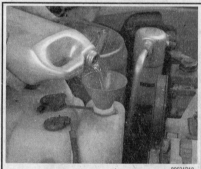

Fig. 189 Be sure to also refill the coolant recovery reservoir with a 50/50 mix of DEX-COOL® and clean water

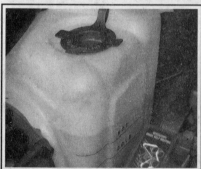

Fig. 190 Another coolant recovery reservoir showing the upper and lower limit marks. This tank is stained because of coolant contamination due to a gasket failure

b. Then slowly add clean water to the system until the level of the coolant mixture has reached the base of the radiator neck.

c. Wait for two minutes and recheck the level of the coolant mixture, and add clean water if necessary to restore the coolant mixture level to the base of the radiator neck.

8. If the cooling system is being refilled ONLY (no flush), simply use a 50/50 mix of coolant and water to refill.

9. Install the radiator cap making certain that the arrows line up with the overflow tube.

10. Close the air bleed valve(s). DO NOT OVER-TIGHTEN. The bleed valve is made of brass and easily damaged.

11. Fill the coolant reservoir as required to bring the 50/50 mix to the COLD level mark on the reservoir.

12. Start the engine and check for leaks.

✳✳ CAUTION

When checking for leaks with the system at normal operating temperature, BE EXTREMELY CAREFUL not to touch any moving or hot engine parts. Once operating temperature has been reached, shut the engine OFF, and check for leaks around the hose fittings and connections that were removed earlier.

➡The low coolant indicator lamp may come on after this procedure. After operating the vehicle so that the engine heats up and cools down three times, if the low coolant indicator lamp does NOT go out, or fails to come on at ignition check, and the coolant is at the proper level, further diagnosis may be required. If at any time the "TEMP" warning indicator comes on, immediate action is required.

FLUSH & CLEANING

1. Refer to the drain and fill procedure in this section, then drain the cooling system.

2. Close the drain valve.

➡Your GM W-Body vehicle uses an aluminum radiator with plastic tanks, and the coolant comes into contact with numerous aluminum parts in the cooling system. Many coolant system flushing chemicals are extremely caustic and will attack aluminum parts. Make absolutely sure any chemical flushing solution is compatible with and safe to use with aluminum cooling system components. Follow the directions on the container.

3. If using a flushing solution, remove the thermostat. Reinstall the thermostat housing.

4. Add sufficient water to fill the system.

5. Start the engine and run for a few minutes. Shut the engine OFF. Drain the cooling system.

6. With the engine OFF, and if using a flushing solution, disconnect the heater hose to the heater core, usually at the firewall. Connect a water hose to end of the heater hose and run water into the system until it begins to flow out of the top of the radiator.

7. Allow the water to flow out of the radiator until it is clear.

8. Reconnect the heater hose.

9. Drain the cooling system again.

10. Reinstall the thermostat.

11. Empty the coolant reservoir or surge tank and flush it.

12. Fill the cooling system using the correct ratio of antifreeze and water, to the bottom of the radiator filler neck. Fill the reservoir or surge tank to the FULL mark.

13. Install the radiator cap, making sure the arrows align with the overflow tube.

Brake Master Cylinder

The brake master cylinder is designed for use in diagonally split hydraulic systems. It incorporates the functions of the standard dual master cylinder plus a fluid level sensor and integral proportioner valves. In a diagonally split system, the left rear brake and the right front brake are on the same hydraulic circuit in the master cylinder, and the left front brake and the right front brake on the other circuit.

The master cylinder is equipped with a fluid level sensor switch located in the side of the reservoir. The switch activates the BRAKE warning lamp if the fluid level is low. Once the fluid level is corrected, the BRAKE warning lamp will go out.

FLUID RECOMMENDATION

◗ See Figure 192

The brake system in these vehicles is a complex system dependent on absolutely clean brake fluid of the proper type. Use only SUPREME 11 or equivalent DOT 3 brake fluid from a clean, sealed container. Do not use fluid from an open container that may be contaminated with water. Using the wrong fluid or contaminated fluid could result in damage to expensive components, or loss of braking, with possible personal injury.

➡Avoid spilling brake fluid on any of the vehicle's painted surfaces, wiring cables or electrical connectors. Brake fluid will damage paint and electrical connections. If any fluid is spilled on the vehicle, flush the area with water to lessen damage.

✳✳ WARNING

Do not use power steering or transmission fluid in the brake system. Do not reuse brake fluid accumulated during brake system bleeding. Always store brake fluid in a closed container. Reseal brake fluid containers immediately after use. Do not use brake fluid left in an open or improperly sealed container, because it absorbs moisture, or can become contaminated.

LEVEL CHECK

◗ See Figures 193, 194 and 195

The brake hydraulic system is a closed system. Low levels of fluid may indicate a need for service as there may be a leak in the system. It is good practice to check the brake fluid level during oil changes or whenever under the hood.

✳✳ CAUTION

Overfilling the reservoir must be avoided due to the potential for overflow onto the nearby catalytic converters in the exhaust system. Brake fluid is flammable, and contact with hot exhaust components could result in a fire and possible personal injury.

93171P34

Fig. 191 The screwdriver is shown on the coolant bleed valve. It is made of brass and easily damaged so do not over-tighten—3.1L engine shown

93171P12

Fig. 192 Pay attention to the brake fluid specification on the fluid reservoir cap. Use DOT 3 brake fluid only, NEVER silicone fluid or any other type of oil

88001P41

Fig. 193 Remove the brake master cylinder reservoir cap . . .

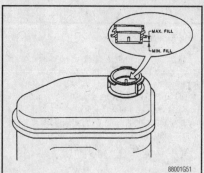

Fig. 194 . . . then check the fluid level against the marks on the neck of the reservoir

Fig. 195 When adding brake fluid, use only DOT 3 brake fluid from a clean, fresh, sealed container

Fig. 196 Close-up view of the fluid level marks on the power steering fluid reservoir cap/dipstick

The master cylinder reservoir is on the master cylinder and is located under the hood on the driver's side of the vehicle. The master cylinder reservoir contains enough fluid so that it never needs service under normal conditions. A low fluid level sensor in the master cylinder reservoir will warn of low fluid level, which could indicate a leak.

Thoroughly clean the reservoir cap before removal to avoid getting dirt in the reservoir. Remove the twist cap and diaphragm under the cap. The fluid level should be at the MAX fill mark on the reservoir when full. Reinstall the cap and diaphragm assembly when the reservoir is full.

Power Steering

FLUID RECOMMENDATIONS

⁑ WARNING

The steering systems on these vehicles, including the Variable Effort Steering (VES) system are sophisticated and complex. They depend on cleanliness and the proper fluid. Use no substitutes. NEVER use automatic transmission fluid in the power steering system!

LEVEL CHECK

▶ **See Figures 196, 197 and 198**

The power steering fluid level is indicated by marks on a fluid level indicator on the fluid reservoir cap. When adding fluid or making a complete fluid change, always use the proper fluid. Failure to use the proper fluid will cause hose and seal damage and fluid leaks. If the fluid is warm; about 150°F (66°C) or hot to the touch, the level should be between the HOT and COLD marks. If the fluid is cooler than 150° F (66°C), the fluid level should be between the ADD and COLD marks.

In conventional, or moderate, climates, use only GM Power Steering Fluid Part Number #1050017 (1 quart size). In cold weather climates, use only GM Power Steering Fluid Part Number #12345867 (1 quart size). Many vehicle owners will purchase a quart or two of GM Power Steering Fluid from an authorized GM dealer so the correct power steering fluid is always available.

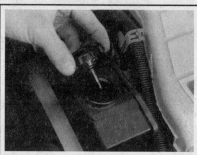

Fig. 197 Make sure the cap and surrounding area is clean before removing the cap. Keep dirt and contamination out of this system

⁑ WARNING

Use care when working on a vehicle equipped with the 3.4L (VIN X) engine. Power steering fluid will damage the secondary timing belt.

Chassis Greasing

There are very few places where the chassis and steering can or should be greased. Most modern vehicle use factory-lubricated sealed joints. Normally only the lower ball joints and the outer tie rod ends can be lubricated and even then, often the factory components are sealed and only aftermarket replacement items will have grease fittings. Where possible, lubricate the chassis lubrication points every 7,500 miles (12,000 km) or 12 months with a quality chassis grease. Lubricate the transaxle shift linkage, park brake cable guides, under body contact points and linkage with white lithium grease.

Body Lubrication and Maintenance

LOCK CYLINDERS, DOOR HINGES AND HINGE CHECKS

GM recommends their Multi-Purpose Lubricant, Super-Lube, part no. 12346241, or equivalent general purpose silicone lubricant. Apply any lock lubricant sparingly.

Fig. 198 Add the correct amount of power steering fluid. Make sure to use the proper type, which will depend upon the climate where you live

HOOD LATCH, PIVOTS, SPRING ANCHOR AND RELEASE PAWL

Use Lubriplate®brand lubricant in an aerosol container, GM Part Number 12346293, or equivalent. This type of NLGI #2 lubricant is commonly referred to as "white grease" and is a relatively thin grease. It is also available in small cans and can be applied with a brush.

WEATHERSTRIPS

Apply a thin coating of Dielectric Silicone Grease GM Part Number 12345579, or equivalent. Apply sparingly and buff with a soft, dry cloth.

UNDERBODY FLUSHING

Use plain water to flush any corrosive materials (road salt, etc.) from the underbody. Take care to clean thoroughly any area where mud and other debris can collect. Check that any drain holes in the doors and rocker panels are open. Use a small screwdriver to clear them of any debris.

Wheel Bearings

The GM W-Body models covered by this book, like most Front Wheel Drive (FWD) vehicles, are equipped with sealed hub and bearing assemblies. The hub and bearing cannot be separated for regreasing. If the assembly is damaged, the complete hub and bearing assembly must be replaced. Please see Section 8 for the hub and bearing removal and installation procedure.

TOWING THE VEHICLE

For maximum safety to the components of your drive train and chassis, it is most desirable to have your vehicle towed by on a flatbed or whole vehicle trailer. The only way to properly place the vehicle on a flatbed is to have it pulled on from the front.

If a flatbed is unavailable, your vehicle can be towed using a wheel lift wrecker. In this case, the front wheels must be off the ground, as this will prevent wear and tear on the drivetrain. Tow vehicle speed should not exceed 35 mph (56 km/h) when using this method.

If absolutely necessary, you can tow your vehicle on a wheel lift wrecker from the rear. The front wheels must be placed on a dolly. Tow vehicle speed should not exceed 35 mph (56 km/h) when using this method.

Towing Your Vehicle Behind Another Vehicle

♦ See Figures 199 and 200

At times, you may want to tow your vehicle behind another vehicle such as a recreational

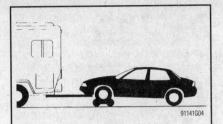

Fig. 199 When towing with an automatic transaxle, the front wheels must be on a dolly

Fig. 200 NEVER tow the vehicle with the rear wheels first

vehicle (RV), a truck, or another car. Before the vehicle is towed a few steps must be taken:

- The front wheels must be placed on a dolly
- Set the parking brake
- Turn the ignition key to **OFF** to unlock the steering wheel
- Clamp the steering wheel in a straight ahead position with a suitable device
- Release the parking brake

When towing your vehicle behind another vehicle a few precautions must be taken:

- Do not tow your vehicle at a speed faster than 55 mph (90 km/h) or the vehicle can be damaged
- Do not tow your vehicle at a speed faster than 55 mph (90 km/h) if you have a manual transaxle

JUMP STARTING A DEAD BATTERY

♦ See Figure 201

Whenever a vehicle is jump started, precautions must be followed in order to prevent the possibility of personal injury. Remember that batteries contain a small amount of explosive hydrogen gas which is a by-product of battery charging. Sparks should always be avoided when working around batteries, especially when attaching jumper cables. To minimize the possibility of accidental sparks, follow the procedure carefully.

✳✳ CAUTION

NEVER hook the batteries up in a series circuit or the entire electrical system will go up in smoke, including the starter!

Vehicles equipped with a diesel engine may utilize two 12 volt batteries. If so, the batteries are connected in a parallel circuit (positive terminal to positive terminal, negative terminal to negative terminal). Hooking the batteries up in parallel circuit

increases battery cranking power without increasing total battery voltage output. Output remains at 12 volts. On the other hand, hooking two 12 volt batteries up in a series circuit (positive terminal to negative terminal, positive terminal to negative terminal) increases total battery output to 24 volts (12 volts plus 12 volts).

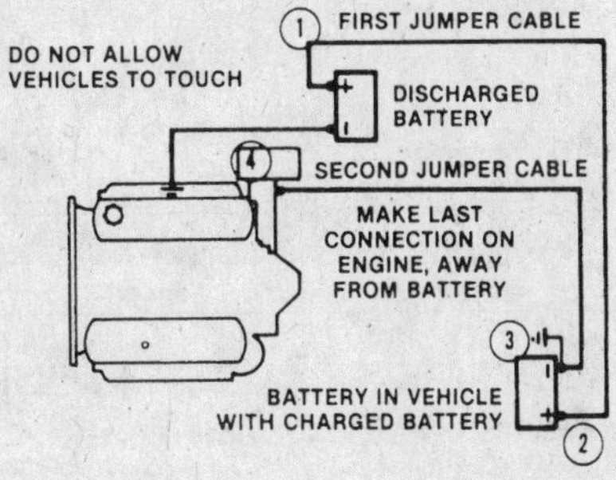

Jump Starting Precautions

- Be sure that both batteries are of the same voltage. Vehicles covered by this manual and most vehicles on the road today utilize a 12 volt charging system.
- Be sure that both batteries are of the same polarity (have the same terminal, in most cases NEGATIVE grounded).
- Be sure that the vehicles are not touching or a short could occur.
- On serviceable batteries, be sure the vent cap holes are not obstructed.
- Do not smoke or allow sparks anywhere near the batteries.
- In cold weather, make sure the battery electrolyte is not frozen. This can occur more readily in a battery that has been in a state of discharge.
- Do not allow electrolyte to contact your skin or clothing.

Jump Starting Procedure

♦ See Figures 202, 203 and 204

✳✳ CAUTION

Do not connect a jumper cable directly to the negative battery to prevent sparking and possible explosion of battery gases.

➡ When jump starting a vehicle with charging equipment, be sure equipment used is 12 volt

Fig. 202 Because the battery is difficult to access, on the passenger side, under this cover at the underhood electrical center is the remote battery-positive connector for jump starting—Grand Prix with 3.8L engine

Fig. 203 On this 3.1L Lumina, the remote auxiliary battery positive terminal is on the driver's side, but still clearly marked

MAKE CONNECTIONS IN NUMERICAL ORDER

DO NOT ALLOW VEHICLES TO TOUCH

① FIRST JUMPER CABLE

DISCHARGED BATTERY

④ SECOND JUMPER CABLE

MAKE LAST CONNECTION ON ENGINE, AWAY FROM BATTERY

③

BATTERY IN VEHICLE WITH CHARGED BATTERY

②

TCCS1080

Fig. 201 Connect the jumper cables to the batteries and engine in the order shown

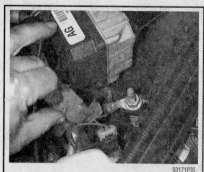

Fig. 204 Lift the protective cover to access the remote auxiliary battery positive— Lumina with 3.1L engine

and negative ground. **Do not use 24-volt charging equipment. Using such equipment can cause serious damage to the electrical system or electronic parts.**

The GM W-Body vehicles covered by this book have a number of sophisticated electronic systems and several sensitive on-board computers that can be damaged and are expensive to replace. Follow this factory procedure to avoid vehicle damage. In addition, the battery on most of these vehicles is usually hidden by other components, usually the windshield washer reservoir. For that rear, a remote battery positive terminal is provided.

1. Position the vehicle with the good battery so that the jumper cables will reach, but do not let the vehicles touch. Be sure the jumper cables are in good condition and do not have loose or missing insulation.

2. Turn the ignition switch to the **OFF** position. Turn all lamps and electrical loads on both vehicles off. Note that the hazard flashers and any lamps needed (underhood light, etc.) should be left on as needed.

3. Apply the parking brake on both vehicles. Verify that the automatic transaxle is in PARK. The vehicle with the good battery should also be in PARK, or NEUTRAL, if a manual transmission.

4. Check the built-in hydrometer "eye" (factory-type battery). If it is clear or light yellow, replace the battery.

5. On these vehicles, a remote positive stud is provided for jump starting. This is much more convenient, and safer, than trying to get a jumper cable on the small side terminal bolt head at the battery, especially when it is hidden by another underhood component. The remote positive stud is covered by a red plastic flap and is located near the underhood electrical center. Clamp one end of the first jumper cable to the positive terminal remote stud. Making sure the jumper cable does not touch any other metal parts, clamp the other end of the same booster cable to the booster battery positive terminal (or its remote stud, if so equipped). NEVER connect positive to negative.

6. Clamp one end of the second cable to the negative terminal of the booster battery. Make the final connection to a solid engine ground (metal bracket on the engine, etc.) at least 18 inches from the discharged battery. Make sure the cables are not on or near pulleys, fans or other parts that will move when the engine is started.

7. Start the engine of the vehicle with the good battery. Run the engine at a moderate speed (approximately 1500 rpm) for several minutes. Then, start the engine of the vehicle which has the discharged battery.

8. Remove the jumper cables by reversing the above sequence. Remove the negative cable from the vehicle with the discharged battery first. While removing each clamp, take care that it does not touch any other metal surfaces while the other end remains attached.

JACKING

▶ **See Figures 205 thru 210**

Your vehicle was supplied with a jack for emergency tire changing. This jack is adequate for changing a flat tire or other short term procedures NOT REQUIRING YOU TO GO UNDER THE VEHICLE. If it is used in an emergency situation, carefully follow the instructions provided either with the jack, in the owner's manual or on an instruction sticker near where the spare tire is stowed. DO NOT attempt to use this jack on any portion of the vehicle other than specified by the vehicle manufacturer as outlined in the owner's manual. Always block the diagonally opposite wheel when using a jack.

A more convenient way of jacking is the use of a garage type floor jack. You may use the floor jack to lift the front of the vehicle by positioning the jack in the center of the front crossmember. When raising the rear of the vehicle, position the jack on the rear jack pad.

Never place the jack under the radiator, engine or transmission components. Severe and expensive damage will result when the jack is raised. Additionally, never jack under the floorpan or bodywork; the metal will deform.

On the vehicles covered by this book, do not place any jack under the engine oil pan, even with a so-called "protective" block of wood. The clearance between the oil pan the oil pickup assembly is very

Fig. 205 When raising the front of your vehicle, position the jack in the center of the crossmember

Fig. 206 Another view of a floor jack lifting at the front crossmember

Fig. 207 Position the floor jack on the rear jack pad to raise the rear of the car

Fig. 208 Another view of a floor jack lifting at the rear crossmember jacking pad

Fig. 209 This safety stand has been solidly placed under a boxed section of the front sub-frame

93171PB1

Fig. 210 This safety stand has been placed where several pieces of sheetmetal come together to form a seam, called a "pinchweld". Some safety stands have a pronounced groove to accommodate pinchwelds

small and attempting to jack under the engine, for any reason, will cause damage to the engine oil pump pickup.

Whenever you plan to work under the vehicle, you must support it on jackstands (safety stands) or ramps. Never use cinder blocks (they crumble easily) or stacks of wood to support the vehicle, even if you are only going to be under it for a few minutes. Never crawl under the vehicle when it is supported only by the tire-changing jack or the floor jack.

Drive-on ramps are a handy and safe way to raise and support the vehicle. Use caution, since some ramps may be steep enough that some portion of the lower front bodywork may scrape when driving onto the ramps. Never support the vehicle on any suspension member (unless instructed to do so by a repair manual) or by an underbody panel.

JACKING PRECAUTIONS

The following safety points cannot be overemphasized:

- Always block the opposite wheel or wheels to keep the vehicle from rolling off the jack.
- When raising the front of the vehicle, firmly apply the parking brake, which works on the back wheels.
- When the front drive wheels are to remain on the ground, place the shift lever in the PARK position to lock the transaxle, to keep the front wheels from rolling.
- Always use jackstands to support the vehicle while you are working underneath. Place the stands beneath the vehicle's jacking brackets. Before getting under the vehicle, rock the vehicle a small amount to make sure it is firmly supported.
- When supporting the vehicle with jackstands, the supports should be placed under the body

pinchwelds or similar strong and stable structure. The vehicle should be on a clean, hard, level surface before any lifting procedure begins. All lifting equipment MUST be in good working order. Make sure all vehicle loads are equally distributed and secure. Note that the center of gravity of front wheel drive cars is further forward than on rear-drive vehicles.

- When jacking or lifting a vehicle at the prescribed lift points, be certain that the jack and/or safety stands do not contact the exhaust system, brake pipes, cables, fuel lines or underbody. Such contact may result in damage or unsatisfactory vehicle performance.

CAPACITIES

Year	Model	Engine Displacement Liters (cc)	Engine ID/VIN	Engine Oil with Filter (qts.)	Transaxle (qts.) Auto.	Fuel Tank (gal.)	Cooling System (qts.)
1997	Cutlass Supreme	3.1 (3135)	M	4.5	7.0	16.1	11.6
	Cutlass Supreme	3.4 (3350)	X	5.5	7.0	17.1	12.3
	Grand Prix	3.1 (3135)	M	4.5	7.4	18.0	11.0
	Grand Prix	3.4 (3350)	X	5.5	7.4	18.0	12.3
	Grand Prix	3.8 (3791)	1	5.0	7.4	18.0	10.2
	Grand Prix	3.8 (3791)	K	5.0	7.4	18.0	10.2
	Lumina	3.1 (3135)	M	4.5	7.0	16.1	11.6
	Lumina	3.4 (3350)	X	5.5	7.0	17.1	12.3
	Monte Carlo	3.1 (3135)	M	4.5	7.0	16.1	11.6
	Monte Carlo	3.4 (3350)	X	5.5	7.0	17.1	12.3
	Regal	3.1 (3135)	M	4.5	7.4	18.0	11.0
	Regal	3.8 (3791)	1	5.0	7.4	18.0	10.2
	Regal	3.8 (3791)	K	4.5	7.4	18.0	10.2
	Century	3.1 (3135)	M	4.5	7.4	18.0	11.0
1998	Grand Prix	3.1 (3137)	M	4.5	8.0	18.0	11.0
	Grand Prix	3.8 (3791)	1	4.5	8.0	18.0	12.3
	Grand Prix	3.8 (3137)	K	4.5	8.0	18.0	12.3
	Lumina	3.1 (3137)	M	4.5	7.0	16.6	11.6
	Lumina	3.8 (3791)	K	4.5	7.4	16.6	11.6
	Monte Carlo	3.1 (3137)	M	4.5	7.0	16.6	11.6
	Monte Carlo	3.8 (3791)	K	4.5	7.4	16.6	11.6
	Regal	3.1 (3137)	M	4.5	7.0	18.0	11.6
	Regal	3.8 (3791)	1	4.5	7.4	17.0	12.3
	Regal	3.8 (3791)	K	4.5	7.4	17.0	12.3
	Century	3.1 (3137)	M	4.5	7.0	17.0	11.6
	Intrigue	3.8 (3791)	K	4.5	7.4	17.0	12.3
1999	Grand Prix	3.1 (3135)	M	4.5	8.0	17.7	11.0
	Grand Prix	3.8 (3791)	1	4.5	8.0	17.7	12.3
	Grand Prix	3.8 (3791)	K	4.5	8.0	17.7	12.3
	Lumina	3.1 (3135)	M	4.5	7.0	16.6	11.6
	Lumina	3.8 (3791)	K	4.5	7.4	16.6	11.7
	Monte Carlo	3.1 (3135)	M	4.5	7.4	16.6	11.7
	Monte Carlo	3.8 (3791)	K	4.5	7.4	16.6	11.7
	Regal	3.8 (3791)	1	4.5	7.4	17.5	12.3
	Regal	3.8 (3791)	K	4.5	7.4	17.5	12.3
	Century	3.1 (3135)	M	4.5	7.0	17.5	11.6
	Intrigue	3.8 (3791)	K	4.5	7.4	17.0	12.3
	Intrigue	3.5 (3474)	H	6.0	7.4	17.0	12.3
2000	Grand Prix	3.1 (3137)	M	4.5	8.0	17.0	11.6
	Grand Prix	3.8 (3791)	1	5.5	8.0	17.0	12.3
	Grand Prix	3.8 (3791)	K	5.5	8.0	17.0	12.3
	Lumina	3.1 (3137)	M	4.5	7.0	16.6	12.2
	Monte Carlo	3.4 (3348)	E	4.5	7.4	17.0	11.3
	Monte Carlo	3.8 (3791)	K	4.5	7.4	17.0	11.3
	Regal	3.8 (3791)	1	5.0	7.4	17.5	12.3
	Regal	3.8 (3791)	K	5.0	7.4	17.5	12.3
	Century	3.1 (3137)	M	5.0	7.4	17.5	12.3
	Intrigue	3.5 (3474)	H	6.0	7.4	17.0	12.3

NOTE: All capacities are approximate. Add fluid gradually to ensure a proper fluid level. Capacities given are service, not overhaul capacities

93171C04

MANUFACTURER RECOMMENDED MAINTENANCE INTERVALS
(NORMAL CONDITIONS)

VEHICLE MAINTENANCE INTERVALS

Component	Procedure	miles (x1000) 7.5	15	22.5	30	37.5	45	52.5	60	67.5	75	82.5	90	97.5	105	112.5	120
		km (x1000) 12	24	36	48	60	72	84	96	108	120	132	144	156	168	180	192
		months	12		24		36		48		60		72		84		96
Check engine oil		Check engine oil level at each fuel stop.															
Engine oil and filter	Replace	✔	✔	✔	✔	✔	✔	✔	✔	✔	✔	✔	✔	✔	✔	✔	✔
Outer tie rod ends	Lubricate																
Tires	Rotate	✔	✔	✔	✔	✔	✔	✔	✔	✔	✔	✔	✔	✔	✔	✔	✔
Brake system	Inspect					✔		✔		✔		✔		✔		✔	
Air filter	Replace				✔				✔				✔				✔
Coolant level	Inspect	✔	✔	✔	✔	✔	✔	✔	✔	✔	✔	✔	✔	✔	✔	✔	✔
Coolant Change	Replace																✔
Fuel lines, fittings, and hoses	Inspect				✔				✔				✔				✔
Spark plugs	Replace													✔			
Spark plug wires	Inspect													✔			
Timing belt	Inspect								✔		✔		✔		✔		
Drive belts	Inspect								✔								✔
PCV valve	Inspect				✔				✔				✔				✔
Fluid levels and condition	Inspect		✔		✔		✔		✔		✔		✔		✔		✔
Exhaust system	Inspect		✔		✔		✔		✔		✔		✔		✔		✔
CV joint boots	Inspect		✔		✔		✔		✔		✔		✔		✔		✔

93171C05

MANUFACTURER RECOMMENDED MAINTENANCE INTERVALS
(SEVERE CONDITIONS)

VEHICLE MAINTENANCE INTERVALS

Component	Service	miles (x1000) 3	6.0	9.0	12	15.0	18	21.0	24	27.0	30.0	33.0	36.0	39.0	42.0	45.0	48.0
		km (x1000) 5.0	6	9	20	25	30	35	40	45	50	55	60	65	70	75	80
		months 3.0	6.0	9	12	15	18	21	24	27	30	33	36	39	42	45	48
Check engine oil	Inspect	Inspect engine oil level at every fuel stop.															
Engine oil and filter	Replace	✔	✔	✔	✔	✔	✔	✔	✔	✔	✔	✔	✔	✔	✔	✔	✔
Tires	Rotate		✔		✔		✔		✔		✔		✔		✔		✔
Check tire pressure	Inspect	Check the tire pressure at least once a month.															
Outer Tie Rod Ends	Lubricate		✔		✔		✔		✔		✔		✔		✔		✔
Brake system	Inspect		✔		✔		✔		✔		✔		✔		✔		✔
Air filter	Replace					✔					✔					✔	
Coolant level	Inspect	✔	✔	✔	✔	✔	✔	✔	✔	✔	✔	✔	✔	✔	✔	✔	✔
Change coolant	Replace								✔							✔	✔
Fuel lines, fittings, and hoses	Inspect		✔		✔		✔		✔		✔		✔		✔		✔
Spark plugs	Replace	Change spark plugs at 100,000 miles															
Spark plug wires	Inspect																✔
Timing belt	Replace										✔						
Drive belts	Inspect				✔				✔				✔				✔
PCV valve	Inspect				✔				✔				✔				✔
Fluid levels and condition	Inspect		✔				✔		✔		✔		✔		✔		✔
Exhaust system	Inspect		✔		✔		✔		✔		✔		✔		✔		✔
CV joint boots	Inspect	✔	✔	✔	✔	✔	✔	✔	✔	✔	✔	✔	✔	✔	✔	✔	✔
Transmission fluid	Inspect		✔		✔		✔		✔		✔		✔		✔		✔

93171C06

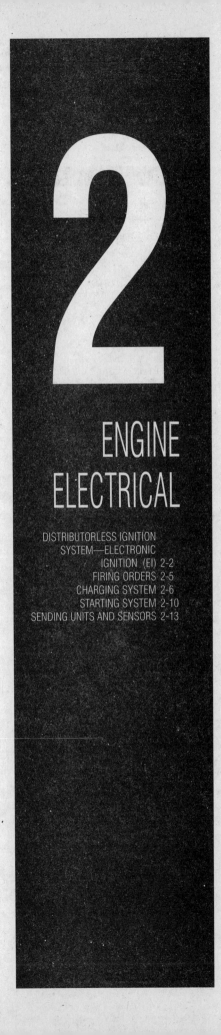

2

ENGINE ELECTRICAL

DISTRIBUTORLESS IGNITION SYSTEM—ELECTRONIC IGNITION (EI)

➡ For information on understanding electricity and troubleshooting electrical circuits, please refer to Section 6 of this manual.

General Information

EXCEPT 3.5L (VIN H) ENGINE

▶ See Figures 1 and 2

The Electronic Ignition (EI) systems used on the 3.1L (VIN M), 3.4L (VIN X and VIN E) and 3.8L (VIN K and VIN 1) engines use a coil pack with one ignition coil for each two cylinders in the engine. Mounted under the ignition coils on each system is an Ignition Control Module (ICM) that performs the ignition coil switching functions and interacts with the Powertrain Control Module (PCM) to optimize ignition system operation.

On these engine systems, the spark timing is controlled electronically. The ICM controls the spark timing during engine start up, and provides a back up timing system that will allow the engine to run in the event of an open or ground in the Ignition Control (IC) circuit. Once the engine starts and is running above the approximate engine speed of 400 RPM, the PCM takes over the spark timing and sends signals to the ICM for ignition coil switching.

The electronic ignition system used on most of these engines uses a "waste spark" method of spark distribution. Each cylinder is paired with its opposing cylinder in the firing order, so that one cylinder on compression fires simultaneously with the opposing cylinder on exhaust. The spark that occurs in the cylinder that is on the exhaust stroke is referred to as the "waste spark".

The spark plugs in the two opposing cylinders are connected to the two secondary terminals of the same ignition coil. The spark voltage appears at the center electrode of one of the spark plugs and jumps to the side electrode, then passes through the engine to the other spark plug. At the second spark plug, the spark jumps from the side electrode to the center electrode and completes the series circuit back to the ignition coil. The high level of energy available from the ignition coil is more than sufficient to fire both plugs simultaneously. Since the waste spark requires very little of the available voltage to fire, most of the coil output voltage is available to fire the cylinder that is on the compression stroke.

Engine speed (RPM) and cylinder position in the intake-compression-power-exhaust sequence are sensed electronically and are used by the ICM and PCM to control timing. A magnetic Crankshaft Position (CKP) sensor mounted in the engine block provides these parameters. The magnetic CKP sensor consists of a wire coil wound around a permanent magnet. The sensor is positioned near a reluctor ring on the crankshaft. The reluctor ring has notches, which trigger signals in the magnetic sensor to indicate Crankshaft Position (CKP), and crankshaft speed (RPM). These signals are used by the ICM during start up, then passed on to the PCM to help determine optimum timing while the engine is running. The PCM also uses other inputs separate from the ignition system itself, to determine

optimum timing. More information is available in Section 4, Electronic Engine Controls.

The 3.8L engines use a dual Crankshaft Position (CKP) sensor to monitor engine speed and stroke sequence. It is mounted on the engine beside the harmonic balancer/crankshaft pulley. The sensor has dual Hall-Effect switches that sense interrupter rings on the harmonic balancer. Gaps in the interrupter rings cause signals to be generated by the sensor to indicate crankshaft position and speed (RPM). These signals are sent to the ICM for use during start up, then on to the PCM for use in timing as the engine runs. The PCM also uses other inputs separate from the ignition system itself, to determine optimum timing. The 3.4L (VIN E) engine uses a 7X Crankshaft Position (CKP) sensor that reads off a toothed portion of the crankshaft and a 24X CKP sensor that reads off the crankshaft pulley

The 3.8L engines also use a Camshaft Position (CMP) sensor which is mounted on the front engine

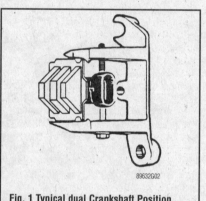

Fig. 1 Typical dual Crankshaft Position (CKP) sensor

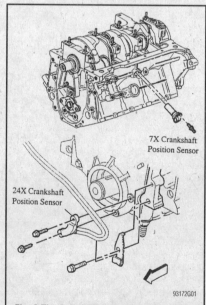

Fig. 2 The 3.4L (VIN E) engine uses a 7X CKP sensor that reads off a toothed portion of the crankshaft and a 24X CKP sensor that reads off the crankshaft pulley

cover above the crankshaft balancer and below the coolant pump. The signal from this sensor passes through the ICM to the PCM, and is used for fuel synchronization.

3.5L (VIN H) ENGINE

▶ See Figure 3

The Electronic Ignition (EI) system on the 3.5L (VIN H) engine used in the 2000 Intrigue is different from the other V6 applications covered by this manual. The ignition system on this engine uses an individual ignition coil for each cylinder. An ignition coil assembly consisting of three coils and an ignition control module, is located in the center of each cam cover. This arrangement allows the ignition coil to connect directly to the spark plug using only a boot. This eliminates the need for secondary spark plug wires. There are separate ignition modules for Bank 1 and Bank 2. Each module controls the three ignition coils for that bank of cylinders. The PCM controls ignition module operation. There are six Ignition Control (IC) units, one per cylinder, that connect the PCM and the ignition modules. The ignition modules also have a power feed, a chassis ground circuit and a Reference Low circuit each. The PCM causes spark to occur by pulsing the IC circuit, which signals the ignition module to trigger the ignition coil and fire the spark plug. Sequencing and timing are PCM controlled. The ignition feed circuits are fused separately for each bank of the engine. The two fuses also supply the injectors for that bank of the engine. This system puts out very high ignition energy for plug firing. Because there are no ignition wires, there is no energy loss due to ignition wire resistance. Also, since the firing is sequential, each coil has five events to saturate as opposed to the two in a waste spark arrangement. Furthermore, no energy is lost to the resistance of a waste spark system. The ignition timing on this engine is not adjustable and, in fact, there are no timing marks on the crankshaft pulley.

The Crankshaft Position (CKP) sensor on the 3.5L (VIN H) engine is actually two sensors in a single housing. Each sensor has a separate power, ground and signal circuit. The Powertrain Control Module (PCM) supplies 12 volts to both sensors. The PCM provides the ground path, or sensor return circuit, from both sensors. These power and ground circuits are also connected to the Camshaft Position sensor. Two separate signal circuits connect the CKP sensor and the PCM. The PCM can use three different modes of decoding crankshaft position. During normal operation, the PCM performs an Angle Based calculation using both signals to determine crankshaft position. The dual sensor allows the engine to run even if one signal is lost. If either signal is lost, the PCM switches to a Time Based method of calculating crankshaft position. If the system is operating in Time A mode, the PCM is using only the signal from Sensor A. Time B indicates that the Sensor B signal is being used. If the lost signal is restored, the PCM will continue to operate in Time Based mode for the remainder of the current key cycle. The PCM will revert back to the Angle mode on the next start if the fault is no longer present. A scan tool can display the Crank Position Sensing Decode Mode and any fault-based

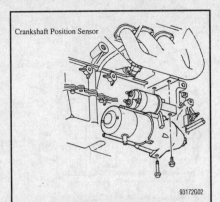

Fig. 3 The 3.5L (VIN H) engine's Crankshaft Position sensor, hidden behind the starter motor, reads off a toothed portion of the crankshaft—2000 Intrigue

Diagnostic Trouble Codes. The CKP sensor is considered the most critical part of the ignition system. If the sensor is damaged so that pulses are not generated, the engine will not start. In addition, CKP sensor clearance is very important. Excessive clearance can result from improper installation, dirt/debris or the old O-ring left in the block cavity when a new sensor is installed. Insufficient clearance will damage the sensor. The sensor must not contact the rotating crankshaft reluctor wheel at any time. The reluctor wheel is cast integrally with the crankshaft. Sensor to reluctor wheel clearance is not adjustable.

The Camshaft Position (CMP) sensor on the 3.5L (VIN H) engine produces a signal, which, when combined with the CKP sensor signal, enables the PCM to determine exactly which cylinder is on a firing stroke. The PCM can then properly synchronize the ignition system, fuel injectors and knock control. The CMP sensor has a power, ground and signal circuit. The PCM supplies 12 volts to the sensor. The PCM provides the ground path, or sensor return circuit, from the sensor. These power and ground circuits are also connected to the CKP sensor. If a problem is detected with the CMP circuit. A Diagnostic Trouble Code will be set that can be read by a scan tool.

IGNITION SYSTEM PRECAUTIONS

There are important considerations to point out when working around the ignition system.
- The ignition coils' secondary voltage output capabilities are very high—more than 40,000 volts. Avoid body contact with ignition high voltage secondary components (including spark plug wires) when the engine is running, or personal injury may result.
- The Crankshaft Position sensor is the most critical part of the ignition system. If the sensor is damaged so that pulses are not generated, the engine will not start.
- Crankshaft position sensor clearance is very important. The sensor must not contact the rotating interrupter ring at any time, or sensor damage will result. If the crankshaft balancer interrupter ring is bent, the interrupter ring blades will destroy the sensor.
- Ignition timing is not adjustable. There are no

timing marks on the crankshaft balancer or timing chain cover.
- If crankshaft position sensor replacement is necessary, the crankshaft balancer must be removed first. The balancer is a press fit onto the crankshaft; removing the serpentine accessory drive belt and balancer attaching bolt should allow its removal with a short balancer removal tool (GM tool J 38197 or equivalent). When reinstalled, proper torquing of the balancer attachment bolt is critical to ensure the balancer stays attached to the crankshaft.
- If a crankshaft position sensor assembly is replaced, check the crankshaft balancer interrupter ring for any blades being bent. If this is not checked closely and a bent blade exists, the new crankshaft position sensor can be destroyed by the bent blade within only one crankshaft revolution. This should be checked closely, especially if repairs are being made after front-end collision work.
- Neither side of the ignition coil primary or secondary windings is connected to engine ground. Although the ignition coil packs are secured to the ignition control module, it is not an electrical connection to ground.
- Be careful not to damage the secondary ignition wires or boots when servicing the ignition system. Rotate each boot to dislodge it from the plug or coil tower before pulling it from either a spark plug or the ignition coil. Never pierce a secondary ignition wire or boot for any testing purpose. Future problems are guaranteed if pinpoints or test lights are pushed through the insulation for testing.
- The ignition control module is grounded to the engine block through 3 mounting studs used to secure the module to its mounting bracket. If servicing is required, ensure that good electrical contact is made between the module and its mounting bracket, including proper hardware and torque.

Diagnosis and Testing

Due the sophistication and complexity of the systems on these vehicles, the testing a non-professional can accomplish is limited. The factory recommends their special tools and test equipment for even the most basic testing. These tools, such as a Tech 1® or equivalent scan tool, take advantage of the On-Board Diagnostic capability built into the Powertrain Control Module (PCM), reading out Diagnostic Trouble Codes (DTCs) that will point the technician in the right direction. A scan tool also taps into the PCM's data stream, giving the technician a wealth of information on voltages, resistances, engine speed, temperatures and much more. Their data capturing capabilities can greatly assist in detecting difficult-to-find intermittent problems. With labor rates in most areas well over a dollar-per-minute, quick, efficient and accurate diagnosis is in everyone's best interest.

Early in the factory testing procedures is a requirement to check for factory-issued Technical Service Bulletins (TSBs), service newsletters and factory training material. This allows the factory to get up-to-date service and testing information to their technicians, much of it based on warranty claims which may show a trend, such as a weak or defective component that should be checked first. Such information and the factory testing tools are just not available to the non-professional.

One factory recommendation that makes particularly good sense is to Verify The Complaint. Is there

really a problem or a misunderstanding on the part of the vehicle operator of how a system should operate? Another recommendation is to start with a thorough Visual Check. Some of the items to look for include:
- For example, although wiring connectors have a good reputation for high reliability, on occasion, a connector could become loose, especially if that connector or component was recently serviced. Are all connectors properly mated, with no broken locks or damaged terminals?
- Vacuum lines crack and fail with age and heat or even get disconnected in the course of other service work and so they should be checked carefully.
- Was other major work recently done on the vehicle? Most W-Body vehicles will have at least four ground straps commonly used to provide an electrical connection to the following: body, frame, engine, transaxle. Always reinstall any disconnected ground straps and replace any broken ground straps to make sure that all electrical components have adequate ground paths to the battery. A forgotten ground strap disconnected during major service work could affect the operation of a number of systems.
- Has the vehicle recently had major body repair? In some cases, components may not be restored to their pre-accident condition.
- Is the fuel of acceptable quality and proper octane?
- Has the vehicle seen regular service so that it can be reasonably assumed that the internal engine components are in good condition?
- Are there any unusual sounds or odors? A sulfur-like smell at the tailpipe when the vehicle is running could indicate a fuel delivery problem.
- Is the battery in good condition, properly connected with clean, tight terminals, and fully charged?
- Are there any fuel, coolant or oil leaks?
- Have non-factory components been installed? Over-size or under-size tires, for example, will affect the Vehicle Speed Sensor (VSS) which was calibrated for that particular vehicle and original tire size. Changing the tire size affects the VSS output, a major input to the vehicle's PCM. Some add-on electrical accessories can affect the vehicle's electrical system.
- Are all of the fuses in good condition?
- Are all of the relays in the underhood power center properly seated? Are there signs of corrosion or damage?
- Is the air intake duct plugged or air filter dirty?
- Are any wires or hoses misrouted too close to high voltage wires such as the spark plug leads?

All of these are things that should be checked on a regular basis and especially if there is a problem.

SECONDARY SPARK TEST

Except 3.5L Engine

One test that can be performed is checking for spark at the plugs. This is an old test, especially when checking on a Will Crank But Won't Start condition. The question has always been, 'Is the trouble in the fuel system or in the ignition system?' If there is a healthy spark at the spark plug, it can be assumed (but not guaranteed) that the problem is in the fuel system. The new twist is that with the high power ignition systems in use today, great care must be used. An older electrical system, if allowed to, might give you a shock as a reward for inattentive work. Today's electrical systems with 40,000 volts or more available to the spark plugs, could cause cardiac arrest, if mishandled.

1. Locate and remove the fuel injection fuse from the underhood electrical center. This will keep the fuel system from spraying fuel into the engine when cranking the engine over with the starter.

2. Install a spark plug tester. GM recommends their tester J 26792. This is similar to a spark plug with a wide gap and an alligator clip fastened to its metal shell. Similar spark plug testers are available at most auto supply stores. Connect the alligator clip to a good engine ground. Disconnect one spark plug wire and plug it onto the tester.

3. Crank the engine while observing the spark tester. A crisp, blue spark should be observed.

4. If a healthy spark appears, reconnect the spark plug and install the fuel injection system fuse. It can be assumed the ignition system is in good condition.

Adjustments

All adjustments in the ignition system are controlled by the Powertrain Control Module (PCM) and Ignition Control Module (ICM) for optimum performance. No adjustments are possible.

Ignition Coil

TESTING

Except 3.5L (VIN H) Engine

1. Remove the ignition coil(s).
2. Using an ohmmeter, check the resistance between the primary terminals on the underside of the coil. The resistance should be 0.50–0.90 ohms.
3. Check the resistance between the secondary terminals. It should be 5,000–8,000 ohms.
4. If the coil failed either test, replace the coil.

REMOVAL & INSTALLATION

Except 3.5L (VIN H) Engine

▶ See Figures 4, 5, 6 and 7

All of the vehicles covered by this book use V6 engines and, with the exception of the 3.5L engine, similar ignition systems. The ignition coil removal procedures are similar, differing only in the types of wiring connections.

1. Disconnect the negative battery cable.
2. Note the position of the spark plug wires for installation. Numbered tags of masking tape or other identification will save time at installation. Spark plug wires MUST be returned to their original and proper locations. Unplug the spark plug wires from the ignition coils.
3. Remove the 2 screws securing the each ignition coil to the ignition control module and remove the ignition coil(s).

To install:

4. Position the ignition coil(s) to the ignition control module.

5. Install the 2 retaining screws for each coil, then tighten to 40 inch lbs. (5 Nm).

6. Attach the spark plugs wires as noted during removal.

7. Connect the negative battery cable.

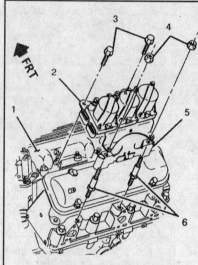

1. Upper intake manifold assembly
2. Ignition coil assembly
3. Bolt/screw
4. Nut
5. Evap purge solenoid valve bracket
6. Stud

88002G30

Fig. 4 Tag and detach the connectors, unfasten the retaining bolts, then remove the coil and module assembly from the vehicle

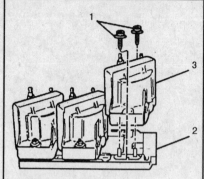

1. Screws (6) - 4-5 N.m (40 lb. in.)
2. Ignition control module (ICM)
3. Ignition coils (3)

88002G43

Fig. 6 The ignition coils are secured to the Ignition Control Module (ICM) with retaining screws

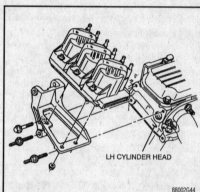

LH CYLINDER HEAD

88002G44

Fig. 7 Ignition control module/coil assembly mounting

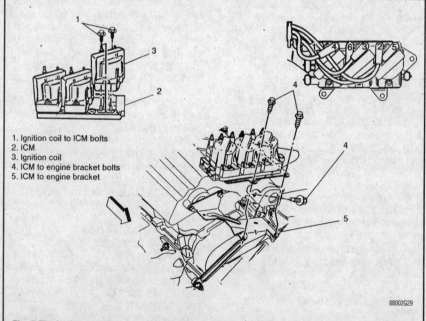

1. Ignition coil to ICM bolts
2. ICM
3. Ignition coil
4. ICM to engine bracket bolts
5. ICM to engine bracket

88002G29

Fig. 5 The ignition coils are secured to the module with retaining bolts/screws—3.4L shown

3.5L (VIN H) Engine

▶ See Figure 8

➡The 2000 Intrigue with the 3.5L (VIN H) engine has a direct-mount coil ignition system and uses no spark plug wires.

1. Verify that the ignition switch is in the **OFF** position.

2. Remove the engine cosmetic/acoustic shield (technically called the injector sight shield). Remove the two mounting nuts and then lift the cover off the mounting studs by lifting at the front of the cover.

3. Unplug the ignition coil module electrical connector.

4. Remove the seven ignition coil assembly (GM calls it the `ignition cassette') to cam cover mounting bolts.

5. Gently pry the cassette away from the cam cover using a screwdriver (protect the finished surfaces from scratches with a shop cloth). Pry a small amount in several locations around the edge of the cassette in order to lift the assembly as evenly as possible. Do not insert the screwdriver far enough to tear the perimeter seal on the cassette.

6. On some vehicles, the oil level indicator (dipstick) tube may interfere with the removal of the front bank coil cassette. Remove the oil level indicator tube retaining bolt and move the oil tube, as necessary.

7. Lift the coil cassette straight up off of the spark plugs.

8. Remove the secondary boots from the spark plugs or the ignition coils, using a twisting motion

to break the seal. Use tool J 43094 Spark Plug Boot Removal Tool or its equivalent. This is a long, padded gripping tool designed to reach down into the spark plug well to remove the boots. GM cautions against the use of pliers, screwdrivers or any unauthorized tool to remove the boots.

To install:

9. Do not re-install any component that has visible signs of damage. Check the boots for a missing or damaged internal spring. Make sure the boots are installed right side up. Make sure the ignition cassette to cam cover ground spring is in places. If necessary, repair a torn perimeter seal with RTV sealant. Clean all mounting surfaces before re-installing components.

10. Install the boots onto the ignition coils (until bottomed out).

11. Install the cassette assembly straight down onto the spark plug boots. If this is not possible due to space limitations (rear bank), just start the boots onto the spark plugs and then align and start the ignition coil towers into the boots. Press the coil assembly as straight down onto the plugs as possible.

12. Install the seven ignition cassette to cam cover mounting bolts and tighten to 84 inch lbs. (9.5 Nm).

13. Plug in the ignition control module electrical connector.

14. If the oil level indicator tube was moved during disassembly, move the tube back into position, then install the retaining bolt and tighten to 80 inch lbs. (9 Nm).

15. Keeping the engine cosmetic/acoustic cover as level as possible, place the rear of the shield

under the mounting bracket, and align and press the cover onto the mounting studs. Install the nuts and snug down to just 27 inch lbs. (3 Nm).

Ignition Control Module

REMOVAL & INSTALLATION

Except 3.5L (VIN H) Engine

All of the vehicles covered by this book use V6 engines and, with the exception of the 3.5L (VIN H) engine, similar ignition systems. The ignition control module removal procedures are similar, differing only in the types of wiring connections.

1. Disconnect the negative battery cable.

2. Tag and detach all the electrical connectors at the ignition control module.

3. Note the position of the spark plug wires for installation. Numbered tags of masking tape or other identification will save time at installation. Spark plug wires MUST be returned to their original and proper locations.

4. Disconnect the spark plug wires from the ignition coils.

5. Remove the screws securing the coil assemblies to the ignition control module.

6. Disconnect the coils from the ignition control module.

7. Remove the fasteners securing the ignition control module assembly to the engine.

8. Remove the ignition control module.

To install:

9. Position the ignition control module to the engine and secure with the retaining screws. Tighten the fasteners to 70 inch lbs. (8 Nm).

10. Install the coils to the ignition module. Install the coil retaining screws and tighten to 40 inch lbs. (5 Nm).

11. Install the spark plugs wires as noted during removal.

12. Install the electrical connectors to the ignition control module. Verify all connections are secure.

13. Connect the negative battery cable.

Crankshaft (CKP) and Camshaft (CMP) Position Sensors

For information and procedures on the position sensors, please refer to Section 4, under Emission Controls, in this manual.

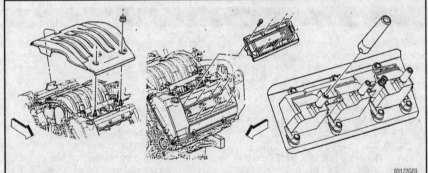

93172G03

Fig. 8 Remove the engine acoustic/cosmetic cover, the seven bolts, then carefully remove the ignition coil "cassette"—3.5L (VIN H) engine

FIRING ORDERS

▶ See Figures 9 thru 14

➡To avoid confusion, remove and tag the spark plug wires one at a time, for replacement.

The 3.5L (VIN H) engine's unique ignition system has the ignition coils directly over each plug. No spark plug wires are used.

If a coil is replaced on any of the 3.1L, 3.4L or

3.8L engines, it may not be numbered, as is the factory coil. For this reason it is imperative that you label all wires before disconnecting any of them. Also, before removal, compare the current wiring with the accompanying illustrations. If the current wiring does not match, make notes in your book to reflect how your engine is wired.

The firing order for the 3.1L VIN M, 3.4L VIN E, 3.4L VIN X and 3.5L VIN H engines is 1-2-3-4-5-6.

The right bank cylinders are on the cowl side (rear) of the engine compartment and are numbered 1,3,5, left bank cylinders on the front side of the vehicle, are numbered 2,4,6.

The firing order for the 3.8L VIN K and 3.8L VIN 1 engines is 1-6-5-4-3-2. Starting at the front of the engine, cylinders in the left bank are numbered 1,3,5 and cylinders in the right bank are numbered 2,4,6.

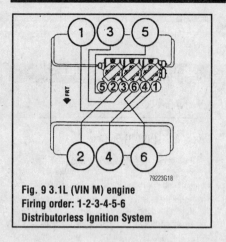

Fig. 9 3.1L (VIN M) engine
Firing order: 1-2-3-4-5-6
Distributorless Ignition System

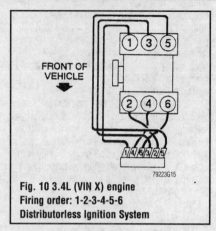

Fig. 10 3.4L (VIN X) engine
Firing order: 1-2-3-4-5-6
Distributorless Ignition System

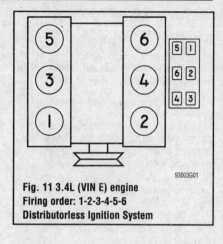

Fig. 11 3.4L (VIN E) engine
Firing order: 1-2-3-4-5-6
Distributorless Ignition System

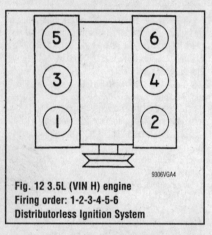

Fig. 12 3.5L (VIN H) engine
Firing order: 1-2-3-4-5-6
Distributorless Ignition System

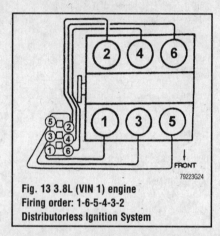

Fig. 13 3.8L (VIN 1) engine
Firing order: 1-6-5-4-3-2
Distributorless Ignition System

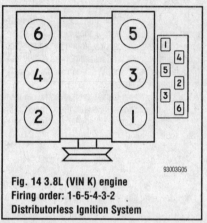

Fig. 14 3.8L (VIN K) engine
Firing order: 1-6-5-4-3-2
Distributorless Ignition System

CHARGING SYSTEM

General Information

The automobile charging system provides electrical power for operation of the vehicle's ignition system, starting system and all electrical accessories. The battery serves as an electrical surge or storage tank, storing (in chemical form) the energy originally produced by the engine driven generator. The system also provides a means of regulating output to protect the battery from being overcharged and to avoid excessive voltage to the accessories.

The storage battery is a chemical device incorporating parallel lead plates in a tank containing a sulfuric acid/water solution. Adjacent plates are slightly dissimilar, and the chemical reaction of the two dissimilar plates produces electrical energy when the battery is connected to a load such as the starter motor. The chemical reaction is reversible, so that when the alternator is producing a voltage (electrical pressure) greater than that produced by the battery, electricity is forced into the battery, and the battery is returned to its fully charged state.

Newer automobiles use alternating current alternators, because they are more efficient, can be rotated at higher speeds, and have fewer brush problems. In an alternator, the field usually rotates while all the current produced passes only through the stator winding. The brushes bear against continuous slip rings. This causes the current produced to periodically reverse the direction of its flow. Diodes (electrical one way valves) block the flow of current from traveling in the wrong direction. A series of diodes is wired together to permit the alternating flow of the stator to be rectified back to 12 volts DC for use by the vehicle's electrical system.

The voltage regulating function is performed by a regulator. The regulator is often built in to the alternator; this system is termed an integrated or internal regulator.

An alternator differs from a DC shunt generator in that the armature is stationary, and is called the stator, while the field rotates and is called the rotor. The higher current values in the alternator's stator are conducted to the external circuit through fixed leads and connections, rather than through a rotating commutator and brushes as in a DC generator. This eliminates a major point of maintenance.

The rotor assembly is supported in the drive end frame by a ball bearing and at the other end by a roller bearing. These bearings are lubricated during assembly and require no maintenance. There are six diodes in the end frame assembly. These diodes are electrical check valves that also change the alternating current developed within the stator windings to a Direct Current (DC) at the output (BAT) terminal. Three of these diodes are negative and are mounted flush with the end frame while the other three are positive and are mounted into a strip called a heat sink. The positive diodes are easily identified as the ones within small cavities or depressions.

The alternator charging system is a negative (-) ground system which consists of an alternator, a regulator, a charge indicator, a storage battery and wiring connecting the components, and fuse link wire.

The alternator is belt-driven from the engine. Energy is supplied from the alternator/regulator system to the rotating field through two brushes to two slip-rings. The slip-rings are mounted on the rotor shaft and are connected to the field coil. This energy supplied to the rotating field from the battery is called excitation current and is used to initially energize the field to begin the generation of electricity. Once the alternator starts to generate electricity, the excitation current comes from its own output rather than the battery.

The alternator produces power in the form of alternating current. The alternating current is rectified by 6 diodes into direct current. The direct current is used to charge the battery and power the rest of the electrical system.

When the ignition key is turned **ON**, current flows from the battery, through the charging system indicator light on the instrument panel, to the voltage regulator, and to the alternator. Since the alternator is not producing any current, the alternator warning light comes on. When the engine is started, the alternator begins to produce current and turns the alternator light off. As the alternator turns and produces current, the current is divided in two ways: part to the battery (to charge the battery and power the electrical components of the vehicle), and part is returned to the alternator (to enable it to increase its output). In this situation, the alternator is receiving current from the battery and from itself. A voltage regulator is wired into the current supply to the alternator to prevent it from receiving too much current which would cause it to put out too much current. Conversely, if the voltage regulator does not allow the alternator to receive enough current, the battery will not be fully charged and will eventually go dead.

The battery is connected to the alternator at all times, whether the ignition key is turned **ON** or not. If the battery were shorted to ground, the alternator would also be shorted. This would damage the alternator. To prevent this, a fuse link is installed in the wiring between the battery and the alternator. If the battery is shorted, the fuse link melts, protecting the alternator.

An alternator is better that a conventional, DC shunt generator because it is lighter and more compact, because it is designed to supply the battery and accessory circuits through a wide range of engine speeds, and because it eliminates the necessary maintenance of replacing brushes and servicing commutators.

Alternator Precautions

Several precautions must be observed when performing work on alternator equipment.

• If the battery is removed for any reason, make sure that it is reconnected with the correct polarity. Reversing the battery connections may result in damage to the one-way rectifiers.

• Never operate the alternator with the main circuit broken. Make sure that the battery, alternator, and regulator leads are not disconnected while the engine is running.

• Never attempt to polarize an alternator.

• When charging a battery that is installed in the vehicle, disconnect the negative battery cable.

• When utilizing a booster battery as a starting aid, always connect it in parallel; negative to negative, and positive to positive.

• When arc (electric) welding is to be performed on any part of the vehicle, disconnect the negative battery cable and alternator leads.

• Never unplug the PCM while the engine is running or with the ignition in the **ON** position. Severe and expensive damage may result within the solid state equipment.

Alternator

CHARGING SYSTEM INSPECTION

1. Make sure the battery connections are clean and tight and that the battery is in good condition and fully charged.

2. On a factory-type battery with the built-in hydrometer (eye), the green dot must be showing. Voltage across the terminals with loads off, should be above 12 volts.

3. Check the drive belt for damage or looseness.

4. Check the wiring harness at the alternator. The harness connector should be tight and latched. Make sure that the output terminal of the alternator is connected to the vehicle battery positive lead.

5. Verify that all charging system related fuses

and electrical connections are tight and free of damage.

GM's testing procedures for this alternator involves a clamp-on ammeter Digital Volt/Ohm Meter (DVOM), GM's MetriPack terminal probes and an adjustable carbon pile load tester. Some basic testing is given below, however, since it is unlikely the non-professional has access to these tools, it is recommended that a professional shop test the alternator if, after a preliminary inspection rules out the items listed above, charging system problems are suspected.

The alternator does not require period lubrication. The rotor shaft is mounted on bearings at the drive end and the slip ring end. Each bearing contains its own permanent grease supply.

The Delphi CS130D and Delphi AD-237 alternator and voltage regulator combinations are serviced only as a complete unit. It should not be disassembled as no internal repair is possible.

TESTING

Voltage Test

1. Make sure the engine is **OFF**, and turn the headlights on for 15–20 seconds to remove any surface charge from the battery.

2. Using a DVOM set to volts DC, probe across the battery terminals.

3. Measure the battery voltage.

4. Write down the voltage reading and proceed to the next test.

No-Load Test

1. Connect a tachometer to the engine.

✳✳ CAUTION

Ensure that the transmission is in Park and the emergency brake is set. Blocking a wheel is optional and an added safety measure.

2. Turn off all electrical loads (radio, blower motor, wipers, etc.)

3. Start the engine and increase engine speed to approximately 1500 rpm.

4. Measure the voltage reading at the battery with the engine holding a steady 1500 rpm. Voltage should have raised at least 0.5 volts, but no more than 2.5 volts.

5. If the voltage does not go up more than 0.5 volts, the alternator is not charging. If the voltage goes up more than 2.5 volts, the alternator is overcharging.

➥Usually under and overcharging is caused by a defective alternator, or its related parts (regulator), and replacement will fix the problem; however, faulty wiring and other problems can cause the charging system to malfunction. Further testing, which is not covered by this book, will reveal the exact component failure. Many automotive parts stores have alternator bench testers available for use by customers. An alternator bench test is the most definitive way to determine the condition of your alternator.

6. If the voltage is within specifications, proceed to the next test.

Load Test

1. With the engine running, turn on the blower motor and the high beams (or other electrical accessories to place a load on the charging system).

2. Increase and hold engine speed to 2000 rpm.

3. Measure the voltage reading at the battery.

4. The voltage should increase at least 0.5 volts from the voltage test. If the voltage does not meet specifications, the charging system is malfunctioning.

➥Usually under and overcharging is caused by a defective alternator, or its related parts (regulator), and replacement will fix the problem; however, faulty wiring and other problems can cause the charging system to malfunction. Further testing, which is not covered by this book, will reveal the exact component failure. Many automotive parts stores have alternator bench testers available for use by customers. An alternator bench test is the most definitive way to determine the condition of your alternator.

REMOVAL AND INSTALLATION

✳✳ CAUTION

Before serving any electrical component, the ignition switch must be in the OFF or LOCK position and all electrical loads must be off, unless instructed otherwise. Since a tool or piece of equipment could come into contact with a live exposed electrical terminal, always disconnect the negative battery cable. Failure to do these precautions may cause personal injury and/or damage to the vehicle or its components. The BAT+ terminal is always electrically "hot", even with the ignition switch OFF.

3.1L (VIN M) Engine

▶ See Figures 15, 16, 17 and 18

➥The CS 130 alternator, used on this engine, cannot be disassembled for repair. Service by replacing the complete assembly.

1. Record all of the vehicle preset radio stations (if applicable).

2. Record your radio Theftlock® codes (if applicable).

3. Turn off all the maps and accessories.

4. Make sure the ignition switch is **OFF**.

5. Disconnect the battery ground (negative) cable with the battery ground terminal bolt from the battery.

6. Remove the drive belt from the alternator.

7. Remove the bolts holding the alternator to the engine bracket.

8. Detach the electrical connector from the alternator.

9. Loosen the alternator front and rear braces at the engine intake manifold.

10. Remove the nut and battery positive lead from the alternator output "BAT" terminal.

11. Remove the alternator from the vehicle.

To install:

12. Position the replacement alternator to the engine bracket.

13. Connect the battery positive lead to the alternator output "BAT" terminal and install the nut. Tighten the nut to 15 ft. lbs. (20 Nm).

14. Hand start the alternator front and rear brace nuts to the engine intake manifold.

15. Plug in the electrical connector to the alternator.

16. Hand start the alternator rear brace bolt to the alternator.

17. Install the alternator through bolts and tighten to 37 ft. lbs. (50 Nm).

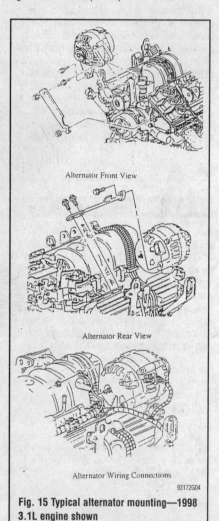

Fig. 15 Typical alternator mounting—1998 3.1L engine shown

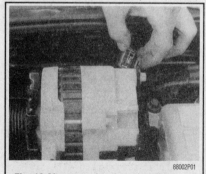

Fig. 16 After removing the serpentine drive belt, detach the electrical connector from the rear of the alternator

Fig. 17 Unfasten the front and rear mounting bolts . . .

Fig. 18 . . . then remove the brace-to-alternator bolt

18. Tighten the alternator front and rear brace nuts at the intake manifold to 18 ft. lbs. (25 Nm).

19. Tighten the rear brace stud to 18 ft. lbs. (25 Nm).

20. Connect the serpentine drive belt to the alternator pulley.

21. Connect the battery negative cable to the battery.

22. Reset the radio codes (if applicable).

3.4L (VIN X) Engine

▶ See Figure 19

➡This is a complicated procedure requiring numerous components to be removed and the sub-frame containing the engine and transaxle to be loosened and lowered for clearance. This is not a job for the inexperienced or ill-equipped. Be very sure that the alternator really needs to be replaced before attempting this procedure. Be very sure of the lifting and jacking equipment you have available before attempting this procedure or the vehicle could be damaged and you could be injured. In addition, the factory specifies that whenever frame to body bolts are loosened or removed, they must be replaced with new bolts and retainers. Procure the bolts before beginning this procedure. Failure to replace frame to body bolts and retainers may result in damage to the frame, powertrain or suspension.

1. Disconnect the negative battery cable.
2. Remove the ignition control module with its

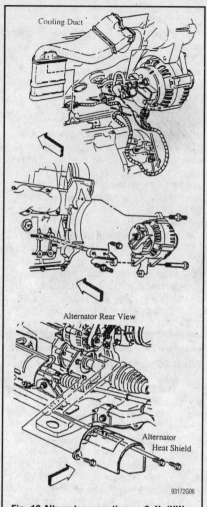

Fig. 19 Alternator mounting on 3.4L (VIN X) engine

mounting bracket and position forward for clearance.

3. Raise and safely support the vehicle.
4. Remove both front wheels.
5. Remove the right engine splash shield
6. Remove the intermediate steering shaft lower pinch bolt and disengage the intermediate shaft from the rack and pinion steering gear assembly.

7. Detach the oxygen sensor electrical connector from the wiring harness. Note that the oxygen sensor uses a permanently attached pigtail and connector. This pigtail should not be removed from the oxygen sensor. Damage or removal of the pigtail or connector will affect proper operation of the sensor. Keep the connector free of grease and contaminates.

8. Disconnect the catalytic converter from the rear exhaust.

9. Install a suitable lifting/jacking device to support the rear of the sub-frame.

10. Remove the rear sub-frame bolts. Discard the bolts. They must be replaced with new bolts.

11. Using the lifting/jacking device, lower the rear of the sub-frame.

✳✳ WARNING

Do not lower the frame more than 4 inches.

12. Disconnect the alternator cooling duct from the alternator by releasing the clip.

13. Unplug the electrical connector from the alternator.

14. Remove the alternator "BAT" terminal nut and lead from the alternator.

15. Remove the serpentine drive belt using the procedure found in Section 1.

16. Remove the alternator rear brace.

17. Disconnect the power steering gear pipe clip from the alternator stud.

18. Remove the alternator to mounting bracket bolts and remove the alternator from the vehicle.

To install:

19. Install the replacement alternator to the brackets on the engine and tighten the bolts and stud to 37 ft. lbs. (50 Nm).

20. Install the alternator rear brace and connect the steering pipe clip to the alternator stud.

21. Install the serpentine drive belt to the alternator pulley.

22. Connect the heavy "BAT" terminal lead to the alternator stud, install the nut and tighten to 15 ft. lbs. (20 Nm).

23. Plug the electrical connectors to the alternator.

24. Clip the cooling duct back in place on the alternator.

25. Using the lifting/jacking device, raise the frame rear until the frame contacts the body. Install new replacement body bolts observing the following:

a. Position the frame with aid of an assistant. A $^{19}\!/_{32}$ (15mm) guide pin or drill bit can be inserted into the alignment holes located on the right side.

b. Proper clamping by the mount depends on clean and dry surfaces. If the frame isolator bolt does not screw in smoothly, it may be necessary to run a tap through the cage nut in the body to remove foreign material. Take care that the tap does not punch through the underbody. If the cage nut cannot be used, the cage nut retainer spot welds will have to be chiseled away with air chisel, the cage nut replaced and the retainer welded back into its original location. Clean and prime the area with catalyzed primer to protect the area from corrosion.

26. Torque the four new frame isolator bolts to 133 ft. lbs. (180 Nm). Do not over-tighten the body mounts; a collapsed spacer or stripped bolt may result. Tighten in the following order:

a. RH Rear

b. RH Front

c. LH Rear

d. LH Front

27. Connect the catalytic converter to the rear exhaust.

28. Attach the oxygen sensor wiring connector.

✳✳ CAUTION

When installing the intermediate shaft, make sure the shaft is seated prior to pinch bolt installation. If the pinch bolt is inserted into the coupling before shaft installation, the two mating shafts may disengage, with a loss of steering.

29. Connect the intermediate steering shaft to the rack and pinion steering assembly stub shaft. Verify that the two shafts are properly coupled. Insert the pinch bolt and torque carefully to 35 ft. lbs. (47 Nm).

30. Install the right side engine splash shield.

31. Install both front wheels.

32. Lower the vehicle.

33. Install the ignition control module with its retaining bracket to the engine.

34. Connect the negative battery cable.

3.4L (VIN E) Engine

1. Disconnect the negative battery cable.

2. At the cowl, there is a 'cross vehicle brace' that runs across the car, to the strut towers. Remove the nuts from the cross brace and remove the cross brace from the vehicle.

✳✳ WARNING

The cross brace nuts thread onto stud plates that are under the strut tower sheetmetal. When the cross brace nuts are removed, the plates will likely fall out and could get caught under the vehicle. Have a helper hold the stud plates during removal.

3. Remove the drive belt from the alternator.

4. Remove the coolant reservoir using the following procedure:

a. Remove the reservoir hose clamp and the hose from the radiator overflow neck fitting.

b. Remove the reservoir retainer nuts from the strut tower studs.

c. Remove the reservoir lower retainer and remove the coolant reservoir. Set it aside.

5. Remove the bolts from the alternator.

6. Unplug the electrical connector.

7. Reposition the protective boot from the output "BAT" terminal, remove the nut and disconnect the heavy "BAT" wire from the alternator.

8. Remove the alternator from the vehicle.

To install:

9. Install the replacement alternator to the engine.

10. Connect the heavy "BAT" lead to the alternator stud terminal, install the nut and tighten to 15 ft. lbs. (20 Nm). Press the protective boot back into place.

11. Plug the electrical terminal back into the alternator.

12. Install the bolts into the alternator and finger start, but do not tighten. Install the pivot bolt and finger start. Tighten the bolts in the following order:

a. Tighten the pivot bolt to 37 ft. lbs. (50 Nm).

b. Tighten the bolt closest to the center of the alternator to 37 ft. lbs. (50 Nm).

13. Tighten the bolt closest to the front of the alternator to 37 ft. lbs. (50 Nm).

14. Install the coolant recovery reservoir.

15. Install the serpentine drive belt.

16. Install the engine compartment cross brace. A helper will be required to hold the stud plates in place during installation of the nuts. Torque the brace nuts to 29 ft. lbs. (40 Nm).

17. Connect the battery negative cable.

3.5L (VIN H) Engine

♦ See Figure 20

The Delphi AD237 125 amp alternator, used on this engine, is serviced as a complete unit only.

1. Disconnect the negative, then the positive battery cables.

2. Remove the battery from the vehicle.

3. Remove the battery tray using the following procedure:

a. Remove the four battery tray bolts.

b. Remove the battery tray from the vehicle.

4. Remove the serpentine drive belt using the procedure outline in Section 1.

5. Remove the cooling fan assembly using the following procedure:

a. Remove the wishbone-shaped engine mount strut by removing the bolts and nuts at the engine mount bracket and on the upper radiator support.

b. Remove the strut from the vehicle.

c. Disconnect the cooling fan harness from the engine wiring harness.

d. Reposition the wiring harness at the upper radiator support.

e. Remove the cooling fan shroud bolts.

f. Remove the right side radiator bracket.

g. Remove the cooling fan shroud with the electric cooling fan motors and fans as an assembly.

6. Remove the thermostat housing and the radiator hose using the following procedure.

a. Partially drain the engine coolant.

b. Use hose clamp pliers to remove the radi-

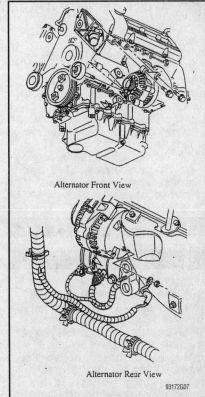

Alternator Front View

Alternator Rear View

93172G07

Fig. 20 Alternator mounting—3.5L (VIN H) engine shown

ator hose clamp to the water inlet housing and disconnect the radiator hose.

　c. Use hose clamp pliers to remove the heater hose clamp to the water inlet housing and disconnect the heater hose from the water inlet housing.

　d. Use hose clamp pliers to remove the surge tank inlet hose clamp from the water inlet housing and disconnect the surge tank hose from the water inlet housing.

　e. Remove the water inlet housing bolts and remove the water inlet housing.

7. Remove the outboard generator bolt and loosen the inboard bolt.

8. Remove the idler pulley bolt and idler pulley.

9. Unplug the electrical connector from the alternator.

10. Pull back the protective boot from the alternator "BAT" terminal, remove the nut and disconnect the heavy "BAT" wire from the alternator terminal stud.

11. Remove the alternator from the vehicle.

To install:

12. Position the alternator to the engine.

13. Plug in the electrical connectors and install the heavy "BAT" wire to the alternator terminal stud. Tighten the nut to 15 ft. lbs. (20 Nm). Press the protective boot back in place over the stud terminal and nut assembly.

14. Install the outboard alternator bolt into the alternator housing.

15. Install the inboard alternator bolt and then finger-tighten the outboard bolt.

16. Install the idler pulley and idler pulley bolt.

17. Tighten the bolts in the following torque sequence:

　a. Tighten the idler pulley bolt to 37 ft lbs. (50 Nm).

　b. Tighten the alternator bolts to 37 ft. lbs. (50 Nm).

18. Install the water inlet and thermostat housing and the radiator hose, observing the following:

　a. Inspect and clean the mating surfaces on the thermostat cover and its mounting surface on the engine.

　b. Use RTV Sealer GM #1052366 or equivalent on the mounting bolts since the threaded openings are open to the cooling system and the torque requirement is low.

　c. Install the water inlet and thermostat housing and tighten the bolts to 80 inch lbs. (9 Nm).

　d. Connect the surge tank inlet hose to the water inlet housing.

　e. Connect the heater hose to the water inlet housing.

　f. Connect the radiator hose to the water inlet housing.

19. Install the cooling fan assembly and tighten the radiator bracket bolts to 80 inch lbs. (9 Nm). Plug in the wiring harness at the upper radiator support. Plug in the cooling fan wiring harness to the engine wiring harness.

20. Install the engine mount strut bracket to the upper radiator support first, insert the through bolt.

Alternator Front View

Alternator Rear View

93172G05

Fig. 21 Typical alternator mounting—1998 3.8L (VIN K) engine shown

Attach the engine side of the strut to the engine mount strut bracket on the engine and install the through bolt. Thread the nuts on the through bolts and tighten to 35 ft. lbs. (48 Nm).

21. Install the battery tray and tighten the bolts to 44 inch lbs. (5 Nm).

22. Install the battery.

23. Install the serpentine drive belt.

24. Connect the positive, then the negative battery cables.

3.8L (VIN K and 1) Engines

▶ **See Figure 21**

The CS130D alternator, used on these engines, is serviced as a complete assembly only.

1. Disconnect the negative battery cable.

2. Remove the serpentine drive belt.

3. Remove the alternator from brace.

4. Remove the electrical connector from the alternator.

5. Remove the retaining bolts from the alternator.

6. Remove the protective boot from the alternator output "BAT" terminal and remove the nut. Disconnect the battery positive lead from the alternator.

7. Remove the alternator from the vehicle.

To install:

8. Position the replacement alternator to the engine bracket.

9. Connect the battery positive lead to the alternator output "BAT" terminal and install the nut. Tighten the nut to 15 ft. lbs. (20 Nm). Install the protective boot over the terminal.

10. Hand start the alternator front lower bolt and tighten to 37 ft. lbs. (50 Nm).

11. Install the alternator brace stud through the alternator flange and the bracket and tighten the brace stud to 22 ft. lbs. (30 Nm).

12. If equipped with the CS 144 alternator, install the inboard alternator bolt through the flange and into the alternator brace assembly and tighten to 37 ft. lbs. (50 Nm).

13. If equipped with the CS 130D alternator, tighten the rear brace bolt to 22 ft. lbs. (30 Nm).

14. Plug in the electrical connector to the alternator.

15. Install the alternator front brace.

16. Install the serpentine drive belt to the alternator pulley.

17. Connect the negative battery terminal.

STARTING SYSTEM

General Information

The starting, or cranking system consists of the battery, starter motor, ignition switch and related wiring. These components are connected electrically. When the ignition switch is turned to the **START** position (and the theft protection module recognizes the key code, as equipped) battery voltage is applied to the starter solenoid (through the theft deterrent relay, as equipped) **S** terminal and the solenoid windings are energized. This causes the plunger to move the shift lever, which engages the pinion with the engine flywheel ring gear. The plunger also closes the solenoid contacts, applying battery voltage to the starter motor, which cranks the engine.

When the engine starts, the pinion will over-run and spin at engine speed (rather than starter motor speed) to help prevent flywheel and starter motor damage. When the ignition switch is released (removing the voltage from the solenoid) the plunger return spring disengages the pinion. In order to prevent excessive over-run, the ignition switch should be released as soon as the engine starts.

✳✳ WARNING

Never operate the starter motor for more than 30 seconds at a time. Allow it to cool for at least two minutes. Overheating, caused by too much cranking, will damage the starter motor.

The vehicles covered by this book use several different starter motor applications. When obtaining a replacement starter motor, make sure you get the correct unit. In nearly every case, the starter motor is considered non-serviceable which means they are not user-serviceable and must be replaced as an assembly.

Starter motors do not require lubrication. In general, starter motors give little trouble. Most no-start or hard cranking complaints can be traced to a low battery, poor connections, defective fusible link, engine oil too thick for the weather conditions and other non-starter related causes.

Although different starter motors are used on different engines, the removal and installation procedures are very similar. The main differences are getting to the starter (air dam removal or radiator baffle removal requirements on some applications).

STARTER MOTOR NOISE DIAGNOSIS

High-Pitched Whine During Cranking

A high-pitched whine during cranking (before the engine fires), although the engine cranks and starts okay, means the distance it too great between the starter pinion and flywheel. This distance is governed by thin metal shims between the starter motor and the engine block. Likely a shim needs to be removed. This is often the case after a starter motor has been changed. The replacement starter may not fit exactly as the original so shims are normally used to adjust the starter in or out to get proper tooth meshing.

High-Pitched Whine After Engine Fires

A high-pitched whine after the engine fires, as the key is being released, although then engine cranks and starts okay, is sometime an intermittent complaint. It is often diagnosed as starter "hang-in" or a weak solenoid. This usually means the distance is too small between the starter pinion and flywheel. Flywheel runout (out-of-round) contributes to the intermittent nature of the complaint. Again, shimming the starter correctly should cure the problem. The GM shims are generally 0.040 inch (1mm) thick. Install the shims, one at a time, until the noise is gone. GM recommends that you use no more than two shims and do not exceed 0.080 inch (2mm).

Loud "Whoop" Noise

A loud "whoop" after the engine starts, while the starter is still engaged, often sounding like a siren as the engine RPM is increased while the starter is engaged, is usually a starter drive problem. On starters that can be serviced (very few on the vehicles covered by this book), a new starter drive should solve the problem. On non-serviceable starters, replace the starter assembly.

Rumble, Growl or Knock

A rumble, growl or in severe cases, a knock as the starter is coasting down to a stop after starting the engine may be traced to a bent starter armature. On starters that can be serviced (very few on the vehicles covered by this book), a new armature (if available) should solve the problem. On non-serviceable starters, replace the starter assembly.

TESTING

Before removing any component of the cranking circuit, check the following:
- Inspect the battery and cables, as outlined in Section 1.
- Inspect the wiring for damage
- Inspect all connections to the starter motor, solenoid, ignition switch, battery and all ground connections. Clean and tighten as required.
- Inspect the starter motor and ignition switches to determine their condition.

If the battery, wiring and switches are in satisfactory condition, and the engine is known to be functioning properly, the starter may be at fault.

Voltage Drop Test

➥The battery must be in good condition and fully charged prior to performing this test.

1. Disable the ignition system by unplugging the coil pack. Verify that the vehicle will not start.
2. Connect a voltmeter between the positive terminal of the battery and the starter **B+** circuit.
3. Turn the ignition key to the **START** position and note the voltage on the meter.
4. If voltage reads 0.5 volts or more, there is high resistance in the starter cables or the cable ground, repair as necessary. If the voltage reading is ok proceed to the next step.
5. Connect a voltmeter between the positive terminal of the battery and the starter **M** circuit.
6. Turn the ignition key to the **START** position and note the voltage on the meter.
7. If voltage reads 0.5 volts or more, there is high resistance in the starter. Repair or replace the starter as necessary.

➥Many automotive parts stores have starter bench testers available for use by customers. A starter bench test is the most definitive way to determine the condition of your starter.

REMOVAL & INSTALLATION

3.1L, 3.4L (VIN X) and 3.8L Engines

◆ See Figures 22 thru 29

❊❊ WARNING

Remember that the positive battery cable to the starter motor is electrically "hot" all the time. You must open the circuit by disconnecting the negative battery cable before servicing the starter motor.

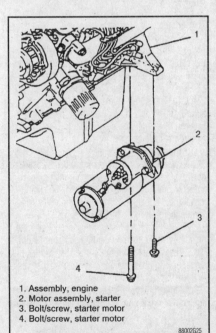

1. Assembly, engine
2. Motor assembly, starter
3. Bolt/screw, starter motor
4. Bolt/screw, starter motor

88002G25

Fig. 22 Typical starter motor mounting— 3.1L engine shown

1. Disconnect the negative battery cable.
2. Raise and safely support the vehicle.
3. Remove the electrical connections at the starter.
4. Remove the torque converter cover. Usually this is just a few small screws and/or small bolts
5. Remove the starter motor mounting bolts. Use care as the starter is relatively heavy. Do not

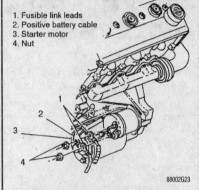

1. Fusible link leads
2. Positive battery cable
3. Starter motor
4. Nut

88002G23

Fig. 23 Detach the starter electrical connections . . .

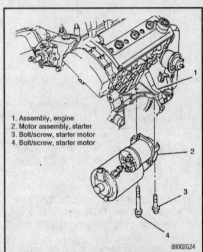

1. Assembly, engine
2. Motor assembly, starter
3. Bolt/screw, starter motor
4. Bolt/screw, starter motor

88002G24

Fig. 24 . . . then unfasten the retaining bolts and remove the starter from the vehicle

88002P11

Fig. 25 Most starter removal requires unfastening the flywheel cover screws . . .

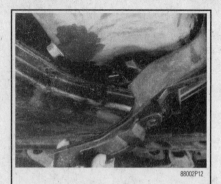

Fig. 26 . . . then removing the plastic fly-wheel cover

Fig. 27 A socket wrench extension is often required to reach the starter motor retaining bolts

Fig. 28 When removing the starter motor, retain the thin sheetmetal shim(s) as they may be required at installation

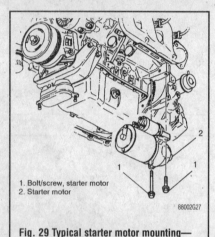

1. Bolt/screw, starter motor
2. Starter motor

Fig. 29 Typical starter motor mounting—3.8L engines shown

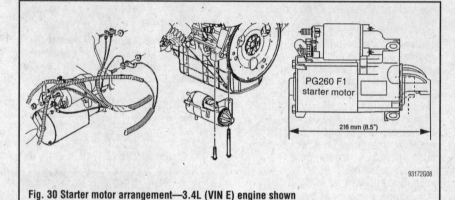

Fig. 30 Starter motor arrangement—3.4L (VIN E) engine shown

allow it to fall. Take note of any thin metal shims between the starter and engine block. They may be required during installation.

To install:

6. Position the starter motor, including any shims found at removal, to the engine block and install the mounting bolts. Tighten the bolts to 32 ft. lbs. (43 Nm).

7. Install the torque converter cover and tighten the torque converter cover screws to 89 inch lbs. (10 Nm).

8. Position the wires to the starter. Tighten the starter solenoid "BAT" (heavy cable) nut to 84 inch lbs. (9 Nm). Tighten the starter solenoid **S** terminal nut to just 27 inch lbs. (3 Nm).

9. Lower the vehicle.

10. Connect the battery negative cable. Start the engine to verify correct operation.

3.4L (VIN E) Engine

♦ See Figure 30

✳✳ WARNING

Remember that the positive battery cable to the starter motor is electrically "hot" all the time. You must open the circuit by disconnecting the negative battery cable before servicing the starter motor.

1. Disconnect the negative battery cable.
2. Raise and safely support the vehicle.

3. Remove the front lower air deflector panel by locating the deflector retainers. These are push-in retainers and should be carefully pried loose. Remove the ambient temperature sensor, if equipped.

4. Remove the two torque converter covers. They are retained by small screws.

5. Remove the starter solenoid "BAT" terminal nut (the large one) and disconnect the battery positive cable from the starter motor. Remove the **S** terminal nut and disconnect the solenoid wire.

6. Remove the starter motor mounting bolts. Use care. The starter is relatively heavy. Do not allow it to fall. Take note of any thin metal shims between the starter and engine block. They may be required at installation.

To install:

7. Verify the correct starter motor has been obtained. Position the starter motor, including any shims found at removal, to the engine block and install the mounting bolts finger-tight until seated. Torque the bolts to 32 ft. lbs. (43 Nm).

8. Position the wires to the starter. Install the nuts finger-tight, then tighten the starter solenoid "BAT" (heavy cable) nut to 84 inch lbs. Tighten the starter solenoid **S** terminal nut to just 20 inch lbs. (2.5 Nm).

9. Install the torque converter covers and tighten the torque converter cover screws to 89 inch lbs. (10 Nm).

10. Install the front lower air deflector panel by pressing in the plastic retainers.

11. Lower the vehicle.

12. Connect the battery negative cable. Start the engine to verify correct operation

3.5L (VIN H) Engine

♦ See Figure 31

The PG260 M1 starter motor used on this engine is not serviceable and must be replaced as a complete unit.

1. Disconnect the negative battery cable.
2. Raise and safely support the vehicle.
3. Remove the front radiator lower air deflector (sometimes called an 'air dam' or 'spoiler'). The bolts should go through the deflector vertically to the substructure.
4. Remove the **S** terminal nut and disconnect the solenoid wire. Remove the starter solenoid "BAT" terminal nut (the large one) and disconnect the battery positive cable from the starter motor.

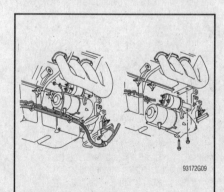

Fig. 31 Exploded view of the starter motor—3.5L (VIN H) engine shown

5. Remove the torque converter cover, retained by small screws.

6. Remove the starter motor mounting bolts. Use care. The starter is relatively heavy. Do not allow it to fall. Take note of any thin metal shims between the starter and engine block. They may be required at installation.

To install:

7. Verify the correct starter motor has been obtained. Position the starter motor, including any shims found at removal, to the engine block and install the mounting bolts finger-tight until seated. Torque the bolts to 37 ft. lbs. (50 Nm).

8. Install the torque converter cover, tightening the screws to 89 inch lbs. (10 Nm).

9. Position the wires to the starter. Install the nuts finger-tight, then tighten the starter solenoid "BAT" (heavy cable) nut to 84 inch lbs. (9 Nm) Tighten the starter solenoid **S** terminal nut to just 20 inch lbs. (2.5 Nm).

10. Install the front radiator lower air deflector. Tighten the bolts to 15 ft. lbs. (20 Nm).

11. Lower the vehicle.

12. Connect the battery negative cable. Start the engine to verify correct operation

SOLENOID REPLACEMENT

All of the starter motor and solenoid assemblies used by vehicles covered by this book are non-serviceable starter assemblies, with the exception of some 3.8L engines using GM's SD255 starter motor.

3.8L Engine With SD255 Starter Motor Only

1. Remove the starter motor from the engine as outlined earlier in this section.

2. Remove the starter solenoid screws.

3. Rotate the solenoid 90 degrees (¼ turn) and pull the solenoid out of the starter.

To install:

➡**Use only GM Part Number 10477431 grease to lubricate the solenoid core. This grease is specially formulated to aid plunger movement and dampen vibration of the plunger as the engine runs. Other greases may eventually degrade and prevent proper plunger movement, causing starter failure.**

4. Clean all parts well. Lubricate the solenoid core. Apply one complete packet (1 gram) of GM Part Number 10477431 grease evenly around the inside edge of the solenoid core. Apply all grease thickly to the first ½ inch (13mm) inside the edge of the core. Plunger movement will distribute grease properly. Avoid getting dirt or other contamination in the grease before installing the solenoid to the starter.

5. Assemble the solenoid over the plunger by compressing the spring and aligning the solenoid motor field terminal with the field lead on the starter.

6. Tighten the starter solenoid to starter motor screws to 58 inch lbs. (6.5 Nm). Tighten the solenoid motor solenoid to field terminal screw to 65 inch lbs. (7.3 Nm).

7. Install the starter motor using the procedure described above.

SENDING UNITS AND SENSORS

➡**This section describes the operating principles of sending units, warning lights and gauges. Sensors which provide information to the Electronic Control Module (ECM) are covered in Section 4 of this manual.**

Instrument panels contain a number of indicating devices (gauges and warning lights). These devices are composed of two separate components. One is the sending unit, mounted on the engine or other remote part of the vehicle, and the other is the actual gauge or light in the instrument panel.

Several types of sending units exist, however most can be characterized as being either a pressure type or a resistance type. Pressure type sending units convert liquid pressure into an electrical signal which is sent to the gauge. Resistance type sending units are most often used to measure temperature and use variable resistance to control the current flow back to the indicating device. Both types of sending units are connected in series by a wire to the battery (through the ignition switch). When the ignition is turned **ON**, current flows from the battery through the indicating device and on to the sending unit.

Low Coolant Sensor (Module)

The low coolant module activates a light in the instrument cluster when coolant in the radiator goes below a certain level (closed with low coolant level). It has two terminals. Terminal B is the connection from the sensor to the instrument panel. Terminal C is the sensor's ground connection. The sensor is located in the radiator's right side tank.

TESTING

"LOW COOLANT" Indicator ON, Coolant Level OK

1. Disconnect the engine coolant level indicator module at the radiator.

2. Place the ignition switch in the **ON** position. Check if the "Low Coolant" indicator is ON.

a. If the indicator is no longer ON, replace the coolant level indicator module.

b. If the indicator is still ON, check the circuit for a short to ground, between the instrument cluster connection and the module connector terminal B (usually a yellow/black wire, to instrument cluster).

c. If the circuit is okay, the instrument cluster may need to be serviced.

"LOW COOLANT" Indicator OFF, Coolant Level LOW

1. Disconnect the engine coolant level indicator module at the radiator.

2. Place the ignition switch in the **ON** position.

3. Connect a 3 Amp fused jumper between the engine coolant level indicator module terminal B and ground.

4. Is the "Low Coolant" indicator ON?

a. If the indicator is still ON, connect the fused jumper between terminal B and terminal C (the ground wire, usually black with a white tracer). If the indicator stays ON, check the module terminal C for a poor connection. If okay, replace the module. If the indicator is OFF, check the coolant module terminal C for a poor connection. If okay, look for an open in the circuit between the coolant module and its ground connection, at the flywheel end of the engine.

b. If, after jumping terminal B and C together, the indicator is now OFF, look for a bad connection at the instrument cluster, an open in the circuit between the coolant level module and instrument cluster connection and/or also a possible bad bulb or bulb connection.

REMOVAL & INSTALLATION

▶ **See Figure 32**

1. Partially drain the radiator to a level below the sensor. See Section 1.

2. Unplug the electrical connector from the low coolant sensor.

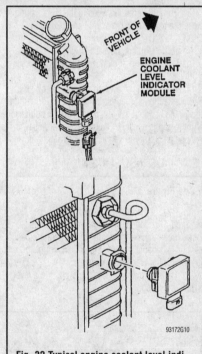

Fig. 32 Typical engine coolant level indicator module arrangement

3. The sensor is retained by a snap clip. To unlock the sensor, lift one leg of the snap clip from its locked position and pull outward with a slight twisting motion.

To install:

4. Inspect the O-ring on the sensor. If serviceable, lubricate with coolant.

5. Place the snap clip in place and install the sensor to the radiator.

6. Plug the electrical connector to the sensor.

7. Refill the cooling system with the proper mix of DEX-COOL® and water and properly bleed the cooling system. Please see Section 1.

8. Check for leaks.

Temperature Gauge/Lamp Switch

The temperature gauge/lamp switch activates a warning lamp in the instrument cluster if the engine overheats. With optional instrumentation, a temperature gauge replaces the warning lamp and the temperature switch is replaced with a transducer. These sensors are self-grounded to the engine. During installation, no sealer tape should be used since it can interfere with the sensor's ground path. As a general specification, this resistance-based sensor should show about 1365 ohms at 100°F (38°C) and 44 ohms at 280°F (138°C). A special tester is recommended by the factory. Resistors of equal value may be used.

TESTING

Temperature Gauge Inoperative or Inaccurate

1. Disconnect the engine coolant temperature (gauge) sensor (usually a dark green wire).
2. Insert a 44 ohm resistor between the connector and ground.
3. Turn the ignition switch to the **ON** position. Does the gauge now read high, approximately 260°F (127°C)?
   a. If the gauge now reads high, check for a poor connection. If okay, replace the gauge sensor.
4. If the gauge shows no change, check for a bad connection at the instrument cluster, or a short to voltage between the instrument cluster connector and the gauge sensor. If these circuits are okay, it may be necessary to service the instrument cluster.

REMOVAL & INSTALLATION

▶ **See Figure 33**

1. Record any radio anti-theft codes, as required. Disconnect the negative battery cable.
2. Locate the engine coolant temperature gauge sensor. It is usually below the coolant connection, just below the bleeder connection.
3. Partially drain the cooling system to a level below the sensor.

4. Unplug the electrical connector.
5. Unscrew the sensor from the engine.

To install:

6. Thread the sensor into the engine. Use care not to damage the "pigtail" wire.
7. Reconnect the lead wire.
8. Refill the cooling system with the proper mix of DEX-COOL® and water and properly bleed the cooling system. Please see Section 1.
9. Check for leaks.

Engine Oil Level Switch

The engine oil level sensor is used on several different engines and they all work in a similar manner. It is a simple float switch that is grounded when the engine oil level is okay. The Powertrain Control Module (PCM) checks the engine oil level switch circuit at start up. If the engine has been running, the PCM performs a test routine based on engine coolant temperature to ensure that the engine oil has drained back into the sump before checking the state of the engine oil level switch. If the engine coolant is between 59–284°F (15–140°C), the PCM compares the engine coolant temperature at the last key **OFF** to the engine coolant temperature at the current key **ON**. If the difference between the recorded temperature values is at least 54° (12°C), the PCM will test the engine oil level.

TESTING

"LOW OIL" Indicator ON, Oil Level OK

1. Unplug the engine oil level sensor connector.
2. Using a 3 Amp fused jumper, connect terminal A to terminal B.
3. With the ignition switch **ON**, is the "LOW OIL" indicator now on?
4. If yes, check the circuit from the oil sensor to the Powertrain Control Module (PCM) and the circuit from the oil sensor to ground for an open. Another remote possibility is an open in the circuit from the PCM to the instrument panel.
5. If no, replace the engine oil level sensor.

REMOVAL & INSTALLATION

▶ **See Figures 34 and 35**

The engine oil level switch is mounted to the side or bottom of the oil pan, depending on the engine.

1. Raise and safely support the vehicle.
2. Drain the engine oil into a suitable container.
3. Unplug the electrical connector from the engine oil level switch.
4. Unthread the switch from the oil pan.

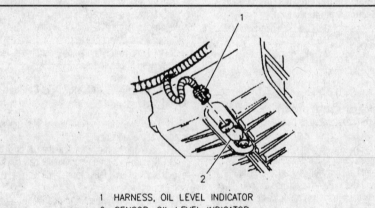

1 HARNESS, OIL LEVEL INDICATOR
2 SENSOR, OIL LEVEL INDICATOR

88002GA2

Fig. 34 Typical oil level sensor and harness location—3.1L engine shown

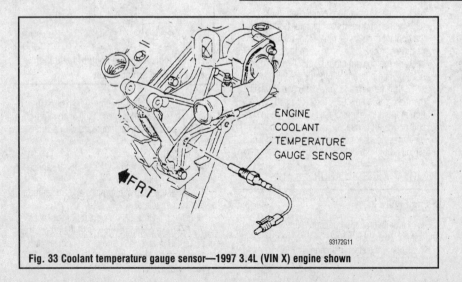

ENGINE COOLANT TEMPERATURE GAUGE SENSOR

93172G11

Fig. 33 Coolant temperature gauge sensor—1997 3.4L (VIN X) engine shown

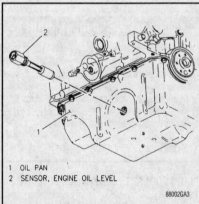

1 OIL PAN
2 SENSOR, ENGINE OIL LEVEL

88002GA3

Fig. 35 This oil level sensor is mounted on the side of the oil pan—3.4L (VIN X) engine shown

To install:

5. Install the oil level switch to the oil pan and tighten to 13–20 ft. lbs. (17–27 Nm).
6. Plug in the electrical connector.
7. Lower the vehicle.
8. Add engine oil to the correct level.

Engine Oil Pressure Warning Indicator Switch

The oil pressure warning indicator switch (also called a sender unit) receives battery voltage with the ignition switch in the **RUN, BULB TEST** or **START** position. The instrument cluster will turn the indicator ON during engine startup for a bulb check. The indicator is grounded by the fuel pump/oil pressure switch with a low oil pressure condition.

TESTING

"OIL" Pressure Indicator Stays ON, With Engine Running and Normal Oil Pressure

1. Disconnect the fuel pump/engine oil pressure indicator switch at the engine.
2. With the ignition switch in the **ON** position, and with the engine running, is the "OIL" indicator ON?
    a. If not, replace the indicator switch.
    b. If the "OIL" indicator is still ON, check the circuit for a short to ground somewhere between the instrument cluster connection and the oil pressure switch terminal A. If okay, the instrument cluster may need to be serviced.

"OIL" Pressure Indicator Not ON, With Ignition in ON Position, Engine Not Running

1. Disconnect the fuel pump/engine oil pressure indicator switch.
2. Connect a fused (3 Amp) jumper between terminal A (tan wire) and ground. With the ignition switch in the **ON** position, is the "OIL" indicator ON?
3. If yes, check for a poor connection at the switch terminal. If okay, replace the switch.
4. If no, look for an open between the instrument cluster connection and the oil pressure switch terminal. If okay, the instrument cluster may need to be serviced.

REMOVAL & INSTALLATION

▶ **See Figures 36, 37, 38 and 39**

1. Raise and safely support the vehicle.
2. Drain the engine oil into a suitable container.
3. Unplug the electrical connector from the oil pressure warning switch.
4. Unthread the and remove the switch.
To install:
5. Install the oil pressure warning switch and tighten securely.
6. Plug in the electrical connector.
7. Lower the vehicle.
8. Add the proper type and amount of engine oil.

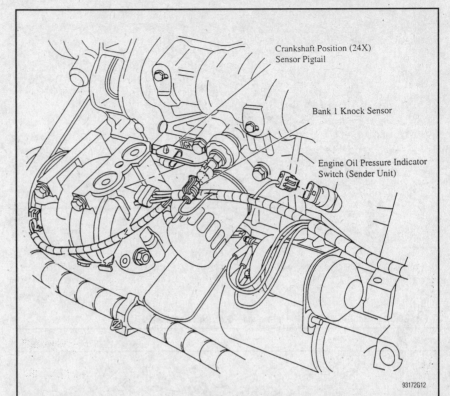

Fig. 36 This oil pressure warning switch is located on the side of the engine block, near the oil filter—3.1L engine shown, 3.4L (VIN X) engine similar

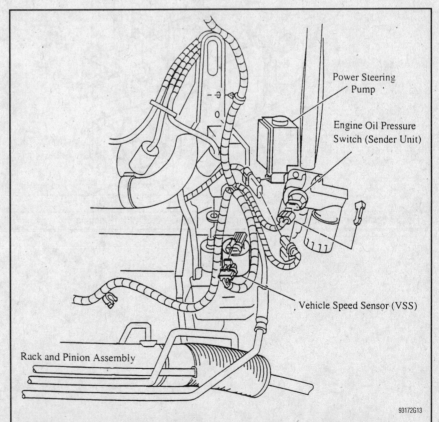

Fig. 37 This oil pressure warning switch is located on the oil filter adapter assembly—3.8L engine

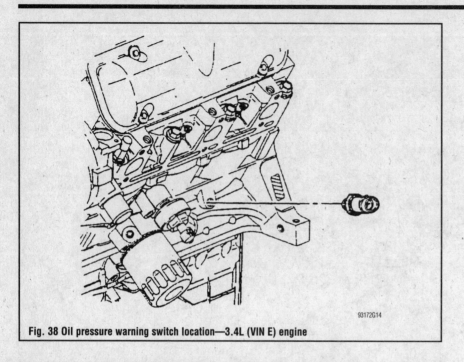

93172G14

Fig. 38 Oil pressure warning switch location—3.4L (VIN E) engine

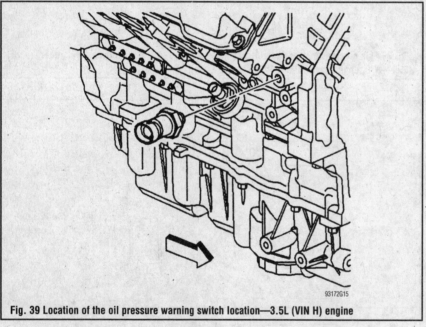

93172G15

Fig. 39 Location of the oil pressure warning switch location—3.5L (VIN H) engine

3

ENGINE AND ENGINE OVERHAUL

ENGINE MECHANICAL 3-2
EXHAUST SYSTEM 3-50
ENGINE RECONDITIONING 3-52

ENGINE MECHANICAL

Engine

GENERAL INFORMATION

Cleanliness and Care

An automobile engine is a combination of many machined, honed, polished and lapped surfaces with tolerances that are measured in the ten-thousandths of an inch. When any internal engine parts are serviced, care and cleanliness are important. A liberal coating of engine oil should be applied to friction areas during assembly in order to protect and lubricate the surfaces on initial operation. Throughout this section, it should be understood that proper cleaning and protection of machined surfaces and friction areas is part of the repair procedure. This is considered standard shop practice even if not specifically stated.

✳✳ WARNING

Engine damage may result is an abrasive paper, pad or motorized wire brush is used to clean any engine gasket surfaces.

Whenever the valve train components are removed for service, they should be kept in order. This should be done in order to install the parts in the same locations and with the same mating surfaces as when removed.

The battery cables should be disconnected before any major work is performed on the engine. Failure to disconnect the cables may result in damage to the wire harness or other electrical parts.

Replacing Engine Gaskets

Do not reuse any gasket unless otherwise specified. Gaskets that can be reused will be identified. Do not apply sealant to any gasket or sealing surface unless directed to do so.

Use a rubber mallet to separate components. Bump the part sideways to loosen the components. Bumping should be done at bends or reinforced areas to prevent distortion of parts.

Remove all gasket and sealing material from the part using a plastic or wood scraper. Care must be used to avoid gouging or scraping sealing surfaces. Do not use any other method or technique to remove gasket material from a part. Do not use abrasive pads, sand paper or power tools to clean gasket surfaces. These methods of cleaning can damage the part. Abrasive pads also produce a fine grit that the oil filter cannot remove from the oil. The grit is abrasive and has been known to cause internal engine damage.

When assembling components, use only the sealant specified. Sealing surfaces should be clean and free of debris or oil. When applying sealant to a component, apply a bead size as specified in the service procedure. Do not allow the sealant to enter into any blind threaded holes, as it may prevent the bolt from seating properly or cause damage when the bolt is tightened.

Tighten bolts to specification. Do not over-tighten.

Use of RTV and Anaerobic Sealer

Two types of sealer are commonly used in engines: Room Temperature Vulcanizing (RTV) sealer and anaerobic gasket eliminator sealer. The correct sealer must be used in the proper place to prevent oil leaks. Do not interchange the two types of sealers. Use the sealer recommended.

APPLYING RTV SEALER

1. Do not use RTV sealant in areas where extreme temperatures are expected. These areas include the exhaust manifold, head gasket and other areas where gasket eliminator is specified.
2. Use a rubber mallet to separate components sealed with RTV. Bump the part sideways to shear the RTV sealer. Bumping should be done at bends or reinforced areas to prevent distortion of components. RTV is weaker in shear (lateral) strength than in tensile (vertical) strength.
3. Remove all gasket material from the part using a plastic or wood scraper. GM recommends Loctite®brand Gasket Remover P/N 4MA or equivalent. Follow all safety recommendations and directions that are on the container. Do not use any other method or technique to remove gasket material from a part. Do not use abrasive pads, since they leave a fine grit that will not filter out of the oil.
4. Apply RTV to a clean surface. Use the proper bead size, if specified. Do not allow sealer to run into blind threaded holes as it may prevent the bolt from seating properly or cause damage when the bolt is tightened.
5. Assemble components while the RTV is still wet (within 3 minutes). Do not wait for the RTV to skin over.
6. Tighten bolts to specifications. Do not over tighten.

APPLYING ANAEROBIC SEALER

1. Anaerobic gasket eliminator hardens in the absence of air. This type of sealer is used where two rigid parts (such as castings) are assembled together. When two rigid parts are disassembled and you do not see any gasket or obvious sealer, the parts were probably originally assembled with an anaerobic gasket eliminator.
2. Remove all gasket material from the part using a plastic or wood scraper. GM recommends Loctite®brand Gasket Remover P/N 4MA or equivalent. Follow all safety recommendations and directions that are on the container. Do not use any other method or technique to remove gasket material from a part. Do not use abrasive pads, since they leave a fine grit that will not filter out of the oil.
3. Apply a continuous bead of gasket eliminator to one flange. Surfaces to be resealed must be clean and dry.

✳✳ WARNING

Anaerobic sealed joints that are partially torqued and allowed to cure more than five minutes may result in incorrect shimming and sealing of the joint. Do not allow sealer to run into blind threaded holes as it may prevent the bolt from seating properly or cause damage when the bolt is tightened.

4. Spread the sealer evenly with your finger to get a uniform coating on the sealing surface.
5. Tighten bolts to specifications. Do not over tighten.
6. Remove the excess sealer from the outside of the joint.

Separating Parts

In addition to its sealing capabilities, RTV sealants can form an adhesive bond between parts that can make them difficult to remove or separate. RTV is weakest in shear strength and parts should be bumped sideways if possible, rather than using prying tools to remove them. This technique should prevent part damage when the bonding strength of the RTV is stronger than the part itself. Any bumping should be done at bends or reinforced areas to prevent part distortion.

General Engine Service Precautions

✳✳ CAUTION

Before removing or installing any electrical unit on the vehicle, or when a tool or equipment could easily come in contact with "live" or "hot at all times" exposed electrical terminals, disconnect the negative battery cable to prevent personal injury and/or damage to the vehicle or components. Unless instructed otherwise, the ignition switch must be in the OFF or LOCK positions. Many technicians performing heavy engine work will remove the battery and place it on a battery charger so it can be fully charged when the repaired engine is first started.

When raising or supporting the engine for any reason, do not use a jack under the oil pan. Due to the small clearance between the oil pan and the oil pump screen, jacking against he oil pan may cause the pan to be bent against the pump screen resulting in a damaged oil pickup unit.

Anytime the air cleaner and ducting is disconnected, the intake opening should be covered. This is to protect against accidental entrance of foreign material which should follow the intake passage into the cylinder and cause extensive damage when the engine is started.

Work in a clean and well lit area. You should have on hand: a suitable parts cleaning tank, compressed air supply, tray to keep parts and fasteners organized and an adequate set of hand tools. An approved engine repair stand will help prevent personal injury or damage to the engine components. Precision measuring tools are required for inspection of certain critical components. Torque wrenches are necessary for the correct assembly of various parts.

REMOVAL & INSTALLATION

In the process of removing the engine, you will come across a number of steps which call for the removal of a separate component or system, such as "disconnect the exhaust system" or "remove the radiator." In most instances, a detailed removal process can be found elsewhere in this manual.

It is virtually impossible to list each individual wire and hose which must be disconnected, simply because so many different model and engine combinations have been manufactured. Careful observation and common sense are the best possible approaches to any repair procedure.

Removal and installation of the engine can be made easier if you follow these basic points:

- If you have to drain any fluids, use a suitable container.
- Always tag any wires or hoses and, if possible, the components they came from before disconnecting them.
- Because there are so many bolts, washers, retainers, clips and other fasteners involved, store and label these components separately in suitable cans and containers. They should save time at installation.
- After unbolting the transaxle, make sure it is properly supported.
- If it is necessary to disconnect the air conditioning system, have the system properly discharged by a qualified technician using a refrigerant recovery/recycling station. If the system does not have to be disconnected, unbolt the compressor and set it aside.
- When unbolting the engine mounts, always make sure the engine is properly supported. When removing the engine, make sure that any lifting devices are properly attached to the engine. It is recommended that if your engine is supplied with lifting hooks, your lifting equipment be attached to them.
- Lift the engine slowly, checking that no wires, hoses or other components are still connected.
- After the engine is clear of the vehicle, place it on a suitable engine stand or workbench.
- After the engine has been removed, you can perform a partial or full teardown of the engine using the procedures outlined in this manual.

3.1L Engine

▶ See Figure 1

The cylinder block is made of cast alloy iron and has six cylinders arranged in a V shape with three cylinders in each bank. The cylinders are set at a 60 degree angle from each other. The right bank cylinders are 1,3,5 and the left bank cylinders are 2,4,6 starting from the front of the engine.

1. Disconnect the negative battery cable.
2. Remove the hood panel using the following procedure and observing the following cautions:

✱✱ WARNING

DO NOT allow the hood to fold back onto the windshield. Windshield and paint damage will result from improper handling of the hood. When removing any body panel, apply tape to the corners of the panel and adjacent surfaces to help prevent paint damage.

　　a. Open and support the hood.
　　b. Disconnect the underhood lamp wire.
　　c. Mark the upper hood hinge location with a grease pencil to aid in reassembly alignment.
　　d. With an assistant, remove the hood hinge bolts and carefully lift the hood from the vehicle.

3. Remove the air cleaner duct.
4. Drain the engine coolant into a suitable container.
5. Remove the engine mount struts The struts are wish-bone shaped pieces that, on one end, attach to the cylinder head and on the other end, to the radiator support. Both ends attach with a through-bolt that should be removed, then the struts can be removed.
6. Remove the right side strut bracket using the following procedure:
　　a. Remove the horizontal bolts from the air conditioning compressor and set the compressor aside.
　　b. Remove the vertical bolt from the right side engine mount strut bracket.
7. Carefully tag for identification all engine wiring harness connectors. Be neat and accurate. A minute spent now will save much time later. Unplug these connectors from engine components, the engine sensors and the engine grounds.
8. Remove the accelerator control and cruise control servo cables from the throttle body
9. Remove the accelerator control cable bracket with the accelerator control and cruise control servo cables and set aside.
10. Remove the power steering pump with the lines still attached and set aside.
11. Disconnect the heater outlet hose from the thermostat bypass pipe.
12. Disconnect the heater inlet hose from the inlet pipe.
13. Disconnect the lower radiator hose from the water pump.
14. Disconnect the power brake vacuum booster hose from the upper intake manifold.
15. Carefully tag for identification all engine vacuum hoses. Disconnect the vacuum hoses from the engine to the body.
16. Disconnect the fuel lines.
17. Remove the automatic transaxle vacuum modulator pipe. This is a piece of steel tubing bent to conform to the engine, that allows engine vacuum to reach the transaxle vacuum modulator, to help smooth shifting. It has rubber connectors on

both ends. A clip should hold the pipe to the engine about halfway up the pipe.
18. Raise and safely support the vehicle
19. Drain the engine oil.
20. Disconnect the three-way catalytic converter pipe from the right side (rear) exhaust manifold.
21. Remove the automatic transaxle fluid filler tube using the following procedure:
　　a. Disconnect the front exhaust manifold pipe.
　　b. Remove the power steering gear heat shield.
　　c. Remove the bolt from the filler tube bracket and remove the filler tube.
22. Remove the transaxle brace. This is a small bracket at the top of the transaxle bellhousing.
23. Remove the engine mount lower nuts using the following procedure:

✱✱ WARNING

Use a block of wood under the oil pan when raising or supporting the engine. Jacking against the oil pan may cause the oil pan to bend against the pump screen and result in a damaged pickup unit.

　　a. Remove the right front wheel and tire.
　　b. Remove the right engine splash shield. Use care since the Anti-lock Brake System (ABS) harness runs through the splash shield. Remove the push-in retainers to release the ABS harness.
24. Remove the push-in retainers from the splash shield and remove the splash shield from the lower flange of the engine compartment side rail.

　　a. The engine mount rests on the drivetrain cradle and two studs face downward from the mount, through the cradle. Remove the engine mount lower nuts from the studs.
25. Remove the starter motor. Please see the procedure in Section 2.
26. Remove the torque converter-to-flywheel bolts.
27. Remove the lower engine-to-transaxle bolts.

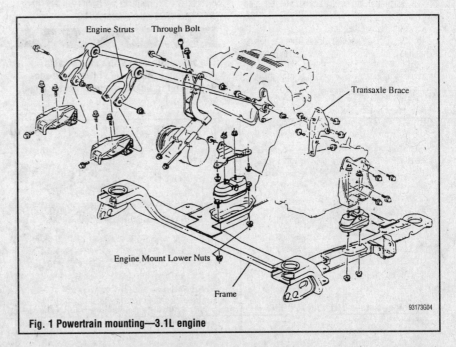

Fig. 1 Powertrain mounting—3.1L engine

28. Lower the vehicle.

29. Remove the upper engine to transaxle bolts.

30. Suitably support the transaxle with safety stands.

31. Attach a suitable engine lifting device.

32. Remove the engine from the vehicle.

To install:

33. Verify that the transaxle torque converter is properly seated in the transaxle pump. Install the engine to the vehicle, using care to align the studs on the transaxle bellhousing with the correct openings in the engine block. Make sure the engine mount studs correctly fit the drivetrain cradle. Install the upper engine-to-transaxle bolts. When satisfied with the fit, torque the upper engine to transaxle bolts to 55 ft. lbs. (75 Nm).

34. Remove the engine lifting rig.

35. Raise and safely support the vehicle.

36. Install the lower engine-to-transaxle bolts and torque to 55 ft. lbs. (75 Nm).

37. Install the torque converter-to-flywheel bolts and torque to 45 ft. lbs. (63 Nm).

38. Install the starter motor. Please see Section 2.

39. Install the engine mount lower nuts and torque to 32 ft. lbs. (43 Nm). Install the splash shield using the push-in fasteners.

40. Install the transaxle brace.

41. Install the transaxle fluid filler tube, observing the following:

   a. When installing the filler tube, inspect the condition of the filler tube seal. Replace if the seal is damaged.

   b. Place the seal in the transaxle case. Do not place the seal on the tube or the seal will be damaged at installation.

   c. Install the retainer bolt and torque to 115 inch lbs. (13 Nm).

   d. If removed, install the power steering gear heat shield.

42. Connect the three-way catalytic converter pipe to the right (rear) exhaust manifold. Always use a new gasket. Tighten the nuts to the manifold to 26 ft. lbs. (35 Nm).

43. Lower the vehicle.

44. Install the automatic transaxle vacuum modulator pipe.

45. Connect the fuel lines.

46. Connect the vacuum hoses from the engine to the body, following the identification tags made at removal.

47. Connect the power brake vacuum booster hose to the upper intake manifold.

48. Connect the lower radiator hose to the water pump and connect the upper radiator hose to the engine.

49. Connect the heater inlet hose to the inlet pipe and the heater outlet hose to the thermostat bypass pipe.

50. Install the power steering pump. Addition information may be found in Section 8.

51. Install the accelerator control cable bracket with the cables attached. Connect the accelerator and cruise control cables to the throttle body.

52. Plug in all engine electrical connectors to the engine components, sensors and the grounds, following the identification tags made at removal.

53. Install the right engine mount strut bracket, then install the struts, tightening the through bolts to 35 ft. lbs. (48 Nm).

54. Install the air cleaner duct.

55. Install the hood assembly, using the grease pencil marks made at removal to aid alignment. If necessary, fore-aft adjustment may be made by elongating the hood-side hinge holes. Vertical adjustment at the front may be made by adjusting the hood bumpers up or down. Gap tolerances are 0.10–0.22 inch (2.54–5.58mm) and flush tolerances are 0.0–0.06 inch (0–1.5mm). Adjust as required.

56. Fill the cooling system with DEX-COOL®coolant.

57. Fill the engine with oil. Verify that the a new oil filter is properly installed.

58. Connect the battery negative cable.

59. Inspect all fluid levels.

60. Inspect for leaks.

3.4L Engines

VIN X ENGINE

▶ **See Figures 2, 3 and 4**

On this engine, the cylinder block is made of cast iron and has six cylinders arranged in a V-shape with three cylinder in each bank. The cylinder banks are set at a 60 degree angle from each other. The right bank cylinders (cowl, or firewall side) are numbered 1,3,5 while the left bank cylinders (front, or radiator side) are numbered 2,4,6.

✳✳ CAUTION

The automatic transaxle range selector lever cable is made out of two cable sections. After initial connection, never sepa-rate the two metal couplings from one another. Integrity of the connection of the two metal couplings will be lost if separation of the two metal couplings occurs. When servicing the transaxle, remove the cable at the automatic transaxle range selector lever and at the lever cable bracket, If either section of the cable needs to be replaced, replace both of the cable sections. Loss of connection integrity of the two metal couplings can cause loss of transaxle shift control which could result in personal injury.**

1. Disconnect the negative battery cable.

2. Remove the engine cosmetic/acoustic cover (also called the fuel injector sight shield). It clips to the fuel rail. Pull the shield up from the rear intake manifold side. Pivot the shield forward and remove from the engine.

3. Remove the air cleaner duct.

4. Remove the hood panel using the following procedure and observing the following cautions.

✳✳ WARNING

DO NOT allow the hood to fold back onto the windshield. Windshield and paint damage will result from improper handling of the hood. When removing any body panel, apply tape to the corners of the panel and adjacent surfaces to help prevent paint damage.

   a. Open and support the hood.

   b. Disconnect the underhood lamp wire, if equipped.

   c. Mark the upper hood hinge location with a grease pencil to aid reassembly alignment.

   d. Disconnect the hood support struts by unsnapping the upper ball stud using a small, flat bladed tool to lift up on (but do not remove) the clip

   e. With an assistant, remove the hood hinge bolts and carefully lift the hood from the vehicle.

5. Drain the coolant into a suitable container.

6. Remove the coolant recovery reservoir by removing the hose clamp and disconnecting the hose, then removing the mounting clips.

7. Disconnect the heater hoses from the engine.

8. Remove the engine mount strut The strut is a dog-bone shaped piece that, on one end, attaches

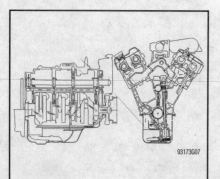

Fig. 2 Views of the 3.4L (VIN X) DOHC engine

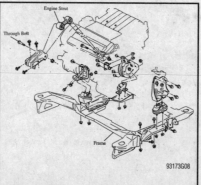

Fig. 3 Powertrain mounting—3.4L (VIN X) DOHC engine

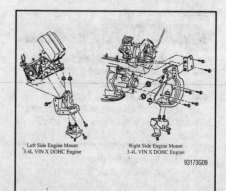

Fig. 4 Engine mounts—3.4L (VIN X) DOHC engine

to the engine, and on the other end, to the radiator support. Both ends attach with a through-bolt that should be removed, then the strut can be removed. Unbolt the strut bracket from the radiator support.

9. Remove the engine cooling fan assemblies.

10. Disconnect the radiator hoses from the engine.

11. Disconnect the transaxle fluid cooler lines at the radiator.

12. Remove the radiator.

13. Disconnect the control cables from the throttle body bracket and from the throttle body.

14. Relieve the fuel system pressure, as outlined in Section 5.

15. Disconnect the fuel lines from the rail and the mounting bracket, observing the following.

   a. When servicing the fuel rail assembly or disconnecting the fuel lines, precautions must be taken to prevent dirt and other contaminates from entering the fuel passages. It is recommended that the fittings be capped, and the holes plugged during servicing.

   b. Clean the fuel rail assembly and connections.

16. Remove the fuel feed and return pipes from the fuel rail tubes by squeezing the tabs and pulling the lines apart.

17. Remove the exhaust crossover. A liberal application of penetrating oil may be required on the retaining nuts.

18. Disconnect the electrical ground straps from the transaxle bellhousing.

✳✳ WARNING

Siphon power steering fluid from the reservoir before disconnecting the power steering lines to avoid spilling fluid on the secondary timing belt cover. Use clean shop cloths when disconnecting to lines to make sure any remaining power steering fluid DOES NOT contact the secondary timing belt cover. Power steering fluid WILL DAMAGE the secondary timing belt.

19. Siphon as much power steering fluid as possible from the reservoir. Disconnect the power steering lines at the pump and at the front cover. Plug the lines or drain into a container to keep fluid off the timing belt.

20. Remove the accessory drive belt. Please see Section 1.

21. Remove the upper air conditioning compressor bolts and detach the electrical connector from the compressor.

22. Raise and safely support the vehicle.

23. Remove the right front tire assembly and remove the right front splash shield (fender liner).

24. Remove the lower air conditioning compressor bolts. Reposition and wire the compressor out of the way. Do NOT disconnect the refrigerant lines.

25. Remove the flywheel inspection cover.

26. Remove the oil filter.

27. Remove the starter motor. Please refer to Section 2.

28. Remove the front exhaust pipe and the catalytic converter.

29. The engine mount nuts are removed next, observing the following.

   a. Set up the engine hoist and take the weight off the engine mounts.

   b. Remove the engine mount nuts at the frame and brackets. Use care when working around the drive axle boot. Some sort of protector shield is recommended to keep from damaging the boot.

   c. On the right side, disconnect the right ball joint is from the control arm. Please see Section 8.

   d. Remove the right side drive axle steel shield.

   e. Remove the right side drive axle from the transaxle. Please see Section 7.

   f. Remove the right side engine mount nuts.

   g. On the left side, it will likely be necessary to disconnect the engine oil cooler hose from the 3-way fitting at the oil cooler.

30. Carefully tag for identification all engine wiring harness connectors. Be neat and accurate. A minute spent now will save much time later. Unplug these connectors from engine components, the engine sensors and the engine grounds.

31. Remove the torque converter-to-flywheel bolts.

32. Remove the outer tie rod end.

33. Suitably support the transaxle with a jacking fixture.

34. Remove the engine mount bracket bolts and nuts from the transaxle.

35. Remove the transaxle support.

36. Lower the vehicle.

37. Remove the plastic cover from the shock tower.

38. Remove the electrical connectors from the Powertrain Control Module (PCM). Use care. The connectors have small pins that are easily damaged.

39. Tag for identification and then remove the necessary vacuum lines.

40. Suitably support the transaxle.

41. Lift the engine. The alternator, normally inaccessible, may still have its electrical connections intact. If so, disconnect the alternator harness as soon as there is room to do so.

42. Carefully lift and remove the engine.

To install:

43. Inspect the engine mounts. Broken or deteriorated engine mounts should be replaced. Replace an engine mount if: the hard rubber surface is covered with heat cracks; the rubber has separated from the metal plate of the mount; the rubber has split through the center; there is fluid leaking from any of the hydraulic mounts.

44. Verify that the transaxle torque converter is properly seated in the transaxle pump. Install the engine to the vehicle. Connect the alternator harness while the alternator is still accessible. When setting the engine in place, use care to align the transaxle dowel pins with the correct openings in the engine block. Make sure the engine mount studs correctly fit the drivetrain cradle. Install the engine-to-transaxle bolts. When satisfied with the fit, torque the engine to transaxle bolts to 55 ft. lbs. (75 Nm).

45. Remove the engine lifting rig.

46. Connect any vacuum lines removed, noting the reference tags made at removal.

47. Connect the electrical harness to the PCM and reinstall the plastic cover on the shock tower.

48. Raise and safely support the vehicle. Suitable support the transaxle with jack.

49. Install the engine mount bracket bolts and nuts on the transaxle. When satisfied with the

transaxle to mount fit, remove the transaxle support.

50. Install the drive axle. Please see Section 7.

51. Install the ball joint into the control arm. Install the right ball joint nut. Connect the outer tie rod end. Please see

52. Reconnect all electrical harnesses noting the reference tags made at removal.

53. Install the torque converter-to-flywheel bolts and torque to 60 ft. lbs. (82 Nm).

54. Install the engine mount nuts at the frame and torque to 32 ft. lbs. (43 Nm).

55. Install the front exhaust pipe and the catalytic converter.

56. Install the starter motor. Please see Section 2.

57. Install the flywheel cover.

58. Position the air conditioning compressor to the bracket and install the lower bolts.

59. Install a new oil filter.

60. Install the right front splash shield and then the tire assembly.

61. Lower the vehicle.

62. Connect the wiring harness to the air conditioning compressor and install the upper compressor bolts.

63. Install the accessory drive belt.

64. Connect the power steering lines at the pump and the front cover.

65. Install the engine cover.

66. Connect the ground straps to the bell housing.

67. Install the exhaust crossover.

68. Connect the fuel lines using new O-rings. Make sure all fuel line retaining clips and brackets are properly installed.

69. Connect the control cables to the throttle body bracket and to the throttle body.

70. Install the radiator and connect the transaxle cooler lines. Connect the radiator and heater hoses to the engine.

71. Install the cooling fans.

72. Install the engine strut (sometimes called the "dogbone", or "wishbone") and bracket.

73. Connect the heater hoses to the engine. Install the coolant recovery reservoir.

74. Refill the engine with oil.

75. Refill the cooling system with the proper mix of DEX-COOL®and water. Please see Section 1

76. Refill the power steering fluid.

77. Check the transaxle fluid level and add, as required.

78. With an assistant, install the hood assembly, using the grease pencil marks made at removal to aid alignment. If necessary, fore-aft adjustment may be made by elongating the hood-side hinge holes. Vertical adjustment at the front may be made by adjusting the hood bumpers up or down. Gap tolerances are 0.10–0.22 inch (2.54–5.58mm) and flush tolerances are 0.0–0.06 inch (0–1.5mm). Adjust as required. Snap the hood struts into place.

79. Install the air cleaner duct.

80. Check and adjust all fluid levels as required.

81. Connect the negative battery cable.

82. Start the engine and check for leaks. Bleed the cooling system. Bleed the power steering system.

VIN E ENGINE

◆ **See Figures 5 and 6**

This engine was introduced with the 2000 model year. The cylinder block is made of cast alloy iron.

The cylinder block has 6 cylinders that are arranged in a V shape. There are 3 cylinders in each bank. The cylinder banks are set at a 60 degree angle from each other. Starting at the front of the engine, the right bank cylinders are 1,3,5. The left bank cylinders are 2,4,6.

1. Disconnect the negative battery cable.
2. Remove the hood panel using the following procedure and observing the following cautions.

✳✳ WARNING

DO NOT allow the hood to fold back onto the windshield. Windshield and paint damage will result from improper handling of the hood. When removing any body panel, apply tape to the corners of the panel and adjacent surfaces to help prevent paint damage.

  a. Open and support the hood.
  b. Disconnect the underhood lamp wire, if equipped.
  c. Mark the upper hood hinge location with a grease pencil to aid reassembly alignment.
  d. Disconnect the hood support struts by unsnapping the upper ball stud using a small, flat bladed tool to lift up on (but do not remove) the clip
  e. With an assistant, remove the hood hinge bolts and carefully lift the hood from the vehicle.

3. Remove the cross vehicle brace.
4. Remove the throttle body air inlet duct and the air cleaner assembly.
5. Remove the engine mount struts from their brackets. The struts are "wish-bone" shaped pieces that, on one end, attach to the engine, and on the other end, to the radiator support. Both ends attach with a through-bolt that should be removed, then the struts can be removed.

6. Remove the accessory drive belt. Please see Section 1.
7. Carefully tag for identification the following engine wiring harness connectors. Be neat and accurate. A minute spent now will save much time later. Unplug the connectors from the following:

- Camshaft Position (CMP) sensor
- Manifold Absolute Pressure (MAP) sensor
- Exhaust Gas Recirculation (EGR) valve
- Evaporative Emissions Canister Purge Solenoid valve
- Throttle Position (TP) sensor
- Idle Air Control (IAC) valve
- Alternator
- Ignition coil pack
- Wiring harness grounds
- Two wiring harness-to-engine harness connectors

8. Raise and safely support the vehicle.
9. Drain the cooling system and the engine oil. Remove the oil filter.
10. Carefully tag for identification the following engine wiring harness connectors. Unplug the connectors from: the Knock Sensor (KS), the Heated Oxygen Sensor (HO2S), the Crankshaft Position (CKP) sensor, the starter motor, the air conditioning compressor and the wiring harness grounds.
11. Remove the engine mount lower nuts.
12. Remove the starter motor. Please see Section 2.

13. Remove the air conditioning compressor bolts. Relocate and secure the compressor out of the way. Do not disconnect the refrigerant hoses.
14. Remove the torque converter-to-flywheel bolts.
15. Remove the right engine splash shield. A door trim pad and garnish clip remover tool is recommended to remove the push-in retainers.
16. Remove the transaxle brace. It will be necessary to remove the right front tire for access to the brace bolts.
17. Remove the lower transaxle-to-engine bolts and the stud.
18. Disconnect the radiator outlet hose from the engine.
19. Lower the vehicle.

✳✳ CAUTION

In order to avoid possible injury or vehicle damage, always replace the accelerator control cable with a NEW cable whenever you remove the engine from the vehicle. In order to avoid cruise control cable damage, position the cable out of the way while you remove or install the engine. Do not pry or lean against the cruise control cable and do not kink the cable. You must replace a damaged cable.

20. Disconnect the accelerator control and cruise control cable from the throttle body and the cable bracket. Use the following procedure:
  a. Take note of the cable routing before removal. Correct cable routing is important.
  b. Remove the accelerator cable shield, if equipped.
  c. Disconnect the accelerator cable from the retaining clip.
  d. Disconnect the accelerator cable from the throttle body lever.
  e. Disconnect the accelerator cable from the cable bracket
21. Tag for identification and remove the vacuum hoses from the upper intake manifold. Also disconnect the power brake booster vacuum hose.

✳✳ CAUTION

Observe all applicable safety precautions when working around fuel. Whenever servicing the fuel system, always work in a well ventilated area. Do not allow fuel spray or vapors to come in contact with a spark or open flame. Keep a dry chemical fire extinguisher near the work area. Always keep fuel in a container specifically designed for fuel storage; also, always properly seal fuel containers to avoid the possibility of fire or explosion.

22. Disconnect the fuel feed and return hoses using the following procedure. Tool J 37088-A or equivalent is required to separate the fuel pipe quick connectors.
  a. Relieve the fuel system pressure at the fuel rail pressure test port. Please see Section 5.
  b. Clean all engine fuel pipe connections.
  c. Using the quick connector separator tool, disconnect the fuel feed and fuel return pipe fittings in the engine compartment
23. Disconnect the Air Injection (AIR) system from the right side exhaust manifold.

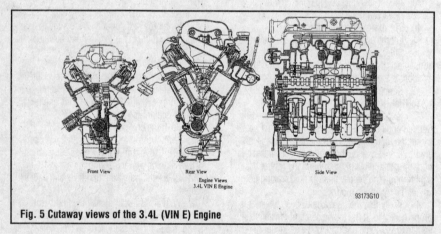

Front View   Rear View   Side View
Engine Views
3.4L VIN E Engine

93173G10

Fig. 5 Cutaway views of the 3.4L (VIN E) Engine

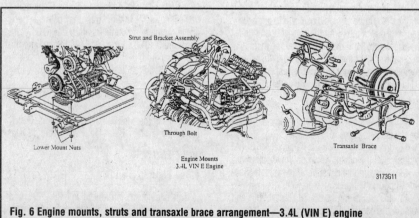

Strut and Bracket Assembly

Lower Mount Nuts   Through Bolt   Transaxle Brace
Engine Mounts
3.4L VIN E Engine

3173G11

Fig. 6 Engine mounts, struts and transaxle brace arrangement—3.4L (VIN E) engine

24. Remove the power steering hoses from the power steering pump. Siphon as much fluid from the reservoir as possible to reduce spillage. Remove the power steering pump.

25. Disconnect the heater and remaining radiator hose(s). If disconnecting the heater hoses at the firewall, note the placement and position of the heater hose clamps. GM recommends that at installation, the clamps be positioned exactly as originally installed.

26. Suitably support the transaxle with safety stands.

27. Attach a suitable engine lift.

28. Remove the upper transaxle-to-engine bolts.

29. Carefully lift the engine from the vehicle, checking that all electrical, fuel, vacuum and mechanical attachments have been separated.

To install:

30. Inspect the engine mounts. Broken or deteriorated engine mounts should be replaced. Replace an engine mount if: the hard rubber surface is covered with heat cracks; the rubber has separated from the metal plate of the mount; the rubber has split through the center; there is fluid leaking from any of the hydraulic mounts.

31. Verify that the transaxle torque converter is properly seated in the transaxle pump. Install the engine to the vehicle. Connect the alternator harness while the alternator is still accessible. When setting the engine in place, use care to align the transaxle dowel pins with the correct openings in the engine block. Make sure the engine mount studs correctly fit the drivetrain cradle. Install the upper engine to transaxle bolts. When satisfied with the fit, torque the engine to transaxle bolts to 55 ft. lbs. (75 Nm).

32. Remove the engine lifting rig.

33. Remove the safety stands from the transaxle.

34. Connect the radiator inlet hose and the heater hoses to the engine. Place the clamps in the same position as originally installed.

35. Install the power steering pump and connect the power steering hoses.

36. Connect the AIR System to the exhaust manifold.

37. Before connecting the fuel pipe fittings, always apply a few drops of clean engine oil to the male pipe ends. This should ensure proper reconnection and prevent a possible fuel leak. The reason for this is, during normal operation, the O-rings located in the female connector will swell and may prevent proper reconnection if not lubricated. Connect the fuel feed and return pipes to their quick-connect fittings.

38. Connect the brake booster hose to the upper intake manifold. Connect all other vacuum lines previously removed, following the reference tags made at removal.

✱✱ CAUTION

In order to avoid possible injury or vehicle damage, always replace the accelerator control cable with a NEW cable whenever you remove the engine from the vehicle. In order to avoid cruise control cable damage, position the cable out of the way while you remove or install the engine. Do not pry or lean against the cruise control cable and do not kink the cable. You must replace a damaged cable.

39. Connect the accelerator and cruise control cables to the throttle body lever. Install the retainer clip(s) and make sure the cable properly fits the bracket. Inspect the throttle operation. The throttle should operate freely, without binding, between full closed and wide open throttle.

➡**Do not route flexible components (hoses, wires, conduits, etc.) within 2 inches of moving parts unless flexible components can be securely fastened. This is necessary to prevent possible interference and damage to the component.**

40. Raise and safely support the vehicle.

41. Install the radiator outlet hose to the engine.

42. Install the lower engine-to-transaxle bolts and torque to 55 ft. lbs. (75 Nm).

43. Install the transaxle brace. Torque the transaxle brace-to-transaxle bolts to 32 ft. lbs. (43 Nm) and the brace-to-engine bolts to 46 ft. lbs. (63 Nm).

44. Install the splash shield and press the retaining clips back in place. Install the right front tire.

45. Install the torque converter bolts and tighten to 47 ft. lbs. (63 Nm).

46. Install the air conditioning compressor.

47. Install the starter motor. Please see Section 2. Install the torque converter cover.

48. Install the engine mount lower nuts and torque to 32 ft. lbs. (43 Nm).

49. Connect the three-way catalytic converter pipe to the right exhaust manifold. Use a new gasket.

50. Install a new oil filter.

51. Referring to the identification tags made at removal, connect the wiring harness connectors to the KS, HO2S, CKP sensor, starter motor, air conditioning compressor and the wiring harness grounds.

52. Lower the vehicle.

53. Fill the engine with new engine oil.

54. Fill the cooling system with the correct mix of DEX-COOL®and water. Please see Section 1

55. Referring to the identification tags made at removal, connect the wiring harness connectors to the CMP sensor, MAP sensor, EGR valve, Evaporative Emissions Canister Purge Solenoid valve, TP sensor, IAC valve, the alternator, ignition coil pack, wiring harness grounds and the two wiring harness to engine harness connectors.

56. Install the accessory drive belt. Please refer to Section 1.

57. Inspect the rubber in the engine mount struts for hardness, splitting and cracking. Replace, if necessary. Install the struts and torque all bolts to 35 ft. lbs. (48 Nm).

58. Install the air inlet duct and the air cleaner assembly.

59. Install the cross vehicle brace.

60. Refill the power steering fluid.

61. Check the transaxle fluid level and add, as required.

62. With an assistant, install the hood assembly, using the grease pencil marks made at removal to aid alignment. If necessary, fore-aft adjustment may be made by elongating the hood-side hinge holes. Vertical adjustment at the front may be made by adjusting the hood bumpers up or down. Gap tolerances are 0.10–0.22 inch (2.54–5.58mm) and flush tolerances are 0.0–0.06 inch (0–1.5mm). Adjust as required. Snap the hood struts into place.

63. Check and adjust all fluid levels as required.

64. Connect the negative battery cable.

65. Start the engine and check for leaks. Bleed the cooling system. Bleed the power steering system.

3.5L Engine

▶ **See Figures 7, 8, 9 and 10**

The 3.5L (VIN H) engine is a Dual Over Head Camshaft (DOHC) engine and uses two intake and two exhaust valves per cylinder with individual cylinder head mounted camshafts for intake and exhaust functions. The cylinder bore is 3.52 inch (89.5mm) and the stroke is 3.62 inch (92mm). The cylinders are arranged in two banks of three on a 90 degree angle. The right (rear) bank of cylinders are numbered 1,3,5 and the left (front) bank of cylinders are 2,4,6. The Engine firing order is 1-2-3-4-5-6.

When servicing the engine, which is constructed largely of aluminum, particular care must be exercised to accommodate the characteristics of this material. Fasteners which thread into aluminum must not be over-torqued or damage to the threads may result. Tightening procedures must be strictly observed in order to assure proper gasket sealing. When cleaning gasket surfaces on aluminum or magnesium parts, tools specifically designed for these materials should be used. Soft wire brushes and dull scrapers are recommended to prevent gouging of the machined surfaces. To obtain valid bolt torque readings, excessive oil or coolant accumulations in the bolt holes must be avoided. Blow out the bolt holes with compressed air prior to installing the fasteners.

✱✱ WARNING

The factory recommended procedure for removing this engine is a lengthy and difficult procedure requiring special lifting and support equipment. The steering shaft must be separated and the vehicle subframe must be loosened and lowered. The vehicle's powertrain assembly, including the entire engine/transaxle/subframe assembly is lowered out of the bottom of the engine compartment and then the vehicle is lifted up away from the removed powertrain. Careful work is required for reassembly. This is not a job for the inexperienced or ill-equipped.

1. Disconnect the negative and positive battery cables. Remove the battery from the vehicle and place in a safe location.

2. Remove the drive belt. Please see Section 1.

3. Remove the cosmetic/acoustic engine cover by removing the two retaining nuts at the front of the shield, then lifting the shield up at the front and sliding it out of the engine bracket.

4. Remove the power steering pump from the engine using the following procedure:

   a. Place a drain pan under the vehicle.

   b. Remove the coolant surge tank.

   c. Remove the accessory junction block and move aside.

   d. Try to siphon as much power steering fluid as possible from the reservoir to reduce spillage.

   e. Disconnect the power steering lines and allow to drain into a container.

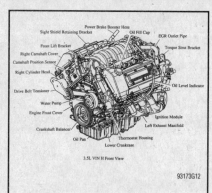

93173G12

Fig. 7 Major external components of the engine, front view—3.5L (VIN H) engine

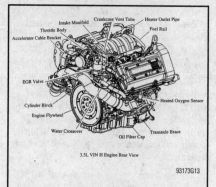

93173G13

Fig. 8 Major external components of the engine, rear view—3.5L (VIN H) engine

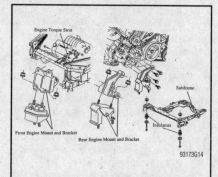

93173G14

Fig. 9 Exploded view of the engine mounts and subframe—3.5L (VIN H) engine

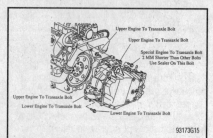

93173G15

Fig. 10 Engine-to-transaxle attachment—3.5L (VIN H) engine

f. Remove the pump mounting bolts and remove the pump from the vehicle. Cover the hose ports to keep out dirt. The hose ends should also be capped or taped shut to prevent dirt entry.

5. Remove the throttle body air duct.

6. Remove the wishbone-shaped engine mount strut from the bracket on the engine.

✳✳ CAUTION

Observe all applicable safety precautions when working around fuel. Whenever servicing the fuel system, always work in a well ventilated area. Do not allow fuel spray or vapors to come in contact with a spark or open flame. Keep a dry chemical fire extinguisher near the work area. Always keep fuel in a container specifically designed for fuel storage; also, always properly seal fuel containers to avoid the possibility of fire or explosion.

7. Disconnect the fuel feed and return hoses using the following procedure. Tool J 37088-A or equivalent is required to separate the fuel pipe quick connectors.

a. Relieve the fuel system pressure at the fuel rail pressure test port. Please see Section 5.

b. Clean all engine fuel pipe connections.

c. Using the quick connector separator tool, disconnect the fuel feed and fuel return pipe fittings in the engine compartment. Disconnect the fuel vapor line.

✳✳ CAUTION

In order to avoid possible injury or vehicle damage, GM insists you always replace the accelerator control cable with a NEW cable

whenever you remove the engine from the vehicle. In order to avoid cruise control cable damage, position the cable out of the way while you remove or install the engine. Do not pry or lean against the cruise control cable and do not kink the cable. You must replace a damaged cable.

8. Disconnect the throttle and cruise control cables with the mounting bracket from the throttle body.

9. Disconnect the automatic transaxle range selector cable from the range switch on the transaxle.

10. Disconnect the power brake booster vacuum hose from the engine.

11. Disconnect the air conditioning system vacuum hose from the engine.

12. Tag for identification the wiring harness connections from the engine and transaxle. Be neat and accurate. A minute spent now will save much time later. Unplug these connectors.

13. Drain the cooling system into a suitable container.

14. Disconnect the radiator inlet hose from the engine.

15. Disconnect the transaxle cooler lines from the radiator.

16. Disconnect the radiator hose from the thermostat housing then remove the thermostat housing from the engine.

17. Disconnect the heater hoses from the engine, from the connection pipes at the top of cam cover.

18. Raise and safely support the vehicle.

19. Drain the engine oil into a suitable container.

20. Remove the lower radiator air deflector (also called an air dam or spoiler) from under the front of the vehicle. It should be retained by five bolts.

21. Disconnect the Air Injection (AIR) system pipe from the AIR inlet valve.

22. Remove the battery cables from their retainers.

23. Disconnect the radiator outlet hose from the engine.

24. Remove the alternator using the following procedure:

a. Remove the battery tray.

b. Remove the cooling fan assembly.

c. The thermostat housing should have already been removed. If not, remove the thermostat housing now.

d. Remove the outboard alternator bolt first, then loosen inboard bolt.

e. Remove the idler pulley bolt and the idler pulley.

f. Detach the electrical connectors from the alternator.

g. Remove the alternator from the vehicle.

25. Without disconnecting the refrigerant lines, remove the air conditioning compressor and secure it out of the way. The left front diagonal brace will likely need to be removed. The right side splash shield may also need to be removed for access.

26. Remove the torque converter cover and then remove the starter motor. Please see Section 2.

27. To retain the balance, scribe a mark on both the torque converter and the flywheel so they can be reassembled in the same relationship. Remove the flywheel-to-torque converter bolts.

28. Disconnect the three-way catalytic converter pipe from the rear exhaust manifold.

29. Remove the lower transaxle-to-engine bolts.

30. Remove both front tires.

31. The inner fender engine splash shield is held in place with push-in retainer clips. A door trim pad and garnish clip remover is recommended to remove these clips. Use care. A front brake Antilock Brake System (ABS) wheel speed sensor harness is attached to the splash shield. Remove the retainers holding the ABS lead to the splash shield then remove the splash shield from the lower flange of the engine compartment side rail.

32. Unplug the fog lamp harness connectors.

33. Remove the ABS wheel speed sensor harness conduits from the retainers in the lower control arms.

34. Remove the tie rod ends from the steering knuckles. Please see Section 8.

35. Remove the lower ball joints from the steering knuckles. Please see Section 8.

36. Disconnect both drive axles (halfshafts). Please see Section 7. Secure the axles.

✳✳ CAUTION

Failure to disconnect the steering intermediate shaft from the rack and pinion stub shaft can result in damage to the steering gear and/or damage to the intermediate shaft. This damage may cause loss of steering control which could result in personal injury.

The steering wheel must be maintained in the straight ahead position and the steering column must be in the LOCK position before disconnecting the steering column or intermediate shaft. Failure to follow these instructions will cause improper alignments of some components during installation and result in damage to the air bag SIR coil assembly in the steering column.

37. Remove the pinch bolt at the intermediate steering shaft using the following procedure:

   a. Reposition the steering column shaft seal (cover) to provide access to the intermediate steering shaft lower pinch bolt.

   b. Remove the pinch bolt and disengage the steering shaft from the stub shaft on the rack and pinion assembly.

To avoid any vehicle damage, serious personal injury or death when major components such as these are removed from the vehicle while the vehicle is supported by a hoist, the following steps must be performed. Chain the vehicle to the hoist at the same end as the components that are being removed. Support the vehicle at the opposite end from which the components are being removed. To avoid any vehicle damage, serious personal injury or death, always use suitable safety stands and/or frame stands to support the vehicle when lifting the vehicle with a jack. Remove or secure all of the vehicle's contents to avoid any shifting or any movement that may occur during the vehicle lifting or jacking procedure. Failure to perform these steps could result in damage to the lifting equipment, the vehicle and/or the vehicle's contents.

38. Place a suitable jack assembly under the engine/transaxle/frame assembly. The factory tool recommended by GM is called a Frame Table and looks like a large, open rack with properly place supports for the powertrain, on casters for mobility. Use extreme care when using substitutes. It MUST support the engine/transaxle/frame assembly safely and be mobile enough to allow the powertrain assembly to be wheeled out from under the vehicle, for further service work.

39. Lower the entire vehicle onto the frame table or other suitable lifting/jacking equipment.

The powertrain makes up a large percentage of the vehicle's weight. Once this weight is removed, the vehicle will tend to pitch nose upward and will want to fall off the hoist to the rear. Chain the vehicle to the hoist at the front and safely support the vehicle at the rear or it will fall off the hoist and may cause serious injury, or death and damage to the vehicle. THIS IS A MUST.

40. With the powertrain secure on a suitable stand and the vehicle chained securely to the hoist, remove the frame to body bolts.

41. Carefully raise the vehicle on the hoist, checking for any overlooked wires, hoses or other components.

➡ **The air conditioning compressor will need to be readjusted for clearance as the vehicle is raised.**

42. Once the vehicle is safely raised, remove the frame table or equivalent with the engine/transaxle/subframe assembly from under the vehicle.

43. Attach an engine crane or other suitable engine lifting device and lift slightly, just enough to take the weight off the engine mounts.

44. Remove the engine mount bracket-to-engine bolts.

45. Remove the transaxle brace.

Before removing the engine-to-transaxle bolts, note that the bolts MUST be returned to their original locations. One of the bolts is 2mm shorter than the other bolts and requires the use of thread sealer. One technique is to make a reasonably accurate drawing of the transaxle bellhousing on cardboard. Poke holes through the cardboard where the bolts should go and push the bolts through the cardboard as they are removed, one by one. This should keep the bolts organized so they can be reinstalled in their proper locations.

46. Remove the engine-to-transaxle bolts taking care to keep the bolts organized since they are not all the same length. Separate the engine from the transaxle and place in an engine stand or other suitable work fixture.

To install:

47. Verify that the transaxle torque converter is properly seated in the transaxle pump. Install the engine to the vehicle using care to align the engine with the engine to transaxle dowels pins. Make sure the engine mount studs correctly fit the subframe. Install the engine to transaxle bolts, taking care to see that the bolts are returned to their original location. Apply a thin coat of sealer to the bolt that is 2mm shorter than the rest. When satisfied with the fit, torque the engine to transaxle bolts to 55 ft. lbs. (75 Nm).

➡ **If the lower bolts are difficult to torque while the powertrain is on the frame table, tighten the top bolts for now and wait until the powertrain is installed to the vehicle. Working from underneath the vehicle, final torque the lower engine to transaxle bolts.**

48. Install the transaxle brace and torque the bolts to 32 ft. lbs. (43 Nm). Install the engine mount bracket bolts and tighten to 43 ft. lbs. (58 Nm). The engine mount nuts are tightened to 35 ft. lbs. (47 Nm).

49. The entire engine/transaxle/subframe assembly should now be on a frame table or other suitable lifting device. Roll the powertrain assembly under the vehicle.

50. Carefully and slowly, lower the vehicle over the powertrain. The air conditioning compressor may need to be repositioned for clearance as the body gets closer to the subframe. Carefully align the frame to body bolt holes with two 19mm pins at least 8 inches long in the alignment holes on the right side of the frame. GM specifies that new body bolts must be installed When the frame is in alignment and the body insulators and spacers are in place, install the new frame to body bolts. Torque the bolts to 133 ft. lbs. (180 Nm).

51. Raise and safely support the vehicle. Remove the frame table from under the vehicle.

When installing the intermediate steering shaft, make sure that the shaft is properly seated prior to pinch bolt installation. If the pinch bolt is inserted into the coupling before shaft installation, the two mating shafts may disengage. Disengagement of the two mating shafts will cause loss of steering control which could result in personal injury.

The steering wheel must be maintained in the straight ahead position and the steering column must be in the LOCK position before connecting the steering column or intermediate shaft. Failure to follow these instructions will cause improper alignments of some components and result in damage to the air bag SIR coil assembly in the steering column.

52. Position the intermediate steering shaft onto the rack and pinion assembly stub shaft. Make absolutely certain that the two shafts are properly mated. When satisfied with the steering shaft fit, install the pinch bolt and tighten to 35 ft. lbs. (48 Nm). Reposition the steering shaft seal (cover) onto the rack and pinion steering gear.

53. Install the drive axles (halfshafts) to the transaxle. Please see Section 7.

54. Install the lower ball joints to the steering knuckles. Please see Section 8.

55. Install the tie rod ends to the steering knuckles. Please see Section 8.

56. Attach the ABS wheel speed sensor harness conduits to the retainers in the lower control arms.

57. Install the inner fender engine splash shields.

58. Plug in the fog lamp electrical connectors.

59. Install the front tires.

60. Install the three-way catalytic converter pipe to rear exhaust manifold.

61. Align the mark scribed on the torque converter to the mark scribed on the flywheel. Install the bolts and torque to 47 ft. lbs. (63 Nm).

62. Install the starter motor and then the torque converter cover. Please see Section 2.

63. Install the air conditioning compressor. The cast groove on the back of the compressor must capture the stud sticking out of the front of the block. Make sure the compressor is properly positioned. Tighten the front and rear nuts as well as the top bolts to 37 ft. lbs. (50 Nm). Attach the electrical connector.

64. Install the alternator. Attach the electrical connections. Tighten the output BAT terminal to 15 ft. lbs. (20 Nm). Press the protective boot on the BAT terminal. Install the outboard alternator bolt into the alternator housing. Install the alternator on

the inboard bolt and finger-tighten the outboard bolt. Install the idler pulley and idler pulley bolt. Tighten the bolts in the following mandatory torque sequence:

    a. Tighten the idler pulley bolt to 37 ft. lbs. (50 Nm).

    b. Tighten the alternator bolts to 37 ft. lbs. (50 Nm).

65. Install the thermostat housing and radiator hose to the engine.

66. Install the battery cables to their retainers.

67. Install the cooling fan assembly.

68. Connect the AIR pipe to the AIR inlet valve.

69. Install the lower radiator air deflector. Tighten the bolts to 15 ft. lbs. (20 Nm).

70. Lower the vehicle and remove the security devices (chains, etc.) that secured the vehicle to the hoist while the powertrain was removed.

71. Install the heater hoses to the engine.

72. Install the surge tank and connect the inlet hose.

73. Connect the transaxle oil cooler lines to the radiator.

74. Connect the radiator inlet hose to the engine.

75. Attach all of the wiring connectors to the engine and transaxle, referring to the identification tags made at removal.

76. Connect the air conditioning vacuum hose to the engine.

77. Connect the vacuum booster hose to the engine.

78. Connect the automatic transaxle selector cable to the switch on the transaxle.

✶✶ CAUTION

In order to avoid possible injury or vehicle damage, GM insists that you always replace the accelerator control cable with a NEW cable whenever the engine is removed from the vehicle. To avoid cruise control cable damage, position the cable out of the way when the engine is removed and installed. Do not pry or lean against the cruise control cable and do no kink the cable. You must replace a damaged cable.

79. Install a new replacement throttle cable using the following procedure:

    a. Remove the trim panel under the left instrument panel and detach the throttle cable from the top of the pedal, then squeeze the retainer and push the cable through the bulkhead to remove it.

    b. Thread the replacement throttle cable through the bulkhead opening and secure to the bulkhead.

    c. Attach the end of the replacement throttle cable to the accelerator pedal.

80. Connect the throttle and cruise control cables with the mounting bracket to the throttle body.

81. Connect the fuel vapor line.

82. Connect the fuel lines to the fuel rail. Pull on the quick connect fittings after assembly to verify correct installation.

83. Inspect the rubber portion of the engine mount strut for hardness, splitting and cracking. Replace as necessary. Install the engine mount strut to the strut bracket and torque the bolts to 35 ft. lbs. (48 Nm).

84. Install the throttle body air inlet duct to the throttle body air intake.

85. Install the power steering pump to the engine and tighten the mounting bolts to 25 ft. lbs. (34 Nm). Connect the fluid lines and install the pulley. Install the wiring junction block.

86. Install the engine cover.

87. Install the drive belt. Please see Section 1.

88. Install the battery tray, battery and connect the cables.

89. Fill the cooling system with the correct mix of DEX-COOL®and water. Please see Section 1.

90. Install a new oil filter and refill the engine with oil.

91. Inspect all fluid levels and adjust as required.

92. Start the engine and check for leaks.

3.8L Engines

▶ See Figures 11 and 12

Starting at the front of the engine, cylinders in the left bank are numbered 1,3,5 and the cylinders in the right bank are numbered 2,4,6.

1. Remove the hood panel using the following procedure and observing the following cautions.

✶✶ WARNING

DO NOT allow the hood to fold back onto the windshield. Windshield and paint damage will result from improper handling of the hood. When removing any body panel, apply tape to the corners of the panel and adjacent surfaces to help prevent paint damage.

    a. Open and support the hood.

    b. Disconnect the underhood lamp wire.

    c. Mark the upper hood hinge location with a grease pencil to aid reassembly alignment.

    d. With an assistant, remove the hood hinge bolts and carefully lift the hood from the vehicle.

2. Disconnect the negative battery cable.

3. Drain the coolant.

4. Drain the engine oil.

5. Remove the cosmetic/acoustic engine cover (properly called the fuel injector sight shield). Use the following procedure:

    a. VIN K engine: Twist counter-clockwise to unlock the tube/oil fill cap from the rocker arm cover. Lift the shield up at the front and slide the tab out of the engine bracket. Install the oil fill cap to keep out dirt.

    b. VIN 1 engine: Twist counter-clockwise to unlock the tube/oil fill cap from the rocker arm cover. Remove the nut that is on top of the shield, holding the shield to the fuel injector rail brace stud. Lift the shield up at the front and slide the tab out of the engine bracket. Install the oil fill cap to keep out dirt.

6. Remove the air cleaner duct.

7. Relieve the fuel system pressure, as outlined in Section 5.

8. Disconnect the fuel lines from the rail and the mounting bracket, observing the following.

    a. When servicing the fuel rail assembly or disconnecting the fuel lines, precautions must be taken to prevent dirt and other contaminates from entering the fuel passages. It is recommended that the fittings be capped, and the holes plugged during servicing.

    b. Clean the fuel rail assembly and connections.

9. Remove the fuel feed and return pipes from the fuel rail tubes by squeezing the tabs and pulling the lines apart.

10. Disconnect the throttle and cruise control cables, along with the mounting bracket from the throttle body.

11. Remove the engine mount struts. The struts are "wish-bone" shaped pieces that, on one end, attach to the cylinder head and on the other end, to the radiator support. Both ends attach with a through-bolt that should be removed, then the struts can be removed.

12. Remove the engine cooling fan assemblies, as outlined in this section.

13. On vehicles with the 3.8L VIN K engine (non-supercharged), remove the automatic transaxle vacuum modulator pipe. This is a piece of steel tubing bent to conform to the engine, that allows engine vacuum to reach the transaxle vacuum mod-

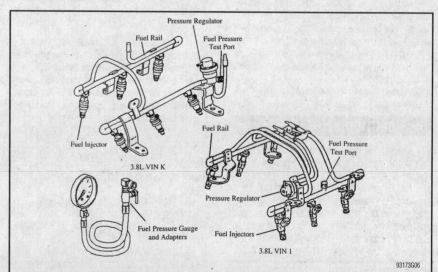

Fig. 11 Fuel system pressure can be relieved by attaching a hose to the fuel pressure test port on the fuel rail—3.8L engines shown

93173G06

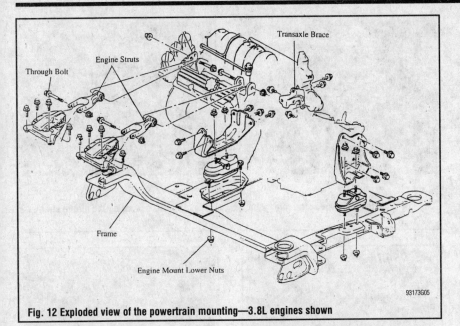

93173G05

Fig. 12 Exploded view of the powertrain mounting—3.8L engines shown

Labels in figure: Transaxle Brace, Engine Struts, Through Bolt, Frame, Engine Mount Lower Nuts

ulator, to help smooth shifting. It has rubber connectors on both ends.

14. Disconnect the power brake vacuum booster hose from the engine.

15. Remove the power steering pump assembly from the engine. It should not be necessary to disconnect the fluid lines. Use a piece of wire to hold the pump aside.

16. Remove the air conditioning compressor assembly from the engine. It should not be necessary to disconnect the refrigerant lines. Use a piece of wire to hold the compressor aside, securing it to the frame.

17. Carefully tag for identification all engine wiring harness connectors. Be neat and accurate. A minute spent now will save much time later. Unplug these connectors from engine components, the engine sensors and the engine grounds.

18. Remove the upper and lower radiator hoses.

19. Disconnect the heater hoses from the engine.

20. Raise and safely support the vehicle.

21. Remove the lower flywheel cover. It should be retained by just a few screws.

22. Remove the starter motor. Save any shims for reassembly. Please see Section 2.

23. To keep rotating parts in balance, scribe a mark on the torque converter and the flywheel so they can later be reassembled in the same relationship. This helps avoid vibration problems after assembly. Remove the torque converter bolts.

24. Remove the transaxle brace. This is a small bracket at the top of the transaxle bellhousing.

25. Remove the engine mount to frame retaining nuts.

26. Disconnect the three-way catalytic converter pipe from the manifold. This is the pipe from the rear (firewall side) of the engine. It is retained by nuts and uses a gasket which must be replaced with a new gasket at assembly.

27. Remove the lower transaxle to engine bolts.

28. Lower the vehicle.

29. Remove the upper transaxle to engine bolts.

30. Attach a suitable engine lifting device.

31. Remove the engine from the vehicle.

To install:

32. Verify that the transaxle torque converter is properly seated in the transaxle pump. Install the engine to the vehicle using care to align the transaxle dowel pins with the correct openings in the engine block. Make sure the engine mount studs correctly fit the drivetrain cradle. Install the upper engine to transaxle bolts. When satisfied with the fit, torque the upper engine-to-transaxle bolts to 55 ft. lbs. (75 Nm).

33. Remove the engine lifting rig.

34. Raise and safely support the vehicle.

35. Install the lower engine to transaxle bolts and torque to 55 ft. lbs. (75 Nm).

36. Raise the vehicle again and safely support.

37. Install the three-way catalytic converter pipe to the rear exhaust manifold using a new gasket. Torque the nuts to 26 ft. lbs. (35 Nm).

38. Install the engine mount nuts to the studs and torque to 32 ft. lbs. (43 Nm).

39. Install the transaxle brace at the top of the transaxle bellhousing.

40. Carefully align the scribe marks on the flywheel and the torque converter made at removal. Install the torque converter to flywheel bolts and torque to 45 ft. lbs. (63 Nm).

41. Install the starter motor following the procedure in Section 2.

42. Install the flywheel cover.

43. Lower the vehicle.

44. Connect the heater hoses to the engine and install the radiator hoses.

45. Plug in all engine electrical connectors to the engine components, sensors and the grounds, following the identification tags made at removal.

46. Install the air conditioning compressor to the engine.

47. Install the power steering pump to the engine.

48. Connect the power brake booster vacuum hose to the engine.

49. If equipped with the VIN K engine, install the vacuum line to the transaxle vacuum modulator.

50. Install the cooling fans.

51. Install the right engine mount strut bracket, then install the struts, tightening the through bolts to 35 ft. lbs. (48 Nm).

52. Connect the throttle and cruise control cables with the mounting bracket to the throttle body.

53. Connect the fuel lines to the fuel rail and the mounting bracket.

54. Install the air cleaner duct.

55. Install the engine cover (fuel injector sight shield).

56. Connect the battery ground cable.

57. Install the hood assembly, using the grease pencil marks made at removal to aid alignment. If necessary, fore-aft adjustment may be made by elongating the hood-side hinge holes. Vertical adjustment at the front may be made by adjusting the hood bumpers up or down. Gap tolerances are 0.10–0.22 inch (2.54–5.58mm) and flush tolerances are 0.0–0.06 inch (0–1.5mm). Adjust as required.

58. Fill the cooling system with the proper mix of DEX-COOL®coolant and water. Please see Section 1.

59. Fill the engine with oil. Verify that the a new oil filter is properly installed.

60. Inspect all fluid levels and adjust, if necessary.

61. Inspect for leaks.

Rocker Arm (Valve) Cover

REMOVAL & INSTALLATION

3.1L Engine

LEFT SIDE (FRONT)

▶ **See Figures 13 thru 19**

1. Disconnect the negative battery cable.

2. Drain the engine coolant into a suitable container for reuse, if the coolant is not contaminated.

3. Tag for identification and remove the left side (front) spark plug wires.

4. Remove the automatic transaxle vacuum modulator pipe.

5. Remove the right engine mount strut through bolt at the engine side and then swing the strut forward out of the way.

6. Remove the PCV valve from the rocker arm cover by pulling the valve from its rubber grommet.

7. Remove the thermostat bypass pipe.

8. Remove the valve cover bolts and remove the cover from the engine. Do not pry it off. Bump the cover sideways with a rubber mallet if it is stuck. Discard the gasket.

To install:

9. Clean all parts well including the sealing surfaces on both the cylinder head and the cover gasket flange.

10. Install a new gasket. Apply sealant, GM #12345739, or equivalent, at the cylinder head to lower intake manifold joint.

11. Install the rocker arm cover and hand tighten the cover bolts. Torque to 89 inch lbs. (10 Nm).

12. Install the remaining components in the reverse order of the removal process.

13. Refill the cooling system and check the engine oil level. Add as necessary.

14. Connect the negative battery cable. Start the engine and verify no coolant or oil leaks.

Fig. 13 Remove the PCV (crankcase vent tube) from the rubber grommet

Fig. 14 Unfasten the torque strut through bolt . . .

Fig. 15 . . . and swing the torque strut up out of the way

Fig. 16 Remove the spark plug wire guide, if necessary

Fig. 17 Unfasten the rocker arm (valve) cover retaining bolts . . .

Fig. 18 . . . then remove the cover from the cylinder head. Do not pry on the cover during removal

Fig. 19 Remove and discard the cover gasket

RIGHT SIDE (REAR)

1. Disconnect the negative battery cable.
2. Remove the accessory drive belt. Please see Section 1.
3. Remove the alternator and brackets. Please see Section 2.
4. Remove the rear spark plug wires.
5. Remove the ignition coil bracket with the coils, the purge solenoid and the vacuum canister solenoid.
6. Remove the vacuum hose from the air duct at the rear cylinder head cover.
7. Remove the rocker arm cover bolts and remove the cover from the engine. Do not pry it off. Bump the cover sideways with a rubber mallet if it is stuck. Discard the gasket.

To install:

8. Clean all parts well including the sealing surfaces on both the cylinder head and the cover gasket flange.
9. Install a new gasket. Apply sealant, GM #12345739, or equivalent, at the cylinder head to lower intake manifold joint.
10. Install the rocker arm cover and hand tighten the cover bolts. Torque to 89 inch lbs. (10 Nm).
11. Install the remaining components in the reverse order of the removal process.

3.4L (VIN E) Engine

LEFT SIDE (FRONT)

▶ See Figure 20

1. Disconnect the negative battery cable.
2. Drain the engine coolant.
3. Tag for identification and remove the left (front) spark plug wires. Please see Section 1.
4. Remove the AIR check valve/pipe.
5. Remove the thermostat bypass hose and pipe.
6. Remove the PCV valve from the rubber grommet in the rocker arm cover.
7. Remove the rocker arm cover bolts and remove the cover from the engine. Do not pry it off. Bump the cover sideways with a rubber mallet if it is stuck. Discard the gasket.

To install:

8. Clean all parts well including the sealing surfaces on both the cylinder head and the cover gasket flange. Install a new cover gasket. Apply

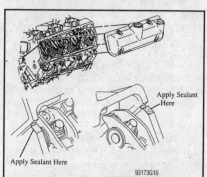

Fig. 20 Left side (front) rocker arm cover and sealant locations—3.4L (VIN E) engine

Apply Sealant Here

Apply Sealant Here

sealant GM #12345739 or equivalent at the cylinder head to lower intake manifold joint at both ends of the lower intake manifold.

9. Install the rocker arm cover and install the cover bolts. Torque to 89 inch lbs. (10 Nm).
10. Install the remaining components in the reverse order of the removal process.
11. Refill the cooling system.

RIGHT SIDE (REAR)

1. Disconnect the negative battery cable.
2. Remove the accessory drive belt. Please see Section 1.
3. Remove the alternator and the alternator brackets. Please see Section 2.
4. Tag for identification and remove the right side spark plug wires.

5. Tag for identification and remove the vacuum hoses from the evaporative canister purge solenoid valve.

6. Remove the evaporative canister purge solenoid valve and the AIR check valve/pipe.

7. Remove the ignition coil bracket with the coils in place.

8. Remove the vacuum hose from the grommet in the right rocker arm cover.

9. Remove the rocker arm cover bolts and remove the cover from the engine. Do not pry it off. Bump the cover sideways with a rubber mallet if it is stuck. Discard the gasket.

To install:

10. Clean all parts well including the sealing surfaces on both the cylinder head and the cover gasket flange. Install a new cover gasket. Apply sealant GM #12345739 or equivalent at the cylinder head to lower intake manifold joint at both ends of the lower intake manifold.

11. Install the rocker arm cover and install the cover bolts. Torque to 89 inch lbs. (10 Nm).

12. Install the remaining components in the reverse order of the removal process.

3.8L Engines

LEFT SIDE (FRONT)

▶ **See Figure 21**

1. Disconnect the negative battery cable.

2. Remove the engine lift bracket from the exhaust manifold studs.

3. Remove the acoustic/cosmetic engine cover.

4. Remove the right side "wish bone" shaped engine strut by removing the through bolts.

5. Tag for identification and remove the left (front) spark plug wires. Please see Section 1.

6. Remove the spark plug wire cover retainer clip from the rocker arm cover.

7. Remove the rocker arm cover bolts and remove the cover from the engine. Do not pry it off. Bump the cover sideways with a rubber mallet if it is stuck. Discard the gasket.

To install:

8. Clean all parts well including the sealing surfaces on both the cylinder head and the cover gasket flange. Clean any thread-locking compound from the rocker arm cover bolts.

9. Install a new gasket making sure the gasket is properly seated in the cover groove. Install the cover. Apply thread-locking compound GM #12345493 or equivalent to the bolt threads and

install the cover bolts. Torque to 89 inch lbs. (10 Nm).

10. Install the remaining components in the reverse order of the removal process.

RIGHT SIDE (REAR)

▶ **See Figure 21**

1. Disconnect the negative battery cable

2. Remove the acoustic/cosmetic engine cover.

3. Remove the rear alternator brace.

4. Tag for identification and remove the right (rear) spark plug wires.

5. Remove the engine cover retaining bracket from the exhaust manifold studs.

6. Remove the right (rear) engine lift bracket from the exhaust manifold studs.

7. Remove the rocker arm cover bolts and remove the cover from the engine. Do not pry it off. Bump the cover sideways with a rubber mallet if it is stuck. Discard the gasket.

To install:

8. Clean all parts well including the sealing surfaces on both the cylinder head and the cover gasket flange. Clean any thread-locking compound from the rocker arm cover bolts.

9. Install a new gasket making sure the gasket is properly seated in the cover groove. Install the cover. Apply thread-locking compound GM #12345493 or equivalent to the bolt threads and install the cover bolts. Torque to 89 inch lbs. (10 Nm).

10. Install the remaining components in the reverse order of the removal process.

Camshaft Carrier Cover

REMOVAL & INSTALLATION

3.4L (VIN X) Engine

LEFT SIDE (FRONT)

▶ **See Figure 22**

1. Remove the oil/air breather hose from the cover.

2. Remove the spark plug wires from the plugs. Please see Section 1.

3. Remove the camshaft carrier cover bolts and remove the cover from the engine.

4. Remove the gasket and the O-ring seals from the cover.

To install:

5. Clean all parts well.

6. Install new O-rings and gasket to the camshaft carrier cover.

7. Install the cover and the retaining bolts. Torque to 97 inch lbs. (11 Nm).

8. Install the remaining components in the reverse order of the removal process.

RIGHT SIDE (REAR)

▶ **See Figure 22**

1. Disconnect the negative battery cable.

2. Remove the upper intake manifold using the procedure in this section.

3. Remove the right timing belt cover using the procedure in this section.

4. Tag and disconnect the right spark plug wires.

5. Disconnect the oil/air separator hose at the camshaft carrier cover.

6. Remove the camshaft carrier cover bolts and remove the cover from the engine.

7. Remove the gasket and the O-ring seals from the cover.

To install:

8. Clean all parts well.

9. Install new O-rings and gasket to the camshaft carrier cover.

10. Install the cover and the retaining bolts. Torque to 97 inch lbs. (11 Nm).

11. Install the remaining components in the reverse order of the removal process.

3.5L Engine

LEFT SIDE (FRONT)

▶ **See Figure 23**

1. Disconnect the negative battery cable.

2. Remove the acoustic/cosmetic engine cover.

3. Remove the dipstick tube bolt and adjust the tube for access.

4. Disconnect the PCV valve and feed tube from the front cover.

5. Remove the ignition coil assembly from the cover.

6. Remove the engine wiring harness channel bolt from the cover and reposition the wiring harness and the channel. Remove and set aside the wiring harness with retainers from the cover.

7. Remove the camshaft cover retaining bolts and lift the cover from the cylinder head evenly.

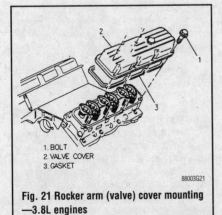

1. BOLT
2. VALVE COVER
3. GASKET

88003G21

Fig. 21 Rocker arm (valve) cover mounting —3.8L engines

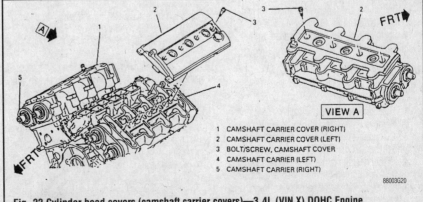

VIEW A

1 CAMSHAFT CARRIER COVER (RIGHT)
2 CAMSHAFT CARRIER COVER (LEFT)
3 BOLT/SCREW, CAMSHAFT COVER
4 CAMSHAFT CARRIER (LEFT)
5 CAMSHAFT CARRIER (RIGHT)

88003G20

Fig. 22 Cylinder head covers (camshaft carrier covers)—3.4L (VIN X) DOHC Engine

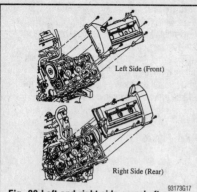

Fig. 23 Left and right side camshaft carrier covers—3.5L (VIN H) engine

Fig. 24 Unfasten the rocker arm nuts . . .

Fig. 25 . . . then remove the rocker arm nut, ball and rocker arm

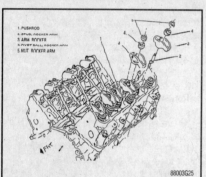

1. PUSHROD
2. STUD, ROCKER ARM
3. ARM ROCKER
4. PIVOT BALL ROCKER ARM
5. NUT ROCKER ARM

Fig. 26 Exploded view of the valve rocker arms, pushrods and pivot assemblies—3.1L engine

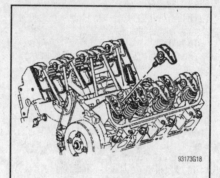

Fig. 27 Rocker arm and pivot assembly—3.4L (VIN E) engine

➡ **Work carefully. The camshaft cover seals (perimeter seal and the spark plug seals) should be reused unless they are damaged or if the perimeter seal is pulled from its groove during removal.**

8. Rotate and remove the spark plug boots. Replace if necessary. GM recommends only tool J 43094 be used to handle the spark plug boots. Please see

To install:

9. Clean all parts well. Clean the camshaft carrier and the cover sealing surfaces with a clean cloth. Inspect the perimeter and spark plug seals for damage. Make sure the perimeter seal is not pulled from its groove. Replace any damaged or worn seals.

10. Place the camshaft carrier cover on the camshaft carrier and install the bolts. Torque carefully to 80 inch lbs. (9 Nm).

11. Install the spark plugs and ignition coil assembly. Please see Section 1.

12. Install the remaining components in the reverse order of the removal process.

RIGHT SIDE (REAR)

▶ **See Figure 23**

1. Disconnect the negative battery cable.
2. Remove the acoustic/cosmetic engine cover.
3. Disconnect the PCV valve and feed tube from the rear cover.
4. Disconnect the surge tank inlet hose from the surge tank and plug the hose. Remove the surge tank nuts and reposition the surge tank. Remove the surge tank inlet hose bracket bolt, and reposition

the bracket.

5. Release the clips at the power steering lines. Reposition the lines as necessary.

6. Remove the engine wiring harness channel bolt from the rear camshaft cover, remove the channel and set aside. Remove the harness retainers from the cover.

7. Detach the oxygen sensor electrical connector.

8. Remove the rear bank ignition coil assembly from the camshaft cover. Please see Section 1.

9. Remove the camshaft cover bolts and lift the cover evenly from the camshaft carrier.

➡ **Work carefully. The camshaft cover seals (perimeter seal and the spark plug seals) should be reused unless they are damaged or if the perimeter seal is pulled from its groove during removal.**

10. Rotate and remove the spark plug boots. Replace if necessary. GM recommends only tool J 43094 be used to handle the spark plug boots. Please see Section 1.

To install:

11. Clean all parts well. Clean the camshaft carrier and the cover sealing surfaces with a clean cloth. Inspect the perimeter and spark plug seals for damage. Make sure the perimeter seal is not pulled from its groove. Replace any damaged or worn seals.

12. Place the camshaft carrier cover on the camshaft carrier and install the bolts. Torque carefully to 80 inch lbs. (9 Nm).

13. Install the spark plugs and ignition coil assembly. Please see Section 1.

14. Install the remaining components in the reverse order of the removal process.

Rocker Arms

REMOVAL & INSTALLTION

3.1L Engine

▶ **See Figures 24, 25 and 26**

1. Remove the valve rocker arm cover(s).
2. Remove the rocker arm bolt(s)/nut(s).
3. Remove the rocker arm(s).

❊❊ WARNING

The pushrods are different lengths and must not be mixed up. Place the valve train parts in a rack to make sure they are installed in the same location from which they were removed. Intake pushrods measure 5.68 inches and the exhaust pushrods measure 6.0 inches. Take care that the pushrods do not fall down in the lifter valley.

To install:

4. Coat the bearing surface of the rocker arms, rocker arm bolts and pushrods with GM prelube #1052365 or equivalent engine assembly lubrication. Install all of the components in their original locations. Make sure the intake and exhaust pushrods are in their proper locations. Torque the rocker arm bolt to 14 ft.lbs. (19 Nm). Then, using a torque angle meter, rotate the bolts an additional 30 degrees.

5. Install the remaining components in the reverse order of the removal process.

3.4L (VIN E) Engine

▶ **See Figure 27**

1. Remove the valve rocker arm cover(s).
2. Remove the rocker arm bolt(s).
3. Remove the rocker arm(s) and the pushrods.

To install:

4. Coat the bearing surface of the rocker arms, rocker arm bolts and pushrods with GM prelube #1052365 or equivalent engine assembly lubrication. Install all of the components in their original locations. Torque the rocker arm bolt to 14 ft.lbs. (19 Nm). Then, using a torque angle meter, rotate the bolts an additional 30 degrees.

5. Install the remaining components in the reverse order of the removal process.

3.8L Engines

▶ See Figure 28

➡ GM requires a torque angle meter for this procedure.

1. Remove the valve rocker arm cover(s).
2. Remove the rocker arm pedestal retaining bolt(s) and remove the rocker arm(s).

➡ Place all the parts on a clean surface. Store the components in order so they can be reassembled in the same location and with the same mating surfaces as when removed.

3. Remove the rocker arm bearing(s) and the retainer plate, if necessary.

To install:

4. Clean all parts well. Clean all thread-locking compound from the bolts. Use compressed air to blow oil out of the threaded holes in the cylinder head.
5. Install the pushrod(s).
6. Install the retainer(s). Make sure the arrows on the retainer(s) point toward the center of the engine.
7. Install the rocker arm(s) and the bearing(s) and the pedestal bolt(s).
8. Tighten the bolts to 18 ft. lbs. (15 Nm). Then, using a torque angle meter, rotate the bolts an additional 90 degrees.
9. Install the remaining components in the reverse order of the removal process.

Thermostat

The thermostat is used to control the flow of engine coolant. When the engine is cold, the thermostat is closed to prevent coolant from circulating from the engine to the radiator. As the engine begins to warm up, the thermostat opens to allow the coolant to flow through the radiator and the engine warms evenly to its normal operating temperature. Fuel economy and engine durability is increased when operated at normal operating temperature.

REMOVAL & INSTALLATION

❈❈❈ CAUTION

Never open the radiator cap or the cooling system when the engine is hot. The system is under pressure and will release scalding hot coolant and steam which can cause severe burns and other bodily harm. After the engine has cooled, drain the coolant into a suitable container. Coolant should be reused unless it is contaminated or several years old.

3.1L, 3.4L (VIN X) and 3.8L Engines

▶ See Figures 29 thru 37

1. Disconnect the negative battery cable.
2. Partially drain the cooling system into a suitable container, to a level below the thermostat.
3. It is usually possible to leave the radiator

hose attached and simply remove the thermostat housing (also called a water outlet) and flex the radiator hose enough to service the thermostat. It is good practice, however, to remove the radiator hose so the thermostat housing can be given a thorough cleaning. Debris on the thermostat housing sealing surface can cause leaks.

4. Some applications may have electrical connections to sensors which mount in the thermostat housing. Use care when detaching these connectors.
5. Unfasten the thermostat housing bolts and remove the housing.
6. Remove the thermostat by simply pulling out. Discard the gasket.

To install:

7. Clean all parts well. Make sure the sealing surfaces on both the thermostat housing gasket flange and the intake manifold are clean and free of corrosion damage. It is good practice to run a thread cutting tap or a clean bolt into the threaded holes in the manifold to clean out old sealer and dirt. The threads should be clean so the thermostat cover clamps the gasket evenly at assembly.
8. Position the thermostat in the intake manifold. Make sure it is seated.
9. Position a new gasket over the thermostat. If no gasket is used, apply a 0.125 in. (3mm) bead of RTV sealer to the thermostat housing and install the housing. Lightly lubricate the bolts with clean engine oil. Torque to 18–20 ft. lbs. (23–27 Nm).
10. If removed, attach the radiator hose to the thermostat housing.
11. Refill the engine with the proper mix of DEX-COOL® and water. Connect the negative battery cable, start the engine and check for leaks.

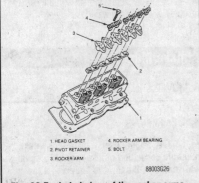

Fig. 28 Exploded view of the rocker arms, lifters and pushrods—3.8L engine

Fig. 29 Unfasten the water outlet attaching bolts, then remove the outlet—3.1L engine shown

Fig. 30 View of the thermostat in its seat in the intake manifold—3.1L engine shown

Fig. 31 Remove the thermostat from the housing . . .

Fig. 32 . . . then remove and discard the gasket from the thermostat

Fig. 33 Remove the radiator cap . . .

Fig. 34 . . . then fill the cooling system with the proper type and amount of coolant

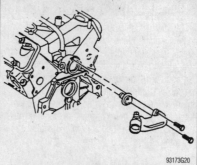

Fig. 35 The thermostat on this 3.1L is mounted horizontally and uses an offset housing/water outlet

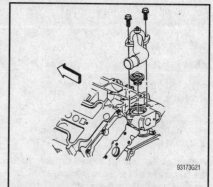

Fig. 36 Thermostat location arrangement—1997 3.4L (VIN X) engine

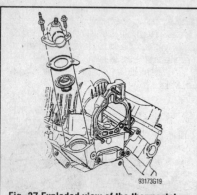

Fig. 37 Exploded view of the thermostat arrangement—3.8L engines

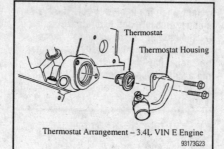

Fig. 38 Thermostat arrangement—3.4L (VIN E) engine

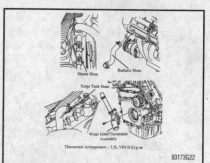

Fig. 39 The thermostat and water inlet assembly are combined in one assembly and must be serviced together—3.5L (VIN H) engine

3.4L (VIN E) Engine

♦ See Figure 38

1. Partially drain the cooling system.
2. Using hose clamp pliers, reposition the hose clamp at the thermostat housing. Disconnect the radiator hose from the thermostat housing.
3. Remove the exhaust crossover pipe using the following procedure:
    a. Carefully remove the throttle body air duct.
    b. Reposition the AIR pipe for access.
    c. Remove the exhaust crossover heat shield bolts and remove the heat shield.
    d. Remove the crossover bolts and lift the crossover from the engine.
    e. Remove the thermostat housing bolts and remove the thermostat from the engine. Discard the gasket.

To install:

4. Clean all parts well. Make sure the sealing surfaces on both the thermostat housing gasket flange and the intake manifold are clean and free of corrosion damage. It is good practice to run a thread cutting tap or a clean bolt into the threaded holes in the manifold to clean out old sealer and dirt. The threads should be clean so the thermostat cover clamps the gasket evenly at assembly.
5. Position the thermostat in the intake manifold. Make sure it is seated.
6. Install the thermostat housing and bolts. Torque the bolts to 18 ft. lbs. (25 Nm).
7. Connect the hoses and reposition the clamps.
8. Install the exhaust crossover pipe. Torque the bolts to 18 ft. lbs. (25 Nm).

9. Install the exhaust crossover pipe heat shield and tighten the bolts to 89 inch lbs. (10 Nm).
10. Install the AIR pipe.
11. Install the throttle body air duct.
12. Refill the engine with the proper mix of DEX-COOL®and water. Check for leaks.

3.5L Engine

♦ See Figure 39

➡This engine uses a combination water inlet housing and thermostat assembly. If replacement is required, the entire assembly must be replaced.

1. Partially drain the cooling system into a suitable container.
2. Using hose clamp pliers, remove the hose clamps from the water inlet housing.
3. Disconnect the radiator hose and the heater hose from the water inlet housing.
4. Remove the surge tank inlet hose clamp and disconnect the surge tank inlet hose from the water inlet housing.
5. Remove the water inlet housing bolts and remove the water inlet/thermostat assembly

To install:

6. Clean all parts well. Make sure there are no traces of dirt or debris on the sealing surfaces.
7. Install the inlet/thermostat assembly to the engine. Install the housing bolts using RTV Sealer GM #1052366, or equivalent. Torque the housing bolts to 80 inch lbs. (9 Nm). Do not over-torque.
8. Connect the surge tank hose, heater hose and radiator hose to the inlet housing.

9. Refill the cooling system with the correct mix of DEX-COOL®and water.
10. Inspect for leaks.

Intake Manifold

REMOVAL & INSTALLATION

3.1L Engine

➡The 3.1L engine uses a two-piece intake manifold consisting of an upper air plenum which mounts the throttle body and a lower intake manifold assembly which houses the fuel injectors.

✷✷ WARNING

This engine uses a sequential multiport fuel injection system. The fuel injector electrical connectors MUST connected to their proper injectors or engine performance will be seriously affected. Identify and tag all injector connectors that are removed. This is most important.

UPPER INTAKE MANIFOLD (PLENUM)

♦ See Figure 40

1. Disconnect the negative battery cable.
2. Remove the air cleaner duct.
3. Drain the cooling system into a suitable container.
4. Remove the accelerator control and cruise

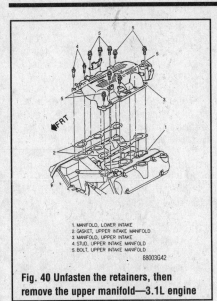

1. MANIFOLD, LOWER INTAKE
2. GASKET, UPPER INTAKE MANIFOLD
3. MANIFOLD, UPPER INTAKE
4. STUD, UPPER INTAKE MANIFOLD
5. BOLT, UPPER INTAKE MANIFOLD

88003G42

Fig. 40 Unfasten the retainers, then remove the upper manifold—3.1L engine

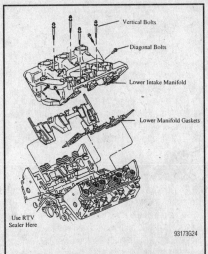

Use RTV Sealer Here

93173G24

Fig. 41 Exploded view of the lower intake manifold arrangement—3.1L engine

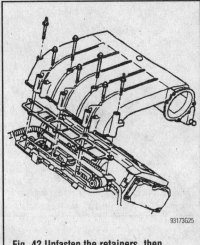

93173G25

Fig. 42 Unfasten the retainers, then remove the upper manifold—1997 3.4L (VIN X) engine shown

control cables with the bracket from the throttle body.

5. Detach the wiring harness connectors from the throttle body.

6. Remove the thermostat bypass pipe coolant hoses from the throttle body.

7. Tag for identification and remove the vacuum hoses from the throttle body and the upper intake manifold.

8. Tag and disconnect the front spark plug wires.

9. Remove the ignition coil bracket with the coils, the purge solenoid and the vacuum canister solenoid.

10. Remove the Manifold Absolute Pressure (MAP) sensor and bracket.

11. Remove the alternator rear brace.

12. Remove the Exhaust Gas Recirculation (EGR) valve.

13. Remove the upper intake manifold bolts and nuts and lift the upper intake manifold off the engine. Remove the gaskets. The throttle body can be removed, if necessary. Otherwise, do not disturb the throttle body assembly. Cover the lower intake manifold with a clean cloth to keep debris out of the intake ports.

To install:

14. Clean all parts well with a degreaser, especially all sealing surfaces.

15. Install new upper intake manifold gaskets

16. Install the upper intake manifold and the bolts and nuts. Torque all fasteners to 18 ft. lbs. (25 Nm).

17. Install the remaining components in the reverse order of the removal process.

LOWER INTAKE MANIFOLD

▶ See Figure 41

1. Disconnect the negative battery cable.

2. Remove the upper intake manifold as outlined earlier.

3. Remove both valve rocker arm covers as outlined in this section.

4. Relive the fuel system pressure. Please see Section 5.

5. Disconnect the fuel injector feed and return pipes from the fuel rail. Please see Section 5.

6. Without disconnect the fluid lines, remove the power steering pump from the front engine cover and reposition aside.

7. Disconnect the heater inlet pipe from the lower intake manifold.

8. Disconnect the upper radiator hose from the engine.

9. Remove the lower intake manifold bolts and carefully lift the manifold from the engine. Discard the gaskets.

To install:

10. Clean all parts well with degreaser, especially the gasket seal surfaces on the cylinder heads and the engine block. Remove all the loose RTV sealer.

11. Apply a bead of RTV sealant approximately ¼inch in diameter on each ridge where the front and rear of the lower intake manifold contacts the engine block. Install new lower intake manifold gaskets and carefully lower the lower intake manifold into place.

12. Bolt installation requires some care. Note that some bolts are "vertical" when installed, others are "diagonal" when installed. Apply a thin, even coat of sealer GM #12345382 or equivalent, to all of the bolt threads. Hand tighten the vertical bolts first, then tighten the diagonal bolts. Note that an oil leak will result if the vertical bolts are not tightened before the diagonal bolts. Now torque the vertical bolts to 115 inch lbs. (13 Nm), followed by the diagonal bolts, also to 115 inch lbs. (13 Nm).

13. Install the remaining components in the reverse order of the removal process.

3.4L (VIN X) Engine

➡The 3.4L (VIN X) engine uses a two-piece intake manifold consisting of an upper air plenum which mounts the throttle body and a lower intake manifold assembly which houses the fuel injectors.

UPPER INTAKE MANIFOLD (PLENUM)

▶ See Figure 42

1. Disconnect the negative battery cable.

2. Remove the air cleaner duct.

3. Drain the cooling system into a suitable container.

4. Disconnect the throttle and cruise control cables from the throttle body.

5. Remove the cosmetic/acoustic engine cover.

6. Remove the evaporative emission canister purge solenoid bracket bolts and remove the solenoid.

7. Tag for identification, then disconnect the spark plug wires.

8. Remove the ignition control module mounting bolts and remove the module with the coil assemblies. Remove the bolts and then remove the ignition module mounting bracket.

9. Tag for identification, then disconnect all vacuum lines from the upper intake manifold.

10. Remove the upper intake manifold bolts and carefully lift the manifold from the engine. Discard the gaskets.

To install:

11. Clean all parts well with degreaser, especially the gasket seal surfaces on both the upper manifold and the lower manifold.

12. Install a new upper manifold gasket, carefully set the manifold into place and then install the bolts. Torque the bolts evenly to 19 ft. lbs. (26 Nm).

13. Install the remaining components in the reverse order of the removal process.

LOWER INTAKE MANIFOLD

▶ See Figure 43

1. Remove the upper intake manifold using the earlier procedure, including draining the cooling system.

2. Remove the fuel rail. Please see Section 5.

3. Disconnect the radiator hose from the thermostat housing.

4. Detach the electrical connector at the temperature sensor.

5. Remove the heater pipe nut at the throttle body.

➡Installing the intake manifold will take some care. As the bolts are removed, make note of their original locations and hardware (washers, etc.) so they can be returned to their original locations.

6. Remove the lower intake manifold mounting bolts and carefully lift off the lower manifold. Discard the gaskets.

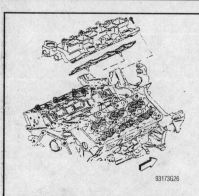

Fig. 43 Lower intake manifold arrangement—1997 3.4L (VIN X) engine shown

To install:

7. Clean all parts well with degreaser, especially the gasket seal surfaces on the cylinder heads and the engine block.

8. Install new lower intake manifold gaskets and carefully lower the lower intake manifold into place.

9. Bolt installation requires some care. Use the following procedure:

a. Install two spare 8mm x 1.25 x 50mm bolts with washers to the vertical holes in the intake manifold. Tighten gently to 62 inch lbs. (7 Nm). The reason for this is, that installing the bolts in the vertical holes of the manifold will align the intake bolt grommet bores with the threaded holes in the cylinder heads. This will minimize the possibility of cross-threading and damage to the grommets resulting in a leak at the intake manifold gaskets.

b. Install the lower intake mounting bolts. Insert the rubber isolators fully into the manifold mounting flange before tightening any fasteners.

c. Draw the lower intake manifold in place by tightening the bolts gradually, starting with the middle bolts and working in a circular pattern. Do not tighten one side or one end fully.

d. Final torque the bolts to 116 inch lbs. (13 Nm).

e. Remove the two bolts in the vertical holes of the intake manifold.

10. Install the remaining components in the reverse order of the removal process. Use care when installing the fuel rail with the fuel injectors. Please see Section 5.

3.4L (VIN E) Engine

➡The 3.4L VIN E engine uses a two-piece intake manifold consisting of an upper air plenum which mounts the throttle body and a lower intake manifold assembly which houses the fuel injectors.

✳✳ WARNING

This engine uses a sequential multiport fuel injection system. The fuel injector electrical connectors MUST connected to their proper injectors or engine performance will be seriously affected. Identify and tag all injector connectors that are removed. This is most important.

UPPER INTAKE MANIFOLD (PLENUM)

▶ **See Figure 44**

1. Disconnect the negative battery cable.
2. Tag for identification and disconnect all vacuum lines that connect to the upper intake manifold.
3. Detach the wiring harness connection from the Intake Air Temperature (IAT) sensor in the throttle body air inlet duct. Then remove the throttle body air inlet duct.
4. Drain the cooling system into a suitable container.
5. Remove the accelerator control and cruise control cables, with the bracket, from the throttle body.
6. Tag for identification and detach the wiring harness connectors from the Throttle Position (TP) sensor and the Idle Air Control (IAC) valve.
7. Disconnect the wiring harness attachment clips from the Camshaft Position (CMP) sensor harness and the left side spark plug wire harness.
8. Disconnect the thermostat bypass pipe coolant hoses from the throttle body.
9. Remove the alternator rear brace and the alternator bracket.
10. Remove the Manifold Absolute Pressure (MAP) sensor and Exhaust Gas Recirculation (EGR) valve.
11. Tag for identification and remove the spark plug wires.
12. Remove the ignition control module. Please see
13. Remove the upper intake manifold bolts and carefully remove the upper intake manifold. Discard the gaskets.

To install:

14. Clean all parts well with degreaser, especially the gasket seal surfaces on both the upper manifold and the lower manifold.

15. Install a new upper manifold gasket, carefully set the manifold into place and then install the bolts. Torque the bolts evenly to 19 ft. lbs. (26 Nm), starting from the center and working outward.

16. Install the remaining components in the reverse order of the removal process.

LOWER INTAKE MANIFOLD

1. Disconnect the negative battery cable.
2. Remove the upper intake manifold assembly using the procedure in this section.
3. Remove the valve rocker arm covers using the procedures in this section.

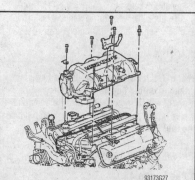

Fig. 44 Unfasten the retainers, then remove the upper manifold—3.4L (VIN E) engine shown

4. Detach the Engine Coolant Temperature (ECT) wiring harness from the sensor in the thermostat housing.

5. Tag for identification and detach the fuel injector and Manifold Absolute Pressure (MAP) sensor wiring harness connectors.

6. Remove the fuel pipe clip bolt, remove the clip, then disconnect the fuel feed pipe from the fuel rail. Also disconnect the fuel return pipe from the fuel rail. Please see Section 5.

7. Remove the fuel injector rail. Please see Section 5.

8. Without disconnecting the fluid lines, remove the power steering pump from the front engine cover and reposition aside.

9. Disconnect the heater inlet pipe from lower intake manifold and reposition aside.

10. Disconnect the radiator inlet hose from the engine. Also disconnect the small thermostat bypass hose that runs between the thermostat pipe and the lower intake manifold pipe.

11. Remove the lower intake manifold bolts and carefully lift the lower intake manifold from the engine.

12. Remove the rocker arms and pushrods as outlined in this section.

13. Remove and discard the gaskets.

To install:

14. Clean all parts well with degreaser, especially the gasket seal surfaces on the cylinder heads and the engine block. Remove all the loose RTV sealer.

15. Install the lower intake manifold gaskets.

16. Install the valve rocker arms and pushrods, following the procedure in this section.

17. Apply a bead of RTV sealant approximately ¼inch in diameter on each ridge where the front and rear of the lower intake manifold contacts the engine block. Install new lower intake manifold gaskets and carefully lower the lower intake manifold into place.

18. Bolt installation requires some care. Note that some bolts are "vertical" when installed, others are "diagonal" when installed. Apply a thin, even coat of sealer GM #12345382, or equivalent, to all of the bolt threads. Hand tighten the vertical bolts first, then tighten the diagonal bolts. Note that an oil leak will result if the vertical bolts are not tightened before the diagonal bolts. Now torque the vertical bolts to 115 inch lbs. (13 Nm), followed by the diagonal bolts, also to 115 inch lbs. (13 Nm).

19. Install the remaining components in the reverse order of the removal process.

3.5L Engine

▶ **See Figure 45**

➡It is important to correctly identify the source of an oil leak. A power steering fluid leak or spillage can travel across the valley area of the engine and run out the weep hole, which is located at the back of the block. Failure to correctly identify the source of an oil leak can lead to the incorrect or unnecessary replacement of components.

1. Disconnect the negative battery cable.
2. Carefully remove the throttle body air inlet duct from the throttle body.
3. Partially drain the cooling system into a suitable container.

4. Remove the cosmetic/acoustic engine cover.

5. Disconnect the accelerator and cruise control cables from the bracket.

6. Disconnect the coolant hoses to the throttle body.

7. Relieve the fuel system pressure and disconnect the fuel rail quick-connect fittings. Please see Section 5.

8. Disconnect the following vacuum lines from the intake manifold:

   a. The vapor line from the EVAP canister purge solenoid.

   b. The power brake booster vacuum hose.

   c. The air conditioning vacuum hose.

9. Disconnect the surge tank inlet pipe from the fuel rail.

10. Tag for identification then detach the fuel injector wiring harness connectors.

11. Tag for identification then detach the Throttle Position (TP) sensor, Idle Air Control (IAC) valve, EVAP purge solenoid and Manifold Absolute Pressure (MAP) sensor wiring harness connectors.

12. Remove the engine wiring harness channel bolts from the camshaft covers and set the harness and channel assemblies.

13. Disconnect the fuel pressure regulator vacuum tube from the regulator and the throttle body.

14. Disconnect and remove the PCV valve and both feed tubes from the camshaft covers and intake manifold.

15. Remove the EGR valve outlet pipe retaining bolts from the intake manifold and the water crossover, then remove the EGR outlet pipe.

16. Disconnect the four fuel rail snap-lock retainers by pushing toward the camshaft covers and lifting. Remove the fuel rail and fuel injectors as an assembly by lifting straight up. Store is a clean, safe place. Since the rail still contains gasoline, keep it away from any heat sources.

17. Remove the throttle body heater hose insulator plate.

18. Remove the intake manifold bolts.

19. Using pliers to loosen the clamp, disconnect the throttle body coolant hoses from the water crossover feed tube.

20. Remove the intake manifold assembly.

To install:

21. Clean all parts well with degreaser, especially the gasket seal surfaces on the cylinder heads and the engine block.

22. Install the intake manifold gaskets. Carefully lower the intake manifold into place.

23. Before bolting the manifold down, connect the throttle body heater hose to the water crossover feed tube. Install the hose clamp.

24. Hand tighten the bolts first. Then torque the bolts to 62 inch lbs. (7 Nm). Tighten the bolts in a circular pattern starting from the center and working outward.

25. Install the remaining components in the reverse order of the removal process, observing the following.

   a. Inspect the fuel injector O-rings or misalignment or damage. Replace the O-rings if necessary. Install the fuel rail and fuel injectors by aligning the fuel injectors with their respective ports and pressing the four fuel rail snap-lock connectors into the intake manifold until they lock in place. DO NOT apply excessive pressure to the fuel rail. The need for excessive pressure may be caused by misalignment of a fuel injector and could cause damage to the seal or even the manifold.

   b. GM recommends that a new replacement EGR outlet pipe be installed.

   c. Use care to make sure all vacuum hoses are properly installed.

   d. Take care to make sure the fuel injector harness connectors are properly installed. This engine uses sequential fuel injectors and the harness connectors MUST be attached to the proper injector.

3.8L Engine

➡The 3.8L (VIN K) non-supercharged engine uses a two-piece intake manifold consisting of an upper air plenum which mounts the throttle body and a lower intake manifold assembly which houses the fuel injectors. The 3.8L (VIN 1) supercharged engine uses a similar lower intake manifold. The supercharger serves as the upper manifold.

UPPER INTAKE MANIFOLD (PLENUM)

▶ See Figure 46

1. Disconnect the negative battery cable.

2. On 3.8L (VIN 1) engines, remove the supercharger assembly. Please see the procedure in this section.

3. Tag for identification, then remove the right side spark plug wires.

4. Disconnect the ignition wires from the fuel rail.

5. Remove the fuel rail. Please see Section 5.

6. Remove the cable bracket from the intake manifold.

7. Remove the throttle body.

➡Two bolts which fasten the lower intake manifold to the cylinder head are accessible are accessible only after the upper intake manifold is removed. These bolts are located in the right front and left rear corners of the lower intake manifold.

8. Remove the upper intake manifold bolts and carefully lift the upper intake manifold from the engine.

To install:

9. Clean all parts well with degreaser, especially the gasket seal surfaces on the upper and lower manifold pieces.

10. Install new gaskets to the cylinder heads and new seals to the engine block. Carefully lower the manifold into place. Make sure to install the two hidden bolts in the lower intake manifold. Hand start all bolts, then torque evenly to 89 inch lbs. (10 Nm). Follow the torque sequence, starting in the center, then working outwards in a circle.

11. Install the remaining components in the reverse order of the removal process.

LOWER INTAKE MANIFOLD

▶ See Figure 47

➡Two bolts which fasten the lower intake manifold to the cylinder head are accessible only after the upper intake manifold is removed. These bolts are located in the right front and left rear corners of the lower intake manifold. Remove the upper intake manifold to service the lower intake.

The 3.8L (VIN 1) supercharged engine uses a manifold similar to the 3.8L (VIN K), but the supercharger serves as the upper manifold.

1. Disconnect the negative battery cable.

2. On 3.8L (VIN 1) engines, remove the supercharger assembly. Please see the procedure in this section.

3. Remove the upper intake manifold using the procedure above.

4. Remove the EGR outlet pipe from the intake manifold.

5. Detach the engine coolant temperature sensor wiring harness from the sensor.

6. Remove the lower intake manifold bolts and carefully lift off the manifold.

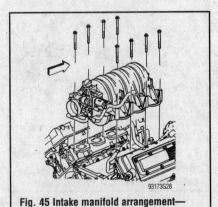

Fig. 45 Intake manifold arrangement—3.5L (VIN H) engine

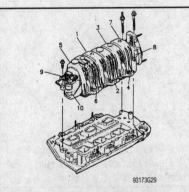

Fig. 46 Upper intake manifold and bolt torque sequence—3.8L (VIN K) engine

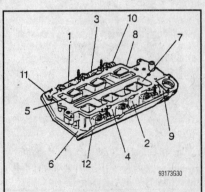

Fig. 47 Lower intake manifold bolt torque sequence—3.8L (VIN K) engine

To install:

7. Clean all parts well with degreaser, especially the gasket seal surfaces on the upper and lower manifold pieces and between the lower manifold and the cylinder heads..

8. Install new gaskets to the cylinder heads and new seals to the engine block. Carefully lower the manifold into place. Apply thread-locking compound to the bolt threads. Make sure to install the two hidden bolts in the lower intake manifold. Hand start all bolts, then torque evenly to 11 ft. lbs. (15 Nm). Follow the toque sequence, starting in the center, then working outwards in a circle.

9. Install the remaining components in the reverse order of the removal process.

Exhaust Manifold

REMOVAL & INSTALLATION

3.1L and 3.4L (VIN E) Engines

LEFT SIDE (FRONT)

▶ See Figure 48

1. Disconnect the negative battery cable.
2. Remove the air cleaner duct.
3. Drain the coolant into a suitable container.
4. Remove the right side engine mount strut bracket.
5. Disconnect the upper radiator hose from the engine.
6. Remove the automatic transaxle vacuum modulator pipe.
7. Remove the thermostat bypass pipe.
8. Remove the exhaust crossover pipe heat shield and then remove the crossover pipe.
9. Remove the left side (front) exhaust manifold heat shield bolts and remove the heat shield.
10. Remove the manifold bolts and nuts and remove the manifold. Discard the gasket.

To install:

11. Clean all parts well. Clean the manifold and cylinder head sealing surfaces.

12. Using a new gasket, position the exhaust manifold to the cylinder head. Install the bolts and nuts. Torque to 12 ft. lbs. (16 Nm).

13. Install the remaining components in the reverse order of the removal process.

RIGHT SIDE (REAR)

▶ See Figure 49

1. Disconnect the negative battery cable.
2. Remove the air cleaner duct.
3. Drain the coolant.
4. Disconnect the upper radiator hose from the engine.
5. Remove the upper radiator hose from the engine.
6. Remove the automatic transaxle vacuum modulator pipe.
7. Remove the exhaust crossover pipe heat shield and then remove the crossover pipe.
8. Detach the oxygen sensor electrical connector.
9. Raise and safely support the vehicle.
10. Disconnect the three-way catalytic converter pipe from the right side (rear) manifold.
11. Remove the automatic transaxle fluid filler tube and move the tube aside.
12. Remove the EGR tube from the rear exhaust manifold.
13. Remove the oxygen sensor.
14. Remove the right side (rear) exhaust manifold upper heat shield bolts and remove the upper heat shield.
15. Remove lower heat shield bolts and remove the lower heat shield.
16. Remove the manifold and nuts and remove the manifold. Discard the gasket.

To install:

17. Clean all parts well. Clean the manifold and cylinder head sealing surfaces.

18. Using a new gasket, position the exhaust manifold to the cylinder head. Install the bolts and nuts. Torque to 12 ft. lbs. (16 Nm).

19. Install the heat shields and tighten the bolts to 89 inch lbs. (10 Nm).

20. Install the remaining components in the reverse order of the removal process.

3.4L (VIN X) Engine

LEFT SIDE (FRONT)

▶ See Figure 50

1. Disconnect the negative battery cable.
2. Remove the air cleaner ducts.
3. Remove the exhaust crossover pipe.

4. Remove the electric cooling fan assembly.
5. Remove the exhaust manifold retaining nuts, the heat shield and the manifold. Discard the gasket.

To install:

6. Using a new gasket, position the exhaust manifold with the heat shield to the cylinder head. Install the nuts and torque to 115 inch lbs. (13 Nm).

7. Install the remaining components in the reverse order of the removal process.

RIGHT SIDE (REAR)

▶ See Figure 50

✷✷ CAUTION

This is a complicated procedure requiring numerous components to be removed and the subframe containing the engine and transaxle to be loosened and lowered for clearance. This is not a job for the inexperienced or ill-equipped. Be very sure that the exhaust manifold and/or manifold gasket really needs to be replaced before attempting this procedure. Be very sure of the lifting and jacking equipment you have available before attempting this procedure or the vehicle could be damaged and you could be injured. In addition, the factory specifies that whenever frame to body bolts are loosened or removed, they must be replaced with new bolts and retainers. Procure the bolts before beginning this procedure. Failure to replace frame to body bolts and retainers may result in damage to the frame, powertrain or suspension.

1. Disconnect the negative battery cable.
2. Remove the air cleaner duct.
3. Remove the exhaust crossover pipe.
4. Disconnect the Exhaust Gas Recirculation (EGR) tube from the exhaust manifold.
5. Raise and safely support the vehicle.
6. Remove the front pipe and the converter assembly.
7. Disconnect the oxygen sensor electrical connector from the wiring harness. Note that the oxygen sensor uses a permanently attached pigtail and connector. This pigtail should not be removed from the oxygen sensor. Damage or removal of the

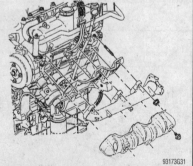

Fig. 48 Left side (front) exhaust manifold and heat shield—3.1L engine shown, 3.4L (VIN E) is similar

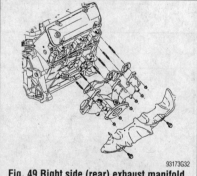

Fig. 49 Right side (rear) exhaust manifold and lower heat shield—3.1L engine shown, 3.4L (VIN E) is similar

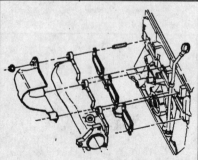

Fig. 50 Exploded view of the exhaust manifold and heat shield; left side shown, right side similar—3.4L (VIN X) engine

pigtail or connector will affect proper operation of the sensor. Keep the connector free of grease and contaminates.

8. Remove the exhaust pipe front heat shield.

9. Remove the alternator rear brace.

10. Remove the automatic transaxle dipstick tube.

11. Remove the intermediate steering shaft lower pinch bolt and disengage the intermediate shaft from the rack and pinion steering gear assembly.

12. Remove the exhaust manifold nuts.

13. Install a suitable lifting/jacking device to support the rear of the subframe.

14. Remove the rear subframe bolts. Discard the bolts. They must be replaced with new bolts.

15. Using the lifting/jacking device, lower the rear of the subframe not more that 4 inches.

✷✷ WARNING

Do not lower the frame more than 4 inches.

16. Remove the rack and pinion steering gear heat shield.

17. Remove the exhaust manifold heat shield.

18. Remove the exhaust manifold. Discard the gasket.

To install:

19. Clean all parts well, especially the sealing surfaces between the manifold and the cylinder head.

20. Using a new gasket, position the exhaust manifold with the heat shield to the cylinder head. Install the nuts and torque to 115 inch lbs. (13 Nm).

21. Install the remaining components in the reverse order of the removal process, paying attention to the following points;

a. When using the lifting/jacking device, raise the frame rear until the frame contacts the body. Install new replacement body bolts. Note the following:

b. Position the frame with aid of an assistant. A ¹⁹⁄₃₂(15mm) guide pin or drill bit can be inserted into the alignment holes located on the right side.

c. Proper clamping by the mount depends on clean and dry surfaces. If the frame isolator bolt does not screw in smoothly, it may be necessary to run a tap through the cage nut in the body to remove foreign material. Take care that the tap does not punch through the underbody. If the cage nut cannot be used, the cage nut retainer spot welds will have to be chiseled away with an air chisel, the cage nut replaced and the retainer welded back into its original location. Clean and prime the area with catalyzed primer to protect the area from corrosion.

22. Torque the four new frame isolator bolts to 133 ft. lbs. (180 Nm). Do not over-tighten the body mounts; a collapsed spacer or stripped bolt may result. Tighten in the following manner:

a. RH Rear, first

b. RH Front, second

c. LH Rear, third

d. LH Front, fourth

23. Connect the catalytic converter to the rear exhaust.

24. Attach the oxygen sensor wiring connector.

✷✷ CAUTION

When installing the intermediate shaft, make sure the shaft is seated prior to pinch bolt installation. If the pinch bolt is inserted into the coupling before shaft installation, the two mating shafts may disengage, with a loss of steering.

25. Connect the intermediate steering shaft to the rack and pinion steering assembly stub shaft. Verify that the two shafts are properly coupled. Insert the pinch bolt and torque carefully to 35 ft. lbs. (47 Nm).

26. Install the remaining components in the reverse order of the removal process.

3.5L Engine

LEFT SIDE (FRONT)

▶ See Figure 51

1. Disconnect the negative battery cable.

2. Remove the cosmetic/acoustic engine cover.

3. Remove the engine mount strut and bracket.

4. Remove the engine cooling fans.

5. Drain the coolant from the engine into a suitable container.

6. Remove both radiator hoses and disconnect the automatic transaxle cooling lines from the radiator.

7. Remove the radiator.

8. Remove the alternator. Please see Section 2.

9. Remove the exhaust manifold heat shield retaining bolts and remove the heat shield.

10. Remove the dipstick and tube.

11. Locate the AIR control valve just over the exhaust crossover and disconnect the vacuum tube and the feed pipe nut from the exhaust manifold. Remove the AIR valve retaining bolt and remove the valve from the engine mount strut bracket.

12. Loosen the exhaust manifold bolts.

13. Remove the exhaust manifold to crossover pipe flange retaining bolts and the flange gasket. Discard the flange gasket.

14. Remove the exhaust manifold bolts and separate the manifold from the cylinder head. Discard the gaskets.

To install:

15. Clean all parts well, especially the sealing

surfaces between the manifold and the cylinder head.

16. Install a new manifold to crossover flange gasket onto the manifold flange, then tighten the manifold-to-crossover pipe flange bolts to 18 ft. lbs. (25 Nm).

17. Using a new gasket, position the exhaust manifold to the cylinder head. Install the nuts and torque to 18 ft. lbs. (25 Nm). The exhaust crossover fasteners are tightened to 15 ft. lbs. (20 Nm).

18. Install the remaining components in the reverse order of the removal process.

RIGHT SIDE (REAR)

▶ See Figure 52

✷✷ WARNING

This is a difficult and complicated procedure. The entire engine/transaxle/subframe assembly must be removed to access the rear exhaust manifold. Be very sure the exhaust manifold and/or gasket really needs to be serviced. The factory recommended procedure for removing this engine is a lengthy and difficult procedure requiring special lifting and support equipment. The steering shaft must be separated and the vehicle subframe must be loosened and lowered. The vehicle's powertrain assembly, including the entire engine/transaxle/subframe assembly is lowered out of the bottom of the engine compartment and then the vehicle is lifted up away from the removed powertrain. Careful work is required for reassembly. This is not a job for the inexperienced or ill-equipped.

1. Remove the engine/transaxle/subframe from the vehicle using the procedure found in this section.

2. With the powertrain assembly secure on a frame table or other suitable, safe work stand and the body lifted and secured away from the powertrain assembly, remove the right side (rear) exhaust manifold crossover pipe bolts from the left side (front) exhaust manifold.

3. Disconnect the EGR valve pipe from the exhaust crossover pipe.

4. Remove the right side (rear) exhaust mani-

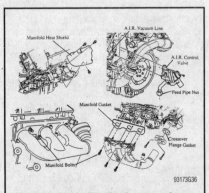

Fig. 51 Left side (front) exhaust manifold—3.5L (VIN H) engine

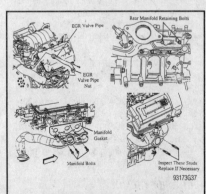

Fig. 52 Right side (rear) exhaust manifold—3.5L (VIN H) engine

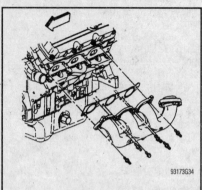

Fig. 53 Left side (front) exhaust manifold—3.8L engine

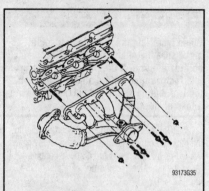

Fig. 54 Right side (rear) exhaust manifold—3.8L engine

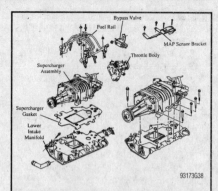

Fig. 55 Supercharger and related components—3.8L (VIN 1) Engine

fold retaining bolts and separate the manifold from the cylinder head. Discard the gasket.

To install:

5. Clean all parts well, especially the sealing surfaces between the manifold and the cylinder head. This is also a good time to remove the oxygen sensor and inspect for excessive deposits. Replace it if necessary. Inspect the exhaust manifold studs and replace if necessary.

6. Install a new manifold to crossover flange gasket onto the manifold flange, then tighten the manifold to crossover pipe flange bolts to 18 ft. lbs. (25 Nm).

7. Position a new gasket onto the exhaust manifold, install the bolts and place the manifold, gasket and bolts, as an assembly, in position on the cylinder head. Install the nuts and torque to 18 ft. lbs. (25 Nm). The exhaust crossover fasteners are tightened to 15 ft. lbs. (20 Nm).

8. Install the remaining components in the reverse order of the removal process. Please see the engine installation procedure in this section.

3.8L Engines

LEFT SIDE (FRONT)

▶ **See Figure 53**

1. Disconnect the negative battery cable.
2. Tag for identification and remove the front side spark plug wires.
3. Remove the exhaust crossover heat shield nuts and remove the shield.
4. Remove the nuts and bolts from the exhaust crossover and remove the crossover pipe.
5. Remove the exhaust manifold nuts and bolts. Remove the manifold. Discard the gasket.

To install:

6. Clean all parts well, especially the sealing surfaces between the manifold and the cylinder head.

7. Using a new gasket, position the exhaust manifold to the cylinder head. Install the nuts and torque to 22 ft. lbs. (30 Nm). Tighten the exhaust crossover fasteners to 15 ft. lbs. (20 Nm).

8. Install the remaining components in the reverse order of the removal process.

RIGHT SIDE (REAR)

▶ **See Figure 54**

1. Disconnect the negative battery cable.
2. Remove the EGR outlet pipe from the manifold.

3. Remove the exhaust crossover heat shield nuts and remove the shield.
4. Remove the nuts and bolts from the exhaust crossover and remove the crossover pipe.
5. Raise and safely support the vehicle.
6. Disconnect the three-way catalytic converter pipe from the manifold.
7. Disconnect the oxygen sensor lead.
8. Remove the exhaust manifold nuts and bolts. Remove the manifold. Discard the gasket.

To install:

9. Clean all parts well, especially the sealing surfaces between the manifold and the cylinder head.

10. Using a new gasket, position the exhaust manifold to the cylinder head. Install the nuts and torque to 22 ft. lbs. (30 Nm). Tighten the exhaust crossover fasteners to 15 ft. lbs. (20 Nm).

11. Install the remaining components in the reverse order of the removal process.

Supercharger

REMOVAL & INSTALLATION

3.8L (VIN 1) Engine

▶ **See Figure 55**

The 3.8L (VIN 1) engine is equipped with a belt-driven supercharger. Note that the supercharger has no user-replaceable parts inside and, if defective must be replaced as a unit. Use care when handling the supercharger to keep debris from entering the air intake. The supercharger lubrication system is sealed and separate from the engine oil system. If it is necessary to add oil, use only GM Supercharger Oil #12345982.

1. Remove the accessory drive belt. Please see Section 1.
2. Remove the engine cover and disconnect the air intake duct.
3. Relieve the fuel system pressure. Please see Section 5.
4. Remove the Ignition Control Module (ICM) harness from the fuel rail.
5. Remove the spark plug wire clips from the supercharger.
6. Remove the vacuum lines from the fuel rail.
7. Remove the fuel rail. Please see Section 5.
8. Remove the booster bypass nut.
9. Remove the regulator valve and harness bolt.

10. Remove the boost solenoid bolts.
11. Remove the bolts from the vacuum block.
12. Remove the MAP sensor bracket bolts.

➡**There are different size bolts and spacers used to retain the supercharger. Take note of the locations as they are being removed so they can be installed in the proper locations.**

13. Remove the bolts, nuts and spacers from the supercharger and carefully lift the supercharger assembly from the engine. Discard the gasket. Cover the manifold with a clean cloth to keep debris out of the intake manifold.

To install:

14. Clean all parts well. Install the supercharger gasket and carefully lower the supercharger into place. Install the bolts, nuts and spacers in their proper locations, as noted at removal.

15. Torque the supercharger retainer bolts to 17 ft. lbs. (23 Nm).

16. Install the remaining components in the reverse order of the removal process.

Radiator

REMOVAL & INSTALLATION

▶ **See Figures 56 thru 66**

The radiator removal procedure is similar among all of the GM W-Body vehicles. A variety of bolts, nuts, clips and fasteners are used. The following procedure should suffice for all W-Body vehicles.

✳✳ CAUTION

Use care when working underhood around the cooling fans. The fans are controlled by the Powertrain Control Module (PCM) to come on at a certain temperature, even with the engine turned off. Always disconnect the negative battery cable to prevent the fans from starting without warning.

1. Disconnect the negative battery cable.
2. Drain the coolant from the radiator.

✳✳ CAUTION

Never open, service or drain the radiator or cooling system when hot; serious burns can occur from the steam and hot coolant. Also, when draining engine coolant, keep in mind

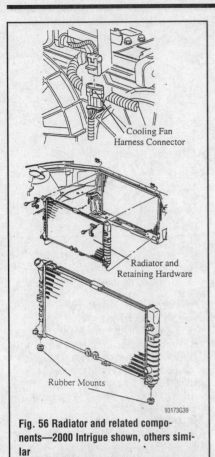

Fig. 56 Radiator and related components—2000 Intrigue shown, others similar

that cats and dogs are attracted to ethylene glycol antifreeze and could drink any that is left in an uncovered container or in puddles on the ground. This will prove fatal in sufficient quantities. Always drain coolant into a sealable container. Coolant should be reused unless it is contaminated or is several years old.

3. Remove the engine mount strut. Some technicians will disconnect just one and swing the strut out of the way. In this case, loosen the through bolts to prevent shearing the rubber bushings when the strut is moved out of the way for radiator removal. In some cases, it is best to remove the strut and its mounting bracket completely.

4. Separate the cooling fan harness connector from the engine harness.
5. Separate the low coolant level module harness connector at the module.
6. Disconnect the radiator hoses.
7. Remove the cooling fan assembly from the vehicle, as outlined in this section.
8. Disconnect the automatic transaxle cooling lines from the radiator
9. There should be two small retaining brackets at both ends of the radiator that are removed.
10. Carefully lift the radiator up and out of the vehicle. Note that the bottom should have locating pins on each end which should fit into grommet-like rubber mounts at installation.

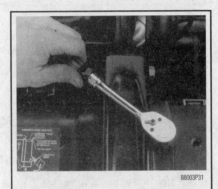

Fig. 57 Unfasten the engine strut brace bolts . . .

Fig. 58 . . . then swing the strut and brace out of the way

Fig. 59 Remove the upper panel mounting bolts and other retainers

Fig. 60 Unfasten the fan electrical connector

Fig. 61 Remove the electric cooling fan assemblies

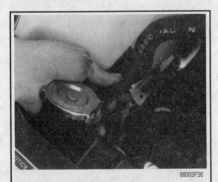

Fig. 62 Disconnect the upper, then the lower radiator hoses

Fig. 63 Detach the transaxle cooler lines from the radiator

Fig. 64 Unfasten the radiator mounting bolts

Fig. 65 If necessary, remove the radiator shroud . . .

Fig. 66 . . . then remove the radiator from the vehicle

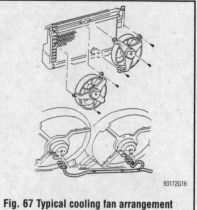

Fig. 67 Typical cooling fan arrangement

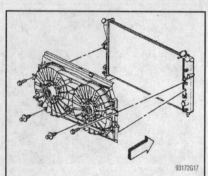

Fig. 68 Some cooling fans are removed along with the shroud assembly—3.4L (VIN E) engine shown

To install:

11. Use care when handling the radiator. It is constructed of aluminum and should be handled carefully. Install the radiator, making sure that the lower locating pins on each end fit into the grommet-like rubber mounts.

12. Connect the transaxle cooling lines to the radiator.

13. Assemble both the cooling fan harness connector and the low coolant level module harness connectors.

14. Install the remaining components in the reverse order of the removal process. When refilling the cooling system, use the proper mix of DEX-COOL® and water. Check for leaks.

Electric Cooling Fans

☀☀ CAUTION

An electric fan under the hood can start up even when the engine is not running and can injure you. Keep hands, clothing and tools away from any underhood electric fans. To help avoid personal injury or damage to the vehicle, a bent, cracked, or damaged fan blade or housing should always be replaced.

All vehicles use two fans to aid airflow through the radiator and air conditioning condenser. Each fan is driven by an electric motor and is attached to the radiator. Motor size varies with engine option.

The fan motors are activated by a coolant temperature switch, or, in the latest models, by the

Powertrain Control Module (PCM). The fans are activated through a relay, when coolant temperature reaches about 230°F (110°C). A transducer can also activate the circuit, depending upon A/C request or A/C compressor head pressure to the condenser.

The engine cooling fan relays provide the high current required for the cooling fan motors using a low current signal coming from the PCM. This signal is a function of various inputs.

REMOVAL & INSTALLATION

Except 3.4L (VIN E) and 3.5L Engines

▶ See Figures 67 and 68

➡**Some applications require the fans to be removed with the shroud assembly**

1. Before replacing a fan motor assembly due to noise or vibration complaints, check for dirt or mud buildup on the fan blades. Clean as required.

2. Record any radio anti-theft codes, as applicable. Disconnect the negative battery cable.

3. Remove the air cleaner assembly and duct as required for access.

4. Disconnect the wiring harness from the fan motors and the clips.

5. Remove the fan mounting bolts.

6. Remove the fans.

To install:

7. Install the fan assembly(s) to the vehicle. Install the mounting bolts and tighten to 53 inch lbs. (6 Nm).

8. Connect the wiring harness to the fan motors and the clips.

9. Install the air clean and duct assembly, as required.

10. Connect the negative battery cable.

3.4L (VIN E) Engine

1. Disconnect the negative battery cable.

2. With the engine cool, partially drain the cooling system.

➡**The engine struts must be rotated. To prevent shearing of the rubber bushings, loosen the bolts on the engine struts before swinging the struts.**

3. Remove the engine strut brace bolts from the upper tie bar and rotate the struts and the braces rearward.

4. Carefully disconnect the throttle body air

inlet and adjust the air cleaner assembly for access.

5. Disconnect the radiator inlet hose from the radiator.

6. Disengage the cooling fan shroud retainers, and remove the shroud bolts.

7. Disconnect the transmission oil cooler lines from the retainers at the bottom of the shroud. Disengage the shroud clip from the top of the radiator.

8. Reposition the cooling fan shroud for access and detach the electrical connector.

9. Remove the fan shroud with the electric cooling fans as an assembly.

To install:

10. Attach the cooling fan electrical connector.

11. Install the cooling fan and shroud assembly. Engage the shroud clip at the top of the radiator. Some pressure is needed to completely engage the clip onto the radiator.

12. Connect the transaxle cooler lines to the retainers at the bottom of the fan shroud.

13. Install the shroud bolts and torque to 80 inch lbs. (9 Nm). Install the shroud retainers.

14. Connect the radiator hose to the radiator.

15. Install the air cleaner assembly and air inlet ducts, as required.

16. Rotate the struts and braces forward to their proper position and install the engine strut brace bolts to the upper tie bar.

17. Refill the cooling system with the proper mix of DEX-COOL® and water. Please see Section 1 for more information.

18. Connect the negative battery cable.

3.5L (VIN H) Engine

1. Obtain anti-theft radio codes, as required. Disconnect the negative battery cable.

2. Remove the engine mount strut from the engine mount strut bracket at the upper radiator support. Remove the four bolts from the strut bracket and remove the bracket from the radiator support.

3. Disconnect the cooling fan wiring harness from the engine wiring harness.

4. Remove the cooling fan shroud bolts.

5. Remove the right side radiator bracket.

6. Remove the cooling fan shroud with the electric cooling fan motors.

To install:

7. Install the cooling fan shroud with the electric cooling fan motors to the radiator.

8. Install the right side radiator bracket and tighten the bolt to 80 inch lbs. (9 Nm). Tighten the shroud bolts to 53 inch. lbs. (6 Nm).

9. Connect the cooling fan wiring harness to the engine wiring harness.

10. Install the engine mount strut bracket to the upper radiator support, using care to correctly align the holes. Install the four bolts and tighten to 21 ft. lbs. (28 Nm). Install the strut to the bracket, and insert the through bolt. Tighten the nut to 35 ft. lbs. (48 Nm).

11. Connect the negative battery cable.

Water Pump

REMOVAL & INSTALLATION

3.1L and 3.4L (VIN E) Engines

▶ See Figure 69

1. Disconnect the negative battery cable.
2. Partially drain the cooling system into a suitable container.
3. Remove the drive belt guard.
4. Loosen the water pump pulley bolts before removing the drive belt. This should help keep the pulley from turning as the bolts are loosened.
5. Remove the drive belt. Please see Section 1.
6. Remove the water pump pulley bolts and remove the pulley.
7. Remove the water pump bolts and separate the pump from the engine front cover.

To install:

8. Clean all parts well. Use care when scraping gasket material from the front cover and the pump. Do not gouge aluminum parts. Clean the bolt threads well. The torque specification is low and if the bolt threads are dirty, an accurate torque is not possible and leaks are likely to develop.
9. Using a new gasket, install the water pump to the front cover. Install the cleaned and lightly lubricated water pump bolts. Torque to 89 inch lbs. (10 Nm).
10. Install the water pump pulley and bolts and torque to 18 ft. lbs. (25 Nm).
11. Install the remaining components in the reverse order of the removal process. When refilling the cooling system, use the proper mix of DEX-COOL®and water. Check for leaks.

3.4L (VIN X) Engine

▶ See Figure 70

1. Disconnect the negative battery cable.
2. Partially drain the cooling system into a suitable container.

3. Remove the coolant recovery reservoir.
4. Remove the drive belt. Please see Section 1.
5. Remove the pulley bolts and separate the pulley from the water pump.
6. Remove the water pump bolts and remove the pump from the engine.

To install:

7. Clean all parts well. Use care when scraping gasket material from the front cover and the pump. Do not gouge aluminum parts. Clean the bolt threads well. The torque specification is low and if the bolt threads are dirty, an accurate torque is not possible and leaks are likely to develop.
8. Using a new gasket, install the water pump to the front cover. Install the cleaned and lightly lubricated water pump bolts. Torque to 89 inch lbs. (10 Nm).
9. Install the water pump pulley and bolts and finger-tighten the bolts.
10. Install the drive belt, then torque the pulley bolts to 18 ft. lbs. (25 Nm).
11. Install the remaining components in the reverse order of the removal process. When refilling the cooling system, use the proper mix of DEX-COOL®and water. Check for leaks.

3.5L Engine

▶ See Figure 71

1. Disconnect the negative battery cable.
2. Partially drain the cooling system into a suitable container.
3. Loosen the water pump pulley bolts before removing the drive belt. This should help keep the pulley from turning as the bolts are loosened.
4. Remove the drive belt. Please see Section 1.
5. Remove the idler pulley bolt and remove the idler pulley.
6. Remove the water pump pulley bolts and remove the pulley.
7. Remove the water pump bolts and separate the pump from the engine. Note that bolt lengths vary. There are long and short bolts. Use care to note the length of bolts as they are removed and the location from which they were removed so they can be returned to their proper locations. Discard the gasket.

To install:

8. Clean all parts well. Use care when scraping gasket material from the front cover and the pump. Do not gouge aluminum parts. Clean the bolt threads well. The torque specification is low and if the bolt threads are dirty, an accurate torque is not possible and leaks are likely to develop.

9. Using a new gasket, install the water pump to the front cover. Install the cleaned and lightly lubricated water pump bolts, then torque to 124 inch lbs. (14 Nm).
10. Install the water pump pulley and bolts and finger-tighten the bolts.
11. Install the idler pulley and bolt. Tighten the idler pulley bolt to 37 ft. lbs. (50 Nm).
12. Install the drive belt, then, with the drive belt holding the pulley from turning, torque the water pump pulley bolts to 18 ft. lbs. (25 Nm).
13. Install the remaining components in the reverse order of the removal process. When refilling the cooling system, use the proper mix of DEX-COOL®and water. Check for leaks.

3.8L Engines

▶ See Figure 72

1. Disconnect the negative battery cable.
2. Loosen the retainers on the underhood electrical center and reposition out of the way.
3. Partially drain the cooling system into a suitable container.
4. Loosen the water pump pulley bolts before removing the drive belt. This should help keep the pulley from turning as the bolts are loosened.
5. Remove the drive belt. Please see Section 1.
6. Remove the power steering pumps and reposition the pump out of the way. Do not disconnect the fluid lines.
7. Remove the water pump bolts and separate the pump from the engine. Note that bolt lengths vary. Use care to note the length of bolts as they are removed and the location from which they were

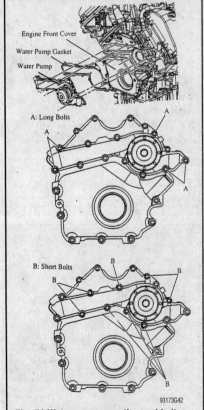

A: Long Bolts

B: Short Bolts

Fig. 71 Water pump mounting and bolt locations—3.5L (VIN H) Engine

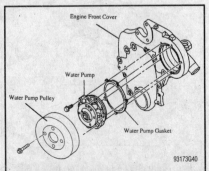

Fig. 69 Exploded view of the water pump and front cover arrangement—3.1L and 3.4L (VIN E) engines

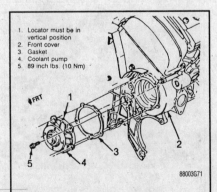

1. Locator must be in vertical position
2. Front cover
3. Gasket
4. Coolant pump
5. 89 inch lbs. (10 Nm)

Fig. 70 Exploded view of the water pump mounting—3.4L (VIN X) engine

removed so they can be returned to their proper locations.

To install:

8. Clean all parts well. Use care when scraping gasket material from the front cover and the pump. Do not gouge aluminum parts. Clean the bolt threads well. These bolts are called 'torque to yield' which means they are tightened to a specific torque, then turned an additional number of degrees. GM recommends a torque angle meter be used for final bolt torque.

9. Using a new gasket, install the water pump to the engine. Install the bolts, taking care to return the bolts to their original location. Tighten the long bolts to 15 ft. lbs. (20 Nm) plus an additional 40 degrees. Tighten the short bolts to 11 ft. lbs. (15 Nm) plus an additional 80 degrees.

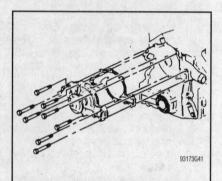

Fig. 72 Water pump mounting—3.8L engines

Fig. 73 Unfasten the cylinder head bolts, then remove the head

Fig. 74 Remove and discard the cylinder head gasket

10. Install the water pump pulley finger-tight, but do not final tighten the bolts yet.

11. Install the remaining components in the reverse order of the removal process. After the drive belt is in place, final tighten the pump pulley bolts to 115 inch lbs. (13 Nm).

12. Refill the cooling system, using the proper mix of DEX-COOL® and water. Check for leaks.

Cylinder Head

REMOVAL & INSTALLATION

3.1L and 3.4L (VIN E) Engines

▶ **See Figures 73, 74, 75 and 76**

Before removing a cylinder head, perform a compression test and/or leakdown test to verify is head removal is required.

➥**With some minor variations, this procedure can be used on both the left and right cylinder heads.**

1. Raise and safely support the vehicle.
2. Drain the engine coolant and the engine oil. Lower the vehicle.
3. Remove the upper and lower intake manifold using the procedures found in this section.
4. Remove the rocker arm and pushrods using the procedures found in this section.
5. Remove the exhaust crossover pipe.
6. Remove the engine mount strut bracket.
7. If removing the left side (front) head, remove the dipstick tube.
8. Tag for identification, then remove the spark plug wires. Remove the spark plugs. Please see
9. Remove the exhaust manifold using the procedures found in this section.
10. Remove the eight cylinder head bolts, then remove the cylinder head. There are locator pins that align the head to the block. Pull upwards on the head to disengage the pins, then remove the cylinder head to a suitable work area.
11. If the head is be overhauled, remove any remaining components such as the engine lift hook, the fuel line bracket bolts, the engine coolant temperature sensor, etc., as required.

To install:

➥**The cylinder head should be cleaned and inspected before installation. Please see the Engine Reconditioning section.**

Fig. 75 Use a suitable scraper to thoroughly clean the gasket mating surfaces

12. If the head gasket failed, determine the cause. Gasket failure is caused by the following conditions: improper installation; overheating due to a failure in the electric cooling fan system or a leak in the cooling system; loose or warped cylinder head; missing, off location or not fully seated locator dowel pins; low torque on the cylinder head bolts; warped block surface; scratched or gouged gasket surfaces; excessive intake manifold torque and even cracked engine block tapped holes.

13. Clean all parts well. Remove all foreign material to the bare metal. Do not use a motorized wire brush on any gasket sealing surface. It is good practice to use the proper size thread-cutting tap to clean the threaded bolt holes in the block. This helps assure an accurate torque reading.

14. Place a new head gasket on the clean engine block deck surface. Many gaskets will have some sort of marking denoting TOP or THIS SIDE UP. Make sure the gasket sits flat and is not hung up on the locator dowel pins. Use no sealer on the head gasket.

15. Carefully set the cylinder head in place, using care not to damage the gasket. Make certain that the head engages the locator dowel pins that properly position the head.

16. The bolts should be very clean since dirt built-up on the bolt threads makes it difficult to get an accurate torque reading. These are 'torque to yield' bolts which stretch a small amount when tightened; new bolts are always recommended. On a used vehicle, especially a high-mileage vehicle, it may be difficult to determine if the heads have been removed before and how many cycles the bolts have been removed and tightened. New bolts should be part of any cylinder head service. Use GM Sealer #1052080, or equivalent, on the threads of the head bolts and install all eight bolts, finger-tight.

17. With an accurate torque wrench, tighten the bolts gradually, in sequence, working from the center outwards. Final torque should be 33 ft. lbs. (45 Nm), plus an additional 90 degrees (1/4-turn). A torque angle meter is recommended.

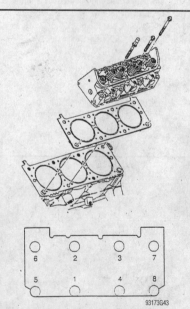

Fig. 76 Position a new gasket, install the head, then tighten the bolts in the sequence shown—3.1L engine shown, 3.4L (VIN E) similar

18. Install the remaining components in the reverse order of the removal process.

3.4L (VIN X) Engine

⚠️ **WARNING**

As with many procedures on the 3.4L (VIN X) DOHC engine, cylinder head removal is a long and complicated task. Be very sure of your diagnosis before attempting to remove the heads on this engine, especially with the engine still in the vehicle. A compression test and/or leakdown test should be performed. A pair of special tools, GM #J 38613-A Camshaft Timing Clamps, is required to hold the camshafts in place once the timing belt is removed and the head bolts loosened. Remember, the valve timing must be reset if the camshaft drive sprockets are removed from their camshafts. Once lost, there are no pins or keys to help you re-establish valve timing. In addition, use care when working with light alloy parts.

LEFT SIDE (FRONT)

▶ See Figure 77

1. Remove the upper and lower intake manifolds, following the procedures given in this section.
2. Remove the left camshaft carrier using the following procedure.
   a. Remove the camshaft timing belt following the procedures given in this section.
   b. Disconnect the exhaust crossover pipe and reposition out of the way.
   c. Remove the engine mount strut.
   d. Remove the front engine lift bracket.
   e. The camshaft carrier covers should have been removed as part of the timing belt removal procedure. From shop stock, cut and install six pieces of rubber hose under the camshaft and between the lifters to hold the lifters in the carrier. The exhaust side uses six pieces of tubing 3/16 x 6 inches long. The intake side uses six pieces of tubing 5/32 x 6 inches long.

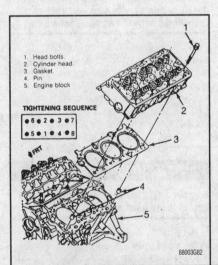

1. Head bolts.
2. Cylinder head.
3. Gasket.
4. Pin.
5. Engine block

TIGHTENING SEQUENCE

Fig. 77 Cylinder head bolt tightening sequence—3.4L (VIN X) engine

88003G82

   f. Remove the camshaft carrier mounting bolts and remove the camshaft carrier. Set aside in a safe place. Discard the gasket.
3. Remove the left side exhaust manifold following the procedures given in this section.
4. Remove the dipstick tube.
5. Detach the electrical connector from the temperature sending unit.
6. Remove the cylinder head bolts and carefully lift the head from the vehicle.

To install:

➡ **The cylinder head should be cleaned and inspected before installation. Please see the Engine Reconditioning section.**

7. Clean all parts well. Use care when working with light alloy parts not to gouge or scratch the gasket sealing surfaces. Clean the head bolts well. New replacement bolts are recommended. Clean the cylinder block bolt threads. Make sure all of the oil is removed from the bolt holes.
8. Carefully lay a new gasket on the engine block deck. Some brands of gaskets may say TOP or have some other marking indicating the surface that should face the cylinder head. Make sure the gasket sits flat on the block deck.
9. Carefully install the cylinder head to the block. Align any dowel pins or other locators. Install the head bolts and finger-tighten. Tighten gradually and in sequence, working up to 44 ft. lbs. (60 Nm). After achieving final torque, use a torque angle meter to turn the bolts an additional 90 degrees (¼ turn).
10. Connect the temperature sensor wire and install the dipstick tube.
11. Install the left exhaust manifold following the procedures given in this section.
12. Install the left camshaft carrier using the following procedure:
   a. Remove the oil from the camshaft carrier to cylinder head bolts, the holes closest to the exhaust manifold.
   b. Install a new camshaft carrier gasket.

⚠️ **WARNING**

Remove the oil from the camshaft hold-down tool hole in the carrier before installing and tightening the bolt.

   c. Install J 38613-A or equivalent camshaft hold-down tool. Tighten the bolt to 22 ft. lbs. (30 Nm).

➡ **The use of petroleum jelly (never chassis grease) in the lifter bores, along with the use of the lifter hold-down hoses mentioned above, will help keep the lifters in place.**

   d. Install the camshaft carrier to the cylinder head and position the hold-down bolts.
   e. Tighten the camshaft carrier bolts to 20 ft. lbs. (27 Nm).
   f. Remove the lifter hold-down hoses. Install the front engine lift bracket.
13. Install the lower and upper intake manifold following the procedures given in this section.
14. Install the remaining components in the reverse order of the removal process. Since coolant will run down into the engine oil system when the head is removed, it is most important to drain the engine oil and refill with clean engine oil. A filter change is also recommended.

RIGHT SIDE (REAR)

▶ See Figure 77

1. Remove the upper and lower intake manifolds following the procedures given in this section.
2. Remove the right camshaft carrier using the following procedure.
   a. Remove the camshaft timing belt following the procedures given in this section.
   b. The camshaft carrier covers should have been removed as part of the timing belt removal procedure. From shop stock, cut and install six pieces of rubber hose under the camshaft and between the lifters to hold the lifters in the carrier. The exhaust side uses six pieces of tubing 3/16 x 6 inches long. The intake side uses six pieces of tubing 5/32 x 6 inches long.
   c. Remove the camshaft carrier mounting bolts and remove the camshaft carrier. Set aside in a safe place. Discard the gasket.
3. Remove the exhaust crossover pipe.
4. Raise and suitably support the vehicle.
5. Disconnect the front exhaust pipe at the manifold.
6. Lower the vehicle.
7. Detach the electrical connector from the oxygen sensor.
8. Remove the rear timing belt tensioner actuator using the following procedure
   a. Remove the timing belt tensioner actuator pulley.
   b. Remove the timing belt tensioner mounting bracket bolts. Do this by aligning the tool to the socket in the bolt head.
   c. Remove the timing belt tensioner mounting bracket. Use care as there is a mounting base gasket. Reattach the gasket to the mounting bracket is the gasket is loose.
9. Remove the cylinder head bolts and carefully lift the head along with the exhaust manifold from the vehicle. Discard the gasket.

To install:

➡ **The cylinder head should be cleaned and inspected before installation. Please see the Engine Reconditioning section.**

10. Clean all parts well. Use care when working with light alloy parts not to gouge or scratch the gasket sealing surfaces. Clean the head bolts well. New replacement bolts are recommended. Clean the cylinder block bolt threads. Make sure all of the oil is removed from the bolt holes.
11. Carefully lay a new gasket on the engine block deck. Some brands of gaskets may say TOP or have some other marking indicating the surface that should face the cylinder head. Make sure the gasket sits flat on the block deck.
12. Carefully install the cylinder head to the block. Align any dowel pins or other locators. Install the head bolts and finger-tighten. Tighten gradually and in sequence, working up to 44 ft. lbs. (60 Nm). After achieving final torque, use a torque angle meter to turn the bolts an additional 90 degrees (¼ turn).
13. Install the timing belt tensioner making sure the gasket is in place. Tighten the bolts to 37 ft. lbs. (50 Nm). Install the timing belt tensioner pulley.
14. Connect the oxygen sensor wire.
15. Raise and safely support the vehicle.
16. Install the front exhaust pipe to the rear manifold. Lower the vehicle.
17. Install the exhaust crossover pipe.

18. Install the right camshaft carrier using the following procedure.

a. Make sure that the pieces of rubber tubing are in place under the camshaft and in between the lifter to hold the lifters in carrier.

b. Remove the oil from the camshaft carrier-to-cylinder head bolts.

c. Install a new camshaft carrier gasket.

✳✳ WARNING

Remove the oil from the camshaft hold-down tool hole in the carrier before installing and tightening the bolt.

d. Install J 38613-A or equivalent camshaft hold-down tool. Tighten the bolt to 22 ft. lbs. (30 Nm).

➡**The use of petroleum jelly (never chassis grease) in the lifter bores, along with the use of the lifter hold-down hoses mentioned above, will help keep the lifters in place.**

e. Install the camshaft carrier to the cylinder head and position the hold-down bolts.

f. Tighten the camshaft carrier bolts to 20 ft. lbs. (27 Nm).

g. Remove the lifter hold-down hoses.

19. Install the lower and upper intake manifold following the procedures given in this section.

20. Install the remaining components in the reverse order of the removal process. Since coolant will run down into the engine oil system when the head is removed, it is most important to drain the engine oil and refill with clean engine oil. A filter change is also recommended.

3.5L Engine

LEFT SIDE (FRONT)

▶ See Figure 78

✳✳ WARNING

As with many procedures on the 3.5L (VIN H) DOHC engine, cylinder head removal is a long and complicated task. Be very sure of your diagnosis before attempting to remove the heads on this engine, especially with the engine still in the vehicle. A compression test and/or leakdown test should be performed. A pair of special tools, GM #J 42042 Camshaft Timing Clamps, is required to hold the camshafts in place once the timing chain is removed and the head bolts loosened. This tool, when properly installed, will be fully seated on the camshaft ends with the camshaft flats parallel to the cam cover sealing surfaces. This tool prevents unexpected camshaft rotation caused by valve spring pressure. This tool must be installed immediately after cam cover removal. Remember, the valve timing must be reset if the camshaft drive sprockets are removed from their camshafts. Once lost, there are no pins or keys to help you re-establish valve timing. In addition, GM specifies that new service replacement head bolts must be used. Do not reuse the head bolts. Procure the necessary parts before beginning this procedure.

➡**This engine is constructed primarily of aluminum. Use care when working with light alloy parts.**

1. Disconnect the negative battery cable.

2. Drain the coolant and the engine oil into suitable containers.

3. Remove the upper and lower intake manifolds using the procedures found in this section.

4. Remove the water outlet housing (thermostat housing). Adjust the water crossover pipe for access.

5. Remove the engine mount strut bracket.

6. Remove the left side (front) exhaust manifold using the procedures found in this section.

7. Remove both camshaft covers using the procedures found in this section.

8. Install special tool J 42038, or equivalent on the camshafts. There should be two flat portions on the camshafts. The tool fits down on these flats to keep valve spring pressure from rotating the camshafts. Proceed no further if you do not have this tool or its functional equivalent.

9. Remove the primary camshaft drive chain using the procedures found in this section.

10. Remove the left side (front) cylinder head camshafts using the procedures found in this section.

➡**Place the valve train parts in a rack in the order in which they are being removed so that they can be installed in the same location from which they were removed.**

11. Remove the valve rocker arms and lifters.

➡**The head bolts are different sizes. While the head bolts must not be reused, it is good practice to note the location of each removed bolt so its correct replacement can be installed. Some technicians will place a replacement head gasket on a clean piece of cardboard and trace out the head bolt holes. The head bolts are punched through the cardboard in their corresponding locations as they are removed.**

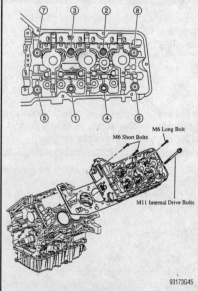

93173G45

Fig. 78 Left side (front) cylinder head, gasket and bolt torque sequence—3.5L (VIN H) engine

In this way, the replacement bolts can be compared to the originals and the new replacement bolts eventually installed in their correct locations.

12. Remove the head bolts observing the following:

a. Remove the M6 external drive bolts from the front portion of the cylinder head. Note the location of the longer M6 bolt.

b. Remove and discard the M11 internal drive head bolts. DO NOT reuse the cylinder head bolts.

13. Remove the cylinder head. Make sure the locating dowel guide pins are not pulled from the engine block and stuck in the head. Place the head on a flat, clean surface with the combustion chambers face-up to prevent damage to the deck face. Discard the gasket.

To install:

➡**The cylinder head should be cleaned and inspected before installation. Please see the Engine Reconditioning section.**

14. Clean all parts well. The heads are aluminum. Use care not to gouge or scratch the gasket sealing surfaces. It is good practice to clean the head bolt threaded holes in the engine block. This cleans out old sealer, rust and other debris which could interfere with getting an accurate torque reading. Use the correct size thread cutting tap, but use care since the engine block is also aluminum. Make sure all of the oil is removed from the bolt holes.

✳✳ WARNING

This engine uses special torque to yield head bolts. This design bolt requires a special tightening procedure. Failure to follow the given procedure will cause head gasket failure and possible engine damage. The head bolts used on this engine are designed to permanently stretch when tightened. The correct part number fastener must be used to replace this type of fastener. Do not use a bolt which is stronger in this application. If the correct bolt is not used, the parts will not be tightened correctly. The components may be damaged. In addition, the factory specifies new service replacement head bolts of the correct part number be used.

15. Carefully lay a new head gasket on the engine block deck. Verify that the arrow or whatever marking is used on the gasket indicating which side is up and/or forward, is correctly aligned. Make sure the gasket sits flat on the block deck, not hung up on the alignment dowels. The alignment dowels (locating pins) should hold the gasket in place. Check that all the bolt holes and water passages line up correctly. Use no sealer on head gaskets.

✳✳ WARNING

A torque angle meter must be used to tighten these head bolts.

16. Carefully install the cylinder head to the block. Align the dowel pins. Install the new head bolts and finger-tighten. The M11 bolts MUST NOT be reused. Tighten gradually, in the proper sequence, in the following steps.

a. Using a torque angle meter, tighten the

M11 bolts in sequence to 22 ft. lbs. (30 Nm) plus 60 degrees.

b. Repeat the sequence turning each bolt an additional 60 degrees.

c. Repeat the sequence again, turning each bolt an additional 60 degrees (total 180 degrees).

d. Tighten the long M6 bolt to 22 ft. lbs. (30 Nm).

e. Tighten the two short M6 bolts to 106 inch lbs. (12 Nm).

17. Install the lifters and the rocker arms.

18. Install the camshafts using the procedures found in this section.

19. Install the primary camshaft drive using the procedures found in this section.

20. Remove tool J 42038, or equivalent, from the camshafts.

21. Install the camshaft covers.

22. Install the remaining components in the reverse order of the removal process. Since coolant will run down into the engine oil system when the head is removed, it is most important to drain the engine oil and refill with clean engine oil. A filter change is also recommended.

RIGHT SIDE (REAR)

♦ See Figure 79

✳✳ WARNING

As with many procedures on the 3.5L (VIN H) DOHC engine, cylinder head removal is a long and complicated task. Be very sure of your diagnosis before attempting to remove the heads on this engine, especially with the engine still in the vehicle. A compression test and/or leakdown test should be performed. A pair of special tools, GM #J 42042 Camshaft Timing Clamps, is required to hold the camshafts in place once the timing chain is removed and the head bolts

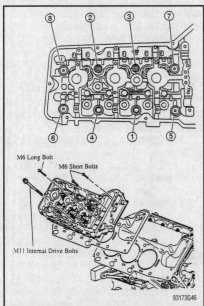

Fig. 79 Right side (rear) cylinder head, gasket and bolt torque sequence—3.5L (VIN H) engine

loosened. This tool, when properly installed, will be fully seated on the camshaft ends with the camshaft flats parallel to the cam cover sealing surfaces. This tool prevents unexpected camshaft rotation caused by valve spring pressure. This tool must be installed immediately after cam cover removal. Remember, the valve timing must be reset if the camshaft drive sprockets are removed from their camshafts. Once lost, there are no pins or keys to help you re-establish valve timing. In addition, GM specifies that new service replacement head bolts must be used. Do not reuse the head bolts. Procure the necessary parts before beginning this procedure.

➡**This engine is constructed primarily of aluminum. Use care when working with light alloy parts.**

1. Disconnect the negative battery cable.
2. Drain the coolant and the engine oil.
3. Remove the upper and lower intake manifolds using the procedures found in this section.

✳✳ WARNING

DO NOT remove the right side (rear) exhaust manifold from the cylinder head.

4. Remove the water outlet housing (thermostat housing). Adjust the water crossover pipe for access.

5. Remove both camshaft covers using the procedures found in this section.

6. Install tool J 42038 on the camshafts. There should be two flat portions on the camshafts. The tool fits down on these flats to keep valve spring pressure from rotating the camshafts. Proceed no further if you do not have this tool or its functional equivalent.

7. Remove the primary camshaft drive chain using the procedures found in this section.

8. Remove the right side (rear) cylinder head camshafts using the procedures found in this section.

➡**Place the valve train parts in a rack in the order in which they are being removed that that they can be installed in the same location from which they were removed.**

9. Remove the valve rocker arms and lifters.

10. Remove the coolant temperature sensor from the right side (rear) cylinder head.

➡**The head bolts are different sizes. While the head bolts must not be reused, it is good practice to note the location of each removed bolt so its correct replacement can be installed. Some technicians will place a replacement head gasket on a clean piece of cardboard and trace out the head bolt holes. The head bolts are punched through the cardboard in their corresponding locations as they are removed. In this way, the replacement bolts can be compared to the originals and the new replacement bolts eventually installed in their correct locations.**

11. Remove the head bolts observing the following.

a. Remove the M6 external drive bolts from

the front portion of the cylinder head. Note the location of the longer M6 bolt.

b. Remove and discard the M11 internal drive head bolts. DO NOT reuse the cylinder head bolts.

12. Remove the cylinder head. Make sure the locating dowel guide pins are not pulled from the engine block and stuck in the head. Place the head on a flat, clean surface with the combustion chambers face-up to prevent damage to the deck face. Discard the gasket.

To install:

➡**The cylinder head should be cleaned and inspected before installation. Please see the Engine Reconditioning section.**

13. Clean all parts well. The heads are aluminum. Use care not to gouge or scratch the gasket sealing surfaces. It is good practice to clean the head bolt threaded holes in the engine block. This cleans out old sealer, rust and other debris which could interfere with getting an accurate torque reading. Use the correct size thread cutting tap, but use care since the engine block is also aluminum. Make sure all of the oil is removed from the bolt holes.

✳✳ WARNING

This engine uses special torque to yield head bolts. This design bolt requires a special tightening procedure. Failure to follow the given procedure will cause head gasket failure and possible engine damage. The head bolts used on this engine are designed to permanently stretch when tightened. The correct part number fastener must be used to replace this type of fastener. Do not use a bolt which is stronger in this application. If the correct bolt is not used, the parts will not be tightened correctly. The components may be damaged. In addition, the factory specifies new service replacement head bolts of the correct part number be used.

14. Carefully lay a new head gasket on the engine block deck. Verify that the arrow or whatever marking is used on the gasket indicating which side is up and/or forward, is correctly aligned. Make sure the gasket sits flat on the block deck, not hung up on the alignment dowels. The alignment dowels (locating pins) should hold the gasket in place. Check that all the bolt holes and water passages line up correctly. Use no sealer on head gaskets.

✳✳ WARNING

A torque angle meter must be used to tighten these head bolts.

15. Carefully install the cylinder head to the block. Align the dowel pins. Install the new head bolts and finger-tighten. The M11 bolts MUST NOT be reused. Tighten gradually and in the following sequence.

a. Using a torque angle meter, tighten the M11 bolts in sequence to 22 ft. lbs. (30 Nm) plus 60 degrees.

b. Repeat the sequence turning each bolt an additional 60 degrees.

c. Repeat the sequence again, turning each bolt an additional 60 degrees (total 180 degrees).

d. Tighten the long M6 bolt to 22 ft. lbs. (30 Nm).

e. Tighten the two short M6 bolts to 106 inch lbs. (12 Nm).

16. Install the coolant temperature sensor into the cylinder head.

17. Install the lifters and rocker arms using the procedures found in this section.

18. Install the right side (rear) camshaft using the procedures found in this section.

19. Install the primary camshaft drive using the procedures found in this section.

20. Remove tool J 42038, or equivalent, from the camshafts.

21. Install the camshaft covers.

22. Install the remaining components in the reverse order of the removal process. Since coolant will run down into the engine oil system when the head is removed, it is most important to drain the engine oil and refill with clean engine oil. A filter change is also recommended.

3.8L Engines

LEFT SIDE (FRONT)

▶ See Figure 80

1. Disconnect the negative battery cable.

2. Drain the coolant and the engine oil into suitable containers.

3. Remove the cosmetic/acoustic engine cover.

4. Remove the air cleaner duct.

5. Remove the right engine mount strut.

6. Remove the upper and lower intake manifolds, using the procedures found in this section.

7. Remove the left side (front) rocker arms and pushrods.

8. Remove the cylinder head bolts and lift the cylinder head from the engine. Discard the gasket.

To install:

➡The cylinder head should be cleaned and inspected before installation. Please see the Engine Reconditioning section.

9. Clean all parts well. Use care not to gouge or scratch the gasket sealing surfaces. It is good practice to clean the head bolt threaded holes in the engine block. This cleans out old sealer, rust and other debris which could interfere with getting an accurate torque reading. Use the correct size thread cutting tap. Most 3.8L engines will require a 7/16-14 tap. Make sure all of the oil is removed from the bolt holes.

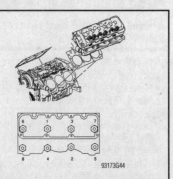

Fig. 80 Cylinder head and gasket arrangement and bolt tightening sequence—3.8L engines

93173G44

This engine uses special torque to yield head bolts. This design bolt requires a special tightening procedure. Failure to follow the given procedure will cause head gasket failure and possible engine damage. The head bolts used on this engine are designed to permanently stretch when tightened. The correct part number fastener must be used to replace this type of fastener. Do not use a bolt which is stronger in this application. If the correct bolt is not used, the parts will not be tightened correctly. The components may be damaged. In addition, the factory recommends new service replacement head bolts of the correct part number be used.

➡The head gaskets on the 3.8L engine are not interchangeable. The head gasket must be installed with the arrow (or noting any other mark, depending on the gasket manufacturer) pointing to the front of the engine. Installing the gasket in any other direction will cause gasket failure and possible engine failure.

10. Carefully lay a new head gasket on the engine block deck. Verify that the arrow or whatever marking is used on the gasket indicating which side is up and/or forward, is correctly aligned. Make sure the gasket sits flat on the block deck, not hung up on the alignment dowels. Check that all the bolt holes and water passages line up correctly. Use no sealer on head gaskets.

11. Carefully install the cylinder head to the block. Align any dowel pins or other locators. Install the head bolts and finger-tighten. Tighten gradually in the following sequence:

a. Tighten the bolts in sequence to 37 ft. lbs. (50 Nm).

b. Using a torque angle meter, rotate each bolt an additional 130 degrees, in sequence.

c. Rotate the center four bolts an additional 30 degrees, in sequence.

12. Install the pushrods and rocker arms using the procedures found in this section.

13. Install the lower and upper intake manifold following the procedures given in this section.

14. Install the remaining components in the reverse order of the removal process. Since coolant will run down into the engine oil system when the head is removed, it is most important to drain the engine oil and refill with clean engine oil. A filter change is recommended.

RIGHT SIDE (REAR)

▶ See Figure 80

1. Disconnect the negative battery cable.

2. Drain the coolant and the engine oil into suitable containers.

3. Remove the cosmetic/acoustic engine cover.

4. Remove the air cleaner duct.

5. Remove the accessory drive belt tensioner.

6. Remove the EGR valve.

7. Remove the upper and lower intake manifold using the procedures found in this section.

8. Remove the right side (rear) exhaust manifold using the procedures found in this section.

9. Remove the right side (rear) rocker arms and pushrods.

10. Remove the cylinder head bolts and lift the cylinder head from the engine. Discard the gasket.

To install:

➡The cylinder head should be cleaned and inspected before installation. Please see the Engine Reconditioning section.

11. Clean all parts well. Use care not to gouge or scratch the gasket sealing surfaces. It is good practice to clean the head bolt threaded holes in the engine block. This cleans out old sealer, rust and other debris which could interfere with getting an accurate torque reading. Use the correct size thread cutting tap. Most 3.8L engines will require a 7/16-14 tap. Make sure all of the oil is removed from the bolt holes.

This engine uses special torque to yield head bolts. This design bolt requires a special tightening procedure. Failure to follow the given procedure will cause head gasket failure and possible engine damage. The head bolts used on this engine are designed to permanently stretch when tightened. The correct part number fastener must be used to replace this type of fastener. Do not use a bolt which is stronger in this application. If the correct bolt is not used, the parts will not be tightened correctly. The components may be damaged. In addition, the factory recommends new service replacement head bolts of the correct part number be used.

➡The head gaskets on the 3.8L engine are not interchangeable. The head gasket must be installed with the arrow (or noting any other mark, depending on the gasket manufacturer) pointing to the front of the engine. Installing the gasket in any other direction will cause gasket failure and possible engine failure.

12. Carefully lay a new head gasket on the engine block deck. Verify that the arrow or whatever marking is used on the gasket indicating which side is up and/or forward, is correctly aligned. Make sure the gasket sits flat on the block deck, not hung up on the alignment dowels. Check that all the bolt holes and water passages line up correctly. Use no sealer on head gaskets.

13. Carefully install the cylinder head to the block. Align any dowel pins or other locators. Install the head bolts and finger-tighten. Tighten gradually and in the following sequence:

a. Tighten the bolts in sequence to 37 ft. lbs. (50 Nm).

b. Using a torque angle meter, rotate each bolt an additional 130 degrees, in sequence.

c. Rotate the center four bolts an additional 30 degrees, in sequence.

14. Install the pushrods and rocker arms using the procedures found in this section.

15. Install the lower and upper intake manifold using the procedures found in this section.

16. Install the remaining components in the reverse order of the removal process. Since coolant will run down into the engine oil system when the head is removed, it is most important to drain the engine oil and refill with clean engine oil. A filter change is also strongly recommended.

Oil Pan

REMOVAL & INSTALLATION

3.1L and 3.4L (VIN E) Engines

▶ See Figures 81, 82 and 83

❈❈ WARNING

A number of special tools are required for this procedure. The working clearance is very tight. The transaxle mounts are loosened so the engine can be repositioned.

Without the support of the transaxle mounts, the engine must be suspended from above in such a way the vehicle can still be raised for the undercar work. The factory engine support fixture has legs which extend across the engine compartment and rest on the shock towers with additional legs resting on the radiator support. Other engine support fixtures are similar in design. It may be possible to rent a similar device locally. Use care if using any type of substitute. Damage to the vehicle and/or personal injury is possible if the powertrain shifts or is dislodged from the vehicle.

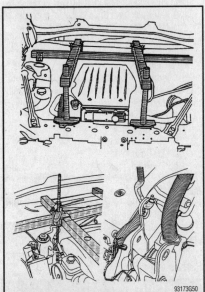

Fig. 81 An engine support fixture like this supports the engine so the mounts can be loosened for undercar engine work—typical for front wheel drive vehicles

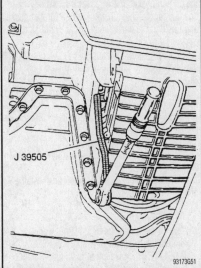

Fig. 82 This special wrench is recommended by GM for removing and installing the right side (rear) oil pan side bolts. A box wrench with a slight offset may also be used

1. Disconnect the negative battery cable.
2. Remove the hood.
3. Remove the engine mount struts from the engine.
4. Without disconnecting the refrigerant lines, remove the air conditioning compressor mounting bolts and set the compressor aside.
5. Remove the right engine mount strut bracket from the engine.
6. Install a suitable engine support fixture. Verify that the engine will be safely supported.
7. Raise and safely support the vehicle.
8. Disconnect the three-way catalytic converter pipe from the right side (rear) exhaust manifold.
9. Drain the engine oil into a suitable container.
10. Detach the oil level sensor wiring harness connector from the sensor in the oil pan.
11. Remove the starter motor. Please see Section 2.
12. Remove the transaxle brace from the oil pan.
13. Remove the lower transaxle mount nuts.
14. Remove the lower engine mount nuts.
15. Raise the engine using the adjustable hooks on the engine support fixture, to gain access for oil pan removal.
16. There are bolts that go through the side of the oil pan and thread into the main bearing caps. GM recommends their special tool J 39505 be used on the right side (rear) oil pan side bolts, to reach up in the narrow area between the engine oil pan and the transaxle case to remove these bolts. This special tool is also used at assembly so the bolts can be properly tightened. Use care is using a substitute wrench to remove the right side (rear) oil pan side bolts.
17. Remove the left side (front) oil pan side bolts.
18. Remove the oil pan side rail mounting bolts.
19. Remove the oil pan from the vehicle.

To install:

20. Clean all parts well. If the engine has high mileage, evaluate changing the oil pump at this time. Please see the procedure in this section. Make sure the oil pan gasket rails and the engine gasket sealing surfaces are clean.
21. Apply a small amount of sealer GM #1234579, or equivalent, on either side of the rear main bearing cap, where the seal surface on the cap meets the engine block. Press sealant into the gap with a putty knife.
22. Install the oil pan gasket, then position the oil pan to the engine. Hand-start a few side rail bolts. Install, then finger-tighten all side rail bolts. Then torque to 18 ft. lbs. (25 Nm).
23. Install the left side (front) oil pan side bolts. Torque to 37 ft. lbs. (50 Nm).
24. Install the right side (rear) oil pan side bolts, using special tool J 39505 or equivalent. Torque to 37 ft. lbs. (50 Nm).
25. Using the adjustable hooks on the engine support fixture, lower the engine enough so the lower transaxle mount nuts can be installed. Also install the lower engine mount nuts and the transaxle brace to the oil pan.
26. Install the remaining components in the reverse order of the removal process. Refill the engine with clean engine oil. A filter change is also recommended.

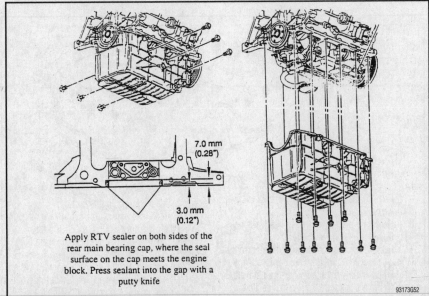

Apply RTV sealer on both sides of the rear main bearing cap, where the seal surface on the cap meets the engine block. Press sealant into the gap with a putty knife

Fig. 83 Engine oil pan bolt arrangement and main bearing cap sealing locations—3.1L and 3.4L (VIN E) engines

3.4L (VIN X) Engine

♦ See Figure 84

✳✳ WARNING

This is a complicated procedure. In this procedure, the subframe that supports the entire powertrain is loosened and removed so the engine oil pan can be removed. This is not a job for the inexperienced or ill-equipped. Be very sure that the oil pan really needs to be removed before attempting this procedure. Be very sure of the lifting and jacking equipment you have available before attempting this procedure or the vehicle could be damaged and you could be injured. Without the support of the subframe, the engine must be suspended from above in such a way the vehicle can still be raised for the undercar work. The factory engine support fixture has legs which extend across the engine compartment and rest on the shock towers with additional legs resting on the radiator support. Other engine support fixtures are similar in design. It may be possible to rent a similar device locally. Use care if using any type of substitute. Extensive and expensive damage to the vehicle and its major components and/or personal injury is possible if the powertrain drops from the vehicle. In addition, the factory specifies that whenever frame to body bolts are loosened or removed, they must be replaced with new bolts and retainers. Procure the bolts before beginning this procedure. Failure to replace frame-to-body bolts and retainers may result in damage to the frame, powertrain or suspension.

1. Disconnect the negative battery cable.
2. Remove the hood assembly.
3. Remove the air cleaner duct.
4. Drain the coolant and remove the coolant recovery reservoir.
5. Install the engine support fixture. Verify that the engine and transaxle assembly will be safely supported when the subframe is removed.
6. With the engine support fixture in place, raise and safely support the vehicle.
7. Remove both front wheels. Remove the splash shield.
8. Drain the engine oil into a suitable.
9. Remove the intermediate steering shaft lower pinch bolt and disengage the intermediate shaft from the rack and pinion steering gear assembly.
10. Remove the power steering rack and pinion steering gear retaining bolts. Without disconnecting the fluid lines, hang the steering gear on the body.
11. Remove the right and left lower ball joint nuts. Separate the lower ball joints from the control arms. Please see Section 8.
12. Remove the power steering cooler line clamps at the frame.
13. Remove the engine mount nuts at the subframe. Support the subframe.
14. Have an assistant hold the subframe or use a suitable lifting/jacking device to safely support the subframe while removing the body mount bolts. Remove the subframe retaining bolts. Discard the

bolts. They must be replaced with new bolts upon assembly. Carefully lower the subframe with both the lower control arms and the stabilizer shaft attached. Work the subframe downward toward the rear of the vehicle.
15. Remove the oil filter, the engine oil cooler and the oil level sensor.
16. Remove the flywheel cover and the starter motor. Please see Section 2.
17. Remove the oil pan retaining nuts and bolts. Remove the oil pan. Discard the gasket.

To install:

18. Clean all parts well. Make sure the oil pan gasket rails, the engine front cover, rear main bearing cap and the engine gasket sealing surfaces are clean. Clean all threaded holes.
19. Apply sealer GM #12345739 to the tabs of the oil pan gasket that insert next to the rear main bearing cap notches. Install the new oil pan gasket and position the pan to the engine. Hand start a few retaining bolts.
20. Install and finger-tighten the oil pan mounting nuts. Then torque the nuts to 97 inch lbs. (11 Nm).
21. Install and finger-tighten the oil pan mounting bolts. Then torque the rear bolts to 20 ft. lbs. (27 Nm). Torque the rest of the bolts to 97 inch lbs. (11 Nm).
22. Install the oil level sensor.
23. Install the starter motor and flywheel cover. Please see Section 2.
24. Install the engine oil cooler and install a new oil filter.
25. Install the subframe to the vehicle, observing the following:

a. If the rubber frame isolators were removed, lubricate with rubber lube GM #1051717 or equivalent at installation. Failure to lubricate may prevent proper seating of insulators in the frame. Make sure the insulators are completely sealed against the frame.

b. Using the lifting/jacking device and an assistant, raise the frame until it frame contacts the body. Install new replacement body bolts, but do not tighten yet, observing the following:

c. Alignment pins are required. Do not remove the alignment pins until all of the body mount bolts are torqued to specifications. The alignment pins must be kept perpendicular to the frame. The right side mounts (nearest the alignment pins) should be tightened first, to maintain correct front wheel alignment. Align the frame by inserting two 0.74 inch (19mm) diameter by 8.0 inch (200mm) long pins in the alignment holes on the right side of the frame.

d. Proper clamping by the mount depends on clean and dry surfaces. If the frame isolator bolt does not screw in smoothly, it may be necessary to run a tap through the cage nut in the body to remove foreign material. Take care that the tap does not punch through the underbody. If the cage nut cannot be used, the cage nut retainer spot welds will have to be chiseled away with air chisel, the cage nut replaced and the retainer welded back into its original location. Clean and prime the area with catalyzed primer to protect the area from corrosion.
26. Torque the four new frame isolator bolts to 133 ft. lbs. (180 Nm). Do not over-tighten the body mounts; a collapsed spacer or stripped bolt may result. Tighten in the following manner:

a. RH Rear, first
b. RH Front, second
c. LH Rear, third
d. LH Front, fourth
27. Install the engine mount nuts at the subframe.
28. Connect the three-way catalytic convert pipe to the exhaust manifold.
29. Install the power steering cooler line clamps at the frame.
30. Connect the ball joints to the control arms. Please see Section 8.

✳✳ CAUTION

When installing the intermediate shaft, make sure the shaft is seated prior to pinch bolt installation. If the pinch bolt is inserted into the coupling before shaft installation,

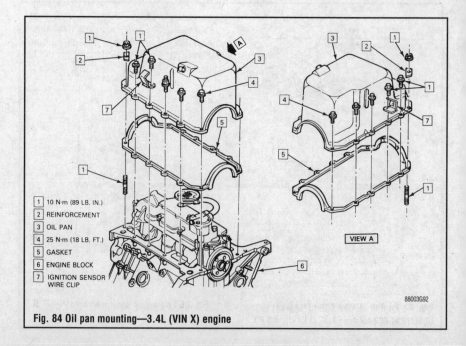

1	10 N·m (89 LB. IN.)
2	REINFORCEMENT
3	OIL PAN
4	25 N·m (18 LB. FT.)
5	GASKET
6	ENGINE BLOCK
7	IGNITION SENSOR WIRE CLIP

88003G92

Fig. 84 Oil pan mounting—3.4L (VIN X) engine

the two mating shafts may disengage, with a loss of steering.

31. Connect the intermediate steering shaft to the rack and pinion steering assembly stub shaft. Verify that the two shafts are properly coupled. Insert the pinch bolt and torque carefully to 35 ft. lbs. (47 Nm).

32. Install the power steering rack and pinion steering gear assembly on the steering gear mounts. Please see Section 8.

33. Install the right side engine splash shield and both front wheels.

34. Lower the vehicle.

35. Remove the engine support fixture.

36. Install the air conditioning compressor.

37. Install the hood assembly.

38. Install the air cleaner duct.

39. Refill the engine with clean engine oil.

40. Connect the negative battery cable.

3.5L Engine

▶ See Figure 85

➡ The engine oil filter is built into the oil pan.

1. Raise and safely support the vehicle.

2. Drain the engine oil. Remove the oil filter cap, remove and discard the oil filter.

3. Detach the oil level sensor/switch wiring harness connector.

4. Remove the automatic transaxle brace.

5. Remove the oil pan retaining bolts and separate the oil pan from the lower crankcase.

To install:

6. Clean all parts well. Make sure the oil pan gasket rails, the engine front cover, the rear main bearing cap and the engine gasket sealing surfaces are clean. Use care. The engine crankcase is aluminum. Do not scratch or gouge the sealing surfaces. Clean all threaded holes.

7. If changing out the oil pan with a service replacement part, move the oil level switch to the new oil pan. Tighten the sensor bolt to 80 inch lbs. (9 Nm).

8. There is a rather specific installation sequence for the oil pan and transaxle brace bolts. Carefully follow the next steps.

a. Using a new gasket, install the oil pan to the engine and hand start a few oil pan bolts. With the pan properly positioned, install and finger-tighten all of the oil pan bolts.

b. Install the automatic transaxle brace and the two brace-to-cylinder block bolts. DO NOT install the brace-to-oil pan bolts. Tighten the transaxle brace-to-cylinder block bolts first, to 18 ft. lbs. (25 Nm).

c. Loosely install the transaxle brace to oil pan bolts.

d. To ensure proper mounting of the transaxle, align the cast boss on the rear of the oil pan so it is flush with the rear of the cylinder block face. Use a straightedge to check the pan alignment from the rear of the block face to the bolt boss on the oil pan.

e. Press the forward part of the oil pan against the transaxle brace. Be sure to keep the rear of the oil pan flush with the rear face of the cylinder block.

f. Torque the transaxle brace-to-oil pan bolts to 18 ft. lbs. (25 Nm).

g. Keep the rear of the oil pan flush with the rear cylinder block and tighten the oil pan retaining bolts. Use the sequence illustrated, working from the center outward, similar to installing an intake manifold or cylinder head. Torque the oil pan bolts to 18 ft. lbs. (25 Nm).

9. Tighten the remaining transaxle brace bolts to the transaxle.

10. Connect the oil level sensor to the harness, install the oil drain plug and install a new oil filter.

11. Lower the vehicle.

12. Refill with clean engine oil and inspect for leaks.

3.8L Engines

▶ See Figure 86

✳✳ CAUTION

A special engine support fixture as well as a transaxle jack are required for this procedure. The reason is that the engine mount brackets wrap around the oil pan and must be removed for access to the oil pan. This means the engine must be suspended from above in such a way the vehicle can still be raised for the undercar work. The factory

engine support fixture has legs which extend across the engine compartment and rest on the shock towers with additional legs resting on the radiator support. Other engine support fixtures are similar in design. It may be possible to rent a similar device locally. Use care if using any type of substitute. Damage to the vehicle and/or personal injury is possible if the powertrain shifts or is dislodged from the vehicle.

1. Disconnect the negative battery cable.

2. Remove the wish bone-shaped engine mount struts from the engine

3. Install an engine support fixture to safely support the weight of the engine when the engine mount brackets are removed.

4. Raise and safely support the vehicle.

5. Disconnect the front exhaust pipe the manifold.

6. Remove the right front tire and right inner fender splash shield.

7. Drain the engine oil and remove the oil filter.

8. Verify that the engine support fixture is in place and engine properly and safely supported. Remove the U-shaped metal engine mount brackets from the front of the engine and the rear of the engine.

9. Remove the flywheel cover.

10. Position a transaxle jack under the transaxle, to raise the engine by lifting the transaxle.

11. Remove the oil level sensor, located in the oil pan, before the oil pan is removed. The sensor may be damaged if the oil pan is removed first.

12. Remove the oil pan retaining bolts and lower the oil pan.

To install:

13. Clean all parts well. Make sure the oil pan gasket rails, the engine front cover, the rear main bearing cap and the engine gasket sealing surfaces are clean. Clean all threaded holes. Some engines may use a "windage tray" which is a sheetmetal shield designed to keep oil from the spinning crankshaft. This reduces oil foaming and helps cut drag from the oil on the crankshaft. This sheetmetal shield may have a formed-in-place seal that acts as an oil pan gasket.

14. Prepare a few cleaned engine oil pan bolts with GM # 12345382, or equivalent thread-locking compound. Install the oil pan gasket (or sheetmetal shield, if equipped), and install the oil pan. Hand start a few of the thread-locking compound treated oil pan bolts. With the pan secure, install the remainder of the oil pan bolts, all of which should be treated with the thread-locking compound. Tighten the bolts to just 125 inch lbs. (14 Nm). DO NOT OVERTIGHTEN THE OIL PAN BOLTS. Over-tightening the oil pan bolts can damage the oil pan, resulting in an oil leak.

15. Install the oil pan level sensor after the oil pan has been installed. Tighten the sensor to 15 ft. lbs. (20 Nm). Attach the connector.

16. Install the flywheel cover.

17. Install the engine mount brackets to the engine. Tighten the bolts to 75 ft. lbs. (102 Nm).

18. Install a new oil filter.

19. Install the inner fender splash shield then install the tire assembly.

20. Connect the front exhaust pipe to the manifold.

21. Lower the vehicle

22. Remove the engine support fixture.

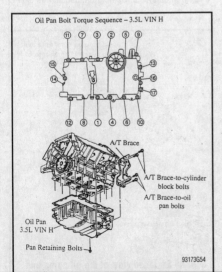

Oil Pan Bolt Torque Sequence – 3.5L VIN H

A/T Brace

A/T Brace-to-cylinder block bolts

A/T Brace-to-oil pan bolts

Oil Pan 3.5L VIN H

Pan Retaining Bolts

93173G54

Fig. 85 Oil pan arrangement and bolt tightening sequence—3.5L (VIN H) Engine

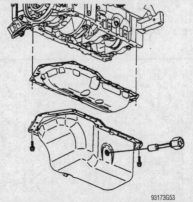

93173G53

Fig. 86 Engine oil pan arrangement—3.8L engines

23. Install the "wish bone" shaped engine struts.

24. Fill the engine with clean engine oil

25. Connect the negative battery cable.

Oil Pump

REMOVAL & INSTALLATION

3.1L and 3.4L Engines

▶ See Figure 87

➡ The oil pump is located in the oil pan.

1. Remove the oil pan using the procedure found in this section.

2. Some engines, such as the may have a crankshaft oil deflector (also called a "windage tray"). Remove the retaining nuts and remove the oil deflector.

3. Remove the bolt attaching the oil pump to the rear crankshaft bearing cap.

4. Remove the oil pump and driveshaft.

To install:

5. Clean all parts well. Inspect the driveshaft at both ends for rounding of the corners. Replace, if necessary. If the original pump is being considered for reuse, inspect the pump body and the pump cover for cracks, scoring, casting imperfections, or any obvious damage.

6. Rotate the pump driveshaft as necessary to engage the with the oil pump. Make sure it turns smoothly. Some technicians will fill the oil pump through the opening next to the driveshaft to shorten the time it take the engine to buildup oil pressure on initial startup after an oil pump replacement. Turning the driveshaft as oil is being added fills the pump cavity.

7. Install the pump and driveshaft assembly to the engine. Install the retaining bolt and tighten to:

    a. 3.1L engines: 30 ft. lbs. (41 Nm)

    b. 3.4L engines: 40 ft. lbs. (54 Nm)

8. Install the oil pan using the procedure found in this section.

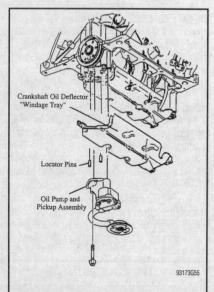

Fig. 87 Oil pump arrangement—3.1L and 3.4L engines

3.5L Engine

▶ See Figures 88, 89 and 90

✳✳ WARNING

As with many procedures on the 3.5L (VIN H) DOHC engine, oil pump removal is a long and complicated task The oil pump is located behind the engine front cover. The engine front cover must be removed. Part of the procedure is lowering the powertrain cradle, or subframe, requiring special lifting and support equipment. The steering shaft must be separated so the vehicle subframe can be loosened and lowered. Careful work is required for reassembly. This is not a job for the inexperienced or ill-equipped. Be very sure of your diagnosis before attempting to remove the oil pump on this engine, especially with the engine still in the vehicle. In addition, a pair of special tools, GM #J 42042 Camshaft Timing Clamps, is required to hold the camshafts in place once the timing chain is removed. This tool, when properly installed, will be fully seated on the camshaft ends with the camshaft flats parallel to the cam cover sealing surfaces. This tool prevents unexpected camshaft rotation caused by valve spring pressure. This tool must be installed immediately after cam cover removal. This engine has no valve timing marks. Once lost, there are no pins or keys to help you re-establish valve timing. If valve timing is lost, it is very difficult to restore.

➡ This engine is constructed primarily of aluminum. Use care when working with light alloy parts.

1. Remove the engine front cover using the procedures found in this section.

2. Remove both camshaft covers. Immediately install Camshaft Holding Fixtures J 42038, or equivalent onto the ends of the camshafts. Rotate the engine to align the camshafts with the tool using the hex on the camshaft and an open end wrench. When installed properly, tool J 42038 will be fully seated on the camshaft ends with the camshaft flats parallel to the cam cover sealing surface.

3. Remove the oil pan using the procedures found in this section.

4. Remove the oil pump pipe and screen.

5. Remove the camshaft drive chain tensioner in order to remove the primary camshaft drive chain from the drive sprocket.

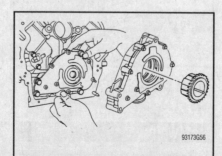

Fig. 88 Removing the oil pump with the crankshaft sprocket—3.5L (VIN H) engine

6. Remove the four oil pump assembly retaining bolts identified by the larger head size.

7. Slide the oil pump off the nose of the crankshaft with the drive sprocket in place.

8. Remove the crankshaft sprocket from the oil pump assembly.

9. Clean all parts well. Please note that the internal parts of this oil pump are not serviced separately. If wear or damage is noted, replace the entire oil pump assembly. To disassemble the pump, use the following procedure:

    a. Remove the eight screws holding the pump housing halves together.

    b. Remove the inner (drive) and the outer (driven) rotors from the housing. Note the orientation of the pump rotors. The outer rotor has a dimple identifying its outer surface. The dimpled side of the outer rotor must always be facing outward.

    c. Remove the threaded pressure relief valve cap and slide the pressure relief spring and valve piston out of the bore.

    d. Clean all pump components with a suitable non-corrosive solvent such as Safety-Kleen®, or equivalent.

    e. Dry the oil pump components with compressed air.

    f. Inspect the housing and the cover for nicks, scoring, casting imperfections and damaged threads. Inspect the gerotor gears for chipping, galling or excessive wear. Inspect the pressure relief valve components for embedded particles and/or wear.

    g. Assemble the pump by installing the inner and outer rotors in the pump cover in the same orientation as removed. The outer rotor and a dimple to indicate the outer surface. The dimpled surface must be face-up in the pump body.

    h. Install the pressure relief valve piston first, followed by the spring, in the pump housing bore. Install the valve cap and torque to 97 inch lbs. (11 Nm).

    i. Lubricate the gears with petroleum jelly, packing all the spaces around the gears, filling the pump cavity. This is important. The petroleum jelly seals the pump cavity to help "prime" the pump. The reduces the time the engine will run with little oil pressure on initial start up after

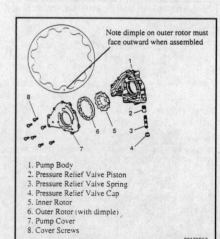

1. Pump Body
2. Pressure Relief Valve Piston
3. Pressure Relief Valve Spring
4. Pressure Relief Valve Cap
5. Inner Rotor
6. Outer Rotor (with dimple)
7. Pump Cover
8. Cover Screws

Fig. 89 Exploded view of the oil pump and outer rotor identification—3.5L (VIN H) engine

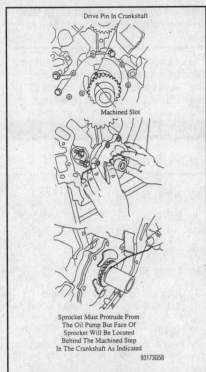

Fig. 90 Verify the sprocket engages the drive pin and that the sprocket face is behind the machined step on the crankshaft—3.5L (VIN H) engine

oil pump installation. DO NOT use chassis grease because it will clog the oil system passages. Petroleum jelly, after it has accomplished its job of acting as a seal so the pump can prime and draw oil, melts at a low temperature and will "go away" as the engine warms.

   j. Assemble the housing and the cover. Install the bolts and torque to 124 inch lbs. (14 Nm).

To install:

10. Align the crankshaft sprocket splines with the oil pump gerotor and install the sprocket in the oil pump.

11. Place the pump and sprocket assembly in position by rotating the crankshaft sprocket until the machined slot is indexed with the drive pin in the crankshaft.

12. Slide the pump and sprocket onto the crankshaft until a positive stop is felt. Make sure the crankshaft sprocket is aligned with the drive pin in the crankshaft. When properly installed, the crankshaft sprocket will protrude from the oil pump but the face of the sprocket will be located behind the machined step in the crankshaft. Align the pump body with the mounting holes in the cylinder block, install the bolts and tighten evenly to 18 ft. lbs. (25 Nm).

13. Install the primary camshaft drive chain over the drive sprocket, using the procedures found in this section.

14. Install the remaining components in the reverse order of removal, following procedures found in this section.

3.8L Engines

▸ See Figure 91

➡ The oil pump is located inside the engine front cover.

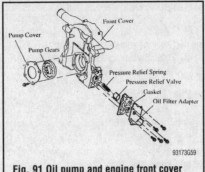

Fig. 91 Oil pump and engine front cover arrangement—3.8L engines

✳✳ WARNING

When troubleshooting a low oil pressure complaint, another possibility is a clogged screen on the oil pickup pipe, damaged pipe or gasket. The oil pan will have to be removed to check this. Running the engine without measurable oil pressure will cause extensive and expensive damage.

1. Remove the engine front cover using the procedure found in this section.

2. Remove the oil pump cover attaching screws and remove the cover.

3. Remove the oil pump gears.

4. If desired, remove the oil filter adapter and remove the pressure regulator valve and the spring for cleaning.

To install:

5. Clean all parts well.

6. Lubricate the gears with petroleum jelly, packing all the spaces around the gears, filling the pump cavity. This is important. The petroleum jelly seals the pump cavity to help "prime" the pump. The reduces the time the engine will run with little oil pressure on initial start up after oil pump installation. DO NOT use chassis grease. Petroleum jelly melts at a low temperature and will "go away" as the engine warms.

7. If the oil pressure relief valve was removed, inspect the valve and bore for burrs. Check the spring for loss of tension. Replace the spring if in doubt.

8. Install the pump cover and tighten the screws evenly to 98 inch lbs. (11 Nm).

9. If removed, thoroughly clean the oil pressure relief valve of all varnish and install the spring first, the valve. Use a new oil filter adapter gasket. Install the adapter. Tighten the oil filter adapter bolts evenly to 22 ft. lbs. (30 Nm).

10. Install the engine front cover using the procedures found in this section.

Crankshaft Balancer

REMOVAL & INSTALLATION

3.1L and 3.4L Engines

▸ See Figure 92

✳✳ WARNING

The inertial weight section of the crankshaft balancer (also called a Crankshaft Damper, or Torsional Damper) is assembled to the

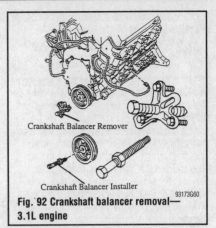

Fig. 92 Crankshaft balancer removal—3.1L engine

hub with a rubber type material. The correct installation procedures, with the proper tools, must be followed or movement of the inertial weight section of the hub will destroy the tuning of the crankshaft balancer.

1. Remove the drive belt. Please see Section 1.

2. Raise and safely support the vehicle.

3. Remove the right front tire assembly. Locate and remove the right splash shield.

4. On the 3.4L (VIN X) engine, remove the three bolts holding the crankshaft pulley and remove the pulley.

5. Remove the crankshaft balancer bolt and washer.

6. Remove the crankshaft balancer using a three-leg puller such as J 24420-B, or equivalent.

To install:

7. Clean all parts well. Apply a thin coat of sealer GM #12345739, or equivalent, to the keyway of the balancer. This is to help prevent oil from wicking along the keyway and causing a leak.

8. Install the crankshaft balancer using tool J 29113 Crankshaft Balancer Installer or equivalent, to draw the balancer onto the crankshaft. Do not hammer on the balancer.

9. Install the crankshaft bolt and washer and torque to 76–80 ft. lbs. (103–108 Nm).

10. Install the remainder of the components in the reverse order of removal.

3.5L Engine

▸ See Figures 93 and 94

✳✳ WARNING

The factory recommended procedure for removing the crankshaft balancer is a lengthy and difficult procedure requiring special lifting and support equipment. The steering shaft must be separated and the vehicle subframe must be loosened and lowered for access to the crankshaft balancer. Careful work is required for reassembly. This is not a job for the inexperienced or ill-equipped.

1. Disconnect the negative battery cable.

2. Remove the accessory drive belt. Please see Section 1.

3. Raise and safely support the vehicle.

4. Remove the right front tire assembly. Locate and remove the right engine splash shield.

5. Place adjustable safety stands on the right side of the frame.

6. Remove the two right side frame bolts.

7. Lower the right side of the frame and engine using the adjustable safety stands to allow access to attach the three-legged puller to the crankshaft balancer.

8. GM recommends a device be used to lock the flywheel to keep the crankshaft from turning when the balancer center bolt is being removed. Their tool, J 43442 is a toothed device that, after removing the torque converter cover, bolts to the block with its teeth engaging the teeth of the flywheel, effectively locking the crankshaft in place. Use care if using substitutes.

9. Loosen and remove the crankshaft balancer bolt.

10. Mount a three-legged puller into the recesses cast into the backside of the balancer inner hub. The factory recommended tool, J 41816, has an accessory piece J 43010 which goes into the nose of the crankshaft to protect the retainer bolt threads. Use care if using substitutes. If the crankshaft threads are damaged, repairs will be lengthy and expensive. Tighten the center screw on the puller until the balancer is drawn clear of the crankshaft end. Remove the balancer from the puller.

To install:

11. Clean all parts well. Inspect the balancer for signs of damage. Do not lubricate the crankshaft front oil seal or the crankshaft balancer sealing surfaces. The crankshaft balancer is installed into a dry seal.

12. Place the balancer in position on the crankshaft. A special tool, J 4201, is recommended to thread into the end of the crankshaft and then draw the balancer back into position. GM recommends engaging at least ten threads of the tool to the crankshaft, before pressing the balancer in place by tightening the nut on the tool until the large washer bottoms out on the crankshaft end. Use care if using substitutes.

✳✳ WARNING

DO NOT attempt to hammer the balancer into place. It will be damaged.

13. Install the crankshaft balancer bolt. Using a torque angle meter, tighten to 37 ft. lbs. (50 Nm), plus as additional 125 degrees.

14. Remove the flywheel locking tool and install the torque converter cover.

15. Raise the right side of the frame with the engine, using the adjustable safety stands.

16. Install the two right side frame bolts.

17. Remove the adjustable safety stands.

18. Install the engine splash shield and right tire assembly. Lower the vehicle.

19. Install the remainder of the components in the reverse order of removal.

3.8L Engine

▶ **See Figure 95**

1. Disconnect the negative battery cable.

2. On the 3.8L (VIN 1) engine, remove the supercharger belt.

3. Remove the accessory drive belt. Please see Section 1.

4. Raise and safely support the vehicle. Remove the right front tire assembly and inner fender splash shield.

5. Remove the flywheel cover.

6. GM recommends a device be used to lock the flywheel to keep the crankshaft from turning when the balancer center bolt is being removed. Their tool, J 37096 is a toothed device that, after removing the torque converter cover, is positioned so its teeth engage the teeth of the flywheel. This particular tool requires an assistant to hold the tool with a breaker bar. Use care if using substitutes.

7. Remove the crankshaft balancer retaining bolt.

➡**Service the balancer as a unit. Do not separate the pulley from the balancer hub.**

8. Install an appropriate puller and draw the balancer from the crankshaft. Use care not to damage the end of the crankshaft.

To install:

9. Coat the front cover seal contact area on the crankshaft balancer and the seal surface with engine oil.

10. Install the balancer and push on as far as it will go.

✳✳ WARNING

This bolt is designed to permanently stretch when tightened. The correct part number fastener must be used to replace this type of fastener. Do not use a bolt that is stronger in this application. If the correct

bolt is not used, the parts will not be tightened correctly. Components may be damaged.

11. Install the crankshaft balancer retainer bolt and, with the flywheel restrained from turning, tighten the bolt with a torque angle meter to 111 ft. lbs. (150 Nm) plus an additional 76 degrees.

REMOVAL & INSTALLATION

3.4L (VIN X) Engine

No oil seals need to be disturbed to perform these cover removal procedures.

UPPER RIGHT SIDE COVER

▶ **See Figure 96**

1. Disconnect the negative battery cable.

2. Remove the mounting bolts, then remove the cover.

To install:

3. Position the cover, then secure with the retaining bolts. Tighten the bolts to 89 inch lbs. (10 Nm).

4. Connect the negative battery cable.

UPPER LEFT SIDE COVER

1. Disconnect the negative battery cable.

2. Remove the ignition coil pack and harness. Please see Section 2.

3. Remove the ignition coil pack bracket and brace.

4. Remove the mounting bolts, then remove the cover.

To install:

5. Position the cover, then secure with the retaining bolts. Tighten the bolts to 89 inch lbs. (10 Nm).

6. Install the ignition coil pack bracket, brace, the coil pack and harness.

7. Connect the negative battery cable.

CENTER COVER

▶ **See Figure 97**

1. Disconnect the negative battery cable.

2. Remove the PCM harness cover.

3. Remove the drive belt tensioner.

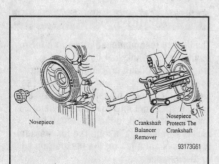

Fig. 93 Use care when rigging a puller on the balancer. Note the nosepiece to protect the balancer bolt threads in the end of the crankshaft—3.5L (VIN H) engine

Fig. 94 This tool installs the balancer by threading into the crankshaft then by turning the nut, the tool presses the balancer into place—3.5L (VIN H) engine

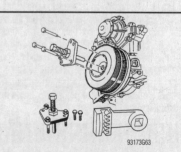

Fig. 95 A puller is needed to draw the balancer from the crankshaft. Also shown is a tool to hold the flywheel to keep the engine from turning when the retaining bolt is loosened or tightened

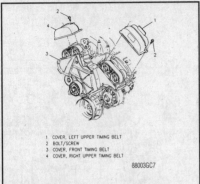

1 COVER, LEFT UPPER TIMING BELT
2 BOLT/SCREW
3 COVER, FRONT TIMING BELT
4 COVER, RIGHT UPPER TIMING BELT

88003GC7

Fig. 96 Left and right upper timing belt cover removal—3.4L (VIN X) engine

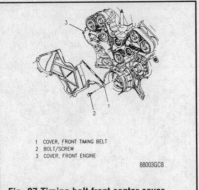

1 COVER, FRONT TIMING BELT
2 BOLT/SCREW
3 COVER, FRONT ENGINE

88003GC8

Fig. 97 Timing belt front center cover removal—3.4L (VIN X) engine

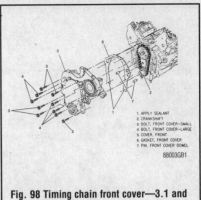

1: APPLY SEALANT
2: CRANKSHAFT
3: BOLT, FRONT COVER-SMALL
4: BOLT, FRONT COVER-LARGE
5: COVER, FRONT
6: GASKET, FRONT COVER
7: PIN, FRONT COVER DOWEL

88003GB1

Fig. 98 Timing chain front cover—3.1 and 3.4L (VIN E) engines

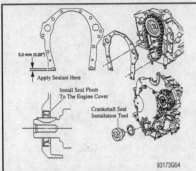

5.0 mm (0.20")

Apply Sealant Here

Install Seal Flush
To The Engine Cover

Crankshaft Seal
Installation Tool

93173G64

Fig. 99 Timing chain cover gasket and seal arrangement—3.1L and 3.4L (VIN E) engines

4. Remove the left and right upper timing belt covers.

5. Remove the power steering pipe retaining clip nut at the alternator stud.

6. Remove the center timing belt cover bolts and remove the cover.

To install:

7. Position the cover, then secure with the retaining bolts. Tighten the bolts to 89 inch lbs. (10 Nm).

8. Install the power steering pipe retaining clip nut.

9. Install the left and right upper belt covers.

10. Install the drive belt tensioner and the PCM harness cover.

11. Connect the negative battery cable.

Timing Chain Front Cover and Seal

REMOVAL & INSTALLATION

3.1L and 3.4L (VIN E) Engines

▶ See Figures 98 and 99

❋❋ WARNING

The timing chain front cover (also called the engine front cover) is made of aluminum. Use care when working with light alloy parts.

➡ **The crankshaft front oil seal can be replaced without removing the timing chain front cover.**

1. Disconnect the negative battery cable.

2. Drain the engine coolant and engine oil into suitable containers.

3. Remove the crankshaft balancer using the procedures found in this section.

4. Remove the drive belt tensioner.

5. Without disconnecting the fluid lines, remove the power steering pump and set aside.

6. Remove the thermostat pipe from the front engine cover.

7. Remove the lower radiator hose from the water pump.

8. Remove the drive belt shield and remove the water pump pulley.

9. Remove the crankshaft position sensor from the engine timing chain front cover.

10. Remove the front cover bolts. Note that they are different lengths. Use care to note the position of the bolts at removal so they can be returned to their original locations. Separate the engine timing chain front cover from the engine. Discard the gasket. If the cover if being replaced with a new one, transfer the water pump to the replacement cover.

To install:

11. Clean all parts well, especially the gasket sealing surfaces. Inspect the water pump shaft and vanes for looseness. Inspect the front cover seal for damage. If the front seal is to be replaced, use the following procedure.

a. Note that the crankshaft front oil seal can be replaced without removing the timing chain front cover.

b. With the front cover on or off the engine, after removing the crankshaft balancer, pry the seal out with an appropriate prying tool.

c. Inspect the crankshaft, the balancer and the front cover for scratches. Replace or repair as necessary.

d. Lubricate the replacement crankshaft seal with clean engine oil to make installation easier.

e. A seal driver is recommended. Install the seal making sure the seal lip faces the engine. Tap into place with a seal driver. Support the aluminum cover underneath to prevent distortion and do not hammer on the seal. Tap in lightly until it seats.

12. Coat both sides of the lower tabs of the new cover gasket for about ¼ inch with sealer, GM #1052080, or equivalent. Install the gasket to the engine block taking care to align the gasket with the dowel pins in the block.

13. Install the front timing chain cover. Install the bolts into their original locations, as noted at removal. Tighten the large bolts to 35 ft. lbs. (47 Nm) and the small bolts to 15 ft. lbs. (21 Nm).

14. Install the crankshaft position sensor to the engine timing chain front cover.

15. Install the remainder of the components in the order in which they were removed.

16. Refill the engine with coolant and engine oil. A filter change is recommended.

17. Connect the negative battery cable.

3.4L (VIN X) Engine

▶ See Figures 100 and 101

➡ **This is a long process and requires the removal of the engine timing belt as well as the alternator. The alternator removal procedure calls for lowering the sub-frame, requiring special lifting and jacking equipment. Special tools are required. Please review the timing belt removal procedure, found in this section, before attempting to service the engine front cover (also called the Cam Interdrive Shaft Chain and Sprocket Cover). This is not a job for the inexperienced or ill-equipped.**

1. Remove the camshaft timing belt and tensioner actuator using the procedures found in this section.

2. Remove the camshaft timing belt idler pulleys.

3. Remove the engine lift bracket.

4. Remove both cooling fans.

5. Drain the cooling system into a suitable container and remove the coolant hoses from the water pump.

6. Remove the heater pipe retaining screws from the frame.

7. Remove the starter motor. Please see Section 2.

8. Remove the crankshaft balancer using the procedures found in this section.

9. Remove the alternator and set aside.

10. Remove the oil filter and the oil cooler from the engine.

11. Remove the oil pan front retaining nuts and bolts, and loosen the remainder of the oil pan bolts.

12. Without disconnecting the refrigerant lines, remove the air conditioning compressor and set aside.

13. Remove the front cover bolts. Please note that different length bolts are used. Some techni-

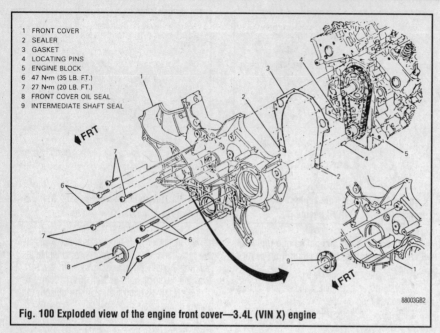

1 FRONT COVER
2 SEALER
3 GASKET
4 LOCATING PINS
5 ENGINE BLOCK
6 47 N·m (35 LB. FT.)
7 27 N·m (20 LB. FT.)
8 FRONT COVER OIL SEAL
9 INTERMEDIATE SHAFT SEAL

88003GB2

Fig. 100 Exploded view of the engine front cover—3.4L (VIN X) engine

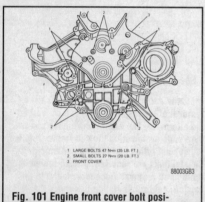

1 LARGE BOLTS 47 N·m (35 LB. FT.)
2 SMALL BOLTS 27 N·m (20 LB. FT.)
3 FRONT COVER

88003GB3

Fig. 101 Engine front cover bolt positions—3.4L (VIN X) engine

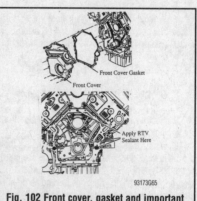

Front Cover Gasket
Front Cover
Apply RTV Sealant Here

93173G65

Fig. 102 Front cover, gasket and important sealing points—3.5L (VIN H) engine

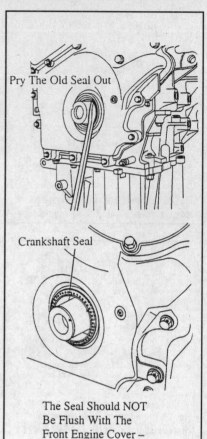

Pry The Old Seal Out

Crankshaft Seal

The Seal Should NOT
Be Flush With The
Front Engine Cover –
It Should Protrude 1-2mm

93173G66

Fig. 103 Prying out the crankshaft front oil seal. The installed new seal should protrude 0.039–0.078 inch (1-2mm)—3.5L (VIN H) engine

cians will trace the bolt pattern of the front cover onto a piece of cardboard, using the replacement gasket as a template. As the bolts are removed, they can be poked through the cardboard in the appropriate places for assembly.

14. Install a device to lock the flywheel in place. GM recommends their J 37096 Flywheel Holder. Use care if using substitutes.

15. Lower the vehicle.

16. Remove the intermediate shaft belt sprocket.

17. Remove the forward lamp relay center screws and position the relay center aside.

18. Remove the water pump pulley.

19. Remove the front cover bolts, noting their location for installation.

20. Separate the front cover from the engine block. Use care when working with light alloy parts. Discard the gasket.

To install:

21. Clean all parts well. Use care not to damage the sealing surfaces.

22. Apply sealer GM #1052080, or equivalent, to the lower edges of the sealing surfaces on the front cover. Using a new gasket, install the front cover. Apply the same sealer to the front cover bolts and install the front cover bolts, taking care the bolts are returned to their original locations. Tighten the bolts

enough to pull the cover against the engine block. Do not finish tightening the bolts at this time.

23. Install the water pump pulley.

24. Install the oil cooler hose at the front cover.

25. Install the forward lamp relay center screws.

26. Install the upper alternator retaining bolts.

27. Install the intermediate drive shaft sprocket.

28. Raise and safely support the vehicle.

29. Final torque the front cover bolts. The large bolts should be tightened to 35–37 ft. lbs. (47–50 Nm) and the small bolts to 18–20 ft. lbs. (27–25 Nm).

30. Install the oil pan retainer bolts using the procedures found in this section.

31. Install the crankshaft balancer using the procedures found in this section.

32. Install the alternator and starter motor. Please see Section 2.

33. Install the remainder of the components in the reverse order of removal.

3.5L Engine

▶ See Figures 102, 103 and 104

✳✳ WARNING

The factory recommended procedure for removing the timing chain engine front

requires special lifting and support equipment. The steering shaft must be separated and the vehicle subframe must be loosened and lowered for access to the crankshaft balancer so the front cover can be removed. Careful work is required for reassembly. This is not a job for the inexperienced or ill-equipped.

➡The crankshaft front oil seal can be replaced without removing the timing chain front cover.

1. Disconnect the negative, then the positive battery cables.

2. Remove the right diagonal brace.

3. Remove the battery hold-down and remove the battery and the battery tray.

4. Remove the engine coolant reservoir (surge tank).

5. Reposition the underhood accessory wiring junction block for access.

6. Remove the drive belt. Please see Section 1.

7. Remove the drive belt idler pulley and the drive belt tensioner.

8. Drain the coolant into a suitable container.

9. Remove the water pump pulley bolts and pull off the pulley.

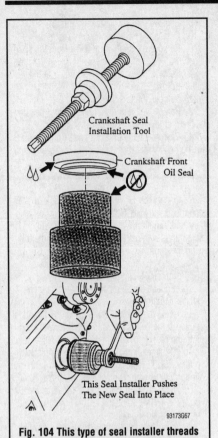

Fig. 104 This type of seal installer threads into the crankshaft and then presses the seal into place—3.5L (VIN H) engine

10. Remove the water pump bolts and the water pump drive belt shield.

11. Remove the water pump bolts and separate the pump from the engine. Note that bolt lengths vary. There are long and short bolts. Use care to note the length of bolts as they are removed and the location from which they were removed so they can be returned to their proper locations. Discard the gasket.

12. Raise and safely support the vehicle.

13. Remove the right front tire assembly. Locate and remove the right engine splash shield.

14. Place adjustable safety stands on the right side of the frame.

15. Remove the two right side frame bolts.

16. Lower the right side of the frame and engine using the adjustable safety stands to allow access to attach the three-legged puller to the crankshaft balancer. Remove the balancer following the procedures found in this section.

17. Remove the ten front cover perimeter bolts. Carefully separate the front cover from the engine. Use care. Both the front cover and the engine block are made of aluminum and are easily damaged.

To install:

18. Clean all parts well. Some gasket material may remain on the engine block. Use care when scraping gasket material from the front cover, engine block and the water pump. GM recommends a plastic scraper. Do not gouge aluminum parts. Clean the bolt threads well. The torque specification is low and if the bolt threads are dirty, an accurate torque is not possible and leaks are likely to develop.

19. Place a short bead of RTV sealant, GM #12345739, or equivalent, on the engine block as illustrated. Align the front cover gasket to the front cover bolt holes and insert two bolts through the front cover to hold the gasket in position. Install the front cover and gasket hand start all of the front cover retaining bolts. Evenly tighten the bolts to 124 inch lbs. (14 Nm).

20. Install the crankshaft balancer following the procedures found in this section.

21. Jack the cradle back into position. Install the cradle bolts side bolts and remove the cradle support.

22. Using a new gasket, install the water pump to the front cover. Install the cleaned and lightly lubricated water pump bolts finger-tight, then torque to 124 inch lbs. (14 Nm).

23. Install the water pump pulley and bolts and finger-tighten the bolts.

24. Install the idler pulley and bolt. Tighten the idler pulley bolt to 37 ft. lbs. (50 Nm).

25. Install the drive belt, then, with the drive belt holding the pulley from turning, torque the water pump pulley bolts to 18 ft. lbs. (25 Nm).

26. Install the remaining components in the reverse order of the removal process. When refilling the cooling system, use the proper mix of DEX-COOL® and water. Check for leaks.

3.8L Engines

▸ See Figure 105

➡ The crankshaft front oil seal can be replaced without removing the timing chain front cover.

1. Disconnect the negative battery cable.
2. Drain the cooling system into a suitable container.
3. Remove the drive belt. Please see Section 1. Remove the drive belt tensioner.
4. Remove the crankshaft balancer using the procedures found in this section.
5. Detach the electrical connections from the front cover.
6. Remove the crankshaft position sensor shield and remove the crankshaft position sensor.
7. Remove the oil pan to front cover bolts.
8. Remove the oil filter.
9. Remove the lower radiator hose.
10. Remove the water pump pulley.
11. Remove the front cover attaching bolts and separate to front cover and oil filter adapter as one assembly from the engine block. Discard the gasket.

To install:

12. Clean all parts well, especially the gasket sealing surfaces. Clean the sealing surfaces with a degreaser. Inspect the front cover seal for damage. If the front seal is to be replaced, use the following procedure:

a. Note that the crankshaft front oil seal can be replaced without removing the timing chain front cover.

b. With the front cover on or off the engine, after removing the crankshaft balancer, pry the seal out with an appropriate prying tool. Use care not to scratch the crankshaft or damage the seal bore.

c. Inspect the crankshaft, the balancer and the front cover for scratches. Replace or repair as necessary.

d. Lubricate the replacement crankshaft seal with clean engine oil to make installation easier.

e. A seal driver is recommended. Install the seal making sure the seal lip faces the engine. Tap into place with a seal driver. Support the aluminum cover underneath to prevent distortion and do not hammer on the seal. Tap in lightly until it seats.

13. If the front cover is being replaced with a new service replacement part, transfer the oil filter adapter, pressure relief valve and water pump to the new cover.

14. Inspect the timing chain for overall in and out movement. Maximum movement is 1 inch (25.4mm). Inspect the sprockets for wear.

➡ The oil pan can be dropped slightly for front cover clearance if all pan bolts are loosened and the oil level sensor is removed.

15. With all sealing surfaces clean, install a new front cover gasket. Apply sealer GM #1052080, or equivalent, to the bolt threads. Install the front cover taking care to align the cogs on the crankshaft sprocket with the cogs on the oil pump in the front cover. When satisfied with the fit and alignment, install the upper front cover bolts finger-tight. Using a torque angle meter, tighten the bolts to 11 ft. lbs. (15 Nm) plus an additional 40 degrees.

16. Inspect the oil pan gasket and replace, if necessary. Install the oil pan to front cover bolts and tighten any oil pan bolts that were removed. Tighten the bolts to 125 inch lbs. (14 Nm).

17. Install the water pump pulley, and the lower radiator hose.

18. Install a new oil filter. Carefully install the crankshaft position sensor and the sensor shield.

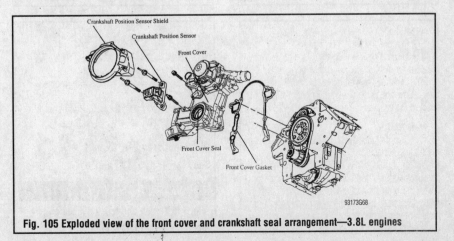

Fig. 105 Exploded view of the front cover and crankshaft seal arrangement—3.8L engines

19. Install the remainder of the components in the reverse order of removal.

20. Refill the engine with oil and the cooling system with the proper mix of DEX-COOL® and water.

Timing Belt and Sprockets

REMOVAL & INSTALLATION

3.4L (VIN X) Engine

▶ See Figures 106 thru 115

The 3.4L (VIN X) DOHC engine uses a two-stage camshaft drive. The first stage transfers power from the crankshaft to an intermediate shaft by means of a chain drive. The second stage uses a cogged belt between the intermediate shaft and the individual camshafts. Special care must be taken during timing belt handling and storage to avoid kinks, cuts, etc., which may cause reduced durability. Both chain and belt tension is set by fully automatic tensioners. Timing must be reset if the sprockets are removed from their camshafts. Pins or keys are NOT uses to establish camshaft to crankshaft timing. This is a long procedure, and requires careful work as well as GM's J 38613-A Camshaft Timing Clamps and J 38614 Camshaft Sprocket Holding Tools or their exact equivalents.

1. Disconnect the negative battery cable.
2. Remove the air cleaner duct.
3. Drain the coolant into a suitable container.
4. Disconnect the throttle and cruise control cables from the throttle body.

5. Remove the engine cosmetic/acoustic cover.
6. Relieve the fuel system pressure and disconnect the fuel lines from the fuel rail. Please see Section 5.
7. Remove the fuel mounting bracket.
8. Remove the heater hose and the bracket at lower intake manifold.
9. Remove the PCV valve and vacuum line from the throttle body.
10. Remove the EGR valve electrical connector, then unbolt the EGR valve from the upper intake manifold.
11. Detach the canister purge solenoid and MAP sensor harness connectors.
12. Disconnect the vacuum lines from the upper intake manifold tee.
13. Remove the wiring loom bracket from the rear bank spark plug wires.
14. Disconnect the power brake booster hose.
15. Remove the upper intake manifold.
16. Remove the coolant recovery reservoir.
17. Remove the accessory drive belt and the drive belt tensioner.

✷✷ WARNING

Siphon the power steering fluid from the reservoir before disconnecting the fluid lines to avoid spilling fluid on the timing belt cover. Use shop rags when disconnecting the lines to make sure any remaining fluid does not contact the timing belt cover. Power steering fluid will damage the timing belt.

18. Remove the power steering pump.
19. Detach the PCM connectors.
20. Remove the spark plug wires from the spark plugs.
21. Remove the wiring harness cover at the right strut tower.
22. Remove the fuel line bracket.
23. Remove left and right upper timing belt covers, then remove the center cover.
24. Disconnect the breather hose from the rear camshaft cover and disconnect the crankcase vent from the breather manifold.
25. Remove the left and right camshaft carrier covers.
26. Inspect the camshaft drive and the camshaft components for wear. Note any evidence of oil or other fluid intrusion. Verify if the camshaft timing belt length is within specification by using the following methods:

a. Insert a flat, narrow ruler 0.020 inch (0.5mm) thick along the tensioner pulley.

b. Engage the steps in the timing belt tensioner actuator base.

c. Note the reading at the top of the tensioner pulley. If the belt is too long, the ruler will drop into the cast groove in the tensioner bracket.

d. If the reading at the top of the tensioner pulley is 1.56–1.68 inch (39.6–42.7mm), the timing belt is within an acceptable range.

e. If the reading at the top of the tensioner pulley is 1.70–1.84 inch (43.2–46.7mm), replace the timing belt.

f. If the belt is less than 1.20 inch (30 mm) wide, it is worn and should be replaced.

g. Measure the timing belt tensioner actuator

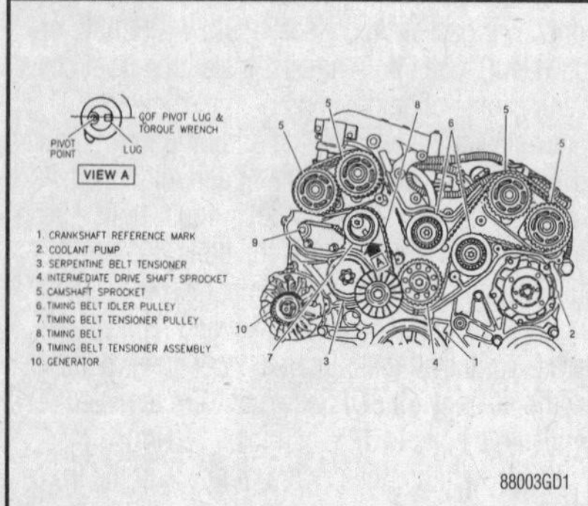

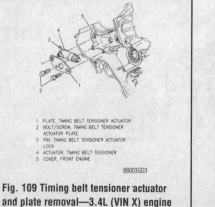

Fig. 106 Timing belt routing—3.4L (VIN X) engine

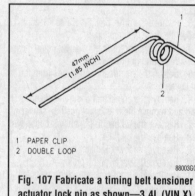

Fig. 107 Fabricate a timing belt tensioner actuator lock pin as shown—3.4L (VIN X) engine

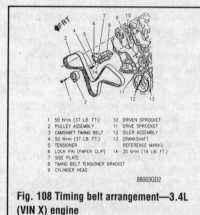

Fig. 108 Timing belt arrangement—3.4L (VIN X) engine

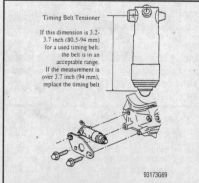

Timing Belt Tensioner

If this dimension is 3.2-3.7 inch (80.5-94 mm) for a used timing belt, the belt is in an acceptable range. If the measurement is over 3.7 inch (94 mm), replace the timing belt

Fig. 110 Timing belt tensioner dimensions—3.4L (VIN X) engine

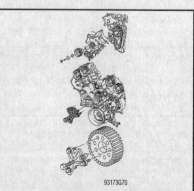

Fig. 111 Intermediate shaft belt sprocket removal—3.4L (VIN X) engine

Fig. 109 Timing belt tensioner actuator and plate removal—3.4L (VIN X) engine

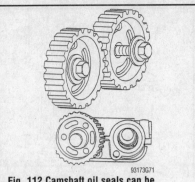

Fig. 112 Camshaft oil seals can be replaced after sprocket removal—3.4L (VIN X) engine

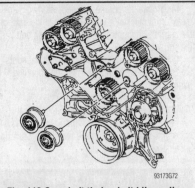

Fig. 113 Camshaft timing belt idler pulley removal—3.4L (VIN X) engine

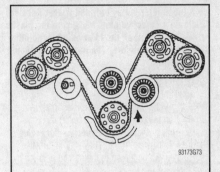

Fig. 114 When installing the camshaft timing belt, work counterclockwise—3.4L (VIN X) engine

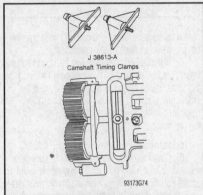

Fig. 115 The camshafts must be locked across their flats with these camshaft timing clamps—3.4L (VIN X) engine

from the centerline of the actuator to the end of the rubber boot. If the measurement reads from 3.20–3.70 inch (80.5–94mm) for a used belt, the belt is in an acceptable range. If the measurement read over 3.7 inch (94mm) for a used timing belt, replace the belt.

h. Also check for a broken or cracked tooth or tooth root (especially after 70,000 miles), signs of a leaking camshaft or crankshaft seal, coolant contamination, cracks on the back side of the belt worn teeth so the canvas is showing or breaks across the fibers.

27. Remove the timing belt tension actuator using the following procedure.

a. Remove the bolts and the side plate from the timing belt tensioner actuator. Rotate the drive belt tensioner actuator from the pulley socket and out of the mounting base. Remove the tensioner actuator pulley.

❊❊ WARNING

Do not install the rod tip or the tensioner actuator boot in the jaws of a vise or damage to the assembly may occur.

b. Position the timing belt tensioner actuator in a vertical position (rod tip down) in a bench vise. CLAMP LIGHTLY.

c. Drain the oil in the tensioner actuator to the boot end for at least 5 minutes before refilling the actuator at assembly.

❊❊ WARNING

Do not lose or damage the tapered bushing between the tensioner actuator and the mounting base while removing the tensioner actuator.

d. Straighten out a standard paper clip (0.032 inch diameter with no serrations) to a minimum straight length of 1.85 inch (47mm).

e. Form a double loop in the remaining end of the paper clip.

f. Remove the rubber plug from the rear of the tensioner actuator. Do not remove the vent plug.

g. Push the paper clip through the center hole in the vent plug and into the pilot hole.

h. Insert a small screwdriver into the screw slot inside the tensioner actuator and behind the rubber plug end.

i. Retract the tensioner actuator plunger by rotating the screw in a clockwise direction until it is fully retracted.

j. Push on the paper clip and slowly rotate the screw in a counterclockwise motion until the paper clip engages.

28. Remove the timing belt.

❊❊ WARNING

Remove the timing marks from the camshaft and the intermediate shaft sprockets.

29. Rotate the crankshaft so the number one cylinder (right side or cowl side, front) is at TDC (Top Dead Center). Mark the timing indicator with white paint (or equivalent permanent mark) on the crankshaft balancer and the front cover.

❊❊ WARNING

Before installing the Camshaft Timing Clamps, make sure the bolt hole into which the clamp bolt will thread is free of oil and debris before installing the tool or the camshaft carrier may be damaged.

30. Position the camshafts so that the flat spots are "up" for the installation of J 38613-A Camshaft Timing Clamps. Install J 38613-A Camshaft Timing Clamps on both camshaft carriers.

31. Remove the camshaft sprocket bolts and the taper lock rings. Remove the sprockets by lightly tapping on them with a soft-faced hammer.

To install:

32. Clean all parts well. Oil will damage the replacement timing belt. Work as cleanly as possible.

33. If the camshaft intermediate drive sprocket is to be serviced, use the following procedure:

a. Remove the camshaft intermediate drive sprocket retaining bolt.

❊❊ WARNING

Use care when working on the camshaft intermediate drive sprocket. Hitting the nose of the shaft and/or prying on the sprocket will cause thrust bearing damage.

b. Remove the camshaft intermediate drive sprocket using a three-arm puller, similar the a steering wheel puller, and three self-tapping bolts of appropriate size (GM suggests seat belt anchor bolts or an equivalent).

c. If the seal is to be replaced, pry out the intermediate drive sprocket shaft oil seal. Replace the seal by tapping in a replacement seal with a seal driver or a suitable socket.

d. To install the camshaft intermediate drive sprocket, lubricate the seal or the seal running surface of the sprocket.

❊❊ WARNING

Use care not to damage the camshaft intermediate drive sprocket shaft oil seal during sprocket installation.

e. Install the sprocket into position on the drive shaft through the oil seal.

f. Engage the locating tangs on the shaft sprocket into the mating sockets of the intermediate drive chain sprocket.

g. Measure the distance from the front face of the intermediate shaft sprocket to the front cover. If the measurement is more than 1.65 inch (42mm), the tangs are not engaged.

h. Lightly lubricate the sprocket retaining bolt and washer and install the bolt. Hold the crankshaft to keep the bolt from rotating. Tighten to 96 ft. lbs. (130 Nm).

34. If the timing belt idler pulleys are to be serviced, use the following procedure:

a. Remove the idler pulley bolts and remove the idler pulleys.

b. To install, install the idler pulleys.

➡A loose idler pulley bolt and spacer does not indicate a defective part. Make sure the plastic ridge by the bolt on the idler pulley is pointing away from the engine. The part number should face outward.

　　c. Tighten the idler pulley bolt to 37 ft. lbs. (50 Nm).

　　d. Verify that the pulley rotates freely and is tight on the timing belt front cover.

35. Install the camshaft sprockets, lock rings and the bolts, finger-tight. They should turn freely since they will be turned to their timed position by the timing belt.

✳✳ WARNING

As the timing belt is being installed, check to make sure that the timing belt teeth are fully engaged with the camshaft sprockets.

36. Install the timing belt by routing the belt in a counterclockwise motion around the camshaft sprockets.

37. Install the timing belt tensioner actuator pulley and tighten the bolt to 37 ft. lbs. (50 Nm).

38. Prepare the tensioner actuator for installation using the following procedure.

　　a. If any tensioner actuator oil has been lost, refill the tensioner actuator with SAE 5W30 Mobil 1® synthetic engine oil, or equivalent, through the end hole.

　　b. Fill the tensioner actuator to the bottom of the plug hole only when the tensioner actuator is fully retracted and the pin installed.

　　c. Install the rubber plug at the rear of the tensioner actuator. Push the rubber end plug until it is flush and snapped into place.

　　d. Check to make sure that the rubber end plug has sealed against the tensioner actuator case.

　　e. Check to make sure that the tapered fulcrum of the tensioner actuator is properly seated in the bracket bushing. Rotate the tensioner pulley into the timing belt a maximum of 11 ft. lbs. (15 Nm) in order to allow the engagement of the actuator shaft into the pulley arm socket.

　　f. Install the timing belt tensioner actuator busing into the side plate.

　　g. Inspect the tensioner bushings and the appropriate holes for dirt or any foreign material. Do not lubricate the tensioner bushings or the holes.

39. Install the tensioner actuator and the side plate. Tighten the bolts to 18 ft. lbs. (25 Nm). Pull out and discard the pin. Retighten the tensioner pulley 11 ft. lbs. (15 Nm) counterclockwise to seat the pulley into the timing belt.

40. Install both right side (rear bank) camshaft sprockets and tighten the sprocket bolts to 96 ft. lbs.(130 Nm). Remove tool J 38613-A Camshaft Timing Clamp from the right side (rear bank) camshaft carrier.

41. Rotate the crankshaft 360 degrees clockwise while looking at the front of the engine. Align the crankshaft reference marks made earlier.

42. Verify that both of the right side (rear bank) camshaft flats are down.

43. Install the left side (front bank) camshaft sprockets. Tighten the bolts to 96 ft. lbs. (130 Nm). Remove tool J 38613-A Camshaft Timing Clamp from the left side (front bank) camshaft carrier.

44. Rotate the engine 720 degrees (two complete turns) clockwise while looking at the front of the engine. Do this to seat the timing belt and verify the correct timing.

45. Verify that both of the camshaft flat spots are up on one bank and down on the opposing bank.

46. Install both camshaft carriers.

47. Install the remaining components in the reverse order of installation. Timing belt covers, crankshaft balancer and intake manifold installation are all covered in this section.

Timing Chain and Gears

REMOVAL & INSTALLATION

3.1L and 3.4L (VIN E) Engines

▶ **See Figures 116 and 117**

1. Remove the timing chain front cover using the procedures found in this section.

2. Rotate the crankshaft until the timing marks in the following locations are aligned:

　　a. The camshaft alignment is at 3 o'clock.

　　b. The timing chain damper and crankshaft sprocket marks are aligned at 12 o'clock.

　　c. The crankshaft key is at 11 o'clock.

　　d. The timing chain damper and camshaft sprocket locator hole are next to each other.

3. Remove the camshaft sprocket bolt and remove the sprocket along with the timing chain.

4. A puller is recommended to draw the crankshaft sprocket from the nose of the crankshaft. Use

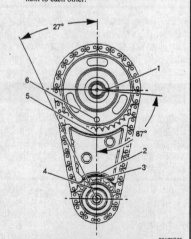

Timing Chain Alignment

Rotate the crankshaft until the timing marks in the following locations are aligned:
The camshaft alignment pin (1) is at 3 o'clock
The timing chain damper (2) and the crankshaft sprocket (3) marks are aligned at 12 o'clock
The crankshaft key (4) is at 11 o'clock
The timing chain damper (5) and camshaft sprocket locator hole (6) are next to each other.

Fig. 116 The camshaft and crankshaft timing marks MUST be properly aligned—3.1L and 3.4L (VIN E) engines

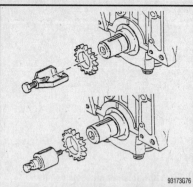

93173G76

Fig. 117 Special tools are recommended for removing and installing the timing chain sprockets—3.1L and 3.4L (VIN E) engines

care if using substitutes. Be careful not to mar the balancer bolt threads in the crankshaft.

5. If desired, remove the two bolts and remove timing chain dampener. The damper is the roughly triangular piece bolted to the block between the crankshaft sprocket and the camshaft sprocket. Look for small timing mark alignment notches in the top and bottom.

To install:

6. Clean all parts well. Inspect the sprockets for wear. While individual parts may be replaced, in actual practice, a timing chain is usually installed with new camshaft and crankshaft sprockets, as a set. If removed, install the timing chain dampener.

7. A special tool, J 38612, or equivalent, is recommended for installing the crankshaft sprocket. It threads into the nose of the crankshaft and the sprocket is pressed in. Use care is using substitutes. Before installation, coat the thrust face (back side) of the crankshaft sprocket with GM EOS #1052367, or equivalent engine assembly lube.

8. Align the crankshaft timing mark at 12 o'clock to the timing mark on the bottom of the chain dampener.

9. Hold the camshaft sprocket and drape the timing chain over the sprocket. With the chain hanging down, install the chain to the crankshaft gear.

10. Align the timing mark on the camshaft gear (centerline of the locator hole) at 6 o'clock with the timing mark on the top of the chain dampener.

11. Align the dowel in the camshaft with the dowel hole in the camshaft sprocket (should be at 3 o'clock).

12. Draw the camshaft sprocket onto the camshaft using the mounting bolt.

13. Coat the crankshaft and camshaft sprocket with engine oil. Install the camshaft sprocket retaining bolt and torque to 81 ft. lbs. (110 Nm).

14. Install the engine front cover using the procedures found in this section.

3.4L (VIN X) Engine

▶ **See Figures 118 thru 124**

The camshaft drive is a two-stage system. The first stage is a chain and sprocket arrangement that transfers power from the crankshaft to an intermediate shaft. The intermediate shaft then transfers power to the camshafts by means of a

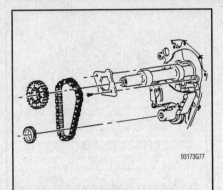

Fig. 118 Cam Inter Drive Shaft Chain and Sprockets—3.4L (VIN X) engine

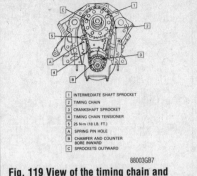

1 INTERMEDIATE SHAFT SPROCKET
2 TIMING CHAIN
3 CRANKSHAFT SPROCKET
4 TIMING CHAIN TENSIONER
5 25 Nm (18 LB. FT.)
A SPRING PIN HOLE
B CHAMFER AND COUNTER BORE INWARD
C SPROCKETS OUTWARD

Fig. 119 View of the timing chain and related components with the front cover removed—3.4L (VIN X) engine

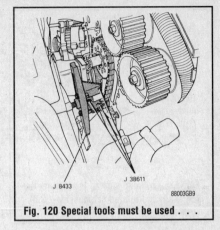

Fig. 120 Special tools must be used . . .

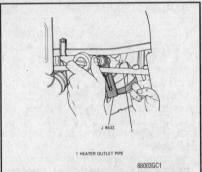

1 HEATER OUTLET PIPE

Fig. 121 . . . to remove the timing chain, crankshaft sprocket and intermediate shaft sprocket—3.4L (VIN X) engine

Fig. 122 This shop-made tool is used to retract the chain tensioner so it can be pinned in place—3.4L (VIN X) engine

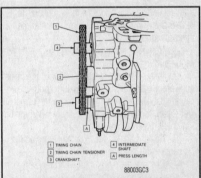

1 TIMING CHAIN
2 TIMING CHAIN TENSIONER
3 CRANKSHAFT
4 INTERMEDIATE SHAFT
A PRESS LENGTH

Fig. 123 Slide the sprocket and chain on the shafts, maintaining the proper alignment—3.4L (VIN X) engine

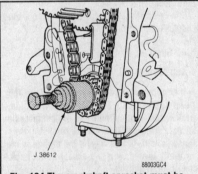

Fig. 124 The crankshaft sprocket must be pressed on using this special tool—3.4L (VIN X) engine

cogged belt and the second stage of the system. To service the chain and sprockets, the first stage of the system, (GM calls it the Cam Inter Drive Shaft Chain and Sprockets), use the following procedure.

1. Remove the engine front cover using the procedures found in this section.
2. Retract the timing chain tensioner and remove the tensioner bolts.
3. Raise and safely support the vehicle.
4. Remove the timing chain, the crankshaft sprocket and the intermediate shaft sprocket as an assembly. A gear puller may be required. If the intermediate gear does not slide off easily with the timing chain, rotate the crankshaft back and forth to help loosen the tight fit.
5. Remove the timing chain tensioner.

6. Inspect the crankshaft alignment key for burrs or marks that could affect assembly.

To install:

7. Make sure the crankshaft key is installed and fully seated, and that the chain tensioner is installed and the blade retracted. Use the following procedures:

a. Inspect the timing chain tensioner for signs of wear.

b. DO NOT use a sharp or narrow point or nylon blade to retract the timing chain tensioner. A shop-made retracting tool, described here, must be used to retract the blade.

c. Install the timing chain tensioner on the engine block. Use the upper attaching hole as the primary locator. Hand-tighten the tensioner retaining bolts.

d. Install the slotted hole bolt and tighten to 18 ft. lbs. (25 Nm). Install the other retaining bolts. Tighten the intermediate drive shaft retaining bolts to 18 ft. lbs. (25 Nm).

e. Fabricate a tool to retract the tensioner. Bend a 12-inch length of 1/8-inch welding rod or equivalent, in half, to a U-shape, leaving a 1 inch gap between the two ends. Make two more U-shaped bends 1-inch from each end.

f. Using the tool, retract the shoe on the timing chain tensioner. Compress the tensioner spring and insert a cotter pin, a nail or equivalent pin strong enough to keep the timing chain tensioner spring compressed.

g. Lightly oil or apply lithium grease to the chain contact surfaces of the tensioner nylon pad and blade.

8. With the chain tensioner retracted, slip both

sprockets and the chain over the proper shaft and engage the slot in the key. The intermediate shaft may move against the rear cover. Slide the sprocket and chain on the shafts maintaining the parallel alignment of the sprockets.

9. Make sure that the rubber and the tension blade of the tensioner does not become caught, misaligned or dislodged.

10. The larger chamfer and the counterbore of the crankshaft sprocket are installed toward the crankshaft. The intermediate sprocket spline sockets are installed away from the case. The crankshaft sprocket must be pressed on for the final 3/8 inch (8mm) or so to the seated position. GM recommends their tool J 38612.

11. Verify that the timing is maintained.

12. Pull the retaining pin from the tensioner

13. Install the front cover using the procedures found in this section.

3.5L Engine

▶ See Figures 125, 126 and 127

The four overhead camshafts are driven by three separate 8mm, single-row, fine pitch chains. The primary drive chain connects the crankshaft with both large intake camshaft sprockets, the balance shaft sprockets and the intermediate shaft sprocket. The exhaust camshafts are driven by the secondary chains which are short chains from the intake camshafts. Primary camshaft timing chain service is covered here. For secondary chain and sprocket service, please see Camshaft Removal and Installation in this section. Careful work will be required to line up all of the timing marks. As with most valve-

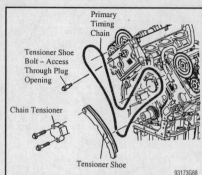

Fig. 125 Exploded view of the primary timing chain and related components—3.5L (VIN H) engine

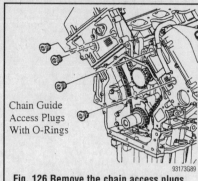

Fig. 126 Remove the chain access plugs. Make sure the O-rings are in good condition—3.5L (VIN H) engine

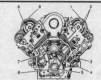

1. Timing Mark, LH Intake Camshaft
2. Paired Darkened Timing Links
3. Darkened Link For Balance Shaft
4. Primary Camshaft Drive Chain
5. Darkened Link For Crankshaft
6. Crankshaft Sprocket Timing Mark At 4 O'clock Position
7. Balance Shaft Timing Mark At 5 O'clock Position
8. Right Intake Camshaft Darkened Link
9. Timing Mark, RH Intake Camshaft

Timing Mark Alignments – 3.5L VIN H Engine

Fig. 127 All of these timing marks and marked (darkened) chain links must be aligned—3.5L (VIN H) engine

train-related service on this engine, Special Tools J 42038 Camshaft Holding Fixtures are required for this procedure.

1. Remove the camshaft covers using the procedures found in this section.

2. Install Special Tools J 42038, or their exact equivalent Camshaft Holding Fixtures onto the camshafts. This is important because the camshafts will rotate from valve spring pressure when the timing chain tension is released.

3. Remove the engine front cover using the procedures found in this section.

4. Remove the front engine lift bracket and the camshaft position sensor next to it

5. Remove the right side (rear) exhaust camshaft sprocket bolt to allow clearance for the right cylinder head chain guide.

6. Remove the four chain guide access plugs located in the cylinder heads. Note the O-ring seal on each access plug.

7. Loosen both primary timing chain tensioner bolts. Remove the lower tensioner bolt allowing the tensioner to swing downward and expand. This will release tension on the chain. Now remove the upper bolt and remove the primary drive chain tensioner.

8. Remove the primary timing chain tensioner shoe retaining bolt and remove the tensioner shoe by pushing the guide downward slightly and then pulling it up through the cylinder head.

9. Remove the primary timing chain from the right side (rear) camshaft sprocket and allow the chain to fall into the oil pump area of the engine block. Remove the chain from the engine.

To install:

10. Clean all parts well. Remove all dirt and old sealer from gasket sealing surfaces. Use care not to gouge the soft light alloy parts.

11. Examine the timing chain. There should be some links chemically darkened to distinguish them from the other links. They will be important in setting up the engine timing. With the Camshaft Holding Fixtures still securely in place, install the timing chain to the engine. Make sure the darkened timing links on the timing chain are facing toward the engine. An open-end wrench can be used on the hex-shape formed into the camshaft to provide minor adjustments to the secondary sprocket position.

12. When installing the primary timing chain, you must set the base engine timing. Base engine timing is set with cylinder #1 (right side, rear, forward cylinder) at Top Dead Center (TDC) starting the intake stroke and with the correct camshaft to

balance shaft to crankshaft relationship. To set the correct base engine timing, proceed as follows:

a. Rotate the crankshaft until cylinder #1 is at TDC and crankshaft sprocket timing mark is at the 4 o'clock position. A Special Tool, J 43032 Crankshaft Rotation Socket, is recommended since it may be difficult to turn the crankshaft since the crankshaft dampener has already been removed for front cover removal. Use care is using substitutes.

b. Rotate the balance shaft until its timing mark is at the 5 o'clock position.

13. Verify that the timing chain has been installed with the darkened timing links on the timing chain facing toward the engine.

14. Center the timing mark on the left side (front) intake camshaft between the paired darkened timing links and wrap the chain around the sprocket. Allow the remainder of the chain to drop into the crankcase area once the timing mark is aligned.

15. Fabricate a hook out of wire and feed it down through the right side (rear) cylinder head. Use the hook to pull the remainder of the timing chain up to the right intake camshaft sprocket.

16. While pulling the timing chain up to the right cylinder head, align the marked timing chain links with the balance shaft and crankshaft sprockets.

17. Wrap the timing chain around the right intake camshaft sprocket and align the marked links with the sprocket's timing mark.

18. Make sure all the timing marks are properly aligned with the marked timing chain links.

19. When satisfied with the timing chain fit and the engine timing, install the timing chain tensioner shoe. To install the retaining bolt, use the access hole in the cylinder head. Tighten the bolt to 22 ft. lbs. (30 Nm).

20. Collapse the timing chain tensioner using the following procedure:

a. Rotate the ratchet release lever counterclockwise and hold.

b. Collapse the tensioner shoe and hold.

c. Release the ratchet lever and slowly release the pressure on the shoe.

21. As the ratchet moves to its first click, hold the tensioner shoe inward. Insert a pin through the hole in the release lever. The locked ratchet mechanism should hold the shoe in a collapsed position.

22. Making sure the tensioner release lever faces toward you, install the tensioner and the

retaining bolts. Tighten the bolts to 18 ft lbs. (25 Nm).

23. Verify once again that all the timing marks are properly aligned. Make any adjustments as necessary.

24. Remove the pin holding the tensioner to tighten any slack in the timing chain.

25. Verify that each of the four chain guide access plugs has an O-ring installed. Install the plugs and snug down to 44 inch lbs. (5 Nm).

26. Install the front engine lift bracket. Tighten the hex-head bolt to 37 ft. lbs. (50 Nm) and the internal drive bolt to 18 ft. lbs. (25 Nm).

27. Install the camshaft position sensor.

28. Remove the camshaft holding fixtures from both banks of camshafts.

29. Verify once again that all the timing marks are properly aligned.

30. Install the camshaft covers using the procedures found in this section.

31. Install the engine front cover using the procedures found in this section.

3.8L Engines

♦ See Figure 128

➡**It is good practice to set the engine to Top Dead Center (TDC), No. 1 cylinder (left side, or front bank, front cylinder) on the compression stroke (firing position) before removing the timing chain. In this way, if the engine is inadvertently turned, you can always come back to the original setting.**

1. Remove the engine front cover using the procedures found in this section.

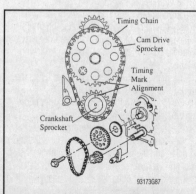

Fig. 128 Timing chain, sprockets and timing mark alignment—3.8L engines

2. Align the timing marks on the sprockets so that they are as close as possible. The cam drive sprocket should be at the 6 o'clock position and the crankshaft sprocket should be at 12 o'clock.

3. Remove the timing chain dampener.

4. Before removing the timing chain, check for wear. Inspect the timing chain for overall in and out movement. Movement should not exceed 1 inch (25mm).

5. Remove the camshaft sprocket bolts and remove the sprocket and timing chain.

➥If the sprocket does not come off easily, a light blow on the lower edge of the sprocket with a plastic mallet should dislodge the sprocket.

6. Remove the crankshaft sprocket.

To install:

7. Clean all parts well. Inspect the chain and sprockets for wear. While it may be possible to replace individual parts, in actual practice, timing chains and sprockets are normally replaced as a set.

8. If the crankshaft has been turned, rotate the crankshaft so that the number one piston is at TDC. Turn the camshaft so that, with the sprocket temporarily installed, the timing mark is straight down (6 o'clock position).

9. Install the crankshaft sprocket. Drape the timing chain over the cam drive sprocket and install the sprocket with the timing marks on the two sprockets as close to each other as possible.

10. Install the camshaft sprocket bolt. A new replacement bolt is recommended. Torque to 74 ft. lbs. (100 Nm) then turn an additional 90 degrees.

➥This bolt is designed to permanently stretch when tightened. The correct part number fastener must be used to replace this type of fastener. Do not use a bolt that is stronger in this application. If the correct bolt is not used, the parts will not be tightened correctly. The system may be damaged.

11. Install the chain dampener and tighten the bolt to 16 ft. lbs. (22 Nm).

※※ WARNING

Rotate the crankshaft two revolutions and check the timing marks. Ensure that, after two full turns, the timing marks come back into alignment.

12. Install the engine front cover using the procedures found in this section.

Camshaft, Bearings and Lifters

REMOVAL & INSTALLATION

3.1L, 3.4L (VIN E) and 3.8L Engines

▶ See Figures 129, 130, 131 and 132

The engine must be removed from the vehicle to service the camshaft.

1. With the engine out of the vehicle, secure the engine in a suitable workstand.

2. Remove the rocker cover, the rocker arms, the pushrods and intake manifolds using the procedures found in this section

3. The roller lifters use guide plates to keep the lifters from rotating off of the cam lobes. Remove the lifter guide bolts and remove the lifter guide. The lifters can be pulled from their bores. All lifters must be removed before the camshaft can be pulled out.

※※ WARNING

Any valve train parts that have been removed with the intention of reinstallation must be marks so that they can be returned to their original locations.

4. Remove the oil pump drive. This is a stub shaft located in the back of engine in the location where the distributor resided in older versions of this engine. It is driven by a gear on the camshaft and is necessary to drive the oil pump. Like a distributor, it is retained by a hold-down clamp. Remove the clamp and lift the oil pump drive straight up and out of the engine.

5. Remove the crankshaft balancer and the engine timing chain front cover, following procedures found in this section.

6. Remove the timing chain and camshaft sprocket, following procedures found in this section.

※※ WARNING

All of the camshaft bearing journals are the same diameter so care must be used when removing the camshaft so the sharp edges of the cam lobes do not gouge the soft metal of the camshaft bearings.

7. Remove the two screws that hold the

camshaft thrust plate to the block and remove the thrust plate.

8. Insert a large screwdriver in the camshaft to act as a handle and to help support the camshaft as it is withdrawn from the block. Pull the camshaft out slowly, rotating the camshaft to help it clear the bearings.

9. Normally, if an engine requires a new camshaft, it likely also needs a complete overhaul. In actual practice, the engine block is stripped of components and sent to an automotive machine shop where the block can have the cylinders refinished or overbored and other checks can be made. Most shops will "hot-tank" the block in a caustic solvent for thorough cleaning. The solution in a hot tank destroys the soft metal in camshaft bearings. In nearly every case, as part of their engine block prepping service, the automotive machine shop will install new replacement cam bearings. If, for some reason, you choose to attempt camshaft bearing replacement yourself, the following should be helpful.

a. A special tool called a Camshaft Bearing Remover/Installer is required. This tool normally consists of a bearing driver and a number of different size expanders, or collets to hold the bearings of a wide variety of engines. These tools vary in quality and cost but are all designed to install the bearing straight, parallel to the engine's centerline. This type of tool can often be rented. Use great care if using substitutes since the block can easily be damaged beyond repair with use of improper tools and methods. Note too, that sometimes if a defective lifter wears a just a lobe or two, and not too much metal has circulated in the oil, it may be possible to replace a camshaft and use the original bearings without removal. Typically, camshaft bearings show little wear, especially in contrast to connecting rod bearings or crankshaft main bearings.

➥Camshaft bearings, once removed, must never be reinstalled.

b. Remove the camshaft rear cover (plug). This is a round plug, similar to a so-called "freeze-plug." The engine flywheel must be removed to access the rear camshaft cover (plug).

c. From a camshaft bearing remover tool kit, select the expander assembly and driving washer. Install the tool into the camshaft bore and drive out the bearings, one by one.

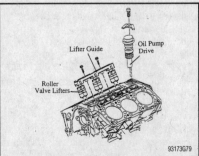

Fig. 129 Internal components that must be removed before the camshaft can be pulled out—3.1L, 3.4L (VIN E) and 3.8L engines

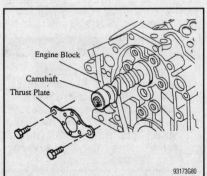

Fig. 130 Remove the thrust plate and pull out the camshaft—3.1L, 3.4L (VIN E) and 3.8L engines

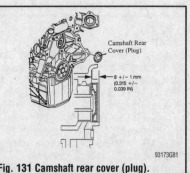

Fig. 131 Camshaft rear cover (plug). Install flush to the block or slightly recessed, as shown—3.1L, 3.4L (VIN E) and 3.8L engines

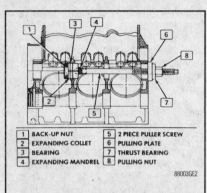

1	BACK-UP NUT	5	2 PIECE PULLER SCREW
2	EXPANDING COLLET	6	PULLING PLATE
3	BEARING	7	THRUST BEARING
4	EXPANDING MANDREL	8	PULLING NUT

88003GE2

Fig. 132 Typical camshaft bearing removal and installation tool

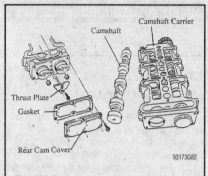

93173G82

Fig. 133 Exploded view of the camshaft and cam carrier arrangement—3.4L (VIN X) engine

To install:

10. Clean all parts well. If the camshaft bearings were removed, examine the bores in the block. Note that there are oil holes which MUST line up with the oil holes in the bearings or the camshaft will quickly fail. Severe engine damage will result if the oil holes are not correctly aligned. If the camshaft bearings were removed, and you attempting to install them, use the following as a guide. A short piece of ³⁄₃₂ inch brass rod with a 90 degree bend in the end, or an appropriate size Allen wrench can be used to probe the bearing holes to ensure the holes are proper aligned with the holes in the block. Use care not to scratch the bearing surfaces.

  a. With the new bearings, select the proper expander and driver washer from the camshaft installation kit.

  b. Index the camshaft bearing oil hole so it will line up with the oil hole in the block.

  c. Install all of the intermediate camshaft bearings first. Make sure the oil hole in the bearing lines up with the oil hole in the block.

  d. Install the #1 camshaft bearing. Make sure the oil hole in the bearing lines up with the oil hole in the block.

  e. Install the #4 camshaft bearing. Make sure the oil hole in the bearing lines up with the oil hole in the block.

  f. Apply sealer, GM #12345493, or equivalent, to the camshaft cover (rear plug) and install the plug until flush with the engine block.

✳✳ WARNING

All camshaft journals are the same diameter so care must be used in removing the camshaft to avoid damage to the bearings.

11. Coat the camshaft bearing journals with engine oil or engine assembly lube. Coat the camshaft lobes with GM lubricant #1052365. Special cam lobe lubricants are also available. The reason a camshaft needs special attention with its lubricant is that it is usually a long time between camshaft installation and initial start-up. This is especially true on front wheel drive vehicles where the engine must be removed and installed. Thin lubricants will drain away. Camshaft lubes or special oils like GM Engine Oil Supplement (EOS) will cling to the camshaft lobes. In addition, camshaft lobes are lubricated by crankshaft and connecting rod throw-off oil. When an engine first starts, it may not run fast enough to supply the oil needed to lubricate the camshaft lobes. A

special camshaft·lube protects a new camshaft in the first few critical minutes at start-up and break-in. Do not neglect to properly lubricate the camshaft or it could be ruined in minutes.

12. Start the camshaft into the bore. Often, with all the lube on it, it can be too slippery to handle conveniently. Some technicians will temporarily install the cam drive sprocket to give them something to grip. Turn the camshaft as you install it and use care to keep the camshaft lobes from gouging the soft metal of the bearings.

13. Install the thrust plate and torque the screws to 89 inch lbs. (10 Nm).

14. Lubricate the driven gear of the oil pump driven gear assembly with GM lubricant #1052365. Coat the rest of the assembly with clean engine oil. Install the oil pump drive and tighten the hold-down bolt to 27 ft. lbs. (36 Nm).

15. Install the timing chain and sprockets using the procedures found in this section.

16. Install the remainder of the components in the reverse order of assembly.

3.4L (VIN X) Engine

♦ See Figure 133

The 3.4L (VIN X) engine uses a direct-acting Double Over Head Camshaft (DOHC) layout. Motion is transmitted from the camshaft lobe through the hydraulic lifter directly to the valve tip. The camshafts are not interchangeable. The right (rear) camshafts are shorter than the left (front) camshafts.

The aluminum camshaft carriers each contain one intake and one exhaust camshaft. The actual aluminum in the carrier serves as the camshaft bearing surface. The camshaft thrust plates, which control the camshaft location, are mounted on the rear of the carriers.

✳✳ WARNING

Timing must be reset if the camshaft sprockets are removed from their shafts. Pins or keys are not used to establish camshaft to crankshaft timing. Please refer to the Timing Belt Removal and Installation and Cylinder Head Removal and Installation procedures for more information, cautions and the special tools required.

1. Remove the camshaft carrier using the procedure found under Cylinder Head Removal and Installation.

✳✳ WARNING

Keep the valve lifters in order so the lifters may be installed in their original locations.

2. Remove the lifters.

3. Remove the oil from the camshaft hold-down tool hole in the camshaft carrier. Install tool J 38613-Camshaft Hold-down Tool or exact equivalent.

4. Remove the camshaft sprockets.

5. Remove the rear cover plate (also called the thrust plate cover) and gasket. Remove the thrust plate bolts and the thrust plates.

6. Remove the camshaft hold-down tool.

✳✳ WARNING

All camshaft journals are the same diameter so care must be used in removing the camshaft to avoid damage to the bearings. In addition, there are no removable bearings since the camshafts ride in the aluminum camshaft carrier.

7. Carefully remove the camshaft out of the back of the camshaft carrier.

8. Pry out the oil seal using care not to damage the aluminum surfaces around the seal.

To install:

9. Clean all parts well. Coat the seal and the camshaft lobes and journals with GM's #1052367 Engine Oil Supplement (EOS), or equivalent camshaft lube. This is very important.

10. Install a replacement oil seal using a suitable driver.

11. Install the camshaft to the carrier, working from the rear of the carrier. Use care not to damage the seal.

12. Inspect the thrust plates and locate the marking arrow. Install the thrust plates with the arrow on the thrust plate "UP". Torque the thrust plate bolts to 89 inch lbs. (10 Nm). Using a new gasket, install the thrust plate cover. Torque the thrust plate cover bolts to 89 inch lbs. (10 Nm).

13. Lubricate the lifters with GM's #1052367 Engine Oil Supplement (EOS), or equivalent camshaft lube. Install the lifters. From shop stock, cut and install six pieces of rubber hose under the camshaft and between the lifters to hold the lifters in the carrier. The exhaust side uses six pieces of tubing 3/16 x 6 inches long. The intake side uses six pieces of tubing 5/32 x 6 inches long.

14. Install the camshaft carrier to the cylinder head using the procedure found under Cylinder Head Removal and Installation.

15. Remove the oil from the camshaft hold-down tool hole in the camshaft carrier. Install Camshaft Hold-down Tool J 38613, or exact equivalent.

16. Install the camshaft sprockets. Please refer to Timing Belt and Sprocket Removal and Installation found in this section.

17. Install the remaining components in the reverse order of removal. Pay particular attention to the information in this section on timing belt installation since this retimes the sprockets to the camshafts. Please see the Timing Belt and Sprocket Removal and Installation procedure. This is most important.

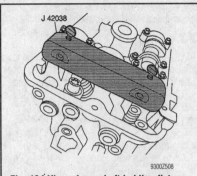

Fig. 134 View of camshaft holding fixture J 42038 installed on the camshafts—3.5L (VIN H) engine

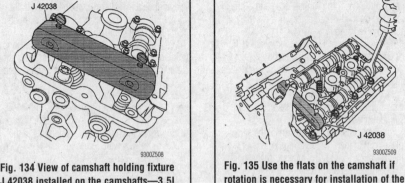

Fig. 135 Use the flats on the camshaft if rotation is necessary for installation of the holding tool—3.5L (VIN H) engine

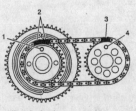

Fig. 136 Before installation, compress the tensioner and lock it in place with a piece of wire—3.5L (VIN H) engine

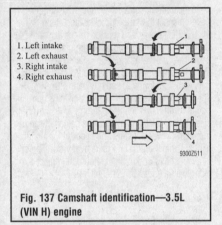

1. Left intake
2. Left exhaust
3. Right intake
4. Right exhaust

Fig. 137 Camshaft identification—3.5L (VIN H) engine

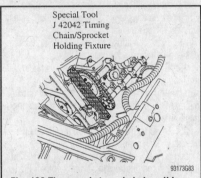

Special Tool J 42042 Timing Chain/Sprocket Holding Fixture

Fig. 138 The sprockets and chains slide off the camshafts onto this fixture—3.5L (VIN H) engine

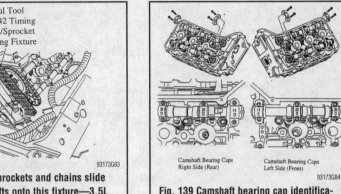

Camshaft Bearing Caps Right Side (Rear)   Camshaft Bearing Caps Left Side (Front)

Fig. 139 Camshaft bearing cap identification—3.5L (VIN H) engine

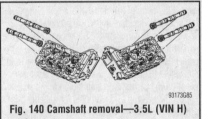

Fig. 140 Camshaft removal—3.5L (VIN H) engine

3.5L Engine

▶ **See Figures 134 thru 141**

The four overhead camshafts are driven by three separate 8mm, single-row, fine pitch chains. The primary drive chain connects the crankshaft with both large intake camshaft sprockets, the balance shaft sprocket and the intermediate shaft sprocket. The exhaust camshafts are driven by short chains from the intake camshafts. Primary timing chain tension is held by a tensioner that hydraulically applies pressure to a pivoting tensioner shoe/chain guide. The intake-to-exhaust camshaft chain tensioner contains an internal spring that provides a constant load on the secondary timing chains.

✷✷ WARNING

This engine is constructed primarily of aluminum. Use care when working with light alloy parts. Fasteners which thread into aluminum must not be over-torqued or damage to the threads may result. Tighten specifica-
tions must be strictly observed to assure proper gasket sealing. When cleaning gasket surfaces on aluminum or magnesium parts, tools specifically designed for these materials should be used. Soft wire brushes and dull scrapers are recommended to prevent gouging of the machined surfaces. In order to obtain valid bolt torque readings, excessive oil or coolant accumulations in the bolt holes should be avoided. Blow out the bolt holes using compressed air prior to installing the fastener.

➡ **In general, this procedure can be used for both the left side (front) and right side (rear) camshafts.**

1. Partially drain the cooling system into a suitable container.
2. Rotate the crankshaft until the engine is positioned at Top Dead Center (TDC) for number 1 cylinder (right side, rear bank, forward cylinder) on the compression stroke (firing position)

✷✷ WARNING

Special Tools J 42038 Camshaft Holding Fixture, J 42042 Timing Chain/Sprocket Holding Fixture and J 36660-A Electronic Angle Meter, or their exact equivalents, are required for this procedure.

3. Disconnect the thermostat housing for access to mount special tool J 42042 Chain/Sprocket Holding Fixture.

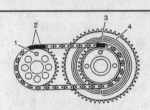

Align the exhaust sprocket drive pin (1) between the two darkened links (2). Align the intake sprocket drive pin (4) with the single darkened link (3)

Left Side (Front)

Align the intake sprocket drive pin (1) with the two darkened links (2). Align the exhaust sprocket drive pin (3) between the single darkened link (4)

Right Side (Rear)

Fig. 141 Secondary camshaft sprocket drive chain and alignment pins—3.5L (VIN H) engine

4. Remove the camshaft cover using the procedures found in this section.

You must install the J 42038 Camshaft Holding Fixture immediately after cam cover removal. This tool prevents unexpected camshaft rotation caused by valve spring pressure.

5. Install special tool J 42038 on the camshafts. When properly installed, this fixture will be fully seated on the camshaft ends with the camshaft flats parallel to the cam cover sealing surface.

6. If working on the right side (rear) camshafts, remove the camshaft position sensor.

7. Remove the camshaft sprocket bolts.

8. Install special tool J 42042 on the cylinder head. Evenly slide the secondary drive chain and camshaft sprockets off the camshafts and onto J 42042. This fixture keeps the sprockets and chain in tension and in the correct relationship.

9. Observe the markings on the camshaft bearing caps. Each bearing cap is marked to identify its locations. It is important that the bearing caps be installed in their correct locations. Look for:

a. The raised feature on the camshaft bearing cap must always be oriented toward the outboard of the engine.

b. The letter I indicates the intake camshaft.

c. The letter E indicates the exhaust camshaft.

d. The number indicates the journal position from the front of the engine.

10. Remove the camshaft bearing cap retaining bolts and remove the bearing caps. Use care to note the position of each bearing cap. Store them in such a way that there will be no mix-up at assembly. The cap closest to the front of the engine is the thrust cap and must not be installed in any other location.

11. Remove special tool J 42038 from the camshafts. Allow the camshaft lobes to find a neutral position by rotating each camshaft, if necessary. DO NOT rotate the camshafts more than 10 degrees. Lift the camshafts from the engine. To prevent corrosion, the camshafts should be covered by an oil soaked shop towel while they are out of the engine.

12. If necessary, remove the camshaft followers. Keep them in the order in which they were removed and store in a clean place.

To install:

13. Clean all parts well. Inspect the camshaft and all related components. If there is any question as to a component's condition, replace the part.

The camshaft follower must be positioned squarely on the valve tip so that the full width of the roller will completely contact the camshaft lobe. If the camshaft followers are being reused, you must put them back in their original locations.

14. If the camshaft followers were removed, apply a liberal amount of clean engine oil or engine assembly lube to the valve lifter roller, the lash adjuster and valve tip areas of the camshaft follow-ers. Place the camshaft followers in position on the valve tip and lifter. The rounded head end of the follower goes on the lash adjuster while the flat end goes on the valve tip.

15. Verify that the No.1 cylinder is still at TDC of its compression stroke (firing position).

16. Select the proper camshafts for installation noting the following:

a. The left side (front) cylinder head camshafts are longer than those on the right cylinder head.

b. Both sets of camshafts share the same placement of identification rings. However the identification ring for the intake camshafts is between the first and second sets of lobes. The identification ring for the exhaust camshafts is located between the second and third sets of lobes.

17. Apply a liberal amount of clean engine oil or engine assembly lube to the camshaft journals and cylinder head camshaft carriers.

18. Place the intake and exhaust camshafts in position in the cylinder head.

19. Position the camshaft lobes in a neutral position with the front notch for the camshaft sprocket drive pins neat the top of their rotation and the rear flats of the camshaft near the installation position of Special Tool J 42038.

20. Observe the markings on the camshaft bearing caps. Each bearing cap is marked to identify its locations. It is important that the bearing caps be installed in their correct locations. Look for the following:

a. The raised feature on the camshaft bearing cap must always be oriented toward the outboard of the engine.

b. The letter I indicates the intake camshaft.

c. The letter E indicates the exhaust camshaft.

d. The number indicates the journal position from the front of the engine.

21. Install the camshaft bearing thrust caps in the first journal of each camshaft. The thrust caps are wider than the others and have machined undercuts not present on the other caps. Make sure the orientation marking is closest to the engine valley. Install the remaining bearing caps with their orientation mark closest to the engine valley. Hand start all of the bearing cap bolts.

22. Tighten the camshaft bearing caps to just 71 inch lbs. (8 Nm). Use J 36660-A or equivalent torque angle meter to tighten the bolts an additional 22 degrees.

23. Using the hex cast into the camshaft, rotate the camshaft so that the rear camshaft flat is facing the cylinder head. It should not be necessary to rotate the camshaft more than 10 degrees. Install J 42038 Camshaft Holding Fixture at the rear of the cylinder head. The camshafts must be locked in place using this fixture before installation of the secondary timing chain.

24. Compress the secondary timing chain tensioner shoes with your hand. Lock the tensioner by inserting a piece of wire into the access hole in the side of the tensioner. Slowly release pressure on the tensioner shoes. The tensioner should remain compressed.

25. Slide the intake and exhaust camshaft sprockets off of special tool J 42042 and onto their respective camshafts and align the drive pins in the camshafts. With the sprockets correctly in place, remove tool J 42042 from the cylinder head. Tighten the camshaft sprocket bolts to 18 ft. lbs. (25 Nm) then, using a torque angle meter, tighten the bolts an additional 45 degrees.

26. Remove the locking wire from the secondary timing chain tensioner allowing the tensioner shoes to expand and apply pressure to the timing chain.

27. Remove tool J 42038 from the camshafts.

28. Install the front camshaft cover and the thermostat housing, following procedures in this section.

29. Install the remaining components in the reverse order they were removed.

CAMSHAFT INSPECTION

3.1L, 3.4L (VIN E) and 3.8L Engines

Inspect all of the camshaft and drive components. Inspect the drive sprockets and chain. Inspect the keyway and threads on the camshaft. Check the cam lobes and the bearing surfaces for wear. The camshaft cannot be repaired, and, if damaged, must be replaced. Measure the camshaft journals with a micrometer and compare with specifications. Replace if worn. Camshafts normally operate with 0.001 inch (0.025mm) or less bearing clearance. If a lathe is available, a camshaft can be mounted between centers and checked for straightness. In actual practice, if there is any question as to a camshaft's condition, it should be replaced along with a complete set of lifters.

3.4L (VIN X) Engine

Inspect the camshaft for wear or deformation. Inspect the lobes for wear. Replace if necessary. Inspect the nose of the camshaft for brinelling from the lock ring. Pressure marks are acceptable. Grooves on the camshaft are not acceptable and the camshaft must be replaced. Inspect the carrier for scratches and/or burrs around the seal surface and also where the camshaft journals rest (bearing surfaces) on the carrier. Clean all the oil holes and inspect the bearing oil feed holes for metal debris, blockage and dirt. In actual practice, if there is any question as to a camshaft's condition, it should be replaced.

3.5L Engine

Clean the camshaft(s) in an appropriate solvent such as Safety-Kleen®. Dry the camshaft(s) with compressed air. Inspect the camshaft sprocket locating notch for damage or wear. Inspect the lobes and bearing journals for excessive scoring or pitting, discoloration from overheating and deformation from excessive wear, especially on the camshaft lobes. If any of these conditions exist, replace the camshaft. Measure the camshaft bearing journals for diameter and out-of-round using a micrometer. If the bearing journal diameter is smaller than 1.061 inch (26.948mm), replace the camshaft. If bearing journal out-of-round exceeds 0.0009 inch (0.022mm), replace the camshaft. If a lathe is available, a camshaft can be mounted between centers and checked for straightness. Camshaft runout cannot exceed 0.002 inch (0.051mm). No machining of the camshaft is allowed. In actual practice, if there is any question as to a camshaft's condition, it should be replaced.

Intermediate Shaft

REMOVAL & INSTALLATION

3.4L (VIN X) Engine

➡ The engine must be removed from the vehicle to service the intermediate shaft.

1. Remove the engine from the vehicle using the procedures found in this section.
2. Remove the right side (rear) cylinder head and oil pump drive assembly using the procedures found in this section.
3. Remove the timing chain assembly using the procedures found in this section.
4. Unfasten the thrust plate screws, then remove the plate.
5. Remove the intermediate shaft, using care not to damage the journals or bearings.

To install:

6. Clean all parts well. Lubricate the intermediate shaft journals and gear with engine oil or engine assembly lube. Install the intermediate shaft, thrust plate and retainer screws. Tighten the screws to 80 inch lbs. (10 Nm).
7. Replace the O-ring after the sprocket is installed, then install the timing chain and gear assembly using the procedures found in this section.
8. Install the oil pump drive assembly and cylinder head using the procedures found in this section.
9. Install the engine assembly using the procedures found in this section.

Balance Shaft

REMOVAL & INSTALLATION

3.8L Engine

1. Remove the engine from the vehicle using the procedures found in this section. Secure the engine to a suitable workstand.

➡ Before removing any of the engine timing components, it is good practice to set the crankshaft so that the #1 cylinder (left side, front, forward cylinder) is at Top Dead Center (TDC) of its compression stroke (firing position). This should align all timing marks and serves as a reference for all later work.

2. Remove the flywheel-to-crankshaft bolts and remove the flywheel.
3. Remove the engine front cover (timing chain cover) using the procedures found in this section.
4. Remove the cam drive sprocket and the timing chain using the procedures found in this section.
5. To remove the balance shaft, perform the following:
   a. Remove the balance shaft gear-to-shaft bolt and the gear.
   b. Remove the balance shaft retainer-to-engine bolts and the retainer.
   c. Using a slide hammer tool, pull the balance shaft from the front of the engine.
6. If replacing the rear balance shaft bearing, perform the following procedures:

   a. Drive the rear plug from the engine.
   b. Using a camshaft bearing tool, press the rear bearing from the engine.
   c. Dip the replacement bearing in engine oil.
   d. Using a camshaft bearing tool, press the new rear bearing into the engine.
   e. Install the rear cup plug. Use sealer around the edges.

To install:

7. Clean all parts well. Inspect all moving parts for wear and clean all gasket sealing surfaces.
8. Lubricate the balance shaft with clean engine oil or engine assembly lube and carefully work the balance shaft back into the engine. Use care not to damage the bearings in the engine block. Install the retainer and torque the bolts to 27 ft. lbs. (37 Nm).
9. Align the balance shaft gear with the camshaft gear timing marks and install the gear onto the balance shaft. Tighten the bolt to 15 ft. lbs. (20 Nm) plus an additional 35 degrees.
10. Align the marks on the balance shaft gear and the camshaft gear by turning the balance shaft.
11. Verify that the crankshaft is still at TDC #1 cylinder. If not, rotate the crankshaft so the #1 piston is at TDC (firing position).
12. Install the timing chain and cam drive sprocket using the procedures found in this section.
13. Replace the balance shaft front bearing retainer and torque the bolts to 26 ft. lbs. (35 Nm).
14. Install the front engine cover using the procedures found in this section.
15. Install the remainder of the components in the reverse order of removal
16. Install the engine into the vehicle using the procedures found in this section.

Rear Crankshaft Seal

REMOVAL & INSTALLATION

3.1L, 3.4L and 3.8L Engines

▶ See Figure 142

Please note that the entire transaxle assembly must be removed to perform this procedure. Make very sure of the diagnosis before beginning work.

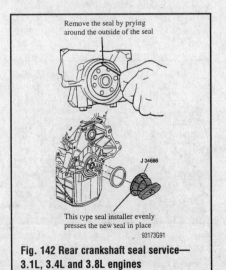

Fig. 142 Rear crankshaft seal service—3.1L, 3.4L and 3.8L engines

Remove the seal by prying around the outside of the seal

J 34686

This type seal installer evenly presses the new seal in place

93173G91

1. Remove the transaxle from the vehicle. Please see Section 7.
2. Remove the engine flywheel using the procedures found in this section.
3. Remove the rear oil seal by prying out of the engine block. Use care not to nick the crankshaft when removing the seal. Pry the seal a little at a time, repeating as necessary around the crankshaft rear oil seal.

To install:

4. Clean all parts well. Coat the new seal entirely with clean engine oil.
5. GM recommends their seal installer J 34686 which presses the replacement seal into place. Many replacement seal kits come with a plastic driver suitable for one-time use. Use care if using substitutes. The goal is to get the seal installed squarely, bottomed in its bore, without damage. If there is any question about the condition of the seal after installation, remove and discard it and try again with another seal. Much time and effort are spend getting access to the rear crankshaft seal. Take the time to make sure it is correctly installed.
6. When satisfied with the seal installation, install the flywheel using the procedures found in this section.
7. Install the transaxle using the procedures found in Section 7.

3.5L Engine

▶ See Figures 143 and 144

Please note that the entire transaxle assembly must be removed to perform this procedure. Make very sure of the diagnosis before beginning work.

1. Remove the transaxle from the vehicle. Please see Section 7.

✳✳ WARNING

Rear crankshaft seal removal cannot be performed on an engine stand. If the engine is out of the vehicle, properly support the engine on a bench or on the floor, keeping in mind that the major components including the oil pan are made of aluminum.

2. Remove the flywheel assembly using the procedures found in this section.
3. GM recommends their Special Tool J 42841

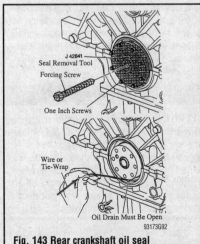

Fig. 143 Rear crankshaft oil seal removal—3.5L (VIN H) engine

J 42841 Seal Removal Tool
Forcing Screw
One Inch Screws
Wire or Tie-Wrap
Oil Drain Must Be Open
93173G92

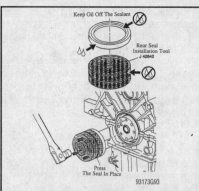

Fig. 144 Rear crankshaft oil seal installation—3.5L (VIN H) engine

to remove the crankshaft rear oil seal. Essentially this is a metal plate with a center hole threaded for a center forcing screw. The plate has eight holes around the outside edge through which 1 inch long self-drilling sheetmetal screws are installed. When the center forcing screw is turned, the plate pulls the seal out. Use care if using substitutes.

To install:

4. Clean all parts well. It is important to make sure the drain is clear before installing the new crankshaft rear oil seal. Failure to clear the drain could cause the crankshaft oil seal to leak. Probe the drain hole with wire or a long plastic tie-wrap.

5. Place a small amount of sealer, GM #1052942 Gasket Maker, or equivalent, at the crankcase split line across the end of the upper/lower crankcase seal.

6. Coat the outer diameter of the crankshaft where the seal will ride, with clean engine oil. DO NOT allow any engine oil on the area where the oil seal is to be pressed onto the rear crankshaft. The factory replacement seal has a green coating pre-applied to the inner diameter of the oil seal and must not be contaminated.

7. Wipe the outer diameter of the flywheel flange clean with a lint-free cloth.

8. DO NOT put any engine oil on the green coating pre-applied to the inner diameter of the oil seal. This coating is a sealant that must not be contaminated. Lubricate the outer rubber surface of the oil seal with clean engine oil.

9. GM recommends their J 42842 oil seal installer. This plate holds the seal and three bolts thread into the rear of the crankshaft and pull the seal into place. Use care if using substitutes. The goal is to get the seal installed squarely, bottomed in its bore, without damage. If there is any question about the condition of the seal after installation, remove and discard it and try again with another seal. Much time and effort are spend getting access to the rear crankshaft seal. Take the time to make sure it is correctly installed.

10. When satisfied with the seal installation, install the flywheel using the procedures found in this section.

11. Install the transaxle as outlined in Section 7.

Flywheel

REMOVAL & INSTALLATION

▶ **See Figure 145**

Please note that the entire transaxle assembly must be removed to perform this procedure. Make very sure of the diagnosis before beginning work. New service replacement flywheel bolts are recommended.

1. Remove the transaxle from the vehicle. Please see Section 7.

2. A flywheel locking tool may be helpful to keep the crankshaft from rotating when the flywheel bolts are loosened. Remove the flywheel bolts. New service replacement bolts are recommended.

3. Remove the flywheel from the vehicle.

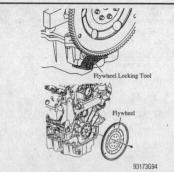

Fig. 145 This typical flywheel locking tool keeps the flywheel from turning when the bolts are loosened or tightened

To install:

4. Clean all parts well. If there is evidence of oil leaking past the rear crankshaft oil seal, replace the oil seal using the procedures found in this section. Examine the teeth around the other edge of the wheel where the starter engages. If they are worn or damaged, replace the flywheel.

5. Flywheel bolts may have thread-locking adhesive on the threads. If the bolts must be reused, clean the threads on the bolts and in the crankshaft.

6. Apply fresh thread-locking compound to all of the flywheel-to-crankshaft bolts.

7. The remaining installation steps are the reverse of the removal procedure. Tighten the flywheel bolts evenly. Final torque should be:

   a. 3.1L and 3.4L engines: 60 ft. lbs. (82 Nm)

   b. 3.5L and 3.8L engines: Tighten to 11 ft. lbs. (15 Nm) plus an additional 50 degrees. NEW BOLTS ARE MANDATORY.

8. Install the transaxle as outlined in Section 7.

EXHAUST SYSTEM

Inspection

▶ **See Figures 146 thru 152**

➡**Safety glasses should be worn at all times when working on or near the exhaust system. Older exhaust systems will almost always be covered with loose rust particles which will shower you when disturbed. These particles are more than a nuisance and could injure your eye.**

✲✲ CAUTION

DO NOT perform exhaust repairs or inspection with the engine or exhaust hot. Allow the system to cool completely before attempting any work. Exhaust systems are noted for sharp edges, flaking metal and rusted bolts. Gloves and eye protection are required. A healthy supply of penetrating oil and rags is highly recommended.

When inspecting or replacing exhaust system components, make sure there is adequate clearance from all points on the underbody to prevent over-

heating of the floor pan and possible damage to the passenger compartment insulation and trim materials.

Check the complete exhaust system and nearby body areas and rear compartment lid for broken, damaged, missing or mis-positioned parts, open seams, holes, loose connections or other deteriora-

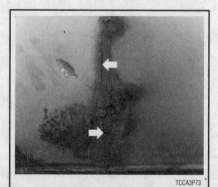

Fig. 146 Cracks in the muffler are a guaranteed leak

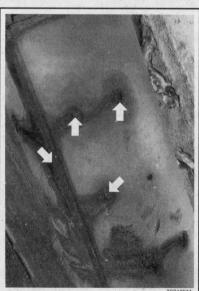

Fig. 147 Check the muffler for rotted spot welds and seams

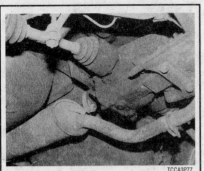

Fig. 148 Make sure the exhaust components are not contacting the body or suspension

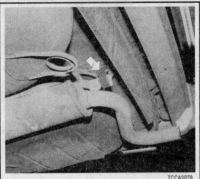

Fig. 149 Check for overstretched or torn exhaust hangers

Fig. 150 Example of a badly deteriorated exhaust pipe

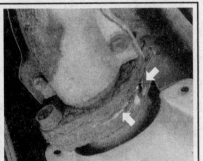

Fig. 151 Inspect flanges for gaskets that have deteriorated and need replacement

Fig. 152 Some systems, like this one, use large O-rings (doughnuts) in between the flanges

tion which could permit fumes to seep into the rear compartment or passenger compartment. Dust or water in the rear compartment may be an indication of a problem in one of these areas. Any faulty area should be corrected immediately. To help insure continued integrity, the exhaust system pipe rearward of the muffler must be replaced whenever a new muffler is installed.

Your GM W-Body vehicle will have one of several types of exhaust systems. On single exhaust systems, for some engines, the entire exhaust system (comprised of a resonator, an exhaust pipe, a muffler and a tailpipe) is serviced as one prewelded part. Some components may be available in the aftermarket but that will require cutting the one piece system to install the parts.

Other W-Body vehicles may use a dual exhaust system serviced as five different components, clamped together. Always replace the catalytic converter gasket at the flanged joint between the exhaust system and the three-way catalytic converter whenever this joint is disturbed. Never reuse a catalytic converter gasket.

Various types of hangers are used to support exhaust systems. These include conventional rubber straps, rubber rings and rubber blocks. The installation of exhaust system hangers is very important as improperly installed hangers can cause annoying vibrations which can be difficult to diagnose.

When servicing a welded connection, it should be cut and the new connection clamped when installing replacement parts. GM recommends you coat slip joints with exhaust system sealer before assembling and that you use new nuts when assembling components. Always wire brush clean

the manifold stud threads with a wire brush before installing new nuts.

Three-Way Catalytic Converter

The three-way catalytic converter is an emission control device added to the exhaust system to reduce pollutants from the exhaust gas stream. It requires the use of unleaded fuel only. Periodic maintenance is not required but the condition of the entire system should be checked whenever the vehicle is raised for any kind of service.

The three-way catalytic converter is serviced by replacing the entire assembly. Always replace the exhaust manifold pipe, gasket and catalytic converter gaskets at the front and rear flanges when serving the catalytic converter.

✴✴ WARNING

To prevent internal damage to the flexible coupling used on most of the catalytic converters, the converter must be supported. The vertical movement at the rear of the converter assembly must not exceed 6 degrees up or down. Also, use caution handling the pipe that contains the oxygen sensor. DO NOT cut the wire. Detach the electrical connector if the pipe needs to be removed or repositioned.

Exhaust System Inspection

The exhaust system (including the catalytic converter heat shield) must be free of leaks, binding, grounding (touching a body or suspension compo-

nent) and excessive vibration. These conditions may occur is any of the following are loose or damaged: flange bolts or flange nuts, heat shield, brackets, pipes, and mis-aligned or defective components. Inspect for cracks on and around the seals and gaskets, exhaust hanger insulators, around the converter, exhaust pipe and tailpipe. Inspect for stripped bolt threads, corroded fasteners and broken welds. If any component is severely rusted or rusted through, it should be replaced.

Your vehicle must be raised and supported safely to inspect the exhaust system properly. By placing 4 safety stands under the vehicle for support should provide enough room for you to slide under the vehicle and inspect the system completely. Start the inspection at the exhaust manifold or turbocharger pipe where the header pipe is attached and work your way to the back of the vehicle. On dual exhaust systems, remember to inspect both sides of the vehicle. Check the complete exhaust system for open seams, holes loose connections, or other deterioration which could permit exhaust fumes to seep into the passenger compartment. Inspect all mounting brackets and hangers for deterioration, some models may have rubber O-rings that can be overstretched and non-supportive. These components will need to be replaced if found. It has always been a practice to use a pointed tool to poke up into the exhaust system where the deterioration spots are to see whether or not they crumble. Some models may have heat shield covering certain parts of the exhaust system , it will be necessary to remove these shields to have the exhaust visible for inspection also.

REPLACEMENT

▶ See Figure 153

There are basically two types of exhaust systems. One is the flange type where the component ends are attached with bolts and a gasket in-between. The other exhaust system is the slip joint type. These components slip into one another using clamps to retain them together.

✴✴ CAUTION

Allow the exhaust system to cool sufficiently before spraying a solvent exhaust fasteners. Some solvents are highly flammable and could ignite when sprayed on hot exhaust components.

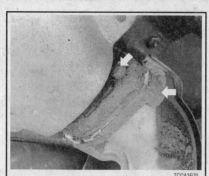

Fig. 153 Nuts and bolts will be extremely difficult to remove when deteriorated with rust

Fig. 154 Example of a flange type exhaust system joint

Fig. 155 Example of a common slip joint type system

Before removing any component of the exhaust system, ALWAYS squirt a liquid rust dissolving agent onto the fasteners for ease of removal. A lot of knuckle skin will be saved by following this rule. It may even be wise to spray the fasteners and allow them to sit overnight.

Flange Type

▶ See Figure 154

☀☀ CAUTION

Do NOT perform exhaust repairs or inspection with the engine or exhaust hot. Allow the system to cool completely before attempting any work. Exhaust systems are noted for sharp edges, flaking metal and rusted bolts. Gloves and eye protection are required. A healthy supply of penetrating oil and rags is highly recommended. Never spray liquid rust dissolving agent onto a hot exhaust component.

Before removing any component on a flange type system, ALWAYS squirt a liquid rust dissolving

agent onto the fasteners for ease of removal. Start by unbolting the exhaust piece at both ends (if required). When unbolting the headpipe from the manifold, make sure that the bolts are free before trying to remove them. if you snap a stud in the exhaust manifold, the stud will have to be removed with a bolt extractor, which often means removal of the manifold itself. Next, disconnect the component from the mounting; slight twisting and turning may be required to remove the component completely from the vehicle. You may need to tap on the component with a rubber mallet to loosen the component. If all else fails, use a hacksaw to separate the parts. An oxy-acetylene cutting torch may be faster but the sparks are DANGEROUS near the fuel tank, and at the very least, accidents could happen, resulting in damage to the under-car parts, not to mention yourself.

Slip Joint Type

▶ See Figure 155

Before removing any component on the slip joint type exhaust system, ALWAYS squirt a liquid rust dissolving agent onto the fasteners for ease of

removal. Start by unbolting the exhaust piece at both ends (if required). When unbolting the head-pipe from the manifold, make sure that the bolts are free before trying to remove them. if you snap a stud in the exhaust manifold, the stud will have to be removed with a bolt extractor, which often means removal of the manifold itself. Next, remove the mounting U-bolts from around the exhaust pipe you are extracting from the vehicle. Don't be surprised if the U-bolts break while removing the nuts. Loosen the exhaust pipe from any mounting brackets retaining it to the floor pan and separate the components.

Slight twisting and turning may be required to remove the component completely from the vehicle. You may need to tap on the component with a rubber mallet to loosen it. In many cases, trying to save and/or salvage exhaust system parts may be more trouble than they are worth. Sawing tailpipes into pieces for easy removal and then installing new parts may make the most sense.

When installing exhaust components, loosely position all components before tightening any of the joints. Once you are satisfied with the fit, begin tightening the fasteners at the front and work your way back.

ENGINE RECONDITIONING

Determining Engine Condition

Anything that generates heat and/or friction will eventually burn or wear out (for example, a light bulb generates heat, therefore its life span is limited). With this in mind, a running engine generates tremendous amounts of both; friction is encountered by the moving and rotating parts inside the engine and heat is created by friction and combustion of the fuel. However, the engine has systems designed to help reduce the effects of heat and friction and provide added longevity. The oiling system reduces the amount of friction encountered by the moving parts inside the engine, while the cooling system reduces heat created by friction and combustion. If either system is not maintained, a breakdown will be inevitable. Therefore, you can see how regular maintenance can affect the service life of your vehicle. If you do not drain, flush and refill your cooling system at the proper intervals, deposits will begin to accumulate in the radiator, thereby reducing the amount of heat it can extract

from the coolant. The same applies to your oil and filter; if it is not changed often enough it becomes laden with contaminates and is unable to properly lubricate the engine. This increases friction and wear.

There are a number of methods for evaluating the condition of your engine. A compression test can reveal the condition of your pistons, piston rings, cylinder bores, head gasket(s), valves and valve seats. An oil pressure test can warn you of possible engine bearing, or oil pump failures. Excessive oil consumption, evidence of oil in the engine air intake area and/or bluish smoke from the tailpipe may indicate worn piston rings, worn valve guides and/or valve seals. As a general rule, an engine that uses no more than one quart of oil every 1000 miles is in good condition. Engines that use one quart of oil or more in less than 1000 miles should first be checked for oil leaks. If any oil leaks are present, have them fixed before determining how much oil is consumed by the engine, especially if blue smoke is not visible at the tailpipe.

COMPRESSION TEST

▶ See Figure 156

A noticeable lack of engine power, excessive oil consumption and/or poor fuel mileage measured over an extended period are all indicators of internal engine wear. Worn piston rings, scored or worn cylinder bores, blown head gaskets, sticking or burnt valves, and worn valve seats are all possible culprits. A check of each cylinder's compression will help locate the problem.

➡**A screw-in type compression gauge is more accurate than the type you simply hold against the spark plug hole. In the case of a V6 where access to the rear spark plug holes is difficult, a screw-in gauge may be only type practical. Although it takes slightly longer to use, it's worth the effort to obtain a more accurate reading.**

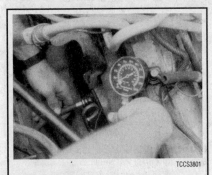

Fig. 156 A screw-in type compression gauge is more accurate and easier to use without an assistant

1. Make sure that the proper amount and viscosity of engine oil is in the crankcase, then ensure the battery is fully charged.

2. Warm-up the engine to normal operating temperature, then shut the engine **OFF**.

3. Disable the ignition system.

4. Label and disconnect all of the spark plug wires from the plugs.

5. Thoroughly clean the cylinder head area around the spark plug ports, then remove the spark plugs.

6. Set the throttle plate to the fully open (wide-open throttle) position. You can block the accelerator linkage open for this, or you can have an assistant fully depress the accelerator pedal.

7. Install a screw-in type compression gauge into the No. 1 spark plug hole until the fitting is snug.

✳✳ WARNING

Be careful not to crossthread the spark plug hole.

8. According to the tool manufacturer's instructions, connect a remote starting switch to the starting circuit.

9. With the ignition switch in the **OFF** position, use the remote starting switch to crank the engine through at least five compression strokes (approximately 5 seconds of cranking) and record the highest reading on the gauge.

10. Repeat the test on each cylinder, cranking the engine approximately the same number of compression strokes and/or time as the first.

11. Compare the highest readings from each cylinder to that of the others. The indicated compression pressures are considered within specifications if the lowest reading cylinder is within 75 percent of the pressure recorded for the highest reading cylinder. For example, if your highest reading cylinder pressure was 150 psi (1034 kPa), then 75 percent of that would be 113 psi (779 kPa). So the lowest reading cylinder should be no less than 113 psi (779 kPa).

12. If a cylinder exhibits an unusually low compression reading, use a squirt-type oil can and introduce about a tablespoon of clean engine oil into the cylinder through the spark plug hole and repeat the compression test. If the compression rises after adding oil, it means the oil has made a temporary seal where the rings meet the cylinder walls. It shows that the cylinder's piston rings and/or cylinder bore are damaged or worn. If, on the other hand, the pressure remains low, the valves may not be seating properly (a valve job is needed), or the head gasket may be blown near that cylinder. If compression in any two adjacent cylinders is low, and if the addition of oil doesn't help raise compression, there is leakage past the head gasket. A quick of the oil dipstick is another indicator. If the dipstick has a light-brown foamy substance looking like melted ice cream, it's a dead giveaway that there is water in the oil and the engine has major problems, such as a blown head gasket. Oil in the cooling system is another indicator of a blown head gasket. Oil and coolant in the combustion chamber, combined with blue or constant white smoke from the tailpipe, may be yet another symptom of this problem. However, don't be alarmed by the normal white smoke emitted from the tailpipe during engine warm-up or from cold weather driving.

OIL PRESSURE TEST

Check for proper oil pressure at the sending unit passage with an externally mounted mechanical oil pressure gauge (as opposed to relying on a factory installed dash-mounted gauge). A tachometer may also be needed, as some specifications may require running the engine at a specific rpm.

1. With the engine cold, locate and remove the oil pressure sending unit. On some engines, this may be a real challenge. In general, accessibility to the oil pressure sending unit determines whether this test can be done.

2. Following the manufacturer's instructions, connect a mechanical oil pressure gauge and, if necessary, a tachometer to the engine.

3. Start the engine and allow it to idle.

4. Check the oil pressure reading when cold and record the number. You may need to run the engine at a specified rpm, so check the specifications.

5. Run the engine until normal operating temperature is reached (upper radiator hose will feel warm).

6. Check the oil pressure reading again with the engine hot and record the number. Turn the engine **OFF**.

7. Compare your hot oil pressure reading to that given in the chart. If the reading is low, check the cold pressure reading against the chart. If the cold pressure is well above the specification, and the hot reading was lower than the specification, you may have the wrong viscosity oil in the engine. Change the oil, making sure to use the proper grade and quantity, then repeat the test.

Low oil pressure readings could be attributed to internal component wear, pump related problems, a low oil level, or oil viscosity that is too low. High oil pressure readings could be caused by an overfilled crankcase, too high of an oil viscosity or a faulty pressure relief valve.

Buy or Rebuild?

Now that you have determined that your engine is worn out, you must make some decisions. The question of whether or not an engine is worth rebuilding is largely a subjective matter and one of personal worth. Is the engine a popular one, or is it an obsolete model? Are parts available? Are special tools available? The Dual Over Head Camshaft engines (3.4L VIN X and 3.5L VIN H) covered in this manual require special camshaft holding fixtures for most procedures. If they are not available, you will have great difficulty servicing these engines. Will it get acceptable gas mileage once it is rebuilt? Is the car it's being put into worth keeping? Would it be less expensive to buy a new engine, have your engine rebuilt by a pro, rebuild it yourself or buy a used engine from a salvage yard? Or would it be simpler and less expensive to buy another car? If you have considered all these matters and more, and have still decided to rebuild the engine, then it is time to decide how you will rebuild it.

➡**The editors at Chilton feel that most engine machining should be performed by a professional machine shop. Don't think of it as wasting money, rather, as an assurance that the job has been done right the first time. There are many expensive and specialized tools required to perform such tasks as boring and honing an engine block or having a valve job done on a cylinder head. Even inspecting the parts requires expensive micrometers and gauges to properly measure wear and clearances. Also, a machine shop can deliver to you clean, and ready to assemble parts, saving you time and aggravation. Your maximum savings will come from performing the removal, disassembly, assembly and installation of the engine and purchasing or renting only the tools required to perform the above tasks. Depending on the particular circumstances, you may save 40 to 60 percent of the cost doing these yourself.**

A complete rebuild or overhaul of an engine involves replacing all of the moving parts (pistons, rods, crankshaft, camshaft, etc.) with new ones and machining the non-moving wearing surfaces of the block and heads. Unfortunately, this may not be cost effective. For instance, your crankshaft may have been damaged or worn, but it can be machined undersize for a minimal fee.

So, as you can see, you can replace everything inside the engine, but, it is wiser to replace only those parts which are really needed, and, if possible, repair the more expensive ones.

In the real world, where time and convenience often count more than money, a worn out engine can be simply replaced with one of the following choices:

• A good used engine from an automotive dismantler. In some cases, a reputable automotive recycler may even offer a limited warranty on the used engine.

• A "short block", or "short engine" is a rebuilt engine that includes a reconditioned engine block, crankshaft, connecting rods, pistons, usually the camshaft and maybe the timing set, depending on the engine. This may be an option if the cylinder heads are in good condition and/or may have been recently reconditioned (a "valve job") themselves, but the engine's "bottom end" is damaged. A rebuilt short block from a reputable dealer should have a warranty.

• A "long block" is a completely assembled, rebuilt engine that includes all the parts in a short block plus reconditioned cylinder heads. Normally you will need to transfer your intake and exhaust manifolds, fuel and ignition systems and other engine accessories. A rebuilt long block from a reputable dealer should have a warranty.

Swapping in a rebuilt long block or good used engine is the solution most individuals and even professional shops will use. It is the quickest, and often the least expensive way to return the vehicle to service. On today's front-wheel drive cars, removing and installing an engine can be long, arduous task. Most individuals and certainly all professional shops will only want to do the job once. Installing an engine rebuilt at home, then having to remove it again (perhaps several times) because some component failed, was incorrectly installed, is out of specification or some leak needs to be corrected, can be most discouraging. Professional engine builders deal in such volume that their prices for an assembled, reconditioned engine may be less than the cost of buying parts, having other components reconditioned and then assembling the engine yourself. Dealership parts departments can often order a so-called "crate motor" which is a factory reconditioned or even brand new engine, at surprisingly reasonable prices. You simply open the "crate", transfer a few components from your engine, and you're ready for installation. A new engine (keep the receipt) should have a warranty and may even enhance the resale value of your vehicle.

If you choose to recondition the engine yourself, look into engine rebuild kits. Most popular engines have kits available containing the major components. The crankshaft is generally reconditioned to a standard undersize and matching oversize bearings are included. Pistons and rings, oil pumps, timing chain sets and gasket sets are available. Since the major components in a rebuild kit are reconditioned, or even new, it takes the guesswork out of precision measuring (if you have the proper tools) and evaluating used parts. These kits, purchased from a reliable supplier and carefully installed in your clean and prepared engine block, can produce a successful overhaul.

Later in this section, we will break the engine down into its two main components: the cylinder head and the engine block. We will discuss each component, and the recommended parts to replace during a rebuild on each.

Engine Overhaul Tips

Most engine overhaul procedures are fairly standard. In addition to specific parts replacement procedures and specifications for your individual engine, this section is also a guide to acceptable rebuilding procedures. Examples of standard rebuilding practice are given and should be used along with specific details concerning your particular engine.

Competent and accurate machine shop services will ensure maximum performance, reliability and engine life. In most instances it is more profitable for the do-it-yourself mechanic to remove, clean and inspect the component, buy the necessary parts and deliver these to a shop for actual machine work.

Much of the assembly work (crankshaft, bearings, piston rods, and other components) is well within the scope of the do-it-yourself mechanic's tools and abilities. You will have to decide for yourself the depth of involvement you desire in an engine repair or rebuild.

TOOLS

The tools required for an engine overhaul or parts replacement will depend on how much work you will be doing yourself. With a few exceptions, they will be the tools found in a mechanic's tool kit (see Section 1 of this manual). More in-depth work will require some or all of the following:
- A dial indicator (reading in thousandths) mounted on a universal base
- Micrometers and telescope gauges
- Jaw and screw-type pullers
- Scraper
- Valve spring compressor
- Ring groove cleaner
- Piston ring expander and compressor
- Ridge reamer
- Cylinder hone or glaze breaker
- Plastigage®
- Engine stand

The use of most of these tools is illustrated in this section. Many can be rented for a one-time use from a local parts jobber or tool supply house specializing in automotive work.

Occasionally, the use of special tools is called for. See the information on Special Tools and the Safety Notice in the front of this book before substituting another tool.

OVERHAUL TIPS

Aluminum has become extremely popular for use in engines, due to its low weight. Observe the following precautions when handling aluminum parts:

- Never hot tank aluminum parts (the caustic hot tank solution will eat the aluminum.
- Remove all aluminum parts (identification tag, etc.) from engine parts prior to the tanking.
- Always coat threads lightly with engine oil or anti-seize compounds before installation, to prevent seizure.
- Never overtighten bolts or spark plugs especially in aluminum threads.

When assembling the engine, any parts that will be exposed to frictional contact must be prelubed to provide lubrication at initial start-up. Any product specifically formulated for this purpose can be used, but engine oil is not recommended as a pre-lube in most cases.

When semi-permanent (locked, but removable) installation of bolts or nuts is desired, threads should be cleaned and coated with Loctite® or another similar, commercial non-hardening sealant.

CLEANING

▶ **See Figures 157, 158, 159 and 160**

Before the engine and its components are inspected, they must be thoroughly cleaned. You will need to remove any engine varnish, oil sludge and/or carbon deposits from all of the components to insure an accurate inspection. A crack in the engine block or cylinder head can easily become overlooked if hidden by a layer of sludge or carbon.

Most of the cleaning process can be carried out with common hand tools and readily available solvents or solutions. Carbon deposits can be chipped away using a hammer and a hard wooden chisel. Old gasket material and varnish or sludge can usually be removed using a scraper and/or cleaning solvent. Extremely stubborn deposits may require the use of a power drill with a wire brush. If using a wire brush, use extreme care around any critical machined surfaces (such as the gasket surfaces, bearing saddles, cylinder bores, etc.). Use of a wire brush is NOT RECOMMENDED on any aluminum components. Always follow any safety recommendations given by the manufacturer of the tool and/or solvent. You should always wear eye protection during any cleaning process involving scraping, chipping or spraying of solvents.

An alternative to the mess and hassle of cleaning the parts yourself is to drop them off at a local garage or machine shop. They will, more than likely, have the necessary equipment to properly clean all of the parts for a nominal fee.

Fig. 157 Use a gasket scraper to remove the old gasket material from the mating surfaces

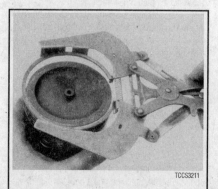

Fig. 158 Use a ring expander tool to remove the piston rings

Fig. 159 Clean the piston ring grooves using a ring groove cleaner tool, or . . .

Fig. 160 . . . use a piece of an old ring to clean the grooves. Be careful, the ring can be quite sharp

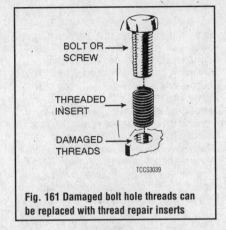

Fig. 161 Damaged bolt hole threads can be replaced with thread repair inserts

Fig. 162 Standard thread repair insert (left), and spark plug thread insert

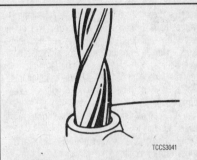

Fig. 163 Drill out the damaged threads with the specified size bit. Be sure to drill completely through the hole or to the bottom of a blind hole

Fig. 164 Using the kit, tap the hole in order to receive the thread insert. Keep the tap well oiled and back it out frequently to avoid clogging the threads

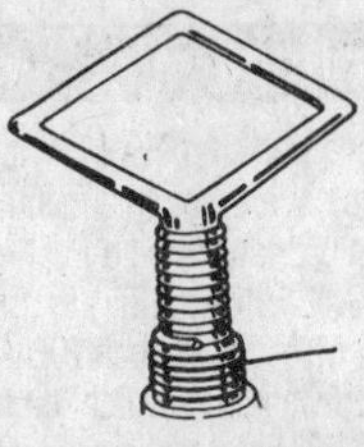

Fig. 165 Screw the insert onto the installer tool until the tang engages the slot. Thread the insert into the hole until it is ¼–½ turn below the top surface, then remove the tool and break off the tang using a punch

✳✳ CAUTION

Always wear eye protection during any cleaning process involving scraping, chipping or spraying of solvents.

Remove any oil galley plugs, freeze plugs and/or pressed-in bearings and carefully wash and degrease all of the engine components including the fasteners and bolts. Small parts such as the valves, springs, etc., should be placed in a metal basket and allowed to soak. Use pipe cleaner type brushes, and clean all passageways in the components. Use a ring expander and remove the rings from the pistons. Clean the piston ring grooves with a special tool or a piece of broken ring. Scrape the carbon off of the top of the piston. You should never use a wire brush on the pistons. After preparing all of the piston assemblies in this manner, wash and degrease them again.

✳✳ WARNING

Use extreme care when cleaning around the cylinder head valve seats. A mistake or slip may cost you a new seat.

When cleaning the cylinder head, remove carbon from the combustion chamber with the valves installed. This will avoid damaging the valve seats.

REPAIRING DAMAGED THREADS

▶ **See Figures 161, 162, 163, 164 and 165**

Several methods of repairing damaged threads are available. Heli-Coil®(shown here), Keenserts®and Microdot®are among the most widely used. All involve basically the same principle—drilling out stripped threads, tapping the hole and installing a prewound insert—making welding, plugging and oversize fasteners unnecessary.

Two types of thread repair inserts are usually supplied: a standard type for most inch coarse, inch fine, metric course and metric fine thread sizes and a spark lug type to fit most spark plug port sizes. Consult the individual tool manufacturer's catalog to determine exact applications. Typical thread repair kits will contain a selection of prewound threaded inserts, a tap (corresponding to the outside diameter threads of the insert) and an installation tool. Spark plug inserts usually differ because they require a tap equipped with pilot threads and a combined reamer/tap section. Most manufacturers also supply blister-packed thread repair inserts separately in addition to a master kit containing a variety of taps and inserts plus installation tools.

Before attempting to repair a threaded hole, remove any snapped, broken or damaged bolts or studs. Penetrating oil can be used to free frozen threads. The offending item can usually be removed with locking pliers or using a screw/stud extractor. After the hole is clear, the thread can be repaired, as shown in the series of accompanying illustrations and in the kit manufacturer's instructions.

Engine Preparation

To properly rebuild an engine, you must first remove it from the vehicle, then disassemble and diagnose it. Ideally you should place your engine on an engine stand. This affords you the best access to the engine components. Follow the manufacturer's directions for using the stand with your particular engine. Remove the flywheel before installing the engine to the stand.

Now that you have the engine on a stand, and assuming that you have drained the oil and coolant from the engine, it's time to strip it of all but the necessary components. Before you start disassembling the engine, you may want to take a moment to draw some pictures, or fabricate some labels or containers to mark the locations of various components and the bolts and/or studs which fasten them. Modern day engines use a lot of little brackets and clips which hold wiring harnesses and such, and these holders are often mounted on studs and/or bolts that can be easily mixed up. The manufacturer spent a lot of time and money designing your vehicle, and they wouldn't have wasted any of it by haphazardly placing brackets, clips or fasteners on the vehicle. If it's present when you disassemble it, put it back when you assemble, you will regret not remembering that little bracket which holds a wire harness out of the path of a rotating part.

You should begin by unbolting any accessories still attached to the engine, such as the water pump, power steering pump, alternator, etc. Then, unfasten any manifolds (intake or exhaust) which were not removed during the engine removal procedure. Finally, remove any covers remaining on the engine such as the rocker arm, front or timing cover and oil pan. Some front covers may require the vibration damper and/or crank pulley to be removed beforehand. The idea is to reduce the engine to the bare necessities (cylinder head(s), valve train, engine block, crankshaft, pistons and connecting rods), plus any other 'in block' components such as oil pumps, balance shafts and auxiliary shafts.

Finally, remove the cylinder head(s) from the engine block and carefully place on a bench. Disassembly instructions for each component follow later in this section.

Cylinder Head

There are two basic types of cylinder heads used on the vehicles covered by this manual: the Over Head Valve (OHV, also called a Pushrod Engine) (3.1L VIN M, 3.4L VIN E, 3.8L VIN 1 and 3.8L VIN K) and the Over Head Camshaft (OHC) (in this case, Dual Over Head Camshaft which, on these V6 engines, use a total of four camshafts) which are the 3.4L VIN X and 3.5L Vin H.

Most cylinder heads are made of an aluminum alloy due to its light weight, durability and heat transfer qualities. However, cast iron is still used on many vehicles today. Whether made from aluminum or iron, all cylinder heads have valves and seats. Some use two valves per cylinder, while the more hi-tech engines will utilize a multi-valve configuration using 4 valves per cylinder. When the valve contacts the seat, it does so on precision machined surfaces, which seals the combustion chamber. All cylinder heads have a valve guide for each valve. The guide centers the valve to the seat and allows it to move up and down within it. The clearance between the valve and guide can be critical. Too much clearance and the engine may consume oil, lose vacuum and/or damage the seat. Too little, and the valve can stick in the guide causing the engine to run poorly if at all, and possibly causing severe damage. The last component all cylinder heads have are valve springs. The spring holds the valve against its seat. It also returns the valve to this position when the valve has been opened by the valve train or camshaft. The spring is fastened to the valve by a retainer and valve locks (sometimes called keepers). Aluminum heads will also have a valve spring shim to keep the spring from wearing away the aluminum.

An ideal method of rebuilding the cylinder head would involve replacing all of the valves, guides, seats, springs, etc., with new parts. However, depending on how the engine was maintained, this might not be not necessary. Springs fall victim to the driving habits of the individual. A driver who often runs the engine rpm to the redline will wear out or break the springs faster then one that stays well below it. Unfortunately, mileage takes it toll on all of the parts. Generally, the valves, guides, springs and seats in a cylinder head can be machined and re-used, saving you money. However, if a valve is burnt, it may be wise to replace all of the valves, since they were all operating in the same environment. The same goes for any other component on the cylinder head. Think of it as an insurance policy against future problems related to that component.

Unfortunately, the only way to find out which components need replacing, is to disassemble and carefully check each piece. After the cylinder head(s) are disassembled, thoroughly clean all of the components.

DISASSEMBLY

3.1L, 3.4L (VIN E) and 3.8L Engines

▶ See Figures 166 thru 171

Before disassembling the cylinder head, you may want to fabricate some containers to hold the various parts, as some of them can be quite small (such as keepers) and easily lost. Also keeping yourself and the components organized will aid in assembly and reduce confusion. Where possible, try to maintain a components original location; this is especially important if there is not going to be any machine work performed on the components.

1. If you haven't already removed the rocker arms do so now.
2. Position the head so that the springs are easily accessed.
3. Use a valve spring compressor tool, and relieve spring tension from the retainer.

➡ **Due to engine varnish, the retainer may stick to the valve locks. A gentle tap with a hammer may help to break it loose.**

Fig. 166 When removing an OHV valve spring, use a compressor tool to relieve the tension from the retainer

Fig. 167 A small magnet will help in removal of the valve locks

Fig. 168 Be careful not to lose the small valve locks (keepers)

Fig. 169 Remove the valve seal from the valve stem—O-ring type seal shown

Fig. 170 Removing an umbrella/positive type seal

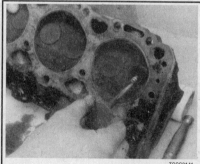
Fig. 171 Invert the cylinder head and withdraw the valve from the valve guide bore

4. Remove the valve locks from the valve tip and/or retainer. A small magnet may help in removing the locks.

5. Lift the valve spring, tool and all, off of the valve stem.

6. If equipped, remove the valve seal. If the seal is difficult to remove with the valve in place, try removing the valve first, then the seal. Follow the steps below for valve removal.

7. Position the head to allow access for withdrawing the valve.

➡Cylinder heads that have seen a lot of miles and/or abuse may have mushroomed the valve lock grove and/or tip, causing difficulty in removal of the valve. If this has happened, use a metal file to carefully remove the high spots around the lock grooves and/or tip. Only file it enough to allow removal.

8. Remove the valve from the cylinder head.

9. If equipped, remove the valve spring shim. A small magnetic tool or screwdriver will aid in removal.

10. Repeat Steps 3 though 9 until all of the valves have been removed.

3.4L (VIN X) and 3.5L Engines

◆ See Figures 172, 173, 174, 175 and 176

Use care when working on these heads. The aluminum alloy is relative soft and easily damaged. Pay attention to careful labeling of the parts on the dual camshaft cylinder head. There will be an intake camshaft and followers as well as an exhaust camshaft and followers and they must be labeled as such. In some cases, the components are identical and could easily be installed incorrectly. DO NOT MIX THEM UP! Determining which is which is very

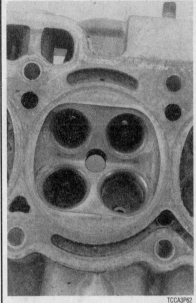

Fig. 173 Example of a multi-valve cylinder head. Note how it has 2 intake and 2 exhaust valve ports

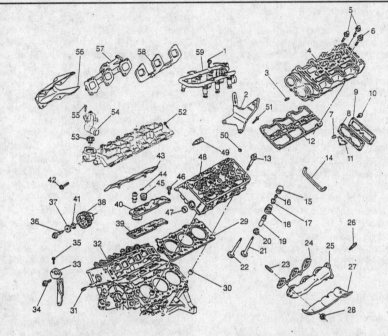

1. Fuel Rail Bolt
2. Engine Mount Strut Brace
3. Camshaft Housing Oil Gallery Bolts
4. Camshaft Housing
5. Camshaft Housing Bolt
6. Camshaft Housing Bolt
7. Camshaft Oil Hole End Plug
8. Camshaft Rear Cover Gasket
9. Camshaft Rear Cover
10. Camshaft Rear Cover Bolt
11. Camshaft Thrust Plate
12. Camshaft Housing Gasket
13. Cylinder Head Bolt (use new bolts)
14. Camshaft Housing End Seal
15. Lifter
16. Valve Stem Keys (locks)
17. Valve Spring Cap
18. Valve Spring
19. Intake Valve Stem Oil Seal
20. Valve Spring Seat
21. Intake Valve
22. Exhaust Valve
23. Exhaust Manifold Stud
24. Exhaust Manifold Gasket
25. Exhaust Manifold
26. Exhaust Crossover Pipe Stud
27. Exhaust Manifold Heat Shield
28. Exhaust Manifold Nut
29. Cylinder Head Gasket
30. Cylinder Head Locating Pin
31. Camshaft Housing Oil Gallery Plug
32. Cylinder Head
33. Engine Lift Front Bracket
34. Engine Lift Front Bracket Screw
35. Engine Lift Front Bracket Bolt
36. Camshaft Intermediate Drive Shaft Sprocket Bolt
37. Camshaft Intermediate Drive Shaft Sprocket Washer
38. Camshaft Intermediate Drive Shaft Sprocket
39. Oil Distribution Cover Gasket
40. Oil Distribution Cover
41. Camshaft Intermediate Drive Shaft Seal
42. Heater Water Engine Inlet Nipple
43. Intake Manifold Gasket
44. Engine Oil Manifold Hole Plug
45. Engine Oil Manifold Check Valve
46. Engine Oil Manifold Bolt
47. Cylinder Head Core Hole Plug
48. Cylinder Head
49. Heater Outlet Hose Nipple
50. Camshaft Housing Locating Pin
51. Engine Mount Strut Bracket Bolt
52. Intake Manifold Lower Bolt
53. Engine Coolant Thermostat
54. Water Outlet
55. Water Outlet Bolt
56. Exhaust Manifold Heat Shield
57. Exhaust Manifold
58. Exhaust Manifold Gasket
59. Fuel Rail

93173G95

Fig. 172 Exploded view the cylinder head and components on a DOHC engine—3.4L (VIN X) engine shown

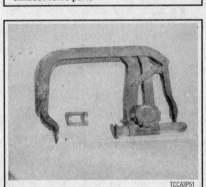

Fig. 174 This type of spring compressor and adapter can be used on OHC engines

Fig. 175 The camshafts are retained by bearing caps similar to this

Fig. 176 Using a spring compressor on a DOHC head

simple; the intake camshaft and components are on the same side of the head as was the intake manifold; the exhaust camshaft and components are on the same side of the head as was the exhaust manifold.

CAMSHAFT FOLLOWERS

Most cylinder heads with rocker arm-type camshaft followers are easily disassembled using a standard valve spring compressor. However, certain models may not have enough open space around the spring for the standard tool and may require you to use a C-clamp style compressor tool instead.

1. If not already removed, remove the rocker arms and/or shafts and the camshaft. If applicable, also remove the hydraulic lash adjusters. Mark their positions for assembly.

2. Position the cylinder head to allow access to the valve spring.

3. Use a valve spring compressor tool to relieve the spring tension from the retainer.

➡Due to engine varnish, the retainer may stick to the valve locks. A gentle tap with a hammer may help to break it loose.

4. Remove the valve locks from the valve tip and/or retainer. A small magnet may help in removing the small locks.

5. Lift the valve spring, tool and all, off of the valve stem.

6. If equipped, remove the valve seal. If the seal is difficult to remove with the valve in place, try removing the valve first, then the seal. Follow the steps below for valve removal.

7. Position the head to allow access for withdrawing the valve.

➡Cylinder heads that have seen a lot of miles and/or abuse may have mushroomed the valve lock grove and/or tip, causing difficulty in removal of the valve. If this has happened, use a metal file to carefully remove the high spots around the lock grooves and/or tip. Only file it enough to allow removal.

8. Remove the valve from the cylinder head.

9. If equipped, remove the valve spring shim. A small magnetic tool or screwdriver will aid in removal.

10. Repeat Steps 3 though 9 until all of the valves have been removed.

INSPECTION

Now that all of the cylinder head components are clean, it's time to inspect them for wear and/or damage. To accurately inspect them, you will need some specialized tools:

- A 0–1 in. micrometer for the valves
- A dial indicator or inside diameter gauge for the valve guides
- A spring pressure test gauge

If you do not have access to the proper tools, you may want to bring the components to a shop that does.

Valves

▶ See Figures 177 and 178

The first thing to inspect are the valve heads. Look closely at the head, margin and face for any cracks, excessive wear or burning. The margin is the best place to look for burning. It should have a squared edge with an even width all around the diameter. When a valve burns, the margin will look melted and the edges rounded. Also inspect the valve head for any signs of tulipping. This will show as a lifting of the edges or dishing in the center of

the head and will usually not occur to all of the valves. All of the heads should look the same, any that seem dished more than others are probably bad. Next, inspect the valve lock grooves and valve tips. Check for any burrs around the lock grooves, especially if you had to file them to remove the valve. Valve tips should appear flat, although slight rounding with high mileage engines is normal. Slightly worn valve tips will need to be machined flat. Last, measure the valve stem diameter with the micrometer. Measure the area that rides within the guide, especially towards the tip where most of the wear occurs. Take several measurements along its length and compare them to each other. Wear should be even along the length with little to no taper. If no minimum diameter is given in the specifications, then the stem should not read more than 0.001 in. (0.025mm) below the unworn area of the valve stem. Any valves that fail these inspections should be replaced.

Springs, Retainers and Valve Locks

▶ See Figures 179 and 180

The first thing to check is the most obvious, broken springs. Next check the free length and squareness of each spring. If applicable, insure to distinguish between intake and exhaust springs. Use a ruler and/or carpenter's square to measure the length. A carpenter's square should be used to check the springs for square. If a spring pressure test gauge is available, check each springs rating and compare to the specifications chart. Check the readings against the specifications given. Any springs that fail these inspections should be replaced.

The spring retainers rarely need replacing, however they should still be checked as a precaution. Inspect the spring mating surface and the valve lock retention area for any signs of excessive wear. Also check for any signs of cracking. Replace any retainers that are questionable.

Valve locks should be inspected for excessive wear on the outside contact area as well as on the inner notched surface. Any locks which appear worn or broken and its respective valve should be replaced.

Cylinder Head

There are several things to check on the cylinder head: valve guides, seats, cylinder head surface flatness, cracks and physical damage.

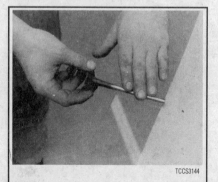

Fig. 177 Valve stems may be rolled on a flat surface to check for bends

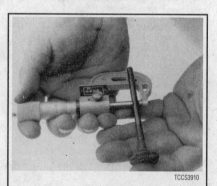

Fig. 178 Use a micrometer to check the valve stem diameter

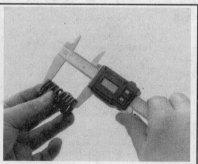

Fig. 179 Use a caliper to check the valve spring free-length

Fig. 180 Check the valve spring for square on a flat surface; a machinist's square can be used

Fig. 181 A dial gauge may be used to check valve stem-to-guide clearance; read the gauge while moving the valve stem

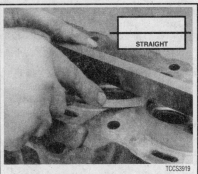

Fig. 182 Check the head for flatness across the center of the head surface using a straightedge and feeler gauge

Fig. 183 Checks should also be made along both diagonals of the head surface

VALVE GUIDES

▶ See Figure 181

Now that you know the valves are good, you can use them to check the guides, although a new valve, if available, is preferred. Before you measure anything, look at the guides carefully and inspect them for any cracks, chips or breakage. Also if the guide is a removable style (as in most aluminum heads), check them for any looseness or evidence of movement. All of the guides should appear to be at the same height from the spring seat. If any seem lower (or higher) from another, the guide has moved. Mount a dial indicator onto the spring side of the cylinder head. Lightly oil the valve stem and insert it into the cylinder head. Position the dial indicator against the valve stem near the tip and zero the gauge. Grasp the valve stem and wiggle towards and away from the dial indicator and observe the readings. Mount the dial indicator 90 degrees from the initial point and zero the gauge and again take a reading. Compare the two readings for a out of round condition. Check the readings against the specifications given. An Inside Diameter (I.D.) gauge designed for valve guides will give you an accurate valve guide bore measurement. If the I.D. gauge is used, compare the readings with the specifications given. Any guides that fail these inspections should be replaced or machined.

VALVE SEATS

A visual inspection of the valve seats should show a slightly worn and pitted surface where the valve face contacts the seat. Inspect the seat carefully for excess pitting or cracks. Also, a seat that is badly worn will be recessed into the cylinder head. A severely worn or recessed seat may need to be replaced. All cracked seats must be replaced. A seat concentricity gauge, if available, should be used to check the seat run-out. If run-out exceeds specifications the seat must be machined (if no specification is given use 0.002 in. or 0.051mm).

CYLINDER HEAD SURFACE FLATNESS

▶ See Figures 182 and 183

Engine performance and life depends a great deal on how well the cylinder head gasket seals to the engine block. There are number of concerns when it appears a cylinder head needs to be removed.

Make sure that the valve train components are kept together when disassembling the cylinder head. Identify the valve train components. Any valve train components that are being reused must be installed in their original locations.

If the head is be overhauled, remove any remaining components such as the engine lift hook, the fuel line bracket bolts, the engine coolant temperature sensor, etc., as required.

If the head gasket failed, determine the cause. Gasket failure is caused by the following conditions: improper installation; loose or warped cylinder head; missing, off location or not fully seated locator dowel pins; low torque on the cylinder head bolts; warped block surface; scratched or gouged gasket surfaces; excessive intake manifold torque and even cracked engine block tapped holes.

Clean all parts well. Remove all foreign material to the bare metal. Do not use a motorized wire brush on any gasket sealing surface.

Clean all threaded holes with a thread-cutting tap to remove rust, old sealer or thread-locking compound and other debris. Use care when using a tap on aluminum parts. Thread the tap in by hand to start so not enough leverage can be applied to damage threads if the tap is started incorrectly.

Inspect the cylinder head for cracks. Check between the valve seats and inspect the inside of the exhaust ports. Inspect the cylinder head for corrosion. Do not attempt to weld the cylinder head. If the head is damaged, it must be replaced.

Inspect the following locations for flatness: the cylinder head deck and the intake and exhaust manifold mating surfaces. Within limits, a head can be reconditioned at an automotive machine shop using a milling machine. On the engines covered by this manual, replace the head if more than 0.010 inch (0.254mm) must be removed to true up the head.

Inspect all of threaded holes for damage. If necessary repair the holes with threaded inserts, if possible. If not, replace the head.

Inspect the cooling jacket plugs (sometimes called freeze plugs). Normally, these should be replaced when a head is removed since access to them once assembled in the vehicle is usually impossible.

If you have the equipment to remove the valve springs, the head can be completely disassembled and the valve seats checked. In most all cases, even professionals technicians leave this job to an automotive machine shop. In many cases, a worn cylinder head can be exchanged for a reconditioned head, saving time and money.

1. With the valves still in place to protect the valve seats, remove the carbon deposits from the combustion chambers and valve heads. Use care. If the head is made of cast iron, a drill-mounted wire brush can be used. Do not use a wire brush on an aluminum head. Use care not to damage the gasket surfaces. If the head is be disassembled, proceed to Step 3. If the head is not to be disassembled, proceed to Step 2.

2. Remove all dirt, oil and old gasket material from the cylinder head with a suitable solvent such as Safety-Kleen®. Clean all the bolt holes and oil and coolant passages. Use care to keep solvent off the valve seals as the solvent may damage them. Dry the cylinder head with compressed air, if available. Check the head for cracks or other damage, and check the gasket surface for burrs, nicks and flatness. If you are in doubt about the head's serviceability, consult a reputable automotive machine shop.

3. If you have the equipment available, remove the valves, springs and retainers, then clean the

valve guide bores with a valve guide cleaning tool. Remove all dirt, oil and gasket material from the cylinder head with a suitable such as Safety-Kleen®. Clean the bolt holes and the oil and coolant passages.

4. Remove all deposits from the valves with a wire brush of buffing wheel. Inspect the valves as described later in this section.

5. Check the head for cracks using a dye penetrant in the valve seat area and port, head surfaces and top. Check the gasket surface for burrs, nicks and flatness. If you are in doubt about the head's serviceability, consult a reputable automotive machine shop.

➡**If the cylinder head was removed to replace a blown head gasket due to an overheating condition and a crack is suspected, do not assume the head is not cracked because a crack is visually found. A crack can be so small that it cannot be seen by eye, but can pass coolant when the engine is at operating temperature. Consult an automotive machine shop that has testing equipment to make sure the head is not cracked.**

After you have cleaned the gasket surface of the cylinder head of any old gasket material, check the head for flatness.

Place a straightedge across the gasket surface. Using feeler gauges, determine the clearance at the center of the straightedge and across the cylinder head at several points. Check along the centerline and diagonally on the head surface. If the warpage exceeds 0.003 in. (0.076mm) within a 6.0 in. (15.2cm) span, or 0.006 in. (0.152mm) over the total length of the head, the cylinder head must be resurfaced. After resurfacing the heads of a V-type engine, the intake manifold flange surface should be checked, and if necessary, milled proportionally to allow for the change in its mounting position.

CRACKS AND PHYSICAL DAMAGE

Generally, cracks are limited to the combustion chamber, however, it is not uncommon for the head to crack in a spark plug hole, port, outside of the head or in the valve spring/rocker arm area. The first area to inspect is always the hottest: the exhaust seat/port area.

A visual inspection should be performed, but just because you don't see a crack does not mean it is not there. Some more reliable methods for inspecting for cracks include Magnaflux®, a magnetic process or Zyglo®, a dye penetrant. Magnaflux® is used only on ferrous metal (cast iron) heads. Zyglo® uses a spray on fluorescent mixture along with a black light to reveal the cracks. It is strongly recommended to have your cylinder head checked professionally for cracks, especially if the engine was known to have overheated and/or leaked or consumed coolant. Contact a local shop for availability and pricing of these services.

Physical damage is usually very evident. For example, a broken mounting ear from dropping the head or a bent or broken stud and/or bolt. All of these defects should be fixed or, if unrepairable, the head should be replaced.

Camshaft and Followers

Inspect the camshaft(s) and followers as described earlier in this section.

REFINISHING & REPAIRING

Many of the procedures given for refinishing and repairing the cylinder head components must be performed by a machine shop. Certain steps, if the inspected part is not worn, can be performed yourself inexpensively. However, you spent a lot of time and effort so far, why risk trying to save a small amount of money if you might have to do it all over again?

Valves

Any valves that were not replaced should be refaced and the tips ground flat. Unless you have access to a valve grinding machine, this should be done by a machine shop. If the valves are in extremely good condition, as well as the valve seats and guides, they may be lapped in without performing machine work.

Springs, Retainers and Valve Locks

There is no repair or refinishing possible with the springs, retainers and valve locks. If they are found to be worn or defective, they must be replaced with new (or known good) parts.

Cylinder Head

Most refinishing procedures dealing with the cylinder head must be performed by a machine shop. Read the sections below and review your inspection data to determine whether or not machining is necessary.

VALVE GUIDE

➡**If any machining or replacements are made to the valve guides, the seats must be machined.**

Unless the valve guides need machining or replacing, the only service to perform is to thoroughly clean them of any dirt or oil residue.

There are only two types of valve guides used on automobile engines: the replaceable-type (all aluminum heads) and the cast-in integral-type (most cast iron heads). There are four recommended methods for repairing worn guides.

*   Knurling
*   Inserts
*   Reaming oversize
*   Replacing

Knurling is a process in which metal is displaced and raised, thereby reducing clearance, giving a true center, and providing oil control. It is the least expensive way of repairing the valve guides. However, it is not necessarily the best, and in some cases, a knurled valve guide will not stand up for more than a short time. It requires a special knurling tool and precision reaming tools to obtain proper clearances. It would not be cost effective to purchase these tools, unless you plan on rebuilding several of the same cylinder head.

Installing a guide insert involves machining the guide to accept a bronze insert. One style is the coil-type which is installed into a threaded guide. Another is the thin-walled insert where the guide is reamed oversize to accept a split-sleeve insert. After the insert is installed, a special tool is then run through the guide to expand the insert, locking it to the guide. The insert is then reamed to the standard size for proper valve clearance.

Reaming for oversize valves restores normal clearances and provides a true valve seat. Most cast-in type guides can be reamed to accept an valve with an oversize stem. The cost factor for this can become quite high as you will need to purchase the reamer and new, oversize stem valves for all guides which were reamed. Oversizes are generally 0.003 to 0.030 in. (0.076 to 0.762mm), with 0.015 in. (0.381mm) being the most common.

To replace cast-in type valve guides, they must be drilled out, then reamed to accept replacement guides. This must be done on a fixture which will allow centering and leveling off of the original valve seat or guide, otherwise a serious guide-to-seat misalignment may occur making it impossible to properly machine the seat.

Replaceable-type guides are pressed into the cylinder head. A hammer and a stepped drift or punch may be used to install and remove the guides. Before removing the guides, measure the protrusion on the spring side of the head and record it for installation. Use the stepped drift to hammer out the old guide from the combustion chamber side of the head. When installing, determine whether or not the guide also seals a water jacket in the head, and if it does, use the recommended sealing agent. If there is no water jacket, grease the valve guide and its bore. Use the stepped drift, and hammer the new guide into the cylinder head from the spring side of the cylinder head. A stack of washers the same thickness as the measured protrusion may help the installation process.

VALVE SEATS

➡**Before any valve seat machining can be performed, the guides must be within factory recommended specifications. If any machining or replacements were made to the valve guides, the seats must be machined.**

If the seats are in good condition, the valves can be lapped to the seats, and the cylinder head assembled. See the valves section for instructions on lapping.

If the valve seats are worn, cracked or damaged, they must be serviced by a machine shop. The valve seat must be perfectly centered to the valve guide, which requires very accurate machining.

CYLINDER HEAD SURFACE

If the cylinder head is warped, it must be machined flat. If the warpage is extremely severe, the head may need to be replaced. In some instances, it may be possible to straighten a warped head enough to allow machining. In either case, contact a professional machine shop for service.

➡**Any OHC cylinder head that shows excessive warpage should have the camshaft bearing journals align bored after the cylinder head has been resurfaced.**

✳✳ WARNING

Failure to align bore the camshaft bearing journals could result in severe engine damage including but not limited to: valve and piston damage, connecting rod damage, camshaft and/or crankshaft breakage.

CRACKS AND PHYSICAL DAMAGE

Certain cracks can be repaired in both cast iron and aluminum heads. For cast iron, a tapered threaded insert is installed along the length of the crack. Aluminum can also use the tapered inserts, however welding is the preferred method. Some physical damage can be repaired through brazing or welding. Contact a machine shop to get expert advice for your particular dilemma.

ASSEMBLY

The first step for any assembly job is to have a clean area in which to work. Next, thoroughly clean all of the parts and components that are to be assembled. Finally, place all of the components onto a suitable work space and, if necessary, arrange the parts to their respective positions.

OHV Engines

1. Lightly lubricate the valve stems and insert all of the valves into the cylinder head. If possible, maintain their original locations.
2. If equipped, install any valve spring shims which were removed.
3. If equipped, install the new valve seals, keeping the following in mind:
   - If the valve seal presses over the guide, lightly lubricate the outer guide surfaces.
   - If the seal is an O-ring type, it is installed just after compressing the spring but before the valve locks.
4. Place the valve spring and retainer over the stem.
5. Position the spring compressor tool and compress the spring.
6. Assemble the valve locks to the stem.
7. Relieve the spring pressure slowly and insure that neither valve lock becomes dislodged by the retainer.
8. Remove the spring compressor tool.
9. Repeat Steps 2 through 8 until all of the springs have been installed.

ROCKER ARM TYPE CAMSHAFT FOLLOWERS

1. Lightly lubricate the valve stems and insert all of the valves into the cylinder head. If possible, maintain their original locations.
2. If equipped, install any valve spring shims which were removed.
3. If equipped, install the new valve seals, keeping the following in mind:
   - If the valve seal presses over the guide, lightly lubricate the outer guide surfaces.
   - If the seal is an O-ring type, it is installed just after compressing the spring but before the valve locks.
4. Place the valve spring and retainer over the stem.
5. Position the spring compressor tool and compress the spring.
6. Assemble the valve locks to the stem.
7. Relieve the spring pressure slowly and insure that neither valve lock becomes dislodged by the retainer.
8. Remove the spring compressor tool.
9. Repeat Steps 2 through 8 until all of the springs have been installed.
10. Install the camshaft(s), rockers, shafts and

any other components that were removed for disassembly.

Engine Block

GENERAL INFORMATION

A thorough overhaul or rebuild of an engine block would include replacing the pistons, rings, bearings, timing belt/chain assembly and oil pump. For OHV engines also include a new camshaft and lifters. The block would then have the cylinders bored and honed and the crankshaft would be reground to a standard undersize to provide new wearing surfaces and acceptable clearances. However, your particular engine may not have everything worn out. What if only the piston rings have worn out and the clearances on everything else are still within factory specifications? You could just replace the rings and put it back together, but this would be a very rare example. Chances are, if one component in your engine is worn, other components are sure to follow, and soon. At the very least, you should always replace the rings, bearings and oil pump.

Cylinder Ridge Removal

Because the top piston ring does not travel to the very top of the cylinder, a ridge of unworn cylinder wall is left between the end of the travel and the top of the cylinder bore.

Pushing the piston and connecting rod assembly past the ridge can be difficult, and damage to the piston ring lands could occur. If the ridge is not removed before installing a new piston or not removed at all, piston ring breakage and piston damage may occur.

➡ It is always recommended that you remove any cylinder ridges before removing the piston and connecting rod assemblies. If you know that new pistons are going to be installed and the engine block will be bored oversize, you may be able to forego this step. However, some ridges may actually prevent the assemblies from being removed, necessitating its removal.

There are several different types of ridge reamers on the market, none of which are inexpensive. Unless a great deal of engine rebuilding is anticipated, borrow or rent a cylinder ridge reamer.
1. Turn the crankshaft until the piston is at the bottom of its travel.
2. Cover the head of the piston with a rag.
3. Follow the tool manufacturers instructions and cut away the ridge, exercising extreme care to avoid cutting too deeply.
4. Remove the ridge reamer, the rag and as many of the cuttings as possible. Continue until all of the cylinder ridges have been removed.

DISASSEMBLY

▶ **See Figures 184 and 185**

The engine disassembly instructions following assume that you have the engine mounted on an engine stand. If not, it is easiest to disassemble the engine on a bench or the floor with it resting on the bell housing or transmission mounting sur-

face. You must be able to access the connecting rod fasteners and turn the crankshaft during disassembly. Also, all engine covers (timing, front, side, oil pan, whatever) should have already been removed. Engines which are seized or locked up may not be able to be completely disassembled, and a core (salvage yard) engine should be purchased.

Pushrod Engines

If not done during the cylinder head removal, remove the pushrods and lifters, keeping them in order for assembly. Remove the timing gears and/or timing chain assembly, then remove the oil pump drive assembly and withdraw the camshaft from the engine block. Remove the oil pick-up and pump assembly. If equipped, remove any balance or auxiliary shafts. If necessary, remove the cylinder ridge from the top of the bore. See the cylinder ridge removal procedure earlier in this section.

TCCS3803

Fig. 184 Place rubber hose over the connecting rod studs to protect the crankshaft and cylinder bores from damage

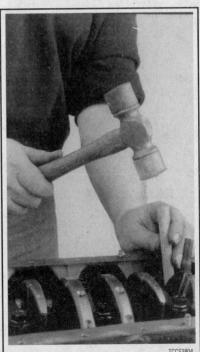

TCCS3804

Fig. 185 Carefully tap the piston out of the bore using a wooden dowel

OHC Engines

If not done during the cylinder head removal, remove the timing chain/belt and/or gear/sprocket assembly. Remove the oil pick-up and pump assembly and, if necessary, the pump drive. If equipped, remove any balance or auxiliary shafts. If necessary, remove the cylinder ridge from the top of the bore. See the cylinder ridge removal procedure earlier in this section.

All Engines

Rotate the engine over so that the crankshaft is exposed. Use a number punch or scribe and mark each connecting rod with its respective cylinder number. The cylinder closest to the front of the engine is always number 1. However, depending on the engine placement, the front of the engine could either be the flywheel or damper/pulley end. Generally the front of the engine faces the front of the vehicle. Use a number punch or scribe and also mark the main bearing caps from front to rear with the front most cap being number 1 (if there are five caps, mark them 1 through 5, front to rear).

✳✳ WARNING

Take special care when pushing the connecting rod up from the crankshaft because the hardened, sharp threads of the rod bolts/studs will score the crankshaft journal. Insure that special plastic caps are installed over them, or cut two pieces of rubber hose to do the same.

With the engine still on a rotating engine stand, turn the engine to position the #1 cylinder bore (head surface) up. Turn the crankshaft until the #1 piston is at the bottom of its travel. This should allow the maximum access to its connecting rod. Remove the #1 connecting rod's fasteners and cap and place two lengths of rubber hose over the rod bolts/studs to protect the crankshaft from damage. Using a sturdy wooden dowel and a hammer, push the connecting rod up about 1 in. (25mm) from the crankshaft and remove the upper bearing insert. Continue pushing or tapping the connecting rod up until the piston rings are out of the cylinder bore. Remove the piston and rod by hand, put the upper half of the bearing insert back into the rod, install the cap with its bearing insert installed, and hand-tighten the cap fasteners. If the parts are kept in order in this manner, they will not get lost and you will be able to tell which bearings came from what cylinder if any problems are discovered and diagnosis is necessary. Remove all the other piston assemblies in the same manner. On the V6 engines covered by this manual, remove all of the pistons from one bank, then reposition the engine with the other cylinder bank head surface up, and remove that banks piston assemblies.

The only remaining component in the engine block should now be the crankshaft. Loosen the main bearing caps evenly until the fasteners can be turned by hand, then remove them and the caps. Remove the crankshaft from the engine block. Thoroughly clean all of the components.

INSPECTION

With the engine block and all of its components clean, inspect for wear and/or damage. To accurately inspect them, you will need some specialized tools:

- Two or three separate micrometers to measure the pistons and crankshaft journals
- A dial indicator
- Telescoping gauges for the cylinder bores
- A rod alignment fixture to check for bent connecting rods.

If you do not have access to the proper tools, you may want to bring the components to a shop that does.

Generally, you shouldn't expect cracks in the engine block or its components unless it was known to leak, consume or mix engine fluids, it was severely overheated, or there was evidence of bad bearings and/or crankshaft damage. A visual inspection should be performed on all of the components, but just because you don't see a crack does not mean it is not there. Some more reliable methods for inspecting for cracks include Magnaflux®, a magnetic process or Zyglo®, a dye penetrant. Magnaflux®is used only on ferrous metal (cast iron). Zyglo®uses a spray on fluorescent mixture along with a black light to reveal the cracks. It is strongly recommended to have your engine block checked professionally for cracks, especially if the engine was known to have overheated and/or leaked or consumed coolant. Contact a local shop for availability and pricing of these services.

Engine Block

ENGINE BLOCK BEARING ALIGNMENT

Remove the main bearing caps and, if still installed, the main bearing inserts. Inspect all of the main bearing saddles and caps for damage, burrs or high spots. If damage is found, and it is caused from a spun main bearing, the block will need to be align-bored or, if severe enough, replacement. Any burrs or high spots should be carefully removed with a metal file.

Place a straightedge on the bearing saddles, in the engine block, along the centerline of the crankshaft. If any clearance exists between the straightedge and the saddles, the block must be align-bored.

Align-boring consists of machining the main bearing saddles and caps by means of a flycutter that runs through the bearing saddles.

DECK FLATNESS

The top of the engine block where the cylinder head mounts is called the "deck." Insure that the deck surface is clean of dirt, carbon deposits and old gasket material. Place a straightedge across the surface of the deck along its centerline and, using feeler gauges, check the clearance along several points. Repeat the checking procedure with the straightedge placed along both diagonals of the deck surface. If the reading exceeds 0.003 in. (0.076mm) within a 6.0 in. (15.2cm) span, or 0.006 in. (0.152mm) over the total length of the deck, it must be machined.

CYLINDER BORES

◆ See Figure 186

The cylinder bores house the pistons and are slightly larger than the pistons themselves. A com-

mon piston-to-bore clearance is 0.0015–0.0025 in. (0.0381mm–0.0635mm). Inspect and measure the cylinder bores. The bore should be checked for out-of-roundness, taper and size. The results of this inspection will determine whether the cylinder can be used in its existing size and condition, or a rebore to the next oversize is required (or in the case of removable sleeves, have replacements installed).

The amount of cylinder wall wear is always greater at the top of the cylinder than at the bottom. This wear is known as taper. Any cylinder that has a taper of 0.0012 in. (0.305mm) or more, must be rebored. Measurements are taken at a number of positions in each cylinder: at the top, middle and bottom and at two points at each position; that is, at a point 90 degrees from the crankshaft centerline, as well as a point parallel to the crankshaft centerline. The measurements are made with either a special dial indicator or a telescopic gauge and micrometer. If the necessary precision tools to check the bore are not available, take the block to a machine shop and have them mike it. Also if you don't have the tools to check the cylinder bores, chances are you will not have the necessary devices to check the pistons, connecting rods and crankshaft. Take these components with you and save yourself an extra trip.

For our procedures, we will use a telescopic gauge and a micrometer. You will need one of each, with a measuring range which covers your cylinder bore size.

1. Position the telescopic gauge in the cylinder bore, loosen the gauges lock and allow it to expand.

➡**Your first two readings will be at the top of the cylinder bore, then proceed to the middle and finally the bottom, making a total of six measurements.**

2. Hold the gauge square in the bore, 90 degrees from the crankshaft centerline, and gently tighten the lock. Tilt the gauge back to remove it from the bore.

3. Measure the gauge with the micrometer and record the reading.

4. Again, hold the gauge square in the bore, this time parallel to the crankshaft centerline, and gently tighten the lock. Again, you will tilt the gauge back to remove it from the bore.

5. Measure the gauge with the micrometer and record this reading. The difference between these two readings is the out-of-round measurement of the cylinder.

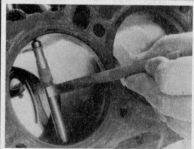

TCCS3209

Fig. 186 Use a telescoping gauge to measure the cylinder bore diameter—take several readings within the same bore

6. Repeat steps 1 through 5, each time going to the next lower position, until you reach the bottom of the cylinder. Then go to the next cylinder, and continue until all of the cylinders have been measured.

The difference between these measurements will tell you all about the wear in your cylinders. The measurements which were taken 90 degrees from the crankshaft centerline will always reflect the most wear. That is because at this position is where the engine power presses the piston against the cylinder bore the hardest. This is known as thrust wear. Take your top, 90 degree measurement and compare it to your bottom, 90 degree measurement. The difference between them is the taper. When you measure your pistons, you will compare these readings to your piston sizes and determine piston-to-wall clearance.

Crankshaft

Inspect the crankshaft for visible signs of wear or damage. All of the journals should be perfectly round and smooth. Slight scores are normal for a used crankshaft, but you should hardly feel them with your fingernail. When measuring the crankshaft with a micrometer, you will take readings at the front and rear of each journal, then turn the micrometer 90 degrees and take two more readings, front and rear. The difference between the front-to-rear readings is the journal taper and the first-to-90 degree reading is the out-of-round measurement. Generally, there should be no taper or out-of-roundness found, however, up to 0.0005 in. (0.0127mm) for either can be overlooked. Also, the readings should fall within the factory specifications for journal diameters.

If the crankshaft journals fall within specifications, it is recommended that it be polished before being returned to service. Polishing the crankshaft insures that any minor burrs or high spots are smoothed, thereby reducing the chance of scoring the new bearings.

Pistons and Connecting Rods

PISTONS

▶ See Figure 187

The piston should be visually inspected for any signs of cracking or burning (caused by hot spots or detonation), and scuffing or excessive wear on the skirts. The wrist pin attaches the piston to the

connecting rod. The piston should move freely on the wrist pin, both sliding and pivoting. Grasp the connecting rod securely, or mount it in a vise, and try to rock the piston back and forth along the centerline of the wrist pin. There should not be any excessive play evident between the piston and the pin. If there are C-clips retaining the pin in the piston then you have wrist pin bushings in the rods. There should not be any excessive play between the wrist pin and the rod bushing. Normal clearance for the wrist pin is approx. 0.001–0.002 in. (0.025mm–0.051mm).

Use a micrometer and measure the diameter of the piston, perpendicular to the wrist pin, on the skirt. Compare the reading to its original cylinder measurement obtained earlier. The difference between the two readings is the piston-to-wall clearance. If the clearance is within specifications, the piston may be used as is. If the piston is out of specification, but the bore is not, you will need a new piston. If both are out of specification, you will need the cylinder bored and oversize pistons installed. Generally if two or more pistons/bores are out of specification, it is best to bore the entire block and purchase a complete set of oversize pistons.

CONNECTING ROD

You should have the connecting rod checked for straightness at a machine shop. If the connecting rod is bent, it will unevenly wear the bearing and piston, as well as place greater stress on these components. Any bent or twisted connecting rods must be replaced. If the rods are straight and the wrist pin clearance is within specifications, then only the bearing end of the rod need be checked. Place the connecting rod into a vice, with the bearing inserts in place, install the cap to the rod and torque the fasteners to specifications. Use a telescoping gauge and carefully measure the inside diameter of the bearings. Compare this reading to the rods original crankshaft journal diameter measurement. The difference is the oil clearance. If the oil clearance is not within specifications, install new bearings in the rod and take another measurement. If the clearance is still out of specifications, and the crankshaft is not, the rod will need to be reconditioned by a machine shop.

➡You can also use Plastigage®to check the bearing clearances. The assembling section has complete instructions on its use.

Camshaft

Inspect the camshaft and lifters/followers as described earlier in this section.

Bearings

All of the engine bearings should be visually inspected for wear and/or damage. The bearing should look evenly worn all around with no deep scores or pits. If the bearing is severely worn, scored, pitted or heat blued, then the bearing, and the components that use it, should be brought to a machine shop for inspection. Full-circle bearings (used on most camshafts, auxiliary shafts, balance shafts, etc.) require specialized tools for removal and installation, and should be brought to a machine shop for service.

Oil Pump

➡The oil pump is responsible for providing constant lubrication to the whole engine and so it is recommended that a new oil pump be installed when rebuilding the engine.

Completely disassemble the oil pump and thoroughly clean all of the components. Inspect the oil pump gears and housing for wear and/or damage. Insure that the pressure relief valve operates properly and there is no binding or sticking due to varnish or debris. If all of the parts are in proper working condition, lubricate the gears and relief valve, and assemble the pump.

REFINISHING

▶ See Figures 188, 189 and 190

Almost all engine block refinishing must be performed by a machine shop. If the cylinders are not to be bored, then the cylinder glaze should be removed with a cylinder hone. Two types are in general use. A "ball hone" uses round marble-like balls of hard abrasive on flexible wire arms. Driven

Fig. 187 Measure the piston's outer diameter, perpendicular to the wrist pin, with a micrometer

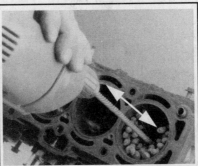

TCCS3913

Fig. 188 This type of cylinder hone is called a "ball hone" and it will remove cylinder wall glaze, providing a new surface for seating the piston rings

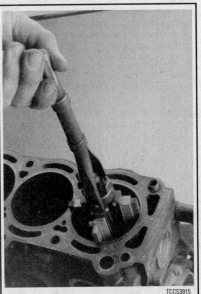

TCCS3915

Fig. 189 This type of cylinder hone uses hard abrasive stones to recondition the cylinder walls

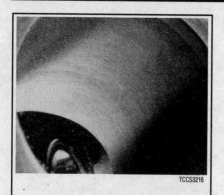

Fig. 190 A properly refinished cylinder displays a "cross-hatch" pattern

Fig. 191 Most pistons are marked to indicate positioning in the engine (usually a mark means the side facing the front)

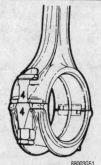

Fig. 192 Always keep the connecting rod and caps in matching sets. Never mix connecting rod caps or the engine will fail

by a power drill, it breaks up the glazing on the cylinder walls. The second, more expensive type of hone uses abrasive stones to perform the same job. Hones using abrasive stones, when used by a skilled automotive machine shop technician using special power hone equipment, can produce precisely reconditioned cylinder walls equal to or better than factory-original finish. Both types of hones will leave very tiny scratches in the cylinder walls which trap and hold engine oil to provide piston ring lubrication, always important, but especially during engine break-in. When removing cylinder glaze with any hone, use a light or penetrating type oil to lubricate the hone. Do not allow the hone to run dry as this may cause excessive scoring of the cylinder bores and wear on the hone. If new pistons are required, they will need to be installed to the connecting rods. This should be performed by a machine shop as the pistons must be installed in the correct relationship to the rod or engine damage can occur.

Pistons and Connecting Rods
▶ See Figures 191, 192, 193 and 194

None of the engines covered by this manual use pistons with wrist pins retained by any type of clip.

Press fit pistons require special presses and/or heaters to remove/install the connecting rod and this operation should only be performed by a machine shop.

All pistons will have a mark indicating the direction to the front of the engine and the must be installed into the engine in that manner. Usually it is a notch or arrow on the top of the piston, or it may be the letter F cast or stamped into the piston. This is important because pistons aren't exactly round; they are made slightly oval, or barrel shape. The reason for this is that the piston's shape changes slightly under the heat and stress of engine operation. Too, the loads on the piston are not uniform. So the piston is designed with a slight offset and in a shape that works best when the engine is running. This reduces running friction and a cold-start noise called "piston slap." The pistons absolutely must be installed in the proper orientation or you will fail the engine.

ASSEMBLY

Before you begin assembling the engine, first give yourself a clean, dirt free work area. Next, clean every engine component again. The key to a good assembly is cleanliness.

Mount the engine block into the engine stand and wash it one last time using water and detergent (dishwashing detergent works well). While washing it, scrub the cylinder bores with a soft bristle brush and thoroughly clean all of the oil passages. Completely dry the engine and spray the entire assembly down with an anti-rust solution such as WD-40® or similar product. Take a clean lint-free rag and wipe up any excess anti-rust solution from the bores, bearing saddles, etc. Repeat the final cleaning process on the crankshaft. Replace any freeze or oil galley plugs which were removed during disassembly.

Crankshaft
▶ See Figures 195, 196, 197 and 198

1. Remove the main bearing inserts from the block and bearing caps.

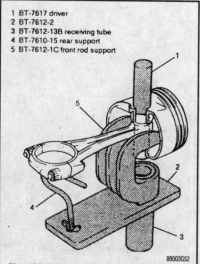

1 BT-7617 driver
2 BT-7612-2
3 BT-7612-13B receiving tube
4 BT-7610-15 rear support
5 BT-7612-1C front rod support

Fig. 193 This type of special tooling fixture is what the factory recommends to remove a piston wrist pin

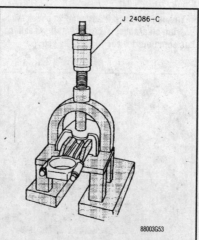

Fig. 194 This type of special tooling fixture is what the factory recommends to install a piston wrist pin. Automotive machine shops can do the job quickly and inexpensively

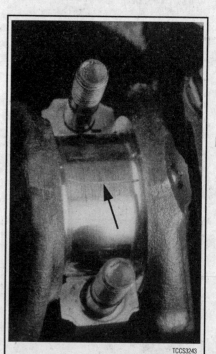

Fig. 195 Apply a strip of gauging material to the bearing journal, install the bearing and cap and torque to specification, squeezing the wax-like gauge strip. Its thickness is the bearing clearance

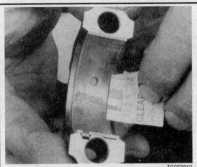

Fig. 196 After the cap is removed again, use the scale supplied with the gauging material to check the clearance

Fig. 197 A dial gauge may be used to check crankshaft end-play

Fig. 198 Carefully pry the crankshaft back and forth while reading the dial gauge for end-play

2. If the crankshaft main bearing journals have been refinished to a definite undersize, install the correct undersize bearing. Be sure that the bearing inserts and bearing bores are clean. Foreign material under inserts will distort bearing and cause failure.

3. Place the upper main bearing inserts in bores with tang in slot.

➡ The oil holes in the bearing inserts must be aligned with the oil holes in the cylinder block.

4. Install the lower main bearing inserts in bearing caps.

5. Clean the mating surfaces of block and rear main bearing cap.

6. Carefully lower the crankshaft into place. Be careful not to damage bearing surfaces.

7. Check the clearance of each main bearing by using the following procedure:

   a. Place a piece of Plastigage® or its equivalent, on bearing surface across full width of bearing cap and about ¼in. off center.

   b. Install cap and tighten bolts to specification. Do not turn crankshaft while Plastigage® is in place.

   c. Remove the cap. Using the supplied Plastigage® scale, check width of Plastigage® at widest point to get maximum clearance. Difference between readings is taper of journal.

   d. If clearance exceeds specified limits, it may be possible to special-order a 0.001 in. or 0.002 in. undersize bearing. Bearing clearance must be within specified limits. If standard and 0.002 in. undersize bearing does not bring clearance within desired limits, the crankshaft will

have to be sent to an automotive machine shop to refinish the crankshaft journal, then install undersize bearings. A more likely solution is to exchange to damaged crankshaft for a reconditioned crankshaft kit that should come with matching bearings, and usually, reconditioned connecting rods, too.

8. After the bearings have been fitted, apply a light coat of engine oil to the journals and bearings. Install the rear main bearing cap. Install all bearing caps except the thrust bearing cap. The thrust bearing has side flanges on it an it absorbs the wear of the crankshaft moving slightly forward and backward in the engine block during operation. Be sure that main bearing caps are installed in original locations. This is very important. If the bearing caps are install out-of-position or backwards, you will quickly fail the engine, if it turns over at all. Tighten the bearing cap bolts to specifications.

9. Install the thrust bearing cap with bolts finger-tight.

10. Pry the crankshaft forward against the thrust surface of upper half of bearing.

11. Hold the crankshaft forward and pry the thrust bearing cap to the rear. This aligns the thrust surfaces of both halves of the bearing.

12. Retain the forward pressure on the crankshaft. Tighten the cap bolts to specifications.

13. Measure the crankshaft end-play as follows:

   a. Mount a dial gauge to the engine block and position the tip of the gauge to read from the crankshaft end.

   b. Carefully pry the crankshaft toward the rear of the engine and hold it there while you zero the gauge.

   c. Carefully pry the crankshaft toward the front of the engine and read the gauge.

   d. Confirm that the reading is within specifications. If not, install a new thrust bearing and repeat the procedure. If the reading is still out of specifications with a new bearing, have a machine shop inspect the thrust surfaces of the crankshaft, and if possible, repair it.

14. Rotate the crankshaft so as to position the first rod journal to the bottom of its stroke.

Pistons and Connecting Rods

▶ See Figures 199, 200, 201 and 202

1. Before installing the piston/connecting rod assembly, oil the pistons, piston rings and the cylinder walls with light engine oil. Install connecting rod bolt protectors or rubber hose onto the connecting rod bolts/studs. Also perform the following:

   a. Select the proper ring set for the size cylinder bore.

   b. Position the ring in the bore in which it is going to be used.

   c. Push the ring down into the bore area where normal ring wear is not encountered.

   d. Use the head of the piston to position the ring in the bore so that the ring is square with the cylinder wall. Use caution to avoid damage to the ring or cylinder bore.

   e. Measure the gap between the ends of the ring with a feeler gauge. Ring gap in a worn cylinder is normally greater than specification. If the ring gap is greater than the specified limits, try an oversize ring set.

   f. Check the ring side clearance of the com-

Fig. 199 Checking the piston ring-to-ring groove side clearance using the ring and a feeler gauge

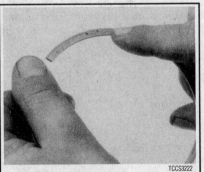

Fig. 200 Most rings are marked to show which side of the ring should face up when installed in the piston

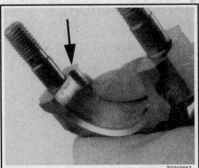

Fig. 201 The notch on the side of the bearing cap matches the tang on the bearing insert

Fig. 202 Install the piston and rod assembly into the block using a ring compressor and tap into place lightly with a hammer handle

TCCS3914

pression rings with a feeler gauge inserted between the ring and its lower land according to specification. The gauge should slide freely around the entire ring circumference without binding. Any wear that occurs will form a step at the inner portion of the lower land. If the lower lands have high steps, the piston should be replaced.

2. Unless new pistons are installed, be sure to install the pistons in the cylinders from which they were removed. The numbers on the connecting rod and bearing cap must be on the same side when installed in the cylinder bore. If a connecting rod is ever transposed from one engine or cylinder to another, new bearings should be fitted and the connecting rod should be numbered to correspond with the new cylinder number. The notch on the piston head goes toward the front of the engine.

3. Install all of the rod bearing inserts into the rods and caps.

4. Install the rings to the pistons. Install the oil control ring first, then the second compression ring and finally the top compression ring. Use a piston ring expander tool to aid in installation and to help reduce the chance of breakage.

5. Make sure the ring gaps are properly spaced around the circumference of the piston. Fit a piston ring compressor around the piston and slide the piston and connecting rod assembly down into the cylinder bore, pushing it in with the wooden hammer handle. Push the piston down until it is only slightly below the top of the cylinder bore. Don't forget to install some short lengths of rubber hose on the connecting rod bolts to protect the crankshaft. The connecting rod bolts are hardened and the threads are sharp enough to nick the crankshaft journal. That will ruin the bearing and fail the

engine shortly after start-up. Guide the connecting rod onto the crankshaft bearing journal carefully, to avoid damaging the crankshaft.

6. Check the bearing clearance of all the rod bearings, fitting them to the crankshaft bearing journals. Follow the procedure in the crankshaft installation above.

7. After the bearings have been fitted, apply a light coating of assembly oil to the journals and bearings.

8. Turn the crankshaft until the appropriate bearing journal is at the bottom of its stroke, then push the piston assembly all the way down until the connecting rod bearing seats on the crankshaft journal. Be careful not to allow the bearing cap screws to strike the crankshaft bearing journals and damage them.

9. After the piston and connecting rod assemblies have been installed, check the connecting rod side clearance on each crankshaft journal.

10. If required, install the balance shaft following the procedures found earlier in this section.

11. Install the rear crankshaft oil seal.

OHV Engines

CAMSHAFT, LIFTERS AND TIMING ASSEMBLY

The installation procedures for the following components may be found earlier in this section.
1. Install the camshaft.
2. Install the lifters/followers into their bores.
3. Install the timing gears/chain assembly.

CYLINDER HEAD(S)

The installation procedures for the following components may be found earlier in this section.
1. Install the cylinder head(s) using new gaskets.
2. Assemble the rest of the valve train (pushrods and rocker arms and/or shafts).

OHC Engines

CYLINDER HEAD(S)

The installation procedures for the following components may be found earlier in this section.
1. Install the cylinder head(s) using new gaskets.
2. Install the timing sprockets/gears and the belt/chain assemblies.

Engine Covers and Components

The installation procedures for the following components may be found earlier in this section.

Install the timing cover(s) and oil pan. Refer to your notes and drawings made prior to disassembly and install all of the components that were removed. Install the engine into the vehicle.

Engine Start-up and Break-in

STARTING THE ENGINE

With the engine installed and every wire and hose is properly connected, take the time to go back and double check that all coolant and vacuum hoses are connected. Check that your oil drain plug is installed and properly tightened. If not already done, install a new oil filter onto the engine. Fill the crankcase with the proper amount and grade of engine oil. Fill the cooling system with a 50/50 mixture of coolant/water.

1. Connect the vehicle battery.
2. Start the engine. Keep your eye on your oil pressure indicator; if it does not indicate oil pressure within 10 seconds of starting, turn the vehicle off.

✷✷ WARNING

Damage to the engine can result if it is allowed to run with no oil pressure. Check the engine oil level to make sure that it is full. Check for any leaks and if found, repair the leaks before continuing. If there is still no indication of oil pressure, you may need to prime the system.

3. Confirm that there are no fluid leaks (oil or other).

4. Allow the engine to reach normal operating temperature (the upper radiator hose will be hot to the touch).

5. At this point you can perform any necessary checks or adjustments, such as checking the ignition timing.

6. Install any remaining components or body panels which were removed.

ENGINE BREAK-IN

Make the first miles on the new engine, easy ones. Vary the speed but do not accelerate hard. Most importantly, do not lug the engine, and avoid sustained high speeds until at least 100 miles. Check the engine oil and coolant levels frequently. Expect the engine to use a little oil until the piston rings seat. Change the oil and filter at 500 miles, 1500 miles, then every 3000 miles after that.

3.1L ENGINE SPECIFICATIONS

Description	English	Metric
General Information		
Type	60° V-type OverHead Valve (OHV)	
Displacement	191	3.1 (3135)
Number of Cylinders	6	
Bore	3.50 in.	89mm
Stroke	3.31 in.	84mm
Compression ratio	9.5:1	
Cylinder Bore		
Diameter	3.5046-3.5053 in.	89.016-89.034mm
Out-of-round (max.)	0.0005 in.	0.014mm
Taper	0.0008 in.	0.020mm
Piston		
Diameter	3.5029-3.5040 in.	88.974-89.001mm
Piston clearance	0.0013-0.0027 in.	0.032-0.068mm
Pin bore	0.9057-0.9060 in.	23.006-23.013mm
Piston Rings		
Top groove side clearance	0.002-0.0033 in.	0.05-0.085mm
Second groove side clearance	0.002-0.0033 in.	0.05-0.085mm
Top ring gap	0.006-0.014 in.	0.15-0.36mm
Second ring gap	0.0197-0.0280 in.	0.50-0.71mm
Groove Clearance	0.008 in.	0.20mm
Gap with segment at 89.0mm	0.0098-0.0500 in.	0.25-1.27mm
Piston pin		
Diameter	0.9052-0.9054 in.	22.9915-22.9964mm
Fit in piston	0.0004-0.0008 in.	0.0096-0.0215mm
Fit in rod	0.0006-0.0018 in.	0.0165-0.0464mm
Crankshaft		
Main journal diameter	2.6473-2.6483 in.	67.239-67.257mm
Main journal taper	0.0002 in.	0.005mm
Out-of-round	0.0002 in.	0.005mm
Flange runout (max.)	0.0016 in.	0.04mm
Cylinder block main bearing bore diameter	2.8407-2.8412 in.	72.155-72.168mm
Main bearing inside diameter	2.6492-2.6502 in.	67.289-67.316mm
Main bearing clearance	0.0008-0.0025 in.	0.019-0.064mm
Main thrust bearing clearance	0.0012-0.0030 in.	0.032-0.077mm
Crankshaft end play	0.0024-0.0083 in.	0.060-0.210mm
Crankshaft flange runout (max.)	0.0016 in.	0.04mm
Connecting Rod		
Connecting rod bearing journal diameter	1.9987-1.9994 in.	50.768-50.784mm
Connecting rod bearing journal taper	0.0002 in.	0.005mm
Connecting rod bearing journal out-of-round	0.0002 in.	0.005mm
Connecting rod bearing bore diameter	2.124-2.125 in.	53.962-53.984mm
Connecting rod inside bearing diameter	2.000-2.002 in.	50.812-50.850mm
Connecting rod bearing journal clearance	0.0007-0.0024 in.	0.018-0.062mm
Connecting rod side clearance	0.007-0.017 in.	0.18-0.44mm

93173C01

3.1L ENGINE SPECIFICATIONS

Description	English	Metric
Camshaft		
Lobe lift (intake and exhaust)	0.2727 in.	6.9263mm
Journal diameter	1.868-1.869 in.	47.45-47.48mm
Camshaft bearing bore diameter (front and rear)	2.009-2.011 in.	51.03-51.08mm
Camshaft bearing bore diameter (middle #2 and #3)	1.999-2.001 in.	50.77-50.82mm
Camshaft bearing inside diameter	1.871-1.872 in.	47.523-47.549mm
Journal clearance	0.001-0.0039 in.	0.026-0.101mm
Journal runout (max.)	0.001 in.	0.025mm
Valve System		
Roller lifter	Hydraulic	
Rocker arm ratio	1.50:1	
Valve face angle	45°	
Seat angle	45°	
Valve seat runout	0.001 in.	0.025mm
Seat width		
Intake	0.061-0.071 in.	1.55-1.80mm
Exhaust	0.067-0.079 in.	1.70-2.0mm
Valve margin		
Minimum intake	0.083 in.	2.10mm
Minimum exhaust	0.106 in.	2.70mm
Valve stem clearance	0.0010-0.0027 in.	0.026-0.068mm
Valve Spring		
Spring free length	1.89 in.	48.5mm
Spring load		
Closed	75 lbs. @ 1.701 in.	320 N @ 43.2mm
Open	230 lbs. @ 1.26 in.	1036 N @ 32mm
Installed height (intake and exhaust)	1.701 in.	43.2mm
Approx. # of coils	6.55	
Oil Pump		
Gear lash	0.0037-0.0077 in.	0.094-0.195mm
Gear pocket depth	1.202-1.204 in.	30.52-30.58mm
Gear pocket diameter	1.503-1.505 in.	38.176-38.226mm
Oil Pump Gear		
Length	1.199-1.200 in.	30.45-30.48mm
Diameter	1.498-1.500 in.	38.05-38.10mm
Side clearance	0.001-0.003 in.	0.038-0.088mm
End clearance	0.002-0.005 in.	0.040-0.125mm
Valve-to-bore clearance	0.0015-0.0035 in.	0.038-0.089mm

93173C02

3.4L (VIN X) ENGINE SPECIFICATIONS

Description	English	Metric
General Information		
Type	60° V-type Dual OverHead Cam (DOHC)	
Displacement	204	3.4 (3350)
Number of Cylinders	6	
Bore	3.622 in.	92mm
Stroke	3.307 in.	84mm
Compression ratio	9.5:1	
Cylinder Bore		
Diameter	3.6228-3.6235 in.	92.019-92.037mm
Out-of-round (max.)	0.0004 in.	0.010mm
Taper, thrust side (max.)	0.00051 in.	0.013mm
Center distance	4.4 in.	111.76mm
Piston		
Diameter (10.5mm below centerline of piston pin bore)	3.6215-3.6220 in.	91.985-92.000mm
Piston clearance	0.0008-0.0020 in.	0.020-0.052mm
Pin bore	0.9056-0.9059 in.	23.003-23.010mm
Piston Rings		
Compression groove clearance, 1st and 2nd	0.0013-0.0031 in.	0.033-0.079mm
Gap (at gauge diameter)		
1st	0.008-0.018 in.	0.20-0.45mm
2nd	0.022-0.032 in.	0.56-0.81mm
Oil groove clearance	0.0011-0.0081 in.	0.028-0.206mm
Gap (segment at gauge diameter)	0.0098-0.0299 in.	0.25-0.76mm
Tension		
1st	6.2 lbs.	27.6 N
2nd	4.5 lbs.	19.8 N
Oil	7.0 lbs.	31.2 N
Piston pin		
Diameter	0.9052-0.9054 in.	22.9915-22.9964mm
Fit in piston	0.00026-0.00073 in.	0.0066-0.0185mm
Fit in rod	0.0006-0.0018 in.	0.0165-0.0464mm
Crankshaft		
Main journal diameter - all	2.6472-2.6479 in.	67.239-67.257mm
Main journal taper (max.)	0.0002 in.	0.005mm
Out-of-round (max.)	0.0002 in.	0.005mm
Cylinder block main bearing bore diameter	2.8407-2.8412 in.	72.155-72.168mm
Main bearing inside diameter	2.6492-2.6502 in.	67.289-67.316mm
Main bearing clearance	0.0008-0.0025 in.	0.019-0.064mm
Main thrust bearing clearance	0.0013-0.0030 in.	0.032-0.077mm
Crankshaft end play	0.002-0.008 in.	0.06-0.21mm
Crank Pin		
Diameter	1.9987-1.9994 in.	50.768-50.784mm
Taper (max.)	0.0002 in.	0.005mm
Out-of-round (max.)	0.0002 in.	0.005mm
Rod bearing bore diameter	2.124-2.125 in.	53.962-53.984mm
Rod inner bearing diameter	2.000-2.002 in.	50.812-50.850mm
Rod bearing clearance	0.0007-0.0024 in.	0.018-0.062mm
Rod side clearance	0.007-0.017 in.	0.18-0.44mm

93173C03

3.4L (VIN X) ENGINE SPECIFICATIONS

Description	English	Metric
Camshaft		
Lobe lift		
Intake (@ 108 deg. Crank ATDC)	0.370 in.	9.398mm
Exhaust (@ 115 deg. Crank BTDC)	0.370 in.	9.398mm
Journal diameter	2.1643-2.1654 in.	54.973-55.001mm
Bore inside diameter	2.1673-2.1683 in.	55.050-55.075mm
Journal clearance	0.0019-0.0040 in.	0.049-0.102mm
Valve System		
Lifter	Hydraulic	
Face angle	45°	
Seat angle	46°	
Valve seat runout (max.)	0.0030 in.	0.075mm
Seat width		
Intake	0.0492-0.0591 in.	1.25-1.50mm
Exhaust	0.063-0.0748 in.	1.60-1.90mm
Valve margin (minimum)	0.029 in.	0.75mm
Stem clearance		
Intake	0.0011-0.0026 in.	0.028-0.066mm
Exhaust	0.0018-0.0033 in.	0.046-0.084mm
Valve Spring		
Spring free length	1.6551 in.	42.04mm
Spring load		
Open	160 lbs. @ 1.030 in.	711 N @ 26.16mm
Closed (all)	65 lbs. @ 1.400 in.	289 N @ 35.56mm
Approx. # of active coils	4	
Oil Pump		
Gear lash	0.0037-0.0077 in.	0.094-0.195mm
Gear pocket depth	1.202-1.204 in.	30.52-30.58mm
Gear pocket diameter	1.504-1.506 in.	38.202-38.252mm
Oil Pump Gear		
Length	1.199-1.200 in.	30.45-30.48mm
Diameter	1.498-1.500 in.	38.05-38.10mm
Side clearance	0.003-0.004 in.	0.08-0.10mm
End clearance	0.002-0.006 in.	0.05-0.152mm
Valve-to-bore clearance	0.0015-0.0035 in.	0.038-0.089mm

93173C04

3.4L (VIN E) ENGINE SPECIFICATIONS

Description	English		Metric
General Information			
Type	60° V-type OverHead Valve (OHV)		
Displacement	204	3.4 (3350)	
Number of Cylinders	6		
Bore	3.62 in.		92mm
Stroke	3.13 in.		84mm
Compression ratio		9.5:1	
Cylinder Bore			
Diameter	3.6228-3.6235 in.		92.019-92.037mm
Out-of-round (max.)	0.0003 in.		0.007mm
Taper	0.0004 in.		0.010mm
Piston			
Diameter (13mm below centerline of piston pin bore)	3.6209-3.6216 in.		91.970-91.988mm
Piston clearance	0.0013-0.0027 in.		0.032-0.068mm
Pin bore	0.9057-0.9060 in.		23.006-23.013mm
Piston Rings			
Top groove side clearance	0.002-0.0033 in.		0.05-0.085mm
Second groove side clearance	0.002-0.0035 in.		0.05-0.09mm
Top ring gap	0.006-0.014 in.		0.15-0.36mm
Second ring gap	0.0197-0.0280 in.		0.50-0.71mm
Groove Clearance	0.008 in.		0.20mm
Gap with segment at 89.0mm	0.0098-0.0500 in.		0.25-1.27mm
Piston pin			
Diameter	0.9052-0.9054 in.		22.9915-22.9964mm
Fit in piston	0.0004-0.0008 in.		0.0096-0.0215mm
Fit in rod	0.0006-0.0018 in.		0.0165-0.0464mm
Crankshaft			
Main journal diameter	2.6473-2.6483 in.		67.239-67.257mm
Main journal taper	0.0002 in.		0.005mm
Out-of-round	0.0002 in.		0.005mm
Flange runout (max.)	0.0016 in.		0.04mm
Cylinder block main bearing bore diameter	2.8407-2.8412 in.		72.155-72.168mm
Main bearing inside diameter	2.6492-2.6502 in.		67.289-67.316mm
Main bearing clearance	0.0012-0.0025 in.		0.019-0.064mm
Main thrust bearing clearance	0.0012-0.0030 in.		0.032-0.077mm
Crankshaft end play	0.0024-0.0083 in.		0.060-0.210mm
Crankshaft flange runout (max.)	0.0016 in.		0.04mm
Connecting Rod			
Connecting rod bearing journal diameter	1.9987-1.9994 in.		50.768-50.784mm
Connecting rod bearing journal taper	0.0002 in.		0.005mm
Connecting rod bearing journal out-of-round	0.0002 in.		0.005mm
Connecting rod bearing bore diameter	2.124-2.125 in.		53.962-53.984mm
Connecting rod inside bearing diameter	2.000-2.002 in.		50.812-50.850mm
Connecting rod bearing journal clearance	0.0007-0.0024 in.		0.018-0.062mm
Connecting rod side clearance	0.007-0.017 in.		0.18-0.44mm

93173C05

3.4L (VIN E) ENGINE SPECIFICATIONS

Description	English	Metric
Camshaft		
Lobe lift (intake and exhaust)	0.2727 in.	6.9263mm
Journal diameter	1.868-1.869 in.	47.45-47.48mm
Camshaft bearing bore diameter (front and rear)	2.009-2.011 in.	51.03-51.08mm
Camshaft bearing bore diameter (middle #2 and #3)	1.999-2.001 in.	50.77-50.82mm
Camshaft bearing inside diameter	1.871-1.872 in.	47.523-47.549mm
Journal clearance	0.001-0.0039 in.	0.026-0.101mm
Journal runout (max.)	0.001 in.	0.025mm
Valve System		
Roller lifter	Hydraulic	
Rocker arm ratio	1.60:1	
Valve face angle	45°	
Seat angle	45°	
Valve seat runout	0.001 in.	0.025mm
Seat width		
Intake	0.061-0.071 in.	1.55-1.80mm
Exhaust	0.067-0.079 in.	1.70-2.0mm
Valve margin		
Minimum intake	0.083 in.	2.10mm
Minimum exhaust	0.106 in.	2.70mm
Valve stem clearance	0.0010-0.0027 in.	0.026-0.068mm
Valve Spring		
Spring free length	1.89 in.	48.5mm
Spring load		
Closed	75 lbs. @ 1.701 in.	320 N @ 43.2mm
Open	230 lbs. @ 1.26 in.	1036 N @ 32mm
Installed height (intake and exhaust)	1.701 in.	43.2mm
Approx. # of coils	6.55	
Oil Pump		
Gear lash	0.0037-0.0077 in.	0.094-0.195mm
Gear pocket depth	1.202-1.204 in.	30.52-30.58mm
Gear pocket diameter	1.503-1.505 in.	38.176-38.226mm
Oil Pump Gear		
Length	1.199-1.200 in.	30.45-30.48mm
Diameter	1.498-1.500 in.	38.05-38.10mm
Side clearance	0.001-0.003 in.	0.038-0.088mm
End clearance	0.002-0.005 in.	0.040-0.125mm
Valve-to-bore clearance	0.002-0.005 in.	0.038-0.089mm

93173C06

3.5L ENGINE SPECIFICATIONS

Description	English	Metric
General Information		
Type	60° V-type Dual OverHead Cam (DOHC)	
Displacement	212	3.5 (3473)
Number of Cylinders	6	
Bore (@ 1.56 in. from deck surface)	3.523 in.	89.5mm
Stroke	3.62 in.	92mm
Compression ratio	9.3:1	
Balance Shaft		
Bearing clearance	0.0006-0.0015 in.	0.015-0.037mm
Bearing journal diameter	1.9995-2.0005 in.	50.787-50.813mm
Bearing diameter	2.0010-2.0025 in.	50.838-50.864mm
Retaining plate-to-balance shaft clearance	0.0027-0.0067 in.	0.068-0.170mm
Cylinder Block		
Bore spacing - centerline-to-centerline	4.016 in.	102.0mm
Deck height	8.976 in.	228.0mm
Deck clearance (below deck)	0.0236 in.	0.60mm
Length	17.427 in.	442.65mm
Piston clearance (1.614 in. from deck face)	0.001-0.0025 in.	0.028-0.062mm
Deck face flatness	0.004 in.	0.101mm
Cylinder Bore		
Out-of-round		
New	0.0004 in.	0.010mm
Max.	0.004 in.	0.100mm
Taper		
New	0.0004 in.	0.010mm
Max.	0.004 in.	0.100mm
Cylinder Head		
Head flatness max. without resurfacing	0.002 in.	0.05mm
Worn limit	0.008 in.	0.20mm
Piston		
Piston clearance (1.496 in. from top of piston)	3.521-3.522 in.	89.446-89.464mm
Piston pin diameter	0.8265-0.8267 in.	20.995-21.000mm
Piston pin bore diameter	0.8269-0.8272 in.	21.004-21.011mm
Piston pin-to-piston clearance	0.0001-0.0006 in.	0.004-0.016mm
Piston Rings		
Clearance between rings and sides of groove in piston		
Compression rings	0.0016-0.0037 in.	0.040-0.095mm
Oil rings	None - side sealing	
Ring Gap		
Top compression ring	0.010-0.016 in.	0.25-0.40mm
2nd compression ring	0.014-0.020 in.	0.35-0.50mm
Oil rings	0.010-0.030 in.	0.25-0.76mm
Number of compression rings	2	
Number of oil rings	2 rails - 1 expander	
Width of groove ring		
Top ring	0.048-0.049 in.	1.230-1.255mm
2nd ring	0.060-0.061 in.	1.530-1.555mm
Oil ring	0.099-0.100 in.	2.530-2.555mm
Piston pin		
Diameter	0.9052-0.9054 in.	22.9915-22.9964mm
Fit in piston	0.00026-0.00073 in.	0.0066-0.0185mm
Fit in rod	0.0006-0.0018 in.	0.0165-0.0464mm

93173G07

3.5L ENGINE SPECIFICATIONS

Description	English	Metric
Crankshaft and Bearings		
Main bearing clearance limit		
New	0.0006-0.0018 in.	0.017-0.047mm
Worn	0.0021 in.	0.055mm
Main bearing journal diameter	2.755-2.756 in.	69.994-70.006mm
Main bearing journal out-of-round	0.00016 in.	0.004mm
Main bearing journal taper	0.00015 in.	0.004mm
Main bearing journal length		
No. 1	0.9350 in.	23.75mm
No. 2	0.9449 in.	24.00mm
No. 3	1.0039 in.	25.50mm
No. 4	0.9449 in.	24.00mm
Crankpin journal diameter	2.1829-2.1835 in.	55.448-55.462mm
Maximum crankpin journal out-of-round	0.00016 in.	0.004mm
Maximum crankpin journal taper	0.00016 in.	0.004mm
Crankshaft end play		
New limit	0.005-0.014 in.	0.13-0.37mm
Worn limit	0.020 in.	0.50mm
Flywheel pilot runout	0.001 in.	0.025mm
Rear crankshaft seal diameter	3.77-3.78 in.	95.88-95.98mm
Connecting Rods		
Clearance between bearing and crankshaft		
New	0.0009-0.002 in.	0.025-0.057mm
Worn	0.0025 in.	0.065mm
Lower end diameter without bearing	2.328-2.329 in.	59.134-59.154mm
Piston pin bore diameter without bushing	0.923-0.925 in.	23.453-23.493mm
Center-to-center length	6.039 in.	153.4mm
Side clearance on crankshaft	0.004-0.013 in.	0.11-0.33mm
Camshaft		
Number of bearings	4	
Bearing journal diameter	1.061-1.062 in.	26.948-26.972mm
Bearing bore diameter (in head)	1.0635-1.0642 in.	27.013-27.033mm
Bearing clearance		
New	0.0016-0.0033 in.	0.041-0.085mm
Worn	0.003 in.	0.085mm
Out-of-round	0.0002 in.	0.007mm
Camshaft runout (max.)	0.002 in.	0.05mm
Valve timing		
Intake centerline	112 degrees ATDC	
Exhaust centerline	104 degrees BTDC	
Valve lift		
Intake	0.413 in.	10.5mm
Exhaust	0.394 in.	10.0mm
Camshaft Drive		
Primary drive type	Endless chain	
Adjustment	Hydraulic pressure (automatic)	
Pitch	0.315 in.	8mm
Width	0.484 in.	12.3mm
Secondary drive type	Endless chain	
Adjustment	Hydraulic pressure (automatic)	
Pitch	0.315 in.	8mm
Width	0.484 in.	12.3mm

93173G08

3.5L ENGINE SPECIFICATIONS

Description	English	Metric
Valve System		
Face angle	45°	
Seat angle	45.75°	
Valve stem-to-guide, new limits (constant top to bottom)		
Intake	0.001-0.003 in.	0.028-0.068mm
Exhaust	0.002-0.004 in.	0.050-0.100mm
Intake worn limits	0.003 in.	0.068mm
Exhaust worn limits	0.004 in.	0.100mm
Head diameter		
Intake	1.42 in.	36.2mm
Exhaust	1.10 in.	28mm
Valve seat width		
Intake	0.0165-0.0322 in.	0.420-0.820mm
Exhaust	0.0511-0.0668 in.	1.300-1.700mm
Seat eccentricity runout (max.)	0.002 in.	0.05mm
Valve face runout	0.0014 in.	0.038mm
Valve margin		
Intake	0.0354 in.	0.900mm
Exhaust	0.0432 in.	1.100mm
Stem diameter	0.2331-0.2339 in.	5.920-5.941mm
Valve guide diameter (in head)	0.235 in.	5.979mm
Valve length		
Intake	4.354-4.364 in.	110.60-110.86mm
Exhaust	3.611-3.621 in.	91.73-91.99mm
Valve Lifters		
Type	Stationary Hydraulic	
Diameter	0.4716-0.4721 in.	11.979-11.993mm
Lifter bore diameter (in head)	0.4727-0.4736 in.	12.008-12.030mm
Clearance	0.0014-0.0016 in.	0.037-0.041mm
Valve Spring		
Spring free length	1.663 in.	42.24mm
Force required to compress		
Valve closed	47-52 lbs. @ 1.377 in.	209-231 N @ 35.0mm
Valve open	130-142 lbs. @ 0.964 in.	580-631 N @ 24.5mm
Installed height	1.377 in.	35.0mm
Oil Pump		
Type	Gerotor	
Minimum pressure at norm. operating temp @ idle	8 psi	55 kPa
Minimum pressure at norm. operating temp @ 2000 rpm	29 psi	200 kPa

93173C09

3.8L (VIN K & 1) ENGINE SPECIFICATIONS

Description	English	Metric
General Information		
Type	90° V-type OverHead Valve (OHV)	
Displacement	231	3.8 (3786)
Number of Cylinders	6	
Bore	3.800	96.52mm
Stroke	3.400	86.36mm
Compression ratio		
VIN K engine	9.4:1	
VIN 1 engines	8.5:1	
Oil Pump		
Gear pocket depth	0.461-0.4625 in.	11.71-11.75mm
Gear pocket diameter	3.508-3.512 in.	89.10-89.20mm
Inner gear tip clearance	0.006 in.	0.152mm
Outer gear diameter clearance	0.008-0.015 in.	0.203-0.381mm
End clearance	0.001-0.0035 in.	0.025-0.089mm
Valve-to-bore clearance	0.0015-0.0030 in.	0.038-0.076mm
Cylinder Bore		
Diameter	3.8 in.	96.5mm
Out-of-round (max.)		
1996 vehicles	0.0004 in.	0.010mm
1997-99 vehicles	0.001 in.	0.0254mm
Taper		
1996 vehicles	0.0005 in.	0.013mm
1997-99 vehicles	0.001 in.	0.0254mm
Piston		
Piston clearance (39mm from top of piston)	0.0004-0.0020 in.	0.010-0.051mm
Piston Rings		
Ring groove depth		
Top compression	0.158-0.163 in.	4.019-4.146mm
2nd compression	0.0166-0.171 in.	4.214-4.341mm
Oil control	0.150-0.155 in.	3.814-3.941mm
End gap		
Top compression	0.012-0.022 in.	0.305-0.559mm
2nd compression	0.030-0.040 in.	0.762-1.016mm
Oil control	0.010-0.030 in.	0.254-0.762mm
Side clearance		
Top compression	0.0013-0.0031 in.	0.033-0.079mm
2nd compression	0.0013-0.0031 in.	0.033-0.079mm
Oil control	0.0009-0.0079 in.	0.023-0.201mm
Ring width		
Top compression	0.0463-0.0471 in.	1.176-1.197mm
2nd compression	0.0581-0.0589 in.	1.476-1.497mm
Oil control	0.073-0.079 in.	1.854-2.007mm
Piston pin		
Diameter	0.8659-0.8661 in.	21.9950-22.0000mm
Fit in piston	0.00008-0.00051 in.	0.0020-0.0130mm
Fit in rod	0.0003-0.0009 in.	0.0066-0.0217mm
Crankshaft and Connecting Rods		
Crankshaft main bearings		
Journal		
Diameter (all)	2.4988-2.4998 in.	63.470-63.495mm
Taper (max.)	0.0003 in.	0.076mm
Runout (max.)	0.0003 in.	0.076mm

93173C10

3.8L (VIN K & 1) ENGINE SPECIFICATIONS

Description	English	Metric
Crankshaft and Connecting Rods (cont.)		
Bearing-to-journal clearance		
1996-97 vehicles	0.0008-0.0022 in.	0.020-0.055mm
1998-99 vehicles		
Main bearing-to-journal clearance 1	0.0007-0.0016 in.	0.0178-0.0406mm
Main bearing-to-journal clearance 2 & 3	0.0010-0.0020 in.	0.0254-0.0508mm
Main bearing-to-journal clearance 4	0.0009-0.0018 in.	0.0229-0.0457mm
Crankshaft end play	0.003-0.011 in.	0.076-0.276mm
Connecting rod bearings		
Rod side clearance	0.003-0.015 in.	0.076-0.381mm
Rod journal diameter (all)	2.2487-2.2499 in.	57.1170-57.1475mm
Rod journal taper (max.)	0.0003 in.	0.076mm
Rod journal out-of-round (max.)	0.003 in.	0.076mm
Rod bearing clearance	0.0005-0.0026 in.	0.0127-0.0660mm
Connecting rod large end bore I.D.	2.37378-2.3745 in.	60.295-60.312mm
Camshaft		
Lobe lift		
Intake		
1996-97 vehicles	0.250 in.	6.43mm
1998-99 vehicles	0.258 in.	6.55m
Exhaust	0.255 in.	6.48mm
Journal diameter		
1996-97 vehicles	1.785-1.786 in.	45.339-45.364mm
1998 vehicles	1.8462-1.8448 in.	47.655-46.858mm
Bearing inside diameter		
1996-97 vehicles	1.7865-1.7885 in.	45.377-45.428mm
1998-99 vehicles		
1 & 4 inside diameter	1.8462-1.8448 in.	47.655-46.858mm
2 & 3 inside diameter	1.8481-1.8492 in.	46.977-46.942mm
Bearing-to-journal clearance		
1996-97 vehicles	0.0005-0.0035 in.	0.013-0.089mm
1998-99 vehicles	0.0016-0.0047 in.	0.041-0.119mm
Balance Shaft		
End play		
1996-97 vehicles	0.0-0.008 in.	0.0-0.203mm
1998-99 vehicles	0.0-0.0067 in.	0.0-0.171mm
Radial play		
Front		
1996-97 vehicles	0.0-0.0011 in.	0.0-0.028mm
1998-99 vehicles	0.0-0.0010 in.	0.0-0.026mm
Rear	0.0005-0.0047 in.	0.0127-0.119mm
Rear journal diameter	1.4994-1.5002 in.	38.085-38.105mm
Rear bearing-to-journal clearance	0.0005-0.0043 in.	0.0127-0.109mm
Drive gear lash		
1996-97 vehicles	0.002-0.005 in.	0.050-0.127mm
1998-99 vehicles	0.002-0.0049 in.	0.050-0.125mm
Bearing bore diameter		
Front	2.0462-2.0472 in.	51.973-51.999mm
Rear		
1996-97 vehicles	1.950-1.952 in.	49.530-49.580mm
1998-99 vehicles (in block)	1.8735-1.8745 in.	47.584-47.612mm
Bearing inside diameter (rear)	1.5007-1.5037 in.	38.118-38.194mm

93173C11

3.8L (VIN K & 1) ENGINE SPECIFICATIONS

Description	English	Metric
Valve System		
Lifter	Hydraulic	
Rocker arm ratio	1.6:1	
Face angle	45°	
Seat angle	45°	
Minimum margin	0.025 in.	0.635mm
Seat runout (max.)	0.002 in.	0.050mm
Seat width		
Intake	0.060-0.080 in.	1.53-2.03mm
Exhaust	0.090-0.110 in.	2.29-2.79mm
Stem height (all)	1.935-1.975 in.	49.15-50.17mm
Stem clearance (all)	0.0015-0.0032 in.	0.038-0.089mm
Valve spring		
Free length		
1996-97 vehicles	1.981 in.	50.32mm
1998-99 vehicles	1.960 in.	49.78mm
Load - closed		
1996-97 vehicles	80 lbs. @ 1.75 in.	356 N @ 43.69mm
1998-99 vehicles	75 lbs. @ 1.72 in.	334 N @ 43.69mm
Load - open		
1996-97 vehicles	210 lbs. @ 1.315 in.	935 N @ 33.4mm
1998-99 vehicles	228 lbs. @ 1.277 in.	1014 N @ 32.4mm
Installed height	1.690-1.720 in.	42.93-44.45mm
Approximate # of coils		
1996-97 vehicles		4
1998-99 vehicles		
Active coils	4.48	
Total coils	6.60	
Flywheel		
Runout (max.)	0.015 in.	0.38mm

93173C12

TORQUE SPECIFICATIONS

Components	English	Metric
Engine		
3.1L & 3.4L (VIN E) engines		
Upper engine-to-transaxle bolts	55 ft. lbs.	75 Nm
Lower engine-to-transaxle bolts	55 ft. lbs.	75 Nm
Torque converter-to-flywheel bolts	45 ft. lbs.	63 Nm
Engine mount lower nuts	32 ft. lbs.	43 Nm
3.4L (VIN X) engine		
Engine-to-transaxle bolts	55 ft. lbs.	75 Nm
Torque converter-to-flywheel bolts	60 ft. lbs.	82 Nm
Engine mount-to-frame nuts	32 ft. lbs.	43 Nm
3.5L engine		
Engine-to-transaxle bolts	55 ft. lbs.	75 Nm
Transaxle brace bolts	32 ft. lbs.	43 Nm
Engine mount bracket bolts	43 ft. lbs.	58 Nm
Engine mount nuts	35 ft. lbs.	47 Nm
Frame-to-body bolts	133 ft. lbs.	180 Nm
Torque converter-to-flywheel bolts	47 ft. lbs.	63 Nm
3.8L engines		
Upper engine-to-transaxle bolts	55 ft. lbs.	75 Nm
Lower engine-to-transaxle bolts	55 ft. lbs.	75 Nm
Engine mount-to-stud nuts	32 ft. lbs.	43 Nm
Torque converter-to-flywheel bolts	45 ft. lbs.	63 Nm
Rocker arm (valve) cover bolts		
3.1L, 3.4L (VIN E) and 3.8L engines	89 inch lbs.	10 Nm
Camshaft carrier cover bolts		
3.4L (VIN X) engine	97 inch lbs.	11 Nm
3.5L engine	80 inch lbs.	9 Nm
Rocker arm (shaft) bolts		
3.1L engine & 3.4L (VIN E) engines (plus an additional 30 degrees)	14 ft. lbs.	10 Nm
3.8L engines (plus an additional 90 degrees)	15 ft. lbs.	20 Nm
Thermostat		
3.1L, 3.4L (VIN X) and 3.8L engines	18-20 ft. lbs.	25-27 Nm
3.4L (VIN E) engine	18 ft. lbs.	25 Nm
Thermostat housing bolts	18 ft. lbs.	25 Nm
Exhaust crossover pipe bolts	80 inch lbs.	9 Nm
Intake Manifold		
3.1L and 3.4L engines		
Upper intake manifold bolts and nuts	18 ft. lbs.	25 Nm
Lower intake manifold vertical and diagonal bolts	115 inch lbs.	13 Nm
3.5L engine	62 inch lbs.	7 Nm
3.8L engines		
Upper intake manifold bolts	89 inch lbs.	10 Nm
Lower intake manifold bolts	11 ft. lbs.	15 Nm

93173C13

TORQUE SPECIFICATIONS

Components	English	Metric
Exhaust Manifold		
3.1L and 3.4L (VIN E) engines		
Exhaust manifold bolts	12 ft. lbs.	16 Nm
Heat shields bolts	89 inch lbs.	10 Nm
3.4L (VIN X) engine		
Exhaust manifold bolts	115 inch lbs.	13 Nm
3.5L (VIN H) engine		
Manifold-to-crossover pipe flange bolts	18 ft. lbs.	25 Nm
Exhaust manifold nuts	18 ft. lbs.	25 Nm
Exhaust crossover fasteners	15 ft. lbs.	20 Nm
3.8L engines		
Exhaust manifold nuts	22 ft. lbs.	30 Nm
Exhaust crossover fasteners	15 ft. lbs.	20 Nm
Supercharger retaining bolts		
3.8L (VIN 1) engine	17 ft. lbs.	23 Nm
Engine Fan		
Except 3.4L (VIN E) and 3.5L engines	53 inch lbs.	6 Nm
3.4L (VIN E) engine	80 inch lbs.	9 Nm
3.5L engine		
Right side radiator bracket bolt	80 inch lbs.	9 Nm
Fan shroud bolts	53 inch lbs.	6 Nm
Engine mount strut bracket-to-upper radiator support bolts	21 ft. lbs.	28 Nm
Strut-to-bracket through bolt	35 ft. lbs.	48 Nm
Water Pump		
3.1L and 3.4L engines		
Water pump-to-front cover bolts	89 inch lbs.	10 Nm
Water pump pulley bolts	18 ft. lbs.	25 Nm
3.5L (VIN H) engine		
Water pump bolts	124 inch lbs.	14 Nm
Idler pulley bolt	37 ft. lbs.	50 Nm
Water pump pulley bolts	18 ft. lbs.	25 Nm
3.8L engines		
Water pump-to-engine bolts		
Long bolts, plus an additional 40 degrees	15 ft. lbs.	20 Nm
Short bolts, plus an additional 80 degrees	11 ft. lbs.	15 Nm
Water pump pulley bolts	115 inch lbs.	13 Nm
Cylinder Head (see procedure for sequence)		
3.1L and 3.4L (VIN E) engines		
Cylinder head bolts, plus an additional 90 degrees	33 ft. lbs.	45 Nm
3.4L (VIN X) engine		
Cylinder head bolts, plus an additional 90 degrees	44 ft. lbs.	60 Nm
3.5L (VIN H) engine		
M11 bolts, plus 60 degrees	22 ft. lbs.	30 Nm
Long M6 bolt	22 ft. lbs.	30 Nm
Two short M6 bolts	106 inch lbs.	12 Nm
3.8L engines		
Cylinder head bolts	37 ft. lbs.	50 Nm

93173C14

TORQUE SPECIFICATIONS

Components	English	Metric
Oil Pan		
3.1L & 3.4L (VIN E) engines		
Side rail bolts	18 ft. lbs.	25 Nm
Left side (front) and right side (rear) oil pan side bolts	37 ft. lbs.	50 Nm
3.4L (VIN X) engine		
Oil pan mounting nuts	97 inch lbs.	11 Nm
Rear oil pan mounting bolts	20 ft. lbs.	27 Nm
Remaining oil pan mounting bolts	97 inch lbs.	11 Nm
3.5L (VIN H) engine		
Transaxle brace-to-cylinder block bolts	18 ft. lbs.	25 Nm
Transaxle brace-to-oil pan bolts	18 ft. lbs.	25 Nm
Oil pan bolts	18 ft. lbs.	25 Nm
3.8L engines		
Oil pan mounting bolts	125 inch lbs.	14 Nm
Oil Pump		
3.1L engines, pump mounting bolt	30 ft. lbs.	41 Nm
3.4L engines, pump mounting bolt	40 ft. lbs.	54 Nm
3.5L (VIN H) engine		
Oil pump housing and the cover bolts	124 inch lbs.	14 Nm
Oil pump body-to-cylinder block bolts	18 ft. lbs.	25 Nm
3.8L engines		
Oil pump cover screws	98 inch lbs.	11 Nm
Oil filter adapter bolts	22 ft. lbs.	30 Nm
Crankshaft Balancer		
3.1L and 3.4L engines, balancer bolt	76-80 ft. lbs.	103-108 Nm
3.5L engine, balancer bolt (plus an additional 125 degrees)	37 ft. lbs.	50 Nm
3.8L engines, balancer bolt (plus an additional 76 degrees)	111 ft. lbs.	150 Nm
Timing Belt Cover		
3.4L (VIN X) engine, cover bolts	89 inch lbs.	10 Nm
Timing Chain Cover		
3.1L and 3.4L (VIN E) engines		
Large cover bolts	35 ft. lbs.	47 Nm
Small cover bolts	15 ft. lbs.	20 Nm
3.4L (VIN X) engine		
Large cover bolts	35-37 ft. lbs.	47-50 Nm
Small cover bolts	18-20 ft. lbs.	25-27 Nm
Timing Chain Cover (cont.)		
3.5L engine		
Timing chain (front) cover bolts	124 inch lbs.	14 Nm
3.8L engines		
Upper front cover bolts, plus an additional 40 degrees	11 ft. lbs.	15 Nm
Oil pan-to-front cover bolts	125 inch lbs.	14 Nm

93173C15

TORQUE SPECIFICATIONS

Components	English	Metric
Timing Belt and Sprockets		
3.4L (VIN X) engine		
Crankshaft sprocket bolt	96 ft. lbs.	130 Nm
Idler pulley bolt	37 ft. lbs.	50 Nm
Timing belt tensioner actuator pulley bolt	37 ft. lbs.	50 Nm
Tensioner actuator bolts	18 ft. lbs.	25 Nm
Tensioner pulley bolts	11 ft. lbs.	15 Nm
Camshaft sprocket bolts	96 ft. lbs.	130 Nm
Timing Chain and Gears		
3.1L and 3.4L (VIN E) engines		
Camshaft sprocket retaining bolt	81 ft. lbs.	110 Nm
3.4L (VIN X) engine		
Timing chain tensioner slotted hole bolt	18 ft. lbs.	25 Nm
Intermediate drive shaft retaining bolts	18 ft. lbs.	25 Nm
3.5L engine		
Timing chain tensioner shoe retaining bolt	22 ft. lbs.	30 Nm
Tensioner retaining bolts	18 ft. lbs.	25 Nm
Chain guide access plug retainers	44 inch lbs.	5 Nm
Front engine lift bracket hex-head bolt	37 ft. lbs.	50 Nm
3.8L engines		
Camshaft sprocket bolt, plus an additional 90 degrees.	74 ft. lbs.	100 Nm
Timing chain dampener bolt	16 ft. lbs.	22 Nm
Camshaft		
3.1L, 3.4L & 3.8L engines		
Thrust plate screws to 89 inch lbs. (10 Nm)	89 inch lbs.	10 Nm
Thrust plate bolts to 89 inch lbs. (10 Nm)	89 inch lbs.	10 Nm
Thrust plate cover bolts to 89 inch lbs. (10 Nm)	89 inch lbs.	10 Nm
3.5L (VIN H) engine		
Camshaft bearing caps, plus an additional 22 degrees	71 inch lbs.	8 Nm
Camshaft sprocket bolts, plus an additional 45 degrees.	18 ft. lbs.	25 Nm
Balance Shaft		
3.8L engine		
Balance shaft retainer	27 ft. lbs.	37 Nm
Balance shaft gear bolt, plus an additional 35 degrees.	15 ft. lbs.	20 Nm
Balance shaft front bearing retainer bolts	26 ft. lbs.	35 Nm
Intermediate shaft		
3.4L (VIN X) engine		
Thrust plate retainer screws	89 inch lbs.	10 Nm
Flywheel		
Flywheel retaining bolts		
3.1L and 3.4L engines	60 ft. lbs.	82 Nm
3.5L and 3.8L engines, plus an additional 50 degrees	11 ft. lbs.	15 Nm

93173C16

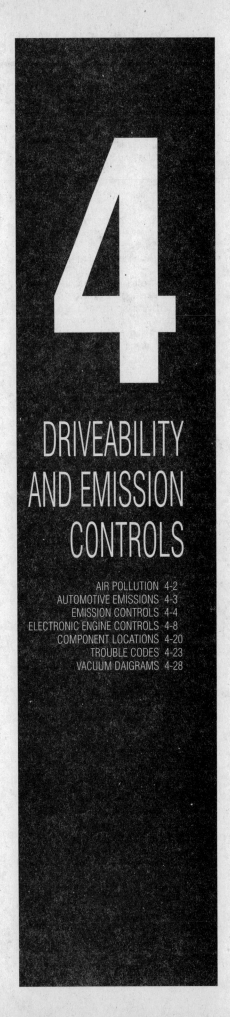

4

DRIVEABILITY AND EMISSION CONTROLS

AIR POLLUTION

The earth's atmosphere, at or near sea level, consists approximately of 78 percent nitrogen, 21 percent oxygen and 1 percent other gases. If it were possible to remain in this state, 100 percent clean air would result. However, many varied sources allow other gases and particulates to mix with the clean air, causing our atmosphere to become unclean or polluted.

Some of these pollutants are visible while others are invisible, with each having the capability of causing distress to the eyes, ears, throat, skin and respiratory system. Should these pollutants become concentrated in a specific area and under certain conditions, death could result due to the displacement or chemical change of the oxygen content in the air. These pollutants can also cause great damage to the environment and to the many man made objects that are exposed to the elements.

To better understand the causes of air pollution, the pollutants can be categorized into 3 separate types, natural, industrial and automotive.

Natural Pollutants

Natural pollution has been present on earth since before man appeared and continues to be a factor when discussing air pollution, although it causes only a small percentage of the overall pollution problem. It is the direct result of decaying organic matter, wind born smoke and particulates from such natural events as plain and forest fires (ignited by heat or lightning), volcanic ash, sand and dust which can spread over a large area of the countryside.

Such a phenomenon of natural pollution has been seen in the form of volcanic eruptions, with the resulting plume of smoke, steam and volcanic ash blotting out the sun's rays as it spreads and rises higher into the atmosphere. As it travels into the atmosphere the upper air currents catch and carry the smoke and ash, while condensing the steam back into water vapor. As the water vapor, smoke and ash travel on their journey, the smoke dissipates into the atmosphere while the ash and moisture settle back to earth in a trail hundreds of miles long. In some cases, lives are lost and millions of dollars of property damage result.

Industrial Pollutants

Industrial pollution is caused primarily by industrial processes, the burning of coal, oil and natural gas, which in turn produce smoke and fumes. Because the burning fuels contain large amounts of sulfur, the principal ingredients of smoke and fumes are sulfur dioxide and particulate matter. This type of pollutant occurs most severely during still, damp and cool weather, such as at night. Even in its less severe form, this pollutant is not confined to just cities. Because of air movements, the pollutants move for miles over the surrounding countryside, leaving in its path a barren and unhealthy environment for all living things.

Working with Federal, State and Local mandated regulations and by carefully monitoring emissions, big business has greatly reduced the amount of pollutant introduced from its industrial sources, striving to obtain an acceptable level. Because of the mandated industrial emission clean up, many land areas and streams in and around the cities that were formerly barren of vegetation and life, have now begun to move back in the direction of nature's intended balance.

Automotive Pollutants

The third major source of air pollution is automotive emissions. The emissions from the internal combustion engines were not an appreciable problem years ago because of the small number of registered vehicles and the nation's small highway system. However, during the early 1950's, the trend of the American people was to move from the cities to the surrounding suburbs. This caused an immediate problem in transportation because the majority of suburbs were not afforded mass transit conveniences. This lack of transportation created an attractive market for the automobile manufacturers, which resulted in a dramatic increase in the number of vehicles produced and sold, along with a marked increase in highway construction between cities and the suburbs. Multi-vehicle families emerged with a growing emphasis placed on an individual vehicle per family member. As the increase in vehicle ownership and usage occurred, so did pollutant levels in and around the cities, as suburbanites drove daily to their businesses and employment, returning at the end of the day to their homes in the suburbs.

It was noted that a smoke and fog type haze was being formed and at times, remained in suspension over the cities, taking time to dissipate. At first this "smog," derived from the words "smoke" and "fog," was thought to result from industrial pollution but it was determined that automobile emissions shared the blame. It was discovered that when normal automobile emissions were exposed to sunlight for a period of time, complex chemical reactions would take place.

It is now known that smog is a photo chemical layer which develops when certain oxides of nitrogen (NOx) and unburned hydrocarbons (HC) from automobile emissions are exposed to sunlight. Pollution was more severe when smog would become stagnant over an area in which a warm layer of air settled over the top of the cooler air mass, trapping and holding the cooler mass at ground level. The trapped cooler air would keep the emissions from being dispersed and diluted through normal air flows. This type of air stagnation was given the name "Temperature Inversion."

TEMPERATURE INVERSION

In normal weather situations, surface air is warmed by heat radiating from the earth's surface and the sun's rays. This causes it to rise upward, into the atmosphere. Upon rising it will cool through a convection type heat exchange with the cooler upper air. As warm air rises, the surface pollutants are carried upward and dissipated into the atmosphere.

When a temperature inversion occurs, we find the higher air is no longer cooler, but is warmer than the surface air, causing the cooler surface air to become trapped. This warm air blanket can extend from above ground level to a few hundred or even a few thousand feet into the air. As the surface air is trapped, so are the pollutants, causing a severe smog condition. Should this stagnant air mass extend to a few thousand feet high, enough air movement with the inversion takes place to allow the smog layer to rise above ground level but the pollutants still cannot dissipate.

This inversion can remain for days over an area, with the smog level only rising or lowering from ground level to a few hundred feet high. Meanwhile, the pollutant levels increase, causing eye irritation, respiratory problems, reduced visibility, plant damage and in some cases, even disease. This inversion phenomenon was first noted in the Los Angeles, California area. The city lies in terrain resembling a basin and with certain weather conditions, a cold air mass is held in the basin while a warmer air mass covers it like a lid.

Because this type of condition was first documented as prevalent in the Los Angeles area, this type of trapped pollution was named Los Angeles Smog, although it occurs in other areas where a large concentration of automobiles are used and the air remains stagnant for any length of time.

HEAT TRANSFER

Consider the internal combustion engine as a machine in which raw materials must be placed so a finished product comes out. As in any machine operation, a certain amount of wasted material is formed. When we relate this to the internal combustion engine, we find that through the input of air and fuel, we obtain power during the combustion process to drive the vehicle. The by-product or waste of this power is, in part, heat and exhaust gases with which we must dispose.

The heat from the combustion process can rise to over 4000°F (2204°C). The dissipation of this heat is controlled by a ram air effect, the use of cooling fans to cause air flow and a liquid coolant solution surrounding the combustion area to transfer the heat of combustion through the cylinder walls and into the coolant. The coolant is then directed to a thin-finned, multi-tubed radiator, from which the excess heat is transferred to the atmosphere by 1 of the 3 heat transfer methods, conduction, convection or radiation.

The cooling of the combustion area is an important part in the control of exhaust emissions. To understand the behavior of the combustion and transfer of its heat, consider the air/fuel charge. It is ignited and the flame front burns progressively across the combustion chamber until the burning charge reaches the cylinder walls. Some of the fuel in contact with the walls is not hot enough to burn, thereby snuffing out or quenching the combustion process. This leaves unburned fuel in the combustion chamber. This unburned fuel is then forced out of the cylinder and into the exhaust system, along with the exhaust gases.

Many attempts have been made to minimize the amount of unburned fuel in the combustion chambers due to quenching, by increasing the coolant temperature and lessening the contact area of the coolant around the combustion area. However, design limitations within the combustion chambers prevent the complete burning of the air/fuel charge, so a certain amount of the unburned fuel is still expelled into the exhaust system, regardless of modifications to the engine.

AUTOMOTIVE EMISSIONS

Before emission controls were mandated on internal combustion engines, other sources of engine pollutants were discovered along with the exhaust emissions. It was determined that engine combustion exhaust produced approximately 60 percent of the total emission pollutants, fuel evaporation from the fuel tank and carburetor vents produced 20 percent, with the final 20 percent being produced through the crankcase as a by-product of the combustion process.

Exhaust Gases

The exhaust gases emitted into the atmosphere are a combination of burned and unburned fuel. To understand the exhaust emission and its composition, we must review some basic chemistry.

When the air/fuel mixture is introduced into the engine, we are mixing air, composed of nitrogen (78 percent), oxygen (21 percent) and other gases (1 percent) with the fuel, which is 100 percent hydrocarbons (HC), in a semi-controlled ratio. As the combustion process is accomplished, power is produced to move the vehicle while the heat of combustion is transferred to the cooling system. The exhaust gases are then composed of nitrogen, a diatomic gas (N_2), the same as was introduced in the engine, carbon dioxide (CO_2), the same gas that is used in beverage carbonation, and water vapor (H_2O). The nitrogen (N_2), for the most part, passes through the engine unchanged, while the oxygen (O_2) reacts (burns) with the hydrocarbons (HC) and produces the carbon dioxide (CO_2) and the water vapors (H_2O). If this chemical process would be the only process to take place, the exhaust emissions would be harmless. However, during the combustion process, other compounds are formed which are considered dangerous. These pollutants are hydrocarbons (HC), carbon monoxide (CO), oxides of nitrogen (NOx) oxides of sulfur (SOx) and engine particulates.

HYDROCARBONS

Hydrocarbons (HC) are essentially fuel which was not burned during the combustion process or which has escaped into the atmosphere through fuel evaporation. The main sources of incomplete combustion are rich air/fuel mixtures, low engine temperatures and improper spark timing. The main sources of hydrocarbon emission through fuel evaporation on most vehicles used to be the vehicle's fuel tank and carburetor float bowl.

To reduce combustion hydrocarbon emission, engine modifications were made to minimize dead space and surface area in the combustion chamber. In addition, the air/fuel mixture was made more lean through the improved control which feedback carburetion and fuel injection offers and by the addition of external controls to aid in further combustion of the hydrocarbons outside the engine. Two such methods were the addition of air injection systems, to inject fresh air into the exhaust manifolds and the installation of catalytic converters, units that are able to burn traces of hydrocarbons without affecting the internal combustion process or fuel economy.

To control hydrocarbon emissions through fuel evaporation, modifications were made to the fuel tank to allow storage of the fuel vapors during periods of engine shut-down. Modifications were also made to the air intake system so that at specific times during engine operation, these vapors may be purged and burned by blending them with the air/fuel mixture.

CARBON MONOXIDE

Carbon monoxide is formed when not enough oxygen is present during the combustion process to convert carbon (C) to carbon dioxide (CO_2). An increase in the carbon monoxide (CO) emission is normally accompanied by an increase in the hydrocarbon (HC) emission because of the lack of oxygen to completely burn all of the fuel mixture.

Carbon monoxide (CO) also increases the rate at which the photo chemical smog is formed by speeding up the conversion of nitric oxide (NO) to nitrogen dioxide (NO_2). To accomplish this, carbon monoxide (CO) combines with oxygen (O_2) and nitric oxide (NO) to produce carbon dioxide (CO_2) and nitrogen dioxide (NO_2). ($CO + O_2 + NO = CO_2 + NO_2$).

The dangers of carbon monoxide, which is an odorless and colorless toxic gas are many. When carbon monoxide is inhaled into the lungs and passed into the blood stream, oxygen is replaced by the carbon monoxide in the red blood cells, causing a reduction in the amount of oxygen supplied to the many parts of the body. This lack of oxygen causes headaches, lack of coordination, reduced mental alertness and, should the carbon monoxide concentration be high enough, death could result.

NITROGEN

Normally, nitrogen is an inert gas. When heated to approximately 2500°F (1371°C) through the combustion process, this gas becomes active and causes an increase in the nitric oxide (NO) emission.

Oxides of nitrogen (NOx) are composed of approximately 97–98 percent nitric oxide (NO). Nitric oxide is a colorless gas but when it is passed into the atmosphere, it combines with oxygen and forms nitrogen dioxide (NO_2). The nitrogen dioxide then combines with chemically active hydrocarbons (HC) and when in the presence of sunlight, causes the formation of photo-chemical smog.

Ozone

To further complicate matters, some of the nitrogen dioxide (NO_2) is broken apart by the sunlight to form nitric oxide and oxygen. (NO_2 + sunlight = NO + O). This single atom of oxygen then combines with diatomic (meaning 2 atoms) oxygen (O_2) to form ozone (O_3). Ozone is one of the smells associated with smog. It has a pungent and offensive odor, irritates the eyes and lung tissues, affects the growth of plant life and causes rapid deterioration of rubber products. Ozone can be formed by sunlight as well as electrical discharge into the air.

The most common discharge area on the automobile engine is the secondary ignition electrical system, especially when inferior quality spark plug cables are used. As the surge of high voltage is routed through the secondary cable, the circuit builds up an electrical field around the wire, which acts upon the oxygen in the surrounding air to form the ozone. The faint glow along the cable with the engine running that may be visible on a dark night, is called the "corona discharge." It is the result of the electrical field passing from a high along the cable, to a low in the surrounding air, which forms the ozone gas. The combination of corona and ozone has been a major cause of cable deterioration. Recently, different and better quality insulating materials have lengthened the life of the electrical cables.

Although ozone at ground level can be harmful, ozone is beneficial to the earth's inhabitants. By having a concentrated ozone layer called the "ozonosphere," between 10 and 20 miles (16–32 km) up in the atmosphere, much of the ultra violet radiation from the sun's rays are absorbed and screened. If this ozone layer were not present, much of the earth's surface would be burned, dried and unfit for human life.

OXIDES OF SULFUR

Oxides of sulfur (SOx) were initially ignored in the exhaust system emissions, since the sulfur content of gasoline as a fuel is less than $\frac{1}{10}$ of 1 percent. Because of this small amount, it was felt that it contributed very little to the overall pollution problem. However, because of the difficulty in solving the sulfur emissions in industrial pollution and the introduction of catalytic converters to automobile exhaust systems, a change was mandated. The automobile exhaust system, when equipped with a catalytic converter, changes the sulfur dioxide (SO_2) into sulfur trioxide (SO_3).

When this combines with water vapors (H_2O), a sulfuric acid mist (H_2SO_4) is formed and is a very difficult pollutant to handle since it is extremely corrosive. This sulfuric acid mist that is formed, is the same mist that rises from the vents of an automobile battery when an active chemical reaction takes place within the battery cells.

When a large concentration of vehicles equipped with catalytic converters are operating in an area, this acid mist may rise and be distributed over a large ground area causing land, plant, crop, paint and building damage.

PARTICULATE MATTER

A certain amount of particulate matter is present in the burning of any fuel, with carbon constituting the largest percentage of the particulates. In gasoline, the remaining particulates are the burned remains of the various other compounds used in its manufacture. When a gasoline engine is in good internal condition, the particulate emissions are low but as the engine wears internally, the particulate emissions increase. By visually inspecting the tail pipe emissions, a determination can be made as to where an engine defect may exist. An engine with light gray or blue smoke emitting from the tail pipe normally indicates an increase in the oil consumption through burning due to internal engine wear. Black smoke would indicate a defective fuel delivery system, causing the engine to operate in a rich mode. Regardless of the color of the smoke, the internal part of the engine or the fuel delivery system should be repaired to prevent excess particulate emissions.

Diesel and turbine engines emit a darkened plume of smoke from the exhaust system because of the type of fuel used. Emission control regulations are mandated for this type of emission and more stringent measures are being used to prevent excess emission of the particulate matter. Electronic components are being introduced to control the injection of the fuel at precisely the proper time of piston travel, to achieve the optimum in fuel ignition and fuel usage. Other particulate after-burning components are being tested to achieve a cleaner emission.

Good grades of engine lubricating oils should be used, which meet the manufacturer's specification. Cut-rate oils can contribute to the particulate emission problem because of their low flash or ignition temperature point. Such oils burn prematurely during the combustion process causing emission of particulate matter.

The cooling system is an important factor in the reduction of particulate matter. The optimum combustion will occur, with the cooling system operating at a temperature specified by the manufacturer. The cooling system must be maintained in the same manner as the engine oiling system, as each system is required to perform properly in order for the engine to operate efficiently for a long time.

Crankcase Emissions

Crankcase emissions are made up of water, acids, unburned fuel, oil fumes and particulates. These emissions are classified as hydrocarbons (HC) and are formed by the small amount of unburned, compressed air/fuel mixture entering the crankcase from the combustion area (between the cylinder walls and piston rings) during the compression and power strokes. The head of the compression and combustion help to form the remaining crankcase emissions.

Since the first engines, crankcase emissions were allowed into the atmosphere through a road draft tube, mounted on the lower side of the engine block. Fresh air came in through an open oil filler cap or breather. The air passed through the crankcase mixing with blow-by gases. The motion of the vehicle and the air blowing past the open end of the road draft tube caused a low pressure area (vacuum) at the end of the tube. Crankcase emissions were simply drawn out of the road draft tube into the air.

To control the crankcase emission, the road draft tube was deleted. A hose and/or tubing was routed from the crankcase to the intake manifold so the blow-by emission could be burned with the air/fuel mixture. However, it was found that intake manifold vacuum, used to draw the crankcase emissions into the manifold, would vary in strength at the wrong time and not allow the proper emission flow. A regulating valve was needed to control the flow of air through the crankcase.

Testing, showed the removal of the blow-by gases from the crankcase as quickly as possible, was most important to the longevity of the engine. Should large accumulations of blow-by gases remain and condense, dilution of the engine oil would occur to form water, soots, resins, acids and lead salts, resulting in the formation of sludge and varnishes. This condensation of the blow-by gases occurs more frequently on vehicles used in numerous starting and stopping conditions, excessive idling and when the engine is not allowed to attain normal operating temperature through short runs.

Evaporative Emissions

Gasoline fuel is a major source of pollution, before and after it is burned in the automobile engine. From the time the fuel is refined, stored, pumped and transported, again stored until it is pumped into the fuel tank of the vehicle, the gasoline gives off unburned hydrocarbons (HC) into the atmosphere. Through the redesign of storage areas and venting systems, the pollution factor was diminished, but not eliminated, from the refinery standpoint. However, the automobile still remained the primary source of vaporized, unburned hydrocarbon (HC) emissions.

Fuel pumped from an underground storage tank is cool but when exposed to a warmer ambient temperature, will expand. Before controls were mandated, an owner might fill the fuel tank with fuel from an underground storage tank and park the vehicle for some time in warm area, such as a parking lot. As the fuel would warm, it would expand and should no provisions or area be provided for the expansion, the fuel would spill out of the filler neck and onto the ground, causing hydrocarbon (HC) pollution and creating a severe fire hazard. To correct this condition, the vehicle manufacturers added overflow plumbing and/or gasoline tanks with built in expansion areas or domes.

However, this did not control the fuel vapor emission from the fuel tank. It was determined that most of the fuel evaporation occurred when the vehicle was stationary and the engine not operating. Most vehicles carry 5–25 gallons (19–95 liters) of gasoline. Should a large concentration of vehicles be parked in one area, such as a large parking lot, excessive fuel vapor emissions would take place, increasing as the temperature increases.

To prevent the vapor emission from escaping into the atmosphere, the fuel systems were designed to trap the vapors while the vehicle is stationary, by sealing the system from the atmosphere. A storage system is used to collect and hold the fuel vapors from the carburetor (if equipped) and the fuel tank when the engine is not operating. When the engine is started, the storage system is then purged of the fuel vapors, which are drawn into the engine and burned with the air/fuel mixture.

EMISSION CONTROLS

Crankcase Ventilation System

OPERATION

▶ See Figures 1 and 2

The Positive Crankcase Ventilation (PCV) system, also referred to as the Crankcase Ventilation (CV) system, is used on all vehicles to evacuate the crankcase vapors. Fresh air from the air cleaner or intake duct is supplied to the crankcase, mixed with

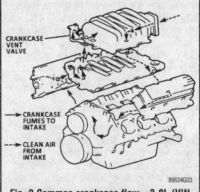

Fig. 2 Common crankcase flow—3.8L (VIN K) engine shown, others similar

blow-by gases and then passed through a Positive Crankcase Ventilation (PCV) valve into the Air Plenum (upper intake manifold).

When manifold vacuum is high, such as at idle, the orifice or valve restricts the flow of blow-by gases allowed into the manifold. If abnormal operating conditions occur, the system will allow excessive blow-by gases to back flow through the hose into the air cleaner. These blow-by gases will then be mixed with the intake air in the air cleaner instead of in the manifold. The air cleaner has a small filter attached to the inside wall that connects to the breather hose to trap impurities flowing in either direction.

A plugged PCV valve, orifice or hose may cause rough idle, stalling or slow idle speed, oil leaks, oil in the air cleaner or sludge in the engine. A leak could cause rough idle, stalling or high idle speed. The condition of the grommets in the valve cover will also affect system and engine performance.

TESTING

PCV Valve

▶ See Figures 3 thru 9

1. Remove the PCV valve. Please see Section 1.
2. With the engine at normal operating temperature, run at idle.
3. With the PCV removed from its seat, place a finger over the end to check if vacuum is present. If vacuum is not present, check for plugged hoses or manifold port. Repair or replace as necessary.
4. Stop the engine and remove the valve. Shake and listen for the rattle of the check valve needle. If no rattle is heard, replace the valve.

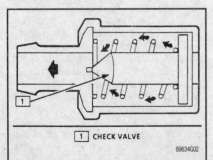

| 1 | CHECK VALVE |

89634G02

Fig. 1 Cross-sectional view of a typical PCV valve

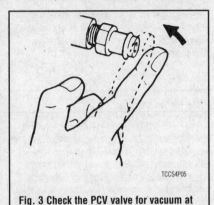

Fig. 3 Check the PCV valve for vacuum at idle

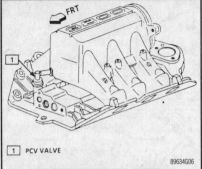

Fig. 4 In this application, the PCV valve is mounted in the rear of the intake manifold—3.8L (VIN K) engine

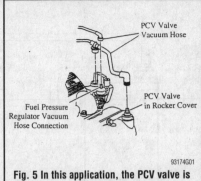

Fig. 5 In this application, the PCV valve is mounted in one of the rocker arm covers—3.1L and 3.4L (VIN E) engines

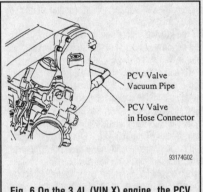

Fig. 6 On the 3.4L (VIN X) engine, the PCV valve is mounted in the connection hose

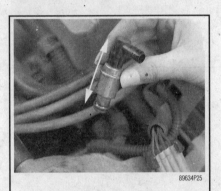

Fig. 7 Remove and shake the PCV valve; if a rattling noise is heard, the valve is OK

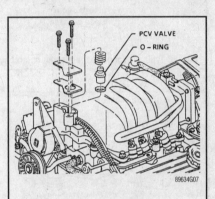

Fig. 8 Exploded view of the PCV valve mounting—3.8L (VIN K) engine

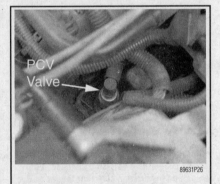

Fig. 9 On some vehicles, the PCV valve is mounted in the intake manifold

PCV System

1. Check to make sure the engine has the correct PCV valve.
2. Start the engine and bring to normal operating temperature.
3. Block off PCV system fresh air intake passage.
4. Remove the engine oil dipstick and install a vacuum gauge on the dipstick tube.
5. Run the engine at 1500 rpm for 30 seconds then read the vacuum gauge with the engine at 1500 rpm.
   a. If vacuum is present, the PCV system is functioning properly.
   b. If there is no vacuum, the engine may not

be sealed and/or is drawing in outside air. Check the grommets and valve cover or oil pan gasket for leaks.
   c. If the vacuum gauge registers a pressure or the vacuum gauge is pushed out of the dipstick tube, check for the correct PCV valve, a plugged hose or excessive engine blow-by.

Evaporative Emission Control System

OPERATION

▶ See Figures 10, 11, 12 and 13

The Evaporative Emission Control (EVAP) System is designed to prevent fuel tank vapors from being emitted into the atmosphere. Changes in atmospheric temperature cause fuel tanks to breathe, that is, the air within the tank expands and contracts with outside temperature changes. If an unsealed system was used, when the temperature rises, air would escape through the tank vent tube or the vent in the tank cap. The air which escapes contains gasoline vapors.

The Evaporative Emission Control System provides a sealed fuel system with the capability to store and condense fuel vapors. When the fuel evaporates in the fuel tank, the vapor passes through the pressure control valve, through vent hoses or tubes to a carbon filled evaporative canister. When the engine is operating, and at normal operating temperature, the vapors are drawn into

the intake manifold and burned during combustion..

A sealed, maintenance free evaporative canister is used. The canister is filled with granules of an activated carbon mixture. Fuel vapors entering the canister are absorbed by the charcoal granules. A vent cap is located on the top of the canister to provide fresh air to the canister when it is being purged. The vent cap opens to provide fresh air into the canister, which circulates through the charcoal, releasing trapped vapors and carrying them to the engine to be burned.

Fuel tank pressure vents fuel vapors into the canister. They are held in the canister until they can be drawn into the intake manifold. The canister purge valve allows the canister to be purged at a pre-determined time and engine operating conditions.

The fuel tank is sealed with a pressure-vacuum relief filler cap. The relief valve in the cap is a safety feature, preventing excessive pressure or vacuum in the fuel tank. If the cap is malfunctioning, and needs to be replaced, ensure that the replacement is the identical cap to ensure correct system operation.

The fuel tank pressure sensor is a three-wire strain gauge sensor much like that of the common GM MAP sensor. However, this sensor has very different electrical characteristics due to the pressure differential design. The sensor measures the difference between the air pressure (or vacuum) in the fuel tank and the outside air pressure. The sensor mounts at the top of the fuel tank. A three-wire electrical harness connects it to the Powertrain Control Module (PCM). The PCM supplies a five volt reference voltage and ground to the sensor. The sensor

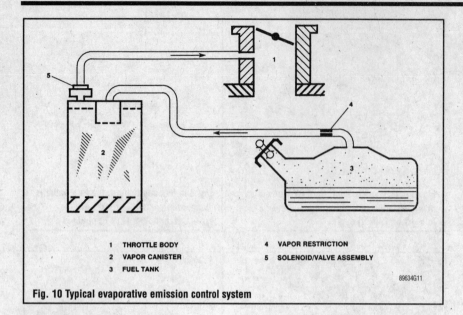

1	THROTTLE BODY	4 VAPOR RESTRICTION
2	VAPOR CANISTER	5 SOLENOID/VALVE ASSEMBLY
3	FUEL TANK	

89634G11

Fig. 10 Typical evaporative emission control system

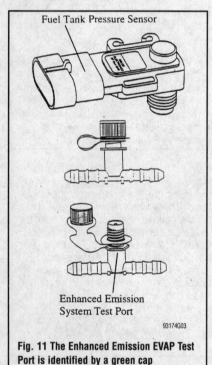

Fuel Tank Pressure Sensor

Enhanced Emission
System Test Port

93174G03

Fig. 11 The Enhanced Emission EVAP Test Port is identified by a green cap

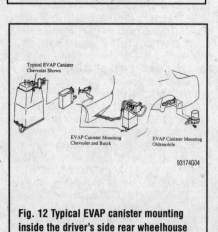

Typical EVAP Canister
Chevrolet Shown

EVAP Canister Mounting
Chevrolet and Buick

EVAP Canister Mounting
Oldsmobile

93174G04

Fig. 12 Typical EVAP canister mounting inside the driver's side rear wheelhouse

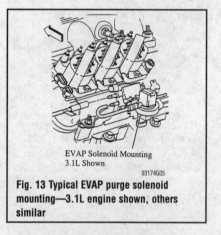

EVAP Solenoid Mounting
3.1L Shown

93174G05

Fig. 13 Typical EVAP purge solenoid mounting—3.1L engine shown, others similar

will return a voltage between 0.1 and 4.9 volts. When the air pressure in the fuel tank is equal to the outside air pressure, such as when the fuel fill cap is removed, the output voltage of the sensor will be 1.3 to 1.7 volts. This sensor is the reason the fuel filler door is usually placarded to remind motorists to tighten the fuel filler cap after refueling. If the tank pressure sensor doesn't see a difference between the air pressure (or vacuum) in the fuel tank and the outside air pressure, the PCM will set a Diagnostic Trouble Code (DTC) and may light up the Malfunction Indicator Lamp (MIL) on the instrument panel.

Enhanced emission testing requires that vehicles be equipped with an EVAP test port. This is located in the evaporative purge hose, located between the purge solenoid and the canister. The service port is identified by a green color cap. The port contains a schrader valve and fittings which allow connections to an EVAP Diagnostic Station, now required in many emission tests.

Poor engine idle, stalling and poor driveability can be caused by an inoperative canister purge solenoid, a damaged canister or split, damaged or improperly connected hoses.

The most common symptom of problems in this system is fuel odors coming from under the hood. If there is no liquid fuel leak, check for a cracked or damaged vapor canister, inoperative or always open

canister control valve, disconnected, misrouted, kinked or damaged vapor pipe or canister hoses; or a damaged air cleaner or improperly seated air cleaner gasket.

TESTING

▶ **See Figure 11**

The EVAP and Enhanced EVAP system monitor is incorporated in the OBD-II engine control system. A pressure sensor is mounted on the fuel tank which measures pressure inside the tank, and a purge flow sensor measures the flow of the gases from the canister into the engine. The vent valve for the canister is now controlled by the PCM. It performs the same functions as the purge valve, however it looks slightly different. A canister vent solenoid is mounted on the canister, taking the place of the vent cap, providing a source of fresh air to the canister.

The PCM can store trouble codes for EVAP system performance, a list of the codes is provided later in this section.

As part of the OBD-II diagnostic system, a test port is installed in the purge line connecting the purge solenoid to the canister. This test port is used to connect a special tester that pressurizes the EVAP system and measure the leakage rate. This tool is very expensive and requires training to operate or you could do damage to the vehicle, however, many professional shops have this device. If you suspect a leak in your EVAP system, you may want to consult a professional shop about performing this test on your car.

A visual inspection is one of the best checks of a EVAP or Enhanced EVAP system operation.
  1. Check for the following conditions:
    a. Poor connection at the PCM. Inspect the PCM harness connectors for backed out terminals, improper or loose connections, broken clips or locks, damaged or corroded terminals, and poor terminal to wire connection.
    b. Inspect the wiring harness for damage.
    c. Inspect for incorrect purge or vacuum source line routing.

Evaporative Emission Canister

➡**On all of the vehicles covered by this manual, the evaporative emission canister is hidden behind the driver's side rear fender well. Please see Section 1 for service procedures.**

  1. Visually check the canister for cracks or damage.
  2. If fuel is leaking from the bottom of the canister, replace canister and check for proper hose routing.
  3. If so equipped, check the filter at the bottom of the canister. If dirty, replace the filter.

REMOVAL & INSTALLATION

Evaporative Emission Canister

▶ **See Figure 12**

  1. Raise and safely support the vehicle.
  2. Remove the left (driver's side) rear tire assembly.
  3. Remove the left rear wheel hose liner (inner fender).

4. Tag for identification the multiple hoses and disconnect the hoses from the canister.

5. Loosen the latch and/or retaining screw(s) on the canister bracket.

6. Remove the canister from the vehicle.

7. Installation is the reverse of the removal procedure, taking care to connect the hoses properly, referencing the identification tags made at removal. If necessary, refer to the Vehicle Emission Control Information (VECI) label, located in the engine compartment, for proper routing of the vacuum hoses.

Exhaust Gas Recirculation System

OPERATION

The Exhaust Gas Recirculation (EGR) system is used to reduce Oxides of Nitrogen (NOx) emission levels caused by high combustion chamber temperatures. It does this by decreasing combustion temperature. The main element of this system is the linear EGR valve. The EGR valve feeds small amounts of exhaust gas back into the combustion chamber. With the fuel/air mix thus diluted, combustion temperatures are reduced.

The linear EGR valve, used on the vehicles covered by this manual, is designed to accurately supply EGR to an engine independent of intake manifold vacuum. The valve controls EGR flow from the exhaust to the intake manifold through an orifice with a PCM controlled pintle. During operation, the PCM controls pintle position by monitoring the pintle position feedback signal. The PCM uses information from the Engine Coolant Temperature (ECT) sensor, Throttle Position (TP) sensor and Mass Air Flow (MAF) sensor to determine the appropriate rate of flow for a particular engine operating condition.

A technician with a scan tool can monitor the feedback signal. The reading on the scan tool is ACTUAL EGR POS. which should always be near the commanded EGR position (DESIRED EGR POS). If a problem with the EGR system will not allow the PCM to control pintle position properly, a DTC should set. The PCM also tests for EGR flow. If flow is incorrect, a DTC should set.

TESTING

A scan tool is required to retrieve DTCs and monitor the EGR system. The testing a non-professional can reasonably perform is limited to visual checks.

If the EGR valve shows signs of excessive heat, check the exhaust system for blockage (possibly a plugged catalytic converter). The following should also be checked:

1. Remove the EGR valve and look for excessive deposits on the EGR pintle or seat. Check for deposits that may interfere with the EGR valve pintle extending completely or cause the pintle to stick.

2. Look for a poor connection or damaged harness. Inspect the wiring harness for damage. If the harness appears to be okay, a scan tool will be required to observe the EGR actual position display while moving the wiring and harness, trying to locate and intermittent wiring fault.

REMOVAL & INSTALLATION

▶ See Figures 14, 15, 16, 17 and 18

1. Disconnect the negative battery cable.
2. Detach the electrical connector from the EGR valve.
3. On the 3.5L (VIN H) engine, remove the fuel lines from the EGR valve bracket.
4. Remove the two base-to-flange nuts (or bolts) and lift the EGR valve assembly from the vehicle. Discard the gasket.

To install:
5. Take the time to thoroughly clean the gasket sealing surfaces to avoid raw exhaust gas leaks
6. Installation the reverse of removal. Always use a new gasket and torque the retaining fasteners to 22 ft. lbs. (30 Nm).
7. Verify the electrical connector is secure.
8. Connect the negative battery cable.

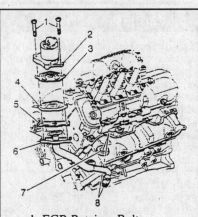

1. EGR Retainer Bolts
2. EGR Valve
3. EGR Valve Gasket
4. EGR Adapter Plate
5. EGR Adapter Gasket
6. EGR Tube
7. EGR Manifold Fitting
8. EGR Pipe Fitting

Fig. 14 Exploded view of the EGR valve mounting—3.1L engine

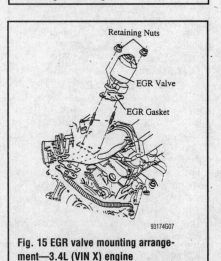

Fig. 15 EGR valve mounting arrangement—3.4L (VIN X) engine

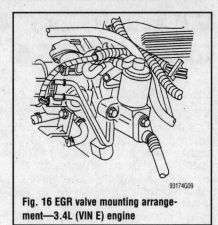

Fig. 16 EGR valve mounting arrangement—3.4L (VIN E) engine

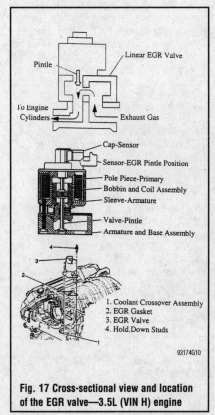

Fig. 17 Cross-sectional view and location of the EGR valve—3.5L (VIN H) engine

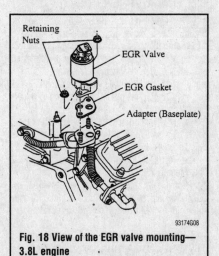

Fig. 18 View of the EGR valve mounting—3.8L engine

ELECTRONIC ENGINE CONTROLS

Powertrain Control Module

OPERATION

The vehicle's Powertrain Control Module (PCM), is a powerful on-board computer that controls most powertrain related functions, hence its name. Earlier versions were often called the Engine Control Module (ECM) but as the computers have become more advanced and, as more and more demands have been placed on them to control more driveline functions, the computers have come to be called Powertrain Control Modules, more accurately reflecting its increased role in vehicle operations.

The PCM in your W-Body vehicle is located underhood, in front of the right strut tower near the engine coolant reservoir. It is the control center for the fuel injection system and constantly looks at the information from various sensors and it controls the systems that affect vehicle performance. It controls the fuel metering system, automatic transaxle shifting, the engine's ignition timing, and also contains a powerful on-board diagnostic system for powertrain functions.

The PCM constantly looks at the information from various sensors and controls the systems that affect vehicle performance. The PCM also performs the diagnostic function of the system. It can recognize operational problems, alert the driver through the MIL (Malfunction Indicator Lamp, also known as the Service Engine Soon light), and store Diagnostic Trouble Codes (DTCs) which identify the problem areas to aid the technician in making repairs. A qualified technician with a piece of equipment called a scan tool, can connect into the system and read the data stream, getting real-time information on the engine's operation. In addition, the technician can interrogate the system and retrieve any DTCs to aid in diagnosing many driveability problems.

For service (replacement parts), the PCM consists of two parts:
- The controller (the PCM body without the Knock Sensor module)
- The Knock Sensor (KS) module

The PCM supplies either 5 or 12 volts to power various sensors or switches. This is done through resistances in the PCM which are so high in value that a test light will not light when connected to the circuit. In some cases, even an ordinary shop voltmeter will not give an accurate reading because its resistance is too low. Therefore, a digital voltmeter with at least 10 megaohms input resistance is required to ensure accurate voltage readings.

The PCM controls output circuits such as the fuel injectors, Idle Air Control (IAC), cooling fan relays, etc., by controlling either the ground or the power feed circuit through transistors or a device called a Driver.

The Electrically Erasable Programmable Read Only Memory (EEPROM) is a permanent memory that is physically soldered within the PCM. The EEPROM contains program and calibration information that the PCM needs to control powertrain operation.

Unlike the Programmable Read Only Memory (PROM) used in certain past applications, the EEP-

ROM is not replaceable. If the PCM is replaced, the new PCM will need to be programmed. This can only be done at a GM dealership. A scan tool such as GM's Tech 1®, or Tech 2®, containing the correct program and calibration for the vehicle is required to program the replacement PCM.

REMOVAL & INSTALLTION

♦ **See Figures 19 thru 22**

✳✳ WARNING

The service PCM EEPROM will not be programmed. This procedure must be done at an authorized dealership with the correct equipment. In most cases, this is not a job for the non-professional.

✳✳ CAUTION

To prevent possible Electrostatic Discharge damage to the PCM, DO NOT touch the connector pins or the soldered components on the circuit board. To prevent internal PCM damage, make sure the ignition switch is in the OFF position when installing or removing the PCM connectors and disconnecting or reconnecting the power to the PCM (battery cable, PCM pigtail, PCM fuse, jumper cables, etc.).

Service of the PCM should normally consist of either replacement of the PCM or EEPROM programming. A replacement PCM should first be checked to verify it is the correct part. If so, remove the faulty PCM and install a new service PCM.

➡ **When replacing the production PCM with a service PCM, it is important to transfer the broadcast code and production PCM number to the service PCM label. Do not record on the PCM cover. This will allow positive identification of PCM parts throughout the service life of the vehicle.**

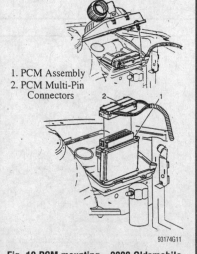

1. PCM Assembly
2. PCM Multi-Pin Connectors

Fig. 19 PCM mounting—2000 Oldsmobile Intrigue shown, others similar

1. Disconnect the negative battery cable.
2. Remove the engine coolant reservoir, if required, for access to the PCM.
3. On the Intrigue, remove the left strut brace and disconnect the air duct for access to the PCM.

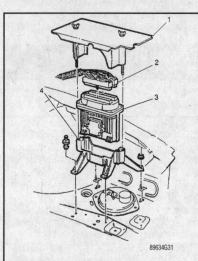

Fig. 20 Some applications may have a shield (1) over top to protect the harness connectors (2) at the PCM (3), all held underhood by a bracket (4)

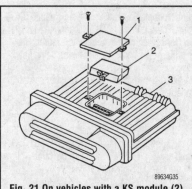

Fig. 21 On vehicles with a KS module (2), remove the module cover (1) from the PCM (3)

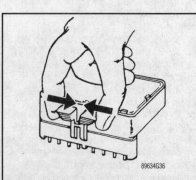

Fig. 22 For the KS module, gently squeeze the retaining tabs together, then carefully lift the module from the PCM

4. Remove the PCM attaching hardware and detach the electrical connectors.

5. Remove the PCM from the engine compartment.

6. Remove the PCM access cover and remove the Knock Sensor (KS) module. This module must be transferred to the replacement PCM.

To install:

7. Installation is a reverse of the removal process.

8. Take great care handling the multi-pin electrical connectors as they are easily damaged.

9. Reprogram the new PCM's EEPROM, using a Tech 1® or equivalent scan tool and the latest available software, and also initiate the PCM Replacement/Programming Crankshaft Position Sensor Variation Learn Procedure. In all likelihood, the vehicle must be towed to a dealer or repair shop containing the suitable equipment for this service.

Oxygen Sensors

OPERATION

All of the models covered by this manual have two Oxygen sensors, one before the catalyst and one after. This is done for a catalyst efficiency monitor that is a part of the OBD-II engine controls that are on your vehicle. Each type of sensor is describe below.

Heated Oxygen Sensor (HO2S 1)

▶ See Figure 23

The fuel control Heated Oxygen Sensor (HO2S 1) is mounted in the exhaust manifold where it can monitor the oxygen content of the exhaust gas stream. The oxygen present in the exhaust gas reacts with the sensor to produce a voltage output. This voltage should constantly fluctuate from approximately 100mV (high oxygen content—lean mixture) to 900mV (low oxygen content—rich mix-

ture). The heated oxygen sensor voltage can be monitored with a scan tool. By monitoring the voltage output of the oxygen sensor, the PCM calculates what fuel mixture command to give the injectors. For example, if the PCM reads a low HO2S voltage, it senses a lean mixture and commands more fuel. If the PCM reads a high HO2S voltage, it senses a rich mixture and commands less fuel.

Catalyst Monitor Heated Oxygen Sensor (HO2S 2)

▶ See Figure 23

To control emissions of Hydrocarbons (HC), Carbon Monoxide (CO), and Oxides of Nitrogen (NOx), a three-way catalytic converter is used. The catalyst within the converter promotes a chemical reaction which oxidizes the HC and CO present in the exhaust gas, converting them into harmless water vapor and carbon dioxide. The catalyst also reduces NOx, converting it to nitrogen. The PCM has the ability to monitor this process using the HO2S 1 and the HO2S 2 heated oxygen sensors. The HO2S 1 sensor produces an output signal which indicates the amount of oxygen present in the exhaust gas entering the three-way converter. The HO2S 2 sensor produces an output signal which indicates the oxygen storage capacity of the catalyst; this, in turn, indicates the catalyst's ability to convert exhaust gases efficiently. If the catalyst is operating efficiently, the HO2S 1 signal will be far more active than the signal produced by the HO2S 2 sensor.

The catalyst monitor sensors operate the same as the fuel control sensors. Although the HO2S 2 sensor's main function is catalyst monitoring, it also plays a limited role in fuel control. If the sensor output indicates a voltage either above or below the 450 millivolt bias voltage for an extended period of time, the PCM will make a sight adjustment to fuel trim to ensure that fuel delivery is correct for catalyst monitoring.

TESTING

▶ See Figure 24

As with most all engine control sensors used in your vehicle, a thorough and proper test can only be performed by a qualified technician using a Scan Tool to read the data stream from the PCM. There are a few items a non-professional should check before taking the vehicle to a qualified technician for diagnosis and repair.

• Because of the proximity of the oxygen sensors and their wiring to the hot exhaust system components, a careful check should be made of the oxygen sensor wiring. The sensor pigtail may be routed incorrectly and contacting the exhaust system.

• Check for poor PCM to engine block ground connections, especially on high-mileage vehicles or where there has been some major work such as engine removal and it is possible the ground connections were not properly installed.

• If the fuel system pressure is too low, the system could go lean. While the PCM can compensate to some degree, if the fuel pressure is too low, an

Fig. 24 The HO2S can be monitored with an appropriate and Data-stream capable scan tool

oxygen sensor DTC may set. A bad fuel injector could also cause an oxygen sensor related DTC.

• Check for vacuum leaks. Look for disconnected or damaged vacuum hoses and for vacuum leaks at the intake manifold, throttle body, EGR system and crankcase ventilation system.

• Check for exhaust leaks. An exhaust leak may cause outside air to be pulled into the exhaust gas stream past the oxygen sensor, causing the system to appear lean. Check for exhaust leaks that may cause a false lean condition to be indicated.

• A faulty MAF sensor could cause a problem with the oxygen sensor system. A technician may disconnect the MAF sensor while watching his scan tool display. If, after disconnecting the MAF sensor, the lean condition is corrected, the MAF sensor likely needs to be replaced.

• Fuel contamination could be a problem. Water, even in small amounts, can be delivered to the fuel injectors. The water can cause a leak exhaust to be indicated. Excessive alcohol in the fuel can also cause this condition.

• Check the EVAP canister for fuel saturation, causing a rich mixture condition.

• A leaking fuel pressure regulator can raise the fuel pressure, causing a rich mixture condition.

• An intermittent TP sensor output could cause the system to go rich due to a false indication of the engine accelerating.

• If, after removing an oxygen sensor, a white powdery deposit on the end of the sensor is found, it indicates silicon contamination, sometimes due to over-use of silicone sealers, or use of sealers in the wrong location. Replace the sensor.

• Check for damaged or otherwise poor connections at the PCM. Inspect the harness for abrasion and/or heat damage.

1. Perform a visual inspection on the sensor as follows:

    a. Remove the sensor from the exhaust.

    b. If the sensor tip has a black/sooty deposit, this may indicate a rich fuel mixture.

    c. If the sensor tip has a white gritty deposit, this may indicate an internal anti-freeze leak.

    d. If the sensor tip has a brown deposit, this could indicate oil consumption.

➡**All these contaminates can destroy the sensor, if the problem is not repaired the new sensor will also be damaged.**

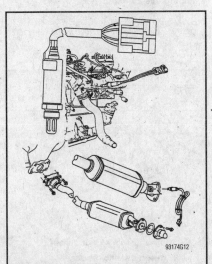

Fig. 23 Locations of the heated oxygen sensors in the exhaust manifold and the three-way catalytic converter—3.4L (VIN E) engine shown, others similar

REMOVAL & INSTALLATION

▶ **See Figures 23 and 25**

> ### ❊❊ WARNING
>
> **The oxygen sensors each use a permanently attached pigtail and connector. This pigtail should not be removed from the oxygen sensor. Damage or removal of the pigtail or connector could affect proper operation of the oxygen sensor.**

➡ Take care when handling an oxygen sensor. The in-line electrical connector and louvered end must be kept free of grease, dirt or other contaminants. Avoid using cleaning solvents of any type. DO NOT drop or roughly handle any oxygen sensor. GM says, "A dropped sensor is a bad sensor." A special anti-seize compound is used on the oxygen sensor threads. The compound consists of graphite suspended in fluid and glass beads. The graphite will burn away, but the glass beads will remain, hopefully making the sensor easier to remove. New or service sensors will already have the compound applied to the threads. If a sensor is removed from an engine and if for any reason is to be reinstalled, the threads must have anti-seize compound applied before reinstallation.

> ### ❊❊ WARNING
>
> **The heated oxygen sensor may be difficult to remove when the engine temperature is less than 120°F. Excessive force may damage the threads in the exhaust manifold or the exhaust pipe.**

1. Disconnect the negative battery cable.
2. Raise and safely support the vehicle.
3. If working on the HO2S 1, remove the intermediate exhaust pipe and the heat shield.
4. Detach the electrical connector and carefully remove the oxygen sensor. Because the permanently attached pigtail may be difficult to work around, note that there are special wrench sockets made with the side removed to accommodate the pigtail.

To install:

5. Coat the threads of the oxygen sensor with a suitable anti-seize compound, if necessary.
6. Install the sensor and torque to 30 ft. lbs. (41 Nm).

7. Install the remainder of the components in the reverse order of removal.
8. Connect the negative battery cable.

Idle Air Control (IAC) Valve

OPERATION

▶ **See Figure 26**

The Idle Air Control (IAC) is a bi-directional motor driven by two coils. The purpose of the IAC valve is to control engine idle speed, while preventing stalls due to changes in the engine load. The IAC valve, mounted in the throttle body, controls bypass air around the throttle plate. The PCM controls engine idle speed by adjusting the position of the IAC motor pintle. The PCM pulses current to the IAC coils in small steps (counts) to extend the pintle into a passage in the throttle body to decrease air flow. The PCM reverses the current pulses to retract the pintle, increasing air flow. This method allows highly accurate control of idle speed and quick response to changes in engine load. If RPM is too low, the PCM will retract the IAC pintle, resulting in more air being bypassed around the throttle plate to increase RPM. If the RPM is too high, the PCM will extend the IAC pintle, allowing less air to be bypassed around the throttle plate, decreasing RPM.

During idle, the proper position of the of the IAC pintle is calculated by the PCM based on the battery voltage, coolant temperature, engine load and engine RPM. If the RPM drops below a specified value, and the throttle plate is closed (TP sensor voltage is between 0.20–0.74), the PCM senses a near stall condition. The PCM will then calculate a new IAC pintle position to prevent stalls.

If the IAC valve is disconnected and reconnected with the engine running, the idle RPM will be wrong. In this case, the IAC has to be reset. The IAC resets when the ignition switch is cycled **ON** and then **OFF**. When servicing the IAC, it should be disconnected or connected with the ignition switch **OFF** in order to keep from having to reset the IAC valve.

The position of the IAC pintle affects engine start up and the idle characteristics of the vehicle. If the IAC pintle is fully open, too much air will be allowed into the manifold. This results in high idle speed, along with possible hard starting and a lean air/fuel ratio. A Diagnostic Trouble Code (DTC) may set. If the IAC pintle is stuck closed, too little air

will be allowed in the manifold. This results in a low idle speed, along with hard starting and a rich air/fuel ratio. Again, a Diagnostic Trouble Code (DTC) may set. If the IAC pintle is stuck part way open, the idle may be high or low and will not respond to changes in engine load.

TESTING

As with most all engine control sensors used in your vehicle, a thorough and proper test can only be performed by a qualified technician using a scan tool to read the data stream from the PCM. There are a few items a non-professional should check before taking the vehicle to a qualified technician for diagnosis and repair.

- Check for a poor connection at the PCM or IAC motor. Inspect the harness connectors for backed out terminals, improper mating, broken locks, improperly formed or damaged terminals and poor terminal-to-wire connection.
- Inspect for a damaged wiring harness, especially if heavy work has recently been performed (intake manifold removal, engine removal, etc.) where the throttle body has been disturbed.
- Inspect for a restricted air intake system. Check for a possible collapsed air intake duct, restricted air filter element or foreign objects blocking the air intake system.
- Inspect the throttle body. Check for objects blocking the IAC passage or throttle bore. Excessive deposits, especially on high-mileage engines, can build up in the IAC passage and on the IAC pintle. Excessive deposits can also build up on the throttle plate, so check for a sticking throttle plate.
- Check for vacuum leaks such as disconnected hoses, leaks at the EGR valve and EGR pipe to the intake manifold, leaks at the throttle body, faulty or incorrectly installed PCV valve, leaks at the intake manifold brake booster hose connection, etc.

REMOVAL & INSTALLATION

▶ **See Figures 26 and 27**

1. Disconnect the negative battery cable.
2. Detach the electrical connector from the IAC valve.

Fig. 25 Note this special socket with a cutaway slot to accommodate the oxygen sensor's wire harness (pigtail)

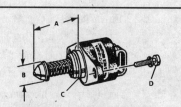

A	DISTANCE OF PINTLE EXTENSION
B	DIAMETER OF PINTLE
C	IACV O-RING
D	IACV ATTACHING SCREW ASSEMBLY

Fig. 26 Typical Idle Air Control (IAC) valve components

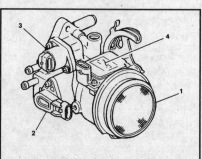

1	THROTTLE BODY AIR INLET SCREEN
2	THROTTLE POSITION SENSOR
3	IAC VALVE
4	MAF SENSOR

Fig. 27 The Idle Air Control (IAC) valve is mounted on the throttle body—3.8L (VIN K) engine shown, others similar

3. Remove the 2 attaching screws and remove the IAC valve from the engine. Remove the O-ring from the housing.

To install:

➡Before installing a new IAC valve, measure the distance that the valve is extended. The measurement should be made from the motor housing to the end of the valve cone (pintle). The distance should be no greater than 1⅛ inch (28mm). If the pintle is extended too far, adjustment is required, otherwise damage may occur when the IAC valve is installed. Adjust the IAC valve by compressing the pintle to achieve the correct length.

4. Use a new O-ring, install the IAC valve and tighten the retaining screws to 18 inch lbs. (2 Nm).
5. Attach the electrical connector.
6. Connect the negative battery cable.
7. The PCM will reset the IAC valve the next time the ignition switch is turned **ON** and then **OFF**.
8. Start the engine and allow to warm to operating temperature to check idle quality.

Engine Coolant Temperature (ECT) Sensor

OPERATION

The Engine Coolant Temperature (ECT) sensor is a thermistor (a resistor which changes value based on temperature) mounted in the engine coolant stream. Low coolant temperature produces a high resistance (100,000 ohms at −40°F.) while high temperature causes low resistance (70 ohms at 266°F.). The PCM supplies a voltage (about 5.0V) through a pull up resistor to the PCM's ECT signal circuit and measures the voltage. When the engine coolant is cold, the sensor (thermistor) resistance is high, therefore the PCM will measure a high signal voltage. As the engine coolant warms, the sensor resistance becomes less, and the ECT signal voltage measured at the PCM drops. With a fully warmed up engine, the ECT signal voltage should measure about 1.5–2.0 volts. By measuring the voltage, the PCM calculates the engine coolant temperature and engine coolant temperature affects most systems the PCM controls.

A technician's scan tool displays engine coolant temperature in degrees. After engine start up, the temperature should rise steadily to about 195°F (90°C), then stabilize and the thermostat opens. If the engine has not been run for several hours (overnight), the engine coolant temperature and intake air temperature displays should be close to each other. A hard or even an intermittent fault in the engine coolant temperature sensor circuit will set a hard Diagnostic Trouble Code (DTC).

Most ECT sensor also contain another circuit which is used to operate the engine coolant temperature gauge (if equipped) located in the instrument panel.

TESTING

There are a few items you should check before beginning more extensive testing.
- Check for poor connection at the PCM.

Inspect harness connectors for backed out terminals, improper mating, broken locks, improperly formed or damaged terminals and poor terminal-to-wire connections.
- Look for a damaged harness or damaged wiring going to the ECT sensor, especially if heavy work has recently been done where the connector could have been damaged.

Sensor Installed in Vehicle

▸ See Figure 28

1. Disconnect the engine wiring harness from the ECT sensor.
2. Connect an ohmmeter between the ECT sensor terminals.
3. With the engine cold and the ignition switch in the **OFF** position, measure and note the ECT sensor resistance.
4. Connect the engine wiring harness to the sensor.
5. Start the engine and allow the engine to reach normal operating temperature.
6. Once the engine has reached normal operating temperature, turn the engine **OFF**.

°C	°F	OHMS
Temperature vs Resistance Values (Approximate)		
100	212	177
90	194	241
80	176	332
70	158	467
60	140	667
50	122	973
45	113	1188
40	104	1459
35	95	1802
30	86	2238
25	77	2796
20	68	3520
15	59	4450
10	50	5670
5	41	7280
0	32	9420
-5	23	12300
-10	14	16180
-15	5	21450
-20	-4	28680
-30	-22	52700
-40	-40	100700

88254G69

Fig. 28 ECT sensor resistance value chart

7. Once again, disconnect the engine wiring harness from the ECT sensor.
8. Measure and note the ECT sensor resistance with the engine hot.
9. Compare the cold and hot ECT sensor resistance measurements with the accompanying chart.
10. If readings do not approximate those in the chart, the sensor may be faulty.

Sensor Removed from Vehicle

▸ See Figure 29

1. Remove the ECT sensor from the vehicle.
2. Immerse the tip of the sensor in a container of water.
3. Connect a digital ohmmeter to the two terminal of the sensor.

TCCS4P02

Fig. 29 Submerge the end of the temperature sensor in cold or hot water and check resistance

4. Using a calibrated thermometer, compare the resistance of the sensor to the temperature of the water. Refer to the accompanying resistance value chart.
5. Repeat the test at two other temperature points, heating or cooling the water as necessary.
6. If the sensor does not meet specifications, it must be replaced.

REMOVAL & INSTALLATION

✳✳ WARNING

Care must be taken when handling the ECT sensor. Damage to the ECT sensor will affect proper operation of the fuel injection system.

3.1L and 3.4L (VIN E) Engines

▸ See Figure 30

1. Disconnect the negative battery cable.
2. With the engine cold, relieve the coolant pressure by opening the radiator cap or opening the bleed screw near the thermostat.
3. Remove the air intake duct.
4. Detach the electrical connector from the ECT sensor.
5. Using a deep well socket and extension, remove the sensor.

To install:
6. Coat the ECT sensor threads with a suitable sealant.

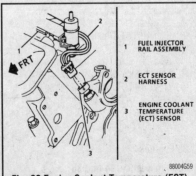

1	FUEL INJECTOR RAIL ASSEMBLY
2	ECT SENSOR HARNESS
3	ENGINE COOLANT TEMPERATURE (ECT) SENSOR

88004G59

Fig. 30 Engine Coolant Temperature (ECT) sensor and harness arrangement—3.1L and 3.4L (VIN E) engines

7. Install the ECT sensor, and using a deep well socket and extension tighten the sensor to 17 ft. lbs. (23 Nm).

8. Install the remaining components in the order of removal.

9. Check for leaks and replenish the coolant, as required.

3.4L (VIN X) Engine

▶ See Figure 31

1. Disconnect the negative battery cable.
2. Remove the rear intake duct and MAF sensor assembly.
3. Drain the engine coolant, into a suitable container, to a level below the sensor.
4. Remove the exhaust crossover pipe.
5. Detach the ECT sensor electrical harness.
6. Using a 19mm deep well socket and a 6-inch extension, remove the ECT sensor.

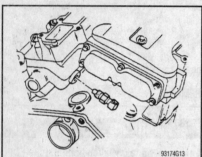

Fig. 31 On this engine, the exhaust crossover must be removed to access the ECT sensor—3.4L (VIN X) Engine

To install:

7. Coat the ECT sensor threads with a suitable sealant. Attach the electrical connector.
8. Install the sensor into the engine and tighten to 22 ft. lbs. (30 Nm).
9. Install the exhaust crossover pipe.
10. Install the rear intake duct and the MAF sensor assembly.
11. Connect the negative battery cable.
12. Check the coolant level and adjust as necessary. Start the engine and check for leaks.

3.5L (VIN H) Engine

▶ See Figure 32

1. Partially drain the engine coolant, into a suitable container, to a level below the sensor.
2. Locate and detach the ECT sensor harness.
3. Remove the ECT sensor.
To install:
4. Apply a suitable non-hardening sealer to the ECT sensor threads to prevent coolant leaks.
5. Install the ECT sensor and tighten to 15 ft. lbs. (20 Nm). Do not over-tighten. The cylinder head is made of aluminum. Attach the electrical connector.
6. Refill the cooling system.

3.8L Engines

▶ See Figures 33, 34 and 35

1. Disconnect the negative battery cable.
2. Drain the engine coolant, into a suitable container, to a level below the sensor.

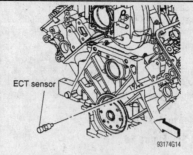

Fig. 32 The ECT sensor is located on the flywheel end of the engine, on the right side (rear) cylinder head—3.5L (VIN H) engine

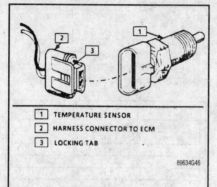

1	TEMPERATURE SENSOR
2	HARNESS CONNECTOR TO ECM
3	LOCKING TAB

89634G46

Fig. 33 Typical Engine Coolant Temperature (ECT) sensor

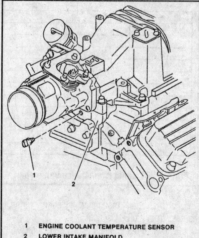

| 1 | ENGINE COOLANT TEMPERATURE SENSOR |
| 2 | LOWER INTAKE MANIFOLD |

89634G49

Fig. 34 Location of the ECT sensor—3.8L (VIN 1) engine

3. Detach the electrical connector.
4. Using a 19mm deep well socket and an extension, remove the ECT sensor.
To install:
5. Hand-start the ECT sensor into the engine, then tighten to 22 ft. lbs. (30 Nm).
6. Attach the electrical connector.
7. Refill the system with coolant.
8. Connect the negative battery cable.
9. Start the engine and check for leaks.

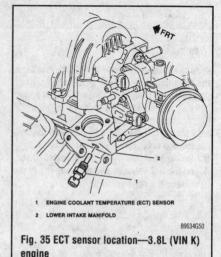

| 1 | ENGINE COOLANT TEMPERATURE (ECT) SENSOR |
| 2 | LOWER INTAKE MANIFOLD |

89634G50

Fig. 35 ECT sensor location—3.8L (VIN K) engine

Intake Air Temperature (IAT) Sensor

OPERATION

The Intake Air Temperature (IAT) sensor is a thermistor which changes value based on the temperature of the air entering the engine. Low temperature produces a high resistance (100,000 ohms at -40°F.) while high temperature causes low resistance (70 ohms at 266°F.). The PCM supplies a voltage (about 5.0V) through a pull up resistor to the PCM's IAT signal circuit and measures the voltage. The voltage will be high when the in coming air is cold, and low when the air is hot. By measuring the voltage, the PCM calculates the in coming air temperature. The IAT sensor signal is used to adjust spark timing according to incoming air density.

A technician's scan tool displays the temperature of the air entering the engine, which should read close to the ambient air temperature when the engine is cold, and rise as the underhood temperature increases. If the engine has not been run for several hours (overnight), the IAT sensor temperature and engine coolant temperature displays should be close to each other. A failure in the IAT sensor circuit should set a Diagnostic Trouble Code.

TESTING

▶ See Figure 36

Check the following items before beginning more in depth diagnosis and testing.
• Check for poor connection at the PCM. Inspect harness connectors for backed out terminals, improper mating, broken locks, improperly formed or damaged terminals and poor terminal-to-wire connections.
• Look for a damaged harness or damaged wiring going to the IAT sensor, especially if heavy work has recently been done where the connector could have been damaged.
1. Turn the ignition switch **OFF**.
2. Disconnect the wiring harness from the IAT sensor.
3. Measure the resistance between the sensor terminals.

°C	°F	OHMS
Temperature vs Resistance Values (Approximate)		
100	212	177
90	194	241
80	176	332
70	158	467
60	140	667
50	122	973
45	113	1188
40	104	1459
35	95	1802
30	86	2238
25	77	2796
20	68	3520
15	59	4450
10	50	5670
5	41	7280
0	32	9420
-5	23	12300
-10	14	16180
-15	5	21450
-20	-4	28680
-30	-22	52700
-40	-40	100700

88254G69

Fig. 36 IAT sensor resistance value chart

4. Compare the resistance reading with the accompanying chart.

5. If the resistance is not within specification, the IAT may be faulty.

6. Connect the wiring harness to the sensor.

REMOVAL & INSTALLATION

▶ **See Figure 37**

✳✳ WARNING

Care must be taken when handling the IAT sensor. Damage to the IAT sensor will affect proper operation of the fuel injection system.

➡ The IAT sensor is located on the air intake housing, near the Mass Air Flow (MAF) sensor.

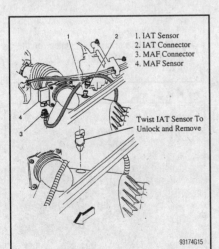

1. IAT Sensor
2. IAT Connector
3. MAF Connector
4. MAF Sensor

Twist IAT Sensor To Unlock and Remove

93174G15

Fig. 37 The IAT sensor is located upstream in the air intake system and is usually close to the Mass Air Flow sensor—3.5L (VIN H) engine shown, other similar

1. Detach the electrical connector.
2. Carefully grasp the sensor and twisting counterclockwise, remove the IAT sensor from the air intake duct.
3. Installation is the reverse of removal.

Mass Air Flow (MAF) Sensor

OPERATION

▶ **See Figures 38 and 39**

The Mass Air Flow (MAF) sensor measures the amount of air which passes through it into the engine during a given time. The PCM uses the mass air flow information to monitor engine operating conditions for fuel delivery calculations. A large quantity of air indicates acceleration, while a small quantity of air indicates deceleration or idle.

The MAF sensor produces a frequency signal which can be monitored using a scan tool. The frequency will vary within a range around 2000 Hz at idle to about 10,000 Hz at maximum engine load.

A technician's scan tool reads the MAF value and displays it in grams per second (gm/s). At idle, it should read between 4 gm/s–7gm/s on a fully warmed up engine. Values should change rather quickly on acceleration but values should remain fairly stable at any given RPM. A failure in the MAF sensor circuit should set a Diagnostic Trouble Code (DTC).

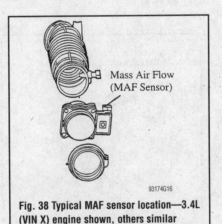

Mass Air Flow (MAF Sensor)

93174G16

Fig. 38 Typical MAF sensor location—3.4L (VIN X) engine shown, others similar

Mass Air Flow (MAF Sensor)

93174G17

Fig. 39 MAF sensor location—3.8L engines

TESTING

As with most all engine control sensors used in your vehicle, a thorough and proper test can only be performed by a qualified technician using a scan tool to read the data stream from the PCM. There are a few items you should check before taking the vehicle to a qualified technician for diagnosis and repair.

• Look for a skewed or stuck Throttle Position (TP) sensor. A malfunctioning TP sensor or TP circuit can cause the PCM to incorrectly calculate the predicted mass air flow value. A scan tool is required to check the Throttle Angle but you can still check for a sticking throttle plate from excessive deposit build up on the throttle plate or in the throttle bore. A poor TP sensor connection, the TP signal circuit shorted to ground or high resistance in the TP sensor ground circuit are also problem areas to check.

• Inspect harness connectors for backed out terminals, improper mating, broken locks, improperly formed or damaged terminals and poor terminal-to-wire connections.

• Look for a misrouted or damaged harness or damaged wiring going to the IAT sensor, especially if heavy work has recently been done where the connector could have been damaged.

• Check the MAF sensor harness to make sure it is not routed too close to high voltage wires such as spark plug leads.

• Check for a plugged intake duct or dirty air filter element.

• Check for a skewed or unresponsive MAP sensor. The barometric pressure used to calculate the default Mass Air Flow value is based on the MAP sensor reading. A skewed MAP sensor at key **ON** will cause the BARO reading to be incorrectly calculated. Also, with the engine running, an unresponsive MAP sensor (due to poor vacuum connections, damaged vacuum source, defective vacuum hoses, unmetered air getting into the intake manifold) will cause inaccurate BARO reading updates during wide-open throttle conditions. Both of these conditions result in a difference between the actual MAF sensor signal and the predicted MAF value (PCM calculated). If a large difference between these two values occurs, a DTC will be set. This condition may also cause abnormal IAC counts and hard starts.

➡ If there is a failure on the MAF sensor circuit, A DTC will set. Refer to Trouble Codes in this section.

• Visually check the connector, making sure it is connected properly and all of the terminals are straight, tight and free of corrosion.

• With the engine running, lightly tap on the MAF sensor and wiggle the wires at the connector, while watching for a change in idle speed. A common problem is MAF sensor wire damage.

REMOVAL & INSTALLATION

▶ **See Figures 38 and 39**

➡ The MAF sensor is located on the air intake housing. Most MAF sensors have a fine mesh screen in front. Use care not to damage the screen when working around the MAF sensor and/or the air intake ducting. Do not allow the sensing elements to touch anything (including solvents and lubricant). Do not drop or handle roughly the MAF sensor. A damaged screen could restrict airflow and lead to a driveability problem.

1. Disconnect the negative battery cable.
2. Detach the electrical connector.
3. Remove the air inlet duct from the MAF sensor and remove the MAF from the air intake duct.

To install:

4. Installation is the reverse of removal.
5. Note that the MAF sensor may have an air flow direction arrow (usually located on top of the MAF sensor). The MAF sensor must be mounted with the arrow pointing towards the throttle body.
6. Take care to ensure that the MAF sensor locating tabs and the locating slots of the intake air ducts line up before connecting the MAF sensor and the intake air ducts.
7. Make sure the MAF sensor is seated in the air inlet grommet and that the electrical connection is secure.

Manifold Absolute Pressure (MAP) Sensor

OPERATION

The Manifold Absolute Pressure (MAP) sensor responds to changes in intake manifold pressure (vacuum). The MAP sensor signal voltage to the PCM varies from below 2 volts at idle (high vacuum) to above 4 volts with the ignition switch **ON**, engine not running or at wide-open throttle (low vacuum).

If the PCM detects a voltage that is lower than the possible range of the MAP sensor, a Diagnostic Trouble Code (DTC) will be set. A signal voltage higher than the possible range of the sensor will also set a DTC. An intermittent low or high voltage will also set DTCs. The PCM can also detect a shifted MAP sensor. The PCM compares the MAP sensor signal to a calculated MAP based on throttle position and various engine load factors. If the PCM detects a MAP signal that varies excessively above or below the calculated value, a DTC will be set. The MAP sensor is also used to measure barometric pressure under certain conditions, which allows the PCM to automatically adjust for different altitudes.

TESTING

As with most all engine control sensors used in your vehicle, a thorough and proper test can only be performed by a qualified technician using a scan tool to read the data stream from the PCM. There are a few items a non-professional should check before taking the vehicle to a qualified technician for diagnosis and repair.

• Check for poor connection at the PCM. Inspect harness connectors for backed out terminals, improper mating, broken locks, improperly formed or damaged terminals and poor terminal-to-wire connections.

• Look for a damaged harness or damaged wiring going to the MAP sensor, especially if heavy work has recently been done where the connector could have been damaged.

• The vacuum hose can deteriorate with age and should always be checked carefully if a MAP problem is suspected.

REMOVAL & INSTALLATION

◆ **See Figures 40 thru 45**

1. Disconnect the negative battery cable.
2. Locate the MAP sensor and remove the retaining screws
3. Detach the electrical connector.
4. Remove the vacuum hose and lift the MAP sensor from the engine.
5. Installation is reverse of the removal procedure.

Throttle Position (TP) Sensor

OPERATION

The Throttle Position (TP) sensor is a potentiometer connected to the throttle shaft on the throttle body. It provides a voltage signal that changes relative to throttle blade angle. The signal voltage will vary from less than 1 volt at closed throttle to about 4 volts at Wide Open Throttle (WOT). By monitoring the voltage on the signal line, the PCM calculates throttle position. As the throttle

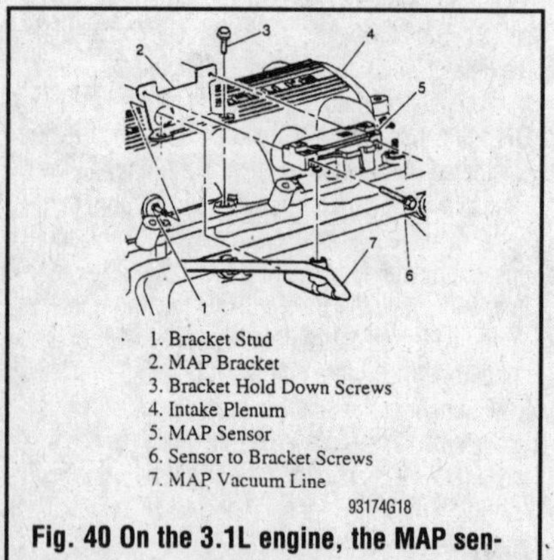

1. Bracket Stud
2. MAP Bracket
3. Bracket Hold Down Screws
4. Intake Plenum
5. MAP Sensor
6. Sensor to Bracket Screws
7. MAP Vacuum Line

93174G18

Fig. 40 On the 3.1L engine, the MAP sensor is located alongside the intake manifold

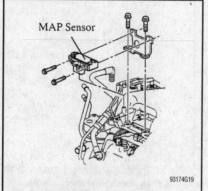

93174G19

Fig. 41 MAP sensor and its bracket arrangement—3.4L (VIN E) engine

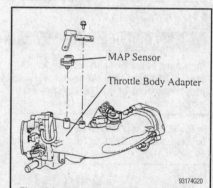

93174G20

Fig. 42 Location of the MAP sensor on the throttle body adapter—3.4L (VIN X) Engine

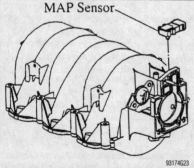

93174G23

Fig. 43 The MAP sensor is located just behind the throttle body mounting base—3.5L (VIN H) engine

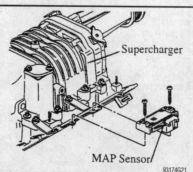

93174G21

Fig. 44 MAP sensor and its location alongside the supercharger—3.8L (VIN 1) Engine

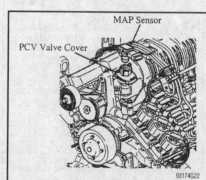

93174G22

Fig. 45 On the 3.8L (VIN K) engine, the MAP sensor is located on top of the PCV valve cover

valve angle is changed (accelerator pedal moved), the TP sensor signal also changes. At a closed throttle position, the output of the TP sensor is low. As the throttle valve opens, the output increases so that at WOT, the output voltage should be above 4 volts.

The PCM calculates fuel delivery based on throttle valve angle (driver demand). A broken or loose TP sensor may cause intermittent bursts of fuel from an injector and unstable idle because the PCM thinks the throttle is moving. A failure in the TP sensor 5 volt reference or signal circuits or ground circuit will set Diagnostic Trouble Codes (DTCs). Once a DTC is set, the PCM will use an artificial default value based on engine RPM and mass air flow for throttle position and some vehicle performance will return. A high idle may result when a circuit ground fault is present.

The PCM can detect intermittent TP sensor faults. The PCM can also detect a shifted TP sensor. The PCM monitors throttle position and compares the actual TP sensor reading to a predicted TP value calculated from engine speed. If the PCM detects an out of range condition, a DTC will be set.

TESTING

There are a few items you should check before getting into more in-depth testing.
• Check for a skewed MAP signal or faulty MAP sensor. An incorrect MAP signal may cause the PCM to incorrectly calculate the predicted TP sensor value during high engine load situations. A qualified technician using a Scan Tool will want to check for an abnormally low MAP reading.
• Check for poor connection at the PCM. Inspect harness connectors for backed out terminals, improper mating, broken locks, improperly formed or damaged terminals and poor terminal-to-wire connections.
• Look for a damaged harness or damaged wiring going to the MAP sensor, especially if heavy work has recently been done where the connector could have been damaged.

1. With the engine **OFF** and the ignition **ON**, check the voltage at the signal return circuit of the TP sensor by carefully backprobing the connector using a DVOM.
2. Voltage should be between 0.2 and 1.4 volts at idle.
3. Slowly move the throttle pulley to the wide open throttle (WOT) position and watch the voltage on the DVOM. The voltage should slowly rise to slightly less than 4.8v at Wide Open Throttle (WOT).
4. If no voltage is present, check the wiring harness for supply voltage (5.0v) and ground (0.3v or less), by referring to your corresponding wiring guide. If supply voltage and ground are present, but no output voltage from TP, replace the TP sensor. If supply voltage and ground do not meet specifications, make necessary repairs to the harness or PCM.

REMOVAL & INSTALLATION

▶ See Figure 46

1. Disconnect the negative battery cable.
2. Remove the air inlet tube to access the throttle body.

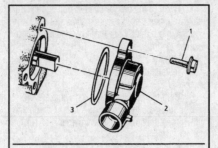

1	SCREW - TP SENSOR ATTACHING
2	SENSOR - THROTTLE POSITION (TP)
3	O-RING - TP SENSOR

88004G80

Fig. 46 Typical Throttle Position (TP) sensor mounting

3. Detach the TP sensor electrical connector.
4. Remove the TP sensor screws and carefully pull the sensor from the throttle shaft stub end.
To install:
5. With the throttle in the normal closed idle position, install the TP sensor on the throttle body assembly
6. Apply a suitable thread-locking compound to the TP sensor attaching screws, install the screws and tighten to just 18 inch lbs. (2 Nm).
7. Install the air inlet tube.
8. Connect the negative battery cable.

Camshaft Position (CMP) Sensor

OPERATION

The PCM uses the Camshaft Position (CMP) sensor signal to determine the position of the No. 1 cylinder piston during its power stroke. The signal is used by the PCM to calculate fuel injection mode of operation. If the cam signal is lost while the engine is running, the fuel injection system will shift to a calculated fuel injected mode based on the last fuel injection pulse, and the engine will continue to run.

On the 3.1L and 3.4L (VIN E) engines, the Camshaft Position (CMP) sensor is located on the timing chain cover behind the water pump near the camshaft sprocket. As the camshaft sprocket turns, a magnet in it activates the Hall-Effect switch in the CMP sensor. When the Hall-Effect switch is activated, it grounds the signal line to the PCM, pulling the CMP sensor circuit's applied voltage low. This is interpreted as a CAM signal. The cam signal is created as piston #1 is on the intake stroke. If the correct CAM signal is not received by the PCM, a DTC will be set.

On the 3.4L (VIN X) engine, the Camshaft Position (CMP) sensor is mounted to the left bank camshaft carrier, towards #6 cylinder. A 3-wire harness connector plugs into the sensor, connecting it to the Powertrain Control Module (PCM). The PCM applies a signal voltage to the sensor. The left bank exhaust camshaft has a tooth machined into the casting. The camshaft position sensor is separated from the exhaust camshaft by an air gap. As the exhaust camshaft rotates, the machined tooth aligns with the sensor. The signal voltage to the sensor is pulled low. The PCM interprets the change in signal

voltage as an indication of camshaft position. The CAM signal is created as piston #1 is on the intake stroke. If the correct CAM signal is not received by the PCM, a DTC will set.

On the 3.5L (VIN H) engine, the Camshaft Position (CMP) sensor is located at the rear of the forward camshaft carrier, near the engine lift ring bracket. The sensor signal, when combined with the Crankshaft Position sensor signal, enables the PCM to determine exactly which cylinder is on a firing stroke. The PCM can then properly synchronize the ignition system, fuel injectors and knock control. The camshaft position sensor has a power, ground and signal circuit. The PCM supplies 12 volts to the sensor. The PCM also supplies the ground path, or sensor return circuit, from the sensor. These power and ground circuits are also connected to the crankshaft position sensor. If a problem is detected in the camshaft position circuit, a DTC will set.

On 3.8L engine, the Camshaft Position (CMP) sensor is mounted on the engine timing chain front cover. The camshaft position sensor sends a cam signal to the PCM which uses it as a sync pulse to trigger the injectors in the proper sequence. The CAM signal is passed through the ignition control module. The PCM uses the CAM signal to indicate the position of the #1 piston during its power stroke, allowing the PCM to calculate true Sequential Fuel Injection. If the PCM detects an incorrect CAM signal, a DTC will set.

TESTING

Perform the following checks before getting into more complicated diagnosis and repair.
• Some faults in the CMP circuit can be the result of secondary ignition components leaking high voltage into the ignition module. Check for incorrect harness routing too near secondary ignition components. Examine the ignition coils for signs of coil arcing to the wiring harness or to the ICM. Check the coils for cracks, carbon tracking or other signs of damage. Check the secondary wiring (spark plug wires) for arcing to the wiring harness.
• An intermittent may be caused by a poor connection, rubbed through wire insulation or a wire broken inside the insulation.
• Inspect for a faulty coil.
• Inspect for poor connections. Check the PCM harness and connectors for improper mating, broken locks, improperly formed or damaged terminals and poor terminal-to-wire connection.
• Look for a damaged harness or damaged wiring going to the CMP sensor, especially if heavy work has recently been done where the connector could have been damaged.

➡**The best method to test this sensor is with the use of an oscilloscope.**

1. Visually check the connector, making sure it is connected properly and all of the terminals are straight, tight and free of corrosion.
2. With the ignition in the **ON** position, check the sensor voltage using an oscilloscope. When the starter is briefly operated, a square wave pattern, alternating from 0–12 volts should be seen at terminal A. If the voltage is within specification, the sensor is functional.

REMOVAL & INSTALLATION

3.1L and 3.4L (VIN E) Engines

▶ See Figure 47

1. Disconnect the negative battery cable.
2. Remove the serpentine drive belt, as outlined in Section 1 of this manual.
3. Remove the power steering pump assembly and set aside with the lines attached.
4. Detach the CMP sensor electrical connector.
5. Unfasten the retainer bolt, then remove the CMP sensor.
6. Installation is the reverse of the removal procedure.

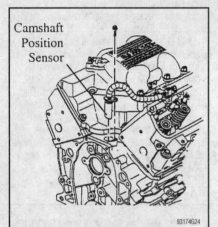

Fig. 47 Camshaft Position (CMP) sensor removal—3.1L and 3.4L (VIN E) engines

3.4L (VIN X) Engine

▶ See Figure 48

1. Disconnect the negative battery cable.
2. Detach the electrical connector from the camshaft position sensor.

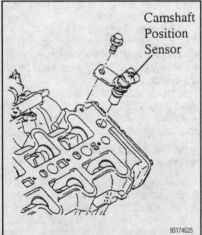

Fig. 48 Camshaft Position (CMP) sensor removal—3.4L (VIN X) engine

3. Remove the sensor retainer bolt and carefully pull the sensor from the camshaft carrier. An O-ring seal may hold the sensor in place. Use care not to lose the O-ring.

To install:
4. Installation is the reverse of the removal procedure.
5. Before installing a replacement camshaft sensor, lubricate the new O-ring with clean engine oil. Tighten the bolt to just 88 inch lbs. (10 Nm). Do not over-tighten.
6. Connect the negative battery cable.

3.5L (VIN H) Engine

▶ See Figure 49

1. Disconnect the negative battery cable.
2. Remove the two coolant recovery tank mounting nuts and lift out the tank to gain access to the camshaft position sensor.
3. Detach the electrical connector from the camshaft position sensor.
4. Remove the retaining screw. Remove the sensor by pulling on the sensor connector. Do not pry on the bracket. Do not rotate (twist) the sensor or damage the mounting bracket, if the sensor is to be reused.

To install:
5. Installation is the reverse of the removal process, observing the following points:
    a. Make sure the sensor bore is completely free of any foreign material (old O-ring, dirt, burrs, etc.).
    b. Make sure that the flange of the sensor bore is not damaged.
    c. Clean all mounting surfaces before reinstalling any components.
    d. If the sensor is being reused, check for damage. Inspect the face of the sensor (bottom of the brass housing) for damage.
    e. Never install a sensor that has been dropped.
    f. Lubricate the O-ring with clean engine oil.

6. Install the camshaft position sensor and fully seat into its bore. Install the retaining screw and torque to just 80 inch lbs. (9 Nm). Do not over-tighten. Verify the electrical connector is secure.
7. Install the coolant recovery tank, then connect the negative battery cable.

3.8L Engines

▶ See Figure 50

1. Disconnect the negative battery cable.
2. Detach the electrical connector from the camshaft position sensor.
3. Remove the retaining screw and separate the sensor from the front cover.

To install:
4. Installation is the reverse of the removal process.
5. Tighten the bolt to just 44 inch lbs. (5 Nm). Do not over-tighten. Verify the electrical connector is secure.
6. Connect the negative battery cable.

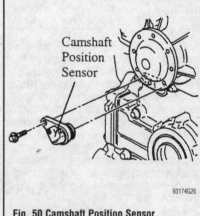

Fig. 50 Camshaft Position Sensor removal—3.8L Engines

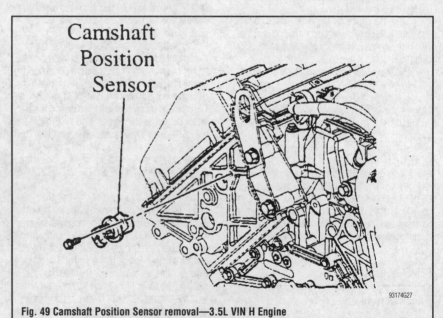

Fig. 49 Camshaft Position Sensor removal—3.5L VIN H Engine

Crankshaft Position (CKP) Sensor

OPERATION

7X Crankshaft Position Sensor

EXCEPT 3.5L (VIN H) AND 3.8L ENGINES

The 7X Crankshaft Position (CKP) sensor provides a signal used by the ignition control module. The ignition control module also uses the 7X CKP sensor to generate 3X reference pulses which the PCM uses to calculate RPM and crankshaft position.

The 7X CKP sensor is the most critical part of the ignition system. If the sensor is damaged so that pulses are not generated, the engine will not start!

The 7X CKP sensor is a Hall-Effect switch, mounted on the outside of the engine block, close to the crankshaft. The interrupter ring is a special wheel cast on the crankshaft that has seven machined slots, six of which are equally spaced 60 degrees apart. The seventh slot is spaced 10 degrees from one of the other slots. As the interrupter ring rotates with the crankshaft, the slots change the magnetic field. This will cause the 7X Hall-Effect switch to ground the 3X signal voltage that is supplied by the ignition control module. The ignition control module interprets the 7X ON-OFF signals as an indication of crankshaft position. The ignition control module must have the 7X signal to fire the correct ignition coil.

The 7X CKP sensor uses a two wire connector at the sensor and a three-way connector at the ignition control module.

24X Crankshaft Position Sensor

EXCEPT 3.5L (VIN H) AND 3.8L ENGINES

The 24X Crankshaft Position (CKP) sensor is used to improve idle spark control at engine speeds up to approximately 1250 RPM. The 24X CKP sensor contains a Hall-Effect switch. The magnet and Hall-Effect switch are separated by an air gap. A Hall-Effect switch reacts like a solid state switch, grounding a low current signal voltage when a magnetic field is present. When the magnetic field is shielded from the switch by a piece of steel placed in the air gap between the magnet and the switch, the signal voltage is not grounded. If the piece of steel (called an interrupter) is repeatedly moved in and out of the air gap, the signal voltage will appear to go ON-OFF-ON-OFF-ON-OFF. Compared to a conventional mechanical distributor, the ON-OFF signal is similar to the signal that a set of breaker points in the distributor would generate as the distributor shaft turned and the points opened and closed.

In the case of the electronic ignition system, the piece of steel is a concentric interrupter ring mounted to the rear of the crankshaft balancer. The interrupter ring has blades and windows that, with crankshaft rotation, either block the magnetic field or allow it to reach the Hall-Effect switch. The Hall-Effect switch is called a 24X Crankshaft Position sensor because the interrupter ring has 24 evenly spaced blades and windows. The 24X CKP sensor

produces 24 ON-OFF pulses per crankshaft revolution.

The 24X interrupter ring and Hall-Effect switch react similarly. The 24X signal is used for better resolution at a calibrated RPM.

The 24X CKP sensor clearance is very important. The sensor must not contact the rotating interrupter rings on the crankshaft balancer at any time, or sensor damage will result. If the balancer interrupter rings are bent, the interrupter ring blades will destroy the sensor. If the 24X CKP sensor replacement is necessary, the crankshaft balancer must be removed first (as outlined in Section 3 of this manual). When reinstalling the balancer, torque the balancer attachment bolt to specification. This is critical to ensure the balancer stays attached to the crankshaft. If the 24X CKP sensor assembly is replaced, check the crankshaft balancer interrupter rings for any blades being bent. If this is not checked closely and a bent blade exists, the new crankshaft position sensor can be destroyed by the bent blade with only one crankshaft revolution!

Dual Crankshaft Position Sensor

3.5L (VIN H) ENGINE

The Crankshaft Position (CKP) sensor used on this engine is actually two sensors within a single housing. Each sensor has a separate power, ground and signal circuit. The PCM supplies 12 Volts to both sensors. The PCM provides the ground path, or sensor return circuit, from both sensors. These power and ground circuits are also connected to the Camshaft Position sensor. Two separate signal circuits connect the CKP sensor and the PCM. The PCM can use three different modes of decoding crankshaft position. During normal operation, The PCM performs an Angle Based calculation using both signals to determine crankshaft position. The dual sensor allows the engine to run even if one signal is lost. If either signal is lost, the PCM switches to a Time Based method of calculating crankshaft position. If the system is operating in Time A mode, the PCM is using only the signal from Sensor A. Time B indicates that the Sensor B signal is being used. If the lost signal is restored, the PCM will continue to operate in Time based mode for the remainder of the current key cycle. The PCM will revert back to the Angle mode on the next start if the fault is no longer present. A technician's scan tool can display the Crank Position Sensing Decode Mode. A problem with either Sensor A or Sensor B will set a Diagnostic Trouble Code.

The Crankshaft Position Sensor Learn Procedure must be performed after replacing the CKP sensor.

Even if the original sensor is reinstalled, the Learn Procedure must be performed. This procedure must be performed with a scan tool. The crankshaft position system variation compensating values are stored in the PCM non-volatile memory after a learn procedure has been performed. If the actual crankshaft position system variation is not within the crankshaft position system variation compensating values stored in the PCM, a diagnostic trouble code may set.

The Crankshaft Position System Variation Learn Procedure should be performed after any of the following conditions:

- DTC P1336 is set
- The PCM has been changed
- The PCM has been reprogrammed
- The engine has been replaced
- The crankshaft has been replaced
- The Crankshaft Position Sensor has been replaced

3.8L ENGINES

◆ See Figures 51 and 57

On the 3.8L engines, the Crankshaft Position (CKP) sensor provides a signal used by the ignition control module to calculate the ignition sequence. The ignition control module also uses the crankshaft position sensor signals to initiate 18X and 3X reference pulses which the PCM uses as reference to calculate RPM and crankshaft position.

The dual crankshaft position sensor used on 3.8L engines is secured in an aluminum mounting bracket and bolted to the front left side of the engine timing chain cover, partially behind the crankshaft balancer. A 4-wire harness connector plugs into the sensor, connecting it to the ignition control module. The dual crankshaft position sensor contains two Hall-Effect switches with one shared magnet mounted between them. The magnet and each Hall-Effect switch are separated by an air gap. A Hall-Effect switch reacts like a solid state switch, grounding a low current signal voltage when a magnetic field is present. When the magnetic field is shielded from the switch by a piece of steel placed in the air gap between the magnet and the switch, the signal voltage is not grounded. If the piece of steel (called an interrupter) is repeatedly moved in and out of the air gap, the signal voltage will appear to go ON-OFF-ON-OFF-ON-OFF. In the case of the electronic ignition system, the piece of steel is two concentric interrupter rings mounted to the rear of the crankshaft balancer.

Each interrupter ring has blades and windows that either block the magnetic field or allow it to

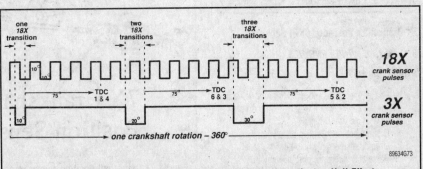

Fig. 51 Because of their different blade and window configurations, the two Hall-Effect switches generate 18 and 3 CHP pulses for each crankshaft revolution—3.8L Engines

close one of the Hall-Effect switches. The outer Hall-Effect switch produces a signal called the CKP 18X because the outer interrupter ring has 18 evenly spaced blades and windows. The CKP 18X portion of the crankshaft position sensor produces 18 ON-OFF pulses per crankshaft revolution. The Hall-Effect switch closest to the crankshaft, the CKP Sync portion of the sensor, produces a signal that approximates the inside interrupter ring. The inside interrupter ring has 3 unevenly spaced blades and windows of different widths. The CKP Sync portion of the crankshaft position sensor produces 3 different length ON-OFF pulses per crankshaft revolution. When a CKP Sync interrupter ring window is between the magnet and inner switch, the magnetic field will cause the CKP Sync Hall-Effect switch to ground the CKP Sync signal voltage supplied from the ignition control module. The CKP 18X interrupter ring and Hall-Effect switch react similarly. The ignition control module interprets the CKP 18X and CKP Sync ON-OFF signals as an indication of crankshaft position, and the ignition control module must have both signals to fire the correct ignition coil. The ignition control module determines crankshaft position for correct ignition coil sequencing by counting how many CKP 18X signal transitions occur, that is, how many ON-OFF or OFF-ON, during a CKP Sync pulse.

TESTING

As with most all engine control sensors used in your vehicle, a thorough and proper test can only be performed by a qualified technician using a scan tool to read the data stream from the PCM. Following is a basic test to check for a 5 volt reference signal.

1. Turn the ignition key **OFF**.
2. Unplug the sensor electrical harness and check the terminals for corrosion and damage.
3. Check the sensor wiring harness wires for continuity and repair as necessary.
4. Attach the sensor harness making sure it is firmly engaged.
5. Using a Digital Volt Ohm Meter (DVOM) set on the DC scale, backprobe the sensor signal terminal (terminal A) with the positive lead of the meter and backprobe the sensor ground terminal (terminal B) with the negative lead of the meter.
6. Have an assistant crank the engine and observe the meter.
7. You should have approximately a 5 volt reference signal pulse. If not, the sensor may be defective.

REMOVAL & INSTALLATION

7X Crankshaft Position (CKP) Sensor

3.1L & 3.4L (VIN E) ENGINES

▶ See Figure 52

The 7X CKP sensor is mounted to an opening in the side of the engine block where it can read off a special area of the crankshaft.

1. Disconnect the negative battery cable.
2. Crank the steering wheel fully to the left.
3. Raise and safely support the vehicle.
4. Locate the 7X CKP sensor on the side of

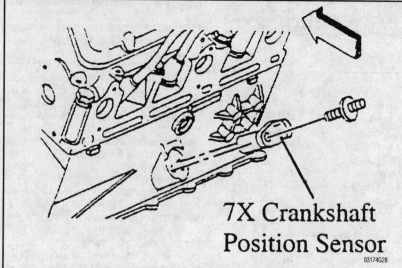

7X Crankshaft Position Sensor

93174G28

Fig. 52 7X Crankshaft Position (CKP) sensor removal—3.1L and 3.4L (VIN E) engines

the block just above the oil pan gasket rail on the block.

5. Detach the electrical connector.
6. Remove the retaining bolt and pull the sensor from the engine.

To install:

7. Inspect the sensor for wear, cracks or leakage. Replace the O-ring as necessary.
8. Lubricate the new O-ring with clean engine oil before installing.
9. Install the engine to the block and snug up the retainer bolt to 71 inch lbs. (8 Nm).
10. Connect the wiring harness and lower the vehicle.
11. Connect the negative battery cable.

3.4L (VIN X) ENGINE

▶ See Figure 53

1. Disconnect the negative battery cable.
2. Raise and safely support the vehicle.
3. Remove the intermediate exhaust pipe.

4. Remove the rack and pinion heat shield.
5. Detach the 7X crankshaft position sensor electrical connector
6. Remove the sensor retainer bolt and separate the sensor from the engine block.

To install:

7. It is important to lubricate the sensor O-ring with clean engine oil. Install the sensor and tighten the bolt to 70 inch lbs. (8 Nm). Do not over-tighten.
8. Install the remainder of the components in the reverse order of removal.
9. Connect the negative battery cable.

24X Crankshaft Position (CKP) Sensor

3.1L AND 3.4L (VIN E & X) ENGINES

▶ See Figures 54 and 55

The 24X CKP sensor is secured in an aluminum mounting bracket and bolted to the front side of the engine timing cover, and is partially behind the crankshaft balancer.

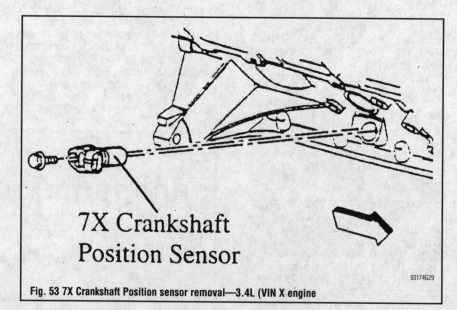

7X Crankshaft Position Sensor

93174G29

Fig. 53 7X Crankshaft Position sensor removal—3.4L (VIN X engine

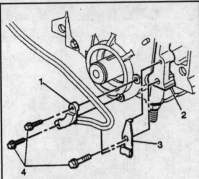

1. Crankshaft Position Sensor
2. Engine Block Face
3. Harness Clip
4. Retainer Bolts

93174G32

Fig. 54 24X Crankshaft Position Sensor arrangement—3.1L and 3.4L (VIN E) engines

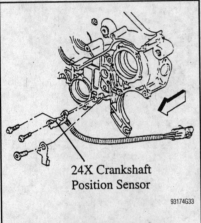

24X Crankshaft Position Sensor

93174G33

Fig. 55 24X Crankshaft Position Sensor arrangement—3.4L (VIN X) engine

1. Disconnect the negative battery cable.
2. Remove the serpentine drive belt, as outlined in Section 1.
3. Raise and safely support the vehicle.
4. Remove the crankshaft balancer, as outlined in Section 3.
5. Take note of the crankshaft position sensor harness routing before removal.
6. Remove the harness retaining clip and detach the electrical connector.
7. Remove the two retaining bolts and remove the sensor.

To install:
8. Install the 24X CKP sensor with the two bolts and route the harness as noted during removal. Torque the bolt to 96 inch lbs. (10 Nm). Install the harness connector
9. Install the crankshaft balancer. Use thread sealer GM #1052080 or equivalent on the balancer through bolt and torque to 110 ft. lbs. (150 Nm). Please see Section 3.
10. Install the remainder of the components in the reverse order of removal.
11. Connect the negative battery cable.

Dual Crankshaft Position (CKP) Sensors

3.5L (VIN H) ENGINE

▶ **See Figure 56**

1. Disconnect the negative battery cable.
2. Raise and safely support the vehicle.
3. Remove the starter motor, as outlined in Section 2.
4. Detach the crankshaft position sensor electrical connector
5. Remove the sensor retainer bolt and separate the sensor from the engine block. Remove by pulling on the sensor connector. Do not pry on the bracket. Do not rotate (twist) the sensor or damage the mounting bracket, if the sensor is to be reused.
6. Installation is the reverse of the removal process, observing the following points.
   a. Make sure the sensor bore is completely free of any foreign material (old O-ring, dirt, burrs, etc.).
   b. Make sure that the flange of the sensor bore is not damaged.
   c. Clean all mounting surfaces before reinstalling any components.
   d. If the sensor is being reused, check for damage. Inspect the face of the sensor (bottom of the brass housing) for damage.
   e. Never install a sensor that has been dropped.
   f. Lubricate the O-ring with clean engine oil.
7. Install the crankshaft position sensor and fully seat into its bore. Install the retaining screw and tighten to 80 inch lbs. (9 Nm). Do not overtighten. Verify that the electrical connection is secure.
8. Install the starter motor, as outlined in Section 2.
9. The Crankshaft Position Sensor Learn Procedure must be performed after replacing the CKP sensor. Even if the original sensor is reinstalled, the Learn Procedure must be performed.

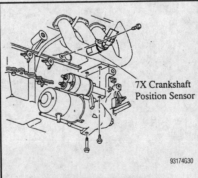

7X Crankshaft Position Sensor

93174G30

Fig. 56 Dual Crankshaft Position sensor removal—3.5L (VIN H) engine

3.8L ENGINES

▶ **See Figure 57**

1. Disconnect the negative battery cable.
2. Remove the serpentine belt(s) from the crankshaft pulley. Please see Section 1.
3. Raise and safely support the vehicle.

4. Remove the right front tire assembly. Remove the right inner fender access cover.
5. A flywheel holding device such as GM's J 37096 is required to keep the crankshaft from turning as the crankshaft balancer is being removed. Install this holding tool or its equivalent. Please see Section 3 for more information.
6. Using a 28mm socket, remove the crankshaft harmonic balancer retaining bolt. Using special tool J 38197 or equivalent balancer removal tools, drawn the balancer from the end of the crankshaft. Please see Section 3 for more information.
7. There is a roughly circular aluminum shield that protects the crankshaft position sensor; remove this shield. Use care not to damage it. Do not pry to remove.
8. Detach the electrical connector from the crankshaft position sensor, remove the attaching bolts and separate the sensor from the engine block face.

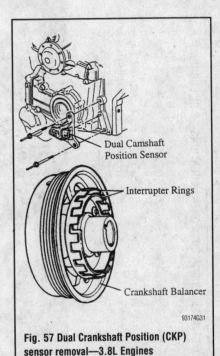

Dual Camshaft Position Sensor

Interrupter Rings

Crankshaft Balancer

93174G31

Fig. 57 Dual Crankshaft Position (CKP) sensor removal—3.8L Engines

To install:
9. Clean all parts well. Position the crankshaft sensor to the block face and tighten the bolts to 14–28 ft. lbs. (20–40 Nm).
10. Install the crankshaft position sensor shield. Verify that the electrical connector is secure.
11. Install the crankshaft balancer. Please see Section 3.
12. Torque the crankshaft balancer center bolt to 110 ft. lbs. (150 Nm), plus an additional 76 degrees.
13. Install the inner fender access cover and the right front tire assembly. Wheel nut torque is 104 ft. lbs. (140 Nm).
14. Lower the vehicle.
15. Install the serpentine belt(s), as outlined in Section 1.
16. Connect the negative battery cable.

COMPONENT LOCATIONS

UNDERHOOD EMISSION COMPONENT LOCATIONS—3.5L ENGINE

1. Fuel injector (1 of 6)
2. Front bank ignition control module and cover assembly
3. Crankshaft Position (CKP) sensor (in block, just above starter motor)
4. Ignition "cassette"
5. PCV valve
6. PCM (in air cleaner housing)
7. Mass Air Flow (MAF) sensor
8. EGR valve
9. Manifold Absolute Pressure (MAP) sensor
10. Camshaft Position (CMP) sensor (just below cam cover gasket rail, front of cam carrier)
11. Underhood relay and fuse center

UNDERHOOD EMISSION COMPONENT LOCATIONS—3.8L (VIN K) ENGINE

1. Ignition coil packs
2. Fuel rail
3. Fuel injector (1 of 6)
4. Fuel pressure regulator
5. Engine Coolant Temperature (ECT) sensor (under hose connection)
6. Throttle Position (TPS) sensor
7. PCM (in air cleaner housing)
8. Intake Air Temperature (IAT) sensor
9. Mass Air Flow (MAF) sensor
10. Rear spark plug wires
11. Alternator
12. Manifold Absolute Pressure (MAP) sensor (under PCV valve)
13. Underhood relay and fuse center

UNDERHOOD EMISSION COMPONENT LOCATIONS—3.8L (VIN 1) ENGINES

1. Ignition coil packs
2. Fuel rail
3. Fuel injector (1 of 6)
4. Fuel pressure regulator
5. Engine Coolant Temperature (ECT) sensor (under hose connection)
6. Throttle Position (TPS) sensor
7. PCM (in air cleaner housing)
8. Intake Air Temperature (IAT) sensor
9. Mass Air Flow (MAF) sensor
10. Supercharger
11. Manifold Absolute Pressure (MAP) sensor (beside Supercharger base)
12. Rear spark plug wires
13. Alternator
14. Underhood relay and fuse center

TROUBLE CODES

General Information

The Powertrain Control Module (PCM) controls most all engine and transmission related operations. Its ability to receive information from various sensors, perform rapid calculations and output commands to the ignition and fuel injection allow the engine to achieve low exhaust emissions while maintaining surprising engine performance. The PCM is a complex, sophisticated on-board solid state computer which receives signals from many sources and sensors; it uses these data to make judgements about operating conditions and then control output signals to the fuel and emission systems to match the current requirements. It is factory programmed with the vehicle's Vehicle Identification Number (VIN) to match its computing ability to a specific platform/powertrain/option combination.

Inputs are received from many sources to form a complete picture of Powertrain operating conditions. Some inputs are simply Yes or No messages, such as that from the Park/Neutral switch; the vehicle is either in gear or in Park/Neutral; there are no other choices. Other data is sent in quantitative input, such as engine RPM or coolant temperature. The PCM is programmed to recognize acceptable ranges or combinations of signals and control the outputs to control emissions while providing good driveability and economy. The PCM also monitors some output circuits, making sure that the components function as commanded. For proper engine operation, it is essential that all input and output components function properly and communicate properly with the PCM.

Since the PCM is programmed to recognize the presence and value of electrical inputs, it will also note the lack of a signal or a radical change in values. It will, for example, react to the loss of signal from the vehicle speed sensor or note that engine coolant temperature has risen beyond acceptable (programmed) limits. Once a fault is recognized, a Diagnostic Trouble Code (DTC) is assigned and held in memory. The dashboard Malfunction Indicator Lamp (MIL)—CHECK ENGINE or SERVICE ENGINE SOON—will illuminate to advise the operator that the system has detected a fault.

More than one DTC may be stored. Although not every engine uses every code, there is a large range of codes. Additionally, the same code may carry different meanings relative to each engine or engine family.

In the event of a PCM failure, the system will default to a pre-programmed set of values. These are compromise values which allow the engine to operate, although likely at a reduced efficiency. This is variously known as the default, limp-in or backup mode. Driveability is almost always affected when the PCM enters this mode.

LEARNING ABILITY

The PCM can compensate for minor variations within the fuel system through the block learn and fuel integrator systems. The fuel integrator monitors the oxygen sensor output voltage, adding or subtracting fuel to drive the mixture rich or lean as needed to reach the ideal air fuel ratio of 14.7:1. The integrator values may be read with a scan tool; the display will range from 0–255 and should center on 128 if the oxygen sensor is seeing a 14.7:1 mixture.

The temporary nature of the integrator's control is expanded by the block learn function. The name is derived from the fact that the entire engine operating range (load vs. rpm) is divided into 16 sections or blocks. Within each memory block is stored the correct fuel delivery value for that combination of load and engine speed. Once the operating range enters a certain block, that stored value controls the fuel delivery unless the integrator steps in to change it. If changes are made by the integrator, the new value is memorized and stored within the block. As the block learn makes the correction, the integrator correction will be reduced until the integrator returns to 128; the block learn then controls the fuel delivery with the new value.

The next time the engine operates within the block's range, the new value will be used. The block learn data can also be read by a scan tool; the range is the same as the integrator and should also center on 128. In this way, the systems can compensate for engine wear, small air or vacuum leaks or reduced combustion.

Any time the battery is disconnected, the block learn values are lost and must be relearned by the PCM. This loss of corrected values may be noticed as a significant change in driveability. To re-teach the system, make certain the engine is fully warmed up. Drive the vehicle at part throttle using moderate acceleration and idle until normal performance is felt.

DASHBOARD WARNING LAMP

The primary function of the dash warning lamp (properly called the Malfunction Indicator Lamp, or MIL) is to advise the operator and that a fault has been detected, and, in most cases, a code stored. Under normal conditions, the dash warning lamp will illuminate when the ignition is turned **ON**. Once the engine is started and running, the PCM will perform a system check and extinguish the warning lamp if no fault is found.

SCAN TOOLS

▶ See Figures 58 and 59

On the vehicles covered by this manual, the DTCs can only be read using a scan tool, such as GM's Tech 1® or Tech 2®, or equivalent. These tools are so-called OBD-II Compliant. This means they are compatible with the federal-mandated On-Board Diagnostic, Second Generation systems. Almost from the beginning of computer controlled vehicles, some sort of on-board diagnostic ability has been built into the vehicle's computer to assist the technician. At one time, the vehicle's instrument panel Malfunction Indicator Lamp could be used to read some codes. Even a vehicle owner could read the flashing MIL lamp and interpret the trouble code. Scan tools became available to the profession technician. A scan tool allows any stored codes to be read from the PCM memory. The tool also allows the technician to view the data being sent to the PCM while the engine is running. While the scan

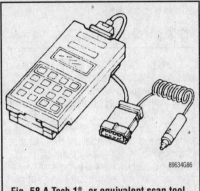

Fig. 58 A Tech 1®, or equivalent scan tool is recommended for reading trouble codes

Fig. 59 Inexpensive scan tools, such as this Auto Xray®, are available to interface with your General Motors vehicle

tool makes collecting information easier, the data must be correctly interpreted by a technician familiar with the system.

As emission regulations get more stringent and vehicles get more complex, the vehicle's on-board computers have evolved into powerful diagnostic tools. The vehicles covered by this manual require the use of OBD-II compliant Scan Tools for efficient troubleshooting, reading DTCs and reading the PCM's data stream. These vehicles use what is called a Class II Serial Data circuit to a Diagnostic Link Connector which allows bi-directional communication between the PCM and the scan tool.

An example of the usefulness of the scan tool may be seen in the case of a temperature sensor which has changed its electrical characteristics. The PCM is reacting to an apparently warmer engine (causing a driveability problem), but the sensor's voltage has not changed enough to set a fault code. Connecting the scan tool, the voltage signal being sent to the PCM may be viewed. Comparison to either factory published information of normal values or a known good vehicle may reveal the problem quickly.

Diagnosis and Testing

Diagnosis of a driveability and/or emissions problems requires attention to detail and following the diagnostic procedures in the correct order. Resist the temptation to perform any repairs before performing the preliminary diagnostic steps. In many cases this will shorten diagnostic time and often cure the problem without electronic testing.

The proper troubleshooting procedure for these vehicles is as follows:

VISUAL/PHYSICAL INSPECTION

This is possibly the most critical step of diagnosis and should be performed immediately after retrieving any codes. A detailed examination of connectors, wiring and vacuum hoses can often lead to a repair without further diagnosis. Performance of this step relies on the skill of the technician performing it; a careful inspector will check the undersides of hoses as well as the integrity of hard-to-reach hoses blocked by the air cleaner or other component. Wiring should be checked carefully for any sign of strain, burning, crimping, or terminal pull-out from a connector. Checking connectors at components or in harnesses is required; usually, pushing them together will reveal a loose fit.

INTERMITTENTS

If a fault occurs intermittently, such as a loose connector pin breaking contact as the vehicle hits a bump, the PCM will note the fault as it occurs and energize the dash warning lamp. If the problem self-corrects, as with the terminal pin again making contact, the dash lamp will extinguish after 10 seconds but a code will remain stored in the computer control module's memory.

When an unexpected code appears during diagnostics, it may have been set during an intermittent failure that self-corrected; the codes are still useful in diagnosis and should not be discounted.

CIRCUIT/COMPONENT REPAIR

The fault codes and the scan tool data will lead to diagnosis and checking of a particular circuit. It is important to note that the fault code indicates a fault or loss of signal in an PCM-controlled system, not necessarily in the specific component.

Refer to the appropriate Diagnostic Code chart to determine the codes meaning. The component may then be tested following the appropriate component test procedures found in this section. If the component is OK, check the wiring for shorts or opens. Further diagnoses should be left to an experienced driveability technician.

If a code indicates the PCM to be faulty and the PCM is replaced, but does not correct the problem, one of the following may be the reason:
- There is a problem with the PCM terminal connections: The terminals may have to be removed from the connector in order to check them properly.
- The PCM is not correct for the application: The incorrect PCM may cause a malfunction and may or may not set a code.
- The problem is intermittent: This means that the problem is not present at the time the system is being checked. In this case, make a careful physical inspection of all portions of the system involved.
- Shorted solenoid, relay coil or harness: Solenoids and relays are turned on and off by the PCM using internal electronic switches called drivers. Each driver is part of a group of four called Quad-Drivers. A shorted solenoid, relay coil or harness

may cause an PCM to fail, and a replacement PCM to fail when it is installed. Use a short tester, J34696, BT 8405, or equivalent, as a fast, accurate means of checking for a short circuit.
- The replacement PCM may be faulty: After the PCM is replaced, the system should be rechecked for proper operation. If the diagnostic code again indicates the PCM is the problem, substitute a known good PCM. Although this is a very rare condition, it could happen.

Diagnostic Connector

▶ See Figure 60

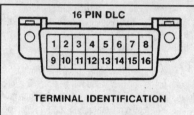

TERMINAL IDENTIFICATION

5	GROUND
9	SERIAL DATA (UART)
16	B +

89634G89

Fig. 60 All of the vehicles covered by this manual use a 16-pin DLC, which is located under the driver's side of the instrument panel

Reading Codes

▶ See Figures 58 and 59

Following is a list of the OBD-II Diagnostic Trouble Codes (DTCs) for the vehicles covered by this manual. An OBD-II compliant scan tool, such as a Tech 1® or equivalent, must be used to retrieve the trouble codes. Follow the scan tool manufacturer's instructions on how to connect the scan tool to the vehicle and how to retrieve the codes.

P0100 Mass or Volume Air Flow Circuit Malfunction

P0101 Mass or Volume Air Flow Circuit Range/Performance Problem

P0102 Mass or Volume Air Flow Circuit Low Input

P0103 Mass or Volume Air Flow Circuit High Input

P0104 Mass or Volume Air Flow Circuit Intermittent

P0105 Manifold Absolute Pressure/Barometric Pressure Circuit Malfunction

P0106 Manifold Absolute Pressure/Barometric Pressure Circuit Range/Performance Problem

P0107 Manifold Absolute Pressure/Barometric Pressure Circuit Low Input

P0108 Manifold Absolute Pressure/Barometric Pressure Circuit High Input

P0109 Manifold Absolute Pressure/Barometric Pressure Circuit Intermittent

P0110 Intake Air Temperature Circuit Malfunction

P0111 Intake Air Temperature Circuit Range/Performance Problem

P0112 Intake Air Temperature Circuit Low Input

P0113 Intake Air Temperature Circuit High Input

P0114 Intake Air Temperature Circuit Intermittent

P0115 Engine Coolant Temperature Circuit Malfunction

P0116 Engine Coolant Temperature Circuit Range/Performance Problem

P0117 Engine Coolant Temperature Circuit Low Input

P0118 Engine Coolant Temperature Circuit High Input

P0119 Engine Coolant Temperature Circuit Intermittent

P0120 Throttle/Pedal Position Sensor/Switch "A" Circuit Malfunction

P0121 Throttle/Pedal Position Sensor/Switch "A" Circuit Range/Performance Problem

P0122 Throttle/Pedal Position Sensor/Switch "A" Circuit Low Input

P0123 Throttle/Pedal Position Sensor/Switch "A" Circuit High Input

P0124 Throttle/Pedal Position Sensor/Switch "A" Circuit Intermittent

P0125 Insufficient Coolant Temperature For Closed Loop Fuel Control

P0126 Insufficient Coolant Temperature For Stable Operation

P0130 O_2 Circuit Malfunction (Bank #1 Sensor #1)

P0131 O_2 Sensor Circuit Low Voltage (Bank #1 Sensor #1)

P0132 O_2 Sensor Circuit High Voltage (Bank #1 Sensor #1)

P0133 O_2 Sensor Circuit Slow Response (Bank #1 Sensor #1)

P0134 O_2 Sensor Circuit No Activity Detected (Bank #1 Sensor #1)

P0135 O_2 Sensor Heater Circuit Malfunction (Bank #1 Sensor #1)

P0136 O_2 Sensor Circuit Malfunction (Bank #1 Sensor #2)

P0137 O_2 Sensor Circuit Low Voltage (Bank #1 Sensor #2)

P0138 O_2 Sensor Circuit High Voltage (Bank #1 Sensor #2)

P0139 O_2 Sensor Circuit Slow Response (Bank #1 Sensor #2)

P0140 O_2 Sensor Circuit No Activity Detected (Bank #1 Sensor #2)

P0141 O_2 Sensor Heater Circuit Malfunction (Bank #1 Sensor #2)

P0142 O_2 Sensor Circuit Malfunction (Bank #1 Sensor #3)

P0143 O_2 Sensor Circuit Low Voltage (Bank #1 Sensor #3)

P0144 O_2 Sensor Circuit High Voltage (Bank #1 Sensor #3)

P0145 O_2 Sensor Circuit Slow Response (Bank #1 Sensor #3)

P0146 O_2 Sensor Circuit No Activity Detected (Bank #1 Sensor #3)

P0147 O_2 Sensor Heater Circuit Malfunction (Bank #1 Sensor #3)

P0150 O_2 Sensor Circuit Malfunction (Bank #2 Sensor #1)

P0151 O_2 Sensor Circuit Low Voltage (Bank #2 Sensor #1)

P0152 O_2 Sensor Circuit High Voltage (Bank #2 Sensor #1)

P0153 O_2 Sensor Circuit Slow Response (Bank #2 Sensor #1)

P0154 O_2 Sensor Circuit No Activity Detected (Bank #2 Sensor #1)

P0155 O_2 Sensor Heater Circuit Malfunction (Bank #2 Sensor #1)

P0156 O_2 Sensor Circuit Malfunction (Bank #2 Sensor #2)

P0157 O_2 Sensor Circuit Low Voltage (Bank #2 Sensor #2)

P0158 O_2 Sensor Circuit High Voltage (Bank #2 Sensor #2)

P0159 O_2 Sensor Circuit Slow Response (Bank #2 Sensor #2)

P0160 O_2 Sensor Circuit No Activity Detected (Bank #2 Sensor #2)

P0161 O_2 Sensor Heater Circuit Malfunction (Bank #2 Sensor #2)

P0162 O_2 Sensor Circuit Malfunction (Bank #2 Sensor #3)

P0163 O_2 Sensor Circuit Low Voltage (Bank #2 Sensor #3)

P0164 O_2 Sensor Circuit High Voltage (Bank #2 Sensor #3)

P0165 O_2 Sensor Circuit Slow Response (Bank #2 Sensor #3)

P0166 O_2 Sensor Circuit No Activity Detected (Bank #2 Sensor #3)

P0167 O_2 Sensor Heater Circuit Malfunction (Bank #2 Sensor #3)

P0170 Fuel Trim Malfunction (Bank #1)
P0171 System Too Lean (Bank #1)
P0172 System Too Rich (Bank #1)
P0173 Fuel Trim Malfunction (Bank #2)
P0174 System Too Lean (Bank #2)
P0175 System Too Rich (Bank #2)
P0176 Fuel Composition Sensor Circuit Malfunction

P0177 Fuel Composition Sensor Circuit Range/Performance

P0178 Fuel Composition Sensor Circuit Low Input

P0179 Fuel Composition Sensor Circuit High Input

P0180 Fuel Temperature Sensor "A" Circuit Malfunction

P0181 Fuel Temperature Sensor "A" Circuit Range/Performance

P0182 Fuel Temperature Sensor "A" Circuit Low Input

P0183 Fuel Temperature Sensor "A" Circuit High Input

P0184 Fuel Temperature Sensor "A" Circuit Intermittent

P0185 Fuel Temperature Sensor "B" Circuit Malfunction

P0186 Fuel Temperature Sensor "B" Circuit Range/Performance

P0187 Fuel Temperature Sensor "B" Circuit Low Input

P0188 Fuel Temperature Sensor "B" Circuit High Input

P0189 Fuel Temperature Sensor "B" Circuit Intermittent

P0190 Fuel Rail Pressure Sensor Circuit Malfunction

P0191 Fuel Rail Pressure Sensor Circuit Range/Performance

P0192 Fuel Rail Pressure Sensor Circuit Low Input

P0193 Fuel Rail Pressure Sensor Circuit High Input

P0194 Fuel Rail Pressure Sensor Circuit Intermittent

P0195 Engine Oil Temperature Sensor Malfunction

P0196 Engine Oil Temperature Sensor Range/Performance

P0197 Engine Oil Temperature Sensor Low
P0198 Engine Oil Temperature Sensor High
P0199 Engine Oil Temperature Sensor Intermittent

P0200 Injector Circuit Malfunction
P0201 Injector Circuit Malfunction—Cylinder #1

P0202 Injector Circuit Malfunction—Cylinder #2

P0203 Injector Circuit Malfunction—Cylinder #3

P0204 Injector Circuit Malfunction—Cylinder #4

P0205 Injector Circuit Malfunction—Cylinder #5

P0206 Injector Circuit Malfunction—Cylinder #6

P0207 Injector Circuit Malfunction—Cylinder #7

P0208 Injector Circuit Malfunction—Cylinder #8

P0209 Injector Circuit Malfunction—Cylinder #9

P0210 Injector Circuit Malfunction—Cylinder #10

P0211 Injector Circuit Malfunction—Cylinder #11

P0212 Injector Circuit Malfunction—Cylinder #12

P0213 Cold Start Injector #1 Malfunction
P0214 Cold Start Injector #2 Malfunction
P0215 Engine Shutoff Solenoid Malfunction
P0216 Injection Timing Control Circuit Malfunction

P0217 Engine Over Temperature Condition
P0218 Transmission Over Temperature Condition

P0219 Engine Over Speed Condition
P0220 Throttle/Pedal Position Sensor/Switch "B" Circuit Malfunction

P0221 Throttle/Pedal Position Sensor/Switch "B" Circuit Range/Performance Problem

P0222 Throttle/Pedal Position Sensor/Switch "B" Circuit Low Input

P0223 Throttle/Pedal Position Sensor/Switch "B" Circuit High Input

P0224 Throttle/Pedal Position Sensor/Switch "B" Circuit Intermittent

P0225 Throttle/Pedal Position Sensor/Switch "C" Circuit Malfunction

P0226 Throttle/Pedal Position Sensor/Switch "C" Circuit Range/Performance Problem

P0227 Throttle/Pedal Position Sensor/Switch "C" Circuit Low Input

P0228 Throttle/Pedal Position Sensor/Switch "C" Circuit High Input

P0229 Throttle/Pedal Position Sensor/Switch "C" Circuit Intermittent

P0230 Fuel Pump Primary Circuit Malfunction
P0231 Fuel Pump Secondary Circuit Low
P0232 Fuel Pump Secondary Circuit High
P0233 Fuel Pump Secondary Circuit Intermittent

P0234 Engine Over Boost Condition

P0261 Cylinder #1 Injector Circuit Low
P0262 Cylinder #1 Injector Circuit High
P0263 Cylinder #1 Contribution/Balance Fault
P0264 Cylinder #2 Injector Circuit Low
P0265 Cylinder #2 Injector Circuit High
P0266 Cylinder #2 Contribution/Balance Fault
P0267 Cylinder #3 Injector Circuit Low
P0268 Cylinder #3 Injector Circuit High
P0269 Cylinder #3 Contribution/Balance Fault
P0270 Cylinder #4 Injector Circuit Low
P0271 Cylinder #4 Injector Circuit High
P0272 Cylinder #4 Contribution/Balance Fault
P0273 Cylinder #5 Injector Circuit Low
P0274 Cylinder #5 Injector Circuit High
P0275 Cylinder #5 Contribution/Balance Fault
P0276 Cylinder #6 Injector Circuit Low
P0277 Cylinder #6 Injector Circuit High
P0278 Cylinder #6 Contribution/Balance Fault
P0279 Cylinder #7 Injector Circuit Low
P0280 Cylinder #7 Injector Circuit High
P0281 Cylinder #7 Contribution/Balance Fault
P0282 Cylinder #8 Injector Circuit Low
P0283 Cylinder #8 Injector Circuit High
P0284 Cylinder #8 Contribution/Balance Fault
P0285 Cylinder #9 Injector Circuit Low
P0286 Cylinder #9 Injector Circuit High
P0287 Cylinder #9 Contribution/Balance Fault
P0288 Cylinder #10 Injector Circuit Low
P0289 Cylinder #10 Injector Circuit High
P0290 Cylinder #10 Contribution/Balance Fault
P0300 Random/Multiple Cylinder Misfire Detected
P0301 Cylinder #1—Misfire Detected
P0302 Cylinder #2—Misfire Detected
P0303 Cylinder #3—Misfire Detected
P0304 Cylinder #4—Misfire Detected
P0305 Cylinder #5—Misfire Detected
P0306 Cylinder #6—Misfire Detected
P0307 Cylinder #7—Misfire Detected
P0308 Cylinder #8—Misfire Detected
P0309 Cylinder #9—Misfire Detected
P0310 Cylinder #10—Misfire Detected
P0320 Ignition/Distributor Engine Speed Input Circuit Malfunction

P0321 Ignition/Distributor Engine Speed Input Circuit Range/Performance

P0322 Ignition/Distributor Engine Speed Input Circuit No Signal

P0323 Ignition/Distributor Engine Speed Input Circuit Intermittent

P0325 Knock Sensor #1—Circuit Malfunction (Bank #1 or Single Sensor)

P0326 Knock Sensor #1—Circuit Range/Performance (Bank #1 or Single Sensor)

P0327 Knock Sensor #1—Circuit Low Input (Bank #1 or Single Sensor)

P0328 Knock Sensor #1—Circuit High Input (Bank #1 or Single Sensor)

P0329 Knock Sensor #1—Circuit Input Intermittent (Bank #1 or Single Sensor)

P0330 Knock Sensor #2—Circuit Malfunction (Bank #2)

P0331 Knock Sensor #2—Circuit Range/Performance (Bank #2)

P0332 Knock Sensor #2—Circuit Low Input (Bank #2)

P0333 Knock Sensor #2—Circuit High Input (Bank #2)

P0334 Knock Sensor #2—Circuit Input Intermittent (Bank #2)

P0335 Crankshaft Position Sensor "A" Circuit Malfunction

P0336 Crankshaft Position Sensor "A" Circuit Range/Performance

P0337 Crankshaft Position Sensor "A" Circuit Low Input

P0338 Crankshaft Position Sensor "A" Circuit High Input

P0339 Crankshaft Position Sensor "A" Circuit Intermittent

P0340 Camshaft Position Sensor Circuit Malfunction

P0341 Camshaft Position Sensor Circuit Range/Performance

P0342 Camshaft Position Sensor Circuit Low Input

P0343 Camshaft Position Sensor Circuit High Input

P0344 Camshaft Position Sensor Circuit Intermittent

P0350 Ignition Coil Primary/Secondary Circuit Malfunction

P0351 Ignition Coil "A" Primary/Secondary Circuit Malfunction

P0352 Ignition Coil "B" Primary/Secondary Circuit Malfunction

P0353 Ignition Coil "C" Primary/Secondary Circuit Malfunction

P0354 Ignition Coil "D" Primary/Secondary Circuit Malfunction

P0355 Ignition Coil "E" Primary/Secondary Circuit Malfunction

P0356 Ignition Coil "F" Primary/Secondary Circuit Malfunction

P0357 Ignition Coil "G" Primary/Secondary Circuit Malfunction

P0358 Ignition Coil "H" Primary/Secondary Circuit Malfunction

P0359 Ignition Coil "I" Primary/Secondary Circuit Malfunction

P0360 Ignition Coil "J" Primary/Secondary Circuit Malfunction

P0361 Ignition Coil "K" Primary/Secondary Circuit Malfunction

P0362 Ignition Coil "L" Primary/Secondary Circuit Malfunction

P0370 Timing Reference High Resolution Signal "A" Malfunction

P0371 Timing Reference High Resolution Signal "A" Too Many Pulses

P0372 Timing Reference High Resolution Signal "A" Too Few Pulses

P0373 Timing Reference High Resolution Signal "A" Intermittent/Erratic Pulses

P0374 Timing Reference High Resolution Signal "A" No Pulses

P0375 Timing Reference High Resolution Signal "B" Malfunction

P0376 Timing Reference High Resolution Signal "B" Too Many Pulses

P0377 Timing Reference High Resolution Signal "B" Too Few Pulses

P0378 Timing Reference High Resolution Signal "B" Intermittent/Erratic Pulses

P0379 Timing Reference High Resolution Signal "B" No Pulses

P0380 Glow Plug/Heater Circuit "A" Malfunction

P0381 Glow Plug/Heater Indicator Circuit Malfunction

P0382 Glow Plug/Heater Circuit "B" Malfunction

P0385 Crankshaft Position Sensor "B" Circuit Malfunction

P0386 Crankshaft Position Sensor "B" Circuit Range/Performance

P0387 Crankshaft Position Sensor "B" Circuit Low Input

P0388 Crankshaft Position Sensor "B" Circuit High Input

P0389 Crankshaft Position Sensor "B" Circuit Intermittent

P0400 Exhaust Gas Recirculation Flow Malfunction

P0401 Exhaust Gas Recirculation Flow Insufficient Detected

P0402 Exhaust Gas Recirculation Flow Excessive Detected

P0403 Exhaust Gas Recirculation Circuit Malfunction

P0404 Exhaust Gas Recirculation Circuit Range/Performance

P0405 Exhaust Gas Recirculation Sensor "A" Circuit Low

P0406 Exhaust Gas Recirculation Sensor "A" Circuit High

P0407 Exhaust Gas Recirculation Sensor "B" Circuit Low

P0408 Exhaust Gas Recirculation Sensor "B" Circuit High

P0410 Secondary Air Injection System Malfunction

P0411 Secondary Air Injection System Incorrect Flow Detected

P0412 Secondary Air Injection System Switching Valve "A" Circuit Malfunction

P0413 Secondary Air Injection System Switching Valve "A" Circuit Open

P0414 Secondary Air Injection System Switching Valve "A" Circuit Shorted

P0415 Secondary Air Injection System Switching Valve "B" Circuit Malfunction

P0416 Secondary Air Injection System Switching Valve "B" Circuit Open

P0417 Secondary Air Injection System Switching Valve "B" Circuit Shorted

P0418 Secondary Air Injection System Relay "A" Circuit Malfunction

P0419 Secondary Air Injection System Relay "B" Circuit Malfunction

P0420 Catalyst System Efficiency Below Threshold (Bank #1)

P0421 Warm Up Catalyst Efficiency Below Threshold (Bank #1)

P0422 Main Catalyst Efficiency Below Threshold (Bank #1)

P0423 Heated Catalyst Efficiency Below Threshold (Bank #1)

P0424 Heated Catalyst Temperature Below Threshold (Bank #1)

P0430 Catalyst System Efficiency Below Threshold (Bank #2)

P0431 Warm Up Catalyst Efficiency Below Threshold (Bank #2)

P0432 Main Catalyst Efficiency Below Threshold (Bank #2)

P0433 Heated Catalyst Efficiency Below Threshold (Bank #2)

P0434 Heated Catalyst Temperature Below Threshold (Bank #2)

P0440 Evaporative Emission Control System Malfunction

P0441 Evaporative Emission Control System Incorrect Purge Flow

P0442 Evaporative Emission Control System Leak Detected (Small Leak)

P0443 Evaporative Emission Control System Purge Control Valve Circuit Malfunction

P0444 Evaporative Emission Control System Purge Control Valve Circuit Open

P0445 Evaporative Emission Control System Purge Control Valve Circuit Shorted

P0446 Evaporative Emission Control System Vent Control Circuit Malfunction

P0447 Evaporative Emission Control System Vent Control Circuit Open

P0448 Evaporative Emission Control System Vent Control Circuit Shorted

P0449 Evaporative Emission Control System Vent Valve/Solenoid Circuit Malfunction

P0450 Evaporative Emission Control System Pressure Sensor Malfunction

P0451 Evaporative Emission Control System Pressure Sensor Range/Performance

P0452 Evaporative Emission Control System Pressure Sensor Low Input

P0453 Evaporative Emission Control System Pressure Sensor High Input

P0454 Evaporative Emission Control System Pressure Sensor Intermittent

P0455 Evaporative Emission Control System Leak Detected (Gross Leak)

P0460 Fuel Level Sensor Circuit Malfunction

P0461 Fuel Level Sensor Circuit Range/Performance

P0462 Fuel Level Sensor Circuit Low Input

P0463 Fuel Level Sensor Circuit High Input

P0464 Fuel Level Sensor Circuit Intermittent

P0465 Purge Flow Sensor Circuit Malfunction

P0466 Purge Flow Sensor Circuit Range/Performance

P0467 Purge Flow Sensor Circuit Low Input

P0468 Purge Flow Sensor Circuit High Input

P0469 Purge Flow Sensor Circuit Intermittent

P0470 Exhaust Pressure Sensor Malfunction

P0471 Exhaust Pressure Sensor Range/Performance

P0472 Exhaust Pressure Sensor Low

P0473 Exhaust Pressure Sensor High

P0474 Exhaust Pressure Sensor Intermittent

P0475 Exhaust Pressure Control Valve Malfunction

P0476 Exhaust Pressure Control Valve Range/Performance

P0477 Exhaust Pressure Control Valve Low

P0478 Exhaust Pressure Control Valve High

P0479 Exhaust Pressure Control Valve Intermittent

P0480 Cooling Fan #1 Control Circuit Malfunction

P0481 Cooling Fan #2 Control Circuit Malfunction

P0482 Cooling Fan #3 Control Circuit Malfunction

P0483 Cooling Fan Rationality Check Malfunction

P0484 Cooling Fan Circuit Over Current

P0485 Cooling Fan Power/Ground Circuit Malfunction

P0500 Vehicle Speed Sensor Malfunction

P0501 Vehicle Speed Sensor Range/Performance

P0502 Vehicle Speed Sensor Circuit Low Input

P0503 Vehicle Speed Sensor Intermittent/Erratic/High

P0505 Idle Control System Malfunction

P0506 Idle Control System RPM Lower Than Expected

P0507 Idle Control System RPM Higher Than Expected

P0510 Closed Throttle Position Switch Malfunction

P0520 Engine Oil Pressure Sensor/Switch Circuit Malfunction

P0521 Engine Oil Pressure Sensor/Switch Range/Performance

P0522 Engine Oil Pressure Sensor/Switch Low Voltage

P0523 Engine Oil Pressure Sensor/Switch High Voltage

P0530 A/C Refrigerant Pressure Sensor Circuit Malfunction

P0531 A/C Refrigerant Pressure Sensor Circuit Range/Performance

P0532 A/C Refrigerant Pressure Sensor Circuit Low Input

P0533 A/C Refrigerant Pressure Sensor Circuit High Input

P0534 A/C Refrigerant Charge Loss

P0550 Power Steering Pressure Sensor Circuit Malfunction

P0551 Power Steering Pressure Sensor Circuit Range/Performance

P0552 Power Steering Pressure Sensor Circuit Low Input

P0553 Power Steering Pressure Sensor Circuit High Input

P0554 Power Steering Pressure Sensor Circuit Intermittent

P0560 System Voltage Malfunction

P0561 System Voltage Unstable

P0562 System Voltage Low

P0563 System Voltage High

P0565 Cruise Control On Signal Malfunction

P0566 Cruise Control Off Signal Malfunction

P0567 Cruise Control Resume Signal Malfunction

P0568 Cruise Control Set Signal Malfunction

P0569 Cruise Control Coast Signal Malfunction

P0570 Cruise Control Accel Signal Malfunction

P0571 Cruise Control/Brake Switch "A" Circuit Malfunction

P0572 Cruise Control/Brake Switch "A" Circuit Low

P0573 Cruise Control/Brake Switch "A" Circuit High

P0574 Through P0580 Reserved for Cruise Codes

P0600 Serial Communication Link Malfunction

P0601 Internal Control Module Memory Check Sum Error

P0602 Control Module Programming Error

P0603 Internal Control Module Keep Alive Memory (KAM) Error

P0604 Internal Control Module Random Access Memory (RAM) Error

P0605 Internal Control Module Read Only Memory (ROM) Error

P0606 PCM Processor Fault

P0608 Control Module VSS Output "A" Malfunction

P0609 Control Module VSS Output "B" Malfunction

P0620 Generator Control Circuit Malfunction

P0621 Generator Lamp "L" Control Circuit Malfunction

P0622 Generator Field "F" Control Circuit Malfunction

P0650 Malfunction Indicator Lamp (MIL) Control Circuit Malfunction

P0654 Engine RPM Output Circuit Malfunction

P0655 Engine Hot Lamp Output Control Circuit Malfunction

P0656 Fuel Level Output Circuit Malfunction

P0700 Transmission Control System Malfunction

P0701 Transmission Control System Range/Performance

P0702 Transmission Control System Electrical

P0703 Torque Converter/Brake Switch "B" Circuit Malfunction

P0704 Clutch Switch Input Circuit Malfunction

P0705 Transmission Range Sensor Circuit Malfunction (PRNDL Input)

P0706 Transmission Range Sensor Circuit Range/Performance

P0707 Transmission Range Sensor Circuit Low Input

P0708 Transmission Range Sensor Circuit High Input

P0709 Transmission Range Sensor Circuit Intermittent

P0710 Transmission Fluid Temperature Sensor Circuit Malfunction

P0711 Transmission Fluid Temperature Sensor Circuit Range/Performance

P0712 Transmission Fluid Temperature Sensor Circuit Low Input

P0713 Transmission Fluid Temperature Sensor Circuit High Input

P0714 Transmission Fluid Temperature Sensor Circuit Intermittent

P0715 Input/Turbine Speed Sensor Circuit Malfunction

P0716 Input/Turbine Speed Sensor Circuit Range/Performance

P0717 Input/Turbine Speed Sensor Circuit No Signal

P0718 Input/Turbine Speed Sensor Circuit Intermittent

P0719 Torque Converter/Brake Switch "B" Circuit Low

P0720 Output Speed Sensor Circuit Malfunction

P0721 Output Speed Sensor Circuit Range/Performance

P0722 Output Speed Sensor Circuit No Signal

P0723 Output Speed Sensor Circuit Intermittent

P0724 Torque Converter/Brake Switch "B" Circuit High

P0725 Engine Speed Input Circuit Malfunction

P0726 Engine Speed Input Circuit Range/Performance

P0727 Engine Speed Input Circuit No Signal

P0728 Engine Speed Input Circuit Intermittent

P0730 Incorrect Gear Ratio

P0731 Gear #1 Incorrect Ratio

P0732 Gear #2 Incorrect Ratio

P0733 Gear #3 Incorrect Ratio

P0734 Gear #4 Incorrect Ratio

P0735 Gear #5 Incorrect Ratio

P0736 Reverse Incorrect Ratio

P0740 Torque Converter Clutch Circuit Malfunction

P0741 Torque Converter Clutch Circuit Performance or Stuck Off

P0742 Torque Converter Clutch Circuit Stuck On

P0743 Torque Converter Clutch Circuit Electrical

P0744 Torque Converter Clutch Circuit Intermittent

P0745 Pressure Control Solenoid Malfunction

P0746 Pressure Control Solenoid Performance or Stuck Off

P0747 Pressure Control Solenoid Stuck On

P0748 Pressure Control Solenoid Electrical

P0749 Pressure Control Solenoid Intermittent

P0750 Shift Solenoid "A" Malfunction

P0751 Shift Solenoid "A" Performance or Stuck Off

P0752 Shift Solenoid "A" Stuck On

P0753 Shift Solenoid "A" Electrical

P0754 Shift Solenoid "A" Intermittent

P0755 Shift Solenoid "B" Malfunction

P0756 Shift Solenoid "B" Performance or Stuck Off

P0757 Shift Solenoid "B" Stuck On

P0758 Shift Solenoid "B" Electrical

P0759 Shift Solenoid "B" Intermittent

P0760 Shift Solenoid "C" Malfunction

P0761 Shift Solenoid "C" Performance Or Stuck Off

P0762 Shift Solenoid "C" Stuck On

P0763 Shift Solenoid "C" Electrical

P0764 Shift Solenoid "C" Intermittent

P0765 Shift Solenoid "D" Malfunction

P0766 Shift Solenoid "D" Performance Or Stuck Off

P0767 Shift Solenoid "D" Stuck On

P0768 Shift Solenoid "D" Electrical

P0769 Shift Solenoid "D" Intermittent

P0770 Shift Solenoid "E" Malfunction

P0771 Shift Solenoid "E" Performance Or Stuck Off

P0772 Shift Solenoid "E" Stuck On

P0773 Shift Solenoid "E" Electrical

P0774 Shift Solenoid "E" Intermittent

P0780 Shift Malfunction

P0781 1–2 Shift Malfunction

P0782 2–3 Shift Malfunction

P0783 3–4 Shift Malfunction

P0784 4–5 Shift Malfunction

P0785 Shift/Timing Solenoid Malfunction

P0786 Shift/Timing Solenoid Range/Performance

P0787 Shift/Timing Solenoid Low

P0788 Shift/Timing Solenoid High

P0789 Shift/Timing Solenoid Intermittent

P0790 Normal/Performance Switch Circuit Malfunction

P0801 Reverse Inhibit Control Circuit Malfunction

P0803 1–4 Upshift (Skip Shift) Solenoid Control Circuit Malfunction

P0804 1–4 Upshift (Skip Shift) Lamp Control Circuit Malfunction

P1106 MAP Sensor Voltage Intermittently High

P1107 MAP Sensor Voltage Intermittently Low

P1111 IAT Sensor Circuit Intermittent High Voltage

P1112 IAT Sensor Circuit Intermittent Low Voltage

P1114 ECT Sensor Circuit Intermittent Low Voltage

P1115 ECT Sensor Circuit Intermittent High Voltage

P1121 TP Sensor Voltage Intermittently High

P1122 TP Sensor Voltage Intermittently Low

P1133 HO2S Insufficient Switching Bank #1, Sensor #1

P1134 HO2S Transition Time Ratio Bank #1, Sensor #1

P1153 HO2S Insufficient Switching Sensor Bank #2, Sensor #1

P1154 HO2S Transition Time Ratio Bank #2, Sensor #1

P1171 Fuel system lean during acceleration

P1200 Injector control circuit

P1222 Injector control circuit intermittent

P1345 Crankshaft/Camshaft (CKP/CMP) Correlation

P1350 Ignition Control (IC) Circuit Malfunction

P1351 Ignition Control (IC) Circuit High Voltage

P1361 Ignition Control (IC) Circuit Not Toggling

P1361 Ignition Control (IC) Circuit Low Voltage

P1374 3X Reference circuit

P1380 Electronic Brake Control Module (EBCM) DTC Detected Rough Road Data Unusable

P1381 Misfire Detected, No EBCM/PCM/VCM Serial Data

P1406 EGR Pintle Position Circuit Fault

P1415 AIR System Bank #1

P1416 AIR System Bank #2

P1441 EVAP Control System Flow During Non-Purge

P1442 EVAP Vacuum Switch Circuit

P1450 Barometric Pressure Sensor Circuit Fault

P1451 Barometric Pressure Sensor Performance

P1460 Cooling Fan Control System Fault

P1500 Starter Signal Circuit Fault

P1510 Back-up Power Supply Fault

P1508 IAC System Low RPM

P1509 IAC System High RPM

P1520 PNP Circuit

P1530 Ignition Timing Adjustment Switch Circuit

P1554 Cruise control status circuit

P1600 PCM Battery Circuit Fault

P1626 Theft Deterrent System Fuel Enable Circuit

P1629 Theft Deterrent Crank Signal Malfunction

P1635 5-Volt Reference "A" Circuit

P1639 5-Volt Reference "B" Circuit

P1641 MIL Control Circuit

P1642 FC Relay 2 and Relay 3 Control Circuit

P1643 Engine Speed Output Circuit

P1651 Fan #1 Relay Control Circuit

P1652 Fan #2 Relay Control Circuit

P1654 A/C Relay Control

P1655 EVAP Purge Solenoid Control Circuit

P1657 Skip Shift Solenoid Control Circuit

P1661 MIL Control Circuit

P1662 Cruise Control Inhibit Control Circuit

P1664 Skip Shift Lamp Control Circuit

P1667 Reverse Inhibit Solenoid Control Circuit

P1672 Low Engine Oil Level Light Control Circuit

Clearing Codes

Stored fault codes may be erased from memory at any time by using a suitable scan tool, or removing power from the PCM for at least 30 seconds. It may be necessary to clear stored codes during diagnosis to check for any recurrence during a test drive, but the stored codes must be written down when retrieved. The codes may still be required for subsequent troubleshooting. Whenever a repair is complete, the stored codes must be erased and the vehicle test driven to confirm correct operation and repair.

❊❊ WARNING

The ignition switch must be OFF any time power is disconnected or restored to the PCM. Severe damage may result if this precaution is not observed.

When using a scan tool to clear the codes, make sure to follow all of the instructions provided by the manufacturer.

Depending on the electrical distribution of the particular vehicle, power to the PCM may be disconnected by removing the PCM fuse in the fuse box, disconnecting the in-line fuse holder near the positive battery terminal or disconnecting the PCM power lead at the battery terminal. Disconnecting the negative battery cable to clear codes is not recommended as this will also clear other memory data in the vehicle such as radio presets.

VACUUM DIAGRAMS

▶ **See Figures 61 thru 73**

Following are vacuum diagrams for most of the engine and emissions package combinations covered by this manual. Because vacuum circuits will vary based on various engine and vehicle options, always refer first to the underhood Vehicle Emission Control Information (VECI) label, if present. Should the label be missing, or should the vehicle be equipped with a different engine from the vehicle's original equipment, refer to the following diagrams for the same or similar configuration.

If you wish to obtain a replacement emissions label, most manufacturers make the labels available for purchase. The labels can usually be ordered from a local dealer.

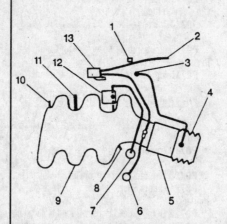

1. EVAP Service Port
2. To EVAP Canister (At Rear of Vehicle)
3. To Rocker Arm Cover
4. Air Intake Duct
5. Throttle Body
6. PCV Valve
7. Fuel Pressure Regulator
8. To Transaxle
9. Intake Manifold
10. To Accessory
11. To Vacuum Brake Booster
12. MAP Sensor
13. EVAP Canister Purge Valve

93174G34

Fig. 61 1997–99 Chevrolet & Buick with 3.1L (VIN M) engine

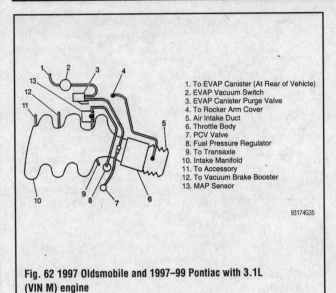

1. To EVAP Canister (At Rear of Vehicle)
2. EVAP Vacuum Switch
3. EVAP Canister Purge Valve
4. To Rocker Arm Cover
5. Air Intake Duct
6. Throttle Body
7. PCV Valve
8. Fuel Pressure Regulator
9. To Transaxle
10. Intake Manifold
11. To Accessory
12. To Vacuum Brake Booster
13. MAP Sensor

93174G35

Fig. 62 1997 Oldsmobile and 1997–99 Pontiac with 3.1L (VIN M) engine

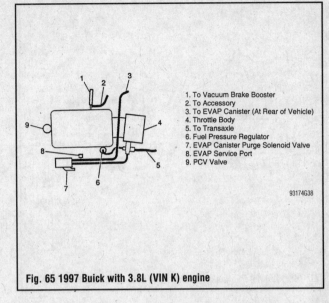

1. To Vacuum Brake Booster
2. To Accessory
3. To EVAP Canister (At Rear of Vehicle)
4. Throttle Body
5. To Transaxle
6. Fuel Pressure Regulator
7. EVAP Canister Purge Solenoid Valve
8. EVAP Service Port
9. PCV Valve

93174G38

Fig. 65 1997 Buick with 3.8L (VIN K) engine

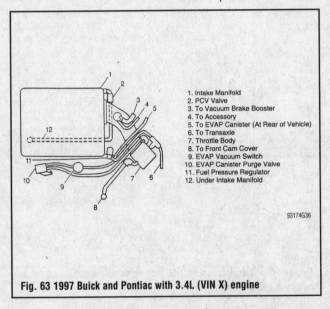

1. Intake Manifold
2. PCV Valve
3. To Vacuum Brake Booster
4. To Accessory
5. To EVAP Canister (At Rear of Vehicle)
6. To Transaxle
7. Throttle Body
8. To Front Cam Cover
9. EVAP Vacuum Switch
10. EVAP Canister Purge Valve
11. Fuel Pressure Regulator
12. Under Intake Manifold

93174G36

Fig. 63 1997 Buick and Pontiac with 3.4L (VIN X) engine

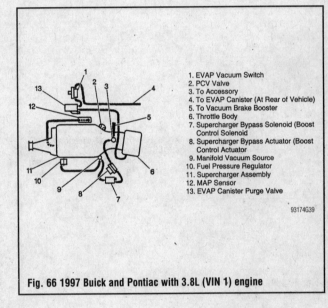

1. EVAP Vacuum Switch
2. PCV Valve
3. To Accessory
4. To EVAP Canister (At Rear of Vehicle)
5. To Vacuum Brake Booster
6. Throttle Body
7. Supercharger Bypass Solenoid (Boost Control Solenoid)
8. Supercharger Bypass Actuator (Boost Control Actuator)
9. Manifold Vacuum Source
10. Fuel Pressure Regulator
11. Supercharger Assembly
12. MAP Sensor
13. EVAP Canister Purge Valve

93174G39

Fig. 66 1997 Buick and Pontiac with 3.8L (VIN 1) engine

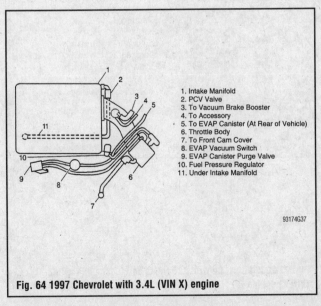

1. Intake Manifold
2. PCV Valve
3. To Vacuum Brake Booster
4. To Accessory
5. To EVAP Canister (At Rear of Vehicle)
6. Throttle Body
7. To Front Cam Cover
8. EVAP Vacuum Switch
9. EVAP Canister Purge Valve
10. Fuel Pressure Regulator
11. Under Intake Manifold

93174G37

Fig. 64 1997 Chevrolet with 3.4L (VIN X) engine

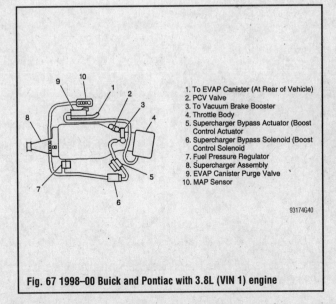

1. To EVAP Canister (At Rear of Vehicle)
2. PCV Valve
3. To Vacuum Brake Booster
4. Throttle Body
5. Supercharger Bypass Actuator (Boost Control Actuator)
6. Supercharger Bypass Solenoid (Boost Control Solenoid)
7. Fuel Pressure Regulator
8. Supercharger Assembly
9. EVAP Canister Purge Valve
10. MAP Sensor

93174G40

Fig. 67 1998–00 Buick and Pontiac with 3.8L (VIN 1) engine

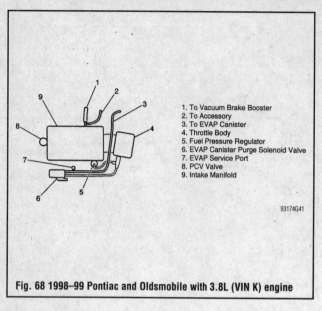

1. To Vacuum Brake Booster
2. To Accessory
3. To EVAP Canister
4. Throttle Body
5. Fuel Pressure Regulator
6. EVAP Canister Purge Solenoid Valve
7. EVAP Service Port
8. PCV Valve
9. Intake Manifold

93174G41

Fig. 68 1998–99 Pontiac and Oldsmobile with 3.8L (VIN K) engine

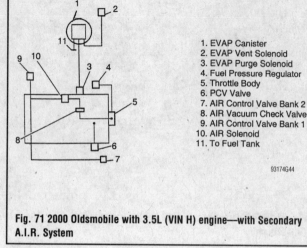

1. EVAP Canister
2. EVAP Vent Solenoid
3. EVAP Purge Solenoid
4. Fuel Pressure Regulator
5. Throttle Body
6. PCV Valve
7. AIR Control Valve Bank 2
8. AIR Vacuum Check Valve
9. AIR Control Valve Bank 1
10. AIR Solenoid
11. To Fuel Tank

93174G44

Fig. 71 2000 Oldsmobile with 3.5L (VIN H) engine—with Secondary A.I.R. System

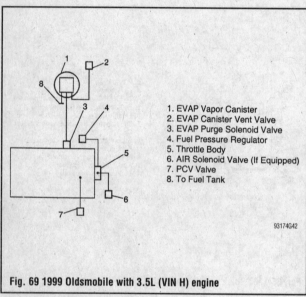

1. EVAP Vapor Canister
2. EVAP Canister Vent Valve
3. EVAP Purge Solenoid Valve
4. Fuel Pressure Regulator
5. Throttle Body
6. AIR Solenoid Valve (If Equipped)
7. PCV Valve
8. To Fuel Tank

93174G42

Fig. 69 1999 Oldsmobile with 3.5L (VIN H) engine

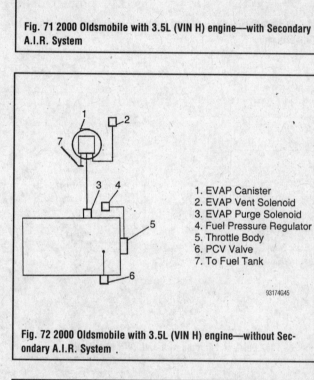

1. EVAP Canister
2. EVAP Vent Solenoid
3. EVAP Purge Solenoid
4. Fuel Pressure Regulator
5. Throttle Body
6. PCV Valve
7. To Fuel Tank

93174G45

Fig. 72 2000 Oldsmobile with 3.5L (VIN H) engine—without Secondary A.I.R. System

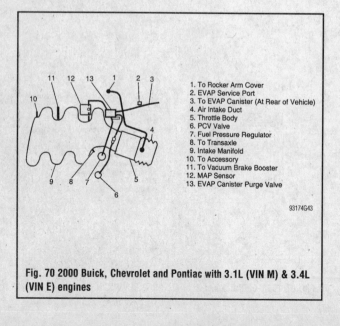

1. To Rocker Arm Cover
2. EVAP Service Port
3. To EVAP Canister (At Rear of Vehicle)
4. Air Intake Duct
5. Throttle Body
6. PCV Valve
7. Fuel Pressure Regulator
8. To Transaxle
9. Intake Manifold
10. To Accessory
11. To Vacuum Brake Booster
12. MAP Sensor
13. EVAP Canister Purge Valve

93174G43

Fig. 70 2000 Buick, Chevrolet and Pontiac with 3.1L (VIN M) & 3.4L (VIN E) engines

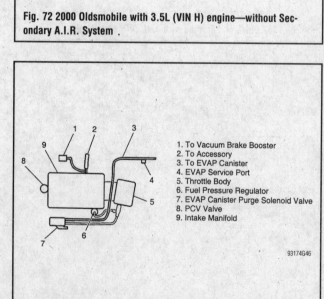

1. To Vacuum Brake Booster
2. To Accessory
3. To EVAP Canister
4. EVAP Service Port
5. Throttle Body
6. Fuel Pressure Regulator
7. EVAP Canister Purge Solenoid Valve
8. PCV Valve
9. Intake Manifold

93174G46

Fig. 73 2000 Buick, Chevrolet, Pontiac and Oldsmobile with 3.8L (VIN K) engine

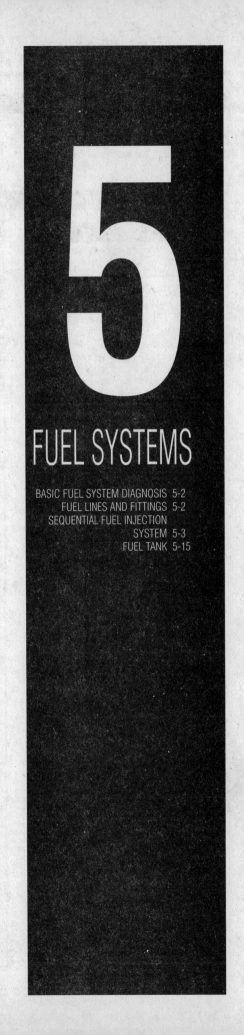

5

FUEL SYSTEMS

BASIC FUEL SYSTEM DIAGNOSIS

When there is a problem starting or driving a vehicle, two of the most important checks involve the ignition and the fuel systems. The questions most technicians attempt to solve first are, "Is there spark?" and "Is there fuel?" Answering these questions often lead to solving many basic problems. For ignition system diagnosis and testing, please see Section 2. If the ignition system checks out and there is a spark at the spark plugs, then you must determine if the fuel system is operating properly and that fuel is getting to the injectors.

FUEL LINES AND FITTINGS

Fuel Lines

DESCRIPTION

Fuel injected vehicles are designed to supply more than an engine needs with the excess being returned to the fuel tank. Your GM W-Body vehicle has both fuel feed and fuel return pipes to carry fuel from the fuel sensor assembly to the fuel injection system and back to the fuel sender assembly.

Many vehicles now use nylon fuel pipes, designed to perform the same job as steel or rubber fuel lines used in older vehicles. Care is required when working around the fuel feed and return pipes. Nylon pipes are constructed to withstand the maximum fuel system pressure, exposure to fuel additives and changes in temperature. Two sizes are used: 5/16 in. for the fuel return and 3/8 in. for the fuel feed.

The fuel feed and fuel return pipes are assembled as a harness. Retaining clips hold the fuel pipes together and provide a means for attaching the fuel pipes to the vehicle. Sections of the fuel pipes that are exposed to chafing, high temperature or vibration are protected with heat resistant rubber hose and/or corrugated plastic conduit. The fuel feed and fuel return pipe connections are sealed with replaceable O-ring seals. These O-ring seals are made of special material and should only be serviced with the correct service part.

Nylon fuel pipes are somewhat flexible and can be formed around gradual turns. However, if forced into sharp bends, nylon pipes will kink and restrict fuel flow. In addition, once exposed to fuel, nylon pipes may become stiffer and are more likely to kink if bent too far. Special care should be taken when working on a vehicle with nylon pipes.

Quick-Connect Fittings

REMOVAL & INSTALLATION

Your GM W-Body vehicle is equipped with Quick-Connect fuel lines. Quick-connect type fittings provide a simplified means of installing and connecting fuel system components. These fittings require some care when handling. Remember that the Sequential Fuel Injection (SFI) system used on these vehicles is a high-pressure system. Normal operating pressure averages around 45 psi, much the same as the water pressure in an average house. Gasoline under pressure like this requires sound, leak-proof fittings to avoid leaks, creating a fire hazard.

Depending on the vehicle model and the system components being connected, there are two types of quick-connect fittings: plastic and metal. Each is used at different locations in the fuel system. Each type of quick-connect fitting consists of a unique female connector and a compatible male fuel pipe end. O-rings, located inside the female connector, provide the fuel seal. Integral locking tabs, or fingers, hold the quick-connect fitting together.

✳✳ CAUTION

To reduce the risk of fire and personal injury, it is necessary to relieve the fuel system pressure before servicing any fuel system component. If this procedure is not performed, fuel may be sprayed out of the connection under pressure. Cover the fuel hose connections with a shop cloth before disconnecting to catch any residual fuel that may still be in the line. Always keep a dry chemical (Class B) fire extinguisher near the work area.

Servicing Plastic Collar Quick Connect Fittings

▶ See Figure 1

1. Disconnect the negative battery cable.
2. Remove the engine cosmetic/acoustic cover (also called the fuel injection sight shield).

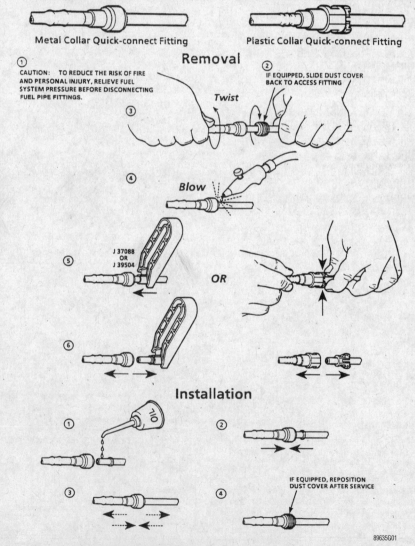

Fig. 1 Two types of fittings are used: metal and plastic. Use care when servicing fittings to maintain system integrity on these high-pressure fuel injection systems

89635G01

3. Relieve the fuel system pressure using the procedures listed later in this section.

4. Grasp both sides of the quick-connect fitting. Twist the quick-connect fitting ¼ turn in each direction to loosen any dirt within the fitting.

5. Repeat for other fuel pipe fitting.

6. Using compressed air, blow out dirt from the quick-connect fittings at both ends.

7. Squeeze the plastic tabs of the male end connector.

8. Pull the connection apart. Repeat for the fitting at the other end of the line, if necessary.

9. Wipe off the male pipe end using a clean shop towel.

10. Inspect and replace components/assemblies as required.

To assemble:

✳✳ CAUTION

To reduce the risk of fire and personal injury, before connecting fuel pipe fittings, always apply a few drops of clean engine oil to the male pipe ends. This will ensure proper reconnection and prevent a possible fuel leak. During normal operation, the O-rings located in the female connector will swell and may prevent proper reconnection if not lubricated.

11. Apply a few drops of clean engine oil to the male pipe end.

12. Push both sides of the quick-connect fitting together causing the retaining tabs/fingers to snap into place.

13. Pull on both sides of the quick-connect fitting to verify the connection is secure.

14. Connect the negative battery cable.

15. Check for leaks using the following procedure:

a. Turn the ignition switch to the **ON** position for 2 seconds, pressurizing the fuel system.

b. Turn the ignition switch to the **OFF** position for 10 seconds.

c. Turn the ignition switch to the **ON** position.

d. Inspect the connection for leaks.

16. Install the engine cosmetic/acoustic cover (fuel injector sight shield).

Servicing Metal Collar Quick Connect Fittings

▶ **See Figure 1**

➡ **This procedure requires a special tool, GM J37088, or equivalent, to release the locking tabs.**

1. Disconnect the negative battery cable.

2. Remove the engine cosmetic/acoustic cover (called the Fuel Injection Sight Shield).

3. Relieve the fuel system pressure using the procedures listed later in this section.

4. Grasp both sides of the quick-connect fitting. Twist the quick-connect fitting ¼ turn in each direction to loosen any dirt within the fitting.

5. Repeat for other fuel pipe fitting.

6. Using shop compressed air, blow out dirt from the quick-connect fittings at both ends.

7. Using special tool J 37088, or equivalent Fuel Line Fitting Service Tool, insert the end of the tool into the female connector, then push forward to release the locking tabs.

8. Pull the connection apart. Repeat for the fitting at the other end of the line, if necessary.

9. Wipe off the male pipe end using a clean

shop towel. If it is necessary to remove rust or burrs from a fuel pipe, use fine emery cloth in a radial motion with the fuel pipe to prevent damage to the O-ring sealing surface.

10. Inspect and replace components/assemblies as required.

To assemble:

✳✳ CAUTION

To reduce the risk of fire and personal injury, before connecting fuel pipe fittings, always apply a few drops of clean engine oil to the make pipe ends. This will ensure proper reconnection and prevent a possible fuel leak. During normal operation, the O-rings located in the female connector will swell and may prevent proper reconnection if not lubricated.

11. Apply a few drops of clean engine oil to the male pipe end.

12. Push both sides of the quick-connect fitting together causing the retaining tabs/fingers to snap into place.

13. Pull on both sides of the quick-connect fitting to verify the connection is secure.

14. Connect the negative battery cable.

15. Check for leaks using the following procedure:

a. Turn the ignition switch to the **ON** position for 2 seconds, pressurizing the fuel system.

b. Turn the ignition switch to the **OFF** position for 10 seconds.

c. Turn the ignition switch to the **ON** position.

d. Inspect the connection for leaks.

16. Install the engine cosmetic/acoustic cover.

SEQUENTIAL FUEL INJECTION SYSTEM

General Information

A number of components make up the fuel injection system. Some meter fuel, others meter air. All must work together for proper engine operation. The major components are discussed here.

FUEL SUPPLY COMPONENTS

▶ **See Figure 2**

Fuel Tank

The fuel tank, naturally enough, is used to store fuel for the vehicle. The tank also houses the fuel pump, the primary fuel strainer and the instrument panel fuel gauge sending unit, all packaged together in one module. The tank is located in the rear of the vehicle and is held in place by two metal straps that are attached to the underbody. The fuel tank is made of steel and is coated internally with a special corrosion inhibitor. Due to the internal coating of the fuel tank, the tank is not repairable. The fuel tank shape includes a reservoir to maintain a constant supply of fuel around the fuel pump strainer during low fuel conditions and aggressive vehicle maneuvers. A fuel tank filler pipe check-ball tube is attached to the fuel tank and extends from the fuel tank inlet to the reservoir. The fuel tank filler pipe check-ball is located inside the fuel tank filler pipe check-ball tube and

prevents fuel from splashing back out of the fuel tank filler pipe during refueling.

The tank is designed as part of a sealed system, to help prevent fuel vapors from entering the atmo-

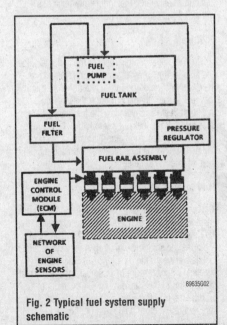

Fig. 2 Typical fuel system supply schematic

89635G02

sphere. The fuel tank cap is an important part of this system. This threaded-type cap requires several turns counterclockwise before it can be removed. A built-in torque limiting device prevents over-tightening. To properly install, turn the cap until at least three clicking noises are heard. The clicking noises signal that the correct torque has been reached and that the fuel tank filler cap is properly seated. This is important. If a fuel tank filler cap requires replacement, use only the correct fuel tank cap. Failure to use the correct cap can result in a serious malfunction of the fuel system. The Enhanced EVAP fuel tank pipe cap may have a tether connected to the fuel filler door. To prevent refueling with leaded gasoline, which will ruin the catalytic converter, the fuel tank filler pipe has a built-in restrictor and deflector.

Fuel Sender/Pump Assembly

▶ **See Figure 3**

The fuel metering system starts with the fuel in the fuel tank. The fuel sender assembly consists of the following major components: a fuel sender, a fuel pump, a fuel pump strainer, a fuel pulse dampener and a roll-over valve. The fuel sender consists of the float, the wire float arm, the rheostat and the roll-over valve. The fuel level is sensed by the position of the float and float arm, which operate the 90 ohm rheostat. As the float position changes, the

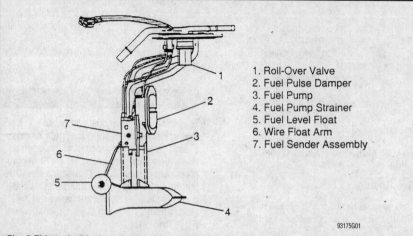

1. Roll-Over Valve
2. Fuel Pulse Damper
3. Fuel Pump
4. Fuel Pump Strainer
5. Fuel Level Float
6. Wire Float Arm
7. Fuel Sender Assembly

93175G01

Fig. 3 This typical fuel sender combines the fuel gauge float and the electric fuel pump in one assembly

amount of current passing through the rheostat varies, sending the signal to the fuel quantity gauge or the Body Control Module (BCM), thus changing the gauge reading on the instrument panel. The roll-over valve is pressed into the EVAP pipe of the fuel sender and is not service separately. The roll-over valve prevents fuel from entering the engine compartment if the vehicle rolls over, by shutting OFF the EVAP pipe to the evaporative emission canister.

A high pressure fuel pump is mounted to the sender. Again, use care ordering replacement parts. Some W-Body vehicles use a roller-vane pump and others use a gerotor fuel pump. Both have the same job, to supply gasoline under high pressure to the system. The fuel is pumped to the engine at a specified flow and pressure. A fuel pressure regulator in the fuel rail keeps fuel available to the injectors at a constant pressure. Excess fuel is returned to the tank by a return pipe. The fuel pump delivers a constant flow of fuel to the engine even during low fuel condition and aggressive vehicle maneuvers. A woven plastic fuel pump strainer is attached to the lower end of the fuel pump. It is designed to filter the fuel and protect the pump from foreign matter. Servicing the in-tank fuel strainer when troubleshooting a low-fuel pressure complaint could prove to be a challenge. On some W-Body vehicles, the fuel module is accessible through an access panel in the trunk floor. On other W-Body models, the fuel tank must be removed to service the fuel sender module assembly. The life of the fuel pump strainer is generally considered to be that of the fuel pump. The fuel pump strainer is self-cleaning and normally requires no maintenance. Fuel stoppage at this point indicates that the fuel tank contains an abnormal amount of sediment or water, in which case the tank should be removed and thoroughly cleaned. If the fuel pump strainer is plugged, replace it with a new one. The fuel pulse dampener is installed between the fuel pump and the fuel sender in order to dampen fuel pulsation and to reduce noise generated by the fuel pump.

A fuel filter is used in the fuel feed pipe ahead of the fuel injection system. The fuel filter is mounted directly in front of the fuel tank, on the underbody. The fuel filter is constructed of steel with a quick-connect fitting at the inlet and a threaded fitting at the outlet. The threaded fitting is sealed with a replaceable O-ring. The filter element is made of paper and is designed to trap particle suspended in the fuel that may damage the injection system. There is no service interval for in-pipe fuel filter replacement. Only change the filter if it is restricted or troubleshooting indicates low fuel pressure.

When the key is first turned **ON**, with the engine **OFF**, the PCM energizes the fuel pump relay for two seconds to quickly build fuel pressure. If the engine is not started within two seconds, the PCM shuts the fuel pump off and waits until the engine is cranked. When the engine is cranked and the RPM signal has been detected by the PCM, the PCM supplies 12 volts to the fuel pump relay to energize the electric in-tank fuel pump. An inoperative fuel pump relay can result in long cranking times, particularly if the engine is cold. An inoperative fuel pump would cause a No-Start condition. A fuel pump which does not provide enough pressure can result in poor performance.

As a back-up system to the fuel pump relay, the fuel pump can also be energized by the engine oil pressure indicator switch. The normally open switch closes when oil pressure reaches about 4 psi. If the fuel pump relay fails, the engine oil indicator switch will close and run the fuel pump.

Fuel Rail

The fuel rail assembly mounts the fuel injectors and also the fuel pressure regulator. It mounts to the lower portion of the intake manifold and distributes fuel to the cylinders through the individual injectors. Fuel is delivered to the fuel inlet tube and goes through the fuel rail to the fuel pressure regulator. The pressure regulator maintains a constant fuel pressure at the fuel injectors. Remaining fuel is then returned to the fuel tank.

Fuel Injectors

The Sequential Multiport Fuel Injection (SFI) fuel injector is a solenoid operated device controlled by the Powertrain Control Module (PCM). The PCM energizes the solenoid which opens a valve to allow fuel delivery onto the director plate. The fuel is injected under pressure in a conical spray pattern at the opening of the intake valve. Excess fuel not used by the injectors passes through the fuel pressure regulator before being returned to the fuel tank. A fuel injector which is stuck partly open will cause

a loss of fuel pressure after engine shut down, causing long crank times to be noticed on some engines.

Fuel Pressure Regulator

The fuel pressure regulator is a diaphragm-operated relief valve with fuel pump pressure on one side and manifold pressure on the other. The function of the fuel pressure regulator is to maintain the fuel pressure available to the fuel injectors at 3 times barometric pressure, adjusted for engine load. The fuel pressure regulator is mounted on the fuel rail and may be serviced separately. If fuel pressure is too low, poor performance and a Diagnostic Trouble Code (DTC) may be set. If the pressure is too high, excessive odor and another DTC may result.

INTAKE AIR METERING COMPONENTS

Throttle Body Unit

The throttle body has a throttle plate to control the amount of air delivered to the engine. The Throttle Position (TP) sensor and Idle Air Control (IAC) valve are mounted on the throttle body. Vacuum ports located behind the throttle plate provide the vacuum signals needed by various components. Engine coolant is directed through a coolant cavity in the throttle body to warm the throttle valve and prevent icing.

Idle Air Control (IAC) Valve

The purpose of the Idle Air Control (IAC) valve is to control engine idle speed, while preventing stalls due to changes in engine load. The IAC valve, mounted in the throttle body, controls bypass air around the throttle plate. By moving a conical valve, known as a pintle, IN (to decrease air flow) or OUT (to increase air flow), a controlled amount of air can move around the throttle plate. If RPM is too low, the PCM will retract the IAC pintle, resulting in more air being bypassed around the throttle plate to increase RPM. If RPM is too high, the PCM will extend the IAC pintle, allowing less air to be bypassed around the throttle plate, decreasing RPM. The IAC pintle moves in small steps, called Counts.

During idle, the proper position of the IAC pintle is calculated by the PCM based on battery voltage, coolant temperature, engine load and engine RPM. If the RPM drops below a specified value, and the throttle plate is closed (TP sensor voltage is between 0.20–0.74), the PCM senses a near stall condition. The PCM will then calculate a new IAC pintle position to prevent stalls.

If the IAC valve is disconnected and reconnected with the engine running, the idle RPM will be wrong. In this case, the IAC has to be reset. The IAC resets when the ignition switch is cycled **ON** then **OFF**. When servicing the IAC, it should only be disconnected or connected with the ignition switch in the **OFF** position to keep from having to reset the IAC.

The position of the IAC pintle affects engine start up and the idle characteristics of the vehicle. If the IAC pintle is open fully, too much air will be allowed into the manifold. This results in high idle speed, along with possible hard starting and a lean air/fuel ratio. DTCs may be set. If the IAC pintle is stuck closed, too little air will be allowed in the manifold. This results in a low idle speed, along with possible hard starting and a rich air/fuel ratio. Another DTC may set. If the IAC pintle is stuck part way open, the idle may be high or low and will not respond to changes in engine load.

Throttle Position (TP) Sensor

The Throttle Position (TP) sensor is mounted on the side of the throttle body opposite the throttle lever. It senses the throttle valve angle and relays that information to the PCM. Knowledge of the throttle angle is needed by the PCM to generate the required injector control signals (pulses). More information on the TP sensor is in @4 Alone:Mass Air Flow (MAF) Sensor

The Mass Air Flow (MAF) sensor is located between the throttle body and air cleaner assembly. The MAF sensor is used to measure the amount of air entering the engine. The PCM uses this information to determine the operating condition of the engine and to control fuel delivery. Refer to Section 4 of this manual for more information on the MAF sensor.

FUEL METERING MODES OF OPERATION

The basic function of the air/fuel metering system is to control air/fuel delivery to the engine. The best air/fuel mixture to minimize exhaust emissions is 14.7 to 1, which allows the catalytic converter to operate most efficiently. Fuel is delivered to the engine by individual fuel injectors mounted in the intake manifold near each intake valve.

The main sensor control is the Heated Oxygen Sensor (HO2S) located in the exhaust manifold. The HO2S tells the Powertrain Control Module (PCM) how much oxygen is in the exhaust gas and the PCM changes the air/fuel ratio to the engine by controlling the fuel injector on time. Because of the constant measuring and adjusting of the air/fuel ratio, the fuel injection system is called a Closed Loop System.

The PCM monitors voltages from several sensors to determine the engine's fuel needs. Fuel is delivered under one of several conditions called modes. All modes are controlled by the PCM and are described here.

Starting Mode

When the ignition is first turned **ON** the PCM energizes the fuel pump relay for two seconds, allowing the fuel pump to build up pressure. The PCM then checks the Engine Coolant Temperature (ECT) sensor and the Throttle Position (TP) sensor. During cranking, the PCM checks the crankshaft and camshaft position signals to determine the proper injector synchronization. The PCM controls the amount of fuel delivered in the starting mode by changing how long the fuel injectors are energized. This is done by pulsing the fuel injectors for very short times.

Clear Flood Mode

If the engine floods, clear it by pushing the accelerator pedal down all the way and then crank the engine. The PCM then de-energizes the fuel injectors. The PCM holds the fuel injectors de-energized as long as the throttle remains above 80% and the engine speed is below 600–800 RPM. If the

throttle position becomes less than 80%, the PCM again begins to pulse the fuel injectors ON and OFF, allowing fuel into the cylinders.

Run Mode

The run mode has two conditions called Open Loop and Closed Loop. When the engine is first started and engine speed is above a predetermined RPM, the system begins in Open Loop operation. In Open Loop, the PCM ignores the signal from the HO2S and calculates the air/fuel ratio based on inputs from the ECT, MAF, MAP and TP sensors. The system remains in Open Loop until the following conditions are met:

• Both HO2S sensors have a varying voltage output, showing that they are hot enough to operate properly (this depends on temperature).

• The ECT is above a specified temperature.

• A specific amount of time has elapsed since starting the engine.

The specific values for the above conditions vary with different engines, and are stored in the Electrically Erasable Programmable Read Only Memory (EEPROM). The system begins Closed Loop operation after reaching these values. In Closed Loop, the PCM calculates the air/fuel ratio based on the signal from various sensors, but mainly the HO2S. This allows the air/fuel ratio to stay very close to 14.7:1 mixture.

Acceleration Mode

When the accelerator is depressed, air flow into the cylinders increases rapidly and the PCM increases the pulse width to the injectors to increase flow. The PCM determines the amount of fuel required based on throttle position, coolant temperature, manifold air pressure, mass air flow and engine speed. The system goes Open Loop.

Deceleration Mode

Deceleration mode indicates that the PCM has detected conditions appropriate to operate in Deceleration Fuel Mode. The PCM will command deceleration fuel mode when a sudden decrease in throttle position has been detected while the vehicle is traveling over 25 mph. While in Deceleration Fuel Mode, the PCM will decrease the amount of fuel delivered by entering Open Loop and decreasing the injector pulse width. When deceleration is very past, the PCM may cut off fuel completely for short periods.

Battery Voltage Correction Mode

When battery voltage is low, the PCM will compensate for the weak spark by:
• Increasing the amount of fuel delivered.
• Increasing the idle RPM.
• Increasing the ignition dwell time.

Fuel Cut Off Mode

The PCM has the ability to shut OFF the fuel injectors completely or selectively when certain conditions are met. The fuel shut off mode allows the powertrain to protect itself from damage and also improve its driveability. The PCM will disable the injectors under the following conditions:
• Ignition **OFF** (prevents engine run-on).
• Ignition **ON** but no ignition reference signal (prevents flooding or backfiring).

• High engine speed (above red line).
• High vehicle speed (above rated tire speed).
• VSS above 106 mph (tire dependent, may vary).

Catalytic Converter Protection Mode

The PCM constantly monitors engine operation and estimates conditions that could result in high catalytic converter temperatures. If the PCM determines the catalytic converter may overheat, it causes the system to return to Open Loop operation and enriches the fuel mixture.

Service Precautions

When working around any part of the fuel system, take precautionary steps to prevent fire and/or explosion:

• Disconnect the battery terminal from the battery (except when testing with battery voltage is required).

• When ever possible, use a flashlight instead of a drop light. Even a few drops of cold fuel on a hot light bulb can cause the bulb to explode and start a fuel flash fire.

• Keep all open flame and smoking material out of the area.

• Use a shop cloth or similar to catch fuel when opening a fuel system.

• Relieve the fuel system pressure before servicing.

• Use eye protection.

• Always keep a dry chemical (Class B) fire extinguisher near the work area.

Relieving Fuel System Pressure

PROCEDURE

▶ **See Figures 4, 5 and 6**

The factory recommended fuel pressure relief procedure requires the use of a hose with a special fitting that threads onto the pressure test port (also called a Schrader Valve and looks similar to a tire valve stem) on the fuel rail. This type of tool usually has a pressure gauge as part of the tool so it can also be used to test the fuel system pressure. Although this special tool is available at automotive tool stores and it is recommended, it may also be possible to use a small screwdriver to depress the valve, allowing the fuel to run out onto a shop cloth. Use care and wear eye protection. The system normally operates at about 45 psi.

✳✳ WARNING

To prevent damaging the electrical systems, make sure the ignition switch is in the OFF position when disconnecting or reconnecting the negative battery cable.

1. Disconnect the negative battery cable to avoid possible fuel discharge if an accidental attempt is made to start the engine.
2. Remove the cosmetic/acoustic engine cover.
3. Loosen the fuel filler cap to relieve the fuel tank vapor pressure.
4. GM recommends their tool J 34730-1A, or equivalent, be used. Attach the tool to the fuel pres-

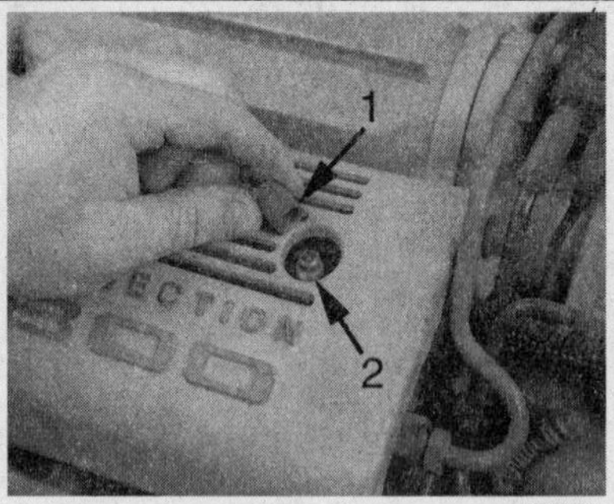

89635P03

Fig. 4 Remove the cap (1) from the fuel rail pressure valve (also called the fuel pressure test port) on the fuel rail

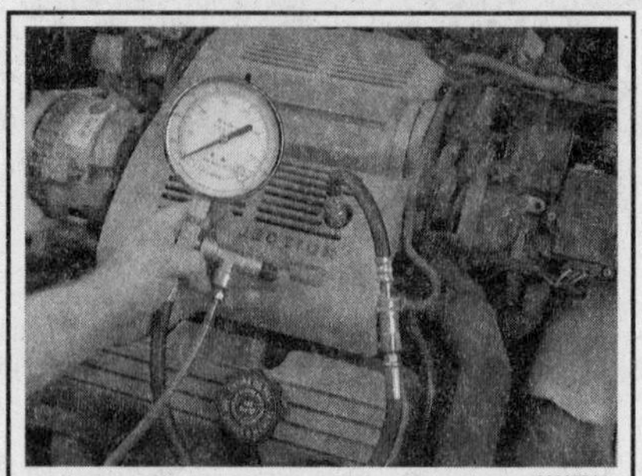

89635P04

Fig. 5 This tool combines a fuel pressure test gauge with the special hose fitting required to connect to the fuel rail pressure valve to relieve the fuel system pressure

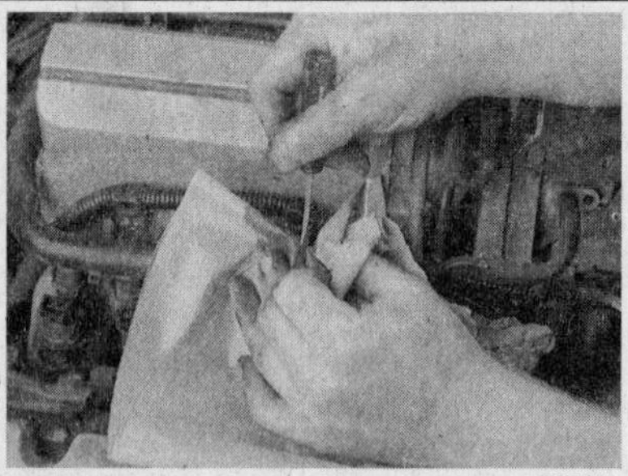

89635P11

Fig. 6 Although a special tool is available, it is possible to use a small screwdriver to depress the fuel pressure connection, to relieve fuel pressure

sure connection. Wrap a shop cloth around the fuel pressure connection while connecting the fuel pressure hose fitting to avoid spillage. This tool has a bleed hose that should be placed in an approved container to catch the fuel the will be expelled when the valve is opened.

5. Open the valve to bleed the fuel system pressure. The fuel connections are now safe for servicing.

6. Drain any fuel remaining in the tool into an approved container.

Electric Fuel Pump

REMOVAL & INSTALLATION

The fuel pump is located inside the fuel tank. It is part of a so-called `fuel pump module' or `fuel sender assembly' which includes the fuel pump, the fuel tank gauge sending unit, the fuel pump strainer and related components. These fuel pump module assemblies are expensive. Be sure of the diagnosis before attempting this procedure to replace a fuel pump.

On some vehicles covered by this manual, the fuel sender assembly can be accessed through a removable panel on the trunk floor. On others, the fuel tank must be removed. The spare tire and trunk carpet have to be removed to expose the trunk floor access panel to see which is the proper procedure to use on your vehicle.

With Trunk Access Panel

See Figure 7

CAUTION

Observe all applicable safety precautions when working around fuel. Whenever servicing the fuel system, always work in a well ventilated area. Do not allow fuel spray or vapors to come in contact with a spark or open flame. Keep a dry chemical fire extinguisher near the work area. Always keep fuel in a container specifically designed for fuel storage; also, always properly seal fuel containers to avoid the possibility of fire or explosion. Wear safety glasses to protect the eyes from fuel splash.

➡Always replace the fuel sender O-rings when reinstalling the fuel sender assembly. Note that the module assembly is spring loaded and it will spring-up when the retaining snapring is removed.

WARNING

When removing the modular fuel sender assembly from the fuel tank, the reservoir bucket on the fuel sender assembly is full of fuel. The sender assembly must be tipped slightly during removal to avoid damage to the float. Place any remaining fuel into an approved container once the sender assembly is removed from the fuel tank.

1. Relieve the fuel system pressure using the procedures found in this section.
2. Disconnect the negative battery cable.
3. Drain the fuel tank to no more than ¼ of a tank full.

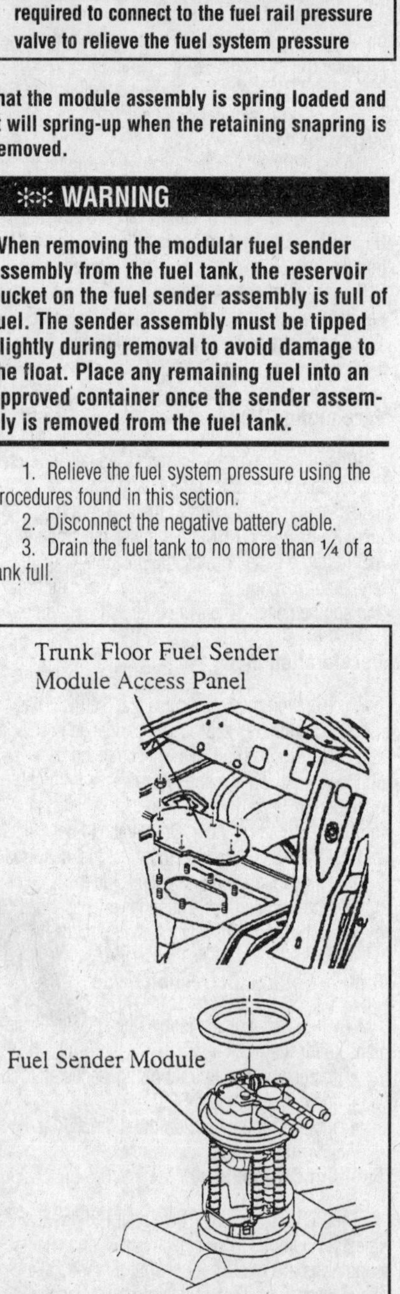

93175G02

Fig. 7 Some vehicles have access panels built into the trunk floor so the fuel pump/sender module can be removed without having to remove the fuel tank

4. Remove the spare tire cover, the jack and the spare tire.
5. Remove the trunk liner.
6. Remove the seven access panel retaining nuts, then lift off the panel.
7. Detach the fuel pump/sender electrical connector.
8. Clean the fuel pipes and the fuel sender assembly to prevent possible fuel contamination during removal.
9. Remove the quick-connect fittings at the fuel sender assembly. Information on servicing these fittings is found earlier in this section.
10. Remove the fuel sender assembly retaining snapring. Expect the sender to spring-up when the snapring is removed.

CAUTION

Do not handle the fuel sender assembly by the fuel pipes. The pipe joints are very fragile. The amount of leverage generated by handling the fuel pipes could damage the joints.

11. Carefully remove the sender assembly. Inspect and clean the O-ring sealing surfaces.

To install:

➡Care should be taken not to fold over or twist the fuel pump strainer when installing the fuel sender assembly as this will restrict fuel flow. Also, make sure that the fuel pump strainer does not block the full travel of the fuel gauge float arm.

12. Position the new fuel sender assembly O-ring on the tank and carefully install the sender assembly into the fuel tank.
13. Install the retaining snapring. Be sure the snapring is fully seated within the tab slots on the fuel tank.
14. Assemble the electrical connector to the sender assembly.
15. Install the quick-connect fittings to the sender assembly.
16. Connect the negative battery cable and install the fuel filler cap.
17. Inspect for leaks using the following procedure:
    a. Turn the ignition switch to the **ON** position for 2 seconds.
    b. Turn the ignition switch to the **ON** position for 10 seconds.
    c. Turn the ignition switch to the **ON** position again.

d. Check for fuel leaks.

18. When satisfied with the fuel sender installation and that connections are secure, install the access cover and the retaining nuts. Snug down the nuts to 96 inch lbs. (10 Nm).

19. Install the trunk liner, spare tire, jack and tire cover.

Without Trunk Access Panel

▶ **See Figure 8**

※ CAUTION

Observe all applicable safety precautions when working around fuel. Whenever servicing the fuel system, always work in a well ventilated area. Do not allow fuel spray or vapors to come in contact with a spark or open flame. Keep a dry chemical fire extinguisher near the work area. Always keep fuel in a container specifically designed for fuel storage; also, always properly seal fuel containers to avoid the possibility of fire or explosion. Wear safety glasses to protect the eyes from fuel splash.

➡ On Oldsmobile models, a special tool, J 35731 Fuel Sender Spanner Wrench is required to disengage the fuel sender assembly. On Chevrolet models, a snapring is usually used to retain the spring-loaded module assembly which will spring-up when the retaining snapring is removed. Always replace the fuel sender O-ring when reinstalling the fuel sender assembly.

※ WARNING

When removing the modular fuel sender assembly from the fuel tank, the reservoir bucket on the fuel sender assembly is full of fuel. The sender assembly must be tipped slightly during removal to avoid damage to the float. Place any remaining fuel into an approved container once the sender assembly is removed from the fuel tank.

1. Relieve the fuel system pressure using the procedures found in this section.

Fuel Sender With Long Fuel Pipes Requires Fuel Tank Removal for Service

93175G03

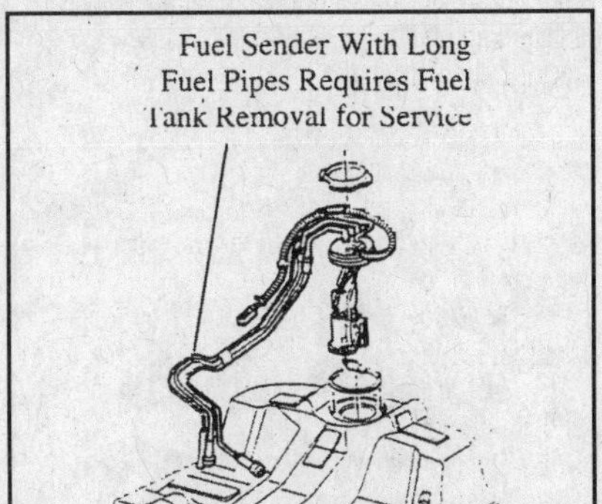

Fig. 8 On applications with extra-long fuel pipes, the fuel tank has to be removed to service the fuel sender module

2. Disconnect the negative battery cable.

3. Drain the fuel tank into a suitable container.

4. Raise and safely support the vehicle.

5. Remove the fuel tank using the procedures found in this section. As the tank is being lowered, clean the fuel pipes and the fuel sender assembly to prevent possible fuel contamination. Remove the quick-connect fittings at the fuel sender assembly. Information on servicing these fittings is found in the section. Detach the electrical connector and with an assistant, lower the fuel tank to the floor.

6. On Oldsmobile vehicles use J-35731 Fuel Sender Spanner Wrench, or equivalent, to remove the fuel sender assembly retaining cam (lock ring). Then remove the sender assembly and O-ring. Discard the O-ring.

7. On Chevrolet vehicles, remove the fuel sender assembly retaining snapring. Expect the sender to spring-up when the snapring is removed.

※ CAUTION

Do not handle the fuel sender assembly by the fuel pipes. The joints are very fragile. The amount of leverage generated by handling the fuel pipes could damage the joints. This is especially true of some Oldsmobile application which use long fuel pipes which are easily damaged.

8. Carefully remove the sender assembly. Inspect and clean the O-ring sealing surfaces.

To install:

9. Care should be taken not to fold over or twist the fuel pump strainer when installing the fuel sender assembly as this will restrict fuel flow. Also, make sure that the fuel pump strainer does not block the full travel of the fuel gauge float arm.

10. Position the new fuel sender assembly O-ring on the tank and carefully install the sender assembly into the fuel tank.

a. On Oldsmobile applications use a suitable fuel sender spanner wrench, to properly tighten the sender assembly retainer cam.

b. On Chevrolet applications, install the retaining snapring. Be sure the snapring is fully seated within the tab slots on the fuel tank.

11. With an assistant, raise the tank and assemble the electrical connector to the sender assembly. Install the quick-connect fittings to the sender assembly. Finish installing the fuel tank using the procedures found in this section. Take care that all insulators and heat shields are in place.

12. Lower the vehicle. Add fuel, connect the negative battery cable and install the fuel filler cap.

13. Inspect for leaks using the following procedure:

a. Turn the ignition switch to the **ON** position for 2 seconds.

b. Turn the ignition switch to the **OFF** position for 10 seconds.

c. Turn the ignition switch to the **ON** position again.

d. Inspect all areas for fuel leaks.

TESTING

When the ignition switch is first turned **ON**, the PCM energizes the fuel pump relay which applies power to the fuel pump. The fuel pump relay will remain ON as long as the engine is running or

cranking and the PCM is receiving reference pulses. If no reference pulses are present, the PCM de-energizes the fuel pump relay within 2 seconds after the ignition is turned **ON** or the engine is stopped. The fuel pump delivers fuel to the fuel rail and injectors, then to the fuel pressure regulator. The fuel pressure regulator controls the fuel pressure by allowing excess fuel to be returned to the fuel tank. With the engine stopped, the fuel pump can be turned ON by using the scan tool output controls function.

An intermittent can be caused by a poor connection, rubbed through wire insulation or a wire broken inside the insulation. Check for a poor connection or a damaged harness, Inspect the PCM harness and connectors for improper mating, broken locks, improperly formed or damaged terminals, poor terminal-to-wire connections and damaged harness.

The fuel pump relay is located in the underhood electrical center.

1. A quick-check is to remove the fuel tank cap. Have an assistant listen at the fuel filler opening while you turn the ignition switch to the **ON** position. Do not crank the engine. The fuel pump should run for two seconds and the assistant should be able to hear the pump run briefly. If no noise is heard, there may be a fault in the pump, relay or wiring.

Pressure Check

1. Locate the fuel pressure test port. It may be necessary to remove the cosmetic/acoustic engine cover to access the test port.

2. Connect a fuel pressure test gauge J-34730-1A, or equivalent, to the fuel pressure connection test port. Wrap a shop cloth around the fuel pressure connection while connecting the fuel pressure hose fitting to avoid spillage. This tool has a bleed hose that should be placed in an approved container to catch the fuel the will be expelled when the valve is opened.

3. Turn the ignition switch to the **ON** position. The fuel pump should run for two seconds. The pressure on the gauge should read 48–55 psi (333–376 kPa).

4. Start the engine and allow to idle. The fuel pressure should drop about 3–10 psi (21–69 kPa). The idle pressure may vary somewhat, depending on barometric pressure. Look for a big drop in fuel pressure, rather than a specific number.

5. If the fuel pressure drops more than a few pounds when you shout the engine **OFF**, there may be a problem in the pump coupling, fuel pressure regulator or the injectors.

6. Before attempting to remove or service any fuel system component, it is necessary to relieve the fuel system pressure, as outlined above.

Throttle Body

The throttle body is part of the air intake system. It is basically a simple butterfly air valve (throttle plate) which controls the amount of air being delivered into the engine. The throttle body also mounts the Idle Air Control (IAC) valve, the Throttle Position (TP) sensor, Mass Air Flow (MAF) sensor on some engines, some vacuum line connections and water connections which heat the throttle body to prevent icing.

REMOVAL & INSTALLATION

▶ **See Figures 9, 10 and 11**

➡**All of the engines covered by this manual use similar procedures for removing the throttle body. Some slight procedure variance (small clips or brackets, etc.) may exist. The following procedure should suffice for all vehicles.**

1. Disconnect the negative battery cable.
2. Drain the cooling system into a suitable container.
3. Remove the air intake tube (runs from the air cleaner to the throttle body).
4. Detach the Idle Air Control (IAC) valve and Throttle Position (TP) sensor electrical connectors. Tag for identification and remove vacuum lines, as necessary.
5. Remove the accelerator control and cruise control cables from the accelerator control cable bracket. Remove the bracket.
6. Disconnect the throttle body coolant by-pass hoses.
7. Remove the heater pipe nut at the throttle body.
8. Remove the nuts and bolts holding the throttle body to the intake manifold and remove the throttle body from the vehicle. On some vehicles (3.8L engine in particular) a wrench should be used the manifold side of the threaded inserts to keep the inserts from rotating in the manifold casting.

✳✳ WARNING

Do not use solvent of any type when cleaning the gasket surfaces on the intake manifold and the throttle body assembly, as damage to the gasket surfaces and the throttle body assembly may result. Take great care not to damage the soft aluminum surfaces when cleaning the gasket surfaces. Sharp tools will damage the sealing surfaces.

To install:

9. Clean all parts well, especially the gasket sealing surfaces on the throttle body and the intake manifold. Inspect the retaining studs and the threaded inserts in the intake manifold, if used. Replace any damaged components as required.
10. Using a new gasket, install the throttle body assembly and tighten the retaining bolts evenly to 19 ft. lbs. (25 Nm).

11. Install all remaining components in the reverse order of removal. It is important that the throttle should operate freely without binding between full closed and wide open throttle. Inspect and check for complete throttle opening and closing positions by operating the accelerator pedal. Also check the carpet fit under the accelerator pedal.

Fuel Rail Assembly

The fuel rail assembly has two sides, to deliver fuel to the injectors on each bank of cylinders. The fuel rail assembly includes the fuel injectors, which are retained by clips to the fuel rail, the fuel pressure regulator and connections for the fuel feed pipe and the fuel return pipe. The fuel rail assembly is installed to the lower half of the intake manifold and the rail must be removed to service the fuel injectors.

✳✳ CAUTION

When servicing any fuel rail component, precautions must be taken to prevent dirt and other contaminates from entering the fuel passages. It is recommended that the fittings be capped and the holes plugged during servicing.

REMOVAL & INSTALLATION

3.1L and 3.4L (VIN E) Engines

▶ **See Figure 12**

If replacing a damaged fuel rail, look for an eight digit identification number stamped on the left side fuel rail. Refer to this number if servicing or part replacement is required.

1. Disconnect the negative battery cable.
2. Relieve the fuel system pressure using the procedures found in this section.
3. Remove the upper intake manifold, as outlined in Section 3 of this manual.
4. Disconnect the engine fuel feed pipe at the fuel rail.
5. Remove the fuel pressure regulator from the fuel rail using the procedures found in this section.
6. Remove the fuel inlet pipe and fuel pressure regulator O-rings and discard.
7. Detach the main injector harness electrical connector.
8. Unplug the ECT sensor harness connector.

9. Remove the fuel rail retaining bolts and gently lift up on the rail assembly to loosen the injector O-rings from the lower intake manifold.
10. Remove and discard the lower O-ring from each injector, taking care to retain the nylon O-ring back-up piece.

To install:

11. Clean all parts well. Care must be taken not to damage or dirty the fuel injector electrical connectors, the fuel injector tips, the O-rings and the inlet and the outlet of the fuel rail. Compressed air must not be used to clean the fuel rail assembly, as this may damage the fuel rail components. The fuel rail must not be immersed in solvent to avoid damage to the fuel rail assembly. Make sure that O-ring back-ups are on the injectors before installing the new O-rings on the injectors. Lubricate the new O-rings with clean engine oil and install on the spray tip end of each injector.
12. Install the fuel rail and injector assembly to the lower intake manifold. Tilt the rail assembly as required to get all of the injectors properly installed. Install the rail attaching bolts and tighten to 84 inch lbs. (10 Nm).
13. Attach the main injector harness connector, as well as the ECT sensor connector.
14. Install new O-rings on the fuel rail inlet line and fuel pressure regulator. Install the fuel feed pipe and tighten the nut to 13 ft. lbs. (17 Nm).
15. Install the fuel pressure regulator using the procedures found in this section.
16. Install the upper intake manifold. Please see Section 3.
17. Connect the negative battery cable.

3.4L (VIN X) Engine

▶ **See Figure 13**

1. Disconnect the negative battery cable.
2. Relieve the fuel system pressure using the procedures found in this section.
3. Remove the upper intake manifold, as outlined in Section 3 of this manual.
4. Disconnect the engine fuel feed and return pipes from the fuel rail tubes by squeezing the tabs and pulling the lines apart.
5. Disconnect the fuel pressure regulator vacuum line.
6. Detach the main injector harness electrical connector.
7. Remove the fuel rail retaining bolts and gently lift up on the rail assembly to loosen the injector O-rings from the lower intake manifold.

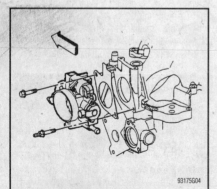

Fig. 9 Typical throttle body arrangement— 3.1L and 3.4L (VIN E) engines

93175G04

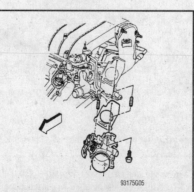

Fig. 10 Exploded view of the throttle body mounting—3.4L (VIN X) engines

93175G05

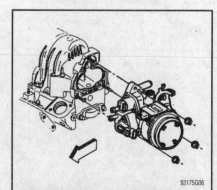

Fig. 11 Typical throttle body arrangement—3.5L (VIN H) and 3.8L engines

93175G06

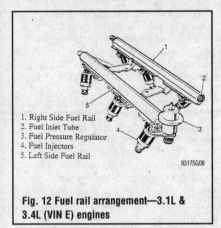

1. Right Side Fuel Rail
2. Fuel Inlet Tube
3. Fuel Pressure Regulator
4. Fuel Injectors
5. Left Side Fuel Rail

93175G08

Fig. 12 Fuel rail arrangement—3.1L & 3.4L (VIN E) engines

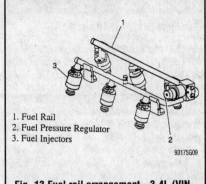

1. Fuel Rail
2. Fuel Pressure Regulator
3. Fuel Injectors

93175G09

Fig. 13 Fuel rail arrangement—3.4L (VIN X) engine

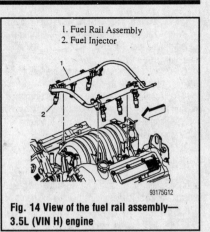

1. Fuel Rail Assembly
2. Fuel Injector

93175G12

Fig. 14 View of the fuel rail assembly—3.5L (VIN H) engine

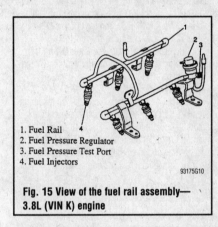

1. Fuel Rail
2. Fuel Pressure Regulator
3. Fuel Pressure Test Port
4. Fuel Injectors

93175G10

Fig. 15 View of the fuel rail assembly—3.8L (VIN K) engine

8. Remove and discard the lower O-ring from each injector, taking care to retain the nylon O-ring back-up piece.

To install:

9. Clean all parts well. Care must be taken not to damage or dirty the fuel injector electrical connectors, the fuel injector tips, the O-rings and the inlet and the outlet of the fuel rail. Compressed air must not be used to clean the fuel rail assembly, as this may damage the fuel rail components. The fuel rail must not be immersed in solvent to avoid damage to the fuel rail assembly. Make sure that O-ring back-ups are on the injectors before installing the new O-rings on the injectors. Lubricate the new O-rings with clean engine oil and install on the spray tip end of each injector.

10. Install the fuel rail and injector assembly to the lower intake manifold. Tilt the rail assembly as required to get all of the injectors properly installed. Install the rail attaching bolts and tighten to 84 inch lbs. (10 Nm).

11. Attach the main injector harness connector and connect the pressure regulator vacuum line.

12. Connect the fuel feed and return lines.

13. Install the upper intake manifold. Please see Section 3.

14. Connect the negative battery cable.

3.5L (VIN H) Engine

▶ **See Figure 14**

1. Disconnect the negative battery cable.
2. Relieve the fuel system pressure using the procedures found in this section.
3. Clean the fuel rail assembly and connections.
4. Disconnect the engine fuel feed pipe quick connect fitting from the fuel rail tubes by squeezing the tabs and pulling the lines apart.
5. Disconnect the return fuel pipe quick connect fitting from the fuel rail.
6. Disconnect the vacuum lines to the fuel pressure regulator, the PCV valve and the throttle body.
7. Remove the snap bracket on the throttle body coolant hose.
8. Remove the engine electrical harness bolts on the camshaft covers.
9. Tag for identification, then detach the injector harness electrical connectors.
10. Release the four snap locking tabs on the fuel rail assembly by pushing toward the camshaft covers and lifting.

11. Remove the fuel rail by gently lifting up to loosen the injector O-rings from the lower intake manifold. Work with equal force on both sides of the fuel rail to avoid bending the fuel rail.

To install:

12. Clean all parts well. Care must be taken not to damage or dirty the fuel injector electrical connectors, the fuel injector tips, the O-rings and the inlet and the outlet of the fuel rail. Compressed air must not be used to clean the fuel rail assembly, as this may damage the fuel rail components. The fuel rail must not be immersed in solvent to avoid damage to the fuel rail assembly. Make sure that O-ring back-ups are on the injectors before installing the new O-rings on the injectors. Lubricate the new O-rings with clean engine oil and install on the spray tip end of each injector.

13. Install the fuel rail and injector assembly onto the lower intake manifold. A snap will be heard when the injectors are properly seated.

14. Using the identification tags made at removal, attach the electrical connectors to the fuel injectors. Install the harness bolts on the camshaft covers. Tighten to 80 inch lbs. (9 Nm).

15. Install the snap bracket on the throttle body coolant tube.

16. Connect the vacuum hoses to the throttle body, the PCV valve and the fuel pressure regulator.

17. Connect the fuel return pipe and fuel feed pipe to their quick-connect fittings using the procedures found in this section.

18. Connect the negative battery cable.

3.8L (VIN K) Engine

▶ **See Figure 15**

1. Disconnect the negative battery cable.
2. Relieve the fuel system pressure using the procedures found in this section.
3. Clean the fuel rail assembly and connections.
4. Disconnect the engine fuel feed and return pipes from the fuel rail tubes by squeezing the tabs and pulling the lines apart.
5. Disconnect the vacuum lines to the fuel pressure regulator and the throttle body.
6. Detach the ignition coil wires.
7. Tag for identification, then detach the injector harness electrical connectors.
8. Remove the fuel rail retaining bolts and gently lift up on the rail assembly to loosen the injector O-rings from the lower intake manifold. Work with equal force on both sides of the fuel rail to avoid bending the fuel rail.

9. Remove and discard the lower O-ring from each injector, taking care to retain the nylon O-ring back-up piece.

To install:

10. Clean all parts well. Care must be taken not to damage or dirty the fuel injector electrical connectors, the fuel injector tips, the O-rings and the inlet and the outlet of the fuel rail. Compressed air must not be used to clean the fuel rail assembly, as this may damage the fuel rail components. The fuel rail must not be immersed in solvent to avoid damage to the fuel rail assembly. Make sure that O-ring back-ups are on the injectors before installing the new O-rings on the injectors. Lubricate the new O-rings with clean engine oil and install on the spray tip end of each injector.

11. Install the fuel rail and injector assembly to the lower intake manifold. Seat the fuel injectors by hand. Install the rail attaching bolts and tighten to 84 inch lbs. (10 Nm).

12. Using the identification tags made at removal, attach the electrical connectors to the fuel injectors.

13. Connect the fuel feed and return lines to the fuel rail.

14. Connect the vacuum lines to the pressure regulator vacuum line and the throttle body.

15. Install the ignition coil wires.

16. Connect the negative battery cable.

3.8L (VIN 1) Engine

▶ **See Figure 16**

1. Disconnect the negative battery cable.
2. Relieve the fuel system pressure using the procedures found in this section.

3. Clean the fuel rail assembly and connections.

4. Disconnect the engine fuel feed and return pipes from the fuel rail tubes by squeezing the tabs and pulling the lines apart.

5. Detach the vacuum lines from the fuel pressure regulator and the throttle body.

6. Disconnect the ignition coil wires from the coil and retainer clips on top of the supercharger.

7. Remove the alternator and rear bracket. Please see Section 2.

8. Remove the supercharger bypass valve actuator.

9. Tag for identification, then detach the injector harness electrical connectors. Remove the fuel injector electrical harness clips holding the harness to the front of the fuel rail.

10. Remove the fuel rail retaining fasteners (4 bolts, 1 stud) and gently lift up on the rail assembly to loosen the injector O-rings from the lower intake manifold. Work with equal force on both sides of the fuel rail to avoid bending the fuel rail.

11. Remove and discard the lower O-ring from each injector, taking care to retain the nylon O-ring back-up piece.

To install:

12. Clean all parts well. Care must be taken not to damage or dirty the fuel injector electrical connectors, the fuel injector tips, the O-rings and the inlet and the outlet of the fuel rail. Compressed air must not be used to clean the fuel rail assembly, as this may damage the fuel rail components. The fuel rail must not be immersed in solvent to avoid damage to the fuel rail assembly. Make sure that O-ring back-ups are on the injectors before installing the new O-rings on the injectors. Lubricate the new O-rings with clean engine oil and install on the spray tip end of each injector.

13. Install the fuel rail and injector assembly to the lower intake manifold. Seat the fuel injectors by hand. Install the rail attaching bolts and tighten to 84 inch lbs. (10 Nm). Tighten the stud to 18 ft. lbs. (25 Nm).

14. Install the supercharger bypass valve actuator.

15. Install the alternator and rear bracket. Please see Section 2.

16. Using the identification tags made at removal, attach the electrical connectors to the fuel injectors. Install the harness clips to the font of the fuel rail.

17. Install the ignition coil wires to the coil and to the retainer clips on top of the supercharger.

18. Connect the fuel feed and return lines to the fuel rail.

19. Connect the vacuum lines to the pressure regulator vacuum line and the throttle body.

20. Connect the negative battery cable.

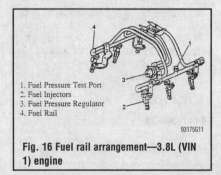

1. Fuel Pressure Test Port
2. Fuel Injectors
3. Fuel Pressure Regulator
4. Fuel Rail

93175G11

Fig. 16 Fuel rail arrangement—3.8L (VIN 1) engine

Fuel Injectors

▶ See Figures 17, 18, 19 and 20

The fuel injectors used on these Sequential Multiport Fuel Injection (SFI) systems are solenoid operated devices controlled by the PCM. The PCM energizes the solenoid which opens a valve to allow fuel delivery. The fuel is injected under pressure in a cone-shaped spray pattern at the opening of the intake valve. Excess fuel not used by the injectors passes through the fuel pressure regulator before being returned to the fuel tank.

A fuel injector which is stuck partially open will cause a loss of fuel pressure after engine shut down, causing long crank times to be noticed on some engines. Excess fuel can also cause dilution of the engine lubricating oil.

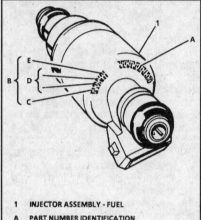

1	INJECTOR ASSEMBLY - FUEL	
A	PART NUMBER IDENTIFICATION	
B	BUILD DATE CODE	
C	MONTH 1-9 (JAN-SEPT) O, N, D (OCT, NOV, DEC)	
D	DAY	
E	YEAR	

89635G14

Fig. 17 Refer to the part number inscribed on the injector to make sure you get the correct part

The fuel injectors are mounted in components known as fuel rails. The injectors press into the fuel rail, are sealed by O-rings and secured by simple clips.

Use care when removing the fuel injectors to prevent damage to the electrical connector pins on the injector. The fuel injector is serviced as a complete assembly only and should not be immersed in any kind of cleaner. Support the fuel rail to avoid damaging any components while removing the injectors. Note too, that different injectors have different calibration, or flow rates. When ordering new fuel injectors, be sure to order the identical part number that is inscribed on the old injector.

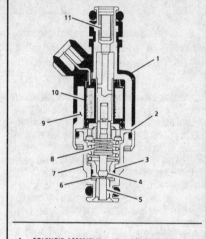

1	SOLENOID ASSEMBLY	7	HOUSING - SPRAY
2	SPACER AND GUIDE ASSEMBLY	8	SPRING - CORE
3	CORE SEAT	9	HOUSING - SOLENOID
4	VALVE - BALL	10	SOLENOID
5	SPRAY TIP	11	FILTER - FUEL INLET
6	PLATE - DIRECTOR		

88005G30

Fig. 19 Cross-section of a typical fuel injector

1. Retaining Clip
2. Upper O-ring
3. Fuel Injector Body
4. Lower O-ring

Fuel Injector

Part Number Identification

25166922

93175G07

Fig. 18 Another form of fuel injector identification

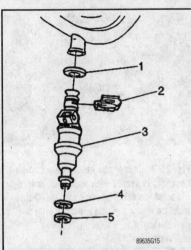

Fig. 20 Fuel injector components: upper O-ring (1), retaining clip (2), fuel injector body (3), back-up ring (4) and lower O-ring (5)

On a sequential injected engine, as are all of the engines covered by the manual, it is most important not to mix up the injector connectors. The electrical connectors MUST be installed on the proper injector. Tag for identification all electrical connectors before detaching.

TESTING

▶ See Figures 21 and 22

The injectors can be tested by installing a "noid light," (a headlamp bulb may work) into the injector electrical connector, which confirms voltage when the light flashes.

1. Start the engine and listen to each fuel injector individually for a clicking sound.
2. Turn the engine **OFF** and detach the electrical connector from the injector(s) that did not have a clicking sound.
3. Check the injector for continuity across the terminals. Compare the resistance value to a known good injector. The readings should be similar, if so proceed to the next step. If readings differ greatly, replace the injector.
4. Check between each injector terminal and ground. If continuity exists, replace the injector.
5. Detach the fuel injector connector and con-

nect a noid light to the wiring harness connector. Crank the engine, while watching the light. Perform this test on at least two injectors before proceeding. If the light does not flash, check the injector power supply and ground control circuitry. If the light flashes proceed to the next step.

6. If the light flashes, remove the fuel rail from the engine and following the procedure below check the injector operation:

   a. Using mechanic's wire, secure the injector to the fuel rail.

   b. Place a clear plastic container around each injector.

✳✳ CAUTION

Prior to performing this test, all fuel safety precautions must be followed. Make certain the container is approved to handle fuel and is securely positioned around the injector. Do NOT use a glass container. Glass containers can be easily damaged, resulting in a serious fire hazard.

   c. With the help of an assistant or using a remote starter button, crank the engine for 15 seconds while observing the injector operation. The injector should produce a cone shaped spray pattern and all containers should retain equal amounts of fuel.

   d. Once the cranking test is complete, leave the fuel rail pressurized and observe the injectors for leakage.

7. Replace any injector which is leaking or fails to provide a cone shaped spray pattern when energized.

REMOVAL & INSTALLATION

The fuel rail must be removed to service the fuel injectors.

✳✳ CAUTION

To reduce the risk of fire and personal injury that may result from a fuel leak, always install the fuel injector O-rings in the proper position. If the upper and lower O-rings are different colors (black and brown), be sure to install the black O-ring in the upper position and the brown O-ring in the lower position on the fuel injector. The O-rings are the same size but are made of different materials. The fuel injector lower O-ring uses a

nylon collar, called the O-ring Back-up, to properly position the O-ring on the fuel injector. Be sure to reinstall the O-ring back-up or the sealing O-ring may move out of position on the injector at installation. If the sealing O-ring is not seated properly, a vacuum leak is possible and driveability problems may occur.

➡When servicing the fuel rail and injector assembly, precautions must be taken to prevent dirt and other contaminants from entering the fuel passages. It is recommended that all areas around fuel fittings be cleaned before disassembly and when disassembled, the fittings be capped and the holes plugged during servicing.

3.1L and 3.4L (VIN E & X) Engines

▶ See Figures 23 thru 28

1. Disconnect the negative battery cable.
2. Relieve the fuel system pressure using the procedures found in this section.
3. Remove the fuel rail as outlined earlier in this section and place on a suitable workbench.
4. On a clean work surface, remove each injector O-ring seal from the spray tip end of each injector. Discard the seals. Fuel injector O-rings should always be replaced whenever fuel injectors are serviced. With the O-ring removed, the nylon O-ring back-up may slip off the injector. Be sure to retain the O-ring back-up for reuse

✳✳ WARNING

Use care when removing the fuel injectors to prevent damage to the small electrical connector pins or the fuel injection nozzles. Do not immerse the fuel injector in any type of cleaner. The fuel injector is an electrical component and may be damaged by this cleaning method. The fuel injector is serviced as a complete assembly only. If the fuel injectors are found to be leaking, the engine oil may be contaminated with fuel.

5. Remove the fuel injector retaining clips and remove the injectors by simply pulling out of the fuel rail.

   To install:

6. Clean all parts well. Fuel injector O-rings should always be replaced whenever the fuel injectors are serviced. Use the following procedure:

Fig. 21 Detach the fuel injector electrical connector . . .

Fig. 22 . . . then use an ohmmeter to check injector resistance. Compare with specifications from a known good injector

Fig. 23 Detach the fuel injector electrical connector

Fig. 24 The fuel injectors are usually retained to the fuel rail by a small clip

Fig. 25 With the retainer removed, the fuel injector can simply be pulled from the fuel rail

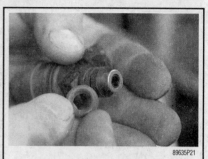

Fig. 26 Whenever any fuel system component that is sealed with an O-ring, including a fuel injector, is removed, the O-ring must be discarded and replaced with a new O-ring. The top O-ring is being removed here

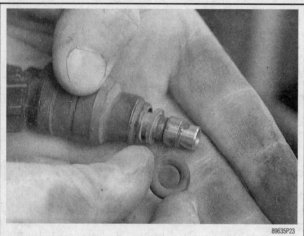

Fig. 27 There is an O-ring and a nylon O-ring back-up piece used on the bottom of the injector. Discard the O-ring but retain the nylon O-ring back-up piece

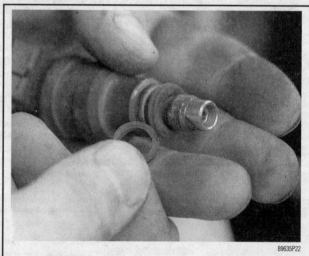

Fig. 28 Retain the nylon O-ring back-up piece, but install new O-rings at assembly

a. Coat all O-rings with clean engine oil before installing.

b. Install the fuel injector nylon O-ring back-up ring first, then install the lower O-ring.

c. Install the fuel injector upper O-ring.

7. Install the fuel injector to the fuel rail. When seated, install the retaining clip. Repeat for each injector that was removed.

8. Install the fuel rail with the injectors attached, as outlined earlier in this section.

9. Connect the negative battery cable.

10. Inspect for leaks using the following procedure:

a. Turn the ignition switch to the **ON** position for 2 seconds.

b. Turn the ignition switch to the **OFF** position for 10 seconds.

c. Turn the ignition switch to the **ON** position again.

d. Inspect all areas for fuel leaks.

3.5L (VIN H) Engine

▶ See Figures 23 thru 28

1. Disconnect the negative battery cable.

2. Relieve the fuel system pressure using the procedures found in this section.

3. Tag for identification and detach the electrical connectors from the fuel injectors.

4. Disconnect the fuel pressure regulator vacuum hose from the fuel pressure regulator.

5. Remove the PCV valve hose and the throttle body port hose.

6. Remove the wiring harness bolt and harness.

➡It may be necessary to remove the fuel rail from the intake manifold to allow increased fuel rail movement for fuel injector access.

7. Release the fuel rail-to-intake manifold locking tab by pushing away toward the center of the intake manifold.

8. Remove the fuel injector up out of the intake manifold. GM recommends using tool J 43013 which is basically a small prying tool with a tapered end and a semi-circular cutout to accommodate the fuel injector. It is designed to fit between the bottom of the injector and the intake manifold, so the injector can be gently levered out of the lower intake manifold. Use care if using substitutes.

➡It may be necessary to release the adjacent injectors from the intake manifold to allow

increased fuel rail movement for injector access.

9. Spread the injector retainer clip to release the injector from the fuel rail. Remove and discard the O-rings. They must be replaced with new seals.

To install:

✳✳ CAUTION

To reduce the risk of fire and personal injury that may result from a fuel leak, always install the fuel injector O-rings in the proper position. If the upper and lower O-ring are different colors (black and brown), be sure to install the black O-rings in the upper position and the brown O-ring in the lower position on the fuel injector. The O-rings are the same size but are made of different materials. The fuel injector O-rings should always be replaced whenever fuel injectors are serviced.

10. Lubricate the new upper and lower O-rings with clean engine oil.

11. Install the new upper and lower O-rings on the fuel injector.

12. Install the fuel injector(s) onto the fuel rail.

Make sure the injectors are aligned properly with the electrical connector in the correct orientation. Push in the retainer clip(s) far enough to engage the retainer clip with the machined slots on the rail socket.

13. Snap the fuel rail down onto the intake manifold.

14. Connect the fuel injector harness to the injectors using care to get the connectors on their proper injector. Install the wiring harness hold down bolt.

15. Connect the throttle body, PCV hose and fuel pressure regulator vacuum hoses.

16. Connect the negative battery cable.

17. Inspect for leaks using the following procedure:

    a. Turn the ignition switch to the **ON** position for 2 seconds.

    b. Turn the ignition switch to the **OFF** position for 10 seconds.

    c. Turn the ignition switch to the **ON** position again.

    d. Inspect all areas for fuel leaks.

3.8L (VIN K) Engine

▶ See Figures 23 thru 28

1. Disconnect the negative battery cable.

2. Remove the cosmetic/acoustic engine cover.

3. Relieve the fuel system pressure using the procedures found in this section.

4. Clean the fuel rail assembly and connections.

5. Remove the fuel rail as outlined earlier in this section.

6. On a clean work surface, remove each injector O-ring seal from the spray tip end of each injector. Discard the seals. Fuel injector O-rings should always be replaced whenever fuel injectors are serviced. With the O-ring removed, the nylon O-ring back-up may slip off the injector. Be sure to retain the O-ring back-up for reuse

7. Use care when removing the fuel injectors to prevent damage to the small electrical connector pins or the fuel injection nozzles. Do not immerse the fuel injector in any type of cleaner. The fuel injector is an electrical component and may be damaged by this cleaning method. The fuel injector is serviced as a complete assembly only. If the fuel injectors are found to be leaking, the engine oil may be contaminated with fuel.

8. Remove the fuel injector retaining clips and remove the injectors by simply pulling out of the fuel rail.

To install:

9. Clean all parts well. Fuel injector O-rings should always be replaced whenever the fuel injectors are serviced. Use the following procedure:

    a. Coat all O-rings with clean engine oil before installing.

    b. Install the fuel injector nylon O-ring back-up ring first, then install the lower O-ring (brown).

    c. Install the fuel injector upper O-ring (black).

10. Install the fuel injectors to the fuel rail.

11. Assemble the fuel rail with the fuel injectors to the lower intake manifold. Seat the fuel injectors by hand. Install the fuel rail as outline earlier in this section.

12. Connect the negative battery cable.

13. Inspect for leaks using the following procedure:

    a. Turn the ignition switch to the **ON** position for 2 seconds.

    b. Turn the ignition switch to the **OFF** position for 10 seconds.

    c. Turn the ignition switch to the **ON** position again.

    d. Inspect all areas for fuel leaks.

3.8L (VIN 1) Engine

▶ See Figures 23 thru 28

1. Disconnect the negative battery cable.

2. Remove the cosmetic/acoustic engine cover.

3. Relieve the fuel system pressure using the procedures found in this section.

4. Clean the fuel rail assembly and connections.

5. Remove the fuel rail, as outlined earlier in this section.

6. On a clean work surface, remove each injector O-ring seal from the spray tip end of each injector. Discard the seals. Fuel injector O-rings should always be replaced whenever fuel injectors are serviced. With the O-ring removed, the nylon O-ring back-up may slip off the injector. Be sure to retain the O-ring back-up for reuse

7. Use care when removing the fuel injectors to prevent damage to the small electrical connector pins or the fuel injection nozzles. Do not immerse the fuel injector in any type of cleaner. The fuel injector is an electrical component and may be damaged by this cleaning method. The fuel injector is serviced as a complete assembly only. If the fuel injectors are found to be leaking, the engine oil may be contaminated with fuel.

8. Remove the fuel injector retaining clips and remove the injectors by simply pulling out of the fuel rail.

To install:

9. Clean all parts well. Fuel injector O-rings should always be replaced whenever the fuel injectors are serviced. Use the following procedure:

    a. Coat all O-rings with clean engine oil before installing.

    b. Install the fuel injector nylon O-ring back-up ring first, then install the lower O-ring (brown).

    c. Install the fuel injector upper O-ring (black).

10. Install the fuel injectors to the fuel rail.

11. Assemble the fuel rail with the fuel injectors to the lower intake manifold. Seat the fuel injectors by hand. Install the fuel rail, as outlined earlier in this section.

12. Connect the negative battery cable.

13. Inspect for leaks using the following procedure:

    a. Turn the ignition switch to the **ON** position for 2 seconds.

    b. Turn the ignition switch to the **OFF** position for 10 seconds.

    c. Turn the ignition switch to the **ON** position again.

    d. Inspect all areas for fuel leaks.

Fuel Pressure Regulator

▶ See Figure 29

The fuel pressure regulator is a diaphragm-operated relief valve with fuel pump pressure on one side and regulator spring pressure and intake manifold vacuum on the other side. The regulator's function is to maintain a constant fuel pressure across the injectors at all times. The pressure regulator compensates for engine load by increasing fuel pressure as engine vacuum drops.

The fuel pressure regulator is serviced as a separate component. When servicing the pressure regulator, make sure that the O-ring back-up, large O-ring, filter screen and small O-ring are properly positioned on the pressure regulator.

REMOVAL & INSTALLATION

The need to work as cleanly as possible cannot be over-emphasized. Even the smallest amount of dirt, if allowed into the fuel pressure regulator and/or the fuel rail, will find its way to the fuel injectors. The nozzle openings of the injectors are very small. Keep hands and tools clean. Clean the areas to be disconnected with a suitable solvent. Carefully cover open fittings and connections to keep out foreign material. Dirt in the injectors almost guarantees a clogged fuel injector and engine performance problems.

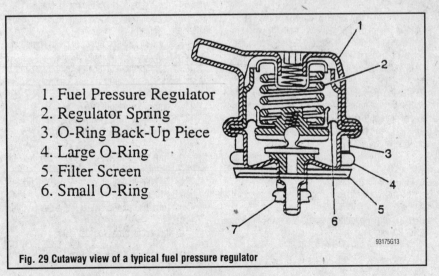

1. Fuel Pressure Regulator
2. Regulator Spring
3. O-Ring Back-Up Piece
4. Large O-Ring
5. Filter Screen
6. Small O-Ring

93175G13

Fig. 29 Cutaway view of a typical fuel pressure regulator

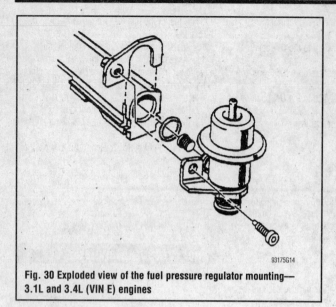

Fig. 30 Exploded view of the fuel pressure regulator mounting—3.1L and 3.4L (VIN E) engines

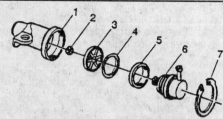

1. Fuel Pressure Regulator Housing
2. Regulator Small O-Ring
3. Fuel Filter Screen
4. Regulator Large O-Ring
5. O-Ring Back-Up Piece
6. Fuel Pressure Regulator
7. Snap Ring

Fig. 31 Exploded view of the fuel pressure regulator—3.4L (VIN X) engine shown, 3.8L engines similar

3.1L and 3.4L (VIN E) Engines

♦ See Figure 30

1. Disconnect the negative battery cable.
2. Relieve the fuel system pressure using the procedures found in this section.
3. Remove the upper intake manifold assembly. Please see Section 3.
4. Disconnect the vacuum line from the pressure regulator.
5. Remove the regulator retaining screw and remove the retainer bracket. Using a clean shop cloth to catch fuel spillage, carefully pull the regulator from the fuel rail. Twist the regulator slightly while removing to ease removal. Discard the O-ring.

To install:

6. Clean all parts well. DO NOT use shop compressed air to test or clean a fuel pressure regulator. Clean the fuel pressure regulator screen, if necessary. DO NOT immerse the fuel pressure regulator in a solvent bath or it will be damaged.
7. If the filter screen has been contaminated, it should be removed and the pressure regulator replaced.
8. Lubricate a new pressure regulator O-ring with clean engine oil and install on the regulator inlet.
9. Install the fuel return pipe to the regulator.
10. Install a new retainer and spacer bracket into the slot on the fuel rail and install the pressure regulator to the fuel rail. Tighten the fuel return line nut to 13 ft. lbs. (17 Nm).
11. Connect the vacuum line to the pressure regulator and install the retainer screw. Tighten to 76 inch lbs. (8.5 Nm).
12. Inspect and verify that the retainer and spacer bracket is engaged in the slots in the fuel rail. Grasp and pull on the regulator to ensure that it is properly seated.
13. Install the upper intake manifold. Please see Section 3.
14. Connect the negative battery cable.
15. Inspect for leaks using the following procedure:

   a. Turn the ignition switch to the **ON** position for 2 seconds.

   b. Turn the ignition switch to the **OFF** position for 10 seconds.

   c. Turn the ignition switch to the **ON** position again.

   d. Inspect all areas for fuel leaks.

3.4L (VIN X) Engine

♦ See Figure 31

1. Disconnect the negative battery cable.
2. Relieve the fuel system pressure using the procedures found in this section.
3. Remove the upper intake manifold. Please see Section 3.
4. Clean any dirt from the fuel pressure regulator retaining ring, and disconnect the vacuum hose.
5. Remove the snapring.
6. Place a clean shop cloth under the fuel pressure regulator to catch spillage. Lift and twist the pressure regulator to pull it from its housing.
7. Remove and discard the O-rings. Save the back-up ring

To install:

8. Clean all parts well. Clean the fuel pressure regulator filter screen. Do not immerse the fuel pressure regulator in a solvent bath to prevent damage to the regulator.
9. Lubricate new O-rings with clean engine oil and install the O-rings on the regulator.
10. Assemble the regulator to its housing and install the snapring. Verify that the snapring is properly seated.
11. Connect the vacuum line.
12. Connect the negative battery cable.
13. Inspect for leaks using the following procedure:

   a. Turn the ignition switch to the **ON** position for 2 seconds.

   b. Turn the ignition switch to the **OFF** position for 10 seconds.

   c. Turn the ignition switch to the **ON** position again.

   d. Inspect all areas for fuel leaks.

3.5L (VIN H) Engine

♦ See Figure 32

1. Disconnect the negative battery cable.
2. Relieve the fuel system pressure using the procedures found in this section.
3. Disconnect the pressure regulator vacuum hose.
4. Remove the regulator assembly retainer clip.
5. Lift and twist the fuel pressure regulator and pull it from its housing. Use a clean shop cloth to catch fuel spillage.
6. Remove and discard the regulator lower O-ring.
7. Remove the regulator assembly filter.
8. Remove and discard the regulator upper O-ring and back-up ring.

To install:

9. Clean all parts well. Clean the fuel pressure regulator filter screen. Do not immerse the fuel pressure regulator in a solvent bath to prevent damage to the regulator.
10. Lubricate new O-rings with clean engine oil and install the O-rings on the regulator.
11. Assemble the regulator to its housing and install the retainer clip.
12. Connect the vacuum line.
13. Connect the negative battery cable.
14. Inspect for leaks using the following procedure:

   a. Turn the ignition switch to the **ON** position for 2 seconds.

   b. Turn the ignition switch to the **OFF** position for 10 seconds.

   c. Turn the ignition switch to the **ON** position again.

   d. Inspect all areas for fuel leaks.

3.8L Engines

♦ See Figure 31

1. Disconnect the negative battery cable.
2. Relieve the fuel system pressure using the procedures found in this section.

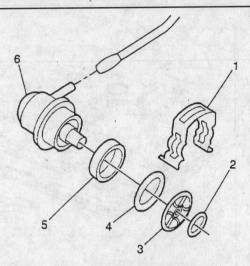

1. Regulator Assembly Retainer Clip
2. Regulator Small O-Ring
3. Regulator Assembly Filter
4. Regulator Large O-Ring
5. O-Ring Back-Up Piece
6. Fuel Pressure Regulator

93175G16

Fig. 32 Fuel pressure regulator mounting—3.5L (VIN H) Engine

3. Clean any dirt from the fuel pressure regulator retaining ring.

4. Remove the vacuum hose from the pressure regulator.

5. Remove the snaprings. Twist the regulator slightly and pull the pressure regulator from the fuel rail. Use a shop towel to catch fuel spillage as the regulator is removed.

6. Remove the O-rings and O-ring back-up.

To install:

7. Clean all parts well. DO NOT use shop compressed air to test or clean a fuel pressure regulator. Clean the fuel pressure regulator screen, if necessary. DO NOT immerse the fuel pressure regulator in a solvent bath or it will be damaged.

8. If the filter screen has been contaminated, it should be removed and the pressure regulator replaced.

9. Lubricate the new pressure regulator O-rings with clean engine oil. Install the O-ring back-up, the large O-ring and then the small O-ring. Install the pressure regulator and secure with the snapring.

10. Attach the vacuum hose.

11. Connect the negative battery cable.

12. Inspect for leaks using the following procedure:

   a. Turn the ignition switch to the **ON** position for 2 seconds.

   b. Turn the ignition switch to the **OFF** position for 10 seconds.

   c. Turn the ignition switch to the **ON** position again.

   d. Inspect all areas for fuel leaks.

FUEL TANK

Tank Assembly

DRAINING

> ✳✳ **CAUTION**

Observe all applicable safety precautions when working around fuel. Whenever servicing the fuel system, always work in a well ventilated area. Do not allow fuel spray or vapors to come in contact with a spark or open flame. Keep a dry chemical fire extinguisher near the work area. Always keep fuel in a container specifically designed for fuel storage; also, always properly seal fuel containers to avoid the possibility of fire or explosion.

> ✳✳ **WARNING**

Never drain fuel through the fuel tank filler pipe in order to prevent damage to the fuel tank filler pipe check-ball.

1. Disconnect the negative battery cable.
2. Loosen the fuel tank filler pipe cap.
3. Raise and safely support the vehicle.
4. Remove the fuel tank filler pipe EVAP pipe restraints.

5. Clean the fuel tank filler pipe EVAP pipe connection and the surrounding area before disconnecting the fuel tank filler pipe to avoid possible contamination of the fuel system. Loosen the fuel tank filler pipe EVAP pipe hose clamp.

6. Wrap a clean shop cloth around the EVAP pipe and slowly remove the pipe from the filler pipe.

7. GM recommends a hand-operated fuel pump device to drain the fuel through the EVAP pipe into an approved container.

REMOVAL & INSTALLATION

▶ See Figures 33 and 34

> ✳✳ **CAUTION**

GM considers a fuel tank to be a major component and they caution that additional support is required if the vehicle is on a hoist. Support the opposite end of the vehicle, chaining the vehicle frame rails to the hoist pads to avoid the vehicle tipping off the hoist. Failure to follow these precautions could lead to vehicle damage, serious personal injury or death.

➡ Do not attempt to straighten any kinked nylon fuel lines. Replace any kinked nylon fuel feed or return lines to prevent damage to the vehicle. Do not attempt to repair damaged lines; replace any damaged lines. Do not bend the fuel tank straps as this may damage the straps and make installation difficult. There are a number of fuel tank and evaporative emission lines that have to be disconnected. Tag for identification all lines to avoid installation mistakes. Due to model variations, some procedures for some vehicles may differ slightly. The following should suffice for all W-Body vehicles.

1. Disconnect the negative battery cable.

2. Relieve the fuel system pressure using the procedures found in this section.

3. Drain the fuel tank using the procedures found in this section.

4. Raise and safely support the vehicle.

5. Remove the EVAP hose from the fuel tank

6. Remove the fuel tank filler hose from the fuel tank.

7. Separate the quick-connect fittings at the fuel tank using the procedures found in this section.

8. Remove the EVAP pipe from the connection at the front of the tank.

9. Remove the rubber exhaust pipe hangers, allowing the exhaust system to drop slightly.

10. With the aid of an assistant, support the fuel tank and remove the fuel tank strap bolts. Lower the tank enough to detach the electrical connector. Carefully lower the tank and remove to a safe, suitable work area.

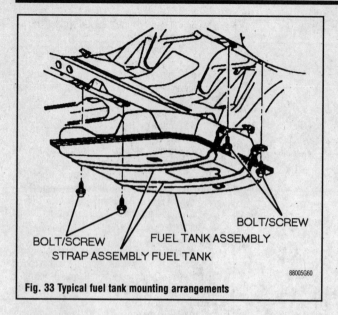

Fig. 33 Typical fuel tank mounting arrangements

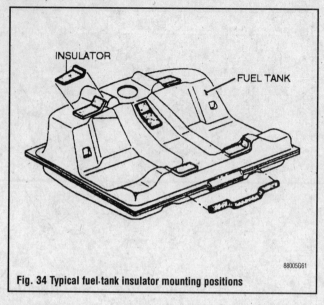

Fig. 34 Typical fuel tank insulator mounting positions

11. If the tank is being replaced with a new tank, transfer any components as required including any insulator pads, fuel line clips and the fuel sender assembly.

To install:

12. Clean all parts well. Inspect the tank for dents, rust or other damage. On high-mileage vehicles, it may be good practice to either replace the fuel sender module as an assembly (includes a new fuel pump) or at least replace the flexible fuel strainer on the bottom of the module.

13. Position the tank to the vehicle and install the quick-connecting fittings using the procedures found in this section. Secure the electrical connection. With the aid of an assistant, position and support the tank and connect the EVAP pipe to the rear of the fuel tank and to the fuller filler pipe. Position the tank straps and tighten the strap bolts to 35 ft. lbs. (47 Nm).

14. Install the exhaust hangers and make sure the exhaust system is properly positioned and supported.

15. Lower the vehicle. Add fuel and connect the negative battery cable. Test for leaks.

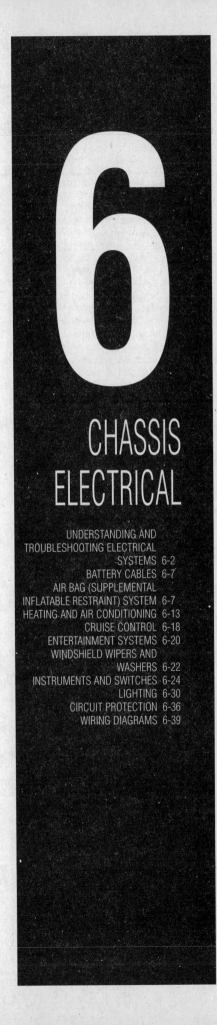

6

CHASSIS ELECTRICAL

UNDERSTANDING AND TROUBLESHOOTING ELECTRICAL SYSTEMS

Basic Electrical Theory

▶ See Figure 1

For any 12 volt, negative ground, electrical system to operate, the electricity must travel in a complete circuit. This simply means that current (power) from the positive (+) terminal of the battery must eventually return to the negative (-) terminal of the battery. Along the way, this current will travel through wires, fuses, switches and components. If, for any reason, the flow of current through the circuit is interrupted, the component fed by that circuit will cease to function properly.

Perhaps the easiest way to visualize a circuit is to think of connecting a light bulb (with two wires attached to it) to the battery—one wire attached to the negative (-) terminal of the battery and the other wire to the positive (+) terminal. With the two wires touching the battery terminals, the circuit would be complete and the light bulb would illuminate. Electricity would follow a path from the battery to the bulb and back to the battery. It's easy to see that with longer wires on our light bulb, it could be mounted anywhere. Further, one wire could be fitted with a switch so that the light could be turned on and off.

The normal automotive circuit differs from this simple example in two ways. First, instead of having a return wire from the bulb to the battery, the current travels through the frame of the vehicle. Since the negative (-) battery cable is attached to the frame (made of electrically conductive metal), the frame of the vehicle can serve as a ground wire to complete the circuit. Secondly, most automotive circuits contain multiple components which receive power from a single circuit. This lessens the amount of wire needed to power components on the vehicle.

HOW DOES ELECTRICITY WORK: THE WATER ANALOGY

Electricity is the flow of electrons—the sub-atomic particles that constitute the outer shell of an

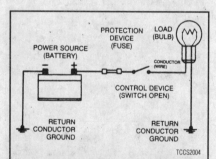

TCCS2004

Fig. 1 This example illustrates a simple circuit. When the switch is closed, power from the positive (+) battery terminal flows through the fuse and the switch, and then to the light bulb. The light illuminates and the circuit is completed through the ground wire back to the negative (-) battery terminal. In reality, the two ground points shown in the illustration are attached to the metal frame of the vehicle, which completes the circuit back to the battery

atom. Electrons spin in an orbit around the center core of an atom. The center core is comprised of protons (positive charge) and neutrons (neutral charge). Electrons have a negative charge and balance out the positive charge of the protons. When an outside force causes the number of electrons to unbalance the charge of the protons, the electrons will split off the atom and look for another atom to balance out. If this imbalance is kept up, electrons will continue to move and an electrical flow will exist.

Many people have been taught electrical theory using an analogy with water. In a comparison with water flowing through a pipe, the electrons would be the water and the wire is the pipe.

The flow of electricity can be measured much like the flow of water through a pipe. The unit of measurement used is amperes, frequently abbreviated as amps (a). You can compare amperage to the volume of water flowing through a pipe. When connected to a circuit, an ammeter will measure the actual amount of current flowing through the circuit. When relatively few electrons flow through a circuit, the amperage is low. When many electrons flow, the amperage is high.

Water pressure is measured in units such as pounds per square inch (psi); The electrical pressure is measured in units called volts (v). When a voltmeter is connected to a circuit, it is measuring the electrical pressure.

The actual flow of electricity depends not only on voltage and amperage, but also on the resistance of the circuit. The higher the resistance, the higher the force necessary to push the current through the circuit. The standard unit for measuring resistance is an ohm. Resistance in a circuit varies depending on the amount and type of components used in the circuit. The main factors which determine resistance are:

- Material—some materials have more resistance than others. Those with high resistance are said to be insulators. Rubber materials (or rubber-like plastics) are some of the most common insulators used in vehicles as they have a very high resistance to electricity. Very low resistance materials are said to be conductors. Copper wire is among the best conductors. Silver is actually a superior conductor to copper and is used in some relay contacts, but its high cost prohibits its use as common wiring. Most automotive wiring is made of copper.

- Size—the larger the wire size being used, the less resistance the wire will have. This is why components which use large amounts of electricity usually have large wires supplying current to them.

- Length—for a given thickness of wire, the longer the wire, the greater the resistance. The shorter the wire, the less the resistance. When determining the proper wire for a circuit, both size and length must be considered to design a circuit that can handle the current needs of the component.

- Temperature—with many materials, the higher the temperature, the greater the resistance (positive temperature coefficient). Some materials exhibit the opposite trait of lower resistance with higher temperatures (negative temperature coefficient). These principles are used in many of the sensors on the engine.

OHM'S LAW

There is a direct relationship between current, voltage and resistance. The relationship between current, voltage and resistance can be summed up by a statement known as Ohm's law.

Voltage (E) is equal to amperage (I) times resistance (R): $E = I \times R$

Other forms of the formula are $R = E/I$ and $I = E/R$

In each of these formulas, E is the voltage in volts, I is the current in amps and R is the resistance in ohms. The basic point to remember is that as the resistance of a circuit goes up, the amount of current that flows in the circuit will go down, if voltage remains the same.

The amount of work that the electricity can perform is expressed as power. The unit of power is the watt (w). The relationship between power, voltage and current is expressed as:

Power (w) is equal to amperage (I) times voltage (E): $W = I \times E$

This is only true for direct current (DC) circuits; The alternating current formula is slightly different, but since the electrical circuits in most vehicles are DC type, we need not get into AC circuit theory.

Electrical Components

POWER SOURCE

Power is supplied to the vehicle by two devices: The battery and the alternator. The battery supplies electrical power during starting or during periods when the current demand of the vehicle's electrical system exceeds the output capacity of the alternator. The alternator supplies electrical current when the engine is running. Just not does the alternator supply the current needs of the vehicle, but it recharges the battery.

The Battery

In most modern vehicles, the battery is a lead/acid electrochemical device consisting of six 2 volt subsections (cells) connected in series, so that the unit is capable of producing approximately 12 volts of electrical pressure. Each subsection consists of a series of positive and negative plates held a short distance apart in a solution of sulfuric acid and water.

The two types of plates are of dissimilar metals. This sets up a chemical reaction, and it is this reaction which produces current flow from the battery when its positive and negative terminals are connected to an electrical load. The power removed from the battery is replaced by the alternator, restoring the battery to its original chemical state.

The Alternator

An alternator supplies alternating current which is then changed to direct current for use on the vehicle. Alternators tend to be more efficient than the old generators used years ago and that is why they are used.

Alternators and generators are devices that consist of coils of wires wound together making big electromagnets. One group of coils spins within another set and the interaction of the magnetic fields causes a current to flow. This current is then drawn off the coils and fed into the vehicles electrical system.

GROUND

Two types of grounds are used in automotive electric circuits. Direct ground components are grounded to the frame through their mounting points. All other components use some sort of ground wire which is attached to the frame or chassis of the vehicle. The electrical current runs through the chassis of the vehicle and returns to the battery through the ground (-) cable; if you look, you'll see that the battery ground cable connects between the battery and the frame or chassis of the vehicle.

➡ **It should be noted that a good percentage of electrical problems can be traced to bad grounds.**

PROTECTIVE DEVICES

▸ **See Figure 2**

It is possible for large surges of current to pass through the electrical system of your vehicle. If this surge of current were to reach the load in the circuit, the surge could burn it out or severely damage it. It can also overload the wiring, causing the harness to get hot and melt the insulation. To prevent this, fuses, circuit breakers and/or fusible links are connected into the supply wires of the electrical system. These items are nothing more than a built-in weak spot in the system. When an abnormal amount of current flows through the system, these protective devices work as follows to protect the circuit:

• Fuse—when an excessive electrical current passes through a fuse, the fuse "blows" (the conductor melts) and opens the circuit, preventing the passage of current.

• Circuit Breaker—a circuit breaker is basically a self-repairing fuse. It will open the circuit in the same fashion as a fuse, but when the surge subsides, the circuit breaker can be reset and does not need replacement.

• Fusible Link—a fusible link (fuse link or main link) is a short length of special, high temperature insulated wire that acts as a fuse. When an excessive electrical current passes through a fusible link, the thin gauge wire inside the link melts, creating an intentional open to protect the circuit. To repair the circuit, the link must be replaced. Some newer type fusible links are housed in plug-in modules, which are simply replaced like a fuse, while older type fusible links must be cut and spliced if they melt. Since this link is very early in the electrical path, it's the first place to look if nothing on the vehicle works, yet the battery seems to be charged and is properly connected.

✳✳ CAUTION

Always replace fuses, circuit breakers and fusible links with identically rated components. Under no circumstances should a component of higher or lower amperage rating be substituted.

SWITCHES & RELAYS

▸ **See Figures 3 and 4**

Switches are used in electrical circuits to control the passage of current. The most common use is to open and close circuits between the battery and the various electric devices in the system. Switches are rated according to the amount of amperage they can handle. If a sufficient amperage rated switch is not used in a circuit, the switch could overload and cause damage.

Some electrical components which require a large amount of current to operate use a special switch called a relay. Since these circuits carry a large amount of current, the thickness of the wire in the circuit is also greater. If this large wire were connected from the load to the control switch, the switch would have to carry the high amperage load

and the fairing or dash would be twice as large to accommodate the increased size of the wiring harness. To prevent these problems, a relay is used.

Relays are composed of a coil and a set of contacts. When the coil has a current passed though it, a magnetic field is formed and this field causes the contacts to move together, completing the circuit. Most relays are normally open, preventing current from passing through the circuit, but they can take any electrical form depending on the job they are intended to do. Relays can be considered "remote control switches." They allow a smaller current to operate devices that require higher amperages. When a small current operates the coil, a larger current is allowed to pass by the contacts. Some common circuits which may use relays are the horn, headlights, starter, electric fuel pump and other high draw circuits.

LOAD

Every electrical circuit must include a "load" (something to use the electricity coming from the source). Without this load, the battery would attempt to deliver its entire power supply from one pole to another. This is called a "short circuit." All this electricity would take a short cut to ground and cause a great amount of damage to other components in the circuit by developing a tremendous amount of heat. This condition could develop sufficient heat to melt the insulation on all the surrounding wires and reduce a multiple wire cable to a lump of plastic and copper.

WIRING & HARNESSES

The average vehicle contains meters and meters of wiring, with hundreds of individual connections. To protect the many wires from damage and to keep them from becoming a confusing tangle, they are organized into bundles, enclosed in plastic or taped together and called wiring harnesses. Different harnesses serve different parts of the vehicle. Individual wires are color coded to help trace them through a harness where sections are hidden from view.

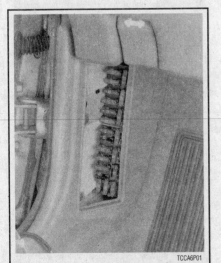

TCCA6P01

Fig. 2 Most vehicles use one or more fuse panels. This one is located on the driver's side kick panel

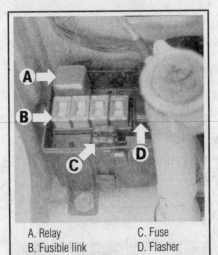

A. Relay   C. Fuse
B. Fusible link   D. Flasher

TCCA6P02

Fig. 3 The underhood fuse and relay panel usually contains fuses, relays, flashers and fusible links

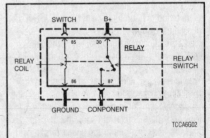

TCCA6G02

Fig. 4 Relays are composed of a coil and a switch. These two components are linked together so that when one operates, the other operates at the same time. The large wires in the circuit are connected from the battery to one side of the relay switch (B+) and from the opposite side of the relay switch to the load (component). Smaller wires are connected from the relay coil to the control switch for the circuit and from the opposite side of the relay coil to ground

Automotive wiring or circuit conductors can be either single strand wire, multi-strand wire or printed circuitry. Single strand wire has a solid metal core and is usually used inside such components as alternators, motors, relays and other devices. Multi-strand wire has a core made of many small strands of wire twisted together into a single conductor. Most of the wiring in an automotive electrical system is made up of multi-strand wire, either as a single conductor or grouped together in a harness. All wiring is color coded on the insulator, either as a solid color or as a colored wire with an identification stripe. A printed circuit is a thin film of copper or other conductor that is printed on an insulator backing. Occasionally, a printed circuit is sandwiched between two sheets of plastic for more protection and flexibility. A complete printed circuit, consisting of conductors, insulating material and connectors for lamps or other components is called a printed circuit board. Printed circuitry is used in place of individual wires or harnesses in places where space is limited, such as behind instrument panels.

Since automotive electrical systems are very sensitive to changes in resistance, the selection of properly sized wires is critical when systems are repaired. A loose or corroded connection or a replacement wire that is too small for the circuit will add extra resistance and an additional voltage drop to the circuit.

The wire gauge number is an expression of the cross-section area of the conductor. Vehicles from countries that use the metric system will typically describe the wire size as its cross-sectional area in square millimeters. In this method, the larger the wire, the greater the number. Another common system for expressing wire size is the American Wire Gauge (AWG) system. As gauge number increases, area decreases and the wire becomes smaller. An 18 gauge wire is smaller than a 4 gauge wire. A wire with a higher gauge number will carry less current than a wire with a lower gauge number. Gauge wire size refers to the size of the strands of the conductor, not the size of the complete wire with insulator. It is possible, therefore, to have two wires of the same gauge with different diameters because one may have thicker insulation than the other.

It is essential to understand how a circuit works before trying to figure out why it doesn't. An electrical schematic shows the electrical current paths when a circuit is operating properly. Schematics break the entire electrical system down into individual circuits. In a schematic, usually no attempt is made to represent wiring and components as they physically appear on the vehicle; switches and other components are shown as simply as possible. Face views of harness connectors show the cavity or terminal locations in all multi-pin connectors to help locate test points.

CONNECTORS

▶ **See Figures 5 and 6**

Three types of connectors are commonly used in automotive applications—weatherproof, molded and hard shell.

• Weatherproof—these connectors are most commonly used where the connector is exposed to the elements. Terminals are protected against moisture and dirt by sealing rings which provide a weathertight seal. All repairs require the use of a

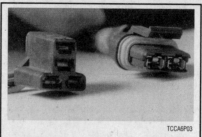

Fig. 5 Hard shell (left) and weatherproof (right) connectors have replaceable terminals—if you can get the parts and have special tools

Fig. 6 Weatherproof connectors are most commonly used in the engine compartment or where the connector is exposed to the elements

special terminal and the tool required to service it. Unlike standard blade type terminals, these weatherproof terminals cannot be straightened once they are bent. Make certain that the connectors are properly seated and all of the sealing rings are in place when connecting leads.

• Molded—these connectors require complete replacement of the connector if found to be defective. This means splicing a new connector assembly into the harness. All splices should be soldered to insure proper contact. Use care when probing the connections or replacing terminals in them, as it is possible to create a short circuit between opposite terminals. If this happens to the wrong terminal pair, it is possible to damage certain components. Always use jumper wires between connectors for circuit checking and NEVER probe through weatherproof seals.

• Hard Shell—unlike molded connectors, the terminal contacts in hard-shell connectors can be replaced. Replacement usually involves the use of a special terminal removal tool that depresses the locking tangs (barbs) on the connector terminal and allows the connector to be removed from the rear of the shell. The connector shell should be replaced if it shows any evidence of burning, melting, cracks, or breaks. Replace individual terminals that are burnt, corroded, distorted or loose.

Test Equipment

Pinpointing the exact cause of trouble in an electrical circuit is most times accomplished by the use of special test equipment. The following describes different types of commonly used test equipment

and briefly explains how to use them in diagnosis. In addition to the information covered below, the tool manufacturer's instructions booklet (provided with the tester) should be read and clearly understood before attempting any test procedures.

JUMPER WIRES

✳✳ CAUTION

Never use jumper wires made from a thinner gauge wire than the circuit being tested. If the jumper wire is of too small a gauge, it may overheat and possibly melt. Never use jumpers to bypass high resistance loads in a circuit. Bypassing resistances, in effect, creates a short circuit. This may, in turn, cause damage and fire. Jumper wires should only be used to bypass lengths of wire or to simulate switches.

Jumper wires are simple, yet extremely valuable, pieces of test equipment. They are basically test wires which are used to bypass sections of a circuit. Although jumper wires can be purchased, they are usually fabricated from lengths of standard automotive wire and whatever type of connector (alligator clip, spade connector or pin connector) that is required for the particular application being tested. In cramped, hard-to-reach areas, it is advisable to have insulated boots over the jumper wire terminals in order to prevent accidental grounding. It is also advisable to include a standard automotive fuse in any jumper wire. This is commonly referred to as a "fused jumper". By inserting an in-line fuse holder between a set of test leads, a fused jumper wire can be used for bypassing open circuits. Use a 5 amp fuse to provide protection against voltage spikes.

Jumper wires are used primarily to locate open electrical circuits, on either the ground (-) side of the circuit or on the power (+) side. If an electrical component fails to operate, connect the jumper wire between the component and a good ground. If the component operates only with the jumper installed, the ground circuit is open. If the ground circuit is good, but the component does not operate, the circuit between the power feed and component may be open. By moving the jumper wire successively back from the component toward the power source, you can isolate the area of the circuit where the open is located. When the component stops functioning, or the power is cut off, the open is in the segment of wire between the jumper and the point previously tested.

You can sometimes connect the jumper wire directly from the battery to the "hot" terminal of the component, but first make sure the component uses 12 volts in operation. Some electrical components, such as fuel injectors or sensors, are designed to operate on about 4 to 5 volts, and running 12 volts directly to these components will cause damage.

TEST LIGHTS

▶ **See Figure 7**

The test light is used to check circuits and components while electrical current is flowing through them. It is used for voltage and ground tests. To use a 12 volt test light, connect the ground clip to a good ground and probe wherever necessary with

Fig. 7 A 12 volt test light is used to detect the presence of voltage in a circuit

TCCS2006

the pick. The test light will illuminate when voltage is detected. This does not necessarily mean that 12 volts (or any particular amount of voltage) is present; it only means that some voltage is present. It is advisable before using the test light to touch its ground clip and probe across the battery posts or terminals to make sure the light is operating properly.

✳✳ WARNING

Do not use a test light to probe electronic ignition, spark plug or coil wires. Never use a pick-type test light to probe wiring on computer controlled systems unless specifically instructed to do so. Any wire insulation that is pierced by the test light probe should be taped and sealed with silicone after testing.

Like the jumper wire, the 12 volt test light is used to isolate opens in circuits. But, whereas the jumper wire is used to bypass the open to operate the load, the 12 volt test light is used to locate the presence of voltage in a circuit. If the test light illuminates, there is power up to that point in the circuit; if the test light does not illuminate, there is an open circuit (no power). Move the test light in successive steps back toward the power source until the light in the handle illuminates. The open is between the probe and a point which was previously probed.

The self-powered test light is similar in design to the 12 volt test light, but contains a 1.5 volt penlight battery in the handle. It is most often used in place of a multimeter to check for open or short circuits when power is isolated from the circuit (continuity test).

The battery in a self-powered test light does not provide much current. A weak battery may not provide enough power to illuminate the test light even when a complete circuit is made (especially if there is high resistance in the circuit). Always make sure that the test battery is strong. To check the battery, briefly touch the ground clip to the probe; if the light glows brightly, the battery is strong enough for testing.

➡ **A self-powered test light should not be used on any computer controlled system or component. The small amount of electricity transmitted by the test light is enough to damage many electronic automotive components.**

MULTIMETERS

Multimeters are an extremely useful tool for troubleshooting electrical problems. They can be purchased in either analog or digital form and have a price range to suit any budget. A multimeter is a voltmeter, ammeter and ohmmeter (along with other features) combined into one instrument. It is often used when testing solid state circuits because of its high input impedance (usually 10 megaohms or more). A brief description of the multimeter main test functions follows:

• Voltmeter—the voltmeter is used to measure voltage at any point in a circuit, or to measure the voltage drop across any part of a circuit. Voltmeters usually have various scales and a selector switch to allow the reading of different voltage ranges. The voltmeter has a positive and a negative lead. To avoid damage to the meter, always connect the negative lead to the negative (-) side of the circuit (to ground or nearest the ground side of the circuit) and connect the positive lead to the positive (+) side of the circuit (to the power source or the nearest power source). Note that the negative voltmeter lead will always be black and that the positive voltmeter will always be some color other than black (usually red).

• Ohmmeter—the ohmmeter is designed to read resistance (measured in ohms) in a circuit or component. Most ohmmeters will have a selector switch which permits the measurement of different ranges of resistance (usually the selector switch allows the multiplication of the meter reading by 10, 100, 1,000 and 10,000). Some ohmmeters are "auto-ranging" which means the meter itself will determine which scale to use. Since the meters are powered by an internal battery, the ohmmeter can be used like a self-powered test light. When the ohmmeter is connected, current from the ohmmeter flows through the circuit or component being tested. Since the ohmmeter's internal resistance and voltage are known values, the amount of current flow through the meter depends on the resistance of the circuit or component being tested. The ohmmeter can also be used to perform a continuity test for suspected open circuits. In using the meter for making continuity checks, do not be concerned with the actual resistance readings. Zero resistance, or any ohm reading, indicates continuity in the circuit. Infinite resistance indicates an opening in the circuit. A high resistance reading where there should be none indicates a problem in the circuit. Checks for short circuits are made in the same manner as checks for open circuits, except that the circuit must be isolated from both power and normal ground. Infinite resistance indicates no continuity, while zero resistance indicates a dead short.

✳✳ WARNING

Never use an ohmmeter to check the resistance of a component or wire while there is voltage applied to the circuit.

• Ammeter—an ammeter measures the amount of current flowing through a circuit in units called amperes or amps. At normal operating voltage, most circuits have a characteristic amount of amperes, called "current draw" which can be measured using an ammeter. By referring to a specified current draw rating, then measuring the amperes and comparing the two values, one can determine what is happening within the circuit to aid in diagnosis. An open circuit,

for example, will not allow any current to flow, so the ammeter reading will be zero. A damaged component or circuit will have an increased current draw, so the reading will be high. The ammeter is always connected in series with the circuit being tested. All of the current that normally flows through the circuit must also flow through the ammeter; if there is any other path for the current to follow, the ammeter reading will not be accurate. The ammeter itself has very little resistance to current flow and, therefore, will not affect the circuit, but it will measure current draw only when the circuit is closed and electricity is flowing. Excessive current draw can blow fuses and drain the battery, while a reduced current draw can cause motors to run slowly, lights to dim and other components to not operate properly.

Troubleshooting Electrical Systems

When diagnosing a specific problem, organized troubleshooting is a must. The complexity of a modern automotive vehicle demands that you approach any problem in a logical, organized manner. There are certain troubleshooting techniques, however, which are standard:

• Establish when the problem occurs. Does the problem appear only under certain conditions? Were there any noises, odors or other unusual symptoms? Isolate the problem area. To do this, make some simple tests and observations, then eliminate the systems that are working properly. Check for obvious problems, such as broken wires and loose or dirty connections. Always check the obvious before assuming something complicated is the cause.

• Test for problems systematically to determine the cause once the problem area is isolated. Are all the components functioning properly? Is there power going to electrical switches and motors. Performing careful, systematic checks will often turn up most causes on the first inspection, without wasting time checking components that have little or no relationship to the problem.

• Test all repairs after the work is done to make sure that the problem is fixed. Some causes can be traced to more than one component, so a careful verification of repair work is important in order to pick up additional malfunctions that may cause a problem to reappear or a different problem to arise. A blown fuse, for example, is a simple problem that may require more than another fuse to repair. If you don't look for a problem that caused a fuse to blow, a shorted wire (for example) may go undetected.

Experience has shown that most problems tend to be the result of a fairly simple and obvious cause, such as loose or corroded connectors, bad grounds or damaged wire insulation which causes a short. This makes careful visual inspection of components during testing essential to quick and accurate troubleshooting.

Testing

OPEN CIRCUITS

◆ See Figure 8

This test already assumes the existence of an open in the circuit and it is used to help locate the open portion.

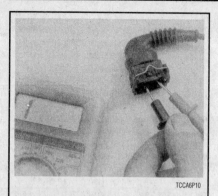

TCCA6P10

Fig. 8 The infinite reading on this multi-meter indicates that the circuit is open

1. Isolate the circuit from power and ground.
2. Connect the self-powered test light or ohmmeter ground clip to the ground side of the circuit and probe sections of the circuit sequentially.
3. If the light is out or there is infinite resistance, the open is between the probe and the circuit ground.
4. If the light is on or the meter shows continuity, the open is between the probe and the end of the circuit toward the power source.

SHORT CIRCUITS

➡**Never use a self-powered test light to perform checks for opens or shorts when power is applied to the circuit under test. The test light can be damaged by outside power.**

1. Isolate the circuit from power and ground.
2. Connect the self-powered test light or ohmmeter ground clip to a good ground and probe any easy-to-reach point in the circuit.
3. If the light comes on or there is continuity, there is a short somewhere in the circuit.
4. To isolate the short, probe a test point at either end of the isolated circuit (the light should be on or the meter should indicate continuity).
5. Leave the test light probe engaged and sequentially open connectors or switches, remove parts, etc. until the light goes out or continuity is broken.
6. When the light goes out, the short is between the last two circuit components which were opened.

VOLTAGE

This test determines voltage available from the battery and should be the first step in any electrical troubleshooting procedure after visual inspection. Many electrical problems, especially on computer controlled systems, can be caused by a low state of charge in the battery. Excessive corrosion at the battery cable terminals can cause poor contact that will prevent proper charging and full battery current flow.

1. Set the voltmeter selector switch to the 20V position.
2. Connect the multimeter negative lead to the battery's negative (-) post or terminal and the positive lead to the battery's positive (+) post or terminal.
3. Turn the ignition switch **ON** to provide a load.
4. A well charged battery should register over 12 volts. If the meter reads below 11.5 volts, the battery power may be insufficient to operate the electrical system properly.

VOLTAGE DROP

◆ **See Figure 9**

When current flows through a load, the voltage beyond the load drops. This voltage drop is due to the resistance created by the load and also by small resistances created by corrosion at the connectors and damaged insulation on the wires. The maximum allowable voltage drop under load is critical, especially if there is more than one load in the circuit, since all voltage drops are cumulative.

1. Set the voltmeter selector switch to the 20 volt position.
2. Connect the multimeter negative lead to a good ground.
3. Operate the circuit and check the voltage prior to the first component (load).
4. There should be little or no voltage drop in the circuit prior to the first component. If a voltage drop exists, the wire or connectors in the circuit are suspect.
5. While operating the first component in the circuit, probe the ground side of the component with the positive meter lead and observe the voltage readings. A small voltage drop should be noticed. This voltage drop is caused by the resistance of the component.
6. Repeat the test for each component (load) down the circuit.

7. If a large voltage drop is noticed, the preceding component, wire or connector is suspect.

RESISTANCE

◆ **See Figures 10 and 11**

⁂ WARNING

Never use an ohmmeter with power applied to the circuit. The ohmmeter is designed to operate on its own power supply. The normal 12 volt electrical system voltage could damage the meter!

1. Isolate the circuit from the vehicle's power source.
2. Ensure that the ignition switch is **OFF** when disconnecting any components or the battery.
3. Where necessary, also isolate at least one side of the circuit to be checked, in order to avoid reading parallel resistances. Parallel circuit resistances will always give a lower reading than the actual resistance of either of the branches.
4. Connect the meter leads to both sides of the circuit (wire or component) and read the actual measured ohms on the meter scale. Make sure the selector switch is set to the proper ohm scale for the circuit being tested, to avoid misreading the ohmmeter test value.

Wire and Connector Repair

Almost anyone can replace damaged wires, as long as the proper tools and parts are available. Wire and terminals are available to fit almost any need. Even the specialized weatherproof, molded and hard shell connectors are now available from aftermarket suppliers.

Be sure the ends of all the wires are fitted with the proper terminal hardware and connectors. Wrapping a wire around a stud is never a permanent solution and will only cause trouble later. Replace wires one at a time to avoid confusion. Always route wires exactly the same as the factory.

➡**If connector repair is necessary, only attempt it if you have the proper tools. Weatherproof and hard shell connectors require special tools to release the pins inside the connector. Attempting to repair these connectors with conventional hand tools will damage them.**

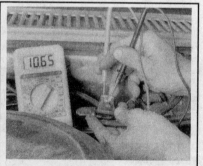

TCCA6P07

Fig. 9 This voltage drop test revealed high resistance (low voltage) in the circuit

TCCA6P08

Fig. 10 Checking the resistance of a coolant temperature sensor with an ohmmeter. Reading is 1.04 kilohms

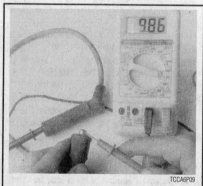

TCCA6P09

Fig. 11 Spark plug wires can be checked for excessive resistance using an ohmmeter

BATTERY CABLES

Disconnecting the Cables

The sophistication of the electrical systems on vehicles such as your GM W-Body car as covered by this manual, means that care and forethought need to be used when working on the electrical system. While it is true that for many years, the first step on most repair procedures involved disconnecting the negative battery cable, some caution must be used. The reason to disconnect the negative battery cable is to prevent short circuits, sparks and voltage spikes that can damage the vehicle and even harm the technician working on the vehicle. To a great extent, this rule is still valid. When working on any electrical component on the vehicle, it is always a good idea (and in many cases, mandatory) to disconnect the negative (-) battery cable. This will prevent potential damage to many sensitive electrical components such as the Powertrain Control Module (PCM), radio, alternator, etc.

However, some W-Body vehicles may be equipped with audio systems that have a Theft Deterrent Feature. The radio has this feature if it shows THEFTLOCK™ on its face. THEFTLOCK™ is designed to discourage theft of the radio. It works by using a secret code to disable all radio functions whenever battery power is removed (as when a battery cable is disconnected). If THEFTLOCK™ is active, the THEFTLOCK™ indicator will flash when the ignition switch is in the **OFF** position. The THEFTLOCK™ feature for the radio may be used or ignored. If ignored, the system plays normally and the radio is not protected by this feature. If THEFT-LOCK™ is activated, the radio will not operate if stolen. When THEFTLOCK™ is activated, the radio will display "LOC" to indicate a locked condition anytime battery power is removed. If the battery loses power for any reason, you must unlock the radio with the secret code before it will operate.

So think before disconnecting the negative battery cable. It is still important to do so for many procedures, but make sure any necessary codes are available or that the THEFTLOCK™ feature has been disabled. More information on THEFTLOCK™ can be found later in this section. The following is GM's recommended procedure.

1. Record all of the vehicle preset radio codes (if applicable).
2. Record the THEFTLOCK™ code (if applicable).
3. Disconnect the negative battery cable first.
4. Clean any existing oxidation from the contact face of the battery terminal and battery cable using a wire brush before installing the battery cable to the battery terminal.
5. At installation, the retaining bolt should be tightened to 11 ft. lbs. (15 Nm). Do not overtighten, or the threads in the battery may strip.
6. Unlock the THEFTLOCK™ radio (if applicable).
7. Program the radio stations back into the radio as recorded at the beginning of this procedure (if applicable).

➡Any time you disengage the battery cables, it is important that you disconnect the negative (-) battery cable first. This will prevent your accidentally grounding the positive (+) terminal to the body of the vehicle when disconnecting it, thereby preventing damage to the above mentioned components.

Before you disconnect the cable(s), first turn the ignition switch to the **OFF** position. This will prevent a draw on the battery which could cause arcing (electricity trying to ground itself to the body of a vehicle, just like a spark plug jumping the gap) and, of course, damaging some components such as the alternator diodes.

When the battery cable(s) are reconnected (negative cable last), be sure to check that the lights, windshield wipers and other electrically operated safety components are all working correctly. If your vehicle contains a THEFTLOCK™ Radio, and it has been activated, it will be necessary to unlock the radio with the code before it will operate.

AIR BAG (SUPPLEMENTAL INFLATABLE RESTRAINT) SYSTEM

General Information

▶ **See Figures 12, 13 and 14**

The Supplemental Inflatable Restraint (SIR) system (also called the air bag system) helps supplement the protection offered by the driver and front passenger seat belts by deploying an air bag from the center of the steering wheel and from the top of the right side of the instrument panel.

The air bag deploys when the vehicle is involved in a frontal crash of sufficient force up to 30 degrees off the centerline of the vehicle. To further absorb the crash energy there is a knee bolster located beneath the instrument panel for both the driver and the passenger, and the steering column is collapsible.

Beginning in 2000, side impact air bags were introduced on selected models. The side impact air bag system consists of the following additional components that interface with the inflatable restraint Sensing and Diagnostic Module (SDM):

• An inflatable restraint Side Impact Sensor

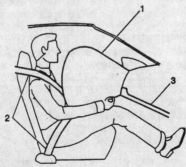

(1) Deployed Air Bag
(2) Seat Belt
(3) Knee Bolster

89636G02

Fig. 13 The SIR system components, when used with a seat belt/shoulder harness, can provide additional protection during an accident

89636G01

Fig. 12 SIR system "deployment window"

93176G01

Fig. 14 Introduced on some 2000 vehicles, the side impact air bags are designed to further enhance the effectiveness of the vehicle's air bag system

(SIS) inside the driver side B-pillar (also called the door post).

• An inflatable restraint front side impact module in the driver's seat.

SYSTEM COMPONENTS

The SIR system consists of the following components:

• An inflatable restraint Sensing and Diagnostic Module (SDM)
• An inflatable restraint steering wheel module (driver's side air bag)
• An inflatable restraint steering wheel module coil
• An inflatable restraint instrument panel module (passenger side air bag)
• An inflatable restraint side impact module (selected 2000 models)
• An AIR BAG warning lamp in the instrument cluster.

Sensing and Diagnostic Module (SDM)

▶ **See Figure 15**

The inflatable restraint Sensing and Diagnostic Module (SDM), inflatable restraint steering wheel module coil (SIR coil assembly), inflatable restraint steering wheel module (driver inflator module), inflatable restraint instrument panel module (passenger inflator module) and connector wires make up the deployment loops. The function of the deployment loops is to supply current through the inflator modules, which will cause deployment of the air bags. Deployment occurs when the SDM detects vehicle velocity changes severe enough to warrant deployment.

The SDM contains a sensing device (accelerometer) that converts vehicle velocity changes to an electrical signal. The SDM compares this electrical signal to a value stored in memory. When the generated signal exceeds the stored value, the SDM performs additional signal processing and compares the generated signals to values stored in memory. When two of the generated signals exceed the stored values, the SDM will cause current to flow through the inflator modules, deploying the air bags.

The SDM performs the following functions in the SIR system.

- Energy Reserve—The SDM maintains 23 Volt Loop Reserve (23 VLR) energy supplies to provide deployment energy. Ignition voltage can provide deployment energy if the 23 Volt Loop Reserves malfunction.
- Frontal Crash Detection—The SDM monitors vehicle velocity changes to detect frontal crashes that are severe enough to warrant deployment.
- Air Bag Deployment—During a frontal crash of sufficient force, the SDM will cause enough current to flow through the inflator modules to deploy the air bags.
- Frontal Crash Recording—The SDM records information regarding the SIR system status during a frontal crash.
- Malfunction Detection—The SDM performs diagnostic monitoring of the SIR system electrical components. Upon detection of a circuit malfunction, the SDM will set a diagnostic trouble code.
- Driver Notification—The SDM warns the vehicle driver of SIR system malfunctions by controlling the AIR BAG warning lamp.

The SDN connects to the SIR wiring harness using a 12-way connector. The SDM harness connector uses a shorting bar across certain terminals in the contact area. Removal of the SDM Connector Position Assurance (CPA) or the harness connector itself will connect the AIR BAG warning lamp to ground through the shorting bar.

The AIR BAG warning lamp will come ON steady with power applied to the SDM when either one of the following two conditions exist:

- You remove the SDM CPA.
- You disconnect the SDM harness connector.

The SDM receives power whenever the ignition switch is at the **ON** or **START** positions. In addition, the SDM can maintain sufficient voltage to cause a deployment for up to ten minutes after the ignition switch is turned to the **OFF** position, the battery is disconnected or the fuse powering the SDM is removed. Many of the SIR service procedures require removal of the "AIR BAG-1" fuse and disconnection of the deployment loops to avoid an accidental deployment.

AIR BAG Warning Lamp

The AIR BAG warning lamp indicates the words "AIR BAG" for domestic vehicles. For Canadian and some export models, the AIR BAG warning lamp is an icon graphic. The ignition switch applies ignition voltage to the AIR BAG warning lamp. The AIR BAG warning lamp receives power whenever the ignition switch is at the **ON** or **START** positions. The inflatable restraint SDM controls the lamp by providing ground with a lamp driver. The SIR system uses the AIR BAG warning lamp to do the following:

- Verify lamp and SDM operation by flashing the lamp seven times when the ignition switch is first turned to the **ON** position.
- Warn the vehicle driver of SIR electrical system malfunctions which could potentially affect the operation of the SIR system. These malfunctions could result in non-deployment in case of a frontal crash or deployment for conditions less severe than intended.

The AIR BAG warning lamp is the key to driver notification of SIR system malfunctions.

Inflatable Restraint Steering Wheel Module Coil

The inflatable restraint steering wheel module coil consists of two or more current-carrying coils. The inflatable restraint steering wheel module coil attaches to the steering column. Two of the current-carrying coils allow rotation of the steering wheel while maintaining continuous contact of the driver deployment loop to the inflatable restraint steering wheel module (the air bag itself).

There is a shorting bar on the yellow 2-way connector near the base of the steering column that connects the inflatable restraint steering wheel module coil to the SIR wiring harness. The shorting bar shorts the circuits to the steering wheel module coil and steering wheel module (air bag) during disconnection of the yellow 2-way connector. The shorting of this circuitry is designed to help prevent unwanted deployment of the air bag when servicing the steering column or other SIR system components.

Inflator Modules

The inflator modules consist of an inflatable bag and an inflator. An inflator consists of a canister of gas-generating material and an initiating device. The initiator is part of the deployment loop. When the vehicle is in a frontal crash of sufficient force, the inflatable restraint SDM causes current to flow through the deployment loops. Current passing through the initiator ignites the material in the inflator module. The gas produced from this reaction rapidly inflates the air bag.

There is a shorting bar on the inflatable restraint steering wheel module side of the upper steering column connector that connects the inflatable restraint steering wheel module coil to the inflatable restraint steering wheel module (air bag). The shorting bar shorts across the steering wheel module circuits during disconnection of the upper steering column connector. The shorting of the steering wheel module circuitry will help prevent unwanted deployment of the air bag when servicing the steering wheel module, the steering column or other SIR system components.

There is a shorting bar on the inflatable restraint instrument panel module (passenger side air bag) connector that connects to the SIR wiring harness. The shorting bar shorts across the inflatable restraint instrument panel module circuits during disconnection of the instrument panel module connector. The shorting of the instrument panel module circuitry will help prevent unwanted deployment of the air bag when servicing the instrument panel module, the instrument panel or other SIR system components.

Side Impact Air Bags

Introduced on selected 2000 models, the Side Impact Air Bag System is designed to further enhance the effectiveness of the vehicle's inflatable restraint system. The Side Impact Air Bag System supplements the protection offered by the driver door, the front passenger door, and the vehicle structure. The Side Impact Air Bag system deploys an air bag from the side of the driver or front passenger seat. A side crash of sufficient force will deploy a side air bag.

The inflatable restraint Side Impact Sensor (SIS), the inflatable restraint front side impact module and the connecting wires make up the side impact deployable loop. The function of the side impact deployment loop is to supply current through the side impact inflator module, which will cause deployment of the side impact air bag. Deployment occurs when the SIS detects a side impact severe enough to warrant deployment.

The SIS contains a sensing device (accelerometer) that converts acceleration into an electrical (analog) signal. This signal is converted by a microprocessor in the SIS into acceleration and velocity data. This data is used by a sensing algorithm and compared to various predetermined boundary conditions. When the acceleration value exceeds the predetermined threshold, and the velocity boundary is crossed, the SIS signals the SDM to cause current to flow through the appropriate inflatable restraint front side impact module, deploying the front side impact air bag.

SERVICE PRECAUTIONS

▶ **See Figures 16 and 17**

Special care is necessary when handling and storing a live (undeployed) inflator module (air bag assembly). If, for example, steering column service is required (turn signal switch, ignition lock repair, etc.) the air bag assembly must be removed for access. Caution is required. The rapid gas generation produced during deployment of the air bag could cause the air bag module, or an object in front of the air bag module, to be thrown through the air in the unlikely event of an accidental deployment.

Inflatable Restraint Sensing
And Diagnostic Module (SDM)

Floorpan, Below Right Side Front Seat

93176G07

Fig. 15 Mounting location for the air bag Sensing and Diagnostic Module (SDM)

☀ CAUTION

When carrying a live inflator module (air bag), make sure the bag opening is pointed away from you. In case of an accidental deployment, the bag will then deploy with minimal chance of injury. Never carry the air bag module by the wires or connector on the underside of the air bag. When placing a live air bag on a bench or other surface, always face the bag and trim cover up, away from the surface. This is necessary so that a free space is provided to allow the air bag to expand in the unlikely event of accidental deployment. Never rest a steering column on the steering wheel with air bag face down and the column vertical. Otherwise, personal injury may result.

• Do not expose the inflator modules to temperatures above 150°F (65°C).
• Verify the correct replacement part number. Do not substitute a component from a different vehicle.
• Do not attempt to repair the SDM, the inflatable restraint inflator module, the air bag, or the steering wheel module coil. Service these components by replacement only.
• Use only new or remanufactured parts from an authorized original equipment manufacturer dealer. Do not use salvaged parts for repairs to the SIR system.
• Discard the following components if they have been dropped from more than a height of 3

feet: the SDM, the inflatable restraint inflator module, the air bag, and the steering wheel module coil.
• Never disconnect any electrical connection with the ignition switch in the **ON** or **RUN** position.
• Avoid touching module connector pins.
• Always wear a grounded wrist static strap when servicing any control module or component labeled with a Electrostatic Discharge (ESD) sensitive device symbol.
• Due to the complexity and critical nature of this system, it should only be serviced by an authorized technician with the proper test equipment. The components are expensive and easily damaged if the wrong equipment or techniques are used, resulting in a compromise of the system's ability to protect the vehicle's passengers and/or expensive and unnecessary component replacement.

DISARMING THE SYSTEM

☀ CAUTION

When performing service on or around SIR components or SIR wiring, follow the procedures listed below to temporarily disable the SIR system. Failure to follow procedures could result in possible air bag deployment, personal injury or otherwise unneeded SIR system repairs.

The inflatable restraint Sensing and Diagnostic Module (SDM) maintains a reserve energy supply. When the vehicle power is insufficient to cause deployment of the air bags, the reserve energy supply provides the deployment power. Deployment power is available for as many as 10 minutes after disconnecting the vehicle power by any of the following methods:

• You turn **OFF** the ignition switch.
• You remove the AIR BAG fuse (also identified as SIR or SDM fuse) that provides power to the SDM.
• You disconnect the vehicle battery from the vehicle electrical system.

Performing the following procedure prevents deploying of the air bags from the reserve energy supply power.

1997–99 Vehicles

▶ **See Figures 18, 19, 20, 21 and 22**

1. Turn the steering wheel to the straight ahead position.
2. Turn the ignition switch to the **OFF** position and remove the key from the ignition switch.

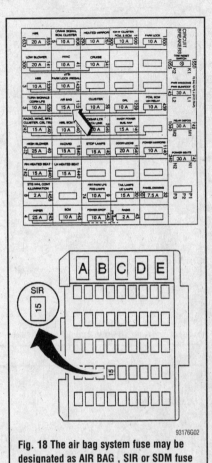

Fig. 18 The air bag system fuse may be designated as AIR BAG, SIR or SDM fuse in the instrument panel fuse block

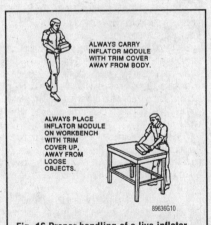

Fig. 16 Proper handling of a live inflator module

Fig. 17 This symbol indicates that a component is sensitive to Electrostatic Discharge (ESD)

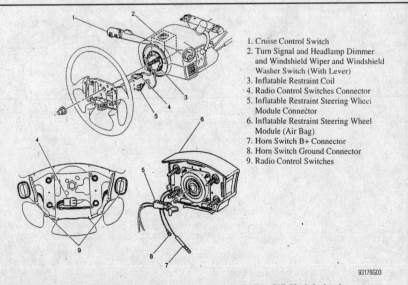

1. Cruise Control Switch
2. Turn Signal and Headlamp Dimmer and Windshield Wiper and Windshield Washer Switch (With Lever)
3. Inflatable Restraint Coil
4. Radio Control Switches Connector
5. Inflatable Restraint Steering Wheel Module Connector
6. Inflatable Restraint Steering Wheel Module (Air Bag)
7. Horn Switch B+ Connector
8. Horn Switch Ground Connector
9. Radio Control Switches

Fig. 19 Typical steering wheel electrical connections, including SIR Module leads

3. Open the instrument panel fuse block access door. Locate and remove the AIR BAG fuse (it may also identified as SIR or SDM fuse, depending on the vehicle) from the instrument panel fuse block.

4. Remove the driver's side instrument panel insulator, a trim panel under the steering column. This normally requires a trim clip removal tool to detach the plastic panel retainers from the steering

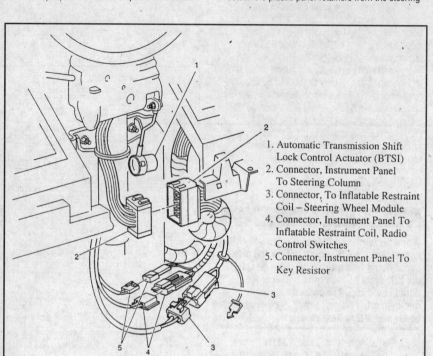

1. Automatic Transmission Shift Lock Control Actuator (BTSI)
2. Connector, Instrument Panel To Steering Column
3. Connector, To Inflatable Restraint Coil – Steering Wheel Module
4. Connector, Instrument Panel To Inflatable Restraint Coil, Radio Control Switches
5. Connector, Instrument Panel To Key Resistor

93176G04

Fig. 20 Typical steering column electrical connections, including SIR Module leads

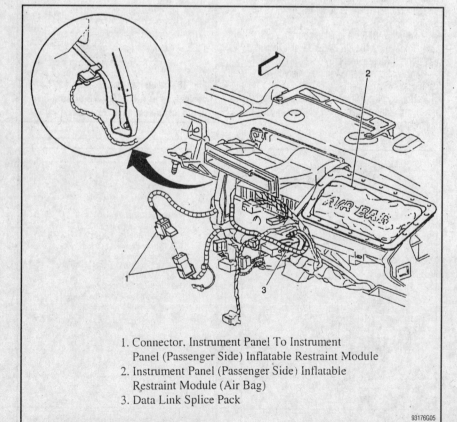

1. Connector, Instrument Panel To Instrument Panel (Passenger Side) Inflatable Restraint Module
2. Instrument Panel (Passenger Side) Inflatable Restraint Module (Air Bag)
3. Data Link Splice Pack

93176G05

Fig. 21 Typical instrument panel (passenger side) air bag electrical connections

column opening filler panel. Disconnect the courtesy lamp, as required, by turning ¼ turn counterclockwise.

5. On the driver's side, a yellow 2-way connector is located at the base of the steering column. First locate, then remove the Connector Position Assurance (CPA) pin. The CPA is a small wedge-shaped plastic piece designed to lock the connector together. With the CPA removed, detach the driver's side yellow 2-way connector.

6. To disable the passenger side instrument panel air bag, remove the instrument panel compartment door.

7. Remove the Connector Position Assurance (CPA) pin and separate the passenger's side yellow 2-way connector located behind the instrument panel door.

2000 Century, Regal, Grand Prix and Intrigue

▶ **See Figures 23, 24 and 25**

1. Turn the steering wheel to center the front wheels in the straight ahead position.
2. Turn the ignition switch to the **OFF** position and remove the key.

➡ **With the AIR BAG fuse removed, if, for some reason, the ignition switch is turned to the ON position, the AIR BAG warning lamp illuminates. This is normal operation and does not indicate an SIR system malfunction.**

3. Remove the instrument panel fuse block access door.
4. Remove the AIR BAG fuse (may also be identified as a numbered fuse or as the SIR or SDM fuse) from the fuse block.
5. Remove the left instrument panel insulator, the trim panel under the steering column.
6. Locate and remove the Connector Position Assurance (CPA) pin which locks the connector together, and separate the driver side yellow 2-way connector located at the base of the steering column.
7. Locate and remove the Connector Position Assurance (CPA) pin which locks the connector together, and separate the passenger side yellow 2-way connector located to the right of the steering column.
8. On vehicles equipped with a driver's side impact air bag, the air bag is built into the side of the seat facing the door. Move the driver's seat back as far as possible to gain access to the driver side air bag yellow 2-way connector. Detach the driver's side impact air bag yellow 2-way connector.

2000 Monte Carlo

▶ **See Figure 26**

1. Turn the steering wheel to center the front wheels in the straight ahead position.
2. Turn the ignition switch to the **OFF** position and remove the key.

➡ **With the AIR BAG fuse removed, if, for some reason, the ignition switch is turned to the ON position, the AIR BAG warning lamp illuminates. This is normal operation and does not indicate an SIR system malfunction.**

3. Remove the left side instrument panel access hole cover.

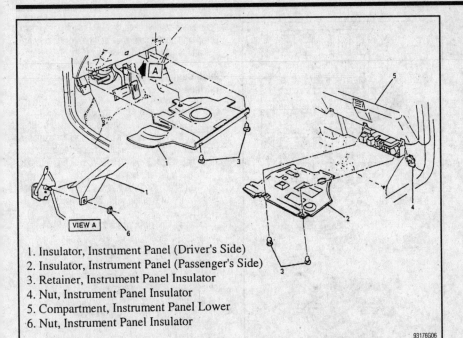

1. Insulator, Instrument Panel (Driver's Side)
2. Insulator, Instrument Panel (Passenger's Side)
3. Retainer, Instrument Panel Insulator
4. Nut, Instrument Panel Insulator
5. Compartment, Instrument Panel Lower
6. Nut, Instrument Panel Insulator

93176G06

Fig. 22 Usually, these insulator panels must be removed to access the air bag connections

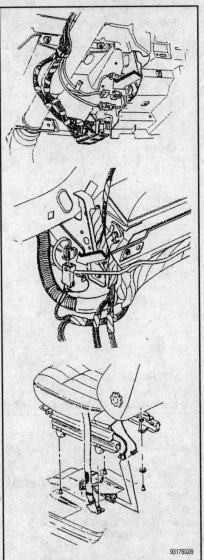

93176G09

Fig. 24 SIR system connector locations, including vehicles with side impact air bag module—2000 vehicles

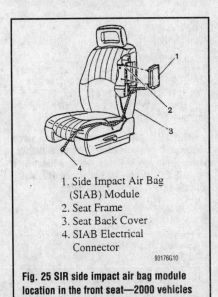

1. Side Impact Air Bag (SIAB) Module
2. Seat Frame
3. Seat Back Cover
4. SIAB Electrical Connector

93176G10

Fig. 25 SIR side impact air bag module location in the front seat—2000 vehicles

1. Steering Wheel
2. Inflatable Restraint Steering Wheel Module
3. Inflatable Restraint Steering Wheel Module Coil
4. Cross-car Beam
5. Inflatable Restraint IP Module
6. Inflatable Restraint Sensing and Diagnostic Module (SDM)
7. Floor Pan
8. Inflatable Restraint Side Impact Module - LH
9. Driver Front Seat
10. Inflatable Restraint Side Impact Sensor – LH
11. Center Pillar – LH
12. SIR Wiring Harness

93176G08

Fig. 23 Major SIR system component locations, including vehicles with side impact air bags

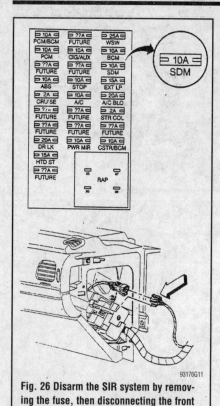

Fig. 26 Disarm the SIR system by removing the fuse, then disconnecting the front air bag connector—2000 Monte Carlo

4. Remove the AIR BAG fuse (may also be identified as SIR or SDM fuse) from the fuse block.

5. Remove the right side instrument panel access hole cover.

6. Unclip the frontal air bag's yellow 4-way connector from the metal rail.

7. Locate and remove the Connector Position Assurance (CPA) pin which locks the connector together, and separate the front air bag's yellow 4-way connector.

8. On vehicles equipped with a driver's side impact air bag, the air bag is built into the side of the seat facing the door. Move the driver's seat back as far as possible to gain access to the driver side air bag yellow 2-way connector. Detach the driver's side impact air bag yellow 2-way connector.

2000 Lumina

▶ See Figure 27

1. Turn the steering wheel to center the front wheels in the straight ahead position.

2. Turn the ignition switch to the **OFF** position and remove the key.

➡With the AIR BAG fuse removed, if, for some reason, the ignition switch is turned to the ON position, the AIR BAG warning lamp illuminates. This is normal operation and does not indicate an SIR system malfunction.

3. Remove the instrument panel fuse block access door.

4. Remove the AIR BAG fuse (may also be identified as Fuse 21, or SIR or SDM fuse) from the fuse block.

5. Remove the left instrument panel insulator, the trim panel under the steering column.

6. Locate and remove the Connector Position

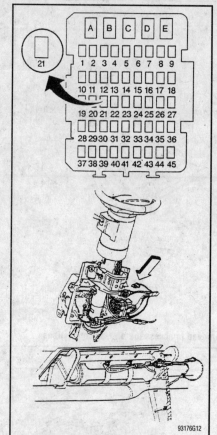

Fig. 27 Disarm the SIR system by removing the fuse and disconnecting the front air bag connector—2000 Lumina

Assurance (CPA) pin which locks the connector together, and separate the driver side yellow 2-way connector located at the base of the steering column.

7. Remove the right side sound insulator from under the instrument panel

8. Locate and remove the Connector Position Assurance (CPA) pin which locks the connector together, and separate the passenger side yellow 2-way connector located behind the instrument panel compartment door.

ARMING THE SIR SYSTEM

1997–99 Vehicles

1. Remove the key from the ignition switch.

2. Attach the yellow 2-way connector located behind the instrument panel compartment door and insert the CPA to verify the connection is secure. Install the instrument panel compartment door.

3. Attach the yellow 2-way connector located at the base of the steering column and insert the CPA pin to verify the connection is secure. Install the driver's side instrument panel insulator.

4. Install the AIR BAG fuse (also identified as SIR or SDM fuse) to the instrument panel fuse block.

5. Staying well away from both air bags, turn the ignition switch to the **ON** position. Verify that the AIR BAG warning lamp flashes seven times and then stays off. If the AIR BAG warning lamp does

not operate as described, an SIR Diagnostic System Check will be required at an authorized dealership. A scan tool is required to check out the SIR system.

2000 Century, Regal, Grand Prix and Intrigue

1. Remove the key from the ignition switch.

2. If equipped with a driver's side impact air bag:
   a. Move the driver's seat back as far as possible to gain access to the driver's side impact air bag yellow 2-way connector which is located under the driver's seat.
   b. Attach the yellow 2-way connector and insert the CPA pin to verify the connection is secure.

3. Attach the passenger's side yellow 2-way connector located to the right of the steering column and insert the CPA pin to verify the connection is secure.

4. Attach the yellow 2-way connector located at the base of the steering column and insert the CPA pin to verify the connection is secure. Install the driver's side instrument panel insulator.

5. Install the AIR BAG fuse (also identified as SIR or SDM fuse) to the instrument panel fuse block.

6. Staying well away from both air bags, turn the ignition switch to the **ON** position. Verify that the AIR BAG warning lamp flashes seven times and then stays off. If the AIR BAG warning lamp does not operate as described, an SIR Diagnostic System Check will be required at an authorized dealership. A scan tool is required to check out the SIR system.

2000 Monte Carlo

1. Turn the ignition switch to the **OFF** position and remove the key.

2. On vehicles equipped with a driver's side impact air bag, the air bag is built into the side of the seat facing the door. Move the driver's seat back as far as possible to gain access to the driver side air bag yellow 2-way connector. Attach the driver's side impact air bag yellow 2-way connector and install the CPA pin to verify the connection is secure.

3. Attach the frontal air bags yellow 4-way connector located at the right side of the instrument panel and install the CPA pin to verify the connection is secure. Attach the 4-way connector to the metal rail.

4. Install the right side instrument panel access hole cover.

5. Install the AIR BAG fuse (may also be identified as SIR or SDM fuse) to the left side fuse block. Install the instrument panel access hole cover.

6. Staying well away from both air bags, turn the ignition switch to the **ON** position. Verify that the AIR BAG warning lamp flashes seven times and then stays off. If the AIR BAG warning lamp does not operate as described, an SIR Diagnostic System Check will be required at an authorized dealership. A scan tool is required to check out the SIR system.

2000 Lumina

1. Remove the key from the ignition switch.

2. Attach the passenger's side air bag yellow 2-way connector which is located behind the instrument panel compartment door and install the CPA pin to verify the connection is secure.

3. Attach the driver's side air bag yellow 2-way connector which is located at the base of the steering column and install the CPA pin to verify the connection is secure.

4. Install the sound insulator trim panels.

5. Install the AIR BAG fuse (may also be identified by a number or as the SIR or SDM fuse) to the instrument panel fuse block. Install the instrument panel fuse block door.

6. Staying well away from both air bags, turn the ignition switch to the **ON** position. Verify that the AIR BAG warning lamp flashes seven times and then stays off. If the AIR BAG warning lamp does not operate as described, an SIR Diagnostic System Check will be required at an authorized dealership. A scan tool is required to check out the SIR system.

HEATING AND AIR CONDITIONING

❄❄ CAUTION

When performing service on or around the SIR (air bag) components or SIR wiring, follow the procedures listed above to temporarily disable the SIR system. Failure to do so may result in possible air bag deployment, personal injury or unneeded SIR system repairs.

➡**The Sensing and Diagnostics Module (SDM) can maintain sufficient voltage to cause deployment for up to ten minutes after the ignition switch is turned to the OFF position or the battery is disconnected.**

Many of the vehicle controls are electronic. Use care when working around solid-state electronic components. Do not open the package on an electronic component until time to install it. Avoid touching electrical terminals of the part. Before removing an electronic part from its packaging, ground the package to a known good ground on the vehicle. Always touch a known good ground before handling the part. This should be repeated while handling the part. Do it more often after sliding across the seat (static electricity danger).

Blower Motor

DESCRIPTION & OPERATION

▶ **See Figures 28 and 29**

The blower motor is a variable speed motor. The higher the voltage applied to the motor, the faster the speed. Depending on the HVAC (Heater Ventilation Air Conditioning) option installed in the vehicle, blower speed control could be through a set of resistors or through a solid-state blower motor control module.

Battery voltage to the blower motor is supplied by the heater & A/C control by way of the blower resistor (or blower motor control module). At low and medium speeds, the voltage is stepped down by the blower motor resistors. At high speed, the blower motor relay is energized, removing the blower motor resistors from the circuit. Battery voltage is then applied directly to the blower motor through the relay. The motor will then run at maximum speed.

Several types of HVAC systems were available on these vehicles, from manual to fully automatic electronic control. The blower motor speed can be adjusted manually by pushing the fan switch up or down or automatically by placing the heater & A/C control in the AUTO mode.

In general, this system is reliable. Because so many of the control operations are electronic, special diagnostic equipment really should be used for system diagnostics and check-out. An authorized technician using a scan tool can most quickly locate HVAC problems.

An inoperative blower motor could be caused by the following:

• Blown fuse(s). The fuse should be replaced. There may be both a LOW BLOWER and HIGH BLOWER fuse. Some models may also call it the HVAC fuse. Even the RADIO fuse is used in some applications. Check them all. If a fuse is blown there may be a short to ground in one of the power supply circuits.

• Open Circuit. Check the circuit between the ignition switch and the blower motor, and the blower motor ground circuit. Repair as necessary.

• Faulty blower switch. A faulty blower switch should be replaced.

• Most heater blower circuits also include a blower motor relay (look in the underdash convenience center), as well as a blow motor resistor. These items should be checked especially if the blower runs in one or two speeds, but not all speeds selected.

REMOVAL & INSTALLATION

▶ **See Figure 30**

1. Disconnect the negative battery cable.

2. The blower motor is located on the passenger side of the vehicle, under the instrument panel. Remove the right side sound insulator (trim panel) by removing the retainers and disconnecting the courtesy lamp.

3. Detach the blower motor electrical connector. Some applications may have cooling hose to the motor which should be disconnected.

4. Unfasten the blower motor mounting screws, then remove the blower motor from the vehicle.

5. If the blower motor fan (also called a `squirrel cage') must be replaced, use the following procedure:

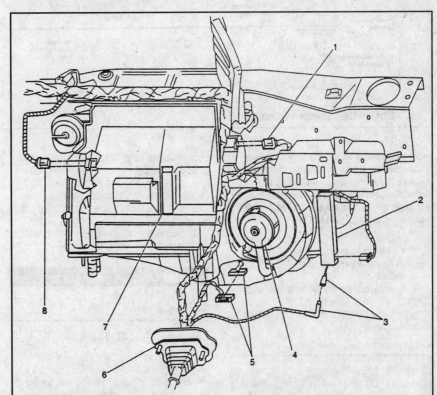

1. Right Side Electric Actuator
2. Vacuum/Electric Solenoid
3. Engine Vacuum Hose
4. Blower Motor
5. Blower Motor Control Module/ Blower Resistors
6. Main Harness Connector
7. Heater A/C Module Assembly
8. Left Side Electric Actuator

93176G13

Fig. 28 Typical behind-the-instrument panel view of HVAC related components. Depending on the HVAC option, not all components are used on all vehicles

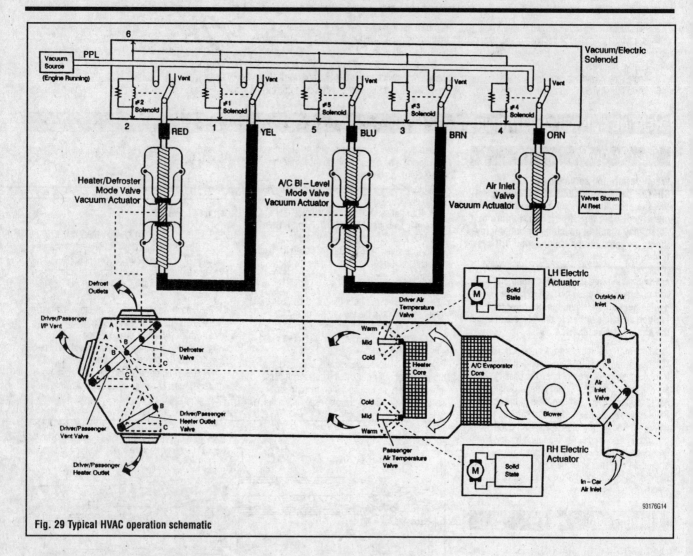

Fig. 29 Typical HVAC operation schematic

➡Do not hammer on the motor to remove or install the fan. Do not apply force to the motor housing to seat the fan on the motor, or motor/shaft bearing damage could result. Do not apply pressure to the fan rim. Be sure the correct replacement part is used.

    a. Remove the metal star clip retaining the fan cage to the motor shaft.
    b. Remove the fan by pulling straight out.
To install:
6. If removed, install the blower motor fan, as follows:
    a. Install the replacement fan cage onto the motor shaft.

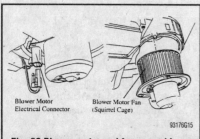

Fig. 30 Blower motor and fan assembly removal

    b. Adjust the fan cage to get a clearance of 0.30 inch (7.5mm) to the motor mount plate.
7. Install the remaining components in the reverse of the removal procedure. Make sure the electrical connection is secure. Tighten the motor screws to 14 ft. lbs. (20 Nm).
8. Connect the negative battery cable, then test the blower motor for proper operations

Heater Core

REMOVAL & INSTALLATION

▶ **See Figures 31, 32, 33 and 34**

    The heater core heats the air before it enters the vehicle. Engine coolant is circulated through the core to heat the outside air passing over the fins of the core. The core is functional at all times (no water shut-off valve is used) and may be used to temper conditioned air in the A/C mode, as well as the heat or vent mode.
1. Disconnect the negative battery cable.
2. Remove the cosmetic/acoustic engine cover, as equipped.
3. Remove the air cleaner and duct assembly.
4. Drain the engine coolant into a suitable container.

5. On the 3.4L (VIN X) engine, remove the throttle body and the throttle body tube to which it mounts.
6. Disconnect both heater hoses from the heater core. On some vehicles, accessing the firewall side heater hoses can be a challenge due to limited working space. In addition, some vehicles equipped with the 3.1L engine may have quick-connect fittings on the hose, requiring special tool J 38723 Heater Line Quick Connect Separator, or equivalent.
7. Remove the lower center console, if equipped. Additional information may be found in the Control Panel service instructions, found in this section.
8. Remove both left and right underdash sound insulator panels.
9. Disconnect the lower heater duct.
10. Remove the heater core cover. The sealer usually should be discarded and replaced with new sealer. Evaluate the condition of the existing sealer and the availability of new sealer.
11. Locate and remove the heater core mounting clip and bracket and remove the heater core from the vehicle. Use care as it will likely have coolant inside and could drip onto the rugs or seats.
12. Installation is the reverse of the removal process. After refilling the cooling system, bleed out the air and check for leaks as outlined in Section 1 of this manual.
13. Connect the negative battery cable.

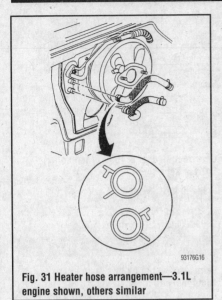

Fig. 31 Heater hose arrangement—3.1L engine shown, others similar

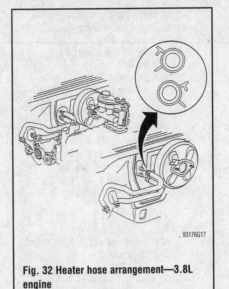

Fig. 32 Heater hose arrangement—3.8L engine

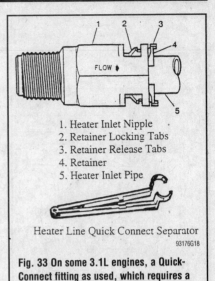

1. Heater Inlet Nipple
2. Retainer Locking Tabs
3. Retainer Release Tabs
4. Retainer
5. Heater Inlet Pipe

Heater Line Quick Connect Separator

Fig. 33 On some 3.1L engines, a Quick-Connect fitting as used, which requires a special tool to separate the fitting

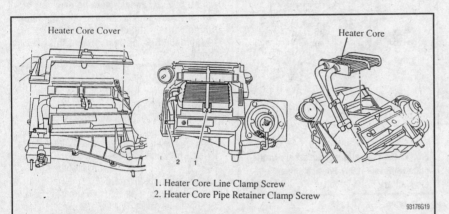

1. Heater Core Line Clamp Screw
2. Heater Core Pipe Retainer Clamp Screw

Fig. 34 Opening the heater core case for heater core removal

Air Conditioning Components

REMOVAL & INSTALLATION

Repair or service of air conditioning components is not covered by this manual, because of the risk of personal injury or death, and because of the legal ramifications of servicing these components without the proper EPA certification and experience. Cost, personal injury or death, environmental damage, and legal considerations (such as the fact that it is a federal crime to vent refrigerant into the atmosphere), dictate that the A/C components on your vehicle should be serviced only by a Motor Vehicle Air Conditioning (MVAC) trained, and EPA certified automotive technician.

➡The refrigeration system on this vehicle uses R-134a which is not compatible with refrigerant R-12. Do not allow this vehicle to be serviced with R-12 or the entire air conditioning system will be severely damaged.

Control Panel

GM recommends that because so many of the control operations are electronic, special diagnostic equipment really should be used for system diagnostics and check-out. An authorized technician using a scan tool can quickly locate most HVAC problems. GM recommends that the heater & A/C control panel be replaced only if specific diagnostic procedures points to the control panel as the only possible source of faults. Even then, the control panel does not automatically need to be replaced if a short is found in the wiring. Repair the wiring first, then check the system for further concerns. Most system malfunctions are traceable to faulty wiring and connectors, and occasionally, components. GM claims the heater & A/C control panel is very reliable and usually not the cause of a system malfunction. A heater & A/C control panel replacement before a complete and thorough diagnosis will usually result in a recurrence of the original complaint.

REMOVAL & INSTALLATION

➡Although the removal procedures for the heater & A/C control panel is similar across the W-Body car line, there are big differences in the shape and size of the trim panel that must be removed to access the control panel screws. On some vehicles, the trim panel is relatively small and easily removed. On other vehicles, the trim panel goes all the way across the instrument panel and may require removal of the center console, too. The trim panels are designed to be retained with a few screws and a number of clips. Trim panels change from year to year and there have been numerous audio panel and heater & A/C control options, but with some minor variations, the following procedures should suffice for the vehicles covered here. Work slowly and carefully. The clips are typically mounted to plastic tabs and are easily broken if handled roughly.

Buick Models

♦ See Figures 35 and 36

✷✷ CAUTION

Vehicles covered by this manual are equipped with a Supplemental Inflatable Restraint (SIR) system, which uses an air bag. Whenever working near any of the SIR components, such as air bag module, steering column and instrument panel, disable the SIR, as described in this section.

1. Disconnect the negative battery cable.
2. Remove the instrument cluster trim plate, using the following as a guide:
   a. Remove the instrument panel access hole

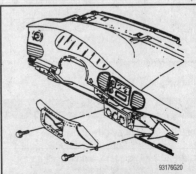

Fig. 35 Instrument panel accessory trim plate removal—1997 Buick shown, others similar

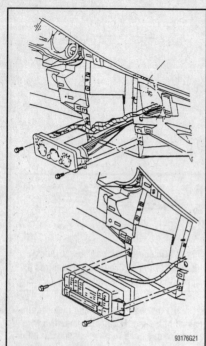

Fig. 36 Heater & A/C control panel removal. Top: Standard system; Bottom: Automatic System—1997 Buick shown, others similar

covers from the instrument panel using a small flat-bladed tool. Remove the screws from each end of the instrument panel cluster trim plate.

b. Remove the screws from the lower edge of the right lower instrument panel trim plate.

c. Open the instrument panel compartment door.

d. Pull the right lower instrument panel trim plate from the instrument panel.

e. Pull steering column tilt level and tilt the steering column to the lowest position.

f. Grasp the instrument panel cluster trim plate at the right edge, slowly pull an working from left to right, release the retainer clips. Lift the trim panel from the vehicle.

3. Remove the screws holding the heater & A/C control panel to the instrument panel and gently pull the assembly from the instrument panel. Detach the electrical connector(s) from the back of the panel. Some models may have a vacuum line connection that must also be removed.

4. Installation is the reverse of the removal process. Use care to make sure the retaining clips are properly seated and all screws are in place. This helps avoid rattles and squeaks later.

Pontiac Models

▶ **See Figures 37 and 38**

✳✳ **CAUTION**

Vehicles covered by this manual are equipped with a Supplemental Inflatable Restraint (SIR) system, which uses an air bag. Whenever working near any of the SIR components, such as air bag module, steering column and instrument panel, disable the SIR, as described in this section.

1. Disconnect the negative battery cable.
2. Remove the instrument cluster trim plate, using the following as a guide:

a. Remove the left instrument panel insulator.

b. Remove the under-steering column opening filler panel.

c. Remove the knee bolster (knee pad) bracket.

d. Remove the nuts holding the steering column bracket to the instrument panel frame and allow the steering column to drop down.

e. Grasp the instrument panel trim plate bottom edge on both sides of the steering column and pull to release the retainer clips. Continue pulling to release the remainder of the clips.

f. Detach the electrical connector from the fog lamp switch, if equipped.

g. Remove the instrument panel cluster trim plate from the instrument panel.

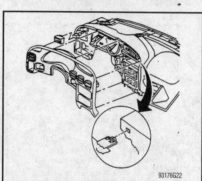

Fig. 37 Instrument panel accessory trim plate removal—1997 Pontiac shown, others similar

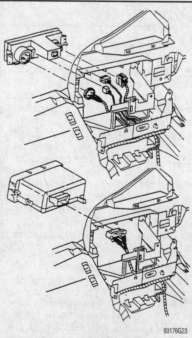

Fig. 38 Heater & A/C control panel removal. Top: Standard system; Bottom: Automatic System—1997 Pontiac shown, others similar

3. Remove the screws holding the heater & A/C panel to the instrument panel and gently pull the assembly from the instrument panel. Detach the electrical connector(s) from the back of the panel. Some models may have a vacuum line connection that must also be removed.

4. Installation is the reverse of the removal process. Use care to make sure the retaining clips are properly seated and all screws are in place. This helps avoid rattles and squeaks later.

Chevrolet Models & 1997 Oldsmobile Cutlass Supreme

▶ **See Figures 39 and 40**

The heater & A/C controls are in the center of the instrument panel, above the audio system.

✳✳ **CAUTION**

Vehicles covered by this manual are equipped with a Supplemental Inflatable Restraint (SIR) system (SIR), which uses an air bag. Whenever working near any of the SIR components, such as air bag module, steering column and instrument panel, disable the SIR, as described in this section.

1. Disconnect the negative battery cable.
2. Remove the instrument cluster trim plate, as follows:

a. Remove the retaining screws from the instrument panel accessory trim plate.

b. Pull the instrument panel accessory trim plate rearward to release the retainers.

c. Rotate the trim panel rearward and up to release the tabs at the top edge.

3. Remove the retaining screws from the heater & A/C control panels. Pull the control panel forward and unsnap the retainers at the ends. Detach the electrical connector(s) from the back of the panel. Some models may have a vacuum line connection that must also be removed.

4. Installation is the reverse of the removal process. Use care to make sure the retaining clips are properly seated and all screws are in place. This helps avoid rattles and squeaks later.

1998–00 Oldsmobile Intrigue

▶ **See Figures 41 and 42**

✳✳ **CAUTION**

Vehicles covered by this manual are equipped with a Supplemental Inflatable Restraint (SIR) system, which uses an air bag. Whenever working near any of the SIR components, such as air bag module, steering column and instrument panel, disable the SIR, as described in this section.

1. Disconnect the negative battery cable.
2. Remove the instrument panel accessory trim plate, as follows:

a. Remove the front floor console trim plate by removing the traction control switch. Use a small flat-bladed tool to carefully pry the traction control switch from the front console trim plate. Detach the electrical connector.

b. Open the front floor console compartment.

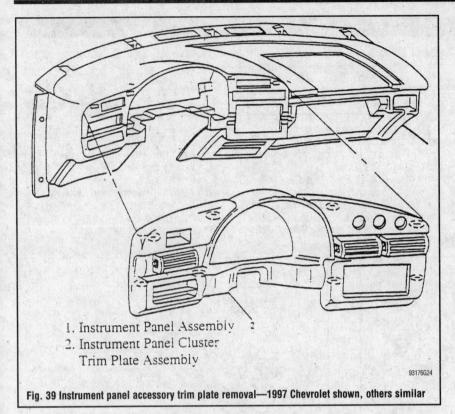

1. Instrument Panel Assembly
2. Instrument Panel Cluster Trim Plate Assembly

93176G24

Fig. 39 Instrument panel accessory trim plate removal—1997 Chevrolet shown, others similar

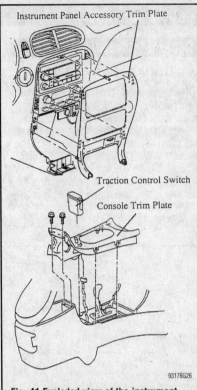

93176G26

Fig. 41 Exploded view of the instrument panel accessory trim plate and console trim plate—2000 Oldsmobile Intrigue shown

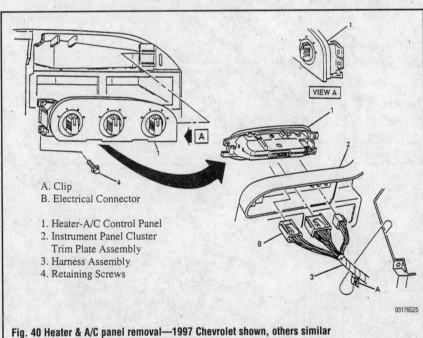

A. Clip
B. Electrical Connector

1. Heater-A/C Control Panel
2. Instrument Panel Cluster Trim Plate Assembly
3. Harness Assembly
4. Retaining Screws

93176G25

Fig. 40 Heater & A/C panel removal—1997 Chevrolet shown, others similar

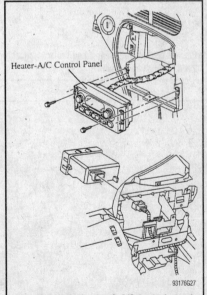

93176G27

Fig. 42 Pull the heater & A/C control panel partially out, detach the electrical connector then remove the control panel—2000 Intrigue shown

Locate and remove the screws from the trim plate.

c. Pull up on the front floor console trim plate to release the retainer clips. Lift the trim plate up and over the transaxle shift lever and remove the trim plate from the vehicle.

3. Remove the instrument panel accessory trim plate from the instrument panel by releasing the retainers.

4. Remove the retaining screws and pull the heater & A/C control panel forward. Detach the electrical connectors from the rear of the panel and remove the control panel from the vehicle.

5. Installation is the reverse of the removal procedure. Use care when aligning the instrument panel accessory trim plate retainers in the slots in the instrument panel. Make sure the retainers are pushed into their slots until fully seated. The instru-

ment panel trim plate is installed in the same manner. When installing the traction control switch, attach the electrical connector and press the switch into the front floor console trim plate until fully seated.

CRUISE CONTROL

General Information

▶ **See Figures 43, 44, 45, 46 and 47**

The Stepper Motor Cruise Control (SMCC) is a speed control system which maintains a desired vehicle speed under normal driving conditions. However, steep grades up or down may cause variations in the selected speeds. The system has the capability to CRUISE, COAST, RESUME SPEED, ACCELERATE, TAP-UP and TAP-DOWN.

An electronic controller and electric motor are combined in the cruise control module. The controller monitors vehicle speed and operates the electric motor. In response to the controller, the motor

moves a connecting strap that is attached to the cruise control cable. The cable moves the throttle linkage to vary throttle position in order to maintain the desired cruise speed. The cruise control module contains a low speed limit which will prevent system engagement below a minimum speed, approximately 25 mph. The module is controlled by mode control switches. Cruise Control is in a "Standby Disabled" mode until all conditions inconsistent with cruise control operation are cleared.

The cruise control inhibit criteria where the PCM will "inhibit" cruise control are:
• When the vehicle speed is less than 25 mph.
• When PARK, REVERSE, NEUTRAL, or 1st GEAR is indicated by the Transaxle Range Switch.

• When an over/under battery voltage condition exists.
• With low engine RPM.
• With high engine RPM (fuel cut-off).

As with most of the computer-controlled systems on these vehicles, troubleshooting requires a qualified technician using a scan tool to extract Diagnostic Trouble Codes (DTCs) and to input test commands to the system. There are, however, some basic checks that can be made.

• Note the cruise control inhibit criteria listed above. Verify that a cruise control complaint really exists, and that the system is not being asked to operate at a time when the parameters for cruise control "enable" are not being met.

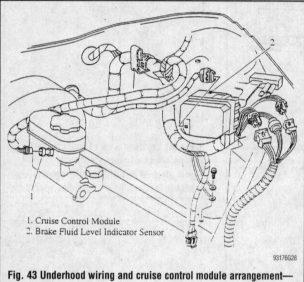

1. Cruise Control Module
2. Brake Fluid Level Indicator Sensor

93176G28

Fig. 43 Underhood wiring and cruise control module arrangement—2000 Grand Prix shown

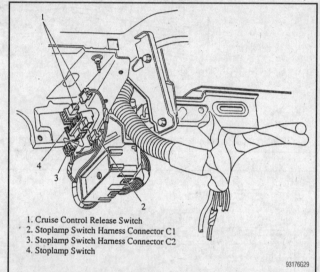

1. Cruise Control Release Switch
2. Stoplamp Switch Harness Connector C1
3. Stoplamp Switch Harness Connector C2
4. Stoplamp Switch

93176G29

Fig. 44 Underdash wiring and cruise switch arrangement—2000 Grand Prix shown

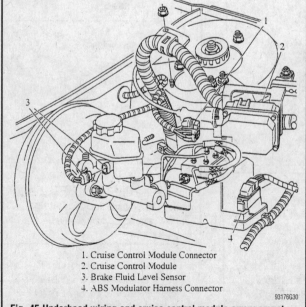

1. Cruise Control Module Connector
2. Cruise Control Module
3. Brake Fluid Level Sensor
4. ABS Modulator Harness Connector

93176G30

Fig. 45 Underhood wiring and cruise control module arrangement—2000 Intrigue shown

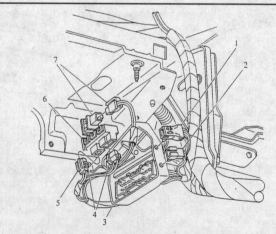

1. Connector C203 (Inline from Windshield Wiper Jumper to IP Harness)
2. Connector C205 (Inline from Steering Wheel Radio Controls to IP Harness)
3. Connector C210 (Inline from Steering Column to IP Harness)
4. Cruise Control Release Switch Connector
5. Stoplamp Switch Connector
6. Brake Pedal Switch
7. Cruise Control Release Switch

93176G31

Fig. 46 Underdash wiring and cruise switch arrangement—2000 Intrigue shown

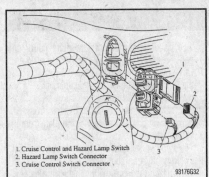

1. Cruise Control and Hazard Lamp Switch
2. Hazard Lamp Switch Connector
3. Cruise Control Switch Connector

93176G32

Fig. 47 Cruise control and hazard lamp switch, LH side of instrument panel—2000 Intrigue shown

- Check that the cruise control module linkage is connected and moving freely.
- Check the stoplamp switch for proper adjustment/alignment. More information on the stoplamp switch is available in Section 9.
- Make sure that the center high mounted stoplamp is working. If this lamp is inoperative, the cruise control module will be disabled.
- Check for a broken (or partially broken) wire inside of the insulation which could cause system malfunction but prove "GOOD" in a continuity/voltage check with a system disconnected. These circuits may be intermittent when loaded, and, if possible, should be checked by monitoring for a voltage drop with the system operational (under load).
- Check the fuses. The cruise control system uses at least one system fuse. The stoplamps are also fused, there may be more than one fuse in the stoplamp circuit and those fuses should also be checked. Don't rely on a visual check. Remove the fuse and check for continuity with an ohmmeter. Remember, the stoplamps and the center high mounted stoplamp must be working for the circuit to the cruise control system to be complete.
- Check the ground. Most of these system use a black wire with an eyelet crimped on the end. A sheetmetal screw secures this ground to the inner fender, usually on the strut tower, and usually under the cruise control module itself.
- Check for proper installation of aftermarket electronic equipment which may affect the integrity of other systems.
- If, after these preliminary checks are made and no problem is found, the vehicle should have the system checked by a qualified technician with a scan tool, interrogating the system through the vehicle's Data Link Connector (DLC).

MAJOR SYSTEM COMPONENTS

Cruise Control Module

The cruise control system uses a cruise control module to obtain and hold any desired vehicle cruise speed above a minimum speed of 25 mph. The module contains the following components:

- An Electronic Controller the monitors the vehicle speed, mode control (switch) inputs, cruise control release inputs, brake switch inputs and it operates the electric stepper motor.
- The Stepper Motor moves the internal band in response to the controller to maintain the desired

cruise speed. The cruise control cable links the internal band to the throttle lever.

Cruise Control Cable

▶ **See Figures 48, 49 and 50**

The cable provides a physical connection between the cruise control module and the engine

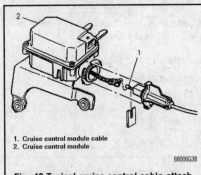

1. Cruise control module cable
2. Cruise control module

88006G38

Fig. 48 Typical cruise control cable attachment to module

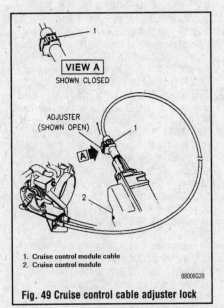

VIEW A
SHOWN CLOSED

ADJUSTER
(SHOWN OPEN)

1. Cruise control module cable
2. Cruise control module

88006G39

Fig. 49 Cruise control cable adjuster lock

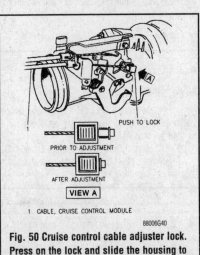

PUSH TO LOCK

PRIOR TO ADJUSTMENT

AFTER ADJUSTMENT

VIEW A

1 CABLE, CRUISE CONTROL MODULE

88006G40

Fig. 50 Cruise control cable adjuster lock. Press on the lock and slide the housing to adjust

throttle lever. The cruise control cable is adjustable. Simply spread the adjuster lock tabs and pull out the adjuster lock to disengage the cruise control cable adjuster lock. Slide the adjuster forward, away from the module. Without moving the throttle lever, remove as much cable slack as possible. Push in on the adjuster lock to lock up the adjustment.

Vehicle Speed Sensor

The Vehicle Speed Sensor (VSS) is mounted to the automatic transaxle. The VSS provides a low voltage Alternating Current (AC) signal to the Powertrain Control Module (PCM). The PCM converts the AC signal to a pulse width modulated Direct Current (DC) signal. The signal is sent to the cruise control module at a rate of 4,000 pulse per mile.

Cruise Control Release and Stoplamp Switches

▶ **See Figure 51**

The cruise control release switch and the stoplamp switch are used to disengage the cruise control system. The switches are mounted on the brake pedal bracket. The switches disengage the system electrically when the brake pedal is pressed.

The cruise control release switch and stop-lamp switch are adjusted together. Incorrect adjustment of either of these switches may cause premature brake lining wear or incorrect cruise control system operation. Remove the underdash insulator panel at the brake pedal. Press the brake pedal fully. Push the switches into their retainers until the switches are fully seated. Pull the brake pedal fully rearward against the pedal stop until the audible click can no longer be heard. Verify that the cruise release switch and stoplamp switch contacts actuate at 0.125–0.500 inch of brake travel. Nominal activation of the stoplamp switch contacts occurs about 0.200 inch beyond the point of the cruise control switch activation.

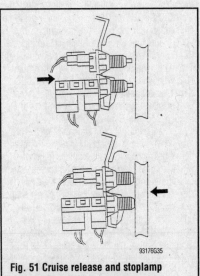

93176G35

Fig. 51 Cruise release and stoplamp switch adjustment at the brake pedal arm—2000 Buick Century and Regal shown, others similar

ENTERTAINMENT SYSTEMS

Radio Receiver/Amplifier/Tape Player/CD Player

SYSTEM COMPONENTS

A number of different types and packages of entertainment systems were available on these vehicles, including:

- AM/FM Stereo
- AM/FM Stereo with Cassette Tape Player
- AM/FM Stereo with Cassette Tape Player and Automatic Tone Control
- AM/FM Stereo with Cassette Tape Player, Compact Disc Player and Automatic Tone Control

A base radio system consists of the following components:

- A radio receiver
- Four speakers
- An appropriate antenna installation

Depending on the make, model and year of your vehicle, the radio system may also include the following options:

- A cassette player with or without Automatic Tone Control
- A remote CD changer with or without Automatic Tone Control
- A dual cassette/remote CD changer with Automatic Tone Control
- A 6 or 8 speaker sound system with various mounting options
- A remote CD changer
- A rear-shelf mounted amplifier

Your owner's manual is a good reference for operating information since it is applicable to your exact make, model and year.

Radio

The radio receives battery voltage at all times through the RADIO fuse to keep the clock and preset station memory alive when the ignition switch is in the **OFF** position. When the ignition switch in the **ACCESSORY** or **ON** position, voltage may be applied through another fuse (for example, on the 2000 Monte Carlo, voltage is applied through the REAR PARK LAMP fuse) to enable radio operation. The radio is grounded through the radio ground circuit. When the ignition switch is in the **ACCESSORY** or **ON** position, the Vacuum Fluorescent (VF) display illuminates to display the time or radio frequency setting.

The range for most AM stations is greater that that of FM stations, especially at night. However, the longer range may cause stations to interfere with each other. AM can pick up noise from things like storms and power lines. Reduce the treble to reduce this noise. FM stereo gives the best sound. However, FM signals reach only about 10–40 miles. Tall buildings or hills can interfere with FM signals, causing the sound to come and go. If the reception is poor, tune to a stronger station to improve reception. All factory-equipped sound systems with a FM stereo radio will switch to stereo operation whenever an FM stereo broadcast is being received. One of the following indicators will light on the display: **STEREO** or **ST**. Stereo opera-

tion means the radio is separating a stereo broadcast back into the original two channels, called left and right.

Compact Disc (CD) and Cassette Player

If equipped, the CD or cassette player is part of the radio unit. When operating, the same power required by the radio is necessary for tape or remote CD changer operation.

Remote Compact Disc (CD) Player

The remote CD Changer receives battery voltage at all times through the RADIO fuse circuit. The remote CD changer is grounded through the radio ground circuit.

THEFTLOCK™ SYSTEM

Some W-Body vehicles may be equipped with audio systems that have a Theft Deterrent Feature. The radio has this feature if it shows THEFT-LOCK™® on its face. THEFTLOCK™ is designed to discourage theft of the radio. It works by using a secret code to disable all radio functions whenever battery power is removed (as when a battery cable is disconnected). If THEFTLOCK™ is active, the THEFTLOCK™ indicator will flash when the ignition switch is in the **OFF** position. The THEFTLOCK™ feature for the radio may be used or ignored. If ignored, the system plays normally and the radio is not protected by this feature. If THEFTLOCK™ is activated, the radio will not operate if stolen. When THEFTLOCK™ is activated, the radio will display "LOC" to indicate a locked condition anytime battery power is removed. If the battery loses power for any reason, you must unlock the radio with the secret code before it will operate. Please consult your owner's manual for complete THEFTLOCK™ instructions.

If the vehicle is equipped with a THEFTLOCK™ radio and the radio is locked up but the codes have been lost or are unobtainable (change of vehicle ownership, etc.) the Dealer Communications System and Technical Assistance service available at the dealership can be consulted in obtaining a Factory Backup Code.

REMOVAL & INSTALLATION

Radio Assembly

▶ See Figure 52

1. Obtain the THEFTLOCK™ codes and radio station presets before attempting to remove the radio, if applicable.
2. Disconnect the negative battery cable.
3. Remove the trim plate bezel from around the radio using the following procedure.
   a. Adjust the steering wheel for access.
   b. Remove the ignition switch cylinder bezel.
   c. Remove the left side instrument panel fuse block access opening cover.
   d. Remove the instrument panel cluster trim plate screws.

e. Starting at the right side of the instrument panel cluster trim plate, grasp the trim plate and carefully pull rearward. Continue working around the trim plate until all of the retainers are released from the trim pad.
   f. Detach the electrical connectors from the hazard switch and remove the trim plate from the vehicle.
4. Remove the screws from the radio and pull the radio gently from the instrument panel.
5. Detach the instrument panel wiring harness connector and the antenna cable connector from the radio.

To install:
6. Installation is the reverse of the removal process, noting the following:
   a. After the electrical connection is secure and the antenna cable is connected, find the radio locator tab.
   b. If the locator tab is difficult to align to the instrument panel locator opening, pull the radio towards you and reposition the antenna cable.
   c. Gently install the radio to the instrument panel, aligning the radio locator tab to the instrument panel locator opening while carefully pressing the radio into the instrument panel until fully seated.
7. Install the trim plate bezel.
8. Connect the negative battery cable.
9. Unlock the THEFTLOCK™ radio (if applicable).
10. Program the radio stations back into the radio as recorded at the beginning of this procedure (if applicable).

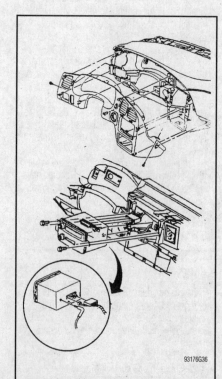

93176G36

Fig. 52 You must remove the instrument panel cluster trim panel in order to remove the radio assembly

Amplifier

♦ See Figure 53

Some vehicles may be equipped with a rear-shelf mounted audio amplifier. To replace the amplifier, use the following procedure.

1. Open the rear compartment (trunk).
2. Locate the amplifier which is mounted to the underside of the rear shelf (also called the rear window panel). Carefully press the spring clip removal tabs to disengage the amplifier retainers from the rear shelf.
3. Detach the electric connectors and remove the amplifier from the vehicle.
4. Installation is the reverse of the removal procedure.

CASSETTE PLAYER CARE AND CLEANING

GM recommends that you clean the cassette player every 15 hours of use for the best performance. In addition, they recommend cleaning the cassette player every 50 hours to prevent damage to the tape head. Clean the head and the capstan on the tape player. Leave the tape player in the vehicle, since you can reach the parts through the tape door. Perform this service at least every 50 hours of cassette operation. After 50 hours of tape play CLN (clean) may appear on the display as a reminder. Although the system will still function when this message is displayed, reduced sound quality and possible damage to the cassette tapes may occur.

After cleaning the cassette tape player, press and

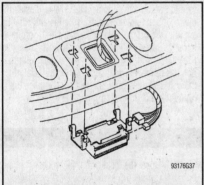

Fig. 53 Removing the rear-shelf mounted audio amplifier

hold EJECT for 5 seconds to reset the CLN indicator. The radio displays to show that the clean feature has been rest.

Keep cassette tapes correctly stored in their plastic cases away from contamination, direct sunlight and extreme heat. Tape cassettes are subject to wear. The sound quality may degrade over time. Before servicing a tape player, verify that the tape is in good condition and that the tape player is clean. If a reduction in sound quality occurs, regardless of when the tape player was last cleaned, play a different tape to see if the tape or the tape player is at fault. If the second cassette tape results in no improvement in sound quality, clean the tape player.

Use a scrubbing action, non-abrasive cleaning cassette (GM J 39916-A, or equivalent) for proper tape player cleaning. This cleaner is a wet-type cleaning system. The wet-type cleaning system uses a cleaning cassette with pads that scrub the tape head as the hubs turn. Using this type of cleaner may cause the radio to display and error and the cartridge to eject. These conditions are normal and is the result of an added feature in the tape player that detects broken tapes. If an error occurs, insert the cleaning cassette at least 3 times to thoroughly clean the tape player. The following steps will enable the radio to accept the tape:

    a. Press and hold the Tape/CD button for 5 seconds.

    b. The radio should display READY.

    c. Insert the cleaner.

    d. Press and hold the Eject button to reset CLN.

1. You can also use a non-scrubbing, wet-type cleaner. This type of cleaner uses a cassette with a fabric belt which cleans the tape head. This type of cleaning cassette will not cause an error, but may not clean the tape player as thoroughly as the scrubbing type cleaner.

Speakers

REMOVAL & INSTALLATION

➡ **Due to differences in optional trim packages and across the car lines, the following procedures, especially for door trim removal, may vary slightly. In general, the door panels are retained in a similar manner across the W-Body car line. The following procedures should suffice for most all W-Body vehicles. It is good**

practice not to rush this job. Take your time when disconnecting the power mirror and power window switches (as equipped). Many of the door panel retainers are clips and a Door Trim Pad and Garnish Clip Remover tool is recommended.

Front

♦ See Figure 54

1. Remove the front door trim panel using the following procedure:

    a. Remove the screw(s) from the upper door trim panel.

2. Remove the screws from the front door pull handle and remove the door handle trim bezel.

➡ **It is important to support the front door trim panel until the power mirror switch and/or power window switch is removed. In addition, GM specifies that the front door trim panel retainers MUST be discarded and replaced with new trim panel retainers. Procure the proper parts before servicing the door trim panel.**

3. Remove the front door trim panel using a trim clip tool to disengage the fasteners from the inner door panel.
4. Detach and reposition the power mirror switch and/or power window switch electrical connectors from the door trim panel, using the following as a guide.

    a. With the inside door handle bezel removed, remove the power door lock switch from the inside door handle bezel using a small flat-bladed tool to release the retainers. Detach the electrical connector from the power door lock switch.

5. Remove the door trim panel from the vehicle.
6. Remove the door speaker screws and remove the speakers. Detach the harness connector.

To install:

7. Installation is the reverse of the removal procedure, noting the following.

    a. Verify correct radio operation before assembly.

    b. GM specifies that the front door trim panel retainers MUST be discarded and replaced with new trim panel retainers. Install the new trim panel retainers to the front door trim panel.

    c. Route the electrical connectors through the openings in the door trim panel and connect to the power mirror and/or power window switches, as equipped.

8. Align the front door trim panel to the front door, guiding the front door handle through the trim panel. Install the upper edge of the door trim panel to the top edge of the inner door panel, firmly pressing down until the retainer clips are fully seated. Align the two locator pins on the door trim panel to the inner door panel. Install the door trim panel by firmly pressing the retainer clips until the flips are fully seated around the perimeter of the door panel.

Rear

♦ See Figures 55 and 56

➡ **To remove the rear shelf for accessing the rear speakers, the rear seat and some side trim must be removed first. This may vary from vehicle to vehicle, so look the job over**

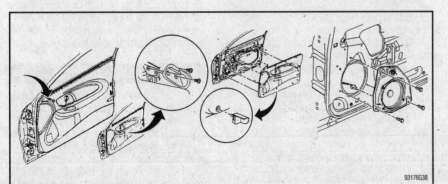

Fig. 54 Remove and disengage the door trip panel retainers, then remove the door panel to service the front speakers

carefully. The following should suffice for most all W-Body vehicles.

1. Remove the rear window (rear shelf) trim panel, using the following as a guide:

  a. Remove the rear seat cushion by pulling the tabs on the rear seat cushion retainers to release the rear seat cushion.

  b. Pull the cushion up and out of its retainers. Remove the rear seat back.

  c. On non-folding seats, remove the nuts from the seat retainer at the bottom of the rear seat back, grasp the rear seat back and swing upward to disengage the offsets on the upper frame bar from the hangers.

  d. On folding seats, remove the nuts from the seat retainer at the bottom of the rear seat back, fold the seat back cushions down, then remove the bolts from the rear seat latches and take the latches off the seat back. Fold the seat back up, reposition the seat belts and remove the seat back from the vehicle.

  e. Remove the rear quarter upper trim panel by first unbolting the seat belt retractor. Remove the coat hook from the rear upper trim panel by removing the plastic cover with a small flat-bladed tool to expose the coat hook screw. Then

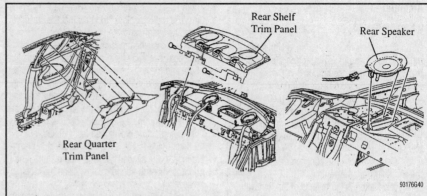

Fig. 56 Remove the rear shelf trim panel to access the rear speakers for removal

remove the rear quarter upper trim panel by disengaging the push-in retainers.

  f. Remove the push-in retainers from the front of the rear window (rear shelf) trim panel.

  g. From inside the trunk, remove the bulbs and holders from the rear High Mount Stop Lamp.

  h. Lift the rear shelf trim panel and remove the seat belts through the slots in the panel.

  i. Slide the rear shelf trim panel forward to disengage the integral hook from the retaining hole, then remove the panel from the vehicle.

2. Disengage the speaker retaining tab. Remove the speaker alignment tabs from the opening in panel. The speaker may have bonded with the shelf metal. Carefully pry the housing away from the metal while holding the speaker retaining tab to remove the speaker.

3. Detach the wiring harness from the speaker and remove the speaker from the vehicle.

To install:

4. Installation is the reverse of the removal process. Make sure the speaker alignment tabs fit the openings in the window panel and that the harness connector is secure. Verify correct radio operation before assembly.

5. Install the remainder of the trim panels using care to line up any alignment tabs. When install the rear seat belt retractors, make sure the anti-rotation tab is in the proper hole in the rear shelf. Torque the retractor bolt and the anchor bolt to 31 ft. lbs. (42 Nm). Make sure the seat belts are aligned with the notches in the rear seat cushion. When installing the rear seat cushion to the retainers, engage the right side first (longer tab) then the left side.

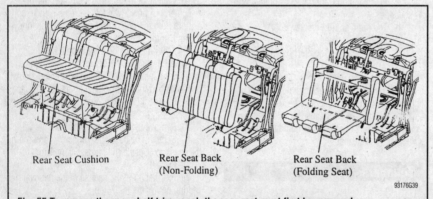

Fig. 55 To remove the rear shelf trim panel, the rear seat must first be removed

WINDSHIELD WIPERS AND WASHERS

Windshield Wiper Blade and Arm

REMOVAL & INSTALLATION

♦ **See Figures 57, 58 and 59**

The wiper arms are attached to an assembly known as the wiper transmission, sometimes also called the wiper pivot or the wiper arm shaft.

1. Turn the ignition switch to the **ACC** position.

2. Set the wiper switch to the PULSE position.

3. Turn the ignition switch **OFF** when the wiper arm is in the innermost wipe position and not moving.

4. Disconnect the washer hose from the nozzle.

5. Remove the protective cover from the wiper arm retaining nut.

6. Remove the nut from the wiper arm and transmission shaft.

7. Remove the wiper arm from the transmission drive shaft. Use a rocking motion. In some cases, a small puller like a battery terminal puller can be used to coax to wiper arm from the transmission shaft.

To install:

8. Clean any metal shavings from the knurls of the wiper transmission shafts.

9. Return the wiper transmission to the PARK position using the following procedure:

  a. Turn the ignition switch to the **ACC** position.

  b. Set the wiper switch ON and then OFF.

  c. Turn the ignition switch **OFF**.

10. Install the wiper arm and position the wiper arm slightly below the stop surface of the park ramp. Push the wiper arm down slightly onto the wiper transmission drive shaft completely,

11. Install the wiper arm retaining nut and tighten to 17 ft. lbs. (23 Nm). Snap the cover back into place. Lubricate the washer hose with windshield wiper fluid to make it easier to connect the washer hose.

12. Inspect the installation. In the parked position, both wiper arm assemblies must be snug against the park ramps. Check the wipe pattern. Wet the glass and run the wipers briefly. There should be 2.17–5.20 inches (55–132mm) from the tip of the driver's side wiper blade on the outerwipe to the edge of the glass. The correct park position and outerwipe dimensions are determined with the wipers operating at low speed on wet glass.

Windshield Wiper Motor

The windshield wiper/washer system consists of a permanent-magnet depressed-park wiper motor assembly, wiper/washer switch, washer solvent container with a pump, wiper arms and blade assemblies and a wiper drive system (also called a wiper transmission). The wiper drive system is installed on the vehicle as a complete assembly called a module. The wiper drive system module consists of a wiper motor assembly and wiper transmission assembly assembled on a tube frame.

Fig. 57 Disconnect the washer hose and remove the protective cap from the wiper arm

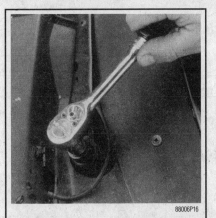

Fig. 58 Remove the wiper arm retaining nut

Fig. 59 Insert a suitable pin through the two holes located next to the arm pivot to hold the arm off the glass, making it easier to rock the arm back and forth and remove it from the pivot shaft

The wiper/washer system is a pulse (delay) type. Pulse timing and demand wash functions are controlled electronically. The pulse type windshield wiper/washer system includes an operating mode in which the wipers make single sweeps with an adjustable time interval between sweeps. The time interval is controlled by a solid state timer in the wiper motor cover assembly. The duration of the delay interval is determined by the delay resistor in the wiper/washer switch assembly. The length of delay time between sweeps is controlled by the variable pulse delay resistor. The delay is adjustable from 0 to 25 seconds.

REMOVAL & INSTALLATION

▶ See Figures 60 thru 65

1. Remove the wiper arms from the vehicle using the procedure found earlier in this section.

2. Remove the air inlet grille panel retaining screws (or plastic push-in retainers) and remove the panel from the vehicle. The panel may be in two pieces, left side and right side.
3. Detach the connectors from the wiper motor assembly.
4. Remove the three screws and the wiper drive system module from the vehicle.
5. The wiper motor crank arm is attached to the wiper drive by a ball-joint type connection that snaps together. GM recommends their special tool J 39232 which is a pliers-like tool with U-shaped jaws that are placed between the components. When the handles are squeezed, the jaws separate the components. Use care if using substitutes.
6. Remove the nut from the wiper motor crank arm.
7. Remove the three screws and separate the wiper motor from the tube frame.

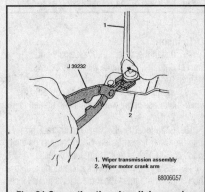

1. Wiper transmission assembly
2. Wiper motor crank arm

Fig. 61 Separating the wiper linkage using GM's special tool

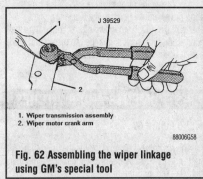

1. Wiper transmission assembly
2. Wiper motor crank arm

Fig. 62 Assembling the wiper linkage using GM's special tool

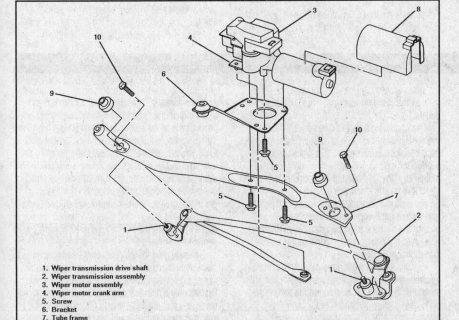

1. Wiper transmission drive shaft
2. Wiper transmission assembly
3. Wiper motor assembly
4. Wiper motor crank arm
5. Screw
6. Bracket
7. Tube frame
8. Cover
9. Boot
10. Screw

Fig. 60 Exploded view of a typical W-Body windshield wiper motor and related components

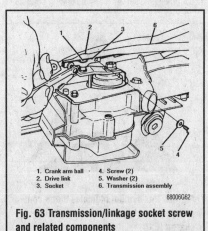

1. Crank arm ball
2. Drive link
3. Socket
4. Screw (2)
5. Washer (2)
6. Transmission assembly

Fig. 63 Transmission/linkage socket screw and related components

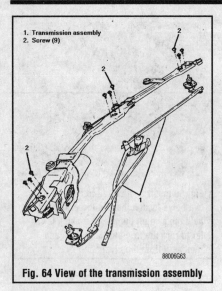

1. Transmission assembly
2. Screw (9)

88006G63

Fig. 64 View of the transmission assembly

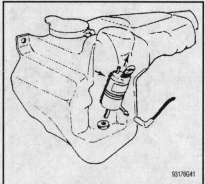

1. Alignment tool
2. Hole in module carrier plate
3. Hole in bell crank

88006G64

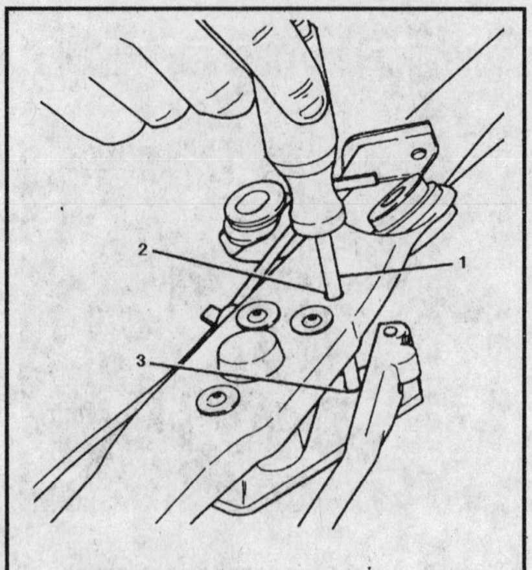

Fig. 65 Use a suitable tool line up the holes in the module carrier plate and bell crank

93176G41

Fig. 66 Most windshield washer pumps are mounted on the washer fluid reservoir

To install

8. Install the wiper motor assembly and bracket onto the tube frame with three screws. Tighten to 106 inch lbs. (12 Nm).

9. Install the wiper motor crank arm onto the wiper motor assembly with the nut and tighten to 18 ft. lbs. (25 Nm).

10. Snap together the wiper motor crank arm onto the wiper transmission. GM recommends their tool J 39529. Use care if using substitutes.

11. Install the wiper drive system module onto the vehicle and tighten the three screws to 106 inch lbs. (12 Nm).

12. Assemble the electrical connectors and verify that they are secure.

13. Install the air inlet grille panel. Use care to align the clearance holes to the wiper arm pivot shafts. If the grilles are in two pieces, look for a small connecting pin which aligns the two pieces and make sure it is correctly registered into its mating opening.

14. Install the wiper arms to the vehicle.

Windshield Washer Pump

When the washer switch is held ON, battery voltage is applied to the wiper motor cover assembly. The park switch is energized and the cover assembly circuitry turns on the washer pump and wiper motor. The cover assembly circuitry turns the wiper motor off approximately six seconds after it interrupts power to the washer pump. If the wipers had been in DELAY, LO or HI, they will return to that operation after the wash cycle.

REMOVAL & INSTALLATION

▶ See Figure 66

The washer pump is mounted to the windshield washer fluid reservoir. On various models, the fluid reservoir may be mounted on either the driver's side or the passenger's side of the engine compartment. Depending on the shape of the reservoir, it may be possible to remove the pump with the reservoir left in place. If the washer reservoir must be removed to service the pump, in nearly all cases, there is a diagonal steel brace running over top of the reservoir that must be removed before the reservoir can be removed.

1. Detach the electrical connector from the pump.

2. Disconnect the washer hose from the pump.

3. The pump is retained by a grommet. Pull the top of the washer pump from the side of the washer solvent reservoir.

4. Installation is the reverse of the removal process. Use care if installing the diagonal brace. On the assembly line, hardened self-tapping screws were used. Use care not to cross-thread the bolts at installation, stripping the threads in the body. Oil the bolt threads and hand start. The brace should have at least some of the holes elongated to allow some adjustment. Make sure all the bolts turn down relatively easily before final tightening.

INSTRUMENTS AND SWITCHES

▶ See Figure 67

The instrument panel contains the operating instruments used by the driver when operating the vehicle. The instrument panel houses the speedometer, heater and air conditioning controls, the audio system controls and convenience items such as the compartment (glove box) and HVAC outlets.

When handling a part that has an "ESD-Sensitive" sticker warning of Electrostatic Discharge (the sticker looks like a hand inside a black triangle with a stripe through it), follow these guidelines to reduce any possible buildup of electrostatic charge.

• If replacing a part that has the warning sticker, do not open the package until just prior to installation. Before removing the part from its package, ground the package to a good ground on the car.

• Avoid touching the electrical terminals of any electronic component.

• Always touch a good ground before handling a parts with an ESD-Sensitive warning sticker. This should be repeated while handling the part; especially after sliding across the seat.

Instrument Cluster

These are electronic units. If one part of the cluster fails, the entire cluster must be replaced. Conventional speedometer cables are not used; the speedometer is a fully electronic unit. Some inputs are hard-wired, such as the turn indicators, high beam indicator and some of the warning lights. All other inputs to the instrument panel cluster are through a Class 2 Serial Data Communications Link. The primary inputs (speedometer, temperature, fuel and tachometer) are driven by information from the data link to the instrument cluster to the cluster microprocessor and then through the stepper motor driver. Although some conventional light bulbs are still being used, Light Emitting Diodes (LEDs) are being used for a number of warning lamps and indicators.

Depending on the vehicle, other information is displayed. Some vehicles may be equipped with a Driver Information Center (DIC) or Message Center. Displays may include the average fuel economy, the range, the fuel used and the oil life remaining. Warning messages may also appear such as Door Ajar, Trunk Ajar, Low Trac, and others. The information is delivered to the driver through tell-tale lamps or the indicators. The tell-tale lamps and indicators illuminate when either a grounding switch is closed or one of the pertinent modules provides a path to

89636G11

Fig. 67 This symbol indicates that a component is sensitive to Electrostatic Discharge (ESD)

ground for the specific indicator. The Driver Information Display does not perform any self-tests or diagnostics and is used only as a communication device for the driver.

Another variation used on some models is the Heads-Up Display (HUD). The instrument cluster HUD system projects the frequently used driver information near the front of the vehicle as viewed from the driver's seat. The instrument cluster HUD system displays speed, turn indicators, high beam indicator, low fuel indicator, the check gauge indicator and radio information. Vehicle using a HUD system have a HUD specific windshield and a special instrument cluster

Although there are many similarities across the W-Body Product Line, there are differences in vehicle equipment, including the instrument panel display and the panel-mounted controls. Your Owner's Manual is a good reference for information specific to your vehicle, what the symbols, lights and chimes mean and what you should look for on the instrument cluster.

REMOVAL & INSTALLATION

➡ **To remove the instrument cluster on these vehicles, the large panel that surrounds the cluster must be removed. The factory calls this panel the instrument panel cluster trim plate and its removal varies from car line, model and vehicle year. Instrument panels and their surrounding pieces use a lot of plastic. The panels are retained by a combination of screws, clips and interlocking tabs. Work carefully to avoid cracking or breaking plastic pieces. Don't force anything or the panels could be damaged. In addition, use care when detaching and attaching the electrical connectors. The connector pins are very small and easily damaged.**

1997–00 Pontiac Models

▶ See Figures 68 and 69

✳✳ CAUTION

All models covered by this manual are be equipped with a Supplemental Inflatable Restraint (SIR) system, which uses an air bag. Whenever working near any of the SIR components, such as the impact sensors, the air bag module, steering column and instrument panel, disable the SIR, as described in this section.

➡ **The steering column must be loosened and lowered for this procedure. Center the front wheels and lock the column. This prevents damage to the coil that feeds power to the air bag module in the steering wheel.**

1. Disconnect the negative battery cable. Disable the SIR system, as outlined earlier in this section.
2. Remove the instrument panel cluster trim plate using the following procedure:
    a. Remove the left instrument panel insulator. This is the piece on the lower left side of the instrument panel adjacent to the driver's knee. This requires a Door Trim Pad and Garnish Clip Remover or similar tool.
    b. Remove the push-in retainers from the left

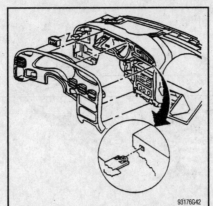

Fig. 68 Removing the instrument panel cluster trim plate—1997–00 Pontiac vehicles

instrument panel insulator using a trim clip remover.
    c. Disconnect the courtesy lamp.
    d. Pull the insulator panel forward from the stud at the accelerator pedal and remove the insulator panel from the vehicle.
    3. Remove the steering column opening filler. This is the panel under the steering column. Use the following procedure:
    a. Remove the screws from the bottom of the steering column opening filler.
    b. Pull the filler rearward and upward, unsnapping it from the instrument panel.
    c. Detach the connector from the low tire reset switch, if equipped.
4. Remove the knee bolster bracket. This piece is below the steering column. Use the following procedure:
    a. With the left instrument panel insulator and the steering column opening filler removed, detach the theft alarm shock sensor, if equipped.
    b. Remove the screws from the knee bolster

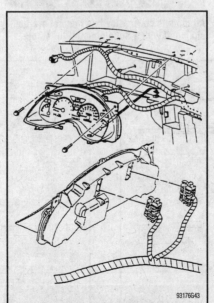

Fig. 69 Front view of the cluster removal and rear view of the wiring harness connectors—1997–00 Pontiac vehicles

bracket at the instrument panel. Also remove the screws from the bracket at the steering column support.
    c. Remove the knee bolster bracket from the steering column.
5. Lower the steering column, using the following procedure:
    a. Locate and remove the nuts that hold the steering column support bracket to the instrument panel structure.
    b. Gently lower the steering column until the steering wheel rests on the driver's seat cushion.
6. Grasp the instrument panel trim plate bottom edge on both sides of the steering column and pull to release the retainer clips. Continue pulling to release all of the clips.
7. Detach the electrical connector from the fog lamp switch.
8. Remove the instrument panel cluster trim plate from the instrument panel.
9. Remove the screws from the top of the instrument cluster.
10. Rotate the top of the cluster rearward and, lifting up, disengage the locating pins on the bottom of the cluster from the instrument panel.
11. Detach the electrical connectors from the instrument cluster and remove the instrument cluster from the vehicle.
12. Installation is the reverse of the removal process, noting the following.
    a. Use care to make sure all installation clips are properly located.
    b. Do not over-tighten any screws or they could force their way through their holes and the panel will not be held properly. Squeaks and rattles may develop later.
    c. Use care when raising the steering column back into position. Tighten the retaining nuts to 18 ft. lbs. (24 Nm).
13. Properly arm the SIR system, as outlined in this section.

1997–00 Buick Models

▶ See Figures 70 and 71

✳✳ CAUTION

All models covered by this manual are be equipped with a Supplemental Inflatable Restraint (SIR) system, which uses an air bag. Whenever working near any of the SIR components, such as the impact sensors, the air bag module, steering column and instrument panel, disable the SIR, as described in this section.

1. Disconnect the negative battery cable. Disarm the SIR system, as outlined in this section.
2. Remove the instrument panel cluster trim plate using the following procedure:
    a. Remove the instrument panel access hole covers from the instrument panel using a small flat-bladed tool.
    b. Remove the screws from each end of the instrument panel cluster trim plate.
    c. Remove the screw(s) from the lower edge of the right side of the trim plate.
    d. Open the instrument panel compartment (glove box) door.
    e. Pull the right lower trim panel plate from the instrument panel.

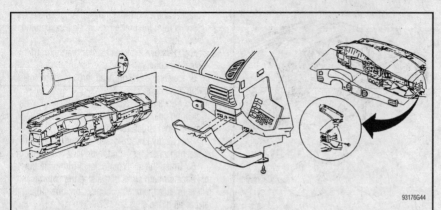

Fig. 70 Instrument panel cluster trim plate and related components—1997–00 Buick models

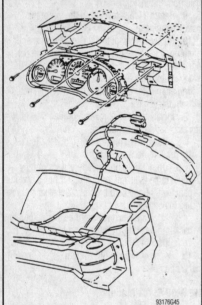

Fig. 71 Front view of instrument cluster removal and rear view of the wiring harness connectors—1997–00 Buick models

f. Pull the steering column tilt lever and tilt the steering column to its lowest position.

g. Grasp the instrument panel cluster trim plate at the right edge and slowly pull, working to the left to release the retainer clips. Remove the instrument panel cluster trim plate from the vehicle.

3. Remove the push-pin retainers from the top of the cluster.

4. Rotate the instrument cluster rearward and disengage the locating pins on the bottom of the cluster from the instrument panel. Detach the electrical connectors and remove the instrument cluster from the vehicle.

5. Installation is the reverse of the removal process. Use care to make sure all installation clips are properly located. Do not over-tighten any screws or they could force their way through their holes and the panel will not be held properly. Squeaks and rattles may develop later.

1997–00 Chevrolet Models

♦ See Figures 72 and 73

❋❋ CAUTION

All models covered by this manual are be equipped with a Supplemental Inflatable Restraint (SIR) system, which uses an air bag. Whenever working near any of the SIR components, such as the impact sensors, the air bag module, steering column and instrument panel, disable the SIR, as described in this section.

1. Disconnect the negative battery cable. Disarm the SIR system, as outlined in this section.

2. Remove the instrument panel cluster trim plate using the following procedure:

a. Move the shift lever from **Park** to **L1**, if equipped with a column shift.

b. Tilt the steering column to its lowest position.

c. Remove the instrument panel cluster trim plate by unsnapping the clips from the instrument panel and lifting the cluster trim panel from the vehicle.

3. Remove the retaining screws from the instrument cluster.

4. Rotate the instrument cluster rearward and disengage the locating pins on the bottom of the cluster from the instrument panel. Detach the electrical connector(s) and remove the instrument cluster from the vehicle.

5. Installation is the reverse of the removal process. Use care to make sure all installation clips are properly located. Do not over-tighten any screws or they could force their way through their holes and the panel will not be held properly. Squeaks and rattles may develop later.

6. Properly arm the SIR system, as outlined in this section.

1997–00 Oldsmobile Models

❋❋ CAUTION

All models covered by this manual are be equipped with a Supplemental Inflatable Restraint (SIR) system, which uses an air bag. Whenever working near any of the SIR components, such as the impact sensors, the air bag module, steering column and instrument panel, disable the SIR, as described in this section.

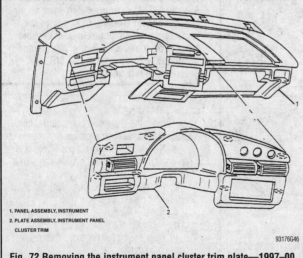

1. PANEL ASSEMBLY, INSTRUMENT
2. PLATE ASSEMBLY, INSTRUMENT PANEL
   CLUSTER TRIM

Fig. 72 Removing the instrument panel cluster trim plate—1997–00 Chevrolet

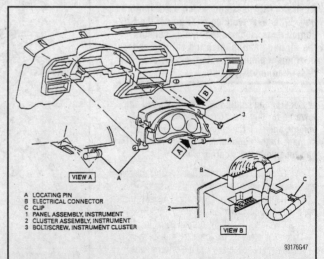

A LOCATING PIN
B ELECTRICAL CONNECTOR
C CLIP
1 PANEL ASSEMBLY, INSTRUMENT
2 CLUSTER ASSEMBLY, INSTRUMENT
3 BOLT/SCREW, INSTRUMENT CLUSTER

Fig. 73 Front view of instrument cluster removal and wiring harness connector—1997–00 Chevrolet

1997 CUTLASS SUPREME

♦ See Figures 74 and 75

➡This is an lengthy procedure and involves removing the front floor console, among other trim parts.

1. Disconnect the negative battery cable. Disarm the SIR system, as outlined in this section.

2. Remove the front floor console, if equipped. Use the following procedure:

a. Remove the transaxle shift handle. Look for a clip just under the top of the **T**handle. This is a horseshoe-shaped clip that retains the shift handle to the shift lever. Carefully pry the clip out with a small flat-blade tool.

b. Remove the screws from the rear compartment of the front floor console.

c. Remove the console transaxle shift opening trim by prying with a small flat-blade tool. Pry gently at the two rear tabs to remove the trim.

d. Remove the front console arm rest by raising it and removing the front console ashtray and steel flame plate. Loosen the two screws inside the ashtray area. Pry the sides of the base apart and remove the armrest at the rear hinge area, from between the base halves.

e. Disconnect the front console wiring and detach the electrical connectors.

f. Remove the screws from the front and rear of the console and remove the console from the vehicle.

3. Remove the instrument panel accessory trim plate. This piece typically surrounds the heater & A/C control panel and/or the radio. Locate and remove the screws from the lower instrument panel accessory trim plate and pull the plate downward to release the retainers. Then rotate the panel rearward and upwards to release the tabs at the top edge.

4. Remove the heater & A/C control panel. Use the procedure found earlier in this section.

5. Set the parking brake.

6. Move the shift lever from Park to L1, if equipped with a column shift.

7. Tilt the steering column to its lowest position and remove the tilt lever by rocking back and forth while pulling it from the steering column.

8. Insert a small flat-bladed tool into the slot in the instrument panel cluster trim plate directly below the headlamp switch. Push the tool handle down, releasing the plastic tab, then pull the trim plate rearward.

9. Grasp the instrument cluster trim plate at the right and below the right center A/C outlet and carefully pull to release the clip.

10. Remove the screw from the steering column wrap seal (below the steering column).

11. Grasp the instrument cluster trim plate bottom edge on both sides of the steering column and pull to release the two additional steel clips.

12. Detach the electrical connector to the cigarette lighter.

13. Insert a small flat-bladed tool into the slot at the left upper corner and raise the handle. Pull rearward at the center of the top edge to disengage the plastic clip on the trim plate. Remove the instrument cluster trim plate from the instrument panel.

14. Remove the two push-in retainers from the top of the instrument panel cluster.

15. Rotate the instrument cluster rearward and disengage the locating pins on the bottom of the cluster from the instrument panel. Detach the electrical connector(s) and remove the instrument cluster from the vehicle.

16. Installation is the reverse of the removal process, noting the following. Make sure the horseshoe-shaped clip is properly installed in the floor shift handle, if equipped. It should seat all the way in, not protruding from the shift handle. Use care to make sure all installation clips are properly located. Do not over-tighten any screws or they could force their way through their holes and the panel will not be held properly. Squeaks and rattles may develop later.

17. Properly arm the SIR system, as outlined earlier in this section.

1998–00 INTRIGUE

♦ See Figure 76

1. Disconnect the negative battery cable. Disarm the SIR system, as outlined in this section.

2. Remove the instrument panel cluster trim plate using the following procedure:

a. Remove the left side instrument panel insulator.

b. Remove the steering column opening filler panel.

c. Remove the screws retaining the instrument panel cluster trim plate to the trim pad.

d. Grasp the cluster trim plate along the bottom edge and carefully pull to release the retainers.

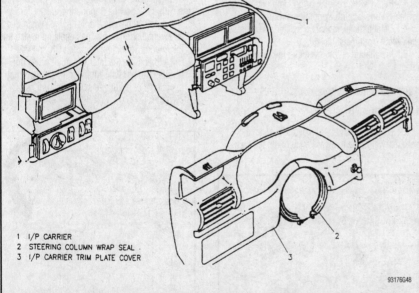

1 I/P CARRIER
2 STEERING COLUMN WRAP SEAL
3 I/P CARRIER TRIM PLATE COVER

93176G48

Fig. 74 Removing the instrument panel cluster trim plate—1997 Oldsmobile Cutlass Supreme

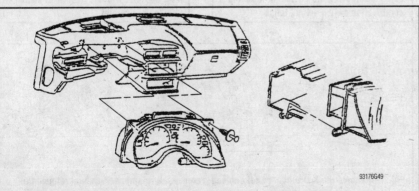

93176G49

Fig. 75 Front view of instrument cluster removal—1997 Oldsmobile Cutlass Supreme

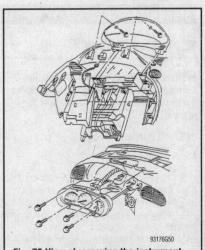

93176G50

Fig. 76 View of removing the instrument panel cluster trim panel (top) and instrument cluster (bottom)

e. Detach the electrical connector from the trip odometer and reset switch.

f. Using a small flat-blade tool, carefully release the switch retainers and remove the switch.

g. Remove the instrument cluster trim plate.

3. Remove the screws retaining the instrument cluster.

4. Detach the electrical connector and remove the instrument cluster from the vehicle.

5. Installation is the reverse of the removal process. Use care to make sure all installation clips are properly located. Do not over-tighten any screws or they could force their way through their holes and the panel will not be held properly. Squeaks and rattles may develop later.

6. Properly arm the SIR system, as outlined in this section.

Gauges

The instrument clusters on these vehicles are sealed electronic units. If a gauge is suspected of failure, it is recommended that the instrument cluster be checked at an authorized dealership using GM's instrument cluster testing equipment. This should verify if the problem is the gauge's sending unit or in the instrument cluster itself. If the cluster is defective, it must be replaced as an assembly.

Windshield Wiper Switch

REMOVAL & INSTALLATION

Dash Mounted Switches

➥**This procedure covers dash mounted switches only. For steering column mounted switches, please refer to Section 8 of this manual.**

1. Disconnect the negative battery cable.
2. Unfasten the screw from the instrument panel, under the switch.
3. Remove the assembly by carefully pulling the switch out to release the two spring clips at the top.
4. Installation is the reverse of the removal procedure.

Headlight Switch

REMOVAL & INSTALLATION

➥**These procedures cover dash mounted switches only. For steering column mounted switches, please refer to Section 8 of this manual.**

1997–00 Pontiac Models

▶ **See Figure 77**

1. Remove the instrument panel cluster trim plate, using the procedure found in this section under Instrument Cluster Removal and Installation.
2. Remove the headlamp switch by unsnapping from the instrument panel.
3. Detach the electrical connector and remove the switch from the vehicle.
4. Installation is the reverse of the removal procedure.

Fig. 77 Removing the headlamp switch—1997–00 Pontiac models

1997 Buick Models

▶ **See Figure 78**

➥**In 1997, the headlamp and fog lamp switch are combined in one unit.**

1. Remove the instrument panel cluster trim plate, using the procedure found in this section under Instrument Cluster Removal and Installation.
2. Remove the screws from the headlamp/ fog lamp combination switch.
3. Remove the headlamp/fog lamp combination switch by unsnapping from the instrument panel.
4. Detach the electrical connector and remove the switch from the vehicle.
5. Installation is the reverse of the removal procedure.

1998–00 Buick Models

▶ **See Figure 79**

1. Using a plastic flat-bladed tool as an aid if necessary, pull the rearward edge of the left side

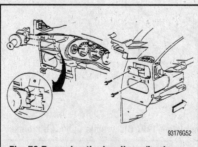

Fig. 78 Removing the headlamp/fog lamp combination switch—1997 Buick

instrument panel access opening cover outboard to release the retainers.

2. Release the forward edge of the left side instrument panel access opening cover from behind the hinge pillar and remove the cover.

3. Remove the screws retaining the headlamp switch.

4. Carefully pull the headlamp switch outboard away from the instrument panel to access the electrical connector.

5. Detach the electrical connector from the headlamp switch.

6. Installation is the reverse of the removal process.

1997–00 Chevrolet Models

▶ **See Figure 80**

1. Remove the instrument panel cluster trim plate, using the procedure found in this section under Instrument Cluster Removal and Installation.

2. Remove the headlamp switch from the instrument panel by depressing the locking tabs with a small flat-blade tool. Note that some Monte Carlo models may have the fog lamp switch share the same bracket as the headlamp switch. Simply pry loose the fog lamp switch, as applicable.

3. Detach the electrical connector and remove the switch from the vehicle.

4. Installation is the reverse of the removal process with the following important point:

a. After replacing the headlamp switch due to an external short, cycle the headlamp switch and the interior light dimmer switch ON and OFF twice to activate the internal circuit protection feature of the switch. All interior lights will not operate if the headlamp switch has not been cycled.

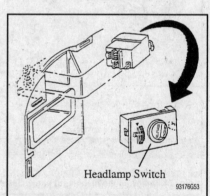

Fig. 80 Removing the headlamp switch—1997–00 Chevrolet

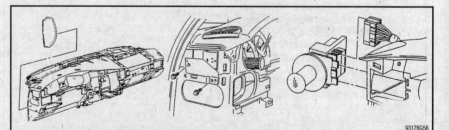

Fig. 79 Remove the instrument panel end cap, remove the retainer screws and remove the headlamp switch—1998–00 Buick

1997–00 Oldsmobile Models

1997 CUTLASS SUPREME

▶ **See Figure 81**

On this model, the headlamp switch, the fog lamp and the Heads Up Display (HUD) switch are all combined into one unit.

1. Remove the instrument panel cluster trim plate, using the procedure found in this section under Instrument Cluster Removal and Installation.
2. Remove the combination headlamp, fog lamp, and HUD control switch from the instrument panel by depressing the locking tabs with a small flat-blade tool.
3. Detach the electrical connector and remove the switch from the vehicle.
4. Installation is the reverse of the removal process.

1998–00 INTRIGUE

The Oldsmobile Intrigue combines the headlamp switch with the turn signal switch into what is often called a multifunction switch. The air bag and steering wheel must be removed to change out the multifunction switch. Please refer to Section 8 for the replacement procedures.

Ignition Switch

The vehicles covered by this manual use one of two types of ignition switches:

• A mechanical key and lock cylinder built into the steering column, that works a pull rod to actuate the separate electrical portion of the ignition switch mounted further down the steering column. For more information and replacement procedures on this type of switch, please see Section 8.

• An instrument panel-mounted ignition switch is also used on some W-Body vehicles. To service this switch, the radio, heater & A/C control panel and the instrument cluster must be removed. All of these procedures are found elsewhere in this section.

REMOVAL & INSTALLATION

Instrument Panel-Mounted Ignition Switch

▶ **See Figure 82**

❋❋ WARNING

You must perform the Body Control Module (BCM) theft deterrent relearn procedure after replacement of the ignition lock cylinder. Failure to perform this relearn procedure means the BCM will not function properly. This means the vehicle will not be theft protected by the Passlock system and the engine may not crank or start. GM recommends that this procedure be performed with their Tech 2® or equivalent scan tool. An alternate relearn procedure is given at the end of this procedure.

1. Disconnect the negative battery cable.
2. Remove the radio assembly following the procedures found in this section.
3. Remove the heater & A/C control head assembly following the procedures found in this section.

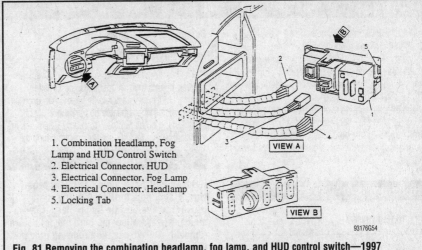

1. Combination Headlamp, Fog Lamp and HUD Control Switch
2. Electrical Connector, HUD
3. Electrical Connector, Fog Lamp
4. Electrical Connector, Headlamp
5. Locking Tab

VIEW A

VIEW B

93176G54

Fig. 81 Removing the combination headlamp, fog lamp, and HUD control switch—1997 Oldsmobile Cutlass Supreme

4. Remove the instrument cluster assembly following the procedures found in this section.
5. Detach the electrical connectors from the ignition switch.
6. Insert the key and turn the ignition switch lock cylinder to the **ACC** position.
7. Depress the transaxle park/lock cable retainer to release, then pull to remove the cable from the ignition switch.

➡**You must perform the Body Control Module theft deterrent relearn procedure after replacement of the ignition lock cylinder.**

8. If it is necessary to remove the ignition lock cylinder from the ignition switch (theft damage, etc.), use the following procedure:
   a. Insert the key and turn the ignition switch lock cylinder to the **ON** position.
   b. Using a small flat-bladed tool, depress and hold the lock cylinder retaining tab.
   c. Using the key as an aid, pull to remove the ignition switch lock cylinder from the switch.
   d. Remove the key from the lock cylinder.
   e. Carefully pull to release the ignition switch bezel from the ignition switch lock cylinder.
9. Remove the ignition switch bracket bolts and remove the ignition switch through the instrument panel cluster opening.
10. Remove the bolts retaining the ignition switch to the bracket and remove the bracket.

To install:

11. Install the ignition switch to its bracket and install the bolts. Install the ignition switch into position through the instrument panel cluster opening and install the bracket retaining bolts.
12. If removed, install the ignition switch lock cylinder to the ignition switch using the following procedure:
   a. Recode the lock cylinder, if necessary.
   b. Align the ignition switch bezel to the tabs on the ignition switch lock cylinder and carefully press to secure in place.
   c. Insert the key and turn the ignition switch lock cylinder to the **ON** position.
   d. Align the ignition switch lock cylinder to the ignition switch, then press into place.
13. Turn the key to the **ACC** position. Align and press into place the transaxle park/lock cable to the ignition switch. Remove the key from the switch.

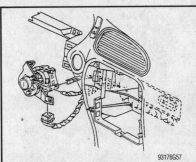

93176G57

Fig. 82 Removing an instrument panel-mounted ignition switch assembly—1998 Oldsmobile Intrigue shown, others similar

14. Attach the electrical connectors to the ignition switch.
15. Install the instrument cluster using the procedures found in this section.
16. Install the heater & A/C control panel using the procedures found in this section.
17. Install the radio assembly using the procedures found in this section.
18. Connect the negative battery cable.
19. If the lock cylinder was removed, perform the BCM Programming/RPO Configuration procedure.

THEFT DETERENT RE-LEARN—WITHOUT TECH 1® SCAN TOOL

This procedure takes approximately 30 minutes. Make sure the battery is fully charged before proceeding.

1. Turn the ignition switch to the **OFF** position.
2. Turn the ignition switch all the way from the **OFF** to the **START** position, then leave it in the **ON** position. The engine will not crank.
3. The SECURITY light should come on and stay on for at lease ten minutes.
4. Turn the ignition switch to the **OFF** position for five seconds.
5. Repeat Steps 2, 3 and 4 again for a second time.
6. Repeat Steps 2, 3 and 4 again for a third time.
7. Turn the ignition switch to the **OFF** position.
8. Turn the ignition switch all the way to the **START** position. The engine should now start.

LIGHTING

The exterior lighting system includes the headlamps and daytime running lamps, backup lamps, fog lamps, license lamps, side marker lamps, front parking/turn signal lamps, tail/stop/turn signal lamps, high-mounted stoplamp and underhood lamp and all related components.

The interior lighting system includes the dome lamps and convenience lamps such as the lower compartment (glove box) lamp, lighted rearview mirror, visor vanity mirror lamp and all related components.

Headlamps

REMOVAL & INSTALLATION

Sealed Beam

▶ See Figure 83

1. Open the hood.
2. Disconnect the negative battery cable.
3. Remove the headlamp bezel retainers and bezel.
4. Remove the spring from the bottom edge of the headlamp assembly.

➡ Do not apply pressure to the plastic bubble of the vertical aim indicator.

5. Detach the electrical connector from the assembly.
6. Unfasten the two screws from the headlamp retaining ring.
7. Rotate the retaining ring away from the headlamp.
8. Remove the headlamp from the vehicle.

To install:
9. Position the headlamp and retaining ring and secure with the two retaining screws. Tighten the screws to 18 inch lbs. (2 Nm).
10. Attach the electrical connector to the assembly.
11. Install the spring to the bottom of the headlamp assembly.
12. Install the headlamp bezel and retainers.
13. Connect the negative battery and test the lights for proper operation.

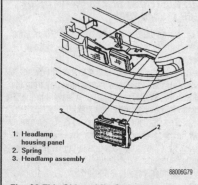

1. Headlamp housing panel
2. Spring
3. Headlamp assembly

88006G79

Fig. 83 This Oldsmobile Cutlass may be equipped with sealed beam headlamps

Composite Headlamps

▶ See Figures 84 thru 95

The headlamps used on the majority of vehicles covered by this manual are called "composite lamps". Unlike the glass sealed beam units used on older vehicles, these headlamps are made of special plastic using small halogen gas bulbs. The bulbs are replaceable, but they do require special handling.

✳✳ CAUTION

Halogen bulbs contain a gas under pressure. Handling a bulb improperly could cause it to shatter into flying glass fragments. Always allow the bulb to cool before removal. Always use the following precautions to help avoid personal injury.

- Turn the light switch OFF and allow the bulb to cool before changing bulbs. Leave the switch OFF until the bulb replacement procedure is complete.
- Always wear eye protection when changing a halogen bulb.
- Handle the bulb only by its base. Avoid touching the glass. Do not drop or scratch the bulb.
- Keep the bulb away from moisture.
- Place the used bulb in the new bulb's carton and dispose of it properly. Keep halogen bulbs out of reach of children.

Depending on the installation, the low-beam and the high-beam halogen bulbs may actually be removable without removing the entire composite headlamp assembly. Look your application over carefully to see there is enough room behind the headlamp to fit your hand to remove the bulb holder. Since removing the composite headlamp assembly is not difficult, the following procedure assumes that the headlamp is being removed from the vehicle for halogen bulb service.

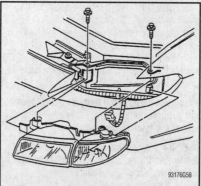

93176G58

Fig. 84 This Pontiac headlamp uses screws as retainers

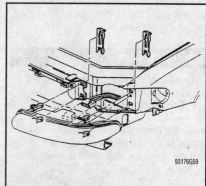

93176G59

Fig. 85 This Buick headlamp uses U-shaped plastic clips as retainers

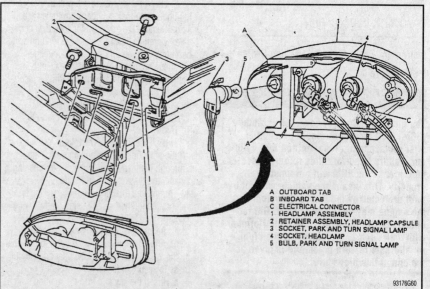

A OUTBOARD TAB
B INBOARD TAB
C ELECTRICAL CONNECTOR
1 HEADLAMP ASSEMBLY
2 RETAINER ASSEMBLY, HEADLAMP CAPSULE
3 SOCKET, PARK AND TURN SIGNAL LAMP
4 SOCKET, HEADLAMP
5 BULB, PARK AND TURN SIGNAL LAMP

93176G60

Fig. 86 This Chevrolet uses multiple special screw type retainers, although it may be possible to remove the halogen bulbs from behind, without removing the headlamp assembly

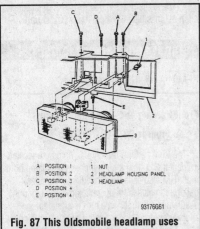

Fig. 87 This Oldsmobile headlamp uses multiple screws as retainers

Fig. 88 This Grand Prix uses two screws to retain the headlamp assembly

Fig. 89 With the two screws removed, the headlamp assembly is gently moved outboard (away from the vehicle center) to disengage the plastic tabs on the back of the lamp from their retainer slots in the sheetmetal mounting bracket

Fig. 90 This halogen bulb has a large, knurled plastic ring that retains the socket to the headlamp. Turn this ring to detach it

Fig. 91 Pull out the socket with the halogen bulb from the headlamp

Fig. 92 This type of halogen headlamp socket is turned to release and remove, or engage and install

Fig. 93 After twisting the socket free, pull the bulb and connector rearward, holding the base, NOT the glass

Fig. 94 Holding the bulb by the base, unplug from the connector

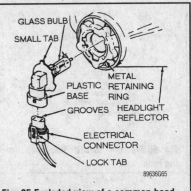

Fig. 95 Exploded view of a common headlamp bulb replacement

1. Raise the hood and look at the headlamp installation. On some applications, the headlamp is retained by screws and some molded tabs that slip into slots in the sheetmetal mounting bracket. On other applications, two U-shaped clips may hold the headlamp in place. Remove the headlamp retainers and gently work the headlamp free of the vehicle.

2. If the wiring harness is so short that it is difficult to work on the headlamp, simply unplug the electrical connector from the headlamp assembly.

3. The halogen bulb may have a large, knurled plastic ring that retains the socket to the headlamp. Turn this ring to detach it and remove the socket with the halogen bulb.

4. Remove the burned-out bulb and discard safely.

✳✳ WARNING

Do not touch the glass bulb with your fingers. Oil from your fingers can severely shorten the life of the bulb. If necessary, wipe off any dirt or oil from the bulb with rubbing alcohol before completing installation.

5. Take great care not to touch the new replacement halogen bulb as oil from your skin will burn when the bulb is turned on and may damage the glass, shortening the life of the bulb. Use a clean, dry paper towel to handle the bulb.

6. Installation is the reverse of the removal procedure.

7. Verify that the lights work correctly.

AIMING THE HEADLAMPS

▶ **See Figures 96, 97 and 98**

The headlamps must be properly aimed to provide the best, safest road illumination. The lights should be checked for proper aim and adjusted as necessary. Certain state and local authorities have requirements for headlamp aiming; these should be checked before adjustment is made.

✳✳ CAUTION

About once a year, when the headlamps are replaced or any time front end work is performed on your vehicle, the headlamp should be accurately aimed by a reputable repair shop using the proper equipment. Headlamps not properly aimed can make it virtually impossible to see and may blind other drivers on the road, possibly causing an accident. Note that the following procedure is a temporary fix, until you can take your vehicle to a repair shop for a proper adjustment.

Headlamp adjustment may be temporarily made using a wall, as described below, or on the rear of another vehicle. When adjusted, the lights should not glare in oncoming car or truck windshields, nor should they illuminate the passenger compartment

of vehicles driving in front of you. These adjustments are rough and should always be fine-tuned by a repair shop which is equipped with headlamp aiming tools. Improper adjustments may be both dangerous and illegal.

Before removing the headlamp bulb or disturbing the headlamp in any way, note the current settings in order to ease headlamp adjustment upon reassembly. If the high or low beam setting of the old lamp still works, this can be done using the wall of a garage or a building:

1. Park the vehicle on a level surface, with the fuel tank about ½ full and with the vehicle empty of all extra cargo (unless normally carried). The vehicle should be facing a wall which is no less than 6 feet (1.8m) high and 12 feet (3.7m) wide. The front of the vehicle should be about 25 feet from the wall.

2. If neither beam on one side is working, and if another like-sized vehicle is available, park the second one in the exact spot where the vehicle was and mark the beams using the same-side light. Then switch the vehicles so the one to be aimed is back in the original spot. It must be parked no closer to or farther away from the wall than the second vehicle.

3. Perform any necessary repairs, but make sure the vehicle is not moved, or is returned to the exact spot from which the lights were marked. Turn the headlamps ON and adjust the beams to match the marks on the wall.

4. Have the headlamp adjustment checked as soon as possible by a reputable repair shop.

Signal and Marker Lights

REMOVAL & INSTALLATION

Front Parking and Turn Signal Lamps

▶ **See Figures 99, 100, 101 and 102**

The front parking/turn signal lamps are located in the left and right side composite headlamp housings (GM also calls them headlamp capsules). The parking lamps can be operated any time using the headlamp switch. When a turn is signaled, the appropriate front parking lamp switches to signal a turn. The turn signals operate only with the ignition switch in the **RUN** position and will not operate during hazard flasher operation.

Look the job over carefully. On some vehicles, the parking and turn signal lamp bulbs can be replaced by simply twisting the socket free and replacing the bulb. On other vehicles, the lamp assembly must be removed.

1. Open the hood.

2. If the parking/turn signal bulb can be accessed, twist the socket to free it from the lamp assembly and withdraw the socket and bulb assembly.

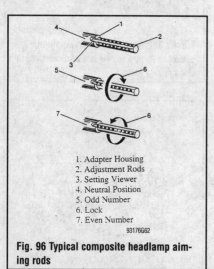

1. Adapter Housing
2. Adjustment Rods
3. Setting Viewer
4. Neutral Position
5. Odd Number
6. Lock
7. Even Number

93176G62

Fig. 96 Typical composite headlamp aiming rods

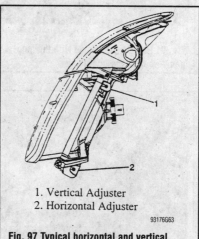

1. Vertical Adjuster
2. Horizontal Adjuster

93176G63

Fig. 97 Typical horizontal and vertical adjuster locations

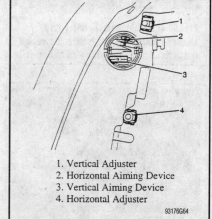

1. Vertical Adjuster
2. Horizontal Aiming Device
3. Vertical Aiming Device
4. Horizontal Adjuster

93176G64

Fig. 98 Vehicle headlamp aiming device (RH)—Buick shown, others similar

93176P20

Fig. 99 This parking lamp/turn signal socket has a locking tab that needs to be depressed to rotate the socket

93176P19

Fig. 100 Depress the locking tab with your thumb, then rotate the socket to remove

93176P21

Fig. 101 With the socket free, the bulb can be replaced

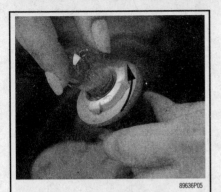

Fig. 102 Carefully push in the bulb and turn it counterclockwise to unlock it

3. If the parking/turn signal bulb cannot be accessed, remove the lamp assembly. Twist the socket to free the locking tabs and withdraw the socket and bulb assembly. Some applications may use a locking tab that needs to be depressed so the socket can be rotated.

Side Marker Lights
▶ See Figures 103, 104 and 105

The side marker lights are located on the sides of the headlamp assemblies. These lamps will light when the headlamp or parking lights are ON. If the headlamp or parking lamps are OFF when a turn is signaled, the appropriate side marker lamp will flash in unison with the with the front turn signal

Fig. 103 On some applications, the side marker bulb socket can be accessed through the engine compartment or from underneath

lamp. If the headlamps or parking lamps are ON when a turn is signaled, the side marker lamp and the front turn signal lamp will flash alternately.

1. On some applications, the marker lamp bulb socket can be accessed through the engine compartment or from under the front valence panel. On other applications, the headlamp assembly should be removed for access.

2. The side marker lamp socket simply twists to remove.

3. The bulb is a baseless bulb and just pulls out of the socket.

4. Inspect the socket. They are often subject to road splash, dirt and corrosion. Clean as required.

5. Install a new bulb and reassemble in the reverse order of removal.

Fig. 104 On this application, the side marker bulb lamp is part of the headlamp assembly

Rear Turn Signal, Brake and Parking Lamps
▶ See Figures 106, 107, 108 and 109

The taillamps, stoplamps and rear turn signals lamps are all incorporated into the rear taillamps. The taillamps are lit whenever the parking lamps or headlamps are in operation. The rear turn signal lamps flash with the front turn signal lamps whenever a turn is indicated with the turn signal/headlamp dimmer switch. The stoplamps light whenever the brake pedal is depressed and the stoplamp switch is closed.

1. Open the rear compartment (trunk).

2. If equipped, unhook the convenience net that stretches between the taillamps. It is attached to hooks molded into the plastic taillamp assembly retaining wingnuts. Loosen the rear compartment trim panel. It is retained by plastic pins with a screw in the center. Back out the screw to release any tension on the plastic pin legs, and pull the trim (thin carpet-like material) for access to the taillamps.

3. Remove the plastic taillamp assembly retaining wingnuts.

4. Remove the taillamp assembly from the vehicle and service the light bulbs as required.

5. Installation is the reverse of the removal process.

6. Test the lights for correct operation.

High-Mounted Stoplamp Bulb
▶ See Figures 110 and 111

The high-mounted stoplamp is in the center of the rear window and lights whenever the brake pedal is depressed and the stoplamp switch is

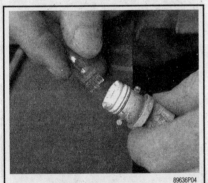

Fig. 105 Twist the socket to unlock it and pull the bulb from the socket

Fig. 106 The trim panel is likely held in place with retainers like this. Back out the screw to release tension on the pin legs and remove the fastener

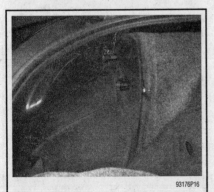

Fig. 107 The taillamp is retained by plastic wingnuts

Fig. 108 Remove the plastic wing nuts from the taillamp housing

Fig. 109 Remove the taillamp housing from the vehicle to service the light bulbs

Fig. 110 This Grand Prix had a slotted vent panel covering the high-mounted stoplamp assembly. Squeeze the ends to remove or install

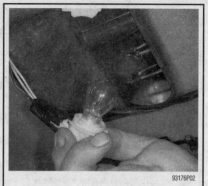

Fig. 111 A quarter-turn removes the socket so the bulb can be serviced

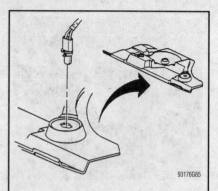

Fig. 112 Removing an under-dash courtesy lamp

closed. The bulbs are accessed from inside the trunk.

1. Open the trunk.

2. If equipped with a slotted vent panel, remove it from the access opening by squeezing the ends and pulling down.

3. Reach through the access opening and turn the bulb socket ¼-turn counterclockwise to remove the socket. Most applications will use two sockets/bulbs. Verify that the correct bulb is being replaced.

4. Replace the bulb as required.

Interior Courtesy Lamps

♦ **See Figures 112 thru 120**

Most W-Body vehicles will have two courtesy lamps under the instrument panel that come on when a door is opened, or when the interior lamps are turned on. Some applications may also have overhead console reading lamps.

Some applications may also have a dome lamp mounted to the headliner between the front seats. The dome lamp will come on when a door is opened or when the interior lamps are turned on.

On vehicles so equipped, the lamps next to the visor mirror will come on when the mirror cover is raised.

Side rail lamps, if equipped, will come on when a door is opened or when the interior lamps are turned on.

Not all vehicles will have all of these interior lights. Application varies from vehicle to vehicle. Service on all of these lamps is similar, differing only in accessing the socket. In most cases, a small flat-bladed prytool is all that is required to unclip or flex a lens cover to remove and/or install. The following should suffice for most all these lamps.

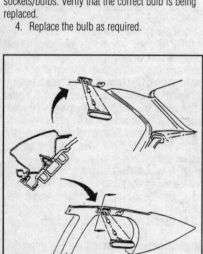

Fig. 113 Removing a side rail lamp

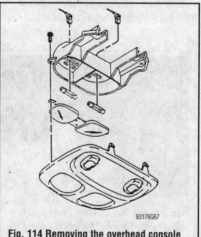

Fig. 114 Removing the overhead console reading lamp—Type 1

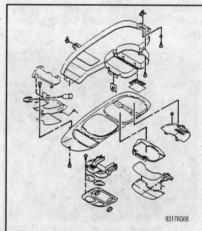

Fig. 115 Removing the overhead console reading lamp—Type 2

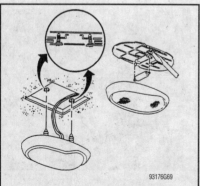

Fig. 116 Removing the dome lamp lens—Type 2

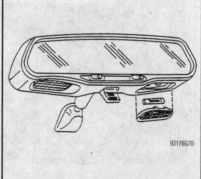

Fig. 117 Removing the lighted rearview mirror lens

Fig. 118 Removing the lighted visor mirror lens

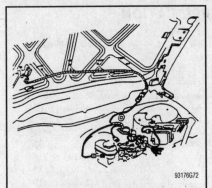

Fig. 119 Underhood lamp arrangement—Pontiac shown, others similar

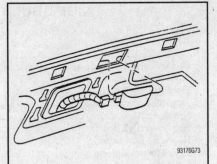

Fig. 120 Trunk compartment lamp arrangement—Pontiac shown, others similar

Fig. 121 Removing the license plate lamp retaining screws with a small socket wrench and a flexible extension

• COURTESY LAMPS: Remove the left or right instrument panel insulator and turn the courtesy lamp socket ¼ turn counterclockwise to remove the socket from the panel. Change the bulb.

• SIDE RAIL LAMPS: Remove the side rail lamp from its retainers using a small flat-bladed prytool. Remove the socket from the panel. Change the bulb. Align the lamp studs to the roof retainers and press the lamp evenly to install.

• OVERHEAD CONSOLE READING LAMPS: Remove the overhead console reading lamp retainers from the housing using a small flat-bladed prytool at the front of the housing. Remove the screws at the housing, remove the housing and lens. Pry out bulb from the socket using a small flat-bladed prytool.

• DOME LAMP: Remove the dome lamp lens by squeezing together until the housing releases from the base plate. It may also be possible to pry the side of the housing using a small flat-bladed prytool. Change the bulb.

• LIGHTED REARVIEW MIRROR: Remove the lens from the lighted rearview mirror using a small flat-bladed prytool. Change the bulb.

• LIGHTED VISOR MIRROR: Remove the lens from the rearview mirror by prying, using a small flat-bladed prytool to flex and release the lens. Pry out bulb from the socket using a small flat-bladed prytool.

• UNDERHOOD LAMP: Using a small flat-bladed prytool, press down on the upper retainer tabs on the upper area of the lens. Pull the lens up and out of the lamp. Change the bulb.

• TRUNK LAMP: Open the trunk. Remove the socket from the lamp. Change the bulb.

License Plate Lamp

▶ **See Figures 121, 122, 123 and 124**

The license lamp(s) are located in the rear fascia license pocket or the trunk lid applique panel. The lamp(s) light whenever the headlamps or parking lamps are activated.

1. If the lamp is mounted to the fascia panel:
   a. Remove the retaining screws.
   b. Remove the socket and change the bulb.

2. If the lamp is mounted to the trunk lid applique panel, perform the following:
   a. Open the trunk and locate the applique harness connector. Detach the connector.
   b. Using a small flat-bladed prytool, remove the grommet at the trunk lid.
   c. Remove the wing nuts from the applique panel.
   d. Remove the applique panel from the trunk link.
   e. Remove the light socket(s) and change the bulb(s).

3. Installation is the reverse of the removal process.

Fog/Driving Lamps

▶ **See Figures 125 and 126**

The fog lamps are operated by a separate instrument panel mounted switch. The fog lamps will go

Fig. 122 Separate the license lamp from the rear panel

Fig. 123 With the license plate lamp removed, unplug the socket and change the bulb

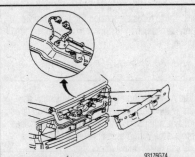

Fig. 124 On some models, the license plate lamp and even back-up lamps are mounted in the trunk-mounted rear fascia panel, detachable by removing the inside fasteners

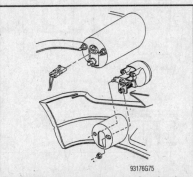

Fig. 125 Fog lamps are mounted under the bumper either in pockets in the bumper or on small brackets—Pontiac shown

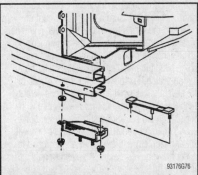

Fig. 126 These fog lamps are mounted under the bumper on small brackets—Buick shown

off whenever the high-beam headlamps are turned on and when you return to low beam headlamps, the fog lamps will come on again. Most installation have provision for vertical (not horizontal) aim by an adjusting nut located on the rear of the fog lamp.

REMOVAL & INSTALLATION

▶ **See Figures 125 and 126**

1. Detach the electrical connector from the rear of the lamp.
2. Remove the lamp mounting nuts.
3. Installation is the reverse of the removal process.

INSTALLING AND WIRING AFTERMARKET EQUIPMENT

GM states "Don't add anything electrical to your (vehicle) unless you check with your dealer first. Some electrical equipment can damage your vehicle and the damage won't be covered by your warranty. Some add-on electrical equipment can keep other components from working as they should."

Because of the extensive computer control of your W-Body vehicle, just "tapping in" to an electrical circuit could produce unforeseen problems, not the least of which is corrosion from where the wiring insulation has been compromised. Always consult with your dealer before adding any aftermarket equipment on your vehicle.

LIGHT BULB APPLICATION

Exterior Lamps	Trade Number
Backup Lamp	3156
Front Fog Lamp	880
Front Parking/Turn Signal Lamps	3357NA or 4157NAK
Front Side Marker Lamp	194
Headlamp	9007
Headlamp High Beam	9005
Headlamp Low Beam	9006
High-Mount Stoplamp	1141 or 3155
License Lamp	194
Rear Side Marker Lamp	194
Taillamp/Stoplamp/Turn Signal Lamp	3057
Trunk Lamp	920
Underhood Lamp	561

Interior Lamps	Trade Number
Ashtray	194
Transaxle Position Indicator Lamp	T-1.0
Courtesy Lamps	194
Driver Information Center	PC74
Headlamp High Beam Indicator	PC195
Heater and A/C Control	T-1.0, T-1.5
Instrument Panel Compartment (Glove Box)	194
Indicator Lamps	PC74
Overhead Console Reading Lamp	168
Side Rail Lamp	168
Turn Signal Indicators	PC74
Vanity Mirror Lamp	74

Note: This is general listing of light bulbs used in the lamps on General Motors W-Body vehicles. Since running changes are always possible, look for a number on the bulb being replaced and replace with the equivalent bulb. Your Owner's Manual should also contain a listing of Replacement Bulbs specific to your vehicle.

93176G77

CIRCUIT PROTECTION

The purpose of circuit protection is to protect the wiring assembly during normal and overload conditions. An overload is defined as a current requirement that is higher than normal. This overload could be caused by a short circuit or system malfunction. The short circuit could be the result of a pinched or cut wire or an internal device short circuit, such as an electronic module failure.

The circuit protection device is only applied to protect the wiring assembly, and not the electrical load at the end of the assembly. For example, if an electronic component short circuits, the circuit protection device will assure a minimal amount of damage to the wiring assembly. However, it will not necessarily prevent damage to the component.

The vehicle's power distribution system consists of fuses, fusible links, circuit breakers and the ignition switch. Fusible links are short pieces of wire several sizes smaller than the circuit wire to which they supply power. They are covered with special high temperature insulation. When conducting an improperly high current flow, they will melt and stop current flow. They are designed to protect the vehicle's electrical system from electrical shorts in circuits not protected by circuit breakers or fuses.

There are three basic types of circuit protection device: Fuses, Fusible links and Circuit breakers.

Fuses

▶ **See Figure 127**

The most common method of automotive wiring circuit protection is the fuse. A fuse is a device that, by the melting of its element, opens an electrical

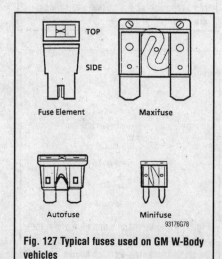

Fig. 127 Typical fuses used on GM W-Body vehicles

circuit when the current exceeds a given level for a sufficient time. The action is non-reversible and the fuse must be replaced each time a circuit is overloaded or after a malfunction is repaired.

Fuses are color-coded with standardized color identification and ratings. For service replacement, non-color fuses of the same respective rating can be used.

Examine a suspect fuse for a break in the element. If the element is broken or melted, replace the fuse with one of equal current rating.

There are additional specific circuits with in-line fuses. These fuses are located within the individual wiring harness and will appear to be an open circuit if blown.

AUTOFUSE

The Autofuse, normally referred to simply as "fuse" is the most common circuit protection device in today's vehicle. The Autofuse is most often used to protect the wiring assembly between the Fuse Block and the system components.

MAXIFUSE

The MaxiFuse was designed to replace the fusible link and Pacific Fuse elements. The Maxi-

Fuse is designed to protect cables, normally between the battery and fuse block, from both direct short circuits and resistive short circuits.

Compared to a fusible link or a Pacific Fuse element, the MaxiFuse performs much more like an Autofuse, although the average opening time is slightly longer. This is because the MaxiFuse was designed to be a slower blowing fuse, with less chance of nuisance blows.

MINIFUSE

The MiniFuse is a smaller version of the Autofuse and has a similar performance. As with the Autofuse, the MiniFuse is usually used to protect the wiring assembly between a fuse block and system components. Since the MiniFuse is a smaller device, it allows for more system specific fusing to be accomplished within the same amount of space as Autofuses.

PACIFIC FUSE ELEMENT/MAXIFUSE

The Pacific Fuse Element and MaxiFuse were developed to be a replacement for the fusible link. Like a fusible link, the fuses are designed to protect wiring from a direct short to ground. These elements are easier to service and inspect than a fusible link and will eventually replace fusible links in future vehicle applications.

REPLACEMENT

▶ **See Figures 128, 129, 130 and 131**

Your vehicle likely has several fuse box locations. There may be one or two underhood electrical centers with fuses and relays. There could also be an underdash fuse box. Some models have removable end caps on the instrument panel harboring a fuse box. Always consult your Owner's Manual for fuse box location specific to your vehicle.

1. Remove the trim panels or covers necessary for access to the fuses.
2. Locate the fuse for the circuit in question.

❊❊ WARNING

When replacing fuses, DO NOT use one with a higher amperage rating.

3. Check the fuse by pulling it from the fuse box and observing the element. If it is broken, install a replacement fuse of the same amperage rating. If the fuse blows again, check the circuit for a short to ground or faulty device in the circuit protected by the fuse.
4. Continuity can also be checked with the fuse installed in the fuse box with the use of a test light connected across the two test points on the end of the fuse. If the test light lights, replace the fuse.

Check the circuit for a short to ground or faulty device in the circuit protected by the fuse.

Fusible Links

▶ **See Figures 132 and 133**

In addition to circuit breakers and fuses, some circuits use fusible links to protect the wiring. Like fuses, fusible links are "one-time" protection devices that will melt and create an open circuit.

Not all fusible link open circuits can be detected by observation. A blown link often, but not always, has "bubbly" appearing insulation making troubleshooting easier. Always inspect that there is battery voltage past the fusible link to verify continuity.

Fusible links are used instead of a fuse in wiring circuits that are not normally fused, such as the ignition circuit. For AWG sizes (wire gauges), each fusible link is four wire gauge sizes smaller than the wire it is designed to protect. For example: to protect a 10 gauge wire, use a 14 gauge link (or for metric, to protect a 5mm wire, use a 2mm link). Links are marked on the insulation with wire-gauge size because the heavy insulation makes the link appear to be a heavier gauge than it actually is. The same wire size fusible link must be used when replacing a blown fusible link.

Fig. 128 This underhood fuse box on a Grand Prix has a diagram on the inside of the fuse box cover identifying the circuit protection devices inside

Fig. 129 This underhood fuse box has its own fuse puller and several spare fuses inside

Fig. 130 This Lumina also has an underhood fuse box. The cover removes by pressing on the retainer clips

Fig. 131 Although there is no identification diagram on this Lumina fuse box, at least access is good. Note the remote battery positive terminal cover next to the fuse box

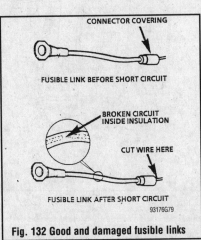

Fig. 132 Good and damaged fusible links

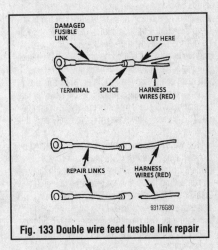

Fig. 133 Double wire feed fusible link repair

Choose the shortest length that is available. A fusible link should NEVER be longer than nine inches. Fusible links longer than this will not provide sufficient overload protection.

To replace a damaged fusible link, cut it off beyond the splice. Replace with a repair link. When connecting the repair link, strip the wire and use staking-type pliers to crimp the splice securely in two places. To replace a damaged fusible link which feeds two harness wires, cut them both off beyond the splice. Use two repair links, one spliced to each wire harness.

Circuit Breakers

A circuit breaker is a protective device designed to open a circuit when a current load is in excess of rated breaker capacity. If there is a short or other type of overload condition in the circuit, the excessive current will open the circuit between the circuit breaker terminals. There are two types of circuit breakers used in GM vehicles: cycling and non-cycling.

The cycling circuit breaker will open due to heat generated when excessive current passes through it for a period of time. Once the circuit breaker cools, it will close again after a few seconds. If the cause of the high current is still present, it will open again. It will continue to cycle open and closed until the condition causing the high current is removed.

There are two types of non-cycling breakers. One type is mechanical and is nearly the same as a cycling breaker. The difference is a small heater wire within the non-cycling circuit breaker. This wire provides enough heat to keep the bimetallic open until the current source is removed.

The other type is solid state, called an Electronic Circuit Breaker (ECB). This device has a Positive Temperature Coefficient. It increases its resistance greatly when excessive current passes through it. The excessive current heats the ECB. As it heats, its resistance increases, therefore having a Positive Temperature Coefficient. Eventually the resistance gets so high that the circuit is opened, removing voltage from its terminals. Once voltage is removed, the circuit breaker will re-close within a second or two.

The primary application of a circuit breaker is the headlights. If the headlamps were protected by a fuse and fault developed driving at night, the headlamps would go out, an unacceptable situation. So a cycling-type circuit breaker is built into the headlamp switch. If a fault develops, the headlamps will go our momentarily, then the breaker quickly resets and the headlamps will come on again. If the fault is still there, the headlamps will go out, the breaker will reset again, and the headlamp will come on again. If the cycle keeps repeating, the result is the headlamps will seem to continuously flash on and off. This at least allows the driver to safely stop the vehicle.

The windshield wiper motor is also protected by a circuit breaker. If the wiper motor overheats (wipers frozen to the windshield or stuck in heavy snow, stalling the motor, for example) the circuit breaker will trip, remaining off until the motor cools or the overload is removed.

There may also be some circuit breakers in the fuse box for the power door locks, power seats and power windows.

Flashers

◆ See Figures 134 and 135

On most W-Body vehicles, the hazard and turn signal flasher is mounted below the steering column.

If the turn signal and/or hazard lamps do not work, first check the fuses. If one of the turn signal lamps goes on when the park lamps are turned on, check the front park/turn lamps on that side for an open or poor connection. If the turn lamps stay on (do not flash) in both turn left and turn right, replace the flasher.

For any of the following symptoms, replace the turn signal switch:
- Turn signal switch will not turn ON/OFF.
- All turn/hazard/stoplamps do not work and all harness connector are secure.

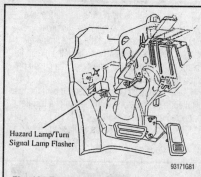

Hazard Lamp/Turn
Signal Lamp Flasher

93171G81

Fig. 134 Typical hazard/turn signal lamp flasher location—1997 Chevrolet shown

- Some turn lamps work and all hazard lamps work.
- Some hazard lamps work and all turn lamps work.
- The hazard lamps do not turn OFF.

If the hazard lamps stay on but do not flash with the hazard switch ON, but the stoplamps operate normally, replace the turn/hazard flasher.

If the stoplamps do not turn OFF, adjust/replace the stoplamp switch.

If a turn signal indicator does not light but the turn signal works, check the bulb connection and wiring to the indicator.

If only one lamp does not operate, check the lamp socket and related wiring for opens and corrosion.

If one front park and/or marker lamp does not light, check that its ground is clean and tight.

If the park lamps do not turn OFF. Check the headlamp switch. If okay, look for a short to battery power in the wiring.

- If one rear lamp is operative, check for an open in the wire. If the wire is okay, the socket may need to be replaced.
- Check for a broken (or partially) broken wire inside of the insulation which could cause a system malfunction but prove good in a continuity/voltage check with a system disconnected. These circuits may be intermittent or resistive when loaded, and if possible, should be checked by monitoring for a voltage drop with the system operational (under load).

Check for improper installation of aftermarket equipment and accessories. For example, a poorly installed trailer towing light connector may affect the rest of the lighting system.

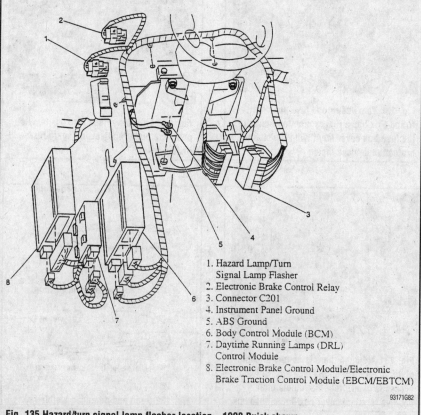

1. Hazard Lamp/Turn
   Signal Lamp Flasher
2. Electronic Brake Control Relay
3. Connector C201
4. Instrument Panel Ground
5. ABS Ground
6. Body Control Module (BCM)
7. Daytime Running Lamps (DRL)
   Control Module
8. Electronic Brake Control Module/Electronic
   Brake Traction Control Module (EBCM/EBTCM)

93171G82

Fig. 135 Hazard/turn signal lamp flasher location—1998 Buick shown

WIRING DIAGRAMS

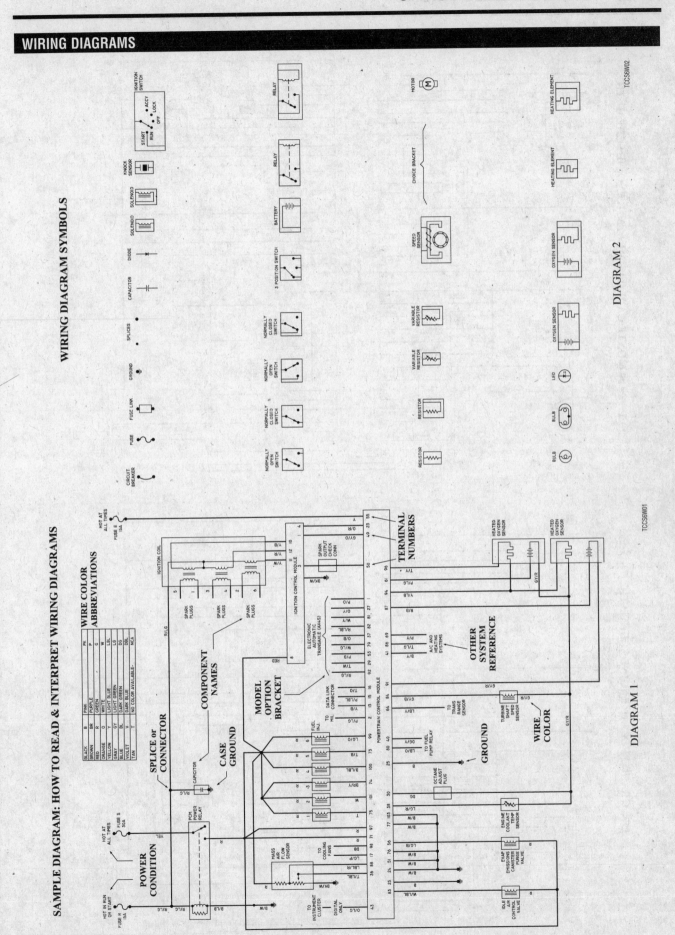

WIRING DIAGRAM SYMBOLS

DIAGRAM 2

SAMPLE DIAGRAM: HOW TO READ & INTERPRET WIRING DIAGRAMS

DIAGRAM 1

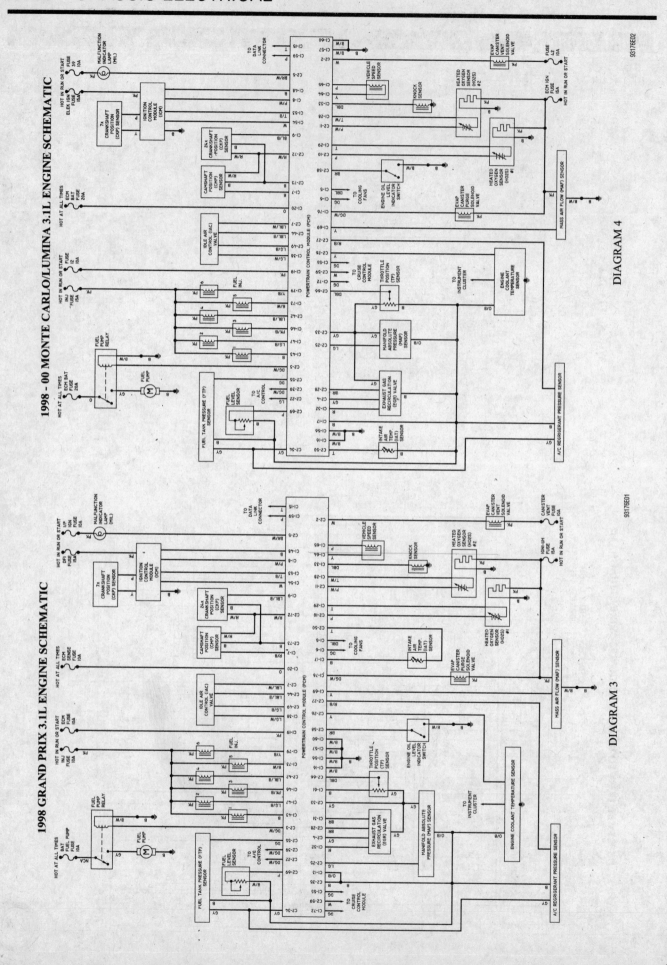

1998 - 00 MONTE CARLO/LUMINA 3.1L ENGINE SCHEMATIC

DIAGRAM 4

1998 GRAND PRIX 3.1L ENGINE SCHEMATIC

DIAGRAM 3

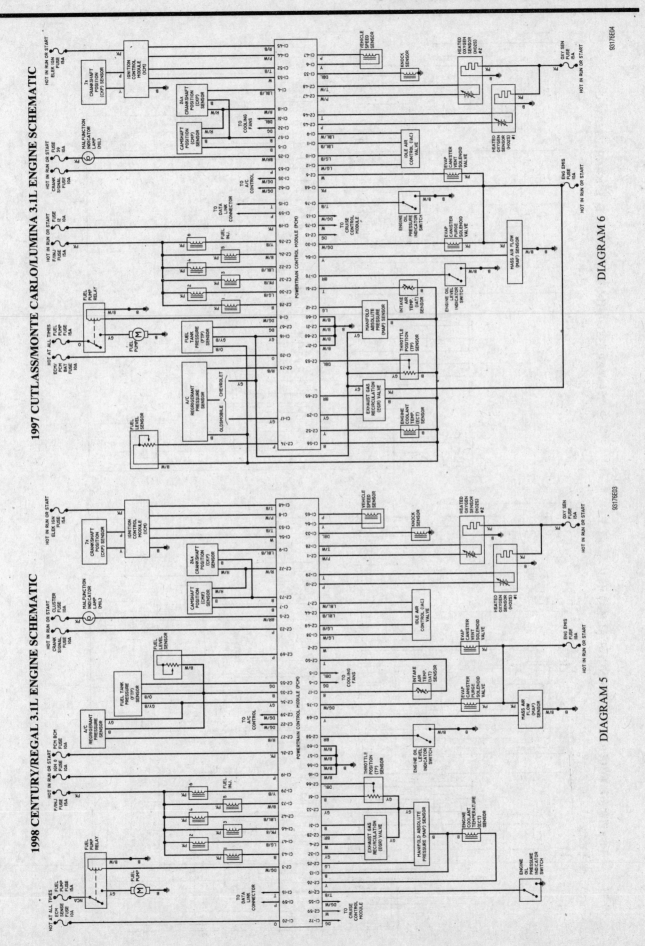

1997 CUTLASS/MONTE CARLO/LUMINA 3.1L ENGINE SCHEMATIC

DIAGRAM 6

1998 CENTURY/REGAL 3.1L ENGINE SCHEMATIC

DIAGRAM 5

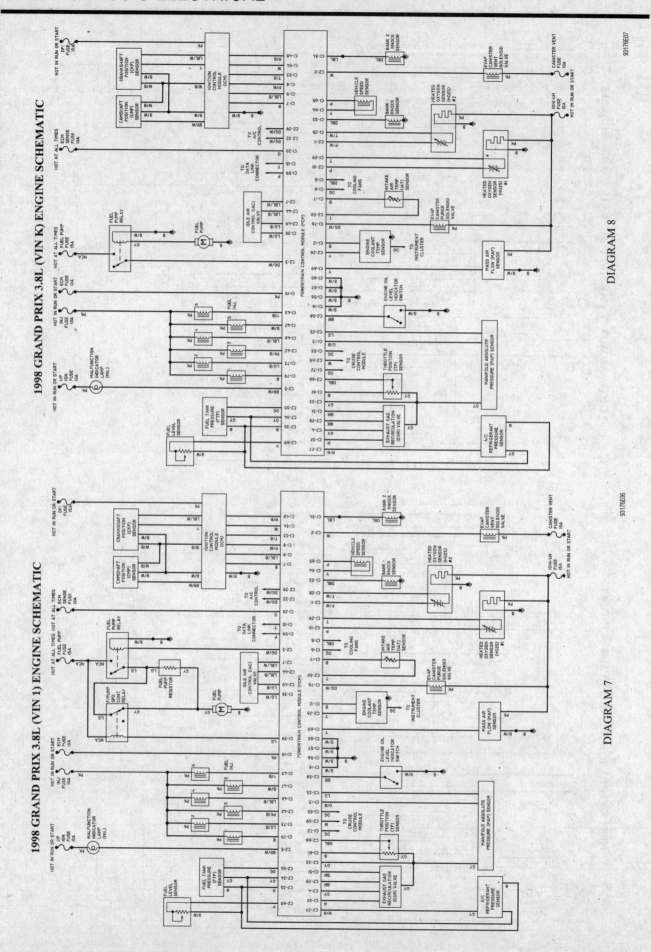

1998 GRAND PRIX 3.8L (VIN K) ENGINE SCHEMATIC

DIAGRAM 8

1998 GRAND PRIX 3.8L (VIN 1) ENGINE SCHEMATIC

DIAGRAM 7

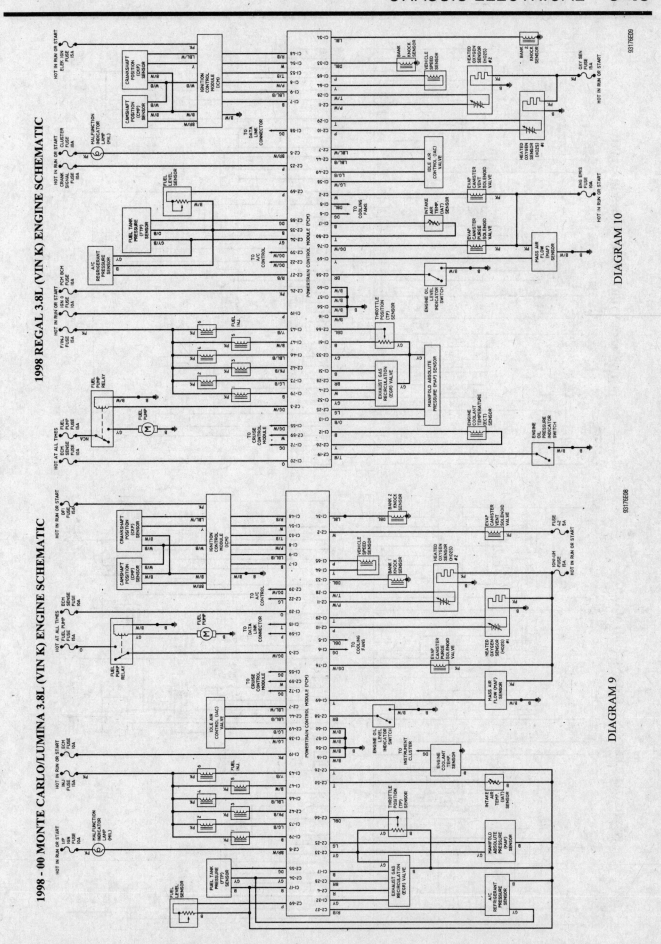

1998 REGAL 3.8L (VIN K) ENGINE SCHEMATIC

DIAGRAM 10

1998 - 00 MONTE CARLO/LUMINA 3.8L (VIN K) ENGINE SCHEMATIC

DIAGRAM 9

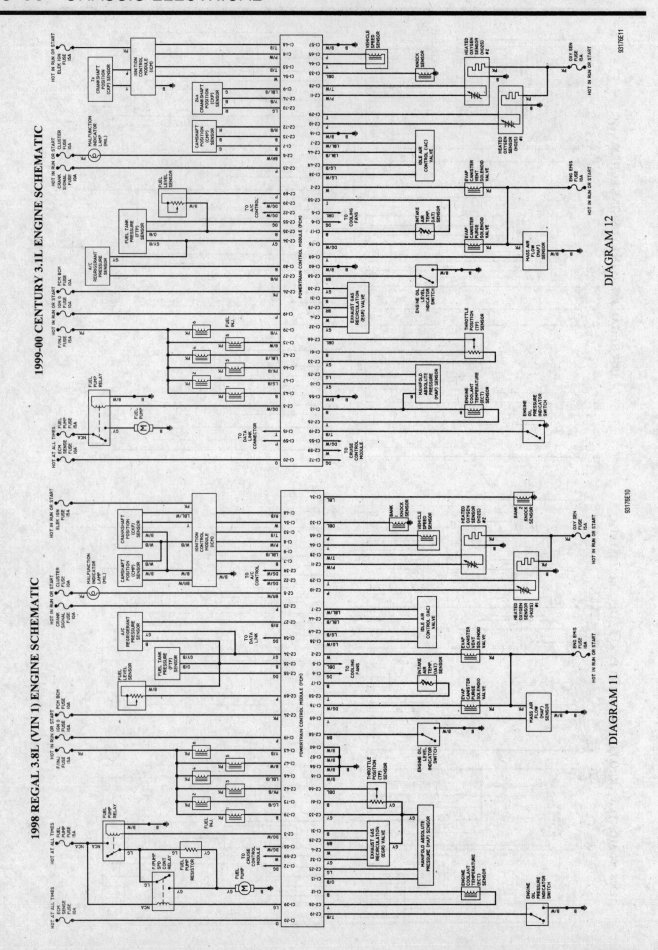

1999-00 CENTURY 3.1L ENGINE SCHEMATIC

DIAGRAM 12

1998 REGAL 3.8L (VIN 1) ENGINE SCHEMATIC

DIAGRAM 11

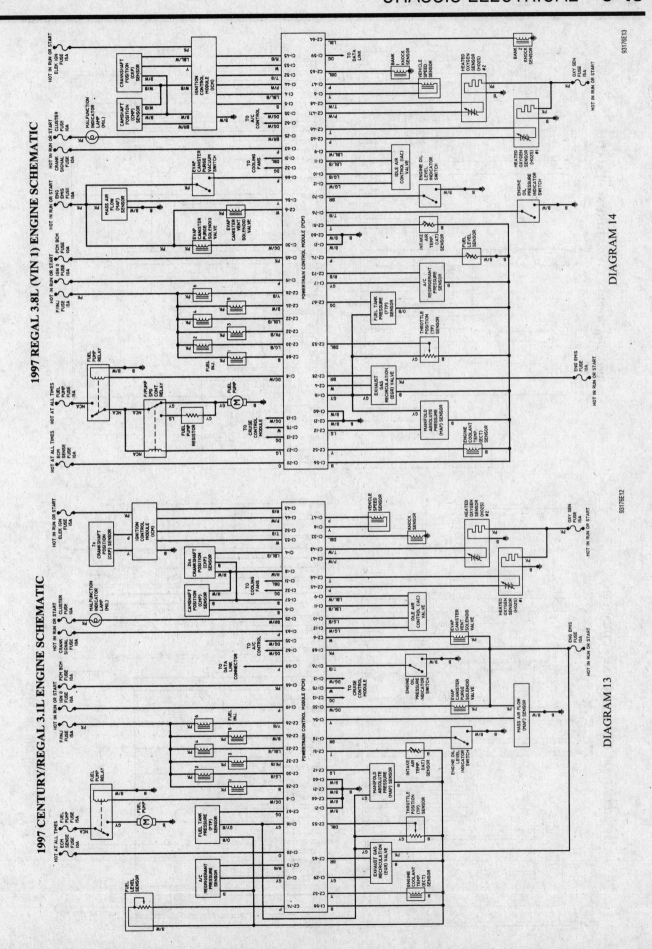

1997 REGAL 3.8L (VIN 1) ENGINE SCHEMATIC

DIAGRAM 14

1997 CENTURY/REGAL 3.1L ENGINE SCHEMATIC

DIAGRAM 13

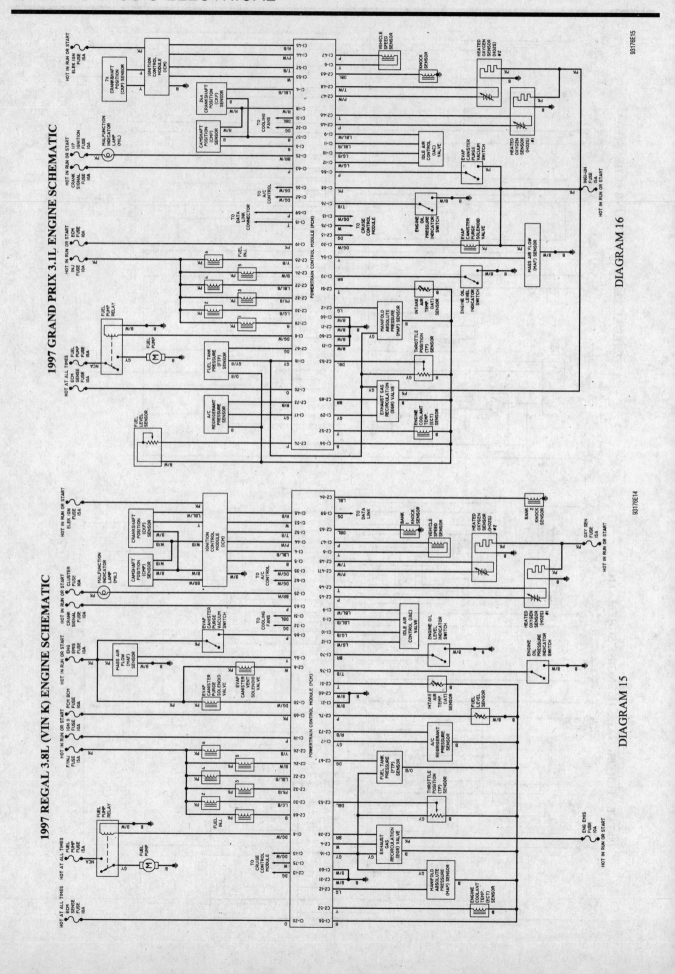

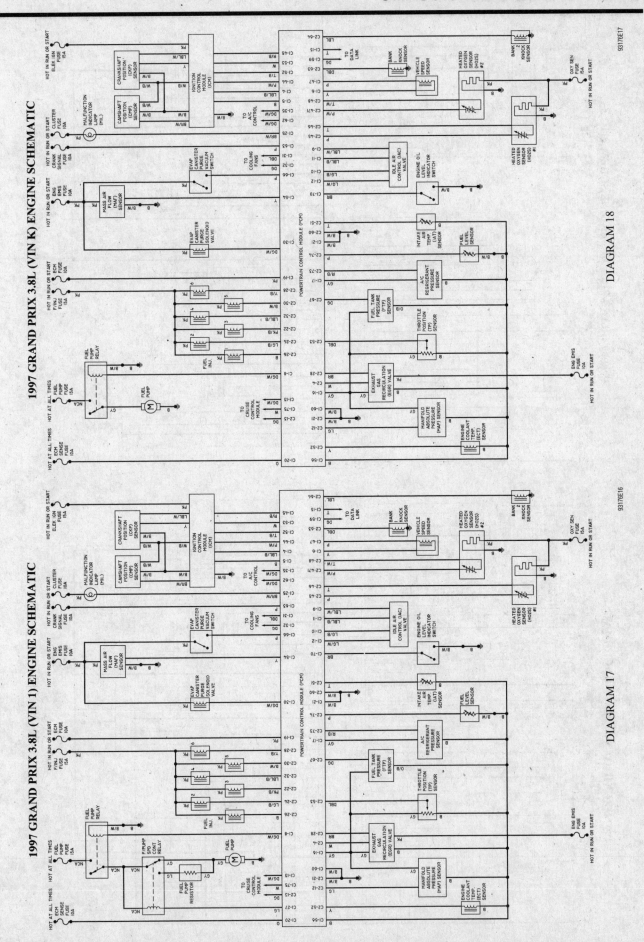

1997 GRAND PRIX 3.8L (VIN K) ENGINE SCHEMATIC

DIAGRAM 18

1997 GRAND PRIX 3.8L (VIN 1) ENGINE SCHEMATIC

DIAGRAM 17

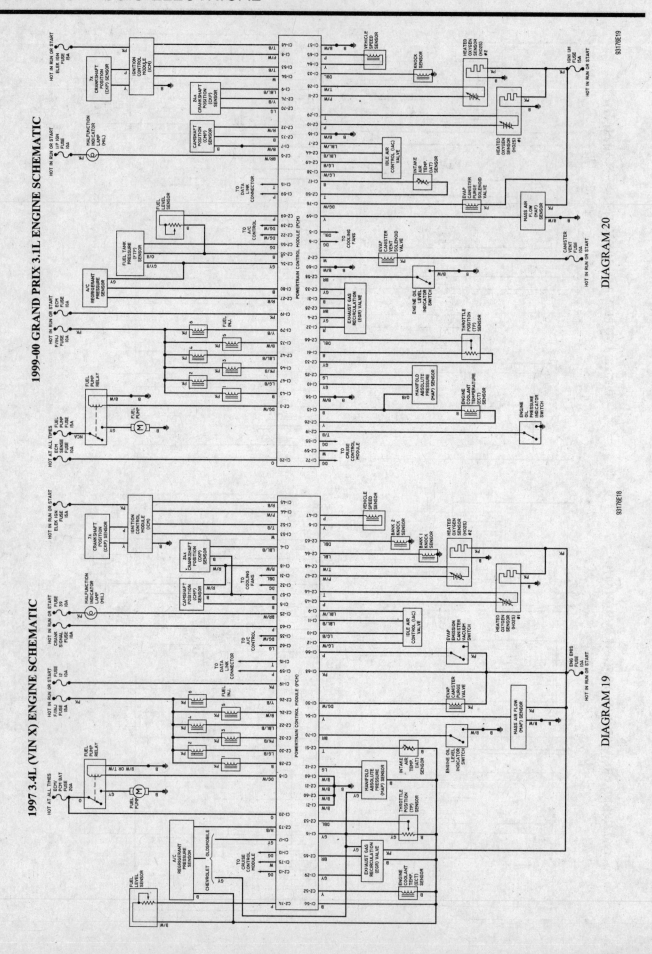

1999-00 GRAND PRIX 3.1L ENGINE SCHEMATIC

DIAGRAM 20

1997 3.4L (VIN X) ENGINE SCHEMATIC

DIAGRAM 19

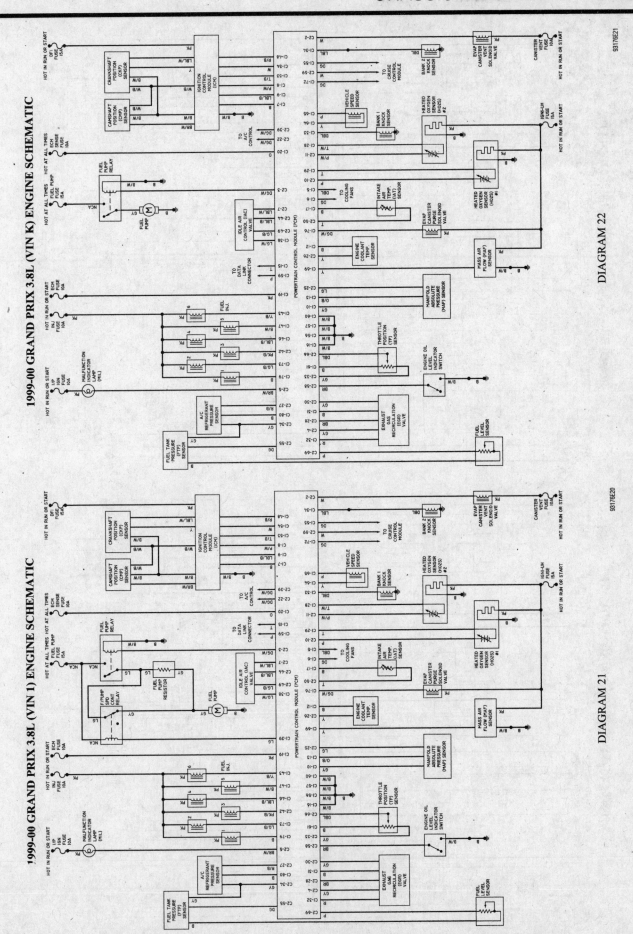

1999-00 GRAND PRIX 3.8L (VIN K) ENGINE SCHEMATIC

DIAGRAM 22

1999-00 GRAND PRIX 3.8L (VIN 1) ENGINE SCHEMATIC

DIAGRAM 21

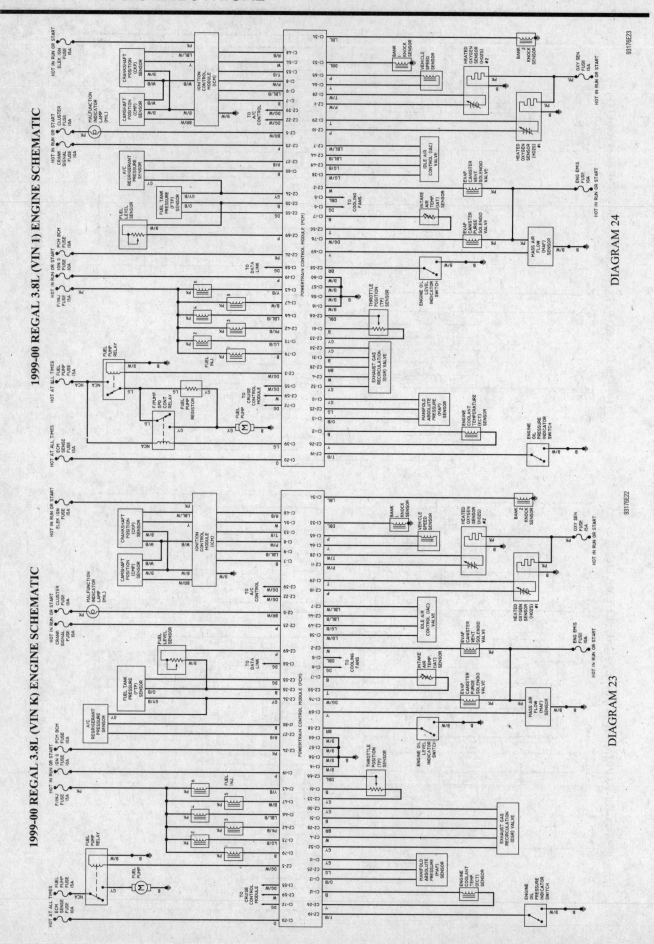

1999-00 REGAL 3.8L (VIN 1) ENGINE SCHEMATIC

DIAGRAM 24

1999-00 REGAL 3.8L (VIN K) ENGINE SCHEMATIC

DIAGRAM 23

1997 - 00 GRAND PRIX/REGAL/CENTURY CHASSIS SCHEMATIC

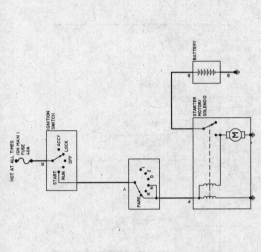

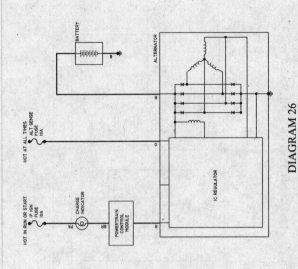

DIAGRAM 26

1997-00 MONTE CARLO/LUMINA/CUTLASS CHASSIS SCHEMATIC

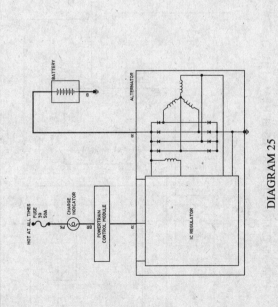

DIAGRAM 25

1997-2000 CHASSIS SCHEMATICS

CUTLASS/
REGAL/
CENTURY/
GRAND PRIX

MONTE CARLO/
LUMINA/
INTRIGUE

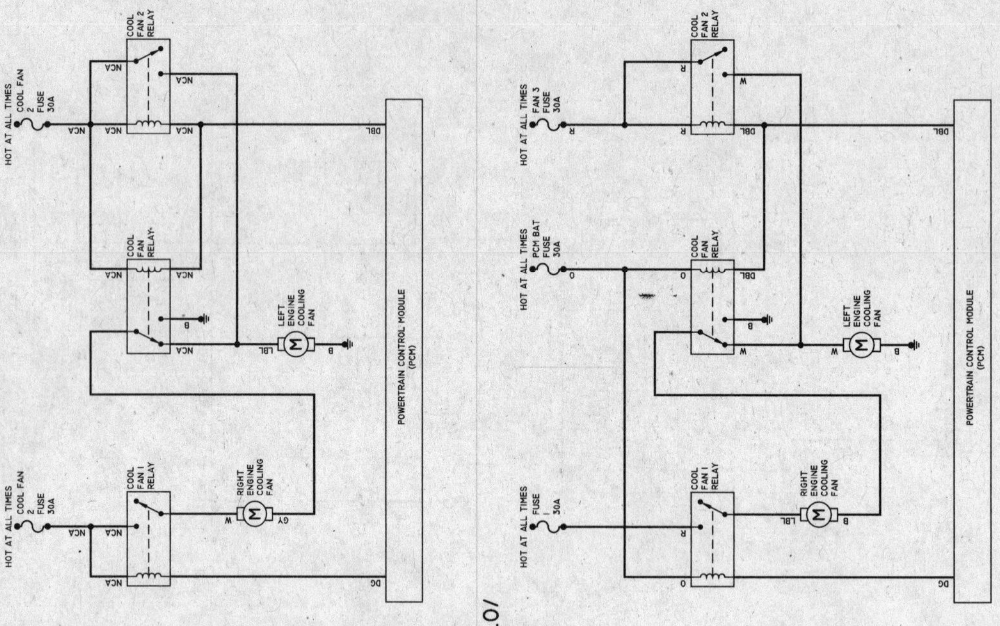

93176B04

DIAGRAM 28

1998 - 00 INTRIGUE CHASSIS SCHEMATIC

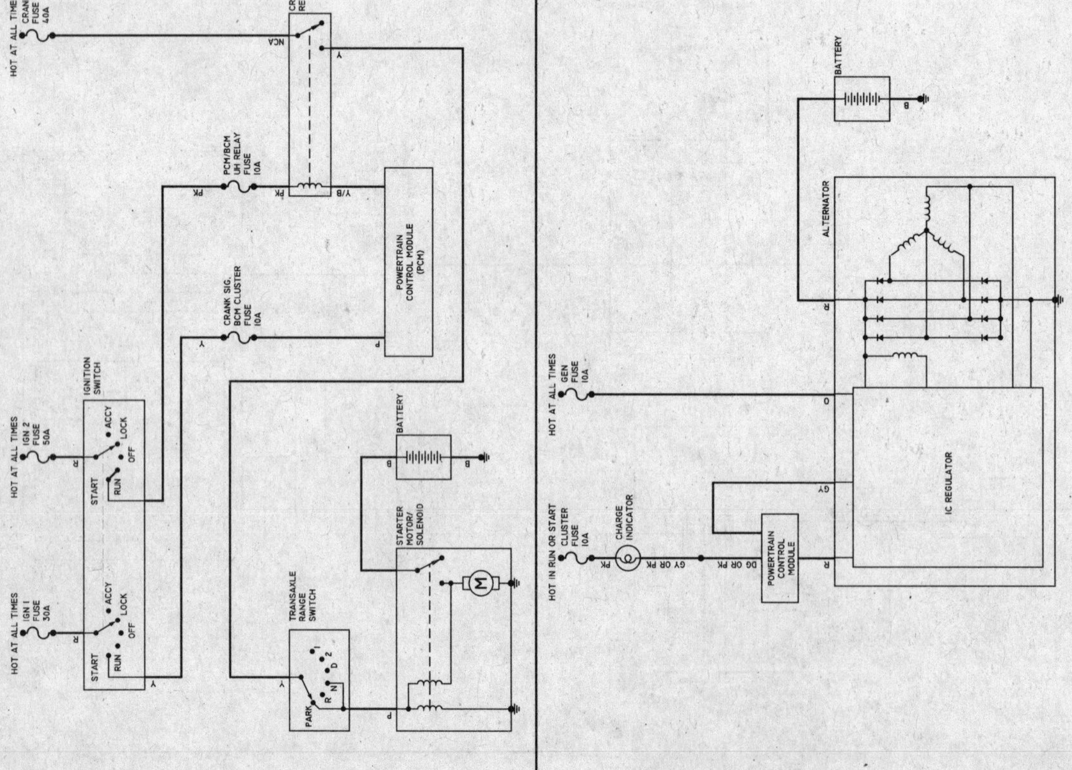

93176B03

DIAGRAM 27

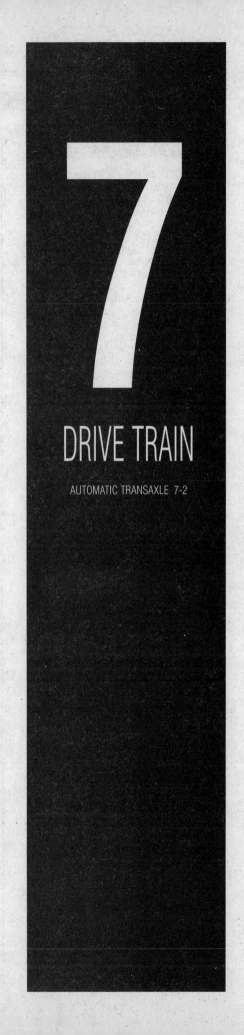

7

DRIVE TRAIN

AUTOMATIC TRANSAXLE

Understanding the Automatic Transaxle

The automatic transaxle allows engine torque and power to be transmitted to the front wheels within a narrow range of engine operating speeds. It will allow the engine to turn fast enough to produce plenty of power and torque at very low speeds, while keeping it at a sensible rpm at high vehicle speeds (and it does this job without driver assistance). The transaxle uses a light fluid as the medium for the transaxle of power. This fluid also works in the operation of various hydraulic control circuits and as a lubricant. Because the transaxle fluid performs all of these functions, trouble within the unit can easily travel from one part to another. For this reason, and because of the complexity and unusual operating principles of the transaxle, a basic understanding of the basic principles of operation will simplify troubleshooting.

TORQUE CONVERTER

♦ See Figure 1

The torque converter has several main functions:
• It allows the engine to idle with the vehicle at a standstill, even with the transaxle in gear.
• It allows the transaxle to shift from range-to-range smoothly, without requiring that the driver close the throttle during the shift.
• It multiplies engine torque to an increasing extent as vehicle speed drops and throttle opening is increased. This has the effect of making the transaxle more responsive and reduces the amount of shifting required.
• The torque lock-up feature reduces slippage when at cruise speed, increasing efficiency and fuel mileage.

The torque converter is a metal case, generally shaped like a sphere flattened on opposite sides. It is bolted to the engine flywheel, rotating at engine speed. The case contains three sets of blades. One set is attached directly to the case. This set forms the torus or pump. Another set is directly connected to the output shaft, and forms the turbine. The third set is mounted on a hub which, in turn, is mounted on a stationary shaft through a one-way clutch. This

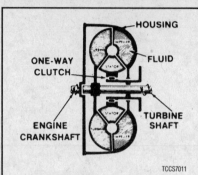

Fig. 1 The torque converter housing is rotated by the engine's crankshaft by means of the flywheel, and turns the impeller. The impeller then spins the turbine, which gives motion to the turbine shaft, driving the gear

third set is known as the stator. A pump, which is driven by the converter hub at engine speed, keeps the torque converter full of transaxle fluid at all times. Fluid flows continuously through the unit to provide cooling. Under low speed acceleration, the torque converter functions as follows:

The torus is turning faster than the turbine. It picks up fluid at the center of the converter and, through centrifugal force, slings it outward. Since the outer edge of the converter moves faster than the portions at the center, the fluid picks up speed. The fluid then enters the outer edge of the turbine blades. It then travels back toward the center of the converter case along the turbine blades. In impinging upon the turbine blades, the fluid loses the energy picked up in the torus. If the fluid was now returned directly into the torus, both halves of the converter would have to turn at approximately the same speed at all times, and torque input and output would both be the same. In flowing through the torus and turbine, the fluid picks up two types of flow, or flow in two separate directions. It flows through the turbine blades, and it spins with the engine. The stator, whose blades are stationary when the vehicle is being accelerated at low speeds, converts one type of flow into another. Instead of allowing the fluid to flow straight back into the

torus, the stator's curved blades turn the fluid almost 90° toward the direction of rotation of the engine. Thus the fluid does not flow as fast toward the torus, but is already spinning when the torus picks it up. This has the effect of allowing the torus to turn much faster than the turbine. This difference in speed may be compared to the difference in speed between the smaller and larger gears in any gear train. The result is that engine power output is higher, and engine torque is multiplied. As the speed of the turbine increases, the fluid spins faster and faster in the direction of engine rotation. As a result, the ability of the stator to redirect the fluid flow is reduced. Under cruising conditions, the stator is eventually forced to rotate on its one-way clutch in the direction of engine rotation. Under these conditions, the torque converter begins to behave almost like a solid shaft, with the torus and turbine speeds being almost equal.

Since some slippage was inherent in former torque converter design, in recent years vehicle manufacturers have gone to a Torque Converter Clutch (TCC) to "lock-up" the sections of a torque converter at certain speeds. This eliminates much of slippage, providing greater efficiency of operation and better fuel mileage. The Torque Converter Clutch used on the vehicles covered by this manual is controlled by an electronic solenoid. The rate of apply/release is controlled by an electronic Pulse Width Modulation solenoid valve to avoid lack of smoothness found in older TCC designs.

PLANETARY GEARBOX

♦ See Figures 2, 3 and 4

The ability of the torque converter to multiply engine torque is limited. Also, the unit tends to be more efficient when the turbine is rotating at relatively high speeds. Therefore, a planetary gearbox is used to carry the power output of the turbine to the driveshaft.

Planetary gears function very similarly to conventional transaxle gears. However, their construction is different in that three elements make up one gear system, and, in that all three elements are different from one another. The three elements are: an outer gear that is shaped like a hoop, with teeth cut into the inner surface; a sun gear, mounted on a

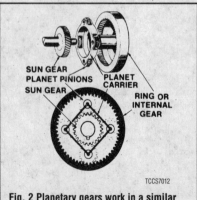

Fig. 2 Planetary gears work in a similar fashion to manual transaxle gears, but are composed of three part

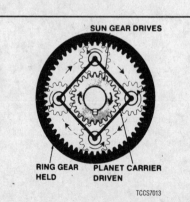

Fig. 3 Planetary gears in the maximum reduction (low) range. The ring gear is held and a lower gear ratio is obtained

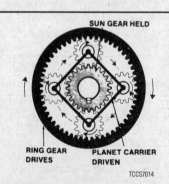

Fig. 4 Planetary gears in the minimum reduction (drive) range. The ring gear is allowed to revolve, providing a higher gear ratio

shaft and located at the very center of the outer gear; and a set of three planet gears, held by pins in a ring-like planet carrier, meshing with both the sun gear and the outer gear. Either the outer gear or the sun gear may be held stationary, providing more than one possible torque multiplication factor for each set of gears. Also, if all three gears are forced to rotate at the same speed, the gearset forms, in effect, a solid shaft.

Most automatics use the planetary gears to provide various reductions ratios. On the transaxles used in the vehicles covered by this manual, both bands and multiple disc wet clutches are used to hold various portions of the gearsets to the transaxle case or to the shaft on which they are mounted. Shifting is accomplished, then, by changing the portion of each planetary gearset which is held to the transaxle case or to the shaft.

SERVOS AND ACCUMULATORS

▶ **See Figure 5**

The servos are hydraulic pistons and cylinders. They resemble the hydraulic actuators used on many other machines, such as bulldozers. Hydraulic fluid enters the cylinder, under pressure, and forces the piston to move to engage the band or clutches.

The accumulators are used to cushion the engagement of the servos. The transaxle fluid must pass through the accumulator on the way to the servo. The accumulator housing contains a thin piston which is sprung away from the discharge passage of the accumulator. When fluid passes through the accumulator on the way to the servo, it must move the piston against spring pressure, and this action smoothes out the action of the servo.

Fig. 5 Servos, operated by pressure, are used to apply or release the bands, to either hold the ring gear or allow it to rotate

HYDRAULIC CONTROL SYSTEM

The hydraulic pressure used to operate the servos comes from the main transaxle oil pump. This fluid is channeled to the various servos through the shift valves. There is a manual shift valve which is operated by the transaxle selector lever and an automatic shift valve for each automatic upshift the transaxle provides.

➡**All of the automatic transaxles on the GM W-Body vehicles are electronically controlled.**

Electrical solenoids are used to better control the hydraulic fluid. The solenoids are regulated by the Powertrain Control Module (PCM).

Only the 4T60-E transaxle uses a vacuum modulator. The slightly more heavy-duty 4T65-E does not. A vacuum modulator responds to the engine's manifold vacuum. In this way, the clutches and bands will be actuated with a force matching the torque output of the engine. The modulator valve helps adjust line boost pressure and affects the 1-2 accumulator valve, a secondary 1-2 accumulator valve, as well as both the 2-3 and 3-4 accumulator valves. A vacuum modulator can be checked with a hand vacuum pump. The modulator should hold approximately 5 in. Hg of vacuum for 30 seconds.

SYSTEM OPERATION

The 4T60-E and 4T65-E transaxles used in the vehicles covered by this manual are fully automatic front wheel drive transaxles. They provide four forward ranges including overdrive.

You can operate the transaxle in any one of the seven following modes:

- P—PARK position prevents the vehicle from rolling either forward or backward. For safety reasons, use the parking brake in addition to the park position.
- R—REVERSE allows the vehicle to be operated in a rearward direction.
- N—NEUTRAL allows the engine to be started and operated while driving the vehicle. If necessary, you may select this position to restart the engine with the vehicle moving.
- OD—OVERDRIVE is used for all normal driving conditions. OVERDRIVE provides four gear ratios plus a converter clutch operation. Depress the accelerator to downshift for safe passing.
- D—DRIVE position is used for city traffic, hilly terrain and trailer towing. DRIVE provides three gear ranges. Depress the accelerator to downshift.
- 2—Manual SECOND provides acceleration and engine braking. You may select this range at any vehicle speed, but, depending on the model, the transaxle will not downshift until the vehicle speed drops below a certain speed (approximately 60 mph).
- 1—Manual LOW provides maximum engine braking. You may select this range at vehicle speeds under 40 mph. but, depending on the model, the transaxle will not downshift until the vehicle speed drops below a certain speed. Manual LOW is not available on some models.

When an automatic transaxle not operating properly, it is likely influenced by one, or a combination of the following items:

- Fluid level too low or two high.
- Engine performance problems.
- Manual linkage adjustment.
- Internal fluid leaks.
- Electrical problems.
- Transaxle or other mechanical components
- Vacuum Modulator, if equipped (4T60-E transaxles).

If noise or vibration is noticeable in PARK and NEUTRAL with the engine at idle, but is less noticeable as RPM increases, the cause may be from poor engine performance. A noise or vibration that is noticeable when the vehicle is in motion, MAY NOT be the result of the transaxle. Inspect:

- Check the tires for uneven wear, imbalance, mixed sizes or mixed radial and bias ply tires.
- Check the suspension for alignment and worn out components or loose fasteners.
- Check the engine and transaxle mounts for damage and loose fasteners.
- Check the transaxle case mounting holes for missing bolts, stripped threads and cracks.
- Check the flywheel for missing or loose bolts, crack and for imbalance.
- Check the torque converter for missing or loose bolts or balance weights.

Fluid Pan

Pan removal, fluid and filter changes are covered in Section 1 of this manual.

Transaxle Range Switch

The backup lamps will light whenever the ignition switch is in the **RUN** position and the transaxle is in REVERSE. On older vehicles, this function was handled by a dedicated switch with a name such as the Neutral/Safety Backup Light Switch, or something similar. This switch was designed to keep the engine from starting in any gear except PARK and/or NEUTRAL. The switch contacts also activated the backup lights when the transaxle was placed in REVERSE.

On the vehicles covered by this manual, the backup lamp control function is part of an integrated switch called the Transaxle Range switch (sometimes also called the Park/Neutral Position or PNP switch). In addition to turning on the backup lights, the Transaxle Range switches primary function is to transmit to the Powertrain Control Module (PCM) the driver's transaxle range selection. The PCM uses this information to control both engine and transaxle functions electronically.

The Transaxle Range switch is mounted externally on the transaxle. New service replacement switches come pinned in the NEUTRAL position and no adjustment should be necessary. Please note that if the switch requires adjustment, GM recommends that their special tool J 41545 Park/Neutral Switch Alignment Tool be used to properly adjust the Transaxle Range switch.

SHIFT TEST

The transaxles used in the vehicles covered by this manual are all electronically controlled, under the command of the Powertrain Control Module (PCM). GM recommends that professional technicians perform this test before any further diagnostic work is done to make sure that the electronic control inputs are connected and operating. If a technician does not check the inputs before operating the transaxle, it is very possible to misdiagnose a simple electrical condition as a major transaxle condition.

1. Start the engine.
2. Firmly depress the brake pedal.
3. Move the gear selector to the following positions:
   a. PARK to REVERSE
   b. REVERSE to NEUTRAL to DRIVE
4. Gear selections should be immediate and not harsh.

Because the transaxle is under the control of the PCM, certain conditions will cause Diagnostic Trouble Codes (DTCs) to set. A qualified technician using a scan tool connected to the vehicle's Data Link Connector (DLC) should be able to read and interpret the codes to help diagnose transaxle performance issues.

✳✳ WARNING

DO NOT, under any circumstances, attempt to diagnose a powertrain condition with basic knowledge of this powertrain; you may misdiagnose the condition and/or damage the powertrain components.

REMOVAL & INSTALLATION

▶ **See Figures 6 and 7**

1. Apply the parking brake and block the front wheels.
2. Place the transaxle gear selector to NEUTRAL.
3. Remove the air intake duct to access the switch located on the top of the transaxle at the range selector cable and arm.
4. Disconnect the transaxle range selector cable.

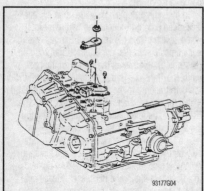

Fig. 6 Remove the selector lever and unbolt the transaxle range selector switch—4T60-E transaxle shown, 4T65-E similar

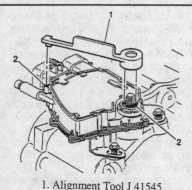

1. Alignment Tool J 41545
2. Alignment Slots

93177G05

Fig. 7 If the transaxle range selector switch must be adjusted, this alignment tool is recommended

5. Detach the electrical connectors from the range selector switch.
6. Remove the range selector lever retaining nut and lift off the lever.
7. Unfasten the range selector switch mounting bolts, then remove the switch from the transaxle manual shaft. Note that the manual shaft should have flat area which registers with a flat area on the switch.

To install:

8. A service replacement range selector switch should come with a small pin holding the switch in NEUTRAL. The transaxle itself should still be in NEUTRAL from the removal procedure. Align the flats of the transaxle manual shaft to the flats in the switch and install the switch. Install, but do not tighten the mounting bolts.

✳✳ WARNING

If the bolt holes on the switch do not align with the mounting boss on the transaxle, verify that the transaxle manual shaft is in the NEUTRAL position. DO NOT ROTATE A NEW SWITCH. A service replacement switch should be already pinned in the NEUTRAL position. If the switch has been rotated and the pin broken or if reusing the old switch, assemble the mounting bolts loosely and use tool J 41545, or equivalent alignment tool, to align the switch, then tighten the bolts.

9. Tighten the mounting bolts to 18 ft. lbs. (25 Nm). Do not overtighten.

10. Install the transaxle range selector lever to the manual shaft, install the nut to 15 ft. lbs. (20 Nm).
11. Attach the electrical connectors.
12. Connect the transaxle range selector cable.
13. After switch installation, verify that the engine will only start in the PARK or NEUTRAL positions. If the engine will start in any other position, readjust the switch and/or check the shifter and shifter cable.

Automatic Transaxle Assembly

REMOVAL & INSTALLATION

▶ **See Figures 8, 9 and 10**

➡ **Special lifting and support equipment is required for this procedure. The engine must be supported from above to hold the weight of the engine. The subframe and transaxle are lowered out from the bottom of the vehicle. This is not a job for the inexperienced or ill-equipped.**

1. Disconnect the negative battery cable.
2. Remove the cosmetic/acoustic engine cover.
3. Remove the air cleaner duct.
4. Tag for identification, if necessary, then detach the electrical connectors from the transaxle. These connectors include the Transaxle Range Switch and the solenoid harness connector.
5. If equipped with the 4T60-E transaxle, disconnect the vacuum hose from the vacuum modulator.

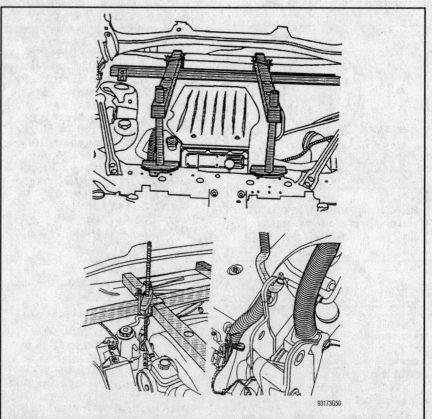

93173G50

Fig. 8 Typical engine support fixture needed to hold the engine in place as the transaxle is being removed from the bottom of the vehicle

6. Disconnect the transaxle range selector lever cable from the transaxle range switch. Unbolt the cable bracket and set aside the bracket with the cable.

7. Remove the fluid filler tube.

8. Remove the upper transaxle bolts including the wiring harness grounds.

9. Install a suitable engine support fixture such as GM engine support fixture tool J 28467-A and J-36462, or equivalent. It must be capable of supporting the weight of the engine and the transaxle.

10. Raise and safely support the vehicle.

11. Remove the front wheel and tire assemblies.

12. Disconnect both tie rod ends from the steering knuckles, as outlined in Section 8 of this manual.

13. Remove the power steering gear heat shield, then remove the power steering gear-to-subframe retaining bolts. Separate the power steering gear from the subframe and secure to the vehicle with wire.

14. Disconnect the power steering cooler line clamps from the subframe.

15. Remove the engine mount-to-frame retaining nuts and washers.

16. Disconnect the lower ball joints from the steering knuckles, as outlined in Section 8.

17. Remove the torque converter cover and then remove the starter motor. Please see Section 2 for more details.

18. Remove the torque converter bolts.

19. Drain the transaxle fluid into a suitable container. Refer to Section 1 for more information.

20. Disconnect the transaxle oil cooler hoses from the transaxle. Use care not to damage the fittings

21. Remove the drive axles (halfshafts) from the vehicle using the procedures found in this section.

22. Detach the wiring connectors from the Vehicle Speed Sensor (VSS) and the wheel speed sensor harness connectors.

23. Support the transaxle/subframe with a transaxle table or equivalent.

24. Disconnect the transaxle brace.

25. Remove the remaining transaxle-to-engine and engine-to-frame transaxle bolts.

26. Remove the frame-to-body bolts. More information is available in Section 3 under Engine Removal and Installation. GM specifies that new replacement subframe bolts must be used.

27. Lower the transaxle and subframe assembly from the vehicle.

To install:

28. Installation is the reverse of removal. Please note the following important steps.

29. If the transaxle failed, the oil cooler in the radiator and all of the pipe must be flushed to removed debris and particles. Although professional transaxle shops have equipment to clean torque converters, in most cases, the torque converter must be replaced.

30. Inspect the flywheel and rear crankshaft seal for leaks. If the flywheel has any cracks or shows signs of worn teeth and/or if there is any question as to the condition of the rear seal, now is the time to replace these parts. Please see Section 3.

31. When reconnecting the transaxle oil cooler hoses, use care. Correct thread engagement is critical. Cross-threaded fittings can achieve proper tightness value but will still leak.

32. Make sure the torque converter is installed all the way. The pump is driven by the tangs on the back of the converter. The converter must be seated all the way in the pump or the transaxle will not fit flush against the back if the engine block.

Halfshafts

The drive axles on front wheel drive vehicles are often called halfshafts. They are flexible shaft assemblies that transmit rotational force from the transaxle to the front wheel assemblies. The halfshaft assembly is made up of an inner and outer Constant-Velocity Joint (CV-Joint) connected to an axle shaft. The inner joint is completely flexible and has the ability of in-and-out movement. The outer joint is also flexible, but cannot move in and out.

Two types of joints are used in the halfshaft, or drive axle. The outboard joint uses what is called a Rzeppa joint design. The shaft end mating with the steering knuckle/hub uses a helical spline to assure a tight, press-type fit. This design provides a no-end play condition between the hub bearing and the driveshaft. With no end play between the hub bearing and driveshaft assembly, the design provides added durability and reduced bearing noise. The inner joint uses what is known as a Tripot design without an over-extension limitation retainer. The left side halfshaft inboard shaft attachment to the transaxle uses a female spline which installs over a stub shaft protruding from the transaxle. The right side halfshaft uses a male spline and interlocks with the transaxle gears using barrel-type snaprings.

The front halfshaft, or drive axle, assemblies use inboard and outboard joint seals made of a thermoplastic material and clamps made of stainless steel. The thermoplastic material performs well against normal handling and operational wear and conditions. However, it is not strong enough to withstand abusive handling or damage due to objects such as

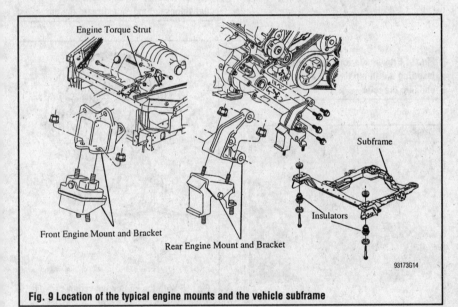

Engine Torque Strut

Subframe

Insulators

Front Engine Mount and Bracket

Rear Engine Mount and Bracket

93173G14

Fig. 9 Location of the typical engine mounts and the vehicle subframe

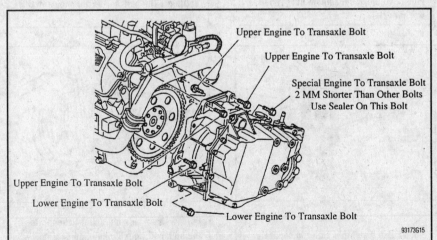

Upper Engine To Transaxle Bolt

Upper Engine To Transaxle Bolt

Special Engine To Transaxle Bolt 2 MM Shorter Than Other Bolts Use Sealer On This Bolt

Upper Engine To Transaxle Bolt

Lower Engine To Transaxle Bolt

Lower Engine To Transaxle Bolt

93173G15

Fig. 10 Transaxle-to-engine bolts may vary in length. Use care so each bolt is returned to its original location

sharp tools or the sharp edge of any surrounding component in the vehicle.

The functions of the seal (most often referred to as the CV-joint boot) are to protect the internal parts of the inboard and outboard joint by protecting the grease from extreme temperatures, stones, dirt, water salt, etc., as well as facilitate the movement of the joints.

The clamps are designed to provide a leak-proof connection at the housing and axle shaft for both the inboard and outboard joints.

The CV-joint boots should be inspected regularly and replace immediately if any defect is found. If the boots are damaged, the special grease will run out, become contaminated and water and dirt will get in an quickly wear out the joint. Refer to Section 1 for CV-boot inspection.

NOISE DIAGNOSIS

CLICKING NOISE IN TURNS indicates a worn or damaged outer joint, probably due to a cut or damaged boot.

CLUNK WHEN ACCELERATING FROM COAST OR DRIVE also indicates a worn or damaged joint.

SHUDDER OR VIBRATION, especially under acceleration could be from a worn or damaged outer joint or it could be from another source. If the CV-boots are in good condition and there is no obvious damage, look for a tire problem, an engine-related vibration or perhaps a damaged wheel with excessive run-out or out of balance.

VIBRATION AT HIGHWAY SPEEDS could be out of balance rear tires or wheels, out of round tires or wheels or a possible worn outer CV-joint binding or tight.

REMOVAL & INSTALLATION

▶ See Figures 11 thru 23

Because the outer joint is essentially a press-fit in the hub and the steering knuckle also needs to be disconnected from the lower control arm, special tools are needed for this job, including a good-quality hub/spindle puller. Use care is using substitutes or expensive damage may result. In general, halfshaft service is not for the inexperienced or ill-equipped.

❊❊ WARNING

Use care when removing the halfshaft. Tripot joints can be damaged if the drive axle is over-extended. It is important to handle the halfshaft in a manner to prevent overextending. Protect the CV-joint boots. Don't let them contact tools or other components. In addition, procure new service replacement hub nuts and tie rod end torque prevailing nuts. The originals, once removed, should not be reused.

1. Raise and safely support the vehicle.
2. Remove the wheel and tire assembly.
3. Disconnect the stabilizer shaft link by removing the through bolt where it passes through the lower control arm and connects to the stabilizer shaft.
4. Remove the front halfshaft, or drive axle, spindle nut. The torque specification on this nut is 150 ft. lbs. (205 Nm). To keep the brake rotor and

hub assembly from turning when removing the nut, insert a suitably sized drift pin or other suitable tool through the brake caliper inspection opening into the brake rotor's ventilation openings. This should lock the assembly in place so the spindle nut can be loosened. It is good practice to wire-brush any exposed threads on the end of the spindle and apply a generous coating of penetrating oil.

5. Detach the tie rod end from the steering knuckle by removing the torque prevailing hex nut. It should be replaced with a new part. This design tie rod has a tapered joint that GM says has been designed to separate easily, unlike previous joints of this type. If required, use a tie rod puller tool to separate the tie rod end from the steering knuckle.

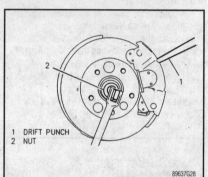

1 DRIFT PUNCH
2 NUT

89637G28

Fig. 11 Prevent the rotor from turning by inserting a drift pin through the caliper and into the rotor

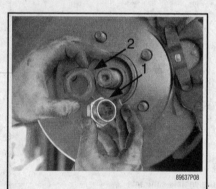

89637P08

Fig. 12 Remove the spindle nut (1) and washer (2)

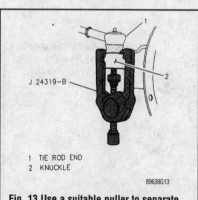

J 24319-B

1 TIE ROD END
2 KNUCKLE

89638G13

Fig. 13 Use a suitable puller to separate the tie rod end from the steering knuckle

❊❊ WARNING

Use care when working around the steering knuckle. If equipped with ABS brakes, there is a wheel speed sensor that reads off a toothed wheel that is part of the outer CV-Joint. The sensor wiring attached to the knuckle should be treated carefully.

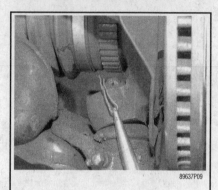

89637P09

Fig. 14 Remove the cotter pin with needlenose pliers, and discard the pin

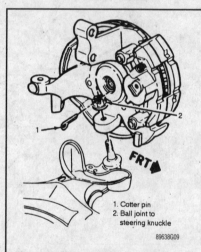

1. Cotter pin
2. Ball joint to steering knuckle

89638G09

Fig. 15 With the slotted nut removed, separate the hub assembly from the lower balljoint. The halfshaft is not shown in this view

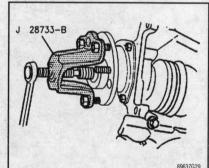

J 28733-B

89637G29

Fig. 16 Use a suitable puller to separate the halfshaft from the hub and bearing assembly

6. Separate the ball joint from the steering knuckle by removing the cotter pin and loosening the nut. Do not remove the nut yet. Install a ball joint puller to separate the joint from the knuckle. By keeping the nut in place as the puller is being used to press the ball stud from the knuckle, the threads on the ball stud are protected so the ball joint can be reused. Now remove the puller and the nut and detach the ball joint stud from the steering knuckle.

Fig. 17 Using a large prytool to carefully separate the inner CV-joint from the transaxle case

Fig. 18 Be very careful to avoid damaging any components when prying the halfshaft from the axle

7. Separate the axle from the hub using a hub puller. Don't try to hammer on the end of the spindle or the outer CV-joint and possibly also the hub bearing will be damaged. Use a hub puller to press the spindle out of the hub. It is good practice to leave the hub nut in place to protect the threads on the spindle as the hub puller presses the spindle free of the hub.

8. Remove the halfshafts (drive axles) from the transaxle, as follows:

   a. Right Side: GM recommends their axle shaft removing set which consists of C-shaped plates that fit behind the inner CV-joint, between the joint and the transaxle housing. A slide hammer attaches to the C-plates so the halfshaft can be popped free of the transaxle.

   b. Left Side: Using the subframe for leverage, carefully separate the halfshaft from the transaxle with a suitable prytool in the groove provided on the inner joint.

✳✳ WARNING

Do not put the wheels back on the vehicle and attempt to move the vehicle with the drive axles removed from the hub and wheel bearings. The wheels could fall off, dropping the vehicle to the ground and causing personal injury and/or expensive damage to the vehicle.

To install:

9. Clean all parts well. Inspect the halfshafts and the CV-boots. Service, if required, using the Overhaul procedures found in this section.

➡**Use care handling the halfshafts to avoid damage to the boots and clamps.**

10. Push the halfshaft into the transaxle. Verify that the halfshaft is seated by grasping the inner joint housing and pulling. It is important to make sure the halfshaft is seated. Do **not** pull on the drive axle shaft, only on the inner CV-joint.

11. Install the halfshaft/drive axle end into the hub and bearing assembly.

12. Connect the ball joint to the steering knuckle. Tighten the nut to 40 ft. lbs. (55 Nm).

Fig. 20 Carefully remove the halfshaft from the vehicle

Fig. 21 The transaxle end of the halfshaft is grooved with a retaining circlip (1)

Fig. 22 While the halfshaft is removed, be sure not to get any dirt or other debris in the transaxle case

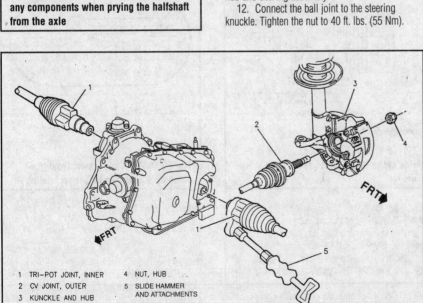

1 TRI-POT JOINT, INNER	4 NUT, HUB	
2 CV JOINT, OUTER	5 SLIDE HAMMER	
3 KNUCKLE AND HUB	AND ATTACHMENTS	

Fig. 19 GM recommends their slide hammers used with C-shaped plates to pull the halfshafts

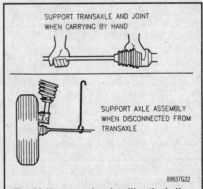

SUPPORT TRANSAXLE AND JOINT WHEN CARRYING BY HAND

SUPPORT AXLE ASSEMBLY WHEN DISCONNECTED FROM TRANSAXLE

Fig. 23 Use care when handling the halfshaft to avoid damaging it

Align the slots in the nut to the cotter pin hole in the ball stud by tightening the nut further, if required. DO NOT loosen the nut to align the holes for the cotter pin. Install a new cotter pin.

13. Connect the tie rod end to the steering knuckle. Use a new service replacement torque prevailing nut and tighten to 18 ft. lbs. (25 Nm) plus an additional 180° of rotation.

14. Install a new service replacement front wheel drive axle nut. To keep the brake rotor and hub assembly from turning when tightening the nut, insert a suitably sized drift pin or other suitable tool through the brake caliper inspection opening into the brake rotor's ventilation openings, locking the assembly in place so the spindle nut can be tightened. Torque the nut to 150 ft. lbs. (205 Nm).

15. Install the stabilizer through bolt from the bottom of the control arm to the stabilizer bar link and tighten the nut to 17 ft. lbs. (23 Nm).

16. Install the front wheel and tire assemblies. Torque the wheel nuts to 100 ft. lbs. (140 Nm).

17. Lower the vehicle.

18. Since some transaxle fluid may be lost when the halfshafts are disconnected, check the fluid level. Please see the procedure in this section.

19. GM recommends that since the steering tie rod and the ball joint were disturbed, that the front end alignment should be checked and adjusted if necessary.

CV- BOOT REPLACEMENT

Outer CV-Boot Assembly

▶ See Figures 24, 25 and 26

➡A number of components will not be reused. Procure the necessary parts before starting this job. CV-Boot Repair Kits normally come with all the parts required, but you should check that all parts are on hand before starting this procedure.

1. Remove the halfshaft from the vehicle, then clamp in a vise. Use soft jaws or wood blocks to protect the finish on the halfshaft.

2. Cut and remove the boot retaining clamps with wire cutters.

3. Separate the boot from the CV-joint race at the large diameter and slide the boot away from the joint along the axle shaft.

4. Wipe the grease from the face of the CV-joint inner race.

5. Locate the retaining ring located on the shaft where is passes through the big end of the joint. It may be under a thick layer of CV-joint grease. Spread the ears of the retaining ring with lock ring pliers and remove the outer joint assembly from the halfshaft.

6. Slide the CV-joint boot from the axle shaft. If just the boot is being replaced, and the joint is still in good condition (the boot is being replaced before the old one failed), it is possible to reassemble using a new boot and the special grease usually found in a CV-boot kit. Flush the grease from the joint and repack the boot with half of the grease provided with the new boot. If, however, the boot was torn and the joint contaminated with water or dirt, the joint will have to be replaced or overhauled, using the procedures found in this section.

7. Install the new boot and clamps (do not tighten yet) on the axle shaft. Make sure the boot is

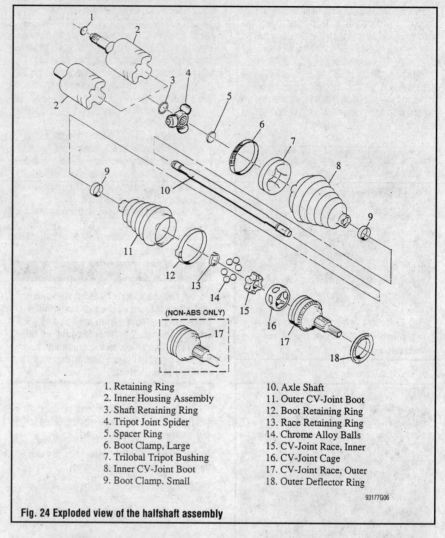

1. Retaining Ring
2. Inner Housing Assembly
3. Shaft Retaining Ring
4. Tripot Joint Spider
5. Spacer Ring
6. Boot Clamp, Large
7. Trilobal Tripot Bushing
8. Inner CV-Joint Boot
9. Boot Clamp, Small
10. Axle Shaft
11. Outer CV-Joint Boot
12. Boot Retaining Ring
13. Race Retaining Ring
14. Chrome Alloy Balls
15. CV-Joint Race, Inner
16. CV-Joint Cage
17. CV-Joint Race, Outer
18. Outer Deflector Ring

93177G06

Fig. 24 Exploded view of the halfshaft assembly

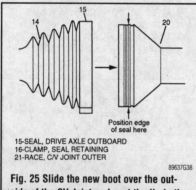

15-SEAL, DRIVE AXLE OUTBOARD
16-CLAMP, SEAL RETAINING
21-RACE, C/V JOINT OUTER

89637G38

Fig. 25 Slide the new boot over the outside of the CV-Joint and seat the lip in the groove

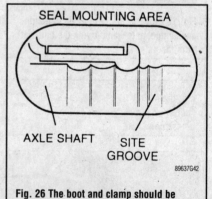

89637G42

Fig. 26 The boot and clamp should be positioned as shown for proper sealing

pointing in the correct direction. With the boot in place, install the joint to the drive axle shaft and snap the race retaining ring into place. Put the remainder of the special CV-Joint grease that came in the boot kit, into the joint. Position the new clamp on the boot. The factory uses a special swaging tool for the original installation. Service replacement CV-boot kits normally come with clamps that can be tightened with pliers.

Inner CV-Boot Assembly

▶ See Figures 27 thru 42

1. Remove the halfshaft from the vehicle, then clamp it in a vise. Use soft jaws or wood blocks to protect the finish on the halfshaft.

2. Cut and remove the boot retaining clamps with wire cutters. Some technicians may use a grinder to cut the bands, especially the smaller swaged band. Use care not to cut through the boot

Fig. 27 Checking the inner CV-joint boot for wear

Fig. 28 Clean the CV-boot and housing prior to removing the boot

Fig. 29 Removing the large, outer clamp band from the CV-boot

Fig. 30 Removing the smaller, inner clamp from the CV-boot using side cutters

Fig. 31 Removing the CV-boot from the inner joint housing

Fig. 32 Removing the CV-joint housing assembly

Fig. 33 On some inner joints, the needle bearings pull right off the spider; on others, the needle bearings are retained by snaprings and can be left on the spider unless damaged

Fig. 34 Inspecting the inner CV-joint housing

Fig. 35 Removing the CV-joint outer snapring

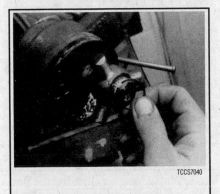

Fig. 36 CV-joint snapring (typical)

Fig. 37 With the snapring removed, slide the spider from the axle shaft

Fig. 38 Locate and remove the CV-joint inner snapring (also called the spacer ring) so the boot can be removed from the shaft

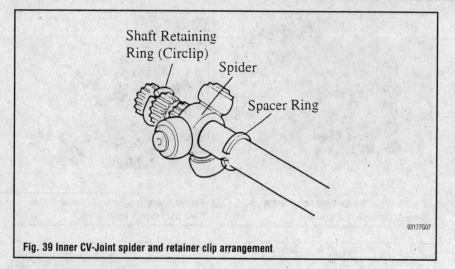

Fig. 39 Inner CV-Joint spider and retainer clip arrangement

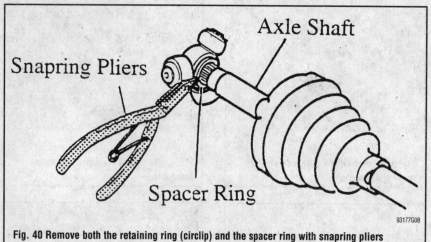

Fig. 40 Remove both the retaining ring (circlip) and the spacer ring with snapring pliers

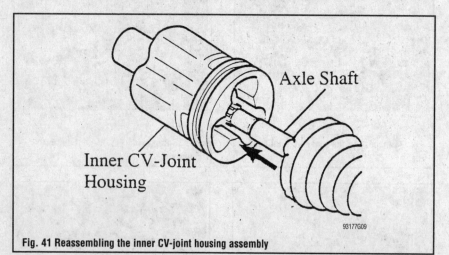

Fig. 41 Reassembling the inner CV-joint housing assembly

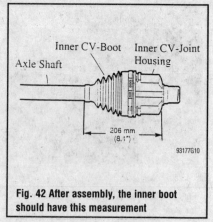

Fig. 42 After assembly, the inner boot should have this measurement

and repack the boot with half of the grease provided with the new boot. If, however, the boot was torn and the joint contaminated with water or dirt, the joint will have to be replaced or overhauled, using the procedures found in this section.

6. Clean all parts well. The spider assembly and the housing must be thoroughly cleaned with a suitable solvent. All traces of old grease and any contaminates must be removed. Dry all parts. Refill the housing with approximately half of the grease from the service kit and provided with the new boot. The other half of the grease goes inside the replacement boot.

7. Install the new boot and clamps (do not tighten yet) on the halfshaft. Make sure the boot is pointing in the correct direction. With the boot in place, install the spacer snapring, the spider assembly and the outer retaining ring. Make sure all retaining snaprings are properly seated in their grooves. Position the new clamps on the boot. The factory uses a special swaging tool for the original installation. Service replacement CV-boot kits normally come with clamps that can be tightened with pliers.

➡The seal must not be dimpled, stretched or out of shape in any way. If the seal is NOT shaped correctly, carefully insert a thin, flat blunt tool (NO SHARP EDGES) between the large seal opening and the tripot bushing to equalize the pressure. Shape the seal properly by hand and remove the tool.

CV-JOINT OVERHAUL

Outer CV-Joint Assembly

♦ See Figures 43, 44, 45, 46 and 47

1. Remove the halfshaft and separate the outer CV-joint from the axle shaft following the CV-boot removal and installation procedure. Clean out the grease from the joint to aid in disassembly.

2. Use a brass drift to gently tap on the cage until tilted enough to remove the first ball. Remove the other balls in a similar manner.

3. Pivot the cage and inner race at 90 degrees to the center line of the outer race with the cage windows aligned with the lands of the outer race. Lift the cage out with the inner race.

4. Rotate the inner race up and out of the cage as in Step 2. Clean all parts with solvent and blow dry with compressed air.

and damage the sealing surface of the CV-joint housing.

3. Separate the boot from the inner CV-joint the large diameter and slide the boot away from the joint along the axle shaft.

4. There is a three-arm bearing called a "spider" that is retained on the halfshaft, or axle shaft, by a snapring. Move the CV-joint housing away from the spider to locate the snapring which is in a groove on the end of the drive axle. Spread the ears

of the ring and remove the retaining ring along with the spider. Use the same pliers to remove the spacer ring which sits next to the spider on the axle shaft.

5. Slide the CV-joint boot from the axle shaft. If just the boot is being replaced, and the joint is still in good condition (the boot is being replaced before the old one failed), it is possible to reassemble using a new boot and the special grease usually found in a Boot Kit. Flush the grease from the joint

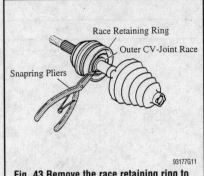

Fig. 43 Remove the race retaining ring to separate the outer CV-Joint from the axle shaft

1. Brass Drift
2. Chrome Alloy Balls
3. Outer CV-Joint Cage
4. Outer CV-Joint Race
5. Outer CV-Joint Race

Fig. 44 Use a brass drift to tap the cage around so the ball bearings can be removed

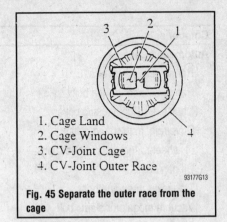

1. Cage Land
2. Cage Windows
3. CV-Joint Cage
4. CV-Joint Outer Race

Fig. 45 Separate the outer race from the cage

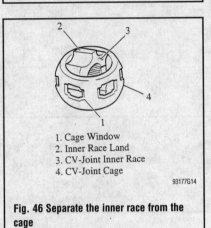

1. Cage Window
2. Inner Race Land
3. CV-Joint Inner Race
4. CV-Joint Cage

Fig. 46 Separate the inner race from the cage

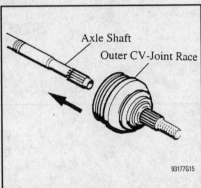

Axle Shaft
Outer CV-Joint Race

Fig. 47 Assembling the overhauled outer CV-joint to the halfshaft

To install:

5. Lightly coat the ball grooves with the provided special CV grease.

6. Install the inner race into the cage, cage into the outer race and balls into the cage as removed.

7. Refill the joint with half the grease provided.

8. Install the joint onto the axle. Make sure the retaining ring is properly seated in its groove.

9. Install the boot and clamps using the procedures for Boot Removal and Installation found in this section. Make sure the lip on the rubber boot is in the proper groove in the outer race.

10. Install the halfshaft in the vehicle, as outlined earlier in this section.

TORQUE SPECIFICATIONS

Components	English	Metric
Automatic transaxle		
Range selector lever nut	15 ft. lbs.	20 Nm
Range selector switch bolts	18 ft. lbs.	25 Nm
Case extension housing bolts	27 ft. lbs.	36 Nm
Drivetrain, front frame bolts	133 ft. lbs.	180 Nm
Flywheel-to-torque converter bolts	46 ft. lbs.	63 Nm
Oil pan bolts	13 ft. lbs.	17 Nm
Transaxle-to-engine bolts	55 ft. lbs.	75 Nm
Vacuum modulator clamp bolt	20 ft. lbs.	27 Nm
Speed sensor bolt	97 inch lbs.	11 Nm
Transaxle brace-to-engine bolts	32 ft. lbs.	43 Nm
Transaxle brace-to-transaxle bolts	32 ft. lbs.	43 Nm
Transaxle bracket-to-transaxle bolts	70 ft. lbs.	95 Nm
Transaxle mount frame bracket bolts	43 ft. lbs.	58 Nm
Transaxle mount nuts	35 ft. lbs.	47 Nm
Halfshaft		
Front drive axle nut	150 ft. lbs.	205 Nm
Ball joint-to-steering knuckle nut	40 ft. lbs.	55 Nm
Tie rod end-to-steering knuckle nut	18 ft. lbs.	25 Nm
Stabilizer bar link nut	17 ft. lbs.	23 Nm

93177C01

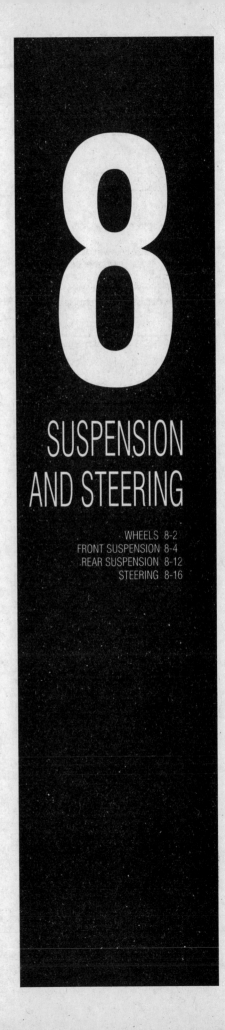

8

SUSPENSION AND STEERING

WHEELS

Wheels

♦ See Figure 1

REMOVAL & INSTALLATION

♦ See Figures 2 thru 7

1. If equipped, remove the hub cap/wheel cover.

2. Many GM W-Body vehicles use styled wheels with cosmetic covers over the wheel retaining nuts (also called lug nuts). Some models may use bright-finished metal caps, others may use a black plastic cap. Use a deep socket to unscrew these cosmetic covers.

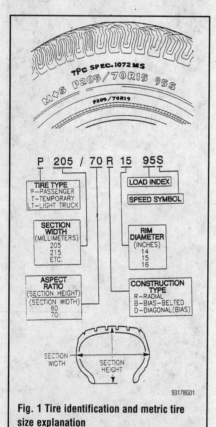

Fig. 1 Tire identification and metric tire size explanation

Fig. 2 Most W-Body vehicles have metal or plastic cosmetic covers over the wheel lug nuts. Use a deep socket to unscrew the lug nut cover

Fig. 3 With the metal or plastic cosmetic cover removed, use a ½ inch breaker bar and a deep socket to remove the lug nut

Fig. 4 Note that the wheel lug nut has external threads to accept a screw-on cosmetic cover

Fig. 5 Note how the cosmetic plastic cover threads onto the steel wheel retaining nut

Fig. 6 Use a torque wrench for final wheel lug nut tightening. Proper torque protects styled alloy wheels and helps prevent distortion of the brake rotor which could cause brake pedal pulsation

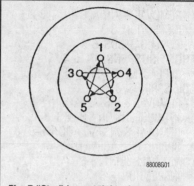

Fig. 7 "Star" lug nut tightening sequence

3. With the vehicle still on the ground, use a deep socket and a suitable breaker bar or ratchet to break loose, but do not unscrew the lug nuts.

4. Raise and safely support the vehicle.

➡Always use a suitable floor jack for raising the vehicle to be serviced. Never use the jacking device supplied with the vehicle for vehicle service. That jacking device is designed for emergency use only to change a flat tire.

5. Remove the wheel lug nuts.

6. Since the tire and wheel assemblies were originally balanced as an assembly on the vehicle and since many professional tire shops may spin balance a tire and wheel assembly while mounted on the vehicle (so the brake rotor and hub are also included in the balance computation), a tire and wheel assembly should always be installed in the same location as removed. Mark the location of the tire and wheel to the hub. Many technicians will chalk the end of the topmost wheel stud and place a another chalk mark on the corresponding wheel opening. In this way, the tire and wheel assembly can be installed in the same relationship as when removed.

7. Remove the tire and wheel assembly.

To install:

✷✷ CAUTION

Before installing a wheel, remove any build-up of corrosion on the wheel mounting surface or brake rotor, by scraping and wire brushing. Installing wheels without good metal-to-metal contact at the mounting surfaces can cause the wheel lug nuts to loosen, which may allow the wheel to come off while the vehicle is in motion.

8. Clean the wheel nuts, studs and the wheel and rotor mounting surfaces.

9. Install the tire and wheel assembly aligning the locating marks made at removal.

✷✷ CAUTION

Never use oil or grease on studs or nuts.

10. Tighten the wheel lug nuts by hand until they are snug. Then tighten the nuts in a `star-shape' sequence, as shown in the accompanying figure, and torque to specification. Improperly tightened wheel lug nuts could eventually allow the

wheel to come off while the vehicle is moving, possibly causing loss of control, personal injury and property damage.

11. Tighten the lug nuts finger-tight. Then tighten in sequence to 100 ft. lbs. (140 Nm). Use of a torque wrench is important. Aluminum wheels will distort under uneven wheel lug nut pressure. Unequal torque can also distort brake rotors, causing uneven brake wear and pulsations in the brake pedal.

12. Install the hub cap, if equipped. Install the lug nut cosmetic covers, if equipped.

13. Lower the vehicle. With the vehicle on the ground, recheck the wheel lug nut torque.

Servicing Difficult To Remove Wheels

General Motors says that penetrating oil has not been found to effective in removing tight wheels. However, if it is to be used, it should be applied sparingly to the hub surface only.

❊❊ CAUTION

If penetrating oil gets on the vertical surfaces between the wheel and the rotor or drum, it could cause the wheel to work loose as the vehicle is driven, resulting in loss of control and an injury accident. Never use heat to loosen a tight wheel. It can shorten the life of the wheel, studs or hub nut and bearing. Wheel nuts must be tightened in sequence and to the proper torque to avoid bending the wheel or rotor.

Excessive force such as hammering the wheel or tire can also cause damage. Use a rubber mallet to lightly tap the tire's sidewall. Sometimes wheels can be difficult to remove from the vehicle due to foreign material or a tight fit between the wheel center hole and the hub or rotor. These wheels can be removed without damage as follows:

1. Tighten all wheel nuts on the affected wheel, then loosen each wheel nut two turns.

2. Lower the vehicle to the floor.

3. Rock the vehicle from side to side as hard as possible using one or more person's body weight to loosen the wheel, and/or rock the vehicle from DRIVE to REVERSE, allowing it to move several feet in each direction. Apply quick, hard jabs on the brake pedal to loosen the wheel.

❊❊ CAUTION

Before installing a wheel, remove any build-up of corrosion on the wheel mounting surface or rotor, by scraping and wire brushing. Installing wheels without good metal-to-metal contact at mounting surfaces can cause wheel nuts to loosen, which may later allow the wheel to come off while the vehicle is in motion. Never use oil or grease on studs and nuts. Tighten the wheel nuts with your fingers until they are snug. Then tighten the nuts in a "star" pattern. The wheel nut torque specification for these vehicles is 100 ft. lbs. (140 Nm). Improperly tightened wheel nuts could eventually allow the wheel to come off while the vehicle is moving, possibly causing loss of control, personal injury and property damage.

INSPECTION

Inspect the tread for abnormal wear, check for nails or other foreign material embedded into the tire. To check for leaks, submerse the wheel assembly into a tub of water and watch for air bubbles.

Wheels must be replaced if they are bent, dented, leak air through welds, have elongated bolt holes, if wheel nuts won't stay tight, or if the wheels are heavily rusted. Replacement wheels must be equivalent to the original equipment wheels in load capacity, diameter, rim width, offset, and mounting configuration.

A wheel of improper size may affect wheel bearing life, brake cooling, speedometer/odometer calibration, vehicle ground clearance and tire clearance to the body and/or chassis.

➡**Replacement with used wheels is not recommended as their service history may have included severe treatment or very high mileage and they could fail without warning.**

Check runout in all directions (up and down, in and out) using a dial indicator. For aluminum wheels, maximum runout is 0.030 in. (0.762mm) For steel wheels, the specification is 0.045 in. (1.143mm). If the wheel causes a vibration and tire balance does not solve the problem, replace the wheel.

Wheel Lug Studs

▸ See Figure 8

All models use metric wheel nuts and studs. The nut will have the word "|`metric" stamped on the face and the stud will have the letter "|`'M" into the threaded end.

The thread size of the metric wheel nuts and wheel studs are M12 X 1.5, this signifies:
- M = Metric
- 12 = Diameter in millimeters
- 1.5 = Millimeters per thread

Fig. 8 The word METRIC is stamped on the wheel retaining nuts (top arrow) and the letter M is stamped in the end of the studs (center arrow)

REPLACEMENT

▸ See Figures 9 and 10

➡**Never try to reuse a wheel stud once it has been removed. Whenever a wheel stud has been removed, discard it and replace it with a new one. GM specifies that only a 1.42 inch (36mm) wheel stud be used for W-Body vehicle front hub service replacement.**

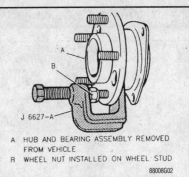

A HUB AND BEARING ASSEMBLY REMOVED FROM VEHICLE
B WHEEL NUT INSTALLED ON WHEEL STUD

88008G02

Fig. 9 This is one recommended tool to remove the wheel stud(s) from a front wheel drive hub

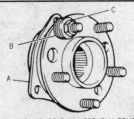

A HUB AND BEARING ASSEMBLY REMOVED FROM VEHICLE
B INSERT WASHER OVER WHEEL STUD
C TIGHTEN NUT TO DRAW WHEEL STUD

88008G03

Fig. 10 Install washers and a nut on the wheel stud, then tighten until the stud is properly seated

1. Raise and safely support the vehicle.

2. Remove the wheel, brake caliper, bracket and rotor. Do not allow the brake caliper to hang by the brake hose. For more information, refer to 3. If using the factory recommended wheel stud removal tool or its exact equivalent, cut about ½in. (13mm) off of the outer end of the stud to accommodate the opening of the stud remover.

3. Position the stud at the 6 o'clock position. Use tool J 6627-A or equivalent to extract the stud from the hub. Do not hammer on the studs to remove, as this could damage the bearing.

To install:

5. Clean the hub and place the replacement stud in the hub.

6. Add enough washers to draw the stud into the hub.

7. Install the lug nut flat side to the washers and tighten until the stud head seats in the hub flange.

8. Remove the nut and washers.

9. Repeat for other studs as required.

10. Install the brake parts and wheel. Tighten the lug nuts to 100 ft. lbs. (140 Nm).

11. Lower the vehicle and recheck the wheel nut torque.

➡**A second method to remove damaged wheel lug studs (and the one most likely to be available to most non-professionals) involves simply removing the wheel hub and bearing assembly from the vehicle and using a hydraulic press to remove the old stud and install the replacement. This task can be handled by most automotive machine shops, once the hub is off the vehicle.**

FRONT SUSPENSION

FRONT SUSPENSION COMPONENT LOCATIONS

1. Lower control arm
2. Ball joint
3. Stabilizer link
4. Strut
5. Tie rod ends
6. Power steering gear
7. Stabilizer shaft

▶ **See Figure 11**

The front suspension is a conventional front-wheel drive strut design. The front spring is mounted between a lower strut spring seat and an upper strut mount spring seat. The spring is cushioned between rubber insulators. The upper and lower coils are tapered to a small diameter.

The front steering knuckle is a machined aluminum casting. Do not use a hammer to loosen suspension components from the knuckle. Suspension components attached to the knuckle (front lower control arm ball stud, ABS sensor bracket and strut damper) are made of steel and have special coatings to prevent corrosion.

The upper steering pivot point (strut bearing) has been placed in the upper spring seat. The bearing is pressed into the front hub and is permanently lubricated and requires no service. The upper spring seat is plastic and is offset at an angle to minimize side loads on the strut and upper strut mount bushing. The dust shield is designed to protect the strut from dirt and corrosion. The shield also contains a strut jounce bumper.

The lower control arm is a two-piece steel welded unit with a riveted ball joint. A conventional rubber bushing is used for the rear lower control arm pivot. The front lower control arm bushing is mounted vertically.

GM W-Body vehicles use non-serviceable wheel hubs and bearings at both the front and rear wheels. The bearing cannot be greased. If a hub bearing is determined to be defective, unit replacement is required.

A stabilizer shaft is mounted to the top rear of the frame and to the lower control arm. The shaft is attached to the frame with clamps and rubber insulators and to the control arm with insulator links.

Suspension components that are bent, worn, or damaged must be replaced with new parts. Do not attempt to heat, quench or straighten parts. Bent or damaged suspension parts are often an indication that the vehicle has been in an accident or driven in an abusive manner. When bent or damaged suspension parts are discovered, a thorough inspection of the knuckle, along with the ball joint and steering tie rod ball attachments should be performed. In addition, fastener torque should be checked at the control arm to frame, strut to knuckle and front lower control arm ball stud to frame.

During component service, if any of the items listed below require replacement, it is not necessary to check or adjust camber and toe.

- Strut bumper
- Strut shield
- Upper spring seat
- Strut bearing
- Spring insulators

If any of the items listed below require replacement during service, GM specifies that a vehicle wheel alignment (check/adjust camber and toe) is required.

- Strut damper
- Knuckle
- Control arm
- Strut mount
- Spring

Coil Springs

REMOVAL & INSTALLATION

The coil springs are part of the front strut assembly. Special spring compressor tools are required to remove the spring from the strut. Please refer to the Front Suspension Struts procedure for coil spring removal.

Front Suspension Struts

The front suspension struts (in previous years, sometimes called MacPherson Struts) combine the functions of a shock absorber (damper) and a spring mount into one structural assembly, a major component of the front suspension and steering systems. While removing the strut assembly is straightforward, disassembling the strut for spring removal and/or strut replacement requires special tools. Older vehicles had struts that could be taken apart and overhauled. The struts on vehicles covered by this manual do not come apart, except for the coil spring which can be replaced. If special tools are not available to disassemble the strut, it may be possible to purchase an aftermarket spring and strut already assembled.

REMOVAL & INSTALLATION

▶ **See Figure 12**

✳✳ WARNING

Use care when servicing the front strut to avoid chipping or scratching the coating on the coil spring. Damage to the coating can cause premature failure.

1. Under the hood, locate and remove the three strut-to-body mount nuts.
2. Raise and safely support the vehicle. Allow the control arms to hang free.
3. Remove the wheel and tire assembly.
4. Scribe a mark around the strut bracket to the knuckle. This will help align the strut at assembly.

✳✳ WARNING

When the strut-to-knuckle bolts are removed, the knuckle will drop and possibly overextend and damage the halfshaft. The ball joint could also be damaged. Support or otherwise restraint the knuckle.

5. Remove the two strut-to-knuckle bolts.
6. Remove the strut from the vehicle.

To install:

7. Install the strut and spring assembly into place taking care to align any scribe marks made at removal.
8. Install three strut-to-body mount nuts and tighten to 30 ft. lbs. (41 Nm).
9. Install the two strut-to-knuckle bolts and tighten to 90 ft. lbs. (123 Nm).

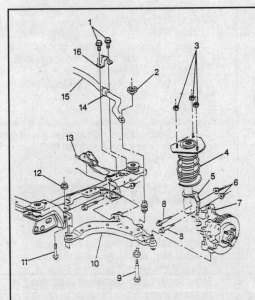

1. Stabilizer Shaft Insulator Clamp Bolts
2. Stabilizer Shaft Link Nut
3. Strut Mount Nuts
4. Front Suspension Spring
5. Front Suspension Strut
6. Strut-To-Knuckle Nut
7. Front Steering Knuckle
8. Strut-To-Knuckle Bolt
9. Stabilizer Shaft Link
10. Front Lower Control Arm
11. Front Lower Control Arm Bolt
12. Front Lower Control Arm Nut
13. Subframe
14. Stabilizer Shaft Insulator
15. Stabilizer Shaft
16. Stabilizer Shaft Clamp

93178G04

Fig. 11 Typical W-Body front suspension arrangement

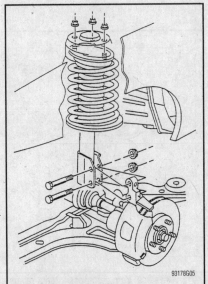

93178G05

Fig. 12 Exploded view of the front strut removal

10. Install the tire and wheel assembly.
11. Lower the vehicle.
12. Take the vehicle to a reputable repair shop to have an alignment performed. A vehicle alignment is mandatory after strut replacement.

SPRING REPLACEMENT

◆ **See Figure 13**

➥ To disassemble the strut for spring replacement, special compressor tools are required to relieve the tension on the top retaining nut. GM recommends their tool set. In your locality, it may be possible to rent a similar tool. Another possibility is to take the strut and spring assembly to a qualified shop with the proper equipment to have the strut disassembled for either spring or strut replacement. The replacement part can then be swapped out and the shop may be able to reassemble the strut for a modest price.

1. Remove the strut from the vehicle using the procedures found in this section.
2. Mount the strut in a strut compressor tool.
3. Use the strut compressor forcing screw to compress the spring just enough to release the tension from the strut mount.
4. Remove the strut shaft nut.
5. Relieve the spring tension and remove the spring from the strut.
To install:
6. Inspect all components for wear or damage.
7. Install the rear spring lower insulator. Make sure the lower spring is visible between the step and the location mark on the insulator.
8. Install the rear suspension spring and the dust shield to the lower insulator. Install the jounce bumper and strut mount.
9. Use a strut compressor to compress the strut, working the strut shaft through the strut mount.
10. Compress the strut and spring assembly enough to install the strut shaft nut. Torque the nut to 55 ft. lbs. (75 Nm).
11. Install the strut into the vehicle using the procedures found in this section.

Lower Ball Joint

INSPECTION

Front lower control arm ball joint stud tightness in the knuckle boss should be checked when inspecting the front lower control arm ball joint. Use the following procedure.
1. Raise and safely support the vehicle, allowing the front suspension to hang free.
2. Grasp the tire at the top and bottom and move the bottom of the tire in an in-and-out motion while checking for movement of the stud end or castellated (slotted) nut at the knuckle boss.
3. A loose castellated nut may indicate a bent stud or a damaged hole in the knuckle boss.
4. Observe any horizontal movement of the knuckle relative to the control arm. Ball joints/studs must be replaced if any looseness is detected in the joint or the ball joint seal is cut.
5. Worn or damaged parts must be replaced with correct service parts. Failure to use the correct ball joint and specified fastener torque may eventually cause a loose joint and may result in loss of steering control which could result in personal injury.

REMOVAL & INSTALLATION

◆ **See Figure 14**

1. Raise and safely support the vehicle.
2. Remove the lower control arm from the vehicle using the procedure found in this section.
3. Drill out the three rivets or grind the heads off the rivets holding the ball joint to the control arm. Remove the ball joint from the control arm.
To install:
4. Align the ball joint to the lower control arm. The replacement ball joint should come with three bolts as replacement for the rivets removed at disassembly. Install the bolts **facing down** and install the nuts. Tighten the nuts to 50 ft. lbs. (68 Nm).
5. Install the control arm to the frame using the procedures found in this section.
6. Lower the vehicle.

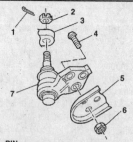

1 PIN
2 NUT BALL JOINT TO KNUCKLE; TIGHTEN TO 10 N-m (88 LB. IN) THEN TIGHTEN 2 FLATS TO 55 N-m (41 LB. FT.), MIN.
3 KNUCKLE
4 BALL JOINT MOUNTING BOLTS MUST FACE DOWN
5 CONTROL ARM
6 BALL JOINT MOUNTING NUTS 68 N-m (50 LB. FT.)
7 SERVICE BALL JOINT

89638G12

Fig. 14 Typical ball joint replacement

7. The vehicle's wheel alignment should be check by a reputable alignment shop.

Stabilizer Shaft

The front stabilizer shaft (sometimes called a sway bar) is mounted to the top rear of the frame and to the lower control arm. The shaft is attached to the frame with clamps and rubber insulators and to the control arms with insulator links.

REMOVAL & INSTALLATION

◆ **See Figure 15**

Because the front stabilizer shaft is mounted to the powertrain subframe, the subframe (with the powertrain) must be lowered to service the stabilizer bar. This is a lengthy and exacting procedure requiring special lifting and jacking equipment. In addition, the rack and pinion steering assembly stub shaft must be disconnected from the steering column. GM specifies that the subframe-to-body bolts, once disturbed, must be replaced with new service replacement parts. Procure the necessary hardware before beginning this procedure. This is not a job for the inexperienced or ill-equipped.
1. Center the front wheels to the straight ahead position and lock the steering column. This is important because it protects the steering wheel airbag coil from damage.
2. Raise and safely support the vehicle.
3. Remove the front wheel and tire assemblies.
4. Locate the steering shaft dust seal and move it back to gain access to the pinch bolt that joins the steering column intermediate shaft to the rack and pinion input shaft (stub shaft).

✳✳ CAUTION

Failure to disconnect the intermediate shaft from the rack and pinion stub shaft can result in damage to the rack and pinion steering gear assembly and/or the steering intermediate shaft. The damage can cause loss of steering control which could result in personal injury.

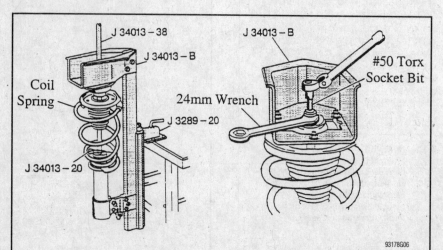

J 34013 - 38
J 34013 - B
Coil Spring
J 3289 - 20
J 34013 - 20
J 34013 - B
24mm Wrench
#50 Torx Socket Bit

93178G06

Fig. 13 Typical strut compressor tools recommended by GM for W-Body front strut disassembly

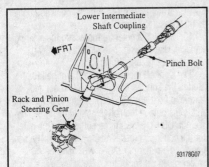

Fig. 15 Remove the pinch bolt and separate the lower intermediate shaft from the rack and pinion stub shaft

5. Remove the pinch bolt from the lower intermediate steering shaft, noting the following:

a. The wheels of the vehicle must be in the straight ahead position and the steering column in the **LOCK** position before disconnecting the steering column or the intermediate shaft from the rack and pinion steering gear.

b. Failure to do this will cause the SIR (airbag) coil, which feeds power to the steering wheel airbag module, to become uncentered, which will cause damage to the airbag coil.

6. Loosen the stabilizer shaft insulator clamp attaching nuts and bolts.

7. Place an adjustable safety stand or hydraulic jack under the center of the rear subframe crossmember.

8. Locate the large subframe-to-body retaining bolts. Remove the two rear frame-to-body bolts.

9. Carefully lower the rear of the subframe just enough to access the stabilizer shaft.

10. Remove the stabilizer shaft insulator clamps and insulators from the subframe.

11. Remove the stabilizer shaft links from the control arms and pull the stabilizer shaft rearward. Swing the stabilizer shaft down and remove from the left side of the vehicle.

To install:

12. Insert the stabilizer shaft from the left side of the vehicle.

❋❋ WARNING

DO NOT tighten the stabilizer link nuts at this time. The weight of the vehicle must be supported by the control arms so the vehicle will have the proper trim heights before tightening the link nuts.

13. Loosely install the stabilizer shaft links at the control arms.

14. Connect the stabilizer shaft insulator clamps to the frame and tighten the bolts to 35 ft. lbs. (48 Nm).

❋❋ WARNING

Make sure the rack and pinion stub shaft is properly seated in the lower intermediate steering shaft coupler prior to installing the pinch bolt. The two mating shafts may disengage if the pinchbolt inserts into the coupling before shaft installation. This is absolutely critical. Otherwise, the vehicle steering will be compromised.

15. Raise the subframe back into position, while guiding the intermediate steering shaft onto the rack and pinion stub shaft. When satisfied with the fit of the intermediate shaft to the rack and pinion stub shaft, install the pinchbolt and torque to 35 ft. lbs. (48 Nm).

16. Install new service replacement frame-to-body attaching bolts noting the following:

a. Do not overtighten the body mount. A collapsed spacer or stripped bolt may result.

b. When subframe insulator bolts are removed, always discard the bolts and replace with new bolts.

c. Proper clamping by the mount depends on clean and dry surfaces. If the subframe bolt does not screw in smoothly, it may be necessary to run a tap through the subframe crossmember nut in the body to remove foreign material. Take care that the tap does not punch through the underbody.

d. If for any reason, the rubber frame insulators were removed, generously lubricate with a suitable rubber lube, at installation. Failure to lubricate may prevent proper seating of the insulators in the frame.

e. Carefully and evenly torque the new subframe-to-body bolts to 133 ft. lbs. (180 Nm).

f. When satisfied with the fit of the subframe, remove the support from under the subframe.

17. Support the weight of the vehicle by the control arms. Tighten the stabilizer shaft link nuts to 17 ft. lbs. (23 Nm).

18. Install the wheel and tire assemblies and lower the vehicle.

Lower Control Arm

The lower control arm is a two-piece welded unit with a riveted ball joint. The rear lower control arm pivot uses a non-replaceable bushing. The front bushing mounts vertically and can be replaced.

❋❋ WARNING

Special tools are recommended for removing both the front hub spindle and the ball joint. Use only the recommended tools for separating the ball joint from the knuckle. Do NOT hammer or pry the ball joint from the knuckle. Remember that the steering knuckle is cast aluminum. Failure to use the recommended tools or their functional equivalent may cause damage to the knuckle, the ball joint and/or the ball joint stud seal.

REMOVAL & INSTALLATION

◆ See Figure 16

1. Raise and safely support the vehicle by the frame. Allow the control arms to hang free.

2. Remove the tire and wheel assembly.

3. Remove the outer tie rod end from the steering knuckle using the procedure found later in this section.

4. Disconnect the stabilizer shaft link (bolt) from the control arm.

5. Detach the ABS speed sensor jumper harness.

6. Remove the control arm mounting bolts.

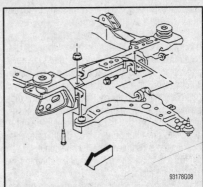

Fig. 16 View of the lower control arm. Note the replaceable vertically mounted front bushing and the non-replaceable horizontally mounted rear bushing

7. Take note of the orientation of the cotter pin. Cotter pin placement may seem insignificant, but at assembly, the bent ends of the cotter pin must not face the ABS wheel speed sensor or the drive axle. Remove the cotter pin and loosen, but do not remove the nut from the ball joint stud.

8. Separate the ball joint stud from the steering knuckle using a ball joint press-type tool. Leaving the ball joint stud nut in place protects the threads on the ball joint stud when the tool presses the stud from the steering knuckle. Do not use a so-called "pickle fork" or any type of wedge to force the ball joint stud from the steering knuckle.

9. Remove the control arm from the frame.

To install:

10. Clean all parts well. If the ball joint is being replaced, use the procedures found in this section.

11. Install the control arm to the frame and install the bolts and nuts. Do not final tighten until the weight of the vehicle is supported by the control arms.

12. Carefully guide the ball joint stud into the bore in the steering knuckle and tighten down the nut. Tighten the nut to 40 ft. lbs. (55 Nm). Align the slots in the nut with the cotter pin hole in the ball joint stud by tightening the nut. DO NOT loosen the nut to align the holes for the cotter pin. Install a new cotter pin. The bent ends of the cotter pin MUST NOT face the ABS wheel speed sensor or the drive axle.

13. Connect the steering tie rod end to the steering knuckle using the procedures found in this section.

14. Install the stabilizer shaft link bolt to the control arm. Torque the nut to 17 ft. lbs. (23 Nm).

15. Assemble the ABS wheel speed sensor harness.

16. Tighten the control arm mounting nuts with the weight of the vehicle supported by the control arms. Tighten the mounting nuts to 83 ft. lbs. (113 Nm).

17. Install the wheel and tire assembly.

18. Lower the vehicle.

19. Take the vehicle to a reputable repair shop to have the wheel alignment checked and adjusted, if necessary.

CONTROL ARM BUSHING REPLACEMENT

The lower control arm uses two types of bushings. The horizontally mounted (rear) bushing is not serviced separately. Service this bushing by replacing the entire lower control arm.

The front bushing is mounted vertically in the control arm. This bushing can be serviced but GM recommends their special tools be used to remove and replace this bushing. The tool set is basically components that look similar to sockets. A heavy bolt passes through the assembly to press the old bushing out and also press the replacement bushing back into place. If these special tools are not available, a hydraulic press, if used with care, could possibly be substituted. Another solution is take the control arm to an automotive machine shop to have the bushing replaced.

1. Remove the lower control arm using the procedures found in this section.

2. Jig together the special tools required to press the bushing out. GM recommends their J 2147-27 puller bolt be used with bushing receiver J 21474-5, installed with the larger diameter end over the bushing against the control arm. Bushing remover J 41014-1 is installed with the large end facing the bushing. Special nut J 21474 threads onto the puller bolt. Tighten the nut until the bushing is driven out of the control arm.

3. Remove the puller tools.

To install:

4. Reassemble the puller tools so that the service replacement bushing will be pressed into the control arm.

5. Lubricate the bushing with soap and water and press it into the control arm.

6. Remove the puller tools.

7. Install the control arm using the procedures found in this section.

Steering Knuckle

The steering knuckle is a machined aluminum casting. Do not use a hammer to loosen suspension components from the knuckle.

REMOVAL & INSTALLATION

▶ **See Figures 17, 18 and 19**

⁑ **WARNING**

Special tools are recommended for removing both the front hub spindle, the tie rod end and the ball joint. Use only the recommended tools for separating the ball joint from the knuckle. Do NOT hammer or pry the ball joint from the knuckle. Remember that the steering knuckle is cast aluminum and can be damaged if care is not used. Failure to use the recommended tools or their functional equivalent may cause damage to the ball joint and seal.

1. Raise and safely support the vehicle.

2. Remove the wheel and tire assembly.

3. Remove the front hub and bearing assembly using the procedures found in this section.

4. Disconnect the lower ball joint using the procedures found in this section.

5. Remove the outer tie rod end using the procedures found in this section.

6. If the knuckle is to be reused, scribe a mark around the strut bracket to the knuckle. This will help align the strut at assembly.

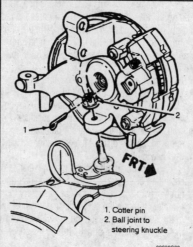

1. Cotter pin
2. Ball joint to steering knuckle

89638G09

Fig. 17 Remove the cotter pin, then loosen the ball joint stud's slotted nut

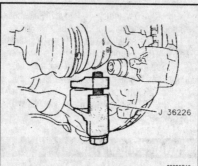

J 36226

89638G10

Fig. 18 Separating the ball joint from the steering knuckle using a special ball joint press tool

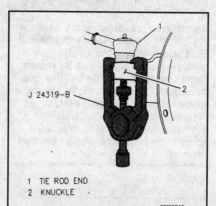

J 24319-B

1 TIE ROD END
2 KNUCKLE

89638G13

Fig. 19 Use a suitable puller to separate the tie rod ends from the steering knuckle

7. Remove the bolts connecting the strut to the knuckle and remove the knuckle from the vehicle.

To install:

8. Install the knuckle to the vehicle. If the original knuckle is being reused, align the scribe marks made at removal to help get the strut-to-knuckle alignment as close as possible to the original location.

9. Install the strut-to-knuckle bolts and tighten to 90 ft. lbs. (123 Nm).

10. Install the outer tie rod end to the steering knuckle. Use a new torque prevailing nut and tighten to 22 ft. lbs. (30 Nm).

11. Connect the lower control arm ball joint stud to the knuckle, install the slotted nut and torque to 40 ft. lbs. (55 Nm). Align the slots in the nut to the hole in the ball joint stud by tightening the nut. DO NOT loosen the nut to align the holes for the cotter pin. Install a new cotter pin. The bent ends of the cotter pin MUST NOT face the ABS wheel speed sensor or the drive axle.

12. Install the front hub and bearing assembly using the procedures found in this section.

13. Install the front wheel and tire assemblies. Torque the wheel nuts to 100 ft. lbs. (140 Nm).

14. Lower the vehicle.

Front Hub and Bearing

GM W-Body vehicles use non-serviceable hubs and bearings at the front and rear wheels. If a hub and bearing is determined to be faulty, replacement is required.

REMOVAL & INSTALLATION

▶ **See Figures 20, 21 and 22**

Because the outer CV-Joint is essentially a press-fit in the front hub and bearing assembly, a good-quality hub/spindle puller is recommended. Use care if using substitutes or expensive damage may result. A new service replacement drive shaft axle nut is specified as well as new hub/bearing retainer bolts. Procure the necessary parts before

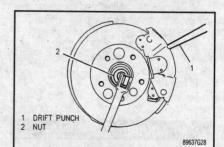

1 DRIFT PUNCH
2 NUT

89637G28

Fig. 20 Prevent the rotor from turning by inserting a drift pin through the caliper and into the rotor

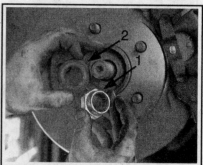

89637P08

Fig. 21 Remove the spindle nut (1) and washer (2)

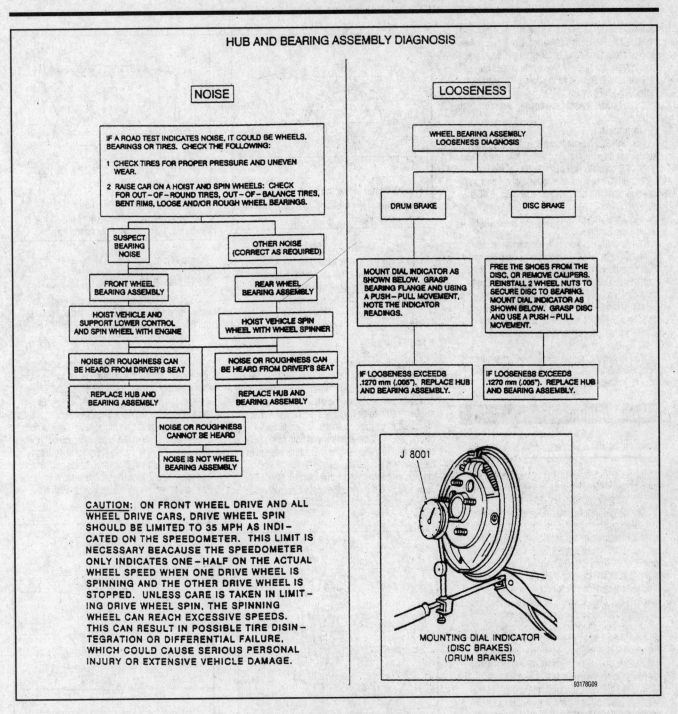

HUB AND BEARING ASSEMBLY DIAGNOSIS

NOISE

IF A ROAD TEST INDICATES NOISE, IT COULD BE WHEELS, BEARINGS OR TIRES. CHECK THE FOLLOWING:

1 CHECK TIRES FOR PROPER PRESSURE AND UNEVEN WEAR.

2 RAISE CAR ON A HOIST AND SPIN WHEELS: CHECK FOR OUT–OF–ROUND TIRES, OUT–OF–BALANCE TIRES, BENT RIMS, LOOSE AND/OR ROUGH WHEEL BEARINGS.

SUSPECT BEARING NOISE

OTHER NOISE (CORRECT AS REQUIRED)

FRONT WHEEL BEARING ASSEMBLY

REAR WHEEL BEARING ASSEMBLY

HOIST VEHICLE AND SUPPORT LOWER CONTROL AND SPIN WHEEL WITH ENGINE

HOIST VEHICLE SPIN WHEEL WITH WHEEL SPINNER

NOISE OR ROUGHNESS CAN BE HEARD FROM DRIVER'S SEAT

NOISE OR ROUGHNESS CAN BE HEARD FROM DRIVER'S SEAT

REPLACE HUB AND BEARING ASSEMBLY

REPLACE HUB AND BEARING ASSEMBLY

NOISE OR ROUGHNESS CANNOT BE HEARD

NOISE IS NOT WHEEL BEARING ASSEMBLY

CAUTION: ON FRONT WHEEL DRIVE AND ALL WHEEL DRIVE CARS, DRIVE WHEEL SPIN SHOULD BE LIMITED TO 35 MPH AS INDICATED ON THE SPEEDOMETER. THIS LIMIT IS NECESSARY BEACAUSE THE SPEEDOMETER ONLY INDICATES ONE–HALF ON THE ACTUAL WHEEL SPEED WHEN ONE DRIVE WHEEL IS SPINNING AND THE OTHER DRIVE WHEEL IS STOPPED. UNLESS CARE IS TAKEN IN LIMITING DRIVE WHEEL SPIN, THE SPINNING WHEEL CAN REACH EXCESSIVE SPEEDS. THIS CAN RESULT IN POSSIBLE TIRE DISINTEGRATION OR DIFFERENTIAL FAILURE, WHICH COULD CAUSE SERIOUS PERSONAL INJURY OR EXTENSIVE VEHICLE DAMAGE.

LOOSENESS

WHEEL BEARING ASSEMBLY LOOSENESS DIAGNOSIS

DRUM BRAKE

DISC BRAKE

MOUNT DIAL INDICATOR AS SHOWN BELOW. GRASP BEARING FLANGE AND USING A PUSH–PULL MOVEMENT, NOTE THE INDICATOR READINGS.

FREE THE SHOES FROM THE DISC, OR REMOVE CALIPERS. REINSTALL 2 WHEEL NUTS TO SECURE DISC TO BEARING. MOUNT DIAL INDICATOR AS SHOWN BELOW. GRASP DISC AND USE A PUSH–PULL MOVEMENT.

IF LOOSENESS EXCEEDS .1270 mm (.005"). REPLACE HUB AND BEARING ASSEMBLY.

IF LOOSENESS EXCEEDS .1270 mm (.005"). REPLACE HUB AND BEARING ASSEMBLY.

J 8001

MOUNTING DIAL INDICATOR (DISC BRAKES) (DRUM BRAKES)

93178G09

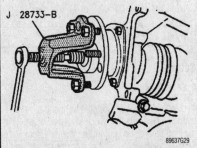

J 28733–B

89637G29

Fig. 22 Use a suitable puller to separate the halfshaft from the hub and bearing assembly

beginning this procedure. GM recommends the following sequence to avoid damage to the bearing.

※※ WARNING

Use care to protect the CV-boots from damage during this procedure.

1. Raise and safely support the vehicle.
2. Remove the wheel and tire assembly.
3. Loosen the drive shaft axle nut (sometimes called a spindle nut) one turn. The torque specification on this nut is 150 ft. lbs. (205 Nm), so expect to need a lot of torque on the wrench to break the nut loose. To keep the brake rotor and hub assembly from turning when loosening the nut, insert a suitably

sized drift pin or other suitable tool through the brake caliper inspection opening into the brake rotor's ventilation openings. This should lock the assembly in place so the spindle nut can be loosened. It is good practice to wire-brush any exposed threads on the end of the spindle and apply a generous coating of penetrating oil. Do not remove the nut yet.

4. Remove the brake caliper, bracket and the rotor. Please see Section 9.
5. Remove the drive shaft nut.
6. Loosen the hub and bearing assembly to knuckle attaching bolts.
7. Using a hub puller, push the axle shaft splines back out of the hub and bearing assembly. Don't try to hammer on the end of the spindle (part

of the outer CV-joint) or the joint and possibly also the hub bearing will be damaged. Use a hub puller to press the spindle out of the hub. It is good practice to leave the hub nut in place to protect the threads on the spindle as the hub puller presses the spindle free of the hub.

8. Remove the hub and bearing assembly from the vehicle.

To install:

9. Install the service replacement hub and bearing to the knuckle, over the splines of the drive axle shaft (actually part of the outer CV-joint).

10. Install new knuckle to front wheel hub and bearing attaching bolts. Tighten the bolts to 96 ft. lbs. (130 Nm).

11. Install the rotor, bracket and brake caliper. Please see Section 9.

12. Install a new service replacement front wheel drive axle nut. To keep the brake rotor and hub assembly from turning when tightening the nut, insert a suitably sized drift pin or other suitable tool through the brake caliper inspection opening into the brake rotor's ventilation openings, locking the assembly in place so the spindle nut can be tightened. Torque the nut to 150 ft. lbs. (205 Nm).

13. Install the front wheel and tire assemblies. Torque the wheel nuts to 100 ft. lbs. (140 Nm).

14. Lower the vehicle.

Wheel Alignment

DESCRIPTION

Wheel alignment refers to the angular relationship between the wheels, the suspension attaching points and the ground.

On the W-Body vehicles covered by this manual, GM specifies that Four Wheel Alignment be used, since the rear suspension is independent and adjustable, not a solid beam axle used on some other Front Wheel Drive vehicles. A complete four wheel alignment check is recommended whenever a service check is deemed necessary (uneven tire wear, the vehicle pulls to one side or a major suspension component has been replaced). This check includes the measurement of all four tires. The fuel economy and tire life increases when the vehicle is geometrically aligned. Additionally, the steering and the vehicle performance is maximized.

Because four wheel alignment is critical to the vehicle's performance and safety, it should be performed by a qualified technician with the proper equipment. The latest alignment equipment uses lasers for accurate sighting and a computer for precise calculations. Below is a description of the various angles used in wheel alignment on these vehicles.

Caster

▶ See Figure 23

Caster is the tilting of the uppermost point of the steering axis, either forward or backward from vertical, when viewed from the side of the vehicle. A backward tilt at the top is called positive caster (+) and a forward tilt is called negative caster (-). Caster influences the directional control of the

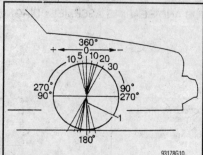

Fig. 23 Caster is the tilting of the uppermost point of the steering axis, either forward or backward

steering, but caster does not affect tire wear. One wheel with more positive caster than the other wheel causes that wheel to pull toward the center of the vehicle. The vehicle will move or lead toward that side with the least amount of caster.

Camber

▶ See Figure 24

Camber is the tilting of the wheels from the vertical when viewed from the front of the vehicle. When the wheels tilt outward at the top, the camber is said to be positive (+). When the wheels tilt inward, the camber is said to be negative (-). The amount of tilt, measured in degrees, from the vertical is known as camber angle. Camber influences both directional control and tire wear. Excessive camber results in tire wear and causes the vehicle to pull or lead to the side with the most positive camber. On GM W-Body vehicles, camber adjustment is available at both the front and rear wheels.

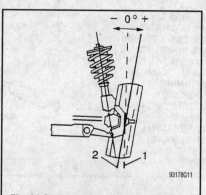

Fig. 24 Camber is the tilting of the wheels from vertical as viewed from the front

Toe

▶ See Figure 25

Toe-in is the turning-in of the wheels, while toe-out is the turning-out of the wheels from the geometric centerline. The purpose of toe is to ensure parallel rolling of the wheels. Toe also serves to offset the small deflections of the wheel support system which occur whenever the vehicle is rolling forward. Even when the wheels are set to toe-in or toe-out, the wheels tend to roll parallel on the road when the vehicle is moving.

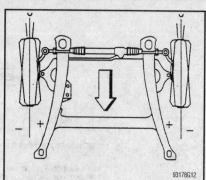

Fig. 25 Toe-in is the turning in of the wheels; toe-out is the turning out of the wheels, from the vehicle centerline

Frame Misalignment

▶ See Figure 26

The frame is a rubber isolated subframe (so-called on these vehicles because it does not run the full length of the vehicle), in the front of the vehicle. The subframe supports the engine and transaxle. The frame provides the mounting point for the front suspension lower control arms. Any misalignment of the subframe (accident damage, improperly performed heavy engine work where the subframe is loosened, lowered and/or removed, etc.) causes a misalignment of the front wheels. Movement of the frame usually causes an increase in caster on one side of the vehicle and decrease in caster on the other side. This can cause the exhaust system to bind up, problems with control cables and unacceptable noise. Check the subframe for any obvious damage, especially on a used vehicle with an unknown history.

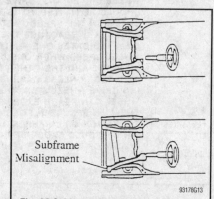

Fig. 26 Subframe misalignment can result from collision damage or poorly performed heavy service work where the subframe is loosened or lowered

Setback

▶ See Figure 27

Setback applies to both the front and the rear wheels. Setback is the amount that one wheel spindle may be aligned behind the other wheel spindle. Setback may be the result of a road hazard (heavily hit pothole, for example) or a collision. The first clue is a caster difference from side-to-side of more than one degree.

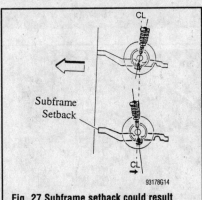

Fig. 27 Subframe setback could result from a road hazard or collision

Thrust Angles

▶ See Figure 28

The front wheels aim or steer the vehicle. The rear wheels control tracking. This tracking action relates to the thrust angle. The thrust angle is the path that the rear wheels take. Ideally the thrust angle is geometrically aligned with the body centerline. If, for example, the toe-in on the left rear wheel is out of specification, it moves the thrust line off center. The resulting deviation from the centerline is the thrust angle.

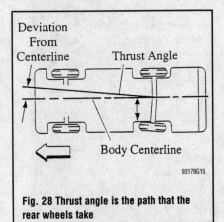

Fig. 28 Thrust angle is the path that the rear wheels take

Lead/Pull

Lead is the deviation of the vehicle from a straight path on a level road, without hand pressure on the steering wheel. Lead is usually the result of tire construction, uneven parking brake adjustment or the wheel alignment. The way in which a tire is built may produce lead. Rear tires do not cause lead.

Torque Steer

▶ See Figure 29

A vehicle pulls or leads in one direction during hard acceleration. A vehicle pulls or leads in the other direction during deceleration. The following

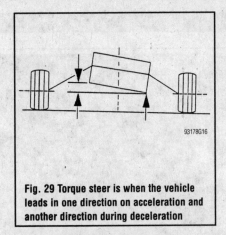

Fig. 29 Torque steer is when the vehicle leads in one direction on acceleration and another direction during deceleration

factors may cause torque steer to be more apparent on a particular vehicle:

• A slightly smaller diameter tire on the right front increases a right torque lead. Inspect the front tires for differences in the brand, the construction or the size. If the tires appear to be similar, change the front tires from side-to-side and retest the vehicle. Tire and wheel assemblies have the most significant effect on torque steer correction.

• A large difference in the right and left front tire pressure.

• Left-to-right differences in the front view axle angle may cause significant steering pull in the vehicle. The pull will be to the side with the most downward sloping axle from the differential to the wheels. Axles (halfshafts) typically slope downward from the differential. The slope of the transaxle pan to level ground may be used as an indication of bias axle angles. The side with the higher transaxle pan has the most downward sloping axle angle.

Memory Steer

Memory steer is when the vehicle wants to lead or pull in the direction the driver previously turned the vehicle. Additionally, after turning in the opposite direction, the vehicle will want to lead or pull in that direction.

Wander

Wander is the undesirable drifting or deviation of a vehicle toward either side from a straight path with hand pressure on the steering wheel. Wander is a symptom of a vehicle's sensitivity to external disturbances, such as road crown and crosswind. A poor, on-center steering feel accentuates a wander condition.

PRELIMINARY ALIGNMENT INSPECTION

▶ See Figure 30

A knowledgeable and competent professional alignment shop will make a number of checks before attempting a vehicle alignment. Loose or worn suspension parts prevents an accurate setting of alignment angles. Checks should include:

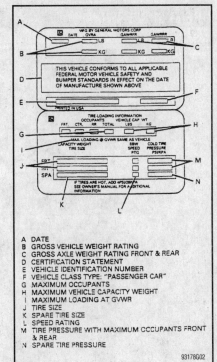

A DATE
B GROSS VEHICLE WEIGHT RATING
C GROSS AXLE WEIGHT RATING FRONT & REAR
D CERTIFICATION STATEMENT
E VEHICLE IDENTIFICATION NUMBER
F VEHICLE CLASS TYPE: "PASSENGER CAR"
G MAXIMUM OCCUPANTS
H MAXIMUM VEHICLE CAPACITY WEIGHT
I MAXIMUM LOADING AT GVWR
J TIRE SIZE
K SPARE TIRE SIZE
L SPEED RATING
M TIRE PRESSURE WITH MAXIMUM OCCUPANTS FRONT & REAR
N SPARE TIRE PRESSURE

Fig. 30 Typical GM Tire Placard as found on the driver's door

• The tires should be checked for proper inflation pressures. Refer to the Tire Placard, referenced in this section.

• Check the tires for normal tread wear.

• Check the front hub and bearing assembly for excessive wear.

• Check the ball joints and tie rods for looseness.

• Inspect the wheels and tires for runout, resulting from bent wheels or faulty tires.

• The vehicle trim height should be checked. If the trim heights are not within specification, it will be necessary to make corrections before adjusting the alignment.

• The steering gear should be checked for looseness.

• The struts should be inspected for wear or damage.

• The control arms should be checked for loose or worn bushings.

• The stabilizer shaft (sometimes called a sway bar) attachments should be checked for loose or missing components.

• The frame fasteners should be checked for proper torque.

• The frame insulators should be checked for wear or damage.

The alignment should be checked with a full tank of fuel. The alignment shop should then check the alignment in the following order:

• Rear wheel camber
• Rear wheel toe and tracking
• Front wheel camber
• Front wheel toe and steering wheel angle

REAR SUSPENSION

REAR SUSPENSION COMPONENT LOCATIONS

1. Rear suspension support
2. Rear stabilizer shaft
3. Adjustable spindle rod
4. Jam nut
5. Adjuster sleeve
6. Rear strut
7. Non-adjustable spindle rod
8. Parking brake cable
9. Trailing arm
10. Trailing arm bracket
11. Fuel tank (fuel pump inside)

93178P07

▶ See Figure 31

All W-Body vehicles use a rear suspension designed around coil springs over struts and lightweight aluminum knuckles. The exception is the 1997 Oldsmobile Cutlass Supreme which uses a fiberglass mono-leaf spring. All vehicles have each rear wheel mounted to a tri-link independent suspension system. The three links are identified as the inverted u-channel trailing arm and the front and rear spindle rods. The spindle rods act as parallel links to allow the rear wheels to deflect upward when the rear wheels hit a road hazard, without moving the toe angle in a positive direction. An advantage of this suspension system is the reduction of unsprung and overall weight. Handling is improved with the independent action of each rear wheel. The spindle rods control the lateral wheel deflection.

The 1997 Oldsmobile Cutlass Supreme uses a composite fiberglass mono-leaf transverse spring. The spring rate is independent of loading. Lightweight cast-iron wheel knuckles are also used. Each wheel is mounted to a tri-link independent suspension system, similar to the other members of the W-Body family.

The tri-link design may be compared to a right angle. The wheel is located at the right angle formed by the spindle rods and the trailing arm. The ends of the tri-links hinge to provide vertical wheel travel. The spindle rods are solid links and force the wheel to travel through a controlled arc whose fore-aft position is determined by the trailing arm and whose lateral position is determined by the spindle rods.

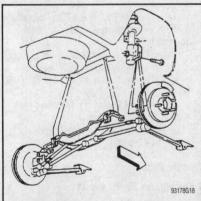

Fig. 31 Typical W-Body rear suspension

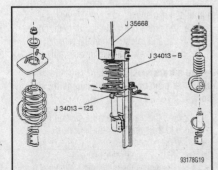

93178G19

Fig. 32 Exploded view of the rear strut and coil spring and the special strut compressor recommended for disassembly

Aside from maintaining geometric wheel location, each portion of the suspension has additional functions. The knuckle supports the brake caliper. All brake torque and braking forces are transmitted through the tri-links and the strut. The final duty of the spindle rods is to maintain the camber angle of the wheel throughout the wheel's travel, and to allow for setting the toe. The overall result of this rear suspension geometry is to maintain the rear wheels in a near vertical position at all times.

The stabilizer shaft attaches to the stabilizer bar drop link and extends rearward, where the stabilizer connects to the rear suspension support by two rubber bushings and mounting brackets.

A non-serviceable hub and bearing bolts to the knuckle. This hub and bearing is a sealed, maintenance-free unit and, if defective, must be replaced as an assembly.

Check the rear suspension system periodically for the following conditions:

- Shock absorbency
- Bushing durability
- Tightness of the attaching bolts
- Visible damage
- Misalignment
- Excessive wear

Coil Springs

The coil springs are mounted to the rear struts. The springs are under high tension. Do not attempt to remove the strut shaft nut without using a spring compressor tool. In addition, a unique nut may be used at the top of the strut and may require a special socket wrench for removal and installation.

REMOVAL & INSTALLATION

▶ See Figure 32

1. Remove the strut from the vehicle using the procedures found in this section.
2. Mount the strut in a strut compressor tool.
3. Use the strut compressor forcing screw to compress the spring just enough to release the tension from the strut mount.
4. Remove the strut shaft nut.
5. Relieve the spring tension and remove the spring from the strut.

To install:

6. Inspect all components for wear or damage.
7. Install the rear spring lower insulator. Make

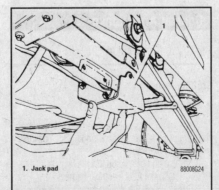

1. Jack pad   88008G24

Fig. 33 Remove the jack pad from the center of the spring

sure the lower spring is visible between the step and the location mark on the insulator.

8. Install the rear suspension spring and the dust shield to the lower insulator. Install the jounce bumper and strut mount.

9. Use a strut compressor to compress the strut, working the strut shaft through the strut mount.

10. Compress the strut and spring assembly enough to install the strut shaft nut. Torque the nut to 55 ft. lbs. (75 Nm).

11. Install the strut into the vehicle using the procedures found in this section.

Transverse Spring Assembly

REMOVAL & INSTALLATION

1997 Oldsmobile Cutlass Supreme

▶ See Figures 33 thru 37

❊❊ CAUTION

Do NOT disconnect any rear suspension components until the transverse spring has been compressed using a rear spring compressor tool J-35778 or equivalent. Failure to follow this procedure may result in personal injury. Wear protective eye equipment when working on the suspension.

➡ Do not use any corrosive cleaning agents, silicone lubricants, engine degreasers, solvents, etc. on or near the rear transverse fiberglass spring. These materials may cause spring strength depletion and consequent damage.

1. Disconnect the negative battery cable.
2. Raise and safely support the vehicle with safety stands.
3. Remove the jack pad from the middle of the spring.
4. If equipped with dual exhaust, remove the exhaust system.
5. Remove the spring retention plates.
6. Disconnect the right trailing arm from the knuckle.
7. If equipped, detach the ABS electrical harness.
8. Separate the rear leaf spring, using compressor tool J 35778 or equivalent, from the center

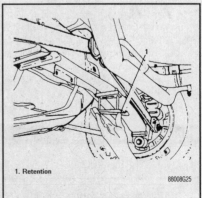

1. Retention   88008G25

Fig. 34 Spring retention plate removal

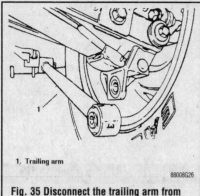

1. Trailing arm

88008G26

Fig. 35 Disconnect the trailing arm from the knuckle

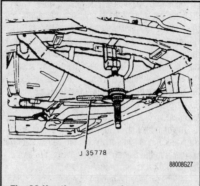

J 35778

88008G27

Fig. 36 Use the proper tool to compress the spring

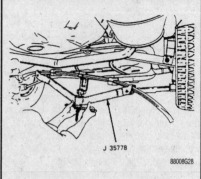

J 35778

88008G28

Fig. 37 Removing the transverse spring from the vehicle

shank and hang the center shank of the tool at the spring center.

> ❊❊❊ **WARNING**
>
> **Attach the center shank of the compressor from the front side of the vehicle only.**

9. Install the compressor body to the center shank and spring. Center the spring on the rollers of the spring compressor only.

10. Fully compress the spring using the spring compressor tool J 35778, or equivalent.

11. Slide the spring to the left side. It may be necessary to pry the spring to the left using a pry-bar against the right knuckle. When prying, be careful not to damage any components.

12. Relax the spring to provide removal clearance from the right side, then remove the spring.

To install:

13. Using the spring compressor tool, compress the spring and install it through the left knuckle. Slide towards the left side as far as possible and raise the right side of the spring as far as possible.

14. Compress the spring fully and install it into right knuckle.

➡ **The rear spring retention plates are designed with tabs on one end. The tabs must be aligned with the support assembly to prevent damage to the fuel tank.**

15. Center the spring to align the holes for the spring retention plate bolts.

16. Install the spring retention plates and bolts. Do NOT tighten at this time.

17. Position the trailing arm and install the bolt. Tighten the bolt to 177 ft. lbs. (239 Nm).

18. Remove the spring compressor tool.

19. Tighten the spring retention plate bolts to 22 ft. lbs. (30 Nm).

20. Install the jack pads and tighten the bolts to 18 ft. lbs. (25 Nm).

21. Carefully lower the vehicle, then tighten the lug nuts to 100 ft. lbs. (140 Nm).

22. Connect the negative battery cable.

Rear Suspension Struts

REMOVAL & INSTALLATION

1. Raise and safely support the vehicle.
2. Remove the wheel and tire assembly.

3. Disconnect the rear stabilizer shaft link.

4. Scribe marks on the strut and knuckle to aid reassembly.

5. Remove the strut mount-to-body nuts.

6. Disconnect the strut from the knuckle.

7. Remove the strut from the vehicle.

To install:

8. Install the strut to the knuckle, aligning the scribe marks made at removal. Install the bolts and nuts and torque the strut-to-knuckle nuts to 82 ft. lbs. (112 Nm).

9. Connect the rear stabilizer shaft links to the strut.

10. Install the wheel and tire assembly.

11. Lower the vehicle.

12. Have the rear wheel alignment checked and adjusted by a reputable alignment shop.

OVERHAUL

The rear suspension struts (in previous years, sometimes called MacPherson Struts) combine the functions of a shock absorber (damper) and a spring mount into one structural assembly. Disassembling the strut for spring removal and/or strut replacement requires special tools. Older vehicles had struts that could be taken apart and overhauled. The struts on vehicles covered by this manual do not come apart, except for the coil spring which can be replaced. If special tools are not available to disassemble the strut, it may be possible to purchase an aftermarket spring and strut already assembled.

For rear strut spring removal, please see the Coil Spring Removal and Installation procedure found in this section.

Control Arms/Links

REMOVAL & INSTALLATION

Trailing Arms

▶ **See Figure 38**

The trailing arms are the inverted U-shape arms that go from the rear suspension knuckle back to a body mount bracket.

1. Raise and safely support the vehicle.
2. Detach the ABS electrical harness.
3. Disconnect the trailing arm from the knuckle.
4. Remove the trailing arm bracket-to-body bolts.

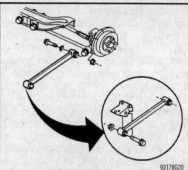

93178G20

Fig. 38 View of the rear trailing arms, which run from the rear wheel knuckles to an underbody bracket

5. Disconnect the trailing arm from the bracket.
6. Remove the trailing arm from the vehicle.

To install:

7. Installation is the reverse of the removal process. Use the following torque specifications:

a. Tighten the bracket bolt to 77 ft. lbs. (105 Nm).

b. Tighten the trailing arm bracket-to-body bolts to 37 ft. lbs. (50 Nm).

c. Tighten the trailing arm-to-knuckle nut to 192 ft. lbs. (260 Nm).

Spindle Rods

▶ **See Figures 39, 40 and 41**

The spindle rods are the suspension members that run from the rear suspension support in the middle of the vehicle to the wheel knuckle. There is a front and rear spindle rod on each side of the vehicle. The procedure is similar for both rods.

1. Raise and safely support the vehicle.
2. Remove the wheel and tire assembly.

➡ **Use a transmission jack or suitable hoist stands to prop up the rear suspension support.**

3. Lower the rear suspension support to gain clearance to the spindle rod-to-knuckle bolt. Use the following procedure:

a. Remove the exhaust pipe.

b. Disengage the hydraulic brake lines from the suspension support.

c. Disconnect the parking brake cables from the suspension support.

d. Disconnect the stabilizer shaft (sway bar) from the links and at the suspension support.

e. Verify that the suspension support is securely support by suitable jack before removing the bolts.

f. Remove the rear suspension support mounting bolts.

Fig. 39 The spindle rod's outboard attachment is at the wheel knuckle. One rod is solid, the other has an adjuster sleeve

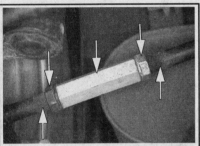

Fig. 40 The adjuster sleeve (center arrow) on this spindle rods allows the rear alignment to be altered and corrected. Note the jam nuts and the adjustment threads

g. Disconnect the rear wheel spindle rods at the wheel knuckle.

h. Lower the rear suspension support to gain access to the inboard spindle rod bolts.

4. With the spindle rod bolts removed from the knuckle and the rear suspension support, remove the spindle rod(s) from the vehicle.

To install:

➡**Threadlocking compound is recommended on all threaded fasteners.**

5. Install the spindle rod to the rear suspension support and install the bolt. Torque the nut to 103 ft. lbs. (140 Nm).

6. Install the rear suspension support to the vehicle. Use the following procedure:

a. Raise the support into place using the hydraulic jack used to lower it. Use care to line up the bolt holes. Install the support mounting bolts and tighten to 77 ft. lbs. (105 Nm).

b. Position the spindle rod(s) to the wheel knuckle. Install the retaining bolts and nuts and torque to 110 ft. lbs. (150 Nm).

c. Install the hydraulic brake lines to the suspension support.

d. Connect the brake cables and the tensioner to the rear suspension support.

e. Install the stabilizer shaft (sway bar) and links to the rear suspension support. More information on the stabilizer shaft may be found in this section. Tighten the bracket bolts to 35 ft. lbs. (48 Nm).

7. Install the wheel and tire assembly.

8. Lower the vehicle.

9. Have the alignment checked and adjusted at a reputable alignment shop.

Stabilizer Shaft

The stabilizer shaft (often called a sway bar) runs across the rear of the suspension and is isolated by rubber bushings.

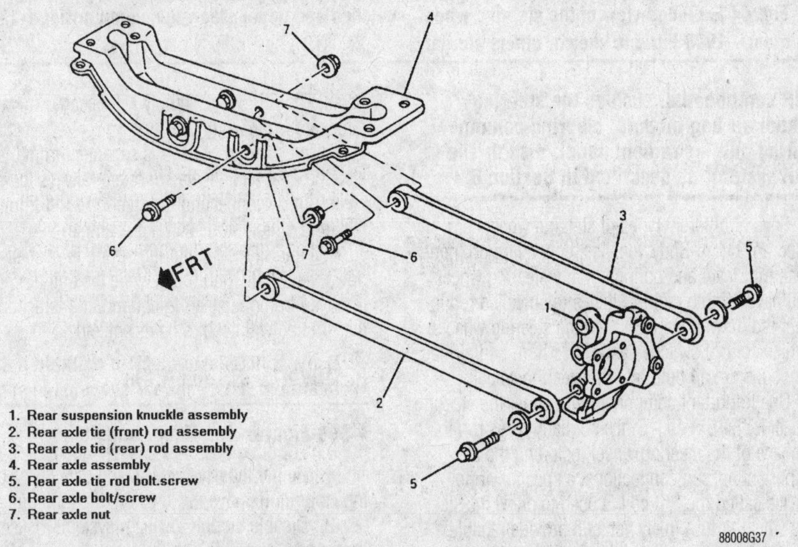

REMOVAL & INSTALLATION

1. Raise and safely support the vehicle.

2. Remove the tire and wheel assemblies from both sides.

3. Remove the right and left side stabilizer shaft link bolts.

4. Remove the insulator brackets and the bolts from the stabilizer shaft.

5. Remove the stabilizer shaft from the rear suspension support.

6. Installation is the reverse of the removal process. Please note that GM specifies that the wheel toe angle should be checked and adjusted as necessary after stabilizer shaft replacement.

Rear Hub and Bearing

The wheel bearings in the rear wheel hubs are integrated into one unit. The hub is non-serviceable. If the bearing is considered worn our or if the hub is damaged, the complete unit must be replaced.

REMOVAL & INSTALLATION

◗ **See Figure 42**

1. Raise and safely support the vehicle.

2. Remove the wheel and tire assembly.

3. Remove the rear caliper and bracket. Please see Section 9.

4. Disconnect the ABS harness and detach the electrical connector.

5. Remove the four rear hub-to-knuckle bolts.

6. Separate the hub from the knuckle.

To install:

7. Install the rear hub and bearing assembly to the knuckle and install the retaining holts. Torque to 55 ft. lbs. (75 Nm).

8. Install the ABS harness and attach the electrical connector.

9. Install the caliper bracket and the caliper. Please see Section 9.

10. Install the wheel and tire assembly.

11. Lower the vehicle.

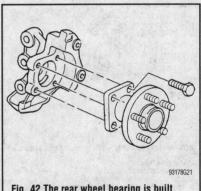

Fig. 42 The rear wheel bearing is built into the hub and, if defective, the entire hub assembly is replaced

1. Rear suspension knuckle assembly
2. Rear axle tie (front) rod assembly
3. Rear axle tie (rear) rod assembly
4. Rear axle assembly
5. Rear axle tie rod bolt.screw
6. Rear axle bolt/screw
7. Rear axle nut

Fig. 41 Front and rear spindle rods—1997 Chevrolet shown

STEERING

The steering column includes three important features in addition to the steering function:

• The column is energy absorbing, designed to compress in a front-end collision to lessen the chance of injury to the driver.

• On most W-Body vehicles, the ignition switch and lock are mounted on the column. With the column-mounted lock, the ignition and steering operations can be locked to inhibit theft of the vehicle.

• The multifunction lever provides for control of the headlamp high-beams, the cruise control and the windshield wiper and washer.

Use care when working around the steering column. Disable the SIR (air bag) system before working on or around the steering wheel and column. Please see Section 6 for the procedure. Do not hammer on the steering column for any reason. The plastic fasteners which maintain column rigidity can be sheared or loosened by using an improper steering wheel puller, striking sharply on the end of the steering shaft, or, if the column has been removed, dropping the column or handling it roughly.

Steering Wheel

▶ See Figures 43 and 44

✷ CAUTION

All models covered by this manual are equipped with a Supplemental Inflatable Restraint (SIR) System, using multiple air bags. Whenever working near any of the

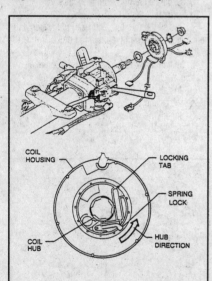

COIL HOUSING

LOCKING TAB

SPRING LOCK

COIL HUB

HUB DIRECTION

PERFORM THE FOLLOWING STEPS TO CENTER COIL ASSEMBLY

A. WHEELS STRAIGHT AHEAD.
B. REMOVE COIL ASSEMBLY.
C. HOLD COIL ASSEMBLY WITH BOTTOM UP.
D. WHILE HOLDING COIL ASSEMBLY, DEPRESS SPRING LOCK TO ROTATE HUB IN DIRECTION OF ARROW UNTIL IT STOPS.
E. THE COIL RIBBON SHOULD BE WOUND UP SNUG AGAINST CENTER HUB.
F. ROTATE COIL HUB IN OPPOSITE DIRECTION APPROXIMATELY TWO AND A HALF (2-1/2) TURNS. RELEASE SPRING LOCK BETWEEN LOCKING TABS.

93178G24

Fig. 43 The SIR coil is located under the steering wheel and if "uncentered" must be reset

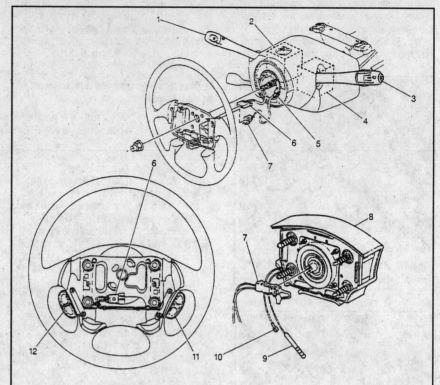

1. Headlamp Switch/Turn Signal Lever
2. Headlamp/Turn Signal Switch
3. Windshield Wiper/Washer Switch Lever
4. Windshield Wiper/Washer Switch
5. Air Bag Steering Wheel Module Coil
6. Remote Radio Control Switch Connector
7. Air Bag Steering Wheel Module Connector
8. Air Bag Steering Wheel Module
9. Horn Switch Connector
10. Horn Switch Ground Connector
11. Cruise Control Switches
12. Remote Radio Switches

93178G25

Fig. 44 Exploded view of the steering wheel, switches and upper steering column arrangement—1998 Intrigue shown, others similar

SIR components, such as the steering wheel air bag module, steering column wiring and instrument panel, disable the SIR system, as described in Section 6.

Several different types of steering wheels are used on GM W-Body vehicles, depending on model year, trim level and options. Many steering wheels will have remote radio switches (also called redundant radio switches) built into the steering wheels. Cruise control switches as well as horn and air bag functions are all built into the steering wheel.

One important component just under the steering wheel is the SIR coil. Since so many wires run to the face of the steering wheel including the all-important air bag connections, a special wiring device called the SIR coil is used to allow the steering wheel to turn freely yet, still provide reliable wiring connections through a "ribbon cable" arrangement. Care must be used to always center the front wheels and lock the steering column when working on the steering wheel and related compo-

nents. The SIR coil assembly will become "uncentered" if:

• The steering column is separated from the steering gear and allowed to rotate (always lock the column if disconnecting the steering shaft from the rack and pinion stub shaft, for example).

• If the SIR coil centering spring is pushed down, letting the hub rotate while the coil is removed from the steering column. If this occurs, the SIR coil will need to be recentered.

REMOVAL & INSTALLATION

▶ See Figures 45, 46, 47 and 48

1. Center the front wheels and lock the steering column. Remove the key from the ignition.

2. Disable the SIR (air bag) system. Please see the procedure in Section 6.

3. Remove the air bag module from the steering wheel using the following procedure:

a. Verify that the SIR system has been disabled.

➡ The air bag can be retained to the steering wheel with several different types of fasteners, depending on Model Year and vehicle equipment. A small mirror may be helpful to examine the back of the steering wheel to determine how the air bag is retained on your vehicle. It could be by Torx® screws which are unscrewed using the proper bit (usually a #30 driver bit). An alternate method of attachment is by small leaf-type springs which are unclipped with a small flat-blade prytool.

b. On the back side of the steering wheel, locate and remove the air bag fasteners.

c. Gently pull on the air bag module to free it from the steering wheel.

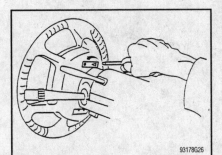

Fig. 45 If leaf-type springs are used to retain the air bag, release the spring clip retainers and separate the air bag module from the steering wheel

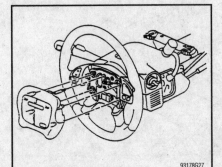

Fig. 46 Carefully pull the air bag module away from the steering wheel, then detach the electrical connector

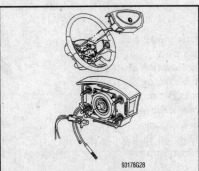

Fig. 47 Exploded view of the air bag module and electrical connections—Buick shown, others similar

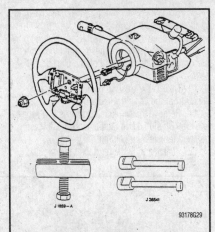

Fig. 48 Typical steering wheel and the recommended puller with special legs to fit steering wheels designed for air bags

d. Detach the electrical connections from the steering wheel to the air bag module.

e. Place the air bag in a safe place, with the trim pad facing upwards.

4. Scribe an alignment mark on the steering wheel hub in line with the existing mark on the steering shaft.

5. Loosen, but do not remove the steering wheel shaft nut, positioning it flush with the end of the steering column shaft. This is protect the steering column shaft threads from the foot of the steering wheel puller center screw.

6. Assemble a suitable steering wheel puller (GM recommends their J 1859-A puller with J 36541 special legs) to the steering wheel and pull the wheel loose from the shaft.

7. Remove the steering wheel shaft nut and the remove the steering wheel. Detach the electrical connectors.

To install:

8. Route the SIR connector through the steering wheel.

9. Align the scribe mark on the steering wheel made at removal with the existing mark on the steering column shaft. Make sure the steering wheel is seated.

10. Install the steering wheel shaft nut and tighten to 33 ft. lbs. (45 Nm).

11. Install the air bag module using the following procedure:

a. Attach the electrical connections to the air bag module.

b. If equipped with leaf-spring type clips, line up the air bag module retainers with the openings in the steering wheel. Gently press the air bag module into place until it `snaps' into place.

c. If equipped with screws to retain the air bag, install the screws using care to line up the screw openings.

12. Enable the SIR system. Please see the procedure in Section 6.

13. Check the operation of the horn and steering wheel. Check the operation of the steering wheel switches, as equipped.

Turn Signal (Combination) Switch

On many W-Body vehicles, the Turn Signal Switch is combined with several other functions including Cruise Control, Washer/Wipers, Headlights and High Beam/Low Beam Control. Because of this, the switch is commonly called a Combination Switch, or as GM calls it, a Multifunction Switch.

REMOVAL & INSTALLATION

Steering Columns With Removable Shrouds

EXCEPT 1998–00 INTRIGUE

▶ See Figure 49

1. Make sure the multifunction lever is in the **OFF** position.

2. Disconnect the negative (ground) battery cable.

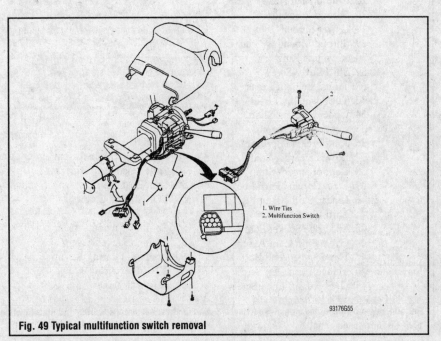

1. Wire Ties
2. Multifunction Switch

Fig. 49 Typical multifunction switch removal

3. Disable the SIR system. Please see Section 6.

4. Remove the air bag module from the steering wheel using the procedures found under steering wheel removal, in this section.

5. Remove the steering wheel using the procedures found in this section.

6. Remove the screws from the lower steering column cover. It may be helpful to tilt the column down and slide the cover back to disengage the plastic locking tabs. Work carefully. The plastic column covers are easily damaged.

7. Remove the screws from the upper steering column cover and lift off the cover.

8. Disconnect the wire harness strap.

9. It is likely that wire ties restrain the multifunction switch harness. Cut off the plastic wire ties.

10. Detach the steering column harness connector from the vehicle wire harness.

11. Remove the two tapping screws and separate the turn signal and multifunction switch assembly from the steering column.

12. Installation is the reverse of the removal process. Use new plastic wire ties to secure the harness as before.

13. Test all multifunction switch operations.

1998–00 INTRIGUE

▶ See Figure 50

Oldsmobile Intrigue combines the headlamp switch with the turn signal switch into what is often called a multifunction switch. The air bag and steering wheel must be removed to change out the multifunction switch.

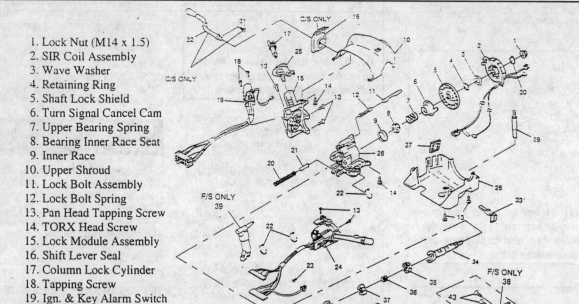

1. Lock Nut (M14 x 1.5)
2. SIR Coil Assembly
3. Wave Washer
4. Retaining Ring
5. Shaft Lock Shield
6. Turn Signal Cancel Cam
7. Upper Bearing Spring
8. Bearing Inner Race Seat
9. Inner Race
10. Upper Shroud
11. Lock Bolt Assembly
12. Lock Bolt Spring
13. Pan Head Tapping Screw
14. TORX Head Screw
15. Lock Module Assembly
16. Shift Lever Seal
17. Column Lock Cylinder
18. Tapping Screw
19. Ign. & Key Alarm Switch
20. Tilt Spring
21. Spring Guide
22. Wire Harness Strap
23. CPA Wedge
24. Multifunction Switch
25. Trim Ring
26. Column Tilt Head
27. Shroud Protector
28. Lower Shroud
29. Shroud Mounting Stud
30. Retaining Ring
31. Shift Lever Screw
32. Transaxle Shift Lever
33. Tilt Assembly Lever
34. Upper Steering Shaft
35. Centering Sphere
36. Joint Preload Spring
37. Lower Steering Shaft
38. Reinforcement Strap
39. Elec. Column Park Lock
40. Linear Shift Assembly
41. Shift Lever Clevis
43. Six-Lobe Socket Screw
44. Cable Shift Cam Assem
45. Hex Flange Head Bolt
46. Flange Head Hex Screw
47. Oval Hd Six-Lobe Screw
48. Park Lock Cable Assem
49. Shift Lever Arm Bracket
50. Cam Bushing
55. TORX Head Screw
56. Pivot Pin
57. Column Support Assem
58. Column Jacket Assem
60. Adapter, Bearing Assem
61. BTSI Electrical Actuator
62. Sensor Retainer
63. Steering Shaft Seal
64. Pinch Bolt
65. Inter. Steering Shaft Joint
66. Inter. Steering Shaft
67. Lower Bearing Seat
68. Lower Bearing Spring
69. Lower Spring Retainer
C/S = Column Shift
F/S = Floor Shift

93178G31

Fig. 50 Exploded view of the shroud-type steering column showing shrouds, wiring and multifunction switch that includes the headlamp function— 1998-00 Oldsmobile Intrigue

1. Verify that the multifunction turn signal lever is in the center of the OFF position.

2. Disconnect the negative battery cable.

3. Disable the SIR (air bag) system, as outlined in Section 6.

4. Remove the air bag module from the steering wheel using the procedures found under steering wheel removal, in this section.

5. Remove the steering wheel using the procedures found in this section.

6. Remove the upper and lower steering wheel trim covers using the following procedure.

   a. Remove the tilt lever assembly.

   b. Remove the two pan head tapping screws from the lower shroud.

   c. Unlock the upper and lower shroud.

   d. Remove the two Torx® head screws from the upper shroud.

   e. Remove the upper shroud.

7. Remove the wire harness straps from the wire harness assembly and detach the wiring harness connectors from the switch side connectors.

8. Remove the two multifunction turn signal switch screws and remove the multifunction switch assembly from the vehicle.

To install:

9. Install the multifunction switch to the steering column. Use a small flat-blade prytool to compress the electrical contact and move the multifunction turn signal switch into position. Verify that the electrical contact rests on the canceling cam. Install the screws and tighten to 62 inch lbs. (7 Nm).

10. Route the wire harness along the steering column jacket assembly and secure into the wire harness strap. Install a new wire tie to the upper tilt head assembly and another lower along the wiring harness, as the original installation.

11. Verify that the lever is in the center of the **OFF** position.

12. Install the upper and lower steering column shrouds.

13. Route the SIR connector through the steering wheel, align the scribe mark on the steering wheel made at removal, with the slash mark on the steering shaft and install the steering wheel. Install the steering shaft nut and torque to 30 ft. lbs. (41 Nm).

14. Install the horn contact leads and the air bag connector to the back of the air bag. Make sure the CPA wedge is in place to secure the connector. Install the air bag by gently pushing on both the right and left sides of the air bag until the retaining springs engage.

15. Enable the SIR system by connecting the yellow 2-way connector at the base of the steering column and installing the air bag fuse.

16. Connect the negative battery cable. Test the horn, turn signals and headlight operation.

Bowl Type Steering Columns (Without Removable Shrouds)

▶ **See Figures 51 thru 56**

These steering columns have a steel anti-theft plate designed to protect the ignition lock, but it also prevents access to the turn signal switch. It requires a special tool for removal.

One important component just under the steering wheel is the SIR Coil. Since so many wires run to the face of the steering wheel including the all-important air bag connections, a special wiring device called the SIR Coil is used to allow the steering wheel to turn freely yet, still provide reliable wiring connections through a "ribbon cable" arrangement. Care must be used to always center the front wheels and lock the steering column when working on the steering wheel and related components. Failure to do so may cause the SIR coil assembly to become uncentered and may result in otherwise unneeded SIR repairs.

✷✷ CAUTION

All models covered by this manual are equipped with a Supplemental Inflatable Restrain (SIR) System using multiple air bags. Whenever working near any of the SIR components, such as the steering wheel, the air bag module, steering column and instrument panel, disable the SIR system, as described in Section 6.

1. Disconnect the negative battery cable.

2. Center the front wheels and lock the steering column. Remove the key from the ignition.

3. Disable the SIR system using the procedures found in Section 6.

4. Remove the steering wheel using the procedures found in this section.

5. Remove the SIR coil retaining ring and remove the assembly. Let the coil hang freely. There should be a wave washer under the coil on the steering shaft. Remove and retain the wave washer.

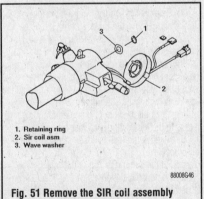

1. Retaining ring
2. Sir coil asm
3. Wave washer

88008G46

Fig. 51 Remove the SIR coil assembly from the steering shaft

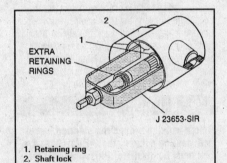

EXTRA RETAINING RINGS

J 23653-SIR

1. **Retaining ring**
2. **Shaft lock**

88008G52

Fig. 52 A special tool is required to depress the lockplate so the retaining ring can be removed

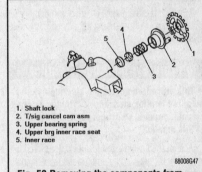

1. **Shaft lock**
2. **T/sig cancel cam asm**
3. **Upper bearing spring**
4. **Upper brg inner race seat**
5. **Inner race**

88008G47

Fig. 53 Removing the components from the upper shaft. Note the steering shaft lock plate (1)

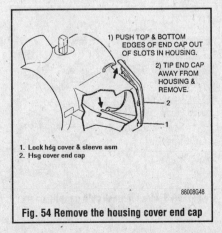

1) PUSH TOP & BOTTOM EDGES OF END CAP OUT OF SLOTS IN HOUSING.

2) TIP END CAP AWAY FROM HOUSING & REMOVE.

1. Lock hsg cover & sleeve asm
2. Hsg cover end cap

88008G48

Fig. 54 Remove the housing cover end cap

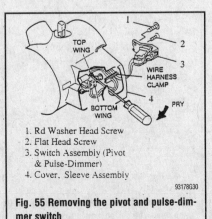

TOP WING

WIRE HARNESS CLAMP

BOTTOM WING

PRY

1. Rd Washer Head Screw
2. Flat Head Screw
3. Switch Assembly (Pivot & Pulse-Dimmer)
4. Cover, Sleeve Assembly

93178G30

Fig. 55 Removing the pivot and pulse-dimmer switch

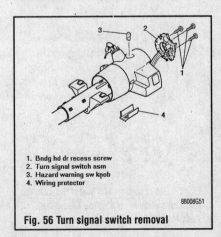

1. **Bndg hd dr recess screw**
2. **Turn signal switch asm**
3. **Hazard warning sw knob**
4. **Wiring protector**

88008G51

Fig. 56 Turn signal switch removal

6. Special tool GM J 23653-SIR or its exact equivalent is required to press down the lockplate against spring pressure so the retaining ring can be removed. Because of the spring pressure against the bottom of the lockplate, this job is difficult without the proper tool. Use care if using any substitute tool since the steering shaft threads and splines can become damaged requiring expensive replacement. Remove the ring, then the lockplate.

7. Remove the upper bearing inner race seat and then remove the inner race.

8. Remove the multi-function lever, as follows:

a. Make sure the lever is in the **OFF** position.

b. Detach the electrical connection behind the lever.

c. Pull the lever straight out.

9. Remove the housing end cap. Using your fingers, pry up and out, tilting the end cap away from the lock housing cover and sleeve assembly, then remove.

10. Unfasten the round washer head screw and the flat head screw.

11. Remove the pivot and pulse dimmer switch assembly. Let the switch hang freely if removal is not needed.

12. Using a suitable prytool, carefully pry off the hazard warning switch knob.

13. Place the turn signal in the right turn position (up). Unfasten the three binding head cross recess screws.

14. Remove the turn signal switch, as follows:

a. Detach the turn signal connector.

b. Remove the wiring protector.

c. Gently pull the wiring harness through the column and remove the switch.

15. Installation is the reverse of the removal procedure.

16. Connect the negative battery cable, then enable the SIR system, using the procedures found in Section 6.

Ignition Switch/Lock Cylinder

➡ **This procedure covers the steering column mounted ignition switch/lock cylinder. For non-column mounted switches, refer to Section 6 of this manual.**

The mechanical key and lock cylinder switch is located in the steering column on the right-hand side, just below the steering wheel.

Two main types of steering columns can be found on the W-Body vehicles covered by this manual. One type uses upper and lower plastic shrouds to cover the upper steering column assembly and its internal components. The other type uses just a bowl-like cover and sleeve assembly under the steering wheel to house the turn signal switch and ignition key lock cylinder. There are also some differences between columns used in floor-shift vehicles and those found in column-shift vehicles, although the differences are mostly in the shift interlock system.

REMOVAL & INSTALLATION

Shroud-Type Steering Column

▶ **See Figures 57, 58 and 59**

While is may be possible to service the ignition switch and lock cylinder with the steering column in the vehicle, on some vehicles, the column may have to be removed so the plastic column shrouds can be disassembled to expose the upper steering column. Look the job over carefully to determine if the ignition lock cylinder can be serviced on your vehicle with the column in place.

If the steering column must be removed, use great care handling the column since the column is extremely susceptible to damage. Remember that the steering column is designed to collapse in a collision. Dropping the steering column assembly on its end could collapse the steering shaft or loosen the plastic injections which maintain column rigidity. Leaning on the column could cause the jacket to bend or deform. Never place the column directly in a vise. GM recommends their holding fixture which is basically just a piece of steel angle. One end of the angle is clamped in the vise. The column then bolts to the other angle, using the column's original mounting bracket. A similar holding tool could be shop-made. Under no conditions should the end of the shaft be hammered on as hammering could loosen the plastic injections which maintain steering column rigidity.

✳✳ CAUTION

Before working around the steering wheel and steering column, the SIR (air bag) system must be disabled. Please refer to the procedure in Section 6.

1. Disconnect the negative battery cable.
2. Disable the SIR (air bag) system using the procedures found in Section 6.

3. Locate the bolts that secure the steering column jacket assembly to the instrument panel sub-frame. The column will tend to drop towards the seat as the bolts are loosened. Use care handling the column. In many cases, simply lowering the column allows enough room for service work.

4. If it is necessary to remove the column from the vehicle, at the bottom of the column, remove the pinch bolt from the intermediate steering shaft assembly universal joint. The intermediate steering shaft is the shaft that goes through the floor/cowl, connecting the steering column to the rack and pinion steering gear assembly. Carefully work the column free of the intermediate steering shaft joint and remove the column from the vehicle.

✳✳ WARNING

Once the steering column is removed from the vehicle, the column is extremely susceptible to damage. Handle the column carefully.

5. If it was necessary to remove the column from the vehicle, secure the steering column so it won't be damaged. Never place the column directly in a vise. GM recommends their holding fixture which is basically just a piece of steel angle. One end of the angle is clamped in the vise. The column then bolts to the other angle, using the column's original mounting bracket. A similar holding tool could be shop-made.

6. If the column is still in the vehicle, and if necessary, the tilt lever can be removed. The tilt lever simply snaps in place. Carefully rock the lever back and forth while pulling it from the steering column

7. Remove the two screws from the lower shroud and remove the lower shroud. It may be helpful to tilt the shroud down and slide it back to disengage the locking tabs.

8. Locate and remove the two screws retaining the upper shroud. If the column is still in the vehicle, the upper shroud likely won't remove all the way since the plastic shroud surrounds the lock cylinder. Just lift the upper shroud enough to gain access to the lock cylinder release hole.

9. Remove the lock cylinder using the following procedure:

a. If the column is still in the vehicle, verify that the negative battery cable has been disconnected.

b. Hold the key in the **START** position.

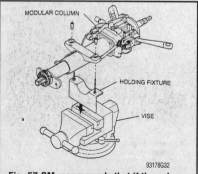

Fig. 57 GM recommends that if the column must be removed, a holding fixture be used to help avoid damage to the column

93178G32

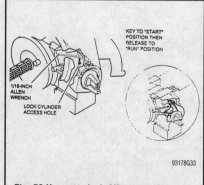

Fig. 58 Use a ¹⁄₁₆ inch Allen wrench to push down the cylinder retaining pin

93178G33

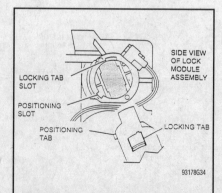

Fig. 59 Sector and lock cylinder alignment position

93178G34

c. Using a 1/16 inch Allen wrench push down on the lock cylinder retaining pin.

d. Release the key to the **RUN** position and pull the steering column lock cylinder set from the lock module assembly.

To install:

10. Position the upper shroud and steering column lock cylinder set observing the following:

a. Place the key in the lock cylinder and in the **RUN** position.

b. Make sure the sector gear in the lock module assembly is in the **RUN** position.

c. Position the lock cylinder to the upper steering column shroud.

d. Line up the locking tabs and positioning tab with the slots in the lock module assembly and push the cylinder into position.

11. Position the upper shroud and install the two retaining screws.

12. Install the lower shroud taking care to align the slots on the lower shroud with the tabs on the upper shroud. Tilt the lower shroud up and snap the two shrouds together. Secure with the retaining screws.

13. Position the shift lever seal and multifunction lever seal into position.

14. Install the tilt lever to the steering column by snapping into place.

15. Install the steering column (or raise back into place, if there was enough room to perform this procedure by simply lowering the column). Install the retaining bolts. Carefully torque to 35 ft. lbs. (47 Nm).

16. If all other service procedures have been performed, enable the SIR system using the procedures found in Section 6.

Bowl-Type Steering Column

▶ See Figures 60, 61, 62, 63 and 64

The electrical switching portion of the assembly is separate from the key and lock cylinder and

1. Lock Nut (M14 x 1.5)
2. Retaining Ring
3. SIR Coil Assem.
4. Wave Washer
5. Connector Cover
6. Lockplate Retaining Ring
7. Lockplate
8. Turn Signal Cancel Cam
9. Upper Bearing Spring
10. Bearing Race Seat
11. Bearing Inner Race
12. Washer Head Screw
13. Flat Head Screw
14. Pulse-Dimmer Pivot Switch
15. Recess Screws
16. Turn Signal Switch
17. Six-Lobe Screws
18. Buzzer Switch Assem.
19. Lock Retaining Screw
20. Hazard Switch Knob
21. Lock Cylinder Set
22. Cover and Sleeve (Bowl)
23. Housing Cover Cap
24. Wiring Protector
30. Steering Column Housing Assem.
31. Bearing Assem.
32. Shaft Lock Bolt
33. Lock Bolt Spring
34. Steering Lock Shoe
35. Steering Lock Shoe
36. Wire Shield
37. Drive Shaft
38. Dowel Pin
39. Pivot Pin
40. Shoe Spring
41. Release Lever Spring
42. Release Lever Pin
43. Shoe Release Lever
44. Switch Actuator Rack
45. Rack Preload Spring
46. Steering Column Housing
47. Switch Actuator Sector
48. Washer Head Screw
50. Guide Spring
51. Wheel Tilt Spring
52. Spring Retainer
55. Steering Shaft Assem.
56. Upper Steering Shaft
57. Centering Sphere
58. Joint Preload Spring
59. Lower Steering Shaft
61. Support Screw
62. Column Housing Support Assem.
63. Column Housing Support
64. Oval Head Screw
65. Shift Lever Gate

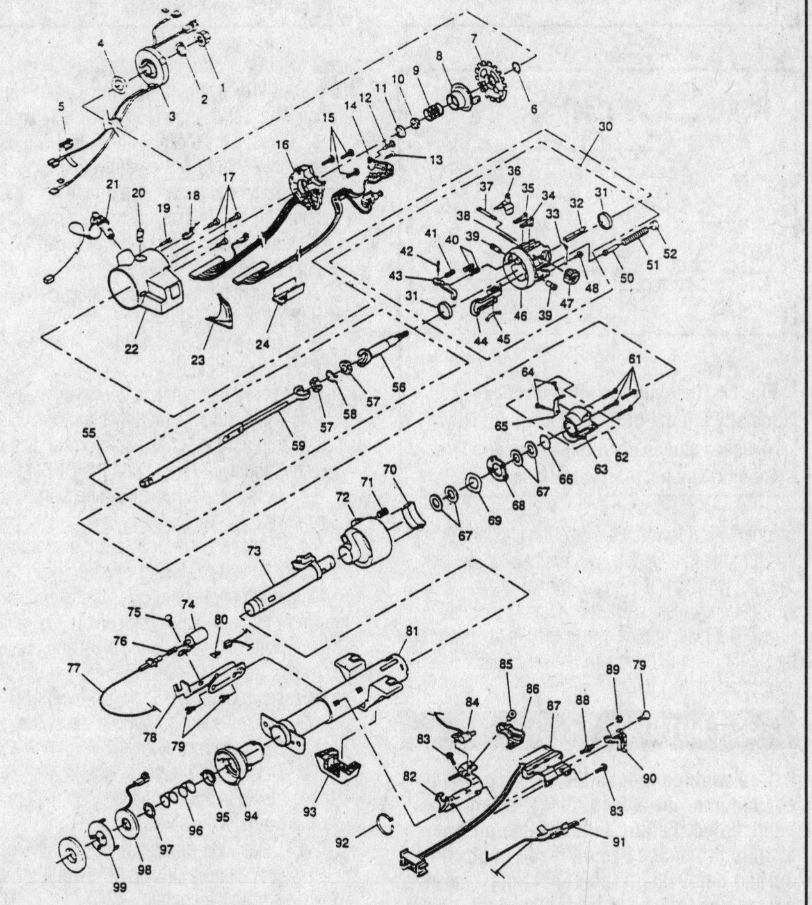

66. Shift Tube Retaining Ring
67. Thrust Washer
68. Lock Plate
69. Wave Washer
70. Shift Bowl Protector
71. Shift Lever Spring
72. Gearshift Lever Bowl Assem.
73. Shift Lever Tube Assem.
74. Interlock Solenoid Assem.
75. Washer Head Screw
76. Ball Joint Spring
77. BTSI Cable Assem.
78. Solenoid Bracket
79. Washer Head Screw
80. CPA Wedge
81. Column Jacket Assem.
82. Stud & Bracket Assem.

83. TORX Washer Head Screw
84. Park Position Switch Assem.
85. Cam Retainer
86. Cable Shift Cam Assem.
87. Ignition Switch Assembly
88. Dimmer Switch Mntg. Stud
89. #10-24 Hex Nut
90. PRNDL Adjuster Assem.
91. Ignition Switch Actuator Assem.
92. Wire Harness Strap
93. Column Support
94. Adapter & Bearing Assem.
95. Lower Bearing Seat
96. Lower Bearing Spring
97. Lower Spring Retainer
98. Strg. Whl. Speed Sensor
99. Sensor Retainer

93178G35

Fig. 60 Typical "bowl-type" GM tilt steering column. GM calls the bowl-like piece housing the ignition switch lock and turn signal switch a cover and sleeve assembly

Fig. 61 Lock housing cover screw positions

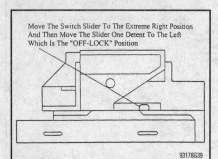

Fig. 64 The ignition switch must be installed in the OFF-LOCK position. New switches should come pinned in position. Remove the pin after installation

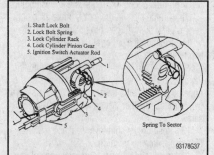

Fig. 62 Turning the key turns the lock cylinder sector, or pinion gear, moving the rack which connects to the ignition switch by a short metal actuator rod

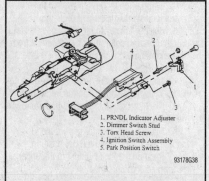

1. PRNDL Indicator Adjuster
2. Dimmer Switch Stud
3. Torx Head Screw
4. Ignition Switch Assembly
5. Park Position Switch

Fig. 63 Location of the ignition and dimmer switches

mounts lower down on the steering column. When you turn the ignition key, you are turning the lock cylinder which turns a small `pinion' gear. The pinion gear engages a small flat toothed piece called a `rack.' The rack, in turn, works the ignition switch by pushing or pulling a short metal actuator rod connected to the ignition switch

✳✳ CAUTION

Before working around the steering wheel and column, the SIR (air bag) system must be disabled. Failure to follow the air bag disable procedures could result in possible air bag deployment, personal injury, or otherwise unneeded SIR system repairs. Please refer to the procedure in Section 6.

➡ **The ignition lock cylinder is protected by a metal lockplate that must be removed to access upper steering column components (turn signal switch, ignition lock cylinder, etc.). This requires a special tool to push the lockplate downwards against spring pressure, so the retaining ring can be removed.**

1. Position the steering wheel so the front tires are pointed straight ahead. This is to protect the SIR coil inside the steering column.
2. Disconnect the negative battery cable.
3. Disable the SIR (air bag) system using the procedures in Section 6.
4. Remove the steering wheel using the procedures in this section.
5. Remove the SIR coil retaining ring from the

upper steering shaft. Lift out the SIR coil and let it hang freely. There should be a wave washer under the coil which should be removed and retained.
6. Remove the lockplate retaining ring using special tool J 23653-SIR or equivalent lockplate compressor tool to push down on the lock plate. The retaining ring is likely just a wire retaining ring which should be replaced with a new part at assembly. Lift out the lockplate.
7. Remove the turn signal cancel cam and the upper bearing under it.
8. Remove the upper bearing inner race seat and inner bearing race.
9. Remove the multifunction lever, as follows:
   a. Make sure the multifunction (turn signal, headlamp dimmer, cruise control, windshield washer and wiper) lever is in the **OFF** position.
   b. Detach the electrical connection behind the lever.
   c. Remove the lever by pulling straight out.
10. Remove the housing cover end cap by using your fingers to pry up and out. Tilt the end cap away from the lock housing (bowl) and remove.
11. Locate and remove the pivot and pulse-dimmer switch assembly retainer screw. Lift out the switch assembly and let the switch hang freely if removal is not needed. To remove the switch:
   a. Remove the wiring.
   b. Detach the dimmer switch from the bowl.
   c. Using a long prytool, pry on the upper and lower wings of the switch body.
   d. Detach the wiring harness clamp from the tab inside the housing and gently pull the wire harness from the column.
12. Remove the hazard warning switch knob by prying with a small blade prytool.
13. Move the turn signal to the RIGHT TURN (up) position. Remove the three turn signal switch retaining screws and lift the switch from the bowl. Let the switch hang freely, if removal is not needed. If the turn signal switch needs to be replaced:
   a. Detach the turn signal switch electrical connector.
   b. Remove the wiring protector.
   c. Gently pull the wire harness through the column.
14. Remove the key from the lock cylinder.
15. Remove the buzzer switch assembly.
16. Reinsert the key in the lock cylinder and place the key in the **LOCK** position.
17. Remove the lock cylinder retaining screw.
18. Remove the lock cylinder and Pass Key harness, as follows:

   a. Note the positioning and routing of the Pass Key wire harness. At installation, it must be installed in the same manner. Failure to route and secure the wire as originally installed may result in component damage and malfunction of the ignition lock set.
   b. Disconnect the terminal of the Pass Key wire harness from the vehicle wire harness.
   c. If not already removed, remove the U-shaped wiring protector.
   d. Attach a length of thin, flexible wire to the Pass Key wire terminal to act as a pull wire to aid in reassembly.
   e. Remove the lock cylinder and retaining clip from the lock housing bowl and gently pull the wire harness through the column.
To install:
19. Route the wire from the Pass Key lock cylinder (ignition lock), routing it in the same position as originally installed. Snap the retaining clip back into the opening in the bowl. Failure to route and secure the wire as originally installed may result in component damage and malfunction of the ignition lock set.
20. Install the ignition lock set cylinder into the steering column bowl and snap the retaining clip into the opening in the bowl. Install the lock cylinder retaining screw and snug up to 22 inch lbs. (2.5 Nm). Do not overtighten.
21. Install the buzzer switch assembly.
22. Reinstall the key in the lock cylinder set. Turn the key to the **OFF-LOCK** position.
23. Install the turn signal switch into the bowl, using care to route the wiring as originally installed. Attach the switch connector and verify a good connection.
24. Install the SIR coil assembly.
25. Install the pivot pulse-dimmer switch assembly, using care to route the wiring as originally installed. Verify the electrical connection is secure and that the dimmer switch is properly installed in the bowl.
26. Install the plastic housing cover end cap.
27. Install the multifunction lever by installing the lever in the OFF position and lining up the aligning tab. Push straight in. If the tilt lever was removed, (it just unsnaps) install by snapping the lever back into the column.
28. Install the hazard warning switch knob by positioning it through the opening in the bowl and snapping into place.
29. Install the upper column bearing inner race and the spring.

30. Install the turn signal canceling cam.

31. Install the lockplate and compress using tool J 23653-SIR, or equivalent lockplate compressor. Note that the inner block tooth of the lockplate must be aligned with the block tooth of the race and upper shaft assembly. When the lockplate has been compressed properly, install a new retaining ring. Verify that the ring is properly and firmly seated in the groove in the upper steering shaft before releasing pressure on the lockplate.

➡Set the upper steering shaft so that the block tooth (largest tooth) on the race and upper steering shaft is at the 12 o'clock position. The front wheels on the vehicle should be straight ahead. Then set the lock cylinder set to the LOCKposition, to ensure no damage will occur to the SIR (air bag) coil assembly. The SIR coil will become uncentered if the steering column is separated from the steering gear and is allowed to rotate, or if the centering spring is pushed down, letting the hub rotate while the coil is removed from the column.

32. Install the wave washer and set the SIR coil into place. Align the opening in the coil with the horn tower and "locating bump" between the two tabs on the bowl. Install the retaining ring, making sure it is properly and firmly seated in the groove in the upper steering shaft. New service replacement SIR coils come pre-centered with a disposable tab to hold it in place until after installation. Use care when routing the SIR coil wires. They should be kept tight with no slack or the wires could become kinked and cut when the steering wheel is turned.

33. Install the wiring protector and any wire ties that need to be installed. Make sure the wiring has no kinks.

34. Install the steering wheel using the procedures found in this section.

35. Enable the air bag system, as outlined in Section 6.

Steering Linkage

The rack piston converts hydraulic pressure to a linear force which moves the rack left or right. The force is then transmitted through the inner and outer tie rods (also called tie rod ends) to the steering knuckles, which turn the front wheels. The tie rod ends determine the front wheel alignment toe-angle, and they are adjustable.

REMOVAL & INSTALLATION

Tie Rod Ends

▸ **See Figures 65 thru 71**

Normally, the only steering linkage components that may require service are the tie rod ends which connect the rack and pinion steering gear to the wheel knuckles.

1. Raise and safely support the vehicle.

2. The outer tie rod ends may be retained to the steering knuckle by either a slotted nut and cotter pin or a torque-prevailing nut. If a slotted nut and cotter pin is used, remove and discard the cotter pin and remove the slotted nut.

3. If a torque prevailing nut is used, remove the nut from the tie rod end's ball stud at the wheel knuckle. GM specifies that this torque prevailing nut be discarded and a new torque prevailing nut be used at assembly. Most service replacement tie rod ends come with new hardware.

4. The position of the tie rod ends determines the toe angle of the steering alignment. To get the replacement tie rod end positioned as closely as possible to the original tie rod end's position, the jam nut's position should be marked. Some technicians, after thoroughly wire-brushing the jam nut and the inner tie rod shaft threads, will mark one flat of the jam nut with paint. Then, the jam nut is loosened exactly one turn.

5. Remove the tie rod end from the wheel knuckle. GM says that the tapered joint of the ball stud has been designed to separate easily, unlike previous joints of this type. If required, use a tie rod puller to separate the tie rod end from the wheel knuckle.

6. Unscrew the tie rod end from the inner tie rod shaft. Do not disturb the jam nut. It should have been loosened one turn only from its original position.

To install:

7. Clean all parts well. Make sure mating surfaces of the stud and knuckle are clean.

8. Thread the replacement tie rod end onto the inner tie rod shaft until it just touches the jam nut. Loosen the tie rod end exactly one turn.

9. Install the tie rod end ball stud to the wheel knuckle. If equipped with a torque prevailing nut, tighten to 18 ft. lbs. (25 Nm). Tighten the nut an additional 180 degrees (one-half turn). If equipped

Fig. 65 Although the outer tie rod ends are supposed to be easy to remove, a puller may be required to separate the joint end from the wheel knuckle

Fig. 66 Separate the tie rod end from the knuckle and inspect for damage

Fig. 67 Unscrew the tie rod end from the tie rod, counting the number of turns for later reference at installation

Fig. 68 Some tie rod ends may have plugs which can be removed so grease fittings can be installed

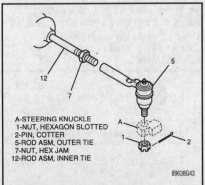

A-STEERING KNUCKLE
1-NUT, HEXAGON SLOTTED
2-PIN, COTTER
5-ROD ASM, OUTER TIE
7-NUT, HEX JAM
12-ROD ASM, INNER TIE

Fig. 69 Exploded view of the outer tie rod end assembly

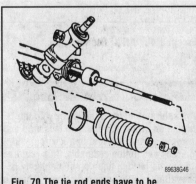

Fig. 70 The tie rod ends have to be removed to renew the rack and pinion steering gear dust boots

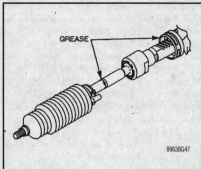

Fig. 71 Apply grease to the areas shown when installing a new rack and pinion dust boot

with a slotted nut for a cotter pin, tighten the retaining nut to 45 ft. lbs. (60 Nm) maximum to align the cotter pin slot. DO NOT back off (loosen) the nut to align the slots in the nut with the cotter pin hole in the ball stud. Install a new cotter pin.

10. Turn the jam nut one turn. This should tighten the jam nut against the end of the tie rod threaded portion. Tighten the jam nut to 50 ft. lbs. (68 Nm).

11. Check that the rubber rack and pinion dust boot is not twisted or puckered.

12. Have a front end alignment performed at a qualified shop.

Power Steering Gear

GM W-Body vehicles all use a Power Rack and Pinion Steering Gear. The movement of the steering wheel is transferred to a small gear called a pinion. The movement of the pinion is then transferred to mesh with the teeth on the rack, causing the rack to move back and forth. The power steering gear system has a rotary control valve which directs hydraulic fluid coming from the power steering pump to one side or the other side of the rack piston. The rack piston converts hydraulic pressure to a linear force which moves the rack left or right. The force is then transmitted through the inner and outer tie rods to the steering knuckles, which turn the front wheels. If hydraulic assist is not available (engine stalls or the pump drive belt breaks), manual control is maintained; however, under these conditions, more steering effort is required. A vane-type pump provides hydraulic pressure for the system.

REMOVAL & INSTALLATION

Except 3.4L (VIN X) Engine

▶ See Figure 72

❊❊ WARNING

The subframe of the vehicle carrying the engine and transaxle must be loosened and lowered a small amount to allow removal the rack and pinion assembly. This requires lifting and jacking equipment that likely is unavailable to the nonprofessional. There is a potential for vehicle damage. This is not a job for the inexperienced or ill-equipped.

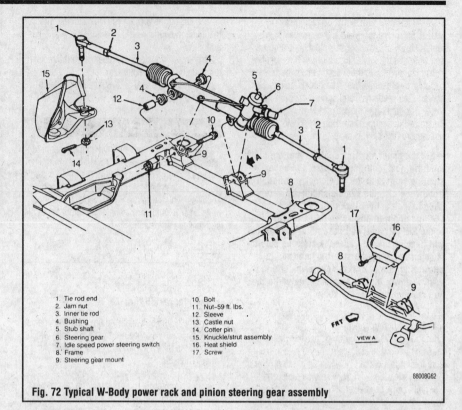

1. Tie rod end
2. Jam nut
3. Inner tie rod
4. Bushing
5. Stub shaft
6. Steering gear
7. Idle speed power steering switch
8. Frame
9. Steering gear mount
10. Bolt
11. Nut–59 ft. lbs.
12. Sleeve
13. Castle nut
14. Cotter pin
15. Knuckle/strut assembly
16. Heat shield
17. Screw

Fig. 72 Typical W-Body power rack and pinion steering gear assembly

1. Disconnect the negative battery cable.
2. Center the front wheels, then remove the key to lock the steering column. This is important to protect the SIR (air bag) coil inside the steering column. This procedure requires the steering intermediate shaft to be disconnected from the rack and pinion stub shaft. If the steering column is allowed to turn, the SIR coil will become uncentered, requiring a rewind procedure or unnecessary SIR coil replacement.
3. Raise and safely support the vehicle with safety stands.

❊❊ CAUTION

Failure to disconnect the intermediate shaft from the rack and pinion stub shaft may result in damage to the steering gear. This damage may cause a loss of steering control and may cause personal injury.

❊❊ WARNING

Verify that the front wheels are straight ahead and that the ignition switch is in the LOCK position. Failure to follow these procedures could result in damage to the SIR coil assembly.

4. Remove the front wheel and tire assemblies.
5. Remove the intermediate shaft lower pinch bolt at the steering gear (end of the steering column shaft).
6. Remove the intermediate shaft from the stub shaft.
7. Remove both tie rod ends from the knuckle using the procedure found in this section.
8. Support the vehicle body with safety stands so that the subframe assembly can be lowered.

❊❊ WARNING

Do NOT lower the frame too far; engine components near the firewall may be damaged.

9. Remove the rear frame bolts and lower the rear of the frame no more than 5 inches (12.7 cm).
10. Remove the heat shield, pipe retaining clip and the fluid pipes from the rack assembly. Use flare nut wrenches to remove the fluid pipes.
11. Remove the rack mounting bolts, nuts and rack assembly. Remove the rack assembly out through the left wheel opening.

To install:

12. Install the rack assembly through the left wheel opening.
13. Install the mounting bolts and nuts. Tighten the bolts to 59 ft. lbs. (80 Nm).
14. Install the fluid pipes with new O-rings using flare nut wrenches. Tighten the fittings to 20 ft. lbs. (27 Nm).
15. Install the pipe retaining clips and heat shield. Tighten the heat shield screws to 54 inch lbs. (6 Nm).
16. Raise the frame and install the rear bolts. Tighten the rear bolts to 103 ft. lbs. (140 Nm).
17. Install the tie rod ends and retaining nut. Tighten the nuts to 40 ft. lbs. (54 Nm). Install a new cotter pin, if your vehicle uses slotted nuts or a new torque-prevailing nut, as applicable.

❊❊ WARNING

When installing the steering column to the intermediate shaft, make sure that the shaft is seated before pinch bolt installation. If the bolt is inserted into the coupling before shaft installation, the two mating shafts

may disengage The vehicle's front wheels should still be straight ahead and the column should still be locked to prevent damage to the SIR coil assembly.

18. Install the intermediate shaft-to-stub shaft. Tighten the lower pinch bolt to 40 ft. lbs. (54 Nm).
19. Install the front wheel and tire assemblies, then carefully lower the vehicle.
20. Fill the power steering pump with the specified GM steering fluid or its equivalent.
21. Bleed the power steering system as outlined later in this section.
22. Connect the negative battery cable.
23. Inspect the system for leaks.
24. Have a qualified alignment technician adjust the front toe angle.

3.4L (VIN X) Engine

> ❈❈ WARNING

The subframe of the vehicle carrying the engine and transaxle must be loosened and lowered a small amount to allow removal the rack and pinion assembly. This requires lifting and jacking equipment that likely is unavailable to the nonprofessional. There is a potential for vehicle damage. This is not a job for the inexperienced or ill-equipped.

1. Remove the air cleaner and duct assembly.
2. Disconnect the negative battery cable.
3. Center the front wheels, then remove the key to lock the steering column. This is important to protect the SIR (air bag) coil inside the steering column. This procedure requires the steering intermediate shaft to be disconnected from the rack and pinion stub shaft. If the steering column is allowed to turn, the SIR coil will become uncentered, requiring a rewind procedure or unnecessary SIR coil replacement.
4. An engine support fixture is required to hold the weight of the powertrain. Install tools J 28467-A, J 28467-90 and J 36462, or equivalent engine support fixtures.
5. Raise and safely support the vehicle.

> ❈❈ WARNING

Verify that the front wheels are straight ahead and that the ignition switch is in the LOCK position. Failure to follow these procedures could result in damage to the SIR coil assembly.

6. Remove the left wheel and tire assembly.
7. Loosen the right side engine splash shield.
8. Remove both tie rod ends from the knuckle using the procedures found in this section.

> ❈❈ CAUTION

Failure to disconnect the intermediate shaft from the rack and pinion stub shaft may result in damage to the steering gear. This damage may cause a loss of steering control and may cause personal injury.

9. Remove the intermediate shaft lower pinch bolt at the steering gear (end of the steering column shaft).
10. Remove the intermediate shaft from the stub shaft.
11. Detach the electrical connection from the steering gear pressure switch.
12. Remove the exhaust pipe and catalytic converter assembly.
13. Using safety stands, securely support the vehicle. A hydraulic jack may be useful to support the subframe and then to lower it after the retaining bolts are loosened. Unfasten the frame retaining bolts, then carefully lower the frame about 3 inches (7.6 cm).
14. Unfasten the steering gear heat shield screws, then remove the heat shield.
15. Remove the power steering line clamp from the steering gear.
16. Unfasten the steering gear bolts.
17. Disconnect and plug the pressure and return lines from the steering gear.
18. Remove the steering gear through the left wheel opening.
19. Replace the stud shaft shields.

To install:
20. Install the rack assembly through the left wheel opening.
21. Unplug and connect the pressure and return lines to the steering gear.
22. Install the steering gear bolts and tighten to 59 ft. lbs. (80 Nm).
23. Fasten the power steering line clamp at the steering gear.
24. Install the steering gear heat shield and secure with the retaining screws. Tighten the screws to 54 inch lbs. (6 Nm).
25. Raise the frame assembly and align the steering gear stub shaft to the intermediate steering shaft.
26. Install the frame retaining bolts and tighten to 125 ft. lbs. (170 Nm). Remove the safety stands supporting the subframe.
27. Install the exhaust pipe and catalytic converter assembly.
28. Attach the electrical connection to the steering gear pressure switch.

> ❈❈ WARNING

When installing the steering column to the intermediate shaft, make sure that the shaft is seated before pinch bolt installation. If the bolt is inserted into the coupling before shaft installation, the two mating shafts may disengage. The front wheels on the vehicle should still be straight ahead and set the column should still be locked. Failure to follow these procedures could result in damage to the SIR (air bag) coil assembly.

29. Install the intermediate steering shaft pinch bolt at the steering gear. Tighten the bolt to 35 ft. lbs. (47 Nm).
30. Install the both tie rod ends, as outlined earlier in this section.
31. Tighten the right side engine splash shield.
32. Install the left tire and wheel assembly.

33. Carefully lower the vehicle.
34. Remove the engine support fixtures. Connect the negative battery cable, then install the air cleaner and duct assembly.
35. Bleed the power steering system, as outlined later in this section.

Power Steering Pump

When servicing the power steering pump, inspect the power steering fluid. Look for foaming, milky power steering fluid, low fluid level and leaks in the hoses and lines.

If the fluid has a foamy or milky appearance, it could be caused by air in the fluid and loss of fluid due to internal pump leakage causing overflow. Extremely low temperatures will cause air bubbles in the system if the fluid level is low. If the fluid level is correct and the pump still foams, look for air entry (cracked housing, etc.).

Your W-Body vehicle may be equipped with the MAGNASTEER® system, a speed-dependent power steering system. The system provides power assist at varying levels depending on need. A bi-directional magnetic rotary actuator in the steering gear adjusts the amount of torque (driver effort) necessary to turn the steering wheel. The MAGNASTEER® system is controlled through software in the Antilock Brake System (ABS) electronic control module or the Electronic Brake Traction Control Module (EBTCM) and varies the amount of torque by adjusting the current flow through the actuator. The amount of adjustment will be directly related to vehicle speed. The controller receives speed-related input signals from the vehicle speed sensor in the transaxle.

GM recommends their Power Steering Fluid 1052884 (pint) or 1050017 (quart) or equivalent. A special cold weather fluid is available under part number 1234586 (pint) and 12345867 (quart). Please note that GM specifies that the system should be flushed and bled prior to switching fluid types.

Power steering fluid level is indicated by marks on the fluid level indicator on the fluid reservoir cap. If the fluid is warmed up (about 150°, hot to the touch), the fluid level should be between the HOT and COLD marks. If the fluid is cool (about 70°), the fluid level should be between the ADD and COLD marks.

REMOVAL & INSTALLATION

3.1L and 3.4L (VIN E) Engines

▶ See Figure 73

1. Disconnect the negative battery cable.
2. Remove the coolant recovery reservoir and position it aside.
3. Remove the serpentine drive belt from the power steering pump assembly.
4. Detach the ignition control wiring harness near the pump assembly.
5. Disconnect the inlet and outlet hoses from the pump assembly.
6. Unfasten the pump retaining bolts/screws.
7. Remove the pump assembly from the vehicle.

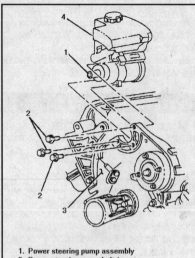

1. Power steering pump assembly
2. Power steering pump bolt /screw
   34 Nm (25 lb. ft.)
3. Engine assembly
4. Power steering fluid reservoir assembly

88008G71

**Fig. 73 Power steering pump mounting—
3.1L and 3.4L (VIN E) engines**

8. Remove the power steering pump pulley from the pump assembly.

9. Remove the reservoir assembly from the pump.

To install:

10. Attach the reservoir to the pump assembly.

11. Install the pulley to the pump.

12. Position the pump to the engine and secure with the retaining bolts/screws. Tighten the bolts/screws to 25 ft. lbs. (34 Nm).

13. Connect the inlet and outlet hoses to the power steering pump.

14. Attach the ignition control wiring harness at the pump assembly.

15. Install the serpentine drive belt over the power steering pump pulley.

16. Install the coolant recovery reservoir.

17. Connect the negative battery cable.

18. Fill and bleed the power steering system.

3.4L (VIN X) Engine

▶ See Figure 74

1. Remove the air cleaner and duct assembly.
2. Disconnect the negative battery cable.
3. Remove the coolant recovery tank.
4. Remove the serpentine drive belt.

➡**Siphon the power steering fluid from the reservoir before disconnecting the lines to avoid spilling fluid on the secondary timing belt cover. Use shop rags when disconnecting the lines to ensure any remaining fluid does NOT contact the secondary timing belt cover. Power steering fluid can damage the timing belt.**

5. Siphon as much fluid as possible from the reservoir.

6. Remove the power steering pump from the bracket.

7. Disconnect the power steering lines. Plug the lines or drain the fluid into a container if changing fluid at this time.

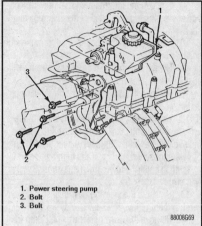

1. Power steering pump
2. Bolt
3. Bolt

88008G69

**Fig. 74 Power steering pump mounting—
3.4L (VIN X) engine**

8. If installing a new pump, transfer the pulley from the old pump to the new one.

To install:

9. Connect the power steering fluid lines.

10. Position the power steering pump in the bracket and secure with the retaining bolts. Tighten the bolts to 25 ft. lbs. (34 Nm).

11. Install the serpentine belt.

12. Install the coolant recovery tank.

13. Connect the negative battery cable.

14. Install the air cleaner and duct assembly.

15. Fill and bleed the power steering system.

16. Check the system for leaks, road test and recheck the fluid level.

3.5L (VIN H) Engine

▶ See Figure 75

Please note that the power steering pump pulley must be removed to access the pump retaining bolts. Special tools are required to draw the pulley off the pump shaft and to later press the pulley onto the pump shaft. A shop press cannot be used to install the pulley or the pump will be damaged.

1. Place a drain pan under the vehicle.

2. Remove the coolant surge tank (coolant reservoir).

3. Remove the cosmetic/acoustic engine cover.

4. Remove the accessory drive belt. Please see Section 1.

5. Remove the accessory wiring junction block and set aside.

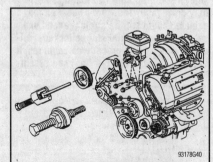

93178G40

**Fig. 75 Power steering pump mounting
and the pulley removal and installation
tool—3.5L (VIN H) engine**

6. Remove the power steering pump pulley from the pump noting the following:

   a. Use a power steering pump pulley remover. These pullers typically have a ridge that surrounds the collar on the pulley center.

   b. Turn the puller screw making sure the center screw is centered in the end of the pump shaft.

   c. Draw the pulley from the pump shaft.

7. Disconnect the pressure line and return hose from the power steering pump.

8. Unfasten the pump retaining bolts and remove the pump from the engine.

To install:

9. Install the pump to the engine. Install the bolts and tighten to 25 ft. lbs. (34 Nm).

10. Connect the power steering return line.

11. Connect the power steering pressure line. Using a "crows foot" adapter and a torque wrench, torque the pressure line fitting to 20 ft. lbs. (27 Nm).

12. Install the power steering pump pulley noting the following:

   a. Use a power steering pump pulley installer such as J 36015, or equivalent. This type of installer threads into the end of the pump shaft. A nut is then turned to press the pulley onto the pump shaft.

   b. The face of the pulley hub must be flush with the end of the pump shaft.

✳✳ WARNING

Do not attempt to use a shop press to install a pump pulley.

13. Install the accessory wiring junction block.

14. Install the accessory drive belt, making sure it is properly routed and seated in all pulley grooves.

15. Install the coolant surge tank.

16. Install the engine cover.

17. Fill the power steering system and bleed the system. Check for leaks.

3.8L Engines

▶ See Figure 76

1. Disconnect the negative battery cable.

2. Remove the coolant recovery reservoir and bracket.

3. Unfasten the ECM retaining nuts, then remove the cover.

4. Remove the serpentine belt from the pulleys by loosening the automatic belt tensioner as outlined in Section 1 of this manual.

5. Disconnect the inlet and outlet hoses from the pump.

6. Unfasten the pump mounting bolts, then remove the pump and reservoir.

7. Using a suitable prybar, remove the retaining clips from the reservoir, then separate the reservoir from the pump.

8. Remove the pump pulley using a power steering pump pulley removing tool J-25034-B or equivalent pulley pullers.

To install:

9. Install the reservoir to the pump with a new O-ring seal and install the retaining clip. Make sure the tabs are fully engaged on the pump.

10. Install the pulley to the power steering pump.

11. Install the pump and retaining bolts. Tighten the retaining bolts to 25 ft. lbs. (34 Nm).

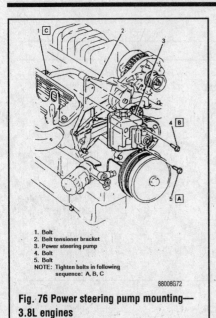

1. Bolt
2. Belt tensioner bracket
3. Power steering pump
4. Bolt
5. Bolt
NOTE: Tighten bolts in following
sequence: A, B, C

88008G72

Fig. 76 Power steering pump mounting—3.8L engines

12. Connect the inlet and outlet hoses to the pump.

13. Install the serpentine drive belt.

14. Install the ECM cover and secure with the retaining nuts.

15. Connect the negative battery cable.

16. Fill and bleed the power steering system as outlined later in this section.

17. Allow the engine to warm up, road test the vehicle and recheck the fluid level.

18. Check the system for leaks, road test and recheck the fluid level.

BLEEDING

♦ See Figure 77

The power steering fluid replacement procedure is a two-stage process: first, flushing the old fluid from the system with new fluid and second, bleeding the system to remove any trapped air. The following sequences outline these procedures.

1. Raise and safely support the front end of the vehicle off the ground until the front wheels are free to turn.

2. Remove the fluid return line at the pump reservoir inlet connector.

3. Plug the inlet connector port on the pump reservoir.

4. Position the fluid return line toward a container (several quart capacity) to catch the draining fluid.

5. When an assistant fills the reservoir with either the standard power steering fluid or optional cold weather power steering fluid, start and run the engine at idle.

6. Turn the steering wheel from stop-to-stop.

❊❊ WARNING

Do not hold the steering wheel against the stops while flushing the system. Holding the steering wheel against the stops will cause high system pressure, overheating and damage to the pump and/or the steering gear assembly.

7. Continue draining until all of the old fluid is cleared from the power steering system. The addition of another quart of fresh fluid will be required to flush the system.

8. Turn the engine **OFF**. Unplug the pump reservoir inlet and reconnect the return line.

9. Fill the reservoir to the FULL COLD mark. After replacing the fluid or servicing the power steering hydraulic system, you must bleed air from the system. Air in the system prevents an accurate fluid level reading, causes pump cavitation noise and over time could damage the pump. To bleed the power steering system, proceed as follows.

10. Begin with the engine **OFF**, front wheels off the ground and the wheels turned all the way to the left.

11. Add either standard power steering fluid or optional cold climate fluid to the FULL COLD mark on the fluid level indicator.

12. With the engine still **OFF**, bleed the system by turning the wheels from stop-to-stop, but without hitting the stops.

➡This may require turning the wheels from side to side up to 40 times. Keep the fluid level at the FULL COLD mark. Fluid with air in it may have a light tan appearance. This air must be eliminated from the fluid before normal steering action can be obtained.

13. Start the engine. With the engine idling, recheck the fluid level. If necessary, add fluid to bring the level to the FULL COLD mark.

14. Return the front wheels to the center position. Verify that the transaxle is in PARK and that the parking brake had been firmly set. Lower the front wheels to the ground. Continue running the engine for two or three minutes.

15. Test drive the vehicle to be sure the power steering functions normally and is free from noise.

➡Inspect for fluid leakage at the connection points along the power steering system.

16. Recheck the fluid level. The fluid level should now be up to the FULL HOT mark after the system has stabilized at operating temperature.

Bleeding Air from Power Steering Systems

Before bleeding: Inspect steering system. Check, and correct as needed:

 Hoses must not touch any other part of vehicle.

 All hose connections must be tight.

- Steering system noise could be caused by hose touching frame, body, or engine
- Loose connections might not leak but could allow air into system

When to bleed:
After any component replacement
After disconnecting fluid line
In case of steering system noise

Why bleed?
To prevent pump damage
To ensure proper system operation
To stop steering system noise

Power Steering Fluid
Use only clean, new power steering fluid. Fluid must be
Conventional Climate
GM #1052984 – 16 ounce
#1050017 – 32 ounce
Cold Climate
GM #12345866 – 16 ounce
#12345867 – 32 ounce

How to bleed:

 ❶ Switch ignition off.

❷ Raise front wheels off ground.

❸ Turn steering wheel full left.

❹ Fill fluid reservoir to "FULL COLD" level. Leave cap off

 ❺ With assistant checking fluid level and condition, turn steering wheel lock-to-lock at least 20 times. Engine remains off.

- On systems with long return lines or fluid coolers, turn steering wheel lock-to-lock at least 40 times
- Trapped air may cause fluid to overflow. Thoroughly clean any spilled fluid to allow for leak check
- Keep fluid level at "FULL COLD"

 ❻ While turning wheel, check fluid constantly

- No bubbles are allowed
- For any sign of bubbles, recheck connections. Repeat step 5

 ❼ Start engine. With engine idling, maintain fluid level. Reinstall cap

 ❽ Return wheels to center Lower front wheels to ground.

 ❾ Keep engine running for two minutes

 ❿ Turn steering wheel in both directions

Verify
☑ Smooth power assist
☑ Noiseless operation
☑ Proper fluid level
☑ No system leaks
☑ Proper fluid condition
- No bubbles, no foam, no discoloration

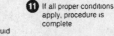 ⓫ If all proper conditions apply, procedure is complete

⓬ If any problem remains, see "Special Conditions"

Special Conditions:
Fluid

- Foam or bubbles in fluid
  Fluid must be completely free of bubbles. In step 5, be alert to periodic bubbles that could indicate a loose connection or leak. O-ring seal in either the return hose or pressure hose
- Discolored fluid
  (milky, opaque, or light tan color)

Switch ignition off. Wait two minutes. Recheck hose connections. Repeat steps 7-10. If condition still exists, replace and check a possible cause

☑ Return hose clamps
☑ Return hose O-ring
☑ Pressure hose O-rings
☑ Gear cylinder line O-rings

Fill system and repeat bleed procedure for each possible cause. Repeat steps 7-10 to verify whether noise has been eliminated

Noise

- Pump whine or groan
  With engine running, recheck hoses for possible contact with frame body or engine. If no contact is found, follow either method below to cool down fluid and repressurize system

Method 1:
Normal Cool Down
Switch engine off
Wait for system to cool
Install reservoir cap

Method 2:
Partial Fluid Replacement
Switch engine off
Use a suction device to remove fluid from reservoir
Refill with cool, clean fluid
Install reservoir cap

After either method of cooling, start engine and allow engine to come up to operating temperature. If noise persists, remove and replace power steering pump. Repeat bleed procedure following pump replacement

88008G73

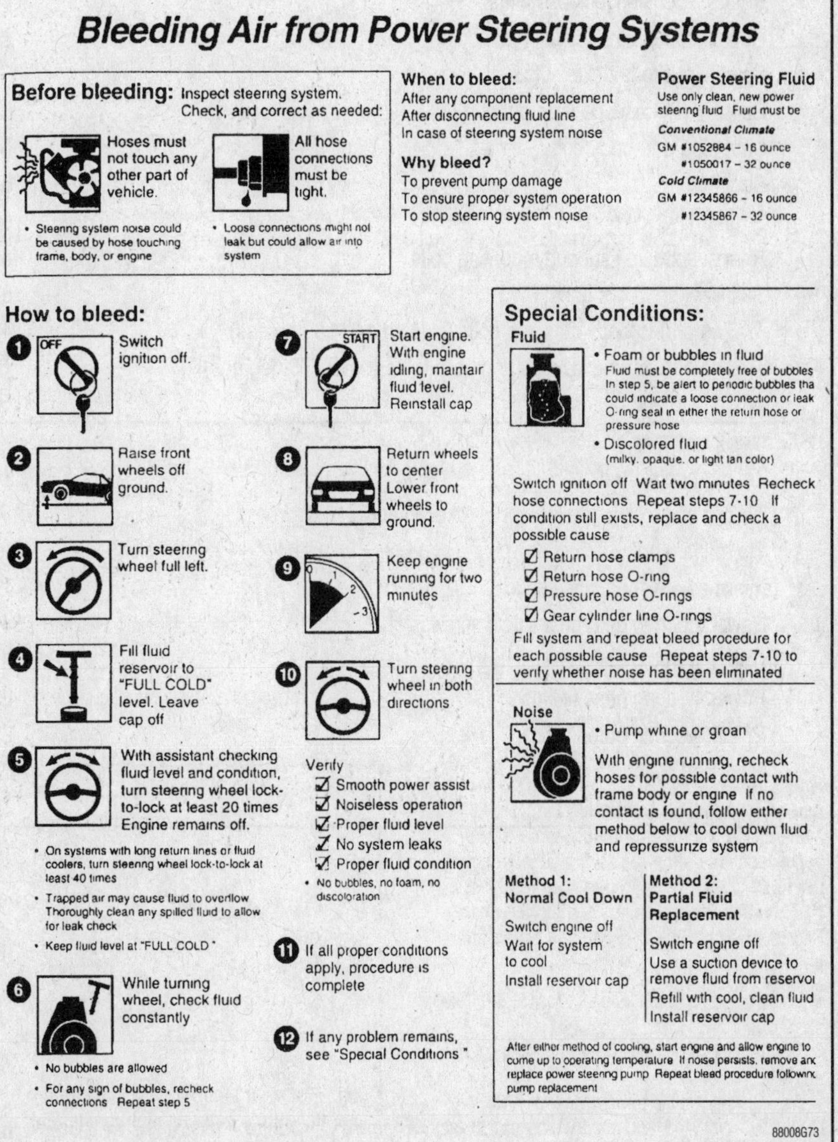

Fig. 77 Power steering system bleeding

TORQUE SPECIFICATIONS

Components	English	Metric
Front Suspension		
Drive axle (halfshaft) nut	151 ft. lbs.	205 Nm
Ball joint nut	63 ft. lbs.	85 Nm
Lower control arm-to-frame bolts	52 ft. lbs.	70 Nm
Strut closure nut	82 ft. lbs.	110 Nm
Strut cover plate bolts	24 ft. lbs.	33 Nm
Strut cover plate nuts	24 ft. lbs.	33 Nm
Strut piston shaft nut	59 ft. lbs.	80 Nm
Strut-to-knuckle nuts	90 ft. lbs.	122 Nm
Stabilizer bar clamp-to-frame nuts	27 ft. lbs.	37 Nm
Stabilizer bar clamp-to-lower control arm bolts	35 ft. lbs.	47 Nm
Wheel hub-to-knuckle bolts	52 ft. lbs.	70 Nm
Rear Suspension		
Rear rod-to-crossmember nuts	111 ft. lbs.	150 Nm
Rear suspension jack pad bolts	18 ft. lbs.	25 Nm
Rear suspension retention plate bolts	22 ft. lbs.	30 Nm
Spindle rod-to-knuckle nuts	177 ft. lbs.	240 Nm
Spindle rod-to-suspension support nut	111 ft. lbs.	150 Nm
Strut mount-to-body bolts	34 ft. lbs.	46 Nm
Strut nut	55 ft. lbs.	75 Nm
Strut-to-knuckle nuts	90 ft. lbs.	122 Nm
Rear suspension support mounting bolts	85 ft. lbs.	115 Nm
Stabilizer shaft link bolts	52 ft. lbs.	70 Nm
Trailing arm-to-body nuts and bolts (plus an adt'l 90 degrees)	44 ft. lbs.	60 Nm
Trailing arm-to-knuckle nuts and bolts (plus an adt'l 75 degrees)	66 ft. lbs	90 Nm
Wheel hub and bearing bolts	52 ft. lbs.	70 Nm
Steering		
Tie rod end slotted nut	40 ft. lbs.	54 Nm
Tie rod end torque prevailing nut (plus an adt'l 210 degrees)	7 ft. lbs.	10 Nm
Tie rod jam nuts	46 ft. lbs.	62 Nm
Intermediate shaft pinch bolt	35 ft. lbs.	47 Nm
Power steering gear heat shield screws	54 inch lbs.	6 Nm
Power steering gear pipe clip nut	54 inch lbs.	6 Nm
Power steering hose fittings	20 ft. lbs.	27 Nm
Power steering pump bolts	25 ft. lbs.	34 Nm
Rack and pinion mounting bolts	59 ft. lbs.	80 Nm
Transaxle mount nuts	35 ft. lbs.	47 Nm

93178C01

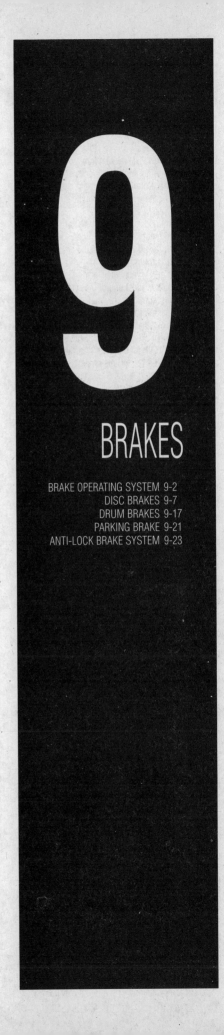

9

BRAKES

BRAKE OPERATING SYSTEM

Basic Operating Principles

Hydraulic systems are used to actuate the brakes of all automobiles. The system transports the power required to force the friction surfaces of the braking system together from the pedal to the individual brake units at each wheel. A hydraulic system is used for two reasons.

First, fluid under pressure can be carried to all parts of an automobile by small pipes and flexible hoses without taking up a significant amount of room or posing routing problems.

Second, a great mechanical advantage can be given to the brake pedal end of the system, and the foot pressure required to actuate the brakes can be reduced by making the surface area of the master cylinder pistons smaller than that of any of the pistons in the wheel cylinders or calipers.

The master cylinder consists of a fluid reservoir and a double cylinder and piston assembly. Double type master cylinders are designed to separate the front and rear braking systems hydraulically in case of a leak.

Steel lines carry the brake fluid to a point on the vehicles frame near each of the vehicles wheels. The fluid is then carried to the calipers and wheel cylinders by flexible tubes in order to allow for suspension and steering movements.

On drum brake systems, now being used on only the rear wheels of some cars, each wheel cylinder contains two pistons, one at either end, which push outward in opposite directions.

In disc brake systems, the cylinders are part of the calipers. One cylinder in each caliper is used to force the brake pads against the disc.

All pistons employ some type of seal, usually made of rubber, to minimize fluid leakage. A rubber dust boot seals the outer end of the cylinder against dust and dirt. The boot fits around the outer end of the piston on disc brake calipers, and around the brake actuating rod on wheel cylinders.

The hydraulic system operates as follows: When at rest, the entire system, from the piston(s) in the master cylinder to those in the wheel cylinders or calipers, is full of brake fluid. Upon application of the brake pedal, fluid trapped in front of the master cylinder piston(s) is forced through the lines to the wheel cylinders. Here, it forces the pistons outward, in the case of drum brakes, and inward toward the disc, in the case of disc brakes. The motion of the pistons is opposed by return springs mounted outside the cylinders in drum brakes, and by spring seals, in disc brakes.

Upon release of the brake pedal, a spring located inside the master cylinder immediately returns the master cylinder pistons to the normal position. The pistons contain check valves and the master cylinder has compensating ports drilled in it. These are uncovered as the pistons reach their normal position. The piston check valves allow fluid to flow toward the wheel cylinders or calipers as the pistons withdraw. Then, as the return springs force the brake pads or shoes into the released position, the excess fluid reservoir through the compensating ports. It is during the time the pedal is in the released position that any fluid that has leaked out of the system will be replaced through the compensating ports.

Dual circuit master cylinders, used on all modern cars, including your GM W-Body vehicle, use two pistons, located one behind the other, in the same cylinder. The primary piston is actuated directly by mechanical linkage from the brake pedal through the power booster. The secondary piston is actuated by fluid trapped between the two pistons. If a leak develops in front of the secondary piston, it moves forward until it bottoms against the front of the master cylinder, and the fluid trapped between the pistons will operate the rear brakes. If the rear brakes develop a leak, the primary piston will move forward until direct contact with the secondary piston takes place, and it will force the secondary piston to actuate the front brakes. In either case, the brake pedal moves farther when the brakes are applied, and less braking power is available.

The W-Body vehicles covered by this manual use proportioner valves which are threaded into the master cylinder. They limit the outlet pressure to the rear brakes after a predetermined rear input pressure has been reached. This is used when less rear apply force is needed to obtain optimum braking and to prevent rear wheel lock-up on vehicles with light rear wheel loads. His feature maintains a proper brake force "balance" during all braking maneuvers.

The hydraulic system may be checked for leaks by applying pressure to the pedal gradually and steadily. If the pedal sinks very slowly to the floor, the system has a leak. This is not to be confused with a springy or spongy feel due to the compression of air within the lines. If the system leaks, there will be a gradual change in the position of the pedal with a constant pressure. Check for leaks along all lines and at wheel cylinders. If no external leaks are apparent, the problem is inside the master cylinder. GM recommends that the brake lines and hoses be checked at least twice a year.

DISC BRAKES

Disc brake systems use a disc (rotor) with brake pads positioned on either side of it. Braking effect is achieved in a manner similar to the way you would squeeze a spinning phonograph record between your fingers. The disc (rotor) is a casting, usually with cooling fins between the two braking surfaces. This enables air to circulate between the braking surfaces making them less sensitive to heat buildup and more resistant to fade. Dirt and water do not affect braking action since contaminants are thrown off by the centrifugal action of the rotor or scraped off the by the pads. Also, the equal clamping action of the two brake pads tends to ensure uniform, straight line stops. Disc brakes are inherently self-adjusting. There are three general types of disc brake:

- A fixed caliper
- A floating caliper
- A sliding caliper

The fixed caliper design uses two pistons mounted on either side of the rotor (in each side of the caliper). The caliper is mounted rigidly and does not move.

The sliding and floating designs are quite similar. In fact, these two types are often lumped together. In both designs, the pad on the inside of the rotor is moved into contact with the rotor by hydraulic force. The caliper, which is not held in a fixed position, moves slightly, bringing the outside pad into contact with the rotor. There are various methods of attaching floating calipers. Some pivot at the bottom or top, and some slide on mounting bolts. In any event, the end result is the same.

All the vehicles covered in this book employ the sliding caliper design.

DRUM BRAKES

Drum brakes use two brake shoes mounted on a stationary backing plate. These shoes are positioned inside a circular drum which rotates with the wheel assembly. On these vehicles, the shoes are held in place by one large retractor spring. This allows the brake shoes to slide toward the drum (when the brake are applied) while keeping the linings and drums in alignment. The shoes are actuated by a wheel cylinder which is mounted at the top of the backing plate. When the brakes are applied, hydraulic pressure forces the wheel cylinder's pistons outward. Since the small projections on the brake shoe bear directly against the wheel cylinder pistons, the tops of the shoes are then forced against the inner side of the drum.

The W-Body vehicles covered by this manual may have either rear disc or drum brakes, depending on the vehicle, model and options. On these vehicles, the drum brake is a leading/trailing design. In the leading/trailing brake, the force from the wheel cylinder is applied equally to both shoes. Torque from the brake shoes is transferred through the backing plate, to the axle flange. Adjustment is automatic when the brakes are applied. When pressure within the wheel cylinder is relaxed, return springs pull the shoes back away from the drum.

Most modern drum brakes are designed to self-adjust themselves during application when the vehicle is moving in reverse. This motion causes both shoes to rotate very slightly with the drum, rocking an adjusting lever, thereby causing rotation of the adjusting screw.

※※ WARNING

Clean, high quality DOT 3 brake fluid is essential to the safe and proper operation of the brake system. You should always buy the highest quality brake fluid that is available. If the brake fluid becomes contaminated, drain and flush the system and fill the master cylinder with new fluid. Never reuse any brake fluid. Any brake fluid that is removed from the system should be discarded. NEVER use DOT 5 (silicone) brake fluid in these vehicles.

Adjustment

DISC BRAKES

The front disc brakes are inherently self-adjusting. No adjustments are either necessary or possible.

DRUM BRAKES

The drum brakes are designed to self-adjust when applied with the car moving in reverse. However, they can also be adjusted manually. This manual adjustment should also be performed whenever the linings are replaced.

1. Raise and safely support the vehicle with safety stands.
2. Matchmark the relationship between the wheel to the axle flange to insure proper balance upon assembly, then remove the tire and wheel assembly.
3. Matchmark the relationship of the drum to the axle flange, then remove the brake drum.
4. Make sure the stops on both parking brake levers are against the edges of the webs on the parking brake shoes. If the parking brake cable is holding the stops off the edge of the shoe webs, loosen the parking brake cable adjustment.
5. Measure the drum inside diameter, using tool J 21177-A or equivalent tool.
6. Turning the star wheel on the adjusting bolt/screw assembly, adjust the shoe and lining diameter to be 0.050 inch (1.27mm) less that the drum inside diameter at each wheel.
7. Install the drums and wheels, aligning the previous marks.
8. Apply and release the brake pedal 30–35 times, with a one second pause between each brake application.

Stop Lamp Switch

REMOVAL & INSTALLATION

◆ See Figures 1 and 2

1. Disconnect the negative battery cable.
2. Remove the driver's side instrument panel sound insulator panel.
3. Detach the switch electrical connectors.
4. Remove the switch from the brake pedal bracket.

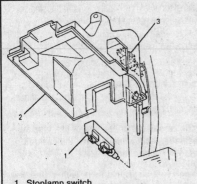

1. Stoplamp switch
2. Brake pedal bracket
3. Cruise control release switch

88009G03

Fig. 1 Typical stop lamp (also called a brake light) switch mounting next to the brake pedal. Note that the cruise control switch is also mounted next to the brake pedal

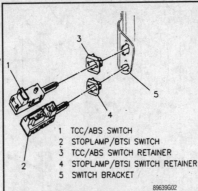

1. TCC/ABS SWITCH
2. STOPLAMP/BTSI SWITCH
3. TCC/ABS SWITCH RETAINER
4. STOPLAMP/BTSI SWITCH RETAINER
5. SWITCH BRACKET

89639G02

Fig. 2 Another view of the stop lamp switch mounted near the torque converter clutch and ABS switch

To install:
5. Position the switch to the brake pedal bracket.
6. Attach the electrical connectors.
7. Install the driver's side instrument panel sound insulator panel.
8. Connect the negative battery cable.

ADJUSTMENT

Proper stop lamp switch adjustment is important. Incorrect adjustment may cause brake drag and excessive brake lining wear. With the brake pedal in the fully released position, the stop lamp switch plunger should be fully depressed against the brake pedal shanks.

1. If installing a replacement stop lamp switch, insert the stop lamp switch into the brake pedal bracket.

2. Push the brake pedal forward to set the brake pushrod into the power brake vacuum booster.
3. Pull the brake pedal to the rear, against the internal pedal stop. The stop lamp switch automatically adjusts due to the movement of the brake pedal.
4. Check the stop lamps for proper operation.

Master Cylinder

◆ See Figures 3 and 4

The master cylinder used on GM W-Body vehicles is a composite design (plastic fluid reservoir and aluminum body) designed to be used in a diagonally split system (one front and one diagonally opposite rear brake served by the primary piston and opposite the front and rear brakes served by the secondary piston). It incorporates the functions of a standard dual master cylinder plus it has a fluid level sensor and integral proportioning valves. Proportioning valves are designed to provide better front to rear braking balance with heavy brake applications.

✳✳ CAUTION

Overfilling the brake fluid reservoir must be avoided due to the potential for overflow onto the nearby catalytic converters in the exhaust system. Brake fluid is flammable and contact with hot exhaust components could result in fire and possible personal injury.

The master cylinder fluid reservoir is on the master cylinder and is located under the hood on the left side of the vehicle. The master cylinder reservoir contains enough fluid so it never needs

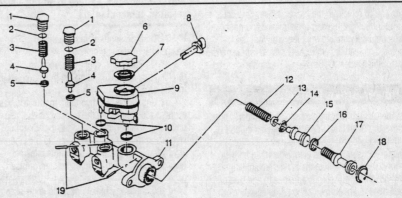

1. Proportioning Valve Cap
2. O-Ring
3. Spring
4. Proportioning Valve Piston
5. Proportioning Valve Seal
6. Reservoir Cap
7. Diaphragm
8. Fluid Level Sensor
9. Fluid Reservoir
10. Reservoir Seals
11. Cylinder Body
12. Spring
13. Spring Retainer
14. Primary Seal
15. Secondary Piston
16. Secondary Seal
17. Primary Piston
18. Retainer
19. Spring Pin

93179G01

Fig. 3 Exploded view of a typical composite master cylinder assembly as used on GM W-Body vehicles

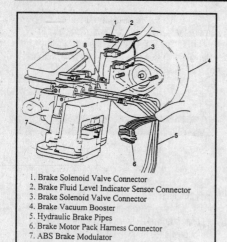

1. Brake Solenoid Valve Connector
2. Brake Fluid Level Indicator Sensor Connector
3. Brake Solenoid Valve Connector
4. Brake Vacuum Booster
5. Hydraulic Brake Pipes
6. Brake Motor Pack Harness Connector
7. ABS Brake Modulator
8. Brake Master Cylinder Attaching Nuts

93179G02

Fig. 4 The master cylinder is mounted to the ABS hydraulic modulator

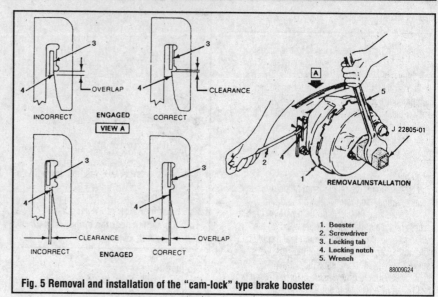

1. Booster
2. Screwdriver
3. Locking tab
4. Locking notch
5. Wrench

88009G24

Fig. 5 Removal and installation of the "cam-lock" type brake booster

service under normal conditions. A low fluid level sensor in the reservoir will warn of low fluid level. Thoroughly clean the reservoir cap before removal to avoid getting dirt into the reservoir.

REMOVAL & INSTALLATION

Because the vehicles covered by this manual are equipped with ABS, please refer to the ABS Hydraulic Modulator/Master Cylinder removal and installation procedure, located later in this section. Please note that a Tech 1® or equivalent scan tool is recommended for bleeding the system. GM specifies that when any brake component is repaired or replaced such that air is allowed to enter the brake system, the entire bleeding procedure MUST be followed. Unapproved or partial bleed procedures can allow air to remain in the brake system. This could result in reduced braking performance and possible personal injury. In addition, the scan tool is required to scan the entire ABS system for Diagnostic Trouble Codes (DTCs).

Power Brake Booster

The vacuum booster system uses a tandem vacuum suspended unit. In a normal operating mode, with the service brakes in the released position, the vacuum booster operates with vacuum on both sides of its diaphragms. When the brakes are applied, air at atmospheric pressure is admitted to one side of each diaphragm to provide the power assist. When the brakes are released, the atmospheric air is shut off from one side of each diaphragm. The air is then drawn from the booster through the vacuum check valve to the vacuum source.

The internal components of this booster are not serviceable. If the booster is proved defective, it must be replaced as a unit.

REMOVAL & INSTALLATION

▶ **See Figure 5**

At one time, vacuum boosters simply bolted to the cowl (firewall) and were easily serviced. These vehicles, however, use a twist-lock (sometimes

called a cam-lock) type of mounting system. A special tool is used that bolts to the master cylinder mounting studs and a large wrench is used to twist the booster to disengage/engage the locking tabs. Use care if using substitute tools.

➡**Inspect the locking flanges on the brake booster and mounting plate. Replace the brake booster and mounting plate if the locking flanges are bent or damaged.**

☀ CAUTION

When replacing the power brake booster, make sure that the cruise control cable is not routed between the booster and the cowl. If the cable is damaged or pinched, it must be replaced. Failure to do this could result in personal injury.

1. On 3.8L engines, remove the cosmetic/acoustic engine cover.
2. On 3.4L (VIN X) engines, remove the throttle body and tube, using the procedures found in Section 5.
3. Unbolt the ABS hydraulic modulator/master cylinder assembly from the booster, as outlined under the ABS portion of this section. On some vehicles, it might not be necessary to disconnect any hydraulic lines. Some brake line clips and retainers may have to be removed and/or disengaged to allow some working room. Use care not to bend and crimp any brake lines. Move the assembly just enough to disengage the master cylinder from the two studs on the front of the booster.
4. Disconnect the transaxle filler tube and remove, if necessary.
5. On 3.8L engines, remove the EGR heat shield.
6. Disconnect the vacuum hose from the brake booster.

➡**Do not attempt to remove the booster until the brake pedal pushrod is disconnected from the brake pedal. When disconnecting the pushrod from the brake pedal, the brake pedal must be held stationary or damage to the brake switch may result.**

7. Disconnect the brake pedal pushrod from the brake pedal. It is retained by a sheetmetal clip. Carefully lift the tab that covers the brake pedal pivot and slide the clips from the brake pushrod. Use care not to distort the clip as it will be needed for installation.
8. Unlock the booster from the front of the cowl (firewall) as follows:
    a. Attach booster holding tool J 22805-01, or equivalent, to the master cylinder mounting studs with the nuts. Tighten the stud nuts to 20 ft. lbs. (27 Nm).
    b. Use a suitable prybar to pry the locking tab on the booster out of the locking notch on the mounting flange.
    c. At the same time, turn the booster counterclockwise with a large wrench on the booster holding tool.
9. Remove the brake booster from the vehicle. Be careful not to damage the insulator boot mounted on the front of the dash when pulling the pushrod end through the hole.

To install:

10. Lightly lubricate the inside and outside diameters of the grommet and front housing seal with silicone grease before installation.
11. Attach tool J 22805-01, or equivalent, to the booster with the nuts. Tighten the nuts to 20 ft. lbs. (27 Nm).
12. Position the booster on the cowl, slightly counterclockwise from the final installation position, so that the locking flanges on the booster and mounted plate engage.

➡**Be careful not to damage or dislodge the insulation boot when passing the pushrod through the cowl opening.**

13. Connect the booster pushrod to the brake pedal. Verify that the retainer clip is properly engaged on the brake pedal pivot pin and that the top of the clip covers the end of the pin.
14. Turn the booster clockwise with a wrench on tool J 22805-01, until the locking flanges are engaged. Make sure the locking tab is fully seated to prevent rotation of the booster. It is not necessary to use a prytool on the locking tab to install the booster. When correctly installed, the locking tab

will slide up the flange and snap in the locking notch.

15. Install the ABS hydraulic modulator/master cylinder assembly.

16. Depending on the vehicle model and engine assembly, install the remaining components.

17. Connect the negative battery cable and bleed the system if the fluid pipes were disconnected from the master cylinder.

Proportioning Valves

REMOVAL & INSTALLATION

▶ See Figure 6

1. Disconnect the negative battery cable.

➡️In order to remove the proportioning valve caps, it may be necessary to remove the reservoir assembly from the master cylinder.

2. Remove the proportioning valve cap assemblies.

3. Remove and discard the O-rings.

4. Remove the springs.

5. Using needle-nosed pliers, remove the proportioning valve pistons. Be very careful not to scratch or damage the piston stems.

6. Remove the proportioning valve seals from the pistons.

7. Inspect the pistons for corrosion or other damage, and replace, if necessary.

To install:

8. Lubricate new O-rings and proportioning valve seals with the silicone grease supplied in the repair kit. Also lubricate the stem of the proportioning valve pistons.

9. Place the new seals on the proportioning valve pistons with the seal lips facing upward toward the cap assembly.

10. Position the proportioning valve pistons and seals into the master cylinder body.

11. Install the springs in the master cylinder body.

12. Place new O-rings in the grooves in the proportioning valve cap assemblies.

13. Install the proportioning valve caps on the master cylinder body. Tighten the caps to 20 ft. lbs. (27 Nm).

14. If removed, install the reservoir assembly to the master cylinder. Refill the system with fresh DOT 3 brake fluid from a sealed container.

15. Connect the negative battery cable.

Brake Hoses and Pipes

▶ See Figures 7 , 8 , 9 and 10

✵✵ CAUTION

Always use double walled steel brake lines when replacing rusted or damaged brake lines. The use of any other tubing is not approved and may cause brake failure. Carefully route and retain replacement brake lines. Always use the correct fasteners and the original location for replace-

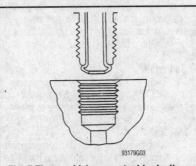

Fig. 7 These vehicles use steel brake lines with an I.S.O. flare. Replacement brake lines must have this flare or the system will leak

ment brake pipes. Failure to properly route and retain brake lines may cause damage to the brake lines and cause brake system failure, resulting in possible personal injury.

The steel brake lines on these vehicles use what is called an I.S.O. Flare. This is different from the flare used on American vehicles for many years. If a brake line is damaged and requires replacement, you must obtain a replacement brake line with the correct flare. Most automotive parts stores stock straight lengths of steel brake line, already flared, with the correct fittings installed. Brake line replacement requires obtaining a piece of brake line as close in length to the original as possible. The brake line must be of the correct diameter and flare. The replacement length of brake line is carefully bent to conform to the shape of the original brake line. GM specifies that a clearance of ¾ inch be maintained from all moving or vibrating components.

One of the major causes of brake line replacement is twisting off or otherwise damaging a piece of brake line when replacing other components. For example, when replacing a rear wheel cylinder, if the brake line is rusted, loosening the brake line fitting backs the fitting over rusted portions of the brake line. This binds up the fitting so it seizes on the brake line. Continuing to loosen the brake line fitting usually results in snapping off the brake line, requiring replacement of that section of brake line. Many technicians take the time to polish off any

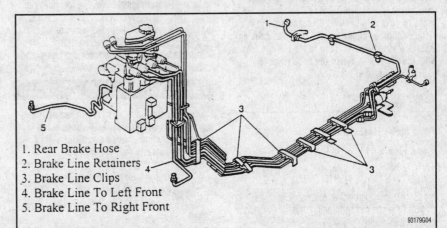

1. Rear Brake Hose
2. Brake Line Retainers
3. Brake Line Clips
4. Brake Line To Left Front
5. Brake Line To Right Front

Fig. 8 ABS systems require a considerable amount of steel brake lines to connect all components

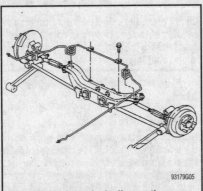

1. Proportioner valve cap assembly
2. O-ring
3. Spring
4. Proportioner valve piston
5. Proportioner valve seal

Fig. 6 Exploded view of a typical proportioning valve assembly

Fig. 9 Typical rear brake line routing— Buick shown, others similar

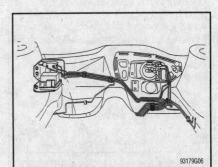

Fig. 10 The tight underhood space constraints of front wheel drive vehicles equipped with ABS means brake lines must be carefully routed and secured

rust and corrosion from the brake line next to the fitting, using fine emery cloth or crocus cloth, then using a penetrating oil to loosen the brake line fitting. The time spent cleaning the brake line before attempting to loosen the fitting pays off by saving the original brake line.

Another condition requiring brake line replacement is when the fittings are damaged. This is almost always caused by using the wrong wrench. Brake line wrenches (sometimes called Flare Nut Wrenches) should be used. These wrenches wrap around the fitting, grasping it on five of the six wrench flats on the fitting. This reduces (but doesn't eliminate) the chance of rounding off the fitting's corners so that it cannot be removed, or, if removed, cannot be adequately tightened at installation. Brake line wrenches are available at most all auto supply stores, in both standard and metric sizes.

Your GM W-Body vehicle also uses brake hoses to carry the brake fluid to parts that are in motion, mainly the front and rear brakes which move with the independent suspension. Generally, brake hoses give little trouble but should be inspected at least twice a year. Check the brake hoses for road hazard damage, crack, chafing of the outer cover, leaks, blisters and for proper routing and mounting. A light and mirror may be needed for an adequate inspection. If any of these conditions are found, it will be necessary to replace the brake hose.

➡**Never allow components to hang from the flexible brake hoses as damage to the hoses may occur. Some brake hoses have protective rings or covers to prevent direct contact of the hose with other chassis parts. Besides causing possible structural damage to the hose, excessive tension could cause the hose rings to move out of proper locations.**

REMOVAL & INSTALLATION

Front Brake Hoses & Lines

▶ **See Figure 11**

1. Raise the vehicle and support with safety stands.
2. Remove the front wheel assembly.
3. Clean all dirt and foreign material from the brake hose and fitting.

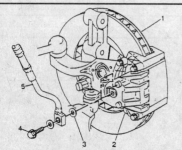

1. Front Brake Rotor
2. Front Brake Caliper
3. Copper Sealing Washer
4. Brake Hose To Caliper Bolt
5. Brake Hose With "Banjo" Fitting

93179G07

Fig. 11 Front disc brake caliper and brake hose arrangement

4. Remove steel brake line from the brake hose at the bracket. Use brake line (flare nut) and back-up wrenches to avoid fitting damage. Generally, one wrench is used to hold the brake hose fitting stationary while another is used to loosen the fitting at the bodyside steel brake line.
5. Remove the brake hose retainer at the mounting bracket. This is usually a U-shaped clip that slides off the end of the brake hose, releasing it from the bracket. Remove the hose from the bracket.
6. Most caliper installations of these vehicle use a "banjo" fitting on the caliper end of the brake hose with a special bolt that goes through the fitting, into the caliper. Remove the inlet fitting bolt at the caliper. There should be two copper sealing washers, one on top of the banjo fitting and one under the fitting. GM recommends that these washers be replaced.

To install:

7. Clean all parts well. Lubricate the caliper bolt threads with clean brake fluid. Using new copper washers, assemble the banjo fitting to the caliper. Carefully tighten the bolt to 30–33 ft. lbs. (40–44 Nm).
8. With the vehicle weight on the suspension, install the brake hose to the bracket and install the U-shaped brake hose retainer clip. Make sure there are NO kinks in the hose. Many brake hoses have a paint stripe on them as a visual aid to help you make sure the hose is not twisted at installation.
9. Hold the brake hose fitting stationary and install the bodyside steel brake line fitting into the brake hose. Tighten with your fingers to make sure the fitting is not cross-threaded, which will cause a fluid leak. When satisfied with the installation of the fitting, use your brake line wrenches to tighten the fitting to 11–15 ft. lbs. (15–20 Nm).

✴✴ WARNING

Make sure the hose is NOT kinked or touching any part of the frame or suspension after installation. These conditions may cause the hose to fail prematurely.

10. Check the hose after turning the steering wheel extreme right and then extreme left. If the hose is tight or touching anything, make the proper adjustments.
11. Install the wheel and tire assembly.
12. Carefully lower the vehicle. The brake system must be bled as outlined later in this section.

✴✴ CAUTION

Do not move the vehicle until a firm brake pedal is obtained. Failure to obtain a firm pedal before moving the vehicle may result in personal injury.

13. Verify that a firm brake pedal has been obtained before moving the vehicle.

Rear Brake Hoses & Lines

WITH REAR DISC BRAKES

▶ **See Figure 12**

1. Raise the vehicle and support with safety stands.
2. Remove the rear wheel and tire assembly.

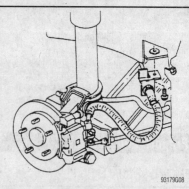

93179G08

Fig. 12 Rear disc brake caliper and hose arrangement

3. Clean all dirt and foreign material from the brake hose and fitting.
4. The rear caliper brake hose is attached to the body with a bracket near the rear strut, that bolts to both the body and the inboard end of the brake hose. Remove the attaching bolt.
5. Remove steel brake line from the brake hose at the bracket. Use brake line (flare nut) and back-up wrenches to avoid fitting damage. Generally, one wrench is used to hold the brake hose fitting stationary while another is used to loosen the fitting at the bodyside steel brake line. Use care not to bend the brake line or the bracket.
6. Remove the brake hose retainer at the mounting bracket. Remove the hose from the bracket.
7. Most caliper installations of these vehicle use a "banjo" fitting on the caliper end of the brake hose with a special bolt that goes through the fitting, into the caliper. Remove the inlet fitting bolt at the caliper. There should be two copper sealing washers, one on top of the banjo fitting and one under the fitting. GM recommends that these washers be replaced.

To install:

8. Clean all parts well. Lubricate the caliper bolt threads with clean brake fluid. Using new copper washers, assemble the banjo fitting to the caliper. Carefully tighten the bolt to 20 ft. lbs. (27 Nm).
9. With the vehicle's weight on the suspension, install the brake hose to the bracket. The hose fitting must align with a notch in the bracket. Make sure there are NO kinks in the hose. Many brake hoses have a paint stripe on them as a visual aid to help you make sure the hose is not twisted at installation.
10. Hold the brake hose fitting stationary and install the bodyside steel brake line fitting into the brake hose. Tighten with fingers to make sure the fitting is not crossthreaded which will cause a fluid leak. When satisfied with the installation of the fitting, use your brake line wrenches to tighten the fitting to 20 ft. lbs. (27 Nm).

✴✴ WARNING

Make sure the hose is NOT kinked or touching any part of the frame or suspension after installation. These conditions may cause the hose to fail prematurely.

11. Install the wheel and tire assembly.
12. Carefully lower the vehicle. The brake system must be bled as outlined later in this section.

Do not move the vehicle until a firm brake pedal is obtained. Failure to obtain a firm pedal before moving the vehicle may result in personal injury.

13. Verify that a firm brake pedal has been obtained before moving the vehicle.

WITH REAR DRUM BRAKES

▶ See Figure 13

Rear drum brakes have flexible rubber hoses from the body to a bracket bolted to the rear struts. A short length of steel brake line connects the wheel-end of the hoses to the wheel cylinders.

1. Raise the vehicle and support with safety stands.
2. Remove the rear wheel assembly.
3. Clean all dirt and foreign material from the brake hose and fittings at both ends of the brake hose.
4. The rear drum brake hoses are attached to the body with a bracket on one end and at the wheel-end, attached to a bracket bolted to the rear of the strut. Remove steel brake lines from both ends of the rear drum brake hose. Use brake line (flare nut) and back-up wrenches to avoid fitting damage. Generally, one wrench is used to hold the brake hose fitting stationary while another is used

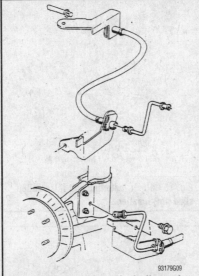

Fig. 13 Rear brake hose, brake line and bracket arrangement for vehicles equipped with rear drum brakes

to loosen the fitting at the bodyside steel brake line. Use care not to bend the brake line or the bracket.

5. Remove the brake hose retainers at the mounting brackets. Remove the hose from the bracket.

To install:

6. Clean all parts well. With the vehicle's weight on the suspension, install the brake hose to the bracket. The hose fitting must align with a notch in the bracket. Make sure there are NO kinks in the hose. Many brake hoses have a paint stripe on them as a visual aid to help you make sure the hose is not twisted at installation.

7. Hold the brake hose fitting stationary and install the bodyside and wheel-end steel brake line fittings into the brake hose. Tighten with fingers to make sure the fittings are not crossthreaded which will cause a fluid leak. When satisfied with the installation of the fitting, use your brake line wrenches to tighten the fitting to 20 ft. lbs. (27 Nm).

Make sure the hose is NOT kinked or touching any part of the frame or suspension after installation. These conditions may cause the hose to fail prematurely.

8. Install the wheel and tire assembly.
9. Carefully lower the vehicle. The brake system must be bled as outlined in this section.

Bleeding Brake System

All vehicles covered by this manual use Antilock Brake Systems (ABS). Please refer to the ABS coverage later in this section.

DISC BRAKES

Older brake pads or shoes may contain asbestos, which has been determined to be a cancer causing agent. Never clean the brake surfaces with compressed air. Avoid inhaling any dust from any brake surface. When cleaning brake surfaces, use a commercially available brake cleaning fluid. GM suggests a water dampened cloth or water-based solution be used to remove any dust on brake parts, to prevent any asbestos fibers from becoming airborne.

Fluid pressure behind the caliper piston(s) increases when applying the brakes. Pressure exerts equally against the bottom of the piston(s) and the bottom of the piston bore(s). The pressure applied to the piston transmits to the inner pad. The pressure forces the pad against the inner rotor surface. The pressure applied to the bottom of the piston bore(s) forces the caliper to slide on the mounting bolts. The caliper slides to the center of the vehicle. Because the caliper is one piece, the sliding movement causes the outer section of the caliper to apply pressure against the back of the outer pad. The pressure then forces the pad against the outer rotor surface. As line pressure builds, the pads press against the rotor surfaces with increased force. The force brings the vehicle to a stop. When releasing the brake pedal, the line pressure releases. The seal and seal groove cause the piston to retract slightly. Piston retraction causes less drag on the rotor by both pads. Outward movement of the piston and inward movement of the caliper

automatically compensate for pad wear. As the pads wear, the increased area behind the piston fills with brake fluid from the master cylinder reservoir.

Brake Pads

The original equipment disc brake pads generally have small sheetmetal wear indicators attached to one of the brake pads. When the brake lining gets too thin, the sheetmetal wear indicator rubs against the brake rotor. The wear indicator does not harm the rotor, but it does makes an irritating screeching noise alerting the vehicle operator that the brake pad replacement is due. This wear indicator is designed to protect the brake rotor from damage from the hard steel backing of the brake pad. In addition, with the brake pads renewed, the vehicle's braking ability stays at its designed level of safety.

REMOVAL & INSTALLATION

Front

▶ See Figures 14 thru 25

Several types of front brake calipers have been used on GM W-Body vehicles. The primary difference is some vehicles use a double-piston front caliper, while others use a single piston. Use care when ordering replacement parts. The caliper is mounted to the support bracket with two mounting bolts.

➡There is no need to disconnect any brake lines or brake hoses for disc brake pad replacement.

1. Using a clean suction gun, remove approximately ⅔ of the brake fluid from the master cylinder. The reason for this is that the caliper pistons must be pushed back into their bores so the caliper can be removed from the rotor. This could cause the brake fluid to overflow from the reservoir onto painted surfaces or wiring.
2. Raise and safely support the vehicle on safety stands.
3. Mark the relationship of the wheel to the hub so it can later be installed in the same relationship. This helps retain the balance of the rotating assembly.
4. Remove the front tire and wheel assembly. Install two wheel lug nuts to keep the rotor on the hub.

Fig. 14 Installed view of the front disc brake assembly—Lumina shown, others similar

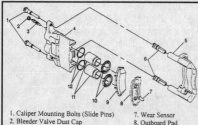

1. Caliper Mounting Bolts (Slide Pins)
2. Bleeder Valve Dust Cap
3. Bleeder Valve
4. Caliper Housing
5. Caliper Mounting Bracket
6. Bushings
7. Wear Sensor
8. Outboard Pad
9. Inboard Pad
10. Caliper Dust Boots
11. Pistons
12. Piston Seals

93179G10

Fig. 15 Exploded view of a typical front caliper and brake pads—Century and Regal shown, others similar

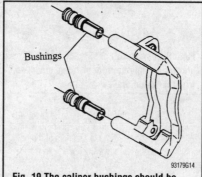

1. Upper Caliper Mounting Bolt
2. Caliper Housing
3. Lower Caliper Mounting Bolt

93179G11

Fig. 16 Caliper mounting bolt (also called slide pin) locations

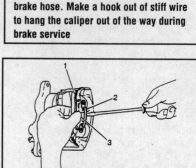

1. Wire Hanger
2. Caliper Housing

93179G12

Fig. 17 Never let a caliper hang by the brake hose. Make a hook out of stiff wire to hang the caliper out of the way during brake service

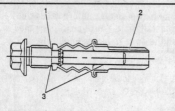

1. Bolt Bearing Surface
2. Inside of Bushing
3. Coat Bushing With Silicone Grease

93179G13

Fig. 18 The caliper mounting bolts (also called slide pins) must be clean and free of corrosion. Replace these bolts if there is any doubt to their condition

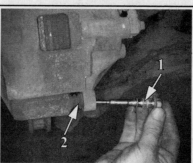

Bushings

93179G14

Fig. 19 The caliper bushings should be lubricated with silicone grease before installation in the caliper bracket

1. Outboard Pad
2. Outboard Pad Retaining Spring
3. Caliper Center Lug

93179G15

Fig. 20 Use a suitable prytool to remove the outboard brake pad and spring

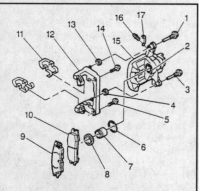

1. Upper Caliper Mounting Bolt
2. Piston Bore
3. Lower Caliper Mounting Bolt
4. Lower Mounting Bolt Boot
5. Caliper Bracket Bolt – Do Not Remove
6. Piston Seai
7. Piston
8. Piston Dust Boot
9. Outer Brake Pad
10. Inner Brake Pad
11. Brake Pad Retainers
12. Caliper Bracket
13. Upper Mounting Bolt Boot
14. Caliper Bracket Bolt – Do Not Remove
15. Caliper Housing
16. Fluid Bleeder Valve
17. Bleeder Valve Dust Cap

93179G16

Fig. 21 The calipers are coded L for Left Side and R for Right Side

93179P06

Fig. 22 Removing the mounting bolts (slide pins). Inspect the threads (1) and the protective rubber boot (2)

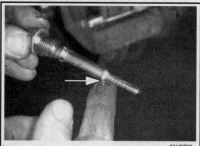

93179P01

Fig. 24 Apply a small amount (arrow) of high-temperature lubricant (disc-brake rated wheel bearing grease) to the area where the caliper and pads rest

93179P03

Fig. 23 Wire brush the surface of the caliper bracket where the caliper and pads rest

93179P09

Fig. 25 Apply a small amount of silicone grease to only the slide pin portion of the mounting bolts. Use care to keep the grease off the bolt threads

Remove the caliper slide pin bolts and carefully work the caliper away from the rotor and caliper mounting bracket.

5. Push the caliper piston(s) back into their bore(s) to provide clearance between the linings and rotor. Use a large C-clamp over the top of the caliper housing and against the back of the outboard pad. Slowly tighten the C-clamp until the piston(s) are pushed back into the caliper bore(s) enough to slide the caliper off the rotor.

6. Remove the outboard brake pad. Use a small prytool to lift up on the outboard pad retaining spring so it will clear the caliper center lug.

7. Remove the inboard brake pad, unsnapping the pad springs from the inside of the piston bores.

8. The caliper mounting bolts (also called slide pins) are important because, in use, the caliper moves (slides) a small amount, along the bolts. This "floating" action is key to the caliper's ability to self-adjust. The bolts must be clean of rust and corrosion. Small rubber boots on the mounting bolts are designed to keep out water and road debris. Inspect the pin boots for cuts, tears or deterioration. If corrosion is found, use new replacement parts including bushings when installing the caliper. GM does not recommend attempting to polish away corrosion. Any protective coating still on the mounting bolts would then be abraded away and corrosion will return in an even shorter time. As insurance against brake problems, many professionals routinely replace the caliper mounting bolts (often sold as "pin kits") during disc brake pad replacements.

9. Inspect the caliper for signs of leaks. While seal kits may be available for caliper overhaul, most professional technicians will simply install a new or factory rebuilt caliper, when required.

To install:

10. Bottom the piston(s) in the caliper bore(s) using a C-clamp, if new brake pads are to be installed. Use a large C-clamp and a metal plate or wooden block across the face of the piston(s). Take care not to damage the piston(s) or caliper rubber dust boot(s). After bottoming the piston(s), carefully lift the inner edge of the caliper boot(s) next to the piston(s) and press out any trapped air. The boots must lay flat below the level of the piston face.

11. Install the inboard brake pad by snapping the pad retainer springs into the hollow of the pistons. Make sure both tangs of the retainer springs are installed inside the hollows (openings) of the pistons. After installing the brake pads, check that the caliper boots are not touching the pads. If there

is any contact, remove the brake pads and reseat or reposition the boots.

12. Install the outboard brake pads by snapping the outboard pad retaining springs over the caliper center lug and into the housing slot. The brake pad wear sensor should be at the trailing edge of the brake pad during forward wheel rotation. The back of the pad must lay flat against the caliper.

13. Install the caliper over the rotor and mounting bracket and work into place. Make sure the bushings in the caliper bracket are still in place.

14. Carefully lubricate the caliper mounting bolts (slide pins) using silicone grease. Do not lubricate the threads or the mounting bolts may tend to work loose. Lubricate the two rubber bushings in the caliper mounting bracket using silicone grease. Install the caliper mounting bolts. Use a small flat-blade tool to push the pin boot over the shoulder of the mounting bolt. The pin boot must be securely in the groove of the mounting bolt. Torque the caliper mounting bolts to 80 ft. lbs. (108 Nm).

15. Install the tire and wheel assembly, aligning the balance marks made at removal.

16. Lower the vehicle.

17. Fill the master cylinder reservoir to the proper level using only fresh, clean DOT 3 brake fluid. Pump the brake pedal firmly to push the pistons back out into operating position and to seat the lining.

18. After the brake pads have been replaced and/or rotors have been refinished, GM recommends that new brake pads be broken in, or "burnished". Use the following procedure:

    a. Make 20 stops from 30 mph using medium to firm brake pedal pressure.

    b. Take care to avoid overheating the brakes.

Rear

Two main types of rear disc brake calipers were used by GM W-Body vehicles: with built-in parking brake mechanism and without built-in parking brake mechanism.

On vehicles with the built-in parking brake mechanism, the rear disc brake calipers have a single piston and the added complexity of a built-in parking brake mechanism. The rear calipers work in a similar fashion to the front calipers and are also mounted by two slide pin bolts.

On vehicles with built-in parking brake mechanism, when the parking brake is applied, the external caliper parking brake lever moves and rotates a

spindle within the caliper housing As the spindle rotates, a connecting rod is pushed against an internal adjusting screw which is threaded into a sleeve nut (cone) in the piston. This causes the piston to move outward bringing the inboard brake pads against the rotor. Since the caliper is free to slide on the mounting pins, as the inboard pads contact the rotor, a reaction force causes the caliper housing to slide inward, pressing the outboard brake pads against the rotor.

The piston contains a self-adjusting mechanism to keep the parking brake in proper adjustment.

As the pads wear, the piston moves through the seal to maintain proper pad-to-rotor clearance. The parking brake adjusts to proper clearances through an internal sleeve nut that rotates and moves as one unit with the piston.

On vehicles with rear disc brake calipers without built-in parking mechanism, the rear caliper is much like a single-piston front caliper and is easily serviced. On these vehicles, the parking brake mechanism uses two small brake shoes that work against the inside of the rear brake rotor (sometimes called the hat). This basic design has been used successfully for many years on the Chevrolet Corvette and many other vehicles.

WITH BUILT-IN PARKING BRAKE MECHANISM

▶ See Figures 26 thru 33

➡ It is not necessary to remove either the brake line or the parking brake cable from the rear disc brake caliper to replace the brake pads. Freeing the cable support bracket allows enough flexibility in the cable to pivot the caliper up and remove the brake pads.

1. Using a suction gun, remove approximately ⅔ of the brake fluid from the master cylinder. The reason for this is that the caliper pistons must be pushed back into their bores so the caliper can be removed from the rotor. This could cause the brake fluid to overflow from the reservoir onto painted surfaces or wiring.

2. Raise and safely support the vehicle on safety stands.

3. Mark the relationship of the wheel to the hub so it can later be installed in the same relationship. This helps retain the balance of the rotating assembly.

4. Remove the rear tire and wheel assembly. Install two wheel lug nuts to keep the rotor on the hub.

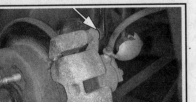

93179P10

Fig. 26 The rear disc brake caliper mounts in the same manner as the front caliper. The arrows indicate the mounting bolts (slider pins)

93179P11

Fig. 27 Remove the two mounting bolts (slider pins) and lift the rear caliper in the direction of the arrow, away from its mounting bracket

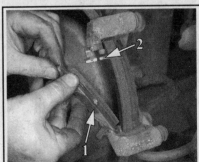

93179P12

Fig. 28 With the rear caliper removed, the outboard (1) and inboard (2) brake pads can be replaced

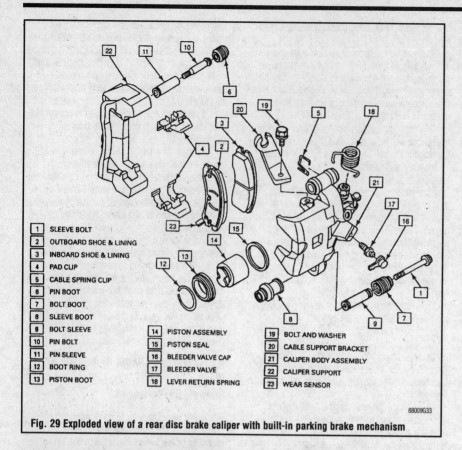

1	SLEEVE BOLT
2	OUTBOARD SHOE & LINING
3	INBOARD SHOE & LINING
4	PAD CLIP
5	CABLE SPRING CLIP
6	PIN BOOT
7	BOLT BOOT
8	SLEEVE BOOT
9	BOLT SLEEVE
10	PIN BOLT
11	PIN SLEEVE
12	BOOT RING
13	PISTON BOOT

14	PISTON ASSEMBLY
15	PISTON SEAL
16	BLEEDER VALVE CAP
17	BLEEDER VALVE
18	LEVER RETURN SPRING

19	BOLT AND WASHER
20	CABLE SUPPORT BRACKET
21	CALIPER BODY ASSEMBLY
22	CALIPER SUPPORT
23	WEAR SENSOR

Fig. 29 Exploded view of a rear disc brake caliper with built-in parking brake mechanism

Fig. 30 Remove the outboard brake pad

Fig. 31 Remove the inboard brake pad and retainer, if necessary

Fig. 32 Before installing the brake pads, retract the piston by turning it with the proper tool or a suitable pair of pliers

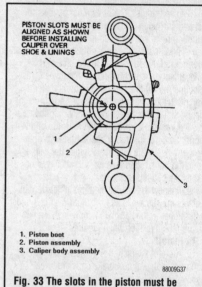

PISTON SLOTS MUST BE ALIGNED AS SHOWN BEFORE INSTALLING CALIPER OVER SHOE & LININGS

1. Piston boot
2. Piston assembly
3. Caliper body assembly

Fig. 33 The slots in the piston must be horizontal when the caliper is in this position

5. Remove the bolt and washer attaching the parking brake cable support bracket to the caliper. It should not be necessary to disconnect the parking brake cable or brake hose to service the rear brake pads.

6. Remove the caliper slide pin bolts and carefully pivot the caliper up. Do not completely remove the caliper.

7. Remove the outboard and inboard brake pads from the caliper support. Remove the two pad clips (sometimes called anti-rattle springs).

To install:

8. Bottom the piston into the caliper bore, noting the following:

 a. There is a special spanner-type tool designed to fit in the piston slots. This allows you to turn the piston and thread it into the caliper, retracting it. Use care if using a substitute tool. Careful work with suitable pliers may enable you to turn the piston back into its bore.

 b. After bottoming the piston, lift the inner edge of the dust boot, next to the piston, and press out any trapped air. The boot must lay flat.

 c. Make sure the slots in the end of the piston are positioned "horizontally" when looking at the caliper with the mounting bolt holes at the 12 o'clock and 6 o'clock position. The slots in the piston must be in this position before pivoting the caliper down over the brake pads in the caliper support.

9. Install the two pad clips in the brake caliper support. Whenever new brake pads are installed, these clips should be in the new disc pad kit.

10. Install the outboard and inboard brake pads in the caliper support. The wear sensor is on the outboard pad. The sensor is positioned downward at the leading edge of the rotor during forward wheel rotation. Hold the metal pad edge against the spring end of the clips in the caliper support. Push the pad in toward the hub, bending the spring ends slightly, and engage the pad notches with the support abutments (the machined edge of the caliper support).

11. Pivot the caliper down over the brake pads. Take care not to damage the piston boot on the inboard side of the caliper. Compress the sleeve boot by hand as the caliper moves into position to prevent boot damage. After the caliper is in position, recheck the installation of the pad clips. If necessary, use a small flat-blade tool to re-seat or center the pad clips on the caliper support.

12. Install the mounting bolts and tighten to 20 ft. lbs. (27 Nm).

13. If removed, install the parking brake support bracket (with cable attached). The bolt is tightened to 32 ft. lbs. (44 Nm).

14. Install the tire and wheel assembly, aligning the balance marks made at removal.

15. Lower the vehicle.

16. Fill the master cylinder reservoir to the proper level using only fresh, clean DOT 3 brake

fluid. Pump the brake pedal firmly to push the pistons back out into operating position and to seat the lining.

17. After the brake pads have been replaced and/or rotors have been refinished, GM recommends that new brake pads be broken in, or "burnished". Use the following procedure:

   a. Make 20 stops from 30 mph using medium to firm brake pedal pressure.

   b. Take care to avoid overheating the brakes.

WITHOUT BUILT-IN PARKING BRAKE MECHANISM

▶ See Figures 34, 35, 36, 37 and 38

1. Using a suction gun, remove approximately ⅔ of the brake fluid from the master cylinder. The reason for this is that the caliper pistons must be pushed back into their bores so the caliper can be removed from the rotor. This could cause the brake fluid to overflow from the reservoir onto painted surfaces or wiring.

2. Raise and safely support the vehicle on safety stands.

3. Mark the relationship of the wheel to the hub so it can later be installed in the same relationship. This helps retain the balance of the rotating assembly.

4. Remove the rear tire and wheel assembly. Install two wheel lug nuts to keep the rotor on the hub.

5. Install a large C-clamp over the brake caliper and against the back of the outboard brake pad. Tighten the C-clamp until the brake caliper

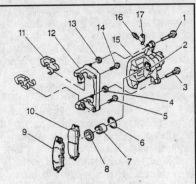

1. Upper Caliper Mounting Bolt
2. Piston Bore
3. Lower Caliper Mounting Bolt
4. Lower Mounting Bolt Boot
5. Caliper Bracket Bolt – Do Not Remove
6. Piston Seal
7. Piston
8. Piston Dust Boot
9. Outer Brake Pad
10. Inner Brake Pad
11. Brake Pad Retainers
12. Caliper Bracket
13. Upper Mounting Bolt Boot
14. Caliper Bracket Bolt – Do Not Remove
15. Caliper Housing
16. Fluid Bleeder Valve
17. Bleeder Valve Dust Cap

93179G19

Fig. 36 Exploded view of a rear disc brake caliper without built-in parking brake— 1998 Oldsmobile Intrigue shown

piston pushes into the brake caliper bore enough to slide the caliper off the rotor. Remove the C-clamp.

6. Remove the upper brake caliper mounting bolt.

7. Rotate the caliper downwards to access the brake pads. Do not remove the brake caliper from the caliper bracket.

8. Remove the brake pads from the caliper bracket. Remove the pad clips (retainers).

To install:

9. To make room for the increased thickness of the new brake pads, the piston must be pushed back all the way into its bore. Insert a block of wood or the old brake pad between the C-clamp and the brake caliper piston to prevent damage to the piston and dust boot. Install the C-clamp over the brake caliper and against the block of wood (or old brake pad). Tighten the C-clamp until the brake caliper piston pushes completely into the brake caliper bore. Remove the C-clamp.

10. Inspect the caliper mounting bolt boots and the piston dust boot for cuts, wear and deterioration. Replace as necessary. When the piston is pushed back into position, air tends to get trapped under the caliper piston dust boot, causing it to bulge outward. Use a small flat-bladed tool to lift the inner edge of the caliper boot next to the piston to release any trapped air. Make sure the piston dust boot is below the level of the piston face. Inspect the caliper bolts for corrosion or damage. If corrosion exists, replace the caliper mounting bolts and the boots. Do not try to polish away corrosion.

11. Install the two brake pad retainers (also called pad clips or anti-rattle springs) to the caliper bracket.

12. Examine the new brake pads. If equipped with a sheetmetal wear indicator, it should be positioned at the leading edge (downward) of the outer pad during forward wheel rotation. Install the brake pads over the pad retainers and onto the caliper bracket.

13. Swing the caliper upward in position around the pads. Use care not to damage the mounting bolt boots when rotating the caliper. Lubricate the mounting bolt and boot with silicone grease. Use care to keep grease off the mounting bolt threads to avoid having the mounting bolt loosen in service. Torque the upper mounting bolt to 33 ft. lbs. (45 Nm).

14. Install the tire and wheel assembly, aligning the balance marks made at removal.

15. Lower the vehicle.

16. Fill the master cylinder reservoir to the proper level using only fresh, clean DOT 3 brake fluid. Pump the brake pedal firmly (¾ of a full stroke) as many times as necessary to push the piston back out into operating position, seat the linings and obtain a firm brake pedal.

> ❋❋ **CAUTION**
>
> **Do not move the vehicle until a firm brake pedal is obtained. Air in the brake system can cause the loss of brakes with possible personal injury.**

17. After the brake pads have been replaced and/or rotors have been refinished, GM recommends that new brake pads be broken in, or "burnished". Use the following procedure:

   a. Make 20 stops from 30 mph using medium to firm brake pedal pressure.

   b. Take care to avoid overheating the brakes.

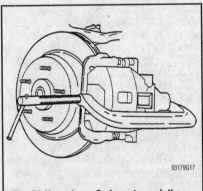

Fig. 34 Use a large C-clamp to push the caliper piston back into its bore

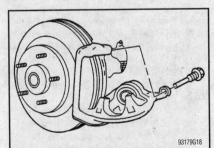

Fig. 35 The caliper does not have to be removed for brake pad replacement. Remove the upper caliper bolt and swing the caliper down for access to the brake pads

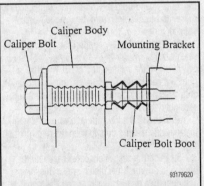

Caliper Body

Caliper Bolt

Mounting Bracket

Caliper Bolt Boot

93179G20

Fig. 37 Inspect the caliper mounting bolts and the rubber boots for deterioration

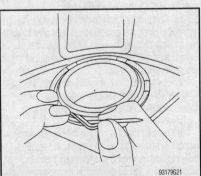

93179G21

Fig. 38 Use a small, flat-bladed tool to carefully lift the piston dust boot to release trapped air

INSPECTION

▶ **See Figure 39**

Brake pads (also called linings) should be inspected every 6,000 miles (9,600 km), anytime the wheels are removed (tire rotation, etc.), and certainly anytime unusual braking action and/or noise is evidenced. The sheetmetal wear indicators used on many brake pads will give a screeching when the brake pads have worn thin, indicating time for brake pad replacement.

Check both ends of the outer brake pad by looking in at each end of the caliper. These are the points at which the highest rate of wear normally occurs. At the same time, check the lining thickness on the inner pad to make sure that it has not worn prematurely. Some inboard brake pads have a thermal layer against the pad, integrally molded with the lining. This extra layer should not be confused with uneven inboard-outboard lining wear. Look down through the inspection hole in the top of the caliper to view the inner pad. Replace the disc brake pads whenever the thickness of any lining is worn to within 0.030 inch (0.762mm) of the pad. In the case of riveted brake pads, replace when the lining is worn to within 0.030 inch (0.762mm) of any rivet head. Replace all disc brake pads at the same time.

➡ **The 0.030 inch (0.762mm) recommended minimum lining thickness is the factory-recommended measurement. Your state's automobile inspection laws may be different, and should be observed.**

The brake pads must have freedom of movement within the brake caliper bracket. If movement is restricted by rust or debris, the brake pads may remain against the rotor after the brake pedal is released. The can contribute to accelerated brake pad wear, brake pulsation and rotor damage.

1. Using a suction gun, remove approximately ⅔ of the brake fluid from the master cylinder.
2. Raise and safely support the vehicle on safety stands.
3. Remove the rear tire and wheel assembly.
4. Install a large C-clamp over the brake caliper and against the back of the outboard brake pad. Tighten the C-clamp until the brake caliper piston pushes into the brake caliper bore as far as possible. Remove the C-clamp.

➡ **The brake pad and the brake caliper should move easily within the brake caliper bracket.**

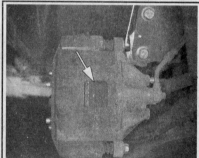

Fig. 39 This opening (arrow) in the brake caliper is for inspecting lining thickness

93179P07

5. Check the outer brake pad for freedom of movement relative to the brake caliper bracket. It should move easily.
6. Use your hands to push the brake caliper inboard as far as possible. If the brake caliper does not move easily, inspect and replace any worn or damaged brake caliper mounting bolts and/or bolt boots.
7. Check the inner brake pad for freedom of movement relative to the brake caliper bracket. If the brake pad movement is restricted, the caliper should be removed for cleaning. Use a wire brush to clean away any rust from the caliper bracket where the pads and retainers contact the bracket. Also clean the ends of the brake pads where they rest on the caliper bracket. Apply a thin coat of silicone grease, GM #18010909 or equivalent, to the brake pad retainers/caliper bracket where the brake pads come in contact with the brake pad retainers and bracket.
8. This same inspection operation should be performed on the opposite side.

Brake Caliper

REMOVAL & INSTALLATION

Front

▶ **See Figures 14, 15, 16 and 21**

1. Using a clean suction gun, remove approximately ⅔ of the brake fluid from the master cylinder. The reason for this is that the caliper pistons must be pushed back into their bores so the caliper can be removed from the rotor. This could cause the brake fluid to overflow from the reservoir onto painted surfaces or wiring.
2. Raise and safely support the vehicle on safety stands.
3. Mark the relationship of the wheel to the hub so it can later be installed in the same relationship. This helps retain the balance of the rotating assembly.
4. Remove the front tire and wheel assembly. Install two wheel lug nuts to keep the rotor on the hub.
5. Push the caliper piston(s) back into their bore(s) to provide clearance between the linings and rotor. Use a large C-clamp over the top of the caliper housing and against the back of the outboard pad. Slowly tighten the C-clamp until the piston(s) are pushed back into the caliper bore(s) enough to slide the caliper off the rotor.
6. Remove the brake hose bolt from the caliper end of the hose. There should be copper seal washers on each side of the hose fitting. Plug the openings in the brake hose to keep the brake fluid reservoir from draining.
7. Remove the caliper slide pin bolts and carefully work the caliper away from the rotor and caliper mounting bracket.
To install:
8. Bottom the piston(s) in the caliper bore(s) using a C-clamp, if new brake pads are to be installed. Use a large C-clamp and a metal plate or wooden block across the face of the piston(s). Take care not to damage the piston(s) or caliper rubber dust boot(s). After bottoming the piston(s), carefully lift the inner edge of the caliper boot(s) next to the

piston(s) and press out any trapped air. The boots must lay flat below the level of the piston face.
9. Install the brake pad using the procedures found in this section.
10. Install the caliper over the rotor and mounting bracket and work into place. Make sure the bushings in the caliper bracket are still in place.
11. Connect the brake hose using new copper seal washers. Tighten the bolt to 32 ft. lbs. (44 Nm).
12. Carefully lubricate the caliper mounting bolts (slide pins) using silicone grease. Do not lubricate the threads or the mounting bolts may tend to work loose. Install the caliper mounting bolts. Use a small flat-blade tool to push the pin boot over the shoulder of the mounting bolt. The pin boot must be securely in the groove of the mounting bolt. Torque the caliper mounting bolts to 80 ft. lbs. (108 Nm).
13. Install the tire and wheel assembly, aligning the balance marks made at removal.
14. Lower the vehicle.
15. Fill the master cylinder reservoir to the proper level using only fresh, clean DOT 3 brake fluid. Pump the brake pedal firmly to push the pistons back out into operating position and to seat the lining.
16. Bleed the brake system using the procedures found at the end of this section.

Rear Disc Brake Calipers

WITH BUILT-IN PARKING BRAKE MECHANISM

▶ **See Figures 26, 27, 29 and 33**

1. Using a suction gun, remove approximately ⅔ of the brake fluid from the master cylinder. The reason for this is that the caliper pistons must be pushed back into their bores so the caliper can be removed from the rotor. This could cause the brake fluid to overflow from the reservoir onto painted surfaces or wiring.
2. Raise and safely support the vehicle on safety stands.
3. Mark the relationship of the wheel to the hub so it can later be installed in the same relationship. This helps retain the balance of the rotating assembly.
4. Remove the rear tire and wheel assembly. Install two wheel lug nuts to keep the rotor on the hub.
5. Disconnect the brake line to the caliper. Plug the opening so all of the brake fluid does not drain from the master cylinder reservoir.
6. Remove the parking brake cable from the parking brake lever. Lift up on one end of the cable spring clip to free the end of the cable from the lever.
7. Remove the caliper slide pin bolts and carefully lift the caliper from its bracket.
To install:
8. Bottom the piston into the caliper bore noting the following:
   a. There is a special spanner-type tool designed to fit in the piston slots. This allows you to turn the piston and thread it into the caliper, retracting it. Use care if using a substitute tool. Careful work with suitable pliers may enable you to turn the piston back into its bore.
   b. After bottoming the piston, lift the inner edge of the dust boot, next to the piston, and press out any trapped air. The boot must lay flat.

9. Install the caliper to the mounting bracket, noting the following:

    a. If not replaced, remove the caliper mounting bolt boot from the caliper and install the small end over the tubular metal sleeve (installed on the caliper bracket). This is to prevent cutting the bolt boot when sliding the caliper body onto the sleeve.

    b. Hold the caliper in position and start over the end of the sleeve. As the caliper approaches the boot, work the large end of the boot into the caliper groove. Then push the caliper fully onto the mounting bolt.

    c. Pivot the caliper down, using care not to damage the piston dust boot on the inboard brake pad. Compress the mounting bolt boot by hand as the caliper moves into position to prevent boot damage.

    d. After the caliper is in position, recheck the installation of the pad clips. If necessary, use a small flat-bladed tool to re-seat or center the pad clips on the mounting bracket.

    e. Tighten the mounting bolts to 20 ft. lbs. (27 Nm).

10. Install the cable support bracket. Connect the parking brake cable to the caliper lever. Lift up on the cable spring clip and work the end of the parking brake cable into the notch in lever.

11. Connect the brake fluid line. Use new copper washers, if equipped. Tighten the brake hose bolt to 32 ft. lbs. (44 Nm).

12. Install the tire and wheel assembly, aligning the balance marks made at removal.

13. Lower the vehicle.

14. Fill the master cylinder reservoir to the proper level using only fresh, clean DOT 3 brake fluid. Pump the brake pedal firmly to push the pistons back out into operating position and to seat the lining.

15. Bleed the brake system using the procedures found at the end of this section.

WITHOUT BUILT-IN PARKING BRAKE MECHANISM

♦ **See Figures 34, 35, 36 and 37**

1. Using a suction gun, remove approximately ⅔ of the brake fluid from the master cylinder. The reason for this is that the caliper pistons must be pushed back into their bores so the caliper can be removed from the rotor. This could cause the brake fluid to overflow from the reservoir onto painted surfaces or wiring.

2. Raise and safely support the vehicle on safety stands.

3. Mark the relationship of the wheel to the hub so it can later be installed in the same relationship. This helps retain the balance of the rotating assembly.

4. Remove the rear tire and wheel assembly. Install two wheel lug nuts to keep the rotor on the hub.

5. Install a large C-clamp over the brake caliper and against the back of the outboard brake pad. Tighten the C-clamp until the brake caliper piston pushes into the brake caliper bore enough to slide the caliper off the rotor. Remove the C-clamp.

6. Disconnect the brake line to the caliper. Plug the opening so all of the brake fluid does not drain from the master cylinder reservoir.

7. Remove the brake caliper mounting bolts

8. Remove the caliper from the mounting bracket.

To install:

9. Install the caliper upward in position. Use care not to damage the mounting bolt boots. Lubricate the mounting bolt and boot with silicone grease. Use care to keep grease off the mounting bolt threads to avoid having the mounting bolt loosen in service. Torque the mounting bolts to 33 ft. lbs. (45 Nm).

10. Install the brake line to the caliper. Use new copper seal washers, if equipped. Torque the brake hose bolt to 40 ft. lbs. (54 Nm).

11. Install the tire and wheel assembly, aligning the balance marks made at removal.

12. Lower the vehicle.

13. Fill the master cylinder reservoir to the proper level using only fresh, clean DOT 3 brake fluid. Pump the brake pedal firmly (¾ of a full stroke) as many times as necessary to push the piston back out into operating position, seat the linings and obtain a firm brake pedal.

14. Bleed the brake system using the procedures found at the end of this section.

✳✳ CAUTION

Do not move the vehicle until a firm brake pedal is obtained. Air in the brake system can cause the loss of brakes with possible personal injury.

OVERHAUL

The decision to overhaul a brake caliper depends on the condition of the caliper and its components, and parts cost and availability. In many cases, a rebuilt brake caliper may be available at slightly more than the cost of overhaul parts, especially if the piston must be replaced. Many professional technicians simply exchange a worn out caliper for a rebuilt unit. This saves time and gets the vehicle back into service in the shortest amount of time. In addition, the rebuilt caliper generally has to pass a factory quality test so there is at least some sort of guarantee in case it leaks or there is some problem with the unit.

If the caliper is to be overhauled, compressed air is almost an absolute necessity to get the piston(s) out of the caliper body without damaging either component.

Front

♦ **See Figures 40 thru 46**

The following sequence shows a typical dual-piston front caliper being disassembled for inspection and overhaul. The overhaul procedure for a single piston front caliper and a rear caliper without a built-in parking brake mechanism overhaul is similar.

1. The first step, even before removing the caliper from the vehicle, is to attempt to open the bleeder valve screw. This fitting is often seized in place in the caliper, especially on high-mileage vehicles or vehicles with aluminum brake calipers and steel bleeder screws. It would be wasted effort to disassemble, clean and overhaul a caliper only to find that it can't be bled because the bleeder screw won't open. It is also very common for a seized

bleeder valve screw to snap off when attempts are made to loosen it. Getting the remainder of a seized bleeder screw out of a caliper without damaging the caliper body is very difficult and a job for an automotive machine shop. The fee to attempt to extract a broken bleeder screw will likely exceed the cost of a rebuilt or even new caliper. Try to open the bleeder screw first. If it loosens and brake fluid does flow from the bleeder screw, the caliper may be suitable for an overhaul. The final decision would depend on the condition of the piston bore(s) and he overall condition of the caliper. Remove the caliper using the procedures found in this section.

2. With the caliper removed from the vehicle, place it on a clean work surface. Brake fluid in the caliper will tend to run out onto the work surface, where it can damage painted components. Placing some cardboard or other disposable covering on the work surface may save time at cleanup.

3. Perform a visual inspection. If the caliper has an obvious crack or shows signs of collision damage, it may not be reusable. Check the tapped openings where the mounting bolts thread. In some cases, the threads can be damaged from corrosion or were cross-threaded during previous brake work. Sometimes threaded inserts can be used to save a caliper, but generally, if the caliper body shows signs of abuse, it should be replaced.

✳✳ CAUTION

Do not place your fingers in front of the caliper piston(s) in an attempt to catch or `protect' the piston(s) when applying compressed air. The piston(s) come out with a surprising amount of force and can serious injure your fingers. In addition, wear eye protection because the brake fluid in the caliper will tend to spray when shop air is applied.

4. Use clean shop cloths to pad the inside of the brake caliper during piston removal. Use just enough shop air to ease the piston(s) out of the bore(s). If the piston(s) is simply blown out, even with padding provided, it may be damaged. Dual piston calipers must have the pistons removed evenly and at the same rate. If one piston pops out before the other, it will be difficult to built enough pressure to remove the other piston. In the event one piston is seized and will not break free, is may be necessary to block the other piston with a piece of wood or C-clamp until the stuck piston can be freed. When working on dual-piston calipers, some technicians use a block of wood to limit the pistons' travel. Once the technician is assured that both pistons are moving, thinner blocks are used, allowing the pistons to come out evenly until both pistons are out. The piston(s) will come out through the piston dust boot(s).

5. Inspect the pistons for scoring, nicks corrosion, and/or worn or damaged chrome plating. Replace the piston, if any of these conditions are found.

6. Remove the caliper boots, being careful not to scratch the housing bore.

✳✳ WARNING

Do not use a metal tool to remove the piston seals. Metal tools may damage the caliper bores or piston seal grooves.

Fig. 40 On dual piston calipers, it is important not to completely remove one piston before the other one is freed

Fig. 41 Do NOT put your fingers in front of the pistons when easing them out with compressed air!

Fig. 42 Remove the pistons from the bores

Fig. 43 When removing the caliper boots, be careful not to scratch the bores

Fig. 44 Never use a metal tool to remove the piston seals

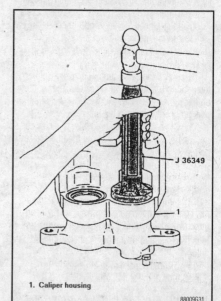

1. Caliper housing

Fig. 45 Use a seal driver or a similar tool to seat the dust boots into the caliper housing

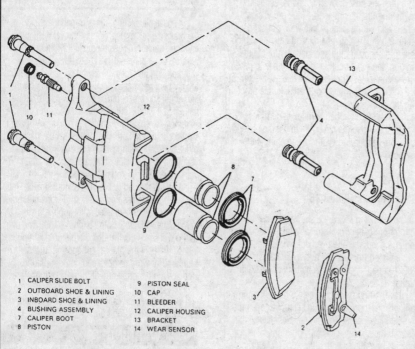

1 CALIPER SLIDE BOLT	9 PISTON SEAL
2 OUTBOARD SHOE & LINING	10 CAP
3 INBOARD SHOE & LINING	11 BLEEDER
4 BUSHING ASSEMBLY	12 CALIPER HOUSING
7 CALIPER BOOT	13 BRACKET
8 PISTON	14 WEAR SENSOR

Fig. 46 Exploded view of a typical dual piston front disc brake caliper assembly

7. Remove the piston seals from the groove in the caliper bore, using a small wood or plastic tool. These seals are usually "square profile". O-rings.

8. Inspect the caliper bores, pistons and mounting threads for scoring or excessive wear.

9. Use crocus cloth (an extremely fine abrasive cloth) to polish out light corrosion from the piston and bore. If the crocus cloth cannot remove the corrosion, do not use a more coarse abrasive. The caliper must be replaced.

10. Clean all parts with denatured alcohol and dry with compressed air.

11. Lubricate the threads of the bleeder valve with a thin coat of anti-seize compound and install just finger tight. It will be final-tightened after the hydraulic system is bled.

12. Lubricate the new piston seals and bore with clean brake fluid or brake assembly lubricant (a special lubricant found in some brands of brake overhaul parts kits).

13. Install the new seals into the caliper bore grooves, making sure they are not twisted.

14. Lubricate the piston bore.

15. Install the piston(s) and dust boot(s) into

the bores of the calipers. Push the piston(s) to the bottom of the bores.

16. Seat the dust boots in the housing using tool J 36349, or equivalent seal installation driver.

17. Install the caliper onto the vehicle, as outlined earlier.

18. Properly bleed the brake system as outlined in this section.

Rear

▶ **See Figures 47, 48, 49, 50 and 51**

1. Remove the rear caliper using the procedures found in this section.

2. With the caliper removed from the vehicle, place it on a clean work surface. Brake fluid in the caliper will tend to run out onto the work surface, where it can damage painted components. Placing some cardboard or other disposable covering on the work surface may save time at cleanup.

3. Perform a visual inspection. If the caliper has an obvious crack or shows signs of collision damage, it may not be reusable. Check the tapped openings where the mounting bolts thread. In some cases, the threads can be damaged from corrosion or were cross-threaded during previous brake work. Sometimes threaded inserts can be used to save a caliper, but generally, if the caliper body shows signs of abuse, it should be replaced.

> **✳✳ CAUTION**
>
> **Do not place your fingers in front of the caliper piston in an attempt to catch or 'protect' the piston when applying compressed air. The piston come out with a surprising amount of force and can serious injure your fingers. In addition, wear eye protection because the brake fluid in the caliper will tend to spray when shop air is applied.**

4. Use clean shop cloths to pad the inside of the brake caliper during piston removal. Use just enough shop air to ease the piston out of the bore.

If the piston is simply blown out, even with padding provided, it may be damaged. The piston will come out through the piston dust boot.

a. An alternate method for piston removal on these calipers is to use a spanner-type tool (or careful work with pliers) in the slots in the end of the piston to thread the piston out of the caliper.

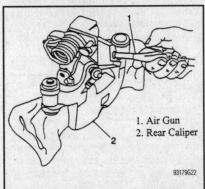

1. Air Gun
2. Rear Caliper

93179G22

Fig. 48 Using an air gun to coax the piston from the caliper bore

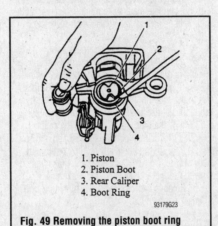

1. Piston
2. Piston Boot
3. Rear Caliper
4. Boot Ring

93179G23

Fig. 49 Removing the piston boot ring

1. Rear Caliper
2. Stopper Pin
3. Lever Return Spring
4. Parking Brake Lever

93179G24

Fig. 50 Removing/installing the parking brake lever return spring

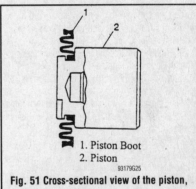

1. Piston Boot
2. Piston

93179G25

Fig. 51 Cross-sectional view of the piston, showing the proper position of the dust boot on the piston

5. Inspect the piston for scoring, nicks corrosion, and/or worn or damaged chrome plating. Replace the piston, if any of these conditions are found.

6. Remove the caliper boot, being careful not to scratch the housing bore. Look for a boot retaining ring. Use a small prying tool to pry up one end of the boot ring. Work the boot ring out of the caliper groove.

> **✳✳ WARNING**
>
> **Do not use a metal tool to remove the piston seals. Metal tools may damage the caliper bores or piston seal grooves.**

7. Remove the piston seal from the groove in the caliper bore, using a small wood or plastic tool. These seals are usually "square profile" O-rings.

8. Remove the bleeder valve screw.

9. Remove the lever return spring only if replacement is required. Use a small prytool to disengage the return spring from the parking brake lever. Then unhook the spring from the stopper pin.

10. Remove the caliper mounting bolt (also called a slider pin) boots and sleeves from the caliper.

11. Inspect the caliper bores, pistons and mounting threads for scoring or excessive wear.

12. Use crocus cloth (an extremely fine abrasive cloth) to polish out light corrosion from the piston and bore. If the crocus cloth cannot remove the corrosion, do not use a more coarse abrasive. The caliper must be replaced.

13. Clean all parts with denatured alcohol and

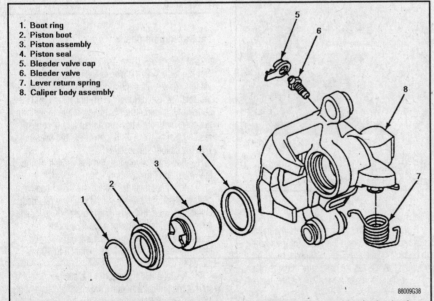

1. Boot ring
2. Piston boot
3. Piston assembly
4. Piston seal
5. Bleeder valve cap
6. Bleeder valve
7. Lever return spring
8. Caliper body assembly

88009G38

Fig. 47 Exploded view of a rear disc brake caliper equipped with built-in parking brake mechanism

dry with compressed air. Inspect all parts for damage and replace as necessary.

14. Lubricate the pin sleeve with silicone grease. Install the pin bolt and pin sleeve to the caliper support. Tighten the bolt to 20 ft. lbs. (27 Nm).

15. Lubricate the sleeve boot with silicone grease to ease installation. Compress the lip sleeve boot and push it all the way through the caliper body until the lip emerges and seats on the inboard face of the caliper ear.

16. Lubricate the sleeve with silicone grease to ease assembly. Push the bolt sleeve in through the lip end of the boot until the boot seats in the sleeve groove at the other end.

17. Install the bolt boot onto the caliper body.

18. Install the pin boot over the pin sleeve (installed on the caliper support).

19. If removed, install a new lever return spring. Position the spring with the hook end around the stopper pin, then pry the other end of the spring over the lever.

20. Lightly lubricate the bleeder valve screw with anti-seize compound and install finger tight. Final tightening will be done after the system is bled.

21. Lubricate a new piston seal with clean brake fluid, then install the seal. Make sure the seal is not twisted.

22. Install the piston boot onto the piston assembly.

23. Lubricate the piston assembly with clean brake fluid, then install the piston and boot into the bore of the caliper body assembly. Start the piston in by hand, then thread it into the bottom of the caliper bore using a suitable spanner-type tool into the slots in the end of the piston assembly.

24. Install the boot ring. Make sure the outside edge of the piston boot is smoothly seated in the counterbore or the caliper body assembly. Work the boot ring into the groove near the open end of the caliper bore, being careful not to pinch the piston boot between the boot ring and the caliper body.

25. After installing the ring, lift the inner edge of the boot next to the piston assembly and press out any trapped air. The boot must lie flat.

26. Install the caliper as outlined earlier in this section. Make sure to properly bleed the brake system.

Brake Rotors

It should not be necessary to refinish the brake rotors when performing routine brake maintenance such as replacing worn disc brake pads. Refinish a rotor only if a pulsation is felt in the brake pedal and/or there is a scoring of the rotor greater than 0.060 inch (1.5 mm).

All brake rotors have a minimum thickness dimension number cast into them. This dimension is the minimum wear dimension and not a refinish dimension. Do not use a brake rotor that, after refinishing, will not meet the specification shown on the rotor. Always replace it with a new rotor.

➡️ It is extremely important that a brake rotor have very little lateral runout. It must turn true or the rotor will wobble on the wheel hub. This wobble will force the brake caliper piston to rapidly pulse in and out of the caliper. This results in a pulsating feel to the brake pedal

when applied. Whenever a rotor has been separated from the wheel bearing flange, clean any rust or contaminants from the wheel flange and brake rotor mating surfaces. Even relatively small particles of dirt, rust or other foreign material between the face of the wheel hub and the back face of the brake rotor is enough to cause problems. Failure to keep the metal contact mating surfaces clean may result in increased lateral runout of the rotor and brake pulsation.

REMOVAL & INSTALLATION

▶ See Figure 52

1. Using a suction gun, remove approximately ⅔ of the brake fluid from the master cylinder. The reason for this is that the caliper pistons must be pushed back into their bores so the caliper can be removed from the rotor. This could cause the brake fluid to overflow from the reservoir onto painted surfaces or wiring.

2. Raise and safely support the vehicle on safety stands.

3. Mark the relationship of the wheel to the hub so it can later be installed in the same relationship. This helps retain the balance of the rotating assembly.

4. Remove the tire and wheel assembly.

5. It is not necessary to remove the brake lines or parking brake cable (as equipped) when removing a caliper to service the brake rotors. It is necessary to use care not to damage the brake hose by letting the caliper hang. The weight of the caliper can damage the brake hose. Remove the caliper using the procedures found in this section and suspend it from the strut with a wire hook or suitable piece of wire. Do NOT disconnect the brake hose or allow the caliper to hang from the brake line.

6. Remove the rotor assembly by simply pulling it off the hub.

Fig. 52 The rotor is removed by sliding it straight off the lug studs

To install:

7. Clean all parts well. Make sure the metal contact surfaces between the brake rotor and the hub bearing flange are clean. Sandpaper and/or wirebrush these areas to make sure they are clean.

8. Install the brake rotor over the hub assembly.

9. Install the brake caliper as outlined in this section.

10. Install the wheel and tire assembly.

11. Carefully lower the vehicle, then fill the master cylinder reservoir to the FULL level with the correct type of DOT 3 brake fluid from a clean, unsealed container.

12. Firmly depress the brake pedal three times before moving the vehicle. This reseats the brake pads and moves the caliper pistons back to their operating positions. Do not attempt to move the vehicle until a firm brake pedal has been established.

INSPECTION

▶ See Figure 53

Thickness Variation Check

The thickness variation can be checked by measuring the thickness of the rotor at four or more points. All of the measurements must be made at the same distance from the edge of the rotor. GM recommends using a micrometer that reads in ten-thousandths of an inch. They feel rotor condition is that critical. A rotor the varies by more than 0.005 inch (0.013 mm) can cause a pulsation in the brake pedal. If these measurement are excessive, the rotor should be refinished or replaced.

Fig. 53 A rotor with grooves this deep will have to be resurfaced or, more likely, replaced

Lateral Runout Check

GM recommends that the best way to check lateral runout is with the wheels still installed on the vehicle. This gives a much more accurate reading of the Total Indicated Runout (TIR) under real braking conditions. If equipment is not available to perform the check with the wheels installed, the next best reading can be made with the wheels removed but with the caliper still installed.

1. Raise and safely support the vehicle. Remove the wheel and tire assembly.

2. It is important that, since the wheel has been removed, that the brake rotor be properly retained. Install the wheel lug nuts (some technicians install them backwards to present a flat face to the rotor, depending on the design of the lug nut). Torque them just as if the wheel were installed to 100 ft. lbs. (140 Nm).

3. Install a dial indicator to the steering knuckle so that the indicator button contacts the rotor about 1 inch (25mm) from the rotor edge.

4. Zero the dial indicator.

5. Turn the rotor one complete revolution and observe the total indicated runout.

6. The Total Indicated Runout (TIR) must not exceed 0.003 inch (0.080mm).

7. If the TIR exceeds specifications, have the rotor refinished or replaced.

Please note that in some cases, excessive lateral runout of the rotor can be improved by indexing the rotor on the hub, one or two bolt positions from the original position. If the lateral runout cannot be corrected by indexing the rotor, remove the rotor and check the wheel hub for excessive lateral runout or

looseness (perhaps the wheel bearings are worn). If the hub lateral runout exceeds 0.0015 inch (0.040 mm), then replace the hub. If the lateral runout of the hub is within specifications, then rotor will have to be refinished at an automotive machine shop or replaced with a new part.

DRUM BRAKES

♦ **See Figure 54**

Some GM W-Body vehicles covered by this manual use an advanced leading/trailing shoe design drum brake on the rear wheels. The parts count is greatly reduced and the operation and servicing is designed to be simpler than other drum brake designs.

The rear drum brake used on some of the W-Body vehicles uses a single universal spring to hold both the shoe and lining assemblies to the backing plate and also acts as the retractor spring for both brake shoes. Force from the brake shoes is transferred through the fixed anchor and backing plate to the axle flange. Adjustment is automatic and occurs on any service brake application.

➡**Use care when servicing this brake assembly as the large spring can pinch fingers.**

Please note that with this design, it is normal for the leading (front) shoe to wear at a faster rate than the trailing (rear) shoe. Do not switch the position of the brake shoes that have been in service as this may render the self-adjustment feature inoperative and may result in increased pedal travel.

✳✳ CAUTION

Some brake shoes contain asbestos, which has been determined to be a cancer causing agent. Never clean the brake surfaces with compressed air. Avoid inhaling any dust from any brake surface. When cleaning brake surfaces, use a commercially available brake cleaning fluid.

Brake Drums

REMOVAL & INSTALLATION

♦ **See Figure 55**

1. Raise and safely support the vehicle with safety stands.

2. Mark the relationship of the wheel to the axle flange to help maintain wheel balance after assembly.

3. Remove the tire and wheel assembly.

4. Mark the relationship of the brake drum to the axle flange.

➡**Do not pry against the splash shield that surrounds the backing plate in an attempt to**

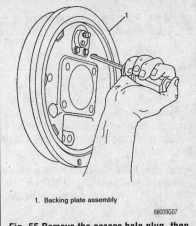

1. Backing plate assembly

88009G07

Fig. 55 Remove the access hole plug, then back off the adjusting screw

free the drum. This will bend the splash shield.

5. If difficulty is encountered in removing the brake drum, the following steps may be of assistance.

    a. Make sure the parking brake is released.

    b. Back off the parking brake cable adjustment.

    c. Remove the access hole plug from the backing plate.

    d. Using a screwdriver, back off the adjusting screw.

    e. Install the access hole plug to prevent dirt or contamination from entering the drum brake assembly.

    f. Use a small amount of penetrating oil applied around the brake drum pilot hole.

    g. Carefully remove the brake drum from the vehicle.

6. After removing the brake drum, it should be checked for the following:

    a. Inspect for cracks and deep grooves.

    b. Inspect for out of round and taper.

    c. Inspecting for hot spots (black in color).

To install:

7. Install the brake drum onto the vehicle aligning the reference marks on the axle flange.

8. Install the tire and wheel assembly and hand-tighten the lug nuts.

9. Carefully lower the vehicle, then tighten the lug nuts to 100 ft. lbs. (140 Nm).

10. Road test the vehicle for proper brake operation.

INSPECTION

Pulsation in the brake pedal is usually corrected by servicing the front brakes. Service the rear brakes only if the problem persists. When the brake

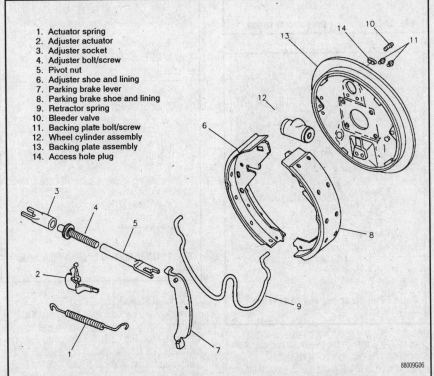

1. Actuator spring
2. Adjuster actuator
3. Adjuster socket
4. Adjuster bolt/screw
5. Pivot nut
6. Adjuster shoe and lining
7. Parking brake lever
8. Parking brake shoe and lining
9. Retractor spring
10. Bleeder valve
11. Backing plate bolt/screw
12. Wheel cylinder assembly
13. Backing plate assembly
14. Access hole plug

88009G06

Fig. 54 Exploded view of the rear drum brake system used on some W-Body vehicles

drums are removed, thoroughly clean and inspect them for cracks, scores, deep grooves, out-of-round and taper. Light scoring of the drum not exceeding 0.020 inch (0.51mm) in depth will not affect brake operation.

Inspect the brake drum for excessive taper and out-of-round. When measuring a drum for out-of-round, taper and wear, take measurements at the open and closed edges of the machined surfaces and at right angles to each other.

Brake Shoes

INSPECTION

1. Remove the wheel and drum.
2. Inspect the shoes for proper thickness. The lining should be at least 1/32 inch (0.8 mm) above the rivet head for riveted brakes and 1/16 inch (1.6 mm) above the mounting surface for bonded brake linings.

➡ Your state inspection brake lining thickness minimum specification may be different, and should be observed if thicker than these specifications.

3. Inspect the linings for even wear, cracking and scoring. Replace as necessary.

REMOVAL & INSTALLATION

▶ **See Figures 56 thru 61**

1. Raise and safely support the vehicle with safety stands.
2. Mark the relationship of the wheel to the axle flange to help maintain wheel balance after assembly.
3. Remove the rear tire and wheel assembly.
4. Remove the brake drum, as outlined earlier in this section.
5. Using tool J-38400, or an equivalent brake spanner and remover, remove the actuator spring from the adjuster lever. Use care not to distort the spring when removing it.

❋❋ CAUTION

During the following steps when removing the retractor spring from either shoe and lining assembly, do not over stretch the spring. This will reduce its effectiveness. Keep fingers away from retractor spring to prevent your fingers from being pinched between the spring and shoe web or spring and the backing plate.

6. Lift the end of the retractor spring from the adjuster shoe assembly. Insert the hook end of the J-38400 between the retractor spring and the shoe. Pry slightly to remove the spring end from the hole in the shoe.
7. Pry the end of the retractor spring toward the axle with the flat end of the tool until the spring snaps down off the shoe web onto the backing plate.
8. Remove the adjuster shoe and lining assembly, adjuster actuator and adjusting bolt/screw assembly.
9. Disconnect the parking brake lever from the

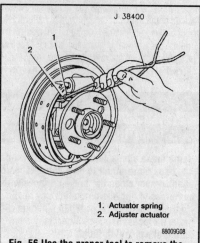

1. Actuator spring
2. Adjuster actuator

88009G08

Fig. 56 Use the proper tool to remove the actuator spring

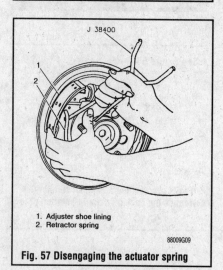

1. Adjuster shoe lining
2. Retractor spring

88009G09

Fig. 57 Disengaging the actuator spring

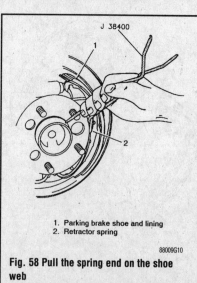

1. Parking brake shoe and lining
2. Retractor spring

88009G10

Fig. 58 Pull the spring end on the shoe web

shoe. DO NOT remove the parking brake lever from the cable end unless it is being replaced.

10. Using J-38400 or the equivalent, lift the end of the retractor spring from the adjuster shoe assembly.

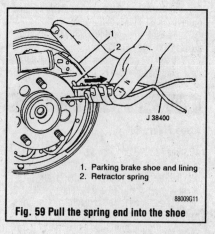

1. Parking brake shoe and lining
2. Retractor spring

88009G11

Fig. 59 Pull the spring end into the shoe

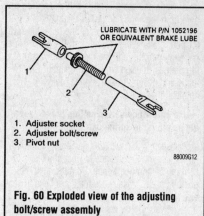

LUBRICATE WITH P/N 1052196 OR EQUIVALENT BRAKE LUBE

1. Adjuster socket
2. Adjuster bolt/screw
3. Pivot nut

88009G12

Fig. 60 Exploded view of the adjusting bolt/screw assembly

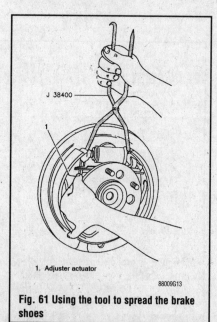

1. Adjuster actuator

88009G13

Fig. 61 Using the tool to spread the brake shoes

11. Insert the hook end of the J-38400 or the equivalent between the retractor spring and the shoe. Pry slightly to remove the spring end from the hole in the shoe. Pry the end of the retractor spring toward the axle with the flat end of the tool until the spring snaps down off the shoe web onto the backing plate.

12. Remove the parking brake shoe and lining assembly.

13. If necessary, remove the retractor spring from the anchor plate. If only the shoe and linings are being replaced, it is not necessary to remove the retractor spring.

To install:

14. Clean all the brake spring completely with brake solvent and allow to air dry.

15. Disassemble, clean and lubricate the adjuster screw. Once lubricated, reassemble.

16. Clean the backing plate and after it is dry apply a thin coat of brake grease to the brake shoe contact points on the backing plate.

17. Position the brake shoe, that connects to the parking brake lever, on the backing plate.

18. Using J-38400 or the equivalent, pull the end of the retractor spring up to rest on the web of the shoe. Pull the end of the retractor spring up until it snaps into the slot in the brake shoe.

19. Connect the parking brake lever.

20. Install the remaining shoe and the adjuster screw assembly.

21. Position the brake shoe, using J-38400 or the equivalent, pull the end of the retractor spring up to rest on the web of the shoe. Pull the end of the retractor spring up until it snaps into the slot in the brake shoe.

22. Using J-38400 or the equivalent, spread the brake shoes and work the adjuster screw into position.

23. Install the actuator spring with the U-shaped end going through the web.

24. Install the brake drum, as outlined earlier in this section.

25. Install the tire and wheel assembly and hand-tighten the lug nuts.

26. Adjust the brakes.

27. Carefully lower the vehicle, then tighten the lug nuts to 100 ft. lbs. (140 Nm).

28. Road test the vehicle for proper brake operation.

Wheel Cylinder

REMOVAL & INSTALLATION

▶ **See Figure 62**

1. Raise and safely support the vehicle.
2. Remove the rear tire and wheel assembly.
3. Remove the brake drum, as outlined earlier in this section.
4. Using tool J-38400, or an equivalent brake spanner and remover, remove the actuator spring from the adjuster lever. Use care not to distort the spring when removing it.

➡**During the following steps when removing the retractor spring from either shoe and lining assembly, do not over stretch the spring. This will reduce its effectiveness.**

✳✳ CAUTION

Keep fingers away from retractor spring to prevent fingers from being pinched between the spring and shoe web or spring and the backing plate.

5. Remove the bleeder screw to gain access to the brake line.
6. Disconnect and cap or plug the wheel cylin-

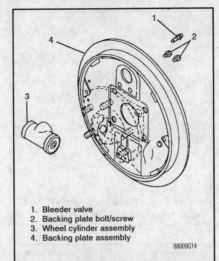

1. Bleeder valve
2. Backing plate bolt/screw
3. Wheel cylinder assembly
4. Backing plate assembly

88009G14

Fig. 62 The wheel cylinder is mounted to the brake backing plate

der brake line to prevent fluid loss and/or brake system contamination.

7. Spread the upper half of the brake shoes and remove the wheel cylinder retaining bolts and remove the wheel cylinder.

To install:

8. Apply Loctite® Master Gasket Maker or equivalent sealer to the wheel cylinder shoulder face that contacts the backing plate.

9. Position the wheel cylinder assembly on the backing plate and hold into place.

10. Install attaching bolts and tighten to 110 inch lbs. (12 Nm).

11. Connect the brake line to the wheel cylinder. Tighten to 12 ft. lbs. (17 Nm).

12. Bleed the wheel cylinder using the recommended procedure.

13. Tighten the bleeder valve to 62 inch lbs. (7 Nm). Do not overtighten.

14. Clean all the brake spring completely with brake solvent and allow to air dry.

15. Install the actuator spring and adjust the brake shoes.

16. Install the brake drum, then the tire and wheel assembly.

17. Add DOT 3 brake fluid to the master cylinder if needed and road test to verify proper brake system performance.

OVERHAUL

▶ **See Figures 63 thru 73**

Wheel cylinder overhaul kits may be available, but often at little or no savings over a reconditioned wheel cylinder. It often makes sense with these components to substitute a new or reconditioned part instead of attempting an overhaul.

If no replacement is available, or you would prefer to overhaul your wheel cylinders, the following procedure may be used. When rebuilding and installing wheel cylinders, avoid getting any contaminants into the system. Always use clean, new, high quality brake fluid. If dirty or improper fluid has been used, it will be necessary to drain the entire system, flush the system with proper brake fluid, replace all rubber components, then refill and bleed the system.

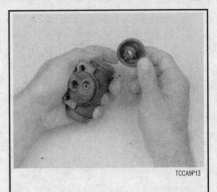

TCCA9P13

Fig. 63 Remove the outer boots from the wheel cylinder

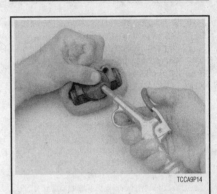

TCCA9P14

Fig. 64 Compressed air can be used to remove the pistons and seals

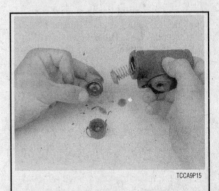

TCCA9P15

Fig. 65 Remove the pistons, cup seals and spring from the cylinder

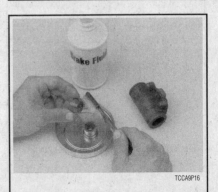

TCCA9P16

Fig. 66 Use brake fluid and a soft brush to clean the pistons . . .

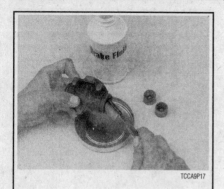

Fig. 67 . . . and the bore of the wheel cylinder

1. Remove the wheel cylinder from the vehicle and place on a clean workbench.

2. First remove and discard the old rubber boots, then withdraw the pistons. Piston cylinders are equipped with seals and a spring assembly, all located behind the pistons in the cylinder bore.

3. Remove the remaining inner components, seals and spring assembly. Compressed air may be useful in removing these components. If no compressed air is available, be VERY careful not to score the wheel cylinder bore when removing parts from it. Discard all components for which replacements were supplied in the rebuild kit.

4. Wash the cylinder and metal parts in denatured alcohol or clean brake fluid.

❋❋ WARNING

Never use a mineral-based solvent such as gasoline, kerosene or paint thinner for cleaning purposes. These solvents will swell rubber components and quickly deteriorate them.

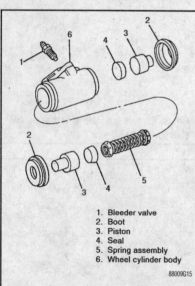

1. Bleeder valve
2. Boot
3. Piston
4. Seal
5. Spring assembly
6. Wheel cylinder body

88009G15

Fig. 68 Exploded view of the wheel cylinder components

Fig. 69 Once cleaned and inspected, the wheel cylinder is ready for assembly

Fig. 70 Lubricate the cup seals with brake fluid

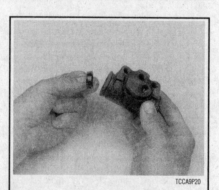

Fig. 71 Install the spring, then the cup seals in the bore

5. Allow the parts to air dry or use compressed air. Do not use rags for cleaning, since lint will remain in the cylinder bore.

6. Inspect the piston and replace it if it shows scratches.

7. Lubricate the cylinder bore and seals using clean brake fluid.

8. Position the spring assembly.

9. Install the inner seals, then the pistons.

10. Insert the new boots into the counterbores by hand. Do not lubricate the boots.

11. Install the wheel cylinder.

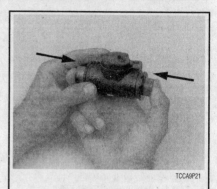

Fig. 72 Lightly lubricate the pistons, then install them

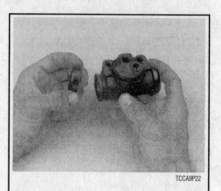

Fig. 73 The boots can now be installed over the wheel cylinder ends

Brake Backing Plate

REMOVAL & INSTALLATION

1. Raise and safely support the vehicle.

2. Mark the relationship of the wheel to the axle flange to help maintain wheel balance after assembly.

3. Remove the tire and wheel assembly.

4. Remove the brake drum, as outlined earlier in this section.

5. Remove the wheel cylinder, as outlined earlier in this section.

6. Disconnect the parking brake cable from the backing plate.

7. Remove the hub and bearing assembly, as outlined in Section 8 of this vehicle.

8. Remove the brake backing plate from the vehicle.

To install:

9. Install the brake backing plate.

10. Install the hub and bearing assembly, as outlined in Section 8 of this manual.

11. Connect the parking brake cable to the backing plate.

12. Install the wheel cylinder, as outlined earlier in this section.

13. Properly bleed the brake hydraulic system, as outlined later in this section.

PARKING BRAKE

Cables

This vehicle is equipped with coated parking brake cable assemblies. The wire strand is coated with a clear plastic material which slides over plastic seals inside the conduit end fittings. This is for corrosion protection and reduced parking brake effort.

Handling of these cables during servicing of the parking brake system requires extra care. Damage to the plastic coating will reduce corrosion protection and if the damaged area passes through the seal, increased parking brake effort could result. Contact of the coating with sharp-edged tools, or with sharp surfaces of the vehicle underbody should be avoided. Do not lubricate the parking brake cables. Lubrication may damage the plastic coating on the parking brake cables.

To prevent damage to the threaded parking brake adjusting rod when servicing the parking brake, the following is recommended: before attempting to turn the adjusting nut, clean the exposed threads on each side of the nut; lubricate the threads of the adjusting rod before turning the nut.

If any one of the parking brake cables has been replaced, it is necessary to pre-stretch the new cable before adjusting the parking brake. To do this, apply the parking brake pedal several times. Fully release it each time. The parking brake pedal assembly, located on the dash panel left of the service brake pedal, is a push-to-release type mechanism which is APPLIED by depressing the pedal once and RELEASED by depressing the pedal again. No release handle is used.

✳✳ WARNING

This is a parking brake NOT a emergency brake. It is designed to hold the vehicle on a flat or an incline and will not stop a vehicle in motion.

REMOVAL & INSTALLATION

▶ **See figures 74, 75, 76, and 77**

Front Cable

1. Remove the lower door sill trim plate.
2. Remove the driver's side sound insulator panel.
3. Fold back the carpeting to expose the parking brake cable.
4. Raise and safely support the vehicle.
5. Loosen the parking brake cable at the equalizer.
6. Pull the front cable at the connector clip and attach the loop of the shear strap to the hook of the parking brake ratcheting.
7. Remove the parking brake front cable at the connector clip.
8. Remove the parking brake front cable clip from the underbody bracket using special tool J 37043 Brake Cable Release Tool or equivalent.
9. Remove the cable button end from the lever clevis.
10. Remove the parking brake cable from the parking brake assembly using special tool J 37043 or equivalent.

To install:

11. Install the cable into the vehicle and from inside the vehicle connect the parking brake cable housing to the parking brake lever assembly and fully seat the locking fingers.
12. Install the parking brake cable end to the lever clevis.
13. Feed the parking brake cable and snap clip to the underbody.
14. Install the carpeting.
15. Install the driver's side sound insulator.
16. Install the lower door sill trim plate.
17. From under the vehicle, connect the front cable to the left rear cable at the connector clip. Tighten the nut on the equalizer to remove the cable slack.
18. Adjust the parking brake cable.
19. Lower the vehicle.

Left Rear Cable

1. Raise and safely support the vehicle.
2. Loosen the cable at the equalizer assembly.
3. Disconnect the left rear cable from the front cable at the connector clip.
4. Disconnect the cable from the bracket.
5. Compress the locking fingers to disconnect the parking brake cable housing from the equalizer assembly using special tool J 37043 or the equivalent Brake Cable Release Tool.
6. Disconnect the parking brake cable end from the parking brake lever on the caliper, if equipped with rear disc brakes. If equipped with rear drum brakes, remove the rear wheel and brake drum. Disconnect the cable end from the brake shoe lever and disengage from the backing plate.

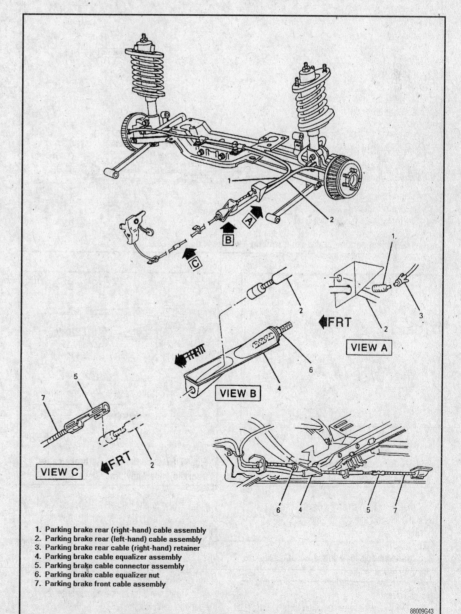

1. Parking brake rear (right-hand) cable assembly
2. Parking brake rear (left-hand) cable assembly
3. Parking brake rear cable (right-hand) retainer
4. Parking brake cable equalizer assembly
5. Parking brake cable connector assembly
6. Parking brake cable equalizer nut
7. Parking brake front cable assembly

88009G43

Fig. 74 Typical parking brake cable routing—with rear drum brakes

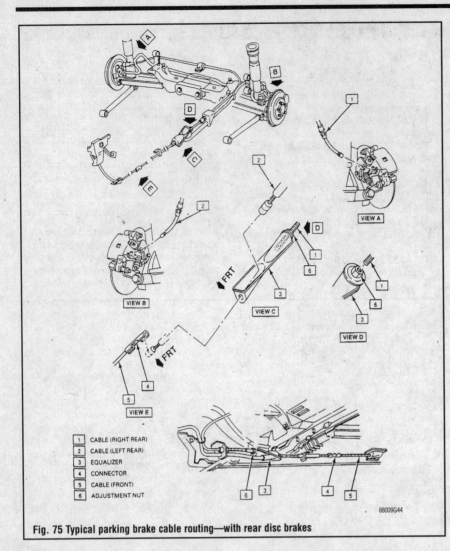

1	CABLE (RIGHT REAR)
2	CABLE (LEFT REAR)
3	EQUALIZER
4	CONNECTOR
5	CABLE (FRONT)
6	ADJUSTMENT NUT

Fig. 75 Typical parking brake cable routing—with rear disc brakes

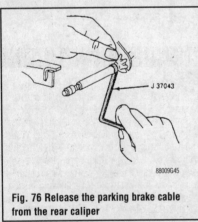

Fig. 76 Release the parking brake cable from the rear caliper

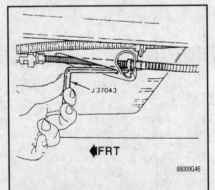

Fig. 77 Release the parking brake cable from the underbody bracket

7. Disconnect the cable from the rear bracket and cable support and remove the cable from the vehicle.

To install:

8. Route the cable through the rear cable bracket and cable support.

9. Feed the cable through the equalizer and front cable bracket.

10. Fully seat the cable housing locking fingers into the equalizer assembly.

11. Connect the parking brake cable to the park-ing brake lever on the caliper, if equipped with rear disc brakes. If equipped with rear drum brakes, thread the cable end through the opening in the backing plate and then connect the cable end to the brake shoe lever.

12. Connect the left rear cable to the front cable at the connector clip.

13. Tighten the nut on the equalizer to remove the parking cable slack.

14. Lower the vehicle.

15. Adjust the parking brakes.

Right Rear Cable

1. Raise and safely support the vehicle.

2. Remove the parking brake cable at the equalizer.

3. Remove the parking brake cable from the brake cable support assembly.

4. Remove the parking brake cable from the rear underbody bracket using special tool J 37043 or the equivalent.

5. Remove the two bolts from clips on the underbody rail.

6. Remove the parking brake cable from the backing plate and parking brake lever for vehicle equipped with drum brakes.

7. Remove the caliper parking brake lever and bracket using special tool J 37043 or the equivalent on vehicles equipped with rear disc brakes.

To install:

8. Install the parking brake cable in position on the underbody rail.

9. Install the two bolts to support clips above the knuckle hub support.

10. Install the parking brake cable to the back-ing plate and the parking brake lever on vehicle equipped with drum brakes.

11. Install the parking brake cable to the caliper parking brake lever and bracket on vehicles equipped with disc brakes. Tighten the bolts to 36 inch lbs. (4 Nm).

12. Feed the parking brake cable through the underbody bracket and snap conduit to the bracket.

13. Install the parking brake cable threaded rod to the equalizer.

14. Tighten the nut on the equalizer to remove the cable slack.

15. Safely lower the vehicle.

16. Adjust the parking brakes as required.

ADJUSTMENT

Rear Disc Brakes

▶ See Figure 78

1. Apply the parking brake pedal three times with heavy force of about 175 lbs. (778 N).

➡ **Do not apply the main/service brake pedal during the next step.**

2. Fully apply and release the parking brake three times.

3. Raise the vehicle and safely support the vehicle with safety stands.

4. Matchmark the position of the wheel to the hub and bearing assembly.

5. Make sure the parking brake is fully released. Turn the ignition switch to the **ON** posi-tion. The BRAKE warning lamp should be off. If the BRAKE warning light is still on, pull downward on the front parking brake to remove the slack from the pedal assembly.

6. Remove the rear wheel and tire assemblies, then reinstall two lug nuts to retain the rotors.

7. The parking brake levers on both calipers should be against the lever stops on the caliper housing. If not against the stops, check for binding in the rear cables and/or loosen the cables at the adjuster until both left and right levers are against their stops.

8. Tighten the parking brake cable at the

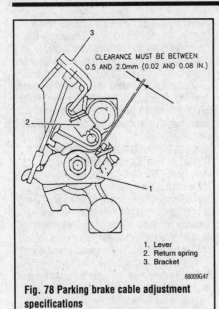

CLEARANCE MUST BE BETWEEN
0.5 AND 2.0mm (0.02 AND 0.08 IN.)

1. Lever
2. Return spring
3. Bracket

88009G47

Fig. 78 Parking brake cable adjustment specifications

adjuster until either the right or left lever reaches the dimensions shown in the accompanying figure.

➡**Do not apply the main/service brake pedal during the next step.**

9. Operate the parking brake several times to check adjustments. A firm pedal should be present. The rear wheels should not rotate forward when the parking brake is fully applies. If necessary, repeat steps 8 and 9.

10. Remove the two wheel lug nuts, then install the rear wheel and tire assemblies.

11. Carefully lower the vehicle.

Rear Drum Brakes

▸ See Figure 78

1. Adjust the rear brakes, as outlined earlier in this section.

2. Apply the parking brake to 10 clicks, then release. Repeat 5 times.

3. Make sure the parking brake is fully released. Turn the ignition switch to the **ON** position. The BRAKE warning lamp should be off. If the BRAKE warning light is still on, pull downward on the front parking brake to remove the slack from the pedal assembly.

4. Raise and safely support the vehicle with safety stands.

5. Adjust the parking brake by turning the nut on the equalizer while spinning both rear wheels. When either rear wheel develops drag, stop adjusting and back off the equalizer one full turn.

6. Apply the parking brake to four clicks and check the rear wheel rotation. The wheel should not move when you attempt to rotate it, by hand, in a forward rotation. The wheel should drag or not move when attempting to rotate it in a rearward direction.

7. Release the parking brake and check for free wheel rotation.

8. Carefully lower the vehicle.

Parking Brake Shoes

REMOVAL & INSTALLATION

On vehicles equipped with rear disc brake calipers without built-in parking brake adjusters, the parking brake assembly is contained inside the rear disc brake rotor. Two small brake shoes press against the inside diameter of the rear brake rotor.

1. Raise and safely support the vehicle with safety stands.

2. Remove the rear caliper using the procedure found in this section. It is not necessary to disconnect the brake line. Use wire to hang the caliper out of the way. Do not allow the caliper to hang by the brake hose.

3. Remove the caliper bracket bolts and remove the caliper. It may take considerable force to remove the bolts. They were factory installed with a thread-locking compound.

4. Remove the rear rotor using the procedures found in this section.

5. Disconnect the parking brake actuator.

6. Remove the rear wheel hub using the procedures found in Section 8.

7. Remove the shoes from the parking brake support plate.

8. Installation is the reverse of the removal process. Note that when the caliper bracket is installed, use thread-locking compound on the bolts. Torque the caliper bracket bolts to 92 ft. lbs. (125 Nm).The parking brake brakes should be adjusted before the rotor is installed. Use the procedure in this section.

ADJUSTMENT

➡**The factory recommends using a Drum To Brake Shoe Clearance Gauge to setup and adjust the parking brake shoes on vehicles equipped with rear disc brake calipers without a built-in parking brake adjuster.**

1. Remove the caliper, caliper bracket and rear disc brake rotor using the procedures found in this section. Slowly turn the rotor while pulling away from the hub.

2. Loosen the parking brake cable adjusting nut until the lever is at its "rest" position.

3. Using a Drum To Brake Shoe Clearance Gauge such as GM's J 41713, or equivalent:

   a. Set the tool so that it contacts the inside diameter of the rotor.

   b. Position the Clearance Gauge over the parking brake shoes at its widest point.

   c. Turn the adjuster nut until the brake shoe lining just touches the Clearance Gauge.

   d. Repeat the procedure for the opposite side.

4. Tighten the parking brake cable adjusting nut.

5. Slowly turn the rotor while installing onto the bearing assembly.

6. Assemble the remaining components using the procedures found in this section.

ANTI-LOCK BRAKE SYSTEM

Description and Operation

▸ See Figure 79

The Delco Anti-lock Braking System (ABS) VI was first introduced on W-body cars in 1992. ABS provides the driver with 3 important benefits over standard braking systems: increased vehicle stability, improved vehicle steerability, and potentially reduced stopping distances during braking. It should be noted that although the ABS-VI system offers definite advantages, the system cannot increase brake pressure above master cylinder pressure applied by the driver and cannot apply the brakes itself.

The ABS-VI Anti-lock Braking System consists of a conventional braking system with vacuum power booster, compact master cylinder, front disc brakes, rear disc or drum brakes and interconnecting hydraulic brake lines augmented with the ABS components. The ABS-VI system includes a hydraulic modulator assembly, Electronic Brake Control Module (EBCM), a system relay, 4 wheel speed sensors, interconnecting wiring and an amber ABS warning light.

The EBCM monitors inputs from the individual wheel speed sensors and determines when a wheel is about to lock up. The EBCM controls the motors on the hydraulic modulator assembly to reduce brake pressure to the wheel about to lock up. When the wheel regains traction, the brake pressure is increased until the wheel approaches lock-up. The cycle repeats until either the vehicle comes to a stop, the brake pedal is released, or no wheels are about to lock up. The EBCM also has the ability to monitor itself and can store diagnostic codes in a non-volatile (will not be erased if the battery is disconnected) memory. The EBCM is serviced as an assembly.

The ABS-VI braking system employs 2 modes: base (conventional) braking and anti-lock braking. Under normal braking, the conventional part of the system stops the vehicle. When in the ABS mode, the Electromagnetic Brakes (EMB) action of the ABS system controls the two front wheels individually and the rear wheels together. If the one rear wheel is about to lock up, the hydraulic pressure to both wheels is reduced, controlling both wheels together.

An Enhanced Traction System (ETS) is used on some W-Body vehicles. The Antilock Brake System and the Enhanced Traction System (ABS/ETS) are both part of the same hydraulic and electric system. Both systems use many of the same components and a problem in either system may disable the other system until it is repaired. Anti-lock braking controls wheel slip when braking. The ETS system provides the capability to control wheel spin at the drive wheels. This improves the ability to maintain vehicle stability and acceleration (drive traction) under changing road and vehicle load conditions.

The Variable Effort Steering (VES) control logic is integrated in the Electronic Brake Control Module/Electronic Brake Traction Control Module (EBCM/EBTCM). Two Diagnostic Trouble Codes (DTCs) are stored in the EBCM/EBTCM for VES malfunctions. The VES and the ABS share the same wheel speed sensors.

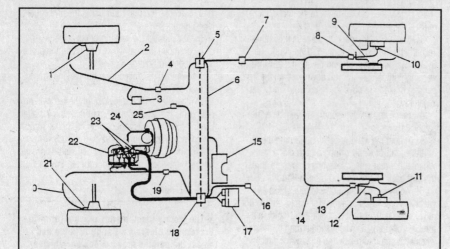

1. Right Front Wheel Speed Sensor
2. Right Front Wheel Speed Sensor Jumper Harness
3. Underhood Electrical Center
4. I/P Harness to Right Front Wheel Speed Sensor Jumper Harness
5. Pass Thru
6. Instrument Panel (I/P) Harness
7. Body Harness to I/P Harness Connector
8. Right Rear Body Pass Thru Connector
9. Right Rear Wheel Speed Sensor Jumper Harness
10. Right Rear Wheel Speed Sensor
11. Left Rear Wheel Speed Sensor
12. Left Rear Wheel Speed Sensor Jumper Harness
13. Left Rear Body Pass Thru Connector
14. Body Harness
15. I/P Warning Indicators
16. Electronic Brake Control Relay
17. Electronic Brake Control Module/Electronic Brake Traction Control Module (EBCM/EBTCM)
18. ABS Pass Thru
19. I/P Harness to Left Front Wheel Speed Sensor Jumper Harness
20. Left Front Wheel Speed Sensor Jumper Harness
21. Left Front Wheel Speed Sensor
22. Brake Modulator (ABS)
23. Brake Solenoid Valves
24. Master Cylinder
25. Power Steering Fluid Flow Actuator

93179G27

Fig. 79 ABS/ETS component locations–typical W-Body applications

BASIC KNOWLEDGE REQUIRED

Before using this section, it is important that you have a basic knowledge of the following items. Without this basic knowledge, it will be difficult to use the diagnostic procedures contained in this section.

Basic Electrical Circuits—You should understand the basic theory of electricity and know the meaning of voltage, current (amps) and resistance (ohms). You should understand what happens in a circuit with an open or shorted wire. You should be able to read and understand a wiring diagram.

Use Of Circuit Testing Tools—You should know how to use a test light and how to use jumper wires to bypass components to test circuits. You should be familiar with the High Impedance Multimeter such as J 34029-A. You should be able to measure voltage, resistance and current and be familiar with the meter controls and how to use them correctly.

ONBOARD DIAGNOSTICS

The ABS-VI contains sophisticated onboard diagnostics that, when accessed with a bi-directional scan tool, are designed to identify the source of any system fault as specifically as possible, including whether or not the fault is intermittent. There are over 58 Diagnostic Trouble Codes (DTCs) to assist with system diagnosis.

The last diagnostic fault code to occur is identified, specific ABS data is stored at the time of this fault, and the first five codes set are stored. Additionally, using a bi-directional scan tool, each input and output can be monitored, thus enabling fault confirmation and repair verification. Manual control of components and automated functional tests are also available when using a GM approved scan tool. Details of many of these functions are contained in the following sections.

ENHANCED DIAGNOSTICS

Enhanced diagnostic information, found in the CODE HISTORY function of the bi-directional scan tool, is designed to provide specific fault occurrence information. For each of the first five (5) and the very last diagnostic fault codes stored, data is stored to identify the specific fault code number, the number of failure occurrences, and the number of drive cycles since the failure first and last occurred (a drive cycle occurs when the ignition is turned **ON** and the vehicle is driven faster than 10 mph). However, if a fault is present, the drive cycle counter will increment by turning the ignition **ON** and **OFF**. These first five (5) diagnostic fault codes are also stored in the order of occurrence. The order in which the first 5 faults occurred can be useful in determining if a previous fault is linked to the most recent faults, such as an intermittent wheel speed sensor which later becomes completely open.

During difficult diagnosis situations, this infor-

mation can be used to identify fault occurrence trends. Does the fault occur more frequently now than it did during the last time when it only failed 1 out of 35 drive cycles? Did the fault only occur once over a large number of drive cycles, indicating an unusual condition present when the fault occurred? Does the fault occur infrequently over a large number of drive cycles, indication special diagnosis techniques may be required to identify the source of the fault?

If a fault occurred 1 out of 20 drive cycles, the fault is intermittent and has not reoccurred for 19 drive cycles. This fault may be difficult or impossible to duplicate and may have been caused by a severe vehicle impact (large pot hole, speed bump at high speed, etc.) that momentarily opened an electrical connector or caused unusual vehicle suspension movement. Problem resolution is unlikely, and the problem may never reoccur (check diagnostic aids proved for that code). If the fault occurred 3 out of 15 drive cycles, the odds of finding the cause are still not good, but you know how often it occurs and you can determine whether or not the fault is becoming more frequent based on an additional or past occurrences visit if the source of the problem can not or could not be found. If the fault occurred 10 out of 20 drive cycles, the odds of finding the cause are very good, as the fault may be easily reproduced.

By using the additional fault data, a trained, qualified technician can also determine if a failure is randomly intermittent or if it has not reoccurred for long periods of time due to weather changes or a repair prior to this visit. Say a diagnostic fault code occurred 10 of 20 drive cycles but has not reoccurred for 10 drive cycles. This means the failure occurred 10 of 10 drive cycles but has not reoccurred since. A significant environmental change or a repair occurred 10 drive cycles ago. A repair may not be necessary if a recent repair can be confirmed. If no repair was made, the service can focus on diagnosis techniques used to locate difficult to recreate problems.

Diagnostic Procedures

When servicing the ABS-VI, the following steps should be followed in order. Failure to follow these steps may result in the loss of important diagnostic data and may lead to difficult and time consuming diagnosis procedures.

1. Connect a bi-directional scan tool, as instructed by the tool manufacturer, then read all current and historical diagnostic codes. Be certain to note which codes are current diagnostic code failures. DO NOT CLEAR CODES unless directed to do so.

2. Using a bi-directional scan tool, read the CODE HISTORY data. Note the diagnostic fault codes stored and their frequency of failure. Specifically note the last failure that occurred and the conditions present when this failure occurred. This last failure should be the starting point for diagnosis and repair.

3. Perform a vehicle preliminary diagnosis inspection. This should include:

   a. Inspection of the compact master cylinder for proper brake fluid level.

   b. Inspection of the ABS hydraulic modulator for any leaks or wiring damage.

   c. Inspection of brake components at all four

(4) wheels. Verify no drag exists. Also verify proper brake apply operation.

d. Inspection for worn or damaged wheel bearings that allow a wheel to wobble.

e. Inspection of the wheel speed sensors (where possible) and their wiring. Verify correct air gap range, solid sensor attachment, undamaged sensor toothed ring, and undamaged wiring, especially at vehicle attachment points. The sensors for the rear wheels are built into the rear wheel hub/bearing assemblies and cannot be inspected or serviced.

f. Verify proper outer CV-joint alignment and operation.

g. Verify tires meet legal tread depth requirements.

4. If no codes are present, or mechanical component failure codes are present, perform the automated modulator test using the Tech 1®, T-100® or equivalent scan tool, to isolate the cause of the problem. If the failure is intermittent and not reproducible, test drive the vehicle while using the automatic snapshot feature of the bi-directional scan tool.

Perform normal acceleration, stopping, and turning maneuvers. If this does not reproduce the failure, perform an ABS stop, on a low coefficient surface such as gravel, from approximately 30–50 mph (48–80 km/h) while triggering any ABS/ETC code. If the failure is still not reproducible, use the enhanced diagnostic information found in CODE HISTORY to determine whether or not this failure should be further diagnosed.

5. Once all system failures have been corrected, clear the ABS codes. The Tech 1® and T-100®, when plugged into the Data Link Connector (DLC), becomes part of the vehicle's electronic system. The Tech 1® and T-100® scan tools can also perform the following functions on components linked by the Serial Data Link (SDL):

- Display ABS data
- Display and clear ABS trouble codes
- Control ABS components
- Perform extensive ABS diagnosis
- Provide diagnostic testing for intermittent ABS conditions

Each test mode has specific diagnostic capabilities which depend upon various keystrokes. In general, five (5) keys control sequencing: YES, NO, EXIT, UP arrow and DOWN arrow. The FO through F9 keys select operating modes, perform functions within an operating mode, or enter trouble code or model year designations.

In general, the Tech 1® has five (5) test modes for diagnosing the anti-lock brake system. The five (5) test modes are as follows:

MODE FO: DATA LIST—In this test mode, the Tech 1® continuously monitors wheel speed data, brake switch status and other inputs and outputs.

MODE F1: CODE HISTORY—In this mode, fault code history data is displayed. This data includes how many ignition cycles since the fault code occurred, along with other ABS information. The first five (5) and last fault codes set are included in the ABS history data.

MODE F2: TROUBLE CODES—In this test mode, trouble codes stored by the EBCM, both current ignition cycle and history, may be displayed or cleared.

MODE F3: ABS SNAPSHOT—In this test

mode, the Tech 1® captures ABS data before and after a fault occurrence or a forced manual trigger.

MODE F4: ABS TESTS—In this test mode, the Tech 1® performs hydraulic modulator functional tests to assist in problem isolation during troubleshooting. Included here is manual control of the motors which is used prior to bleeding the brake system.

Press F7 to covert from English to Metric.

INTERMITTENT FAILURES

As with most electronic systems, intermittent failures may be difficult to accurately diagnose. The following is a method to try to isolate an intermittent failure especially wheel speed circuitry failures.

If an ABS fault occurs, the ABS warning light indicator will be on during the ignition cycle in which the fault was detected. If it is an intermittent problem which seems to have corrected itself (ABS warning light off), a history trouble code will be stored. Also stored will be the history data of the code at the time the fault occurred. The Tech 1® or equivalent scan tool must be used to read ABS history data.

INTERMITTENTS AND POOR CONNECTIONS

Most intermittents are caused by faulty electrical connections or wiring, although occasionally a sticking relay or solenoid can be a problem. Some items to check are:

1. Poor mating of connector halves, or terminals not fully seated in the connector body (backed out).

2. Dirt or corrosion on the terminals. The terminals must be clean and free of any foreign material which could impede proper terminal contact.

3. Damaged connector body, exposing the terminals to moisture and dirt, as well as not maintaining proper terminal orientation with the component or mating connector.

4. Improperly formed or damaged terminals. All connector terminals in problem circuits should be checked carefully to ensure good contact tension. Use a corresponding mating terminal to check for proper tension. Refer to "Checking Terminal Contact" later in this section for the specific procedure.

5. GM's J 35616-A Connector Test Adapter Kit must be used whenever a diagnostic procedure requests checking or probing a terminal. Using the adapter will ensure that no damage to the terminal will occur, as well as giving an idea of whether contact tension is sufficient. If contact tension seems incorrect, refer to "Checking Terminal Contact" later in this section for specifics.

6. Poor terminal-to-wire connection. Checking this requires removing the terminal from the connector body. Some conditions which fall under this description are poor crimps, poor solder joints, crimping over wire insulation rather than the wire itself, corrosion in the wire-to-terminal contact area, etc.

7. Wire insulation which is rubbed through, causing an intermittent short as the bare area touches other wiring or parts of the vehicle.

8. Wiring broken inside the insulation. This condition could cause a continuity check to show a

good circuit, but if only 1 or 2 strands of a multi-strand type wire are intact, resistance could be far too high.

Checking Terminal Contact

When diagnosing an electrical system that uses Metri-Pack 150/280/480/630 series terminals (refer to Terminal Repair Kit J 38125-A for terminal identification), it is important to check terminal contact between a connector and component, or between inline connectors, before replacing a suspect component.

Mating terminals must be inspected to ensure good terminal contact. A poor connection between the male and female terminal at a connector may be the result of contamination or deformation.

Contamination is caused by the connector halves being improperly connected, a missing or damaged connector seal, or damage to the connector itself, exposing the terminals to moisture and dirt. Contamination, usually in underhood or underbody connectors, leads to terminal corrosion, causing an open circuit or an intermittently open circuit.

Deformation is caused by probing the mating side of a connector terminal without the proper adapter, improperly joining the connector halves or repeatedly separating and joining the connector halves. Deformation, usually to the female terminal contact tang, can result in poor terminal contact causing an open or intermittently open circuit.

Follow the procedure below to check terminal contact.

1. Separate the connector halves. Refer to Terminal Repair Kit J 38125-A, if available.

2. Inspect the connector halves for contamination. Contamination will result in a white or green buildup within the connector body or between terminals, causing high terminal resistance, intermittent contact or an open circuit. An underhood or underbody connector that shows signs of contamination should be replaced in its entirety: terminals, seals, and connector body.

3. Using an equivalent male terminal from the Terminal Repair Kit J 38125-A, check the retention force of the female terminal in question by inserting and removing the male terminal to the female terminal in the connector body. Good terminal contact will require a certain amount of force to separate the terminals.

4. Using an equivalent female terminal from the Terminal Repair Kit J 38125-A, compare the retention force of this terminal to the female terminal in question by joining and separating the male terminal to the female terminal in question. If the retention force is significantly different between the two female terminals, replace the female terminal in question, using a terminal from Terminal Repair Kit J 38125-A.

Reading Codes

▶ **See Figures 80 thru 88**

Diagnostic Trouble Codes (DTCs) can be only be read through the use of a bi-directional scan tool, such as a Tech 1® or equivalent. There are no provisions for "Flash Code" diagnostics. Make sure to follow the scan tool manufacturer's directions for tool hook up, and reading codes.

DIAGNOSTIC TROUBLE CODE	DESCRIPTION	DIAGNOSTIC TROUBLE CODE	DESCRIPTION
C1211	ABS Warning Indicator Circuit Malfunction	C1253	RF ABS Channel In Release Too Long
C1213	ABS Active Indicator Circuit Malfunction	C1254	Rear ABS Channel In Release Too Long
C1214	Brake Control Relay Contact Circuit Open	C1255	EBCM/EBTCM Internal Malfunction
C1215	Brake Control Relay Contact Circuit Always Active	C1256	LF ABS Motor Circuit Open
		C1257	LF ABS Motor Circuit Shorted To Ground
C1216	Brake Control Relay Coil Circuit Open	C1258	LF ABS Motor Circuit Shorted To Voltage
C1217	Brake Control Relay Coil Circuit Shorted to Ground	C1261	RF ABS Motor Circuit Open
		C1262	RF ABS Motor Circuit Shorted To Ground
C1218	Brake Control Relay Coil Circuit Shorted to Voltage	C1263	RF ABS Motor Circuit Shorted To Voltage
		C1264	Rear ABS Motor Circuit Open
C1221	LF Wheel Speed Sensor Input Signal = 0	C1265	Rear ABS Motor Circuit Shorted To Ground
C1222	RF Wheel Speed Sensor Input Signal = 0	C1266	Rear ABS Motor Circuit Shorted To Voltage
C1223	LF Wheel Speed Sensor Input Signal = 0	C1273	VES Actuator Circuit Open or Shorted To Ground (if equipped w/VES)
C1224	RF Wheel Speed Sensor Input Signal = 0		
C1225	LF Excessive Wheel Speed Sensor Variation	C1274	VES Actuator Circuit Shorted To Voltage or Solenoid Shorted (if equipped w/VES)
C1226	RF Excessive Wheel Speed Sensor Variation		
C1227	LF Excessive Wheel Speed Sensor Variation	C1275	Serial Data Malfunction
C1228	RF Excessive Wheel Speed Sensor Variation	C1276	LF Solenoid Circuit Open Or Shorted To Ground
C1232	LF Wheel Speed Sensor Circuit Open or Shorted	C1277	LF Solenoid Circuit Shorted To Voltage
C1233	RF Wheel Speed Sensor Circuit Open or Shorted	C1278	RF Solenoid Circuit Open Or Shorted To Ground
C1234	LR Wheel Speed Sensor Circuit Open or Shorted		
C1235	RR Wheel Speed Sensor Circuit Open or Shorted	C1281	RF Solenoid Circuit Shorted To Voltage
C1236	Low System Supply Voltage	C1282	Calibration Malfunction
C1237	High System Supply Voltage	C1286	EBCM/EBTCM Turned On The Red BRAKE Warning Indicator
C1238	LF ESB Will Not Hold Motor		
C1241	RF ESB Will Not Hold Motor	C1287	Red Brake Warning Indicator Circuit Open or Shorted to Voltage
C1242	Rear ESB Will Not Hold Motor		
C1243	VES Steering Wheel Sensor Circuit Malfunction (if equipped w/VES)	C1291	Open Brake Lamp Switch Circuit During Deceleration
		C1292	Open Brake Lamp Switch When ABS Was Required
C1244	LF ABS Channel Will Not Move		
C1245	RF ABS Channel Will Not Move	C1293	DTC C1291 or C1292 Set In Current Or Previous Ignition Cycle
C1246	Rear ABS Channel Will Not Move		
C1247	LF ABS Motor Free Spins	C1294	Brake Switch Contacts Always Closed
C1248	RF ABS Motor Free Spins	C1295	Brake Lamp Switch Circuit Open
C1251	Rear ABS Motor Free Spins		
C1252	LF ABS Channel In Release Too Long		

93179G26

Fig. 80 ABS Diagnostic Trouble Codes—1997 vehicles

DIAGNOSTIC TROUBLE CODE	DESCRIPTION	DIAGNOSTIC TROUBLE CODE	DESCRIPTION
C1214	Brake Control Relay Contact Circuit Open	C1265	Rear ABS Motor Circuit Shorted To Ground
C1215	Brake Control Relay Contact Circuit Active	C1266	Rear ABS Motor Circuit Shorted To Voltage
C1216	Brake Control Relay Coil Circuit Open	C1275	Serial Data Malfunction
C1217	Brake Control Relay Coil Circuit Shorted To Ground	C1276	LF Solenoid Circuit Open Or Shorted To Ground
		C1277	LF Solenoid Circuit Shorted To Voltage
C1218	Brake Control Relay Coil Circuit Shorted to Voltage	C1278	RF Solenoid Circuit Open Or Shorted To Ground
C1221	LF Wheel Speed Sensor Input Signal is 0	C1281	RF Solenoid Circuit Shorted To Voltage
C1222	RF Wheel Speed Sensor Input Signal is 0	C1282	Calibration Malfunction
C1223	LR Wheel Speed Sensor Input Signal is 0	C1286	EBCM/EBTCM Turned On Brake Warning Indicator
C1224	RR Wheel Speed Sensor Input Signal is 0		
C1225	LF Excessive Wheel Speed Variation	C1287	Red BRAKE Warning Indicator Circuit Open
C1226	RF Excessive Wheel Speed Variation	C1291	Open Brake Lamp Switch Contacts During Deceleration
C1227	LR Excessive Wheel Speed Variation		
C1228	RR Excessive Wheel Speed Variation	C1292	Open Brake Lamp Switch When ABS Was Required
C1232	LF Wheel Speed Circuit Open Or Shorted		
C1233	RF Wheel Speed Circuit Open Or Shorted	C1293	Code C1291 or C1292 Set In Current Or Previous Ignition Cycle
C1234	LR Wheel Speed Circuit Open Or Shorted		
C1235	RR Wheel Speed Circuit Open Or Shorted	C1294	Brake Lamp Switch Circuit Always Active
C1236	Low System Supply Voltage	C1295	Brake Lamp Switch Circuit Open
C1237	High System Supply Voltage	C1315	Adjuster Assembly Thermal Model Temperature Exceeded
C1238	LF ESB Does Not Hold Motor		
C1241	RF ESB Does Not Hold Motor	C1323	PCM To EBTCM Delivered Torque Circuit Malfunction
C1242	Rear ESB Does Not Hold Motor		
C1244	LF ABS Channel Does Not Move	C1324	EBTCM To PCM Requested Torque Circuit Malfunction
C1245	RF ABS Channel Does Not Move		
C1246	Rear ABS Channel Does Not Move	C1344	Left TCS Channel Does Not Move
C1247	LF ABS Motor Free Spins	C1345	Right TCS Channel Does Not Move
C1248	RF ABS Motor Free Spins	C1347	Left TCS Motor Free Spins
C1251	Rear ABS Motor Free Spins	C1348	Right TCS Motor Free Spins
C1252	LF ABS Channel In Release Too Long	C1355	EBTCM Malfunction
C1253	RF ABS Channel In Release Too Long	C1356	Left TCS Motor Circuit Open
C1254	Rear ABS Channel In Release Too Long	C1357	Left TCS Motor Circuit Shorted To Ground
C1255	EBCM/EBTCM Internal Malfunction	C1358	Left TCS Motor Circuit Shorted To Voltage
C1256	LF ABS Motor Circuit Open	C1361	Right TCS Motor Circuit Open
C1257	LF ABS Motor Circuit Shorted To Ground	C1362	Right TCS Motor Circuit Shorted To Ground
C1258	LF ABS Motor Circuit Shorted To Voltage	C1363	Right TCS Motor Circuit Shorted To Voltage
C1261	RF ABS Motor Circuit Open	U1016	Loss Of Communications With PCM
C1262	RF ABS Motor Circuit Shorted To Ground	U1255	Generic Loss Of Communications
C1263	RF ABS Motor Circuit Shorted To Voltage	U1300	Class 2 Short To Ground
C1264	Rear ABS Motor Circuit Open	U1301	Class 2 Short To Battery

93179G28

Fig. 81 ABS Diagnostic Trouble Codes—1998 Century and Regal

DIAGNOSTIC TROUBLE CODE	DESCRIPTION
C1214	Brake Control Relay Contact Circuit Open
C1215	Brake Control Relay Contact Circuit Active
C1216	Brake Control Relay Coil Circuit Open
C1217	Brake Control Relay Coil Circuit Shorted To Ground
C1218	Brake Control Relay Coil Circuit Shorted to Voltage
C1221	LF Wheel Speed Sensor Input Signal is 0
C1222	RF Wheel Speed Sensor Input Signal is 0
C1223	LR Wheel Speed Sensor Input Signal is 0
C1224	RR Wheel Speed Sensor Input Signal is 0
C1225	LF Excessive Wheel Speed Variation
C1226	RF Excessive Wheel Speed Variation
C1227	LR Excessive Wheel Speed Variation
C1228	RR Excessive Wheel Speed Variation
C1232	LF Wheel Speed Circuit Open Or Shorted
C1233	RF Wheel Speed Circuit Open Or Shorted
C1234	LR Wheel Speed Circuit Open Or Shorted
C1235	RR Wheel Speed Circuit Open Or Shorted
C1236	Low System Supply Voltage
C1237	High System Supply Voltage
C1238	LF ESB Does Not Hold Motor
C1241	RF ESB Does Not Hold Motor
C1242	Rear ESB Does Not Hold Motor
C1244	LF ABS Channel Does Not Move
C1245	RF ABS Channel Does Not Move
C1246	Rear ABS Channel Does Not Move
C1247	LF ABS Motor Free Spins
C1248	RF ABS Motor Free Spins
C1251	Rear ABS Motor Free Spins
C1252	LF ABS Channel In Release Too Long
C1253	RF ABS Channel In Release Too Long

DIAGNOSTIC TROUBLE CODE	DESCRIPTION
C1254	Rear ABS Channel In Release Too Long
C1255	EBCM/EBTCM Internal Malfunction
C1256	LF ABS Motor Circuit Open
C1257	LF ABS Motor Circuit Shorted To Ground
C1258	LF ABS Motor Circuit Shorted To Voltage
C1261	RF ABS Motor Circuit Open
C1262	RF ABS Motor Circuit Shorted To Ground
C1263	RF ABS Motor Circuit Shorted To Voltage
C1264	Rear ABS Motor Circuit Open
C1265	Rear ABS Motor Circuit Shorted To Ground
C1266	Rear ABS Motor Circuit Shorted To Voltage
C1275	Serial Data Malfunction
C1276	LF Solenoid Circuit Open Or Shorted To Ground
C1277	LF Solenoid Circuit Shorted To Voltage
C1278	RF Solenoid Circuit Open Or Shorted To Ground
C1281	Right Front Solenoid Circuit Shorted To Voltage
C1282	Calibration Malfunction
C1286	EBCM/EBTCM Turned On Brake Warning Indicator
C1287	Red BRAKE Warning Indicator Circuit Open
C1291	Open Brake Lamp Switch Contacts During Deceleration
C1292	Open Brake Lamp Switch When ABS Was Required
C1293	Code C1291 or C1292 Set In Current Or Previous Ignition Cycle
C1294	Brake Lamp Switch Circuit Always Active
C1295	Brake Lamp Switch Circuit Open
U1016	Loss Of Communications With PCM
U1255	Generic Loss Of Communications

93179G29

Fig. 82 ABS Diagnostic Trouble Codes—1998 Intrigue

DIAGNOSTIC TROUBLE CODE	DESCRIPTION
C0035	LF Wheel Speed Circuit Malfunction
C0036	LF Wheel Speed Circuit Range/Performance
C0040	RF Wheel Speed Circuit Malfunction
C0041	RF Wheel Speed Circuit Range/Performance
C0045	LR Wheel Speed Circuit Malfunction
C0046	LR Wheel Speed Circuit Range/Performance
C0050	RR Wheel Speed Circuit Malfunction
C0051	RR Wheel Speed Circuit Range/Performance
C0060	LF ABS Solenoid #1 Circuit Malfunction
C0065	LF ABS Solenoid #2 Circuit Malfunction
C0070	RF ABS Solenoid #1 Circuit Malfunction
C0075	RF ABS Solenoid #2 Circuit Malfunction
C0080	LR ABS Solenoid #1 Circuit Malfunction
C0085	LR ABS Solenoid #2 Circuit Malfunction
C0090	RR ABS Solenoid #1 Circuit Malfunction
C0095	RR ABS Solenoid #2 Circuit Malfunction
C0110	Pump Motor Circuit Malfunction
C0121	Valve Relay Circuit Malfunction
C0141	Left TCS Solenoid #1 Circuit Malfunction
C0146	Left TCS Solenoid #2 Circuit Malfunction
C0151	Right TCS Solenoid #1 Circuit Malfunction
C0156	Right TCS Solenoid #2 Circuit Malfunction
C0161	ABS/TCS Brake Switch Circuit Malfunction
C0236	TCS RPM Signal Circuit Malfunction
C0240	PCM Traction Control Not Allowed
C0241	PCM Indicated Requested Torque Malfunction
C0244	PWM Delivered Torque Malfunction
C0245	Wheel Speed Sensor Frequency Error
C0450	Steer Assist Control Actuator Circuit Malfunction
C0550	ECU Malfunction
C0896	Device Voltage Range Performance
U1304	Lost Communications With UART System

93179G30

Fig. 83 ABS Diagnostic Trouble Codes—1998 Grand Prix

DIAGNOSTIC TROUBLE CODE — DESCRIPTION

CODE	DESCRIPTION
C1211	ABS Warning Indicator Circuit Malfunction
C1213	ABS ACTIVE Indicator Circuit Malfunction
C1214	Brake Control Relay Contact Circuit Open
C1215	Brake Control Relay Contact Circuit Always Active
C1216	Brake Control Relay Coil Circuit Open
C1217	Brake Control Relay Coil Circuit Shorted to Ground
C1218	Brake Control Relay Coil Circuit Shorted to Voltage
C1221	LF Wheel Speed Sensor Input Signal = 0
C1222	RF Wheel Speed Sensor Input Signal = 0
C1223	LR Wheel Speed Sensor Input Signal = 0
C1224	RR Wheel Speed Sensor Input Signal = 0
C1225	LF Excessive Wheel Speed Sensor Variation
C1226	RF Excessive Wheel Speed Sensor Variation
C1227	LR Excessive Wheel Speed Sensor Variation
C1228	RR Excessive Wheel Speed Sensor Variation
C1232	LF Wheel Speed Sensor Circuit Open or Shorted
C1233	RF Wheel Speed Sensor Circuit Open or Shorted
C1234	LR Wheel Speed Sensor Circuit Open or Shorted
C1235	RR Wheel Speed Sensor Circuit Open or Shorted
C1236	Low System Supply Voltage
C1237	High System Supply Voltage
C1238	LF ESB Will Not Hold Motor
C1241	RF ESB Will Not Hold Motor
C1242	Rear ESB Will Not Hold Motor
C1244	LF ABS Channel Will Not Move
C1245	RF ABS Channel Will Not Move
C1246	Rear ABS Channel Will Not Move
C1247	LF ABS Motor Free Spins
C1248	RF ABS Motor Free Spins

CODE	DESCRIPTION
C1251	Rear ABS Motor Free Spins
C1252	LF ABS Channel In Release Too Long
C1253	RF ABS Channel In Release Too Long
C1254	Rear ABS Channel In Release Too Long
C1255	EBCM/EBTCM Internal Malfunction
C1256	LF ABS Motor Circuit Open
C1257	LF ABS Motor Circuit Shorted To Ground
C1258	LF ABS Motor Circuit Shorted To Voltage
C1261	RF ABS Motor Circuit Open
C1262	RF ABS Motor Circuit Shorted To Ground
C1263	RF ABS Motor Circuit Shorted To Voltage
C1264	Rear ABS Motor Circuit Open
C1265	Rear ABS Motor Circuit Shorted To Ground
C1266	Rear ABS Motor Circuit Shorted To Voltage
C1276	LF Solenoid Circuit Open Or Shorted To Ground
C1277	LF Solenoid Circuit Shorted To Voltage
C1278	RF Solenoid Circuit Open Or Shorted To Ground
C1281	RF Solenoid Circuit Shorted To Voltage
C1282	Calibration Malfunction
C1286	EBCM/EBTCM Turned On The Red BRAKE Warning Indicator
C1287	Red Brake Warning Indicator Circuit Open or Shorted to Voltage
C1291	Open Brake Lamp Switch Circuit During Deceleration
C1292	Open Brake Lamp Switch When ABS Was Required
C1293	DTC C1291 or C1292 Set In Current Or Previous Ignition Cycle
C1294	Brake Switch Contacts Always Closed (Active)
C1295	Brake Lamp Switch Circuit Open

93179G31

Fig. 84 ABS Diagnostic Trouble Codes—1998–2000 Lumina and 1998–99 Monte Carlo

DIAGNOSTIC TROUBLE CODE — DESCRIPTION

CODE	DESCRIPTION
C1214	Solenoid Valve Relay Contact Or Coil Circuit Open
C1217	Pump Motor Shorted To Ground
C1218	Pump Motor Circuit Shorted to Voltage
C1221	LF Wheel Speed Sensor Input Signal is 0
C1222	RF Wheel Speed Sensor Input Signal is 0
C1223	LR Wheel Speed Sensor Input Signal is 0
C1224	RR Wheel Speed Sensor Input Signal is 0
C1225	LF Excessive Wheel Speed Variation
C1226	RF Excessive Wheel Speed Variation
C1227	LR Excessive Wheel Speed Variation
C1228	RR Excessive Wheel Speed Variation
C1232	LF Wheel Speed Circuit Open Or Shorted
C1233	RF Wheel Speed Circuit Open Or Shorted
C1234	LR Wheel Speed Circuit Open Or Shorted
C1235	RR Wheel Speed Circuit Open Or Shorted
C1236	Low System Supply Voltage
C1237	High System Supply Voltage
C1238	Brake Thermal Model Exceeded
C1242	Pump Motor Circuit Open
C1243	BPMV Pump Motor Stalled
C1247	Low Brake Fluid Detected
C1254	Abnormal Shutdown Detected

CODE	DESCRIPTION
C1255	EBCM/EBTCM Internal Malfunction
C1256	EBCM/EBTCM Internal Malfunction
C1261	LF Inlet Valve Solenoid Malfunction
C1262	LF Outlet Valve Solenoid Malfunction
C1263	RF Inlet Valve Solenoid Malfunction
C1264	RF Outlet Valve Solenoid Malfunction
C1265	LR Inlet Valve Solenoid Malfunction
C1266	LR Outlet Valve Solenoid Malfunction
C1267	RR Inlet Valve Solenoid Malfunction
C1268	RR Outlet Valve Solenoid Malfunction
C1272	LF TCS Valve Solenoid Malfunction
C1274	RF TCS Valve Solenoid Malfunction
C1275	PCM Requested ETS To Be Disabled
C1276	Delivered Torque Signal Circuit Malfunction
C1277	Requested Torque Signal Circuit Malfunction
C1278	TCS Temporarily Inhibited By PCM
C1291	Open Brake Lamp Switch Contacts During Deceleration
C1293	Code 1291 Set In Previous Ignition Cycle
C1294	Brake Lamp Switch Circuit Always Active
C1295	Brake Lamp Switch Circuit Open
C1298	PCM Class 2 Serial Data Link Malfunction

93179G32

Fig. 85 ABS Diagnostic Trouble Codes—1999 Century and Regal

DIAGNOSTIC TROUBLE CODE	DESCRIPTION
C0035	LF Wheel Speed Circuit Malfunction
C0036	LF Wheel Speed Circuit Range/Performance
C0040	RF Wheel Speed Circuit Malfunction
C0041	RF Wheel Speed Circuit Range/Performance
C0045	LR Wheel Speed Circuit Malfunction
C0046	LR Wheel Speed Circuit Range/Performance
C0050	RR Wheel Speed Circuit Malfunction
C0051	RR Wheel Speed Circuit Range/Performance
C0060	LF ABS Solenoid #1 Circuit Malfunction
C0065	LF ABS Solenoid #2 Circuit Malfunction
C0070	RF ABS Solenoid #1 Circuit Malfunction
C0075	RF ABS Solenoid #2 Circuit Malfunction
C0080	LR ABS Solenoid #1 Circuit Malfunction
C0085	LR ABS Solenoid #2 Circuit Malfunction
C0090	RR ABS Solenoid #1 Circuit Malfunction
C0095	RR ABS Solenoid #2 Circuit Malfunction
C0110	Pump Motor Circuit Malfunction
C0121	Valve Relay Circuit Malfunction
C0141	Left TCS Solenoid #1 Circuit Malfunction
C0146	Left TCS Solenoid #2 Circuit Malfunction
C0151	Right TCS Solenoid #1 Circuit Malfunction
C0156	Right TCS Solenoid #2 Circuit Malfunction
C0161	ABS/TCS Brake Switch Circuit Malfunction
C0236	TCS RPM Signal Circuit Malfunction
C0240	PCM Traction Control Not Allowed
C0241	PCM Indicated Requested Torque Malfunction
C0244	PWM Delivered Torque Malfunction
C0245	Wheel Speed Sensor Frequency Error
C0550	ECU Malfunction
C0896	Device Voltage Range Performance
C1214	Solenoid Valve Relay Contact Circuit Open
C1215	Solenoid Valve Relay Contact Circuit Active
C1216	Solenoid Valve Relay Coil Circuit Open
C1217	Solenoid Valve Relay Coil Circuit Short To Ground
C1218	Solenoid Valve Relay Coil Circuit Short To Voltage
C1221	LF Wheel Speed Sensor Input Signal is 0
C1222	RF Wheel Speed Sensor Input Signal is 0
C1223	LR Wheel Speed Sensor Input Signal is 0
C1224	RR Wheel Speed Sensor Input Signal is 0
C1225	LF Excessive Wheel Speed Variation
C1226	RF Excessive Wheel Speed Variation
C1227	LR Excessive Wheel Speed Variation
C1228	RR Excessive Wheel Speed Variation
C1232	LF Wheel Speed Circuit Open Or Shorted
C1233	RF Wheel Speed Circuit Open Or Shorted
C1234	LR Wheel Speed Circuit Open Or Shorted
C1235	RR Wheel Speed Circuit Open Or Shorted
C1236	Low System Supply Voltage
C1237	High System Supply Voltage
C1238	LF ESB Does Not Hold Motor
C1241	RF ESB Does Not Hold Motor
C1242	Rear ESB Does Not Hold Motor
C1244	LF ABS Channel Does Not Move
C1245	RF ABS Channel Does Not Move
C1246	Rear ABS Channel Does Not Move
C1247	LF ABS Motor Free Spins
C1248	RF ABS Motor Spins Free
C1251	Rear ABS Motor Spins Free
C1252	LF ABS Channel In Release Too Long
C1253	RF ABS Channel In Release Too Long
C1254	Rear ABS Channel In Release Too Long
C1255	EBCM/EBTCM Internal Malfunction
C1256	LF ABS Motor Circuit Open
C1257	LF ABS Motor Shorted To Ground
C1258	LF ABS Motor Shorted To Voltage
C1261	RF ABS Motor Circuit Open
C1262	RF ABS Motor Circuit Shorted To Ground
C1263	RF ABS Motor Circuit Shorted To Voltage
C1264	Rear ABS Motor Circuit Open
C1265	Rear ABS Motor Circuit Shorted To Ground
C1266	Rear ABS Motor Circuit Shorted To Voltage
C1275	Serial Data Malfunction
C1276	LF Solenoid Circuit Open Or Shorted To Voltage
C1277	LF Solenoid Circuit Shorted To Voltage
C1278	RF Solenoid Circuit Open Or Shorted To Ground
C1281	RF Solenoid Circuit Shorted To Voltage
C1282	Calibration Malfunction
C1286	EBCM/EBTCM Turned On Brake Warning Indicator
C1287	Brake Warning Indicator Circuit Open Or Shorted To Voltage
C1291	Open Brake Lamp Switch Contacts During Deceleration
C1292	Open Brake Lamp Switch When ABS Was Required
C1293	Code C1291 Or C1292 Set In Previous Ignition Cycle
C1294	Brake Lamp Switch Circuit Always Active
C1295	Brake Lamp Switch Circuit Open

93179G33

Fig. 86 ABS Diagnostic Trouble Codes—1999 Intrigue

DIAGNOSTIC TROUBLE CODE	DESCRIPTION
C0035	LF Wheel Speed Circuit Malfunction
C0036	LF Wheel Speed Circuit Range/Performance
C0040	RF Wheel Speed Circuit Malfunction
C0041	RF Wheel Speed Circuit Range/Performance
C0045	LR Wheel Speed Circuit Malfunction
C0046	LR Wheel Speed Circuit Range/Performance
C0050	RR Wheel Speed Circuit Malfunction
C0051	RR Wheel Speed Circuit Range/Performance
C0060	LF ABS Solenoid #1 Circuit Malfunction
C0065	LF ABS Solenoid #2 Circuit Malfunction
C0070	RF ABS Solenoid #1 Circuit Malfunction
C0075	RF ABS Solenoid #2 Circuit Malfunction
C0080	LR ABS Solenoid #1 Circuit Malfunction
C0085	LR ABS Solenoid #2 Circuit Malfunction
C0090	RR ABS Solenoid #1 Circuit Malfunction
C0095	RR ABS Solenoid #2 Circuit Malfunction
C0110	Pump Motor Circuit Malfunction
C0121	Valve Relay Circuit Malfunction
C0141	Left TCS Solenoid #1 Circuit Malfunction
C0146	Left TCS Solenoid #2 Circuit Malfunction
C0151	Right TCS Solenoid #1 Circuit Malfunction
C0156	Right TCS Solenoid #2 Circuit Malfunction
C0161	ABS/TCS Brake Switch Circuit Malfunction
C0236	TCS RPM Signal Circuit Malfunction
C0240	PCM Traction Control Not Allowed
C0241	PCM Indicated Requested Torque Malfunction
C0244	PWM Delivered Torque Malfunction
C0245	Wheel Speed Sensor Frequency Error
C0550	ECU Malfunction
C0896	Device Voltage Range Performance

93179G34

Fig. 87 ABS Diagnostic Trouble Codes—1999–2000 Grand Prix and 2000 Intrigue

DIAGNOSTIC TROUBLE CODE	DESCRIPTION	DIAGNOSTIC TROUBLE CODE	DESCRIPTION
B2747	Traction Control Switch Circuit Low	C1254	Abnormal Shutdown Detected
C1214	Valve Relay Contact or Coil Circuit Open	C1255	EBCM/EBTCM Internal Malfunction
C1216	EBCM Commanded Pressure Release Too Long	C1256	EBCM/EBTCM Internal Malfunction
C1217	Pump Motor Shorted To Ground	C1261	LF Inlet Valve Solenoid Malfunction
C1218	Pump Motor Circuit Shorted To Voltage	C1262	LF Outlet Valve Solenoid Malfunction
C1221	LF Wheel Speed Sensor Input Signal = 0	C1263	RF Inlet Valve Solenoid Malfunction
C1222	RF Wheel Speed Sensor Input Signal = 0	C1264	RF Outlet Valve Solenoid Malfunction
C1223	LR Wheel Speed Sensor Input Signal = 0	C1265	LR Inlet Valve Solenoid Malfunction
C1224	RR Wheel Speed Sensor Input Signal = 0	C1266	LF Outlet Valve Solenoid Malfunction
C1225	LF Excessive Wheel Speed Sensor Variation	C1267	RR Inlet Valve Solenoid Malfunction
C1226	RF Excessive Wheel Speed Sensor Variation	C1268	RF Outlet Valve Solenoid Malfunction
C1227	LR Excessive Wheel Speed Sensor Variation	C1272	LF TCS Valve Solenoid Malfunction
C1228	RR Excessive Wheel Speed Sensor Variation	C1274	RF TCS Valve Solenoid Malfunction
C1232	LF Wheel Speed Sensor Circuit Open or Shorted	C1276	Delivered Torque Signal Circuit Malfunction
C1233	RF Wheel Speed Sensor Circuit Open or Shorted	C1277	Requested Torque Signal Circuit Malfunction
C1234	LR Wheel Speed Sensor Circuit Open or Shorted	C1278	TCS Temporarily Inhibited By PCM
C1235	RR Wheel Speed Sensor Circuit Open or Shorted	C1291	Open Brake Lamp Switch Contacts During Deceleration
C1236	Low System Supply Voltage	C1293	Code C1291 Set In Previous Ignition Cycle
C1237	High System Supply Voltage	C1294	Brake Lamp Switch Circuit Always Active
C1238	Brake Thermal Model Exceeded	C1295	Brake Lamp Switch Circuit Open
C1242	Pump Motor Circuit Open	C1298	PCM Class 2 Serial Data Link Malfunction
C1243	BPMV Pump Motor Stalled		
C1247	Low Brake Fluid Detected		

93179G35

Fig. 88 ABS Diagnostic Trouble Codes—2000 Century and Regal and Monte Carlo

Clearing Codes

The Diagnostic Trouble Codes (DTCs) in the EBCM memory are erased in one of two ways:
1. Using a scan tool such as GM's Tech 1®, or equivalent.
2. Ignition cycle default.

These two methods are detailed below. Be sure to verify proper system operation and absence of DTCs when the clearing procedure is completed.

The EBCM will not permit DTC clearing until all of DTCs have been displayed. Also, DTCs cannot be cleared by unplugging the EBCM, disconnecting the battery cables, or turning the ignition **OFF** (except on an ignition cycle default).

SCAN TOOL METHOD

1. Select DTCs for diagnostic trouble codes.
2. After DTCs have been viewed completely, the Scan Tools should ask CLEAR DTCs?
3. Enter YES.
4. The Scan Tool should then read, HISTORY DATA WILL BE LOST CLEAR DTCs?
5. Enter YES and the DTCs will be cleared.

IGNITION CYCLE DEFAULT

If no diagnostic trouble codes occur for 100 drive cycles (a drive cycle occurs when the ignition switch is turned **RUN**, and the vehicle is driven faster then 10 mph (16 km/h), any existing DTCs are automatically cleared from the EBCM memory.

ABS Service Precautions

Failure to observe the following precautions may result in system damage.
• Performing diagnostic work on the ABS-VI requires the use of a Tech 1® or equivalent scan tool. If unavailable, please refer diagnostic work to a qualified technician.
• Before performing electric arc welding on the vehicle, disconnect the Electronic Brake Control Module (EBCM) and the hydraulic modulator connectors.
• When performing painting work on the vehicle, do not expose the Electronic Brake Control Module (EBCM) to temperatures in excess of 185°F (85°C) for longer than 2 hours. The system may be exposed to temperatures up to 200°F (95°C) for less than 15 minutes.
• Never disconnect or connect the Electronic Brake Control Module (EBCM) or hydraulic modulator connectors with the ignition switch **ON** or damage to the system will occur.
• Never disassemble any component of the Anti-Lock Brake System (ABS) which is designated non-serviceable; the component must be replaced as an assembly.
• When filling the master cylinder, always use Delco Supreme 11 brake fluid or equivalent, which meets DOT-3 specifications. Any type of petroleum-base fluid (power steering fluid, automatic transmission fluid; etc.) will destroy the rubber parts.

ABS Brake Modulator/Master Cylinder Assembly

The ABS brake modulator/brake motor pack assembly controls the hydraulic pressure to the front calipers and rear calipers (or rear wheel cylinders, as equipped) by modulating the hydraulic pressure to reduce the tendency of wheel lock-up.

The basic ABS brake modulator configuration consists of gear subassemblies, ball screws, nuts, pistons and hydraulic check valves. The ABS brake motor pack consists of three motors, three drive gears and three Expansion Spring Brakes (ESBs). The ESBs are used to hold the pistons in the upmost (or home) position. An ESB is a spring that is retained in a housing at a close tolerance. One end of the spring is in contact with the motor drive dog and the other end is in contact with the pinion drive dog. In normal braking, brake pressure is present on the top of the piston, applying a downward force. The force applies a counterclockwise torque to the motor pinion which tries to rotate the spring counterclockwise. The counterclockwise torque expands the spring outward within the housing and prevent gear rotation

REMOVAL & INSTALLATION

♦ See Figure 89

✷✷ CAUTION

To avoid personal injury, due to a retained spring load on the brake modulator, the gear tension relief function of a scan tool must be performed prior to removal of the ABS Brake Modulator/Master Cylinder assembly.

✷✷ WARNING

Proper operation of any ABS system depends on clean DOT 3 brake fluid and a system free of moisture and any dirt or foreign material. Clean all of the brake line connections well and use great care to keep the any contamination out of the system.

1. Using a Tech 1® or equivalent scan tool, perform the Gear Tension Relief Sequence.
2. Disconnect the negative battery cable.

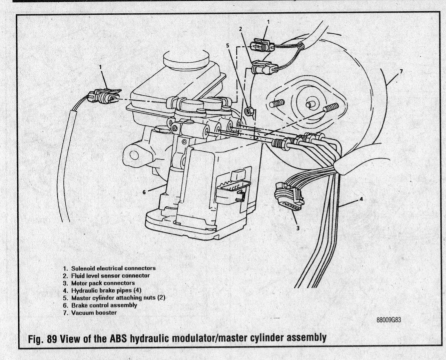

1. Solenoid electrical connectors
2. Fluid level sensor connector
3. Motor pack connectors
4. Hydraulic brake pipes (4)
5. Master cylinder attaching nuts (2)
6. Brake control assembly
7. Vacuum booster

88009G83

Fig. 89 View of the ABS hydraulic modulator/master cylinder assembly

3. Detach the two brake solenoid valve electrical connectors.

4. Detach the brake fluid level indicator sensor electrical connector.

5. Detach the ABS brake motor pack 6-way electrical connector.

6. Using a brake line wrench, disconnect the four brake lines. Cap the disconnected lines to prevent the loss of fluid and the entry of moisture and contaminants.

7. Remove the two nuts holding the ABS brake modulator/master cylinder assembly to the vacuum booster and remove the assembly from the vehicle.

8. Installation is the reverse of the removal process. Torque the nuts holding the ABS brake modulator/master cylinder assembly to the vacuum booster to 20 ft. lbs. (27 Nm) and the brake line tube nuts to 18 ft. lbs. (24 Nm). Verify that all electrical connectors are secure.

9. Properly bleed the system, as outlined later in this section.

10. Connect the negative battery cable.

ABS Hydraulic Modulator Solenoid

REMOVAL & INSTALLATION

▶ **See Figure 90**

1. Detach the solenoid electrical connector.
2. Unfasten the Torx® head bolts, then remove the solenoid assembly.

➡ **Be sure the seal is still attached to the brake solenoid valve when it is removed. If not, check the valve bore in the modulator. Do not attempt to disassemble the brake solenoid valve. It is serviceable only as an assembly.**

To install:

3. Lubricate the O-rings on the new solenoid with clean brake fluid.

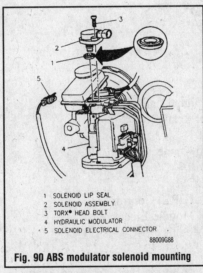

1 SOLENOID LIP SEAL
2 SOLENOID ASSEMBLY
3 TORX® HEAD BOLT
4 HYDRAULIC MODULATOR
5 SOLENOID ELECTRICAL CONNECTOR

88009G88

Fig. 90 ABS modulator solenoid mounting

4. Position the solenoid so the connectors face each other.

5. Press down firmly by hand until the solenoid assembly flange seats on the modulator assembly.

6. Install the Torx® head bolts. Tighten to 40 inch lbs. (4.5 Nm).

7. Attach the solenoid electrical connector. Make sure the connectors are installed on the correct solenoids.

8. Properly bleed the brake system.

Fluid Level Sensor

REMOVAL & INSTALLATION

See Figure 91

1. Disconnect the negative battery cable.
2. Detach the electrical connection from the fluid level sensor.

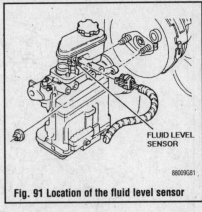

FLUID LEVEL
SENSOR

88009G81

Fig. 91 Location of the fluid level sensor

3. Remove the fluid level sensor, using needlenose pliers to compress the switch locking tabs at the inboard side of the master cylinder.

To install:

4. Insert the fluid level sensor unit until the locking tabs snap in place.

5. Attach the sensor electrical connector.

6. Connect the negative battery cable.

Electronic Brake Control Module (EBCM)

The controlling element of the ABS system is a microprocessor-based Electronic Brake Control Module (EBCM). If the vehicle is equipped with traction control, the microprocessor is called the Electronic Brake Traction Control Module (EBTCM). Inputs to the system include four wheel speed sensors, the brake switch, ignition switch and unswitched battery voltage. Outputs include three bi-directional motor controls, four indicator controls, two solenoid controls, and the system enable relay. A serial data line, located in terminal 9 of the Data Link Connector (DLC), is provided for scan tools.

The EBCM/EBTCM monitors the speed of each wheel. If any wheel begins to approach lock-up and the brake switch is on, the EBCM/EBTCM controls the motors and solenoids to reduce brake pressure to the wheel approaching lock-up. Once the wheel regains traction, brake pressure is increased until the wheel again begins to approach lock-up. This cycle repeats until either the vehicle comes to a stop, the brake is released, or no wheels approach lock-up. Additionally, the EBCM/EBTCM monitors itself, each input (except the serial data line) and each output for proper operation. If any system malfunction is detected, the EBCM/EBTCM will store a DTC in nonvolatile memory (DTCs will not disappear if the battery is disconnected).

➡ **The EBCM/EBTCM has no serviceable or removable PROM. If defective, the EBCM/EBTCM must be replaced as an assembly.**

REMOVAL & INSTALLATION

▶ **See Figure 92**

1. Locate the EBCM/EBTCM under the instrument panel, to the left of the steering column.

2. Release the EBCM/EBTCM from its bracket using the pressure tabs.

3. Detach the electrical harness and remove the EBCM/EBTCM from the vehicle.

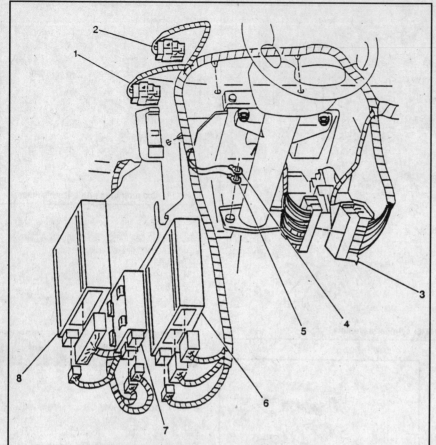

1. Hazard Lamp and Turn Signal Lamp Flasher
2. Electronic Brake Control Relay
3. Electrical Connector C201
4. Instrument Panel Ground Connection
5. ABS Ground Connection
6. Body Control Module (BCM)
7. Daytime Running Lamps (DRL) Control Module
8. Electronic Brake Control Module/Electronic Brake Traction Control Module (EBCM/EBTCM)

Fig. 92 The Anti-lock Brake System EBCM (or EBTCM) is located under the steering column, on the left side

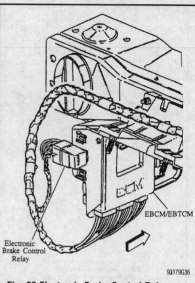

Fig. 93 Electronic Brake Control Relay location

4. Installation is the reverse of the removal process. Verify that all electrical connections are secure.

Electronic Brake Control Relay

The Electronic Brake Control Relay is a normally-open contact type relay. It has special contact material to handle the high currents required for ABS/ETS operation. The relay allows battery voltage and current to be supplied to the Brake Solenoid Valves and the EBCM/EBTCM, which supplies power to the ABS Brake Motors.

REMOVAL & INSTALLATION

◆ See Figure 93

1. Disconnect the negative battery cable.
2. Detach the electrical connection.

3. Unfasten the retainer on the bracket, then slide the relay off the bracket.
To install:
4. Slide the relay onto the bracket and make sure the retainer locks the relay to the bracket. Fasten the retainer.
5. Attach the electrical connection.
6. Connect the negative battery cable.

Wheel Speed Sensors

The front wheel speed sensors consist of a variable reluctance sensor. The sensor and toothed ring are part of the sealed hub and bearing assembly. This allows for improved environmental protection and easier assembly. As teeth pass by the sensor, an AC voltage with a frequency proportional to the speed of the wheel is generated. The sensor is not repairable, nor is the air gap adjustable. The sensor

and toothed ring cannot be serviced separately from the hub and bearing assembly. If a front wheel speed sensor fails, the entire integral hub bearing/sensor assembly must be replaced.

The rear wheel speed sensors operate in the same manner as the front wheel speed sensors. However, the rear wheel speed sensor and toothed ring are contained within the dust cap of the integral rear wheel bearing. This allows for improved environmental protection and easier assembly. Like the front sensors, the rear sensor and toothed ring are not repairable and no provision for air gap adjustment exists. If a rear wheel speed sensor fails, the entire integral hub bearing/sensor assembly must be replaced.

Between each wheel speed sensor and the main wiring harness is a jumper harness made up of highly flexible twisted pair wiring. This wiring is there because the main harness must connect to the suspension of the vehicle. The wiring in this area is subjected to the same motion as a spring or shock absorber. Consequently, any repair to this section of wiring will result in stiffening and therefore, eventual failure due to wire fatigue. Service is by replacement only. Use care when working around the wheel speed sensor and the jumper harness.

※※ WARNING

The wheel speed sensor jumper harnesses are not repairable and must be replaced. Do not attempt to solder, splice or crimp these harnesses as eventual failure will result.

REMOVAL & INSTALLATION

◆ See Figure 94

The wheel speed sensors, front and rear, are built into the non-serviceable wheel bearing/hub assembly. If a wheel speed sensor is proved to be defective, the entire wheel bearing/hub assembly must be replaced. For wheel bearing/hub assembly replacement, please see the procedures in Section 8.

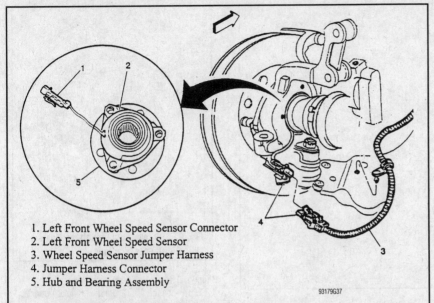

1. Left Front Wheel Speed Sensor Connector
2. Left Front Wheel Speed Sensor
3. Wheel Speed Sensor Jumper Harness
4. Jumper Harness Connector
5. Hub and Bearing Assembly

93179G37

Fig. 94 The wheel speed sensors are built into the wheel bearing hub assemblies—left front wheel speed sensor shown, others similar

Filling And Bleeding The ABS System

✳✳ CAUTION

Use only GM SUPREME 11 (GM #1052542) or equivalent DOT 3 brake fluid from a clean, sealed container. Do not use fluid from an open container that may be contaminated with water. Improper or contaminated fluid could result in damage to components or loss of braking, with possible personal injury.

✳✳ WARNING

Overfilling the brake fluid reservoir must be avoided due to the potential for overflow onto the nearby catalytic converters in the exhaust system. Brake fluid is flammable, and contact with hot exhaust components could result in a fire and possible personal injury. Do NOT allow brake fluid to spill on or come in contact with the vehicle's finish as it will remove the paint. In case of a spill, immediately flush the area with water.

➡If any brake component is repaired or replaced such that air is allowed to enter the brake system, the entire bleeding procedure MUST be followed. Prior to bleeding the brakes, the front and rear displacement cylinder pistons must be returned to the topmost position. The preferred method uses a Tech 1® or equivalent scan tool to perform the rehoming procedure. If a scan tool is not available, a second procedure may be used, but it is extremely important that the procedure be followed exactly as outlined.

A bleeding operation is necessary to remove air when it has been introduced into the hydraulic brake system (by disconnecting brake lines or if the brake fluid reservoir has been allowed to run dry).

It is necessary to bleed the system at all four brakes. If a brake hose or steel brake line has been disconnected at one wheel, only that wheel caliper (or wheel cylinder, as equipped) needs to be bled. If brake lines or hoses are disconnected at any fitting located between the master cylinder and the brakes, then the brake system served by the disconnected brake line must be bled.

SYSTEM FILLING

The master cylinder reservoirs must be kept properly filled to prevent air from entering the system. No special filling procedures are required because of the anti-lock system.

When adding fluid, use only DOT 3 fluid; the use of DOT 5 or silicone fluids is specifically prohibited. Use of improper or contaminated fluid may cause the fluid to boil or cause the rubber components in the system to deteriorate. Never use any fluid with a petroleum base or any fluid which has been exposed to water or moisture.

SYSTEM BLEEDING

Before bleeding the ABS brake system, the front and rear displacement cylinder pistons must be returned to the topmost position. The preferred method uses a Tech 1® or T-100® scan tool to perform the rehoming procedure. If a Tech 1® is not available, the second procedure may be used, but it must be followed EXACTLY.

Rehome Procedure

WITH TECH 1® OR T-100® OR EQUIVALENT SCAN TOOLS

1. Using a Tech 1® or T-100® (CAMS), select "Motor Rehome." The motor rehome function cannot be performed if current DTCs are present. If DTCs are present, the vehicle must be repaired and the codes cleared before performing the motor rehome function.

2. The entire brake system should now be bled using the pressure or manual bleeding procedures outlined later in this section.

WITHOUT TECH 1® OR T-100® R EQUIVALENT SCAN TOOLS

➡**Do not place your foot on the brake pedal through this entire procedure unless specifically instructed to do so.**

This method can only be used if the ABS warning lamp is not illuminated and no DTCs are present.

1. Remove your foot from the brake pedal.
2. Start the engine and allow it to run for at least 10 seconds while observing the amber ABS warning lamp.
3. If the ABS warning lamp turned ON and stayed ON after about 10 seconds, the bleeding procedure must be stopped and a Tech 1® or equivalent scan tool must be used to diagnose the ABS function.
4. If the ABS warning lamp turned ON for about 3 seconds, then turned OFF and stayed OFF, turn the ignition switch to the **OFF** position.
5. Repeat Steps 1–4 one more time.
6. The entire brake system should now be bled by following the manual or pressure bleeding procedure.

Pressure Bleeding

▶ **See Figures 95 and 96**

➡**The pressure bleeding equipment must be of the diaphragm type. It must have a rubber diaphragm between the air supply and the brake fluid to prevent air, moisture and other contaminants from entering the hydraulic system.**

1. Clean the master cylinder fluid reservoir cover and surrounding area, then remove the cover.
2. Add fluid, if necessary to obtain a proper fluid level.
3. Connect bleeder adapter J 35589, or equivalent, to the brake fluid reservoir, then connect the bleeder adapter to the pressure bleeding equipment.
4. Adjust the pressure bleed equipment to 5–10 psi (35–70 kPa) and wait about 30 seconds to be sure there is no leakage.
5. Adjust the pressure bleed equipment to 30–35 psi (205–240 kPa).

✳✳ WARNING

Use a shop rag to catch the escaping brake fluid. Be careful not to let any fluid run down the motor pack base or into the electrical connector.

6. With the pressure bleeding equipment connected and pressurized, proceed as follows:
    a. Attach a clear plastic bleeder hose to the rearward bleeder valve on the hydraulic modulator.
    b. Slowly open the bleeder valve and allow fluid to flow until no air is seen in the fluid.
    c. Close the valve when fluid flows out without any air bubbles.
    d. Repeat Steps 6b and 6c until no air bubbles are present.

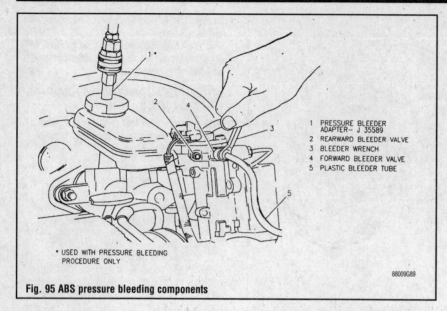

1 PRESSURE BLEEDER ADAPTER- J 35589
2 REARWARD BLEEDER VALVE
3 BLEEDER WRENCH
4 FORWARD BLEEDER VALVE
5 PLASTIC BLEEDER TUBE

* USED WITH PRESSURE BLEEDING PROCEDURE ONLY

Fig. 95 ABS pressure bleeding components

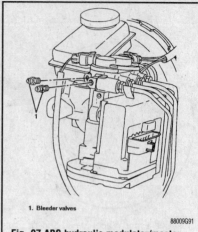

1. Bleeder valves

Fig. 97 ABS hydraulic modulator/master cylinder bleeder locations

Fig. 96 Position a shop rag to catch escaping brake fluid

e. Relocate the bleeder hose on the forward hydraulic modulator bleed valve and repeat Steps 6a through 6d.

7. Tighten the bleeder valve to 80 inch lbs. (9 Nm).

8. Proceed to bleed the hydraulic modulator brake pipe connections as follows with the pressure bleeding equipment connected and pressurized:

a. Slowly open the forward brake pipe tube nut on the hydraulic modulator and check for air in the escaping fluid.

b. When the air flow ceases, immediately tighten the tube nut. Tighten the tube nut to 18 ft. lbs. (24 Nm).

9. Repeat Steps 8a and 8b for the remaining three brake pipe connections moving from the front to the rear.

10. Raise and safely support the vehicle.

11. Proceed, as outlined in the following steps, to bleed the wheel brakes in the following sequence: right rear, left rear, right front, then left front.

a. Attach a clear plastic bleeder hose to the bleeder valve at the wheel, then submerge the opposite hose end in a clean container partially filled with clean brake fluid.

b. Slowly open the bleeder valve and allow the fluid to flow.

c. Close the valve when fluid begins to flow without any air bubbles. Tap lightly on the caliper or backing plate to dislodge any trapped air bubbles.

12. Repeat Step 11 on the other brakes using the earlier sequence.

13. Remove the pressure bleeding equipment, including bleeder adapter J 35589, or equivalent.

14. Carefully lower the vehicle, then check the brake fluid and add if necessary. Secure the reservoir cap onto the reservoir.

15. With the ignition switch turned to the **RUN** position, apply the brake pedal with moderate force and hold it. Note the pedal travel and feel. If the pedal feels firm and constant and the pedal travel is not excessive, start the engine. With the engine running, recheck the pedal travel. If it's still firm and constant and pedal travel is not excessive, go to Step 17.

16. If the pedal feels soft or has excessive travel either initially or after the engine is started, the following procedure may be used:

a. With the Tech 1® or equivalent scan tool, RELEASE then APPLY each motor 2–3 times and cycle each solenoid 5–10 times. When finished, be sure to APPLY the front and rear motors to ensure the pistons are in the upmost position. DO NOT DRIVE THE VEHICLE.

b. If a Tech 1® or equivalent scan tool is not available, remove your foot from the brake pedal, start the engine and allow it run for at least 10 seconds to initialize the ABS. DO NOT DRIVE THE VEHICLE. After 10 seconds, turn the ignition switch to the **OFF** position. The initialization procedure most be repeated 5 times to ensure any trapped air has been dislodged.

c. Repeat the bleeding procedure, starting with Step 1.

17. Road test the vehicle, and make sure the brakes are operating properly.

Manual Bleeding

▶ See Figure 97

1. Clean the master cylinder fluid reservoir cover and surrounding area, then remove the cover.

2. Add fluid, if necessary to obtain a proper

fluid level, then put the reservoir cover back on.

3. Prime the ABS hydraulic modulator/master cylinder assembly as follows:

a. Attach a bleeder hose to the rearward bleeder valve, then submerge the opposite hose end in a clean container partially filled with clean brake fluid.

b. Slowly open the rearward bleeder valve.

c. Depress and hold the brake pedal until the fluid begins to flow.

d. Close the valve, then release the brake pedal.

e. Repeat Steps 3b–3d until no air bubbles are present.

f. Relocate the bleeder hose to the forward hydraulic modulator bleeder valve, then repeat Steps 3a–3e7.

4. Once the fluid is seen to flow from both modulator bleeder valves, the ABS modulator/master cylinder assembly is sufficiently full of fluid. However, it may not be completely purged of air. At this point, move to the wheel brakes and bleed them. This ensures that the lowest points in the system are completely free of air and then the assembly can purged of any remaining air.

5. Remove the fluid reservoir cover. Fill to the correct level, if necessary, then fasten the cover.

6. Raise and safely support the vehicle.

7. Proceed, as outlined in the following steps, to bleed the wheel brakes in the following sequence: right rear, left rear, right front, then left front.

a. Attach a clear plastic bleeder hose to the bleeder valve at the wheel, then submerge the opposite hose end in a clean container partially filled with clean brake fluid.

b. Open the bleeder valve.

c. Have an assistant slowly depress the brake pedal.

d. Close the valve and slowly release the release the brake pedal.

e. Wait 5 seconds.

f. Repeat Steps 7a–7e until the brake pedal feels firm at half travel and no air bubbles are observed in the bleeder hose. To assist in freeing the entrapped air, tap lightly on the caliper or braking plate to dislodge any trapped air bubbles.

8. Repeat Step 7 for the remaining brakes in the sequence given earlier.

9. Carefully lower the vehicle.

10. Remove the reservoir cover, then fill to the correct level with brake fluid and replace the cap.

11. Bleed the ABS hydraulic modulator/master cylinder assembly as follows:

    a. Attach a clear plastic bleeder hose to the rearward bleeder valve on the modulator, then submerge the opposite hose end in a clean container partially filled with clean brake fluid.

    b. Have an assistant depress the brake pedal with moderate force.

    c. Slowly open the rearward bleeder valve and allow the fluid to flow.

    d. Close the valve, then release the brake pedal.

    e. Wait 5 seconds.

    .f. Repeat Steps 11a–11e until no air bubbles are present.

    g. Relocate the bleeder hose to the forward hydraulic modulator bleeder valve, then repeat Steps 11a–11f.

12. Carefully lower the vehicle, then check the brake fluid and add if necessary. Secure the reservoir cap to the reservoir.

13. With the ignition switch placed in the **RUN** position, apply the brake pedal with moderate force and hold it. Note the pedal travel and feel. If the pedal feels firm and constant and the pedal travel is not excessive, start the engine. With the engine running, recheck the pedal travel. If it's still firm and constant and pedal travel is not excessive, road test the vehicle and make sure the brakes are operating properly.

14. If the pedal feels soft or has excessive travel either initially or after the engine is started, the following procedure may be used:

    a. With the Tech 1® or equivalent scan tool, RELEASE then APPLY each motor 2–3 times and cycle each solenoid 5–10 times. When finished, be sure to APPLY the front and rear motors to ensure the pistons are in the upmost position. DO NOT DRIVE THE VEHICLE.

    b. If a Tech 1® or equivalent scan tool is not available, remove your foot from the brake pedal, start the engine and allow it run for at least 10 seconds to initialize the ABS. DO NOT DRIVE THE VEHICLE. After 10 seconds, turn the ignition switch to the **OFF** position. The initialization procedure most be repeated 5 times to ensure any trapped air has been dislodged.

    c. Repeat the bleeding procedure, starting with Step 1.

15. Road test the vehicle, and make sure the brakes are operating properly.

BRAKE SPECIFICATIONS
All measurements in inches unless noted

Year	Model		Master Cylinder Bore	Brake Disc Original Thickness	Brake Disc Minimum Thickness	Maximum Runout	Brake Drum Diameter Original Inside Diameter	Brake Drum Diameter Max. Wear Limit	Brake Drum Diameter Maximum Machine Diameter	Minimum Lining Thickness Front	Minimum Lining Thickness Rear
1997	Cutlass Supreme	F	0.945	1.039	0.987	0.003	-	-	-	0.030	-
		R	0.945	0.492	0.444	0.003	8.863	8.920	8.909	-	0.030
	Grand Prix	F	1.000	1.270	1.250	0.003	-	-	-	0.030	-
		R	1.000	0.430	0.410	0.003	8.863	8.920	8.909	-	0.030
	Lumina	F	0.945	1.039	0.987	0.003	-	-	-	0.030	-
		R	0.945	0.492	0.444	0.003	8.863	8.920	8.909	-	0.030
	Monte Carlo	F	0.945	1.039	0.987	0.003	-	-	-	0.030	-
		R	0.945	0.492	0.444	0.003	8.863	8.920	8.909	-	0.030
	Regal	F	1.000	1.270	1.250	0.003	-	-	-	0.030	-
		R	1.000	0.430	0.410	0.003	8.863	8.920	8.909	-	0.030
	Century	F	1.000	1.270	1.250	0.003	-	-	-	0.030	-
		R	1.000	0.430	0.410	0.003	8.863	8.920	8.909	-	0.030
1998	Intrigue	F	NA	1.270	1.250	0.003	-	-	-	0.030	-
		R	NA	0.430	0.350	0.003	-	-	-	-	0.030
	Grand Prix	F	1.000	1.270	1.250	0.003	-	-	-	0.030	-
		R	1.000	0.430	0.410	0.003	-	-	-	-	0.030
	Lumina	F	0.945	1.039	0.987	0.003	-	-	-	0.030	-
		R	0.945	0.433	0.385	0.003	8.863	8.920	8.909	-	0.030
	Monte Carlo	F	0.945	1.039	0.987	0.003	-	-	-	0.030	-
		R	0.945	0.433	0.385	0.003	8.863	8.920	8.909	-	0.030
	Regal	F	1.000	1.270	1.250	0.003	-	-	-	0.030	-
		R	1.000	0.430	0.410	0.003	8.863	8.920	8.909	-	0.030
	Century	F	1.000	1.270	1.250	0.003	-	-	-	0.030	-
		R	1.000	0.430	0.410	0.003	8.863	8.920	8.909	-	0.030
1999	Intrigue	F	NA	1.270	1.250	0.003	-	-	-	0.030	-
		R	NA	0.430	0.370	0.003	-	-	-	-	0.030
	Grand Prix	F	1.000	1.270	1.250	0.003	-	-	-	0.030	-
		R	1.000	0.430	0.410	0.003	-	-	-	-	0.030
	Lumina	F	0.945	1.039	0.987	0.003	-	-	-	0.030	-
		R	0.945	0.433	0.385	0.003	8.863	8.920	8.909	-	0.030
	Monte Carlo	F	0.945	1.039	0.987	0.003	-	-	-	0.030	-
		R	0.945	0.433	0.385	0.003	8.863	8.920	8.909	-	0.030
	Regal	F	1.000	1.270	1.250	0.003	-	-	-	0.030	-
		R	1.000	0.430	0.410	0.003	8.86	8.920	8.909	-	0.030
	Century	F	1.000	1.270	1.250	0.003	-	-	-	0.030	-
		R	1.000	0.430	0.410	0.003	8.86	8.920	8.909	-	0.030
2000	Intrigue	F	NA	1.270	1.250	0.003	-	-	-	0.030	-
		R	NA	0.430	0.350	0.003	-	-	-	-	0.030
	Grand Prix	F	1.000	1.270	1.250	0.003	-	-	-	0.030	-
		R	1.000	0.430	0.410	0.003	-	-	-	-	0.030
	Lumina	F	0.945	1.270	1.250	0.003	-	-	-	0.030	-
		R	0.945	0.430	0.410	0.003	8.863	8.920	8.909	-	0.030
	Monte Carlo	F	0.945	1.270	1.250	0.003	-	-	-	0.030	-
		R	0.945	0.430	0.410	0.003	8.863	8.920	8.909	-	0.030
	Regal	F	1.000	1.270	1.250	0.003	-	-	-	0.030	-
		R	1.000	0.430	0.410	0.003	8.863	8.920	8.909	-	0.030
	Century	F	1.000	1.270	1.250	0.003	-	-	-	0.030	-
		R	1.000	0.430	0.410	0.003	8.863	8.920	8.909	-	0.030

93179C01

10

BODY
AND TRIM

EXTERIOR

Some production door hardware attaching screws contain an epoxy thread-locking compound to ensure that the original torque setting will be maintained.

Service (replacement parts) attaching screws may not contain a thread-locking compound. To prevent loosening of service screws or to renew thread-locking characteristics of production screws, the threads of the fastener(s) can be treated with GM #12345382 Adhesive/Sealant Compound, or equivalent. Upon installation and drying, the adhesive cures to bond the attachment and to prevent it from backing out. The adhesive bond does not prevent future attachment removal, if required. Adhesive/Sealant Compound or equivalent can be used on any threaded fastener.

Doors

REMOVAL & INSTALLATION

▶ **See Figures 1, 2, 3, 4 and 5**

The door hinges are bolted to the door and body. The door side hinges have elongated holes which allow for some up and down and in and out adjustment. The body side hinges have elongated holes which allow for some fore and aft adjustment.

➡ **The body side door hinge may have four bolts: two 13mm, one Torx® and one 10mm bolt. Do not remove the 10mm bolt. A cone attached to the back side of the hinge may fall off and end up in the bottom of the A-Pillar (forward door post) causing a rattle. This cone is used for assembly purposes only and need not be removed to adjust or remove the door hinge strap (body side hinges). If replacing door hinges, to minimize door realignment, do not remove both door hinges at the same time. Do each hinge separately, and replace any broken hinges first. GM specifies that if a worn or damaged hinge is replaced, both hinges must be replaced at the same time.**

✳✳ WARNING

The negative battery cable should be disconnected because these vehicles are equipped with an air bag system and interior work should only be performed with the air bag system disabled. Please see Section 6 for Air Bag Disarm procedures. In addition, since many GM W-Body vehicles are equipped with Theftlock® radios, this radio protection feature must be turned off. When power is removed from the vehicle, the Theftlock radio is disabled. When the power is later restored, this radio is designed not to play. Take the time to turn off the Theftlock® feature before disconnecting the negative battery cable. Another concern is that, when working around the inside of a door, the express down switch on an electric window controls may be activated, catching and injuring a hand or arm.

➡**The following procedure can be used for both the front doors and the rear doors.**

1. Turn off the radio Theftlock® feature, if equipped.
2. Raise the window all the way.
3. Disconnect the negative battery cable and disarm the air bag system. Please see Section 6 for Air Bag Disarming procedures.
4. Clean the hinge mounting surfaces on the door with a shop cloth and mark the hinge location on the door surface (and on the body pillar, if the hinges are being replaced, too) with a grease pencil or other suitable marker.
5. The electrical connections to the door must be detached. Use the following procedure:
   a. Remove the door trim panel using the procedures found in this section. Please note that GM specifies that when an inner trim panel is

removed, new trim panel retainers MUST be used at assembly.
   b. Remove the plastic water deflector sheet. Work it loose from its pressure-sensitive tape along the bottom and sides and peel it up out of the way.

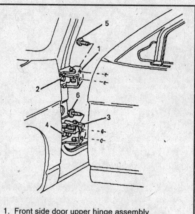

1. Front side door upper hinge assembly
2. Front side door upper body side hinge bolt/screw
3. Front side door lower hinge assembly
4. Front side door lower body side hinge bolt/screw
5. Rear side door upper door side hinge bolt/screw
6. Rear side door lower door side hinge bolt/screw

88000G03

Fig. 1 Typical W-Body door hinge attachment

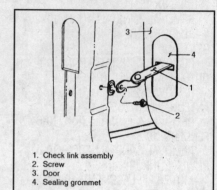

1. Check link assembly
2. Screw
3. Door
4. Sealing grommet

88000G04

Fig. 3 Door check link-to-body arrangement

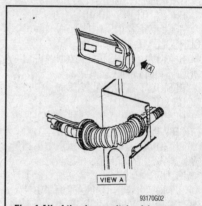

VIEW A

93170G02

Fig. 4 All of the door switch wiring runs through a conduit like this that must be disconnected

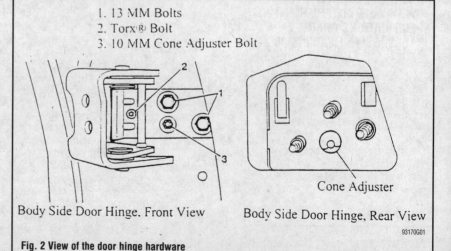

1. 13 MM Bolts
2. Torx® Bolt
3. 10 MM Cone Adjuster Bolt

Body Side Door Hinge, Front View

Cone Adjuster

Body Side Door Hinge, Rear View

93170G01

Fig. 2 View of the door hinge hardware

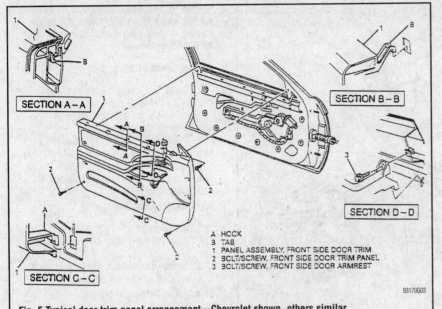

A HOOK
B TAB
1 PANEL ASSEMBLY, FRONT SIDE DOOR TRIM
2 BOLT/SCREW, FRONT SIDE DOOR TRIM PANEL
2 BOLT/SCREW, FRONT SIDE DOOR ARMREST
3 BOLT/SCREW, FRONT SIDE DOOR ARMREST

SECTION A–A
SECTION B–B
SECTION C–C
SECTION D–D

93170G03

Fig. 5 Typical door trim panel arrangement—Chevrolet shown, others similar

c. If equipped, remove the energy absorber pad.

d. Remove the door speaker(s).

e. Tag for identification as necessary and detach the electrical connectors. Use care. There are numerous wires and connectors running to the door.

f. .There is a rubber tube, or conduit, through which the electric wires to the door are routed. Carefully work this conduit loose from the door and pull the wiring harness through the opening in the door.

6. The doors on this vehicle are heavy and difficult to balance. With an assistant or two steadying the door and with some sort of support under the door (many shops use a floor jack with lots of padding on the lift saddle to protect the paint), remove the 13mm bolts on the door side (not the body side) of the hinge and separate the door from the vehicle.

To install:

7. With an assistant or two steadying the door and with an adjustable support (floor jack) under the door, carefully install the door to the vehicle, using care to raise the door to meet and align with the door hinge bolt openings and the grease pencil outlines made earlier. When satisfied with the fit, coat the door hinge bolt threads with Loctite® Blue thread-locking compound (GM # 12345382, or equivalent) then install the 13mm bolts and tighten to 24 ft. lbs. (33 Nm). Remove the support.

8. Feed the door wiring harness through the opening in the door and route to the proper door devices, using the identification tags made at removal. Secure the rubber conduit to the door opening.

9. Align the door, as required, using the procedures found in this section.

10. Install the remaining components removed earlier.

ADJUSTMENT

If the original door is being removed and installed again, one trick is to apply short pieces of masking tape, one piece to bridge the gap between the door and the rocker panel and the second piece to bridge the gap between the door and the rear door or quarter panel, depending on the door being serviced. Cut the tape at the gap using a sharp blade. When the door is being installed, use the tape as an alignment guide to get the door back into position as close as possible to the original location.

Up/Down or In/Out Adjustment

➡Before attempts are made to adjust a door, verify that the door hinges are in good condition. Open the door and have an assistant lift the latch end of the door. If more than about 1/16 inch or movement can be detected at the door, the hinge pin and/or bushings may be worn and the hinge may need to be serviced or replaced.

1. Loosen, but do not remove, the two 13mm door side hinge bolts.

2. Move the door up or down and in or out by reposition the door as necessary. An assistant may be required.

3. When satisfied with the fit, tighten the bolts to 24 ft. lbs. (33 Nm).

Fore/Aft Adjustment

1. Remove the front fender insulator to gain access to the body side hinge bolts. The following may be helpful.

a. The front fender insulator attaches to the fender liner at the rear of the liner. One some models it may be possible to remove the insulator by disengaging the mounting tabs from the studs and pulling it off. On other models, it may be necessary to remove the front fender liner first, using the following as a guide.

b. To remove the front fender liner, it will likely be necessary to first remove the front tire and wheel assembly for access.

c. Remove the screws from the front fender liner. There may be a screw at the front tab of the liner at the lower engine compartment side rail.

2. Remove the screws from the liner at the rear of the fender and work the liner from the vehicle.

3. With access to the body side hinge bolts, loosen, but do not remove the two 13mm body side hinge bolts.

4. Loosen the one 10mm cone adjuster body hide hinge bolt. Do not remove the 10mm bolt. A cone attached to the back side of the hinge may fall off and end up in the bottom of the A-Pillar (forward door post) causing a rattle. This cone is used for assembly purposes only and need not be removed to adjust the door hinge strap (body side hinges).

5. Loosen, but do not remove the one Torx® bolt.

6. Adjust the door fore and aft by repositioning the door as necessary.

7. When satisfied with the fit, tighten the bolts as follows:

a. Tighten the Torx® bolt first to 89 inch lbs. (10 Nm).

b. Tighten the 10mm cone bolt to 89 inch lbs. (10 Nm).

c. Tighten the 13mm bolts to 24 ft. lbs. (33 Nm).

8. Install the fender insulator/fender liner.

Hood

REMOVAL & INSTALLATION

▶ See Figure 6

❋❋ WARNING

DO NOT allow the hood to fold back onto the windshield. Windshield and paint damage may result from improper handling of the hood.

➡It is good practice, when removing body panels, to apply tape to the corners of the panel and adjacent surfaces to help prevent paint damage.

1. Raise and safely support the hood.

2. Disconnect the underhood lamp, if equipped.

3. If the same hood is to be reinstalled, mark the upper hood hinge location to the hood with a grease pencil.

4. With an assistant, remove the bolts from the upper hood hinge.

5. With an assistant, remove the hood from the vehicle.

6. Installation is the reverse of the removal process. With an assistant, place the hood on the vehicle and align the hood hinges with the marks made at removal. Tighten the hinge bolts to 20 ft. lbs. (27 Nm).

7. Adjust the hood alignment.

ALIGNMENT

The hood hinges are bolted to the fender and the hood. Fore/aft adjustment may be made by elongating the hood-side hinge holes. Vertical adjustment at the front may be made by adjusting the hood bumpers up or down. Gap tolerances are 0.10–0.22 inch (2.0–6.0mm) and flush tolerances are 0–6 inch (0–2.0mm).

1. Open the hood.

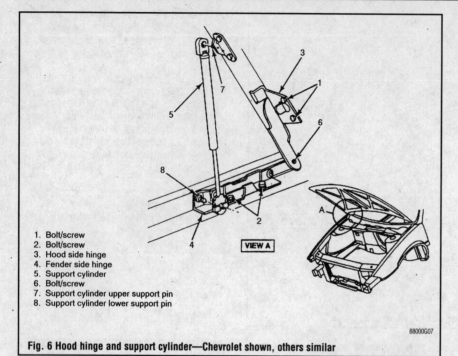

1. Bolt/screw
2. Bolt/screw
3. Hood side hinge
4. Fender side hinge
5. Support cylinder
6. Bolt/screw
7. Support cylinder upper support pin
8. Support cylinder lower support pin

88000G07

Fig. 6 Hood hinge and support cylinder—Chevrolet shown, others similar

2. Loosen the hinge-to-hood bolts.
3. Adjust the hood to the fender position.
4. Close the hood and check the alignment.
5. Open the hood and adjust the hood as needed.
6. When satisfied with the hood alignment, tighten the hinge bolt.
7. Adjust the hood bumpers up or down as required.

Trunk Lid

REMOVAL & INSTALLATION

▶ **See Figure 7**

➡ **It is good practice, when removing body panels, to apply tape to the corners of the panel and/or cover the adjacent surfaces to help prevent paint damage.**

1. Open the trunk lid (GM calls it the Rear Compartment Lid).
2. Place protective coverings over adjacent body panels.

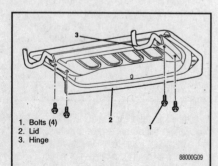

1. Bolts (4)
2. Lid
3. Hinge

88000G09

Fig. 7 Typical trunk lid retaining bolt locations

3. Detach all electrical connectors, as required.
4. If the same trunk lid is to be reinstalled, mark the upper trunk lid hinge location to the lid with a grease pencil.
5. With an assistant, remove the bolts from the upper trunk lid hinge.
6. With an assistant, remove the trunk lid from the vehicle.
7. If the spoiler (if equipped) is to be replaced, remove the nuts from the spoiler mounting studs and lift the spoiler from the trunk lid.
8. Installation is the reverse of the removal process. With an assistant, place the trunk lid on the vehicle and align the lid hinges with the marks made at removal. Tighten the hinge bolts to 18 ft. lbs. (25 Nm).
9. Connect all electrical harnesses and make sure all the body side weather-stripping is in place.
10. Remove the protective coverings and close the trunk lid.

ADJUSTMENT

1. Adjust the trunk lid alignment, as required. Inspect the trunk lid for damage and the hinges for wear.
2. There should be a height adjustment bumper at the front of the hinge. An Allen wrench is used for the adjustment.

Grille

REMOVAL & INSTALLATION

➡ **Although the basic W-Body platform is shared among four GM manufacturers, different grilles and fascia panels give the vehicles their identify. This may change from year to year and depending on the model and may vary between different Regular Production Options (RPOs). Since most all grille panels are retained with a combination of tabs and screws, the following should suffice for most all W-Body vehicles.**

Pontiac Grand Prix

1. Locate and remove the attaching screws from the front bumper fascia panel (with RPO Z7M).
2. Lift up and out on the bottom edge of the grille to release the lower tabs.
3. Pull down on the grille to release the upper grille tabs from the bumper fascia (with RPO Z7K).
4. Remove the grille from the bumper fascia.
5. Installation is the reverse of removal. Do not over-tighten the screws.

Buick Century and Regal

1. Open the hood.
2. Remove the nuts from the grille locating studs.
3. Remove the grille from the bumper fascia.
4. Installation is the reverse of removal.

Oldsmobile Cutlass Supreme

1. Open and support the hood.
2. Remove the parking lamps.
3. Unsnap the grill from the headlamp housing panel.
4. Remove the grille from the vehicle.
5. Installation is the reverse of the removal procedure. Secure one edge of the grille first, snap the center of the grille in place, then snap in the other end of the grille.
6. Install the parking lamps and check lamp operation at completion.

Outside Mirrors

REMOVAL & INSTALLATION

In general, the outside mirrors are mounted with either studs and nuts or bolts, depending on body style. The mirror face should be replaceable without removing the entire mirror. Left side and right side convex mirror faces are different and must be replaced with the same type mirror face when serviced.

Manual Mirror

▶ **See Figure 8**

1. Remove the door trim panel using the procedures found in this section.
2. Remove the mirror reinforcement cover
3. Remove the manual mirror attaching fasteners and remove the mirror from the vehicle.
   To install:
4. Route the mirror control cable through the opening in the door panel at the mirror reinforcement.
5. Position the mirror to the door. On sedan models, the front edge of the mirror should be tucked under the channel. Slide the mirror forward as far as possible so the mirror is flush with the belt molding. Install the fasteners, as equipped and tighten to 89 inch lbs. (10 Nm).
6. Install the mirror reinforcement cover.
7. Install the interior door trim panel.

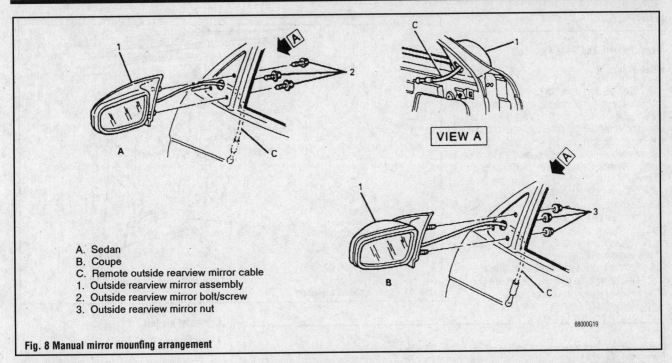

A. Sedan
B. Coupe
C. Remote outside rearview mirror cable
1. Outside rearview mirror assembly
2. Outside rearview mirror bolt/screw
3. Outside rearview mirror nut

88000G19

Fig. 8 Manual mirror mounting arrangement

Electric Mirror

▶ **See Figure 9**

1. Remove the door trim panel using the procedures found in this section.
2. Detach the electric mirror electrical connectors.
3. Remove the mirror reinforcement cover
4. Remove the manual mirror attaching fasteners and remove the mirror from the vehicle.

To install:

5. Route the mirror electrical harness through the opening in the door panel at the mirror reinforcement.
6. Position the mirror to the door. On sedan models, the front edge of the mirror should be tucked under the channel. Slide the mirror forward as far as possible so the mirror is flush with the belt molding. Install the fasteners, as equipped. Start tightening at the lower left fastener (could be a nut or a small bolt) and tighten in a clockwise direction. Tighten to 89 inch lbs. (10 Nm).

7. Install the mirror reinforcement cover.
8. Attach the electrical connectors.
9. Install the interior door trim panel.

Antenna

W-Body vehicles may be equipped with a fixed antenna, a power antenna or an antenna built into the rear window glass, depending on vehicle and model.

A fixed antenna mast can be removed by simply unscrewing from its base. On vehicles equipped with a rear window antenna, if a rear window antenna grid line is broken, the repair procedure is the same as the procedure for repairing a rear window defogger grid line. If a fixed antenna base is to be replaced, use the following procedure. Please note that because of the design of the antenna bezel and nut, a special tool, J 38536 Antenna Bezel Socket, is recommended. Use care if using substitute tools.

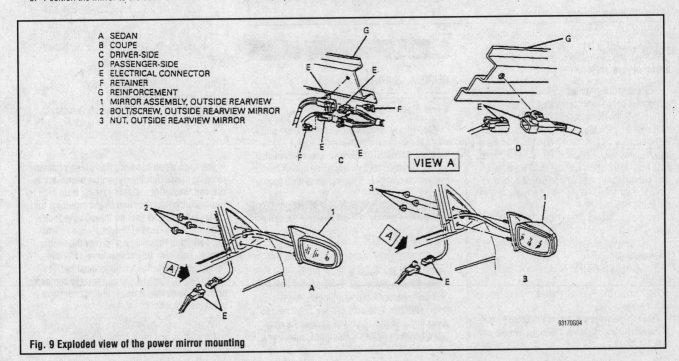

A SEDAN
B COUPE
C DRIVER-SIDE
D PASSENGER-SIDE
E ELECTRICAL CONNECTOR
F RETAINER
G REINFORCEMENT
1 MIRROR ASSEMBLY, OUTSIDE REARVIEW
2 BOLT/SCREW, OUTSIDE REARVIEW MIRROR
3 NUT, OUTSIDE REARVIEW MIRROR

93170G04

Fig. 9 Exploded view of the power mirror mounting

REMOVAL & INSTALLATION

Fixed Antenna and Base Assembly

▶ See Figure 10

1. Open the rear compartment (trunk).
2. Remove the right side rear compartment trim to gain access. First unhook the netting from the tail lamp retainer nuts. Remove the trunk mat. If necessary, remove the spare tire cover and spare tire, then remove the trim panel side panels by folding down and inward. Carefully lift the trim panel from the trunk.
3. Disconnect the antenna cable from the antenna.
4. Unscrew the fixed antenna mast from the base.
5. Remove the antenna bezel nut using J 38536 socket, or equivalent.
6. Remove the antenna base from the vehicle.
7. Installation is the reverse of the removal process.

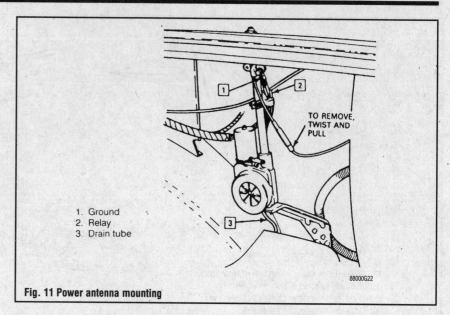

1. Ground
2. Relay
3. Drain tube

88000G22

Fig. 11 Power antenna mounting

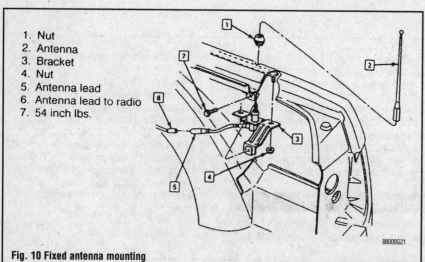

1. Nut
2. Antenna
3. Bracket
4. Nut
5. Antenna lead
6. Antenna lead to radio
7. 54 inch lbs.

88000G21

Fig. 10 Fixed antenna mounting

Power Antenna

▶ See Figure 11

The power antenna mast should be cleaned when it becomes dirty. Do not lubricate the antenna mast.

1. Open the rear compartment (trunk).
2. Remove the right side rear compartment trim to gain access. First unhook the netting from the tail lamp retainer nuts. Remove the trunk mat. If necessary, remove the spare tire cover and spare tire, then remove the trim panel side panels by folding down and inward. Carefully lift the trim panel from the trunk.
3. Disconnect the ground strap to the quarter panel.
4. Detach the electrical connector from the power antenna.
5. Disconnect the lead-in cable from the antenna.
6. Remove the mounting fasteners (nuts, bolts and/or screws).
7. Remove the power antenna from the vehicle.
8. Installation is the reverse of the removal process.

Fenders

REMOVAL & INSTALLATION

▶ See Figure 12

GM W-body vehicles use a unitized body with a separate sub-frame supporting the engine and transaxle. The inner fender panels and the radiator support are also integral parts of the body. Anti-corrosion materials have been applied to the interior surfaces of some metal panels. When servicing these panels, disturbed areas should be properly recoated with a service type anti-corrosion material.

The front fenders on W-Body vehicles basically bolt to the body. There are numerous bolts and screws that must be removed, some hidden by trim pieces. There will be some minor variations to these procedures, depending on model, vehicle year and trim level, but fender removal is reasonably straightforward.

➡Fender and door edges should be covered with masking tape for protection against chipping.

Chevrolet Models

▶ See Figure 12

1. Remove the hood using the procedures found in this section.
2. Remove the hood strut from the fender by unsnapping from the upper ball stud. Use a small, flat-bladed tool to lift up on the clip. Do not remove the clip from the strut. Do the same on the lower clip.
3. If the fender is being removed for replacement, the hood hinge will need to be removed and transferred to the replacement fender. Note that the hood hinge is bolted and spot welded in one place to the front fender. To remove the hood hinge, use the following procedure.
   a. Remove the bolts from the hinge.
   b. Use a center punch to accurately mark the center of the spot weld.
   c. Drill out the spot weld using a ⅜ inch drill bit.
   d. Remove the hood hinge from the fender.
4. Remove the bolts from the upper part of the fender.
5. Raise and safely support the vehicle. Remove the tire and wheel assembly.
6. Remove the fender liner.
7. Remove the rocker panel finish molding from the fender. Use the following procedure:
   a. Remove the sill plate at the lower door opening.

➡Use care when handling this piece of plastic molding. Note that it may not be necessary to remove the entire molding just for front fender removal. Start at the front of the molding, and remove the screws that go through the fender flange into the front of the molding and from the bottom of the molding up into the fender flange. This may be enough to release the fender. If more of the molding must be loosened, or if accident damage requires removal of the rocker panel finish molding, continue with this procedure.

   b. Remove the molding's screws from the front fender and rear quarter panel
   c. Loosen the retainers from the bottom of

the rocker panel finish molding. Use care these are primarily plastic clips. Do not break off the integral molding clips when removing the molding from the body. Gently unsnap the clips and remove the tabs. Some push/pin retainers may also be used to hold the molding to the body.

8. Locate and remove the fascia nuts from the fender.

9. Remove the remaining bolts from the lower and rear part of the fender.

10. Remove the fender from the vehicle

To install:

11. Install the fender to the vehicle and install the upper fender bolts and the screws at the rear of the fender.

12. Install the nuts retaining the front of the fender to the front fascia panel.

13. Install the rocker panel finish molding to the fender. Push the rear of the molding forward to ensure a flush fit with the quarter panel flange at the rear wheel opening. Align the rocker panel molding tabs and snap into the door slots. Push the front of the molding rearward to ensure a flush fit with the front fender flange at the front wheel opening. Install all hardware removed earlier. Install the sill plate at the bottom of the door opening.

14. Install the front fender inner liner, install the tire and wheel assembly and lower the vehicle

15. Install the hood hinge to the fender, and tighten the bolts to 18 ft. lbs. (25 Nm).

16. Install the hood strut by snapping back into place.

17. Install the hood using the procedure found in this section.

Oldsmobile Models

CUTLASS SUPREME

▶ **See Figure 12**

1. Remove the hood using the procedures found in this section.

2. If removing the left fender, perform the following:

   a. Remove the left strut tower brace.

   b. Remove the windshield washer reservoir.

   c. Remove the battery cover.

3. Remove the headlamp access panel.

4. Remove the turn signal lamp.

5. Raise and safely support the vehicle. Remove the tire and wheel assembly and then remove the fender inner liner.

6. Remove the vacuum tank if removing the left fender.

7. Remove the fasteners from the fender at the front fascia panel.

8. The Cutlass Supreme uses a separate piece of rocker panel finish molding that mounts to the lower part of the front fender. It is retained by screws going from the bottom of the molding up into the front fender flange. Remove the fasteners and gently work the molding forward to disengage it from the main piece of the rocker outer finish panel.

9. Remove the fasteners from the fender at the headlamp panel.

10. Remove the splash shield.

11. Remove the nut from the fender support bracket.

12. Lower the vehicle enough to work in the engine compartment.

13. If removing the right fender, perform the following:

   a. Remove the coolant recovery reservoir.

   b. Unbolt the electrical convenience center.

14. Remove the fasteners from the fender support bracket and the bolts from the upper fender.

15. Remove the fender from the vehicle.

To install:

16. Install the fender to the vehicle and install the upper fender bolts as well as the bolts to the fender support bracket.

17. If removed earlier install the electrical convenience center and/or the coolant recovery reservoir

18. Install the splash shield and the fasteners at the headlamp panel.

19. Install the rocker outer finish panel at the bottom rear of the fender.

20. Install the vacuum tank, if removed.

21. Install the front fender liner and the front tire and wheel assembly.

22. Install the turn signal lamp and the headlamp access panel.

23. If removed, install the following:

   a. The battery cover.

   b. The windshield washer reservoir

   c. The left strut tower brace.

24. Install the hood using the procedures found in this section.

INTRIGUE

▶ **See Figure 12**

1. Remove the hood using the procedures found in this section.

2. If the fender is being removed for replacement, the hood hinge will need to be removed and transferred to the replacement fender. Note that the hood hinge is bolted and spot welded in one place to the front fender. To remove the hood hinge, use the following procedure.

   a. Remove the hood rear side seal (weatherstrip) and the hood assist rod.

   b. Remove the bolts from the hinge.

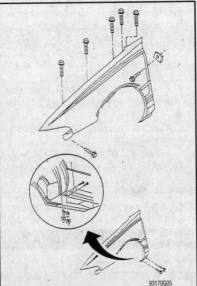

Fig. 12 Typical fender fastener locations—1998 Oldsmobile Intrigue shown, others similar

93170G05

   c. Use a center punch to accurately mark the center of the spot weld.

   d. Drill out the spot weld using a ⅜ inch drill bit.

3. Remove the front fender liner.

4. Remove the windshield washer solvent container if removing the right fender.

5. Remove the rocker finish molding using the following procedure.

   a. Remove the screws from the front edge of the rocker molding at the fender.

   b. Remove the push-in retainers from the bottom of the rocker molding from the rocker panel using a suitable door trim pad and garnish clip remover tool.

   c. Open the doors to access the push-in retainers.

   d. Remove the push-in retainers from the top inside edge of the rocker molding at the sill area, again using a door trim pad and garnish clip removal tool.

   e. Remove the rocker molding from the rocker panel.

6. Remove the bolts from the fender at the door hinge pillar.

7. Remove the bolts from the rocker panel at the bottom of the fender.

8. Remove the bolts from the fender at the front of the engine compartment side rail.

9. Remove the bolts from the fender at the lower engine compartment side rail.

10. Remove the fender from the vehicle.

11. Installation is the reverse of the removal process. Tighten the fender bolts as follows:

   a. Tighten the bolts attaching the front fender to the front engine compartment side rail and to the rocker panel to 53 inch lbs. (6 Nm).

   b. Tighten the bolts attaching the fender to the door hinge pillar to 89 inch lbs. (10 Nm).

   c. Tighten the lower engine compartment bolts to 70 inch lbs. (8 Nm).

Buick and Pontiac Models

▶ **See Figure 12**

1. Remove the headlamp on the side where the fender is being removed (Buick only).

2. Remove the hood using the procedures in the section.

3. Remove the hood hinge.

4. If the fender is being removed for replacement, the hood hinge will need to be removed and transferred to the replacement fender. Note that the hood hinge is bolted and spot welded in one place to the front fender. To remove the hood hinge, use the following procedure.

   a. Remove the bolts from the hinge.

   b. Use a center punch to accurately mark the center of the spot weld.

   c. Drill out the spot weld using a ⅜ inch drill bit.

   d. Remove the hood hinge from the fender.

5. Remove the front fender liner.

6. Remove the screws retaining the front fender to the front bumper fascia.

7. This vehicle uses a separate piece of rocker panel finish molding that mounts to the lower part of the front fender. It is retained by screws at the bottom of the molding. Remove the fasteners and remove it from the fender.

8. Remove the bolts from the fender at the

door hinge pillar, the rocker panel and engine compartment side rail.

9. Remove the fender from the vehicle.

10. Installation is the reverse of the removal procedure.

Power Sunroof

A power sunroof is an option on W-Body vehicles. It features a sliding window panel and a manually operated sunshade. The sunroof is electrically operated from a rocker switch located in the center of the windshield header area. To put the sunroof in the vent position, turn the ignition switch to the **RUN** position and press, then release the control switch rearward position. On Pontiac and Chevrolet vehicles, when the control switch rearward position is pressed and released with the window in the vent position, the window will slide back above the roof panel to the fully open position. On Buick and Oldsmobile vehicles, the window will retract downwards and slide rearward into the storage space between the roof panel and the headliner. Both vehicles are equipped with a wind deflector that extends just above the roof line when the window panel is in the open position. To close, hold the control switch in the forward position until the window completely closes, retracting the wind deflector and sealing against the roof opening flange. An express module at the front of the module causes the window panel to stop in the closed, vent, and fully open positions. An electrical harness is routed along the left portion of the windshield header and down the left windshield pillar.

MOTOR REPLACEMENT

Pontiac Models

◆ See Figure 13

✳✳ WARNING

The sunroof system is timed from the factory so that the actuator (motor) shuts off automatically when the sunroof window reaches a certain position. Extreme care must be taken when removing the actuator from the sunroof module or this timing may be thrown off causing damage to the sunroof system. Anytime the actuator needs to be removed from the module, the sunroof window must be in the fully closed position. GM specifies that their tool set, J 41718 Sunroof Timing Pins, be used when servicing the sunroof actuator.

1. Remove the sunroof window using the following procedure:

a. Slide the sunshade fully rearward.

b. Move the sunroof window to the vent position.

c. Locate and remove the sunroof window screws (3 each side).

d. Remove the sunroof window from the sunroof module assembly.

2. After removing the window, place the sunroof module in the fully closed position.

3. Remove the headliner using the procedure found in this section.

4. Detach the sunroof actuator (motor) electrical connection from the actuator.

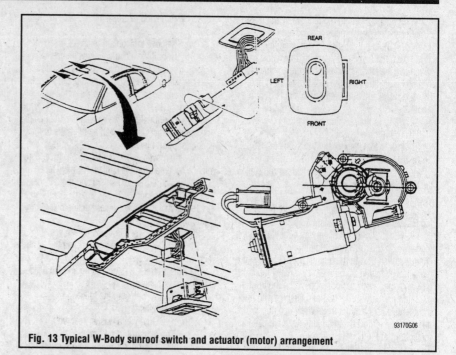

Fig. 13 Typical W-Body sunroof switch and actuator (motor) arrangement

5. Thread J 41718 Sunroof Timing Pins, or equivalent), into the front sunroof window screw holes to retain the cable adjustment. Make sure the Timing Pins (or their equivalent) are tight and holding the cable before removing the actuator.

6. Remove the sunroof actuator retaining screws and separate the actuator from the vehicle.

To install:

7. Install the sunroof actuator to the sunroof module assembly and tighten the screws to 35 inch lbs. (4 Nm).

8. Remove the timing pins, or their equivalent, from the sunroof window screw holes.

9. Attach and secure the electrical connector.

10. Install the headliner using the procedure found in this section.

11. Install the sunroof window using the following procedure:

a. Install the sunroof window to the module assembly making sure the information/logo stencil is towards the rear of the opening.

b. Install the sunroof window screws, starting with the center screws first. Tighten to 35 inch lbs. (4 Nm).

c. Adjust the sunroof window using the procedure found in this section.

d. Open and close the sunroof window to recheck the fit of the window.

Chevrolet Models

◆ See Figure 13

✳✳ WARNING

Use care when servicing the sunroof motor and drive gear assembly. The sunroof motor has an internal microswitch when opens the motor circuit (turns the motor off) when the window reaches the full vent position. If you remove the sunroof motor from the module

(sunroof assembly) and then function the motor or change the position of the sunroof window while the motor is removed, the timing of the sunroof motor will be out of phase. Putting the motor back into the sunroof assembly while out of phase will cause loss of the vent position. Do not run the motor while the motor is hanging loose in the vehicle. If the motor and module become out of phase, the motor will have to be retimed to the sunroof module.

1. Remove the headliner using the procedure found in this section.

2. Remove the sunroof switch by grasping the switch on its left and right side and pulling straight downward to disengage it from its mounting bracket.

3. Remove the motor attaching screws and separate the motor and drive gear assembly from the vehicle.

To install:

4. Install the motor and drive gear assembly to the sunroof. Tighten the screws to 35 inch lbs. (4 Nm).

5. Install the headliner and sunroof switch.

6. Retime the sunroof motor, as follows:

7. With the sunroof motor removed from the vehicle, back-probe the connector with an ohmmeter.

8. Connect the meter leads between the white and yellow wires located at the gear housing portion of the motor.

9. Insert a large, flat-bladed tool into the motor gear slot. Rotate the sunroof motor gear counterclockwise (turning the flat-bladed tool clockwise) until the ohmmeter shows Open Circuit. This positions the gear drive to FULL VENT.

➡It may take up to eleven rotations to reach the Open Circuit position.

10. Continue to turn the motor gear drive exactly 1 ½ additional turns counterclockwise. This

will retime the motor to the fully closed position. Make sure the sunroof window is in the fully closed position.

11. Install the sunroof motor to the vehicle using the procedure found in this section.

Buick Models and 1998–99 Oldsmobile Intrigue

♦ See Figure 13

Before removing the sunroof actuator, position the system in the fully closed position. Do not move the sunroof mechanism while the actuator is not in place.

1. Remove the headliner using the procedure found in this section.
2. Cut the tie straps from the wiring harness.
3. Detach the electrical connector, remove the actuator screws and separate the actuator from the sunroof assembly.

To install:

4. Install the actuator to the sunroof and tighten the screws to 35 inch lbs. (4 Nm).
5. Attach and secure the electrical connector to the actuator. Use nylon wire tires to secure the harness, as required.
6. Install the headliner using the procedures found in this section.

1997 Oldsmobile Cutlass Supreme

♦ See Figure 13

1. Position the sunroof at its maximum vent position.
2. Remove the headliner using the procedure found in this section.
3. Detach the electrical connection from the motor and drive gear assembly.
4. Remove the screws holding the motor to the motor support bracket.
5. Carefully pull the motor down to disengage the gear from the drive cables.

To install:

6. Install the motor to the sunroof.
7. Check that the sunroof is at the maximum vent position by manually pushing the mechanism forward on both sides. This aligns the drive cables.
8. Install the motor in an upward position so the gear engages between the drive cables.
9. Install the motor retaining screws and tighten screws to 35 inch lbs. (4 Nm).
10. Attach the electrical connector.
11. Install the headlining using the procedure found in this section.

2000 Oldsmobile Intrigue

♦ See Figure 14

Starting with model year 2000, the Oldsmobile Intrigue sunroof actuator (motor) is a "dumb motor". Its driveshaft turns in both directions, but it contains no limit switches. The sunroof actuator can be replaced with the glass in any position. The sunroof actuator contains no limit switches and can rotate its driveshaft in either direction.

1. Remove the headliner using the procedure in this section.
2. Remove the tie strap from the wiring harness.

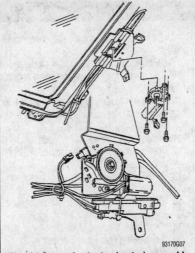

Fig. 14 Sunroof actuator (motor) assembly and fastener arrangement—2000 Oldsmobile Intrigue

93170G07

3. Remove the sunroof actuator retainer screws.
4. Detach the actuator electrical connector Pull the actuator straight down to disengage the drive gear and remove the actuator from the vehicle.

To install:

5. Align the sunroof actuator to the sunroof module.
6. Push the sunroof actuator straight in to engage its drive gear into the Position Encoding System Module. Install the screws just snug. The torque specification is only 24 inch lbs. (2.75 Nm).
7. Attach the electrical connector to the harness. Install tie-straps as required.
8. Check the operation of the sunroof in all positions.
9. Install the headliner.

SUNROOF ADJUSTMENT

Sunroof Vertical Height Adjustment

EXCEPT CUTLASS SUPREME

Adjust the sunroof window vertical height using the following procedure.

1. The sunshade must be fully open and the window fully closed.
2. Loosen the six screws and individually adjust the four corners of the window panel.
3. Adjust the front of the sunroof window to the following specifications:
   a. Buick and Pontiac: 1⁄32 (0.8mm) below the top surface of the roof panel and the rear 1⁄32 (0.8mm) above the top surface.
   b. Chevrolet and Oldsmobile: front of the window should be flush to 0.080 inch (2mm) below the roof surface and the rear of the window should be flush to 0.080 inch (2mm) above the roof surface.
4. Buick and Pontiac: Tighten the screws to 35 inch lbs. (4 Nm).
5. Chevrolet and Oldsmobile: Tighten the screws to 44 inch lbs. (5 Nm).

CUTLASS SUPREME

1. Position the sunroof to vent.
2. Slide the upper half of the mechanism cover

rearward until the cover clips disengage from the side adjustment bracket.
3. Remove the cover.
4. Close the window panel and separately loosen the four adjusting bolts (two on each side) and individually adjust the four corners of the windows.
5. Adjust the front of the window panel to be 1⁄32 (0.8mm) below the top surface of the roof panel and the rear to be 1⁄32 (0.8mm) above the top surface.
6. Tighten the screws just 44 inch lbs. (5 Nm).

Headliner

REMOVAL & INSTALLATION

➡ The one piece formed headlining consists of molded substrate covered with a foam backed cloth facing. The headlining is held in place with retainers at the rear of the headlining and the installation of related hardware and interior trim. The one piece construction requires the headlining be serviced as a complete assembly.

1. Remove the sun visors.
2. Remove the overhead console.
3. Remove the sunshade retainers.
4. Remove the dome lamp.
5. Remove the sunroof trim lace.
6. Remove the coat hook.
7. Remove the rail lamp.
8. Remove the windshield side upper garnish molding.
9. Remove the upper quarter trim panels as well as the upper center pillar trim panels.
10. Pull down on the door opening weather-strip seal on both front and rear doors.
11. Remove the two retainers using a trim clip tool.
12. Hook and loop material (sometimes called Velcro®) is used to retain the headliners. GM recommends their J 2772 C Headliner tool be used, but a rounded, dull tool can be substituted to work between the hook and loop material, working the two side apart, until the headliner is loose.
13. Work the headliner free and out through the right front door.

Use care not to bend the headlining too much when removing or installing.

To install:

14. Install the headliner through the right front door, using care not to bend it too much.
15. Align the sunshade holes in the headlining with their respective holes in the body structure and engage the hook and loop fasteners. Install the two rear retainers.
16. Install the door opening weather-strip seal to hold the headliner in place on both the front and rear doors.
17. Install the upper center pillar trim panels as well as the lower and upper quarter trim panels.
18. Install the windshield side upper garnish molding. The rail lamp, coat hook, sunroof trim lace and dome lamp.
19. Install the sunshade retainers, overhead console and the sunshades.

INTERIOR

Instrument Panel and Pad

PRECAUTIONS

When handling a part that has an "ESD-Sensitive" sticker warning of Electrostatic Discharge (it looks like a hand inside a black triangle with a white stripe through it), follow these guidelines to reduce any possible buildup of electrostatic charge.

• If replacing a part that has the sticker, do not open the package until just prior to installation. Before removing the part from its package, ground the package to a good ground on the car.

• Avoid touching the electrical terminals of the component.

• Always touch a good ground before handling a part with the sticker. This should be repeated while handling the part; do it more often when sliding across the seat, sitting from a standing position, or after walking.

✴✴ WARNING

As always when working on the vehicles, make sure the THEFTLOCK® feature of the radio is turned off before disconnecting the battery. Otherwise the radio will be internally disabled and will not work even after power has been restored.

✴✴ CAUTION

All of the vehicles covered by this manual are equipped with Supplemental Inflatable Restraint (SIR) or air bag systems. Properly disarm the air bag system before beginning work on the interior of the vehicle. Failure to do so can cause accidental deployment and serious injury. Please refer to the Air Bag Disarming procedure in Section 6 of this manual.

REMOVAL & INSTALLATION

Except Oldsmobile Intrigue

◆ See Figures 15 and 16

➡Additional information on working around the instrument panel and cluster may be found in Section 6.

1. Disconnect the front door inside carpet retainers.

2. Remove the underdash sound insulators.

3. Disconnect the negative battery and disarm the air bag system. Please see Section 6.

4. Remove the windshield side upper garnish moldings.

5. Remove the instrument panel upper trim panel as follows:

   a. Insert a flat-bladed tool, downward at the rearmost edge of the upper trim panel.

   b. Carefully pry the panel up to release the 10 panel tabs.

   c. Lift the rear edge approximately 2 inches and pull the panel rearward to remove.

6. Remove the instrument panel lower compartment.

7. Disconnect the theft deterrent module.

8. Disconnect the passenger side air bag inflator module.

9. Remove the steering column opening filler.

10. Remove the instrument panel cluster trim plate.

11. Remove the console, if equipped.

12. Remove the audio system and HVAC control panel, as outlined in Section 6.

13. Remove the instrument panel cluster, as outlined in Section 6.

14. Disconnect the headlamp switch, foglamp, HUD switch and trip calculator, as equipped.

15. Disconnect the fuse block.

16. Remove the knee bolster deflector.

17. Remove the steering column retaining nuts and lower the steering column.

18. Remove the instrument panel carrier mounting bolts and screws.

19. Disconnect the Data Link Connector (DLC), lower compartment light and trunk release switch.

20. Remove the instrument panel carrier clips.

21. Reposition the instrument panel wiring harness and remove the carrier assembly.

To install:

22. Reposition the instrument panel carrier assembly and route the instrument panel wiring.

23. Install the instrument panel carrier clips.

24. Install the Data Link Connector (DLC), lower compartment light and trunk release switch.

25. Install the instrument panel carrier mounting bolts and screws and tighten the bolts to 89 inch lbs. (10 Nm).

26. Raise the steering column and install the retaining nuts.

27. Install the remaining components in the reverse order of the removal procedure.

28. Enable the air bag system as outlined in Section 6.

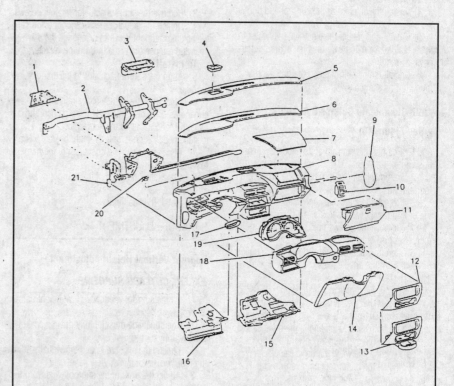

1. Brake pedal bracket
2. Body hinge pillar tie bar
3. Inflatable restraint instrument panel bar
4. Instrument cluster head up display
5. Instrument panel upper trim panel (w hud)
6. Instrument panel upper trim (w/o hud)
7. Inflatable restraint instrument panel module trim cover
8. Instrument panel
9. Instrument panel fuse block accessory cover door
10. Instrument panel outer air outlet
11. Instrument panel compartment
12. Instrument panel accessory trim plate (w console)
13. Instrument panel accessory trim plate (w/o console)
14. Instrument panel steering column opening filler
15. Instrument panel sound insulator (RH)
16. Instrument panel sound insulator (LH)
17. Trip calculator
18. Instrument panel cluster trim plate
19. Instrument cluster
20. Side window defogger outlet
21. Instrument panel lower tie bar

88000G36

Fig. 15 Exploded view of a typical instrument panel assembly—Grand Prix, Regal and Cutlass Supreme shown

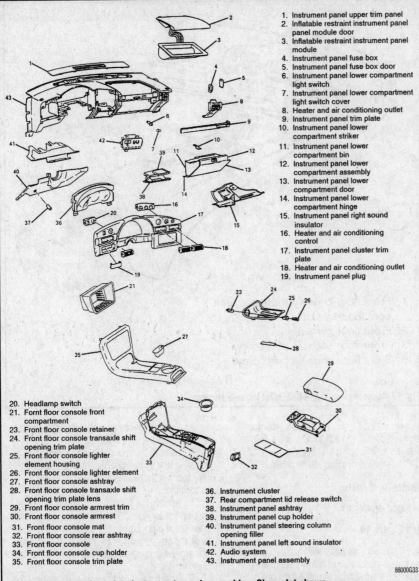

1. Instrument panel upper trim panel
2. Inflatable restraint instrument panel panel module door
3. Inflatable restraint instrument panel module
4. Instrument panel fuse box
5. Instrument panel fuse box door
6. Instrument panel lower compartment light switch
7. Instrument panel lower compartment light switch cover
8. Heater and air conditioning outlet
9. Instrument panel trim plate
10. Instrument panel lower compartment striker
11. Instrument panel lower compartment bin
12. Instrument panel lower compartment assembly
13. Instrument panel lower compartment door
14. Instrument panel lower compartment hinge
15. Instrument panel right sound insulator
16. Heater and air conditioning control
17. Instrument panel cluster trim plate
18. Heater and air conditioning outlet
19. Instrument panel plug

20. Headlamp switch
21. Fornt floor console front compartment
23. Front floor console retainer
24. Front floor console transaxle shift opening trim plate
25. Front floor console lighter element housing
26. Front floor console lighter element
27. Front floor console ashtray
28. Front floor console transaxle shift opening trim plate lens
29. Front floor console armrest trim
30. Front floor console armrest
31. Front floor console mat
32. Front floor console rear ashtray
33. Front floor console
34. Front floor console cup holder
35. Front floor console trim plate

36. Instrument cluster
37. Rear compartment lid release switch
38. Instrument panel ashtray
39. Instrument panel cup holder
40. Instrument panel steering column opening filler
41. Instrument panel left sound insulator
42. Audio system
43. Instrument panel assembly

88000G33

Fig. 16 Exploded view of an instrument panel assembly—Chevrolet shown

Oldsmobile Intrigue

➡Additional information on working around the instrument panel and cluster may be found in Section 6.

1. Disable the SIR (air bag) system. Please refer to Section 6.
2. Disconnect the negative battery cable.
3. Remove the windshield side garnish moldings.
4. Remove the instrument panel upper trim pad. Use care. The retaining clips could possibly come loose and fall into the instrument panel. Raise the rear of the pad about 2 inches, then pull to release the upper trim panel retainers. Rotate the sun load sensor and ambient light sensors ¼ turn counterclockwise to release the sensors from the trim panel.
5. Remove the left and right side carpet retainers.
6. Remove the front floor console using the procedure found in this section.

7. Grasp the instrument panel accessory trim plate and carefully and evenly pull to release the retainers from the instrument panel.
8. Detach the heated seat switch electrical connector, if equipped.
9. Remove the instrument panel accessory trim plate.
10. Remove the radio control assembly. Please see Section 6.
11. Remove the HVAC control panel as outlined in Section 6.
12. Remove the cigarette lighter socket.
13. Remove the left side instrument panel insulator.
14. Remove the screws retaining the Data Link Connector (DLC) and reposition the connector out of the way.
15. Grasp the instrument panel steering column opening filler panel and carefully pull rearward to release the retainers and remove the panel.
16. Remove the bolts retaining the base of the hood release handle and reposition the handle out of the way.

17. Remove the screws retaining the instrument panel switch bank from the instrument panel. Detach the electrical connectors from the switch bank and remove the switch bank.
18. Remove the instrument panel cluster trim plate, remove the cluster screws and detach the instrument cluster connectors. Remove the instrument from the vehicle.
19. Remove the hazard warning and cruise control switches.
20. Remove the ignition switch.
21. Remove the inside air temperature sensor, if equipped.
22. Remove the bolts retaining the knee bolster bracket to the instrument panel and to the steering column bracket. Remove the knee bolster bracket.
23. Remove the steering wheel following all of the cautions given in the procedure in Section 8.
24. Using a small flat-bladed tool, carefully release the front floor console power accessory port from the console. Detach the electrical connector and remove the accessory port.
25. Remove the right side instrument panel insulator.
26. Remove the instrument panel compartment.
27. Remove the instrument panel compartment lamp switch.
28. Remove the right side instrument panel access opening cover.
29. Depress the fuse block upper locking tab and carefully rotate the fuse block inward to release the fuse block from the instrument panel. Reposition the fuse block out of the way.
30. Remove the bolts retaining the instrument panel to the right side hinge pillar.
31. Remove the bolts retaining the center of the instrument panel.
32. Remove the left side instrument panel access opening cover.
33. Remove the bolts retaining the instrument panel to the left side hinge pillar.
34. Remove the bolts retaining the upper edge of the instrument panel.
35. Reposition the instrument panel wiring harness away from the instrument panel.
36. Carefully remove the instrument panel from the vehicle.

To install:
37. Carefully install the instrument panel into the vehicle, positioning the instrument panel wiring harness. Install the following:
    a. Instrument panel upper retaining bolts and tighten to 44 inch lbs. (5 Nm).
    b. Instrument panel to hinge pillar retaining bolts and tighten to 15 ft. lbs. (20 Nm).
    c. Instrument panel center retaining bolts and tighten to 44 inch lbs. (5 Nm).
38. Align the fuse block lower retaining tabs into position in the fuse block cutout on the instrument panel. Carefully rotate the upper edge of the fuse block outward to secure the upper locking tab into position. Install the left and right instrument panel end access opening covers.
39. Install the instrument panel compartment lamp switch and install the compartment (sometimes called a glove box).
40. Install the right side insulator panel.
41. Attach the electrical connector to the front floor console power accessory port. Align the port to the console and press into place to secure.

42. Install the steering column. Please see the procedures and cautions in Section 8.

43. Install the knee bolster bracket to the steering column bracket. Tighten the bolts to 53 inch lbs. (6 Nm).

44. Install the inside air temperature sensor, if equipped.

45. Install the ignition switch.

46. Install hazard warning and cruise control switch.

47. Attach the electrical connector to the instrument panel cluster, position and install the cluster. Install the cluster trim plate.

48. Attach the electrical connectors to the instrument panel switch bank and install the switch bank to the instrument panel.

49. Install the hood release handle to the instrument panel.

50. Align the instrument panel steering column opening filler panel to the instrument panel, then carefully press into place to secure the retainers.

51. Install the Data Link Connector (DLC) and the left side insulator panel.

52. Install the cigarette lighter socket.

53. Install the HVAC control panel and the radio. Please see Section 6 for additional information on these components.

54. Attach the heated seat switch electrical connector, if equipped.

55. Align the instrument panel accessory trim plate retainers to the slots in the instrument panel. Carefully and evenly press the trim plate into place to secure the retainers.

56. Install the front floor console using the procedures found in this section.

57. Install the left and right side front carpet retainers.

58. Install the instrument panel upper trim pad and the windshield side garnish moldings.

59. Connect the negative battery cable and enable the SIR (air bag) system. Please see Section 6.

Console

REMOVAL & INSTALLATION

Chevrolet Lumina and Monte Carlo

▶ **See Figure 17**

1. Disconnect the negative battery cable after first disabling the Theftlock® feature of the radio, if equipped.

2. Remove the front floor console trim plate using the following procedure:

    a. Remove the cigarette lighter.

    b. Remove the transaxle shift handle.

    c. Remove the front floor console trim plate by unsnapping from the console.

    d. Detach the automatic transaxle control indicator socket and bulb from the trim plate and detach the electrical connector from the trim plate.

3. Remove the CD storage bin at the front of the console by unsnapping it.

4. Raise the console armrest and remove the compartment mat. Remove the screws from console.

5. Detach the electrical connectors and remove the front floor console from the vehicle.

6. Installation is the reverse of the removal pro-

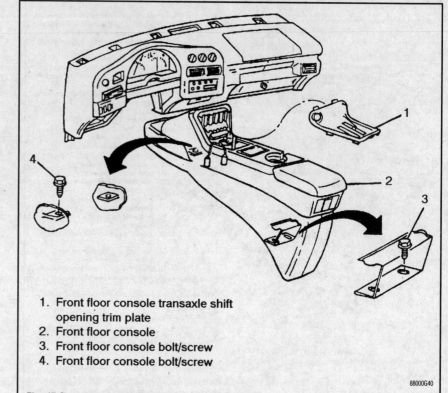

1. Front floor console transaxle shift opening trim plate
2. Front floor console
3. Front floor console bolt/screw
4. Front floor console bolt/screw

88000G40

Fig. 17 Console mounting—Chevrolet models shown

cess. Start with the front right console retaining screws and continue in a clockwise order. Tighten the screws to 106 inch lbs. (12 Nm).

7. Connect the negative battery cable.

Oldsmobile Models

CUTLASS SUPREME

▶ **See Figure 18**

1. Remove the transaxle shift handle. Look for a horseshoe-shaped clip just below the top of the handle. Use a small hook to pull out the retainer so the handle can be lifted from the shifter lever.

2. Remove the screws from the rear compartment in the front floor console.

3. Remove the floor console transaxle shift opening trim by prying with a small flat-bladed tool. Pry gently at the two rear tabs with the same flat-bladed tool.

4. Remove the front floor console armrest by raising the armrest, then removing the ashtray and steel flame plate. Loosen the screws in the ashtray area and pry the sides of the base apart. Remove the armrest at the rear hinge area, from between the base halves.

5. Detach the console wiring and electrical connectors.

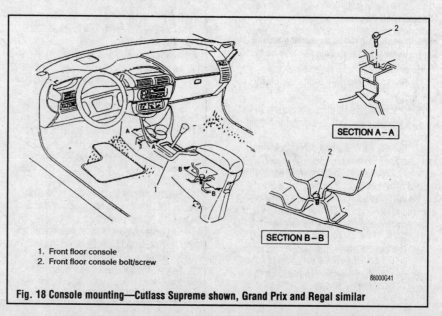

1. Front floor console
2. Front floor console bolt/screw

88000G41

Fig. 18 Console mounting—Cutlass Supreme shown, Grand Prix and Regal similar

6. Remove the screws from the console and remove the console from the vehicle.

7. Installation is the reverse of the removal process. When installing the shifter handle, make sure the retaining clip is fully seated.

INTRIGUE

1. Remove the front console trim plate.
2. Detach the necessary electrical connectors.
3. Remove the screws from the console mounting bracket at the rear of the shift lever.
4. Open the console armrest. Remove the mat from the bottom of the storage compartment.
5. Remove the screws from the of the storage compartment.
6. Remove the screws from the console mounting bracket at the rear of the storage compartment base and from the front mounting point.
7. Remove the console rearward, up and out.
8. Installation is the reverse of the removal process.

Pontiac Grand Prix

▶ See Figure 18

1. Disconnect the negative battery cable after first disabling the Theftlock® feature of the radio, if equipped.
2. Remove the console trim plate using the following procedure.
   a. Raise the armrest and remove the storage compartment and mat from the console base.
   b. Detach the electrical connectors from the driver's seat heater switch, if equipped
   c. Open the cup holder by pulling the cup holder door forward. Pull up on the trim plate starting with the rear two clips behind the cup holder, working forward. Remove the trim plate from the console.
3. Remove the screws from the console mounting bracket at the rear of the storage compartment base and the rear of the transaxle shift lever.
4. Pull the console rearward to release the console from the retainer in the lower instrument panel. Detach any remaining electrical connectors and remove the console from the vehicle.

To install:

5. Installation is the reverse of the removal procedure. Align the locating pins on the console bracket to the instrument panel console retainer hole and slots, Push the console forward into the instrument panel until fully seated.
6. Install the remaining components.
7. Connect the negative battery cable.

Buick Century and Regal

▶ See Figure 18

1. Disconnect the negative battery cable.
2. Apply the parking brake.
3. Reposition the transaxle shift lever to the LOW position.
4. Remove the console trim plate using the following procedure:
   a. Pull the trim plate upwards, starting at the front and working back to release the tabs at the retainers.
   b. Detach the electrical connectors from the driver's seat heater switch, if equipped.
   c. Remove the trim plate from the vehicle.
5. Remove the rubber mat from the storage

compartment in the console. Remove the screws from the storage compartment.
6. Remove the screws from the console mounting bracket at the rear of the transaxle shifter lever.
7. Remove the screws from the forward edge of the console.
8. Detach the electrical connectors and pull the console rearward to release the tabs from the retainers in the instrument panel. Remove the console from the vehicle.
9. Installation is the reverse of the removal process. Align the console over the transaxle shifter and position the console tabs to the retainers in the instrument panel. Press the console forward into the retainers until fully seated. Use care to align the console with the mounting brackets.
10. Once the console is installed, return the transaxle shift lever to PARK. Release the parking brake.
11. Connect the negative battery cable.

Door Trim Panels

REMOVAL & INSTALLATION

▶ See Figure 19

➡Use a door trim panel and garnish clip remover tool such as GM's J38778, or equivalent to remove the door trim panel. Failure to use this tool may cause damage to the retaining clips, panel backing and door.

Door trim panel attachment is similar across the W-Body car line. The only differences may be in whether the vehicle is equipped with power window switches or is equipped with window crank handles, manual or power mirrors and minor differences in pull handles. The following should suffice for most all W-Body vehicles.

1. Remove the door latch trim plate (coupe and sedan front doors).
2. Remove the ashtray (sedan rear doors).
3. Remove the seat belt retractor cover (coupe and sedan front doors). Use a suitable door trim panel removal tool to release the clip retainers

4. Remove the door lock trim plate and the power window switch, if so equipped.
5. Remove the window regulator handle by removing the inner retaining clip, if so equipped.
6. Remove the remote mirror control, if so equipped
7. Remove the trim panel retaining screws
8. Remove the door trim panel using a door trim panel removing to work loose the retainer clips.
9. Detach all electrical and remote mirror controls, as required.

To install:

10. Install the wiring harnesses through the openings in the panel, as equipped.
11. Position the trim panel to the door and align the clips. Press the trim panel to the door until all the clips are fully engaged. Align all the holes before engaging the clips.
12. Install the screws, remote mirror control and inside door handle bezel, as equipped.
13. Install the window regulator handle or power window switch.
14. Install the door trim plate, seat belt retractor cover or ashtray.

Door Locks

To properly evaluate the lock system after a replacement part has been installed, the following operational check may be made.

1. Insert the key into the outside door lock cylinder. While holding the key in the neutral (pullout) position, actuate the key inside the locking button to the fully locked position and back to the fully unlocked position. There must be no forced movement of the key out of the neutral position during the entire cycle. The key must be able to be removed when the inside locking button is held in both the fully locked and unlocked positions.
2. Turn the key to the fully locked position and return it to the neutral (pull-out) position. Actuate both the outside and inside handles to ensure that the door will not open.
3. Turn the key to the fully unlocked position and return it to the neutral (pull-out) position. Actuate both the outside and inside handles to make sure the door will open.

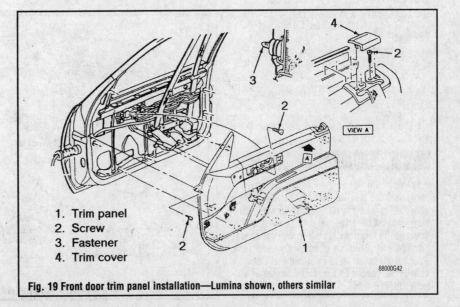

1. Trim panel
2. Screw
3. Fastener
4. Trim cover

88000G42

Fig. 19 Front door trim panel installation—Lumina shown, others similar

REMOVAL & INSTALLATION

Note that the manufacturing process for many inside-the-door uses heavy-duty pull-rivets that must be drilled out to remove components. If heavy-duty pull-type rivets and the tools used to set them are not available, use care when choosing substitute fasteners.

❄ CAUTION

When removing a door trim panel or switch plate, the ignition switch must be in the OFF position. This will eliminate the possibility of shorting out the switch if a flat-bladed tool, awl or metal object is used to remove the switch from the harness. In addition, disconnect the power window switch when working inside the driver's door. When operated, the express down feature allows the door window to drop very quickly, without stopping, which could cause personal injury.

Lock Module

▶ **See Figures 20 and 21**

GM calls the inside-the-door lock components a "Lock Module". Do not attempt repairs to correct door lock problems. Always replace the lock module assembly.

1. If equipped with a Theftlock® radio, disable this anti-theft feature. Disconnect the negative battery cable.

2. Remove the door trim panel as outlined in this section.

3. Loosen the water deflector (plastic sheet) to gain access to the lock module.

4. Remove the screw and nut securing the cover assembly to the door.

5. Remove the door handle cover assembly.

6. Remove the lock cylinder-to-lock rod and outside handle-to-lock rod.

7. Remove the screws securing the lock assembly to the door.

8. Remove the rivets securing the lock module to the door. Use the following procedure:

   a. Use a small pin punch to knock out any remaining rivet mandrel from the center of the rivet(s).

   b. Using a 3/16 inch (5mm) drill bit, drill out the pull rivet(s) securing the lock module to the door.

9. Disconnect the power lock electrical connector and remove the lock module.

To install:

10. Install the lock module through the access hole in the door inner panel.

❄ WARNING

It is important, when performing the next step, that the lock be held tight against the door facing while installing the screws. All screws must be driven at a right angle (90 degrees) to the door facing to prevent cross-threading or stripping of screws or door lock attachment holes. It is required that the screws be tighten to a specific torque of 89 inch lbs. (10 Nm).

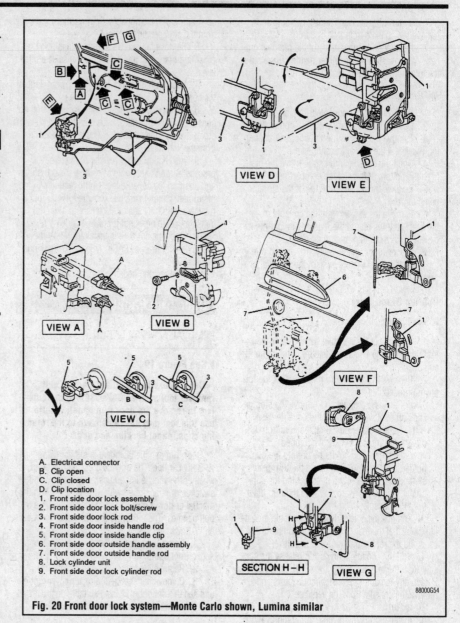

A. Electrical connector
B. Clip open
C. Clip closed
D. Clip location
1. Front side door lock assembly
2. Front side door lock bolt/screw
3. Front side door lock rod
4. Front side door inside handle rod
5. Front side door inside handle clip
6. Front side door outside handle assembly
7. Front side door outside handle rod
8. Lock cylinder unit
9. Front side door lock cylinder rod

88000G54

Fig. 20 Front door lock system—Monte Carlo shown, Lumina similar

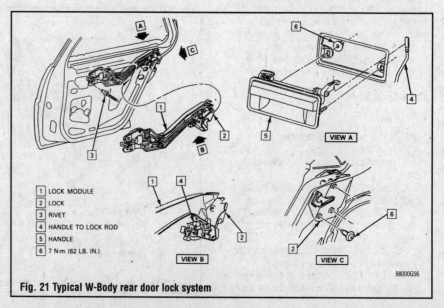

1 LOCK MODULE
2 LOCK
3 RIVET
4 HANDLE TO LOCK ROD
5 HANDLE
6 7 N·m (62 LB. IN.)

88000G56

Fig. 21 Typical W-Body rear door lock system

11. Install the lock assembly screws at a 90 degree angle to prevent cross threading. Torque the screws to 89 inch lbs. (10 Nm).

12. Install the power lock connector, if so equipped.

13. Install the rivets securing the lock module-to-door. Use ³⁄₁₆ inch diameter by ¼ inch long rivets.

14. Install the outside handle and lock cylinder lock rods. Check the locking operation before going any further.

15. Install the door handle cover, retaining screws and nuts.

16. Install the water deflector and door trim panel.

17. Connect the negative battery cable and check all door operations for completion of repair.

Lock Cylinder

▶ See Figure 22

1. If equipped with a Theftlock® radio, disable this anti-theft feature. Disconnect the negative battery cable.

2. Remove the door handle cover.

3. Remove the lock cylinder-to-lock rod.

4. Remove the anti-theft shield.

5. Remove the lock cylinder from the door.

To install:

6. Install the lock cylinder, anti-theft shield and shield retaining screw.

7. Connect the cylinder lock rod and handle cover assembly.

8. Check all door operations.

9. Connect the negative battery cable.

Power Lock Actuator

The optional power door lock system has motor actuators in each door. The system is activated by a control switch on each front door. All locks are activated when any switch is pushed up or down. Each actuator has an internal circuit breaker which may require one to three minutes to reset after service.

1. If equipped with a Theftlock® radio, disable this anti-theft feature. Disconnect the negative battery cable.

2. Remove the door trim panel and water deflector as outlined in this section.

3. If the actuator is retained by pull-rivets, drill out using a ³⁄₁₆ inch drill bit.

4. If the actuator is retained by screws, remove the two actuator retaining screws located at opposite corners.

5. Disconnect the electrical connector and linkage.

6. Remove the actuator through the access hole.

To install:

7. Install the actuator linkage, electrical connector and retaining screws.

8. Check for proper operation by cycling the system.

9. Install the water deflector and trim panel.

10. Connect the negative battery cable.

Door Window Glass

REMOVAL & INSTALLATION

➡GM specifies that before installing a door trim panel to the door, the old trim panel retainers MUST be discarded and replaced

with NEW retainers. If new retainers are not used, the trim panel will not be properly secured to the door.

Front

CHEVROLET MODELS

▶ See Figure 23

1. If equipped with a Theftlock® radio, disable this anti-theft feature. Disconnect the negative battery cable.

2. Remove the door trim panel and water deflector as outlined in this section.

3. Remove the inner belt sealing strip using the following procedure:

a. Lower the window to the bottom of the door.

b. With the door trim panel removed, it may be necessary to remove the outside rear view mirror using the procedures found in this section.

c. Remove the energy absorber (foam pad), if equipped.

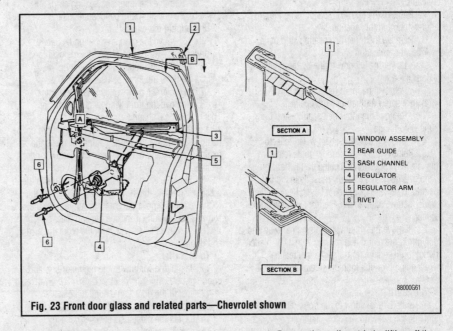

Fig. 23 Front door glass and related parts—Chevrolet shown

1	WINDOW ASSEMBLY
2	REAR GUIDE
3	SASH CHANNEL
4	REGULATOR
5	REGULATOR ARM
6	RIVET

d. Remove the sealing strip by lifting off the weld flange.

4. Remove the outer belt sealing strip by removing the retaining screws from each end.

5. Remove the window run channel. This is the channel (weather-strip) that runs around the door frame. Remove the retainer bolts at the ends of the weather-strip, rotate the legs outboard and pull out from the window frame.

6. Drill out the pull rivets.

7. Remove the window from the regulator sash.

8. Remove the window from the vehicle.

9. Remove the sash insulators, if necessary.

To install:

10. Install the sash insulators to the bottom edge of the window and snap to secure.

11. Position the window between the inner and outer panels. Point the lower front corner of the window down and pass through the belt opening,

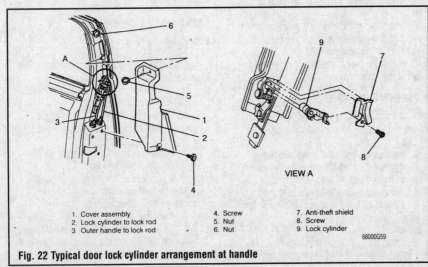

1. Cover assembly
2. Lock cylinder to lock rod
3. Outer handle to lock rod
4. Screw
5. Nut
6. Nut
7. Anti-theft shield
8. Screw
9. Lock cylinder

VIEW A

Fig. 22 Typical door lock cylinder arrangement at handle

aligning the edges with the door window channel. Turn the window to the horizontal position and align the holes in the window with holes in the regulator sash.

12. Install replacement pull rivets.

13. Install the window run channel, the outer, then the inner belt sealing strips.

14. Reposition the plastic sheet water deflector.

15. Reposition the foam energy absorber pad, if equipped.

16. Install the door trim panel.

OLDSMOBILE CUTLASS SUPREME—COUPE

The door window consists of a frameless piece of solid tempered safety glass. The guides on the glass are bonded on and are not serviceable except by replacement of the window. The factory service replacement glass has the guide already installed. The door window and lower sash channel are removed from the door as a unit and replacement glass is installed as a bench operation.

1. If equipped with a Theftlock® radio, disable this anti-theft feature. Disconnect the negative battery cable.

2. Remove the door trim panel using the procedures found in this section.

3. Remove the inner belt sealing strip using the following procedure:

a. Lower the window to the bottom of the door.

b. Remove the inner belt sealing strip retainer screw and remove the retainer.

c. Remove the inner belt sealing strip from the weld flange.

4. Remove the plastic sheet water deflector.

5. Remove the front window guide retainer. This is a vertical channel located on the door hinge side of the door. The window must be in the full up position to remove the guide retainer. Remove the retainer screws and remove the front window guide retainer.

6. Remove the window by raising half way and pushing on the rear guide retainer with a flat-bladed prytool to disengage from the channel retainer. Lift the window up on the inboard side of the door frame.

To install:

7. Install the window to the door, relocating the regulator arm roller to the sash channel.

8. Lower the window halfway and pull rearward on the window to engage the rear guide retainer to the channel retainer.

9. Install the front window guide retainer by lowering the window to 3 inches above the belt line and locating the retainer to the door.

10. Install the front window guide retainer noting the following:

a. Position the front window guide retainer at the forward part of the window.

b. Slowly lower the window to properly align the retainer into position.

c. Install the retainer screws.

➡**For proper operation of the window, adjust as necessary.**

11. Adjust the door glass as follows:

a. With the trim panel and water deflector still removed, loosen the front window guide retainer bolts.

b. Cycle the glass to the full DOWN position.

c. Adjust the top screws and then tighten the top retainer screws to 53 inch lbs. (6 Nm).

d. Cycle the window again to the full DOWN position.

e. Torque the bottom screws to 53 inch lbs. (6 Nm).

f. Recheck the glass for proper operation without binding.

12. Install the inner belt sealing strip, water deflector and trim panel.

13. Connect the negative battery cable and check for proper door operation.

OLDSMOBILE CUTLASS SUPREME—SEDAN

1. If equipped with a Theftlock® radio, disable this anti-theft feature. Disconnect the negative battery cable.

2. Remove the door trim panel using the procedures found in this section.

3. Remove the outside mirror using the procedures found in this section.

4. Remove the door frame garnish moldings. These are the trim parts that run around the inside of the window frame. Use the following procedure.

a. Remove the inner belt sealing strip.

b. Remove the trim panel applique by unsnapping the retainer clips.

c. Remove the garnish molding by gently prying away with a flat-blade trim removal tool.

5. Remove the outer belt sealing strip.

6. Remove the inner belt sealing strip.

7. Remove the plastic sheet water deflector.

8. Remove the front window guide retainer. This is a vertical channel located on the door hinge side of the door. The window must be in the full up position to remove the guide retainer. Remove the retainer screws and remove the front window guide retainer.

9. Remove the door frame applique. This is the outside trim plate that runs from the belt line to the roof drip rail. Remove the screw cover, remove the screws and carefully work free the applique.

10. Remove the window from the regulator arm and door.

To install:

11. Install the window to the regulator arm and door.

12. Install the door frame applique panel.

13. Install the front window guide retainer.

14. Install the plastic sheet water deflector.

15. Install the inner and outer belt sealing strips.

16. Install the window frame garnish moldings.

17. Install the outside mirror using the procedures found in this section.

18. Install the door trim panel using the procedures found in this section.

OLDSMOBILE INTRIGUE

1. If equipped with a Theftlock® radio, disable this anti-theft feature. Disconnect the negative battery cable.

2. Remove the front door inner trim panel.

3. Remove the plastic sheet water deflector.

4. Remove the inner belt sealing strip.

5. Remove the window-to-regulator bolts.

6. Lift and remove the front door window from the door.

To install:

7. Install the front door window between the inner and outer panels.

8. Point the lower front corner of the front door window down and pass through the belt opening.

9. Align the edges with the front door window weather-strips.

10. Turn the window to a horizontal position and align the holes in the window with the holes in the window regulator. Make sure that the window clips are seated on the regulator carrier plate.

11. Install the window-to-regulator bolts, forward bolt first. Tighten to 89 inch lbs. (10 Nm). Then install the rearward window-to-regulator bolt second and also torque to 89 inch lbs. (10 Nm).

12. Inspect both sealing lips on the outer belt sealing strip to make sure they are not rolled over and pointing downwards. If this condition is present, the window will not raise properly.

13. Install the inner sealing strip.

14. Reposition the plastic sheet water deflector.

15. Install the door trim panel.

BUICK AND PONTIAC MODELS

1. If equipped with a Theftlock® radio, disable this anti-theft feature. Disconnect the negative battery cable.

2. Remove the door trim panel using the procedures found in this section.

3. Remove the inner sealing strip.

4. Remove the window-to-regulator bolts

5. Remove the window from the door.

To install:

6. Position the window between the inner and outer panels. Point the lower front corner of the window down and pass through the belt opening, aligning the edges with the door window channel. Turn the window to the horizontal position and align the holes in the window with holes in the regulator sash.

7. Install replacement pull rivets, as required.

8. Inspect both sealing lips on the outer belt sealing strip to make sure they are not rolled over and pointing downwards. If this condition is present, the window will not raise properly.

9. Install the window-to-regulator bolts, forward bolt first. Tighten to 89 inch lbs. (10 Nm). Then install the rearward window-to-regulator bolt second and also torque to 89 inch lbs. (10 Nm).

10. Install the inner sealing strip.

11. Reposition the plastic sheet water deflector.

12. Install the door trim panel.

Rear

CHEVROLET MODELS

▶ **See Figures 24 and 25**

1. Remove the rear door trim panel using the following procedure.

a. Remove the armrest pull cup retaining screw and lift out the pull cup.

b. Remove the inside door handle bezel screw and remove the bezel along with the power window switch, if equipped.

c. Detach the electrical connector, if equipped with power windows.

d. If equipped with window crank handles, remove the rear side door window regulator handle by unsnapping from the spindle.

e. Remove the trim panel screws.

f. Remove the trim panel by carefully prying the top of the trim panel to release the tabs and hooks from the door inner panel. Push up and

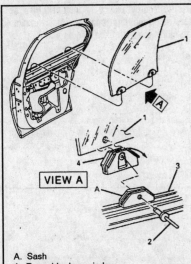

A. Sash
1. Rear side door window
2. Rear side door window rivet
3. Rear side door window regulator assembly
4. Rear side door window sash insulator

88000G64

Fig. 24 Rear door glass and related components—Chevrolet shown

pull the trim panel towards you to remove the trim panel.

2. Remove the energy absorber (foam pad).

3. Remove the plastic sheet water deflector.

4. Remove the outer sealing strip by lifting it off the pinch-weld flange using a trim remover tool.

5. Drill out the pull rivets holding the metal brackets on the glass to the regulator assembly.

6. Disengage the metal brackets on the glass from the regulator assembly and remove the window from the vehicle.

To install:

7. Renew the insulators in the brackets, if necessary.

8. Position the window between the inner and outer panels. Point the lower front corner of the window down and pass it through the belt opening, aligning the edges with the door window channel. Turn the window to the horizontal position and align the holes in the window brackets with the holes in the brackets on the window regulator.

9. Install new pull rivets.

10. Install the outer belt sealing strip by pressing in place.

11. Install the inner belt sealing strip. Engage each end of the sealing strip by pressing firmly onto the front and rear ends of the pinch-weld flange. Seat the entire length of the sealing strip, tapping along the strip with a rubber mallet.

12. Reposition the plastic sheet water deflector and the foam energy absorber pad.

13. Install the door trim panel using the following procedure:

a. Position the trim panel tabs and hooks to the slots in the door inner panel. Press down on the trim panel. Apply enough pressure to fully engage the three top tabs to the door inner panel.

b. Install the trim panel screws.

c. Install the window regulator handle, if equipped,.

d. Install the handle bezel, attaching the

power window switch electrical connector, if equipped.

e. Install the armrest pull cup.

OLDSMOBILE CUTLASS SUPREME

♦ **See Figure 25**

1. Remove the window regulator handle, if equipped.

2. Remove the handle bezel screw (the door lock knob is located within the door handle bezel). Remove the inside handle bezel

3. If equipped with power windows, remove the switch plate mounting screws and remove the switch plate from the trim panel. Detach the electrical connector.

4. Remove the screws from the trim panel. Using a trim panel removal tool, carefully disengage the fasteners from the holes in the door inner panel.

5. Remove the inner belt sealing strip by lowering the window to the bottom of the door and lifting the sealing strip off the pinch flange.

6. Remove the outer belt sealing strip by removing the retaining screw and lifting off the sealing strip off the pinch weld flange.

7. Remove the plastic sheet water deflector.

8. Remove the window regulator sash nuts, washer-like fasteners that hold the glass to the window regulator.

9. Lower the window to the bottom of the door and remove the front portion of the window weather-strip from the front of the door frame.

10. Lift the window upward and outboard of the door frame.

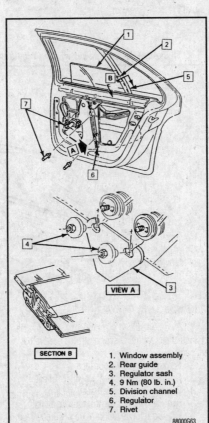

SECTION B

1. Window assembly
2. Rear guide
3. Regulator sash
4. 9 Nm (80 lb. in.)
5. Division channel
6. Regulator
7. Rivet

88000G63

Fig. 25 Rear door glass and related components—Oldsmobile Cutlass shown, others similar

To install:

11. Install the window to the door from the outboard side of the door frame. Lower the window to the bottom of the door. Align the glass to the regulator and install the regulator sash nuts. Tighten to 80 inch lbs. (9 Nm).

12. Reposition the plastic sheet water deflector.

13. Install the outer belt sealing strip by pressing in place.

14. Install the inner belt sealing strip. Engage each end of the sealing strip by pressing firmly onto the front and rear ends of the pinch-weld flange. Seat the entire length of the sealing strip, tapping along the strip with a rubber mallet.

15. Install the door trim panel, noting the following:

a. Position the fasteners to the inner panel, align the trim panel and press in to secure. Install the trim panel screws

b. If equipped with power windows, attach the electrical connector and install the switch plate.

c. Install the handle bezel and retaining screw.

d. If equipped with manual windows, install the window crank handle

OLDSMOBILE INTRIGUE

1. Remove the trim panel using the following procedure.

a. Remove the rear door power window and door lock switch plate assembly from the trim panel. Use a protective layer of tape on a flat-bladed tool. Insert the tool at the rear of the switch plate releasing the switch plate retainer. Lift the rear of the switch plate.

b. Detach the electrical connector(s).

c. Remove the door handle bezel.

d. Remove the door trim panel screw located behind the door handle bezel.

e. Remove the door trim panel screws located by the armrest handle.

f. Using a trim panel tool, carefully work around the panel, disengaging the fasteners.

g. Remove the trim panel by pulling straight off the door. Detach the electrical connectors

2. Remove the plastic sheet water deflector.

3. Remove the inner sealing strip by lifting off the pinch weld flange

4. Remove the retaining screw from the outer sealing strip and using fingers, pull off the door flange.

5. Remove the window-to-regulator bolts and remove the rear door window from the rear door.

To install:

6. Install the rear door window between the inner and outer panels.

7. Point the lower front corner of the rear door window down and pass through the belt opening.

8. Align the edges with the rear door window weather-strips.

9. Turn the window to a horizontal position and align the holes in the window with the holes in the window regulator.

10. Install the window-to-regulator bolts, forward bolt first. Tighten to 89 inch lbs. (10 Nm). Then install the rearward window-to-regulator bolt second and also torque to 89 inch lbs. (10 Nm).

11. Install the inner and outer sealing strips.

Inspect both sealing lips on the outer belt sealing strip to make sure they are not rolled over and pointing downwards. If this condition is present, the window will not raise properly.

12. Reposition the plastic sheet water deflector.

13. Install the rear door trim panel. New panel retainers are recommended. Align the trim panel retainers to the door panel holes and press straight in. Press firmly to properly seat the fasteners into the holes in the door panel. Install the screws. Snap the power window switch back into place.

BUICK AND PONTIAC MODELS

1. Remove the trim panel using the following procedure:

a. Remove the power window and door lock switch plate assembly from the trim panel. Use a protective layer of tape on a flat-bladed tool. Insert the tool at the rear of the switch plate and press forward to release the switch plate retainers.

b. Detach the electrical connector.

c. Locate the trim panel plugs that cover the screw heads. Carefully pry off the plugs and remove the trim panel screws.

d. Using a trim panel tool, carefully work around the panel, disengaging the fasteners.

e. Remove the trim panel by pulling straight off the door.

2. Remove the plastic sheet water deflector.

3. Remove the energy absorber (foam pad).

4. Remove the inner sealing strip by lifting off the pinch weld flange.

5. Remove the retaining screw from the outer sealing strip and using fingers, pull off the door flange.

6. Remove the door frame molding. This is the vertical panel at the front of the door frame. The window should be in the full down position. It may be necessary to pull the door window weather-strip part way from the molding. On Pontiacs, there should be screws retaining the door frame molding. On Buicks, the door frame molding should slide upwards for removal.

7. Remove the window mounting bolts and remove the rear door window from the rear door.

To install:

8. Install the rear door window between the inner and outer panels.

9. Point the lower front corner of the rear door window down and pass through the belt opening.

10. Align the edges with the rear door window weather-strips.

11. Turn the window to a horizontal position and align the holes in the window with the holes in the window regulator.

12. Inspect both sealing lips on the outer belt sealing strip to make sure they are not rolled over and pointing downwards. If this condition is present, the window will not raise properly.

13. Install the window-to-regulator bolts, forward bolt first. Tighten to 89 inch lbs. (10 Nm). Then install the rearward window-to-regulator bolt second and also torque to 89 inch lbs. (10 Nm).

14. Install the inner and outer sealing strips and the energy absorber (foam pad).

15. Reposition the plastic sheet water deflector.

16. Install the rear door trim panel. New panel retainers are recommended. Align the trim panel retainers to the door panel holes and press straight in. Press firmly to properly seat the fasteners into

the holes in the door panel. Install the screws and cover the heads with the trim panel plugs. Snap the power window switch back into place.

Window Regulators and Motors

REMOVAL & INSTALLATION

➡Some window regulators are retained at least in part, by heavy-duty pull rivets. To remove these rivets, the center mandrel must be pushed through with a small punch, and the

rivet(s) drilled out with a ³⁄₁₆ inch drill bit. The factory recommended repair requires the use of the same quality of heavy-duty pull rivet.

Front

CHEVROLET

▶ **See Figures 26 and 27**

Coupe and sedan front doors use a cross arm regulator. The following procedures are required for removal and replacement of both power and manual window regulators.

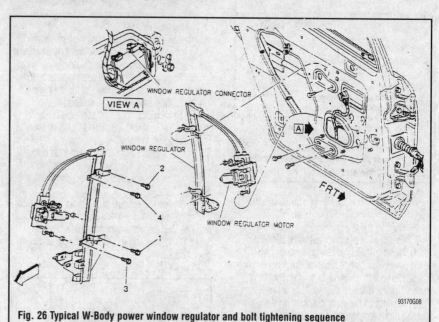

Fig. 26 Typical W-Body power window regulator and bolt tightening sequence

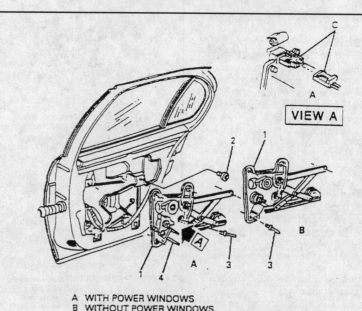

A WITH POWER WINDOWS
B WITHOUT POWER WINDOWS
C ELECTRICAL CONNECTOR
1 REGULATOR ASSEMBLY, REAR SIDE DOOR WINDOW
2 BOLT/SCREW, REAR SIDE DOOR WINDOW REGULATOR
3 RIVET, REAR SIDE DOOR WINDOW REGULATOR
4 MOTOR, REAR SIDE DOOR WINDOW REGULATOR

Fig. 27 Chevrolet models use a cross-arm type window regulator

1. Remove the door trim panel, as outlined in this section.

2. Remove the plastic sheet water deflector and the energy absorber (foam pad).

3. Remove the door window. Please see Door Window Glass, Removal and Installation in this section.

4. Detach the electrical connector, if equipped.

5. Remove the window regulator bolts and the regulator cam nut.

6. Drill out and remove the pull rivets.

7. Remove the window regulator cam bolt.

8. Remove the window regulator from the vehicle.

❋❋ CAUTION

Do not attempt to service the window regulator motor separately. It is part of the window regulator. The regulator lift arm is under tension from the counterbalance spring and can cause personal injury if the motor is removed from the regulator. The door window regulator cannot be serviced separately. If defective, replace the regulator and motor as an assembly.

To install:

9. Position the regulator by inserting the bottom through the access opening in the door, then rotate the top of the regulator through the opening while lowering the regulator to clear the top of the access opening. Align the holes in the regulator with holes in the door inner panel.

10. Install the door window regulator bolts and tighten to 89 inch lbs. (10 Nm).

11. Install new pull rivets. Install the upper left rivet first, followed by the lower right rivet.

12. Install the door window regulator cam bolt and cam nut and tighten both to 89 inch lbs. (10 Nm).

13. Attach the electrical connector, if equipped with power windows.

14. Install the door window. Please see Door Window Glass, Removal and Installation in this section.

15. Install the energy absorber (foam pad) and reposition the plastic sheet water deflector.

16. Install the door trim panel, as outlined in this section.

OLDSMOBILE CUTLASS SUPREME

▶ See Figure 28

Both the coupe and sedan front doors use a single lift arm regulator. The following procedures are required for removal and replacement of both power and manual window regulators.

1. Securely tape the window in the full-up position.

2. Remove the door trim panel, as outlined in this section.

3. Remove the plastic sheet water deflector and the energy absorber (foam pad).

4. Using a ¼ inch bit, drill out and remove the pull rivets.

5. Remove the window regulator by disengaging the regulator arm from the sash channel.

6. Remove the window regulator from the vehicle through the door inner access hole. Detach the electrical connector, if equipped.

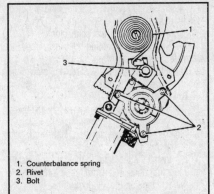

1. Counterbalance spring
2. Rivet
3. Bolt

88000G68

Fig. 28 Front door power window regulator-to-motor attachments. Note location of special bolt to retain the sector gear

7. If the window regulator motor is to be replaced, use the following procedure exactly because the counterbalance spring can cause personal injury.

a. With the window regulator and motor assembly removed from the vehicle, drill a hole through the regulator sector gear and back plate. Do not drill the hole closer than ½ inch to the edge of the sector gear or back plate. This step must be performed once the regulator is removed from the door. The regulator lift arm is under tension from the counterbalance spring and it can cause personal injury if the motor is removed without locking the sector gear in position.

b. Install a bolt and nut to lock the sector gear in position.

c. Drill out the ends of the three rivets using a ¼ inch bit.

To install:

8. If a new motor is being installed to the regulator, use the following procedure.

a. Position the new motor to the back plate.

b. Install one rivet to the motor at the bottom location.

c. Clamp the motor to the back plate using locking pliers.

d. Remove the nut and bolt installed earlier to lock the sector gear.

e. Supply 12 volts of power to the regulator to gain access to the two remaining motor rivets and install both rivets.

f. Remove the locking pliers.

9. Install the window regulator through the door inner access hole and attach the regulator arm to the sash channel. Attach the electrical connector, if equipped.

10. Install replacement rivets to retain the regulator. GM recommends ¼ inch diameter rivets ½ inch long.

11. Install the plastic sheet water deflector and the energy absorber (foam pad).

12. Install the door trim panel, as outlined in this section.

BUICK, PONTIAC AND OLDSMOBILE INTRIGUE

1. Remove the door trim panel, as outlined in this section.

2. Remove the plastic sheet water deflector.

3. Remove the window-to regulator bolts by raising the window far enough to gain access to the bolts through the door metal.

4. Raise and securely tape the window in the full up position.

5. Detach the electrical connector.

6. Remove the mounting bolts and remove the regulator from the door.

7. If the motor is to be replaced, simply unbolt the motor from the regulator.

To install

8. If the motor is to be replaced, install the motor to the regulator. The motor can be installed with the regulator in any position. Tighten the bolts to 89 inch lbs. (10 Nm).

9. Install the regulator to the door and install the mounting bolts. To ensure proper orientation of the window regulator to the door, it is very important that the window regulator bolts are tightened in the specified sequence. For a left side door, tighten the bolts to 89 inch lbs. (10 Nm) in the following sequence. On a right side door, the sequence is reversed.

a. Lower Right
b. Upper Right
c. Lower Left
d. Upper Left

10. Attach the electrical connector.

11. Carefully untape the window and lower the glass far enough to gain access to the bolts through the door metal. Tighten the bolts to 89 inch lbs. (10 Nm).

12. Install the plastic sheet water deflector.

13. Install the door trim panel. Please see Door Window Glass, Removal and Installation in this section for door trim installation information.

Rear

CHEVROLET

The following procedures are required for removal and replacement of both power and manual window regulators.

1. Remove rear door window. Please see Door Window Glass, Removal and Installation in this section.

2. Remove the door window regulator bolts.

3. Remove the pull rivets from the rear side door window regulator.

4. Detach the electrical connector, if equipped.

5. Remove the window regulator from the vehicle.

❋❋ CAUTION

Do not attempt to service the window regulator motor separately. It is part of the window regulator. The regulator lift arm is under tension from the counterbalance spring and can cause personal injury if the motor is removed from the regulator. The door window regulator cannot be serviced separately. If defective, replace the regulator and motor as an assembly.

To install:

6. Position the regulator to the door. Align the holes in the regulator with holes in the door inner panel.

7. Install the door window regulator bolts and tighten to 89 inch lbs. (10 Nm).

8. Install new pull rivets.

9. Attach the electrical connector, if equipped with power windows.

10. Install the door window and trim panel, as outlined in this section.

OLDSMOBILE CUTLASS SUPREME

▶ See Figure 29

The sedan doors use a tape drive regulator. The following procedures are required for removal and installation of both power and manual window regulators.

1. Securely tape the window in the full-up position.

2. Remove the rear door trim panel, as outlined in this section.

3. Remove the plastic sheet water deflector.

4. Remove the window regulator sash nut.

5. Drill out the rivets using a ¼ inch drill bit.

6. Detach the electrical connector from the motor, if equipped with power windows.

7. Remove the rear window regulator through the access hole in the door inner panel.

8. If the motor is defective, the entire motor and regulator assembly must be replaced.

To install:

9. Install the regulator and motor assembly through the access hole in the door inner panel.

10. Attach the electrical connector, if equipped with power windows.

11. Secure the regulator to the door panel with ¼ inch diameter rivets ½ inch long .

12. Install the door window regulator sash nut and tighten to just 80 inch lbs. (9 Nm).

13. Install the plastic sheet water deflector.

14. Install the rear door trim panel, as outlined in this section.

BUICK, PONTIAC AND OLDSMOBILE INTRIGUE

1. Remove the rear door trim panel, as outlined in this section.

2. Remove the plastic sheet water deflector.

3. Remove the window-to regulator bolts by raising the window far enough to gain access to the bolts through the door metal.

4. Raise and securely tape the window in the full up position.

5. Detach the electrical connector.

6. Remove the mounting bolts and remove the regulator from the door.

7. If the motor is to be replaced, simply unbolt the motor from the regulator.

To install

8. If the motor is to be replaced, install the motor to the regulator. The motor can be installed with the regulator in any position. Tighten the bolts to 89 inch lbs. (10 Nm).

9. Install the regulator to the door and install the mounting bolts. To ensure proper orientation of the window regulator to the door, it is very important that the window regulator bolts are tightened in the specified sequence. Tighten the bolts to 89 inch lbs. (10 Nm) in this sequence.

   a. Lower Right

   b. Upper Right

   c. Lower Left

   d. Upper Left

10. Attach the electrical connector.

11. Carefully untape the window and lower the glass far enough to gain access to the bolts through the door metal. Tighten the bolts to 89 inch lbs. (10 Nm).

12. Install the plastic sheet water deflector.

13. Install the door trim panel, as outlined in this section.

Inside Rear View Mirror

REPLACEMENT

▶ See Figure 30

The W-Body rearview mirror snaps onto a small metal tab called the rearview mirror support. The rearview mirror is removed from the support by prying with a small flat-bladed tool. There is also a small wiring connector, under a cover, if it is a lighted rearview mirror.

The rearview mirror is attached to a rearview mirror support which is bonded to the windshield. The support is installed using a plastic-polyvinyl

butyl adhesive. To install a detached mirror support or install a new part, the following items are needed.

• Loctite® Minute-Bond Adhesive 312 two component pack, GM part number #1052369, or equivalent.

• The original rearview mirror support (properly prepared, see below) or a replacement rearview mirror support.

   • Wax marking pencil or crayon.

   • Isopropyl alcohol.

   • Clean paper towel.

   • Fine grit emery cloth or sandpaper (320 or 360)

➡**The following procedure calls for layout lines on the windshield. Make all marks on the outside of the windshield. This keeps the inside of the glass clean of wax marking pencil marks. Simply look through the windshield from the inside when positioning the mirror support, lining up the layout marks on the outside of the glass.**

1. Mark the location of the mirror support on the outside of the windshield and draw a line on the windshield. Start by measuring 3 inches (76mm) down from the top of the windshield and draw a line on the glass.

2. Measure and find the center of the windshield and draw a line.

3. Position the support centered on the center line and with the top of the support aligned under the horizontal line.

4. Outline the support location.

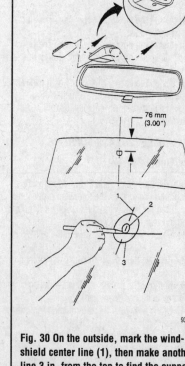

Fig. 30 On the outside, mark the windshield center line (1), then make another line 3 in. from the top to find the support position (2). Mark a larger circle (3), the area on the inside to be cleaned well

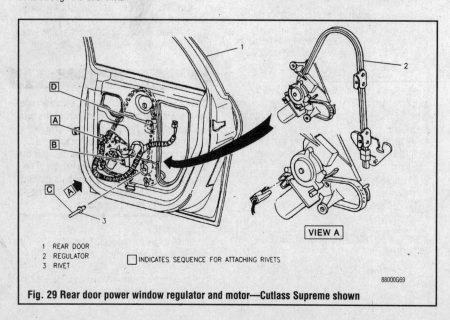

1 REAR DOOR
2 REGULATOR
3 RIVET

☐ INDICATES SEQUENCE FOR ATTACHING RIVETS

VIEW A

88000G69

Fig. 29 Rear door power window regulator and motor—Cutlass Supreme shown

5. Mark a larger diameter circle around the rearview mirror support location on the outside of the windshield.

6. On the inside of the windshield, clean the large circle area with a paper towel and a domestic scouring cleanser, GM Window Cleaner GM #1050427, or polishing compound. Rub until the area is completely clean.

7. Wipe the area with an isopropyl alcohol saturated paper towel to remove any traces of scouring cleanser. Polishing compound or cleaning solution.

8. With a piece of fine grit (320 or 360) emery cloth or sandpaper, sand the bonding surface of the rearview mirror support. If the original rearview mirror support is to be reused, all traces of factory installed adhesive must be removed prior to reinstallation.

9. Wipe the sanded rearview mirror support with a clean paper towel saturated with isopropyl alcohol and allow to dry.

10. Follow the directions on the manufacturer's kit to prepare the rearview mirror support prior to installation on the windshield.

11. Apply the adhesive to the support.

12. Position the rearview mirror support, with its rounded end pointed upward, to its pre-marked location.

13. Press the rearview mirror support against the windshield exerting steady pressure for 30 to 60 seconds.

14. After five minutes, remove any excess adhesive with an isopropyl alcohol moistened paper towel or window cleaning solution.

15. Install the rearview mirror to the support. Make sure it is fully seated. Attach the electrical connector, if it is a lighted rearview mirror.

Seats

On W-Body vehicles, the front seats are secured to the floorpan by two front hook attachments and two rear bolts installed to nuts welded to the floorpan.

The manually operated two-way front adjusters provides only fore and aft movement of the seat. When the seat adjuster handle located on the front seat is pulled up, the seat adjusters unlock, permitting travel of the seat. When the seat is in the desired position and the seat adjuster handle is released, the seat locks in place.

A power operated six-way seat adjuster is available. The adjusters are activated by three 12 volt, reversible, permanent magnet motors with a built-in circuit breaker. The motors are energized by a switch bolted on the seat side panel.

The three motors drive the front seat and rear vertical actuators and a horizontal actuator. When the adjusters reach the limit of travel, torque is absorbed through the rubber mounted grommets located between the motor and the support. An overload relay is provided in the circuit and will open should excessive stall be applied.

The optional 60/40 split bench front seats have seat back head restraints on the driver's and passenger's seat back. The head restraints are designed so they cannot be removed from the seat back without first inserting a small rounded tool inside the head restraint support tube to release the locking tab. The 60/40 split bench seat is equipped with a reclining mechanism on both the driver's and passenger's side. The recliner lever is located on the outboard side of the spring cushion. When the lever

is pulled upward, the spring loaded dual linear reclining unit located in the cushion frame is released, allowing the seat back to be pushed rearward or allowing the spring loaded reclining unit to bring the seat back forward.

Bucket seats are equipped with manual reclining mechanisms. An optional six-way power seat adjuster is available. Some bucket seats are equipped with inertia seat back locks. This system allows the seat back to fold forward without requiring the occupant to release a locking lever or access to the rear seat area. During a sudden stop or deceleration, or if the front of the vehicle is nose down, the inertia system of the seat back lock will engage, holding the seat back in its rest position. A release lever is provided to allow manual release of the seat back lock when the vehicle is in the nose down position. The release lever is located at the lower rear outboard corner of the seat back.

Some W-Body vehicles (notably Pontiac coupes) have passenger front seats equipped with an E-Z Entry device. This is actuated, in an unoccupied

seat, by completely folding the seat back forward disengaging the adjuster, and sliding the front seat forward to gain access to the rear seat area. To return the seat to its normal position, return the seat back to its rest position, and slide the entire seat rearward, engaging the adjuster.

W-Body rear seats are available in several styles including a rear seat with an integral child restraint device.

REMOVAL & INSTALLATION

Front Seats

▶ **See Figure 31**

1. Remove the adjuster track covers, as follows:

   a. Unsnap the track covers from the front of the adjusters (manual and power adjusters).

   b. Remove the track cover screw from the rear of the adjusters (manual seat adjuster only).

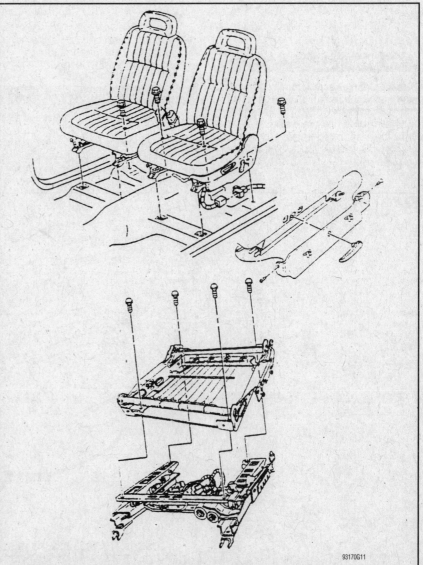

93170G11

Fig. 31 Front seat, side trim and adjuster assembly arrangement—2000 Intrigue shown, other vehicles with 6-way power seats similar

c. Unsnap the track covers from the rear of the adjusters (power adjusters).

2. Move the seat to the full forward and full up position.

3. Remove the retractor side seat belt anchor from the seat.

4. Remove the seat adjuster-to-floorpan bolts.

5. Detach the power seat electrical connector, if equipped.

6. Detach the seat belt reminder electrical connector, driver's side only.

7. Disengage the front hook attachments.

8. Remove the front seat from the vehicle.

➡ **Be careful not to damage the interior and painted surfaces when removing the seat assemblies.**

To install:

9. With an assistant, install the seat assembly into place and engage the front hook attachments.

10. Attach all electrical connectors.

11. Operate the seat to the full forward, full up position.

12. Install the retractor side belt anchor to the seat.

13. Install the adjuster-to-floorpan bolts and tighten to 18 ft. lbs. (24 Nm).

✳✳ WARNING

Do not overtorque adjuster-to-floorpan nuts as a hard seat travel problem could result.

14. Install the adjuster track covers.

15. Cycle the seat (six-way power) to ensure proper operation and synchronization of the left and front adjusters.

Rear Seats

SEAT CUSHION

▶ **See Figure 32**

1. Locate and remove the small bolts at the front lower edge of the seat cushion.

2. Pull the tabs on the rear cushion retainers.

3. Remove the seat cushion by lifting up and pulling out of the retainer.

4. Installation is the reverse of the removal procedure. Make sure the retainer tabs are snapped into place. Tighten the bolts to 18 ft. lbs. (25 Nm).

SEAT BACK

▶ **See Figure 33**

1. Remove the seat cushion as described above.

2. Remove the anchor nuts securing the rear seat retainer at the bottom of the seat back.

3. Grasp the bottom of the seat back and swing upward to disengage the offsets on the upper frame bar from the hangers.

4. Lift the seat back upwards to remove from the vehicle.

5. Installation is the reverse of the removal process. Make sure the hooks on the seat back are properly installed to the hangers. Tighten the anchor nuts to 89 inch lbs. (10 Nm).

Power Seat Motors

The six-way power seat adjusters are actuated by three 12V, reversible permanent magnet motors with built in circuit breakers. The motors drive the front and rear vertical gearnuts and a horizontal actuator. When the adjusters are at their limit of travel, an overload relay provides stall torque so the motors are not overloaded. Each motor can be serviced as a separate unit.

REMOVAL & INSTALLATION

1. Disconnect the negative battery cable.

2. Remove the seat assembly from the vehicle as outlined in this section.

3. Place the seat with the adjuster assembly attached upside down on a clean, protected surface. Do not leave a seat upside down on the cushion or damage to the cushion may occur.

4. Detach the electrical connectors, as equipped.

5. Remove the finish panels using the following procedure:

a. Remove the recliner handle. Use a small flat-bladed tool to carefully release the wire retainer from the base of the recliner handle.

b. Remove the finish panel screws.

c. Pull the finish panel away from the seat cushion frame to release the clips. Discard the clips. GM specifies that new clips must be used at assembly.

d. Detach the power seat electrical connector.

e. Remove the finish panel from the seat.

6. Remove the adjuster-to-seat cushion frame bolts.

7. Separate the adjuster assembly from the seat frame.

8. Disconnect the drive cables by squeezing the oblong connector at the motors and the vertical/horizontal actuators. To gain access to the cable connector at the motor for the inboard (passenger

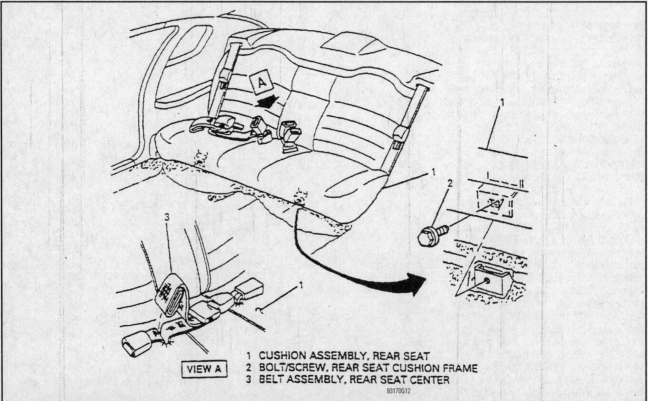

VIEW A

1 CUSHION ASSEMBLY, REAR SEAT
2 BOLT/SCREW, REAR SEAT CUSHION FRAME
3 BELT ASSEMBLY, REAR SEAT CENTER

93170G12

Fig. 32 Typical W-Body rear seat cushion removal

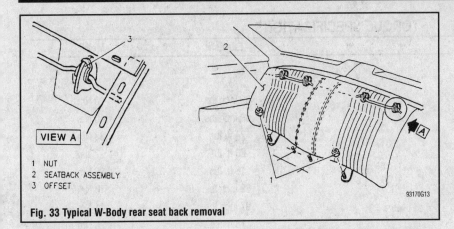

VIEW A

1 NUT
2 SEATBACK ASSEMBLY
3 OFFSET

93170G13

Fig. 33 Typical W-Body rear seat back removal

side) or outboard (driver's side) rear vertical gear-nut, initial removal of the nut securing the motor support bracket is suggested.

9. If necessary, separate the left and right adjusters by unbolting the crossbrace.

10. Tag for identification the electrical connectors. With the electrical wiring harness connectors detached from the motors, remove the nut securing the actuator motor bracket to the seat adjuster assembly.

11. If not already done, remove the cables from the motors.

12. Remove the defective motor as required.

To install:

13. Install the replacement motor(s) as required.

14. Connect the cables to the motors.

15. Install the nut securing the actuator motor bracket to the seat adjuster assembly. Tighten to 89 inch lbs. (10 Nm).

16. Attach the electrical connectors to the motors.

   a. The black connector goes to the front vertical motor.

   b. The blue connector goes to the rear vertical motor.

   c. The white connector goes to the horizontal motor.

17. Installation is the reverse of the removal process. Attach the crossbrace to the left and right adjusters making sure the tab bending downward at the center of the crossbrace faces the rear of the adjusters. Secure with the two bolts, tightened to 53 inch lbs. (6 Nm).

TORQUE SPECIFICATIONS

Components	English	Metric
Exterior		
Door		
Torx bolt	89 inch lbs.	10 Nm
10mm cone bolt	89 inch lbs.	10 Nm
13mm bolts	24 ft. lbs.	33 Nm
Hood hinge bolts	20 ft. lbs.	27 Nm
Trunk lid hinge bolts	18 ft. lbs.	25 Nm
Rear view mirror bolts	89 inch lbs.	10 Nm
Fender	97 inch lbs.	11 Nm
Hood hinge-to-fender bolts	18 ft. lbs.	25 Nm
Front fender-to-front engine compartment side rail and rocker panel	53 inch lbs.	6 Nm
Fender-to-door hinge pillar bolts	89 inch lbs.	10 Nm
Lower engine compartment bolts	70 inch lbs.	8 Nm
Interior		
Sunroof		
Except 2000 Intrigue		
Sunroof actuator-to-the sunroof module assembly screws	35 inch lbs.	4 Nm
Motor and drive gear assembly screws	35 inch lbs.	4 Nm
2000 Intrigue		
Sunroof actuator screws	24 inch lbs.	3 Nm
Instrument panel		
Except Intrigue		
Instrument panel carrier mounting bolts	89 inch lbs.	10 Nm
Intrigue		
Instrument panel upper retaining bolts	44 inch lbs.	5 Nm
Instrument panel-to-hinge pillar retaining bolts	15 ft. lbs.	20 Nm
Instrument panel center retaining bolts	44 inch lbs.	5 Nm
Front console retaining screws	106 inch lbs.	12 Nm
Lock module bolts/screws	89 inch lbs.	10 Nm
Window regulator		
Front		
Except Olds. Cutlass Coupe regulator retaining screws/bolts	89 inch lbs.	10 Nm
Oldsmobile Cutlass Coupe regulator retaining screws/bolts	53 inch lbs.	6 Nm
Rear		
Except Olds. Cutlass Coupe regulator retaining screws/bolts	89 inch lbs.	10 Nm
Oldsmobile Cutlass Coupe regulator retaining screws/bolts	80 inch lbs.	90 Nm
Regulator sash nut	80 inch lbs.	90 Nm
Seats		
Front seat adjuster-to-floorpan bolts	18 ft. lbs.	25 Nm
Rear seat cushion bolts	18 ft. lbs.	25 Nm
Seat back anchor nuts	89 inch lbs.	10 Nm
Power seat motor		
Actuator motor bracket-to-seat adjuster assembly nut	89 inch lbs.	10 Nm
Crossbrace-to-left and right adjuster bolts	53 inch lbs.	6 Nm

93170C01

11

TROUBLE-
SHOOTING

Condition	Section/Item Number

The following troubleshooting charts are divided into 7 sections covering engine, drive train, brakes, wheels/tires/steering/suspension, electrical accessories, instruments and gauges, and climate control. The first portion (or index) consists of a list of symptoms, along with section and item numbers. After selecting the appropriate condition, refer to the corresponding diagnostic procedure in the second portion's specified location.

INDEX

SECTION 1. ENGINE

A. Engine Starting Problems

Gasoline Engines

Engine turns over, but will not start	1-A, 1
Engine does not turn over when attempting to start	1-A, 2
Engine stalls immediately when started	1-A, 3
Starter motor spins, but does not engage	1-A, 4
Engine is difficult to start when cold	1-A, 5
Engine is difficult to start when hot	1-A, 6

Diesel Engines

Engine turns over but won't start	1-A, 1
Engine does not turn over when attempting to start	1-A, 2
Engine stalls after starting	1-A, 3
Starter motor spins, but does not engage	1-A, 4
Engine is difficult to start	1-A, 5

B. Engine Running Conditions

Gasoline Engines

Engine runs poorly, hesitates	1-B, 1
Engine lacks power	1-B, 2
Engine has poor fuel economy	1-B, 3
Engine runs on (diesels) when turned off	1-B, 4
Engine knocks and pings during heavy acceleration, and on steep hills	1-B, 5
Engine accelerates but vehicle does not gain speed	1-B, 6

Diesel Engines

Engine runs poorly	1-B, 1
Engine lacks power	1-B, 2

C. Engine Noises, Odors and Vibrations

Engine makes a knocking or pinging noise when accelerating	1-C, 1
Starter motor grinds when used	1-C, 2
Engine makes a screeching noise	1-C, 3
Engine makes a growling noise	1-C, 4
Engine makes a ticking or tapping noise	1-C, 5
Engine makes a heavy knocking noise	1-C, 6
Vehicle has a fuel odor when driven	1-C, 7
Vehicle has a rotten egg odor when driven	1-C, 8
Vehicle has a sweet odor when driven	1-C, 9
Engine vibrates when idling	1-C, 10
Engine vibrates during acceleration	1-C, 11

D. Engine Electrical System

Battery goes dead while driving	1-D, 1
Battery goes dead overnight	1-D, 2

E. Engine Cooling System

Engine overheats	1-E, 1
Engine loses coolant	1-E, 2
Engine temperature remains cold when driving	1-E, 3
Engine runs hot	1-E, 4

F. Engine Exhaust System

Exhaust rattles at idle speed	1-F, 1
Exhaust system vibrates when driving	1-F, 2
Exhaust system seems too low	1-F, 3
Exhaust seems loud	1-F, 4

Condition	Section/Item Number

SECTION 2. DRIVE TRAIN

A. Automatic Transmission

Transmission shifts erratically	2-A, 1
Transmission will not engage	2-A, 2
Transmission will not downshift during heavy acceleration	2-A, 3

B. Manual Transmission

Transmission grinds going into forward gears while driving	2-B, 1; 2-C, 2
Transmission jumps out of gear	2-B, 2
Transmission difficult to shift	2-B, 3; 2-C, 2
Transmission leaks fluid	2-B, 4

C. Clutch

Clutch slips on hills or during sudden acceleration	2-C, 1
Clutch will not disengage, difficult to shift	2-C, 2
Clutch is noisy when the clutch pedal is pressed	2-C, 3
Clutch pedal extremely difficult to press	2-C, 4
Clutch pedal remains down when pressed	2-C, 5
Clutch chatters when engaging	2-C, 6

D. Differential and Final Drive

Differential makes a low pitched rumbling noise	2-D, 1
Differential makes a howling noise	2-D, 2

E. Transfer Assembly

All Wheel and Four Wheel Drive Vehicles

Leaks fluid from seals or vent after being driven	2-E, 1
Makes excessive noise while driving	2-E, 2
Jumps out of gear	2-E, 3

F. Driveshaft

Rear Wheel, All Wheel and Four Wheel Drive Vehicles

Clunking noise from center of vehicle shifting from forward to reverse	2-F, 1
Excessive vibration from center of vehicle when accelerating	2-F, 2

G. Axles

All Wheel and Four Wheel Drive Vehicles

Front or rear wheel makes a clicking noise	2-G, 1
Front or Rear wheel vibrates with increased speed	2-G, 2

Front Wheel Drive Vehicles

Front wheel makes a clicking noise	2-G, 3
Rear wheel makes a clicking noise	2-G, 4

Rear Wheel Drive Vehicles

Front or rear wheel makes a clicking noise	2-G, 5
Rear wheel shudders or vibrates	2-G, 6

H. Other Drive Train Conditions

Burning odor from center of vehicle when accelerating	2-H, 1; 2-C, 1; 3-A, 9
Engine accelerates, but vehicle does not gain speed	2-H, 2; 2-C, 1; 3-A, 9

SECTION 3. BRAKE SYSTEM

Brakes pedal pulsates or shimmies when pressed	3-A, 1
Brakes make a squealing noise	3-A, 2
Brakes make a grinding noise	3-A, 3
Vehicle pulls to one side during braking	3-A, 4
Brake pedal feels spongy or has excessive brake pedal travel	3-A, 5
Brake pedal feel is firm, but brakes lack sufficient stopping power or fade	3-A, 6

Condition	Section/Item Number
Vehicle has excessive front end dive or locks rear brakes too easily	3-A, 7
Brake pedal goes to floor when pressed and will not pump up	3-A, 8
Brakes make a burning odor	3-A, 9

SECTION 4. WHEELS, TIRES, STEERING AND SUSPENSION

A. Wheels and Wheel Bearings

All Wheel and Four Wheel Drive Vehicles

Front wheel or wheel bearing loose	4-A, 1
Rear wheel or wheel bearing loose	4-A, 2

Front Wheel Drive Vehicles

Front wheel or wheel bearing loose	4-A, 1
Rear wheel or wheel bearing loose	4-A, 2

Rear Wheel Drive Vehicles

Front wheel or wheel bearing loose	4-A, 1
Rear wheel or wheel bearing loose	4-A, 2

B. Tires

Tires worn on inside tread	4-B, 1
Tires worn on outside tread	4-B, 2
Tires worn unevenly	4-B, 3

C. Steering

Excessive play in steering wheel	4-C, 1
Steering wheel shakes at cruising speeds	4-C, 2
Steering wheel shakes when braking	3-A, 1
Steering wheel becomes stiff when turned	4-C, 4

D. Suspension

Vehicle pulls to one side	4-D, 1
Vehicle is very bouncy over bumps	4-D, 2
Vehicle seems to lean excessively in turns	4-D, 3
Vehicle ride quality seems excessively harsh	4-D, 4
Vehicle seems low or leans to one side	4-D, 5

E. Driving Noises and Vibrations

Noises

Vehicle makes a clicking noise when driven	4-E, 1
Vehicle makes a clunking or knocking noise over bumps	4-E, 2
Vehicle makes a low pitched rumbling noise when driven	4-E, 3
Vehicle makes a squeaking noise over bumps	4-E, 4

Vibrations

Vehicle vibrates when driven	4-E, 5

SECTION 5. ELECTRICAL ACCESSORIES

A. Headlights

One headlight only works on high or low beam	5-A, 1
Headlight does not work on high or low beam	5-A, 2
Headlight(s) very dim	5-A, 3

B. Tail, Running and Side Marker Lights

Tail light, running light or side marker light inoperative	5-B, 1
Tail light, running light or side marker light works intermittently	5-B, 2
Tail light, running light or side marker light very dim	5-B, 3

C. Interior Lights

Interior light inoperative	5-C, 1
Interior light works intermittently	5-C, 2
Interior light very dim	5-C, 3

Condition	Section/Item Number

D. Brake Lights

One brake light inoperative	5-D, 1
Both brake lights inoperative	5-D, 2
One or both brake lights very dim	5-D, 3

E. Warning Lights

Ignition, Battery and Alternator Warning Lights, Check Engine Light, Anti-Lock Braking System (ABS) Light, Brake Warning Light, Oil Pressure Warning Light, and Parking Brake Warning Light

Warning light(s) remains on after the engine is started	5-E, 1
Warning light(s) flickers on and off when driving	5-E, 2
Warning light(s) inoperative with ignition on, and engine not started	5-E, 3

F. Turn Signal and 4-Way Hazard Lights

Turn signals or hazard lights come on, but do not flash	5-F, 1
Turn signals or hazard lights do not function on either side	5-F, 2
Turn signals or hazard lights only work on one side	5-F, 3
One signal light does not work	5-F, 4
Turn signals flash too slowly	5-F, 5
Turn signals flash too fast	5-F, 6
Four-way hazard flasher indicator light inoperative	5-F, 7
Turn signal indicator light(s) do not work in either direction	5-F, 8
One turn signal indicator light does not work	5-F, 9

G. Horn

Horn does not operate	5-G, 1
Horn has an unusual tone	5-G, 2

H. Windshield Wipers

Windshield wipers do not operate	5-H, 1
Windshield wiper motor makes a humming noise, gets hot or blows fuses	5-H, 2
Windshield wiper motor operates but one or both wipers fail to move	5-H, 3
Windshield wipers will not park	5-H, 4

SECTION 6. INSTRUMENTS AND GAUGES

A. Speedometer (Cable Operated)

Speedometer does not work	6-A, 1
Speedometer needle fluctuates when driving at steady speeds	6-A, 2
Speedometer works intermittently	6-A, 3

B. Speedometer (Electronically Operated)

Speedometer does not work	6-B, 1
Speedometer works intermittently	6-B, 2

C. Fuel, Temperature and Oil Pressure Gauges

Gauge does not register	6-C, 1
Gauge operates erratically	6-C, 2
Gauge operates fully pegged	6-C, 3

SECTION 7. CLIMATE CONTROL

A. Air Conditioner

No air coming from air conditioner vents	7-A, 1
Air conditioner blows warm air	7-A, 2
Water collects on the interior floor when the air conditioner is used	7-A, 3
Air conditioner has a moldy odor when used	7-A, 4

B. Heater

Blower motor does not operate	7-B, 1
Heater blows cool air	7-B, 2
Heater steams the windshield when used	7-B, 3

DIAGNOSTIC PROCEDURES

1. ENGINE

1-A. Engine Starting Problems

Gasoline Engines

1. Engine turns over, but will not start

a. Check fuel level in fuel tank, add fuel if empty.
b. Check battery condition and state of charge. If voltage and load test below specification, charge or replace battery.
c. Check battery terminal and cable condition and tightness. Clean terminals and replace damaged, worn or corroded cables.
d. Check fuel delivery system. If fuel is not reaching the fuel injectors, check for a loose electrical connector or defective fuse, relay or fuel pump and replace as necessary.
e. Engine may have excessive wear or mechanical damage such as low cylinder cranking pressure, a broken camshaft drive system, insufficient valve clearance or bent valves.
f. Check for fuel contamination such as water in the fuel. During winter months, the water may freeze and cause a fuel restriction. Adding a fuel additive may help, however the fuel system may require draining and purging with fresh fuel.
g. Check for ignition system failure. Check for loose or shorted wires or damaged ignition system components. Check the spark plugs for excessive wear or incorrect electrode gap. If the problem is worse in wet weather, check for shorts between the spark plugs and the ignition coils.
h. Check the engine management system for a failed sensor or control module.

2. Engine does not turn over when attempting to start

a. Check the battery state of charge and condition. If the dash lights are not visible or very dim when turning the ignition key on, the battery has either failed internally or discharged, the battery cables are loose, excessively corroded or damaged, or the alternator has failed or internally shorted, discharging the battery. Charge or replace the battery, clean or replace the battery cables, and check the alternator output.
b. Check the operation of the neutral safety switch. On automatic transmission vehicles, try starting the vehicle in both Park and Neutral. On manual transmission vehicles, depress the clutch pedal and attempt to start. On some vehicles, these switches can be adjusted. Make sure the switches or wire connectors are not loose or damaged. Replace or adjust the switches as necessary.
c. Check the starter motor, starter solenoid or relay, and starter motor cables and wires. Check the ground from the engine to the chassis. Make sure the wires are not loose, damaged, or corroded. If battery voltage is present at the starter relay, try using a remote starter to start the vehicle for test purposes only. Replace any damaged or corroded cables, in addition to replacing any failed components.
d. Check the engine for seizure. If the engine has not been started for a long period of time, internal parts such as the rings may have rusted to the cylinder walls. The engine may have suffered internal damage, or could be hydro-locked from ingesting water. Remove the spark plugs and carefully attempt to rotate the engine using a suitable breaker bar and socket on the crankshaft pulley. If the engine is resistant to moving, or moves slightly and then binds, do not force the engine any further before determining the problem.

3. Engine stalls immediately when started

a. Check the ignition switch condition and operation. The electrical contacts in the run position may be worn or damaged. Try restarting the engine with all electrical accessories in the off position. Sometimes turning the key on an off will help in emergency situations, however once the switch has shown signs of failure, it should be replaced as soon as possible.
b. Check for loose, corroded, damaged or shorted wires for the ignition system and repair or replace.
c. Check for manifold vacuum leaks or vacuum hose leakage and repair or replace parts as necessary.
d. Measure the fuel pump delivery volume and pressure. Low fuel pump pressure can also be noticed as a lack of power when accelerating. Make sure the fuel pump lines are not restricted. The fuel pump output is not adjustable and requires fuel pump replacement to repair.
e. Check the engine fuel and ignition management system. Inspect the sensor wiring and electrical connectors. A dirty, loose or damaged sensor or control module wire can simulate a failed component.
f. Check the exhaust system for internal restrictions.

4. Starter motor spins, but does not engage

a. Check the starter motor for a seized or binding pinion gear.
b. Remove the flywheel inspection plate and check for a damaged ring gear.

5. Engine is difficult to start when cold

a. Check the battery condition, battery state of charge and starter motor current draw.

Replace the battery if marginal and the starter motor if the current draw is beyond specification.
b. Check the battery cable condition. Clean the battery terminals and replace corroded or damaged cables.
c. Check the fuel system for proper operation. A fuel pump with insufficient fuel pressure or clogged injectors should be replaced.
d. Check the engine's tune-up status. Note the tune-up specifications and check for items such as severely worn spark plugs; adjust or replace as needed. On vehicles with manually adjusted valve clearances, check for tight valves and adjust to specification.
e. Check for a failed coolant temperature sensor, and replace if out of specification.
f. Check the operation of the engine management systems for fuel and ignition; repair or replace failed components as necessary.

6. Engine is difficult to start when hot

a. Check the air filter and air intake system. Replace the air filter if it is dirty or contaminated. Check the fresh air intake system for restrictions or blockage.
b. Check for loose or deteriorated engine grounds and clean, tighten or replace as needed.
c. Check for needed maintenance. Inspect tune-up and service related items such as spark plugs and engine oil condition, and check the operation of the engine fuel and ignition management system.

Diesel Engines

1. Engine turns over but won't start

a. Check engine starting procedure and restart engine.
b. Check the glow plug operation and repair or replace as necessary.
c. Check for air in the fuel system or fuel filter and bleed the air as necessary.
d. Check the fuel delivery system and repair or replace as necessary.
e. Check fuel level and add fuel as needed.
f. Check fuel quality. If the fuel is contaminated, drain and flush the fuel tank.
g. Check engine compression. If compression is below specification, the engine may need to be renewed or replaced.
h. Check the injection pump timing and set to specification.
i. Check the injection pump condition and replace as necessary.
j. Check the fuel nozzle operation and condition or replace as necessary.

2. Engine does not turn over when attempting to start

a. Check the battery state of charge and condition. If the dash lights are not visible or very dim when turning the ignition key on, the battery has either failed internally or discharged, the battery cables are loose, excessively corroded or damaged, or the alternator has failed or internally shorted, discharging the battery. Charge or replace the battery, clean or replace the battery cables, and check the alternator output.
b. Check the operation of the neutral safety switch. On automatic transmission vehicles, try starting the vehicle in both Park and Neutral. On manual transmission vehicles, depress the clutch pedal and attempt to start. On some vehicles, these switches can be adjusted. Make sure the switches or wire connectors are not loose or damaged. Replace or adjust the switches as necessary.
c. Check the starter motor, starter solenoid or relay, and starter motor cables and wires. Check the ground from the engine to the chassis. Make sure the wires are not loose, damaged, or corroded. If battery voltage is present at the starter relay, try using a remote starter to start the vehicle for test purposes only. Replace any damaged or corroded cables, in addition to replacing any failed components.
d. Check the engine for seizure. If the engine has not been started for a long period of time, internal parts such as the rings may have rusted to the cylinder walls. The engine may have suffered internal damage, or could be hydro-locked from ingesting water. Remove the injectors and carefully attempt to rotate the engine using a suitable breaker bar and socket on the crankshaft pulley. If the engine is resistant to moving, or moves slightly and then binds, do not force the engine any further before determining the cause of the problem.

3. Engine stalls after starting

a. Check for a restriction in the fuel return line or the return line check valve and repair as necessary.
b. Check the glow plug operation for turning the glow plugs off too soon and repair as necessary.
c. Check for incorrect injection pump timing and reset to specification.
d. Test the engine fuel pump and replace if the output is below specification.
e. Check for contaminated or incorrect fuel. Completely flush the fuel system and replace with fresh fuel.
f. Test the engine's compression for low compression. If below specification, mechanical repairs are necessary to repair.
g. Check for air in the fuel. Check fuel tank fuel and fill as needed.

h. Check for a failed injection pump. Replace the pump, making sure to properly set the pump timing.

4. Starter motor spins, but does not engage
a. Check the starter motor for a seized or binding pinion gear.
b. Remove the flywheel inspection plate and check for a damaged ring gear.

1-B. Engine Running Conditions

Gasoline Engines

1. Engine runs poorly, hesitates
a. Check the engine ignition system operation and adjust if possible, or replace defective parts.
b. Check for restricted fuel injectors and replace as necessary.
c. Check the fuel pump output and delivery. Inspect fuel lines for restrictions. If the fuel pump pressure is below specification, replace the fuel pump.
d. Check the operation of the engine management system and repair as necessary.

2. Engine lacks power
a. Check the engine's tune-up status. Note the tune-up specifications and check for items such as severely worn spark plugs; adjust or replace as needed. On vehicles with manually adjusted valve clearances, check for tight valves and adjust to specification.
b. Check the air filter and air intake system. Replace the air filter if it is dirty or contaminated. Check the fresh air intake system for restrictions or blockage.
c. Check the operation of the engine fuel and ignition management systems. Check the sensor operation and wiring. Check for low fuel pump pressure and repair or replace components as necessary.
d. Check the throttle linkage adjustments. Check to make sure the linkage is fully opening the throttle. Replace any worn or defective bushings or linkages.
e. Check for a restricted exhaust system. Check for bent or crimped exhaust pipes, or internally restricted mufflers or catalytic converters. Compare inlet and outlet temperatures for the converter or muffler. If the inlet is hot, but outlet cold, the component is restricted.
f. Check for a loose or defective knock sensor. A loose, improperly torqued or defective knock sensor will decrease spark advance and reduce power. Replace defective knock sensors and install using the recommended torque specification.
g. Check for engine mechanical conditions such as low compression, worn piston rings, worn valves, worn camshafts and related parts. An engine which has severe mechanical wear, or has suffered internal mechanical damage must be rebuilt or replaced to restore lost power.
h. Check the engine oil level for being overfilled. Adjust the engine's oil level, or change the engine oil and filter, and top off to the correct level.
i. Check for an intake manifold or vacuum hose leak. Replace leaking gaskets or worn vacuum hoses.
j. Check for dragging brakes and replace or repair as necessary.
k. Check tire air pressure and tire wear. Adjust the pressure to the recommended settings. Check the tire wear for possible alignment problems causing increased rolling resistance, decreased acceleration and increased fuel usage.
l. Check the octane rating of the fuel used during refilling, and use a higher octane rated fuel.

3. Poor fuel economy
a. Inspect the air filter and check for any air restrictions going into the air filter housing. Replace the air filter if it is dirty or contaminated.
b. Check the engine for tune-up and related adjustments. Replace worn ignition parts, check the engine ignition timing and fuel mixture, and set to specifications if possible.
c. Check the tire size, tire wear, alignment and tire pressure. Large tires create more rolling resistance, smaller tires require more engine speed to maintain a vehicle's road speed. Excessive tire wear can be caused by incorrect tire pressure, incorrect wheel alignment or a suspension problem. All of these conditions create increased rolling resistance, causing the engine to work harder to accelerate and maintain a vehicle's speed.
d. Inspect the brakes for binding or excessive drag. A sticking brake caliper, overly adjusted brake shoe, broken brake shoe return spring, or binding parking brake cable or linkage can create a significant drag, brake wear and loss of fuel economy. Check the brake system operation and repair as necessary.

4. Engine runs on (diesels) when turned off
a. Check for idle speed set too high and readjust to specification.
b. Check the operation of the idle control valve, and replace if defective.
c. Check the ignition timing and adjust to recommended settings. Check for defective sensors or related components and replace if defective.
d. Check for a vacuum leak at the intake manifold or vacuum hose and replace defective gaskets or hoses.
e. Check the engine for excessive carbon build-up in the combustion chamber. Use a recommended decarbonizing fuel additive or disassemble the cylinder head to remove the carbon.

f. Check the operation of the engine fuel management system and replace defective sensors or control units.
g. Check the engine operating temperature for overheating and repair as necessary.

5. Engine knocks and pings during heavy acceleration, and on steep hills
a. Check the octane rating of the fuel used during refilling, and use a higher octane rated fuel.
b. Check the ignition timing and adjust to recommended settings. Check for defective sensors or related components and replace if defective.
c. Check the engine for excessive carbon build-up in the combustion chamber. Use a recommended decarbonizing fuel additive or disassemble the cylinder head to remove the carbon.
d. Check the spark plugs for the correct type, electrode gap and heat range. Replace worn or damaged spark plugs. For severe or continuous high speed use, install a spark plug that is one heat range colder.
e. Check the operation of the engine fuel management system and replace defective sensors or control units.
f. Check for a restricted exhaust system. Check for bent or crimped exhaust pipes, or internally restricted mufflers or catalytic converters. Compare inlet and outlet temperatures for the converter or muffler. If the inlet is hot, but outlet cold, the component is restricted.

6. Engine accelerates, but vehicle does not gain speed
a. On manual transmission vehicles, check for causes of a slipping clutch. Refer to the clutch troubleshooting section for additional information.
b. On automatic transmission vehicles, check for a slipping transmission. Check the transmission fluid level and condition. If the fluid level is too high, adjust to the correct level. If the fluid level is low, top off using the recommended fluid type. If the fluid exhibits a burning odor, the transmission has been slipping internally. Changing the fluid and filter may help temporarily, however in this situation a transmission may require overhauling to ensure long-term reliability.

Diesel Engines

1. Engine runs poorly
a. Check the injection pump timing and adjust to specification.
b. Check for air in the fuel lines or leaks, and bleed the air from the fuel system.
c. Check the fuel filter, fuel feed and return lines for a restriction and repair as necessary.
d. Check the fuel for contamination, drain and flush the fuel tank and replenish with fresh fuel.

2. Engine lacks power
a. Inspect the air intake system and air filter for restrictions and, if necessary, replace the air filter.
b. Verify the injection pump timing and reset if out of specification.
c. Check the exhaust for an internal restriction and replace failed parts.
d. Check for a restricted fuel filter and, if restricted, replace the filter.
e. Inspect the fuel filler cap vent . When removing the filler cap, listen for excessive hissing noises indicating a blockage in the fuel filler cap vents. If the filler cap vents are blocked, replace the cap.
f. Check the fuel system for restrictions and repair as necessary.
g. Check for low engine compression and inspect for external leakage at the glow plugs or nozzles. If no external leakage is noted, repair or replace the engine.

ENGINE PERFORMANCE TROUBLESHOOTING HINTS

When troubleshooting an engine running or performance condition, the mechanical condition of the engine should be determined *before* lengthy troubleshooting procedures are performed.

The engine fuel management systems in fuel injected vehicles rely on electronic sensors to provide information to the engine control unit for precise fuel metering. Unlike carburetors, which use the incoming air speed to draw fuel through the fuel metering jets in order to provide a proper fuel-to-air ratio, a fuel injection system provides a specific amount of fuel which is introduced by the fuel injectors into the intake manifold or intake port, based on the information provided by electronic sensors.

The sensors monitor the engine's operating temperature, ambient temperature and the amount of air entering the engine, engine speed and throttle position to provide information to the engine control unit, which, in turn, operates the fuel injectors by electrical pulses. The sensors provide information to the engine control unit using low voltage electrical signals. As a result, an unplugged sensor or a poor electrical contact could cause a poor running condition similar to a failed sensor.

When troubleshooting a fuel related engine condition on fuel injected vehicles, carefully inspect the wiring and electrical connectors to the related components. Make sure the electrical connectors are fully connected, clean and not physically damaged. If necessary, clean the electrical contacts using electrical contact cleaner. The use of cleaning agents not specifically designed for electrical contacts should not be used, as they could leave a surface film or damage the insulation of the wiring.

The engine electrical system provides the necessary electrical power to operate the vehicle's electrical accessories, electronic control units and sensors. Because engine management systems are sensitive to voltage changes, an alternator which over or undercharges could cause engine running problems or component failure. Most alternators utilize internal voltage regulators which cannot be adjusted and must be replaced individually or as a unit with the alternator.

Ignition systems may be controlled by, or linked to, the engine fuel management system. Similar to the fuel injection system, these ignition systems rely on electronic sensors for information to determine the optimum ignition timing for a given engine speed and load. Some ignition systems no longer allow the ignition timing to be adjusted. Feedback from low voltage electrical sensors provide information to the control unit to determine the amount of ignition advance. On these systems, if a failure occurs the failed component must be replaced. Before replacing suspected failed electrical components, carefully inspect the wiring and electrical connectors to the related components. Make sure the electrical connectors are fully connected, clean and not physically damaged. If necessary, clean the electrical contacts using electrical contact cleaner. The use of cleaning agents not specifically designed for electrical contacts should be avoided, as they could leave a surface film or damage the insulation of the wiring.

1-C. Engine Noises, Odors and Vibrations

1. Engine makes a knocking or pinging noise when accelerating
a. Check the octane rating of the fuel being used. Depending on the type of driving or driving conditions, it may be necessary to use a higher octane fuel.
b. Verify the ignition system settings and operation. Improperly adjusted ignition timing or a failed component, such as a knock sensor, may cause the ignition timing to advance excessively or prematurely. Check the ignition system operation and adjust, or replace components as needed.
c. Check the spark plug gap, heat range and condition. If the vehicle is operated in severe operating conditions or at continuous high speeds, use a colder heat range spark plug. Adjust the spark plug gap to the manufacturer's recommended specification and replace worn or damaged spark plugs.

2. Starter motor grinds when used
a. Examine the starter pinion gear and the engine ring gear for damage, and replace damaged parts.
b. Check the starter mounting bolts and housing. If the housing is cracked or damaged replace the starter motor and check the mounting bolts for tightness.

3. Engine makes a screeching noise
a. Check the accessory drive belts for looseness and adjust as necessary.
b. Check the accessory drive belt tensioners for seizing or excessive bearing noises and replace if loose, binding, or excessively noisy.
c. Check for a seizing water pump. The pump may not be leaking; however, the bearing may be faulty or the impeller loose and jammed. Replace the water pump.

4. Engine makes a growling noise
a. Check for a loose or failing water pump. Replace the pump and engine coolant.
b. Check the accessory drive belt tensioners for excessive bearing noises and replace if loose or excessively noisy.

5. Engine makes a ticking or tapping noise
a. On vehicles with hydraulic lash adjusters, check for low or dirty engine oil and top off or replace the engine oil and filter.
b. On vehicles with hydraulic lash adjusters, check for collapsed lifters and replace failed components.
c. On vehicles with hydraulic lash adjusters, check for low oil pressure caused by a restricted oil filter, worn engine oil pump, or oil pressure relief valve.
d. On vehicles with manually adjusted valves, check for excessive valve clearance or worn valve train parts. Adjust the valves to specification or replace worn and defective parts.
e. Check for a loose or improperly tensioned timing belt or timing chain and adjust or replace parts as necessary.
f. Check for a bent or sticking exhaust or intake valve. Remove the engine cylinder head to access and replace.

6. Engine makes a heavy knocking noise
a. Check for a loose crankshaft pulley or flywheel; replace and torque the mounting bolt(s) to specification.
b. Check for a bent connecting rod caused by a hydro-lock condition. Engine disassembly is necessary to inspect for damaged and needed replacement parts.
c. Check for excessive engine rod bearing wear or damage. This condition is also associated with low engine oil pressure and will require engine disassembly to inspect for damaged and needed replacement parts.

7. Vehicle has a fuel odor when driven
a. Check the fuel gauge level. If the fuel gauge registers full, it is possible that the odor is caused by being filled beyond capacity, or some spillage occurred during refueling. The odor should clear after driving an hour, or twenty miles, allowing the vapor canister to purge.
b. Check the fuel filler cap for looseness or seepage. Check the cap tightness and, if loose, properly secure. If seepage is noted, replace the filler cap.
c. Check for loose hose clamps, cracked or damaged fuel delivery and return lines, or leaking components or seals, and replace or repair as necessary.
d. Check the vehicle's fuel economy. If fuel consumption has increased due to a failed component, or if the fuel is not properly ignited due to an ignition related failure, the catalytic converter may become contaminated. This condition may also trigger the check engine warning light. Check the spark plugs for a dark, rich condition or verify the condition by testing the vehicle's emissions. Replace fuel fouled spark plugs, and test and replace failed components as necessary.

8. Vehicle has a rotten egg odor when driven
a. Check for a leaking intake gasket or vacuum leak causing a lean running condition. A lean mixture may result in increased exhaust temperatures, causing the catalytic converter to run hotter than normal. This condition may also trigger the check engine warning light. Check and repair the vacuum leaks as necessary.
b. Check the vehicle's alternator and battery condition. If the alternator is overcharging, the battery electrolyte can be boiled from the battery, and the battery casing may begin to crack, swell or bulge, damaging or shorting the battery internally. If this has occurred, neutralize the battery mounting area with a suitable baking soda and water mixture or equivalent, and replace the alternator or voltage regulator. Inspect, service, and load test the battery, and replace if necessary.

9. Vehicle has a sweet odor when driven
a. Check for an engine coolant leak caused by a seeping radiator cap, loose hose clamp, weeping cooling system seal, gasket or cooling system hose and replace or repair as needed.
b. Check for a coolant leak from the radiator, coolant reservoir, heater control valve or under the dashboard from the heater core, and replace the failed part as necessary.
c. Check the engine's exhaust for white smoke in addition to a sweet odor. The presence of white, steamy smoke with a sweet odor indicates coolant leaking into the combustion chamber. Possible causes include a failed head gasket, cracked engine block or cylinder head. Other symptoms of this condition include a white paste build-up on the inside of the oil filler cap, and softened, deformed or bulging radiator hoses.

10. Engine vibrates when idling
a. Check for loose, collapsed, or damaged engine or transmission mounts and repair or replace as necessary.
b. Check for loose or damaged engine covers or shields and secure or replace as necessary.

11. Engine vibrates during acceleration
a. Check for missing, loose or damaged exhaust system hangers and mounts; replace or repair as necessary.
b. Check the exhaust system routing and fit for adequate clearance or potential rubbing; repair or adjust as necessary.

1-D. Engine Electrical System

1. Battery goes dead while driving
a. Check the battery condition. Replace the battery if the battery will not hold a charge or fails a battery load test. If the battery loses fluid while driving, check for an overcharging condition. If the alternator is overcharging, replace the alternator or voltage regulator. (A voltage regulator is typically built into the alternator, necessitating alternator replacement or overhaul.)
b. Check the battery cable condition. Clean or replace corroded cables and clean the battery terminals.
c. Check the alternator and voltage regulator operation. If the charging system is over or undercharging, replace the alternator or voltage regulator, or both.
d. Inspect the wiring and wire connectors at the alternator for looseness, a missing ground or defective terminal, and repair as necessary.
e. Inspect the alternator drive belt tension, tensioners and condition. Properly tension the drive belt, replace weak or broken tensioners, and replace the drive belt if worn or cracked.

2. Battery goes dead overnight
a. Check the battery condition. Replace the battery if the battery will not hold a charge or fails a battery load test.
b. Check for a voltage draw, such as a trunk light, interior light or glove box light staying on. Check light switch position and operation, and replace if defective.
c. Check the alternator for an internally failed diode, and replace the alternator if defective.

1-E. Engine Cooling System

1. Engine overheats
a. Check the coolant level. Set the heater temperature to full hot and check for internal air pockets, bleed the cooling system and inspect for leakage. Top off the cooling system with the correct coolant mixture.
b. Pressure test the cooling system and radiator cap for leaks. Check for seepage caused by loose hose clamps, failed coolant hoses, and cooling system components such as the heater control valve, heater core, radiator, radiator cap, and water pump. Replace defective parts and fill the cooling system with the recommended coolant mixture.
c. On vehicles with electrically controlled cooling fans, check the cooling fan operation. Check for blown fuses or defective fan motors, temperature sensors and relays, and replace failed components.
d. Check for a coolant leak caused by a failed head gasket, or a porous water jacket casting in the cylinder head or engine block. Replace defective parts as necessary.
e. Check for an internally restricted radiator. Flush the radiator or replace if the blockage is too severe for flushing.
f. Check for a damaged water pump. If coolant circulation is poor, check for a loose water pump impeller. If the impeller is loose, replace the water pump.

2. Engine loses coolant
a. Pressure test the cooling system and radiator cap for leaks. Check for seepage caused by loose hose clamps, failed coolant hoses, and cooling system components such as the heater control valve, heater core, radiator, radiator cap, and water pump. Replace defective parts and fill the cooling system with the recommended coolant mixture.
b. Check for a coolant leak caused by a failed head gasket, or a porous water jacket casting in the cylinder head or engine block. Replace defective parts as necessary.

3. Engine temperature remains cold when driving
a. Check the thermostat operation. Replace the thermostat if it sticks in the open position.
b. On vehicles with electrically controlled cooling fans, check the cooling fan operation. Check for defective temperature sensors and stuck relays, and replace failed components.
c. Check temperature gauge operation if equipped to verify proper operation of the gauge. Check the sensors and wiring for defects, and repair or replace defective components.

4. Engine runs hot
a. Check for an internally restricted radiator. Flush the radiator or replace if the blockage is too severe for flushing.
b. Check for a loose or slipping water pump drive belt. Inspect the drive belt condition. Replace the belt if brittle, cracked or damaged. Check the pulley condition and properly tension the belt.
c. Check the cooling fan operation. Replace defective fan motors, sensors or relays as necessary.
d. Check temperature gauge operation if equipped to verify proper operation of the gauge. Check the sensors and wiring for defects, and repair or replace defective components.
e. Check the coolant level. Set the heater temperature to full hot, check for internal air pockets, bleed the cooling system and inspect for leakage. Top off the cooling system with the correct coolant mixture. Once the engine is cool, recheck the fluid level and top off as needed.

NOTE: The engine cooling system can also be affected by an engine's mechanical condition. A failed head gasket or a porous casting in the engine block or cylinder head could cause a loss of coolant and result in engine overheating.

Some cooling systems rely on electrically driven cooling fans to cool the radiator and use electrical temperature sensors and relays to operate the cooling fan. When diagnosing these systems, check for blown fuses, damaged wires and verify that the electrical connections are fully connected, clean and not physically damaged. If necessary, clean the electrical contacts using electrical contact cleaner. The use of cleaning agents not specifically designed for electrical contacts could leave a film or damage the insulation of the wiring.

1-F. Engine Exhaust System

1. Exhaust rattles at idle speed
a. Check the engine and transmission mounts and replace mounts showing signs of damage or wear.
b. Check the exhaust hangers, brackets and mounts. Replace broken, missing or damaged mounts.
c. Check for internal damage to mufflers and catalytic converters. The broken pieces from the defective component may travel in the direction of the exhaust flow and collect and/or create a blockage in a component other than the one which failed, causing engine running and stalling problems. Another symptom of a restricted exhaust is low engine manifold vacuum. Remove the exhaust system and carefully remove any loose or broken pieces, then replace any failed or damaged parts as necessary.
d. Check the exhaust system clearance, routing and alignment. If the exhaust is making contact with the vehicle in any manner, loosen and reposition the exhaust system.

2. Exhaust system vibrates when driving
a. Check the exhaust hangers, brackets and mounts. Replace broken, missing or damaged mounts.
b. Check the exhaust system clearance, routing and alignment. If the exhaust is making contact with the vehicle in any manner, check for bent or damaged components and replace, then loosen and reposition the exhaust system.
c. Check for internal damage to mufflers and catalytic converters. The broken pieces from the defective component may travel in the direction of the exhaust flow and collect and/or create a blockage in a component other than the one which failed, causing engine running and stalling problems. Another symptom of a restricted exhaust is low engine manifold vacuum. Remove the exhaust system and carefully remove any loose or broken pieces, then replace any failed or damaged parts as necessary.

3. Exhaust system hangs too low
a. Check the exhaust hangers, brackets and mounts. Replace broken, missing or damaged mounts.
b. Check the exhaust routing and alignment. Check and replace bent or damaged components. If the exhaust is not routed properly, loosen and reposition the exhaust system.

4. Exhaust sounds loud
a. Check the system for looseness and leaks. Check the exhaust pipes, clamps, flange bolts and manifold fasteners for tightness. Check and replace any failed gaskets.
b. Check and replace exhaust silencers that have a loss of efficiency due to internally broken baffles or worn packing material.
c. Check for missing mufflers and silencers that have been replaced with straight pipes or with non-original equipment silencers.

NOTE: Exhaust system rattles, vibration and proper alignment should not be overlooked. Excessive vibration caused by collapsed engine mounts, damaged or missing exhaust hangers and misalignment may cause surface cracks and broken welds, creating exhaust leaks or internal damage to exhaust components such as the catalytic converter, creating a restriction to exhaust flow and loss of power.

2. DRIVE TRAIN

2-A. Automatic Transmission

1. Transmission shifts erratically
a. Check and if not within the recommended range, add or remove transmission fluid to obtain the correct fluid level. Always use the recommended fluid type when adding transmission fluid.
b. Check the fluid level condition. If the fluid has become contaminated, fatigued from excessive heat or exhibits a burning odor, change the transmission fluid and filter using the recommended type and amount of fluid. A fluid which exhibits a burning odor indicates that the transmission has been slipping internally and may require future repairs.
c. Check for an improperly installed transmission filter, or missing filter gasket, and repair as necessary.
d. Check for loose or leaking gaskets, pressure lines and fittings, and repair or replace as necessary.
e. Check for loose or disconnected shift and throttle linkages or vacuum hoses, and repair as necessary.

2. Transmission will not engage
a. Check the shift linkage for looseness, wear and proper adjustment, and repair as necessary.
b. Check for a loss of transmission fluid and top off as needed with the recommended fluid.
c. If the transmission does not engage with the shift linkage correctly installed and the proper fluid level, internal damage has likely occurred, requiring transmission removal and disassembly.

3. Transmission will not downshift during heavy acceleration
a. On computer controlled transmissions, check for failed sensors or control units and repair or replace defective components.

b. On vehicles with kickdown linkages or vacuum servos, check for proper linkage adjustment or leaking vacuum hoses or servo units.

NOTE: Many automatic transmissions use an electronic control module, electrical sensors and solenoids to control transmission shifting. When troubleshooting a vehicle with this type of system, be sure the electrical connectors are fully connected, clean and not physically damaged. If necessary, clean the electrical contacts using electrical contact cleaner. The use of cleaning agents not specifically designed for electrical contacts could leave a film or damage the insulation of the wiring.

2-B. Manual Transmission

1. Transmission grinds going into forward gears while driving
a. Check the clutch release system. On clutches with a mechanical or cable linkage, check the adjustment. Adjust the clutch pedal to have 1 inch (25mm) of free-play at the pedal.
b. If the clutch release system is hydraulically operated, check the fluid level and, if low, top off using the recommended type and amount of fluid.
c. Synchronizers worn. Remove transmission and replace synchronizers.
d. Synchronizer sliding sleeve worn. Remove transmission and replace sliding sleeve.
e. Gear engagement dogs worn or damaged. Remove transmission and replace gear.

2. Transmission jumps out of gear
a. Shift shaft detent springs worn. Replace shift detent springs.
b. Synchronizer sliding sleeve worn. Remove transmission and replace sliding sleeve.
c. Gear engagement dogs worn or damaged. Remove transmission and replace gear.
d. Crankshaft thrust bearings worn. Remove engine and crankshaft, and repair as necessary.

3. Transmission difficult to shift
a. Verify the clutch adjustment and, if not properly adjusted, adjust to specification.
b. Synchronizers worn. Remove transmission and replace synchronizers.
c. Pilot bearing seized. Remove transmission and replace pilot bearing.
d. Shift linkage or bushing seized. Disassemble the shift linkage, replace worn or damaged bushings, lubricate and reinstall.

4. Transmission leaks fluid
a. Check the fluid level for an overfilled condition. Adjust the fluid level to specification.
b. Check for a restricted transmission vent or breather tube. Clear the blockage as necessary and check the fluid level. If necessary, top off with the recommended lubricant.
c. Check for a porous casting, leaking seal or gasket. Replace defective parts and top off the fluid level with the recommended lubricant.

2-C. Clutch

1. Clutch slips on hills or during sudden acceleration
a. Check for insufficient clutch pedal free-play. Adjust clutch linkage or cable to allow about 1 inch (25mm) of pedal free-play.
b. Clutch disc worn or severely damaged. Remove engine or transmission and replace clutch disc.
c. Clutch pressure plate is weak. Remove engine or transmission and replace the clutch pressure plate and clutch disc.
d. Clutch pressure plate and/or flywheel incorrectly machined. If the clutch system has been recently replaced and rebuilt, or refurbished parts have been used, it is possible that the machined surfaces decreased the clutch clamping force. Replace defective parts with new replacement parts.

2. Clutch will not disengage, difficult to shift
a. Check the clutch release mechanism. Check for stretched cables, worn linkages or failed clutch hydraulics and replace defective parts. On hydraulically operated clutch release mechanisms, check for air in the hydraulic system and bleed as necessary.
b. Check for a broken, cracked or fatigued clutch release arm or release arm pivot. Replace defective parts and properly lubricate upon assembly.
c. Check for a damaged clutch hub damper or damper spring. The broken parts tend to become lodged between the clutch disc and the pressure plate. Disassemble clutch system and replace failed parts.
d. Check for a seized clutch pilot bearing. Disassemble the clutch assembly and replace the defective parts.
e. Check for a defective clutch disc. Check for warpage or lining thicknesses larger than original equipment.

3. Clutch is noisy when the clutch pedal is pressed
a. Check the clutch pedal stop and pedal free-play adjustment for excessive movement and adjust as necessary.
b. Check for a worn or damaged release bearing. If the noise ceases when the pedal is released, the release bearing should be replaced.

c. Check the engine crankshaft axial play. If the crankshaft thrust bearings are worn or damaged, the crankshaft will move when pressing the clutch pedal. The engine must be disassembled to replace the crankshaft thrust bearings.

4. Clutch pedal extremely difficult to press
a. Check the clutch pedal pivots and linkages for binding. Clean and lubricate linkages.
b. On cable actuated clutch systems, check the cable routing and condition. Replace kinked, frayed, damaged or corroded cables and check cable routing to avoid sharp bends. Check the engine ground strap for poor conductivity. If the ground strap is marginal, the engine could try to ground itself via the clutch cable, causing premature failure.
c. On mechanical linkage clutches, check the linkage for binding or misalignment. Lubricate pivots or linkages and repair as necessary.
d. Check the release bearing guide tube and release fork for a lack of lubrication. Install a smooth coating of high temperature grease to allow smooth movement of the release bearing over the guide tube.

5. Clutch pedal remains down when pressed
a. On mechanical linkage or cable actuated clutches, check for a loose or disconnected link.
b. On hydraulically actuated clutches, check the fluid level and check for a hydraulic leak at the clutch slave or master cylinder, or hydraulic line. Replace failed parts and bleed clutch hydraulic system. If no leakage is noted, the clutch master cylinder may have failed internally. Replace the clutch master cylinder and bleed the clutch hydraulic system.

6. Clutch chatters when engaging
a. Check the engine flywheel for warpage or surface variations and replace or repair as necessary.
b. Check for a warped clutch disc or damaged clutch damper hub. Remove the clutch disc and replace.
c. Check for a loose or damaged clutch pressure plate and replace defective components.

NOTE: The clutch is actuated either by a mechanical linkage, cable or a clutch hydraulic system. The mechanical linkage and cable systems may require the clutch pedal free-play to be adjusted as the clutch disc wears. A hydraulic clutch system automatically adjusts as the clutch wears and, with the exception of the clutch pedal height, no adjustment is possible.

2-D. Differential and Final Drive

1. Differential makes a low pitched rumbling noise
a. Check fluid level type and amount. Replace the fluid with the recommended type and amount of lubricant.
b. Check the differential bearings for wear or damage. Remove the bearings, inspect the drive and driven gears for wear or damage, and replace components as necessary.

2. Differential makes a howling noise
a. Check fluid level type and amount. Replace the fluid with the recommended type and amount of lubricant.
b. Check the differential drive and driven gears for wear or damage, and replace components as necessary.

2-E. Transfer Assembly

All Wheel and Four Wheel Drive Vehicles

1. Leaks fluid from seals or vent after being driven
a. Fluid level overfilled. Check and adjust transfer case fluid level.
b. Check for a restricted breather or breather tube, clear and check the fluid level and top off as needed.
c. Check seal condition and replace worn, damaged, or defective seals. Check the fluid level and top off as necessary.

2. Makes excessive noise while driving
a. Check the fluid for the correct type of lubricant. Drain and refill using the recommended type and amount of lubricant.
b. Check the fluid level. Top off the fluid using the recommended type and amount of lubricant.
c. If the fluid level and type of lubricant meet specifications, check for internal wear or damage. Remove assembly and disassemble to inspect for worn, damaged, or defective components.

3. Jumps out of gear
a. Stop vehicle and make sure the unit is fully engaged.
b. Check for worn, loose or an improperly adjusted linkage. Replace and/or adjust linkage as necessary.
c. Check for internal wear or damage. Remove assembly and disassemble to inspect for worn, damaged, or defective components.

2-F. Driveshaft

Rear Wheel, All Wheel and Four Wheel Drive Vehicles

1. Clunking noise from center of vehicle shifting from forward to reverse
a. Worn universal joint. Remove driveshaft and replace universal joint.

2. Excessive vibration from center of vehicle when accelerating
a. Worn universal joint. Remove driveshaft and replace universal joint.
b. Driveshaft misaligned. Check for collapsed or damaged engine and transmission mounts, and replace as necessary.
c. Driveshaft bent or out of balance. Replace damaged components and reinstall.
d. Driveshaft out of balance. Remove the driveshaft and have it balanced by a competent professional, or replace the driveshaft assembly.

NOTE: Most driveshafts are linked together by universal joints; however, some manufacturers use Constant Velocity (CV) joints or rubber flex couplers.

2-G. Axles

All Wheel and Four Wheel Drive Vehicles

1. Front or rear wheel makes a clicking noise
a. Check for debris such as a pebble, nail or glass in the tire or tire tread. Carefully remove the debris. Small rocks and pebbles rarely cause a puncture; however, a sharp object should be removed carefully at a facility capable of performing tire repairs.
b. Check for a loose, damaged or worn Constant Velocity (CV) joint and replace if defective.

2. Front or rear wheel vibrates with increased speed
a. Check for a bent rim and replace, if damaged.
b. Check the tires for balance or internal damage and replace if defective.
c. Check for a loose, worn or damaged wheel bearing and replace if defective.
d. Check for a loose, damaged or worn Constant Velocity (CV) joint and replace if defective.

Front Wheel Drive Vehicles

3. Front wheel makes a clicking noise
a. Check for debris such as a pebble, nail or glass in the tire or tire tread. Carefully remove the debris. Small rocks and pebbles rarely cause a puncture; however, a sharp object should be removed carefully at a facility capable of performing tire repairs.

b. Check for a loose, damaged or worn Constant Velocity (CV) joint and replace if defective.

4. Rear wheel makes a clicking noise
a. Check for debris such as a pebble, nail or glass in the tire or tire tread. Carefully remove the debris. Small rocks and pebbles rarely cause a puncture; however, a sharp object should be removed carefully at a facility capable of performing tire repairs.

Rear Wheel Drive Vehicles

5. Front or rear wheel makes a clicking noise
a. Check for debris such as a pebble, nail or glass in the tire or tire tread. Carefully remove the debris. Small rocks and pebbles rarely cause a puncture; however, a sharp object should be removed carefully at a facility capable of performing tire repairs.

6. Rear wheel shudders or vibrates
a. Check for a bent rear wheel or axle assembly and replace defective components.
b. Check for a loose, damaged or worn rear wheel bearing and replace as necessary.

2-H. Other Drive Train Conditions

1. Burning odor from center of vehicle when accelerating
a. Check for a seizing brake hydraulic component such as a brake caliper. Check the caliper piston for surface damage such as rust, and measure for out-of-round wear and caliper-to-piston clearance. For additional information on brake related odors, refer to section 3-A, condition number 9.
b. On vehicles with a manual transmission, check for a slipping clutch. For possible causes and additional information, refer to section 2-C, condition number 1.
c. On vehicles with an automatic transmission, check the fluid level and condition. Top off or change the fluid and filter using the recommended replacement parts, lubricant type and amount. If the odor persists, transmission removal and disassembly will be necessary.

2. Engine accelerates, but vehicle does not gain speed
a. On vehicles with a manual transmission, check for a slipping or damaged clutch. For possible causes and additional information refer to section 2-C, condition number 1.
b. On vehicles with an automatic transmission, check the fluid level and condition. Top off or change the fluid and filter using the recommended replacement parts, lubricant type and amount. If the slipping continues, transmission removal and disassembly will be necessary.

3. BRAKE SYSTEM

3-A. Brake System Troubleshooting

1. Brake pedal pulsates or shimmies when pressed
a. Check wheel lug nut torque and tighten evenly to specification.
b. Check the brake rotor for trueness and thickness variations. Replace the rotor if it is too thin, warped, or if the thickness varies beyond specification. Some rotors can be machined; consult the manufacturer's specifications and recommendations before using a machined brake rotor.
c. Check the brake caliper or caliper bracket mounting bolt torque and inspect for looseness. Torque the mounting bolts and inspect for wear or any looseness, including worn mounting brackets, bushings and sliding pins.
d. Check the wheel bearing for looseness. If the bearing is loose, adjust if possible, otherwise replace the bearing.

2. Brakes make a squealing noise
a. Check the brake rotor for the presence of a ridge on the outer edge; if present, remove the ridge or replace the brake rotor and brake pads.
b. Check for debris in the brake lining material, clean and reinstall.
c. Check the brake linings for wear and replace the brake linings if wear is approaching the lining wear limit.
d. Check the brake linings for glazing. Inspect the brake drum or rotor surface and replace, along with the brake linings, if the surface is not smooth or even.
e. Check the brake pad or shoe mounting areas for a lack of lubricant or the presence of surface rust. Clean and lubricate with a recommended high temperature brake grease.

3. Brakes make a grinding noise
a. Check the brake linings and brake surface areas for severe wear or damage. Replace worn or damaged parts.
b. Check for a seized or partially seized brake causing premature or uneven brake wear, excessive heat and brake rotor or drum damage. Replace defective parts and inspect the wheel bearing condition, which could have been damaged due to excessive heat.

4. Vehicle pulls to one side during braking
a. Check for air in the brake hydraulic system. Inspect the brake hydraulic seals, fluid lines and related components for fluid leaks. Remove the air from the brake system by bleeding the brakes. Be sure to use fresh brake fluid that meets the manufacturer's recommended standards.
b. Check for an internally restricted flexible brake hydraulic hose. Replace the hose and flush the brake system.
c. Check for a seizing brake hydraulic component such as a brake caliper. Check the caliper piston for surface damage such as rust, and measure for out-of-round wear and caliper-to-piston clearance. Overhaul or replace failed parts and flush the brake system.
d. Check the vehicle's alignment and inspect for suspension wear. Replace worn bushings, ball joints and set alignment to the manufacturer's specifications.
e. If the brake system uses drum brakes front or rear, check the brake adjustment. Inspect for seized adjusters and clean or replace, then properly adjust.

5. Brake pedal feels spongy or has excessive travel
a. Check the brake fluid level and condition. If the fluid is contaminated or has not been flushed every two years, clean the master cylinder reservoir, and bleed and flush the brakes using fresh brake fluid that meets the manufacturer's recommended standards.
b. Check for a weak or damaged flexible brake hydraulic hose. Replace the hose and flush the brake system.
c. If the brake system uses drum brakes front or rear, check the brake adjustment. Inspect for seized adjusters and clean or replace, then properly adjust.

6. Brake pedal feel is firm, but brakes lack sufficient stopping power or fade
a. Check the operation of the brake booster and brake booster check valve. Replace worn or failed parts.
b. Check brake linings and brake surface areas for glazing and replace worn or damaged parts.
c. Check for seized hydraulic parts and linkages, and clean or replace as needed.

7. Vehicle has excessive front end dive or locks rear brakes too easily
a. Check for worn, failed or seized brake proportioning valve and replace the valve.
b. Check for a seized, disconnected or missing spring or linkage for the brake proportioning valve. Replace missing parts or repair as necessary.

8. Brake pedal goes to floor when pressed and will not pump up
a. Check the brake hydraulic fluid level and inspect the fluid lines and seals for leakage. Repair or replace leaking components, then bleed and flush the brake system using fresh brake fluid that meets the manufacturer's recommended standards.
b. Check the brake fluid level. Inspect the brake fluid level and brake hydraulic seals. If the fluid level is ok, and the brake hydraulic system is free of hydraulic leaks, replace the brake master cylinder, then bleed and flush the brake system using fresh brake fluid that meets the manufacturer's recommended standards.

9. Brakes produce a burning odor
a. Check for a seizing brake hydraulic component such as a brake caliper. Check the caliper piston for surface damage such as rust, and measure for out-of-round wear and caliper-to-piston clearance. Overhaul or replace failed parts and flush the brake system.
b. Check for an internally restricted flexible brake hydraulic hose. Replace the hose and flush the brake system.
c. Check the parking brake release mechanism, seized linkage or cable, and repair as necessary.

4. WHEELS, TIRES, STEERING AND SUSPENSION

4-A. Wheels and Wheel Bearings

1. Front wheel or wheel bearing loose

All Wheel and Four Wheel Drive Vehicles
a. Torque lug nuts and axle nuts to specification and recheck for looseness.
b. Wheel bearing worn or damaged. Replace wheel bearing.

Front Wheel Drive Vehicles
a. Torque lug nuts and axle nuts to specification and recheck for looseness.
b. Wheel bearing worn or damaged. Replace wheel bearing.
c. Wheel bearing out of adjustment. Adjust wheel bearing to specification; if still loose, replace.

Rear Wheel Drive Vehicles
a. Wheel bearing out of adjustment. Adjust wheel bearing to specification; if still loose, replace.
b. Torque lug nuts to specification and recheck for looseness.
c. Wheel bearing worn or damaged. Replace wheel bearing.

2. Rear wheel or wheel bearing loose

All Wheel and Four Wheel Drive Vehicles
a. Torque lug nuts and axle nuts to specification and recheck for looseness.
b. Wheel bearing worn or damaged. Replace wheel bearing.

Front Wheel Drive Vehicles
a. Wheel bearing out of adjustment. Adjust wheel bearing to specification; if still loose, replace.
b. Torque lug nuts to specification and recheck for looseness.
c. Wheel bearing worn or damaged. Replace wheel bearing.

Rear Wheel Drive Vehicles
a. Torque lug nuts to specification and recheck for looseness.
c. Wheel bearing worn or damaged. Replace wheel bearing.

4-B. Tires

1. Tires worn on inside tread
a. Check alignment for a toed-out condition. Check and set tire pressures and properly adjust the toe.
b. Check for worn, damaged or defective suspension components. Replace defective parts and adjust the alignment.

2. Tires worn on outside tread
a. Check alignment for a toed-in condition. Check and set tire pressures and properly adjust the toe.
b. Check for worn, damaged or defective suspension components. Replace defective parts and adjust the alignment.

3. Tires worn unevenly
a. Check the tire pressure and tire balance. Replace worn or defective tires and check the alignment; adjust if necessary.

BRAKE PERFORMANCE TROUBLESHOOTING HINTS

Brake vibrations or pulsation can often be diagnosed on a safe and careful test drive. A brake vibration which is felt through the brake pedal while braking, but not felt in the steering wheel, is most likely caused by brake surface variations in the rear brakes. If both the brake pedal and steering wheel vibrate during braking, a surface variation in the front brakes, or both front and rear brakes, is very likely.

A brake pedal that pumps up with repeated use can be caused by air in the brake hydraulic system or, if the vehicle is equipped with rear drum brakes, the brake adjusters may be seized or out of adjustment. A quick test for brake adjustment on vehicles with rear drum brakes is to pump the brake pedal several times with the vehicle's engine not running and the parking brake released. Pump the brake pedal several times and continue to apply pressure to the brake pedal. With pressure being applied to the brake pedal, engage the parking brake. Release the brake pedal and quickly press the brake pedal again. If the brake pedal pumped up, the rear brakes are in need of adjustment. Do not compensate for the rear brake adjustment by adjusting the parking brake, this will cause premature brake lining wear.

To test a vacuum brake booster, pump the brake pedal several times with the vehicle's engine off. Apply pressure to the brake pedal and then start the engine. The brake pedal should move downward about one inch (25mm).

b. Check for worn shock absorbers. Replaced failed components, worn or defective tires and check the alignment; adjust if necessary.
c. Check the alignment settings. Check and set tire pressures and properly adjust the alignment to specification.
d. Check for worn, damaged or defective suspension components. Replace defective parts and adjust the alignment to specification.

4-C. Steering

1. Excessive play in steering wheel
a. Check the steering gear free-play adjustment and properly adjust to remove excessive play.
b. Check the steering linkage for worn, damaged or defective parts. Replace failed components and perform a front end alignment.
c. Check for a worn, damaged, or defective steering box, replace the steering gear and check the front end alignment.

2. Steering wheel shakes at cruising speeds
a. Check for a bent front wheel. Replace a damaged wheel and check the tire for possible internal damage.
b. Check for an unevenly worn front tire. Replace the tire, adjust tire pressure and balance.
c. Check the front tires for hidden internal damage. Tires which have encountered large pot holes or suffered other hard blows may have sustained internal damage and should be replaced immediately.
d. Check the front tires for an out-of-balance condition. Remove, spin balance and reinstall. Torque all the wheel bolts or lug nuts to the recommended specification.
e. Check for a loose wheel bearing. If possible, adjust the bearing, or replace the bearing if it is a non-adjustable bearing.

3. Steering wheel shakes when braking
a. Refer to section 3-A, condition number 1.

4. Steering wheel becomes stiff when turned
a. Check the steering wheel free-play adjustment and reset as needed.
b. Check for a damaged steering gear assembly. Replace the steering gear and perform a front end alignment.
c. Check for damaged or seized suspension components. Replace defective components and perform a front end alignment.

4-D. Suspension

1. Vehicle pulls to one side
a. Tire pressure uneven. Adjust tire pressure to recommended settings.
b. Tires worn unevenly. Replace tires and check alignment settings.
c. Alignment out of specification. Align front end and check thrust angle.
d. Check for a dragging brake and repair or replace as necessary.

2. Vehicle is very bouncy over bumps
a. Check for worn or leaking shock absorbers or strut assemblies and replace as necessary.
b. Check for seized shock absorbers or strut assemblies and replace as necessary.

NOTE: When one shock fails, it is recommended to replace front or rear units as pairs.

3. Vehicle leans excessively in turns
a. Check for worn or leaking shock absorbers or strut assemblies and replace as necessary.
b. Check for missing, damaged, or worn stabilizer links or bushings, and replace or install as necessary.

4. Vehicle ride quality seems excessively harsh
a. Check for seized shock absorbers or strut assemblies and replace as necessary.
b. Check for excessively high tire pressures and adjust pressures to vehicle recommendations.

5. Vehicle seems low or leans to one side
a. Check for a damaged, broken or weak spring. Replace defective parts and check for a needed alignment.
b. Check for seized shock absorbers or strut assemblies and replace as necessary.
c. Check for worn or leaking shock absorbers or strut assemblies and replace as necessary.

4-E. Driving Noises and Vibrations

Noises

1. Vehicle makes a clicking noises when driven
a. Check the noise to see if it varies with road speed. Verify if the noise is present when coasting or with steering or throttle input. If the clicking noise frequency changes with road speed and is not affected by steering or throttle input, check the tire treads for a stone, piece of glass, nail or another hard object imbedded into the tire or tire tread. Stones rarely cause a tire puncture and are easily removed. Other objects may create an air leak when removed. Consider having these objects removed immediately at a facility equipped to repair tire punctures.
b. If the clicking noise varies with throttle input and steering, check for a worn Constant Velocity (CV-joint) joint, universal (U- joint) or flex joint.

2. Vehicle makes a clunking or knocking noise over bumps
a. A clunking noise over bumps is most often caused by excessive movement or clearance in a suspension component. Check the suspension for soft, cracked, damaged or worn bushings. Replace the bushings and check the vehicle's alignment.
b. Check for loose suspension mounting bolts. Check the tightness on subframe bolts, pivot bolts and suspension mounting bolts, and torque to specification.
c. Check the vehicle for a loose wheel bearing. Some wheel bearings can be adjusted for looseness, while others must be replaced if loose. Adjust or replace the bearings as recommended by the manufacturer.
d. Check the door latch adjustment. If the door is slightly loose, or the latch adjustment is not centered, the door assembly may create noises over bumps and rough surfaces. Properly adjust the door latches to secure the door.

3. Vehicle makes a low pitched rumbling noise when driven
a. A low pitched rumbling noise is usually caused by a drive train related bearing and is most often associated with a wheel bearing which has been damaged or worn. The damage can be caused by excessive brake temperatures or physical contact with a pot hole or curb. Sometimes the noise will vary when turning. Left hand turns increase the load on the vehicle's right side, and right turns load the left side. A failed front wheel bearing may also cause a slight steering wheel vibration when turning. A bearing which exhibits noise must be replaced.
b. Check the tire condition and balance. An internally damaged tire may cause failure symptoms similar to failed suspension parts. For diagnostic purposes, try a known good set of tires and replace defective tires.

4. Vehicle makes a squeaking noise over bumps
a. Check the vehicle's ball joints for wear, damaged or leaking boots. Replace a ball joint if it is loose, the boot is damaged and leaking, or the ball joint is binding. When replacing suspension parts, check the vehicle for alignment.
b. Check for seized or deteriorated bushings. Replace bushings that are worn or damaged and check the vehicle for alignment.
c. Check for the presence of sway bar or stabilizer bar bushings which wrap around the bar. Inspect the condition of the bushings and replace if worn or damaged. Remove the bushing bracket and apply a thin layer of suspension grease to the area where the bushings wrap around the bar and reinstall the bushing brackets.

Vibrations

5. Vehicle vibrates when driven
a. Check the road surface. Roads which have rough or uneven surfaces may cause unusual vibrations.
b. Check the tire condition and balance. An internally damaged tire may cause failure symptoms similar to failed suspension parts. For diagnostic purposes, try a known good set of tires and replace defective tires immediately.
c. Check for a worn Constant Velocity (CV-joint) joint, universal (U- joint) or flex joint and replace if loose, damaged or binding.
d. Check for a loose, bent, or out-of-balance axle or drive shaft. Replace damaged or failed components.

NOTE: Diagnosing failures related to wheels, tires, steering and the suspension system can often times be accomplished with a careful and thorough test drive. Bearing noises are isolated by noting whether the noises or symptoms vary when turning left or right, or occur while driving a straight line. During a left hand turn, the vehicle's weight shifts to the right, placing more force on the right side bearings, such that if a right side wheel bearing is worn or damaged, the noise or vibration should increase during light-to-heavy acceleration. Conversely, on right hand turns, the vehicle tends to lean to the left, loading the left side bearings.

Knocking noises in the suspension when the vehicle is driven over rough roads, railroad tracks and speed bumps indicate worn suspension components such as bushings, ball joints or tie rod ends, or a worn steering system.

5. ELECTRICAL ACCESSORIES

5-A. Headlights

1. One headlight only works on high or low beam
a. Check for battery voltage at headlight electrical connector. If battery voltage is present, replace the headlight assembly or bulb if available separately. If battery voltage is not present, refer to the headlight wiring diagram to troubleshoot.

2. Headlight does not work on high or low beam
a. Check for battery voltage and ground at headlight electrical connector. If battery voltage is present, check the headlight connector ground terminal for a proper ground. If battery voltage and ground are present at the headlight connector, replace the headlight assembly or bulb if available separately. If battery voltage or ground is not present, refer to the headlight wiring diagram to troubleshoot.
b. Check the headlight switch operation. Replace the switch if the switch is defective or operates intermittently.

3. Headlight(s) very dim
a. Check for battery voltage and ground at headlight electrical connector. If battery voltage is present, trace the ground circuit for the headlamp electrical connector, then clean and repair as necessary. If the voltage at the headlight electrical connector is significantly less than the voltage at the battery, refer to the headlight wiring diagram to troubleshoot and locate the voltage drop.

5-B. Tail, Running and Side Marker Lights

1. Tail light, running light or side marker light inoperative
a. Check for battery voltage and ground at light's electrical connector. If battery voltage is present, check the bulb socket and electrical connector ground terminal for a proper ground. If battery voltage and ground are present at the light connector, but not in the socket, clean the socket and the ground terminal connector. If battery voltage and ground are present in the bulb socket, replace the bulb. If battery voltage or ground is not present, refer to the wiring diagram to troubleshoot for an open circuit.
b. Check the light switch operation and replace if necessary.

2. Tail light, running light or side marker light works intermittently
a. Check the bulb for a damaged filament, and replace if damaged.
b Check the bulb and bulb socket for corrosion, and clean or replace the bulb and socket.
c. Check for loose, damaged or corroded wires and electrical terminals, and repair as necessary.
d. Check the light switch operation and replace if necessary.

3. Tail light, running light or side marker light very dim
a. Check the bulb and bulb socket for corrosion and clean or replace the bulb and socket.

b. Check for low voltage at the bulb socket positive terminal or a poor ground. If voltage is low, or the ground marginal, trace the wiring to, and check for loose, damaged or corroded wires and electrical terminals; repair as necessary.

c. Check the light switch operation and replace if necessary.

5-C. Interior Lights

1. Interior light inoperative

a. Verify the interior light switch location and position(s), and set the switch in the correct position.

b. Check for battery voltage and ground at the interior light bulb socket. If battery voltage and ground are present, replace the bulb. If voltage is not present, check the interior light fuse for battery voltage. If the fuse is missing, replace the fuse. If the fuse has blown, or if battery voltage is present, refer to the wiring diagram to troubleshoot the cause for an open or shorted circuit. If ground is not present, check the door switch contacts and clean or repair as necessary.

2. Interior light works intermittently

a. Check the bulb for a damaged filament, and replace if damaged.

b. Check the bulb and bulb socket for corrosion, and clean or replace the bulb and socket.

c. Check for loose, damaged or corroded wires and electrical terminals; repair as necessary.

d. Check the door and light switch operation, and replace if necessary.

3. Interior light very dim

a. Check the bulb and bulb socket for corrosion, and clean or replace the bulb and socket.

b. Check for low voltage at the bulb socket positive terminal or a poor ground. If voltage is low, or the ground marginal, trace the wiring to, and check for loose, damaged or corroded wires and electrical terminals; repair as necessary.

c. Check the door and light switch operation, and replace if necessary.

5-D. Brake Lights

1. One brake light inoperative

a. Press the brake pedal and check for battery voltage and ground at the brake light bulb socket. If present, replace the bulb. If either battery voltage or ground is not present, refer to the wiring diagram to troubleshoot.

2. Both brake lights inoperative

a. Press the brake pedal and check for battery voltage and ground at the brake light bulb socket. If present, replace both bulbs. If battery voltage is not present, check the brake light switch adjustment and adjust as necessary. If the brake light switch is properly adjusted, and battery voltage or the ground is not present at the bulb sockets, or at the bulb electrical connector with the brake pedal pressed, refer to the wiring diagram to troubleshoot the cause of an open circuit.

3. One or both brake lights very dim

a. Press the brake pedal and measure the voltage at the brake light bulb socket. If the measured voltage is close to the battery voltage, check for a poor ground caused by a loose, damaged, or corroded wire, terminal, bulb or bulb socket. If the ground is bolted to a painted surface, it may be necessary to remove the electrical connector and clean the mounting surface, so the connector mounts on bare metal. If battery voltage is low, check for a poor connection caused by either a faulty brake light switch, a loose, damaged, or corroded wire, terminal or electrical connector. Refer to the wiring diagram to troubleshoot the cause of a voltage drop.

5-E. Warning Lights

1. Warning light(s) stay on when the engine is started

Ignition, Battery or Alternator Warning Light

a. Check the alternator output and voltage regulator operation, and replace as necessary.

b. Check the warning light wiring for a shorted wire.

Check Engine Light

a. Check the engine for routine maintenance and tune-up status. Note the engine tune-up specifications and verify the spark plug, air filter and engine oil condition; replace and/or adjust items as necessary.

b. Check the fuel tank for low fuel level, causing an intermittent lean fuel mixture. Top off fuel tank and reset check engine light.

c. Check for a failed or disconnected engine fuel or ignition component, sensor or control unit and repair or replace as necessary.

d. Check the intake manifold and vacuum hoses for air leaks and repair as necessary.

e. Check the engine's mechanical condition for excessive oil consumption.

Anti-Lock Braking System (ABS) Light

a. Check the wheel sensors and sensor rings for debris, and clean as necessary.

b. Check the brake master cylinder for fluid leakage or seal failure and replace as necessary.

c. Check the ABS control unit, pump and proportioning valves for proper operation; replace as necessary.

d. Check the sensor wiring at the wheel sensors and the ABS control unit for a loose or shorted wire, and repair as necessary.

Brake Warning Light

a. Check the brake fluid level and check for possible leakage from the hydraulic lines and seals. Top off brake fluid and repair leakage as necessary.

b. Check the brake linings for wear and replace as necessary.

c. Check for a loose or shorted brake warning light sensor or wire, and replace or repair as necessary.

Oil Pressure Warning Light

a. Stop the engine immediately. Check the engine oil level and oil filter condition, and top off or change the oil as necessary.

b. Check the oil pressure sensor wire for being shorted to ground. Disconnect the wire from the oil pressure sensor and with the ignition in the ON position, but not running, the oil pressure light should not be working. If the light works with the wire disconnected, check the sensor wire for being shorted to ground. Check the wire routing to make sure the wire is not pinched and check for insulation damage. Repair or replace the wire as necessary and recheck before starting the engine.

c. Remove the oil pan and check for a clogged oil pick-up tube screen.

d. Check the oil pressure sensor operation by substituting a known good sensor.

e. Check the oil filter for internal restrictions or leaks, and replace as necessary.

WARNING: If the engine is operated with oil pressure below the manufacturer's specification, severe (and costly) engine damage could occur. Low oil pressure can be caused by excessive internal wear or damage to the engine bearings, oil pressure relief valve, oil pump or oil pump drive mechanism.

Before starting the engine, check for possible causes of rapid oil loss, such as leaking oil lines or a loose, damaged, restricted, or leaking oil filter or oil pressure sensor. If the engine oil level and condition are acceptable, measure the engine's oil pressure using a pressure gauge, or determine the cause for the oil pressure warning light to function when the engine is running, before operating the engine for an extended period of time. Another symptom of operating an engine with low oil pressure is the presence of severe knocking and tapping noises.

Parking Brake Warning Light

a. Check the brake release mechanism and verify the parking brake has been fully released.

b. Check the parking brake light switch for looseness or misalignment.

c. Check for a damaged switch or a loose or shorted brake light switch wire, and replace or repair as necessary.

2. Warning light(s) flickers on and off when driving

Ignition, Battery or Alternator Warning Light

a. Check the alternator output and voltage regulator operation. An intermittent condition may indicate worn brushes, an internal short, or a defective voltage regulator. Replace the alternator or failed component.

b. Check the warning light wiring for a shorted, pinched or damaged wire and repair as necessary.

Check Engine Light

a. Check the engine for required maintenance and tune-up status. Verify engine tune-up specifications, as well as spark plug, air filter and engine oil condition; replace and/or adjust items as necessary.

b. Check the fuel tank for low fuel level causing an intermittent lean fuel mixture. Top off fuel tank and reset check engine light.

c. Check for an intermittent failure or partially disconnected engine fuel and ignition component, sensor or control unit; repair or replace as necessary.

d. Check the intake manifold and vacuum hoses for air leaks, and repair as necessary.

e. Check the warning light wiring for a shorted, pinched or damaged wire and repair as necessary.

Anti-Lock Braking System (ABS) Light

a. Check the wheel sensors and sensor rings for debris, and clean as necessary.

b. Check the brake master cylinder for fluid leakage or seal failure and replace as necessary.

c. Check the ABS control unit, pump and proportioning valves for proper operation, and replace as necessary.

d. Check the sensor wiring at the wheel sensors and the ABS control unit for a loose or shorted wire and repair as necessary.

Brake Warning Light
a. Check the brake fluid level and check for possible leakage from the hydraulic lines and seals. Top off brake fluid and repair leakage as necessary.
b. Check the brake linings for wear and replace as necessary.
c. Check for a loose or shorted brake warning light sensor or wire, and replace or repair as necessary.

Oil Pressure Warning Light
a. Stop the engine immediately. Check the engine oil level and check for a sudden and rapid oil loss, such as a leaking oil line or oil pressure sensor, and repair or replace as necessary.
b. Check the oil pressure sensor operation by substituting a known good sensor.
c. Check the oil pressure sensor wire for being shorted to ground. Disconnect the wire from the oil pressure sensor and with the ignition in the ON position, but not running, the oil pressure light should not be working. If the light works with the wire disconnected, check the sensor wire for being shorted to ground. Check the wire routing to make sure the wire is not pinched and check for insulation damage. Repair or replace the wire as necessary and recheck before starting the engine.
d. Remove the oil pan and check for a clogged oil pick-up tube screen.

Parking Brake Warning Light
a. Check the brake release mechanism and verify the parking brake has been fully released.
b. Check the parking brake light switch for looseness or misalignment.
c. Check for a damaged switch or a loose or shorted brake light switch wire, and replace or repair as necessary.

3. Warning light(s) inoperative with ignition on, and engine not started
a. Check for a defective bulb by installing a known good bulb.
b. Check for a defective wire using the appropriate wiring diagram(s).
c. Check for a defective sending unit by removing and then grounding the wire at the sending unit. If the light comes on with the ignition on when grounding the wire, replace the sending unit.

5-F. Turn Signal and 4-Way Hazard Lights

1. Turn signals or hazard lights come on, but do not flash
a. Check for a defective flasher unit and replace as necessary.

2. Turn signals or hazard lights do not function on either side
a. Check the fuse and replace, if defective.
b. Check the flasher unit by substituting a known good flasher unit.
c. Check the turn signal electrical system for a defective component, open circuit, short circuit or poor ground.

3. Turn signals or hazard lights only work on one side
a. Check for failed bulbs and replace as necessary.
b. Check for poor grounds in both housings and repair as necessary.

4. One signal light does not work
a. Check for a failed bulb and replace as necessary.
b. Check for corrosion in the bulb socket, and clean and repair as necessary.
c. Check for a poor ground at the bulb socket, and clean and repair as necessary.

5. Turn signals flash too slowly
a. Check signal bulb(s) wattage and replace with lower wattage bulb(s).

6. Turn signals flash too fast
a. Check signal bulb(s) wattage and replace with higher wattage bulb(s).
b. Check for installation of the correct flasher unit and replace if incorrect.

7. Four-way hazard flasher indicator light inoperative
a. Verify that the exterior lights are functioning and, if so, replace indicator bulb.
b. Check the operation of the warning flasher switch and replace if defective.

8. Turn signal indicator light(s) do not work in either direction
a. Verify that the exterior lights are functioning and, if so, replace indicator bulb(s).
b. Check for a defective flasher unit by substituting a known good unit.

9. One turn signal indicator light does not work
a. Check for a defective bulb and replace as necessary.
b. Check for a defective flasher unit by substituting a known good unit.

5-G. Horn

1. Horn does not operate
a. Check for a defective fuse and replace as necessary.
b. Check for battery voltage and ground at horn electrical connections when pressing the horn switch. If voltage is present, replace the horn assembly. If voltage or ground is not present, refer to Chassis Electrical coverage for additional troubleshooting techniques and circuit information.

2. Horn has an unusual tone
a. On single horn systems, replace the horn.
b. On dual horn systems, check the operation of the second horn. Dual horn systems have a high and low pitched horn. Unplug one horn at a time and recheck operation. Replace the horn which does not function.
c. Check for debris or condensation build-up in horn and verify the horn positioning. If the horn has a single opening, adjust the opening downward to allow for adequate drainage and to prevent debris build-up.

5-H. Windshield Wipers

1. Windshield wipers do not operate
a. Check fuse and replace as necessary.
b. Check switch operation and repair or replace as necessary.
c. Check for corroded, loose, disconnected or broken wires and clean or repair as necessary.
d. Check the ground circuit for the wiper switch or motor and repair as necessary.

2. Windshield wiper motor makes a humming noise, gets hot or blows fuses
a. Wiper motor damaged internally; replace the wiper motor.
b. Wiper linkage bent, damaged or seized. Repair or replace wiper linkage as necessary.

3. Windshield wiper motor operates, but one or both wipers fail to move
a. Windshield wiper motor linkage loose or disconnected. Repair or replace linkage as necessary.
b. Windshield wiper arms loose on wiper pivots. Secure wiper arm to pivot or replace both the wiper arm and pivot assembly.

4. Windshield wipers will not park
a. Check the wiper switch operation and verify that the switch properly interrupts the power supplied to the wiper motor.
b. If the wiper switch is functioning properly, the wiper motor parking circuit has failed. Replace the wiper motor assembly. Operate the wiper motor at least one time before installing the arms and blades to ensure correct positioning, then recheck using the highest wiper speed on a wet windshield to make sure the arms and blades do not contact the windshield trim.

6. INSTRUMENTS AND GAUGES

6-A. Speedometer (Cable Operated)

1. Speedometer does not work
a. Check and verify that the speedometer cable is properly seated into the speedometer assembly and the speedometer drive gear.
b. Check the speedometer cable for breakage or rounded-off cable ends where the cable seats into the speedometer drive gear and into the speedometer assembly. If damaged, broken or the cable ends are rounded off, replace the cable.
c. Check speedometer drive gear condition and replace as necessary.
d. Install a known good speedometer to test for proper operation. If the substituted speedometer functions properly, replace the speedometer assembly.

2. Speedometer needle fluctuates when driving at steady speeds.
a. Check speedometer cable routing or sheathing for sharp bends or kinks. Route cable to minimize sharp bends or kinks. If the sheathing has been damaged, replace the cable assembly.
b. Check the speedometer cable for adequate lubrication. Remove the cable, inspect for damage, clean, lubricate and reinstall. If the cable has been damaged, replace the cable.

3. Speedometer works intermittently
a. Check the cable and verify that the cable is fully installed and the fasteners are secure.
b. Check the cable ends for wear and rounding, and replace as necessary.

6-B. Speedometer (Electronically Operated)

1. Speedometer does not work
a. Check the speed sensor pickup and replace as necessary.
b. Check the wiring between the speed sensor and the speedometer for corroded terminals, loose connections or broken wires and clean or repair as necessary.
c. Install a known good speedometer to test for proper operation. If the substituted speedometer functions properly, replace the speedometer assembly.

2. Speedometer works intermittently
a. Check the wiring between the speed sensor and the speedometer for corroded terminals, loose connections or broken wires and clean or repair as necessary.
b. Check the speed sensor pickup and replace as necessary.

6-C. Fuel, Temperature and Oil Pressure Gauges

1. Gauge does not register
a. Check for a missing or blown fuse and replace as necessary.
b. Check for an open circuit in the gauge wiring. Repair wiring as necessary.

c. Gauge sending unit defective. Replace gauge sending unit.
d. Gauge or sending unit improperly installed. Verify installation and wiring, and repair as necessary.

2. Gauge operates erratically
a. Check for loose, shorted, damaged or corroded electrical connections or wiring and repair as necessary.
b. Check gauge sending units and replace as necessary.

3. Gauge operates fully pegged
a. Sending unit-to-gauge wire shorted to ground.
b. Sending unit defective; replace sending unit.
c. Gauge or sending unit not properly grounded.
d. Gauge or sending unit improperly installed. Verify installation and wiring, and repair as necessary.

7. CLIMATE CONTROL

7-A. Air Conditioner

1. No air coming from air conditioner vents
a. Check the air conditioner fuse and replace as necessary.
b. Air conditioner system discharged. Have the system evacuated, charged and leak tested by an MVAC certified technician, utilizing approved recovery/recycling equipment. Repair as necessary.
c. Air conditioner low pressure switch defective. Replace switch.
d. Air conditioner fan resistor pack defective. Replace resistor pack.
e. Loose connection, broken wiring or defective air conditioner relay in air conditioning electrical circuit. Repair wiring or replace relay as necessary.

2. Air conditioner blows warm air
a. Air conditioner system is discharged. Have the system evacuated, charged and leak tested by an MVAC certified technician, utilizing approved recovery/recycling equipment. Repair as necessary.
b. Air conditioner compressor clutch not engaging. Check compressor clutch wiring, electrical connections and compressor clutch, and repair or replace as necessary.

3. Water collects on the interior floor when the air conditioner is used
a. Air conditioner evaporator drain hose is blocked. Clear the drain hose where it exits the passenger compartment.
b. Air conditioner evaporator drain hose is disconnected. Secure the drain hose to the evaporator drainage tray under the dashboard.

4. Air conditioner has a moldy odor when used
a. The air conditioner evaporator drain hose is blocked or partially re-stricted, allowing condensation to build up around the evaporator and drainage tray. Clear the drain hose where it exits the passenger compartment.

7-B. Heater

1. Blower motor does not operate
a. Check blower motor fuse and replace as necessary.
b. Check blower motor wiring for loose, damaged or corroded contacts and repair as necessary.
c. Check blower motor switch and resistor pack for open circuits, and repair or replace as necessary.
d. Check blower motor for internal damage and repair or replace as necessary.

2. Heater blows cool air
a. Check the engine coolant level. If the coolant level is low, top off and bleed the air from the cooling system as necessary and check for coolant leaks.
b. Check engine coolant operating temperature. If coolant temperature is below specification, check for a damaged or stuck thermostat.
c. Check the heater control valve operation. Check the heater control valve cable or vacuum hose for proper installation. Move the heater temperature control from hot to cold several times and verify the operation of the heater control valve. With the engine at normal operating temperature and the heater temperature control in the full hot position, carefully feel the heater hose going into and exiting the control valve. If one heater hose is hot and the other is much cooler, replace the control valve.

3. Heater steams the windshield when used
a. Check for a loose cooling system hose clamp or leaking coolant hose near the engine firewall or under the dash area, and repair as necessary.
b. Check for the existence of a sweet odor and fluid dripping from the heater floor vents, indicating a failed or damaged heater core. Pressure test the cooling system with the heater set to the fully warm position and check for fluid leakage from the floor vents. If leakage is verified, remove and replace the heater core assembly.

NOTE: On some vehicles, the dashboard must be disassembled and removed to access the heater core.

GLOSSARY

AIR/FUEL RATIO: The ratio of air-to-gasoline by weight in the fuel mixture drawn into the engine.

AIR INJECTION: One method of reducing harmful exhaust emissions by injecting air into each of the exhaust ports of an engine. The fresh air entering the hot exhaust manifold causes any remaining fuel to be burned before it can exit the tailpipe.

ALTERNATOR: A device used for converting mechanical energy into electrical energy.

AMMETER: An instrument, calibrated in amperes, used to measure the flow of an electrical current in a circuit. Ammeters are always connected in series with the circuit being tested.

AMPERE: The rate of flow of electrical current present when one volt of electrical pressure is applied against one ohm of electrical resistance.

ANALOG COMPUTER: Any microprocessor that uses similar (analogous) electrical signals to make its calculations.

ARMATURE: A laminated, soft iron core wrapped by a wire that converts electrical energy to mechanical energy as in a motor or relay. When rotated in a magnetic field, it changes mechanical energy into electrical energy as in a generator.

ATMOSPHERIC PRESSURE: The pressure on the Earth's surface caused by the weight of the air in the atmosphere. At sea level, this pressure is 14.7 psi at 32°F (101 kPa at 0°C).

ATOMIZATION: The breaking down of a liquid into a fine mist that can be suspended in air.

AXIAL PLAY: Movement parallel to a shaft or bearing bore.

BACKFIRE: The sudden combustion of gases in the intake or exhaust system that results in a loud explosion.

BACKLASH: The clearance or play between two parts, such as meshed gears.

BACKPRESSURE: Restrictions in the exhaust system that slow the exit of exhaust gases from the combustion chamber.

BAKELITE: A heat resistant, plastic insulator material commonly used in printed circuit boards and transistorized components.

BALL BEARING: A bearing made up of hardened inner and outer races between which hardened steel balls roll.

BALLAST RESISTOR: A resistor in the primary ignition circuit that lowers voltage after the engine is started to reduce wear on ignition components.

BEARING: A friction reducing, supportive device usually located between a stationary part and a moving part.

BIMETAL TEMPERATURE SENSOR: Any sensor or switch made of two dissimilar types of metal that bend when heated or cooled due to the different expansion rates of the alloys. These types of sensors usually function as an on/off switch.

BLOWBY: Combustion gases, composed of water vapor and unburned fuel, that leak past the piston rings into the crankcase during normal engine operation. These gases are removed by the PCV system to prevent the buildup of harmful acids in the crankcase.

BRAKE PAD: A brake shoe and lining assembly used with disc brakes.

BRAKE SHOE: The backing for the brake lining. The term is, however, usually applied to the assembly of the brake backing and lining.

BUSHING: A liner, usually removable, for a bearing; an anti-friction liner used in place of a bearing.

CALIPER: A hydraulically activated device in a disc brake system, which is mounted straddling the brake rotor (disc). The caliper contains at least one piston and two brake pads. Hydraulic pressure on the piston(s) forces the pads against the rotor.

CAMSHAFT: A shaft in the engine on which are the lobes (cams) which operate the valves. The camshaft is driven by the crankshaft, via a belt, chain or gears, at one half the crankshaft speed.

CAPACITOR: A device which stores an electrical charge.

CARBON MONOXIDE (CO): A colorless, odorless gas given off as a normal byproduct of combustion. It is poisonous and extremely dangerous in confined areas, building up slowly to toxic levels without warning if adequate ventilation is not available.

CARBURETOR: A device, usually mounted on the intake manifold of an engine, which mixes the air and fuel in the proper proportion to allow even combustion.

CATALYTIC CONVERTER: A device installed in the exhaust system, like a muffler, that converts harmful byproducts of combustion into carbon dioxide and water vapor by means of a heat-producing chemical reaction.

CENTRIFUGAL ADVANCE: A mechanical method of advancing the spark timing by using flyweights in the distributor that react to centrifugal force generated by the distributor shaft rotation.

CHECK VALVE: Any one-way valve installed to permit the flow of air, fuel or vacuum in one direction only.

CHOKE: A device, usually a moveable valve, placed in the intake path of a carburetor to restrict the flow of air.

CIRCUIT: Any unbroken path through which an electrical current can flow. Also used to describe fuel flow in some instances.

CIRCUIT BREAKER: A switch which protects an electrical circuit from overload by opening the circuit when the current flow exceeds a predetermined level. Some circuit breakers must be reset manually, while most reset automatically.

COIL (IGNITION): A transformer in the ignition circuit which steps up the voltage provided to the spark plugs.

COMBINATION MANIFOLD: An assembly which includes both the intake and exhaust manifolds in one casting.

COMBINATION VALVE: A device used in some fuel systems that routes fuel vapors to a charcoal storage canister instead of venting them into the atmosphere. The valve relieves fuel tank pressure and allows fresh air into the tank as the fuel level drops to prevent a vapor lock situation.

COMPRESSION RATIO: The comparison of the total volume of the cylinder and combustion chamber with the piston at BDC and the piston at TDC.

CONDENSER: 1. An electrical device which acts to store an electrical charge, preventing voltage surges. 2. A radiator-like device in the air conditioning system in which refrigerant gas condenses into a liquid, giving off heat.

CONDUCTOR: Any material through which an electrical current can be transmitted easily.

CONTINUITY: Continuous or complete circuit. Can be checked with an ohmmeter.

COUNTERSHAFT: An intermediate shaft which is rotated by a mainshaft and transmits, in turn, that rotation to a working part.

CRANKCASE: The lower part of an engine in which the crankshaft and related parts operate.

CRANKSHAFT: The main driving shaft of an engine which receives reciprocating motion from the pistons and converts it to rotary motion.

CYLINDER: In an engine, the round hole in the engine block in which the piston(s) ride.

CYLINDER BLOCK: The main structural member of an engine in which is found the cylinders, crankshaft and other principal parts.

CYLINDER HEAD: The detachable portion of the engine, usually fastened to the top of the cylinder block and containing all or most of the combustion chambers. On overhead valve engines, it contains the valves and their operating parts. On overhead cam engines, it contains the camshaft as well.

DEAD CENTER: The extreme top or bottom of the piston stroke.

DETONATION: An unwanted explosion of the air/fuel mixture in the combustion chamber caused by excess heat and compression, advanced timing, or an overly lean mixture. Also referred to as "ping".

DIAPHRAGM: A thin, flexible wall separating two cavities, such as in a vacuum advance unit.

DIESELING: A condition in which hot spots in the combustion chamber cause the engine to run on after the key is turned off.

DIFFERENTIAL: A geared assembly which allows the transmission of motion between drive axles, giving one axle the ability to turn faster than the other.

DIODE: An electrical device that will allow current to flow in one direction only.

DISC BRAKE: A hydraulic braking assembly consisting of a brake disc, or rotor, mounted on an axle, and a caliper assembly containing, usually two brake pads which are activated by hydraulic pressure. The pads are forced against the sides of the disc, creating friction which slows the vehicle.

DISTRIBUTOR: A mechanically driven device on an engine which is responsible for electrically firing the spark plug at a predetermined point of the piston stroke.

DOWEL PIN: A pin, inserted in mating holes in two different parts allowing those parts to maintain a fixed relationship.

DRUM BRAKE: A braking system which consists of two brake shoes and one or two wheel cylinders, mounted on a fixed backing plate, and a brake drum, mounted on an axle, which revolves around the assembly.

DWELL: The rate, measured in degrees of shaft rotation, at which an electrical circuit cycles on and off.

ELECTRONIC CONTROL UNIT (ECU): Ignition module, module, amplifier or igniter. See Module for definition.

ELECTRONIC IGNITION: A system in which the timing and firing of the spark plugs is controlled by an electronic control unit, usually called a module. These systems have no points or condenser.

END-PLAY: The measured amount of axial movement in a shaft.

ENGINE: A device that converts heat into mechanical energy.

EXHAUST MANIFOLD: A set of cast passages or pipes which conduct exhaust gases from the engine.

FEELER GAUGE: A blade, usually metal, or precisely predetermined thickness, used to measure the clearance between two parts.

FIRING ORDER: The order in which combustion occurs in the cylinders of an engine. Also the order in which spark is distributed to the plugs by the distributor.

FLOODING: The presence of too much fuel in the intake manifold and combustion chamber which prevents the air/fuel mixture from firing, thereby causing a no-start situation.

FLYWHEEL: A disc shaped part bolted to the rear end of the crankshaft. Around the outer perimeter is affixed the ring gear. The starter drive engages the ring gear, turning the flywheel, which rotates the crankshaft, imparting the initial starting motion to the engine.

FOOT POUND (ft. lbs. or sometimes, ft.lb.): The amount of energy or work needed to raise an item weighing one pound, a distance of one foot.

FUSE: A protective device in a circuit which prevents circuit overload by breaking the circuit when a specific amperage is present. The device is constructed around a strip or wire of a lower amperage rating than the circuit it is designed to protect. When an amperage higher than that stamped on the fuse is present in the circuit, the strip or wire melts, opening the circuit.

GEAR RATIO: The ratio between the number of teeth on meshing gears.

GENERATOR: A device which converts mechanical energy into electrical energy.

HEAT RANGE: The measure of a spark plug's ability to dissipate heat from its firing end. The higher the heat range, the hotter the plug fires.

HUB: The center part of a wheel or gear.

HYDROCARBON (HC): Any chemical compound made up of hydrogen and carbon. A major pollutant formed by the engine as a byproduct of combustion.

HYDROMETER: An instrument used to measure the specific gravity of a solution.

INCH POUND (inch lbs.; sometimes in.lb. or in. lbs.): One twelfth of a foot pound.

INDUCTION: A means of transferring electrical energy in the form of a magnetic field. Principle used in the ignition coil to increase voltage.

INJECTOR: A device which receives metered fuel under relatively low pressure and is activated to inject the fuel into the engine under relatively high pressure at a predetermined time.

INPUT SHAFT: The shaft to which torque is applied, usually carrying the driving gear or gears.

INTAKE MANIFOLD: A casting of passages or pipes used to conduct air or a fuel/air mixture to the cylinders.

JOURNAL: The bearing surface within which a shaft operates.

KEY: A small block usually fitted in a notch between a shaft and a hub to prevent slippage of the two parts.

MANIFOLD: A casting of passages or set of pipes which connect the cylinders to an inlet or outlet source.

MANIFOLD VACUUM: Low pressure in an engine intake manifold formed just below the throttle plates. Manifold vacuum is highest at idle and drops under acceleration.

MASTER CYLINDER: The primary fluid pressurizing device in a hydraulic system. In automotive use, it is found in brake and hydraulic clutch systems and is pedal activated, either directly or, in a power brake system, through the power booster.

MODULE: Electronic control unit, amplifier or igniter of solid state or integrated design which controls the current flow in the ignition primary circuit based on input from the pick-up coil. When the module opens the primary circuit, high secondary voltage is induced in the coil.

NEEDLE BEARING: A bearing which consists of a number (usually a large number) of long, thin rollers.

OHM: (Ω) The unit used to measure the resistance of conductor-to-electrical flow. One ohm is the amount of resistance that limits current flow to one ampere in a circuit with one volt of pressure.

OHMMETER: An instrument used for measuring the resistance, in ohms, in an electrical circuit.

OUTPUT SHAFT: The shaft which transmits torque from a device, such as a transmission.

OVERDRIVE: A gear assembly which produces more shaft revolutions than that transmitted to it.

OVERHEAD CAMSHAFT (OHC): An engine configuration in which the camshaft is mounted on top of the cylinder head and operates the valve either directly or by means of rocker arms.

OVERHEAD VALVE (OHV): An engine configuration in which all of the valves are located in the cylinder head and the camshaft is located in the cylinder block. The camshaft operates the valves via lifters and pushrods.

OXIDES OF NITROGEN (NOx): Chemical compounds of nitrogen produced as a byproduct of combustion. They combine with hydrocarbons to produce smog.

OXYGEN SENSOR: Use with the feedback system to sense the presence of oxygen in the exhaust gas and signal the computer which can reference the voltage signal to an air/fuel ratio.

PINION: The smaller of two meshing gears.

PISTON RING: An open-ended ring with fits into a groove on the outer diameter of the piston. Its chief function is to form a seal between the piston and cylinder wall. Most automotive pistons have three rings: two for compression sealing; one for oil sealing.

PRELOAD: A predetermined load placed on a bearing during assembly or by adjustment.

PRIMARY CIRCUIT: the low voltage side of the ignition system which consists of the ignition switch, ballast resistor or resistance wire, bypass, coil, electronic control unit and pick-up coil as well as the connecting wires and harnesses.

PRESS FIT: The mating of two parts under pressure, due to the inner diameter of one being smaller than the outer diameter of the other, or vice versa; an interference fit.

RACE: The surface on the inner or outer ring of a bearing on which the balls, needles or rollers move.

REGULATOR: A device which maintains the amperage and/or voltage levels of a circuit at predetermined values.

RELAY: A switch which automatically opens and/or closes a circuit.

RESISTANCE: The opposition to the flow of current through a circuit or electrical device, and is measured in ohms. Resistance is equal to the voltage divided by the amperage.

RESISTOR: A device, usually made of wire, which offers a preset amount of resistance in an electrical circuit.

RING GEAR: The name given to a ring-shaped gear attached to a differential case, or affixed to a flywheel or as part of a planetary gear set.

ROLLER BEARING: A bearing made up of hardened inner and outer races between which hardened steel rollers move.

ROTOR: 1. The disc-shaped part of a disc brake assembly, upon which the brake pads bear; also called, brake disc. 2. The device mounted atop the distributor shaft, which passes current to the distributor cap tower contacts.

SECONDARY CIRCUIT: The high voltage side of the ignition system, usually above 20,000 volts. The secondary includes the ignition coil, coil wire, distributor cap and rotor, spark plug wires and spark plugs.

SENDING UNIT: A mechanical, electrical, hydraulic or electro-magnetic device which transmits information to a gauge.

SENSOR: Any device designed to measure engine operating conditions or ambient pressures and temperatures. Usually electronic in nature and designed to send a voltage signal to an on-board computer, some sensors may operate as a simple on/off switch or they may provide a variable voltage signal (like a potentiometer) as conditions or measured parameters change.

SHIM: Spacers of precise, predetermined thickness used between parts to establish a proper working relationship.

SLAVE CYLINDER: In automotive use, a device in the hydraulic clutch system which is activated by hydraulic force, disengaging the clutch.

SOLENOID: A coil used to produce a magnetic field, the effect of which is to produce work.

SPARK PLUG: A device screwed into the combustion chamber of a spark ignition engine. The basic construction is a conductive core inside of a ceramic insulator, mounted in an outer conductive base. An electrical charge from the spark plug wire travels along the conductive core and jumps a preset air gap to a grounding point or points at the end of the conductive base. The resultant spark ignites the fuel/air mixture in the combustion chamber.

SPLINES: Ridges machined or cast onto the outer diameter of a shaft or inner diameter of a bore to enable parts to mate without rotation.

TACHOMETER: A device used to measure the rotary speed of an engine, shaft, gear, etc., usually in rotations per minute.

THERMOSTAT: A valve, located in the cooling system of an engine, which is closed when cold and opens gradually in response to engine heating, controlling the temperature of the coolant and rate of coolant flow.

TOP DEAD CENTER (TDC): The point at which the piston reaches the top of its travel on the compression stroke.

TORQUE: The twisting force applied to an object.

TORQUE CONVERTER: A turbine used to transmit power from a driving member to a driven member via hydraulic action, providing changes in drive ratio and torque. In automotive use, it links the driveplate at the rear of the engine to the automatic transmission.

TRANSDUCER: A device used to change a force into an electrical signal.

TRANSISTOR: A semi-conductor component which can be actuated by a small voltage to perform an electrical switching function.

TUNE-UP: A regular maintenance function, usually associated with the replacement and adjustment of parts and components in the electrical and fuel systems of a vehicle for the purpose of attaining optimum performance.

TURBOCHARGER: An exhaust driven pump which compresses intake air and forces it into the combustion chambers at higher than atmospheric pressures. The increased air pressure allows more fuel to be burned and results in increased horsepower being produced.

VACUUM ADVANCE: A device which advances the ignition timing in response to increased engine vacuum.

VACUUM GAUGE: An instrument used to measure the presence of vacuum in a chamber.

VALVE: A device which control the pressure, direction of flow or rate of flow of a liquid or gas.

VALVE CLEARANCE: The measured gap between the end of the valve stem and the rocker arm, cam lobe or follower that activates the valve.

VISCOSITY: The rating of a liquid's internal resistance to flow.

VOLTMETER: An instrument used for measuring electrical force in units called volts. Voltmeters are always connected parallel with the circuit being tested.

WHEEL CYLINDER: Found in the automotive drum brake assembly, it is a device, actuated by hydraulic pressure, which, through internal pistons, pushes the brake shoes outward against the drums.

MASTER·
INDEX